Excerpt From Review in *Teaching Sociology*

"It is exciting to see a new offering such as Our Social World *that is innovative in its pedagogical choices. It is an exceptionally well-organized and well-written text, and as such is an exciting new option for any introductory sociology class. This text strikes us as particularly effective at engaging students. It becomes quite evident that these two award-winning coauthors understand where students are coming from and which questions are most likely to engage them and push them to think analytically."*

—Reviewed by Catherine Fobes and Laura von Wallmenich,
Alma College, in *Teaching Sociology,* Vol. 36, 2008 (April: 161–184)

Student Praise for *Our Social World*

"It's been one of my favorite textbooks to read!"

"I felt the text was speaking 'my language.'"

"I liked that it explains what careers come from sociology. I love the real-life examples to explain key words. This really helped me understand how sociology applies to life."

"I really enjoyed how it started off with a story as an example of what sociology is . . . I formed a picture in my mind that stayed there throughout the chapter."

"It helped me relate my life and personal experiences to the concepts in sociology . . . . It made me concentrate on what was happening to others instead of worrying whether I could get through all the reading. I stayed focused."

"The chapters provide a good overview of the concepts of sociology."

"The charts/diagrams are very helpful in understanding the topics."

"The 'Thinking Sociologically' questions are a great way to stop and reflect because you remember what you read so much better when you have a chance to make it personal."

"It made me become more aware of why people are the way they are and do the things they do. It taught me to view the world with a different outlook. . . . By being aware of the various social groups out there, I can become a better person."

"Overall, I found this to be one of the most interesting things I have ever been forced to read, and I mean that in a good forced way."

"I really enjoy the book. It is clear to understand, funny at times, and has great examples!"

"I enjoyed how a real person's story was told at the opening of the chapters. It made sociology seem pertinent to real life."

To the Instructor

A New Intro Text for a New Generation of Students . . .
Incredibly Successful in Its First Two Editions and Now Even Better!

Written by two award-winning sociology instructors who are passionate about excellence in teaching, this textbook has been adopted at a variety of community colleges, four-year colleges, and comprehensive research universities, and these schools have used it in traditional as well as online Introduction to Sociology courses. Some of the many schools that have adopted the book include

- American River College
- Boise State University
- Buffalo State College
- Cape Cod Community College
- Capital Community College
- Capital University
- Chaffey College
- Cleveland State University
- College of Staten Island, The City University of New York
- Drexel University
- Hanover College
- Hofstra University
- Indiana University of Pennsylvania
- Ithaca College
- La Salle University
- Le Moyne College
- Long Island University
- Messiah College
- Minot State University
- Monroe County Community College
- New Mexico State University
- Ohio State University
- Pennsylvania State University
- Quinebaug Valley Community College
- St. Cloud State University
- San Francisco State University
- Shippensburg University
- Sinclair Community College
- The State University of New York
- Tennessee State University
- Towson University
- University of Central Oklahoma
- University of Maryland
- University of Nebraska
- University of Richmond
- University of Tennessee
- University of the Ozarks
- Villa Julie College
- Wright State University

. . . . and many, many more! We would like to say THANK YOU to our loyal adopters who chose *Our Social World* in its first two editions, making it such an overwhelming success. We hope you find the Third Edition Media Update even more exciting.

Instructor Praise for *Our Social World*

"Unlike most textbooks that I have read, the breadth and depth of coverage . . . is very impressive. This text forces the students deep into the topics covered and challenges them to see the interconnectedness of them."
—Keith Kerr, Texas A&M University

"I love the global emphasis, the applied material, and the emphasis on solutions to social problems."
—Gina Carreno, Florida Atlantic University

"So often students ask, 'What can I do with sociology?' Having this applied information interspersed in the text allows them to get answers to that question over and over again."

"Finally, a text that brings sociology to life! . . . This is so well written that I'm not sure the students will even realize they are learning theory!"
—Martha Shockey, St. Louis University

"This is an excellent textbook. It has definitely made life easier, and the ancillary material is extremely helpful."
—Jamie M. Dolan, Carroll College

...y event on the timeline could be placed in more than one category. Some scholars claim that globalization has been happening for a long time, and others say ...has only been happening for a relatively short time. As you read through this timeline, think about how current events happening in your social world are part ...this larger process of global change.

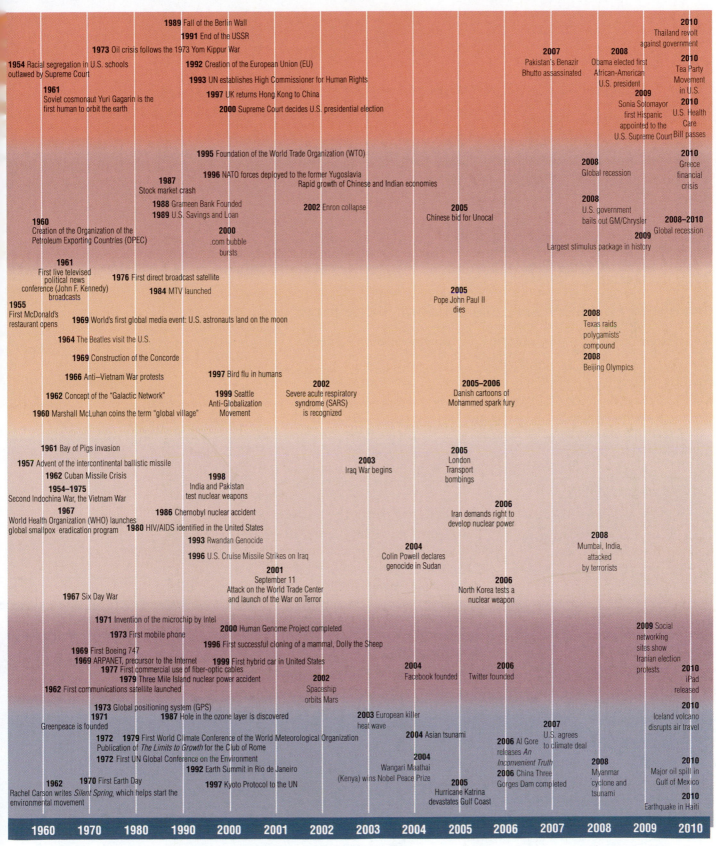

MODERN ERA

THIRD EDITION

OUR SOCIAL WORLD

Introduction to Sociology

Jeanne H. Ballantine | Keith A. Roberts

To the Student

Improve Your Grade With These Student Study Tools!

Our praised student study site at **www.pineforge.com/oswmedia3e** features

- Updated and revised audio episodes of National Public Radio's *This American Life*
- New video links from YouTube, PBS's *Frontline*, and TED
- Updated chapter quizzes, e-flashcards, and Internet exercises
- Updated "Learning From SAGE Journal Articles" features for each chapter with related discussion questions
- New recommended readings
- and much more!

Chapter-opening visual representations of the **Social World Model**—now rendered with particular attention to clarity and simplicity—display the micro, meso, and macro levels for that chapter's topic, with **"Think About It"** questions to focus your thinking on key ideas.

This feature, streamlined for the Third Edition, Media Update provides active learning opportunities to encourage you to further engage with the subject matter.

"Thinking Sociologically" features throughout the text challenge your understanding of core concepts and ask you to apply the material to your own life.

Color bars at the end of each chapter pose important questions for you to consider and provide you with a brief look ahead to what will be covered in the next chapter.

Chapter-ending review material includes **"What Have We Learned?"** features to ensure mastery of each chapter's core material.

Thinking Sociologically

Place the groups to which you belong in a hierarchy from micro, to meso, to macro levels. Note how each social unit and its subunits exist within a larger unit until you reach the level of the entire global community.

Think About It	
Self and Inner Circle	How can sociology help me understand my own life and my sense of self?
Local Community	How can sociology help me to be a more effective employee and citizen in my community?
National Institutions; Complex Organizations; Ethnic Groups	How do sociologists help us understand and even improve our lives in families, classrooms, and health care offices?
National Society	How do national loyalty and national policies affect my life?
Global Community	How might global events affect my life?

The next issue, then, is how we gather data that inform how we understand and influence the social world. When we say we know something about society, how is it that we know?

What is considered evidence in sociology, and what lens (theory) do we use to interpret the data? These are the central issues of the next chapter.

Contributing to Our Social World: What Can We Do?

At the end of this and all subsequent chapters, you will find suggestions for work, service learning, internships, and volunteering that encourage you to apply the ideas discussed in the chapter. Suggestions for Chapter 1 focus on student organizations for sociology majors and nonmajors.

At the Local Level

At the Regional, National, and Global Levels

- *The American Sociological Association (ASA):* This is the leading professional organization of sociologists in the United States. It has several programs and initiatives of special interest to students. Visit the ASA Web site at www.asanet.org, and click on the "Students" link at the top of the page. Read the items and follow the links to additional material on the advantages available to students.

What Have We Learned?

How can sociology help me understand my own life, who I am, and how I relate to others? This question was posed at the beginning of the chapter. Throughout this book you will find ideas and examples that will expand on the *sociological imagination*, illustrating how sociology can help you communicate more effectively and understand your interactions with others.

How do sociologists help us understand and even improve our lives in families, educational systems, or health care systems? Understanding organizations and bureaucracies can make us better family members, more effective citizens, and more adept at getting along with coworkers. As citizens of democracies, we need to understand how to influence our social environments, from city councils, school boards, health care systems, and state legislatures to congressional, presidential, and other organizations.

How do national policies and global events influence my life? As the world changes, we need to be aware of global issues and how they affect us, from our job changes and lost jobs to skills demanded in the 21st century.

We live in a complex social world with many layers of interaction. If we really want to understand our own lives, we need to comprehend the levels of analysis that affect our lives and the connections between those levels. To do so wisely, we need both objective lenses for viewing this

New to This Edition!

- A brand-new feature, "**Engaging Sociology**," appears in every chapter. Each Engaging Sociology exercise encourages active learning, providing students with an opportunity to use sociology to solve a problem or analyze some aspect of society.
- The **Social World Model** has been simplified for greater clarity and increased ease of use.
- "**Think About It**" questions have moved to the first page of each chapter, giving students a framework for understanding what they are about to read.
- Twenty-seven new featured essays and five new "**The Applied Sociologist at Work**" boxes have been added.
- Chapters 2 (**Examining the Social World: How Do We Know?**), 3 (**Society and Culture: Hardware and Software of Our Social World**), and 13 (**Politics: Penetrating Power**) have been reorganized.
- A new section opener in Part IV clearly defines and introduces institutions—a concept that introductory students typically find difficult to understand.
- Dozens of new and updated tables have been added, as have more than 300 new references, more than 120 new photos, and two new Photo Essays.
- The exciting new Interactive eBook version is ideal for students in an online or traditional course who prefer a more contemporary, multimedia-integrated presentation for learning. With the eBook students have immediate access to carefully selected academic and professional handbook articles (placed in margins relevant to the discussion), integrated links to engaging video and audio clips, an interactive glossary, and study tools such as highlighting, book marking, and note-taking. To see a demo visit http://www.pineforge.com/oswmedia3e/demos.

    Your students can get access to this dynamic resource in one of two ways:

1. Order it as a stand-alone access using this ISBN: 978-1-412-99650-1
2. Bundle it with the textbook at no additional cost using this ISBN: 978-1-4129-9946-5

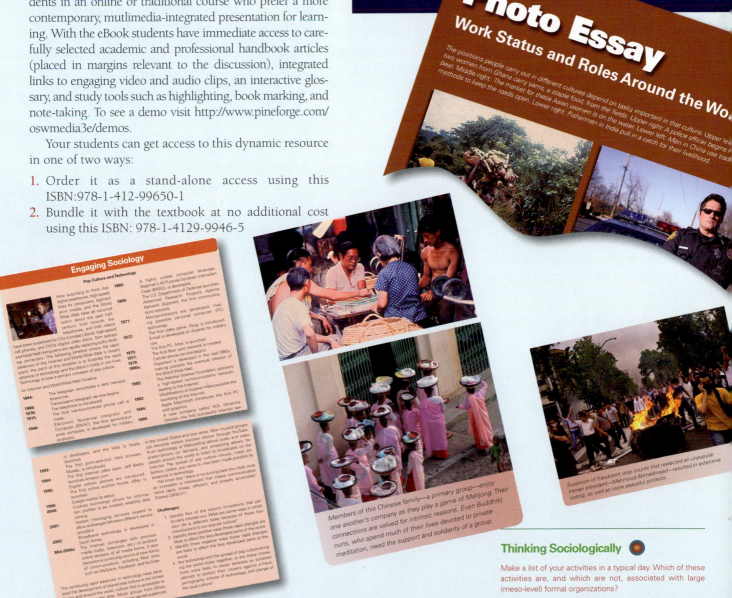

Thinking Sociologically

Make a list of your activities in a typical day. Which of these activities are, and which are not, associated with large (meso-level) formal organizations?

Finally, here is a text that engages students. *Our Social World* uses a unique, dynamic approach to focus on developing sociological skills of analysis rather than simply emphasizing memorization of basic ideas.

The text is both personal and global. It introduces sociology clearly, with the updated Social World Model providing a clear and cohesive framework that lends integration and clarity to the course. With the theme of globalization intertwined throughout the text and an emphasis on deep learning and the applied side of sociology, *Our Social World*, Third Edition Media Update inspires both critical thinking and community participation.

Teach Students the Basics of Sociology via the Newly Simplified, Visually Compelling "Social World Model"

This model, which provides the organizing framework for the text and visually introduces each chapter, illustrates the level of analysis of each topic (from micro to meso to macro), and addresses how each topic is related.

Engage Students . . . With Engaging Sociology

Active learning exercises keep sociology fun, drawing students into an analysis of a relevant table, the application of a population pyramid to the business world, or an interactive survey on the differences in social and cultural capital for first-generation students. This element replaces the last edition's "How Do We Know?" feature, although you will still see your favorite "How Do We Know" examples reprised within "Sociology in Our Social World."

Introduce a Global Perspective, Asking Students to Be Citizens of the World

This text uniquely weaves a truly global perspective into each part of the book, challenging students to think of themselves as global citizens rather than as local citizens looking out at others in the world. "Sociology Around the World" features introduce fascinating historical or global examples of key concepts.

Encourage Deep Learning and Critical Thinking With Uniquely Effective Pedagogy

"Thinking Sociologically" questions, "What Have We Learned?" end-of-chapter summaries, and "Sociology in Our Social World" features encourage critical thought, challenging students to reflect on how the material is relevant and applicable to their lives.

Inspire an Active Engagement in Sociology Using Motivating Chapter Features

"Contributing to Our Social World: What Can We Do?" suggestions include work and volunteer opportunities in which students can apply their newfound sociological knowledge right away. "The Applied Sociologist at Work" boxes—five of which are new to this edition—introduce students to a variety of people with sociological degrees, illuminating post-degree career options.

Sociology Around the World

The McDonaldization of Society

The process of rationalization described by Max Weber—the attempt to reach maximum bureaucratic efficiency—comes in a new modern version, expanded and streamlined, as exemplified by the fast-food restaurant business and the chain "box" stores found around the world. Efficient, rational, predictable sameness is sweeping the world—from diet centers such as NutriSystem to 7-Eleven and from Wal-Mart to Gap clothing stores with their look-alike layouts. Most major world cities feature McDonald's or Kentucky Fried Chicken in the traditional main plazas or train stations for the flustered foreigners and curious native consumers.

The McDonaldization of society, as George Ritzer (2008) calls it, refers to several trends: First, *efficiency* is maximized by the sameness—same store plans, same mass-produced items, same procedures. Second is *predictability*, the knowledge that each hamburger or piece of ___ will be the same, leaving nothing to chance. Third, ___ *calculated* so that the organization can ensure ___ standard—every burger ___

is taking over individual creativity and human interactions. The mom-and-pop grocery, bed and breakfasts, and local craft or clothing shops are rapidly becoming a thing of the past, giving way to the McClones. This process of the McDonaldization of society, meaning principles of efficiency and rationalization exemplified by fast-food chains, is coming to dominate more and more sectors of our social world (Ritzer 1998, 2004, 2008). While there are aspects of this predictability that we all like, there is also a loss of the uniqueness and local flavor that individual entrepreneurs bring to a community.

To try to re-create this culture, Ritzer suggests, there is a movement toward "Starbuckization." Starbucks is unique because of its aesthetic contribution. Starbucks makes customers feel like they are purchasing a cultural product along with their coffee. This culture, however, is as controlled as any other McDonaldized endeavor, making Starbuck ___ ___ ___ ___ predecessors.

Sociology in Our Social World

Bowling Alone Versus Contributing to Your Social World

To join or not to join—that is a question many college students must decide. They are torn between spending time with their computers and video games and joining groups, even doing volunteer work in the community or working on a political campaign. Research on joining organized groups versus engaging in individual activities gives us some insight into choices and the consequences of these choices.

According to one study of group activities, bowling leagues have experienced significant declines in membership in recent years. Yet more people in the United ___ than vote, often enjoying the sport as indi- ___ in organized groups. For soc ___

In a separate study, a team of sociologists from the University of California, Berkeley, also analyzed the relationship between individualism and a sense of community. They concluded that individualism is problematic for Americans living in an interdependent world (Bellah, Madsen, Sullivan, Swidler, and Tipton 1996). As individuals lose contact with others, they face private problems alone. What the United States needs, according to the authors of this study, is a greater sense of community to give individuals a feeling of belonging, to link the micro and macro levels of the social ___ (Bellah ___

What Have We Learned?

Our social lives are lived in small groups and personal networks. The scope of those networks has broadened with the increased complexity of societies and includes the global social world. Indeed, it is easy not to recognize how far our networks reach, even to the global level. Although some of our social experiences are informal (unstructured), we are also profoundly affected by another phenomenon of the past three centuries—highly structured bureaucracies. As a result of both, the intimate experiences of our personal lives are far more extensively linked to meso- and macro-level events and to people and places on the other side of the globe than was true for our parents' generation. If we hope to understand our lives, we must understand this broad context. ___ ___ have been possible to live without global ___ ___ ___ ___ systems several ___

- Many of our behaviors are shaped by the statuses (se ___ positions) we hold and the roles (expectations as ___ ated with a status) we play. However, our multiple-s ___ occupancy can create role conflicts (between the r ___ two statuses) and role strains (between the role ex ___ tions of a single status). (See pp. 145–146.)

- When the norms of behavior are unclear, we may ___ ence anomie (normlessness), and this ambiguity ___ mises our sense of belonging and is linked to the ___ for individuals performing one of the most pe ___ acts—suicide. (See pp. 147–148.)

- Various types of groups affect our behavior— ___

Contributing to Our Social World: What Can We Do?

At the Local Level

Tutoring and mentoring: Most campuses have programs that are designed to help students who are struggling with their studies. Contact the Student Affairs Office and arrange to observe and/or volunteer in a program. Helping students build their *social capital*, which includes their knowledge of ways to obtain the help they need, can increase their chances of success.

At the Organizational or Institutional Level

The social capital theory can also be applied to meso-level ___ ___ organizations:

At the National or Global Level

- *The Anti-Defamation League, the Arab Anti-Defa* ___ *League, and the National Association for the Advance* ___ *Colored People:* These organizations often use vol ___ or interns and can provide you with the opport ___ learn about the extent to which social contacts ___ works play a role in managing social conflict.

- Organize or contribute to a micro-credit organ ___ help women in countries of the developing wo ___

Ancillaries

Compatible With Blackboard and Other Course Management Systems

To facilitate the use of the Third Edition Media Update of *Our Social World* with Blackboard and other course management platforms, SAGE and Pine Forge Press provide the following teaching and learning ancillaries at **www.pineforge.com/oswmedia3e:**

A password-protected **Instructor Teaching Site**

An open-access **Student Study Site**

Instructor Teaching Site

The Instructor Teaching Site features a variety of popular and effective teaching aids, including

Chapter Outlines: Carefully crafted outlines follow the structure of each chapter, providing an essential reference and teaching tool.

Chapter Exercises and Activities: These include lively and stimulating ideas for use both in and out of class to reinforce active learning. The activities apply to individual or group projects.

Course Syllabi: Sample syllabi—for semester, quarter, and online classes—provide suggested models for creating the syllabus for your course.

Web Resources: These links to relevant websites direct both instructors and students to additional resources for further research on important chapter topics.

Photographic Essay Projects: Unique assignments encourage students to observe and evaluate social issues in creative ways.

SAGE Journal Articles: A "Learning From SAGE Journal Articles" feature provides access to recent, relevant full-text articles from SAGE's leading research journals. Each article supports and expands on the concepts presented in the chapter. Also provided are discussion questions to focus and guide student interpretation.

Video Resources: Carefully selected, web-based video resources feature relevant interviews, lectures, personal stories, inquiries, and other content for use in independent or classroom-based explorations of key topics. Discussion questions are provided to guide interpretation of material. The site also includes new video links for YouTube and for PBS's *Frontline.*

Test Bank (Word): This Word test bank offers a diverse set of multiple-choice, true/false, short-answer, and essay test questions and answers for every chapter to aid instructors in assessing students' progress and understanding.

Test Bank (Diploma): This electronic test bank using Diploma software is available for use with a PC or Mac. The test bank offers a diverse set of multiple-choice, true/false, short-answer, and essay test questions and answers for every chapter to aid instructors in assessing students' progress and understanding.

PowerPoint Slides: Chapter-specific slide presentations offer assistance with lecture and review preparation by highlighting essential content, features, and artwork from the book.

Teaching Tips: Teaching Tips provide suggestions and resources for using the Social World Model for traditional and online Introduction to Sociology courses.

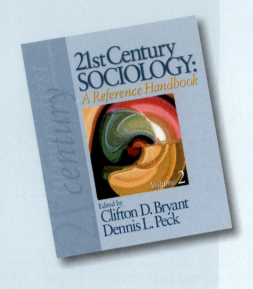

Additional Resource: Adopters will receive free online access to Bryant's *21st Century Sociology: A Reference Handbook* (SAGE, ©2007), to help make teaching globally even more impactful. Contact Customer Care at 1-800-818-SAGE (7243) for more information on this extraordinary teaching aid.

Student Study Site

To further enhance students' understanding of and interest in the course material, we have created a Student Study Site, which includes

Podcasts and Audio Clips: Each chapter includes links to podcasts, which cover important topics and are designed to supplement key points within the text. The site also includes updated and revised audio episodes of National Public Radio's *This American Life*.

Encyclopedia and Handbook Resources: Expanded study site resources include new encyclopedia and handbook material that is relevant to the topics in the book.

Video Resources: Carefully selected, web-based video resources feature relevant interviews, lectures, personal stories, inquiries, and other content for use in independent or classroom-based explorations of key topics. Discussion questions are provided to guide interpretation of material. The site includes new video links for YouTube and for PBS's *Frontline*.

Web Quizzes: Self-quizzes allow students to independently assess their progress in learning course material.

Web Exercises and Activities: These links direct both instructors and students to useful and current web resources, as well as creative activities to extend and reinforce learning.

E-flashcards: This study tool reinforces student understanding of key terms and concepts that have been outlined in the chapters.

SAGE Journal Articles: A "Learning From SAGE Journal Articles" feature provides access to recent, relevant full-text articles from SAGE's leading research journals. Each article supports and expands on the concepts presented in the chapter. Discussion questions focus and guide student interpretation.

Recommended Readings: Interesting and relevant supplements provide a jumping-off point for course assignments, papers, research, group work, and class discussion.

and much more!

SAGE and Pine Forge Press Teaching Innovations and Professional Development Awards Fund

Partly inspired by the authors of *Our Social World*, SAGE and its sociology imprint, Pine Forge Press, have created this awards fund to help graduate students and pretenure faculty attend the annual American Sociological Association preconference, hosted by the Section on Teaching and Learning in Sociology, with grants of approximately $500 per recipient. In its first 4 years there have been 72 recipients selected from more than 320 applicants. In 2010, 19 people were funded. In 2008, the ASA's Section on Teaching and Learning in Sociology awarded SAGE and Pine Forge Press with a glass plaque to honor the publisher and its participating authors and editors—including the authors of *Our Social World*—for their commitment to excellence in teaching.

About the Authors

Jeanne H. Ballantine (far right) is Professor of Sociology at Wright State University, a state university of about 17,000 students in Ohio. She has

also taught at several 4-year colleges, including an "alternative" college and a traditionally Black college, and at international programs in universities abroad. She has been teaching introductory sociology for more than 30 years with a mission to introduce the uninitiated to the field and to help students see the usefulness and value in sociology. She has been active in the teaching movement, shaping curriculum, writing and presenting research on teaching, and offering workshops and consulting in regional, national, and international forums. She is a Fulbright Senior Scholar and serves as a Departmental Resources Group consultant and evaluator.

She has written several textbooks, all with the goal of reaching the student audience. As the original director of the Center for Teaching and Learning at Wright State University, she scoured the literature on student learning and served as a mentor to teachers in a wide variety of disciplines. Local, regional, and national organizations have honored her for her teaching and for her contributions to helping others become effective teachers. In 1986, the American Sociological Association's Section on Undergraduate Education (now called the Section on Teaching and Learning in Sociology) recognized her with the Hans O. Mauksch Award for Distinguished Contributions to Teaching of Sociology. In 2004, she was honored by the American Sociological Association with its Distinguished Contributions to Teaching Award.

Keith A. Roberts (top left) is Professor of Sociology at Hanover College, a private liberal arts college of about 1,100 students in Indiana. He has

been teaching introductory sociology for more than 30 years with a passion for active learning strategies and a focus on "deep learning" by students that transforms the way they see the world. Prior to teaching at Hanover, he taught at a 2-year regional campus of a large university.

He has been active in the teaching movement, writing on teaching and serving as a consultant to sociology departments across the country in his capacity as a member of the American Sociological Association Departmental Resources Group. He has written a very popular textbook in the sociology of religion, has coauthored a book on writing in the undergraduate curriculum, and annually runs workshops for high school sociology teachers. He has chaired the Selection Committee for the SAGE/Pine Forge Innovations and Professional Development Awards since the program's inception. He has been honored for his teaching and teaching-related work at local, state, regional, and national levels. The American Sociological Association's Section on Teaching and Learning awarded him the Hans O. Mauksch Award for Distinguished Contributions to Teaching of Sociology in 2000. He was honored with the American Sociological Association's Distinguished Contributions to Teaching Award in 2010.

2004 AMERICAN SOCIOLOGICAL ASSOCIATION

DISTINGUISHED CONTRIBUTIONS TO TEACHING AWARD

2010 AMERICAN SOCIOLOGICAL ASSOCIATION

DISTINGUISHED CONTRIBUTIONS TO TEACHING AWARD

Visit www.pineforge.com for valuable
Intro to Sociology supplemental texts
1-800-818-SAGE (7243)
www.pineforge.com

Writing this book has been a labor of love,

for we are both passionate about sociology and about teaching sociology.

Still, this labor of love has sometimes come at a steep price to others we love.

Thus, we dedicate this book to two saints of patience, support, and understanding,

Hardy Ballantine

and

Judy Roberts,

our supportive and beloved spouses,

and to our children, who have shared their educational trials and triumphs,

giving us food for thought as we wrote.

media edition

OUR SOCIAL WORLD
Introduction to Sociology
THIRD EDITION

Jeanne H. Ballantine | Keith A. Roberts
Wright State University | *Hanover College*

Los Angeles | London | New Delhi
Singapore | Washington DC

For information:

Pine Forge Press
An Imprint of SAGE Publications, Inc.
2455 Teller Road
Thousand Oaks, California 91320
E-mail: order@sagepub.com

SAGE Publications Ltd.
1 Oliver's Yard
55 City Road
London EC1Y 1SP
United Kingdom

SAGE Publications India Pvt. Ltd.
B 1/I 1 Mohan Cooperative Industrial Area
Mathura Road, New Delhi 110 044
India

SAGE Publications Asia-Pacific Pte. Ltd.
33 Pekin Street #02-01
Far East Square
Singapore 048763

Printed in Canada

A catalog record of this book is available from the Library of Congress.

978-1-4129-9298-5

This book is printed on acid-free paper.

11   12   13   14   15   10   9   8   7   6   5   4   3   2   1

Acquisitions Editor:	David Repetto
Associate Editor:	Julie Nemer
Assistant Editor:	Eve Oettinger
Editorial Assistant:	Maggie Stanley
Production Editor:	Eric Garner
Copy Editor:	QuADS Prepress (P) Ltd.
Typesetter:	C&M Digitals (P) Ltd.
Proofreader:	Theresa Kay
Indexer:	Molly Hall
Cover Designer:	Edgar Abarca
Marketing Manager:	Erica DeLuca
Permissions Editor:	Karen Ehrmann

Brief Contents

Detailed Contents

Chapter 12 • Religion: The Meaning of Sacred Meaning   390

Preface

To Our Readers

This book asks you to think outside the box. Why? The best way to become a more interesting person, to grow beyond the old familiar thoughts and behaviors, and to make life exciting is to explore new ways to view things. The world in which we live is intensely personal and individual in nature, with much of our social interaction occurring in intimate groups of friends and family. Our most intense emotions and most meaningful links to others are at this "micro" level of social life.

However, these intimate micro-level links in our lives are influenced by larger social structures and global trends. At the start of the second decade of the 21st century, technological advances make it possible to connect with the farthest corners of the world. Multinational corporations cross national boundaries, form new economic and political unions, and change job opportunities of people everywhere. Some groups embrace the changes, while others try to protect their members from the rapid changes that threaten to disrupt their traditional lives. Even our most personal relationships or what we eat tonight may be shaped by events on the other side of the continent or the globe. From the news headlines to family and peer interactions, we confront sociological issues daily. The task of this book and of your instructor is to help you see world events and your personal lives from a sociological perspective. Unless you learn how to look at our social world with an analytical lens, many of its most intriguing features will be missed.

The social world you face in the job markets of the 21st century is influenced by changes and forces that are easy to miss. Like the wind, which can do damage even if the air is unseen, social structures are themselves so taken for granted that it is easy to miss seeing them. However, their effects can be readily identified. Sociology provides new perspectives, helping students to understand their families, their work lives, their leisure, and their place in a diverse and changing world.

A few of you will probably become sociology majors. Others will find the subject matter of this course relevant to your personal and professional lives. Some of the reasons the authors of this book and your own professor chose to study sociology many years ago are the factors that inspire undergraduates today to choose a major in sociology: learning about the social world from a new perspective; working with people and groups; developing knowledge, inquiry, and interpersonal skills; and learning about social life, from small groups to global social systems. As the broadest of the social sciences, sociology has a never-ending array of fascinating subjects to study. This book touches only the surface of what the field has to offer and the exciting things you can do with this knowledge. These same considerations motivated us and gave us direction in writing this introductory book.

Where This Book Is Headed

A well-constructed course, like an effective essay, needs to be organized around a central question, one that spawns other subsidiary questions and intrigues the participants. The problem with introductory courses in many disciplines is that there is no central question and thus no coherence to the course. They have more of a flavor-of-the-week approach (a different topic each week), with no attempt at integration. We have tried to correct that problem in this text.

The Social World Model

For you to understand sociology as an integrated whole rather than a set of separate chapters in a book, we have organized the chapters in this book around the *social world model*: a conceptual model that demonstrates the relationships between individuals (micro level); organizations, institutions, and subcultures (meso level); and societies and global structures (macro levels of analysis). At the beginning of each chapter, a visual diagram of the model will illustrate this idea as it relates to the topic of that chapter, including how issues related to the topic have implications at various levels of analysis in the social world, influencing and being affected by other parts of society. No aspect of society exists in a vacuum. On the other hand, this model does not assume that everyone always gets along or that relationships are always harmonious or supportive. Sometimes, different parts of the society are in competition for resources, and intense conflict and hostility may be generated.

This micro- to macro-level analysis is a central concept in the discipline of sociology. Many instructors seek first and foremost to help students develop a *sociological imagination*, an ability to see the complex links between various levels of the social system. This is a key goal of this book. Within a few months, you may not remember all the specific concepts or terms that have been introduced, but if the way you see the world has been transformed during this course, a key element of deep learning has been accomplished. Learning to see things from alternative perspectives is a precondition for critical thinking. This entire book attempts to help you recognize connections between your personal experiences and problems and larger social forces of society. You will be learning to take a new perspective on the social world in which you live.

A key element of that social world is diversity. We live in societies in which there are people who differ in a host of ways: ethnicity, socioeconomic status, religious background, political persuasion, gender, sexual orientation, and so forth. Diversity is a blessing in many ways to a society because the most productive and creative organizations and societies are those that are highly diverse. This is the case because people with different backgrounds solve problems in very different ways. When people with such divergences come together, the outcome of their problem solving can create new solutions to vexing problems. However, diversity often creates challenges as well. Misunderstanding and "we" versus "they" thinking can divide people. These issues will be explored throughout this book. We now live in a global village, and in this book, you will learn something about how people on the other side of the village live and view the world.

We hope you enjoy the book and get as enthralled with sociology as we are. It genuinely is a fascinating field of study.

Jeanne H. Ballantine
Wright State University

Keith A. Roberts
Hanover College

Your authors—teaching "outside the box."

Instructors

How to Make This Book Work for You

Special features woven throughout each chapter support the theme of the book. These will help students comprehend and apply the material and make the material more understandable and interesting. These features are also designed to facilitate deep learning, to help students move beyond rote memorization, and increase their ability to analyze and evaluate information.

For students to understand both the comparative global theme and sociology as an integrated whole rather than as a set of separate chapters in a book, we have organized the chapters in this book around the *social world model:* a conceptual model that demonstrates the relationships between individuals (micro level); organizations, institutions, and subcultures (meso level); and societies and global structures (macro levels of analysis). At the beginning of each chapter, a visual diagram of the model will illustrate this idea as it relates to the topic of that chapter, including how issues related to the topic have implications at various levels of analysis in the social world.

"Think About It"

So that students can become curious, active readers, we have posed questions at the outset of each chapter that we hope are relevant to everyday life, but that are also tied to the micro-meso-macro levels of analysis that serve as the theme of the book. The purpose is to transform students from passive readers who run their eyes across the words into curious active readers who read to answer a question and to be reflective. Active or deep reading is key to comprehension and retention of reading material (Roberts and Roberts 2008). Instructors can also use this feature to encourage students to think critically about the implications of what they have read. Instructors might want to ask students to write a paragraph about one of these questions before coming to class each day. These questions might also provide the basis for in-class discussions.

Students should be encouraged to start each chapter by reading and thinking about these questions, looking at the topics in the chapter, and asking some questions of their own. This will mean that they are more likely to stay focused, remember the material long-term, and be able to apply it to their own lives.

A Global Perspective and the Social World Model

We are part of an ever-shrinking world, a global village. What happens in distant countries is not only news the same day but also affects relatives living in other countries, the cost of goods, work and travel possibilities, and the balance of power in the world. Instead of simply including cross-cultural examples of strange and different peoples, this book incorporates a global perspective throughout. This is done so that students can see not only how others live different but rewarding lives but also the connections between others' lives and their own. Students will need to think and relate to the world globally in future roles as workers, travelers, and global citizens. Our analysis illustrates the interconnections of the world's societies and their political and economic systems and demonstrates that what happens in one part of the world affects others. For instance, if a major company in your area moves much of its operations to another country with cheaper labor, jobs are lost, and the local economy is hurt. Likewise, this new company in a developing country of the world may contribute to deterioration of the local culture as the people adapt to the lifestyles and cultures of Western societies.

This global approach attempts to instill interest, understanding, and respect for different groups of people and their lifestyles. Race, class, and gender are an integral part of understanding the diverse social world, and these features of social life have global implications. The comparative global theme is carried throughout the book in headings and written text, in examples, and in boxes and selection of photos. As students read this book, they should continually think about how the experiences in their private world are influenced by and may influence events at other levels: the community, organizations and institutions, the nation, and the world.

Opening Vignettes

Chapters typically open with an illustration relevant to the chapter content. For instance, in Chapter 2, "Examining the Social World," the case of Hector, a Brazilian teenager living in poverty in a *favela*, is used to illustrate research methods and theory throughout the chapter. Chapter 3, "Society and Culture," begins with scenarios of mealtime scenes from around the world to illustrate the variations in human cultures. In Chapter 4, "Socialization," the case of an immigrant child attending school in his new society and facing a new learning environment is discussed. Chapter 8 begins with an actual account of a girl who is among the 27 million slaves in the modern world. These vignettes are meant to interest students in the upcoming subject matter by helping them relate to a personalized story. In several cases, the vignettes serve as illustrations throughout the chapters.

"Thinking Sociologically" Questions

Following major topics, students will find questions that ask them to think critically and apply the material just read to some aspect of their lives or the social world. The purpose of this feature is to encourage students to apply the ideas and concepts in the text to their lives and to develop critical thinking skills. These questions can be the basis for in-class discussions and can be assigned as questions to start interesting conversations with friends and families to learn how the topics relate to their own lives. Note that some of these questions have a miniature icon—a small version of the chapter-opening model—signifying that these questions reinforce the theme of micro, meso, and macro levels of social influence.

Key Concepts, Examples, and Writing Style

Key terms that are defined and illustrated within the running narrative appear in bold. Other terms that are defined but are of less significance are italicized. The text is rich in examples that bring sociological concepts to life for student readers. Each chapter has been student tested for readability. Both students and reviewers describe the writing style as reader friendly, often fascinating, and accessible, but not watered down.

Special Features

Although there are numerous examples throughout the book, featured inserts provide more in-depth illustrations of the usefulness of the sociological perspective to understand world situations or events with direct relevance to a student's life. There are four kinds of special features. "Sociology in Our Social World" features focus on a sociological issue or story, often with policy implications. "Sociology Around the World" takes readers to another part of the globe to explore how things are different (or how they are the same) from what they might experience in their own lives. "The Applied Sociologist at Work" features appear in many chapters and examine profiles of contemporary sociologists who are working in the field. This helps students grasp what sociologists can actually do with sociology. The most innovative new feature in this edition is called "Engaging Sociology"—and the double entendre is intentional. We want students to think of sociology as engaging and fun, and these features are designed to engage—to draw students into active analysis of a table, application of a population pyramid to the business world, or taking a survey to understand why differences in social and cultural capital make first-generation students feel alienated on a college campus.

Technology and Society

Nearly every chapter examines the issues of technology as they would be relevant to that chapter. We have especially sought out materials that have to do with the Internet and with communications technology.

Social Policy and Becoming an Active Citizen

Most chapters include discussion of some social policy issues: an effort to address the concerns about public sociology and the relevance of sociological findings to current social debates. Furthermore, because students sometimes feel helpless to know what to do about social issues that concern them at macro and meso levels, we have concluded every chapter with a few ideas about how they might become involved as active citizens, even as undergraduate students. Suggestions in the "Contributing to Your Social World: What Can We Do?" section may be assigned as service learning or term projects or simply used as suggestions for ways students can get involved on their own time.

Summary Sections

Each chapter ends with review material: a "What Have We Learned?" feature that includes a "Key Points" bulleted summary of the chapter's core material.

A Little (Teaching) Help From Our Friends

Whether the instructor is new to teaching or an experienced professor, there are some valuable ideas that can help invigorate and energize the classroom. A substantial literature on teaching methodology tells us that student involvement is key to the learning process. Built into this book are discussion questions and projects that students can report on in class. In addition, there are a number of suggestions in the supplements and teaching aids for active learning in large or small classes.

Instructor Teaching Site

The **Instructor Teaching Site** contains a number of helpful teaching aids, from goals and objectives for chapters to classroom lecture ideas, active learning projects, collaborative learning suggestions, and options for evaluating students. Suggestions for the use of visual materials—videos, transparencies, and multimedia—are also included.

Test Bank

Compatible with both PC and Mac computers, the computerized test bank allows for easy question sorting and exam creation. It includes multiple-choice, true/false, short-answer, and essay questions. In keeping with the deep learning thrust of this book, however, the test questions will have more emphasis on application skills rather than rote memorization questions—the latter a too common characteristic of test banks.

PowerPoint Slides

Because visuals are an important addition to classroom lectures, recognizing the varying learning styles of students, PowerPoint slides that include lecture outlines and relevant tables, maps, diagrams, pictures, and short quotes for instructors to use in the classroom are included on the Instructor Teaching Site.

Student Study Site

To further enhance students' understanding of and interest in the material, we have created a student study site to accompany the text. This site includes the following:

- *Flashcards* that allow for easy reviewing of key terms and concepts;
- *Self-quizzes* that can be used to check students' understanding of the material or can be sent in to the professor for a grade;
- *Web exercises* that direct students to various sites on the web and ask them to apply their knowledge to a particular topic;
- *This American Life* radio segments that illustrate each chapter's concepts;
- *"Learning From Journal Articles"* features that include original research from SAGE journal articles and teach students how to read and analyze a journal article;
- A list of *recommended websites* that students can explore for research or their own edification;
- Information on how to create *video and photo essays*;
- and much more!

Visit **www.pineforge.com/oswmedia3e** to view the site.

What Is New in the Third Edition Media Update?

There are 30 new boxed features in this book, including the innovative "Engaging Sociology" feature that was described earlier. Faculty members who have test-driven the "Engaging Sociology" features in class have found them highly engaging to students and deeply enhancing to the learning-teaching process. The one boxed feature that we heard was sometimes less effective for beginning sociology students was the "How Do We Know?" feature. So "Engaging Sociology" replaces that. The content of a few of the most effective "How Do We Know?" features were kept and converted into "Sociology in Our Social World" features. There are also five new "Applied Sociologists at Work"—one such feature per chapter.

Three chapters were substantially reorganized based on feedback from reviewers—Chapter 2 (Examining the Social World), Chapter 3 (Society and Culture), and Chapter 13 (Politics and Economics). Although Chapter 13 still has more focus on politics than economics (with economics discussed in many other chapters—such as Chapter 7 on socioeconomic inequality), the discussion of economics was expanded and more fully integrated into the chapter.

We have also made hundreds of other changes—adding new information, updating data, and in some cases changing topics within chapters. For example, this third edition media update has 315 entirely new references and 120 new photos. We have added a section opener that more clearly presents "institutions"—having discovered that our first and second editions, and almost all other introductory texts, have done a notoriously poor job of defining institutions.

The core elements of the book—with the unifying theme and the social world model at the beginning of every chapter—have not changed. For greater simplicity in understanding the "Social World Model," the "Think About It" questions were moved to the first page of the chapter rather than on the opening page.

Finally, although we had been told that the writing was extraordinarily readable, we have tried to simplify sentence structure in a number of places. In short, we have tried to respond to what we heard from all of you—both students and instructors (and yes, we *do* hear from students)—to make this book more engaging and more accessible.

A Personal Note to the Instructor

We probably share many of the same reasons for choosing sociology as our careers. Our students also share these reasons for finding sociology a fascinating and useful subject: learning about the social world from a new perspective; working with people and groups; developing a range of knowledge, inquiry, and interpersonal skills; and learning the broad and interesting subject matter of sociology, from small groups to societies. In this book, we try to share our own enthusiasm for the subject with students. The following explains what we believe to be unique features of this book and some of our goals and methods for sharing sociology. We hope you share our ideas and find this book helps you meet your teaching and learning goals.

What Is Distinctive About This Book?

What is truly distinctive about this book? This is a text that tries to break the mold of the typical textbook synthesis, the cross between an encyclopedia and a dictionary. *Our Social World* is a unique course text that is *a coherent essay on the sociological imagination—understood globally*. We attempt to radically change the feel of the introductory book by emphasizing coherence, an integrating theme, and current knowledge about learning and teaching, but we also present much traditional content. Instructors will not have to throw out the well-honed syllabus and begin from scratch, but they can refocus each unit so it stresses understanding of micro-level personal troubles within the macro-level public issues framework. Indeed, in this book, we make clear that the public issues must be understood as global in nature.

Here is a text that engages students. *They* say so! From class testing, we know that the writing style, structure of chapters and sections, the "Thinking Sociologically" features, the wealth of examples, and other instructional aids help students stay focused, think about the material, and apply it to their lives. It neither bores them nor insults their intelligence. It focuses on deep learning rather than memorization. It develops sociological skills of analysis rather than emphasizing memorization of vocabulary. Key concepts and terms are introduced but only in the service of a larger focus on the sociological imagination. The text is both personal and global. It speaks to sociology as a science as well as addressing applied aspects of sociology. It has a theme that provides integration of topics as it introduces the discipline. This text is an analytical essay, not a disconnected encyclopedia.

As one of our reviewers noted,

Unlike most textbooks I have read, the breadth and depth of coverage in this one is very impressive. It challenges the student with college-level reading. Too many textbooks seem to write on a high-school level and give only passing treatment to most of the topics, writing in nugget-sized blocks. More than a single definition and a few sentences of support, the text forces the student deep into the topics covered and challenges them to see interconnections.

Normally, the global-perspective angle within textbooks, which seemed to grow in popularity in the mid- to late 1990s, was implemented by using brief and exotic examples to show differences between societies—a purely comparative approach rather than a globalization treatment. They gave, and still give to a large extent, a token nod to diversity. This textbook, however, forces the student to take a broader look at similarities and differences in social institutions around the world, and structures and processes operating in all cultures and societies.

So our focus in this book is on deep learning, especially expansion of students' ability to role-take or "perspective-take." Deep learning goes beyond the content of concepts and terms and cultivates the habits of thinking that allow one to think critically. Being able to see things from the perspective of others is essential to doing sociology, but it is also indispensible to seeing weaknesses in various theories or recognizing blind spots in a point of view. Using the sociological imagination is one dimension of role-taking because it requires a step back from the typical micro-level understanding of life's events and fosters a new comprehension of how meso- and macro-level forces—even global ones—can shape the individual's life. Enhancement of role-taking ability is at the core of this book because it is a *prerequisite* for deep learning in sociology. This may sound daunting for some student audiences, but we have found that instructors at every kind of institution have had great success with the book because of the writing style and instructional tools used throughout.

We have made some strategic decisions based on these principles of learning and teaching. We have focused much of the book on higher-order thinking skills rather than memorization and regurgitation. We want students to learn to think sociologically: to apply, analyze, synthesize, evaluate, and comprehend the interconnections of the world through a globally informed sociological imagination. However, we think it is also essential to do this with an understanding of how students learn.

Many introductory-level books offer several theories and then provide a critique of the theory. The idea is to teach critical thinking. We have purposefully refrained from extensive critique of theory (although some does occur) for several reasons. First, providing critique to beginning-level students does not really teach critical thinking. It trains them to memorize someone else's critique. Furthermore, it simply confuses many of them, leaving students with the feeling that sociology is really just contradictory ideas, and the discipline really does not have anything firm to offer. Teaching critical thinking needs to be done in stages, and it needs to take into account the building steps that occur before effective critique is possible. That is why we focus on the concept of deep learning. We are working toward building the foundations that are necessary for sophisticated critical thought at upper levels in the curriculum.

Therefore, in this beginning-level text, we have attempted to focus on a central higher order or deep learning skill—synthesis. Undergraduate students need to grasp this before they can fully engage in evaluation. Deep learning involves understanding of complexity, and some aspects of complexity need to be taught at advanced levels. While students at the introductory level are often capable of synthesis, complex evaluation requires some foundational skills. Thus, we offer contrasting theories in this text, and rather than telling what is wrong with each one, we encourage students through "Thinking Sociologically" features to analyze the use of each and to focus on honing synthesis and comparison skills.

Finally, research tells us that learning becomes embedded in memory and becomes long-lasting only if it is related to something that learners already know. If they memorize terms but have no unifying framework to which they can attach those ideas, the memory will not last until the end of the course, let alone until the next higher-level course. In this text, each chapter is tied to the social world model that

is core to sociological thinking. At the end of a course using this book, we believe that students will be able to explain coherently what sociology is and construct an effective essay about what they have learned from the course as a whole. Learning to develop and defend a thesis, with supporting logic and evidence, is another component of deep learning. A text that is mostly a dictionary does not enhance that kind of cognitive skill.

Organization and Coverage

Reminiscent of some packaged international tours, in which the travelers figure that "it is Day 7, so this must be Paris," many introductory courses seem to operate on the principle that it is Week 4 so this must be deviance week. Students do not sense any integration, and at the end of the course, they have trouble remembering specific topics. This book is different. A major goal of the book is to show the integration between topics in sociology and between parts of the social world. The idea is for students to grasp the concept of the interrelated world. A change in one part of the social world affects all others, sometimes in ways that are mutually supportive and sometimes in ways that create intense conflict.

Although the topics are familiar, the textbook is organized around levels of analysis, explained through the social world model. This perspective leads naturally to a comparative approach and discussions of diversity and inequality.

Each chapter represents a part of the social world structure (society, organizations and groups, and institutions) or a process in the social world (socialization, stratification, and change). Chapter order and links between chapters clarify this idea. Part I (Chapters 1 and 2) introduces the student to the sociological perspective and tools of the sociologist: theory and methods. Part II examines "Social Structure, Processes, and Control," exploring especially processes such as socialization, interaction, and networks. Part III covers the core issue of inequality in society, with emphasis on class, race or ethnicity, and gender. Part IV turns to the structural dimensions of society, as represented in institutions. Rather than trying to be all-encompassing, we examine family, education, religion, politics, economics, and medicine to help students understand how structures affect their lives. We do not cover sports, science, mass media, or the military in separate chapters, but aspects of emerging institutions are woven into many chapters. It was a painful decision to leave any institution out but attention to length and cost required hard choices. Part V turns to social dynamics: How societies change. Population patterns, urbanization and environmental issues, social movements, technology, and other aspects of change are included.

As instructors and authors, we value books that provide students with a well-rounded overview of approaches to the field. Therefore, this book takes an eclectic theoretical approach, drawing on the best insights of various theories and stressing that multiple perspectives enrich our understanding. We give attention to most major theoretical perspectives in sociology: structural-functional and conflict theories at the meso and macro levels of analysis and symbolic interaction and rational choice theories at the micro to meso levels of analysis. Feminist, postmodern, and ecological theories are discussed where relevant to specific topics. Each of these is integrated into the broad social world model, which stresses development of a sociological imagination.

The book includes 16 chapters plus additional online materials, written to fit into a semester or quarter system. It allows instructors to use the chapters in order, or to alter the order, because each chapter is tied into others through the social world model. We strongly recommend that Chapter 1 be used early in the course because it introduces the integrating model and explains the theme. Also, if any institutions chapters are used, the four-page section opener on "Institutions" may be useful to include as well. Otherwise, the book has been designed for flexible use. Instructors may also want to supplement the core book with other materials, such as those suggested on the Instructor Teaching Site. While covering all the key topics in introductory sociology, the cost and size of a midsized book allows for this flexibility. Indeed, for a colorful introductory-level text, the cost of this book is remarkably low—roughly half the cost of some other very popular introductory texts.

A Unique Program Supporting Teaching of Sociology

There is one more way in which *Our Social World* has been unique among introductory sociology textbooks. In 2007, the authors teamed with SAGE/Pine Forge Press to start a new program to benefit the entire discipline. Using royalties from *Our Social World*, there is a new award program called the SAGE/Pine Forge Teaching Innovations & Professional Development Award. It is designed to prepare a new generation of scholars within the teaching movement in sociology. People in their early-career stages (graduate students, assistant professors, newer PhDs) can be reimbursed $500 each for expenses entailed while attending the day-long American Sociological Association (ASA) Section on Teaching and Learning's preconference workshop. The workshop is the day before ASA meetings. In 2007, 13 young scholars—graduate students or untenured faculty members—received this award and benefited from an extraordinary workshop on learning and teaching. Joined by other SAGE/Pine Forge authors in subsequent years, 72 people had benefited by 2010 because of donations from royalties and the generosity of SAGE/Pine Forge: 19 in 2008, 21 in 2009, and 19 in 2010.

We hope you find this book engaging. If you have questions or comments, please contact us.

Jeanne H. Ballantine
Wright State University

Keith A. Roberts
Hanover College

Acknowledgments

Knowledge is improved through careful, systematic, and constructive criticism. The same is true of all writing. This book is of much greater quality because we had such outstanding critics and reviewers. We, therefore, wish to honor and recognize the outstanding scholars who served in this capacity. These scholars are listed on this page and the next.

We also had people who served in a variety of other capacities: drafting language for us for special features, doing library and Internet research to find the most recent facts and figures, and reading or critiquing early manuscripts. Khanh Nguyen deserves special mention as an amazing research assistant. Other contributors include Kate Ballantine, Kelly Joyce, Justin Roberts, Kent Roberts, Susan Schultheis, and Vanessa M. Simpson. Authors of short sections within the book include Helen Berger, Jeffrey Breese, Jeremiah Castle, Leslie Elrod, Melanie Hughes, Kichiro Iwamoto, Jeffrey Lashbrook, Laura McCloud, Ruth Meizen-Dick, Wendy Ng, Amy Orr, Lynette Osborne, Robert Pellerin, Lynn Richey, Elise Roberts, Susan St. John, David Stadden, and Jay Weinstein. Susan Alexander provided a critique of the visual messages in the first edition and helped select photos for the second edition. Scholars who helped with early drafts of some chapters include James W. Burfiend, Timothy Buzzell, Dora Lodwick, and Gregory Weiss. Thanks also to designer Bruce Stiver.

Both of us are experienced authors, and we have worked with some excellent people at other publishing houses. However, the team at Pine Forge/SAGE Publications was truly exceptional in support, thoroughness, and commitment to this project. Our planning meetings have been fun, intelligent, and provocative. Ben Penner, former Pine Forge acquisitions editor, provided excellent advice and support, and Jerry Westby has been a sustaining member of the team as executive editor. Dave Repetto stepped into the senior acquisitions editor role seamlessly and effectively and has been a great support to us. Elise Caffee, developmental editor, coordinated the work of many people and even managed to keep her sometimes cranky authors in line and in good humor. Other folks who have meant so much to the quality production of this book include Nancy Scrofano and Maggie Stanley, editorial assistants; Eric Garner, production editor; Shankaran Srinivasan and his team at QuADS Prepress, copy editors; Sheri Gilbert, permissions editor; Erica DeLuca, senior marketing manager; Claudia Hoffman, managing editor; Scott Hooper, manufacturing manager; Ravi Balasuriya, art director; Steven Martin, vice president—production; Michele Sordi, vice president and editorial director—books acquisitions; Dory Schrader, director—books marketing; David Horwitz, vice president—sales; and Blaise Simqu, president and chief executive officer. We have become friends and colleagues with the staff at Pine Forge/SAGE Publications. They are all greatly appreciated.

Thanks to the following reviewers:

Sabrina Alimahomed
University of California, Riverside

Fred Beck
Illinois State University

David L. Briscoe
University of Arkansas at Little Rock

James A. Crone
Hanover College

Jamie M. Dolan
Carroll College (MT)

Obi N. I. Ebbe
The University of Tennessee at Chattanooga

Stephanie Funk
Hanover College

Loyd R. Ganey, Jr.
Western International University

Mary Grigsby
University of Missouri–Columbia

Keith Kerr
Blinn College

Elaine Leeder
Sonoma State University

Stephen Lilley
Sacred Heart University

David A. Lopez
California State University, Northridge

Akbar Madhi
Ohio Wesleyan University

Gerardo Marti
Davidson College

Laura McCloud
The Ohio State University

Meeta Mehrotra
Roanoke College

Melinda S. Miceli
University of Hartford

Leah A. Moore
University of Central Florida

R. Marlene Powell
University of North Carolina at Pembroke

Martha L. Shockey-Eckles
Saint Louis University

Toni Sims
University of Louisiana–Lafayette

Frank S. Stanford
Blinn College

Tracy Steele
Wright State University

Rachel Stehle
Cuyahoga Community College

John Stone
Boston University

Stephen Sweet
Ithaca College

Tim Ulrich
Seattle Pacific University

Thomas L. Van Valey
Western Michigan University

Chaim I. Waxman
Rutgers University

Deborah J. White
Collin County Community College

Jake B. Wilson
University of California, Riverside

John Zipp
University of Akron

PART I

Understanding Our Social World

The Scientific Study of Society

Is sociology just common sense? Why would anyone want to study relationships with friends and family, how groups work, and where societies fit into the global system? What can we learn from scientifically studying our everyday lives? What exactly does it mean to see the world sociologically? Can sociology make our lives any better as the study of biology or chemistry does through new medications?

Those are some of the questions we hope to answer as we take a trip to a deeper level of understanding of ourselves and our social world. The first chapter of this book helps answer two questions: What is sociology, and why study it? Like your sociology professor, this book will argue that sociology is valuable because it gives us new perspectives on our personal and professional lives and because sociological insights and skills can help all of us make the world a better place.

The second chapter addresses how sociology began and how sociologists know what they know. When sociologists make a statement about the social world, how do they know it is true? What perspective or lens might sociologists employ to make sense of their information? For example, when sociologists find that education does not treat all children equally, what can be done about it? What evidence would be considered reliable, valid, dependable, and persuasive to support this statement? As we study sociology, we consider how we interact with each other; why we join groups and organizations; why some people are richer than others; why some people commit crimes; how race, class, and gender influence our positions in the social world; the major parts of society; and many other aspects of our social world.

By the time you finish reading the first two chapters, you should have an initial sense of what sociology is, how it can help you understand your social world, why the field is worth taking your time to explore, and how sociologists know what they know. We invite you to take a seat and come on a trip through the fascinating field of sociology and our social world.

Sociology

A Unique Way to View the World

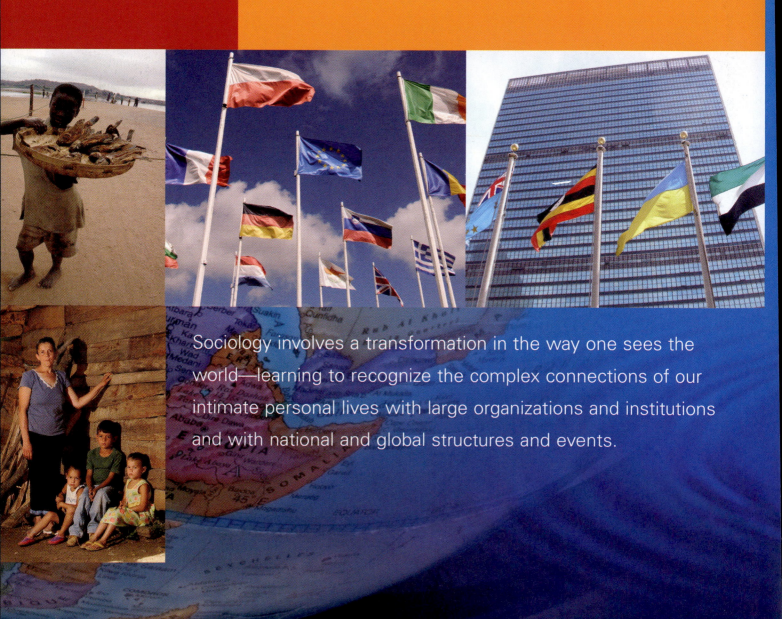

Sociology involves a transformation in the way one sees the world—learning to recognize the complex connections of our intimate personal lives with large organizations and institutions and with national and global structures and events.

Our Social World Model

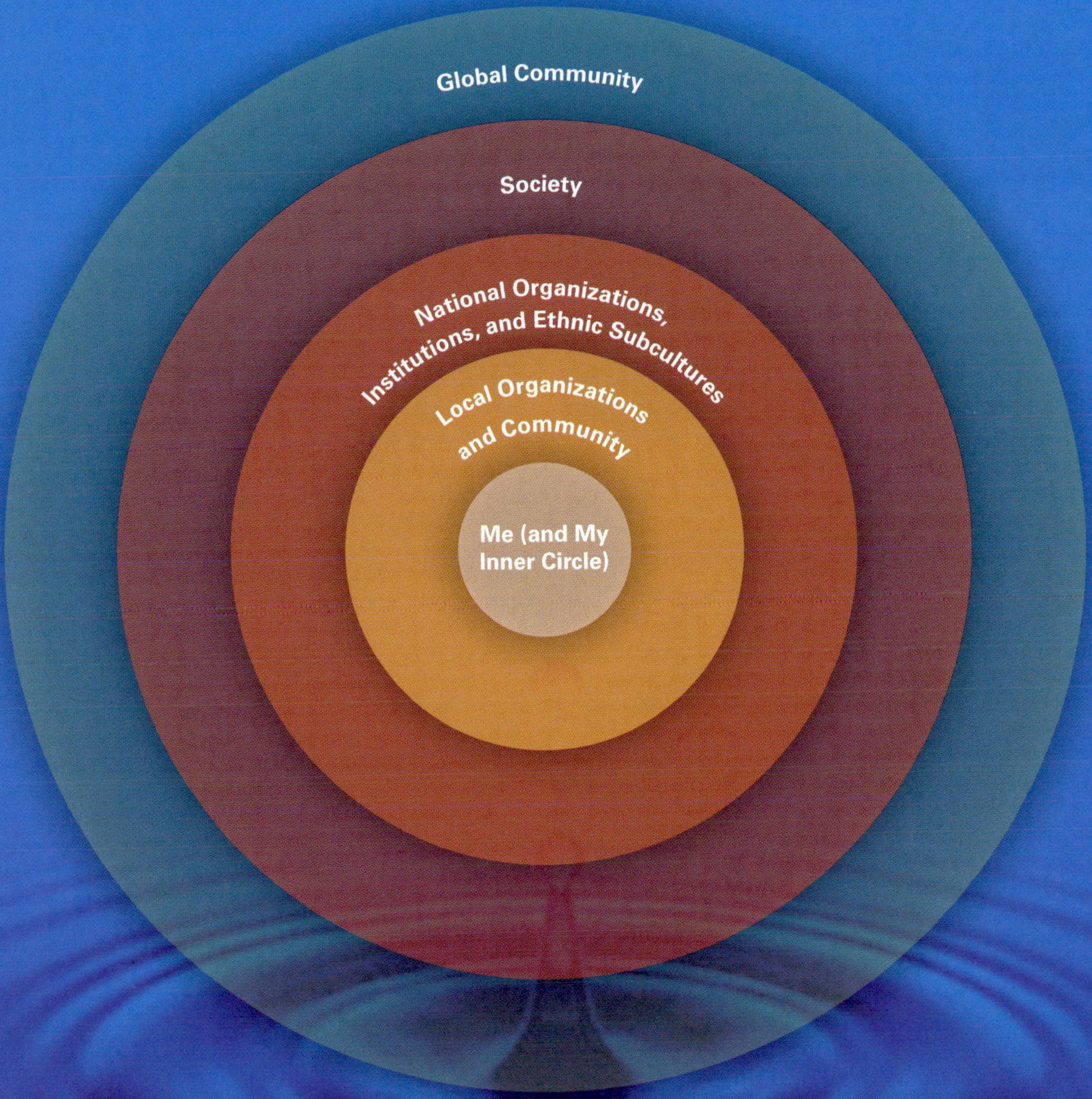

Global Community

Society

National Organizations, Institutions, and Ethnic Subcultures

Local Organizations and Community

Me (and My Inner Circle)

This model expresses a core idea carried throughout the book—the way in which your own life is embedded in, is shaped by, and influences your family, community, society, and world. It is a critically important reality that can make you a more effective person and a more knowledgeable citizen.

Think About It

Self and Inner Circle	How can sociology help me understand my own life and my sense of self?
Local Community	How can sociology help me to be a more effective employee and citizen in my community?
National Institutions; Complex Organizations; Ethnic Groups	How do sociologists help us understand and even improve our lives in families, classrooms, and health care offices?
National Society	How do national loyalty and national policies affect my life?
Global Community	How might global events affect my life?

At 16, Zac Sunderland was the youngest person ever to sail solo around the world. During his 13 months at sea, he faced pirates; a broken boom, tiller, forestay, rigging, and bulkhead; and was almost washed overboard off Grenada. His adventure took him across three oceans, five seas, the equator, and 25,000 miles—alone! To quote his father, "He left thinking he knew a lot about life, and the difference now is, he does." Another adventurer, determined to set a record by sailing across the Atlantic in a tiny, one-person craft powered only by the wind, knew he would be out of contact with other people for the duration of the voyage. He departed from the east coast of the United States, and for 2 months, he sailed in solitude. Although some feared that he was lost at sea, fortune was with him. His craft was spotted off the Irish coast—his destination. As he sailed into port, the media had been alerted to his arrival and awaited him. When the man disembarked to end this remarkable and sometimes painfully lonely journey, a reporter asked him what he had learned on his solitary voyage. The intrepid sailor thought for a moment and calmly replied, "I

learned a lot about people" ("California Teen Youngest" 2009; Thomas 2009).

By being so totally alone for so long, these two intrepid sailors learned how completely social we humans really are. When alone, they spent much of their time reflecting on people and learned how painful and disorienting it can be to live without human contact. In short, their experiences taught them a basic sociological insight: Humans are fundamentally social beings.

Strange as it may seem, the social world is not merely something that exists outside us. As this story illustrates, the social world is also something we carry inside us. We are part of it, we reflect on it, and we are influenced by it, even when we are alone. The patterns of the social world engulf us in ways both subtle and obvious, with profound implications for how we create order and meaning in our lives.

Sometimes it takes a dramatic and shocking event for us to realize just how deeply embedded we are in a social world that we take for granted. "It couldn't happen in the United States," read typical world newspaper accounts. "This is something you see in the Middle East, Central Africa, and other war-torn areas . . . . It's hard to imagine this happening in the economic center of the United States." Yet on September 11, 2001, shortly after 9 a.m., a commercial airliner crashed into a New York City skyscraper, followed a short while later by another pummeling into the paired tower, causing this mighty symbol of financial wealth—the World Trade Center—to collapse. After the dust settled and the rescue crews finished their gruesome work, nearly 3,000 people were dead or unaccounted for. The world as we knew it changed forever that day. This event taught U.S. citizens how integrally connected they are with the international community. Ten years later, we still wonder why the attacks occurred.

Following the events of 9/11, the United States launched its highly publicized War on Terror, and many terrorist strongholds and training camps became targets for destruction. Still, troubling questions remain unanswered. Why did this extremist act occur? How can such actions be deterred in the future? How do the survivors recover from such a horrific event? Why was this event so completely disorienting to Americans and to the world community? Such terrorist acts horrify people because they are unpredicted and unexpected in a normally predictable world. They violate the rules that

Zac Sunderland completed a solo sail around the world, learning a lot about life and about people. We humans are fundamentally social beings.

These signs were put up right after the 9/11 attacks on the World Trade Center by people looking for missing loved ones. The experience of New Yorkers was alarm, fear, grief, and confusion—precisely the emotions that the terrorists sought to create. Terrorism disrupts normal social life and daily routines and undermines security. It provides an effective tool for those with no power or way of lashing out at perceived threats and injustice.

foster our connections to one another. They also bring attention to the discontent and disconnectedness that lie under the surface in many societies—discontent that expressed itself in hateful violence. Such discontent and hostility are likely to continue until the root causes are addressed.

Terrorist acts represent a rejection of modern civil society (Smith 1994). The terrorists themselves see their acts as justifiable, one way they can strike out against injustices and threats to their way of life—but more on that later. Few outside the terrorists' inner circle understand their thinking and behavior. When terrorist acts occur, we struggle to fit such events into our mental picture of a just, safe, comfortable, and predictable social world. The events of 9/11 forced U.S. citizens to realize that although they may see a great diversity among themselves, people in other parts of the world view them as all the same. U.S. citizens are despised by some for what they represent. In other words, terrorists view U.S. citizens as intimately connected. For many U.S. citizens, their sense of loyalty to the nation was deeply stirred by the events of 9/11. Patriotism abounded. So, in fact, the nation's people became more connected as a reaction to an act against the United States.

Most of the time, we live with social patterns that we take for granted as routine, ordinary, and expected. These social patterns are essential in social groups. Unlike our motivations or drives, social expectations come from those around us and guide (or constrain) our behaviors and thoughts. Without shared expectations between humans about proper patterns of behavior, life would be chaotic. Our social interactions require some basic rules, and these rules create routine and safe normalcy in everyday interaction. It would be strange if someone broke the expected patterns. For the people in and around the World Trade Center on 9/11, the social rules governing everyday life broke down that awful day. How could anyone live in society if there were no rules, and can a society exist without rules?

This chapter examines the social ties that make up our social world, as well as sociology's focus on those ties. We will learn what sociology is and why it is valuable to study; how sociologists view the social world and what they do; how studying sociology can help us in our everyday life; and how the social world model is used to understand the social world and present the topics we will study throughout this book.

What Is Sociology?

Whether we are in a coffee shop, classroom, or dining hall, at a party or in our residence hall, at work or at home, we interact with other people. Such interactions are the foundation of social life, and they are the subject of interest to sociologists. According to the American Sociological Association (2009),

Video Link 1.1
Explore sociology.

Sociology is the study of social life, social change, and the social causes and consequences of human behavior. Sociologists investigate the structure of groups, organizations, and societies and how people interact within these contexts. Since all human behavior is social, the subject matter of sociology ranges from the intimate family to the hostile mob; from organized crime to religious traditions; from the divisions of race, gender, and social class to the shared beliefs of a common culture. (p. 5)

Journal Article Link 1.1
Learn about socialization and sports.

As we shall see, sociology is relevant and applicable to our lives in many ways. Sociologists conduct scientific research on social relationships and problems that range from tiny groups of two people to national societies and global social networks.

Unlike the discipline of psychology, which focuses on the attributes, motivations, and behaviors of individuals, sociology tends to focus on group patterns. Whereas a psychologist might try to explain behavior by examining the personality traits of individuals, a sociologist would examine the positions of different people within the group and how these positions influence what people do. Sociologists seek to analyze and explain why people interact with others and belong to groups, how groups work, who has power and who does not, how decisions are made, and how groups deal with conflict and change. From the early beginnings of sociology (discussed in Chapter 2), sociologists have asked questions about the rules that govern group behavior; about the causes of social problems, such as child abuse, crime, or poverty; and about why nations declare war and kill each other's citizens.

Two-person interactions—*dyads*—are the smallest units sociologists study. Examples of dyads include roommates discussing their classes, a professor and student going over an assignment, a husband and wife negotiating their budget, and two children playing. Next in size are small groups consisting of three or more interacting people—a family, a neighborhood or peer group, a classroom, a work group, or a street gang. Then come increasingly larger groups—organizations such as sports or scouting clubs, neighborhood associations, and local religious congregations. Among the largest groups contained within nations are ethnic groups and national organizations or institutions, such as the auto industry, national religious organizations, and the Republican and Democratic national political parties. Nations themselves are still larger and can sometimes involve hundreds of millions of people. In the past several decades, social scientists have also pointed to globalization, the process by which the entire world is becoming a single interdependent entity. Of particular interest to sociologists is how these various groups are organized, how they function, why they conflict, and how they influence one another.

Thinking Sociologically

Identify several dyads, small groups, and large organizations to which you belong. Did you choose to belong, or were you born into membership in these groups? How does each group influence who you are and the decisions you make?

Underlying Ideas in Sociology

All sciences rest on certain fundamental ideas. The idea that one action can cause something else is a core idea in all science—for example, heavy drinking before driving might cause an automobile accident. Sociology is based on several ideas that sociologists tend to take for granted about the social world. These ideas about humans and social life are supported by considerable evidence, and they are no longer matters of debate or controversy—they are assumed at this point to be true. Understanding these core assumptions helps us see how sociologists approach the study of people in groups.

People are social by nature. This means that humans seek contact with other humans, interact with one another,

An athletic team teaches members to interact, cooperate, develop awareness of the power of others, and deal with conflict. Here children experience ordered interaction in the competitive environment of a football game. What values, skills, attitudes, and assumptions about life and social interaction do you think these young boys are learning?

and influence and are influenced by the behaviors of others. Furthermore, humans need groups to survive. Although a few individuals may become socially isolated as adults, they could not have reached adulthood without sustained interactions with others. The central point here is that we become who we are because other people and groups constantly influence us.

People live much of their lives belonging to social groups. It is in social groups that we interact, learn to share goals and to cooperate, develop identities, obtain power, and have conflicts. Our individual beliefs and behaviors, our experiences, our observations, and the problems we face are derived from connections to our social groups.

Interaction between the individual and the group is a two-way process in which each influences the other. Individuals can influence the shape and direction of groups; groups provide the rules and decide the expected behaviors for individuals.

Recurrent social patterns, ordered behavior, shared expectations, and common understandings among people characterize groups. A degree of continuity and recurrent behavior is present in human interactions, whether in small groups, large organizations, or society.

The processes of conflict and change are natural and inevitable features of groups and societies. No group can remain stagnant and hope to perpetuate itself. To survive, groups must adapt to changes in the social and physical environment. Rapid change often comes at a price. It can lead to conflict within a society—between traditional and new ideas and between groups that have vested interests in particular ways of doing things. Rapid change can give rise to protest activities; changing in a controversial direction or failing to change fast enough can spark conflict, including revolution. The 2009 demonstrations following what some saw as a rigged election in Iran and the violence of citizens against what some saw as a corrupt election in Kenya in 2007–2008 illustrate the demand for change that can spring from citizens' discontent with corrupt or authoritarian rule.

As you read this book, keep in mind these basic ideas that form the foundation of sociological analysis: People are social; they live and carry out activities largely in groups; interaction influences both individual and group behavior; people share common behavior patterns and expectations; and processes such as change and conflict are always present. Thus, in several important ways, sociological understandings differ from our everyday views of the social world and provide new lenses for looking at our social world that expand our view.

Sociology Versus Common Sense

Human tragedy can result from inaccurate common-sense beliefs. For example, the Nazi genocide and the existence of slavery both have their roots in false beliefs about racial superiority. Consider for a moment some events that

An East German border guard shakes hands with a West German woman through a hole in the Berlin Wall. Although their governments were hostile to one another, the people themselves often had very different sentiments toward those on the other side of the divide.

have captured media attention, and ask yourself questions about these events: Why do some families remain poor generation after generation? Are kids from certain kinds of neighborhoods more likely to get into trouble with the law than kids from other neighborhoods? Why do political, religious, and ethnic conflicts exist in the Congo, Rwanda, Sudan, the Middle East, and the disputed areas of China, such as Tibet and Uyghurstan? Why do some families experience high levels of violence in the home? Why is the homicide rate in the United States so much higher than that of other developed nations? Our answers to such questions reflect our beliefs and assumptions about the social world. These assumptions often are based on our experiences, our judgments about what our friends and family believe, what we have read or viewed on television, and common stereotypes (rigid beliefs, often untested and unfounded) about a group or a category of people.

Common sense refers to ideas that are so completely taken for granted that they have never been seriously questioned and seem to be sensible to any reasonable person. We all use common sense, based on our personal experiences, to process information and decide how to act. Although all of us base decisions on common sense, that does not mean it is always accurate. The difference between common sense

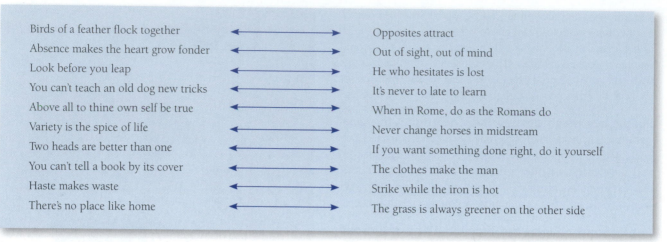

Birds of a feather flock together	Opposites attract
Absence makes the heart grow fonder	Out of sight, out of mind
Look before you leap	He who hesitates is lost
You can't teach an old dog new tricks	It's never to late to learn
Above all to thine own self be true	When in Rome, do as the Romans do
Variety is the spice of life	Never change horses in midstream
Two heads are better than one	If you want something done right, do it yourself
You can't tell a book by its cover	The clothes make the man
Haste makes waste	Strike while the iron is hot
There's no place like home	The grass is always greener on the other side

and sociology is that sociologists use scientific methods to test the accuracy of commonsense beliefs and ideas about human behavior and the social world.

Would our commonsense notions about the social world be reinforced or rejected if examined with scientifically gathered information? Some commonsense notions (above) actually contradict each other, yet all guide behavior at some time.

Audio Link 1.1
Listen to the connection between theory and practice.

These are examples of maxims that people use as "absolute" guides to live by. They become substitutes for real analysis of situations. The fact is that all of them are accurate at *some times, some places, about some things.* Sociological thinking/analysis is about studying the conditions in which they hold and do not hold. (Eitzen and Zinn n.d.)

Wodaabe society in Niger in sub-Saharan Africa illustrates that our notions of masculinity and femininity—which common sense tells us are innate and universal—are actually socially defined, variable, and learned. Wodaabe men are known for their heavy use of makeup to be attractive to women.

Thinking Sociologically

What are some other commonsense sayings that you know that contradict one another? Also, take a look at the commonsense quiz online at www.pineforge.com/oswmedia3e. Do some of the answers surprise you? If so, why?

The difference between common sense and sociology is that sociologists test their beliefs by gathering information and analyzing the evidence in a planned, objective, systematic, and replicable (repeatable) scientific way. Indeed, they set up studies to see if they can disprove what they think is true. This is the way science is done. Consider the following examples of commonsense beliefs about the social world and some research findings about these beliefs.

Commonsense Beliefs and Social Science Findings

Belief: Most of the differences in the behaviors of women and men are based on "human nature"; men and women are just plain different from each other. Research shows that biological factors certainly play a part in the behaviors of men and women, but the culture (beliefs, values, rules, and way of life) that people learn as they grow up determines how biological tendencies are played out. A unique example illustrates this: In the Wodaabe tribe in Africa, women do most of the heavy work, while men adorn themselves with makeup, sip tea, and gossip (Beckwith 1983). Variations in the behavior of men and women around the world are so great that it is impossible to attribute behavior to biology or human nature alone.

Belief: As developing countries modernize, the lives of their female citizens improve. This is generally false.

The commonsense notion is that most children in the world, boys and girls, have equal access to education. Literacy is a major issue for societies around the globe. These Chinese children are learning to read, but in many developing countries, boys have more access to formal education than girls have; many children, especially girls, do not gain literacy.

In fact, the status of women in many developed and developing countries is getting worse. Women make up roughly 51% of the world's approximately 6.8 billion people and account for two thirds of the world's hours-at-work. However, in no country for which data are available do they earn what men earn, and sometimes, the figures show women earning less than 50% of men's earnings for similar work. Women hold many unpaid jobs in agriculture, and they own only 1% of the world's property. Furthermore, of the world's 1 billion illiterate adults, two thirds are women (World Factbook 2009e). Only 77% of the world's women over age 15 can read and write compared with 87% of men. Illiteracy rates for women in South Asia, sub-Saharan Africa, and the Middle East are the highest in the world, implying lack of access to education. These are only a few examples of the continuing poor status of women in many countries (Institute for Statistics 2006a; World Factbook 2009e; youthxchange 2007).

Belief: Given the high divorce rates in the United States and Canada, marriages are in serious trouble. Although the divorce rate in North America is high, the rate of marriage is also one of the highest in the world (Coontz 2005). Moreover, even those who have been divorced tend to remarry. Despite all the talk about the decline of marriage and despite genuine concern about the high levels of

marital failure, Americans now spend more years of their lives in marriage than at any other time in history. Divorce appears to be seen as rejection of a particular partnership rather than as a rejection of marriage itself (Coontz 2005; Wallerstein and Blakeslee 1996). The divorce rate reached a peak in the United States in 1982 and has declined modestly since that time (Newman and Grauerholz 2002).

As these examples illustrate, many of our commonsense beliefs are challenged by social scientific evidence. On examination, the social world is often more complex than our commonsense understanding of events, which is based on limited evidence. Throughout history, there are examples of beliefs that seemed obvious at one time but have been shown to be mistaken through scientific study. The point is that the discipline of sociology provides a method to assess the accuracy of our commonsense assumptions about the social world.

Handbook Link 1.1
Read more about sociological perspective.

To improve the lives of individuals in societies around the world, decision makers must rely on an accurate understanding of the society. Accurate information gleaned from sociological research can be the basis for more rational and just social policies—policies that better meet the needs of all groups in the social world. The sociological perspective, discussed below, helps us gain a reliable understanding of social problems.

Thinking Sociologically

What are some of your commonsense beliefs? How did you develop these beliefs, and what evidence do you have to support these beliefs?

The Sociological Imagination

Happenings in the social world affect our individual lives. If we are unemployed or lack funds for our college education, we may say this is a personal problem. Yet often, broader social issues are at the root of our situation. The sociological perspective holds that we can best understand our personal experiences and problems by examining their broader social context—by looking at the big picture.

Individual problems (or private troubles) are rooted in social or public issues (what is happening in the social world outside one's personal control). C. Wright Mills (1959) called this relationship between individual experiences and public issues the **sociological imagination**. For Mills, many personal experiences can and should be interpreted in the context of large-scale forces in the wider society.

Consider, for example, the personal trauma caused by being laid off of a job, a common situation in today's economy due to the recession. The unemployed person often experiences feelings of inadequacy or lack of worth. This, in turn, may produce stress in a marriage or even result in divorce. These conditions not only are deeply troubling to the person most directly affected but also are related to wider political and economic forces in society. The unemployment may be due to unsound banking practices, to corporate downsizing, or to a corporation taking operations to another country where labor costs are cheaper and where there are fewer environmental regulations on companies. People may blame themselves or each other for personal troubles such as unemployment or a failed marriage, believing that they did not try hard enough. Often, they do not see the connection between their private lives and larger economic and social forces beyond their control. They fail to recognize the public issues that create private troubles.

Families also experience stress as partners have, over time, assumed increasing responsibility for their mate's and their children's emotional and physical needs. Until the second half of the 20th century, the community and the extended family unit—aunts, uncles, grandparents, and cousins—assumed more of that burden. Extended families continue to exist in countries where children settle near their parents, but in modern urban societies, both the sense of community and the connection to the extended family are greatly diminished. There are fewer intimate ties to call on for help and support. Divorce is a very personal condition for those affected, but it can be understood far more clearly when considered in conjunction with the broader social context of economics, urbanization, changing gender roles, lack of external support, and legislated family policies.

As we learn about sociology, we will come to understand how social forces shape individual lives, and this will help us understand aspects of everyday life we take for granted. In this book, we will investigate how group life influences our behaviors and interactions and why some individuals follow the rules of society and others do not. A major goal is to help us incorporate the sociological perspective into our way of looking at the social world and our place in it. Indeed, the notion of *sociological imagination*—connecting events from the global and national levels to the personal and intimate level of our own lives—is the core organizing theme of this book.

Thinking Sociologically

How does poverty, war, or an economic recession cause personal troubles for someone you know? Why is it inadequate to try to explain these personal troubles by examining only the personal characteristics of those affected?

Some sociologists study issues and problems and present their results for others to use. Others become involved in solving the very problems they study. The

following feature on the next page, "Sociology in Our Social World," provides an extension on the sociological imagination, illustrating how some use their sociological knowledge to become involved in their communities or the larger world; these students of sociology advocate an active role in bringing about change.

Questions Sociologists Ask—and Don't Ask

The existence of God, the meaning of life, the ethical implications of stem cell research, or the morality of physician-assisted suicide are philosophical issues that sociologists, like other scientists, cannot answer. Sociologists do ask questions about human behavior in social groups and organizations—questions that can be studied scientifically. What effect does holding certain ideas or adhering to certain ethical standards have on the behavior and attitudes of people? For example, are people more likely to obey rules if they believe that there are consequences for their actions in an afterlife? What are the consequences—positive and negative—of allowing suicide for terminally ill patients who are in pain? Although sociologists may study the philosophical or religious beliefs held by groups, they do not make judgments about what beliefs are right or wrong or about moral issues involving philosophy, religion, values, or opinion. Rather, they focus on issues that can be studied objectively and scientifically to discover the social causes or consequences.

Applied sociologists, those who carry out research to help organizations solve problems, agree that the research itself should be as objective as possible. After the research is completed, the applied sociologists might use the research findings to explore policy implications and make recommendations for change.

Consider the following examples of questions sociologists might ask:

- Who gets an abortion, why do they do so, and how does society as a whole view abortion? These are matters of fact that a social scientist can explore. However, sociologists avoid making ethical judgments about whether abortion is right or wrong. The question about the morality of abortion is very important to many people, but it is based on philosophical or theological rationale and values, not on scientific analysis.
- Who is the most beautiful? Cultural standards of beauty affect individual popularity and social interaction, an issue that interests some social scientists. However, the sociologist would not judge which individuals are more or less attractive. Such questions are matters of aesthetics, a field of philosophy and art.
- What are the circumstances around individuals becoming drunk and drunken behavior? This question is often tied more to the social environment than to alcohol itself. The researcher does not make judgments about

Sociology in Our Social World

How Will You Spend the 21st Century?

By Peter Dreier

Today, Americans enjoy more rights, better working conditions, better living conditions, and more protection from disease in childhood and old age than anyone could have imagined 100 years ago . . . But that doesn't let you off the hook! There are still many problems and much work to do. Like all agents for social change, . . . social reformers such as Martin Luther King Jr., a sociology major, understood the basic point of sociology, that is, to look for the connections between people's everyday personal problems and the larger trends in society.

Things that we experience as personal matters—a woman facing domestic violence, or a low-wage worker who cannot afford housing, or middle-class people stuck in daily traffic jams—are really about how our institutions function. Sociologists hold a mirror up to our society and help us see our society objectively. One way to do this is by comparing our own society to others. This sometimes makes us uncomfortable—because we take so much about our society for granted. Conditions that we may consider "normal," other societies may consider serious problems. For example, if we compare the United States to other advanced industrial countries such as Canada, Germany, France, Sweden, Australia, Holland, and Belgium, we find some troubling things:

- The United States has the highest per capita income among those countries. At the same time, the United States has, by far, the widest gap between the rich and the poor.
- Almost 30 percent of American workers work full-time, year-round, for poverty-level wages.
- The United States has the highest overall rate of poverty. More than 40 million Americans live in poverty.
- Over 13 million of these Americans are children. In fact, one out of six American children is poor. They live in slums and trailer parks, eat cold cereal for dinner, share a bed or a cot with their siblings, and sometimes with their parents, and are often one disaster away from becoming homeless . . .
- Only half to two-thirds of children eligible for the Head Start program are enrolled because of the lack of funding . . .
- The United States has the highest infant mortality rate among the major industrial nations . . .
- The United States is the only one of these nations without universal health insurance.

More than 50 million Americans have no health insurance.

- Americans spend more hours stuck in traffic jams than people of any of these other countries. This leads to more pollution, more auto accidents, and less time spent with families.
- Finally, the United States has a much higher proportion of our citizens in prison than any of these societies . . .

. . . What would you like your grandchildren to think about how you spent the 21st century? . . . No matter what career you pursue, you have choices about how you will live your lives. As citizens, you can sit on the sidelines and merely be involved in your society, or you can decide to become really committed to making this a better world.

Today, there are hundreds of thousands of patriotic Americans committed to making our country live up to its ideals . . . They are asking the same questions that earlier generations of active citizens asked: Why can't our society do a better job of providing equal opportunity, a clean environment, and a decent education for all? They know there are many barriers and obstacles to change, but they want to figure out how to overcome these barriers, and to help build a better society.

So ask yourselves: What are some of the things that we take for granted today that need to be changed? What are some ideas for changing things that today might seem "outrageous," but that—25 or 50 or 100 years from now—will be considered common sense?

. . . A record number of college students today are involved in a wide variety of "community service" activities—such as mentoring young kids in school, volunteering in a homeless shelter, or working in an AIDS hospice. As a result of this student activism, more than 100 colleges and universities have adopted "anti-sweatshop" codes of conduct for the manufacturers of clothing that bear the names and logos of their institutions.

Positive change is possible, but it is not inevitable . . . I am optimistic that your generation will follow a lifelong commitment to positive change.

I know you will not be among those who simply "see things the way they are and ask: why?" Instead, you will "dream things that never were and ask: why not?" [George Bernard Shaw].

What is acceptable or unacceptable drinking behavior varies according to the social setting—a wedding reception versus a fraternity party. Binge drinking, losing consciousness, vomiting, or engaging in sexual acts while drunk may be a source of storytelling at a college party but can be offensive at a wedding reception. Sociologists study different social settings and how the norms of acceptability vary in each, but they do not make judgments about those behaviors.

Sociologists learn techniques to avoid letting their values influence their research designs, data gathering, and analysis. Still, complete objectivity is difficult at best, and what one chooses to study may be influenced by one's interests and concerns about injustice in society. The fact that sociologists know they will be held accountable by other scientists for the objectivity of their research is a major factor in encouraging them to be objective when they do their research.

Thinking Sociologically

From the information you have just read, what are some questions sociologists might ask about divorce or cohabitation or same-sex unions? What are some questions sociologists would not ask about these topics, at least while in their roles as researchers?

The Social Sciences: A Comparison

Not so long ago, our views of people and social relationships were based on stereotypes, intuition, superstitions, supernatural explanations, and traditions passed on from one generation to the next. Natural sciences first used the scientific method, a model later adopted by social sciences. Social scientists, including anthropologists, psychologists, economists, cultural geographers, historians, and political scientists, apply the scientific method to study social relationships, to correct misleading and harmful misconceptions about human behaviors, and to guide policy decisions. Consider the following examples of specific studies various social scientists might conduct. This is followed by a brief description of the focus of sociology as a social science.

One anthropological study focused on garbage, studying what people discard to understand what kind of life they lead and foods they eat—their patterns of life. *Anthropology* is the study of humanity in its broadest context. It is closely related to sociology, and the two areas have common historical roots. There are four major subfields within anthropology: physical anthropology (which is related to biology), archaeology, linguistics, and cultural anthropology (sometimes called *ethnology*). This last field has the most in common with sociology. Cultural anthropologists study the culture, or way of life, of a society.

A psychologist wires research subjects to a machine that measures their physiological reaction to a violent film clip, then asks them questions about what they were feeling. *Psychology* is the study of individual behavior and mental processes (e.g., sensation, perception, memory, and thought processes). It differs from sociology in that it focuses on individuals rather than on groups, institutions, and societies. Although

whether use of alcohol is good or bad, right or wrong, and avoids—as much as possible—opinions regarding responsibility or irresponsibility. The sociologist does, however, observe variations in the use of alcohol in social situations and the resulting behaviors. Note that a person might be very intoxicated at a fraternity party but will behave differently at a wedding reception, where the expectations for behavior are very different. An applied sociologist researching alcohol use on campus for a college or for a national fraternity may, following the research, offer advice based on that research about how to reduce the number of alcohol-related deaths or sexual assault incidents on college campuses (Sweet 2001).

Video Link 1.2
Watch a sociological analysis of the meth epidemic.

there are different branches of psychology, most psychologists are concerned with what motivates individual behavior, personality attributes, attitudes, beliefs, and perceptions. Psychologists also explore abnormal behavior, the mental disorders of individuals, and the stages of normal human development (Wallerstein 1996; Wallerstein and Blakeslee 2004).

A political scientist studies opinion poll results to predict who will win the next election, how various groups of people are likely to vote, or how elected officials will vote on proposed legislation. *Political science* is concerned with government systems and power—how they work, how they are organized, the forms of government, the relations between governments, who holds power and how they obtain it, how power is used, and who is politically active. Political science overlaps with sociology, particularly in the study of political theory and the nature and the uses of power.

An economist studies the banking system and market trends, trying to determine what will remedy the global recession. *Economists* analyze economic conditions and explore how people organize, produce, and distribute material goods. They are interested in supply and demand, inflation and taxes, prices and manufacturing output, labor organization, employment levels, and comparisons between industrial and nonindustrial nations.

What all these social sciences—sociology, anthropology, psychology, economics, political science, cultural geography, and history—have in common is that they study aspects of human behavior and social life. Social sciences share many common topics, methods, concepts, research findings, and theories, but each has a different focus or perspective on the social world. Each of these social sciences relates to topics studied by sociologists, but sociologists focus on human interaction, groups, and social structure, providing the broadest overview of the social world.

Thinking Sociologically

Consider other issues such as the condition of poverty in developing countries or homelessness in North America. What question(s) might different social sciences ask about these problems?

Why Study Sociology . . . and What Do Sociologists Do?

Did you ever wonder why some families are close and others are estranged? Why some work groups are very

Psychology as a discipline tends to focus on individuals, including fields such as sensation, perception, memory, and thought processes. In this study, the researcher is using some equipment and a computer to measure how the eye and the brain work together to help create depth perception.

productive while others are not? Why some people are rich and others remain impoverished? Why some people engage in criminal behaviors and others conform rigidly to rules? Sociologists have the perspective and methods to search for a deeper understanding than common sense can provide about human interaction.

Two ingredients are essential to the study of our social world: (1) a keen ability to observe what is happening in the social world and (2) a desire to find answers to the question of why it is happening. The value of sociology is that it affords us a unique perspective and provides the methods to study systematically important questions about human interaction, group behavior, and social structure. The practical significance of the sociological perspective is that it

Audio Link 1.2
Listen to a sociological analysis of the financial crisis.

- fosters greater self-awareness, which can lead to opportunities to improve one's life;
- encourages a more complete understanding of social situations by looking beyond individual explanations to include group analyses of behavior;
- helps people understand and evaluate problems by enabling them to view the world systematically and objectively rather than in strictly emotional or personal terms;
- cultivates an understanding of the many diverse cultural perspectives and how cultural differences are related to behavioral patterns;

- provides a means to assess the impact of social policies;
- reveals the complexities of social life and provides methods of inquiry to study them; and
- provides useful skills in interpersonal relations, critical thinking, data collection and analysis, problem solving, and decision making.

This unique perspective has practical value as we carry out our roles as workers, friends, family members, and citizens. For example, an employee who has studied sociology may better understand how to work with groups and how the structure of the workplace affects individual behavior, how to approach problem solving, and how to collect and analyze data. Likewise, a school teacher trained in sociology may have a better understanding of classroom management, student motivation, the causes of poor student learning that have roots outside the school, and other variables that shape the professional life of teachers and academic success of students. Consider the example in "Sociology in Our Social World" on the next page, which explores how high school groups such as "jocks" and "burnouts" behave and why each clique's behavior might be quite logical in certain circumstances. "Burnouts and Jocks in a Public High School" explores a social environment very familiar to most of us, the social cliques in a high school.

What Sociologists Do

Sociologists are employed in a variety of settings. Although students may first encounter them as teachers and researchers in higher education, sociologists also hold nonacademic, applied sociology jobs in social agencies, government, and business. Table 1.1 illustrates that a significant portion of sociologists work in business, government, and social service agencies (American Sociological Association 2006; Dotzler and Koppel 1999).

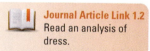
Journal Article Link 1.2
Read an analysis of dress.

The amount of study completed in sociology plus the sociologists' areas of specialization help determine the types of positions they hold. The three typical sociology degrees are bachelor of arts or bachelor of science (BA or BS), master of arts (MA), and doctorate (PhD).

College graduates who seek employment immediately after college (without other graduate work) are most likely to find their first jobs in social services, administrative assistantships, or some sort of management position. The areas of first jobs of sociology majors are indicated in Figure 1.1. With a master's or a doctorate degree, graduates usually become college teachers, researchers, clinicians, and consultants.

Consider your professor. The duties of professors vary depending on the type of institution and the level of courses offered. Classroom time fills only a portion of a professor's

Table 1.1	**Where Sociologists Are Employed**
Places of Employment	Percentage Employed
College or university	75.5
Government (all positions)	7.1
Private, for-profit business	6.2
Not-for-profit public service organizations	7.6
Self-employed	0.4

Source: American Sociological Association (2006).

7%
4%
6%
27%
10%
16%
8%
8%
14%

- Social Services, Counselors
- Administrative Support
- Management
- Teachers/Librarians
- Services
- Sales, Marketing
- Social Science Research
- Other
- Other Professional (includes PR and IT)

Figure 1.1 Occupational Categories for Sociology Graduates' First Jobs

Source: Based on "21st Century Careers With an Undergraduate Degree in Sociology," American Sociological Association, 2009.

Sociology in Our Social World

Burnouts and Jocks in a Public High School

Burnouts and jocks in a public high school

High schools are big organizations made up of smaller friendship networks and cliques; a careful examination can give us insight into the tensions that exist as the groups struggle for resources and power in the school.

Sociologist Penelope Eckert (1989) focused on two categories of students that exist in many high schools in North America: "burnouts" and "jocks." The burnouts defied the authorities, smoked in the restrooms, refused to use their lockers, made a public display of not eating in the school cafeteria, and wore their jackets all day. Their open and public defiance of authority infuriated the jocks—the college prep students who participated in choir, band, student council, and athletics and who held class offices. The burnouts were disgusted with the jocks. In their view, by constantly sucking up to the authorities, the jocks received special privileges, and by playing the goody-two-shoes role, they made life much more difficult for the burnouts.

Despite their animosity toward one another, the goal of both groups was to gain more autonomy from the adult authorities who constantly bossed students around. As the burnouts saw things, if the jocks would have even a slight bit of backbone and stand up for the dignity of students as adults, life would be better for everyone. The burnouts believed that school officials should earn their obedience. The burnouts maintained their dignity by affirming that they did not recognize bossy adults as authorities. Wearing coats all day was another way to emphasize the idea that "I'm just a visitor in this school."

The jocks, for their part, became irritated at the burnouts when they caused trouble and were belligerent with the authorities; then the administration would crack down on everyone, and no one had any freedom. The jocks found that if they did what the adults told them to do—at least while the adults were around—they got a lot more freedom. When the burnouts got defiant, however, the principal got mad and removed everyone's privileges.

Eckert found that the behavior of both groups was quite logical for their circumstances and ambitions. Expending energy as a class officer or participating in extracurricular activities is a rational behavior for college preparatory students because those leadership roles help students get into their college of choice.

However, those activities do not help one get a better job in a town factory. In fact, hanging out at the bowling alley makes far more sense. For the burnouts, having friendship networks and acquaintances in the right places is more important to achieving their goals than a class office listed on their résumé.

Eckert's (1989) method of gathering information was effective in showing how the internal dynamics of schools—conflicts between student groups—were influenced by outside factors such as working- and upper-middle-class status. Recent research upholds Eckert's findings on the importance cliques play in shaping school behavior. Like Eckert, Bonnie Barber, Jacquelynne Eccles, and Margaret Stone (2001) followed various friendship cliques starting in 10th grade in a Michigan high school. The jocks in their study were the most integrated to mainstream society in adult life. The burnouts (or criminals, as they are labeled in Barber's research) were most likely to have been arrested or incarcerated, showing that the propensity to defy authority figures may carry on into adult life.

These studies show that sociological analysis can help us understand some of the ways in which connections between groups—regardless of whether they are in conflict or harmony—shape the perceptions, attitudes, and behaviors of people living in this complex social world.

working day. Other activities include preparing for classes, preparing and grading exams and assignments, advising students, serving on committees, keeping abreast of new research in the field, and conducting research studies and having them published. This last "publish or perish" activity is deemed the most important activity for faculty in some major universities.

In businesses, applied sociologists use their knowledge and research skills in human resources or to address organizational needs or problems. In government jobs, they provide data such as population projections for education and health care planning. In social service agencies, such as police departments, they help address deviant behavior, and in health agencies, they may be concerned with doctor-patient interactions. Applied sociology is an important aspect of the field; you will find featured inserts in some chapters discussing the work of an applied sociologist. These examples will provide a picture of what one can do with a sociology degree. In addition, at the end of some chapters you will find a section discussing policy examples and implications related to that chapter topic. Figure 1.2 provides some ideas of career paths for graduates with a degree in sociology.

Thinking Sociologically

From what you have read so far, how might social interaction skills and knowledge of how groups work be useful to you in your anticipated major and career?

What Employers Want and What Sociology Majors Bring to a Career

Sociologists and other social scientists have studied what job skills and competencies employers seek in new employees, in addition to subject matter expertise. Employers focus on writing, speaking, analytical skills—especially when faced with complex problems, understanding of other cultures and of the diversity within the United States, the ability to work effectively in diverse teams, and the ability to gather and interpret quantitative information. As

Business or Management
Market researcher
Sales manager
Customer relations
Manufacturing representative
Banking or loan officer
Data processor
Attorney

Research
Population analyst
Surveyor
Market researcher
Economic analyst
Public opinion pollster
Interviewer
Policy researcher
Telecommunications researcher

Human Services
Social worker
Criminologist
Gerontologist
Hospital administrator
Charities administrator
Community advocate or organizer

Government
Policy advisor or administrator
Labor relations
Legislator
Census worker
International agency representative
City planning officer
Prison administrator
Law enforcement
FBI agent
Customs agent

Education
Teacher
Academic research
Administration
School counselor
Policy analyst
College professor
Dean of student life

Public Relations
Publisher
Mass communications
Advertising
Writer or commentator
Journalist

Figure 1.2   What Can You Do With a Sociology Degree?

Note: Surveys of college alumni with undergraduate majors in sociology indicate that this field of study prepares people for a broad range of occupations, some of which require graduate or professional training. For further information, contact your department chair or the American Sociological Association in Washington, D.C., for a copy of *Careers in Sociology,* 2009.

Source: American Sociological Association (2006).

Table 1.2 indicates, employers want more of these kinds of skills from college graduates.

Table 1.2 **Percentage of Employers Who Want Colleges to "Place More Emphasis" on Essential Learning Outcomes**	
Knowledge of human culture	
Global issues	72
The role of the United States in the world	60
Cultural values and traditions—U.S. and global	53
Intellectual and practical skills	
Teamwork skills in diverse groups	76
Critical thinking and analytic reasoning	73
Written and oral communication	73
Information literacy	70
Creativity and innovation	70
Complex problem solving	64
Quantitative reasoning	60
Personal and social responsibility	
Intercultural competence (teamwork in diverse groups)	76
Intercultural knowledge (global issues)	72

Source: American Sociological Association (2009).

The following skills and competencies are part of most sociological training:

1. Communication skills (listening, verbal and written communication, working with peers, and effective interaction in group situations)

2. Analytical and research skills

3. Computer and technical literacy (basic understanding of computer hardware and software programs)

4. Flexibility, adaptability, and multitasking (ability to set priorities, manage multiple tasks, adapt to changing situations, and handle pressure)

5. Interpersonal skills (working with coworkers)

6. Effective leadership skills (ability to take charge and make decisions)

7. Sensitivity to diversity in the workplace and with clients

8. Organizing thoughts and information and planning effectively (ability to design, plan, organize, and implement projects and to be self-motivated)

9. Ability to conceptualize and solve problems and be creative (working toward meeting the organization's goals)

Video Link 1.3
Learn about opportunities for sociology majors.

10. Working with others (ability to work toward a common goal)

11. Personal values (honesty, flexibility, work ethic, dependability, loyalty, positive attitude, professionalism, self-confidence, willingness to learn) (Hansen and Hansen 2003)

These competencies reflect skills stressed in the sociology curriculum: the ability to understand and work with others, research and computer skills, planning and organizing skills, oral and written communication skills, and critical thinking skills (WorldWideLearn 2007).

We now have a general idea of what sociology is and what sociologists do. It should be apparent that sociology is a broad field of interest; sociologists study all aspects of human social behavior. The next section of this chapter shows how the parts of the social world that sociologists study relate to each other, and it outlines the model you will follow as you continue to learn about sociology.

Thinking Sociologically

Video Link 1.4
Examine advertising and the link to our social lives.

What are some advantages of mayors, legislators, police chiefs, or government officials making decisions based on information gathered and verified by social scientific research rather than on their own intuition or assumptions?

The Social World Model

Think about the different groups you depend on and interact with on a daily basis. You wake up to greet members of your family or your roommate. You go to a larger group—a class—that exists within an even larger organization—the college or university. Understanding sociology and the approach of

These men carry the supplies for a new school to be built in their local community—Korphe, Pakistan. The trek of more than 20 miles up mountainous terrain was difficult, but their commitment to neighbors and the children of the community made it worthwhile. The project was a local one (micro level), but it was also made possible by an international organization—Central Asia Institute—founded as a charitable organization by Greg Mortenson of Montana.

this book requires a grasp of levels of analysis, that is, social groups from the smallest to the largest. It may be relatively easy to picture small groups, such as a family, a sports team, or a sorority or fraternity. It is more difficult to visualize large groups, such as corporations—The Gap, Abercrombie and Fitch, Eddie Bauer, General Motors Corporation, or Starbucks—or organizations such as local or state governments. The largest groups include nations or international organizations, such as the sprawling networks of the United Nations or the World Trade Organization. Groups of various sizes shape our lives. Sociological analysis requires that we understand these groups at various levels of analysis.

The **social world model** helps us picture the levels of analysis in our social surroundings as an interconnected series of small groups, organizations, institutions, and societies. Sometimes these groups are connected by mutual support and cooperation, but sometimes there are conflicts and power struggles over access to resources. What we are asking you to do here and throughout this book is to develop a sociological imagination—the basic lens used by sociologists. Picture the social world as a linked system made up of increasingly larger circles. To understand the units or parts of the social world model, look at the model shown here.

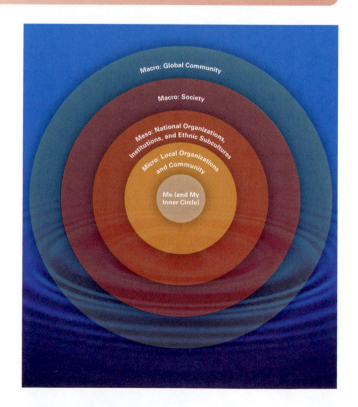

This social world model will be used throughout our book to illustrate how each topic fits into the big picture—our social world. No social unit of our social world can stand alone. All units affect each other, either because they serve the needs of other units in the system or because of the intense conflict and tension affecting different units. The social world is organized into two parts—*social structures* and *social processes*. Now, let us take a trip through our social world.

Social Structures

The social world model is made up of a number of parts that combine to form the **social structure**, like a framework that holds societies together. **Social units**, interconnected parts of the social world, range from interaction in dyads (two people) and small groups to large-scale actions such as negotiating between countries or wars between societies. All these social units combine into a larger social structure that brings order to our lives.

Sometimes, however, the interconnections in the social structure conflict, due to divergent beliefs or the self-interests of units. For example, a religion that teaches that it is wrong to have blood transfusions may conflict with the health care system regarding how to save the life of a child. Business executives want to produce products at the lowest possible cost, but this may mean paying workers low wages and causing damage to the environment. All levels of analysis are linked. Some links are supportive; others are in conflict and cause tension in the system.

Social institutions are the largest units that make up every society—family, education, religion, politics, economics, science, sports, healthcare, and the military. They provide the rules, roles, and relationships to meet human needs and guide human behavior. They are the units through which organized social activities take place, and they provide the setting for activities essential to human and societal survival. For example, we cannot survive without an economic institution to provide guidelines and a structure for meeting our basic needs of food, shelter, and clothing. Likewise, we would never make it to adulthood as functioning members of society without the family, the most basic of all institutions.

Compare this with a picture of our body's skeleton, which governs how our limbs are attached to the torso and how they move. Like the system of organs that make up our bodies—heart, lungs, kidneys, bladder—all social institutions are interrelated. Just as a change in one part of the body affects all others, a change in one institution affects the others. When governments pass laws providing money to schools for children's lunches, requiring standardized testing, or limiting extracurricular activities due to lack of funds, it affects both families and schools. Likewise, if many people are unable to afford medical treatment, the society is less healthy, and there are consequences for families, schools, workplaces, and society as a whole.

The **national society**, one of the largest social units in our model, includes a population of people, usually living within a specified geographic area, who are connected by common ideas and are subject to a particular political authority. It also features a social structure with groups and institutions. Although a national society is one of the largest social units, it is still a subsystem of the interdependent global system. France, Kenya, Brazil, and Laos are all national societies on separate continents, but they are linked as part of the global system of nations. In addition to having relatively permanent geographic and political boundaries, a national society also has one or more languages and a way of life. In most cases, national societies involve countries or large regions where the inhabitants share a common identity as members. In certain other instances, such as contemporary

Handbook Link 1.2
Read more about
social structure.

This refugee mother and child from Mozambique represent the smallest social unit, a dyad. In this case, they are trying to survive with help from larger groups such as the United Nations.

Great Britain, a single national society may include several groups of people who consider themselves distinct nationalities (Welsh, English, Scottish, and Irish within the United Kingdom). Such multicultural societies may or may not be harmonious.

Thinking Sociologically

Think about how a major conflict or change in your family (micro level) might affect your education, economic situation, or health care. How might change in one national institution such as health care affect change in another institution (such as the family or the economy)?

Social Processes

Picture **social processes** as the actions taken by people in social units. Processes keep the social world working, much as the beating heart keeps the body working. For example, the process of socialization teaches individuals how to become productive members of society. It takes place through actions in families, educational systems, religious organizations, and other social units. Socialization is essential for the continuation of any society. Similarly, our social positions in society are the result of stratification, the process of layering people into social strata based on factors such as birth, income, occupation, and education. Conflict occurs between individuals or groups over money, jobs, and other needed resources. The process of change is also a continuous pattern in every social unit; change in one unit affects other units of the social world, often in a chain reaction. For instance, change in the quality of health care can affect the workforce; a beleaguered workforce can affect the economy; instability in the economy can affect families, as breadwinners lose jobs; and family economic woes can affect religious communities because devastated families cannot afford to give money to the churches, mosques, or temples.

Sociologists generally do not judge these social processes as good or bad. Rather, they try to identify and explain the processes that take place within social units. Picture these processes as overlaying and penetrating our whole social world, from small groups to societies. Social units would be lifeless without the action brought about by social processes, just as body parts would be lifeless without the processes of electrical impulses shooting from the brain to each organ or the oxygen transmitted by blood coursing through our arteries to sustain each organ.

Video Link 1.5
Consider a social theory of war.

The Environment

Surrounding each social unit, whether a small family group or a large corporation, is an **environment**. It includes everything that influences the social unit, such as its physical and organizational surroundings and technological innovations. Each unit has its own environment to which it must adjust, just as each individual has a unique social world, including family, friends, and other social units that make up our immediate environment. Some parts of the environment are more important to the social unit than others. Your local church, synagogue, temple, or mosque is located in a community environment. That religious organization may seem autonomous and independent, but it depends on its national organization for guidelines and support, the local police force to protect the building from vandalism, and the local economy to provide jobs to members so that the members, in turn, can support the organization. If the religious education program is going to train children to understand the scriptures, local schools are needed to teach the children to read. A religious group may also be affected by other religious bodies, competing with one another for potential members from the community. These religious groups may work cooperatively—organizing a summer program for children or jointly sponsoring a holy-day celebration—or they may define one another as evil, each trying to stigmatize the other. Moreover, one local religious group may be composed primarily of professional and business people and another group mostly of laboring people. The religious groups may experience conflict in part because they each serve a different socioeconomic constituency.

The point is that to understand a social unit or the human body, we must consider the structure and processes within the unit as well as the interaction with the surrounding environment. No matter what social unit the sociologist studies, the unit cannot be understood without considering the interaction of that unit with its unique environment.

Perfect relationships or complete harmony between the social units is unusual. Social units, be they small groups or large organizations, are often motivated by self-interest and the need for self-preservation, with the result that they compete with other units for resources (time, money, skills, energy of members). Therefore, social units within a society are often in conflict. Whether groups are in conflict or mutually supportive does not change their interrelatedness; units are interdependent. The nature of that interdependence is likely to change over time and can be studied using the scientific method.

Studying the Social World: Levels of Analysis

Picture for a moment your sociology class as a social unit in your social world. Students (individuals) make up the class, the class (small group) is offered by the sociology department, the sociology department (a large group) is part of the college or university, the university (an organization) is located in a community and follows the practices approved by the social institution (education) of which it is a part,

Table 1.3 **The Structure of Society and Levels of Analysis**		
	Level	*Parts of Education*
Micro-level analysis	Interpersonal	Sociology class; study group cramming for an exam
	Local organizations	University; sociology department
Meso-level analysis	Organizations and institutions	State boards of education; National Education Association
	Ethnic groups within a nation	Islamic madrassas or Jewish yeshiva school systems
Macro-level analysis	Nations	Policy and laws governing education
	Global community	World literacy programs

and education is an institution located within a nation. The practices the university follows are determined by a larger accrediting unit that provides guidelines and oversight for institutions. The national society, represented by the national government, is shaped by global events—technological and economic competition between nations, natural disasters, global warming, wars, and terrorist attacks. Such events influence national policies and goals, including policies for the educational system. Thus, global tensions and conflicts may shape the experiences that individuals have with the curriculum in the local sociology classroom.

Each of these social units—from the smallest (the individual student) to the largest (society and the global system)—is referred to as a **level of analysis** (see Table 1.3). These levels are illustrated in the social world model at the beginning of each chapter and relate to that chapter's content as shown through examples in the model.

 MICRO-LEVEL ANALYSIS

Sometimes, sociologists ask questions about face-to-face interactions in small groups. A focus on small-group interaction entails **micro-level analysis**. This level is important because face-to-face interaction forms the basic foundation of all social groups and organizations to which we belong, from families to corporations to societies. We are members of many groups at the micro level.

To illustrate micro-level analysis, consider the problem of spousal abuse. Why does a person remain in an abusive relationship, knowing that each year thousands of people are killed by their lovers or mates and millions more are severely and repeatedly battered? To answer this question, several possible micro-level explanations can be considered. One view is that the abusive partner has convinced the abused person that she is powerless in the relationship or that she "deserves" the abuse. Therefore, she gives up in despair of ever being able to alter the situation. The abuse is viewed as part of the interaction—of action and reaction—and the partners come to see abuse as what comprises "normal" interaction.

Another explanation for remaining in the abusive relationship is that battering is a familiar part of the person's everyday life. However unpleasant and unnatural this may seem to outsiders, it may be seen by the abuser or by the abused as a "normal" and acceptable part of intimate relationships, especially if they grew up in an abusive family.

Another possibility is that an abused woman may fear that her children would be harmed or that she would be harshly judged by her family or church if she "abandoned" her mate. She may have few resources to make leaving the abusive situation possible. To study each of these possible explanations involves analysis at the micro level because each focuses on interpersonal interaction factors rather than on large society-wide trends or forces.

Meso-level analyses lead to quite different explanations for abuse.

 MESO-LEVEL ANALYSIS

Analysis of intermediate-size social units, called **meso-level analysis**, involves looking at units smaller than the nation but larger than the local community or even the region. This level includes national institutions (such as the economy of a country, the national educational system, or the political system within a country), nationwide organizations (such as a political party, a soccer league, or a national women's rights organization), nationwide corporations (such as Ford Motor Company or IBM), and ethnic groups that have an identity as a group (such as Jews, Mexican Americans, or Native Americans in the United States). Organizations, institutions, and ethnic communities are smaller than the nation or global social forces, but they are still beyond the everyday personal experience and control of individuals, unless those individuals organize to collectively change these structures. They are intermediate in the sense of being too large to know everyone in the group, but they are not as large as nation-states at the macro level. For example, meso-level states in the United States, provinces in Canada, or prefectures in Japan are more accessible and easier to change than the national bureaucracies of these countries.

Using meso-level analysis to examine changes in women's status, for example, could include study of women's legal, educational, religious, economic, political, scientific, and sports-related opportunities in society. However, meso-level changes that create new opportunities for women may also cause conflicts and even abuse within individual families at the micro level as women take advantage of expanding opportunities outside the home (Newman and Grauerholz 2002).

In discussing micro-level analysis, we used the example of domestic violence. We must be careful not to "blame the victim"—in this case, the abused person—for getting into an abusive relationship and for failing to act in ways that stop the abuse. To avoid blaming victims for their own suffering, many social scientists look for broader explanations of spousal abuse, such as the social conditions at the meso level of society that cause the problem (Straus and Gelles 1990). When a pattern of behavior in society occurs with increasing frequency, it cannot be understood solely from the point of view of individual cases or micro-level causes. For instance, sociological findings show that fluctuations in spousal or child abuse are related to levels of unemployment. Frustration resulting in abuse erupts within families when poor economic conditions make it nearly impossible for people to find a stable and reliable means of

Audio Link 1.3
Consider the macro ramifications of vaccinations.

supporting themselves and their families. Economic issues must be addressed if violence in the home is to be lessened.

MACRO-LEVEL ANALYSIS

Studying the largest social units in the social world, called **macro-level analysis**, involves looking at entire nations, global forces, and international social trends. Macro-level analysis is essential to our understanding of how larger social forces, such as global events, shape our everyday lives. A natural disaster such as the 2009 earthquake in Sumatra, the 2004 tsunami in Indonesia, the heat waves of the 2006 summer in Europe, the floods in the United States in the summer of 2008, or the frequent earthquakes around the world may change the foods we are able to serve at our family dinner table, since much of our food is now imported from other parts of the world. (Map 1.1 shows some of the most deadly natural disasters of the past few years.) Likewise, a political conflict on the other side of the planet can lead to war, which means that a member of your family may be called up on active duty and sent into harm's way more than 7,000 miles from your home. Each member of the family may experience individual stress, have trouble concentrating, and feel ill with worry. The entire globe has

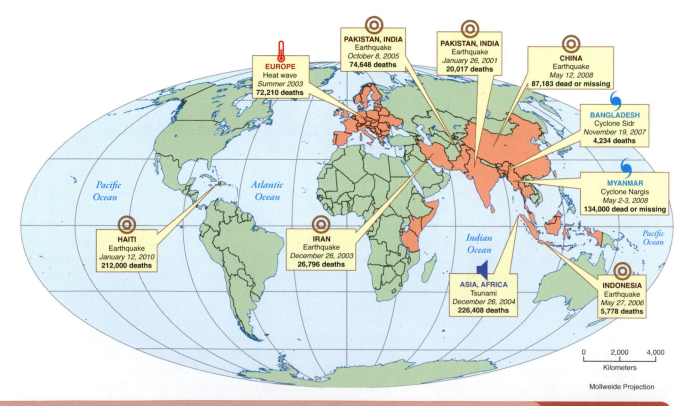

Map 1.1   The Ten Most Deadly Natural Disasters From January 2001 to January 2010

Source: EM-DAT emergency events database, Centre for Research on the Epidemiology of Disasters. Map by Anna Versluis.

become an interdependent social unit. If we are to prosper and thrive in the 21st century, we need to understand connections that go beyond our local communities.

Even patterns such as domestic violence, considered as micro- and meso-level issues above, can be examined at the macro level. A study of 95 societies around the world found that violence against women (especially rape) occurs at very different rates in different societies, with some societies being completely free of rape (Benderly 1982) and others having a "culture of rape." The most consistent predictor of violence against women was a macho conception of masculine roles and personality. Societies that did not define masculinity in terms of dominance and control were virtually free of rape. Some sociologists believe that the same pattern holds for domestic violence: A society or subgroup within society that teaches males that the finest expression of their masculinity is physical strength and domination is very likely to have battered women (Burn 2005). The point is that understanding individual human behavior often requires investigation of the larger societal beliefs that support that behavior. Worldwide patterns may tell us something about a social problem and offer new lenses for understanding that problem. Try the "Engaging Sociology" on the following page to test your understanding of levels of analysis and the sociological imagination.

This photo depicts the damage following the tsunami in Indonesia in 2005. This event not only changed the lives of people living where it struck but had ripple effects on economic exchange, relief efforts around the globe, and international trade that affected the cost of oil and the foods that were available to be served on your dining table.

Thinking Sociologically

What factors at each level of analysis influenced you to take this sociology class? Micro-level factors might include your advisor, your schedule, and your interest in sociology. At the meso and macro levels, what other factors influenced you?

Distinctions between each level of analysis are not sharply delineated. The micro level shades into the meso level, and the lines between the meso level and the macro level are blurry. Still, it is clear that in some micro-level social units, you know everyone, or at least every member of the social unit is only 2 degrees of relatedness away, that is, every person in the social unit knows someone whom you also know. We all participate in meso-level social units that are smaller than the nation but that can be huge. Millions of people may belong to the same religious denomination or the same political party. We share

connections with those people, and our lives are affected by people we do not even know. Consider the political activities in the United States and other countries that take place on the Internet. In political campaigns, millions of individuals join organizations such as Moveon.org and True Majority, participate in dialogues online, and contribute money to political organizations. People living thousands of miles from one another united financially and in spirit to support Obama-Biden or McCain-Palin in the 2008 U.S. election. Thus, the meso level is different from the micro level, but both influence us. The macro level is even more removed from the individual, but its impact can change our lives.

Video Link 1.6
Watch social forces impacting China.

The social world model presented in the chapter opening illustrates the interplay of micro-, meso-, and macro-level forces, and Figure 1.3 illustrates that this micro-to-macro model should be seen as a continuum. In the "Sociology Around the World" on page 25, we examine a village in Tunisia to see how macro-level forces influence a meso-level local community and individual micro-level lives.

Micro social units   Meso social units   Macro social units

Figure 1.3   The Micro-to-Macro Continuum

Engaging Sociology

Micro-Meso-Macro

Look at the list of various groups and other social units below. Identify which group would belong to in each level—(1) micro, (2) meso, or (3) macro. The definitions below should help you make your decisions. Answers are found online at www.pineforge.com/oswmedia3e.

Micro-level groups: Small, local-community social units in which everyone within that group knows everyone else or knows someone whom you also know.

Meso-level groups: Social units of intermediate size, usually so large that many members may never have heard the names of many other members and may have little access to the leaders yet not so large as to make the leaders seem distant or unapproachable. If you do not know the leader yourself, you probably know someone who is friends with the leader.

Macro-level groups: Large social units, usually quite bureaucratic, that operate at a national or a global level. Most members are unlikely to know or have communicated with the leaders personally or know someone who knows the leaders. The "business" of these groups is of international import and implication. Some research indicates that every person on the planet is within 7 degrees of relatedness to every other human being. A macro-level system is one in which *most* of the members are at least 5 degrees of relatedness from one another—that is, you know someone who knows someone who knows someone who knows someone who knows the person in question.

1. Micro social units

_____ Your nuclear family

_____ The United Nations

_____ A local chapter of the Lions Club or the Rotary Club

_____ Your high school baseball team

_____ India

_____ NATO (North Atlantic Treaty Organization)

_____ The First Baptist Church in Muncie, Indiana

_____ World Bank

_____ A family reunion

_____ Google, Inc. (international)

_____ The Department of Education for the Commonwealth of Kentucky

_____ The show choir in your local high school

_____ African Canadians

_____ The Dineh (Navajo) people

2. Meso social units

3. Macro social units

_____ Canada

_____ The Republican Party in the United States

_____ The World Court

_____ A fraternity at your college

_____ International Monetary Fund (IMF)

_____ The Ministry of Education for Spain

_____ The Roman Catholic Church (with its headquarters at the Vatican in Rome)

_____ Australia

_____ The Chi Omega National Sorority

_____ Boy Scout Troop #3 in Marion, Ohio

_____ Al Qaeda (an international alliance of terrorist organizations)

_____ The provincial government for the Canadian province of Ontario

_____ The United States of America

Most of these fall into clear categories, but some are "on the line," and one could legitimately place them in more than one group. It should be viewed as a continuum from micro to macro social units. See how your authors rate these at www.pineforge.com/oswmedia3e.

Sociology Around the World

Tunisian Village Meets the Modern World

This is a story of change as macro-level innovations enter a small traditional village. It illustrates how the social units of the social world model and the three levels of analysis enter into sociological analysis. As you read, try to identify both the units and the levels of analysis being discussed and the impact of globalization on a community that cannot know what these changes will bring.

The workday began at dawn as usual in the small fishing village on the coast of Tunisia, North Africa. Men prepared their nets and boats for the day, while women prepared breakfast and dressed the young children for school. About 10 a.m., it began—the event that would change this picturesque village forever. Bulldozers arrived first, followed by trench diggers and cement mixers, to begin their overhaul of the village.

Villagers had suspected something was afoot when important-looking officials arrived 2 months earlier with foreign businessmen, followed by two teams of surveyors. Without their approval, the government had sold the land that the village had held communally for generations to the foreigners so that they could build a multimillion-dollar hotel and casino. When concerned citizens asked what was happening in their village, they were assured that their way of life would not change. The contractor from the capital city of Tunis said that they would still have access to the beach and ocean for fishing. He also promised them many benefits from the hotel project—jobs, help from the government to improve roads and housing, and a higher standard of living.

The contractor had set up camp in a trailer on the beach, and word soon got around that he would be hiring some men for higher hourly wages than they could make in a day or even month of fishing. Rivalries soon developed between friends over who should apply for the limited number of jobs.

As the bulldozers moved in, residents had mixed opinions about the changes taking place in their village and their lives. Some saw the changes as exciting opportunities for new jobs and recognition of their beautiful village; others viewed the changes as destroying a lifestyle that was all they and generations before them had known.

Today, the village is dwarfed by the huge hotel, and the locals are looked on as quaint curiosities by the European tourists. Fishing has become a secondary source of employment to working in the hotel and casino or selling local crafts and trinkets to souvenir-seeking visitors. Many women are now employed outside the home by the hotel, creating new family structures as grandparents, unemployed men, and other relations take over child-rearing responsibilities.

To understand the changes in this one small village and other communities facing similar change, a sociologist uses the sociological imagination. This involves understanding the global political and economic trends that are affecting this village and its inhabitants (macro-level analysis). It requires comprehension of the transformation of social institutions within the nation (meso-level analysis). Finally, sociological investigation explores how change affects the individual Tunisian villagers (micro-level analysis).

To sociologically analyze the process of change, it is important to understand what is going on in this situation. The government officials and the international business representatives negotiated a lucrative deal to benefit both Tunisia and the business corporation. The community and its powerless residents presented few obstacles to the project from the point of view of the government, and in fact, government officials reasoned that the villagers could benefit from new jobs. However, the economic and family roles of the villagers—how they earned a living and how they raised their children—changed dramatically with the disruption of their traditional ways. The process of change began with the demand of people far from Tunisia for vacation spots in the sun. Ultimately, this process reached the village's local environment, profoundly affecting the village and everyone in it. For this Tunisian village, the old ways are gone forever.

Building and staffing of this resort in Tunisia—which is patronized by affluent people from other continents (global)—changed the economy, the culture, the social structure (meso level), and individual lives (micro level) in the local community.

Thinking Sociologically

Place the groups to which you belong in a hierarchy from micro, to meso, to macro levels. Note how each social unit and its subunits exist within a larger unit until you reach the level of the entire global community.

The Social World Model and This Book

Journal Article Link 1.3
Think about the levels of analysis and "gastronationalism."

The social world engulfs each of us from the moment of our birth until we die. Throughout our lives, each of us is part of a set of social relationships that provides guidelines for how we interact with others and how we see ourselves. This does not mean that human behavior is strictly determined by our links to the social world. Humans are more than mere puppets whose behavior is programmed by social structure. It does mean, however, that the individual and the larger social world influence each other. We are influenced by and we have influence on our social environment. The social world is a human creation, and we can and do change that which we create. It acts on us, and we act on it. In this sense, social units are constantly emerging and changing in the course of human interaction.

The difficulty for most of us is that we are so caught up in our daily concerns that we fail to see and understand the social forces that are at work in our personal lives. What we need are the conceptual and methodological tools to help us gain a more complete and accurate perspective on the social world. The concepts, theories, methods, and levels of analysis employed by sociologists are the very tools that will help give us that perspective. To use an analogy, each different lens of a camera gives the photographer a unique view of the world. Wide-angle lenses, close-up lenses, telephoto lenses, and special filters each serve a purpose in creating a distinctive picture or frame of the world. No one lens will provide the complete picture. Yet the combination of images produced by various lenses allows us to examine in detail aspects of the world we might ordinarily overlook. That is what the sociological perspective gives us: a unique set of tools to see the social world around us with deeper understanding. In seeing the social world from a sociological perspective, we are better able to understand who we are as social beings.

Throughout this book, the social world model will be used as the framework for understanding the social units, processes, and surrounding environment. Each social unit and process is taken out, examined, and returned to its place in the interconnected social world model so that you can comprehend the whole social world and its parts, like putting a puzzle together. Look for the model at the beginning of every chapter. You can also expect the micro-, meso-, and macro-level dimensions of issues to be explored throughout the text. Practice the levels of analysis in the following "Engaging Sociology."

Engaging Sociology

Micro-Meso-Macro: An Application Exercise

Imagine that there has been a major economic downturn (recession) in your local community. Identify four possible events at each level (micro, meso, and macro) that could contribute to the economic troubles in your town.

The micro (local community) level:

1. _____
2. _____
3. _____
4. _____

The meso (intermediate—state, organizational, or ethnic subculture) level:

1. _____
2. _____
3. _____
4. _____

The macro (national/global) level:

1. _____
2. _____
3. _____
4. _____

The next issue, then, is how we gather data that inform how we understand and influence the social world. When we say we know something about society, how is it that we know? What is considered evidence in sociology, and what lens (theory) do we use to interpret the data? These are the central issues of the next chapter.

What Have We Learned?

How can sociology help me understand my own life, who I am, and how I relate to others? This question was posed at the beginning of the chapter. Throughout this book you will find ideas and examples that will expand on the *sociological imagination*, illustrating how sociology can help you communicate more effectively and understand your interactions with others.

How do sociologists help us understand and even improve our lives in families, educational systems, or health care systems? Understanding organizations and bureaucracies can make us better family members, more effective citizens, and more adept at getting along with coworkers. As citizens of democracies, we need to understand how to influence our

social environments, from city councils, school boards, health care systems, and state legislatures to congressional, presidential, and other organizations.

How do national policies and global events influence my life? As the world changes, we need to be aware of global issues and how they affect us, from our job changes and lost jobs to skills demanded in the 21st century.

We live in a complex social world with many layers of interaction. If we really want to understand our own lives, we need to comprehend the levels of analysis that affect our lives and the connections between those levels. To do so wisely, we need both objective lenses for viewing this complex social world and accurate, valid information (facts) about the society. As the science of society, sociology can provide both tested empirical data and a broad, analytical perspective, as you will learn in the next chapter. Here is a summary of points from Chapter 1.

Key Points

- Humans are, at their very core, social animals—more akin to pack or herd animals than to individualistic cats. (See pp. 4–5.)

- Sociology is based on scientific findings, making it more reliable than commonsense beliefs in a particular culture. (See pp. 5–9.)

- A core idea in sociology is *the sociological imagination*. It requires that we see how our individual lives and personal troubles are shaped by historical and structural events outside our everyday lives. It also prods us to see how we can influence our society. (See pp. 9–10.)

- Sociology is a social science and, therefore, uses the tools of the sciences to establish credible evidence to understand our social world. As a science, sociology is scientific and objective rather than value laden. (See pp.12–13.)

- Sociology has pragmatic applications, including those that are essential for the job market. (See pp.13–17.)

- Sociology focuses on social units or groups, on social structures such as institutions, on social processes that give a social unit its dynamic character, and on their environments. (See pp. 17–20.)

- The social world model is the organizing theme of this book. Using the sociological imagination, we can understand our social world best by clarifying the interconnections between micro, meso, and macro levels of the social system. Each chapter of this book will examine society at these three levels of analysis. (See pp. 21–26.)

Contributing to Our Social World: What Can We Do?

At the end of this and all subsequent chapters, you will find suggestions for work, service learning, internships, and volunteering that encourage you to apply the ideas discussed in the chapter. Suggestions for Chapter 1 focus on student organizations for sociology majors and nonmajors.

At the Local Level

- *Student organizations and clubs:* Many sociology departments have organizations through which you can meet other students interested in sociology, get to know faculty members, and attend presentations by guest speakers. These clubs are usually not limited to sociology majors. If no such organization exists, consider forming one with the help of a faculty member. Sociologists also have an undergraduate honors society, Alpha Kappa Delta (AKΔ). Visit the AKΔ Web site at http://sites.google.com/site/alphakappadeltainternational and learn more about it and what it takes to form a chapter.

At the Regional, National, and Global Levels

- *The American Sociological Association (ASA):* This is the leading professional organization of sociologists in the United States. It has several programs and initiatives of special interest to students. Visit the ASA Web site at www.asanet.org, and click on the "Students" link at the top of the page. Read the items and follow the links to additional material on the advantages available to students.

- *State and regional associations:* These groups are especially student friendly and feature publications and sessions at their annual meetings specifically for undergraduates. The organizations and Web site addresses are listed by the ASA, with direct links to their home pages at http://www2.asanet.org/governance/aligned.html.

- *The International Sociological Association (ISA):* This organization serves sociologists from around the world. Every 4 years, they have a large meeting (Gothenburg, Sweden, in July 2010 and Yokohama, Japan, in July 2014). Specialty groups within ISA hold conferences in many different countries the other years. Check out www.isa-sociology.org.

 For chapter-specific resources, including **Frontline**, **TED**, and **YouTube** videos; self-quizzes; web exercises; and more, visit **www.pineforge.com/oswmedia3e**.

Examining the Social World

How Do We Know?

Science is about knowing through careful systematic investigation. Pictured here are scientists: archaeologists, a sociologist, a geologist, and a chemist. Sociology is a social science because of the way we gather scientific evidence to understand society and human interactions.

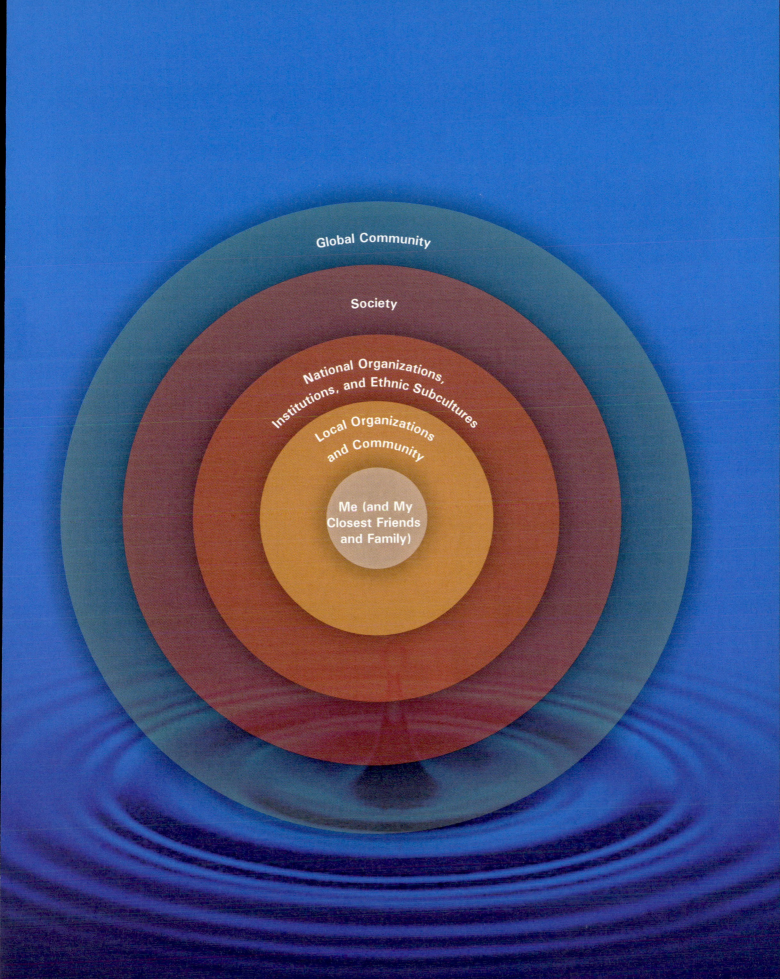

Global Community

Society

National Organizations,
Institutions, and Ethnic Subcultures

Local Organizations
and Community

Me (and My
Closest Friends
and Family)

Think About It	
Me (and My Inner Circle)	When you say that you know something, how do you know?
Local Community	When you are trying to convince neighbors or people in your community of your opinion, why is evidence important?
National Institutions; Complex Organizations; Ethnic Groups	How do sociologists go about gathering dependable data about families, educational institutions, or ethnic groups?
National Society	What does it mean to study national societal patterns scientifically?
Global Community	How can theories about global interactions help us understand our own lives at the micro level?

Let us travel to the Southern Hemisphere to meet a teenage boy, Hector. He is a 16-year-old living in a *favela* (slum) on the outskirts of São Paulo, Brazil. He is a polite, bright boy, but his chances of getting an education and a steady job in his world are limited. Like millions of other children around the world, he comes from a poor family that migrated to the urban area in search of a better life. However, his family ended up in a crowded slum with only a shared spigot for water and one string of electric lights along the dirt road going up the hill on which they live. The sanitary conditions in his community are appalling—open sewers, no garbage collection—which makes the people susceptible to various diseases. His family is relatively fortunate, perhaps, for they have cement walls and wood flooring, although no water or electricity. Many adjacent dwellings are little more than cardboard walls with corrugated metal roofs and dirt floors.

Hector wanted to stay in school but was forced to drop out to help support his family. Since leaving school, he has picked up odd jobs—deliveries, trash pickup, janitorial work, gardening—to help pay the few centavos for the family's dwelling and to buy food to support his parents and six siblings. Even when he was in school, Hector's experience was discouraging. He was not a bad student, and some teachers encouraged him to continue, but other students from the city teased the *favela* kids and made them feel unwelcome. Most of his friends dropped out before he did. Hector often missed school because of other obligations—looking for part-time work, visiting a sick relative, or taking care of a younger sibling. The immediate need to put food on the table outweighed the long-term value of staying in school. What is the bottom line for Hector and millions like him? Because of his limited education and work skills, obligations to his family, and limited opportunities, he most likely will continue to live in poverty.

Sociologists are interested in the factors that influence the social world of children like Hector: family, friends, school, community, and the place of one's nation in the global political and economic structural systems. To understand how sociologists study poverty and many other social issues, we consider the theories and methods they use to do their work. Understanding the *how* helps us see that sociology is more than guesswork or opinion. Rather, it involves the use of scientific methods based on a systematic process for expanding knowledge of the social world.

Whatever our area of study or job interests, we are likely to find ourselves asking sociological questions. All of us will face situations where conducting a research study will help our organization or community; knowing what is involved in a good study and the tools to carry out a study will make us more effective participants. Consider some examples of questions we might ask: Why is there binge drinking on college campuses? Do sexually explicit videos and magazines reinforce

Slum dwellers of São Paulo, Brazil. Hector lives in a neighborhood with shelters made of available materials such as boxes, with no electricity or running water and poor sanitation.

sexist stereotypes or encourage sexual violence? Do tough laws and longer prison sentences deter people from engaging in criminal conduct? How do we develop our religious and political beliefs? Do classroom teachers treat children from different social classes, races, or ethnic groups the same or differently? How are the Internet and other technologies affecting everyday life for people around the world? How are people's lives affected by the globalization of jobs and companies?

This chapter will introduce you to the basic tools used to plan studies and gather dependable information on topics of interest. It will help you understand how sociology approaches research questions. To this end, we will consider the development of sociology as a science, the relationship between sociological theories and research methods, how sociologists study the social world using the process and tools of research methods, the ethics involved in conducting sociological research, and contemporary sociological theories. We start with some ideas underlying sociology as a science.

Ideas Underlying Science

Throughout most of human history, people came to "know" the world by the traditions passed down from one generation to the next. Things were so because authoritative people in the culture said they were so. Often, there was reliance on magical or religious explanations of the forces in nature, and these explanations became part of tradition. People were interested in the natural world and observed it carefully, but with advances in the natural sciences, observations of cause-and-effect processes became more systematic and controlled. As the way of knowing about the world shifted, tradition and magic as the primary means to understand the world were challenged. It was little more than 200 years ago that people thought lightning storms were a sign of an angry god, not electricity caused by meteorological forces.

The scientific approach is based on several core ideas: First, there is a real physical and social world that can be studied scientifically. Second, there is a certain order to the world, with identifiable patterns that result from a series of causes and effects. The world is not merely a collection of unrelated random events but rather events that are systematically sequenced and patterned—that is, *causally* related. Third, the way to gain knowledge of the world is to subject it to empirical testing. **Empirical knowledge** means that the facts have been objectively (without opinion or bias) observed and carefully measured and that the reality of what is being measured is the same for all the people who observe it.

For knowledge to be scientific, it must come from phenomena that can be observed and measured. Phenomena that cannot be subject to measurement are not within the realm of scientific inquiry. The existence of God, the devil, heaven, hell, and the soul cannot be observed and measured and therefore cannot be examined scientifically. While certain religious notions

Lightning has been understood as a form of electricity rather than a message from an angry god only since 1752, thanks to an experiment by Benjamin Franklin.

Encyclopedia Link 2.1
Read more about the scientific method.

cannot themselves be subjects of scientific inquiry, religion can be studied in terms of the role it plays in society and our lives: its impact on our values and behavior (the sociology of religion), the historical development of specific religious traditions (the history of religion), or the emotional comfort and stability it brings to people (the psychology of religion).

Finally, science is rooted in **objectivity**, using methods that limit the impact of the researcher's personal opinions or biases on the study being planned, data collection, and analysis of evidence about the social world. **Evidence** refers to facts and information that are confirmed through systematic testing. This involves use of our five senses, sometimes enhanced with research tools. Moreover, scientists are obliged not to distort their research findings so as to promote a particular point of view. Scientific research is judged first on whether it relies on techniques to be objective.

One way to evaluate objectivity is to see whether the research does or does not support what the researcher thinks is true. For example, if we wish to study whether Hector dropped out of school because of his need to work, then we must plan the research study so that we can either support or disprove our hypothesis (educated guess or prediction) about Hector's situation.

You have probably seen one of the *CSI (Crime Scene Investigation)* series on television. The shows in this series depict the importance of careful collection of data and commitment to objective analysis. Sociologists deal with different issues, but the same concern for accuracy in gathering data guides their work. Failure to meet these standards—empirical knowledge, objectivity, and scientific evidence—means that a study is not scientific. Someone's ideas can seem plausible and logical but may still not be supported by the facts. This is why evidence is so important. Sociology is concerned with having accurate evidence, and it is important to know what is or is not considered accurate, dependable evidence.

Sociologists have come a long way from the early explanations of the social world that were based on the moralizing of the 18th- and 19th-century social philosophers and the guesswork of social planners. Part of the excitement of sociology today comes from the challenge to improve the scientific procedures applied to the study of humans and social behavior and to base policy on carefully collected and analyzed data.

Thinking Sociologically

Imagine that you want to understand people who live in poverty in your own state or province. Why are scientifically gathered data based on a wide sample of people who have or are currently experiencing poverty preferable to explanations based only on anecdotes told by people who made it out of poverty?

Empirical Research and Social Theory

We all have beliefs that we take for granted about how our social world works. Social researchers use the scientific method to examine these views of society. They assume that (a) there are predictable social relationships in the world, (b) social situations will recur in certain patterns, and (c) social situations have causes that can be understood. If the social world were totally chaotic, little would be gained by scientific study.

Just as individuals develop preferences for different religious or political beliefs that guide their lives, sociologists develop preferences for different social theories. The main difference between individual beliefs and social theories is that the latter are subject to ongoing, systematic testing.

Theories are statements or explanations of how two or more facts are related to each other. Sociological theories try to explain social interactions, behaviors, and problems. A good theory should allow the scientist to make predictions about the social world. Different theories are useful at each level of analysis in the social world (micro, meso, and macro); which theory a sociologist uses to study the social world depends on the level of analysis to be studied, as illustrated in the following model.

Each theory discussed in this chapter gives a perspective on the way the social world works. To study Hector's life in Brazil, researchers might focus on the micro-level interactions between Hector and his family members, peers,

What factors—individual, group, institutional, national, and global—cause poverty in the developing world? This grocery store in Ethiopia illustrates poverty in parts of Africa, Latin America, and Asia. Imagine that this is the only place for miles around to buy food.

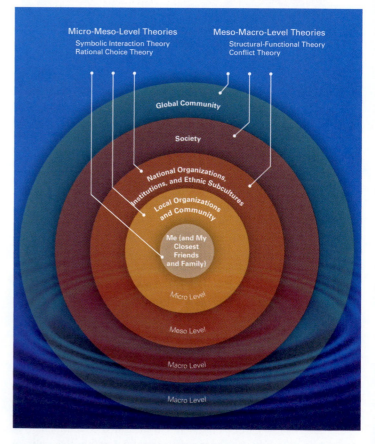

teachers, and employers as factors that contribute to his situation. For example, why does Hector find some activities (working) more realistic or immediately rewarding than others (attending school)? A meso-level focus might examine the organizations and institutions—such as the business world, the schools, and the religious communities in Brazil—to see how they shape the forces that affect Hector's life. Alternatively, the focus might be on macro-level analysis—the class structure (rich to poor) of the society and the global forces, such as trade relations between Brazil and other countries, that influence opportunities for the Brazilian poor.

Sociologists focus on group or societal explanations to understand issues such as the poverty that haunts Hector's life. Different research methods to collect data are appropriate at different levels of analysis (micro, meso, and macro) and depend on the theory being used and the question being researched.

Scientists, including sociologists, often use theories to predict why things happen and under what conditions they are likely to happen. So theory tells the researcher what to look for and what concepts or variables need to be measured. However, explanations about the relationships between social variables need to be tested. This is where research methods—the procedures one uses to gather data—are relevant. If a theory is not supported by the data, it must be reformulated or discarded. These facts (data) collected must be carefully assessed. Theory and research are used together and are mutually dependent. We turn first to the discussion of how we gather data.

How Sociologists Study the Social World

How do we know? Sociologists design research studies using scientific tools to answer sociological questions. What is presented here is a skeleton of the research process that sociologists and other social scientists spend years studying and perfecting. This section will begin to provide a sense of how sociologists study issues and know what they know. If you study more sociology, you will learn more about the research process. It is exciting to collect accurate information and find out answers to important, meaningful questions that can make a difference in people's lives and in your own organization or community.

A researcher follows a number of logically related steps.

A. Planning a research study
- *Step 1:* Define a topic or problem that can be investigated scientifically.
- *Step 2:* Review existing relevant research studies and theory to refine the topic and define variables.
- *Step 3:* Formulate hypotheses or research questions and figure out how to define and measure the variables.

B. Designing the research plan and method for collecting the data

Gathering data—through interviews, direct observations of behavior, experiments, and other methods—is part of the science of sociological investigation.

- *Step 4:* Design the research plan that specifies how the data will be gathered.
- *Step 5:* Select a sample of people or groups to study.
- *Step 6:* Collect the data using appropriate research methods.

C. Making sense of the data
- *Step 7:* Analyze the data, figuring out exactly what the study says about the research question(s) from Step 3.
- *Step 8:* Draw conclusions and present the final report, including suggestions for future research. Recommendations for actions may be part of the report.

Audio Link 2.1
How would you study the kindness of strangers?

Each of these steps is very important, whether you become a professional sociologist or do a study for a local organization or your workplace. To introduce the research process, we provide a quick summary reduced to four central issues: (1) planning a research study, (2) designing the research and collecting data, (3) analyzing the data, and (4) drawing conclusions.

Planning a Research Study

Planning a research study involves four main steps: (1) define the topic or problem clearly, (2) find out what is already known about the topic, (3) formulate hypotheses (educated guesses), and (4) develop clear definitions of variables and ways to measure them.

Step 1, the most important step, is to define a topic or problem that can be investigated scientifically. Without a clear problem, the research will go nowhere. Using poverty as an example of a broad topic area, sociologists could focus on a number of issues—for example, rates of poverty in different countries, poverty and levels of education, the relationship of race or gender to poverty, or the relationship between poverty and drug or alcohol abuse. These broad topic areas are a good start, but they must be more specific and defined before they become suitable topics for research. One must clarify specifically what one wants to know about the topic.

Specific research topics, ones that can be measured and tested, are usually posed in the form of questions: Why is it that, in some countries, large segments of the population live in poverty? Why are there many more women and people of color living in poverty? What causes some students—especially those in poor families—to drop out of school? Are people who are poor more vulnerable to excessive drug or alcohol use? The research question must be asked in a precise way. Otherwise, it cannot be tested empirically. Developing good research questions is extremely important in sound scientific research.

Thinking Sociologically

Pick a topic of interest to you. Now, write a research question based on your topic.

Step 2 in planning the research is reviewing relevant existing research studies and theory to determine what other researchers have already learned about the topic. One needs to know how the previous research was done, how terms such as *poverty* were defined, and the strengths and limitations of that research. Social scientists can then link their study to existing findings and expand what is known about the topic. This step usually involves combing through scholarly journals and books on the topic. In the case of Hector, researchers would need to identify what previous studies have said about why young people living in poverty drop out of school.

In *Step 3* (based on the review of the literature on the topic in Step 2), social scientists often formulate **hypotheses**—educated guesses about the relationship between variables (see definition below) such as amount of education and likelihood of living in poverty. A hypothesis predicts the relationship between two or more variables and the ways in which variables are related to each other. A hypothesis to study Hector's situation might be as follows: "Poverty is a major cause of teenagers in the *favela* dropping out of school because they need to earn money for the family." Another hypothesis could predict the opposite—that dropping out of school leads to poverty. Again, a hypothesis provides a statement that we can then test to see if it is true.

Researchers then identify the key concepts, or ideas, in the hypothesis (e.g., poverty and dropping out of school). These concepts can be measured by collecting facts or data. This process of determining how to measure concepts is called *operationalizing variables*. **Variables** are concepts (ideas) that can vary in frequency of occurrence from one time, place, or

person to another. Examples include levels of poverty, percentage of people living in poverty, or number of years of formal education. Variables can then be measured by collecting data to test the hypothesized relationships between variables.

To operationalize variables, researchers link concepts such as poverty to specific measurements. Using the hypothesis above, concepts such as school dropouts and poverty can be measured by determining the number of times they occur. Dropouts, for instance, might be defined by the number of days of school missed in a designated period of time according to school records. Poverty could be defined as having an annual income that is less than half of the average income for that size of family in Brazil. Measurement of poverty could also include family assets such as ownership of property or other tangible goods such as cattle, automobiles, and indoor plumbing, as well as access to medical care, education, transportation, and other services available to citizens. It is important to be clear, precise, and consistent in how one measures poverty. This is essential so that those reading the study are clear on how the study was done and those doing follow-up studies can critique and improve on the study. Background research—including examination of previous studies of poverty—can provide guidelines or examples for how to operationalize variables.

Thinking Sociologically

Considering your research question, what are your variables, and how could you operationalize them?

At the heart of the research process is the effort to find causal relationships (i.e., one variable causes another one to change) and not just covariations (variables changing together). The following key research terms are important in understanding how two variables are related:

- **Correlation** refers to a relationship between variables in which change in one variable is associated with change in another. The hypothesis above predicts that poverty and teenagers dropping out of school vary together.
- **Cause-and-effect relationships** help establish the relationship between two variables. Once we have determined that there is probably a relationship, or correlation (the fact that the two variables, such as poverty and dropping out of school, both occur in the same situation), we need to take the next step of testing for a causal relationship between variables to see if one variable causes change in another. The **independent variable** is hypothesized to cause the change. In terms of time sequence, it comes first and affects the **dependent variable**. If we hypothesize that poverty causes Hector and others to drop out of school, *poverty* is the independent variable in this hypothesis and *dropping out of school* is the dependent variable,

The months when ice cream is consumed the most are the same months when drownings occur. However, this is not because of a causal connection. Both variables are related to another factor—hot weather.

dependent variables but they vary together, often due to a third variable affecting both of them. For example, if the quantity of ice cream consumed is highest during those weeks of the year when most drownings occur, these two events are correlated. However, eating ice cream did not cause the increase in deaths. Indeed, hot weather may have caused more people both to purchase ice cream and to go swimming, thus resulting in more drowning incidents—a spurious relationship. **Controls** are steps used by researchers to eliminate all variables except those related to the hypothesis—especially those variables that might be spurious. Using controls helps ensure that the relationship is not spurious.

Another important idea in designing the research process is whether to start with the big picture and deduce patterns from this picture or to start with facts from collected data and develop a bigger picture, or theory. Inductive and deductive reasoning lay out these design processes. **Deductive reasoning** begins with broad general ideas, or theories, of human social behavior. From these ideas, more specific patterns are identified or "deduced" using logical reasoning. These educated guesses—which still do not have data to support them—are called hypotheses.

Inductive reasoning, on the other hand, begins with specific facts (data) or evidence and tries to find or develop a theory—a more generalized set of concepts—to explain the facts. The researcher first collects facts and then attempts to explain the relationship between these facts. In so doing, the researcher is building up to a generalization, moving from the concrete facts to the abstract theory. The specific facts give rise to a theory, and that theory can be tested again in the future using new data. Figure 2.1 illustrates the relationship of inductive and deductive reasoning to theory and facts. Research data may confirm a theory, force its modification, require the scientist to abandon it altogether, or lead to an entirely new theory.

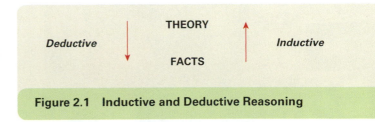

Figure 2.1   Inductive and Deductive Reasoning

Designing the Research Method and Collecting the Data

After the researcher has carefully planned the study, *Step 4* is to select appropriate data collection methods. This selection depends on the levels of analysis of the research question (micro, meso, and macro) the researcher is asking. If

dependent on the poverty. In determining cause and effect, the independent variable must always precede the dependent variable in time sequence if we are to say that one variable causes another.

- **Spurious relationships** occur when there is no causal relationship between the independent and

Micro Level

Individual	Hector
Small group	Hector's family and close friends
Local community	The *favela*; Hector's local school, church, neighborhood organizations

Meso Level

Organizations	Brazilian corporations, Catholic Church, and local school system in Brazil
Institutions	Family; education; political, economic, and health systems in the region or nation of Brazil
Ethnic subcultures	Native peoples, African-Brazilians

Macro Level

National society	Social policies, trends, and programs in Brazil
Global community of nations	Status of Brazil in global economy; trade relations with other countries; programs of international organizations or corporations

Figure 2.2   The Social World Model and Levels of Analysis

researchers want to answer a macro-level research question, such as the effect of poverty on school success nationwide, they are likely to focus on large-scale social and economic data sources. To learn about micro-level issues such as the influence of peers on an individual's decision to drop out of school, researchers will focus on small-group interactions. Figure 2.2 illustrates the different levels of analysis.

The method selected is one of the most important decisions in the research process because the quality of the data collected is directly related to answering the research question. Accuracy in planning can mean the difference between a fruitful scientific study and data that have little meaning.

The primary methods used to collect data for research studies include surveys (both interviews and questionnaires), observation studies, controlled experiments, and use of existing materials. Our discussion cannot go into detail about how researchers use these techniques, but a brief explanation gives an idea of why they use these primary methods.

The **survey method** is used when sociologists want to gather information directly from a number of people regarding how they think or feel or what they do. Two forms of surveys are common: the interview and the questionnaire. Both involve a series of questions asked of respondents.

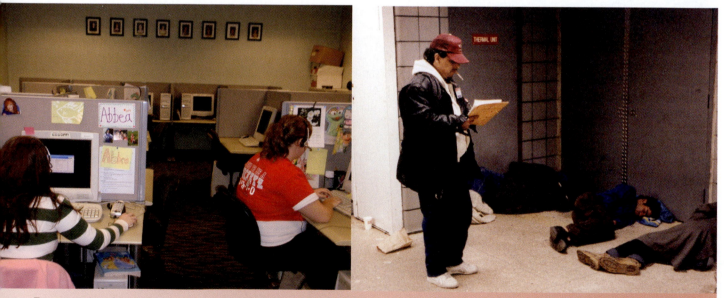

Two examples of the survey are the telephone research lab—like this one on the left at Wright State University in Ohio—and the government census. The university's lab hires out for government or business surveys. The census is taken in the United States and many other countries every 10 years. Sometimes it is difficult to gather accurate data on the entire population, as in the situation with this census worker, who is counting homeless people in Penn Station in New York City.

Interviews are conducted by talking directly with people and asking questions in person or by telephone. *Questionnaires* are written questions to which respondents reply in writing or electronically. In both cases, questions may be open-ended, allowing the respondent to say or write whatever comes to mind, or closed-ended, requiring the respondent to choose from a set of possible answers.

One method to study school dropouts is to survey teenagers about what caused them to leave school. The researcher would have to evaluate whether an interview or questionnaire would provide the best information. Interviews are more time-consuming and labor-intensive than questionnaires but are better for gathering in-depth information. However, if the researcher wants information from a large number of teenagers, questionnaires are often more practical and less costly.

Thinking Sociologically

How would you word questions in a survey about the effects of peer influence on dropping out of school? How could you find out whether your questions are good ones? Would a survey be a good method of data collection to study this research question? Why or why not?

Field studies (also called observational methods) are used when systematic, planned observation of interaction is needed to obtain data. *Observation*—the systematic viewing and recording of behavior or interaction in the settings where the behavior takes place—can take several forms. In *nonparticipant observation*, the researcher is not involved in group activities but observes or videotapes the activity; an example would be observing a classroom that Hector and his friends attend to study the group dynamics without those in the classroom being aware of the researcher's presence. Observation may be done from behind a one-way mirror.

Participant observation occurs when the researcher actually participates in the activities of the group being studied. The researcher, for instance, might hang out with Hector and his friends or join Alcoholics Anonymous to observe group processes as they occur naturally. Participation is particularly useful when studying illegal or deviant activities, where it might be impossible to gain scientifically useful information any other way.

Problems for participant-observers are that they may alter group functioning and interaction by their presence—a process called *research effects*—or they become involved in the group to such a degree that objectivity becomes difficult. Participation is more likely

to be a problem in a smaller group, where the very presence of the researcher may change the group dynamics. Furthermore, the researcher must be aware that interpretation of the social scene is especially subject to bias. Despite these potential problems, observation remains a useful way of obtaining information.

The results from observation studies are referred to as *qualitative* (involving the use of written or verbal language or observation to interpret the meaning of something) rather than *quantitative* (numerical data) research. They provide valuable information that is rich in detail about the context of the situation, such as the *favela* or Hector's classroom, rather than providing hard data such as percentages or other numbers that can be illustrated in neat tables.

Ethnography (also called ethnographic research) is a form of field study involving some unique strategies of data collection and methods of analysis. The researcher pursues any ideas that may shed light on the research problem and uses his or her own self-reflection to determine what might work as the research progresses. Often, the research takes place in a natural setting (home, office, playground) and involves using several different data collection techniques, such as interviewing and observing, with recorded systematic field notes about the observations. Thus, ethnography relies on the researcher pursuing all relevant data to be successful. The research evolves in response to what the researcher learns as the research progresses. Unlike research driven by hypotheses to be tested, this method allows the researcher to respond to new ideas that come up during the research (Creswell 2009).

In **controlled experiments**, researchers manipulate the main variable being studied to determine the social consequences of a change in that variable. All variables except the one being studied are held constant. A controlled experiment usually requires an **experimental group**, in which people are exposed to the variable being studied to test the effects of manipulating the main variable, and a **control group**, in which the participants are not exposed to the variable the experimenter wants to test. The control group provides a baseline with which the experimental group can be compared. Controlled experiments are powerful because they are the most accurate test of cause and effect. By separating the sample into experimental and control groups, the researcher can see if the study's independent variable makes a difference in the behavior of people who are exposed to that variable. For example, researchers may want to determine whether teacher help and support for Hector and other kids from the *favela* affect their classroom achievement. The control group is exposed to the usual teaching, and the experimental group is provided with extra support in the classroom. If there is a more positive effect on achievement in the experimental group than the control group, researchers can conclude that extra help raises achievement.

Journal Article Link 2.1
Think about the sample method used in this study.

Experiments, such as the one pictured above, are especially effective at controlling all the variables to be able to know which outcomes result from the independent variable. Of course, they are not as effective as field studies in terms of being real-life situations, and they are more subject to research effects.

Despite the advantages of controlled experiments, there are some drawbacks to using this method: Many sociological questions cannot be studied in controlled settings because they deal with macro-level organizations and social forces that cannot be placed in a controlled situation. For example, Hector's situation in the *favela* cannot be studied in a laboratory setting. Second, the mere fact of being in a laboratory setting and knowing one is in an experiment may affect the research results—another form of research effect. Third, because of ethical constraints, social scientists cannot do studies that might harm people. Thus, there are many variables that social scientists cannot introduce in the laboratory.

Journal Article Link 2.2
Read about qualitative research.

Existing sources refer to data that already exist but are being employed in a new way or to understand a new relationship. Two main approaches to using existing sources are (1) secondary analysis and (2) content analysis.

Secondary analysis uses existing data, information that has already been collected in other studies. Often, large data-collecting organizations such as the United Nations or a country's census bureau, the national education department, or a private research organization will make data available for use by researchers. Consider the question of the dropout rate in Brazil. Researchers can learn a great deal about the patterns of school dropouts from analysis of information gathered by ministries or departments of education.

Likewise, if we want to compare modern dropout rates with those of an earlier time, we may find data from previous decades to be invaluable. Sometimes secondary analysis is the sole method of data collection, and sometimes it is used along with other methods.

Despite its usefulness, secondary analysis cannot be used in some research studies, and it has several potential weaknesses. First, not all data sets are representative of the total population the researcher is studying, especially when comparing data sets from countries using different data-gathering techniques. Second, secondary analysis does not touch the "human side" of research questions in the way interviews or observation can. Secondary analysis involves no direct observation of the behavior in question or contact with those involved. School dropouts, for example, have individual stories and problems that are not told by large, impersonal data sets. Third, any problems or biases that exist in the original data are carried over to the secondary analysis. Despite such limitations, however, secondary analysis can be an excellent way to do meso- or macro-level studies that reveal large-scale patterns in the social world.

Content analysis involves systematic categorizing and recording of information from written or recorded sources. With content analysis (a common method in historical research and study of organizations), sociologists can gather the data they need from printed materials—books, magazines, video recordings, newspapers, laws, letters, memos, and sometimes even artwork. They develop a coding system to classify the source content. A researcher trying to understand shifts in Brazilian attitudes toward Hector's poverty could do a content analysis of popular magazines to see how many pages or stories were devoted to child poverty in the Brazilian media in 1960, 1970, 1980, 1990, 2000, and 2010. Content analysis has the advantage of being relatively inexpensive and easy to do. It is also unobtrusive, meaning that the researcher does not influence the participants being investigated by having direct contact. Furthermore, using materials in historical sequence can be effective in recognizing patterns over time. However, the accuracy of the study depends on what content is available.

Thinking Sociologically

What methods would be appropriate to collect data on your research question?

An example of historical research using existing materials to examine social patterns is illustrated in "Sociology in Our Social World." In this case, the researcher, Virginia Kemp Fish, studied records and writings of early women sociologists in Chicago to discover the contributions to sociology and to the betterment of society.

Sociology in Our Social World

The Hull House Circle: Historical Content Analysis in Sociology

Jane Addams, social researcher, critic, and reformer.

Hull House was a settlement house in Chicago, one of several residences established in urban immigrant neighborhoods. Settlement houses created a sense of community for residents and offered a multitude of services to help residents and neighbors negotiate poverty. In addition to offering services, Hull House was the location for a group of women social researchers, reformers, and activists. The well-known social activist Jane Addams (1860–1935), who received a Nobel Peace Prize, was one of them. These women had obtained college degrees in some of the few fields then open to women (political science, law, economics), and because they were often excluded from full-time careers in their fields, they used their education and skills to help others and to do research on social conditions, contributing to the development of the science of sociology. Until recently, women sociologists, such as the members of the Hull House Circle, have not received much attention for their contributions to the science of sociology. Yet some of the earliest social survey research was conducted by the women connected with Hull House, sometimes employing the Hull House residents to help collect data. These women led the first systematic attempt to describe an immigrant community in an American city, a study found in *Hull House Maps and Papers* (Residents of Hull House [ca.1895] 1970).

Historical research can be an important source of data for sociological analysis, for history can demonstrate causal events vividly. Historical circumstances help us understand why things evolved to the present state of affairs. Virginia Kemp Fish (1986), who originated the designation Hull House Circle, researched historical literature to learn more about the lives and contributions of these women and their place in the sociological literature. She examined records, letters, biographies, and other historical sources to piece together their stories. By studying their writings and their activist work, Fish showed how they supported each other's work and scholarship and provided emotional encouragement and intellectual stimulation rather than interacting in terms of an unequal power distribution. Fish also made an interesting observation about these women's professional styles as compared with those of men. While men often received their training and support from a mentor (an older, established, and respected man in the field), the women of Hull House operated within a network of egalitarian relationships and interactions.

According to Fish's (1986) research, the data and documents collected by their leader, Jane Addams, and other Hull House women provide baseline information that has been used as a starting point or comparison for later studies—for social researchers in the fields of immigration, ethnic relations, poverty, health care, housing, unemployment, work and occupations, delinquency and crime, war, and social movements.

Social scientists aren't the only professionals who use triangulation. Journalists also consult a variety of sources, including social scientists, to put together news broadcasts.

Triangulation, or multiple methods of social research, combines two or more methods of data collection to enhance the amount of data for analysis and the accuracy of the findings. To study Hector's situation, a research study could use macro-level data on poverty in Brazil and micro-level interviews with Hector and his peers to determine their attitudes and goals. Thus, if all findings point to the same conclusion, the researcher can feel much more confident about the study results. Data collection techniques—survey, field study, controlled experimentation, and analysis of existing sources—represent the dominant methods used to collect data for sociological research.

Step 5 involves selecting a sample. It would be impossible to study the reasons for poverty or for every teenager dropping out of school in Brazil. Researchers must select a representative group to study that will help us understand the larger group. A part of the research design is determining how to make sure the study includes people who are typical of the total group. When the research study involves a survey or field observation, sociologists need to decide who will be observed or questioned to provide responses representative of the whole. This involves careful selection of a **sample**, a small and more manageable group of people to study, systematically chosen to accurately represent the characteristics of the entire group (or population) being studied.

Researchers use many types of samples. A common one, the representative sample, attempts to accurately reflect the group being studied so that the sample results can be generalized or applied to the larger population. In the case of Hector's *favela*, a sample for a study could be drawn from all 13- to 16-year-olds in his region or city of Brazil.

The most common form of representative sample is the *random sample*. People from every walk of life and every group within the population have an equal chance of being selected for the study. By observing or talking with this smaller group selected from the total population under study, the researcher can get an accurate picture of the total population and have confidence that the findings apply to the larger group. Drawing a representative sample is not always simple. In the case of Brazil, people constantly move in and out of the *favela*. Those who have just arrived may not have the same characteristics as those who have been living there a long time. Developing an effective sampling technique is often a complex process, but it is important to have a sample that represents the group being studied. If researchers wanted to know the attitudes of Brazilian teenagers toward school, they would not question only adults from the city of São Paulo, Brazil.

Step 6 involves collecting the data. Now that the appropriate research method for collecting data and the sample to study have been selected, the researcher's next step is to analyze the data collected and see what they say about the research questions and hypotheses.

Analysis: Making Sense of the Data

Once data are gathered, *Step 7* is to analyze the data and evaluate the relationship of variables to each other. Now that we have, say, 500 questionnaires or a notebook full of field observation notes, what do we do with them? Social researchers use multiple techniques to analyze data. First, the variables being tested must be clear: If dropout rates are high among Hector's friends, was their school achievement low? How were they treated by peers and teachers? What other factors are present? This analysis can become quite complex, but the purpose is the same—to determine the relationship between the variables being examined. Second, sociologists determine the most effective tools to analyze the relationships between variables. Sociology is not guesswork or speculation. It involves careful, objective analysis of specific data.

Discussion and criticism are an important part of science and make possible more accurate findings, new ideas and interpretations, and more sophisticated methodological approaches to problems. Interpretation of data involves judgment and opinion, often based on the theory guiding the research. As such, it can be challenged by other researchers, who might interpret the results differently or challenge the methods used to collect and analyze the data. Sociologists grow through these critiques, as does the field of sociology itself. Because every research study should be *replicable*—capable of being repeated—enough information must be given to ensure that another researcher could repeat the study and compare the results.

Step 8 involves discussion of results and drawing conclusions for the analysis. A report is developed, outlining the research project and analysis of the data collected. The final section of the report presents a discussion of the results, draws conclusions as to whether or not the hypotheses were supported, interprets the results, and makes recommendations from the researcher's point of view, if appropriate. As part of the presentation and discussion of results, the report may contain tables or figures presenting summaries of data that are useful in understanding the data. In the next "Engaging Sociology," "How to Read a Research Table" provides useful tips on reading research tables found in journal articles and newspapers.

Video Link 2.1
Watch an interesting presentation of data.

Engaging Sociology

How to Read a Research Table

A statistical table is a researcher's labor-saving device. Quantitative data presented in tabular form are clearer and more concise than the same information presented in several written paragraphs. A good table has clear signposts to help the reader avoid confusion. For instance, Table 2.1 shows many of the main features of a table, and the list that follows explains how to read each feature.

Table 2.1   Educational Attainment by Selected Characteristic: 2007, for Persons 25 Years Old and Over, Reported in Thousands

Characteristic	Population (1,000)	Percentage of Population—Highest Level					
		Not a High School Graduate	High School Graduate	Some College, but No Degree	Associate's Degree[a]	Bachelor's Degree	Advanced Degree
Total persons	194,318	14.3	31.6	16.7	8.6	18.9	9.9
Age years:							
25–34	39,868	12.9	28.6	18.1	9.3	22.8	8.3
35–44	42,762	11.8	29.7	16.4	9.8	22.2	10.4
45–54	43,461	11.2	32.1	17.1	9.8	19.3	10.5
55–64	32,191	12.8	30.9	17.8	9.8	19.3	12.3
65–74	18,998	20.7	36.8	15.0	6.1	12.3	9.2
75 and over	17,037	27.4	38.1	13.2	4.7	9.8	6.9
Sex:							
Male	93,421	15.0	31.7	16.1	7.7	18.7	10.8
Female	100,897	13.6	31.6	17.3	9.5	19.0	9.0
Race:							
White[b]	159,262	13.8	31.7	16.7	8.7	19.1	10.0
Black[b]	21,924	17.7	36.2	18.8	8.7	13.0	5.6
Other	13,132	14.2	23.8	2.9	7.6	25.6	15.7
Hispanic origin:							
Hispanic	24,551	39.7	28.4	13.0	6.2	9.4	3.3
Non-Hispanic	169,767	10.6	32.1	17.2	9.0	20.2	10.8
Region:							
Northeast	36,333	12.9	33.5	12.3	8.1	20.3	12.9
Midwest	42,949	10.8	35.4	17.6	9.4	17.9	9.0
South	70,571	16.2	32.1	16.7	8.3	17.9	8.8
West	44,465	15.6	25.9	19.5	8.9	20.1	9.9

Source: U.S. Census Bureau (2009b).

Note: Features of the table are adapted from Broom and Selznick (1963).

a. Includes vocational degrees.

b. For persons who selected this race group only.

(Continued)

(Continued)

TITLE: The title provides information on the major topic and variables in the table.

"Educational Attainment by Selected Characteristic: 2007"

HEADNOTE (or Subtitle): Many tables will have a headnote or subtitle under the title, giving information relevant to understanding the table or units in the table.

For this table, the reader is informed that it includes all persons over the age of 25 and they will be reported in thousands.

HEADINGS AND STUBS: Tables generally have one or two levels of headings under the title and headnotes. These instruct the reader about what is in the columns below.

In this table, the headings indicate the level of education achieved so that the reader can identify the percentage with a specified level of education.

The table also has a stub: the far-left column under "Characteristic." This lists the items that are being compared according to the categories found in the headings. In this case, the stub indicates population of various characteristics: age, sex, race, Hispanic origin, and region.

MARGINAL TABS: In examining the numbers in the table, try working from the outside in. The marginals, the figures at the margins of the table, often provide summary information.

In this table, the first column of numbers is headed "Population (1,000)," indicating (by thousands) the total number of people in each category who were part of the database. The columns to the right indicate—by percentages—the level of educational attainment for each category.

CELLS: To make more detailed comparisons, examine specific cells in the body of the table. These are the boxes that hold the numbers or percentages.

In this table, the cells contain data on age, sex, racial/ethnic (White, Black, Hispanic), and regional differences in education.

UNITS: Units refer to how the data are reported. It could be in percentages, in number per 100 or 1,000, or in other units.

In this table, the data are reported first in raw number in thousands and then in percentages.

FACTS FROM THE TABLE: After reviewing all the above information, the reader is ready to make some interpretations about what the data mean.

In this table, the reader might note that young adults are more likely to have a college education than older citizens.

Likewise, African Americans and Hispanics are less likely than Whites to have college or graduate degrees, but the rate for "Other" is even higher than that for Whites, probably because it includes Asian Americans. People in the Northeast have the highest levels of education, followed by those in the West. What other interesting patterns do you see?

FOOTNOTES: Some tables have footnotes, usually indicating something unusual about the data or where to find more complete data.

In this table, two footnotes are provided so that the reader does not make mistakes in interpretation.

Source: The source note, found under the table, points out the origin of the data. It is usually identified by the label "Source."

Given that social science research focuses on humans and humans are changeable, it is difficult to say that any single study has definitively proven the hypothesis or answered a research question with finality. Indeed, the word *prove* is never used to describe the interpretation of findings in the social and behavioral sciences. Rather, social scientists say that findings tend to support or reject hypotheses.

Science and Uncertainty

So why bother doing social science research if findings can be challenged, nothing is absolute, and conclusions seem so uncertain? We can base social policy and our understanding of society on information that is as close to the truth as possible, even if we can never claim absolute truth. Systematic, scientific research brings us closer to the reality of the social world than guesswork and opinions. Having supportive findings from numerous studies, not just one, builds a stronger case to support a theory. The search for truth is ongoing—a kind of mission in life for those of us who are scholars. Furthermore, as we get closer to an accurate understanding of society, our social policies can be based on the most accurate knowledge available.

What makes a discipline scientific is not the subject matter. It is how we conduct our research and what we consider valid evidence. The four core features of a science are (1) a commitment to empirically validated evidence, facts, and information that are confirmed through systematic processes of testing using the five senses; (2) a focus on being convinced by the evidence rather than by our preconceived ideas; (3) absolute integrity and objectivity in reporting and in conducting research; and (4) continual openness to having our findings reexamined and new interpretations proposed.

It is the fourth feature that causes us to be open to criticism and alternative interpretations. To have credible findings, we always consider the possibility that we have overlooked alternative explanations of the data and alternative ways to view the problem. This is one of the hardest principles to grasp, but it is one of the most important in reaching the truth. Science—including social science—is not facts to be memorized. Science is a process that is made possible by a social exchange of ideas, a clash of opinions, and a continual search for truth. Knowledge in the sciences is created by vigorous debate. Rather than just memorizing the concepts in this book to take a test, we hope you will engage in the creation of knowledge by entering into these debates.

Ethical Issues in Social Research

Sociologists and other scientists are bound by the ethical codes of conduct governing research. This is to protect any human participants in research from being harmed by the research. The American Sociological Association (ASA) code of ethical conduct outlines standards that researchers are expected to observe when doing research, teaching, and publishing. They include points such as being objective, reporting findings and sources fully, making no promises to respondents that cannot be honored, accepting no support that requires violation of these principles, completing contracted work, and delineating responsibilities in works with multiple authors. Related to these standards are the following key ethical issues for sociologists, each a part of the ASA code of ethics:

- How will the findings from the research be used? Will it hurt individuals, communities, or nations if it gets into the hands of "enemies"? Can it be used to aggravate hostilities? In whose interest is the research being carried out? To illustrate the relevance of these questions, in 1964, a number of U.S. social researchers began a study called Project Camelot. The goal was to predict when revolutions would occur in Latin America and to show how governments could stop them. However, the $6 million project was canceled when social scientists complained that it would be unethical for research findings to be used so that the United States could inter-

Video Link 2.2
Watch more about the role of science.

  vene in the internal affairs of other countries, especially when such interference might short-circuit movements for human rights.

- How can the researcher protect the privacy and identities of respondents and informants? Is the risk to participants justified by an anticipated outcome of improved social conditions? For example, in several instances, courts have subpoenaed journalists and social scientists, forcing them to reveal confidential sources and information. Some researchers have spent time in jail to protect the confidentiality of their respondents (Comarow 1993; Scarce 1999).

- Is there informed consent among the people being studied? How much can and should the researcher tell participants about the purpose of the research without completely biasing the outcome? Does informed consent mean only signing a release form at the beginning of a study? This issue relates to the harm or danger faced by respondents as well as the question of deception by social scientists. Is it acceptable to lie or to mislead participants so that they do not change their behavior when they are responding to the situations that the researcher has created? If the

public learns that social scientists actively deceive them, what will be the consequences for people trusting researchers at a later time when a different study is being conducted?

- Will there be any harm to the participants—including injury to self-esteem or feelings of guilt and self-doubt? Philip Zimbardo and colleagues (1973) conducted a well-known social psychological experiment in which he designed a mock prison and assigned students to roles of prisoners and guards. The purpose of the study was to gauge the degree to which social roles affect attitudes and behaviors. However, the students took the roles so seriously that they no longer distinguished reality from the artificial situation, and some "guards" became violent and abusive toward the "prisoners." Given these negative reactions, the experiment was discontinued, and students were informed about the purpose of the study. Is a research project unethical if it negatively affects a participant's self-esteem? Most social scientists would say yes, such research is beyond the boundaries of ethical conduct.

- How much invasion of privacy is legitimate in the name of research? How much disclosure of confidential information, even in disguised form, is acceptable? For example, a researcher who studies sexual behavior and attitudes may collect data about the most intimate of relationships. How this confidential information is handled to protect respondents is of utmost importance in research ethics.

Codes of ethics provide general guidelines. In addition, most universities and organizations where research is common have Human Subjects Review Boards whose function is to ensure that human participants are not harmed by the research.

Thinking Sociologically

Consider some ethical issues in conducting research. Why is informed consent of participants important? Is it ethical to talk to people when they do not know you are recording their words? Is it ethical to be a researcher in a setting or situation but not inform the group of your research study or that you are studying them? Why?

The Development of Sociology as a Discipline

Throughout recorded history, humans have been curious about how and why people form groups. That should not be surprising because the groups we belong to are so central to human existence and to a sense of satisfaction in life.

Early Sociological Thought

Religion had a major influence on the way individuals thought about the world and their social relationships. Christianity dominated European thought systems during the Middle Ages, from the end of the Roman Empire to the 1500s, while Islamic beliefs were very widespread in much of the Middle East and parts of Africa. The North African Islamic scholar Ibn Khaldun (1332–1406) was probably the first to suggest a systematic approach to explain the social world. Khaldun was particularly interested in understanding the feelings of solidarity that held tribal groups together during his day, a time of great conflict and wars (Alatas 2006; Hozien n.d.). These issues interested philosophers and theologians, but they did not use scientific methods to gather data and test their theories, processes that now allow us to get closer to the facts.

Sociology has its modern roots as a scientific discipline in the ideas of 19th-century social, political, and religious philosophers, mostly European, who laid the groundwork for the scientific study of society. Until the 19th century, social philosophers provided the primary approach to understanding society, one that invariably had a strong moral tone. Their opinions were derived from abstract reflection about how the social world should work. Often, they advocated forms of government that they believed would be just and good, denouncing those they considered inhumane or evil. For instance, Plato's *Republic*, written around 400 BCE, outlines plans for an ideal state—complete with government, family, economic systems, class structure, and education—designed to achieve social justice. Even today, people debate the ideal communities proposed by Plato, Aristotle, Machiavelli, Thomas More, and other philosophers from the past.

Conditions Leading to Modern Sociology

Several conditions in the 19th century gave rise to the emergence of sociology. First, European nations were imperial powers that were establishing oppressive colonies in other cultures (see Map 2.1 on page 48). This exposure to other cultures encouraged at least some Europeans to learn more about the people in their new colonies. Second, they sought to understand the social revolutions taking place and the changes brought about by the Industrial Revolution. Finally, advances in the natural sciences demonstrated the value of the scientific method, and some wished to apply this scientific method to understand the social world.

THE TAKING of the BASTILLE,

By the Citizens of Paris, headed by the National Guards, the 14ᵗʰ July, 1789. This Fortress was begun to be built in 1369, in the Reign of Charles 5ᵗʰ. Hugues Aubrist, at that time Provost of Paris, laid the first stone, it was not completely finished till 1382. He was a Native of DIJON and was the first imprisoned there on a Charge of Heresy.

The Bastille, a state prison in Paris, France, and a symbol of oppression, was seized by the common people in the French Revolution, an upheaval in society that forced social analysts to think differently about society and social stability.

The social backdrop for the earliest European sociologists was the Industrial Revolution (which began around the middle of the 1700s) and the French Revolution (1789–1799). No one had clear, systematic explanations for why the old social structure, which had lasted since the early Middle Ages, was collapsing or why cities were exploding with migrants from rural areas. French society was in turmoil, members of the nobility were being executed, and new rules of justice were taking hold. Churches were subordinated to the state, equal rights under the law were established for citizens, and democratic rule emerged. These dramatic changes marked the end of the traditional monarchy and the beginning of a new social order. With no methods to collect information on the dramatic changes taking place, leaders in France had to rely on the social philosophies of the time to react to the problems that surrounded them, philosophies that were not informed by social science studies.

It was in this setting that the scientific study of society emerged. Two social thinkers, Henri Saint-Simon (1760–1825)

and Auguste Comte (1798–1857), decried the lack of systematic data collection or objective analysis in social thought. These Frenchmen are considered the first to suggest that a science of society could help people understand and perhaps control the rapid changes and unsettling revolutions taking place.

Comte officially coined the term *sociology* in 1838. His basic premise was that religious or philosophical speculation about society did not provide an adequate understanding of how to solve society's problems. Just as the natural sciences provided basic facts about the physical world, so, too, there was a need to gather scientific knowledge about the social world. Only then could leaders systematically apply this scientific knowledge to improve social conditions.

Comte asked two basic questions: What holds society together and gives rise to a stable order rather than anarchy? and Why is there change in society? Comte conceptualized society as divided into two parts: (1) *Social statics*, like

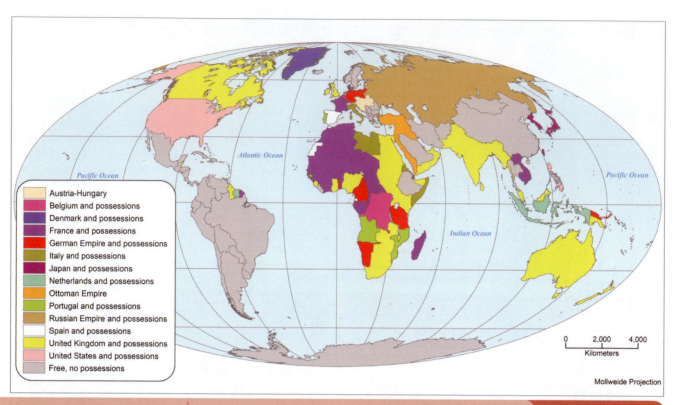

Map 2.1   Colonial Possessions in 1914

Source: Barraclough (1986:100–101), O'Brien (1999:206), Shepherd (1964:166–167), and Stone (1991:243).
Map by Anna Versluis.

social structure, referred to aspects of society that give rise to order, stability, and harmony. (2) *Social dynamics* referred to change and evolution in society over time. Simply stated,

Handbook Link 2.1
Read more about the origins of sociology.

Comte was concerned with what contemporary sociologists and the social world model in this book refer to as *structure* (social statics) and *process* (social dynamics). By understanding these aspects of the social world, Comte felt that leaders could strengthen the society and respond appropriately to change. His optimistic belief was that sociology would be the "queen of sciences," guiding leaders to construct a better social order.

Although he helped found a new discipline, Comte had some ideas that are not above reproach. While advocating the use of science, Comte still maintained strong biases in favor of order and stability, even though the outcomes of that order might reinforce inequality and oppression, including slavery. Nevertheless, the two main contributions of Comte are influential today: (1) the social world can and should be studied scientifically and (2) the knowledge gained should be used to improve the human condition.

Sociology continued its evolution as scholars contemplated further changes brought about by the Industrial

Revolution. Massive social and economic changes in the 18th and 19th centuries brought about restructuring and sometimes the demise of political monarchies, aristocracies, and feudal lords. Scenes of urban squalor were common in Great Britain and other industrializing European nations. Machines replaced both agricultural workers and cottage (home) industries because they produced an abundance of goods faster, better, and cheaper. Peasants were pushed off the land by the new technology and migrated to urban areas to find work at the same time as a powerful new social class of capitalists was emerging.

Industrialization brought the need for a new skilled class of laborers, putting new demands on an education system that had served only the elite. Families now depended on wages from their labor in the industrial sector to stay alive. From its beginning, sociology focused on the relationship between these micro-, meso-, and macro-level processes.

These changes stimulated other social scientists to study society and its problems. The writings of Émile Durkheim, Karl Marx, Harriet Martineau, Max Weber, W. E. B. Du Bois, and many other early sociologists set the stage for the development of sociological theories—statements or explanations of how two or more facts about the social world are related to each other. Accompanying

Industrialization had a number of positive outcomes, including the extension of prosperity to a larger class of people, but it also had some high costs in exploitation of workers and growth of slums in places such as London.

the development of sociological theory was the utilization of the scientific method—the systematic gathering and recording of reliable and accurate data to test ideas. First, let us examine several traditions that emerged during the development of sociology.

Three Sociological Traditions

First, we have the situation of Hector living in poverty (research problem). Then, we have possible explanations to help us understand his situation (theories). Finally, we have methods of collecting information (data) to study his situation. Sociologists put these three parts together to carry out research. Here, we discuss three long-standing traditions in sociology that speak to the relationship between empirical research and social theory (Buechler 2008). All three traditions have been around for as long as the discipline has existed. The founders of sociology tended to combine them, especially the first and third traditions.

One tradition, strongly influenced by the ideas of Auguste Comte, Émile Durkheim, and other early sociologists, stresses *scientific sociology*. The thrust is on objectivity and on modeling the discipline after the natural sciences. For these scholars, the net result of sociological work is pure, unbiased analysis for the purpose of scientific understanding. As they saw it, others would be left to decide how to use the facts. Sociology was to stick to fact-finding and testing hypotheses.

A second tradition is called *humanistic sociology*: "When scientific sociologists do science, they emphasize the word *science*, linking it to other sciences. When humanistic sociologists do social science, they emphasize the word *social*, separating it from other sciences" (Buechler 2008:326). This tradition puts much more emphasis on the unique capacity of humans to create *meaning*—the way humans interpret their social world—and it recognizes the subjective nature of meaning. However, when one is studying meaning—such as what a handshake, a kiss, or a cross symbolizes for people—it is virtually impossible to produce objective quantitative data, which are often the standard of the natural sciences. Humanistic sociologists argue that studying humans is qualitatively different and that focusing only on the standards of objectivity causes researchers to miss some of the most interesting and important dimensions of human social behavior. Studies should be relevant to humans by improving society and the quality of human life, they assert.

A third tradition sees the role of the discipline as *improving society*. This often takes two forms. One approach is to help us think more critically about the society in which we live, with special focus on issues of social justice; this is known as *critical sociology*. Critical sociology was the focus of Karl Marx, and many in this tradition call for rather drastic changes in society to promote fairness. Two other strands of the "social improvement" emphasis are applied sociology and public sociology. These are discussed in more detail at the end of this chapter, but the field's practical applications and its concern for justice for women and other "second-class citizens" have been a central focus since the time of the first president of the American Sociological Association, Lester Ward. All three traditions will be given attention in this book, for they are all part of mainstream sociology today.

Sociology's Major Theoretical Perspectives

Recall the description of the social world model presented in Chapter 1. It stresses the levels of analysis—smaller units existing within larger social systems. We have mentioned that some methods of data collection are better for analyzing micro-level processes of interaction (e.g., participant observation), whereas other methods work more effectively for understanding macro-level social systems (e.g., secondary data analysis). The same is true of theoretical perspectives. Some are especially effective in understanding micro-level interactions, and others illuminate macro-level structures, although the distinctions are not absolute. Either type of theory—those most useful at the micro or macro levels—can be used at the meso level, depending on the research question being asked. To illustrate how a social problem is approached differently by these four major theoretical perspectives, we will further delve into our examination of Hector's circumstances (Ashley and Orenstein 2009; Turner 2003). Keep in mind that sociologists use many theories, some of which will be introduced in future chapters.

Sociologists have several perspectives that can help us understand the poverty Hector experiences in São Paulo, Brazil. For example, Hector's interactions with family, peers, school teachers, employers, and religious leaders can be studied at the micro level of analysis. A micro analysis would stress the small groups and neighborhood of which he is a part.

In contrast, meso-level analysis focuses on institutions, large organizations, and ethnic communities. For instance, the policies of the city of São Paulo regarding transportation, sanitation, education, and health affect what happens to local residents in a *favela*. Migration of native Brazilians ("Indians") from rural areas into the big city of São Paulo is a meso-level issue. These ethnic communities often have little education (due to very inadequate schools in the areas where they live), and residents have few job skills, but they have been displaced from their native areas due to encroachment of corporations and agribusiness in their territories. They may find themselves in urban slums where there is conflict between ethnic groups for the few jobs that do exist. This is not a global issue or a micro-level issue. It has to do with how large corporations and institutions meet the needs of ethnic groups within the nation—or fail to do so.

Handbook Article Link 2.2
Read more about tradition and theory.

Macro-level analysis considers the larger social context—national and global—within which Hector and his family live. From this perspective, Hector's position in society is part of a total system in which the poor in Brazil and other countries constitute a reserve labor force, available to work in unskilled jobs as needed. International trade, or a change in the Brazilian economy, could have an influence on Hector's job prospects quite independent of his individual motivation to work. Macro-level theories would consider questions related to Brazilian policies as a nation and the position of Brazil in the world system.

Sociologists draw on major theoretical perspectives at each level of analysis to guide their research and to help them understand social interactions and social organizations. A **theoretical perspective**, then, is a basic view of society that guides sociologists' research and analysis. Theoretical perspectives are the broadest theories in sociology, providing overall approaches to understanding the social world and social problems. These perspectives help sociologists to develop explanations of social behaviors and systems and to see the relationships between them.

Micro- to Meso-Level Theories

Symbolic Interaction

Symbolic interaction theory (also called social construction or interpretative theory) considers how people create shared meanings regarding symbols and events and then interact on the basis of those meanings. For example, Hector interacts with his family and friends in the *favela* in ways that he has learned are necessary for survival there. In Hector's world of poverty, the informal interactions of the street and the more formal interactions of the school carry different sets of meanings that guide Hector's behavior.

Symbolic interaction theory assumes that groups form around interacting individuals. Through these interactions, people learn to share common understandings and to learn what to expect from others. They make use of **symbols** (actions or objects that represent something else and therefore have meaning beyond their own existence) such as language or verbal and nonverbal communication (words and gestures) to interpret interactions with others. Symbolic communication (e.g., language) helps people construct a meaningful world. This implies that humans are not merely passive agents responding to their environments. Instead, they are actively engaged in creating their own meaningful social world based on their constructions and interpretations of the social world. In some cases, people may passively accept the social definitions and interpretations of others. This saves them the effort of making sense of the stimuli around them and of figuring out interpretations (Blumer 1969; Fine 1990). Still, more than any other theory in the social sciences, symbolic interactionism stresses *human agency*—the active role of individuals in creating their social environment.

Micro-level interactions occur in classrooms every day, both among peers and between teacher and students.

George Herbert Mead (1863–1931) is prominently identified with the symbolic interaction perspective through his influential work *Mind, Self, and Society* (Mead [1934] 1962). Mead believed that humans have the ability to decide how to act—they have *agency* or freedom to act—based on their perceptions of their reality. Mead explored the mental processes associated with how humans define or make sense of situations. He placed special emphasis on human interpretations of gestures and symbols (including language) and the meanings we attach to our actions. He also examined how we learn our social roles in society, such as mother, teacher, and friend, and how we learn to carry out these roles. Indeed, as we will see in Chapter 4, he insisted that our notion of who we are—our self—emerges from social experience and interaction with others. These ideas of how we construct our individual social worlds and have some control over them come from a perspective known as the Chicago School of symbolic interaction.

Another symbolic interaction approach—the Iowa School (named after scholars from the University of Iowa)—makes a more explicit link between individual identities connected to roles and positions within organizations (Kuhn 1964)—the meso level of the social system. If we hold several positions—honors student, club president, daughter, sister, student, athlete, thespian, middle-class person—those positions form a relatively stable core *self*. We will interpret new situations in light of our social positions, some of which are very important and anchor how we see the social world. Once a core self is established, it guides and shapes the way we interact with people in many situations—even new social settings. Thus, if you are president of an organization and have the responsibility for overseeing the organization, part of your self-esteem, your view of responsible citizenship, and your attitude toward life will be shaped by that position. Thus, the Iowa School of symbolic interactionism places a little less emphasis on individual choice, but it does a better job of recognizing the link between the micro, meso, and macro levels of society (Carrothers and Benson 2003; Stryker 1980).

The following principles summarize the modern symbolic interaction perspective and how individual action results in groups, institutions, and societies (Ritzer 2004).

- Humans are endowed with the capacity for thought, shaped by social interaction.
- In social interaction, people learn the meanings and symbols that allow them to exercise thought and participate in human action.
- People modify the meanings and symbols as they struggle to make sense of their situations and the events they experience.
- Interpreting the situation involves seeing things from more than one perspective, examining possible courses of action, assessing the advantages

and disadvantages of each, and then choosing one course of action.

- These patterns of action and interaction make up the interactive relations that we call groups, institutions, and societies.
- Our positions or memberships in these groups, organizations, and societies may profoundly influence the way we define ourselves and may lead to fairly stable patterns of interpretation of our experiences and of social life.

To summarize, the modern symbolic interaction perspective emphasizes the process each individual goes through in creating and altering his or her social reality and identity within a social setting. Without a system of shared symbols, humans cannot coordinate their actions with one another, and hence society as we understand it would not be possible.

Critique of the Symbolic Interaction Perspective. Each theory has its critics, just as each political party or religious group's philosophy has critics. Although symbolic interactionism is widely used by sociologists today (especially the Chicago School), it is often criticized for neglecting the macro-level structures of society that affect human behavior. By focusing on interpersonal interactions, large-scale social forces, such as an economic depression or a political revolution, that shape human destinies are given less consideration. With the focus on individual agency and the ability of each individual to create his or her meaning in social situations, symbolic interaction has often been less attuned to issues of social class position, social power, historical circumstances, or international conflict between societies. Yet these are important issues (Meltzer, Petras, and Reynolds 1975). In addition, critics point out the difficulty in studying ambiguous ideas such as the "development of the self" or "how the mind works."

Despite these limitations, theorists from the symbolic interaction perspective have made significant contributions to understanding the development of social identities and interactions as the basis for groups, organizations, and societies. Many of these studies will be discussed in chapters throughout the book.

Rational Choice (Exchange) Theory

Hector and his friends from the *favela* make decisions to stay in school or drop out, and according to rational choice theory, this is based on the balance of rewards versus costs. Picture it as a mental balance sheet: On the plus side, staying in school may lead to future opportunities not available to the uneducated. On the minus side, school is a negative experience, and the family needs help now to feed its members, so going to school is a "waste of time." Which side will win depends on his friends' assessment of the rewards versus costs.

Rational choice theory states that people make decisions based on a rational calculation of costs and benefits. For some women in violent relationships, the options of leaving and of living on their own without resources seem more costly than the abuse they suffer. The balance of costs and benefits must shift before they are likely to leave the situation.

Consider another example: Women also may decide whether to stay in abusive relationships based on rewards versus costs. In considering a divorce, do the rewards of escaping a conflicted, abusive marriage outweigh the costs of daily economic and emotional stresses related to going it alone? Also, consider homosexual couples. There are potential costs of coming out of the closet to friends, family, and employers. There may also be significant benefits: When applying for health insurance, coverage is often denied to unrecognized partners, and acknowledged

Audio Link 2.2
Apply rational choice theory to our fear of germs.

homosexuals no longer live in hiding with constant fear of being exposed. These cost-and-benefit decisions are the types of questions addressed by rational choice theorists.

A central premise of micro-level rational choice theory is that human behavior involves choices. On what basis do people make their choices? As the term implies, **rational choice** approaches assume that people chart a course of action on the basis of rational decisions. People act in ways that maximize their rewards and minimize their costs. Where the balance lies determines our behavior.

Rational choice, also called exchange theory, has its roots in several disciplines—economics, behavioral psychology, anthropology, and philosophy (Cook, O'Brien, and Kollock 1990). Social behavior is seen as an exchange activity—a transaction in which resources are given and received (Blau 1964; Homans 1974). Every interaction involves an exchange of something valued—money, time, material goods, attention, sex, allegiance, and so on. People stay in relationships because they get something from the exchange, and they leave relationships that cost them without providing adequate benefits. Simply stated, people are more likely to act if they see some reward or success coming from their behavior. The implication is that self-interest for the individual is the guiding element in human interaction.

Critique of the Rational Choice Perspective. Rational choice theorists give little attention to macro-level analysis or micro-level internal mental processes. They see human conduct as self-centered, with rational behavior implying that people seek to maximize rewards and minimize costs. Charitable, unselfish, or altruistic behavior is not easily explained by this view. Why would a soldier sacrifice his or her life to save a comrade? Why would a starving person in a Nazi concentration camp share a crust of bread with another? Proponents of rational choice counter the criticism by arguing that if a person feels good about helping another, that in itself is a benefit that compensates for the cost.

In some U.S. states and school districts, some residents voted against public school levies because they did not want to pay the extra hundred dollars or so per year in taxes. Yet the same voters are dismayed to find when trying to sell their house that their property value has dropped by as much as $15,000 because they live in a district that does not support education (Roberts 2003). In short, acting in what seems to be our own self-interest may not always end up being the best choice.

Some theorists (Denzin 1992; Fiske 1991) have attempted a synthesis between the interaction level of analysis and macro-level theories. For instance, studies of friendships, employee-employer contracts, relations in families, and consumer-salesperson transactions can all be represented as exchange relationships. By combining the millions of exchange relationships, these researchers contend that we can study macro-level patterns in the social world (Fiske 1991).

Rational choice theory assumes that people act in ways that maximize their own self-interests. Some citizens vote against school levies in order to save a few dollars in taxes, only to find that after a school levy fails, their property values fall, sometimes far more than the taxes they would have saved. So people do not always accurately assess their self-interests.

The Tanzanian village elders in this photo continue to have authority to make local (micro-level) decisions about the traditional irrigation canals that are being improved in their village, but their expanded water supply is possible in part because of international financial support (meso- and macro-level decisions).

Thinking Sociologically

How can symbolic interaction and rational choice perspectives help explain dating behavior? For example, what might a goodnight kiss versus sexual intercourse mean to females versus males? How does one learn the cues that indicate attraction to a person of the same or opposite sex? Why are these micro-level questions?

Meso- and Macro-Level Theories

Meso- and macro-level theories consider large units in the social world: organizations, institutions (such as education, politics, or economics), societies, or global systems. For example, Hector lives in a modernizing country, Brazil, which is struggling to raise the standard of living of its people and compete in the world market. The decisions that are made by his government at the national and international levels affect his life in a variety of ways. As Brazil industrializes, the nature of jobs and the modes of communication change. Local village cultures modify as the entire nation gains more uniformity of values, beliefs, and norms. Similarly, resources such as access to clean water may be allotted at the local level, but local communities need national and sometimes international support, as illustrated in the photo of tribal elders from Tanzania. We can begin to understand how the process of modernization influences Hector, this village in Tanzania, and other people around

the globe by looking at two major macro-level approaches: the structural-functional and conflict perspectives.

Structural-Functional Theory

The structural-functional perspective, also called **functional theory**, assumes that all parts of the social structure (including groups, organizations, and institutions), the culture (values and beliefs), and social processes (e.g., social change or socialization—learning to be a member of society) work together to make the whole society run smoothly and harmoniously. To understand the social world from this perspective, we must look at how the parts of society (structure) fit together and how each part contributes (functions) toward the maintenance of society. For instance, two functions of the family include reproducing children and teaching them to be members of society. These and other functions help perpetuate society, for without reproducing and teaching new members to fit in, societies would collapse.

Émile Durkheim (1858–1917) was a key social scientist in developing functionalism. He theorized that society is made up of necessary parts that fit together into a working whole. Durkheim (1947) felt that individuals conform to the rules of societies because of a collective conscience—the shared beliefs in the values of a group. People grow up sharing the same values, beliefs, and rules of behavior as those around them. Gradually, individuals internalize these shared beliefs and rules. A person's behavior is, in a sense, governed from within because it feels right and proper to

A Masai family works together as a unit, and in so doing, they enhance the stability and continuity of their entire society.

Although the microwave oven and fast-food restaurants have had many benefits for a society in a hurry, one dysfunction is the deterioration of health—especially due to obesity.

behave in accordance with what is expected. As such, the functionalist perspective of Durkheim and subsequent theorists places emphasis on societal consensus, which gives rise to stable and predictable patterns of order in society. Because people need groups for survival, they adhere to the group's rules so that they fit in. This means that most societies run in an orderly manner, with most individuals fitting into their positions in society.

Functions can be manifest or latent. **Manifest functions** are the planned outcomes of interactions, social organizations, or institutions. The function of the microwave oven, for instance, has been to allow people to prepare meals quickly and easily, facilitating life in overworked and stressed modern families. **Latent functions** are unplanned or unintended consequences (Merton 1938, [1942] 1973). The unplanned consequences of the microwave oven were creation of a host of new jobs and stimulation of the economy as people wrote new cookbooks and as businesses were formed to produce microwavable cookware and prepared foods for the microwave.

Dysfunctions (Merton 1938) are those actions that undermine the stability or equilibrium of society. By allowing people to cook meals without using a convection oven, the microwave oven has contributed to some young people having no idea how to cook, thus making them highly dependent on expensive technology and processed foods, and in some cases adding to problems of obesity.

Some behaviors may be functional for an individual and dysfunctional socially. From a functionalist perspective, it is important to examine the possible functional and dysfunctional aspects of life in society in order to maintain harmony and balance in society as a whole.

To summarize the structural-functional perspective, the following points are key:

1. It examines the macro-level organizations and patterns in society.

2. It focuses on what holds societies together and enhances social continuity.

3. It considers the consequences or "functions" of each major part in society.

4. It focuses on the way the structure (groups, organizations, institutions), the culture, and social processes work together to make society function smoothly.

5. It considers manifest functions (which are planned), latent functions (which are unplanned or secondary), and dysfunctions (which undermine stability).

Critique of the Structural-Functional Perspective. Some assertions of functionalism are so abstract that they are difficult to test with data. Moreover, functionalism does not explain social changes in society, such as conflict and revolution. As we try to understand the many societal upheavals in the world, from suicide bombings in Iraq to the democracy and economic privatization movements in China, it is clear that dramatic social change is possible. The functionalist assumption is that if a system is running smoothly, it must be working well because it is free from conflict. It assumes that conflict is harmful, even though we know that stability may come about because of ruthless dictators suppressing the population. In short, stability is not always good for the people.

Feminist sociologists criticize functionalism's support of the status quo. If the family or economic system of society seems to be functioning smoothly, it does not mean that these systems are fair and equitable or that women and minorities are content with their roles in them. A paradigm that assumes so is making false assumptions, according to feminist theorists. Feminists and others reject the implicit idea of functionalism that orderly society is necessarily positive. The point is that a stable system is not the same thing as a healthy system.

Functionalism has had a profound impact on social science analysis. Still, functionalism in the 21st century fails to explain many contemporary social situations, according to proponents of a rival macro-level perspective, conflict theory.

Thinking Sociologically

Are the existing social patterns in a society necessarily desirable? Is dramatic change necessarily dysfunctional as suggested by functional theory?

Conflict Theory

Conflict theory contends that conflict is inevitable in any group or society. To support this view, conflict theorists advance the following key ideas:

- Conflict and the potential for conflict underlie all social relations.
- Social change is desirable, particularly changes that bring about a greater degree of social equality.
- The existing social order reflects powerful people imposing their values and beliefs on the weak.

The conflict perspective claims that inequality and injustice are the source of the conflicts that permeate society. Because resources and power are distributed unequally in society, some members have more money, goods, and prestige than others. The rich protect their positions by using the power they have accumulated to keep those less fortunate in their places. From the perspective of poor

people such as Hector, it seems the rich get all the breaks. Because most of us want more of the resources in society (money, good jobs, nice houses, and cars), conflict erupts between the haves and the have-nots. Therefore, conflict sometimes brings about a change in the society.

Modern conflict theory has its origins in the works of Karl Marx (1818–1883), a German social philosopher who lived in England during the height of 19th-century industrial expansion. He recognized the plight of exploited underclass workers in the new industrial states of Europe and viewed the ruling elites and the wealthy industrial owners as exploiters of the working class. Marx wrote about the new working class crowded in urban slums, working long hours every day, not earning enough money for decent housing and food, and living and working in conditions that were appalling. Few of the protections enjoyed by workers today—such as retirement benefits, health coverage, sick leave, the 40-hour workweek, and restrictions against child labor—existed in Marx's time.

Video Link 2.3
Consider private war contractors.

Capitalism emerged as the dominant economic system in Europe. *Capitalism* is an economic system in which (a) the equipment and property for producing goods are owned privately by wealthy individuals, who have the right to use these resources however they want, and (b) the market system (supply and demand) determines the distribution of resources and the levels of income (including wages, rents, and profits). Although there are various forms of capitalism, the core principles involve private ownership of industries and nonintervention by government (Heilbroner and Milberg 2007).

Marx believed that two classes, the capitalists (also referred to as the bourgeoisie or "haves"), who owned the **means of production** (property, machinery, and cash), and the workers (also referred to as the proletariat or "have-nots") would continue to live in conflict until the workers shared more equally in the profits of their labor. The more workers came to understand their plight, the more awareness they would have of the unfairness of the situation. Eventually, Marx believed that workers would rise up and overthrow capitalism, forming a new, classless society. Collective ownership—shared ownership of the means of production—would be the new economic order (Marx and Engels [1848] 1969).

The idea of the bourgeoisie (the capitalist exploiters who own the factories) and the proletariat (the exploited workers who sell their labor) has carried over into analysis of modern-day conflicts between labor and management, between women's and men's interests, and between warring factions within countries such as the Congo, Rwanda, Darfur, Indonesia, and countries in the Middle East. From a conflict perspective, Hector in Brazil and millions like him in other countries are part of the reserve labor force—a cheap labor pool that can be called on when labor is needed and disregarded when demand is low, thus meeting the changing labor needs of industry and capitalism. This pattern results in permanent economic insecurity and poverty for Hector and those like him.

Harriet Martineau (left) *published a critique of America's failure to live up to its democratic principles 11 years before Karl Marx's most famous work, but she was not taken seriously as a scholar for more than a century because she was female—the first feminist theorist.* Karl Marx (center) *was a social analyst who is often identified as the founder of conflict theory.* W. E. B. Du Bois (right) *continued the development of conflict theory and was among the first to apply that theory to American society and to issues of race and ethnicity.*

Many branches of the conflict perspective have grown from the original ideas of Marx. Here, we mention two contributions to conflict theory, those of the American sociologists W. E. B. Du Bois ([1899] 1967) and Ralf Dahrendorf (1959). As you can see, social conflict has been a major focus of sociological investigation for more than a century.

One of the very first American conflict theorists was W. E. B. Du Bois, the first African American to receive a doctorate from Harvard University. Du Bois felt that sociology should be active in bettering society, that although research should be scientifically rigorous and fair-minded, the ultimate goal of sociological work was social improvement—not just human insight. He saw the conflict between the haves and have-nots as being based largely on race in the United States, not just social class.

Du Bois ([1899] 1967) not only wrote on these issues but also acted on them. He was one of the cofounders of the National Association for the Advancement of Colored People (NAACP). He stressed the need for minority ethnic groups to become advocates for their rights, to create conflict where destructive harmony exists, and to change the society toward greater equality and participation. He was—and continues to be—an inspiration to many sociologists who believe that their findings should have real applications and should be used to create a more humane social world (Mills 1956). He was well ahead of his time in recognizing the conflicting nature of American society and the way privilege and self-interest blinded people to the inequities. He really is a part of the third tradition discussed above, an early applied sociologist.

A half-century later, Dahrendorf (1959) argued that society is always in the process of change and affected by forces that bring about change. Dahrendorf refined Marx's ideas in several ways. First, he pointed out that Marx's

predicted overthrow of capitalism had not come about because of changes in conditions for workers (employee organizations, unions). Instead, a middle class developed, some workers became part owners of companies, stockholders dispersed the concentration of wealth, and a higher standard of living was achieved for workers. Second, he proposed that class conflict occurs between the haves and the have-nots but in several additional categories of people: quasi-groups, interest groups, and conflict groups.

Quasi-groups include individuals who have similar social positions and interests but do not belong to an organized group. They therefore have little power. For example, residents who live in poverty like Hector but live in different *favelas* surrounding São Paulo are a quasi-group. People in quasi-groups are vulnerable precisely because they lack a social power base that is well organized and has resources.

Interest groups, such as the members of Hector's *favela*, emerge from the quasi-groups as a way to seek the power to solve problems. They share interests, such as a desire for sanitation, running water, electricity, and a higher standard of living. From within these more organized interest groups, *conflict groups* arise to fight for changes. There is always potential for conflict when those without power realize their common position and form interest groups. How much change or violence is brought about depends on how organized those groups become.

Dahrendorf's major contribution is the recognition that class struggle goes beyond Marx's idea of economic self-interests, control of the means of production by the elite, and distribution of power, authority, and prestige. A split society—consisting of haves and have-nots—becomes sliced in many directions. Thus, conflict over resources results not just in a conflict between the proletariat and the bourgeoisie but in a multitude of divisions including old people versus young people, rich versus poor, one region of the country versus another, Christians versus non-Christians, men versus women, African Americans versus Jews or Hispanics, and so forth. This acknowledges multiple rifts in the society based on interest groups.

Whereas Marx emphasized the divisive nature of conflict, other theorists have offered a modified theory. The American theorist Lewis Coser (1956) took a very different approach to conflict from that of Marx, arguing that it can strengthen societies and the organizations within them. According to Coser, problems in a society or group lead to complaints or conflicts—a warning message to the group that all is not well. Resolution of the conflicts shows that the group is adaptable in meeting the needs of its members, thereby creating greater loyalty to the group. Thus, conflict provides the message of what is not working to meet people's needs, and the system adapts to the needs for change because of the conflict (Coser 1956; Simmel 1955).

Critique of the Conflict Perspective. First, many conflict theorists focus on the macro-level analysis and lose sight of the individuals involved in conflict situations, such as Hector and his family. Second, empirical research to test conflict theory is limited. The conflict perspective often paints a picture with rather broad brushstrokes. Research to test the picture involves interpretations of broad spans of history and is more difficult to claim as scientific. Third, conflict theorists tend to focus on social stress, power plays, and disharmony. Conflict theory is not as effective in explaining social cohesion and cooperation. Fourth, many theorists are not convinced that self-interest is the ultimate motivator of behavior or that altruism and cooperation are uncommon.

The notion that men and women can be seen as interest groups, each looking out for its own self-interests, has resulted in one particular version of conflict theory—feminist theory (discussed next).

Thinking Sociologically

Imagine you are a legislator. You have to decide whether to cut funding for a senior citizens program or slash a scholarship program for college students. You want to be reelected, and you know that approximately 90% of senior citizens are registered to vote and most do actually vote. You also know that less than half of college-age people are likely to vote. These constituencies are about the same size. What would you do, and how would you justify your decision? How does this example illustrate conflict theory?

Feminist Sociological Theory

Feminist theory critiques the hierarchical power structures, which feminists argue treat women and other minorities unequally (Cancian 1992; Collins 2000). Feminists argue that sociology has been dominated by a male perspective and that the male perspective does not give a complete view of the social world. Much of feminist theory, then, has foundations in the conflict perspective. Women are viewed as disadvantaged by the hierarchical way in which society is arranged, whereas men experience privilege because of those arrangements. Men become an interest group intent on preserving its privileges.

Some branches of feminist theory, however, are not based on Marx's writings. Instead, their ideas come from interaction perspectives, emphasizing the way gender cues and symbols shape the nature of much human interaction. Thus, feminist theory moves from meso- and macro-level analysis (e.g., looking at national and global situations that give privileges to men) to micro-level analysis (e.g., the inequality between husbands and wives in marriage). In particular, feminist theory points to the importance of gender as a variable influencing social life (Nagy, Hesse-Biber, and Leavey 2007).

Feminists contend that there is a disparity between what actually goes on in women's lives and many accounts by social scientists of the social relations between males and females. Men's explanations of gender relations often have not presented women's lives in a way that is authentic for women themselves. The ideas, work opportunities, and life experiences of women of color are even less understood by traditional sociology (Collins 2000). Thus, many studies and writing about women are far removed from women's own experiences, and the reality for women becomes distorted.

In general, feminists point out, women's experiences in social relations involve interdependence with others, whereas males have been taught to be competitive and individualistic in sports, business competition, and many other social arenas. Males learn early in their lives that vulnerability must be avoided so that one is not exploited by others. This, according to feminist theorists, is one influence on the way men think about society. For example, rational choice theory maintains that each individual is out to protect self-interests and to make choices that benefit only the self. This theory is based on a male view of society. Men are also more likely to view hierarchical social arrangements as normal, which contributes to their difficulty in recognizing how patriarchal our society is. Also, some feminists claim that we are blind to the fact that gender roles are socially created, not biologically determined. As a result of these differences in experience and in socialization, women's views on issues of justice, morality, and society lend a different interpretation to society (Brettell and Sargent

Patricia Hill Collins is an innovative feminist scholar who has challenged sociologists to look at the ways race, social class, gender, and sexuality can work alone or in combination to provide privilege or disprivilege to certain citizens—sometimes without the awareness of the persons involved.

Michelle Obama has a law degree from an Ivy League university, has had a successful legal career, and also calls herself the "Mom-in-Chief." She is unapologetic about believing that men and women should be treated equally or about being called feminist.

Handbook Article Link 2.3
Read more about feminist theory.

An important contemporary scholar, Patricia Hill Collins, examined the discrimination and oppression people face because of their race, class, gender, sexuality, or nationality, all of which are interconnected. Many people are considered secondary citizens because of any or all these factors, and it is the interplay of these that interested Collins. For example, Black women are often restricted in their opportunities because of others' definitions of who and what they should be. In response, people who are disprivileged due to one or more social traits often create their own self-definitions and self-images. The idea of multiple identities (such as race, class, and gender) being intertwined and affecting individuals' life chances is a particularly powerful concept in sociology (Collins 1990, 2000, 2005).

It is interesting that many women today will begin a sentence with the disclaimer, "I am not a feminist, but . . ." Perhaps this is because some feminists have had a rather strident style and often focused on men as the cause of problems. Not all feminists are strident or focus on men as oppressors. Indeed, many men call themselves feminists, for a feminist is someone who believes that men and women should be given equal standing and equal opportunities in the society. Feminists have opened the door to understanding how social structures can bind and inhibit the freedom of both men and women. They also recognize that males have generally had more privileges than females in societies around the world. To study sociological questions, feminist methodology puts emphasis on qualitative methods that involve empathetic role-taking with respondents in interviews and trying to understand the world from the female or male respondents' point of view.

Critique of the Feminist Sociological Perspective. Feminists are not the only group with concerns about being fairly and accurately represented in theory and research. Race and ethnic groups and social class groups are also affected. Thus, some theorists argue that theory should represent the intersection between race, class, and gender. When trying to understand minority women in minimum-wage jobs or the factors affecting homelessness, this intersection can provide a more complete view.

Multi-Level Analysis: Max Weber's Contributions

Max Weber (1864–1920), a German-born social scientist, has had a lasting effect on sociology and other social sciences. He cannot be pigeonholed easily into one of the theoretical categories, for his contributions include both micro- and macro-level analyses. His emphasis on **Verstehen** (meaning deep empathetic understanding) gives him a place in micro-level theory, and his discussions of Karl Marx and of bureaucracies give him a place in meso- and macro-level theory (Weber 1946).

2001; Kramer 2007) and can present a more inclusive view of the world (Burn 2005; Lengermann and Niebrugge-Brantley 1990).

Verstehen stems from the subjective interpretations or meanings individuals give to parts of their social worlds. Following Weber's footsteps, sociologists try to understand both people's behaviors and the meanings that they attach to their behaviors and their experiences.

The goal-oriented, efficient new organizational form called bureaucracy was the focus of much of Weber's writing at the meso level. This form was based not on tradition but on rationality. In other words, decisions were based on what would best accomplish the organization's goals, not individual benefit. Hiring and promotion on the basis of individual merit (getting the most qualified person rather than hiring a friend or relative) is one example of this rational decision making. This is a principle we take for granted now, but it was not always so. The entire society becomes transformed through a change in how individuals make decisions on behalf of a bureaucratic organization.

Opportunities for jobs were changed, the culture became more geared to merit as a basis for decisions, and organizational life became more governed by rules and routines. All this came from a redefinition of appropriate ways to make decisions. Weber's conceptualizations of society at the meso level have laid the groundwork for a theoretical understanding of modern organizations.

Weber also attempted to understand macro-level processes. For instance, in his famous book *The Protestant Ethic and the Spirit of Capitalism* (Weber [1904–1905] 1958), he asked how capitalists understood the world around them. His work was influenced by Marx's writings, but where Marx focused on economic conditions as the key factor shaping history and power relations, Weber argued that Marx's focus was too narrow. He felt that politics, economics, religion, psychology, and people's

ideas are interdependent—affecting each other. In short, Weber thought that the society was more complex than Karl Marx's core notion that two groups—the haves and the have-nots—are in conflict over economic resources.

Thinking Sociologically

To what extent are human beings free agents who can create their own social world and come up with their own ideas about how to live their lives? To what extent are our lives determined or influenced by the social systems around us and by our positions of power or powerlessness in the economic and political system?

Using Different Theoretical Perspectives

Each of the theoretical perspectives described in this chapter begins from a set of assumptions about humans. Each makes a contribution to our understanding, but each has limitations or blind spots, such as not taking into account the other levels of analysis (Ritzer 2004). Figure 2.3 provides a summary of cooperative versus competitive perspectives to illustrate how the theories differ.

Video Link 2.4
Apply different perspectives to describe the family in this video.

It is important to understand that there are different and viable theoretical perspectives to explain society. None

	Macro analysis	Micro analysis
Humans viewed as cooperative (people interact with others on the basis of shared meanings and common symbols)	*Structural-Functional Theory*	*Symbolic Interactionism Theory*
Humans viewed as competitive (behavior governed by self-interest)	*Conflict Theory* (group interests)	*Rational Choice Theory* (individual interests)

Figure 2.3   Cooperative Versus Competitive Perspectives

of these is right or wrong. Rather, a particular theory may be more or less useful when studying some level of analysis or aspect of society. It is also important to learn how each major theoretical perspective can be used to provide a framework and viewpoint to guide research. The strength of a theory depends on its ability to explain and predict behavior accurately. Each theoretical perspective focuses on a different aspect of society and level of analysis and gives us a different lens through which to view our social world. The social world model helps us picture the whole system and determine which theory or synthesis of theories best suits our needs in analyzing a specific social process or structure.

Thinking Sociologically

Consider the issue of homelessness in cities around the world. How could each of the theories discussed in this chapter be used to help us understand the problem of homelessness?

Putting Sociology to Work

As discussed previously, one of the three traditions in sociology is to put sociology to work in communities, using our theory and methods for the betterment of society. Sociology produces useful knowledge for creating change in our social world. Several approaches focus on making sociology useful.

Applied Sociology

You may have asked yourself, "What can I do with a sociology degree?" Chapter 1 discussed some careers held by sociologists. One career path involves the application of sociological theory and research methods by applied sociologists

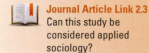

Journal Article Link 2.3
Can this study be considered applied sociology?

to answer questions raised by agencies, organizations, or government. **Applied sociology** (also known as sociological practice) is concerned with practical ways to improve society, sometimes with a major reorganization of society and sometimes with modest policy proposals that will make modern organizations operate more smoothly.

Since the founding of sociology, especially in the United States, some sociologists have had a problem-solving or social reform orientation to the discipline, always asking about the practical implications of sociological findings. They have used their tools and knowledge to help solve organizational problems (Mauksch 1993; Pickard and Poole 2007; Steele and Price 2004). Early sociologists, including the first president of the American Sociological Association, believed that systematic study of society could lead to social

betterment. The relationship between sociology and its application has remained central to sociology ever since but has taken various forms over time.

In the late 19th and early 20th centuries, many sociologists were concerned with the growing disorganization of family and work life that accompanied rapid urbanization and industrialization. They believed that scientific sociology could be used to control such processes and, thus, improve the conditions they considered undesirable. However, this reformist sociology carried the seeds of an internal tension within sociology. Surveys and other techniques used by the reformers to gather data soon became the tools of many sociologists in universities whose focus turned increasingly toward more academically accepted scientific scholarly work: quantitatively sophisticated, objective, and value-free science. This concern for pure scientific analysis existed side by side with reformist sociology, sometimes creating conflict between sociologists about which purposes were primary.

In the late 1920s and during the Great Depression of the 1930s, a large number of sociologists were employed by the government to analyze and address the escalating economic and social distress in the United States. With the start of World War II, the research skills of many of these applied sociologists were directed toward finding ways to boost the morale of the country's armed forces, mobilize civilian support, and demoralize the enemy. After the war, issues such as racism, crime, and illiteracy drew the attention of the action-oriented sociologists. In 1951, a new professional organization, the Society for the Study of Social Problems, was established, and applied sociology was fortified as a major subdiscipline of sociology.

In more recent years, applied sociology has received increased attention due in part to declining opportunities for university employment. Today, sociologists can be found in a wide variety of work situations, and depending on the focus, they may be known as sociological practitioners, applied sociologists, clinical sociologists, policy analysts, program planners, or evaluation researchers, among other titles. This role expansion is not only generating a vigorous new area of employment but also raising the old debate about the role of sociologists: pure scientist or social reformer. Whether the concern is justice in the social system or compassion and humane treatment of all people, a common concern is with the practical uses of sociology in formulating social policy (Pickard and Poole 2007).

Table 2.2 outlines the key differences between basic (pure) and applied sociology. In most chapters, you will find a feature called "The Applied Sociologist at Work," which describes a sociologist with a bachelor's, master's, or doctoral degree working in the topic area being discussed.

Public Sociology

Those advocating for *public sociology* want to move the focus of sociology from the classrooms and labs of universities into communities where they can have a direct impact on social change

Table 2.2	**Basic Versus Applied Sociology**	
	Basic Sociology	*Applied Sociology*
Orientation	Theory building, hypothesis testing	Program effects, focus on consequences of practices
Goal	Knowledge production	Knowledge utilization, problem solving
Source	Self- or discipline generated; supported by grants	Client generated

Source: Adapted with permission from the NTL Institute (DeMartini 1982).

and decision making (ASA 2005). In advocating for public sociology, Burawoy (2005) defines it as follows: "As a mirror and conscience of society, sociology must define, promote and inform public debate about deepening class and racial inequality, new gender regimes, environmental degradation, market fundamentalism, state and non-state violence" (p. 4). Sociology should deal with multiple groups outside the university, from the media to oppressed communities, and at all levels of analysis.

The different "sociologies" include the following:

1. professional academic—such as developing theory, doing research, and teaching in universities;

2. policy and applied sociology—working on problems for organizations and helping to meet goals; and

3. public sociology—implying a new style of sociology, a way of writing for change, of relating to the world through policy initiatives, activism, and social movements. The idea is to consider what *might* be and what would make a better world, using sociological tools of theory and methods. We might say it is a "do something about problems out there" sociology. It puts sociology to work for the improvement of society.

So far, we have focused on what sociology is and how sociologists know what they know. The rest of the book examines what our social world is like. The next chapter explores how you can understand your culture and society at various levels in our social world.

What Have We Learned?

The opening question in "Think About It" asked, "How do you know?" In this chapter, we have outlined the process of research that describes how sociologists and other social scientists "know." The next question asks, "Why is evidence important?" Our simple answer is that it is better to base social policies on evidence (scientifically collected facts and data) than on our untested assumptions or biased opinions. We also asked, "How do sociologists gather dependable facts?" The process of planning and carrying out a scientific study is outlined in the beginning of this chapter and provides a partial answer to this question. Finally, "How can theories help us understand social forces affecting our lives?"

What makes a discipline scientific is not the subject matter, but how we conduct our research and what we consider valid evidence. The core features of a science are (1) commitment to empirically validated evidence, facts, and information that are confirmed through systematic processes of testing using the five senses; (2) an effort to disprove whatever it is

we think is true, allowing us to be convinced by the evidence rather than by our preconceived ideas; (3) absolute integrity and objectivity in reporting and in conducting research; and (4) continual openness to having our findings reexamined and new interpretations proposed. It is the fourth feature that causes us to be open to criticism and alternative interpretations. To have credible findings, we always consider the possibility that we have overlooked alternative explanations of the data and alternative ways to view the problem. This is one of the hardest principles to grasp, but it is one of the most important in reaching the truth. Science—including social science—is not facts to be memorized. Science is a process that is made possible by a social exchange of ideas, a clash of opinions, and a continual search for truth. Knowledge in the sciences is created by vigorous debate. Rather than just memorizing the concepts in this book to take a test, we hope you will engage in the creation of knowledge by entering into these debates.

Theories serve as lenses to help us make sense of the data that we gather with various research strategies. However, the data themselves can be used to test the theories, so there is an ongoing reciprocal relationship between theory (the lens for making sense of the data) and the research (the evidence used to test the theories). The most important ideas in this chapter are what sociology considers evidence and how sociology operates as a science. These ideas form the framework for the content of sociology.

Key Points

- Sociology is a science that studies society, and therefore it is essential to understand what is—and what is not—considered credible evidence; for a scientist, this means that ideas must be tested empirically, that is, scientifically. (See pp. 32–34.)

- As a science, sociology uses eight systematic steps to gather data and test theories about the social world. (See pp. 35–44.)

- In most cases, planning a research study requires that we identify causes (independent variables) and effects (dependent variables) and that we make sure the correlations of variables are not spurious; the simultaneous occurrence of two variables can be accidental or non-causal. (See pp. 35–37.)

- Major methods for gathering data in sociology include surveys (e.g., interviews and questionnaires), field studies (direct observation of a natural setting), controlled experiments, and analysis of existing sources (through secondary sources or through content analyses). (See pp. 37–42.)

- Use of multiple methods—triangulation—increases confidence in the findings. (See p. 42.)

- Scientific confidence in results also requires representative samples, usually drawn randomly. (See p. 42.)

- Responsible research also requires sensitivity to the ethics of research—ensuring that gathering scientific data does no one harm. (See pp. 45–46.)

- Attempts to understand society have existed for at least two and a half millennia, but gathering of scientific evidence to test hypotheses and validate claims is a rather modern idea. (See pp. 46–49.)

- Sociology has three strong traditions: One stresses the objective position taken as a science; another emphasizes the uniquely human qualities, such as humans making meaning, and argues that complete objectivity is never fully attained; and the third stresses practical applications of research to make a more humane, just, and compassionate society. Each of these has a long tradition within sociology, and each will be given attention in this book. (See pp. 49–60.)

- Theories are especially important to science because they raise questions for research, and they explain the relationships between facts. Sociology has four primary, over-riding theoretical perspectives or paradigms: symbolic interactionism, rational choice theory, functionalism, and conflict theory. Other perspectives, such as feminist theory, serve as correctives to the main paradigms. Most of these theories are more applicable at the micro to meso level or at the meso to macro level. (See pp. 49–60.)

- Applied and public sociologists are activists, "putting sociology to work." Their goals are for the betterment of society. (See pp. 60–61.)

Contributing to Our Social World: What Can We Do?

At the Local Level

Local service organizations: These are found in every community and work to provide for the unmet needs of community members: housing, legal aid, medical care, elder care, and so on. United Way works with most local service organizations. Volunteer to work with the organization in its needs assessment research, and practice the sociological principles and research methods described in this chapter.

At the State/Meso Level

State agencies: These agencies often have ongoing projects to gather data for more accurate information about the state and the needs of its citizens. Contact your state or provincial government to see if they need volunteers.

At the National and Global Levels

The U.S. Bureau of the Census (and census bureaus in other countries): The census is best known for its decennial (every 10 years) enumeration of the population, but its work continues each year as it prepares special reports, population estimates, and regular publications (including *Current Population Reports*). Visit the Bureau's Web site at www.census.gov, and explore the valuable and extensive amount of quantitative data and other information available, or visit your local Census Bureau office to discuss volunteer work.

 For chapter-specific resources, including **Frontline**, **TED**, and **YouTube** videos; self-quizzes; web exercises; and more, visit **www.pineforge.com/oswmedia3e**.

PART II

Social Structure, Processes, and Control

Picture a house. First there is the wood frame, then the walls and roof. This provides the framework or structure. Within that structure, activities or processes take place—electricity to turn on lights and appliances, water to wash in and drink, and people to carry out these processes. If something goes wrong in the house, we take steps to control the damage and repair it.

Our social world is constructed in a similar way: Social structure is the framework of society with its groups and organizations, and social processes are the dynamic activities of this society. This section begins with a discussion of the structure of society, followed by the processes of culture and socialization through which individuals are taught cultural rules—how to function and live effectively within their society's structure. Although socialization takes place primarily at the micro level, we will explore its implications at the meso and macro levels as well.

If we break the social structure into parts, such as the wood frame, walls, and roof of a house, it is the groups and organizations (including bureaucracies) that make up the social structure. To work smoothly, these organizations depend on people's loyalty so that they do what society and its groups need to survive. However, smooth functioning does not always happen. Things break down. This means that those in control of societies try to control disruptions and deviant individuals in order to maintain control and smooth functioning.

As we explore the next few chapters, we will continue to examine social life at the micro, meso, and macro levels, for each of us as individuals is profoundly shaped by social processes and structures at larger and more abstract levels, all the way to the global level.

CHAPTER

3

Society and Culture

Hardware and Software of Our Social World

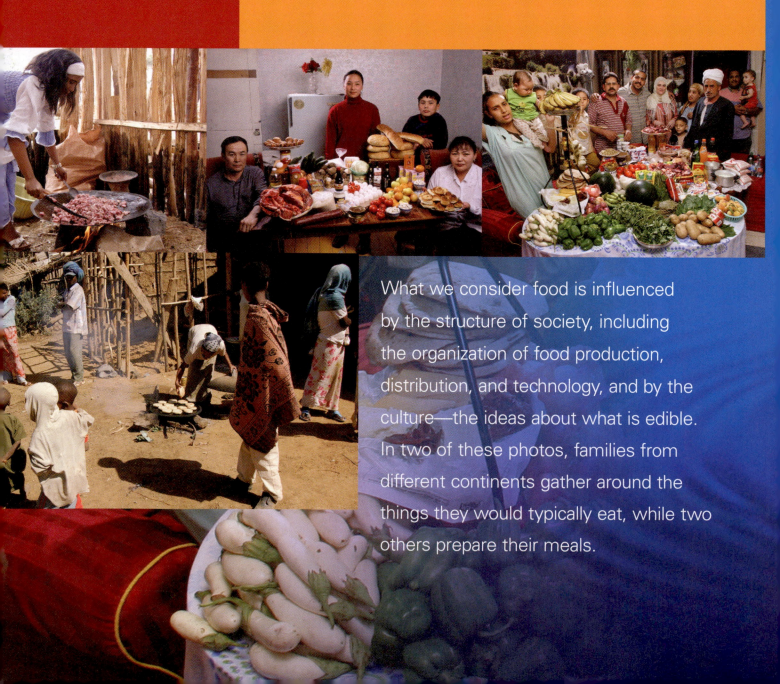

What we consider food is influenced by the structure of society, including the organization of food production, distribution, and technology, and by the culture—the ideas about what is edible. In two of these photos, families from different continents gather around the things they would typically eat, while two others prepare their meals.

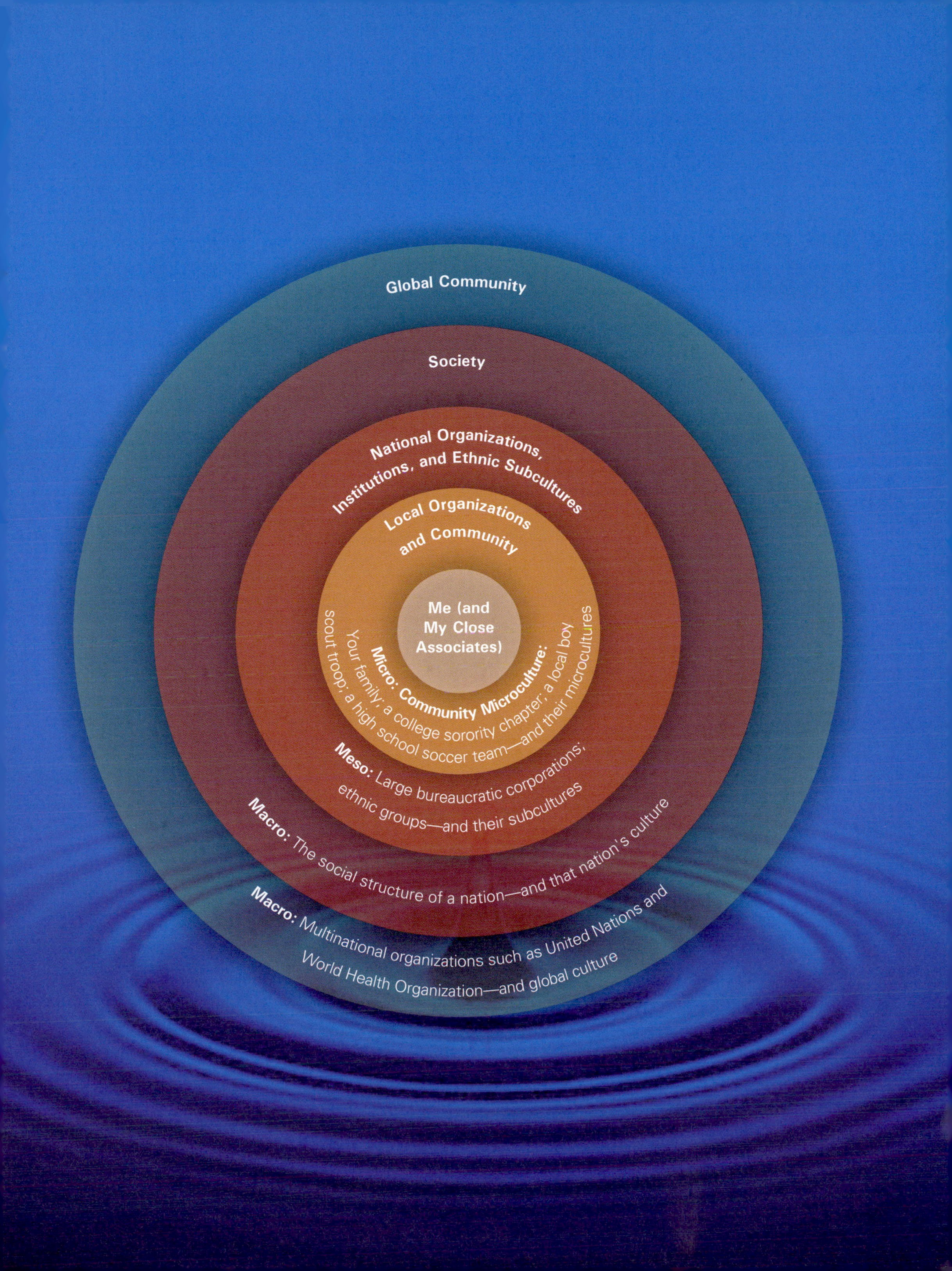

Global Community

Society

National Organizations, Institutions, and Ethnic Subcultures

Local Organizations and Community

Me (and My Close Associates)

Micro: Community Microculture: Your family; a college sorority chapter; a local boy scout troop; a high school soccer team—and their microcultures

Meso: Large bureaucratic corporations; ethnic groups—and their subcultures

Macro: The social structure of a nation—and that nation's culture

Macro: Multinational organizations such as United Nations and World Health Organization—and global culture

Think About It	
Me (and My Inner Circle)	Could you be human without culture?
Local Community	How do microcultures—the values and beliefs of your fraternity, choir, or athletic team—affect you?
National Institutions; Complex Organizations; Ethnic Groups	How do subcultures and countercultures shape the character of the nation and influence your own life?
National Society	How do the nation's social structures and culture influence you, and how can you influence the national structures and culture?
Global Community	Why do people live so differently in various parts of the world, and how can those differences be relevant to your own people?

All animals eat to survive, but what they eat differs tremendously. Two of the photos in the chapter opening show the results when researchers asked families to buy food supplies for a week. They then took pictures of families with their weekly diets laid out. The differences in these foods and what each family paid to eat give us an insight into differences in one aspect common to all cultures around the world—food.

Mrs. Ukita, the mom in the Ukita family, rises early to prepare a breakfast of miso soup and a raw egg on rice. The father and two daughters eat quickly and rush out to catch their early morning trains to work and school in Kodaira City, Japan. The mother cares for the house, does the shopping, and prepares a typical evening meal of fish, vegetables, and rice for the family.

The Ahmed family lives in a large apartment building in Cairo, Egypt. The 12 members of the extended family include the women who shop for and cook the food—vegetables, including peppers, greens, potatoes, squash, tomatoes, garlic, spices, and rice, along with pita bread and often fish or meat. The adult men work in shops in one of the many bazaars, while the school-age children attend school, then help with the chores.

The nine members of the Ayme family live in Tingo, Equador, high in the Andes mountains, where the main occupation of Indian families is herding and growing potatoes and other crops suited to the high altitude and cool climate. Their diet consists of foods that are readily available in the market: plantains, potatoes, onions, carrots, and grains.

In the Breidjing refugee camp in Chad, many Sudanese refugees eat what relief agencies can get to them—and that food source is not always reliable. Typical for the Aboubakar family, a mother and five children, is rice or some other grain, oil for cooking, occasionally some root plants or squash that keep longer than fresh fruits and vegetables, dried legumes, and a few spices. The girls and women go into the desert to fetch firewood for cooking and to get water from whatever source has water at the time. This is a dangerous trip as they may be attacked and raped or even killed outside the camps.

In Sicily, Italy, the Manzo family—mother, father, and three young boys—enjoy fresh bread from the baker for breakfast and often have pasta with sauce, vegetables, and

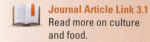

Journal Article Link 3.1
Read more on culture and food.

fish or meat for dinner. Typically, the father works in the family orchard, while the mother takes care of the house, and the boys go to school, helping with chores after school. Although most diets include some form of grain and starch, locally available fruits and vegetables, and perhaps meat or fish, broad variations exist even within one society. Yet all these differences have something in common: Each represents a society that has a unique culture that includes what people eat.

Culture consists of ideas and "things" that are passed on from one generation to the next in a society—the knowledge, beliefs, values, rules or laws, language, customs, symbols, and material products (such as food, houses, and transportation) that help meet human needs. Culture provides guidelines for living. Learning our culture puts our social world in an understandable framework, providing a tool kit we can use to help us construct the meaning of our world (Bruner 1996; Nagel 1994).

A **society** consists of individuals who live together in a specific geographic area, who interact more with each other than they do with outsiders and cooperate for the attainment of common goals. Each society includes key institutions—such as family, education, religion, politics, economics, and health—that meet basic human needs. Members of a society share a common culture over time. The way people think

Two of the photos on the opening page of this chapter show families from Egypt and Japan gathered around a typical week's food supply. Members of the Aboubakar family of Sudan gather here in front of their tent with a week's supply of food. Note the difference.

and behave in any society is largely prescribed by its culture, which is learned, transmitted, and reshaped from generation to generation. All activities in the society, whether educating young members, preparing and eating dinner, selecting leaders for the group, finding a mate, or negotiating with other societies, are guided by cultural rules and expectations. In each society, culture provides the social rules for how individuals carry out necessary tasks, just as software provides the rules for computer applications.

While culture provides the "software" for the way people live, society represents the "hardware"—the structure that gives organization and stability to group life. Society—organized groups of people—and culture—their way of life—are interdependent. The two are not the same thing, but they cannot exist without each other, just as computer hardware and software are each useless without the other.

This chapter explores the ideas of society and culture and discusses how they relate to each other. We will look at what society is and how it is organized, how it influences and is influenced by culture, what culture is, how and why culture develops, and the components that make up culture, cultural theories, and policy issues. After reading this chapter, we will have a better idea of how we as individuals fit into society and learn our culture.

Society: The Hardware

All societies have geographical boundaries or borders and individuals who live together in families and communities and who share a culture. The structures that make up society include the interdependent positions we hold (as parents, workers), the groups to which we belong (family, work group, and clubs), and the institutions in which we participate. This "hardware" (structure) of our social world provides the framework for "software" (culture) to function.

Societies exist in particular places and times, and they change over time. Human societies have become more complex over time, but people have been hunters and gatherers for 99% of human existence. A few groups remain hunter-gatherers today. As Table 3.1 illustrates, if all human history were to be compressed into the lifetime of an 80-year-old person, humans would have started cultivating crops and herding animals for their food supply only a few months ago. Note the incredible rate of change that has occurred just in the past two centuries.

Thinking Sociologically

What major changes took place in your grandparents' lifetimes that affect the way you and your family live today? You may want to look at the timeline inside the cover of this book. It will provide some ideas.

A Chinese family sits outside on the ground enjoying a home-cooked meal.

Societies are organized in particular patterns, patterns that are shaped by a range of factors, including the way people procure food, the availability of resources, contact with other societies, and cultural beliefs. For example, people can change from herding to farming only if they have the knowledge, skills, and desire to do so and only in environments that will support agriculture. As societies develop, changes take place in the social structures and relationships between people that characterize each type of society. For example, in industrialized societies, relationships between people typically must become more formal because people must interact with strangers and not just relatives. It is important to note that not all societies go through all stages. Some are jolted into the future by political events or changes in the global system, and some resist pressures to become modernized and continue to live in simpler social systems.

Evolution of Societies

The Saharan desert life for the Taureg tribe is pretty much as it has been for centuries. In simple traditional societies, individuals are assigned to comparatively few social positions or statuses. Today, however, few societies are isolated from global impact. Even the Taureg are called on to escort adventurous tourists through the desert for a currency unknown to them and unneeded until recently.

In such traditional societies, men teach their sons everything they need to know, for all men do much the same jobs, depending on where they live—hunting, fishing, or farming and protecting the community from danger. Likewise, girls learn their jobs from their mothers—such

Table 3.1   One Million Years of Human History Compressed Into One 80-Year Lifetime

Year	Age	Event	
2,500,000 years ago	Birth	*Homo habilis* is born—the first ancestor to make/use tools and have culture; evidence of sharing food, congregating, and probably sharing housing	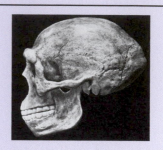
2 million years ago	2 years old	*Homo erectus* shows early evidence of family structures; findings of longer life spans and three generations alive simultaneously	
15,000 years ago	79 years old	Six months ago: North America settled by early humans, hunters and gatherers	
11,000 years ago	79 years old	Five months ago: In the Middle East, the first agricultural communities, indicating food cultivation	
10,000 years ago	79 years old	Twenty weeks ago: the last ice age is over; humans spread more widely over the planet	
5,000 years ago	79 years old	Ten weeks ago: humans began to cast and use metals and built the pyramids	
2,000 years ago	79 years old	Seven weeks ago: beginning of the Common Era (under the Holy Roman Empire)	
220 years ago	79 years old	Two and a half weeks ago: the United States began a new experiment with democracy	
100 years ago	79 years old	Yesterday morning: the airplane was invented	
30 years ago	79 years old	Yesterday afternoon: humans first set foot on the moon; after dinner, we broke the DNA (genetic) code	 

Increasingly in the United States, where both parents work, dinner is a fast-food takeout or a ready-to-cook packaged meal—a quick dash for nourishment in front of the TV rather than a communal event.

The Taureg live a simple traditional life in the Sahara Desert in the Sahel region of Niger (Africa), and their social structure has few social positions except those defined by gender.

A mother in Côte d'Ivoire (West Africa), carrying her load on her head, returns to the village with her daughter after gathering wood. Carrying wood and water is typically women's work. In this society, the primary social cohesion is mechanical solidarity.

as child care, fetching water, food preparation, farming, weaving, and perhaps house building. In contrast, in more complex societies, such as industrial or "modern" societies, thousands of interdependent statuses are based on complex divisions of labor with designated tasks. An interesting question that has intrigued sociologists is how traditional societies change into new types of societies.

Émile Durkheim ([1893] 1947), an early French sociologist, pictured a continuum between simple and complex societies. He described simple premodern societies as held together by *mechanical solidarity*—common beliefs, values, and emotional ties. Furthermore, the division of labor is based largely on male/female distinctions and age groupings. Members of premodern societies tend to think the same way on important matters, and everyone fulfills his or her expected social positions. This provides the glue that holds the society together. The entire society may involve only a few hundred people, with no meso-level institutions, organizations, and subcultures. Prior to the emergence of nation-states, there was no macro level either—only tribal groupings.

According to Durkheim, as societies transformed, they became more complex through increasingly complex divisions of labor and changes in the ways people carried out necessary tasks for survival. Societies in which social positions are specialized and interdependent are held together by *organic solidarity*. Prior to the factory system, for example, individual cobblers made shoes to order. With the Industrial Revolution, factories took over the process, with many individuals carrying out interdependent tasks. The division of labor is critical because it leads to new forms of social cohesion based on interdependence, not on emotional ties. Gradual changes from mechanical (traditional) to organic (modern) society also involve harnessing new forms of energy and finding more efficient ways to use them (Nolan and Lenski 2008). For example, the use of steam engines and coal for fuel triggered the Industrial Revolution, leading to the development of industrial societies.

Also, as societies changed, they added more large organizations and institutions that reached individuals and families as never before. The meso level—institutions and large bureaucratic organizations—became more influential. Still, as recently as 200 years ago, even large societies had little global interdependence, and life for the typical citizen was influenced mostly by events at the micro and meso levels. Keep in mind that it was just over 200 years ago when American colonies selected representatives to form a loosely federated government that came to be called the United States. As communication and transportation around the world developed and expanded, the global level grew.

As you read about each of the following types of societies, from the simplest to the most complex, notice the presence of these variables: (a) division of labor, (b) interdependence of people's positions, (c) increasingly advanced technologies, and (d) new forms and uses of energy. Although none of these variables alone is *sufficient* to trigger evolution to a new type of society, they may all be *necessary* for a transition to occur.

According to Durkheim, then, in traditional societies with mechanical solidarity, interpersonal interaction and community life at the micro level were the most important aspects of social life. Meso- and macro-level societies developed as a result of changes toward more organic solidarity. As societies become more complex, meso- and macro-level institutions become more important and have more profound impacts on the lives of individuals.

Hunter-Gatherer Societies

From the beginning of human experience until recently, hunting and gathering (or foraging) were the sole means of sustaining life. Other types of societies emerged only recently (Nolan and Lenski 2008); yet today, only a handful of societies still rely on hunting and gathering.

In the Kalahari Desert of southwest Africa live hunter-gatherers known as the !Kung. (The ! is pronounced with a click of the tongue.) The !Kung live a nomadic life, moving from one place to another as food supplies become available or are used up. As a result, they carry very few personal possessions and live in temporary huts, settling around water holes for a few months at a time. Settlements are small, rarely more than 20 to 50 people, for food supplies are not plentiful enough to support large, permanent populations (Lee 1984). !Kung women gather edible plants and nuts, while !Kung men hunt. Beyond division of labor by gender and age, however, there are few differences in roles or status.

Life is organized around kinship ties and reciprocity for the well-being of the whole community. When a large animal is killed, people gather from a wide area to share in the bounty, and great care is taken to ensure that the meat is distributed fairly. Resources are shared among the people, but sharing is regulated by a complex system of mutual obligations. A visitor who eats food at another's hearth is expected to repay that hospitality in the future.

The !Kung are a typical **hunter-gatherer society**, in which people rely directly on the plants and animals in their habitat to live. People make their clothing, shelter, and tools from available materials and through trade with other nearby groups. People migrate seasonally to new food sources. Population size remains small as the numbers of births and deaths are balanced.

Today, the hunter-gatherer lifestyle is becoming extinct. For example, much of the wild game on which the !Kung subsisted has been overhunted or is now protected on game preserves. The governments of South Africa and Botswana have attempted to settle such groups on reservations, and contacts with macro-level societies, by choice and by force, have forever changed the !Kung way of life and that of other hunting-and-gathering societies.

Herding and Horticultural Societies

The Masai inhabit the grasslands of Kenya and Tanzania, depending on their herds for survival. Their cattle and goats provide meat, milk, blood (which they drink), and hides. A seminomadic herding society, the Masai move camp to find grazing land for their animals and set up semipermanent shelters for the few months they will remain in one area. Settlements consist of huts constructed in a circle with a perimeter fence surrounding the compound. At the more permanent settlements, the Masai grow short-term crops to supplement their diet. The Masai are under some pressure to become agriculturalists, however, as the government of Kenya—a relatively new macro-level influence in their lives—now restricts their

Masai men in Kenya herd their cattle, leading them to water or better grazing. The strategy of domesticating cattle rather than hunting game has been a survival strategy for the Masai, but it also affects the culture in many other ways.

territory and herding practices that encroach on wild-animal refuges. Tourism also greatly influences their economy.

Herding societies have food-producing strategies based on keeping herds of domesticated animals, whose care is the central focus of their activities. Domesticating animals has replaced hunting them. In addition to providing food and other products, cattle, sheep, goats, pigs, horses, and camels represent forms of wealth on which further changes in roles and status may be built.

Horticultural societies keep domesticated animals but focus on primitive agriculture or gardening. Horticulturalists use digging sticks and wooden hoes to cultivate tree crops, such as date palms or bananas, and to plant and maintain produce in garden plots, such as yams, beans, taro, squash, or corn. This is more efficient than gathering wild vegetables and fruits. Both herding and horticultural societies differ from hunter-gatherer societies in that they make their living by cultivating food and have some control over its production (Ward and Edelstein 2009).

The ability to control food sources was a major turning point in human history. Societies became more settled and built surpluses of food, which led to increases in population size. A community could contain as many as 3,000 individuals. More people, surplus food, and greater accumulation of possessions encouraged the development of private property and created new status differences between individuals and families. Forms of social inequality became even more pronounced in agricultural societies.

The end of the horticultural stage saw advances in irrigation systems, in the fertilization of land, and in crop rotation. The Neolithic Revolution, occurring as early as 14,500 years ago in Egypt, 10,000 years ago in Melanesia, and 9,000 to 7,000 years ago in the Middle East Fertile Crescent and many parts of Asia, was characterized by more permanent settlements, land ownership, human modification of the natural environment, higher population density (cities), changes in diets to more vegetables and cereals, and power hierarchies. However, the technological breakthrough that moved many societies from the horticultural to the agricultural stage was the plow, introduced more than 6,000 years ago. It marked the beginning of the agricultural revolution in Europe, the Middle East, and other parts of the world, and it brought about massive changes in social structures in many societies.

Agricultural Societies

Pedro and Lydia Ramirez, their four young children, and Lydia's parents live as an extended family in a small farming village in Nicaragua. They rise early, and while Pedro heads for the fields to do some work before breakfast, Lydia prepares his breakfast and lunch and sees that their eldest son is up and ready to go to school, while Lydia's mother looks

A fair trade coffee farmer ("fair trade" means no slavery was used in the production, and workers were paid a fair price) picks organic coffee beans in Central America. Producing a crop for cash exchange, rather than growing something to eat locally, is the normal pattern in an agricultural society.

after the younger children. After school, the boy also helps in the fields. Most of the land in the area is owned by a large company that grows coffee, but the Ramirez family is fortunate to have a small garden plot where its members grow some vegetables for themselves. At harvest time, all hands help, including young children. The families receive cash for the crops they have grown, minus the rent for the land. The land is plowed with the help of strong animals such as horses and oxen, and fertilizers are used. Little irrigation is attempted, although the garden plots may be watered by hand in the dry season.

The Ramirez's way of life is typical of that in an **agricultural society**. Like horticulturalists, agrarian farmers rely primarily on raising crops for food. However, agricultural societies are more efficient than horticultural societies: Technological advances such as the plow, irrigation, use of animals, and fertilization allow for intensive and continuous cultivation of the same land, thus permitting permanent settlements and greater food surpluses. Through time, as increasingly sophisticated agricultural technology resulted in surplus food, the size of population centers increased to as much as a million or more.

As surpluses accumulated, land in some societies became concentrated in the hands of a few individuals.

The invention of the plow was essential for agricultural societies to develop, and in the early period of agriculture, the plow was first pushed by people and then pulled by animals. The harnessing of energy was taken to another level when gasoline engines could pull the plow and cultivate thousands of acres. This represents the beginning of industrialization.

Wealthy landowners built armies and expanded their empires. During these periods, fighting for and controlling land took precedence over technological advance. War was prevalent, and societies were divided increasingly into rich and poor classes. Those who held the land and wealth could control the labor sources and acquire serfs or slaves. Thus, the feudal system was born. Serfs (the peasant class) were forced to work the land for their

survival. Food surpluses also allowed some individuals to leave the land and to trade goods or services in exchange for food. For the first time, social inequality became extensive enough to divide society into social classes. At this point, religion, political power, a standing army, and other meso-level institutions and organizations came to be independent of the family. The meso level became well established.

As technology advanced, goods were manufactured in cities, and peasants moved from farming communities, where the land could not support the population, to rapidly growing urban areas, where the demand for labor was great. It was not until the mid-1700s in England that the next major transformation of society took place, resulting largely from technological advances and the harnessing of energy.

Industrial Societies

The Industrial Revolution involved the harnessing of steam power and the manufacture of gasoline engines, permitting machines to replace human and animal power; a tractor can plow far more land in a week than a horse, and an electric pump can irrigate more acres than an ox-driven pump. As a result of the new technologies, raw mineral products, such as ores, raw plant products, such as rubber, and raw animal products, such as hides, could be transformed into mass-produced consumer goods. The Industrial Revolution brought about enormous changes in products and social structures.

Industrial societies rely primarily on mechanized production, resulting in greater division of labor based on expertise. Economic resources were distributed more widely among individuals in industrial societies, but inequities between owners and laborers persisted. Wage earning gradually replaced slavery and serfdom, and highly skilled workers earned higher wages, leading to the rise of a middle class. Farmworkers moved from rural areas to cities to find work in factories, which produced consumer goods such as cars and washing machines. Cities come to be populated by millions of people.

Family and kinship patterns at the micro level also changed. Agricultural societies need large, land-based, extended family units to do the work of farming (recall how the Ramirez parents, grandparents, and children in Nicaragua all help out at harvest time), but industrial societies need individuals with specific skills and smaller families to support. Family roles changed. For example, children are an asset in agrarian societies and begin farmwork at an early age. In an industrial society, however, children become a liability because they contribute less to the finances of the family and ultimately compete with adults for jobs.

Meso- and macro-level dimensions of social life expand in industrializing societies and become more influential in the lives of individuals. National institutions and multinational organizations develop. Today, for example, global organizations such as the World Bank, the World Court, the United Nations, and the World Health Organization address social problems and sometimes even make decisions that change national boundaries or national policies. Medical organizations such as Doctors Without Borders work cross-nationally; corporations become multinational; and voluntary associations such as Amnesty International lobby for human rights around the globe.

Perhaps the most notable characteristic of the industrial age is the rapid rate of change compared with other stages of societal development. The beginning of industrialization in Europe was gradual, based on years of population movement, urbanization, technological development, and other factors of modernization. Today, however, societal change occurs so rapidly that societies at all levels of development are being drawn together into a new age—the postindustrial era.

This Buddhist monk uses modern technology, including a laptop that can connect him with colleagues on the other side of the globe.

Postindustrial or Information Societies

The difference between India and the United States is "night and day"—literally. As Keith and Jeanne finished chapters for this book, the chapters were sent to India in the evening and returned typeset by morning, a feat made possible by the time differences. The efficiency of overnight delivery and the lower cost of production have led many publishing companies to turn to businesses halfway around the world for much of the book production process. As India and other developing countries increase their trained, skilled labor force, they are being called on by national and multinational companies to carry out global manufacturing processes. India has some of the world's best technical training institutes and the most modern **technology**—that is, the knowledge and tools used to extend human abilities. Although many people in India live in poverty, a relatively new middle class is rapidly emerging in major business centers around the country.

After World War II, starting in the 1950s, the transition from industrial to postindustrial society began in the United States, western Europe (especially Germany), and Japan. This shift was characterized by movement from human labor to automated production and from a predominance of manufacturing jobs to a growth in service jobs, such as computer operators, bankers, scientists, teachers, public relations workers, stockbrokers, and salespeople. More than two thirds of all jobs in the United States now reside in organizations that produce and transmit information, thus the reference to an "Information Age." Daniel Bell (1973) describes this transformation of work, information, and communication as "the third technological revolution" after industrialization based on steam (what he calls the first technological revolution) and the invention of electricity (the second technological revolution). According to Bell, the third technological revolution was the development of the computer, which has led to this postindustrial or Information Age.

As in the other types of societies, **postindustrial societies** are undergoing significant structural changes. For example, postindustrial societies require workers with high levels of technical and professional education, such as those in India. Those without technical education are less likely to find rewarding employment in the technological revolution. This results in new class lines being drawn, based in part on skills and education in new technologies.

Inequalities in access to education and technology will create or perpetuate social inequalities. A recent survey indicates that 62% of households in the United States had one or more computers and 88% of computer users had Internet access (U.S. Census Bureau 2005a). Use of computers in 2004 by adults was 85% from ages 18 to 27, 87% from ages 28 to 39, 84% from ages 40 to 49, 76% from ages 50 to 58, 57% from ages 59 to 68, and 24% for age 69 and older (Pew Internet and American Life Project 2004). Note the decline in use with end of work years and among earlier generations, who had less—or no—access to computers when they were growing up. More than half of the adult Internet

Encyclopedia Link 3.1
Explore postindustrial society.

Hybrid buses have been adopted in some cities and in national parks because of the effects of pollution on the globe and its occupants.

In a study of postmodern communities, sociologist Richard Florida links creativity to the local cultural climate and to economic prosperity. His research has important applied dimensions and is useful to policymakers in local communities. As his research in the "Applied Sociologist at Work" on the next page makes clear, the organization of society and the means of providing the necessities of life have a profound impact on values, beliefs, lifestyle, and other aspects of culture.

Thinking Sociologically

What are likely to be the growth areas for jobs in your community and society? What competencies and skills will be essential in the future for you to find employment and be successful on the job?

users in the United States are between 18 and 44. The number of older generations online has been growing steadily, and they are engaging in more varied activities, such as shopping, looking for health information, and making travel reservations online (Pew Internet and American Life Project 2009). Female and male computer users are about equal, at 73%. Among English-speaking Hispanics, 75% use computers; among Whites, 73%; and among Blacks, 62%. Computer usage grows as household incomes and education increase, with more than 90% of households earning above $50,000 using computers (Pew Internet and American Life Project 2004).

Postindustrial societies rely on new sources of power such as atomic, wind, and solar energy and new uses of computer automation, such as computer-controlled robots, which eliminate the need for human labor other than highly skilled technicians. In an age of global climate change, there is also a lot of concern about technologies that reduce pollution, as the photo of the hybrid bus illustrates. The core issue in a postindustrial society is this: The control of information and the ability to develop technologies or provide services have become more important than the control of money or capital.

Values of 21st-century postindustrial societies favor scientific and creative approaches to problem solving, research, and development, along with attitudes that support the globalization of world economies. Satellites, cell phones, fiber optics, and, especially, the Internet are further transforming postindustrial societies of the Information Age, linking people from societies around the world.

What will the future bring? Futurologists predict new trends based on current activities, predictions of new advances and technologies, and inventions on the horizon. Among the many ideas for the future, technological advances dominate the field. Predictions include the use of cell phones, connecting the poorest corners of the globe with the rest of the world. One billion mobile phone users are predicted for China by 2020, with 80% of the population having phones. Alternative energy sources from wind and solar power to hydrogen will replace gasoline. One million hydrogen-fueled cars are predicted for the United States. Rechargeable batteries that will run for 40 hours without recharging will run most home appliances by 2030. Those who are paralyzed will find help from Brain Computer Interfaces, giving them the ability to control their environments. Many advances will occur in space travel; a hotel may open on the moon by 2025, with transport to the moon. Medical advances will result in stem cell breakthroughs that can develop into various types of body tissue (Future for All 2008; News of Future 2007). These are just a few of the many predictions that will affect societies and alter some human interactions. The point is that rapid change is inevitable, and the future looks exciting.

In much of this book, we focus on complex, multi-level societies, for this is the type of system in which most of us reading this book now live. Much of this book also focuses on social interaction and social structures, including interpersonal networking, the growth of bureaucratic structures, social inequality within the structure, and the core institutions necessary to meet the needs of individuals and society. In short, "hardware"—society—is the focus of many subsequent chapters. The remainder of this chapter will focus primarily on the social "software" that complements the hardware of our society.

The Applied Sociologist at Work— Richard Florida	Creativity, Community, and Applied Sociology

Like the transformations of societies from the hunter-gatherer to the horticultural stage or from the agricultural to the industrial stage, our own current transformation seems to have created a good deal of "cultural wobble" within society. How does one identify the elements or the defining features of a new age while the transformation is still in progress? This was one of the questions that intrigued sociologist Richard Florida, who studied U.S. communities.

Dr. Florida (2002) combined several methods. First, he traveled around the country to communities that were especially prosperous and seemed to be on the cutting edge of change in U.S. society. In these communities, he did both individual interviews and focus-group interviews. Focus-group interviews are semistructured group interviews with seven or eight people where ideas can be generated from the group by asking open-ended questions. Professor Florida recorded the discussion and analyzed the transcript of the discussion. The collected data helped Professor Florida identify the factors that caused people to choose the place where they decided to live. His informants discussed quality of life and the way they make decisions. As certain themes and patterns emerged, he tested the ideas by comparing statistical data for regions that were vibrant, had growing economies, and seemed to be integrated into the emerging information economy. He used another method to compare communities and regions of the country— analyzing already existing archival data collected by various U.S. government agencies, especially the U.S. Bureau of Labor Statistics and the U.S. Census Bureau.

Florida argues that the economy of the 21st century is largely driven by creativity, and creative people often decide where to live based on certain features of the society. Currently, more than one third of the jobs in the United States—and almost all the extremely well-paid professional positions—require creative thinking. These include not just the creative arts but scientific research, computer and mathematical occupations, education and library science positions, and many media, legal, and managerial careers. People in this "creative class" are given an enormous amount of autonomy in their work; they have problems to solve and the freedom to figure out how to do so. Florida found that modern businesses flourish when they hire highly creative people. Thus, growing businesses tend to seek out places where creative people locate.

Through his research, Florida identified regions and urban areas that are especially attractive to the creative class. Florida's research led him to collaborate with Gary Gates, a scholar who was doing research on communities that are open and hospitable to gays and lesbians. Gates and Florida were amazed to find that their lists were nearly identical. Florida found that creative people thrive on diversity—ethnic, gender, religious, and otherwise—for when creative people are around others who think differently, it tends to spawn new avenues of thinking and problem solving. Tolerance of difference and even the enjoyment of individual idiosyncrasies are hallmarks of thriving communities.

Florida is now very much in demand as a consultant to mayors and urban-planning teams, and his books have become required reading for city council members. Some elected officials have decided that fostering an environment conducive to creativity that attracts creative people leads to prosperity because business will follow. Key elements for creative communities are local music and art festivals, the presence of organic food grocery stores, legislation that encourages interesting mom-and-pop stores (and keeps out large "box stores" that crush such small and unique endeavors), encouragement of quaint and locally owned bookstores and distinctive coffee shops, provisions for bike and walking paths throughout the town, and ordinances that establish an environment of tolerance for people who are "different."

Note: Richard Florida heads the Prosperity Institute at the Rotman School of Management at the University of Toronto. He also runs a private Creative Class Institute. He earned his bachelor's degree from Rutgers College and his doctorate in urban planning from Columbia University.

Culture: The Software

I sleep on a bed. Perhaps you sleep on a tatami mat or animal skins. I brush my teeth with a toothbrush and toothpaste. Perhaps you chew on a special stick to clean your teeth. I speak English, along with 514 million native English speakers. You may speak one of the many other languages in the world, as do more than 1 billion Mandarin Chinese speakers, 495 million Hindustani speakers, and 425 million Spanish speakers (Information Please 2008). I like meat and veggies. Perhaps you like tofu and grasshoppers. I wear jeans and a T-shirt. Perhaps you wear a sari or burqa. In the United States, proper greetings include a handshake, a wave, or saying "Hello" or "Hi." The greeting ceremony in Japan includes bowing, with the depth of the bow defined by the relative status of each individual. To know the proper bowing behavior, Japanese business people who are strangers exchange business cards on introduction. Their titles, as printed on their cards, disclose each person's status and thus provide clues as to how deeply each should bow. The proper greeting behavior in many European countries calls for men as well as women to kiss acquaintances on both cheeks.

Video Link 3.1
Learn about the impact of the Internet.

The point of these examples is to show that the culture—the ideas and "things" that are passed on from one generation to the next in a society, including their knowledge, beliefs, values, rules and laws, language, customs, symbols, and material products—varies greatly as we travel across the globe. Each social unit of cooperating and interdependent people, whether at the micro, meso, or macro level, develops a unique way of life. This culture provides guidelines for the actions and interaction of individuals and groups within society. The cultural guidelines that people follow when they greet another person are examples.

As you can see, the sociological definition of culture refers to far more than "high culture"—such as fine art, classical music, opera, literature, ballet, or theater—and also far more than "popular culture"—such as reality TV, professional wrestling, YouTube, and other mass entertainment. In fact, much of pop culture has been shaped by technology, as is illustrated in the next "Engaging Sociology." The sociological definition of culture includes both high culture and pop culture and has a much broader meaning besides.

Engaging Sociology

Pop Culture and Technology

How surprising to think that digital telephones, high-speed lines for computers, digitized print media, and the World Wide Web have all occurred within about the past half-century. Vinyl records, dial telephones, and VHS videos have been surpassed by CDs (compact discs), high-speed cell phones, and DVDs (digital video discs). Slim laptops and hand-held computers are rapidly replacing bulky desktop computers. The following timeline shows the rapid advances of the Internet and World Wide Web in recent years; the point of this timeline is to illustrate the rapid advance of technology and the place it holds in our lives. Technology is now a primary conveyer of pop culture.

An Internet and World Wide Web Timeline

1844:	The telegraph constitutes a data network forerunner.
1866:	Transoceanic telegraph service begins.
1876:	The telephone is introduced.
1915:	The first transcontinental phone call is made.
1946:	Electronic Numerical Integrator and Computer (ENIAC), the first general-purpose computer, is developed for military purposes.
1951:	UNIVersal Automatic Computer (UNIVAC) becomes the first civilian computer.
1962:	The first communications satellite and the first digital phone networks are introduced.

1965:	A highly usable computer language, Beginner's All-Purpose Symbolic Instruction Code (BASIC), is developed.
1969:	The U.S. Department of Defense launches Advanced Research Projects Agency Network (Arpanet), the first communications network.
1971:	Microprocessors are developed, making possible personal computer (PC) technology.
1972:	The first video game, *Pong*, is introduced. E-mail is developed on Arpanet for military use.
1975:	The first PC, Altair, is launched.
1977:	The first fiber optic network is created.
1978:	Cellular phone service begins.
1980s:	Hypertext is developed in the mid-1980s, making possible the eventual creation of the World Wide Web.
1982:	The National Science Foundation sponsors a high-speed communications network, leading to the Internet.
1983:	Modifications of Arpanet make possible the launching of the Internet.
1984:	Apple Macintosh introduces the first PC with graphics.
1989:	A new company called AOL (America Online)—the first successful Internet service provider—is formed.
1990:	The first Internet search engine, Archie, is developed.
1991:	The Internet opens to commercial uses, HTML (HyperText Markup Language)

1993: is developed, and the Web is finally launched.

1993: The first point-and-click Web browser, Mosaic, is introduced.

1994: The first Internet cafes open. Jeff Bezos launches Amazon.com.

1995: Digital cellular phones are introduced. The first online auction house, eBay, is launched.

1996: Google makes its debut.

2000: Cookies technology allows for information profiles to be created, enabling data mining.

2001: Instant messaging services expand to allow exchanges between different service providers.

2002: Broadband technology is developed in South Korea.

Mid-2000s: The Internet converges with previous media (radio, television, etc.) to produce online versions of all media forms. It also becomes a continuing source of new forms of communication, including Web sites such as MySpace, Facebook, and YouTube.

The continuing rapid advances in technology have paralleled the development of shared pop culture in the United States and around the world, culture that is accessible to everyone, not just the elite. Music groups from Africa, Asia, the Middle East, and Europe have gained audiences in the United States and vice versa. New musical groups can become instant success stories through YouTube. Push technology or Webcasting allows audio and video presentations on demand, and streaming allows for people around the world to listen to broadcasts on the Internet. The spread of pop culture—music, mass art, fashion, books, you name it—has been made possible by advances in technology.

We know that "there is no turning back the clock once an innovation is introduced that makes communication more rapid, cheap, efficient, and broadly accessible" (Danesi 2008:21).

Challenges:

1. Identify four of the historic innovations that particularly interest you. What are some ways in which your life is different today because of those four introductions to our popular culture?
2. Identify three positive ways these rapid changes are likely to affect the less developed parts of the world.
3. Identify three negative ways these rapid changes are likely to affect the less developed parts of the world.
4. Are technology and the spread of pop culture bringing the world closer together, or are these innovations more likely to cause tensions as societies attempt to protect their citizens against e-fraud, pornography, misuse of technology, and change of the local culture?

Everyone shares a culture with others, although there may be different views within and between cultures about what rules and behaviors are the most important. No one could survive without culture, for without culture, there would be no guidelines or rules of behavior. Societies would be chaotic masses of individuals. Culture provides the routines, patterns, and expectations for carrying out daily rituals and interactions. Within a society, the process of learning how to act is called socialization (discussed in detail in Chapter 4). From birth, we learn the patterns of behavior approved in our society.

Culture evolves over time and is adaptive. What is normal, proper, and good behavior in hunter-gatherer societies, where cooperation and communal loyalty are critical to the hunt, differs from appropriate behavior in the Information Age, where individualism and competition are encouraged and enhance one's well-being.

The creation of culture is ongoing and cumulative because individuals and societies continually build on existing culture to adapt to new challenges and opportunities. The behaviors, values, and institutions that seem natural to you are actually shaped by your culture. Culture is so much a part of life that you may not even notice behaviors that outsiders find unusual or even abhorrent. You may not think about touching someone on the head, putting a baby in a crib, or picking up food with your left hand, but in some other cultures, such acts may be defined as inappropriate or morally wrong.

The transmission of culture is the feature that most separates humans from other animals. Some societies of higher primates have shared cultures but do not systematically enculturate (teach a way of life to) the next generation. Primate cultures focus on behaviors relating to obtaining food, use of territory, and social status. Human cultures have significantly more content and are mediated by language. Humans are the only mammals with cultures that enable them to adapt to and even modify their environments so that they can survive on the equator, in the Arctic, or even beyond the planet.

Thinking Sociologically

Try playing a game of cards with four people in which each player thinks a different suit is trump (a trump is a rule whereby any card from the trump suit wins over any card from a different suit). In this game, one person believes hearts is trump, another assumes spades is trump, and so forth. What would happen? How would the result be similar to a society with no common culture?

Ethnocentrism and Cultural Relativity

As scientists, sociologists must rely on careful use of the scientific method to understand behavior. The scientific method calls for objectivity—the practice of considering observed behavior independently of one's own beliefs and values. The study of social behavior thus requires both sensitivity to a wide variety of human social patterns and a perspective that reduces bias. This is more difficult than it sounds because sociologists themselves are products of society and culture. All of us are raised in a particular culture that we view as normal or natural. Yet not every culture views the same things as "normal."

The Arapesh of New Guinea, a traditional and stable society, encourage premarital sex. It is a way for a girl to prove her fertility, which makes her more attractive as a potential marriage partner (Mead [1935] 1963). Any babies born out of wedlock are simply absorbed into the girl's extended family. The baby's care, support, belonging, and lineage are not major issues for the Arapesh.

The babies are simply accepted and welcomed as new members of the mother's family because the structure is able to absorb them. For the Arapesh and for the Bontoc of the Philippines, sexual behavior outside marriage is not a moral issue.

From studies of 154 societies documented in the *Human Relations Area Files* (Ford 1970; a source of comparative information on many traditional societies around the world), scientists have found that about 42% of the 154 included societies encourage premarital sex, whereas 29% forbid such behavior and punish those who disobey this rule. The remainder fall in between. As you can see, social values, beliefs, and behaviors can vary dramatically from one society to the next. These differences can be threatening and even offensive because most people judge others according to their own perspectives, experiences, and values.

The tendency to view one's own group and its cultural expectations as right, proper, and superior to others is called **ethnocentrism**. If you were brought up in a society that forbids premarital or extramarital sex, for instance, you might judge the Arapesh—or many Americans—to be immoral. In a few Muslim societies, people who violate this taboo may be severely punished or even executed, because premarital sex is seen as an offense against the faith and the family and as a weakening of social bonds. In turn, the Arapesh would find rules of abstinence to be strange and even wrong.

Societies instill some degree of ethnocentrism in their members because ethnocentric beliefs hold groups together and help members feel that they belong to the group. Ethnocentrism promotes loyalty, unity, high morale, and conformity to the rules of society. Fighting for one's country, for instance, requires some degree of belief in the rightness of one's own society and its causes. Ethnocentric attitudes also help protect societies from rapid, disintegrating change. If most people in a society did not

This Japanese schoolgirl might think that eating with a fork or spoon is quite strange. She has been well socialized to know that polite eating involves competent use of chopsticks.

In 1923, the Hollywood Association started a campaign to expel the Japanese from their community. Signs like these were prominent throughout Hollywood and in other California communities. They illustrate ethnocentrism.

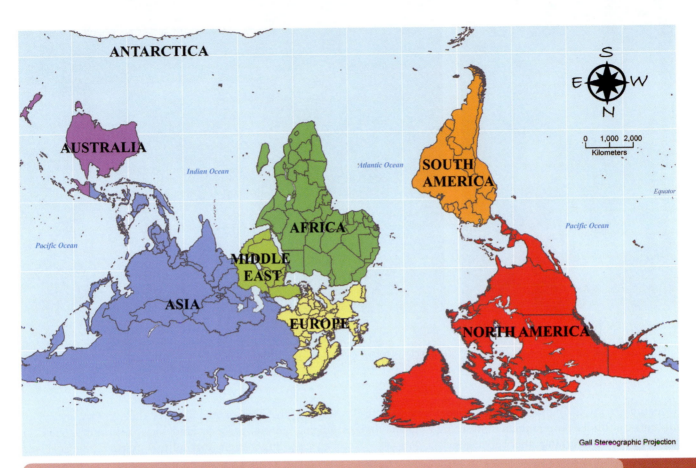

Map 3.1 "Southside Up" Global Map

Source: Map by Anna Versluis.

Note: This map illustrates geographic ethnocentrism. Americans tend to assume it is natural that the north should always be "on top." The fact that this upside-down map of the world, where south is "up," looks incorrect or disturbing is a consequence of an ethnocentric view of the world. Most people think of their countries or regions as occupying a more central and larger part of the world. Does this map change the way you view the world? Why?

believe in the rules and values of their own culture, the result could be widespread dissent, deviance, or crime.

Ethnocentrism can take many forms (see, for example, how you react to Map 3.1). Unfortunately, ethnocentrism often leads to misunderstandings between people of different cultures. In addition, the same ethnocentric attitudes that strengthen societies may also encourage hostility, racism, war, and genocide against others—even others within the society—who are different. Virtually all societies tend to "demonize" their adversary—in movies, the news, and political speeches—while the conflict is most intense. Dehumanizing another group with labels makes it easier to torture or kill them or to perform acts of discrimination and brutality against them. We see this in the current conflicts in Iraq, in which both sides in the conflict feel hatred for each other. However, as we become a part of a global social world, it becomes increasingly important to accept those who are "different." Bigotry and attitudes of superiority do not enhance cross-national cooperation and trade—which is what the global village and globalization entail.

Ethnocentrism can lead to misunderstandings between members of different cultures. Consider the American businesspeople who go to Japan to negotiate deals and sign contracts. The Japanese way of doing business takes time. It involves getting to know the other party by socializing over drinks in the evening. It is important not to rush the deal. To the Japanese, the Americans seem pushy, too concerned about contract details rather than trust, and in too much of a hurry. Many an international business arrangement has fallen through because of such cultural misunderstandings.

U.S. foreign relations also illustrate how ethnocentrism can produce hostility. Many U.S. citizens are surprised to learn that the United States—a great democracy, world power, and disseminator of food, medicine, and technological assistance to developing nations—is despised in many countries. One cause is the political dominance of the United States and the threat it poses to other people's way of life (Hertsgaard 2003). U.S. citizens are regarded by some as thinking ethnocentrically and only about their own welfare as their country exploits weaker nations. U.S. tourists are

In the United States, dogs are family members and are highly cherished, with dog care becoming a growth industry. In Nanking, China, dogs are valued more as a culinary delicacy and a good source of protein. If you feel a twinge of disgust, that is part of the ethnocentrism we may experience as our perspectives conflict with those elsewhere in the world.

sometimes seen as loudmouthed ignoramuses whose ethnocentric attitudes prevent them from seeing value in other cultures or from learning other languages.

Anti-U.S. demonstrations in South America, the Middle East, and Asia have brought this reality to life through television. Indeed, politicians in several Latin American and European countries have run for office on platforms aimed at reducing U.S. influence. Thus, U.S. ethnocentrism may foster anti-American ethnocentrism among people from other countries. Note that even referring to citizens of the United States as "Americans"—as though people from Canada, Mexico, or South America do not really count as Americans—is seen as ethnocentric by many people from these other countries. *America* and the *United States* are not the same thing, but many people in the United States, including some presidents, fail to make the distinction, much to the dismay of other North and South Americans.

Not all ethnocentrism is hostile; some of it is just a reaction to the strange ways of other cultures. An example is making judgments about what is proper food to eat and what is just not edible. While food is necessary for survival, there are widespread cultural differences in what people eat. Some of the New Guinea tribes savor grasshoppers; Europeans and Russians relish raw fish eggs (caviar); Eskimo children find seal eyeballs a treat; some Indonesians eat dog; and some Nigerians prize termites. Whether it is from another time period or another society, variations in food can be shocking to us.

In contrast to ethnocentrism, **cultural relativism** is a view that requires setting aside cultural and personal beliefs and prejudices to understand another group or society

through the eyes of members of that group. Instead of judging cultural practices and social behavior as good or bad according to one's own cultural practices, the goal is to be impartial in learning the purposes and consequences of practices and behaviors of the group under study. Although we may have preferences for certain software programs to do word processing, we can recognize that other software programs are quite good, may have some features that are better than the one we use, and are ingeniously designed.

Yet being tolerant and understanding is not always easy, and even for the most impartial observer, the subtleties of other cultures can be elusive. The idea of being "on time," which is so much a part of the cultures of the United States, Canada, Japan, and parts of Europe, is a rather bizarre concept in many societies. Among many Native American people, such as the Dineh (Apache and Navajo), it is ludicrous for people to let a timepiece that one wears on one's arm—a piece of machinery—govern the way one constructs and lives life. The Dineh orientation to time—that one should do things according to the natural rhythm of the body and not according to an artificial ticking mechanism—is difficult for many North Americans to grasp. Misunderstandings occur when those of European heritage think that "Indians are always late" and jump to the erroneous conclusion that "Indians" are undependable. Native Americans, on the other hand, think Whites are neurotic about letting some instrument control them (Basso 1979; Farrer 1996; Hall 1959, 1983).

Whether it is from another time period or another society, variations in food can be shocking to us, making it hard to understand other people and other times, as the next "Sociology Around the World" illustrates. Cultural relativism

Sociology Around the World

Evolutionary Cuisine

Early Humans' Salad Bar

This is the menu of the early hominids, who lived in the savannahs of eastern and southern Africa from roughly 1.5 million to 5 million years ago. Everything was served raw. Cooking with fire had not been discovered.

Main course: Nuts, birds' eggs, roots, tubers, beans, leaves, gum, sap, greens, insects, worms, grubs, termites, and seasonal berries and fruits. (90% of the diet)

Raw meat appetizer tray: Gathered delicacies include small mammals, birds, reptiles, fish, shellfish, slow game, dead or dying animals, and infants of species such as antelope, pig, giraffe, or baboons when available. Bone marrow or the contents of animal heads and stomachs are delicious additions to this menu. Season with honey, rock salt, or puree of worms and insects. (10% of the diet)

Ancestral Potluck Dinner

The first members of our own genus, *Homo erectus*, used these recipes from about 100,000 to 1.5 million years ago in the tropical and temperate zones of Africa and Eurasia. New technologies in fire making, advanced scavenging, and simple hunting as well as social advances in cooperation, sharing, and the gender division of labor provided some very tasty and nourishing meals for our ancestors.

Main courses: A stew or soup made with vegetables, bird bones, roots, nuts, and foods from the Salad Bar and Raw Meat Appetizer Tray, plus other gathered foods as available. Add leftovers and herbal seasonings. (80% of the diet)

Outdoor barbecue: Sizzling deer haunch, roasted rabbit, shellfish, wild boar, ox, or cattle ribs. (20% of the diet)

Source: Ward (1996).

---

requires that we shrug our shoulders and say, "Well, they are getting vitamins, proteins, and other nutrients, and it seems to work for them."

Cultural relativism does not require that social scientists accept or agree with all the beliefs and behaviors of the societies or groups they study. Certain behaviors, such as infanticide, cannibalism, head-hunting, slavery, female genital mutilation (removal of the clitoris), forced marriage, terrorism, or genocide may be regarded as unacceptable by almost all social scientists. Yet it is still important to try to understand those practices in the social and cultural contexts in which they occur so that abuses of human rights can be challenged. Many social scientists take strong stands against violations of human rights, environmental destruction, and other social policies. They base their judgments on the concept of universal human rights and the potential for harm to human beings and to the world community. Yet note that most Western democracies are adaptations to systems that thrive on values of extreme individualism, differentiation of job positions, and competition, consistent with a very complex society. Not all leaders of other societies agree that these values produce the type of life they wish for their people.

Thinking Sociologically

Small, tightly knit societies with no meso or macro level often stress cooperation, conformity, and personal sacrifice for the sake of the community. Complex societies with established meso- and macro-level linkages are more frequently individualistic, stressing personal uniqueness, individual creativity, and critical thinking. Why might this be so?

The Components of Culture

Things and thoughts—these make up much of our culture. From our things—**material culture**—to our thoughts (feelings, beliefs, values, and attitudes)—**nonmaterial culture**—culture provides the guidelines for our lives.

Material Culture: The Artifacts of Life

Material culture includes all the objects we can see or touch, all the artifacts of a group of people—their grindstones for grinding cassava root, microwave ovens for cooking, bricks of mud or clay for building shelters, hides or woven cloth for making clothing, books or computers for conveying information, tools for reshaping their environments, vessels for carrying and sharing food, and weapons for dominating and subduing others. Material culture includes anything you can touch that is made by humans.

Some material culture is of local, micro-level origin. The kinds of materials with which homes are constructed and the materials used for clothing often reflect the geography and resources of the local area. Houses are an especially good example of material culture, since they both result from local notions of what a "home" looks like and shape the interactions and attitudes toward many aspects of society. Likewise, types of jewelry, pottery, musical instruments, or clothing reflect tastes that emerge at the micro and meso levels of family, community, and subculture. At a more macro level, national and international corporations interested in making profits work hard to establish trends in fashion and style that may cross continents and oceans.

Material culture in many ways drives the globalization process. Many of our clothes are now made in Asia or Central American countries. Our shoes may well have been produced in the Philippines. The oil used to make the plastic water bottles and devices in our kitchens likely came from the Middle East. Even food is imported year-round from around the planet. That romantic diamond engagement ring—a symbol that represents the most intimate tie—may well be imported from a South African mine using low-paid or even slave labor. Our cars are assembled from parts produced on nearly every continent. Moreover, we spend many hours in front of a piece of material culture—our computers—surfing the World Wide Web. Material culture is not just for local homebodies anymore.

Thinking Sociologically

Think of examples of material culture that you use daily: stove, automobile, cell phone, refrigerator, clock, money, and so forth. How do these material objects influence your way of life and the way you interact with others? How would your behavior be different if these material objects, say watches or cars, did not exist?

Multinational corporations know no national barriers. Thousands of products you use every day were likely made or assembled on the other side of the globe. Industrialization in the less developed countries is also changing life for them, as well as affecting jobs and consumption patterns in North America.

Nonmaterial Culture: Beliefs, Values, Rules, and Language

Nonmaterial culture refers to the invisible and intangible parts of culture; they are of equal or even greater importance than material culture for they involve society's rules of behavior, ideas, and beliefs that shape how people interact with others and with their environment. Although we cannot touch the nonmaterial components of our culture, they pervade our life and are instrumental in determining how we think, feel, and behave. Nonmaterial culture is complex, comprising four main elements: values, beliefs, norms or rules, and language. These elements are also expressed in an ideal culture and a real culture.

Each culture has ideals that its members learn are desirable ways to think and act. **Ideal culture** consists of practices, beliefs, and values that

Audio Link 3.1
Listen to more on material culture.

Video Link 3.2
Watch the influence of branding.

Photo Essay

Houses as Part of a Society's Material Culture

Homes are good examples of material culture. Their construction is influenced not only by local materials but also by ideas of what a home is. Homes shape the context in which family members interact, so they can influence the nonmaterial culture. Indeed, in some cases, homes become status symbols that are far larger than the family needs; the family uses the home to make a prestige statement about its socioeconomic standing.

are regarded as most desirable and are consciously taught to children. Not everyone, however, follows the approved cultural patterns. **Real culture** refers to the way things in society are actually done. For the most part, we hardly question these practices and beliefs that we see around us. Rather like animals that have always lived in a rain forest and cannot imagine a treeless desert, we often fail to notice how our culture helps us make sense of things. Because of this, we do not recognize the gap between what we tell ourselves about ourselves and what we actually do.

For example, the ideal in many societies is to ban extramarital sex. Sex outside marriage can raise questions of paternity and inheritance, besides leading to spousal jealousy and family conflict. In the United States, about one fourth of all married men and one in seven married women report that they have had at least one extramarital affair (Newman and Grauerholz 2002). So while we claim that we believe in marital fidelity and that this is at the core of family morality, actual behavior is frequently a bit different.

Values are shared judgments about what is desirable or undesirable, right or wrong, good or bad. They express the basic ideals of any culture. In industrial societies, for instance, a good education is highly valued. Gunnar Myrdal (1964), a Swedish sociologist and observer of U.S. culture, referred to the U.S. value system as the "American creed." Values become a creed when they are so much a part of the way of life that they acquire the power of religious doctrine. We tend to take our core values for granted, including freedom, equality, individualism, democracy, efficiency, progress, achievement, material comfort, and patriotic duty (Macionis 2007; Williams 1970).

At the macro level, conflicts may arise between groups in society because of differing value systems. For example, there are major differences between the values of various Native American groups and the dominant culture—whether that dominant culture is in North, Central, or South America (Lake 1990; Sharp 1991). Consider the story in "Sociology Around the World" about Rigoberta Menchú Tum and the experiences of Native American populations living in Guatemala.

The conflict in values between Native Americans and the national cultures of Canada and the United States has had serious consequences. Cooperation is a cultural value that has been passed on through generations of Native Americans because group survival depends on group cooperation in the hunt, in war, and in daily life. The value of cooperation can place native children at a disadvantage in North American schools that emphasize competition. Native American and Canadian First Nation children experience more success in classrooms that stress cooperation and sociability over competition and individuality (Lake 1990; Mehan 1992).

Another Native American value is the appreciation of and respect for nature. Conservation of resources and protection of the natural environment—Mother Earth—have always been important because of people's dependence on nature for survival. Today, we witness disputes between native tribes and the governments of Canada, the United States, Mexico, Guatemala, Brazil, and other countries over the raw resources found on native reservations. While many other North and South Americans also value cooperation and respect for the environment, these values do not govern decision making in most communities (D. Brown 2001; Marger 2006). The values honored by governments and corporations are those held by the people with power, prestige, and wealth.

Thinking Sociologically

How are different cultural values a source of major problems for native peoples or other minority groups with which you are familiar?

Beliefs are more specific ideas we hold about life, about the way society works, and about where we fit into the world. They are expressed as specific statements that we hold to be true. Beliefs come from traditions established over time, from religious teachings, from experiences people have had, and from lessons given by parents and teachers or other individuals in authority. Beliefs influence the choices we make. Many Hindus, for example, believe that fulfilling behavioral expectations of one's own social caste will be rewarded in one's next birth, or incarnation. In the next life, good people will be born into a higher social status. In contrast, some Christians believe that one's fate in the afterlife depends on whether one believes in certain ideas—for instance, that Jesus Christ is one's personal savior. Beliefs tend to be based on values, which are broader and more abstract notions of something desirable. One value might be that the environment is worth preserving, but a belief might be that humans have caused global warming. Another value might be eternal life, but a belief might be that this occurs through reincarnation and eventually nirvana.

Norms are rules of behavior shared by members of a society and rooted in the value system. Norms range from religious warnings such as "thou shalt not kill" to the expectation that young people will complete their high school education. Sometimes the origins of particular norms are quite clear. Few people wonder, for instance, why there is a norm to stop and look both ways at a stop sign. Other norms, such as the rule in many societies that women should wear skirts but men should not, have been passed

Sociology Around the World

Life and Death in a Guatemalan Village

In her four decades of life, Rigoberta Menchú Tum experienced the closeness of family and cooperation in village life. These values are very important in Chimel, the Guatemalan hamlet where she lives. She also experienced great pain and suffering with the loss of her family and community. A Quiche Indian, Menchú became famous throughout the world in 1992, when she received the Nobel Peace Prize for her work to improve conditions for Indian peoples.

Guatemalans of Spanish origin hold the reins of power and have used Indians almost as slaves. Some of the natives were cut off from food, water, and other necessities, but people in the hamlet helped support each other and taught children survival techniques. Most people had no schooling. Menchú's work life in the sugarcane fields began at age 5. At 14, she traveled to the city to work as a domestic servant. While there, she learned Spanish, which helped her to be more effective in defending the rights of the indigenous population in Guatemala. Her political coming of age occurred at age 16, when she witnessed her brother's assassination by a group trying to expel her people from their native lands.

Her father started a group to fight the repression of the indigenous and poor, and at 20, Menchú joined the movement, Comite de Unidad Campesina (CUC, meaning "Peasant Unity Committee"), which the government claimed was communist inspired. Her father was murdered during a military assault, and her mother was tortured and killed. Menchú moved to Mexico with many other exiles to continue their nonviolent fight for rights and democracy.

The values of the native population represented by Menchú focus on respect for and a profound spiritual relationship with the environment, equality of all people, freedom from economic oppression, the dignity of her culture, and the benefits of cooperation over competition. The landowners tended to stress freedom of people to pursue their individual self-interests (even if inequality resulted), the value of competition, and the right to own property and to do whatever one desired to exploit that property for economic gain. Individual property rights were thought to be more important than preservation of indigenous cultures. Economic growth and profits were held in higher regard than religious connectedness to the earth.

The values of the native population and those of the landowners are in conflict. Only time will tell if the work of Indian activists such as Rigoberta Menchú Tum and her family will make a difference in the lives of this indigenous population.

on through the generations and have become unconsciously accepted patterns and a part of tradition. Sometimes we may not know how norms originated or even be aware of norms until they are violated.

Norms are generally classified into three categories—folkways, mores, and laws—based largely on how important the norms are in the society and people's response to the breach of those norms. *Folkways* are customs or desirable behaviors, but they are not strictly enforced: Some examples are responding appropriately and politely when introduced to someone, speaking quietly in a library, not scratching your genitals in public, using proper table manners, or covering your mouth when you cough. Violation of these norms causes people to think you are weird or even uncouth but not necessarily immoral or criminal.

Mores are norms that most members observe because they have great moral significance in a society. Conforming to mores is a matter of right and wrong, and violations of many mores are treated very seriously. The person who deviates from mores is considered immoral or bordering on criminal. Being honest, not cheating on exams, and being faithful in a marriage are all mores. Table 3.2 provides examples of violations of folkways and mores.

Taboos are the strongest form of mores. They concern actions considered unthinkable or unspeakable in the culture. For example, most societies have taboos that forbid incest (sexual relations with a close relative) and prohibit defacing or eating a human corpse. Taboos are most common and

Encyclopedia Link 3.2
Read more
about folkways.

Table 3.2 Types of Norms

Folkways: Conventional Polite Behaviors

Violations viewed as "weird":

Swearing in house of worship

Wearing blue jeans to the prom

Using poor table manners

Picking one's nose in public

Mores: Morally Significant Behaviors

Violations viewed as "immoral":

Lying or being unfaithful to a spouse

Buying cigarettes or liquor for young teens

Having sex with a professor as a way to increase one's grade

Parking in handicap spaces when one is in good physical condition

incest taboo varies greatly across cultures (Brown 1991). In medieval Europe, if a man and a woman were within 7 degrees of relatedness and wanted to marry, the marriage could be denied by the priest as incestuous. (Your first cousin is a third degree of relatedness from you.) On the other hand, the Balinese permit twins to marry because it is believed they have already been intimately bonded together in the womb (Leslie and Korman 1989). In some African and Native American societies, one cannot marry a sibling but might be expected to marry a first cousin. As Table 3.3 illustrates, the definition of what is and what is not incest varies even from state to state in the United States.

Laws are norms that have been formally encoded by those holding political power in society, such as laws against stealing property or killing another person. The violator of a law is likely to be perceived not just as a weird or immoral person but as a criminal who deserves formal punishment. Many mores are passed into law, and some folkways are also made into law. Formal punishments are imposed. Spitting on the sidewalk is not a behavior that has high levels of moral contempt, yet it is illegal in some cities, resulting in fines to punish violators. Furthermore, behaviors may be folkways in one situation and mores in another. For example, nudity or various stages of near nudity may be only mildly questionable in some social settings (the beach or certain fraternity parties) but would be quite offensive in others (a four-star restaurant or a house of worship) and against the law in still other situations, incurring a penalty.

numerous in societies that do not have centralized governments to establish formal laws and to maintain jails.

Taboos and other moral codes are of the utmost importance to a group because they provide guidelines for what is right and wrong. Yet behaviors that are taboo in one situation may be acceptable at another time and place. The incest taboo is an example found in all cultures, yet the application of the

Table 3.3 Incest Taboos in the United States: States That Allow First-Cousin Marriage

Alabama	Hawaii	Georgia	New Jersey	South Carolina
Alaska	Connecticut	New York	New Mexico	Tennessee
California	District of Columbia	Maryland	North Carolina	Vermont
Colorado	Florida	Massachusetts	Rhode Island	Virginia

States that allow only under certain conditions: The following states also allow first-cousin marriage but only under certain conditions such as marriage after a certain age or inability to bear children: Arizona, Illinois, Indiana, Utah, and Wisconsin.

Marriage of half cousins: Kansas, Maine, Montana, Nebraska, Nevada, and Oklahoma.

Marriage of adopted cousins: Louisiana, Mississippi, Oregon, and West Virginia.

States that do not allow first-cousin marriage: Fifteen other U.S. states disallow marriages to first cousins within the state: Arkansas, Delaware, Idaho, Iowa, Kentucky, Michigan, Minnesota, Missouri, New Hampshire, North Dakota, Ohio, Pennsylvania, South Dakota, Washington, and Wyoming.

Historically, in the United States, incest laws forbid in-law marriages far more than first-cousin marriages.

Source: "State Laws Regarding Marriages" (2010).

Nudity may be considered a violation of law, mores, or folkways, or it may simply be accepted as normal, as in the case of this nude beach.

Sanctions reinforce norms through rewards and penalties. **Formal sanctions** to enforce the most important norms are implemented by official action. Fines for parking illegally, lowered grades on an assignment for plagiarism, or expulsion for bringing drugs or weapons to school are formal negative sanctions your school might impose. Honors and awards are formal positive sanctions. **Informal sanctions** are unofficial rewards or punishments. A private word of praise by your professor after class about how well you did on your exam would be an informal positive sanction; gossip or ostracism by other students because of the clothes you are wearing would be informal negative sanctions. Sanctions vary with the importance of the norm and can range from a parent frowning at a child who fails to use proper table manners (a micro-level setting) to a prison term or death sentence. Similarly, when we obey norms, we are rewarded, sometimes with simple acts such as smiles and jokes and pats on the back that indicate solidarity with others. Most often, adherence to norms is ingrained so deeply that our reward is simply "fitting in." Your reward for polite social behavior—for asking about someone's interests and activities, for not being overly shy or pushy in conversation—is friendship and fitting into the group. Folkways and many mores are enforced through informal sanctions, yet sometimes penalties for deviant behavior can be severe.

Norms concerning sexual behaviors are often very strong and carry powerful sanctions; sometimes they are even imposed by national governments. A woman who becomes pregnant outside marriage in societies that strongly condemn nonmarital sex is likely to be ostracized and her child labeled illegitimate. Such children may be stigmatized for life, living as outcasts in poverty on the streets, begging for food. This was the case in Vietnam during the French colonial period and during the U.S.-Vietnam War, when many biracial children were excluded from participation in society. "Half-breed" children bore the stigma, fueled by xenophobia and nationalism, because they were reminders of interaction with the country's colonial and wartime past. Biracial children are still suffering discrimination in Vietnam (DiversityInc. 2008; Nguyen 2005).

When a society faces change, especially from war, rapid urbanization, industrialization, and modernization, traditional norms that have worked for the society for centuries are challenged. In the past few decades, examples have been seen in many Islamic countries where modernization has been met with a resurgence of religious fundamentalism. A case in point is Iran. The rapid modernization and social changes that took place in the post–World War II era under the Shah of Iran, Mohammed Reza Pahlavi, were met by a backlash from religious fundamentalists. When the Shah was ousted in 1979, Ayatollah Ruhollah Khomeini restored traditional Islamic rule. Strict Muslim laws and swift, often severe punishments were meted out to offenders. Radio music and drinking of alcoholic beverages were banned, and women were required to again wear the veil, as in previous times. Afghanistan and other Muslim nations are currently struggling with the conflicts between traditional religious and cultural values and those related to pressures from the social environment—in this case Western nations—for change and modernization. At the global level, there are newly emerging norms to deal with some areas of technology, such as fraud and theft on the Internet and the World Wide Web. Without norms, there are no guidelines for interactions between individuals and groups. E-mail has been in existence for civilians only since 1994, thus allowing social scientists to watch the emergence of norms in this new social environment.

Communication is often mediated and enhanced through nonverbal indicators such as tone of voice, inflection, facial expressions, or other gestures that communicate emotion. In an e-mail, the words are just words without context. To establish norms, many listservs now have rules for polite communication to avoid "flaming" someone—insulting them with insensitive words by a faceless person. The development of smileys and emoticons adds combinations of characters that represent the emotional context of the message. Norms of Internet communication are still emerging, and you probably have experienced times when messages have been misunderstood because the norms of communication are ambiguous.

Thinking Sociologically

One of the problems of Internet communication has been that many norms of civil discourse are ignored, and new norms emerge. What do you see as the current rules for Internet communication? A related problem is that some young people think these new norms are appropriate in other communication situations—such as communicating with a professor or an employer. What problems might occur when applying Internet norms to communication in other social situations?

Language is the foundation of every culture. The mini-drama between infant and adult is played out every day around the world as millions of infants learn the language of the adults who care for them. In the process, they acquire an important part of culture. Although many animals can communicate with a limited repertoire of sounds, the ability to speak a language is unique to humans. Human infants have the potential for developing language because the human voice box, tongue, and brain make speech biologically possible. In their early months, babies make many sounds—squealing, growling, "raspberries," cooing, and tongue clicks. These become more recognizable as syllables in the second 6 months of life (Oller 2006). At about 1 year of age, most infants begin to pronounce recognizable words in the language of their culture. The human infant is capable of making roughly 1,000 sounds, but any given society considers only about 40 or 50 of these to be language sounds. The baby soon learns that some of those sounds elicit enthusiastic responses from the adult caretakers, reinforcing their use.

Transport a baby from France to the Arapesh tribe in New Guinea and another baby from New Guinea to France, and each will learn to speak the language and adhere to the culture in which it is brought up. The reason is that language, like other components of culture, is learned. Language conveys verbal and nonverbal messages among members of society. Simply put, without language there would be little, if any, culture. Through the use of language, members of a culture can pass on essential knowledge to children and can share ideas with other members of their society. Work can be organized; the society can build on its experiences and plan its future. Through language, members express their ideas, values, beliefs, and knowledge, a key ingredient in the ability of humans to sustain social life.

Language takes three primary forms: spoken, written, and nonverbal. Spoken language allows individuals to produce a set of sounds that symbolize an object or idea. That combination of sounds is learned by all who share a culture, and it generally holds similar meaning for all members. Written language enables humans to store ideas for future generations, accelerating the accumulation of ideas on which to build. It also makes possible communication over distances. Members of a society learn to read these shared symbols, some of which are displayed in Figure 3.1.

Nonverbal language is communication consisting of gestures, facial expressions, and body postures. This mode of communication may carry as much as 90% of the meaning of the message (Samovar and Porter 2003). Every culture uses nonverbal language to communicate, and just like verbal language, those cues may differ widely among cultures. For instance, an A-OK gesture or a hand wave that is positive in one culture may have a negative, even obscene, meaning in another.

The power to communicate nonverbally is illustrated in the American Sign Language, designed for the hearing challenged and the mute. Complex ideas can be transmitted without vocalizing a word. Indeed, one can argue that the deaf have a distinctive culture of their own rooted in large part in the unique language that serves them. In addition, technology has aided communication among the hearing impaired through text messaging.

Misunderstandings occur between ethnic groups because of cultural differences regarding communication. The Apache Indians in the American Southwest tell "Whiteman jokes"—ridiculing White people because they engage in grossly unacceptable actions such as calling one another by name even when they do not know each other intimately, asking about one another's health, complementing one another's clothing, and greeting others who walk into a room. Because so many White U.S. citizens do not understand that these behaviors are viewed as offensive, they may violate expectations and create difficulties for themselves in dealing with the Apaches. They may act in ways that are considered ill-mannered and rude (Basso 1979).

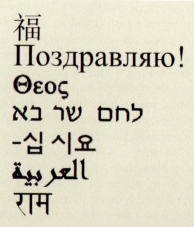

Figure 3.1 Societies Use Various Symbols to Communicate Their Written Language

Language development is extremely important to becoming fully human, and it happens very rapidly from about the first year of life of a baby. Still, babies learn to communicate in a variety of other ways. Note how these infants communicate emotions nonverbally. What does each of them seem to be communicating?

Misinterpretation of nonverbal signals can also occur between male and female microcultures in Western societies. When women nod their heads in response to a person who is talking, they often are encouraging the speaker to continue, signaling that they are listening and that they want the speaker to carry on with the clarification and explanation. It does not signal agreement. When men nod their heads when another person is speaking, they typically assume that the message is "I agree with what you are saying." This can lead to awkward, confusing, and even embarrassing miscues when men and women talk to one another, with the man mistakenly confident that the woman agrees with his ideas (Stringer 2006).

Language also plays a critical role in perception and in thought organization. The *linguistic relativity theory* (Sapir 1929, 1949; Whorf 1956) posits that the people who speak a specific language make interpretations of their reality—they notice certain things and may fail to notice certain other things. "A person's 'picture of the universe' or 'view of the world' differs as a function of the particular language or languages that person knows" (Kodish 2003:384). Children in each different culture will learn about the world within the framework provided by their language. Scientists continue to debate the extent to which language can influence thought, but most agree that while language may contribute to certain ways of thinking, it does not totally determine human thinking (Casasanto 2008; Gumperz and Levinson 1996; Levinson 2000). Although this theory is controversial and aspects have been misinterpreted, the idea of language, culture, consciousness, and behavior affecting each other is influential when studying the role of language.

Consider how language affects the planning of our day: Many nonindustrial peoples in Asia, Africa, Australia, and South and North America do not keep time in the kinds of exact units used in the industrial world—seconds, minutes, and hours. The smallest units might be sunrise, morning, midday, late afternoon, dusk, and night (Hall 1983). Meeting someone for an appointment requires great patience, for there are no words for what we call seconds, minutes, or even hours. Think about how this would change your life and the pace of everything around you. If you showed up at a predesignated location, your friend might appear three hours later but would be on time because the unit of time would include a four- or five-hour time period. In such a culture, one would eat when food is prepared or when one is hungry. One gets up when one is rested. Time-based words cause most of us to organize our days in particular ways and even to become irritated with others who do not adhere to these expectations (Bertman 1998).

Audio Link 3.2
Listen for more on language and labels.

To use another example, in the English language, people tend to associate certain colors with certain qualities in a way that may add to the problem of racist attitudes. In *Webster's Unabridged English Dictionary*, the definition of the word *black* includes "dismal," "boding ill," "hostile," "harmful," "inexcusable," "without goodness," "evil," "wicked," "disgrace," and "without moral light." The word *white*, on the other hand, is defined as "honest," "dependable," "morally pure," "innocent," and "without malice." If the linguistic relativity thesis is correct, it is more than a coincidence that bad things are associated with the *black sheep* of the family, the *blacklist*, or *Black Tuesday* (when the stock market dropped dramatically).

This association of blackness with negative images and meanings is not true of all languages. The societies that have negative images for black and positive images for white are the same societies that associate negative qualities with people of darker skin. The use of *white* as a synonym for "good" or "innocent"—as in reference to a "white noise machine" or a "white lie"—may contribute to a cultural climate that devalues people of color. In essence, English may influence our perception of color in a manner that contributes to racism. Interestingly, there is empirical evidence supporting this claim of color symbolism. Athletic teams that wear black uniforms have more penalties called on them than teams with lighter colored uniforms (Frank and Gilovich 1988).

White and black as colors have symbolic meaning—with phrases such as blackballed from the club or black sheep of the family indicating negative judgment associated with blackness. Research shows that teams wearing black are called for more fouls than teams wearing white, which raises questions about how pervasive this association is in our perception.

context but may be utterly confusing to those not in that microculture.

When grouped together, material and nonmaterial components form cultural patterns. People's lives are organized around these patterns. For example, family life includes patterns of courtship, marriage, child rearing, and care of the elderly. Table 3.4 illustrates some of the more prominent material and nonmaterial cultural components involved in one aspect of Western society—child rearing.

We have seen that material artifacts and nonmaterial beliefs, values, norms, and language are the basic components of culture. Next, we explore the theoretical explanations for culture.

Thinking Sociologically

The words *bachelor* and *spinster* are supposedly synonymous terms, referring to unmarried adult males and females, respectively. Generate a list of adjectives that describe each of these words and that you frequently hear associated with them (e.g., *eligible, swinging, old, unattractive*). Are the associated words positive or negative in each case? How are these related to the position of the unmarried in societies?

Unique language evolves in specific settings. In a prison where inmates are closed off from the larger world, a whole lingo evolves that is incomprehensible to outsiders but essential to survival within the prison: *kites, rats, store, punks, wolves, cops,* and *ballbuster* are examples of prison terms. Even within your own college, there are probably terms used to refer to course sequences, majors, or Greek houses that people at other universities would find bewildering. At the Massachusetts Institute of Technology, for example, students often respond to the question "What is your major?" with the number from the catalog: "I'm majoring in 23." That would be a truly bizarre response at some other campuses. Within the meso-level medical profession, people may discuss magnetic resonance imaging (MRIs), brain scans, heart catheterizations, prostate-specific antigen (PSA) tests, and other processes that are meaningful in that

Language varies from one social setting to another, and one must learn the language to survive. The prison is a society separated from the larger society, and it develops its own microculture. In prison, one must learn the lingo and the associated values that are applied to kites, rats, store, punks, wolves, cops, and ballbusters. Inmates, such as these men in the yard of San Quentin State Prison, develop their own insider lingo.

Table 3.4	**Material and Nonmaterial Cultural Patterns in Western Child Rearing**
Material objects	Toys and children's books; school buildings and playgrounds
Nonmaterial cultural components	
Beliefs	Children should be given as many options and opportunities as can be afforded.
Values	Parents should sacrifice time and money for their children to help them become successful individuals.
Rules	Children should obey parents, teachers, and other adult authority figures.
Language or symbols	Parents should use appropriate language as the child grows; nonverbal language sends messages of approval or disapproval.

Source: "Cousin Marriages" 2008.

Society, Culture, and Our Social World

Whether their people are eating termite eggs, fish eggs, or chicken eggs, societies always have a culture, and culture is always linked to a society. Culture provides guidelines for each level of society, from the global system to the individual family. The social world model at the beginning of the chapter, with its concentric circles, represents the micro to macro levels of society. Smaller social units such as a school operate within larger social units such as the community, which is also part of a region of the country. What takes place in each of these units is determined by the culture. There is a social unit—a structural "hardware"—and a culture or "software" at each level.

⊙ MICROCULTURES: MICRO-LEVEL ANALYSIS

Micro-level analysis focuses on social interactions in small-group or organizational settings. To apply this idea to culture, we look at microcultures. Groups and organizations such as a Girl Scout troop or a local chapter of the Rotary Club or participants in a Facebook chat room involve a small number of people. These organizations influence only a portion of the members' lives. When the culture affects only a small segment of one's life—affecting a portion of one's week or influencing a limited time period in one's life—it is called a **microculture** (Gordon 1970). Other classic examples from sociology include a street gang, a college sorority, a business office, or a

summer camp group. In fact, workplaces have been studied in some detail to explore the climate of these microcultures that we inhabit daily, as we see in the next "Sociology in Our Social World."

Hospitals are social units with microcultures. People in different-colored uniforms scurry around carrying out their designated tasks as part of the organizational culture. Hospital workers interact among themselves to attain goals of patient care. They have a common in-group vocabulary, a shared set of values, a hierarchy

Journal Article Link 3.2 Read more on culture.

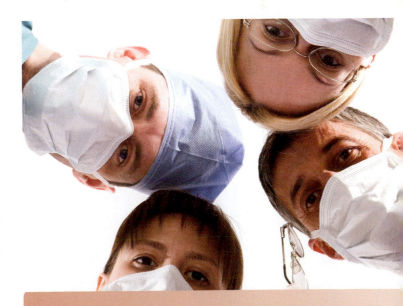
When these people work together in a hospital, they share a common culture: shared terminology, rules of interaction, and values regarding objectifying human body parts so that they are not sexualized. However, the hospital microculture only affects a part of each day and each week for the hospital personnel.

Sociology in Our Social World

Culture in Workplaces

By Lynn Ritchey

Think for a moment about your work environments. Some probably have been enjoyable, and some miserable. In the workplace that was most enjoyable, you might have been working for someone who valued your insights. In the miserable workplace, you may have worked for a tyrant who dictated everything and allowed no flexibility. The workplace is an environment in which most of us will have sustained interactions with people of different cultural backgrounds. With this in mind, it becomes important for us to understand the rules of how work is to be done. Professor Geert Hofstede is a social scientist who understands the impact of the culture of the workplace and also recognizes that different countries have different values when it comes to the workplace. A study of IBM (International Business Machines) employees identified several cultural dimensions and value orientations relative to the workplace: power distance, individualism, masculinity, and avoidance of uncertainty.

The Power Distance Index (PDI) measures the degree to which less powerful people in an organization accept the unequal distribution of power in the organization. In countries with a high score on the PDI, the "followers" expect that the more powerful people in the organizations will dictate what everyone else does in the workplace. The powerful do not seek input from followers. The United States has a low PDI score. This means most workers in the United States expect that they will have input into decisions about their workplace and tasks that they perform.

The Individualism Index (IDV) compares countries on whether they are more individualist or collectivist in their value orientation. This dimension assesses the degree of interrelatedness between individuals. Countries scoring high on individualism, such as the United States, have looser connections with groups, and the employees are working mostly for their own personal benefit. Countries with low scores

on individualism are more collectivist or group oriented and work for the success of the entire group, whether it be the extended family, school community, or work group.

The Masculinity Index (MAS) measures the degree that "masculine" traits are valued in the country more than "feminine" ones. Countries scoring low in the MAS value modesty, caring, group cohesion, personal relationships, and overall quality of life. Competition is not especially valued in low masculinity countries. The United States has a high MAS score because competition and assertiveness are rewarded. We strive for success with little concern about group cohesion or personal relationships. Only the strong survive; dog eat dog.

The Uncertainty Avoidance Index (UAI) measures the degree to which a society socializes it members to feel comfortable in ambiguous settings. Countries with a high score on the UAI have very strict laws and rules governing most areas of life. Everyone knows what is expected, and very little is left to chance. Countries with low scores on the UAI, such as the United States, are more accepting of ambiguous situations. There is more flexibility, creativity, and acceptance of diverse points of view.

Understanding these value orientations is important because many of us will come into contact with people from other cultures in the workplace. When we are aware of our own value orientations and the value orientations of those with whom we work, we can become more successful in our interactions and reduce the frustration and confusion we might experience when we interact with culturally different people. For example, instead of thinking your boss is a tyrant, you might come to understand that your boss is from a high power-distance country. To explore the scores for different countries, visit http://www.geert-hofstede.com.

of positions with roles and behaviors for each position, and a guiding system of regulations for the organization—all of which shape interactions during the hours when each member works in the hospital. Yet the hospital culture may have little relevance to the rest of the employees' everyday lives. Microcultures may survive over time, with individuals coming in and going out from the group, but in a complex society, no one lives his or her entire life within a microculture. The values, rules, and specialized language used by the hospital staff continue as one shift ends and other medical personnel enter and sustain that microculture.

Every organization, club, and association has an organizational microculture—its own set of rules and expectations. Schools develop their own unique cultures and traditions; as students graduate and move out of that microculture, others move into it. Many microcultures exist for a limited period of time or for a special purpose. A summer camp microculture may develop but exists only for that summer. The following summer, a very different culture may evolve because of new counselors and campers. A girls' softball team may develop its own cheers, jokes, insider slang, and values regarding competition or what it means to be a good sport, but next year, the girls may be realigned into different teams, and the transitory culture of the previous year changes. In contrast to microcultures, subcultures continue across a person's life span.

SUBCULTURES AND COUNTERCULTURES: MESO-LEVEL ANALYSIS

A subculture is a way of life in a social unit or group that is smaller than the nation but large enough to sustain people throughout the life span. A subculture is in some ways unique to that group yet at the same time shares the culture of the dominant society (Arnold 1970; Gordon 1970). For example, one can be African Canadian, Chinese Canadian, or Hispanic Canadian, living within an ethnic community that provides food, worship, and many other resources, and still be a good Canadian citizen. One can also be a Mormon and live almost all of one's life in Utah, interacting entirely with other Mormons, and still be a good American citizen.

Subcultures add their own set of conventions and expectations to the general standards of the dominant culture. Subcultures are suitable for meso-level analysis because the social unit plays a more continuous role in the life of members. (Table 3.5 illustrates the connection between the social unit at each level and the type of culture at that level.) One can be born, work, marry, and die in that social unit. Members maintain a feeling of "we" (belonging to the group) versus "they" (for those outside the group). Members also maintain a belief in the rightness of their customs, rituals, religious practices, dress, food, or whatever else distinguishes them as a subculture.

Audio Link 3.3
Listen to stories about culture.

Note that many of the categories into which we group people are not subcultures. For example, redheads, left-handed people, tall people, individuals who read *Wired* magazine, people who are single, visitors to Chicago, and DVD watchers do not make up subcultures because they do not interact as social units or share a common way of life. A motorcycle gang, a college fraternity, and a summer camp are also not subcultures because they affect only a segment of one's life (Gordon 1970; Yablonski 1959). A subculture influences a person's life every day in pervasive ways throughout the person's life.

In the United States, subcultures include ethnic groups, such as Mexican American and Korean American; exclusive religious groups, such as the Mennonites in Ohio and Orthodox Jews in New York City; and social class groups, including the exclusive subculture of the elite upper class on the east and west coasts of the United States. The superwealthy have networks, exclusive clubs, and the Social Register, which lists the names and phone numbers of the elite, so they can maintain contact with one another. They have a culture of opulence that differs from middle-class culture, and this culture is part of their experience throughout their lives.

Another example is Hasidic Jews, who adhere to the same laws as other Americans but follow additional rules specific to their religion. Clothing and hairstyles follow strict rules; men wear beards and temple locks (*payos*), and married women wear wigs. Their religious holidays are different from those of the dominant Christian culture. Hasidic Jews observe dietary restrictions, such as avoiding pork and

Video Link 3.3
Watch more about subcultures.

Table 3.5   Social Units of Society and Level of Culture

Social Unit (the people who interact and feel they belong)	Culture (the way of life of that social unit)
Dyads; small groups; local community	Microculture
Ethnic community or social class community	Subculture
National society	Culture of a nation
Global system	Global culture

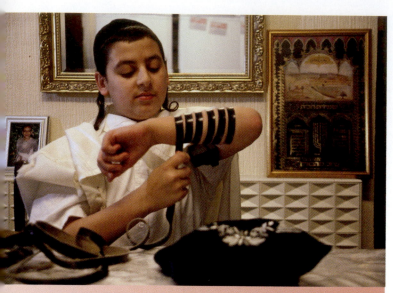

A young Orthodox Jewish boy prepares to pray according to Jewish law by wrapping the leather strap of his Tefillin (amulet) around his arm and a Tallit (prayer shawl) around his shoulders. He is part of a subgroup of the larger society—the Jewish faith community. This community will influence his values throughout his life—from infancy to death. It is a subculture.

shellfish, and they observe the Sabbath from sunset Friday to sunset Saturday. Hasidic Jews are members of a subculture in the larger society of which they are citizens. In today's world, this is a global subculture maintained through Web sites of, by, and for Hasidic Jews. Again, one can live one's entire life under the influence of the values and rules of the subculture, and this is certainly true of the Hasidic Jews.

A give-and-take exists between subcultures and the dominant culture, with each contributing to and influencing the other. Hispanic Americans have brought many foods to American cuisine, for example, including tacos, burritos, and salsa.

Subcultural practices can be the source of tensions with the dominant group, which has the power to determine cultural expectations in society. In direct conflict with the law, a very small faction of Mormons in the United States believe in and practice polygamy. Having more than one wife (polygyny) violates federal laws and state laws in Utah, where many of them live, but some hold onto the old teachings of the founder Joseph Smith and cling to this practice as sanctioned by God.

Video Link 3.4
Learn more about Amish culture.

When conflict with the larger culture becomes serious and laws of the dominant society are violated, a different type of culture emerges. A **counterculture** is a group with expectations and values that contrast sharply with the dominant values of a particular society (Yinger 1960).

One type of counterculture is represented by the Old Order Amish of Pennsylvania and Ohio. The Amish drive horse-drawn buggies and seldom use electricity or modern machines. They reject many mainstream notions of success and replace them with their own work values and

goals. Conflicts between federal and state laws and Amish religious beliefs have produced compromises by the Amish on issues of educating children, using farm machinery, and transportation. The Old Order Amish prefer to educate their children in their own communities, insisting that their children not go beyond an eighth-grade education in the public school curriculum. They also do not use automobiles or conventional tractors. The Amish are pacifists and will not serve as soldiers in the national military.

Other types of countercultures seek to withdraw from society or to operate outside its economic and legal systems or even to bring about the downfall of the larger society. Examples are survivalist groups such as racist militia and skinheads, who reject the principles of democratic pluralism. Countercultures of all types have existed throughout history. The "old believers" of 17th-century Russia committed group suicide rather than submit to the authority of the czar of Russia on matters of faith and lifestyle (Crummey 1970). There are now Russian old-believer communities in Oregon, northern Alberta, and the Kenai Peninsula of Alaska. Some of their villages are so isolated that they are virtually inaccessible by car, and visitors are greeted with "No trespassing" signs. The Ranters—a group that arose in 16th-century England, with its strict puritan attitudes toward sensuality and sex—flaunted their opposition to those attitudes by running naked through the streets and having sex in village squares (Ellens 1971; Hill 1991).

These contrary groups can operate at the meso or the micro level. Some countercultures continue over time and can sustain members throughout their life cycle—such as the Amish. They are like subcultures in that they operate at the meso level but strongly reject the mainstream culture. However, most countercultural groups, such as punk rock groups or violent and deviant teenage gangs, are short-lived or are relevant to people only at a certain age—operating only at the micro level.

A counterculture, such as the Amish, rejects important aspects of the mainstream or dominant culture such as technology and consumerism, replacing it with biblical principles calling for a simple lifestyle.

Members of countercultures do not necessarily reject all the dominant culture, and in some cases, parts of their culture may eventually come to be accepted by the dominant culture. During the Vietnam War, for instance, some antiwar protesters focused their lives on protesting the U.S. involvement in Southeast Asia (and related political and economic issues). By the early 1970s, opposition to the war had become widespread in society, so the antiwar protesters were no longer outside the mainstream. They were less likely to be labeled as anti-American for their beliefs. Following the war, many counterculture antiwar hippies became active in the mainstream culture and developed conventional careers in the society. Thus, their ideas, their protest songs, their emblems, longer hair for men, and the peace symbol from the 1960s were absorbed into the larger culture.

Countercultures are not necessarily bad for society. According to the conflict perspective, which was introduced in Chapter 2, the existence of counterculture groups is clear evidence that there are contradictions or tensions within a society that need to be addressed. Countercultures often challenge the unfair treatment of groups in society that do not hold power and sometimes develop into social organizations or protest groups. Extremist religious and political groups, whether Christian, Islamic, Hindu, or any other, may best be understood as countercultures against Western or global influences that they perceive as threatening to their way of life. Figure 3.2 graphically illustrates the types of cultures in the social world and the relationship of countercultures with their national culture. Countercultures, as depicted, view themselves and are viewed by others as "fringe" groups—partial outsiders within a nation.

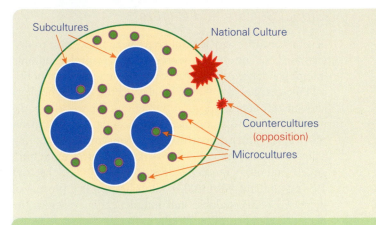

Figure 3.2   Cultures at Various Levels in the Social World

Thinking Sociologically

Describe a counterculture group whose goals are at odds with those of the dominant culture. Do you see any evidence to show that the group is influencing behavioral expectations and values in the larger society? What effect, if any, do they have on your life?

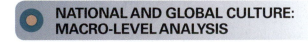

NATIONAL AND GLOBAL CULTURE: MACRO-LEVEL ANALYSIS

Canada is a national society, geographically bounded by the mainland United States on the south, the Pacific Ocean and Alaska on the west, the Atlantic Ocean on the east, and the Arctic on the north. The government in Ottawa passes laws that regulate activities in all provinces (which are similar to states or prefectures), and each province passes its own

laws. These geographic boundaries and political structures make up the national society of Canada.

National Society and Culture

The **national society** is made up of a group of people who interact more with each other than with outsiders and who cooperate for the attainment of certain goals. Within the nation, there may be smaller groups, such as ethnic, regional, or tribal subcultures, made up of people who identify closely with each other. Along with subcultures, most nations have a **national culture** of common values and beliefs that tie citizens together. The national culture affects the everyday lives of all its citizens to some extent. Within some countries of Africa and the Middle East that became self-governing nations during the 20th century, local ethnic or religious loyalties are much stronger than any sense of national culture. Subcultural differences divide many nations. Consider, for example, the loyalties of Shiites, Sunnis, and Kurds in Iraq, where the national culture struggles for influence over its citizens through laws, traditions, and military force.

In colonial America, people thought of themselves as Virginians or Rhode Islanders rather than as U.S. citizens. Even during the "war between the states" of the 1860s, the battalions were organized by states and often carried their state banners into battle. The fact that some southern states still call it the War Between the States rather than the Civil War communicates the struggle over whether to recognize the nation or states as the primary social unit of loyalty and identity. People in the United States today are increasingly likely to think of themselves as U.S. citizens (rather than as Iowans or Floridians), yet the national culture determines only a few of the specific guidelines for everyday life. Still, the sense of nation has grown stronger in most industrialized societies over the past century, and the primary identity is likely to be "American" or "Canadian."

Global Society and Culture

Several centuries ago, it would have been impossible to discuss a global culture, but with expanding travel, economic interdependence of different countries, international political linkages, global environmental concerns, and technology allowing for communication throughout the world, people now interact across continents in seconds. **Globalization** refers to the process by which the entire world is becoming a single interdependent entity—more uniform, more integrated, and more interdependent (Pieterse 2004; Robertson 1997; Stutz and Warf 2005). Globalization is a process of increased connectedness and interdependency across the planet (Eitzen and Zinn 2006).

Western political and economic structures dominate in the development of this global society, largely as a result of the domination of Western (Europe and the United States) worldviews and Western control over resources. For example, the very idea of governing a geographic region with a bureaucratic structure known as a nation-state is a fairly new notion. Formerly, many small bands and tribal groupings dominated areas of the globe. However, with globalization, nation-states now exist in every region of the world.

Global culture refers to behavioral standards, symbols, values, and material objects that have become common across the globe. For example, beliefs that monogamy is normal; that marriage should be based on romantic love; that people have a right to life, liberty, and the pursuit of happiness; that people should be free to choose their leaders; that women should have rights such as voting; that wildlife and fragile environments should be protected; and that everyone should have a television set are spreading across the globe (Leslie and Korman 1989; Newman and Grauerholz 2002). During the 20th century, the idea of the primacy of individual rights, civil liberties, and human rights spread around the world, creating conflicts in nations that traditionally lack democratic institutions and processes. Backlashes against these and other Western ideas also can be seen in the acts of groups that have embraced terrorism (Eitzen and Zinn 2006; Misztal and Shupe 1998; Turner 1991a, 1991b). Still, these trends are aspects of the emerging global culture. Even 100 years ago, notions of global cooperation and competition would have seemed quite bizarre (Lechner and Boli 2005). However, in nations all over the globe, people who travel by plane know they must stand in line, purchase a ticket, negotiate airport security, squeeze their bodies into confined spaces, and stay seated in the airplane until they are told they can get up (Lechner and Boli 2005). Regardless of nationality, we know how to behave in any airport in the world.

Nations are accepted as primary units of social control, and use of coercion is perfectly normal if it is done by the government. We compete in Olympic Games as citizens of nations, and the winner stands on the platform while her or his national anthem is played. Across the globe, this seems "normal," yet only a few centuries ago, the notion of nationhood would have seemed very strange (Lechner and Boli 2005). Global culture probably has a fairly minimal impact on the everyday interactions and lives of the average person, yet it affects nations and, in turn, our lives.

As the world community becomes more interdependent and addresses issues that can only be dealt with at the global level (such as global warming or international terrorism), the idea of a common "software" of beliefs, social rules, and common interests takes on importance. Common ideas for making decisions allow for shared solutions to conflicts that previously would have resulted in war and massive killing of people. Global culture at the macro level will increasingly be a reality in the third millennium.

However, global culture is not the only pattern that is new. Today, we are seeing a counterculture at the global level. Stateless terrorist networks reject the values of the World Court, the Geneva Convention, and other international systems designed to resolve disputes. Terrorists do not recognize the sovereignty of nations and do not acknowledge many values of respect for life or for civil discourse. This counterculture at the global level is a more serious threat than those at the micro and meso levels.

Thinking Sociologically

Make a list of social units of which you are a part. Place these groups into categories of microculture, subculture, national culture, and global culture. Consider which of them affects only a portion of your day or week (such as your place of work) or only a very limited time in your entire life span. Consider which groups are smaller than the nation but which will likely influence you over much of your life. To what cross-national (global) groups do you belong? Do you belong to fewer groups at the national culture and global culture levels? If so, why do you suppose that is the case?

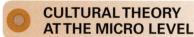

CULTURAL THEORY AT THE MICRO LEVEL

To understand our interactions with family and friends, we turn to the micro level of analysis. When students first read about sociology or other social sciences, the underlying message may seem to be that humans are shaped by the larger society in which they live. External forces do shape us in many ways, but that is not the whole story, as we see when we examine the **symbolic interaction** approach to culture.

Video Link 3.5
Watch how cultures combine.

Symbolic Interaction Theory

How amazing it is that babies learn to share the ideas and meanings of complex cultures with others in those cultures. Symbolic interaction theory considers how we learn to share the meanings of symbols, whether material or nonmaterial. Culture is about symbols, such as rings, flags, and words that stand for or represent something. A ring means love and commitment. A flag represents national identity and is intended to evoke patriotism and love for one's country. A phrase such as *middle class* conjures up images and expectations of what the phrase means, and we share this meaning with others with whom we interact. Together in our groups and societies, we define what is real, normal, and good.

Symbolic interaction theory maintains that our humanness comes from the impact we have on each other through these shared understandings of symbols that humans have created. When people create symbols, such as a new greeting ("Give me five") or a symbolic shield for a fraternity or sorority, symbols come to have an existence and importance for the group. *Step 1:* The symbol is created. Who designed the Star of David and gave it meaning as a symbol of the Jewish people? Who initiated the sign of the cross for Catholics to use before prayer? Who designed the fraternity's or sorority's shield? Who determined that an eagle should symbolize the United States? Most people do not know the answers to these questions, but they do know what the symbol stands for. They share with others the meaning of a particular object. *Step 2:* The symbol is objectified, assuming a reality independent of the creator. In fact, people may feel intense loyalty to the symbol itself. An entire history of a people may be recalled and a set of values rekindled when the symbol is displayed. *Step 3:* The group has internalized the symbol. This may be the case whether the symbol is part of a material culture or a nonmaterial gesture. Members of a culture absorb the ideas or symbols of the larger culture—which were originally created by some individual or small group.

Symbolic interaction theory pictures humans as consciously and deliberately creating their personal and collective histories. The theory emphasizes the part that verbal and nonverbal language and gestures play in the shared symbols of individuals and the smooth operation of society. More than any other theory in the social sciences, symbolic interaction stresses the active decision-making role of individuals—the ability of individuals to do more than conform to the larger forces of the society.

This notion that individuals shape culture and that culture influences individuals is at the core of the symbolic interaction theory. Other social theories tend to focus at the meso and macro levels.

Thinking Sociologically

Recall some of the local "insider" symbols that you used as a preteen, such as friendship bracelets, best-friend necklaces, matching outfits, and secret handshakes. Some individual started each idea, and it spread rapidly from one school to another and from one community to another. How are the three steps in the creation of symbols illustrated by a symbol you and your friends used?

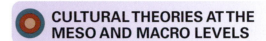

CULTURAL THEORIES AT THE MESO AND MACRO LEVELS

How can we explain such diverse world practices as eating grubs and worshipping cows? Why have some societies allowed men to have four wives, whereas others—such as the Shakers—prohibited sex between men and women entirely? Why do some groups worship their ancestors, while others have many gods, and yet others believe in a single divine being? How can societies adapt to extremes of climate and geographical terrain—hot, cold, dry, wet, mountainous, and flat? Humankind has evolved practices so diverse that it would be hard to find a practice that has not been adopted in some society at some time in history.

Handbook Link 3.1
Read more about symbolic interaction.

To explain these cultural differences, we will examine two perspectives that have made important contributions to understanding culture at the meso and macro levels: structural-functional and conflict theories.

Structural-Functional Theory

Structural-functional theory seeks to explain why members of an ethnic subculture or a society engage in certain practices. To answer, structural-functionalists look at how those practices meet social needs or contribute to the survival or social solidarity of the group or society as a whole. A classic example is the reverence for cattle in India. The "sacred cow" is protected and treated with respect and is not slaughtered for food. The reasons relate to India's ancient development into an agricultural society that required sacrifices (Harris 1989). Cattle were needed to pull plows, and their dried dung was the main source of fuel. To this day, cows are symbols of sacrifice. Cows gained religious significance because of their importance for the survival of early agricultural communities. They must, therefore, be protected from hungry people for the long-term survival of the group.

Functionalists view societies as composed of interdependent parts, each fulfilling certain necessary functions or purposes for the total society (Radcliffe-Brown 1935). Shared norms, values, and beliefs, for instance, serve the function of holding a social group together. At a global macro level, functionalists see the world moving in the direction of having a common culture, potentially reducing "we" versus "they" thinking and promoting unity across boundaries. Synthesis of cultures and even the loss of some cultures are viewed as a natural result of globalization.

Although most cultural practices serve positive functions for the maintenance and stability of society, some practices, such as slavery or child abuse, may be dysfunctional for minority groups or individual members of society. The fact that some societies are weak or have died out suggests that their way of life may not have been functional in the long run. Consider the case of Haiti, where all the forests have been cut down to provide firewood and the resulting erosion is making the land unusable for growing crops. Thus, some of the population have been starving (Diamond 2005). Add to the existing poverty and hunger the devastation brought about by the January 12, 2010, earthquake that damaged or destroyed most buildings. The country and its people must rely on external support from donations from other countries to survive and rebuild.

The functionalist perspective has been criticized because it fails to consider how much dysfunction a society has, how much conflict a society can tolerate, and how much unity is necessary for a society to survive. Some critics argue that functional theory overemphasizes the need for consensus and integration among different parts of society, thus ignoring conflicts that may point to problems in societies (Dahrendorf 1959).

Conflict Theory

Some communities in the United States have absorbed large numbers of immigrants from Mexico—some legal and some illegal. The influx of people who speak another language and whose cultural values are a bit different from those in the dominant society causes some members of the dominant society to be very wary of the newcomers. For one thing, they fear that their religious beliefs and certain social ideas will no longer be the predominant ones in the community. They may not be able to prevent immigrants being issued green cards by the federal government, but they still do not want their own way of life challenged. They will do all they can to stop illegal immigrants from gaining access to U.S. citizenship.

Conflict theorists believe that society is composed of groups, each acting to meet its own self-interests, and those groups struggle to make their own cultural values supreme in the society. The recent conflict over immigration laws is illustrated by protesters who expressed their opinions in this "Day Without an Immigrant" march in Los Angeles.

In some communities in the middle part of the United States—states that depend on agriculture as a major source of productivity—there are intense conflicts over whether animals should be raised in concentrated animal feeding operations (CAFOs). These high-tech operations are more profitable for livestock farmers, and they depend on extensive technology, but many citizens worry about the impact on the environment (especially the water supplies for the community), and others are outraged at the inhumane treatment of animals, who often do not ever get to go outside. They live their lives in pens not much larger than the animal. Some people believe that cruelty to animals has an effect on the people themselves. It should be clear that in both of the foregoing examples there are cultural as well as economic dimensions to the conflicts.

Whereas functionalists assume consensus because all people in society have learned the same cultural values, rules, and expectations, conflict theorists do not view culture as having this uniting effect. Conflict theorists describe societies as composed of groups—class, ethnic, religious, and political groups at the meso level—vying for power. Each group protects its own self-interests and struggles to make its own cultural ways dominant in the society. Instead of consensus, the dominant groups may impose their cultural beliefs on minorities and other subcultural groups, thus laying the groundwork for conflict. Conflict theorists identify tension between meso and macro levels, whereas functionalists tend to focus on harmony and smooth integration between those levels.

Actually, conflict may contribute to a smoother-running society in the long run. The German sociologist Georg Simmel (1955) believed that some conflict could serve a positive purpose by alerting societal leaders to problem areas that need attention. This view is illustrated by the political changes that followed the women's movement or by the organic food industry that has arisen in response to corporate agribusiness, genetically modified foods, and massive use of pesticides.

Conflict theorists argue that the people with privilege and power in society manipulate institutions such as religion and education. In this way, people learn the values, beliefs, and norms of the privileged group and foster beliefs that justify the dominant group's self-interests, power, and advantage. The needs of the privileged are likely to be met, and their status will be secured. For instance, schools that serve lower-class children usually teach obedience to authority, punctuality, and respect for superiors—behaviors that make for good laborers. The children of the affluent, meanwhile, are more likely to attend schools stressing divergent thinking, creativity, and leadership, attributes that prepare them to occupy the most professional, prestigious, and highly rewarded positions in the society. Conflict theorists point to this control of the education process by those with privilege as part of the overall pattern by which the society benefits the rich.

Conflict theory can also help us understand global dynamics. Poor nations feel that the global system protects the self-interests of the richest nations and that those rich nations impose their own culture, including their ideas about

This local community has a farmers' market, and these organic farmers are helping to mobilize the citizens against a state law that would authorize concentrated animal feeding operations—an approach to providing food that these people see as a violation of local cultural values. Here, we see the connection between the micro-level activities at a farmers' market and the state- and national-level policies on agriculture.

economics, politics, and religion, on the less affluent. Some scholars believe there is great richness in local customs that is lost when homogenized by the cultural domination by the powerful in the macro-level trends of globalization (Ritzer 2004).

Conflict theory is useful for analyzing the relationships between societies (at a macro level) and between subcultures (at a meso level) within complex societies. It also helps illuminate tensions in a society when local (micro-level) cultural values clash with national (macro-level) trends. Conflict theory is not as successful, however, in explaining simple, well-integrated societies in which change is slow to come about and cooperation is an organizing principle.

Video Link 3.6
Watch how industry can conflict with values.

Social Policy and Cultural Change

Imagine living in a remote village on Borneo that, due to its location in the East Indies, has remained largely isolated from the outside world for hundreds of years. Traditions are well established, and members seldom question how things are done. Then, television comes to the village—one set located in a central meeting hut. Initially, it is used for educational

Cruise ships such as this one have a huge impact on local communities in the Caribbean or in areas such as Borneo when as many as 3,000 tourists descend on a local community for a day. Sometimes the tourists outnumber the natives. Some ships dump tons of waste into the ocean, endangering the fishing industry and threatening the safety of the beaches.

change in political and economic ideologies and make available raw materials, new products, and growing markets.

The social costs of rapid change can be great. During the period of early industrialization, newly arrived peasants lived in urban squalor hard to imagine today. Even today, these problems exist as people in impoverished regions of the world leave their villages to seek employment in overcrowded urban areas. New technologies have the potential to save lives and to make life less harsh, if they are distributed to those who need them, but introduction of Western technology can also disrupt and even destroy indigenous cultures. This destruction of a culture—called *ethnocide*—can be extremely disorienting to the people (Lukunka 2008). A contributing factor to terrorism is the challenge and threat to traditional cultures and values. Policymakers cannot stop change, but they can determine how to introduce change for the most beneficial and positive results.

Video Link 3.7
Watch more on social change.

Thinking Sociologically

Is it appropriate for powerful countries or organizations to try to change the politics or religion of another culture? Why or why not? Do individual human rights always have supremacy over the rights of a group to determine their own culture? These are tough questions that trouble many people who work in the area of human rights policy.

programs, but the village TV receives its share of Western movies and reruns of American sitcoms (situation comedies). The advertisements also expose people to new consumer products. With the arrival of cruise ships, this village in Borneo will never be the same again. Villagers develop a desire for goods hitherto unknown, and young people leave for cities and new opportunities. Refrigerators, dishwashers, and fancy autos become known commodities. People learn that modern medicines can relieve suffering, cure some illnesses, and extend life, making for a higher quality of life and a longer life for many people. Change also challenges the old traditions. Without new norms to take their place, disorganization can occur.

Technology is bringing change to societies around the world, often with unanticipated consequences. While technology (an example of material culture) advances rapidly, the nonmaterial culture lags behind, resulting in social disruption. Sociologist William Ogburn (1950) used the term **cultural lag** for this change that occurs unequally between material culture (tangible objects) and nonmaterial culture (ideas, beliefs, and values). Rapid change is opposed by people whose lifestyle is threatened and who wish to preserve their native cultures. Should policymakers respect these differences and reduce the impact of change? That is the policy dilemma.

For societies to remain isolated in our global system is rare. Most are drawn into the dynamics of the 21st century, even if they are not full participants. Societies interact constantly through negotiation, trade, alliances, competition, compromise, conflict, and war. External forces bring about

The Fit Between Hardware and Software

Computer software cannot work with incompatible machines. Some documents cannot be easily transferred to another piece of hardware, although sometimes a transfer can be accomplished with significant modification in the formatting of the document. The same is true with the hardware of society and the software of culture. For instance, the value of having large extended families, typically valued in agricultural societies, does not work well in the structure of industrial and postindustrial societies. Other values such as rewarding people based on individual merit, emphasizing the idea that humans are motivated primarily by their own self-interests, or believing that change in cultures is inevitable and equals progress are not particularly compatible with the hardware (structure) of traditional horticultural or herding societies. Values and beliefs ("software") can be transferred to another type of society ("hardware"). However, there are limits to what can be transferred, and the change of "formatting" may mean the new beliefs are barely recognizable.

Attempts to transport U.S.-style "software" (culture)—individualism, capitalism, freedom of religion, and democracy—to other parts of the world illustrate that these ideas are not always successful in other settings. The hardware of other societies may be able to handle more than one type of software or set of beliefs, but there are limits to the adaptability. Thus, we should not be surprised when our ideas are transformed into something quite different when they are imported to another social system. If we are to understand the world in which we live and if we want to improve it, we must first fully understand these societies and cultures.

Thinking Sociologically

Some anthropologists argue that *team sports*, groups playing each other in coordinated competition, were learned by Europeans from certain Native American groups. How has the diffusion of team sports into U.S. culture influenced the nature of U.S. society and culture? How might society be different if we had only individual sports?

Because there is such variation between societies and cultures in what they see as normal, how do any of us ever adjust to our society's expectations? The answer is addressed in the next chapter. Each society relies on the process of socialization to teach the culture to its members. Human life is a lifelong process of socialization to social and cultural expectations. The next chapter discusses the ways in which we learn our culture and become members of society.

What Have We Learned?

Individuals and small groups cannot live without the support of a larger society, the hardware of the social world. Without the software—culture—there could be no society, for there would be no norms to guide our interactions with others in society. Humans are inherently social and learn their culture from others. Furthermore, as society has evolved into more complex and multileveled social systems, humans have learned to live in and negotiate conflicts between multiple cultures, including those at micro (microcultures), meso (subcultures), and macro (global cultures) levels. Life in an Information Age society demands adaptability to different sociocultural contexts and tolerance of different cultures and subcultures. This is a challenge to a species that has always had tendencies toward ethnocentrism.

Key Points

- Society consists of individuals who live together in a specific geographic area, interact with each other more than with outsiders, cooperate to attain goals, and share a common culture over time. Each society has a culture, ideas, and "things" that are passed on from one generation to the next in a society; the culture has both material and nonmaterial components. (See p. 66.)

- Societies evolve from very simple societies to more complex ones, from the simple hunting-gathering society to the information societies of the postindustrial world. (See pp. 67–74.)

- The study of culture requires that we try to avoid ethnocentrism (judging other cultures by the standards of our culture), taking a stance of cultural relativity instead so that the culture can be understood from the standpoint of those inside it. (See pp. 78–81.)

- Just as social units exist at various levels of our social world, from small groups to global systems, cultures exist within different levels of the social system—microcultures, subcultures, national cultures, and global cultures. Some social units at the micro or meso level stand in opposition to the dominant national culture, and they are called countercultures. (See pp. 91–96.)

- Various theories offer different lenses for understanding culture. While symbolic interaction illuminates the way humans bring meaning to events (thus generating culture), the functionalist and conflict paradigms examine cultural harmony/seamless fit and conflict between cultures, respectively. (See pp. 96–99.)

- The metaphor of hardware (society's structure) and software (culture) describes their interdependent relationship, and as with computers, there must be some compatibility between the structure and the culture. If there is none, either the cultural elements that are transported into another society will be rejected or the culture will be "reformatted" to fit the society. (See p. 100.)

Contributing to Our Social World: What Can We Do?

At the Local and National Levels

- *Ethnic group organizations:* Most large (and many smaller) communities have organizations and clubs that focus on the interests of specific ethnic groups: Arabic Americans, Chinese Americans, Italian Americans, Polish Americans, and so on. Contact one of these groups (of your own background or, even more interesting, of a background that differs from your own). Arrange to visit one of the group's meetings, and learn about the activities in which its members are involved.

- *Immigrant aid groups:* Many ethnically oriented organizations assist recent immigrants in dealing with adjustment to American life, especially those from Mexico and other Spanish-speaking countries, Arabic-speaking countries of the Middle East, and eastern and South Asian countries such as China, Vietnam, the Philippines, Korea, and India. Contact one of these groups, and explore the possibility of volunteering or serving as an intern.

At the Global Level

- *UN Permanent Forum on Indigenous Issues:* As the process of globalization accelerates, the cultures, languages, and basic rights of indigenous people around the world are under increasing threat. We have experienced this in North America in relation to Native American and Inuit populations, but it is occurring throughout the world. The United Nations Forum on Indigenous Issues assists affected groups in facing these challenges. Visit their Web site at www .un.org/esa/socdev/unpfii, and contact them about the possibility of volunteering.

- *Nongovernmental organizations:* You might also contact a leading nongovernmental organization engaged in similar, action-oriented programs. One example is Cultural Survival (www.cs.org). The organization partners with indigenous people to secure rights, promote respect, ensure their participation, and assure rights to land.

For chapter-specific resources, including **Frontline**, **TED**, and **YouTube** videos; self-quizzes; web exercises; and more, visit **www.pineforge.com/oswmedia3e.**

CHAPTER 4

Socialization

Becoming Human and Humane

Whether at the micro, meso, or macro level, our close associates and various organizations teach us how to be human and humane in that society. Skills are taught, as well as values such as loyalty and caregiving.

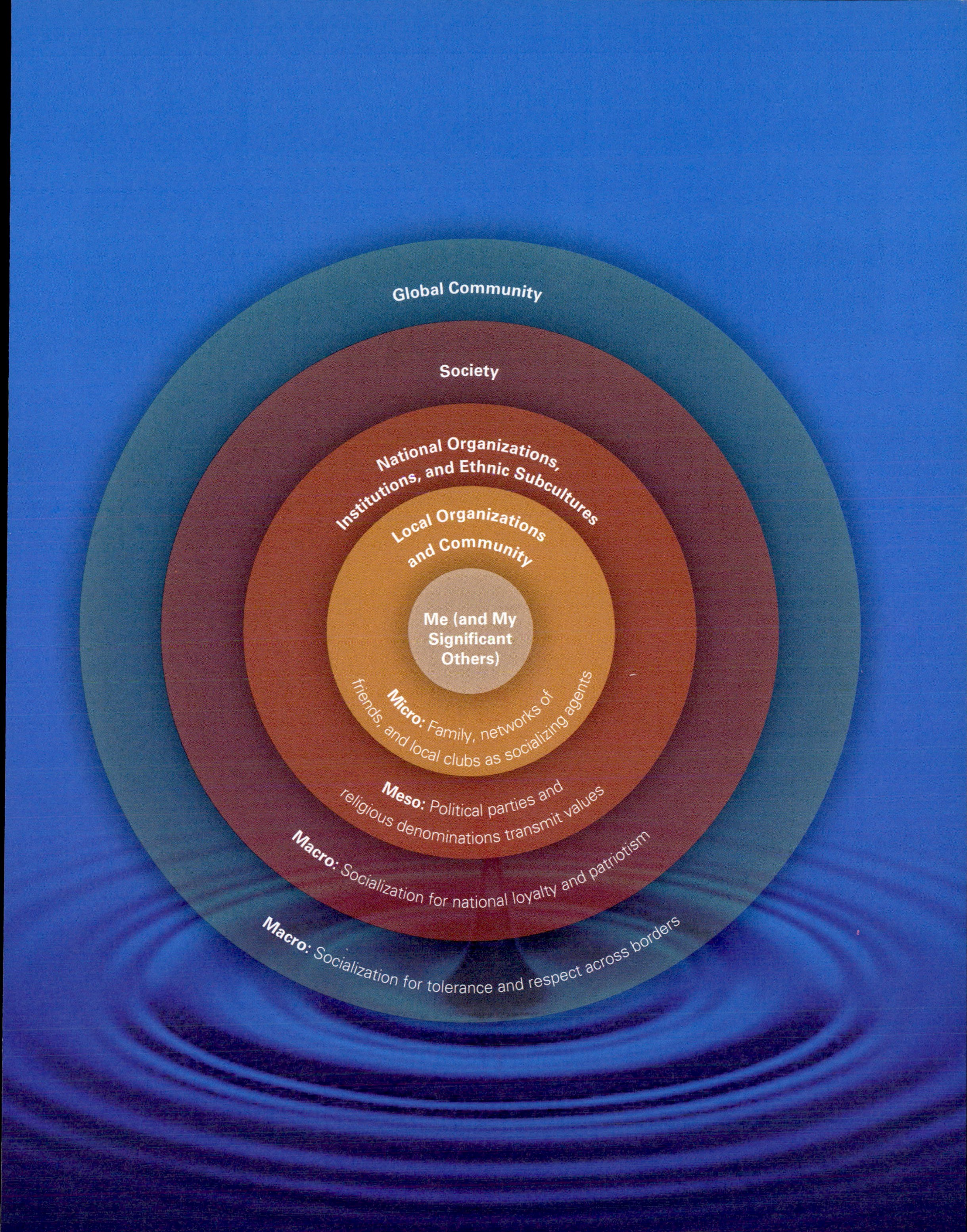

Global Community

Society

National Organizations,
Institutions, and Ethnic Subcultures

Local Organizations
and Community

Me (and My
Significant
Others)

Micro: Family, networks of
friends, and local clubs as socializing agents

Meso: Political parties and
religious denominations transmit values

Macro: Socialization for national loyalty and patriotism

Macro: Socialization for tolerance and respect across borders

Think About It	
Me (and My Inner Circle)	What does it mean to have a "self"? How would you be different if you had been raised in complete isolation from other people?
Local Community	What groups in your community have shaped your values and your beliefs?
National Institutions; Complex Organizations; Ethnic Groups	How do various subcultures or organizations of which you are a member (your political party; your religious affiliation) influence your position in the social world?
National Society	What would you be like if you were raised in a different country? How does your sense of national identity influence the way you see things?
Global Community	How might globalization or other macro-level events impact you and your sense of self?

Ram, a first grader from India, had been in school in Iowa for only a couple of weeks. The teacher was giving the first test. Ram did not know much about what a test meant, but he rather liked school, and the red-haired girl next to him had become a friend. He was catching on to reading a bit faster than she, but she was better at the number exercises. They often helped each other learn while the teacher was busy with a small group in the front of the class.

The teacher gave each child the test, and Ram saw that it had to do with numbers. He began to do what the teacher had instructed the children to do with the worksheet, but after a while, he became confused. He leaned over to look at the page Elyse was working on. She hid her sheet from him, an unexpected response. The teacher looked up and asked what was going on. Elyse said that Ram was "cheating." Ram was

not quite sure what that meant, but it did not sound good. The teacher's scolding of Ram left him baffled, confused, and entirely humiliated.

This incident was Ram's first lesson in the individualism and competitiveness that govern Western-style schools. He was being socialized into a new set of values. In his parents' culture, competitiveness was discouraged, and individualism was equated with selfishness and rejection of community. Athletic events were designed to end in a tie so that no one would feel rejected. Indeed, a well-socialized person would rather lose in a competition than cause someone else to feel bad because they lost.

Socialization is the lifelong process of learning to become a member of the social world, beginning at birth and continuing until death. It is a major part of what the family, education, religion, and other institutions do to prepare individuals to be members of their social world. Like Ram, each of us learns the values and beliefs of our culture. In Ram's case, he literally moved from one cultural group to another and had to adjust to more than one culture within his social world.

From the time they are born, infants are interactive, ready to develop into members of the social world. As they cry, coo, or smile, they gradually learn that their behaviors elicit responses from other humans. This exchange of messages—this **interaction**—is the basic building block of socialization. Out of this process of interaction, a child learns its culture and becomes a member of society. This process of interaction shapes the infant into a human being with a social self—perceptions we have of who we are.

Human biological potential, culture, and individual experiences all provide the framework for socialization. Babies enter this world unsocialized, born totally dependent on others to meet their needs, and completely lacking in social awareness and an understanding of the rules of their society. Despite this complete vulnerability, they have the potential to learn the language, norms, values, and skills needed in their society. They gradually learn who they are and what is expected of them. Socialization is necessary not only for the survival of the individual but also for the survival of society and its groups. The process continues in various forms throughout our lives as we enter and exit various positions—from school to work to retirement to death.

Babies interact intensively with their parents, observing and absorbing everything around them and learning what kinds of sounds or actions elicit response from the adults. Socialization starts at the beginning of life.

In this chapter, we will explore the nature of socialization and how individuals become socialized. We consider why socialization is important. We also look at development of the self, socialization through the life cycle, the agents of socialization, macro-level issues, and a policy example illustrating socialization. First, we briefly examine an ongoing debate: Which is more influential in determining who we are—our genes (nature) or our socialization into the social world (nurture)?

Nature and Nurture

What is it that most makes us who we are? Is it our biological makeup or the environment in which we are raised that guides our behavior and the development of our self? One side of the contemporary debate regarding nature versus nurture seeks to explain the development of the self and human social behaviors—violence, crime, academic performance, mate selection, economic success, gender roles, and other behaviors too numerous to mention here—by examining biological or genetic factors (Harris 2009; Winkler 1991). Sociologists call this sociobiology, and psychologists refer to it as evolutionary psychology. The theory claims that our human genetic makeup wires us for social behaviors (E. Wilson et al. 1978).

Sociobiologists believe that we perpetuate our own biological family lines and the human species through various social behaviors. Human groups develop power structures, are territorial, and protect their kin. A mother ignoring her own safety to help a child, soldiers dying in battle for their comrades and countries, communities feeling hostility toward outsiders or foreigners, and people defending property lines against intrusion by neighbors are all examples of behaviors that sociobiologists claim are rooted in the genetic makeup of the species. Sociobiologists would say that these behaviors continue because they result in an increased chance of survival of the species as a whole (Lerner 1992; Lumsden and Wilson 1981; Wilson 1980, 1987).

Most sociologists believe that sociobiology and evolutionary psychology explanations have flaws. Sociobiology is a *reductionist* theory; that is, it too often reduces complex social behaviors to a single factor—in this case, inherited traits—yet evidence of an altruism gene, an aggression gene, or any other behavioral gene is lacking. Sociologists point to the fact that there are great variations in the way members of different societies and groups behave. People born in one culture and raised in another adopt social behaviors common to the culture in which they are raised (Gould 1997), not based on inherited traits. If specific social behavior is genetically programmed, then it should manifest itself regardless of the culture in which humans are raised. The key is that what makes humans unique is not our biological heritage but our ability to learn the complex social arrangements of our culture.

Most sociologists recognize that individuals are influenced by biology, which limits the range of human responses and creates certain needs and drives, but they believe that nurture is far more important in shaping human social behavior through the socialization process. Some sociologists propose theories that consider both nature and nurture. Alice Rossi, former president of the American Sociological Association, argues that we need to build both biological and social theories—or biosocial theories—into explanations of social processes such as parenting. In the 21st century, a few sociologists are developing an approach called evolutionary sociology, which takes seriously the way our genetic makeup—including a remarkable capacity for language—shapes our range of behaviors. However, it is also very clear from biological research that living organisms are often modified by their environments and the behaviors of others around them—with even genetic structure changing (Lopreato 2001; Machalek and Martin 2010). In short, biology influences human behavior, but interactive behavior can also modify biological traits. Indeed, the nutritional history of grandparents can affect the metabolism of their grandchildren, and what grandparents ate was largely shaped by cultural ideas about food (BBC's Science and Nature 2009; Freese, Powell, and Steelman 1999; Rossi 1984). In short, socialization is key in the process of "becoming human and humane."

Intense interaction by infants and their caregiver, usually a parent, occurs in all cultures and is essential to becoming a part of the society and to becoming fully human. This African father shares a tender moment with his son.

The Importance of Socialization

If you have lived on a farm, watched animals in the wild, or seen television nature shows, you probably have noticed that many animal young become independent shortly after birth. Horses are on their feet in a matter of hours, and by the time turtles hatch from eggs, their parents are long gone. Many species in the animal kingdom do not require contact with adults to survive because their behaviors are inborn and instinctual. Generally speaking, the more intelligent the species, the longer the period of gestation and of nutritional and social dependence on the mother and family. Humans clearly take the longest time to socialize their young. Even among primates, human infants have the longest gestation and dependency period, generally 6 to 8 years. Chimpanzees, very similar to humans in their DNA, take only 12 to 28 months. Table 4.1 compares human infants and other primate babies. This extended dependency period for humans—what some have referred to as the *long childhood*—allows each human being time to learn the complexities of culture. This suggests that biology and social processes work together.

Handbook Link 4.1
Read about socialization and students.

Normal human development involves learning to sit, crawl, stand, walk, think, talk, and participate in social interactions. Ideally, the long period of dependence allows children the opportunity to learn necessary skills, knowledge, and social roles through affectionate and tolerant interaction with people who care about them. Yet what happens if children are deprived of adequate care or even human contact? The following section illustrates the importance of socialization by showing the effect of deprivation and isolation on normal socialization.

Isolated and Abused Children

What would children be like if they grew up without human contact? Among the most striking examples are cases of severely abused and neglected children whose parents kept them isolated in cellars or attics for years without providing even minimal attention and nurturing. When these isolated children were discovered, typically they suffered from profound developmental disorders that endured throughout their lives (Curtiss 1977; Davis 1947). Most experience great difficulty in adjusting to a social world guided by complex rules of interaction learned from infancy onward.

In case studies comparing two girls, Anna and Isabelle, who experienced extreme isolation in early childhood, Kingsley Davis (1947) found that even minimal human contact made some difference in their socialization. Both "illegitimate" girls were kept locked up by relatives who wanted to keep their existence a secret. Both were discovered at about age 6 and moved to institutions where they received intensive training. Yet the cases were different in one significant respect: Prior to her discovery by those outside her immediate family, Anna experienced virtually no human contact. She saw other individuals only when they left food for her. Isabelle lived in a darkened room with her deaf-mute mother, who provided some human contact. Anna could not sit, walk, or talk and learned little in the special school in which she was placed. When she died from jaundice at age 11, she had learned the language and skills of a 2- or 3-year-old. Isabelle, on the other hand, did progress. She learned to talk and played with her peers. After 2 years, she reached an intellectual level approaching normal for her age but remained about 2 years behind her classmates in performance levels (Davis 1940, 1947).

Less extreme than the cases of isolation but equally illustrative are the cases of children who come from war-torn countries (Povik 1994), live in orphanages, or are neglected or abused. Although not totally isolated, these children also experience problems and disruptions in the socialization process. These neglected children's situations have been referred to as abusive, violent, and dead-end

Table 4.1	**Dependence on Adults Among the Primates**			
Primate Form	Pregnancy Period	Period of Absolute Nutritional Dependency on Mother or Mother-Surrogate	Nursing Period	Social Independence
Human	266 days	1 year or more	1–2 years	6–8 years
Ape: chimpanzee	235 days	3–6 months	2–3 months	12–28 months
Monkey: rhesus	166 days	1–3 weeks	2–4 weeks	2–4 months
Lemur	111–145 days	1–3 days	2–14 days	2–3 weeks

Note: Lemurs and monkeys, among the less complex members of the primate order, depend on adults for food for a much shorter time than do apes and humans. The period of dependence affords human infants time to absorb the extensive knowledge important to the survival of the species.

environments that are socially toxic because of their harmful developmental consequences for children.

What is the message? These cases illustrate the devastating effects of isolation, neglect, and abuse early in life on normal socialization. Less extreme but also damaging are the physical, mental, and sexual abuse and neglect suffered by many children around the world. Humans need more from their environments than food and shelter. They need positive contact, a sense of belonging, affection, safety, and someone to teach them knowledge and skills. This is children's socialization into the world, through which they develop a self. Before we examine the development of the self in depth, however, we consider the complexity of socialization in the multileveled social world.

Socialization and the Social World

Sociologists are interested in how individuals become members of their society and learn the norms of the culture to which they belong. Through the socialization process, individuals learn what is expected in their society. At the micro level, most parents teach children proper behaviors to be successful in life, and peers influence children to "fit in" and have fun. Psychologists and social psychologists focus on the individual and group settings: the origins of identity and stages in the development of reasoning (Piaget 1989; Piaget and Inhelder [1955] 1999), morality and gender differences (Gilligan 1982; Kohlberg 1971), or personality (Erikson 1950). However, most recognize that individual development and behavior occur in social settings. In fact, the process of socialization in groups allows the self to develop as individuals learn to interact with others in their culture. Interaction theory, focusing on the micro level, forms the basis of this chapter, as you will see.

Examples of socialization at the meso level include religious denominations espousing their versions of the Truth and schools teaching the knowledge and skills necessary for functioning in society. At the nationwide, macro level, television ads encourage viewers to vote for particular candidates, buy products that will make them better and happier people, and join the military. From interactions with our significant others to dealing with government bureaucracy, most activities are part of the socialization experience that teaches us how to function in our society.

The social world model at the start of the chapter illustrates the levels of analysis in the social world. The process of socialization takes place at each level, linking the parts. Small micro-level groups include families, **peer groups** (whose members are roughly equal in some status within the society, such as the same age or the same occupation), and voluntary groups such as the Girl Scouts. Examples of meso-level institutions are educational institutions and political parties, while an important macro-level unit is the federal government. All these have a stake in how we are socialized because they all need trained and loyal group members to survive. Organizations need citizens who have been socialized to devote the time, energy, and resources

that these groups need to survive and meet their goals. For example, volunteer and charitable organizations cannot thrive unless people are willing to volunteer their energy, time, skills, and money. Lack of adequate socialization increases the likelihood of individuals becoming misfits or social deviants.

Most perspectives on socialization focus on the micro level, as we shall see when we explore the development of the self. For example, an influential microsociologist, Erving Goffman (1922–1982), developed what he referred to as "dramaturgy." Influenced by symbolic interaction, he explored the importance of symbols and ritual in everyday life, using participant observation. His book *Presentation of Self in Everyday Life* ([1959] 2001) analyzes social life as drama, with our onstage behavior played out for an audience and our backstage behavior involving only significant others. Goffman focused on understanding our ritual behavior, what we do in the presence of others, as part of understanding our interactions. We learn to manage the impressions we present to others through the roles we play, much as actors do in a theatrical production. Although Goffman's theory is unique and appealing, he was scientifically unsystematic in his research, so among sociologists who consider sociology as a science, there is less enthusiasm for his approach.

Audio Link 4.1
Listen to why children are mean to each other.

Meso- and macro-level theories add to our understanding of how socialization prepares individuals for their roles in the larger social world. For example, structural-functionalist perspectives of socialization tend to see different levels of the social world operating to support each other. According to this perspective, education in many Western societies reinforces individualism and an achievement ethic. Families often organize holidays around patriotic themes, such as a national independence day, or around religious celebrations. These activities are believed to strengthen family members' commitment to the nation and to buttress the moral values emphasized in churches, temples, and mosques. All these values are compatible with preparing individuals to support national political and economic systems.

Socialization can also be understood from the conflict perspective, with the linkages between various parts of the social world based on competition with or even direct opposition to another part. Consider the following examples. Socialization into a nation's military forces stresses patriotism and ethnocentrism, sometimes generating conflict and hostility toward other groups and countries. Demands from organizations for our resources (time, money, and energy devoted to the Little League, the Rotary Club, and library associations) may leave nothing to give to our religious communities or even our families, setting up a conflict. Each organization and unit competes to gain our loyalty in order to claim some of our resources.

At the meso level, the purposes and values of organizations or institutions are sometimes in direct contrast with one another or are in conflict with the messages at other levels of the social system. Businesses and educational institutions try to socialize their workers and students to be serious, hardworking, sober, and conscientious, with lifestyles focused on the future. In contrast, many fraternal organizations and barroom microcultures favor lifestyles that celebrate frivolity, playfulness, and living for the moment. This creates conflicting values in the socialization process.

Conflict can occur in the global community as well. For example, religious groups often socialize their members to identify with humanity as a whole ("the family of God"). However, in some cases, nations do not want their citizens socialized to identify with those beyond their borders. They may seek to persuade Christians to kill other Christians or Jews or Muslims who are defined as "the enemy," as in the case of Nazi Germany's efforts to exterminate Jews during World War II in Europe. If religion teaches that all people are "brothers and sisters" and if religious people object to killing, the nation may have trouble mobilizing its people to arms when the leaders call for war.

Conflict theorists believe that those who have power and privilege use socialization to manipulate individuals to support the power structure and the self-interests of the elite. Those who have power and privilege are in the best position to get what they need, and they also have significant influence on the socialization of others through schools and political institutions. Most individuals have little power to control and decide their futures. For example, parents decide how they would like to raise their children and what values they want to instill in their children, but as soon as the school enters into socialization, parents must share the socialization process. One reason why some parents choose to home-school their children is to control external influences on the socialization process.

Each theoretical explanation has merit for explaining some situations. Whether we stress harmony in the socialization process or conflict rooted in power differences, the development of a sense of self through the process of socialization is an ongoing, lifelong process. Having considered the multiple levels of analysis and the issues that make socialization complicated, let us focus specifically on the micro level: Where does the sense of self originate?

Thinking Sociologically

Although the socialization process occurs primarily at the micro level, it is influenced by events at each level of analysis shown in the social world model. Give examples of family, community, subcultural, national, or global events that might influence how you were socialized or how you would socialize your child.

DEVELOPMENT OF THE SELF: MICRO-LEVEL ANALYSIS

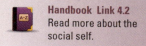
Handbook Link 4.2
Read more about the social self.

The main product of the socialization process is the self. Fundamentally, **self** refers to the

perceptions we have of who we are. Throughout the socialization process, our self is derived from our perceptions of the way others are responding to us. The development of the self allows individuals to interact with other people and to learn to function at each level of the social world.

Humans are not born with a sense of self. It develops gradually, beginning in infancy and continuing throughout adulthood. Selfhood emerges through interaction with others. Individual biology, culture, and social experiences all play a part in shaping the self. The hereditary blueprint each person brings into the world provides broad biological outlines, including particular physical attributes, temperament, and a maturational schedule. However, nature is shaped by nurture. Each person is also born into a family that lives within a particular culture. This hereditary blueprint, in interaction with family and culture, helps create each unique person, different from any other person yet sharing the types of interactions by which the self is formed.

Most sociologists, although not all (Irvine 2004), believe that we humans are distinct from other animals in our ability to develop a self and to be aware of ourselves as individuals or objects. Consider how we refer to ourselves in the first person—*I* am hungry, *I* feel foolish, *I* am having fun, and *I* am good at basketball. We have a conception of who we are, how we relate to others, and how we differ from and are separate from others in our abilities and limitations. We have an awareness of the characteristics, values, feelings, and attitudes that give us our unique sense of self (James [1890] 1934; Mead [1934] 1962).

Thinking Sociologically

Write a character sketch that describes you. Who are some of the people who have been most significant in shaping your *self*? How have their actions and responses helped shape your self-conception as musically talented, athletic, intelligent, kind, assertive, or any of the other hundreds of traits that might make up your *self*?

The Looking-Glass Self and Taking the Role of the Other

The symbolic interaction theory offers important insights into how individuals develop the self. Two of the major scholars in this approach were Charles H. Cooley ([1909] 1983) and George Herbert Mead ([1934] 1962). Cooley believed that the self is a social product, shaped by interactions with others from the time of birth. He likened interaction processes to looking in a mirror wherein each person reflects an image of the other.

Each to each a looking-glass

Reflects the other that doth pass. (Cooley [1909] 1983:184)

For Cooley ([1909] 1983), the **looking-glass self** is a reflective process based on our interpretations of the reactions of others. In this process, Cooley believed that there are three principal elements, shown in Figure 4.1: (1) we imagine how we appear to others, (2) others judge our appearance and respond to us, and (3) we react to that feedback. We experience feelings such as pride or shame based on this imagined judgment and respond based on our interpretation. Moreover, throughout this process, we actively try to manipulate other people's view of us to serve our needs and interests. This is one of the many ways we learn to be boys or girls—the image that is reflected back to us lets us know whether we have behaved in ways that are socially acceptable according to gender expectations. The issue of gender socialization in particular will be discussed in some detail in Chapter 9. Of course, this does not mean our interpretation of the other person's response is correct, but our interpretation does determine how we respond.

Our self is influenced by the many "others" with whom we interact, and each of our interpretations of their reactions feeds into our self-concept. Recall that the isolated children failed to develop this sense of self precisely because they lacked interaction with others. The next "Sociology in Our Social World" illustrates the looking-glass self process for African American males. This situation experienced by Brent Staples vividly illustrates the impact of others on us.

Taking the looking-glass self idea a step further, Mead explained that individuals take others into account by imagining themselves in the position of that other, a process called **role-taking**. When children play mommy and daddy, doctor and patient, or firefighter, they are imagining themselves in

Our sense of self is often shaped by how others see us and what is reflected back to us by the interactions of others. Operating somewhat like a mirror, Cooley called this process the "looking-glass self."

another's shoes. Role-taking allows humans to view themselves from the standpoint of others. This requires mentally stepping out of our own experience to imagine how others experience and view the social world. Through role-taking, we begin to see who we are from the standpoint of others. In short, role-taking allows humans to view themselves as objects, as though they were looking at themselves from outside themselves.

Audio Link 4.2
Listen to people who pretend to be others.

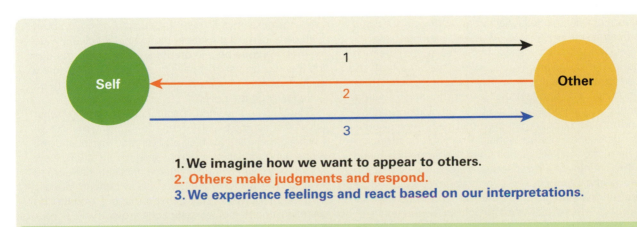

1. **We imagine how we want to appear to others.**
2. **Others make judgments and respond.**
3. **We experience feelings and react based on our interpretations.**

Figure 4.1 The Looking-Glass Process of Self-Development

Sociology in Our Social World

Black Men and Public Space

By Brent Staples

Many stereotypes—rigid images of members of a particular group—surround the young African American male in the United States. How these images influence these young men and their social world is the subject of this feature. Think about the human cost of stereotypes and their effect on the socialization process as you read the following essay. If your sense of self is profoundly influenced by the ways others respond to you, how might the identity of a young African American boy be affected by public images of black males?

My first victim was a woman—white, well dressed, probably in her early-twenties. I came upon her late one evening on a deserted street in Hyde Park, a relatively affluent neighborhood in an otherwise mean, impoverished section of Chicago. As I swung onto the avenue behind her, she cast back a worried glance. To her, the youngish black man—broad, six-feet two-inches tall, with a beard and billowing hair, both hands shoved into the pockets of a bulky military jacket—seemed menacingly close. After a few more quick glimpses, she picked up her pace and was running in earnest. Within seconds, she disappeared into a cross street.

That was more than a decade ago. I was 22 years old, a graduate student newly arrived at the University of Chicago. It was in the echo of that terrified woman's footfalls that I first began to know the unwieldy inheritance I'd come into. . . . It was clear that she thought herself the quarry of a mugger, a rapist, or worse. Suffering a bout of insomnia, however, I was stalking sleep, not defenseless wayfarers. . . . I was surprised, embarrassed, and dismayed all at once. Her flight . . . made it clear that I was indistinguishable from the muggers who occasionally seeped into the area from the surrounding ghetto. That first encounter, and those that followed, signified that a vast, unnerving gulf lay between night-time pedestrians—particularly women—and me. And I soon gathered that being perceived as dangerous is a hazard in itself. I only needed to turn a corner into a dicey situation, or crowd some frightened, armed person in a foyer somewhere, or make an errant move after being pulled over by a policeman. Where fear and weapons meet—and they often do in urban America—there is always the possibility of death.

In that first year, my first away from my hometown, I was to become thoroughly familiar with the language of fear. At dark, shadowy intersections, I could cross in front of a car stopped at a traffic light and elicit the thunk, thunk, thunk, thunk of the driver—black, white, male, or female—hammering down the door locks. On less-traveled streets after dark, I grew accustomed to but never comfortable with people crossing to the other side of the street rather than pass me. Then there was the standard unpleasantness with policemen, doormen, bouncers, cabdrivers, and those whose business it is to screen out troublesome individuals before there is any nastiness.

After dark, on the warren-like streets of Brooklyn where I live, I often see women who fear the worst from me. They seem to have set their faces on neutral, and with their purse straps strung across their chests bandolierstyle, they forge ahead as though bracing themselves against being tackled. I understand, of course, that . . . women are particularly vulnerable to street violence, and young black males are drastically overrepresented among the perpetrators of that violence. Yet these truths are no solace against the kind of alienation that comes of being ever the suspect. . . .

Over the years, I learned to smother the rage I felt at so often being taken for a criminal. Not to do so would surely have led to madness. I now take precautions to make myself less threatening. I move about with care, particularly late in the evening. I give a wide berth to nervous people on the subway platforms during the wee hours. . . . I have been calm and extremely congenial on those rare occasions when I've been pulled over by the police.

And on late-evening constitutionals, I employ what have proved to be excellent tension-reducing measures: I whistle melodies from Beethoven and Vivaldi and the more popular classical composers. Even steely New Yorkers hunching toward nighttime destinations seem to relax, and occasionally they even join in the tune. Virtually everybody seems to sense that a mugger wouldn't be warbling bright, sunny selections from Vivaldi's Four Seasons. It is my equivalent of the cowbell that hikers wear when they know they are in bear country.

Mead also argued that role-taking is possible because humans have a unique ability to use and respond to **symbols**. Symbols, discussed in Chapter 3 on culture, are human creations such as language and gestures that are used to represent objects or actions; they carry specific meaning for members of a culture. Symbols such as language allow us to give names to objects in the environment and to infuse those objects with meanings. Once the person learns to symbolically recognize objects in the environment, the self can be seen as one of those objects. In the most rudimentary sense, this starts with possessing a name that allows us to see our self as separate from other objects. Note that the connection of symbol and object is arbitrary, such as the name Al Gore and a specific human being. When we say that name, most listeners would immediately think of the same person, the former U.S. vice president, congressman and senator, 2000 presidential nominee, environmental activist, and Nobel Peace Prize winner.

Using symbols such as language is unique to humans. In the process of symbolic interaction, we take the actions of others and ourselves into account. Individuals may blame, encourage, praise, punish, or reward themselves. An example would be a basketball player missing the basket because the shot was poorly executed and thinking, *What did I do to miss that shot? I'm better than that!* Reflexive behavior, being able to look at oneself and one's behaviors as though from the outside looking in, includes the simple act of taking mental notes or mentally talking to one's self.

Thinking Sociologically

Brent Staples goes out of his way to reassure others that he is safe and harmless. What might be some other responses to this experience of having others assume one is dangerous and untrustworthy? How might one's sense of self be influenced by these responses of others? How is the looking-glass self at work in this scenario?

Parts of the Self

According to the symbolic interaction perspective, the self is composed of two distinct but related parts—dynamic parts in interplay with one another (Mead [1934] 1962). The most basic element of the self is what George Herbert Mead refers to as the **I**, the spontaneous, unpredictable, impulsive, and largely unorganized aspect of the self. These spontaneous, undirected impulses of the *I* initiate or give propulsion to behavior without considering the possible social consequences. We can see this at work in the "I want it now" behavior of a newborn baby or even a toddler. Cookie Monster on the children's television program *Sesame Street* illustrates the *I* in every child, gobbling cookies at every chance.

The *I* continues as part of the self throughout life, tempered by the social expectations that surround individuals. In stages, humans become increasingly influenced by interactions with others who instill society's rules. Children develop the ability to see the self as others see them (called role-taking) and critique the behavior of the *I*. Mead called this reflective capacity of the self the *Me*. The **Me** is the part of the self that has learned the rules of society through interaction and role-taking, and it controls the *I* and its desires. Just as the *I* initiates the act, the *Me* gives direction to the act. In a sense, the *Me* channels the impulses of the *I* in an acceptable manner according to societal rules and restraints yet meets the needs of the *I* as best it can. When we stop ourselves just before saying something and think to ourselves, *I'd better not say that*, it is our *Me* monitoring and controlling the *I*. Notice that the *Me* requires the ability to take the role of the other, to anticipate the other's reaction.

Stages in the Development of the Self

The process of developing a social self occurs gradually and in stages. Mead identified three critical stages—(1) the imitation stage, (2) the play stage, and (3) the game stage—each

Cookie Monster can be understood as a symbol of Mead's concept of the I—the spontaneous, impulsive aspect of the self that seeks only to meet one's own immediate needs and desires.

By imitating roles she has seen, this child is learning both adult roles and empathy with others. This kind of role enactment is an important prerequisite to the more complex interaction of playing a game with others.

A child who is playing mommy or daddy with a doll is playing at *taking the role* of parent. The child is directing activity toward the doll in a manner imitative of how the parents direct activity toward the child. Though trying to enact another role, that of a parent "going off to work," the child often does not know what to do when playing this role. Children can play only roles they have seen or are familiar with, and they do not know what the absent parent does at work when not in their presence. The point is that this "play" is actually extremely important "work" for children because they need to observe and imitate the relationships between roles to form the adult self (Handel, Cahill, and Elkin 2007).

Society and its rules are initially represented by **significant others**—parents, guardians, relatives, or siblings—whose primary and sustained interactions with the child are especially influential. That is why much of the play stage involves role-taking based on these significant people in the child's life. The child does not yet understand the complex relations and multiple role players in the social world outside the immediate family. Children may have a sense of how Mommy or Daddy sees them, but children are not yet able to comprehend how they are seen by the larger social world. Lack of role-taking ability is apparent when children say inappropriate things such as "Why are you so fat?"

In the **game stage**, the child learns to take the role of multiple others concurrently. Have you ever watched a team of young children play "tee ball" (a pre–Little League baseball game in which the children hit the ball from an upright rubber device that holds the ball), or have you observed a soccer league made up of 6-year-olds? If so, you have seen Mead's point illustrated vividly. In soccer (or football), 5- or 6-year-old children will not play their positions despite constant urging and cajoling by coaches. They all run after the ball, with little sense of their interdependent positions. Likewise,

of which requires the unique human ability to engage in role-taking. In the **imitation stage**, the child under 3 years of age is preparing for role-taking by observing others and imitating their behaviors, sounds, and gestures.

The **play stage** involves a kind of playacting in which the child is actually "playing at" a role. Listen to children who are 3 to 5 years old play together. You will notice that they spend most of their time telling each other what to do. One of them will say something like, "You be the mommy, and Jose can be the daddy, and Julie, you be the dog. Now you say 'good morning dear,' and I'll say, 'How did you sleep?' and Julie, you scratch at the door like you want out." They will talk about their little skit for 15 minutes and then enact it, with the actual enactment taking perhaps 1 minute. Small children mimic or imitate role-taking based on what they have seen.

Video Link 4.1
Watch how music can influence development.

Very young children who play soccer do not understand the role requirements of games. They all—including the goalie—want to chase after the ball. Learning to play positions is a critical step in socialization, for it requires a higher level of role-taking than children can do at the play stage.

a child in a game of tee ball may pick up a ball that has been hit, turn to the coach, and say, "Now what do I do with it?" Most still do not quite grasp throwing it to first base, and the first-base player may actually have left the base to run for the ball. It can be hilarious for everyone except the coach, as a hit that goes 7 feet turns into a home run because everyone is scrambling for the ball.

Prior to the game stage, the vision of the whole process is not possible. When the children enter the game stage at about age 7 or 8, they will be developmentally able to play the roles of various positions and enjoy a complex game. Each child learns what is expected and the interdependence of roles because they are then able to respond to the expectations of several people simultaneously (Hewitt 2007; Meltzer 1978). This allows the individual to coordinate his or her activity with others.

In moving from the play stage to the game stage, children's worlds expand from family and day care to neighborhood playmates, school, and other organizations. This process gradually builds up a composite of societal expectations—what Mead refers to as the **generalized other**. The child learns to internalize the expectations of society—the generalized other—over and above the expectations of any "significant others." Behavior comes to be governed by abstract rules ("no running outside of the baseline" or "no touching the soccer ball with your hands unless you are the goalie") rather than guidance from and emotional ties to a "significant other." Children become capable of moving into new social arenas such as school, organized sports, and (eventually) the workplace to function with others in both routine and novel interactions. Individuals are active in shaping their social contexts, the self, and the choices they make about the future.

Journal Article Link 4.1
Read more on socialization and sports.

An illustration of internalizing the generalized other into one's conception of self is the common human experience of feeling embarrassed. Blushing, a physiological response to feeling embarrassed, may occur when one has violated a social norm and is taking into account how others view that behavior. Making an inappropriate remark at a party or having another call undue attention to one's appearance can cause embarrassment. According to this role-taking view, we see ourselves as objects from the standpoint of others, and we judge ourselves accordingly. Very young children, however, do not feel embarrassment when they do things such as soiling their pants or making inappropriate comments because they have not incorporated the generalized other. They have not yet learned the perspective of others. The capacity to feel embarrassed is not only an indicator of having internalized the generalized other but also a uniquely human outcome of our role-taking ability (Hewitt 2007).

As we grow, we identify with new in-groups such as a neighborhood, a college sorority, or the military. We learn new ideas and expand our understanding. Some individuals ultimately come to think of themselves as part of the global human community. Thus, for many

individuals, the social world expands through socialization. However, some individuals never develop this expanded worldview, remaining narrowly confined and drawing lines between themselves and others who are different. Such narrow boundaries often result in prejudice against others.

Thinking Sociologically

Who are you? Write down 15 or 20 roles or attributes that describe who you are. How many of these items are characteristics associated with the *Me*—nouns such as *son, mother, student, employee*? Which of the items are traits or attributes—adjectives such as *shy, sensitive, lonely, selfish, vulnerable*? How do you think each of these was learned or incorporated into your conception of your *self*?

The Self and Connections to the Meso Level

In the preceding "Thinking Sociologically" exercise, we asked you to think about how you see yourself and what words you might use to portray yourself. If you were describing yourself for a group of people you did not know, we suspect that you would use mostly nouns or adjectives describing a status or a social position within the society: student, employee, athlete, violinist, daughter, sister, Canadian, Lutheran, and so forth. To a large extent, our sense of who we are is rooted in social positions that are part of organizations and institutions in the society (Kuhn 1964; Stryker 1980). This is a key point made by what is referred to as the Iowa School of symbolic interaction: Selfhood is relatively stable because we develop a core self—a stable inner sense of who we are regardless of the immediate setting in which we find ourselves. This core often centers on the most important social positions we hold in the larger structure of society. You may think of yourself as politically or religiously conservative or liberal, and that may influence the way you conduct yourself in a wide range of situations and social settings. It may shape your sexual behavior, the honesty with which you conduct business with others, and whether you are willing to cheat on an exam—even though you may not be around other people of your moral or political persuasion at the time (Turner 2003).

The Iowa School stresses that our identities are linked to our environments: institutions, organizations, and nations. Because of that, we have a vested interest in the stability of society and the survival of those organizations that mean a lot to us—whether it is the college where we are a student, the Greek house that we join, the faith community with which we affiliate, or the nation of which we are a citizen. We will voluntarily give up our resources—time, energy, money, or even our lives—to preserve our beliefs, way of life, institutions, or our nation. Thus, the self and meso-level structures are linked (Kuhn 1964; Stryker 1980, 2000; Stryker and Stratham 1985; Turner 2003).

Other symbolic interactionists belong to the Chicago School, which emphasizes the role of the *I* and focuses on individuals' involvement in their own development and their ability to create their world. The Iowa School places somewhat more emphasis on the *Me*—on the role of others and the external social environment in shaping us (Carrothers and Benson 2003). While we will report on both schools, there is more in this book on the Chicago school, which has become the more dominant voice of symbolic interactionism.

Socialization Throughout the Life Cycle

The ceremony begins with an introduction of the 6-week-old baby, followed by the rituals surrounding the naming and welcoming of the newcomer into his tribe in Nigeria, Africa. By 6 weeks, the baby is considered likely to survive and thus incorporated into the group. Markers such as the naming ceremony point to movement from one stage to the next in the socialization process: birth, naming ceremonies or christenings, starting school at age 5 or 6, rites of passage to mark puberty, obtaining a driver's license at about age 16, becoming eligible for military draft, being able to vote at age 18, and retirement. Most social scientists emphasize the importance of rites of passage—celebrations or public recognitions when individuals shift from one status to another. The importance of this shift resides in how others come to perceive the individual differently, the different expectations that others hold for the person, and changes in how the person sees himself or herself.

Socialization is a lifelong process with many small and large passages. Infants begin the socialization process at birth. In childhood, one rite of passage is a child's first day at school—entrance into the meso-level institution of education. This turning point marks a child's entry into the larger world. The standards of performance are now defined by the child's teachers, peers, friends, and others outside the home. Adolescence is an important stage in Western industrial and postindustrial societies, but this stage is far from universal. Indeed, it is largely an invention of complex societies over the past two centuries, characterized by extensive periods of formal education and dependency on parents (Papalia, Olds, and Feldman 2006). Adolescence is, in a sense, a structurally produced mass identity crisis because Western societies lack clear rites of passage for adolescents. Teens come to view themselves as

Video Link 4.2
Watch how teen socialization and advertising are related.

Children learn many things in school, but one of the first is to master rules such as standing in lines.

a separate and distinct group with their own culture, slang vocabulary, clothing styles, and opinions about appropriate sexual behavior and forms of recreation.

Most of our adult years are spent in work and home life, including marriage and parenting roles. It is not surprising, then, that graduation from one's final alma mater (whether it be high school, college, or graduate school), marriage, and acceptance of one's first full-time job are rites of passage into adulthood in modern societies. Media hype about the aging of the baby boomer generation increases as the number of citizens in the United States older than 65 grows (just over 12% in 2008). The average life expectancy in 1929 was 57 years. Today, it is 78.1 years, with 50 countries out of 224 having higher average life expectancies than the United States (Landau 2009).

Even the retired and elderly members of society are constantly undergoing socialization and resocialization and developing their sense of self. The type of society influences the socialization experience of the elderly and how they carry out their roles, as well as their status in society. Consider the changes that have taken place in the lifetimes of those born before 1945, as described by one group of elders:

If you were born before 1945: We were born before television, before polio shots, frozen foods, Xerox, plastic contact lenses, Frisbees and the Pill. We were born before credit cards, split atoms, laser beams and ballpoint pens; before pantyhose, dishwashers, clothes dryers, electric blankets, air conditioners in our homes, drip-dry clothes and before man walked on the moon. . . . We were before house husbands, gay rights, computer dating, dual careers and commuter marriages. We were before day care centers, group therapy and nursing homes. We never heard of FM radio, tape decks, electric typewriters, artificial hearts, word processors, yogurt, and guys wearing earrings. For us time sharing means togetherness—not computers and condominiums. A chip meant a piece of wood, hardware meant hardware and software wasn't even a word. . . . smoking was fashionable, grass was mowed, coke was a cold drink and pot was something you cooked in. And we were the last generation that was so dumb as to think that you needed a husband to have a baby.

Oh my, how the world has changed! (Grandpa Junior 2006)

Thinking Sociologically

What are the rites of passage from adolescence into adulthood in your family and community? Have you experienced any ambiguity in roles during this transition? Why do some adolescents engage in defiant acts against adults?

The elderly are vitally important to the ongoing group in more settled agricultural societies. They are the founts of wisdom and carry group knowledge, experiences, and traditions that are valued in societies where little change takes place. In industrial and postindustrial countries, the number of the elderly is growing rapidly as medical science keeps people alive longer, diets improve, and diseases are brought under control. Yet in modern systems, social participation by the elderly often drops after retirement. Retirement is a rite of passage to a new status, like that of marriage or parenthood, for which there is little preparation. As a result, retired people sometimes feel a sense of uselessness when they abruptly lose their occupational status. Yet retirees in Western societies generally have 20 or more years of life yet to live. Many retirees develop hobbies, enjoy sports, or have new jobs they can pursue.

Dying is the final stage of life (Kübler-Ross 1997). Death holds different meanings in different cultures: passing into another life, a time of judgment, a waiting for rebirth, or a void and nothingness. In some religious groups, people work hard or do good deeds because they believe that they will be rewarded in an afterlife or with rebirth to a better status in the next life on earth. Thus, beliefs about the meaning of death can affect how people live their lives and how they cope with dying and death.

A policy issue being debated in many countries is physician-assisted suicide, sometimes called euthanasia,

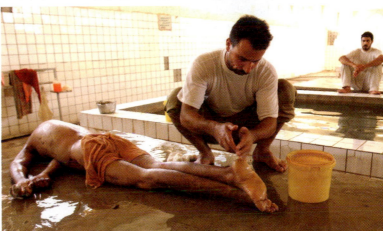

Death rituals differ depending on the culture and religion of the group. The top photo shows a body being cremated by the holy Ganges River in India to release the soul from earthly existence. The closest relative lights the funeral pyre. The middle photo shows the Muslim tradition of washing and wrapping the dead before burial in Najaf, Iraq. At the bottom, a U.S. Honor Guard carries a casket with the remains of U.S. Air Force personnel at Arlington National Cemetery.

or "good death." Currently, the Netherlands permits the practice but with many safeguards. Most U.S. states prohibit the practice under specific physician-assisted suicide laws or general homicide laws (Darr 2007; Nightingale Alliance 2007), although the citizens of Oregon voted in 1994 on measures to allow euthanasia and voted again to uphold this law (Lee and Werth 2000; Nightingale Alliance 2007), and several other states have approved bills (Robinson 2007). These measures are being challenged in courts, but at this time, the laws still stand. So how you die—certainly an intensely personal experience—may be decided by a medical facility, an agency, or a decision-making body of the federal government. Even death involves decisions by macro-level social structures.

Each stage of the life cycle involves socialization into new roles in the social world. Many social scientists have studied these developmental stages and contributed insights into what happens at each stage (Clausen 1986; Erikson 1950; Freud [1923] 1960; Gilligan 1982; Handel et al. 2007; Kohlberg 1971; Papalia et al. 2006; Piaget 1989). Although examination of these valuable theories is beyond the scope of this chapter, developmental theorists have detailed stages in the growth process.

Death ends the lifelong process of socialization, a process of learning social rules and roles and adjusting to them. When the individual is gone, society continues. New members are born, are socialized into the social world, pass through roles once held by others, and eventually give up those roles to younger members. Cultures provide guidelines for each new generation to follow, and except for the changes each generation brings to society, the social world perpetuates itself and outlives the individuals who populate it.

Thinking Sociologically

How were you socialized to view death and dying? What have you learned in your family about how to cope with death?

The Process of Resocialization

If you have experienced life in the military, a boarding school, a convent, a mental facility, or a prison or had a major transition in your life such as divorce or the death of a spouse or child, you have experienced resocialization. **Resocialization** is the process of shedding one or more positions and taking on others. It involves changing from established patterns learned earlier in life to new ones suitable to the newly acquired status (Goffman 1961). Resocialization may take place in a

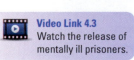
Video Link 4.3
Watch the release of mentally ill prisoners.

total institution in which a group of people are bureaucratically processed, physically isolated from the outside world, and scheduled for all activities. These include prisons, mental hospitals, monasteries, concentration camps, boarding schools, and military barracks. Bureaucratic regimentation and the manipulation of residents for the convenience of the staff is part of the routine (Goffman 1961).

We often associate resocialization with major changes in adult life—divorce, retirement, and widowhood. Following a divorce, one must adjust to raising children alone, living alone, loneliness, and possible financial problems. One divorcee of 3 years told the author, "There are many things to commend the single life, but I still have not adjusted to eating alone and cooking for myself. But worse than that are Sunday afternoons. That is the loneliest time."

Sometimes, resocialization describes individuals' attempts to adjust to new statuses and roles, such as widowhood. In other cases, individuals are forced into resocialization to correct or reform behaviors that are defined as undesirable or deviant. Prison rehabilitation programs provide one example. However, research suggests that the difficulty in resocializing prisoners is rooted in the nature of the prison environment itself. Prisons are often coercive and violent environments, which may not provide the social supports necessary for bringing about change in a person's attitudes and behaviors.

Although resocialization is the goal of self-help groups such as Alcoholics Anonymous, Gamblers Anonymous, Parents Anonymous, drug rehabilitation groups, and weight loss groups, relapse is a common problem among participants. These groups aim to substitute new behaviors and norms for old undesirable ones, but the process of undoing socialization and achieving resocialization is difficult. Some applied sociologists work on projects to resocialize clients, as shown in the next "Applied Sociologist at Work" feature. Jeffrey Breese's work focuses on role transitions and exits for adults.

There are multiple individuals, groups, and institutions involved in the socialization process. These socialization forces are referred to as agents of socialization.

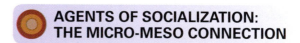

AGENTS OF SOCIALIZATION: THE MICRO-MESO CONNECTION

Agents of socialization are the transmitters of culture—the people, organizations, and institutions that teach us how to thrive in our social world. Agents are the mechanism by which the self learns the values, beliefs, and behaviors of the culture. Agents of socialization help new members find their place, just as they prepare older members for new responsibilities in society. At the micro level, one's family, the peer group, and local groups and organizations help people know what is expected of them. At the meso level, formal sources of learning—education, religion, politics,

The Applied Sociologist at Work— Jeffrey Breese

Role Exit and Resocialization: Researching Adults in the Midst of Change

Individuals constantly wrestle with life events that force them to think and rethink how they define themselves. Sociologists who focus on adult life transitions offer an understanding of the process of making role changes in the lifelong process of socialization. My own research on adult nontraditional women students in the midst of career and personal transitions serves to assist counselors who work with these individuals. In fact, counselors are becoming increasingly interested in life role counseling as a means of assisting clients to cope with changes.

Role exit theory is the sociological ideas that help explain events and changes in adult life. These "exits" can be the result of an act of nature (such as death of a spouse), expulsion by a group (being excommunicated by your church), involuntary action (termination from a job), or voluntary (a chosen career change or divorce). Often, a combination of factors result in a role exit. The social significance of this process is that you literally "exit" a role, yet that past part of your identity continues on into the present and could continue to impact decisions you make, how you approach daily work, and how others perceive and interact with you.

Helen Rose Ebaugh's book (1988), *Becoming an Ex: The Process of Role Exit,* laid the foundation for research into this process by examining groups of individuals undergoing key life-changing events. She considered doctors, teachers, and air traffic controllers who made career changes; widowers, divorcees, and mothers without custody, each wrestling with family life transitions; and ex-nuns who decided to leave their religious lifestyle. Ebaugh's research demonstrates that studying the process of role exit has informative elements for sociology as well as for professionals in related helping professions.

Sociologists who study socialization issues appreciate the complexity of life transitions and role exits. As an example, adult women students now have more options when it comes to selecting a major for study. Although some traditional perceptions of "women's work" remain, many of our society's preconceived notions of what women can do and should do have been washed away, opening more opportunities. Clinical sociologists, who often partner with social workers and professional counselors, can offer professional guidance to individuals making life changes. They offer insights into the complex nature of role transitions. Does the individual have the support of others with this life transition? Is the event a voluntary or involuntary change? Is an individual undergoing the change alone (fired from a job) or as part of a much larger group (the entire factory was shut down)? Adult life transitions, while experienced by an individual, must be understood in the larger cultural context. Sociologists studying career changes, divorce trends, and educational issues look at the bigger picture in assisting the individuals exiting roles that are central to their identity.

Note: Jeffrey Breese is an associate professor of sociology and associate dean of the School of Education and Human Services at Marymount University. He received his doctorate from The University of Akron.

economics, health—and other informal sources of learning such as the media and books are all agents that contribute to socialization. They transmit information to children and to adults throughout people's lives.

Thinking Sociologically

As you read this section, make a list of the socializing agents discussed in these pages. Indicate two or three central messages each agent of socialization tries to instill in people. Consider which agents are micro, meso, and macro agents. Are there different kinds of messages at each level? Do any of them conflict? If so, why, and what are the problems that are caused?

In early childhood, the family acts as the primary agent of socialization, passing on messages about respect for property, authority, and neatness, for example (Handel et al. 2007). Peer groups are also important, especially during the teenage years. Some writers even argue that the peer group is most important in the socialization process of children and teens (Aseltine 1995; Harris 2009). Each agent has its own functions or purposes and is important at different stages of the life cycle, but meso-level institutions play a more active role as one matures. For example, schools and religious bodies become more involved in socialization as children become 6 years old and older compared with when they were preschool age. For us, the authors of this book, other members of the American Sociological Association serve as "significant others" and shape our sense of appropriate behavior for sociologists and professors.

The primary socialization unit for young children is the family, but as they become teenagers, peers become increasingly important as a reference group, shaping the norms, values, and attitudes of adolescents and young adults.

bombardment is a particularly influential part of socialization at young ages.

This distinction between formal, intentional socialization and informal, unplanned socialization has important implications for the kinds of messages that are presented and for how such messages are received.

Thinking Sociologically

What confusion might be created for children when the formal and informal agents of socialization provide different messages about values or acceptable behaviors? Is this contradiction something that we should be concerned about? Why or why not?

Families: Micro-Level Socializing Agents

One way in which families teach children what is right and wrong is through rewards and punishments, called sanctions. Children who lie to their parents may receive a verbal reprimand or a slap on the hand, be sent to their rooms, have "time out," or receive a beating, depending on differences in child-rearing patterns. These are examples of negative sanctions. Conversely, children may be rewarded for good behavior with a smile, praise, a cookie, or a special event. These are examples of positive sanctions. The number and types of sanctions dispensed in the family shape the socialization process, including development of the self and the perceptions we have of who we are and even whether we are good and clever or bad and stupid. Note that family influence varies from one culture to another.

In Japan, the mother is a key agent in the process of turning a newborn into a member of the group, passing on the strong group standards and expectations of family, neighbors, community, and society through the use of language with emotional meaning. The child learns the importance of depending on the group and therefore fears being cast out. The need to belong creates pressure to conform to expectations, and the use of threats and fear of shame help socialize children into Japanese ways (Hendry 1987; Holloway 2001). Nonconformity is a source of shame in Japan. The resulting ridicule is a powerful means of social control. In some cases, the outcast is physically punished by peers. Thus, to bring shame on oneself or the family is to be avoided. In the most extreme cases, young people have committed suicide because they did not conform to group expectations and felt profoundly ashamed as a result. The interaction of family and formal education in Japan is explored in more detail in the next "Sociology Around the World" (see page 123).

The next "Sociology in Our Social World" discusses how we know about socialization in schools by exploring an important and widely cited research project. Note what kind of data are viewed as legitimate evidence for understanding gender socialization.

Lessons from one agent of socialization generally complement those of other agents. Parents work at home to support what school and religion teach. However, at times, agents provide conflicting lessons. For example, family and faith communities often give teens messages that conflict with those of peer groups regarding sexual activity and drug use. This is an example of mixed messages given by formal and informal agents.

For **formal agents**, socialization is the stated goal. Formal agents usually have some official or legal responsibility for instructing individuals. A primary goal of families is to teach children to speak and to learn proper behavior. In addition, school teachers educate by giving formal instruction, and religious training provides moral instruction. (These formal agents of socialization will be discussed in Chapters 10 to 12.)

Informal agents do not have the express purpose of socialization, but they function as unofficial forces that shape values, beliefs, and behaviors. For example, the media, books, the Internet, and advertisements bring us continuous messages even though their primary purpose is not socialization but entertainment or selling products. Children watch countless advertisements on television, many with messages about what is good and fun to eat and how to be more attractive, more appealing, smarter, and a better person through the consumption of products. This

Sociology in Our Social World

Gender Socialization in American Public Schools

Video Link 4.4
Watch children express gender roles.

Pause for a moment as you pass a school yard, and observe the children at play. Children's behavior on the school playground translates into a powerful agent of gender socialization in a world that is very complex. Consider the evidence reported in the ethnographic study of Barrie Thorne (1993), recounted in her award-winning book, *Gender Play*.

Many people assume that gender differences are natural and that we are "born that way." In contrast, Thorne provides evidence that gender differences are social constructions, influenced by the setting, the players involved in the situation, and the control people have over the situation.

As an astute observer and researcher, Thorne suspected that girls and boys have complex relations that play out in the classroom and school yard. She chose the playground as the focus of her observation on the separate worlds of girls and boys (Thorne 1993:12).

Through systematic participant observation, she found that kids and adults play an active role in defining and shaping gender expectations through the collective practices of forming lines, choosing seats, teasing, gossiping, and participating in selected activities. Thorne (1993) used two schools for her research. One school was in a small city on the coast of California and the other on the outskirts of a large city in Michigan. Both schools had about 400 students, mostly from working-class backgrounds. Most students were White, with 12% to 14% Latino and 5% African American. Thorne entered the world of the children, sometimes sitting apart on the playground taking notes, sometimes participating in their activities, such as eating, and talking with them in the lunchroom. In each setting, she recorded her observations and experiences. For example, she noted what children call themselves and how they think of themselves. She was intrigued by the reference to the opposite sex—a term that stresses difference and opposition rather than similarity and the sense of "we." Thorne was struck by the active meaning construction involved as the children gained a notion of "normal" gender behavior. The real focus of her work is in taking seriously how children themselves make sense of sex differences.

Previous studies concluded that boys tend to interact in larger, more age-heterogeneous groups and in more rough-and-tumble play and physical fighting. Thorne also found that boys' play involves a much larger portion of the playground, and their play space was generally farther from the building, making them less subject to monitoring and sanctioning. Boys not only used roughly 90% of the playground, they would also often run "sneak invasions" into the girls' space to take things belonging to the girls. Many boys felt that they had a right to the geographical space that was occupied by girls. Girls played close to the buildings in much smaller areas and rarely ventured into the boys' area.

Girls' play tended to be characterized by cooperation and turn taking. They had more intense and exclusive friendships, which took shape around keeping and telling secrets, shifting alliances, and indirect ways of expressing disagreement. Instead of direct commands, girls more often used words such as "let's" or "we gotta" (Thorne 1993). However, Thorne found that these notions of "separate girls' and boys' worlds" used in most previous studies miss the subtleties of race, class, and other factors in the situation.

In follow-up, Valerie Ann Moore (2001) examined children at a summer day camp. Like Thorne, she watched the children play and interact with one another. Moore found that the children also use play to construct the meaning of race and age. All the boys in the camp showed their age by defying the adults' rules, which unified them across racial and age boundaries. The girls at the camp, on the other hand, were much more likely to separate by age and race when interacting with other campers. Narratives of romance were likely to break the physical boundaries among older campers (Moore 2001). These romances, however, emphasize gender differences. The camp counselors reinforced this difference by constantly creating and maintaining gender boundaries to prohibit romances from forming between the teens.

The major contribution of these two studies is to alert us to the complexity of the gender socialization process, helping us see the extent to which children are active agents creating their own definitions of social relations, not just short automatons who enact adult notions of what gender means.

Japanese fathers and their sons eat lunch during a festival. While mothers are the key agents of socialization in Japan, fathers also have a role, especially during special events in the life of the child.

A Japanese mother helps her son at Heian Shinto Shrine during Shichi-go-san Matsuri, also called 7–5–3 Festival, a celebration with prayers of long life for children aged three to seven.

In the United States, most parents value friendliness, cooperation, orientation toward achievement, social competence, responsibility, and independence as qualities their children should learn, in contrast to the values of conformity and fitting into the group espoused in Japan. However, subcultural values and socialization practices may differ within the diverse groups in the U.S. population. Conceptions of what makes a "good person" or a "good citizen" and different goals of socialization bring about differences in the process of socialization around the world.

In addition, the number of children in a family and the placement of each child in the family structure can influence the unique socialization experience of the child. In large families, parents typically have less time with each additional child. Where the child falls in the hierarchy of siblings can also influence the development of the self. In fact, birth order is a better predictor of social attitudes than race, class, or gender, according to some studies (Benokraitis 2004; Freese et al. 1999), and firstborns are typically the highest achievers ("First Born" 2008; Paulhus, Trapnell, and Chen 1999). Younger children may be socialized by older siblings as much as by parents, and older siblings often serve as models that younger children want to emulate.

Social Class: Meso-Level Socialization

Our educational level, our occupation, the house we live in, what we choose to do in our leisure time, the foods we eat, and our religious and political beliefs are just a few aspects of our lives that are affected by socialization. Applying what we know from sociological research, the evidence strongly suggests that socialization varies by **social class**, or the wealth, power, and prestige rankings that individuals hold in society (Ellison, Bartkowski, and Segal 1996). Meso-level patterns of distribution of resources affect who we become. For example, upper-middle-class and middle-class parents in the United States usually have above-average education and managerial or professional jobs. They tend to pass on to their children the skills and values necessary to succeed in this social class subculture. Autonomy, creativity, self-direction (the ability to make decisions and take the initiative), responsibility, curiosity, and consideration of others are especially important for middle-class success (Kohn 1989). If the child misbehaves, for example, middle-class parents typically analyze the child's reasons for misbehaving, and punishment is related to these reasons. Sanctions often involve instilling guilt and denying privileges.

Working-class parents tend to pass on to children their cultural values of respect for authority and conformity to rules, lessons that will be useful if the children also have blue-collar jobs (Kohn 1989). Immediate punishment with no questions asked if a rule is violated functions to prepare children for positions in which obedience to rules is

Sociology Around the World

Socialization in Japan: The Family and Early Schooling

By Wendy Ng

Each of our families prepares us through the socialization process for the culture we are entering. How families carry out this process differs around the world, just as the cultures for which they are preparing their children differ. Here we consider meso-level family and early schooling in Japanese socialization.

The family is one of the most important socializing influences in Japan. The basis of the family unit in Japan is called the *ie* (pronounced ee-ay). Traditionally, it is made up of blood relatives who reside in the same household, as well as ancestors and descendents not yet born. Thus, family in Japan goes beyond those who belong to the immediate nuclear grouping and includes a broader array of individuals. Compared with the past, the modern *ie* in Japan relies more on the nuclear and living extended family and serves as the major reference group that socializes individuals within the family. Thus, family members within the *ie* are responsible for teaching individuals their family roles, values, and norms within the culture.

A unique feature of interdependence that is found within the family structure is that of *amae* (ah-may), which roughly translated means passive love but is often referred to as an emotional bond usually held between mother and child. Through this relationship, children are socialized to understand that they are an important part of the family, and they also learn that parents are to be respected and obeyed as the adults within the family. Although this appears hierarchical, the emotional bond of *amae* sets up a relationship of interdependency between child and parent for their lifetime. As children grow into adulthood, they will take care of their parents in the way that they were taken care of as children. This bond of loyalty between parent and child within the family structure is translated into other social structures outside the family. For example, in a business organization, there is a similar expectation of group loyalty.

In terms of early childhood socialization, Japanese children learn the distinction between two related, yet distinct concepts: *uchi* (inside) and *soto* (outside). These concepts apply to material distinctions of clean and unclean spaces. In behavior, this means taking one's shoes off outside the house because the inside is clean and the outside is unclean. In Japanese households, the bathroom has similar clean and unclean designations. The bath is "clean" and the toilet, used to dispose of bodily wastes, is "unclean." Thus, one would never wear the same shoes or slippers in the toilet room as the bathroom because that would be mixing clean and unclean elements.

Within the family, immediate members are "insiders" and other people are "outsiders." Children learn that the family is a safe and secure environment where the emphasis is on harmony among the various family members. Interactions between individuals stress cooperation, and interpersonal disputes are avoided. If a disagreement happens, children are taught to apologize to one another. Reciprocity is yet another behavior that is emphasized within the family. Children are taught to put themselves in the role of the other person and to think of the consequences of their behavior before acting out. This type of role behavior suggests that harmony between and among family members is important and sets the foundation for the child's educational socialization.

Whereas the family serves as the central socializing force when children are very young, as they grow, the educational system continues to socialize children through group interaction and learning. When children enter kindergarten they become familiar with participating in a social group with peers. The Japanese kindergarten system emphasizes group equality among children and thus socializes children to be loyal to their classmates and group. Other children now form their new *uchi* or "inside" associations and friendships. The emphasis on group over individual identities is accomplished through wearing identical uniforms or smocks, having similar educational tools for all students, and having children take turns in different duties in the classroom. For example, the responsibility of passing out paper in the classroom, or food at lunchtime, are rotated among all the children in the classroom. Thus, cooperation and group participation becomes an important defining feature of kindergarten socialization.

At first glance, the emphasis on equality among individuals in the kindergarten classroom setting might seem to conflict with the emphasis on hierarchical authority present in much of Japanese society. In fact, the emphasis on group socializing helps to encourage a sense of belonging and group identity that works well within hierarchical authority structures. By learning these behaviors at a young age, the children learn that they are individuals within a larger group, and that their actions reflect not only on themselves but also on their family, school, or whatever social group they belong to as adults.

important to success. They are expected to be neat, clean, well-mannered, honest, and obedient students (MacLeod 1995). Socialization experiences for boys and girls are often different, following traditional gender-role expectations. Moreover, these differences in behavior across social classes and parenting styles are apparent cross-culturally as well (Leung, Lau, and Lam 1998).

What conclusions can we draw from these studies? Members of each class are socializing their children to be successful in their social class and to meet expectations for adults of that class. Schools, like families, participate in this process. Although the extent to which schools create or limit opportunities for class mobility is debated, what is clear is that children's social class position on entering school has an effect on the socialization experiences they have in school (Ballantine and Hammack 2009). Families and schools socialize children to adapt to the settings in which they grow up and are likely to live.

Electronic Media: Meso-Level Agents Within the Home

Television and computers are important informal agents of socialization. In developed countries, there is scarcely a home without a television set, and nearly 75% of homes had computers and Internet access by 2004 ("U.S. Broadband Penetration" 2004).

Video Link 4.5
Watch an analysis of the Internet on children's lives.

Researchers have collected nearly five decades of information on how television has become a way of life in homes. By the time an average child in the United States reaches age 18, he or she will have spent more time watching television than any other single activity besides sleeping. On average, children between ages 8 and 18 spend 3 hours a day watching television, 1 hour and 11 minutes watching videos or DVDs, 1 hour and 44 minutes with audio media, 1 hour using computers, and 49 minutes playing video games, with a total media exposure in a typical day of 8 hours and 33 minutes. The "Engaging Sociology" below shows the total media exposure of children by several variables (Kaiser Family Foundation 2005a). Examine this issue in more depth by answering the questions following Table 4.2.

This father passes on a love for the piano to his young son. Because of the social class of this father, his son is likely to receive many messages about creativity, curiosity, and self-direction.

Engaging Sociology

Media Exposure and Socialization

Examine Table 4.2 and respond to the questions below.

Table 4.2 **Total Media Exposure (average hours per day)**		
		Hours per Day
Age	8–10 years old	8:05
	11–14 years old	8:41
	15–18 years old	8:44
Gender	Boys	8:38
	Girls	8:27
Race	White	7:58
	Black	10:10
	Hispanic	8:52
Parent education	High school or less	8:30
	Some college	8:02
	College graduate	8:55
Income	Less than $35,000	8:40
	$35,000 to $50,000	8:28
	More than $50,000	8:34

Questions:

1. Considering the data in Table 4.2, how would you describe television-watching patterns among different groups?

2. How might television watching affect other aspects of socialization of children?

3. How does this table reflect or differ from your family's viewing patterns?

4. Do your conclusions cause any concerns about our society? Why or why not?

Source: Kaiser Family Foundation (2005).

Between the ages of 2 and 8, children in the United States spend an average of half an hour a day using computers, including computer use at school. Children ages 8 and older spend more than an hour and a half each day on computers: 22% of this time is spent doing schoolwork; 33% is spent on the Internet chatting, surfing the Web, or sending e-mail; and 26% is spent playing games (National Parent Information Network 2000). This means that the moguls of the mass media—a meso-level social system—are able to influence socialization within the most intimate of environments. "Children [in the U.S.] use computers at very young ages—21 percent of children 2 years and younger, 58 percent of 3- to 4-year-olds, and 77 percent of 5- to 6-year-olds" (National Science Foundation 2005:1); 74.1% of the U.S. population use the Internet (Internet World Statistics 2009).

A serious concern related to socialization centers around the messages children receive from television and computer games, along with the behavioral effects of these messages. There is ample evidence that children are affected in negative ways from excessive television viewing, especially television violence (National Science Foundation 2005), but a direct causal link between television viewing and behavior is difficult to establish. Researchers know, however, that parents who play an active role in helping children understand the content of television shows can have a powerful effect on mitigating television's negative impacts and enhancing the positive aspects of television shows. The television-viewing habits of parents—length of viewing time, types of shows watched, times of day—can also influence how their children respond to television.

Perhaps the most important aspect of television and computers is something that we do not fully understand but that has frightening potential. For the first time in human history, we have powerful agents of socialization in the home from a child's birth onward. Time spent watching television or playing computer games means less time spent engaging in interaction with caregivers and peers. Intimate family bonds formed of affection and meaningful interaction are being altered by the dominant presence of electronic media in the home. Television and computer games augment, and potentially compete with, the family as a socializing agent. Those who control the flood of mass media messages received by children may have interests and concerns that are very much at odds with those of parents.

We can conclude that a significant part of the informal socialization process occurs with the assistance of electronic equipment that shares the home with parents and siblings and that commands a significant portion of a child's time and attention. The "Sociology in Our Social World" on pages 126–127 compares formal socialization in schools with informal socialization through television and the Internet.

With globalization, global knowledge and understanding also become important parts of school curricula and media coverage; we move next to a discussion of some of the national and global processes that influence socialization.

Elderly people learn how to use computers in Shanghai, China. Keeping up with the rapid pace of change—especially in technology—is sometimes a challenge for seniors in postindustrial societies. Their grandchildren may know more than they do about technology.

Thinking Sociologically

What agents of socialization in addition to family, social class, and electronic media are important in teaching us our roles, norms, values, and beliefs? What is the impact, for example, of friendship networks or peer groups?

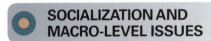

SOCIALIZATION AND MACRO-LEVEL ISSUES

Heterogeneous Societies and Sense of Self Versus "Other"

Immigration patterns and ethnic conflicts around the world have resulted in a fairly new phenomenon: transnationalism. **Transnationalism** involves an individual or a family that has national loyalty to more than one country (Levitt 2001). Often, it occurs after migration of war refugees, when one's roots lie in the country of origin and many of one's close family members continue to live there. Consider children raised in war-torn countries. In the Palestinian territories, especially Gaza, and in Israeli settlements along the border, children grow up with fear and hatred, major influences on their socialization. Some war refugees spend childhoods in refugee camps and may never return to their countries.

For people experiencing transnationalism, there are conflicting messages about culturally appropriate behaviors and

Sociology in Our Social World

Formal and Informal Agents of Socialization: A Comparison of Schooling, Television, and the Internet

By Alan McEvoy and Laurie McCloud

Schooling, television, and the Internet share a basic characteristic: All are purveyors of messages to young people. Despite this similarity, however, there are also many differences. Schools are formal agents of socialization with the expressed purpose of socializing the young. Television and the Internet are informal agents of socialization because their goals are entertaining, selling products, and increasing consumerism. Socialization is a secondary result.

Schools	Television	Internet
Schooling is formal and bureaucratic; it takes place in specially designed buildings.	TV viewing generally takes place in the informal setting of one's home.	The majority of Internet users have home access but others use the Internet in institutional settings such as work and school.
Acquisition of information requires obeying certain rules (e.g., no eating, no talking, no running around).	There are often no rules for watching TV, although parents may put limits on how much time can be spent viewing or what shows can be watched.	There are no rules for Internet viewing, except those imposed by parents. Listserv applications and blogs sometimes develop and impose their own rules of civility. The issue of rules for civil use is an emerging one in this new medium, especially with e-mail.
School is structured around a sequential, age-appropriate curriculum that intends to inform and to build on skills.	TV has no structured curriculum but a random content (channel surfing), which is usually designed to entertain. Watching TV requires no special skills.	The Internet has random content, and it can be user-provided, which means a large variety of information and opinions is represented. Users need access and some skills.
Students are a captive audience, required to attend school for specified periods (usually 8 A.M. to 3 P.M., excluding weekends and certain holidays).	Watching TV is voluntary. Programs are available 24 hours per day throughout the year.	Internet use is voluntary. Web sites are available 24 hours a day throughout the year.
There is a power imbalance between teachers and students; students have a role imposed on them and have little control over the requirements of that role. Students do not directly control the flow of information from teachers.	There are no role requirements imposed on the viewer from the TV. The viewer has power to control the flow of information with the on/off switch and choice of channels.	Many Web sites are interactive or have user content. Most users passively view content. Users can close Web browsers and change pages at will.

Schools	Television	Internet
Schools do not provide information to students for commercial purposes (no profit motive).	TV messages are generally provided to viewers for commercial purposes (excepting public TV).	Commercial Web site messages are generally provided to viewers to generate profit.
Students are grouped in classes by age or ability, and groups of students (15 to 30) together receive instruction.	Viewers watch TV individually or in small groups, and millions may receive the same message.	Internet users typically are individuals, though they may be communicating with people geographically very distant from themselves.
Face-to-face interaction defines the relationship between students and teachers and among students, as each takes the other into account throughout the interaction. Face-to-face interaction allows for mutual influence.	Vicarious interaction with an electronic image (rather than a live person) defines the relationship between viewers and media personalities. Viewers are not able to interact directly with the millions of other people receiving the same messages, hence no mutual influence.	Web sites vary in the ability to interact with the content provider. No face-to-face interaction occurs. Some sites allow users to post comments or edit content. Many sites allow only passive viewing of shared information.
Influence of schooling starts when the child begins school (about age 5).	The influence of TV begins in infancy when children become new members of the family, and the impact of TV is significant even before a child has entered school.	Many individuals are introduced to the Internet at a young age, and the Web appears to have a growing influence throughout the life course.

Journal Article Link 4.2
Read more on cultural socialization.

the obligations of loyalty to family and nation. However, one need not migrate to another country to experience global pressures. The Internet and cell phones have increasingly created a sense of connectedness to other parts of the world and an awareness of global interdependencies (Brier 2004; Roach 2004). Some commentators have even suggested that the Internet is a threat to the nation-state as it allows individuals to maintain traditions and loyalties to relatives and friends in more than one country (Drori 2006). Ideas of social justice or progress in many parts of the world are shaped not just by the government that rules the country but by international human rights organizations and ideas that are obtained from media that cross borders, such as the World Wide Web.

Access to international information and friendships across borders and boundaries are increasingly possible as more people have access to the Internet. Map 4.1 (page 128) on Internet use around the world, illustrates not only variability of access but also how widespread this access is becoming. One interesting question is how access or lack of access will influence the strength of "we" versus "they" feelings.

At a time when people lived in isolated rural communities and did not interact with those unlike themselves, there was little price to pay for being bigoted or chauvinistic toward those who were different. However, we now live in a global village where we or our businesses will likely interact

with very different people in a competitive environment. If we hold people in low regard because they are unlike us or because we think they are destined for hell because of their spiritual beliefs, there may be a high cost for this alienation toward those who are not like us. Among other problems, terrorism is fermented when people feel alienated. Therefore, diversity training and cultural sensitivity to those "others" has become an economic and political issue.

The reality is that children in the 21st century are being socialized to live in a globalized world. Increasingly, children around the world are learning multiple languages to enhance their ability to communicate with others. Some college campuses require experiences abroad as part of the standard curriculum because faculty members and administrators feel that a global perspective is essential in our world today and part of a college education. Global sensitivity and tolerance of those who were once considered "alien" has become a core element of our day (Robertson 1992; Schaeffer 2003; Snarr and Snarr 2008).

Sometimes, global events can cause a different turn: away from tolerance and toward defensive isolation. When 19 young men from Saudi Arabia and other Middle Eastern countries crashed planes into the World Trade Center in New York City and into the Pentagon in Washington, D.C., the United States was shocked and became mobilized to defend itself and its borders. The messages within schools and from the government suddenly took a more patriotic

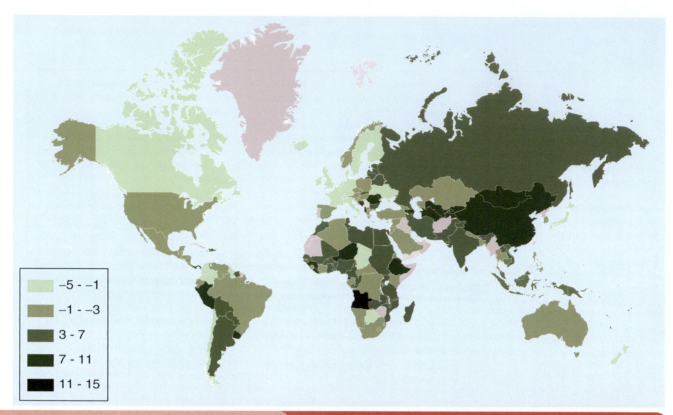

Map 4.1   Internet Users per 100 People in 2005

Source: World Bank.

Legend:
- −5 - −1
- −1 - −3
- 3 - 7
- 7 - 11
- 11 - 15

turn. So this event and other terrorist acts, clearly tragedies rooted in global political conflicts, can intensify the boundaries between people and loyalty to the nation-state. Global forces are themselves complex and do not always result in more tolerance.

Indeed, the only thing that we can predict with considerable certainty is that in this age of sharing a small planet, the socialization of our citizens will be influenced by events at the macro level, whether national or global.

Policy and Practice

Should preschoolers living in poverty be socialized in day care settings? Should adolescents work while going to school? Should new parents be required to take child-rearing classes? How should job-training programs be structured? How can communities use the talents and knowledge of retirees? Can the

Audio Link 4.3
Think about how veterans can be helped when returning from war.

death process be made easier for the dying person and the family? Should we place emphasis in high school and college on in-group loyalty and patriotism or on developing a sense of global citizenship mobilized around common human issues such as global climate change? These are all policy questions—issues of how to establish governing principles that will enhance our common life.

These policy questions rely on an understanding of socialization—how we learn our beliefs and our positions in society. For example, making decisions about how to provide positive early-childhood education experiences at a time when young children are learning the ways of their culture depends on understanding the socialization they receive at home and at school. The quality of child care we provide for young children will affect not only how effective our future workforce is but also whether kids turn out to be productive citizens or a drain on society.

Some sociologists do research to provide policymakers with accurate data and interpretations of the data so that they can make wise decisions. Others are more activist, working in the field as applied sociologists and trying to solve social problems through private foundations, consulting firms, or state agencies.

Now that we have some understanding of the process of socialization, we look next at the process of interaction and how individuals become members of small groups, networks, and large complex organizations.

What Have We Learned?

Human beings are not born to be noble savages or depraved beasts. As a species, we are remarkable in how many aspects of our lives are shaped by learning—by socialization. Human socialization is pervasive, extensive, and lifelong. We cannot understand what it means to be human without comprehending the impact of a specific culture on us, the influence of our close associates, and the complex interplay of pressures at the micro, meso, and macro levels. Indeed, without social interaction, there would not even be a self. We humans are, in our most essential natures, social beings. The purpose of this chapter has been to open our eyes to the ways in which we become the individuals we are.

Key Points

- Human beings come with their biological makeup, but most of what makes us uniquely human we learn from our culture and society—our socialization. Humans who are not socialized and live in isolation from others are tragic—barely human—creatures. (See pp. 106–109.)

- The self consists of the interaction of the *I*—the basic impulsive human with drives, needs, and feelings—and the *Me*—the reflected self one develops by role-taking to see how others might see one. (See pp. 113–114.)

- The self is profoundly shaped by others, but it also has agency—it is an initiator of action and the maker of meaning. (See pp. 110–113.)

- The self develops through stages, from mimicking others (the play stage) to more intellectually sophisticated abilities to role-take and to see how various roles compliment each other (the game stage). (See pp. 113–115.)

- Although the self is somewhat elastic in adjusting to different settings and circumstances, there is also a core self that is often vested in meso-level organizations and institutions in which the self participates. (See pp. 115–116.)

- The self is modified as it moves through life stages, and some of those stages require major resocialization—shedding old roles and taking on new ones as one enters new statuses in life. (See pp. 116–118.)

- A number of agents of socialization are at work on each of us, communicating messages that are relevant at the micro, meso, or macro level of social life. At the meso level, for example, we may receive different messages about what it means to be a "good" person depending on our ethnic, religious, or social-class subculture. (See pp. 118–125.)

- Some of these messages may be in conflict with each other, as when global messages about tolerance for those who are different conflict with a nation's desire to have absolute loyalty and a sense of superiority. (See pp. 125–128.)

Contributing to Our Social World: What Can We Do?

At the Local Levels

In every community, numerous opportunities exist for volunteer work in helping children from economically and otherwise disadvantaged backgrounds to succeed in school.

Helping disadvantaged children succeed in school:

- Tutor or mentor in the local schools. Contact an education faculty member for information.

- Volunteer in Head Start centers for poor preschool children. See Web site at www.nhsa.org.

- Help in a Local Boys and Girls Club that provides socialization experiences for children through their teens.

- Volunteer in care facilities and hospices for people who are ill or dying to help reduce loneliness and provide positive interaction.

- Check these opportunities for Academic Service Learning (ASL) credit in which course assignments include such community work under the supervision of the instructor. Find out about ASL programs on your campus.

At the National and Global Levels

Promoting literacy: Literacy is a vital components of socialization yet remains an unmet need in many parts of the world, especially in the less-developed countries of Africa and Asia.

- World Education Web site at www.worlded.org to learn about its wide variety of projects and volunteer/work opportunities.

- Care International and Save the Children provide funding for families to send children to school and to receive specialized training. Opportunities exist for fundraising, internships, or eventually jobs with these organizations.

 For chapter-specific resources, including **Frontline**, **TED**, and **YouTube** videos; self-quizzes; web exercises; and more, visit **www.pineforge.com/oswmedia3e.**

CHAPTER

5

Interaction, Groups, and Organizations

Connections That Work

Human interaction results in connections—networks—that work to make life more fulfilling and that make our economic efforts more productive. These connections are critical in our social world—from small micro groups to large bureaucratic organizations.

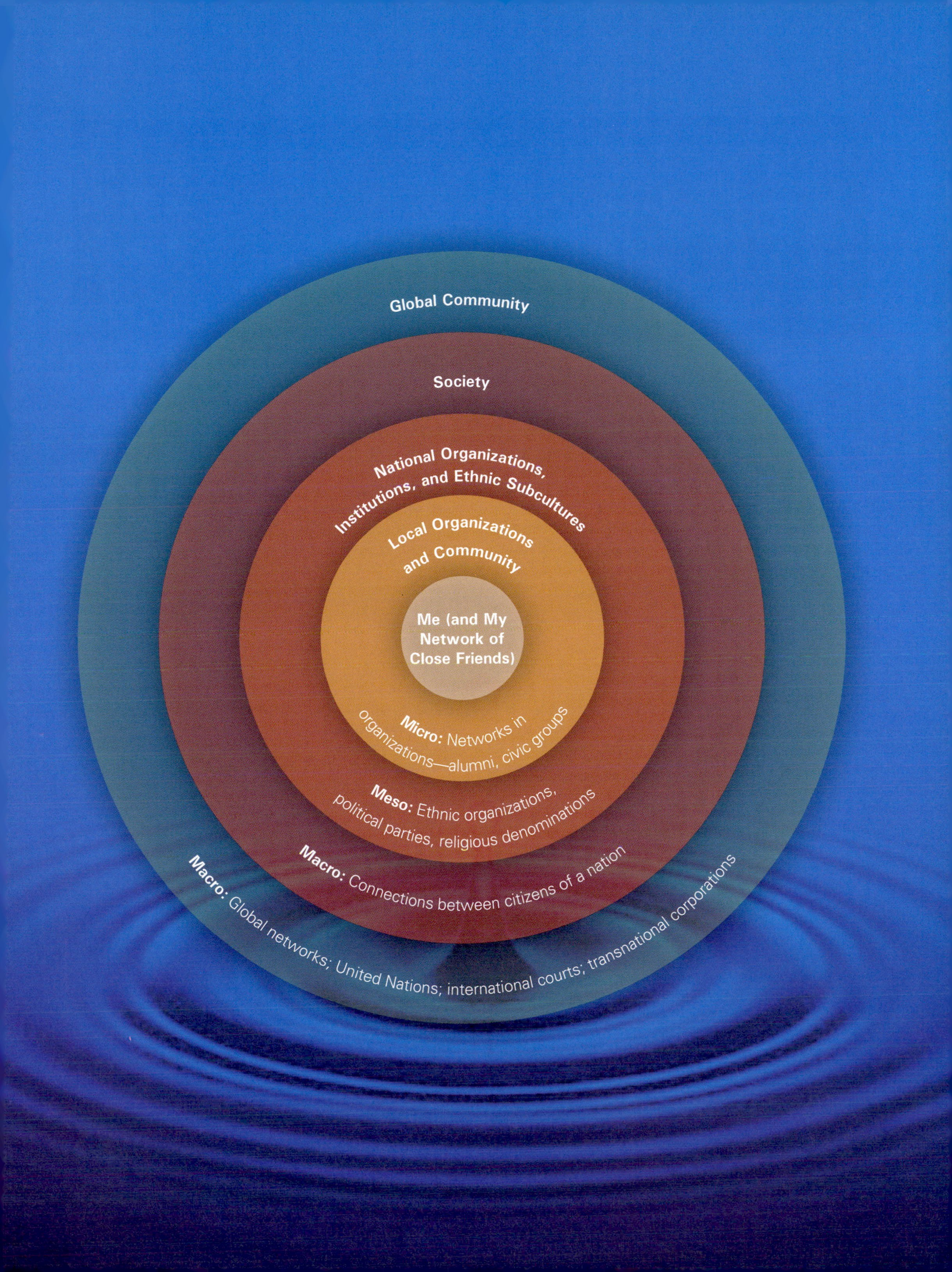

Global Community

Society

National Organizations,
Institutions, and Ethnic Subcultures

Local Organizations
and Community

Me (and My
Network of
Close Friends)

Micro: Networks in
organizations—alumni, civic groups

Meso: Ethnic organizations,
political parties, religious denominations

Macro: Connections between citizens of a nation

Macro: Global networks; United Nations; international courts; transnational corporations

Think About It	
Me (and My Inner Circle)	Are you likely to meet your perfect mate over the Internet?
Local Community	How does interaction with others affect who you are and what you believe?
National Institutions; Complex Organizations; Ethnic Groups	Is bureaucratic "red tape" really necessary?
National Society	How do national trends—such as the spread of fast-food chains and "box stores"—influence your quality of life?
Global Community	How are you connected through the networks with people across the globe?

Peaceful demonstrators who gathered to protest against the 2009 election in Iran were confronted with massive police forces. They were forced to disperse, and many were beaten and arrested. Although there was a news blackout and a crackdown on communications imposed by the government, demonstrators used their cell phones, blogs, Twitter, and Facebook to send pictures and video footage documenting the events around the world. Some have referred to this as "The Twitter Revolution." Cyberspace links people around the world in seconds, and few governments are able to prevent this (Stone and Cohen 2009). There is no need to wait for the mail or even talk on the phone. The information superhighway is opening new communication routes and networking individuals with common interests. Yet only a few decades ago, we read about cyberspace in science fiction novels written by authors with a little science background and a lot of imagination. Indeed, the word *cyberspace* was coined in 1984 by the science fiction writer William Gibson (Brasher 2004).

The implications of the rapidly expanding links in cyberspace are staggering. We cannot even anticipate some of them because change is so rapid. For entertainment, we can talk with friends on Listservs or with people we have "met" through cyber social groups. Some of these acquaintances have never left their own country, which is on the other side of the planet. All of this takes place in the comfort of our homes. Face-to-face communication only occurs on cameras attached to our computers.

Universities now communicate with students and employees by computer. You may be able to register for a class by "talking" to the computer. Computers track your registration and grades, and they may even write you letters about your status. They also monitor employee productivity. For doing certain types of research, library books are becoming secondary to the World Wide Web.

Jeanne, one of the coauthors of this book, took a leave of absence in the mid-1980s to do some research in Japan. A benefit of that leave was that she escaped the distractions of ringing phones and she could concentrate. Fax was almost unknown, and e-mail hardly existed for the civilian population. In 2007, she took a leave of absence to teach on Semester at Sea. Even in the middle of the ocean, she was in instant contact with her office, publisher, and family over the international e-mail superhighway. She could insert earphones into her laptop computer and have a Skype conversation by voice or pick up a mobile phone and call her family or coauthor. What a change in 25 years! Technology is creating a smaller world where time zones are the only thing separating our communication, but it also may be making the world more impersonal because there is less need to meet face-to-face.

Even dating is changing. One of our students recently reported that she was ecstatic about having met the perfect man—over the Internet. She expressed reservations about meeting her perfect man in person because it might change this "perfect" relationship. Dating services have sprung up to introduce people via the Internet, and people put pictures and biographies, like home pages, on the Internet. Whether cyberspace is limiting face-to-face contacts is a subject of much debate, but

No longer are paper and pencil the medium of academics. Most universities are now requiring students to have laptops or access to computers on campus. Most colleges now provide wi-fi Internet access, thus expanding the modes of learning.

individuals do interact, whether through cyberspace or face-to-face, and form networks linking them to the social world.

This chapter continues the discussion of how individuals fit into the social world, exploring the link between the individual and the social structure. Socialization prepares individuals to be part of the social world, and individuals interact with others to form groups and organizations. Interacting face-to-face and belonging to groups and organizations are the primary focus in the following pages. First, we consider how networks and connections link individuals and groups to different levels of analyses. Then, we focus on micro-level interactions, meso-level groups, and meso- and macro-level organizations and bureaucracies. Finally, we consider macro-level national and global networks.

Networks are a bit like a spider's web—with many intersections and connective links.

Networks and Connections in Our Social World

Try imagining yourself at the center of a web, such as a spider's web. Attach the threads that spread from the center first to family members and close friends, on out in the web to peers, then friends of friends. Some thread connections are close and direct. Others are more distant but connect more and more people in an ever-expanding web. Now imagine trying to send a letter to someone you do not know. A researcher actually tried this experiment to discover how people are networked and how far removed citizens are from one another within the United States.

Perhaps you have heard it said that every American is only 6 steps (or degrees) from any other person in the country. This assertion is rooted in a study with evidence to support it. Stanley Milgram and his associates (Korte and Milgram 1970; Milgram 1967; Travers and Milgram 1969) studied social networks by selecting several target people in different cities. Then, they identified "starting persons" in cities more than 1,000 miles away. Each starter person was given a booklet with instructions and the target person's name, address, occupation, and a few other facts. The starter person was instructed to pass the booklet to someone he or she knew on a first-name basis who lived closer to or might have more direct networks with the target person than the sender had. Although many packages never arrived at their destinations, one third did. The researchers were interested in how many steps were involved in the delivery of the packages that did arrive. The number of links in the chain to complete delivery ranged from 2 to 10, with most having 5 to 7 intermediaries. This is the source of the reference to "6 degrees of separation." Clearly, networks are powerful linkages and create a truly small world.

Our **social networks**, then, refer to individuals linked together by one or more social relationships, connecting us to the larger society. We use our social network to get jobs or favors, often from people who are not very far removed from us in the web. Networks begin with micro-level contacts and exchanges between individuals in private interactions and expand to small groups, then to large (even global) organizations (Granovetter 2007; Tolbert and Hall 2008). The stronger people's networks, the more influential they can be in the person's life. However, types of networks differ. For example, women's networks for both getting jobs and promotions and for succeeding in careers are broader (more extensive) than men's but also weaker than men's in helping with promotions. This is because men's networks are more "instrumental," that is, focused on the task at hand (Rothbard and Brett 2000). The web in Figure 5.1 illustrates that individuals are linked to other people, groups, organizations, and nations in the social world through networks.

Handbook Link 5.1
Read more about
social networks.

Although network links can be casual and personal rather than based on official positions and channels, they place a person within the larger social structure, and it is from these networks that group ties emerge. People in networks talk to each other about common interests. This communication process creates linkages between clusters of people. For example, cyber networks on the Internet bring together people with common interests.

Networks at the Micro, Meso, and Macro Levels

At the most micro level, you develop close friends in college—bonds that may continue for the rest of your life. You introduce your friends from theater to your roommate's friends from the soccer team, and the network expands.

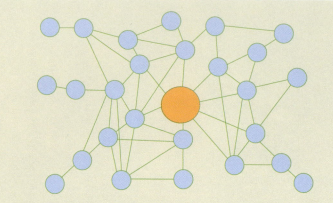

The golden circle represents an individual—perhaps you—and the blue dots represent your friends and acquaintances. Your network looks a bit like a web but is less complete in terms of every point connected to the adjacent point, since some of your friends do not know each other.

Figure 5.1   Networks: A Web of Connections

These acquaintances from the soccer team may have useful information about which professors to avoid, how to make contacts to study abroad, and how to get a job in your field. Food cooperatives, self-help groups such as Alcoholics Anonymous and Weight Watchers, and computer user groups are examples of networks that connect individuals with common interests.

All of you—if you are successful at your university—will eventually become part of the university's alumni association, and this may become important to you for social contacts, business connections, or help with settling in a new location. When people refer to the Old Boy network, they are talking about contacts made through general association with people such as alumni. Men have used networks quite successfully in the past, and networks of working women—New Girl networks—are expanding rapidly. One of the reasons for the persistent inequality in our society is that members of certain groups may not have access to these privilege-enhancing networks.

Thinking Sociologically

Map your social network web. What advantages do you get from your network? What economic or other benefits might your connections have for you?

Network links create new types of organizational forms at the meso level, such as those in the opening example of demonstrations and cyberspace. These networks cross

societal, racial, ethnic, religious, and other lines that otherwise divide people. Networks also link groups at different levels of analysis. In fact, you are linked through networks to (1) local civic, sports, and religious organizations; (2) formal, complex organizations such as a political party or national fraternity and ethnic or social class subcultures; (3) the nation of which you are a citizen and to which you have formal obligations (such as the requirement that you go to war as a draftee if the government so decides); and (4) global entities such as the United Nations that use some of your taxes or donate resources to help impoverished people, tsunami victims, and earthquake survivors elsewhere in the world. These networks may open opportunities, but they also may create obligations that limit your freedom to make your own choices. As we move from micro-level interactions to larger meso- and macro-level organizations, interactions tend to become more formal. Formal organizations will be explored in the latter half of this chapter.

One of the most interesting developments at the beginning of the 21st century is the way Internet technology is influencing networking by linking individuals to people around the globe. Internet users have redefined networking through the creation of blogs, chat rooms, message boards, Listservs, newsgroups, and dozens of Web sites devoted to online networking ("Five Rules" 2005). Web sites such as LinkedIn.com and WorldWIT.org offer business and

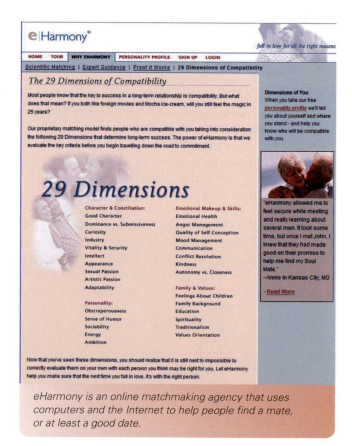

eHarmony is an online matchmaking agency that uses computers and the Internet to help people find a mate, or at least a good date.

professional networking, whereas other sites such as MySpace .com, YouTube, Tribe.net, Xanga.com, Classmates.com, and Facebook.com focus on personal and social networking. Some people even find their partners using the Internet, as the illustration from eHarmony suggests. Together, these Web sites are revolutionizing the way people make friends, acquire information, and go about their daily lives.

Web sites dedicated to social networking focus on sharing mutually interesting information, finding and keeping up with friends, uploading photos and videos, finding activity partners, publishing notes, or establishing professional contacts. One of the largest and most popular, with well over 250 million participants, is Facebook ("Facebook Statistics" 2009), which was launched in February 2004 at Harvard University. It is now used by university students around the world and has spread to high school students, adults, bands, politicians, and businesses. In 2007, Facebook Platform was launched, allowing other software specialists to design new features such as games, music, and photo sharing. These new features have increased the users of Facebook (Stone and Cohen 2009).

Like many other social networking sites, Facebook allows users to post a profile and pictures, create and join groups, and link to the profiles of "friends"—often a mixture of friends, colleagues, relatives, and acquaintances of varying levels and from various periods of life. Users can view the profiles of anyone within 4 degrees of separation—friends of friends of friends of friends—and search the network for people with the same friends, location, hometown, occupation, schools attended, interests, hobbies, or taste in movies, books, or television shows. In many cases, users link to dozens of friends and can access thousands of profiles around the world without reaching beyond the friends-of-friends level of connectivity. Once members are friends, they can view each others' "statuses," or short messages declaring a user's location, recent activities, or personal thoughts. Benefits include getting to know acquaintances' movie preferences, music taste, and even contact information without having to have a face-to-face conversation. One downside is that some critics believe that social networking sites may provide a means for predators such as pedophiles to solicit sex from minors (Bahney 2009). As a way of examining your own networks, try the exercise in the "Engaging Sociology" feature that follows.

Journal Article Link 5.1
Read about the Internet and social capital.

Engaging Sociology

Networking via Facebook

If you are on Facebook, go to your Facebook account and note the number of friends you have listed. Then, look at them carefully to see if you can answer the following questions:

What is the age range of the friends on your list?

What is the gender composition of your list?

How many of each of the following racial or ethic groups are on your list:

___ African Americans

___ Whites of predominantly European heritage

___ Hispanics

___ Asians

___ Other (mixed)

What is the socioeconomic status of your friends?

___ Blue-collar (families where the primary wage earners works for an hourly wage)

___ Middle class (families where the primary wage earners earns a salary of less than $100,000 per year)

___ Professional (families where the primary wage earners earns a salary of $100,000 to $500,000 per year)

___ Highly affluent corporate executive (families where the primary wage earner(s) earns a salary of $500,000 to $10 million)

___ Upper class (where much of the family wealth is inherited and annual income is in multimillions)

What do you conclude about the diversity or homogeneity of your network of friends and acquaintances? You can carry this to the next degree by looking at friends' friends.

An even more recent development is the rapidly increasing popularity of Twitter, a microblogging Web site that allows users to post 140-character messages ("tweets") using their personal computer or the text messaging function on their mobile phone. Interestingly, users have played a crucial role in developing Twitter, including inventing "hash tags" that indicate the subject of the tweet and allowing others to search for all tweets on the same topic (Johnson 2009).

Video Link 5.1
Watch a discussion of social media and marketing.

Thinking Sociologically

How have you or your friends used the Internet to expand social or professional networks? What influence have these networks had on you or your friends?

THE PROCESS OF INTERACTION: CONNECTIONS AT THE MICRO LEVEL

Each morning as you rouse yourself and prepare for the challenges ahead, you consider what the day might bring, what activities and obligations are on your calendar, and who you will talk to. As you lift your limp, listless body from a horizontal to upright position and blood begins coursing through your veins, thoughts of the day's events begin to penetrate your semiconscious state. A cup of caffeine, cold water on the face, and a mouth-freshening brush bring you to the next stage of awareness. You evaluate what is in store for you, what roles you will play during the day, and with whom you are likely to interact.

Should you wear the ragged but comfortable jeans and T-shirt? No, not today. There is that class trip to the courthouse. Something a bit less casual is in order. Then, you are meeting with your English professor to discuss the last essay you wrote. What approach should you take? You could act insulted that she failed to think of you as a future J. K. Rowling. Maybe a meek, mild "Please tell me what I did wrong, I tried so hard" approach would work. She seems a nice, sympathetic sort. After class, there is a group of students who chat in the hall. It would be nice to meet them. What strategy should you use? Try to enter the conversation? Tell a joke? Make small talk? Talk to the students individually so you can get to know each before engaging the whole group? Each of these responses is a strategy for interaction, and each might elicit various reactions.

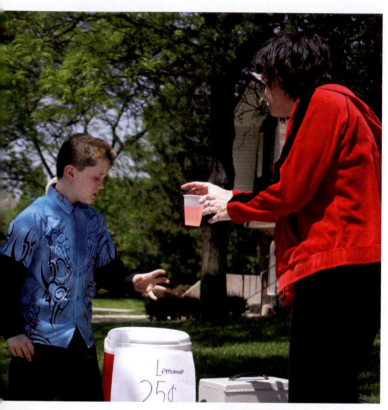

The same words, "Let's have a drink," may have very different meanings in different social interaction contexts. Humans must learn not only the language but also how to read interactional settings.

The Elements of Social Interaction

"Let's have a drink!" Such a simple comment might have many different meanings. We could imagine two children playing together, men going to a bar after work, a couple of friends getting together to celebrate an event, fraternity brothers at a party, or a couple on a date. In all these cases, **social interaction** consists of two or more individuals purposefully relating to each other.

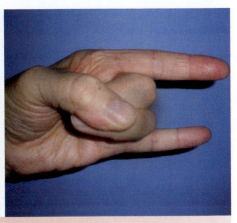

Gestures are symbolic forms of interaction. However, these gestures can have entirely different meanings in different cultures. A friendly gesture in one culture may be considered obscene in another culture.

"Having a drink," like all interaction, involves action on the part of two or more individuals, is directed toward a goal that people hope to achieve, and takes place in a social context that includes cultural norms and rules governing the situation, the setting, and other factors shaping the way people perceive the circumstances. The action, goal, and social context help us interpret the meaning of statements such as "Let's have a drink."

The norms governing the particular social context tell what is right and proper behavior. Recall from Chapter 3 that norms are rules that guide human interactions. People assume that others will share their interpretation of a situation. These shared assumptions about proper behavior provide the cues for your own behavior that become a part of your social self. You look for cues to proper behavior and rehearse in your mind your actions and reactions. In the "Let's have a drink" scenario, you assume that the purpose of the interaction is understood. What dress, mannerisms, speech, and actions you consider appropriate depends on expectations from your socialization and past experience in similar situations (Parsons 1951b), for in modern societies, a range of behaviors and responses is possible in any social situation.

Although most people assume that talking, or verbal communication, is the primary means of communication between individuals, words themselves are actually only a part of the message. In most contexts, they make up less than 35% of the emotional content of the message (Birdwhistell 1970). **Nonverbal communication**—interactions using facial expressions, the head, eye contact, body posture, gestures, touch, walk, status symbols, and personal space—makes up the rest (Drafke and Kossen 2002). These important elements of communication are learned through socialization as we grow up. Although you may master another written and verbal language, it is much more difficult to learn the nonverbal language. People who travel to a country other than their own often use gestures to be understood. Like spoken language, nonverbal gestures vary from culture to culture, as illustrated in the photos above. Communicating with others in one's own language can be difficult enough. Add to this

the complication of individuals with different language, cultural expectations, and personalities using different nonverbal messages, and misunderstandings are likely. Nonverbal messages are the hardest part of another language to master because they are specific to a culture and learned through socialization.

Consider the following example: You are about to wrap up a major business deal. You are pleased with the results of your negotiations, so you give your hosts the thumb-and-finger A-OK sign. In Brazil, you have just grossly insulted your hosts—it is like giving them "the finger" in the United States. In Japan, you have asked for a small bribe. In the south of France, you have indicated the deal is worthless. Although your spoken Portuguese, Japanese, or French may have been splendid, your nonverbal language did not cut the deal. Intercultural understanding is more than being polite and knowing the language.

Audio Link 5.1
Listen to interaction before the Internet.

Consider another example of nonverbal language: personal space. Most people have experienced social situations, such as parties, where someone gets too close. One person backs away, the other moves in again, the first backs away again—into a corner or a table with nowhere else to go. Perhaps the person approaching was aggressive or rude, but it is also possible that the person held different cultural norms or expectations in relation to personal space.

The amount of personal space an individual needs to be comfortable or proper varies with the cultural setting, gender, status, and social context of the interaction. Individuals from Arab countries are comfortable at very close range. However, people from Scandinavia or the United States need a great deal of personal space. Consider the following four categories of social distance and social space based on a study of U.S. middle-class people. Each category applies to particular types of activity (Hall and Hall 1992):

1. *Intimate distance:* from zero distance (touching, embracing, kissing) to 18 inches. Children may play

In North America, friends interact at a close distance—from 1 to 4 feet—as in the top photo. A more formal setting calls for a distance of 4 to 10 feet, and that space can feel cold and intimidating. What is the message at the meeting in the lower photo?

together in such close proximity, and adults and children may maintain this distance, but between adults, this intimate contact is reserved for private and affectionate relationships.

2. *Personal distance:* from 18 inches to 4 feet. This is the public distance for most friends and for informal interactions with acquaintances.

3. *Social distance:* from 4 feet to 12 feet. This is the distance for impersonal business relations, such as a job interview or class discussions between students and a professor. This distance implies a more formal

interaction or a significant difference in the status of the two people.

4. *Public distance:* 12 feet and beyond. This is the distance most public figures use for addressing others, especially in formal settings and in situations in which the speaker has a very high status.

Personal space also communicates one's position in relation to others. The higher the position, the greater the control of space. In social situations, individuals with higher positions spread out, prop their feet up, put their arms out, and use more sweeping gestures (Knapp and Hall 1997). Women and men differ with regard to personal space and other forms of nonverbal language. For instance, women are more sensitive to subtle cues such as status differences and the use of personal space (Henley, Hamilton, and Thorne 2000).

Sociologists study interactions, including verbal and nonverbal communication, to explain this very basic link between humans and the group. The following theoretical perspectives focus on the micro level of analysis in attempting to explain interactions.

Thinking Sociologically

What are some complications that you or your friends have had in interactions involving cross-cultural contacts or male-female miscommunication? What might help clarify communication in these cases?

Theoretical Perspectives on the Interaction Process

How many people do you interact with each day, and what happens in each of these interactions? You probably have not given the question much thought or analysis, but that process is exactly what fascinates interaction theorists. Why do two people interact in the first place? What determines whether the interaction will continue or stop? How do two people know how to behave and what to say around each other? What other processes are taking place as they "talk" to each other? Why do people interact differently with different people? What governs the way they make sense of messages and how they respond to them? These questions interest sociologists because they address the basic interaction processes that result in group formations that range in size from dyads (two people) to large organizations. The following are several theories that provide explanations for interactions.

Rational Choice Theory

Rational choice or exchange theorists look at why relationships continue, considering the rewards and costs of interaction for the individual. They argue that the choices we make are guided by reason. If the benefits of the interaction are high and if the costs are low, the interaction will be valued and sustained. Every interaction involves calculations of self-interest, expectations of reciprocity (a mutual exchange of favors), and decisions to act in ways that have current or eventual payoff for the individual (Smelser 1992).

Reciprocity is a key concept for rational choice theorists. The idea is that if a relationship is imbalanced over a period of time, it will be unsatisfying. As theorists from this perspective see human interaction, each person tends to keep a mental ledger of who "owes" whom. If I have done you a favor, you owe me one. If you have helped me in some way, I have an obligation to you. If I then fail to comply or even do something that hurts you, you will likely view it as a breach in the relationship and have negative feelings toward me. Moreover, if there is an imbalance in what we each bring to the relationship, one person may have more power in the relationship. In the study of families, scholars use the "principle of least interest," which states that the person with the least interest in the relationship has the most power. The person with the least interest is the person who brings more resources (financial, physical, social, personal) to the relationship and receives less. That person could easily leave. The person who offers less to the relationship or who has fewer assets is more dependent on the relationship. This person is likely to give in when there is a disagreement, so the person with less interest gets her or his way. Lack of reciprocity can be important for how relationships develop. It is this idea that particularly interests rational choice theorists.

Sometimes a person may engage in a behavior where there is little likelihood of reciprocity from the other person—as in cases where the behavior is altruistic or self-giving. Rational choice theorists would argue that there is still a benefit. It might be enhanced feelings of self-worth, recognition from others, hope for a place in heaven, or just the expectation of indirect reciprocity. This latter notion is that the person I help might not help me, but if I am in a similar situation, I could hope for and expect someone to come to my assistance (Gouldner 1960; Turner 2003).

Symbolic Interaction Theory

Symbolic interaction theory focuses instead on how individuals interpret situations, such as "Let's have a drink," and how this, in turn, affects their actions. Two other theories that are variations on symbolic interaction theory—ethnomethodology and dramaturgy—explain aspects of symbolic interaction that are part of interpreting situations or manipulating how people perceive interactions.

When a respected person speaks in a public setting, listeners would be expected to keep themselves at a greater distance. Los Angeles Mayor Antonio R. Villaraigosa speaks here in a formal setting with appropriate public distance.

Ethnomethodology

Most people take for granted the underlying interaction rules—norms that govern the expected behaviors and the verbal or nonverbal exchanges. However, ethnomethodologists do not take these norms for granted. They study the formation of ground rules underlying social interaction and people's responses to violation of norms (Riehl 2001). This is often done by violating norms to see how strongly others in the social setting respond to the improper behavior.

Suppose an acquaintance greets you with a friendly, "Hi, how ya' doin'?" and you respond with "Rotten, I want to die!" or "Oh, shut up!" rather than the perfunctory "Fine, how's it goin'?" You may have had a really bad day, but you would get a strong reaction because you would be breaching norms related to casual greetings. Similarly, if you violate elevator behavior by singing in the elevator, trying to sell a product to others in the elevator, sniffing the person next to you, or staring at other occupants rather than at the floor numbers, you are breaching elevator norms. These norms are generally understood, even among strangers.

Encyclopedia Link 5.1
Read more about
rational choice.

Researchers use empirical methods to study how people develop shared meanings and consider how common ground rules originated. They question even the most basic aspects of social interactions.

Dramaturgy

Dramaturgy theorists analyze life as a play or drama on a stage, with scripts and props and scenes to be played. The play we put on creates an impression for our audience. In everyday life, individuals learn new lines to add to their scripts through the socialization process, including influence from family, friends, films, and television. They perform these scripts for social audiences to maintain certain images, much like the actors in a play.

Consider the following familiar example: Every day in high schools around the world, teenagers go on stage—in the classroom or the hallway with friends and peers and with adult authorities who may later be giving grades or writing letters of reference. The props these students use include their style of clothing; a backpack with books, paper, pen, and laptop; and a smile or a "cool" look. The set is the classroom, the cafeteria, and perhaps the athletic field. The script is shaped by the actors: Teachers may establish an authoritarian relationship, classmates engage in competition for grades, or peers seek social status among companions. The actors include hundreds of teens struggling with issues of identity, changing bodies, and attempts to avoid humiliation. Each individual works to assert and maintain an image through behavior, clothing, language, and friends.

As individuals perform according to society's script for the situation, they take into consideration how their actions will influence others. By carefully managing the impression they wish the acquaintance to receive—a process called *impression management*—people hope to create an impression that works to their advantage. In other words, the actor is trying to manipulate how others define the situation, especially as it relates to their opinion of the actor.

Most of the time, we engage in front-stage behavior, the behavior safest with casual acquaintances because it is scripted and acted for the public and it presents a definition of self we hope others will accept as the "real me." A poor or unacceptable performance will be embarrassing both for us and for our audience. People develop strategies to cover up their weaknesses or failures, such as laughing at a joke even though they do not understand it.

Each part or character an individual plays and each audience requires a different script. For example, interacting with peers at a bar differs from meeting a professor in her office. We learn to avoid those performance activities that are likely to result in humiliation or failure or that contradict the image we have worked to create. At home or with close friends with whom we are more intimate, we engage in "backstage behavior," letting our feelings show and behaving in ways that might be unacceptable for other audiences (Goffman 1967, [1959] 2001). Dramaturgical analysis can be a useful approach to broadening our understanding of interactions.

Thinking Sociologically

Describe some ways in which your life feels like a dramatic production. Identify front-stage and backstage behaviors.

Social Status: The Link to Groups

Recall the network web you drew. Now add to that web your **social statuses**, the positions you hold in the social world. Our social statuses define how, for example, we interact with others and how others react to us in a specific situation. We interact differently when in the daughter status with our parents, in a student status with our professor, or in friend status with our peers. Each individual holds many statuses, and this combination held by any individual is called a *status set*: for instance, daughter, mother, worker, teammate, student.

Each individual's unique status set is the product of family relationships and groups that the individual joins (a university or club) or into which she or he is born (an ethnic group or gender). Many statuses change with each new stage of life, such as student, work, marital, or parenthood status. Statuses at each stage of life and the interactions that result from those statuses form each person's unique social world.

Statuses affect the type of interactions individuals have. In some interactions (as with classmates), people are equals. In other situations, individuals have interchanges with people who hold superior or inferior statuses. If you are promoted to supervisor, your interaction with former peers and subordinates will change. Consider the possible interactions shown in Figure 5.2, in which the first relationship is between equals and the others are between those with unequal statuses.

When individuals are in dominant or subordinate positions, power or deference affects interactions, respectively. With a friend, these status relationships are constantly being negotiated and bargained: "I'll do what you want tonight, but tomorrow I choose." Studies of interaction between males and females find that, in addition to gender, power and hierarchical relationships are important in determining interaction patterns. The more powerful person, such as one who has more wealth or privilege, can interrupt in a conversation with his or her partner and show less deference in the interaction (Kim et al. 2007; Reid and Ng 2006; Wood 2008).

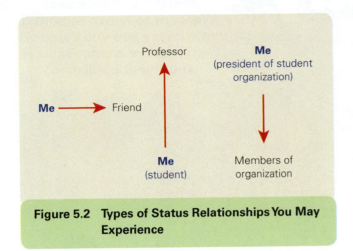

Figure 5.2   Types of Status Relationships You May Experience

People have no control over certain statuses they hold. These **ascribed statuses** are often assigned at birth and do not change during an individual's lifetime. Some examples are gender and race or ethnicity. Ascribed statuses are assigned to a person without regard for personal desires, talents, or choices. In some societies, one's caste or the social position into which one is born (e.g., a slave) is an ascribed status because it is usually impossible to change.

Achieved status, on the other hand, is chosen or earned by the decisions one makes and sometimes by personal ability. Attaining a higher education, for example, improves an individual's occupational opportunities and thus his or her achieved status. Being a guitarist in a band is an achieved status and so is being a prisoner in jail, for both are earned positions based on the person's own decisions and actions.

At a particular time in life or under certain circumstances, one of an individual's statuses may become most important and take precedence over others. Sociologists call this a **master status**. Whether it is an occupation, parental status, or something else, it dominates and shapes much of an individual's life, activities, self-concept, and position in the community for a period of time. For a person who is very ill, for instance, that illness may occupy a master status, needing constant attention from doctors, influencing social relationships, and determining what that person can do in family, work, or community activities.

Thinking Sociologically

What are your statuses? Which ones are ascribed, and which are achieved statuses? Do you have a master status? How do these statuses affect the way you interact with others in your network of relationships?

The Relationship Between Status and Role

Every status (position) in your network includes certain behaviors and obligations as you carry out the expected behaviors, rights, and obligations of the status; these are referred to as **roles**. Roles are the dynamic, action part of statuses in a society. They define how each individual in an interaction is expected to act (Linton 1937). The role of a college student includes behaviors and obligations such as attending classes, studying, taking tests, writing papers, and interacting with professors and other students. Individuals enter most statuses with some knowledge of how to carry out the roles dictated by their culture. Through the process of socialization, individuals learn roles by observing others, watching television and films, reading, and being taught how to carry out the status. Both statuses (positions) and roles (behavioral obligations of the status) form the link with other people in the social world because they must be carried out in relationships with others. A father has certain obligations (or roles) toward his children and their mother. The position of father does not exist on its own but in relationship to significant others who have reciprocal ties.

Your status of student requires certain behaviors and expectations, depending on whether you are interacting with a dean, a professor, an adviser, a classmate, or a prospective employer. This is because the role expectations of the status of student vary as one interacts with specific people in other statuses. In Figure 5.3, the student is the subject, and the others are those with whom the student interacts in the status of student.

Within a group, individuals may hold both formal and informal statuses. One illustration is the formal status of high school students, each of whom plays a number of informal roles in cliques that are not part of the formal school structure. They may be known as jock, nerd, loner, goth, clown, prep, outcast, or life of the party. Each of these roles takes

Journal Article Link 5.2
Read about inequality regimes.

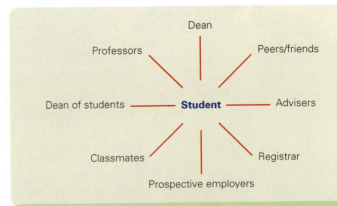

Figure 5.3   Types of Interactions Students Have With Reciprocal Status Holders

Photo Essay

Work Status and Roles Around the World

The positions people carry out in different cultures depend on tasks important in that culture. Upper left: The two women from Ghana carry yams, a staple food, from the fields. Upper right: A police officer begins his local beat. Middle left: Men in Ghana have the traditional role of hand-stamping cloth. Middle right: The market for these Asian women is on the water. Lower left: Men in China use traditional methods to keep the roads open. Lower right: Fishermen in India pull in a catch for their livelihood.

place in a status relationship with others: teacher-student, peer-peer, coach-athlete. The connections between statuses, roles, and environment are illustrated in Table 5.1.

Our statuses connect us and make us integral parts of meso- and macro-level organizations. Sometimes, the link is through a status in a family group, such as son or daughter; sometimes through an employer; and sometimes through our status as citizen of a nation. Social networks may be based on ascribed characteristics, such as age, race, ethnicity, and gender, or on achieved status, such as education, occupation, or common interests. These links, in turn, form the basis for social interactions and group structures (Hall 2002). However, at times, individuals cannot carry out their roles as others expect them to, creating role strain or conflict.

Table 5.1	**The Relationship Between Statuses and Roles**
Status (position in structure)	*Role (behavior, rights, obligations)*
Student	*Formal*
	Study, attend class, turn in assignments
	Informal
	Be a jock, clown, cut-up; abuse alcohol on weekends
Parent	*Formal*
	Provide financial support, child care
	Informal
	Be a playmate, lead family activities
Employee	*Formal*
	Work responsibilities: punctuality, doing one's tasks
	Informal
	Befriend coworkers, join lunch group, represent company in bowling league

Role Strain and Role Conflict

Most people have faced times in their lives when they simply could not carry out all the obligations of a status, such as student—write two papers, study adequately for two exams, complete the portfolio for the studio art class, finish the reading assignments for five classes, and memorize lines for the oral interpretation class, all in the same week. Every status carries role expectations, the way the status is supposed to be carried out according to generally accepted societal or group norms. Yet in these cases, individuals face **role strain**, the tension between roles *within* one of the statuses. Role strain causes the individual to be pulled in many directions by various obligations of the

single status, as in the example regarding the status of "student." Another such strain is often experienced by first-time fathers as they attempt to reconcile their role expectations of fathering with ideas held by their wives.

To resolve role strain, individuals cope in one of several ways: pass the problem off lightly (and thus not do well in classes), consider the dilemma humorous, become highly focused and pull a couple of all-nighters to get everything done, or become stressed, tense, fretful, and immobilized because of the strain. Most often, individuals set priorities based on their values and make decisions accordingly: "I'll work hard in the class for my major and let another slide."

Audio Link 5.2
Listen to a discussion of office politics.

Role conflict differs from role strain in that conflict is *between* the roles of two or more statuses. The conflict can come from within an individual or be imposed from outside. College athletes face role conflicts from competing demands on their time (Adler and Adler 1991, 2004). They must complete their studies on time, attend practices and be prepared for games, perhaps attend meetings of a Greek house to which they belong, and get home for a little brother's birthday. Similarly, a student may be going to school, holding down a part-time job to help make ends meet, and raising a family. If the student's child gets sick, the status of parent comes into conflict with that of student and worker. In the case of role conflict, the person may choose—or be informed by others—which status is the master status. Figure 5.4 on page 146 visually illustrates the difference between role conflict and role strain.

Statuses and the accompanying roles come and go. You will not always be a student, and someday, you may be a parent and hold a professional job. Certainly, you will retire from your job. For instance, as people grow older, they disengage from some earlier statuses in groups and engage in new and different statuses and roles.

Our place within the social world is guaranteed, even obligatory, because of statuses we hold at each level of society— within small groups (family and peers), in larger groups and organizations (school and work organizations), in institutions (political parties or religious denominations), and ultimately as citizens of the society and the world (workers in global corporations). Each of these statuses connects us to a group setting.

Encyclopedia Link 5.2
Read more about role strain.

Thinking Sociologically

Using Figure 5.4, fill in the statuses you hold in your social world and the roles you perform in these statuses. Then, list three examples of role conflicts and three examples of role strains that you experience.

Parenting roles often need to be negotiated. In some traditional families in the past, the status had more explicit role expectations, and fathers were rarely expected to change diapers.

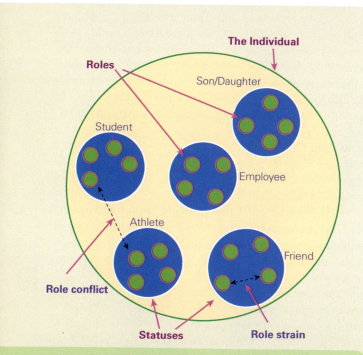

Figure 5.4 Role Strain and Role Conflict

Each individual has many statuses: a status set. Each status has many roles: a role set. A conflict between two roles of the same status is a role strain. A conflict between the roles of two different statuses is a role conflict.

Groups in Our Social World: The Micro-Meso Connection

As we have seen throughout the early chapters of this book, humans are social beings. Few of us can survive without others; we constantly interact with the family we are born into, our socialization occurs in groups, and we depend on the group for survival. Groups are necessary for protection, to obtain food, to manufacture goods, to get jobs done. Groups meet our social needs for belonging and acceptance, support us throughout our lives, and place restrictions on us. Groups can be small, intimate environments—micro-level interactions such as a group of friends—or they can become quite large as they morph into meso-level organizations. In any case, it is through our group memberships that the micro and meso levels are connected.

Groups include two or more people who interact with each other because of shared common interests, goals, experiences, and needs (Drafke 2008). The members feel they belong to the group and are seen by others as thinking, feeling, and behaving with a common goal. Members consider each other's behavior and engage in structured interaction patterns. Groups have defined memberships and ways to take in new members. They also have rules that guide the behavior of members. In this section, we look at several questions: What are groups, and how do they vary? How is interaction carried out in small groups? What is the importance of groups for individuals?

Not all collections of individuals are groups, however. For instance, your family is a group, but people shopping at a mall or waiting for a bus are not a group because they do not interact or acknowledge shared common interests.

Groups form through a series of succeeding steps. Consider people forming a village: The first step is initial interaction. If membership is rewarding and meets individuals' needs, the individuals will attempt to maintain the benefits the group provides (Mills 1984). A group of people live near each other and interact to form this village. In the second step, a collective goal emerges. For example, villagers may work together to build an irrigation system or a school. Groups establish their own goals and pursue them, trying to be free from external controls or constraints. In the third and final step, the group attempts to expand its collective goals by building on the former steps and by pursuing new goals. For example, the irrigation system may improve crop production, so the villagers decide to sell the

Audio Link 5.3
Listen to how we create social groups.

extra produce at the town vegetable market to earn money for the school.

The Importance of Groups for the Individual

Groups are essential parts of human life (micro level) and of organizational structures (meso and macro levels). They establish our place in the social world, providing us with support and a sense of belonging. Few individuals can survive without groups. This becomes clear when we consider two problems: anomie and suicide.

Anomie and Suicide

With the rapid changes and continued breakdown of institutional structures in Afghanistan as rival warlords vie for power over territory and in Iraq as religious groups vie for political and economic power, horrific problems abound. Civil disorder, conflicts for power, suicide bombings, murder of police officers, and looting are frequent occurrences. Social controls (police and military forces) are strained, and leaders struggle to cope. The result of this breakdown in norms is *anomie*, the state of normlessness; the rules for behavior in society break down under extreme stress from rapid social change or conflict (Merton 1938).

Suicide seems like an individual act, committed because of personal problems. However, the early sociologist Émile Durkheim took a unique approach to this problem. In his volume, *Suicide* (Durkheim [1897] 1964), he discussed the social factors contributing to suicide. Using existing statistical data to determine suicide rates in European populations, Durkheim looked at variables such as sex, age, religion, nationality, and the season in which the suicide was committed. His findings were surprising to many, and they demonstrate that individual problems cannot be understood without also understanding the group context in which they occur.

Durkheim found that Protestants committed suicide more often than Catholics, urban folks more often than people living in small communities, people in highly developed and complex societies more frequently than those in simple societies, and people who lived alone more than those situated in families. The key variable linking these findings was the degree to which an individual was integrated into the group, that is, the degree of social bond with others. During war, for instance, people generally felt a sense of common cause and belonging to their country. Thus, suicide rates were greater during peacetime because it offered less cause for feeling that bond.

Durkheim described three distinct types of suicide. *Egoistic suicide* occurs when the individual feels little social bond to the group or society and lacks ties, such as family or friends, that might prevent suicide. Egoistic suicide is the result of personal despair and involves the kind of motive most people associate with suicide. This is what we often think of when we hear about a suicide.

Anomic suicide occurs when a society or one of its parts is in disorder or turmoil and lacks clear norms and guidelines for social behavior. This situation is likely during major social change or economic problems such as a severe depression.

Altruistic suicide differs from the others in that it involves such a strong bond and group obligation that the individual is willing to die for the group. Self-survival becomes less important than group survival (Durkheim [1897] 1964). Examples of altruistic suicide include the young suicide bombers in Iraq, Afghanistan, and Pakistan committing suicide missions against their country's police forces and sometimes against American military forces, which they have defined as invading forces. These suicides usually occur in societies or religious groups that have very clear norms and high levels of consensus about values arising from their religious or political commitments.

Durkheim's analysis provides an excellent example of the importance of the group for individuals by showing what individuals will do for their groups. Many sociologists have studied suicide, confirming the importance of group ties for

This monk committed suicide, setting himself on fire in a public square as a statement against war. He was tightly integrated into his religious community and his people, and his own death seemed a worthy sacrifice if it could help bring attention to or end the suffering that the war had brought to his nation. This illustrates altruistic suicide.

Members of this Chinese family—a primary group—enjoy one another's company as they play a game of Mahjong. Their connections are valued for intrinsic reasons. Even Buddhist nuns, who spend much of their lives devoted to private meditation, need the support and solidarity of a group.

individuals in religious, educational, and social group networks that provide integration of individuals into the society (Tolbert and Hall 2008). Clearly, no individual is an island.

The importance of groups is an underlying theme throughout this text. Groups are essential to human life, but to understand them more fully, we must understand the various kinds of groups in which humans participate.

Types of Groups

Each of us belongs to several types of groups. Some groups provide intimacy and close relationships, whereas others

do not. Some are required affiliations, and others are voluntary. Some provide personal satisfaction, and others are obligatory or necessary for survival. The following discussion points out several types of groups and the reasons why individuals belong to them.

Primary groups are characterized by close contacts and lasting personal relationships—the most micro level. Your family members and best friends, school classmates, and close work associates are all of primary importance in your everyday life. Primary groups provide a sense of belonging and shared identity. Group members care about you, and you care about the other group members, creating a sense of loyalty. Approval and disapproval from the primary group influence the activities you choose to pursue. Belonging rather than accomplishing a task is the main reason for membership. The group is of intrinsic value—enjoyed for its own sake—rather than for some utilitarian value such as making money.

For individuals, primary groups provide an anchor point in society. You were born into a primary group—your family. You play a variety of roles in primary relationships—those of spouse, parent, child, sibling, relative, close friend. You meet with other members face-to-face or keep in touch on a regular basis and know a great deal about their lives. What makes them happy or angry? What are sensitive issues? In primary groups you share values, say what you think, let down your hair, dress as you like, and share your concerns and emotions, your successes and failures (Goffman 1967, [1959] 2001). Charles H. Cooley ([1909] 1983), who first discussed the term *primary group*, saw these relationships as the source of close human feelings and emotions—love, cooperation, and concern.

Secondary groups are those with formal, impersonal, businesslike relationships. In the modern world, people cannot always live under the protective wing of primary group relationships. Secondary groups are usually large and task oriented because they have a specific purpose to achieve and focus on accomplishing a goal. As children grow, they move from the security and acceptance of primary groups—the home and neighborhood peer group—to a secondary group—the large school classroom, where each child is one of many students vying for the teacher's approval and competing for rewards. Similarly, the job world requires formal relations and procedures: applications, interviews, contracts. Employment is based on specific skills, training, and job knowledge, and there may be a trial period. In Western cultures, we assume that people should not be hired because of personal friendship or nepotism but rather for their competence to carry out the role expectations in the position.

Because each individual in a secondary group carries out a specialized task, communication between members is often specialized as well. Contacts with doctors, store clerks, and even professors are generally formal and impersonal parts of organizational life. Sometimes associations with secondary groups are long lasting, sometimes of short duration—as in the courses you are taking this term. Secondary groups operate at the meso and macro levels of our social world, but they affect individuals at the micro level.

As societies modernize, they evolve from small towns and close, primary relationships to predominantly urban areas with more formal, secondary relationships. In the postindustrial world, as family members are scattered across countries and around the world, secondary relationships have come to play ever greater roles in people's lives. Large work organizations may provide day care, health clinics, financial planning, courses to upgrade skills, and sports leagues.

Small micro-level and large macro-level groups often occur together. Behind most successful secondary groups are primary groups. Consider the small work group that eats together or goes out for a beer on Friday afternoons. These relationships help individuals feel a part of the larger organization, just as residents of large urban areas have small groups of neighborhood friends. Megachurches began in the 1950s, and some have more than 10,000 members. In fact, the largest church in the world (in Korea) has 830,000 members. About half of these megachurches are nondenominational Protestant, and the rest are related to evangelical or Pentecostal groups. The focus of programming is on creating small support groups (primary groups) within the huge congregation ("O Come All Ye Faithful" 2007; Sargeant 2000; Thumma and Travis 2007). In a formal setting such as a university or corporation, primary groups can play a major role in making people feel they belong. For instance, many students live with roommates at the university, study with a small group, go out Friday nights with friends, and regularly have meals with close friends. Table 5.2 on page 150 summarizes some of the dimensions of primary and secondary groups.

Problems in primary groups can affect performance in secondary groups. Consider the problems of a student who has an argument with a significant other or roommate or experiences a failure of his or her family support system due to divorce or other problems. Self-concepts and social skills diminish during times of family stress and affect group relationships in other parts of one's life (Drafke 2008).

The residents of Thimpu, Bhutan, visit the vegetable market. Although this is a large, impersonal market, people form primary groups among both the vendors and the shoppers. Shoppers may find their favorite vendors and develop close relationships.

Thinking Sociologically

In the past, raising children was considered a family task, done by the primary family group. Today, many children are in child care settings, often run by secondary groups. What differences do you see between the experiences a child receives in a family versus child care? What might be the advantages and disadvantages of each? Can a secondary group provide care comparable with that provided by a family? Can the secondary group provide better care than do abusive families?

Reference groups are composed of members who act as role models and establish the standards against which all members measure their conduct. Individuals look to reference groups to set guidelines for behavior and decision making. The term is often used to refer to models in one's chosen career field. Students in premed, nursing, computer science, business, or sociology programs watch the behavior patterns of those who have become successful professionals in their chosen career. When people make the transition from student to professional, they adopt clothing, time schedules, salary expectations, and other characteristics from reference groups. Professional organizations such as the American Bar Association or the American Sociological Association set standards for behavior and achievements.

However, it is possible to be an attorney or an athlete and not aspire to be like others in the group if they are unethical or abuse substances such as steroids. Instead, a person might be shaped by the values of a church group or a political group with which he or she identifies. Not every group one belongs to is a reference group. It must provide a standard by which

Table 5.2   Primary and Secondary Group Characteristics

	Primary Group	Secondary Group
Quality of relationships	Personal orientation	Goal orientation
Duration of relationships	Usually long-term	Variable, often short-term
Breadth of activities	Broad, usually involving many activities	Narrow, usually involving few largely goal-directed activities
Subjective perception of relationships	As an end in itself (friendship, belonging)	As a means to an end (to accomplish a task, earn money)
Typical examples	Families, close friendships	Coworkers, political organizations

Bloods gang members in Los Angeles use their in-group hand signal to identify one another.

school one attends, an interest group such as the fraternity or sorority one joins, or the area where one lives. People tend to judge others according to their own in-group identity. Members of the in-group—for example, supporters of a high school team—often feel hostility toward or reject out-group members—boosters of the rival team. The perceived outside threat or hostility is often exaggerated, but it does help create the in-group members' feelings of solidarity.

Unfortunately, these feelings of hostility can result in prejudice and ethnocentrism, overlooking the individual differences of group members. Teen groups or gangs such as the Bloods and the Crips are examples of in-groups and out-groups in action, as are the ethnic and religious conflicts between Sunni and Shiite Muslims in Iraq. In each case, the group loyalty is enhanced by hostility toward the out-group, resulting in gang conflicts and war.

Thinking Sociologically

What are some examples of your own group affiliations: Primary groups? Secondary groups? Peer groups? Reference groups? In-groups and out-groups?

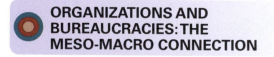

ORGANIZATIONS AND BUREAUCRACIES: THE MESO-MACRO CONNECTION

you evaluate your behavior for it to be a reference group. For example, ethnic groups provide some adolescents with strong reference group standards by which to judge themselves. The stronger the ethnic pride and identification, the more some teens may separate themselves from contact with members of other ethnic groups (Schaefer and Kunz 2007). This can be functional or dysfunctional for the teens, as shown in the next section on in-groups and out-groups.

An **in-group** is one to which an individual feels a sense of loyalty and belonging. It also may serve as a reference group and a primary group; these are different features of groups. An **out-group** is one to which an individual does not belong, but more than that, it is a group that is often in competition or in opposition to an in-group.

Membership in an in-group may be based on sex, race, ethnic group, social class, religion, political affiliation, the

Video Link 5.3
Watch an analysis of the Darfur genocide.

Our days are filled with activities that involve us with complex organizations: from the doctor's appointment to college classes; from the political rally for the issue we are supporting to worship in our church, temple, or mosque; from paying state sales tax for our toothpaste to buying a sandwich at a fast-food franchise. Figure 5.5 shows the institutions of society, each made up of thousands of organizations (your medical organization, educational organization, religious group, economic corporations, political movements, the government itself) and each following the cultural norms of the society. We have statuses and roles in each group, and these link us to networks and the larger social world.

How did these organizational forms develop? Let us consider briefly the transformations of organizations into their modern forms and the characteristics of meso-level organizations today.

Modern Organizations and Their Evolution

Empires around the world have risen and fallen since the dawn of civilization. Some economic, political, and religious systems have flourished. Others such as monarchies and fascism have withered. We cannot understand our social world at any historical or modern time without comprehending the organizational structures and processes present at that time. Recall from Chapter 3 the discussion of types of societies, from hunter-gatherer to postindustrial. Each type of society entails different organizational structures, from early cities and feudal manors to craft guilds, heavy industries, and Web-based companies today (Blau 1956; Nolan and Lenski 2008).

The development of modern organizations and bureaucracies began with industrialization in the 1700s, and they had become the dominant form of industrial organizations by the 1800s. Rationality, the attempt to reach maximum efficiency, became the trend in managing organizations and was thought to be the best way to run organizations—efficiently and with rules that are rationally designed to accomplish goals (Weber 1947). People were expected to behave in purposeful, coordinated ways to reach goals efficiently. No longer were decisions made by tradition, custom, or the whim of a despot. Instead, trained leaders planned policies to achieve organizational efficiency. Tasks became more specialized, and some manual jobs were taken over by machines.

Standardization of products allowed for greater productivity, precision, and speed. These modern "rational" organizations, called formal organizations, are complex secondary groups deliberately formed to pursue and achieve certain goals. The Red Cross, Ford Motor Corporation, Blue Cross/Blue Shield insurance, and your university are all formal organizations. Another example of rational formal organization is found in the fast-food empires springing up around the world. The next "Sociology Around the World" describes the trend toward the "McDonaldization of Society"—Ritzer's pop culture term for rationalization.

Video Link 5.4
Consider recent bank mergers.

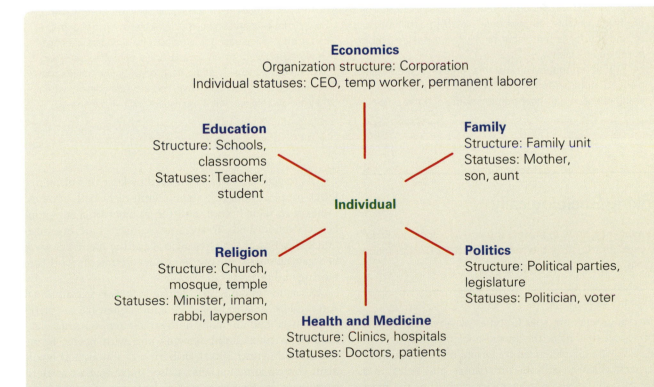

Economics
Organization structure: Corporation
Individual statuses: CEO, temp worker, permanent laborer

Education
Structure: Schools, classrooms
Statuses: Teacher, student

Family
Structure: Family unit
Statuses: Mother, son, aunt

Individual

Religion
Structure: Church, mosque, temple
Statuses: Minister, imam, rabbi, layperson

Politics
Structure: Political parties, legislature
Statuses: Politician, voter

Health and Medicine
Structure: Clinics, hospitals
Statuses: Doctors, patients

Figure 5.5 Our Social World: Institutions, Organizations, and Individual Status

Sociology Around the World

The McDonaldization of Society

The process of rationalization described by Max Weber—the attempt to reach maximum bureaucratic efficiency—comes in a new modern version, expanded and streamlined, as exemplified by the fast-food restaurant business and the chain "box" stores found around the world. Efficient, rational, predictable sameness is sweeping the world—from diet centers such as NutriSystem to 7-Eleven and from Wal-Mart to Gap clothing stores with their look-alike layouts. Most major world cities feature McDonald's or Kentucky Fried Chicken in the traditional main plazas or train stations for the flustered foreigners and curious native consumers.

The McDonaldization of society, as George Ritzer (2008) calls it, refers to several trends: First, *efficiency* is maximized by the sameness—same store plans, same mass-produced items, same procedures. Second is *predictability*, the knowledge that each hamburger or piece of chicken will be the same, leaving nothing to chance. Third, everything is *calculated* so that the organization can ensure that everything fits a standard—every burger is cooked the same number of seconds on each side. Fourth, there is *increased control* over employees and customers so there are fewer variables to consider—including substitution of technology for human labor as a way to ensure predictability and efficiency.

What is the result of this efficient, predictable, planned, automated new world? According to Ritzer, the world is becoming more dehumanized, and the efficiency is taking over individual creativity and human interactions. The mom-and-pop grocery, bed and breakfasts, and local craft or clothing shops are rapidly becoming a thing of the past, giving way to the McClones. This process of the McDonaldization of society, meaning principles of efficiency and rationalization exemplified by fast-food chains, is coming to dominate more and more sectors of our social world (Ritzer 1998, 2004, 2008). While there are aspects of this predictability that we all like, there is also a loss of the uniqueness and local flavor that individual entrepreneurs bring to a community.

To try to re-create this culture, Ritzer suggests, there is a movement toward "Starbuckization." Starbucks is unique because of its aesthetic contribution. Starbucks makes customers feel like they are purchasing a cultural product along with their coffee. This culture, however, is as controlled as any other McDonaldized endeavor, making Starbucks as much a McClone as its predecessors.

McDonaldization is so widespread and influential that many modern universities are McDonaldized. A large lecture hall is a very efficient way of teaching sociology or biology to many students at once. Similarly, distance learning, PowerPoint presentations, multiple-choice exams, and limited textbooks increase the predictability of course offerings. Grade point averages and credit hours completed are very calculated ways to view students. Moreover, universities control students by deciding what courses are offered, when they are offered, and what professors will teach them.

Thinking Sociologically

Can anything be done to protect the non-McClone, individually owned stores, or is the move toward McDonaldization inevitable?

Bureaucracies are specific types of very large formal organizations that have the purpose of maximizing efficiency. They are characterized by formal relations between participants, clearly laid-out procedures and rules, and pursuit of stated goals. Bureaucracies evolved as the most efficient way of producing products economically for mass markets (Ritzer 2004).

As societies became dominated by large organizations, fewer people worked the family farm or owned a cottage industry in their homes, and the number of small shopkeepers diminished. Today, some countries are organizational societies in which a majority of the members work in organizations. Many other societies around the world are moving in this direction.

Societies making the transition between traditional and modern organizational structures often have a blend of the two, and in many industrializing countries, traditional organizational systems mix with newer forms (Nolan and Lenski 2008). Bribery, corruption, and favoritism govern some nations as they move toward modern bureaucracies. People in government jobs are promoted based on whom they are connected to in their family tree, not on the basis of their competence as assessed by formal training, examinations, or criteria derived from the needs of the position and the organization. Breaking down old systems can create disruption, even anomie, in societies undergoing these transitions.

Postindustrial societies feature high dependence on technology and information sharing. Few people live and work on farms. In the United States today, only 1% of the population claim farming as their main occupation, and only 2% live on farms (U.S. Environmental Protection Agency 2009). About one in five citizens lives in a rural area (U.S. Department of Agriculture 2008). This is compared with 15% in farm-related occupations in 1950 (Wright 2007) and 63.7% in 1850 (Europa World Year Book 2005). The number of farms decreased from 5,648,000 in 1950 to 2,090,000 in 2006, while the average size of farms grew from 213 to 445 acres as agribusiness bought up small family farms (Wright 2007).

Some organizations provide us work necessary for survival. Others are forced on us—prisons, mental hospitals, military draft systems, even education to a certain age. Still others are organizations we believe in and voluntarily join—scouts, environmental protest groups, sports leagues (Etzioni 1975). Membership in voluntary organizations is higher in the United States than in many other countries (D. Johnson and Johnson 2006), yet in recent years, membership in many voluntary organizations has dropped, a factor discussed in the next "Sociology in Our Social World." Some analysts argue that new types of affiliations and interactions, including the Internet, are replacing some older affiliations.

The hospital setting is an example of a modern formal organization that not only is governed by formal rules and impersonal relations but also increasingly involves extensive communication via computers.

Thinking Sociologically

Make a list of your activities in a typical day. Which of these activities are, and which are not, associated with large (meso-level) formal organizations?

Organizations and modern life are almost synonymous. Live in one, and you belong to the other. In this section, we consider some characteristics of bureaucracy and some of the processes and problems that occur in organizations.

Think about the many organizations that regularly affect your life: the legal system that passes laws, your college, your workplace, and voluntary organizations to which you belong. Individuals require organizations for human interaction and to meet their needs, and organizations need humans to hold positions and carry out tasks or roles. Some organizations, such as the local chapter of the Rotary Club or a chapter of a sorority, function at the micro level. Everyone is in a face-to-face relationship with every other member of the organization. However, those local chapters are part of a nationwide

These young people come together for the voluntary civic action of cleaning up the community—part of a local service project.

organization that is actually a meso-level corporation. At another level in terms of size, the federal government is a very complex organization that influences the lives of every citizen, and some transnational corporations are global in their reach. Both operate at the macro level.

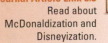

Journal Article Link 5.3
Read about
McDonaldization and
Disneyization.

Sociology in Our Social World

Bowling Alone Versus Contributing to Your Social World

To join or not to join—that is a question many college students must decide. They are torn between spending time with their computers and video games and joining groups, even doing volunteer work in the community or working on a political campaign. Research on joining organized groups versus engaging in individual activities gives us some insight into choices and the consequences of these choices.

According to one study of group activities, bowling leagues have experienced significant declines in membership in recent years. Yet more people in the United States bowl than vote, often enjoying the sport as individuals rather than in organized groups. For sociologists, this pattern points to a broad trend—those who once participated in group activities are turning inward and not joining organized groups (Putnam 1995, 2001).

Does this reflect a breakdown of the U.S. community? Parent-Teacher Associations (PTAs), the Red Cross, bowling leagues, and other civic groups were all down in numbers in the mid-1990s. The result is that people got together less often. The U.S. enthusiasm for organizational participation that de Tocqueville observed some 200 years ago appeared to be dampening. Robert Putnam, the researcher, speculated that loss of faith in institutions and the existence of television and computers, what some call "technological individualizing," in many homes kept people from connecting with others. Staying home and watching TV or surfing the Net replaced a night out with friends or joining organized groups.

In a separate study, a team of sociologists from the University of California, Berkeley, also analyzed the relationship between individualism and a sense of community. They concluded that individualism is problematic for Americans living in an interdependent world (Bellah, Madsen, Sullivan, Swindler, and Tipton 1996). As individuals lose contact with others, they face private problems alone. What the United States needs, according to the authors of this study, is a greater sense of community to give individuals a feeling of belonging and to link the micro and macro levels of the social world (Bellah et al. 1996). In other words, individuals should think about "bowling together" or find other ways to connect and build a sense of community through group affiliation or involvement.

More recently, there is evidence that different types of groups and affiliations—some based on new technologies, some based on volunteering—are emerging to replace bowling leagues and similar organizations (Putnam 2001; Thoits and Hewitt 2001). From college students involved in the 2008 political campaigns to volunteer work on Habitat for Humanity and other work projects, volunteerism has increased in the past decade (Cillizza and Murray 2008). The benefits for those who join groups and volunteer are increased physical and psychological well-being, happiness, greater life satisfaction, higher self-esteem, more sense of control over life, better physical health, and less depression. Thus, contributing to your social world may have many advantages for both you as an individual and those you are helping.

Thinking Sociologically

Think about your friends and their activities. Are they involved in social activities or volunteer work? What differences do you see between your friends based on their involvement? Is lack of involvement a real threat to a local community?

Characteristics of Bureaucracy

To get a driver's license, pay school fees, or buy tickets for a popular concert or game, you may have to stand in a long line. Finally, after waiting in line, you discover that you have forgotten your social security number, or they do not take a credit card. The rules and red tape are irksome. Yet what is the alternative? Some institutions have adopted telephone and online registration or ticket purchases, but even with this automated system, problems can occur. Frustrations with bureaucracy are a part of modern life, but the alternatives (such as bartering) are less efficient and sometimes more frustrating or bewildering to those who are used to bureaucratic efficiency.

If you have been to a Caribbean, African, Asian, or Middle Eastern market, you know that the bartering system is used to settle on a mutually agreeable price. This system is more personal and involves intense interaction between the seller and the buyer, but it also takes more time and is less efficient. Bartering can be frustrating to the uninitiated visitor accustomed to the relative efficiency and predictability of bureaucracy, going to a store, selecting a product, and paying a set price. As societies transition, they tend to adopt bureaucratic forms of organization.

Bureaucracies are a particular form of modern organization, characterized by trained officials who carry out procedures and tasks in an efficient way. Most organizations in modern society—hospitals, schools, churches, government agencies, industries, banks, and even large clubs—are bureaucracies. Therefore, understanding these modern organizations is critical to understanding the modern social world in which we live.

At the beginning of the 20th century, Max Weber (1864–1920) looked for the reasons behind the massive changes taking place in societies that were causing the transition from traditional society to bureaucratic, capitalist society. He wanted to understand why the rate of change was more rapid in some parts of Europe than in others and why bureaucracy came to dominate the forms of organization in some countries. Whereas traditional society looked to the past for guidance, bureaucratic industrial society required a new form of thinking and behavior, a change in attitude toward rationality. Weber observed that leadership in business and government was moving from traditional forms with powerful families and charismatic leaders toward the more efficient and less personal bureaucracy.

Weber's (1947) term, **ideal-type bureaucracy**, refers to the dominant and essential characteristics of organizations that are designed for reliability and efficiency. It describes not a good or perfect organization but merely an organization with a particular set of traits. Any particular bureaucracy is unlikely to have all the characteristics in the ideal type, but the degree of bureaucratization is measured by how closely they resemble the core characteristics of the ideal type. The following shows Weber's ideal-type bureaucracy with examples related to schools:

1. *Division of labor based on technical competence:* Administrators lead but do not teach, and instructors teach only in areas of their certification; staff are assigned positions for which their credentials make them most qualified, and recruitment and promotion are governed by formal policies.

2. *Administrative hierarchy:* There is a specified chain of command and designated channels of communication, from school board to superintendent to principal to teacher.

3. *Formal rules and regulations:* Written procedures and rules—perhaps published in an administrative manual—spell out systemwide requirements, including discipline practices, testing procedures, curricula, sick days for teachers, penalties for student tardiness, field trip policies, and other matters.

4. *Impersonal relationships:* Formal relationships tend to prevail between teachers and students and between teachers and administrative staff (superintendents, principals, counselors); written records and formal communication provide a paper trail for all decisions.

5. *Emphasis on rationality and efficiency to reach goals:* Established processes are used, based on the best interests of the school. Efficiency is defined in terms of the lowest overall cost to the organization in reaching a goal, not in terms of personal consequences.

6. *Provision of life-long careers:* Employees may spend their entire careers working for the same organization, working their way up the hierarchy through promotions.

Although the list of characteristics makes bureaucracies sound formal and rigid, informal structures allow organizational members to deviate from rules both to meet the goals of the organization more efficiently and to humanize an otherwise uncaring and sterile workplace. The **informal structure** includes the unwritten norms and the interpersonal networks that people use within an organization to carry out roles. Likewise, although bylaws, constitutions, or contracts spell out the way things are supposed to be done, people often develop unwritten shortcuts to accomplish goals. The U.S. Postal Service has rules specifying that letter carriers are not supposed to walk across people's lawns, yet if they did not find shortcuts, it would take much longer for mail to be delivered.

Informal norms are not always compatible with those of the formal organization. Consider the following example from a famous classical study. In the Western Electric plant near Chicago, the study found that new workers were quickly socialized to do "a fair day's work," and those who did more or less than the established norm—what the work group thought was fair—were considered "rate busters" or "chiselers" and experienced pressure from the group to conform. These informal mechanisms gave informal groups of workers a degree of power in the organization (Roethlisberger and Dickson 1939).

Thinking Sociologically

How closely does each of Weber's characteristics of ideal-type bureaucracy describe your college or your work setting? Is your college highly bureaucratized, with many rules and regulations? Are decisions based on efficiency and cost-effectiveness, educational quality, or both? To what extent is your work setting characterized by hierarchy, formal rules governing your work time, and impersonality?

Individuals in Bureaucracies

Lindi England, a young woman from a small town in West Virginia, joined the military looking for opportunity and adventure. Instead, she became a victim and a scapegoat. The bureaucracy was the U.S. military; the setting was the Abu Ghraib prison in Iraq; the group pressure was to conform and fit in under stressful conditions by "going along with the guards," who were abusing and humiliating the prisoners (Zimbardo 2004). Caring and humane military officers may allow abuse of prisoners or order bombing strikes even though they know that some innocent people will be killed or maimed. In the military command in a war, a cold, impersonal cost-benefit analysis takes priority. In bureaucracies, self-preservation is the core value, and rational choice is often effective in explaining interactions in these contexts.

Humans can be moral, altruistic, and self-sacrificing for the good of others, but nations and other extremely large organizations (such as corporations or government) are inherently driven by a cost-benefit ratio (Niebuhr 1932). As one moves toward larger and more impersonal bureaucracies, the nature of interaction often changes.

Professionals in bureaucracies include doctors, lawyers, engineers, professors, and others who have certain special attributes: advanced education, knowledge and competency in a field, high levels of autonomy to make decisions based on their expertise, a strong commitment to their field, a service orientation and commitment to the needs of the client, standards and regulations set by the profession, and a sense of intrinsic satisfaction from the work (rather than motivation rooted in external rewards, such as salary). Professionals also claim authority, power, and control in their work area because of their mastery or expertise in a field (Tolbert and Hall 2008). Professionals may face conflicting loyalties to their profession and to the bureaucratic organization in which they are employed. A scientist hired by a tobacco company faced a dilemma when his research findings did not support the company position that nicotine is not addictive. They wanted him to falsify his research, which would be a violation of professional ethics. Should he be a whistle-blower and publicly challenge the organization? Several professionals have done so but lost their jobs as a result.

Bureaucracy, some argue, is the number one enemy of professionalism, for it reduces autonomy. First, bureaucrats insist that authority rests in the person who holds an organizational status or title in the hierarchy rather than the person with the most expertise. Second, bureaucrats tend to reward people with external rewards such as bonuses rather than internal motivations. Third, bureaucrats focus on the needs of the organization as primary rather than on the needs of the client or professional. The potential clash between professionals and bureaucracy raises key concerns as universities, hospitals, and other large organizations are governed increasingly by bureaucratic principles (Roberts and Donahue 2000). Alienation among professionals occurs when they are highly regulated rather than when they have some decision-making authority and are granted some autonomy (Tolbert and Hall 2008). For example, high-tech companies that depend on engineering designers find that hierarchical structures undermine productivity, whereas factors such as intrinsic satisfaction, flexible hours, and relaxed work environments are central to creative productivity (Florida 2002; Friedman 2005; Molotch 2003).

Minorities in bureaucracies may come up against barriers that keep women and minority group members from reaching high levels of management. The result is that individuals from these groups are found disproportionately in midlevel positions with little authority and less pay than others with similar skills and credentials (Arulampalam, Booth, and Bryan 2007; Heilman and Chen 2003). When employees have little chance of promotion, they have less ambition and loyalty to the organization (Kanter 1977).

Women in many countries have low-paid, dead-end jobs that make them feel uninvolved and unconnected. The jobs result in alienation, but these women need the work, and they have little choice but to accept dead-end jobs.

Research indicates that women executives bring valuable alternative perspectives to organizational leadership. They share information readily, give employees greater autonomy, and stress interconnectedness between parts of the organization, resulting in a more democratic type of leadership (Kramer 2007). The more women in an organization's senior positions, the more likely newcomers are to find support.

The interaction of people who see things differently because of religious beliefs, ethnic backgrounds, and gender experiences increases productivity in many organizations. Having a wide range of perspectives can lead to better problem solving (Florida 2004; Molotch 2003). Because diversity actually increases productivity and problem solving, the barriers to promotion have been irrational and dysfunctional to organizations.

Problems in Bureaucracies

Bureaucratic inefficiency and red tape are legendary and have been the theme of many classic novels, from Charles Dickens's *Bleak House*, which describes the legal system in England in the 1800s, to George Orwell's *1984*, which depicts a sterile, controlled environment. Yet bureaucracies are likely to stay, for they are the most efficient form of modern organization yet devised. Nonetheless, several individual and organizational problems created by bureaucratic structures are important to understand.

Alienation, feeling uninvolved, uncommitted, unappreciated, and unconnected, occurs when workers are assigned routine, boring tasks or dead-end jobs with no possibility of advancement. Marx believed that alienation is a structural feature of capitalism, with serious consequences: Workers lose their sense of purpose and seem to become dehumanized and objectified in their work, creating a product that they often do not see completed and for which they do not get the profits (Marx [1844] 1964).

Dissatisfaction comes from low pay and poor benefits; routine, repetitive, and fragmented tasks; lack of challenge and autonomy, leading to boredom; and poor working conditions. Workers who see possibilities for advancement put more energy into the organization, but those stuck in their positions are less involved and put more energy into activities outside the workplace (Kanter 1977).

Thinking Sociologically

How might participation in decision making, increased autonomy for workers, and stockholder shares in the company enhance commitment and productivity in your place of work? What might be some risks or downsides to such worker input and freedom?

Oligarchy, the concentration of power in the hands of a small group, is a common occurrence in organizations. In the early 1900s, Robert Michels, a French sociologist, wrote about the *iron law of oligarchy*, the idea that power becomes concentrated in the hands of a small group of leaders in political, business, voluntary, or other organizations. Initially, organizational needs, more than the motivation for power, cause these few stable leaders to emerge. As organizations grow, a division of labor emerges so that only a few leaders have access to information, resources, and the overall picture. This, in turn, causes leaders who enjoy their elite positions of power to become entrenched (Michels [1911] 1967). How do they do this? Some political leaders attempt to exceed their term limits, as in Honduras and Venezuela, or hold fraudulent elections so they can stay in power, as in Afghanistan and other countries. Corporate executives sometimes also hide information about financial problems from workers and investors to protect their positions.

Goal displacement occurs when the original motives or goals of the organization are displaced by new, secondary goals. Organizations are formed to meet specific goals. Religious organizations are established to worship a deity and serve humanity on behalf of that deity, schools are founded to educate children, and social work agencies are organized to serve the needs of citizens who seem to have fallen between the cracks. Yet, over time, the original goals may be met or become less important as other motivations and interests emerge (Merton 1938; Whyte 1956).

Parkinson's law, which states that in a bureaucracy work expands to fill the time and space available for its completion, is an example of inefficiency (Parkinson 1957). If we build a new room on our house, we are likely to fill it to capacity. If classes are canceled for a day, our free day gets filled up with other activities. If we have two tests to study for, each takes half a day, but if we have one, it may still take most of the day. Despite the expansion of space or time, we still do not seem to have enough time or room. Organizations work similarly. Parkinson's point is that organizations grow automatically, sometimes beyond efficiency or effectiveness.

Video Link 5.5
Watch an analysis of the iron industry.

Policymakers have explored other ways of organizing complex social systems besides hierarchical bureaucracies. Workers' productive behavior is influenced not just by pay and working conditions but by emotions, beliefs, and the norms of the other workers (Roethlisberger and Dickson 1939). To address these factors, many organizations have moved toward workplace democracy, employee participation in decision making, and employee ownership plans. Note the recent plans to provide stock incentives to high-paid employees, increasing their motivation to improve the company.

Alternative organization structures refer to recent approaches that have been developed to deal with some of the problems discussed previously. Employee-owned companies are owned in part or in full by employees, who are given or can buy shares. Profit sharing is generally part of the deal. If the company does well, all workers benefit. Studies show that this increases production and improves dedication, but the decision-making process is slower, and there is increased risk for the individual employees. However, the idea is that employees have a stake in their company and the job they do (Blasi, Kruse, and Bernstein 2003). Other companies, democratic-collective organizations, rely on cooperation, place authority and decision making in the collective group, and use personal appeals to ensure that everyone participates in problem solving. Rules, hierarchy, and status distinctions are minimized, and hiring is often based on shared values and friendships (Deming 2000). Members believe these organizations are more humane, and workers feel connected to the purpose and the product. The hope is that these new forms of organization—nonbureaucratic forms—may actually be a more effective way to organize postindustrial corporations.

Although we may fantasize about escaping from the rat race or about isolating ourselves on an island, groups and bureaucracies are a part of modern life that few can escape.

Thinking Sociologically

In what areas of your college or workplace do you see goal displacement? That is, where do you see decisions being driven by goals other than the original purpose of the university, which was to educate a new generation and expand human knowledge?

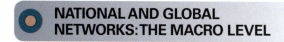

NATIONAL AND GLOBAL NETWORKS: THE MACRO LEVEL

In one sense, learning to understand people who are unlike us, to network with people who have different cultures, and to make allowances for alternative ideas about society and human behavior have become core competencies in our globalizing social world. Increasingly, colleges have study-abroad programs, jobs open up abroad for teaching English as a second language, and corporations seek employees who are multilingual and culturally competent in diverse settings. One rather recent college graduate with a sociology degree found that she could use her sociology skills in leading groups of college-age students in international travel experiences. She explains this use of sociology in the next "The Applied Sociologist at Work."

With modern communication and transportation systems and the ability to transfer ideas and money with a touch of the keyboard, global networks are superseding national

boundaries. Multinational corporations now employ citizens from around the world and can make their own rules because there is no oversight body. National systems and international organizations, from the United Nations to the World Bank to multinational corporations, are typically governed through rational bureaucratic systems.

One complicating factor at the national and global levels is multilingualism, the reality that many languages are used to communicate. Although Spanish, Chinese, and Arabic are widely used in homes across the globe, English has become the language of commerce. This is because much of the political and economic power and control over the expansion of technology has been located in English-speaking countries.

Technology has some interesting implications for human interaction. E-mail, Web pages, chat rooms, and blogs have made it possible for people around the world to talk with each other, exchange ideas, and even develop friendships. In other parts of the world, dictators can no longer keep the citizenry from knowing what people outside their country think. In China, as fast as officials censor information on the World Wide Web, computer experts find ways around the restrictions. Officials in Myanmar try to block satellite communication to restrict access to the information highway, but despite efforts to limit access, the process of change is occurring so rapidly that we cannot know what technology will mean for the global world. It is almost certain that the processes of interaction across national lines will continue despite some efforts to curb communication. The World Wide Web was not invented until 1989, and e-mail has been available to most citizens—even in the affluent countries—only since the early 1990s (Brasher 2004). Countries are still struggling with what this means for change.

Within nations, people with common interests, be it organic food, animal rights, or peace, can contact one another. Hate groups also set up Web pages and mobilize others with their view of the world, and terrorists use the Internet to communicate with terrorist cells around the world. Clearly, the ability to communicate around the globe is transforming the world and our nations in ways that affect local communities and private individuals. Indeed, the Internet has become a major outlet for sellers and a source for consumers. A wide range of products can be obtained through Internet orders from Web sites that have no geographical home base. In some cases, there are no actual warehouses or manufacturing plants, and there might not be a home office. Some businesses are global and exist in the Ethernet, not in any specific nation (Ritzer 2004). This reality makes one rethink national and global loyalties and realities.

From the discussion of rationalization and the McDonaldization of society in the previous section, we see some results: Family loyalties are considered less important

The Applied Sociologist at Work— Elise Roberts

Using Sociology in International Travel and Intercultural Education

By Elise Roberts

After graduating from college with a bachelor's degree in sociology, I left the country to backpack through Mexico and Central America. My studies helped me to be more objective and aware as I experienced other societies. My international travel helped me examine my own societal assumptions and further understand how society creates so much of one's experience and view of the world. Eventually, I found a job leading groups of teenagers on alternative-education trips abroad. I was excited to get the job, but I was soon to learn that leading groups of teenagers in other countries is actually very hard work.

What struck me on meeting my first group was that I had very few students who initially understood this sociological perspective that I took for granted and that was so helpful in dealing with others. At times, my students would make fun of the way things were done in other countries, calling them "weird" or "stupid." They would mock the local traditions, until we discussed comparable traditions in American culture. These students were not mean or unintelligent. In fact, they loved the places we were seeing and the people we were meeting. They just thought everything was factually, officially weird. They had been socialized to understand their own society's ways as "right" and "normal." They were fully absorbed in the U.S. society, and they had never questioned it before.

It was rewarding to apply concepts from my textbooks in the real world. My coleaders and I learned to have fun while encouraging our students to become more socially conscious and analytical about their travel experience. We sent the groups out on scavenger hunts, and they would inevitably come back proudly announcing what they had paid for a rickshaw ride—only to learn that they had paid 10 times the local price. We would use this experience to talk about the role of foreigners, the assumptions that the local population made due to our skin color, and the culture of bartering. They had to learn to understand "odd" gestures, like pointing with the lips or side-to-side nodding. We would use these experiences to discuss nonverbal communication and gestures that we take for granted in U.S. culture.

We would encourage our novice travelers to interact with the people around them, which helped them understand the struggles facing immigrants and non-English speakers in the United States. We would force them to have conversations while standing toe-to-toe with each other, and they would finish with backaches from leaning away from one another. We would not allow them to explain their behavior with "because it's creepy to stand so close together," even though this was the consensus. "Why do you feel uncomfortable?" we would ask. "Why is this weird?" The answer has to do with social constructions of what is "normal" in any society.

Of course, while traveling internationally, one is surrounded by various other sociological issues, such as different racial or ethnic conflicts, gender roles, or class hierarchies, and learning about these issues was a part of our program as well. Without realizing it, many group conversations and meetings began to remind me of some of my favorite undergraduate sociology classes. "Study sociology!" I would say, plugging my major to the most interested students.

I have always thought that travel was an incredibly useful means not only to learn about the society and culture one is visiting but also to learn much about oneself and one's home society. For teenagers who otherwise might never step back to think about the role of being a foreigner or the traditions and social patterns they take for granted, it is even more important. Traveling abroad on my own and leading programs abroad were such extremely rich and rewarding experiences not only due to the cross-cultural exchanges and the intense personal examination that I saw in my students but also because it was fascinating and rewarding to be able to use my sociology degree every day on my job.

Note: Elise Roberts graduated from Macalester College with a major in sociology. Her recent travels took her through Central America, the South Pacific, and many parts of Asia. She recently graduated from Columbia University with a master's degree in international social work.

than the needs of the corporation. Feelings are subordinated to thought processes. Efficiency and calculability are highly prized in the social system. However, as these Western notions of how public life should operate are exported to other countries, a severe backlash has occurred. In many Middle Eastern Islamic countries, for example, these values clash with Muslim loyalties and priorities. The result has been high levels of anger at the United States and Western Europe. Many scholars believe that Middle Eastern anger at the United States is based not on opposition to freedom and democracy, as our politicians sometimes say, but on what some Middle Easterners see as the crass greed and impersonal organizational structures we try to import into their micro-, meso-, and macro-level worlds. They feel that their very culture is threatened. Radical fundamentalist movements—groups that are fueled by religious beliefs and socioeconomic stressors and that cope by seeing the world in absolutes, rejecting all ambiguity—are mostly antimodernization movements turned militant (Antoun 2001; Heilman 2000; Marty and Appleby 2004; Ontario Consultants on Religious Tolerance 2004). They have emerged in Christian, Jewish, Islamic, Sikh, and other groups, largely as a response to a perceived crisis (Armstrong 2000). Some aspects of global terrorism and international conflict are based on the way the Western world organizes its social life and exports it to other parts of the world. These conflicts, in turn, have resulted in mobilization of the military in the United States. The consequence is that members of your own family might be serving abroad even as you read these pages.

Thinking Sociologically

How do you think global interaction will be transformed through Internet technology? How will individual connections between people be affected by macro-level changes in our social world?

Policy Issues: Women and Globalization

Women in many parts of the world are viewed as second-class citizens, the most economically, politically, and socially marginalized people on the planet, caught in expectations of religion, patriarchy, and roles needed to sustain life (Schneider and Silverman 2006). To help their children survive, women do whatever their situation allows to make money: street selling, low-paying factory assembly line work, piecework (i.e., sewing clothing in their homes),

prostitution and sex work, and domestic service. Women also produce 75% to 90% of the food crops in the world, run households, and are often the main support for children in poor countries. Yet, due to the "feminization of poverty," two out of three poor adults are women (Enloe 2006; Robbins 2005). Causes of and policies to address the many problems facing women are found at each level of analysis and will be discussed throughout the book.

One macro-level organization with policies to help raise the status of women through development is the United Nations. Each decade since the 1960s, this global organization has set forth plans to improve conditions in poor countries. Early plans to help poor countries were driven by the interests of capitalist countries in the developed world. This left powerless women out of the equation and planning. Women suffered more under some of these plans because their positions and responsibilities did not change. Conditions got worse as development money went to large corporations with the idea that profits would trickle down to the local level, an idea that did not materialize in most countries (Boulding and Dye 2002).

Around the world, two thirds of the poorest adults are women, even though women produce more than two thirds of the food supplies in the world. A Laotian woman works in the field (top), and an Indian woman transports goods to the market (bottom).

More recently, the United Nations has sponsored conferences on the status of women. The United Nations' Division for the Advancement of Women and other organizations are now developing policies to help educate local women in health, nutrition, basic first aid, and business methods. Many projects have been spawned, including micro-lending organizations (Grameen Bank, SEWA, Finca, Care), allowing individuals and groups of women to borrow money to start cooperatives and other small-business ventures. These organizations can have very beneficial effects if they are used wisely by policymakers who care about the people rather than just about their own interests. In the next few chapters, we will learn about some of the factors that cause some individuals and countries to be poorer than others.

Our networks set norms and curb our behaviors, usually inclining us to conform to the social expectations of our associates. This, of course, contributes to the stability of the entire social system because deviation can threaten the existence of "normal" patterns, as we see in the next chapter.

What Have We Learned?

Our social lives are lived in small groups and personal networks. The scope of those networks has broadened with the increased complexity of societies and includes the global social world. Indeed, it is easy not to recognize how far our networks reach, even to the global level. Although some of our social experiences are informal (unstructured), we are also profoundly affected by another phenomenon of the past three centuries—highly structured bureaucracies. As a result of both, the intimate experiences of our personal lives are far more extensively linked to meso- and macro-level events and to people and places on the other side of the globe than was true for our parents' generation. If we hope to understand our lives, we must understand this broad context. Although it may have been possible to live without global connections and bureaucratic systems several centuries ago, these networks are intricately woven into our lifestyles and our economic systems today. The question is whether we control these networks or they control us.

Key Points

- People in the modern world are connected through one acquaintance to another in a chain of links, referred to as networks. (See pp. 135–136.)

- Increasingly, our electronic technology is creating networks that span the globe, but this same impersonal technology is used to enhance friendship networks and even to meet a romantic life partner. (See pp. 136–138.)

- Interpersonal interactions at the micro level are affected by unspoken assumptions that are understood due to context, by nonverbal communication, and by the symbolism of space between people. (See pp. 138–140.)

- Many of our behaviors are shaped by the statuses (social positions) we hold and the roles (expectations associated with a status) we play. However, our multiple-status occupancy can create role conflicts (between the roles of two statuses) and role strains (between the role expectations of a single status). (See pp. 145–146.)

- When the norms of behavior are unclear, we may experience anomie (normlessness), and this ambiguity compromises our sense of belonging and is linked to the reasons for individuals performing one of the most personal of acts—suicide. (See pp. 147–148.)

- Various types of groups affect our behavior—from primary and secondary groups to peer groups and reference groups. (See pp. 148–150.)

- At the meso level, we find that formal organizations in the contemporary modern world are ruled by rational calculation of the organization's goals rather than by tradition or emotional ties. These modern formal organizations expand, are governed by impersonal formal rules, and stress efficiency and rational decision making. They have come to be called bureaucracies. (See pp. 150–157.)

- Bureaucracies often create certain problems for individuals, and they may actually make them inefficient or destructive. (See pp. 157–158.)

- While bureaucratization emerged at the meso level as the defining element of the modern world, it is also found at the national and global levels, where people do not know each other on a face-to-face basis. (See pp. 158–160.)

- Some scholars think that this impersonal mode of organizing social life—so common in the West for several centuries now—is a critical factor in anti-American and anti-Western resistance movements. (See p. 160.)

Contributing to Our Social World: What Can We Do?

At the Local Level

Tutoring and mentoring: Most campuses have programs that are designed to help students who are struggling with their studies. Contact the Student Affairs Office and arrange to observe and/or volunteer in a program. Helping students build their *social capital*, which includes their knowledge of ways to obtain the help they need, can increase their chances of success.

At the Organizational or Institutional Level

The social capital theory can also be applied to meso-level community organizations:

At the National or Global Level

- *The Anti-Defamation League, the Arab Anti-Defamation League, and the National Association for the Advancement of Colored People:* These organizations often use volunteers or interns and can provide you with the opportunity to learn about the extent to which social contacts and networks play a role in managing social conflict.

- Organize or contribute to a micro-credit organization to help women in countries of the developing world.

 For chapter-specific resources, including **Frontline**, **TED**, and **YouTube** videos; self-quizzes; web exercises; and more, visit **www.pineforge.com/oswmedia3e.**

Deviance and Social Control

Sickos, Perverts, Freaks, and Folks Like Us

Deviants are often thought of as perverts and rule breakers without consciences. We often contrast them to people like us, but the reality is that the line between deviants and conformists is frequently vague, and we may be surprised to learn that often the "deviants are us."

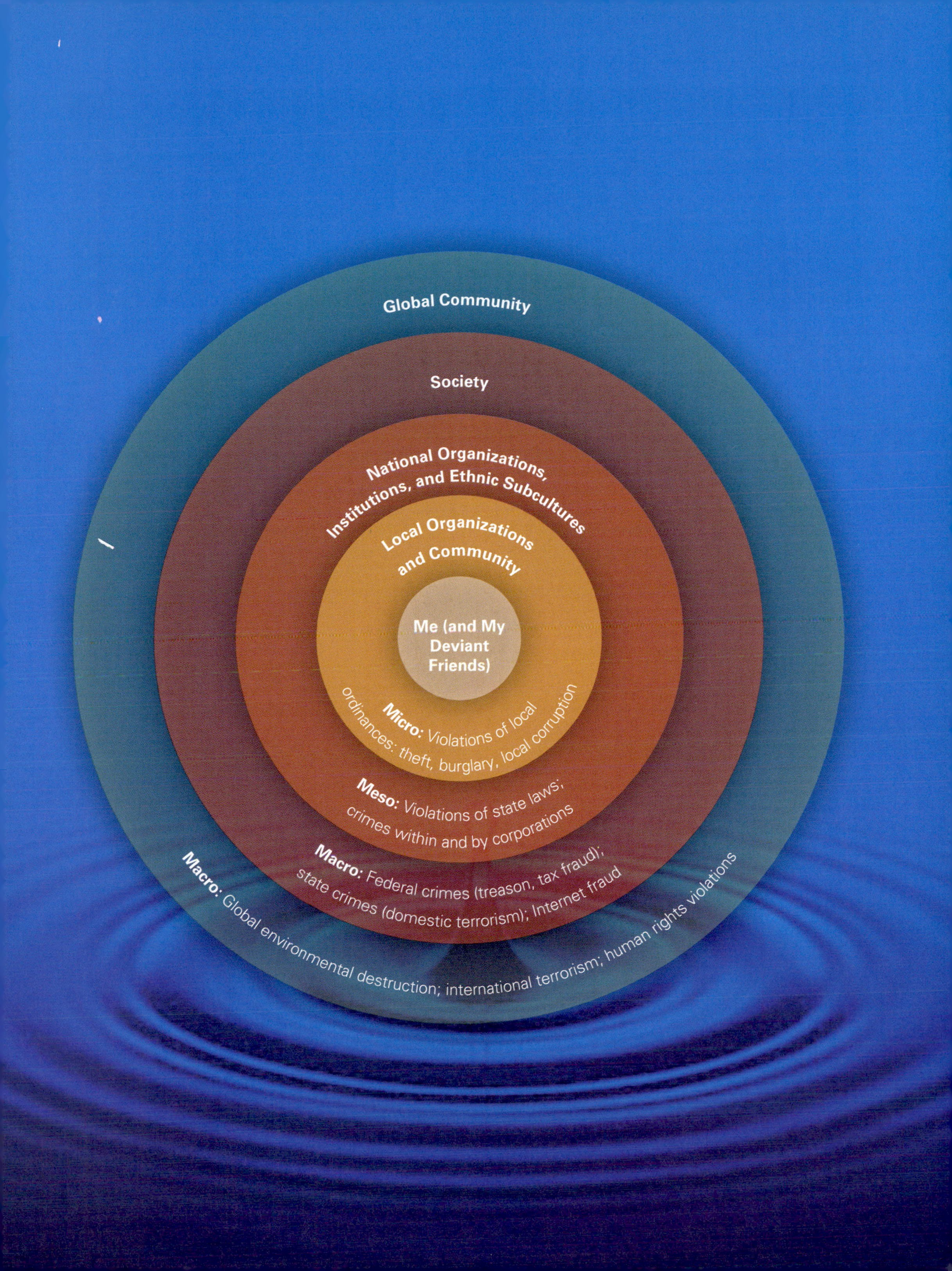

Global Community

Society

National Organizations, Institutions, and Ethnic Subcultures

Local Organizations and Community

Me (and My Deviant Friends)

Micro: Violations of local ordinances: theft, burglary, local corruption

Meso: Violations of state laws; crimes within and by corporations

Macro: Federal crimes (treason, tax fraud); state crimes (domestic terrorism); Internet fraud

Macro: Global environmental destruction; international terrorism; human rights violations

Think About It	
Me (and My Inner Circle)	Are you deviant? Who says so?
Local Community	Why do some people in your community become deviant?
National Institutions; Complex Organizations; Ethnic Groups	What are the implications of organized crime or occupational crime in large bureaucratic organizations?
National Society	What are the costs, and the benefits, of deviance for the nation?
Global Community	How can a global perspective on crime enhance our understanding of international criminal activities?

Wafa grew up as other girls do, but she was destined to make world headlines on January 27, 2002—as the first female suicide bomber in the Palestinian-Israeli conflict. She was the age of most university students reading this book, but she never had an opportunity to attend college. Her chore was to smuggle explosives across the Israeli border for the intended bomber, her brother. Instead, she blew up herself and an Israeli soldier. She was declared a martyr, a *sahida*, by the Al-Aqsa Martyrs Brigade, and they took credit for the attack. Her act was given approval by the group's political leadership, opening the way for other women to follow. Why did this happen? What motivated her to commit suicide and take other lives in the process? Was she driven by ideology to participate in the Palestinian-Israeli struggle? Were there sociological and social structural factors that affected her decision? Most important, was she deviant in carrying out this act, and according to whom?

Wafa Idris grew up in Palestine. She was married at a young age but could not have children. Because this leaves a woman with no role to play in Palestinian society, her husband divorced her and remarried. She had no future, for who would want a barren, divorced woman in a society that values women for their purity and their childbearing ability? She was a burden to her family. Her way out of an impossible and desperate situation was to commit suicide, bringing honor and wealth to her family and redeeming herself in the process. Other women who followed Wafa have similar stories: Most share an inability to control their own lives in the patriarchal society (Handwerk 2004; Victor 2003).

Ironically, terrorist cells in Palestine saw this as an opportunity to recruit other women. Most who joined the cause were vulnerable, broken, with no way out of untenable situations, and they felt they had nothing to lose. For most, this was a way not only to escape the problems in their lives but also to bring honor to their families in the process. It is not a measure of equality that women, too, commit suicide bombings. This development results from a structure of inequality, according to Barbara Victor (2003), who analyzed the lives of these women.

Our question is this: Are these women deviant criminal terrorists, hapless victims of terrorist groups, mentally ill, or martyrs to be honored for their acts? Who says so? Both views are held depending on who is judging the situation. Are they

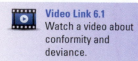

Video Link 6.1
Watch a video about conformity and deviance.

victims of their situations—powerless and lacking status in a patriarchal society? From this opening example, we can begin to see several complexities that arise when considering deviance, and some of these ideas may encourage new ways of looking at what is deviant. In this chapter, we will consider who is deviant, under what circumstances, and in whose eyes. We will find that most people around the world conform to the social norms of their societies most of the time, and we will explore why some turn to deviance.

While most people do conform to the expected norms of their society, occasionally they may violate a norm, and depending on its importance and on the severity of the violation, the violator may or may not be seen as deviant. Wearing strange clothes may be seen as amusing and nonconformist once in a while, but it is labeled deviant if it becomes a regular occurrence. Adorning oneself with tattoos and rings to be distinctive and individualistic may result in widespread adoption of these behaviors, so that they become accepted rather than deviant.

In this chapter, we discuss **deviance**—the violation of social norms—and the social control mechanisms that keep most people from becoming deviant. We also explore crime, the forms of deviance on which formal penalties are imposed by society. The content of this chapter may challenge some of your deeply held assumptions about human behavior and defy some conceptions about deviance. In fact, it may convince you that we are all deviant at some times and in some places. The self-test in the next "Engaging Sociology" illustrates this point. Try taking it to see whether you have committed a deviant act.

What Is Deviance?

Deviance refers to the violation of society's norms, which then evokes negative reactions from others. The definition is somewhat imprecise because of the constantly changing ideas and laws about what acts are considered deviant. Some acts are deviant in most societies most of the time: murder, assault, robbery, and rape. Most societies impose severe penalties on these forms of deviance, and if the government imposes severe formal penalties, then the deviant actions become **crimes**. Occasionally, deviant acts may be overlooked or even viewed

Engaging Sociology

Who Is Deviant?

Please jot down your answers to the following self-test questions. No need to share your responses with others.

Have you ever engaged in any of the following acts?

☐   1. Stolen anything, even if its value was under $10

☐   2. Used an illegal drug

☐   3. Misused a prescription drug

☐   4. Run away from home prior to age 18

☐   5. Used tobacco prior to age 18

☐   6. Drunk alcohol prior to age 21

☐   7. Engaged in a fist fight

☐   8. Carried a knife or a gun

☐   9. Used a car without the owner's permission

☐ 10. Driven a car after drinking alcohol

☐ 11. Forced a girl to have sexual relations against her will (for boys)

☐ 12. Offered sex for money

☐ 13. Damaged property worth more than $10

☐ 14. Played truant from school

☐ 15. Arrived home after your curfew

☐ 16. Been disrespectful to someone in authority

☐ 17. Accepted or transported property that you had reason to believe might be stolen

☐ 18. Taken a towel from a hotel room after renting the room for a night

All the above are delinquent acts (violations of legal standards), and most young people are guilty of at least one infraction. However, few teenagers are given the label of *delinquent*. If you have answered yes to any of the preceding questions, you have committed a crime in the state of Ohio and in many other states. Your penalty or sanction for the infraction could range from a stiff fine to several years in prison—*if* you got caught!

Questions:

1. Do you think of yourself as being deviant? Why or why not?

2. Are deviants only those who get caught? For instance, if someone steals your car but avoids being caught, is he or she deviant?

as understandable, as in the case of looting by citizens following the fall of the Iraqi government in 2003 or following Hurricane Katrina along the Gulf Coast in August 2005. The killing of innocent people, looting, and burning of houses during a civil or tribal war, as occurred in the aftermath of the 2008 presidential election in Kenya, also may have seemed reasonable to those committing the atrocities. Other acts of deviance are considered serious offenses in one society but are tolerated in another. Examples include prostitution, premarital or extramarital sex, gambling, corruption, and bribery. Even within a single society, different groups may define deviance and conformity quite differently. The state legislature may officially define alcohol consumption by 19-year-olds as deviant, but on a Saturday night at the fraternity party, the 19-year-old "brother" who does not drink may be viewed as deviant by his peers. What do these cases tell us about what deviance is?

Deviance is socially constructed. This means that members of groups in societies define what is deviant. Consider the phenomenon of today's young people getting tattoos, tongue studs, and rings anyplace on the body one can place a ring. Is this deviant? It depends on who is judging. Are tattoos and rings symbols of independence and rebellion—a "cool" and unique look? What if many people begin to adopt the behavior? Is it still a sign of independence, or does it indicate conformity to a group? Do such "deviant" acts then become a symbol of conformity? When the Beatles started the long hair rage in the 1960s, this was deviant behavior to many. Today, we pay no special attention to men with long hair.

Some acts are deviant at one time and place and not at others. Stem cell research had been viewed as unacceptable and a violation of U.S. law because of ethical concerns about using or destroying human cells. However, that policy changed with the change of administrations. In many other countries, there are no moral restrictions, and scientists are proceeding with such research.

An individual's status or group may be defined as deviant. Some individuals have a higher likelihood of being labeled deviant because of the group into which they were born, such as a particular ethnic group, or because of a distinguishing mark or characteristic, such as a deformity. Others may escape being considered deviant because of their dominant status in society. The higher one's status, the less likely that one will be suspected of violating norms and the less likely that any violations will be characterized as "criminal." Who would suspect that a respectable white-collar husband and father is embezzling funds? The Société General French bank scandal of 2008 involved massive fraud and attracted extraordinary attention because it seemed like an "impossible" crime.

Even the looting that happened following Hurricane Katrina was addressed differently when it was done by Whites than when it was done by African Americans. (An image of a looter in New Orleans appears in the top right corner of the Photo Essay on p. 168.) The media showed

Photo Essay

Social Construction of Deviance

Are any of these people deviant? Why or why not? How does your answer reflect the "social construction" of deviance?

photos of Black "looters" who "stole food," but the same media described Whites who "broke into grocery stores" in search of food as "resourceful." Likewise, gays and lesbians are often said to be deviant and accused of flaunting their sexuality. Heterosexuals are rarely accused of "flaunting" their sexuality, regardless of how overtly flirtatious or underdressed they may be. So one's group membership or ascribed traits may make a difference in whether or not one is defined as deviant.

Deviance can be problematic or functional for society. It represents a breakdown in norms. However, according to structural-functional theory, deviance serves vital functions by setting examples of what is considered unacceptable behavior, providing guidelines for behavior that is necessary to maintain social order, and bonding people together through their common rejection of the deviant behavior. Deviance is also functional because it provides jobs for those who deal with deviants—police, judges, social workers, and so forth (Gans 2007). Furthermore, deviance can signal problems in society that need to be addressed and can therefore stimulate positive change. Sometimes deviant individuals break the model of conventional thinking, thereby opening society to new and creative paths of thinking. Scientists, inventors, and artists have often been rejected in their time but have been honored later for accomplishments that positively affected society. Vincent Van Gogh, for example, lived in poverty and mental turmoil during his life, but he became recognized as a renowned painter after his death. His paintings now sell for millions of dollars.

Our task in this chapter is to understand what deviance is, what causes it, and where it fits in the social world. We look at theoretical perspectives that help explain deviance, how some deviant acts become crimes, and what policies might be effective in controlling or reducing crime.

Thinking Sociologically

Would there be any negative consequences in a heterogeneous society if everyone conformed and no one ever deviated from social standards?

Misconceptions About Deviance

Many common beliefs about deviance are, in fact, misperceptions. Using scientifically collected data, the sociological perspective helps dispel false beliefs, as shown in the examples given below.

Popular belief: Some acts are inherently deviant.
Fact: Deviance is relative to the time, place, and status of the individual. At some place or time, almost any behavior you can mention has been defined as deviant, just as most acts have been legal or even typical behavior in other times and places. For example, homosexual liaisons were normal for men in ancient Greece and have been acceptable in

Some sociologists point out that crime can be "functional" because it creates jobs for people such as those above and it unifies society against the nonconformists.

various societies throughout time. Deviance is not inherent in certain behaviors but is defined by people and their governments (Erikson 1987, [1966] 2005).

Those in power have great influence over what is defined as deviant and can often determine punishment for deviant behavior. Some individuals are defined as deviant because they do not fit into the dominant system of values and norms. They may be seen as disruptive, a liability, or a threat to the system. In the military dictatorship of Myanmar (Burma) in Asia, political indoctrination controls many

Encyclopedia Link 6.1
Read more about deviance.

aspects of the citizens' lives. The rate of deviance is low because of threats against those who do not conform. Those who commit deviant acts are severely punished. However, ongoing protests against the military by Buddhist monks and dissidents show that not all agree with the norms of the powerful military government. Within dissident groups, antigovernment protests are heroic rather than deviant.

Famous individuals remembered in history books were often considered deviant in their time. In the Middle Ages, for

Handbook Link 6.1
Read about death and deviance.

example, anyone who questioned the concept of a flat earth at the center of the universe (with the sun and stars circling it) was considered a deviant and a religious heretic. In the early 17th century, Galileo, following Copernicus's lead, wrote a treatise based on empirical observations that upheld the concept of the earth revolving around the sun. He was tried by the Inquisition, a Roman Catholic Church court, in Rome and condemned for heresy because of his theory.

Definitions of deviance also vary depending on the social situation or context in which the behavior occurs (McCaghy et al. 2006). If we take the same behavior and place it in a different social context, perceptions of whether the behavior is deviant may well change. In Greece, Spain, and other Mediterranean countries, the clothing norms on beaches are very different from those in most of North America. Topless sunbathing by women and nudity on beaches for men is not at all uncommon, even on beaches designated as family beaches. Along the banks of the Rhein River men stroll and sunbathe in their birthday

suits. On other beaches, the norms vary, however, even within a few feet of the beach. Women will sunbathe topless, lying only 10 feet from the boardwalk where concessionaires sell beverages, snacks, and tourist items. If these women become thirsty, they cover up, walk the 15 feet to purchase a cola, and return to their beach blankets, where they again remove their tops. To walk onto the boardwalk topless would be highly deviant, yet to be topless on the sand is acceptable. Likewise, drunken behavior during spring break or at Mardi Gras in New Orleans may be acceptable but conducting oneself in the same manner while sipping champagne at a wedding reception would be a cause for disgust. The same behavior can be conventional or deviant depending on where it occurs. Even behaviors about which there is much agreement, such as murder and rape, can be justified by the perpetrators during times of war, in feuds, or after conquests.

Popular belief: Those who deviate are socially identified and recognized. Fact: Most of us deviate from some norm at some time or the other, as you saw when completing the questionnaire on deviance. (See the preceding "Engaging Sociology.") However, most behaviors that violate a norm are never socially recognized as deviant. Only about one third of all crime that is reported to the police in the United States ever leads to an arrest. This means that two thirds is never officially handled through the formal, legal structure, and the perpetrators escape being labeled deviant.

Popular belief: Deviants purposely and knowingly break the law. Fact: Although it is a popular notion that those who engage in deviant behavior make a conscious choice to do so, much deviance is driven by emotion, encouraged by friends, caused by disagreements over norms (as in the case of whether marijuana use should be decriminalized), or is the result of conditions in the immediate situation (as in the case of teens spontaneously engaging in a behavior in response to boredom or a struggle for prestige among peers; McCaghy et al. 2006).

Popular belief: Deviance occurs because there is a dishonest, selfish element to human nature. Fact: While surveys show that many of us believe this, most people who commit deviant acts do not attribute their own deviance to basic dishonesty or other negative personality factors. These misperceptions imply that most people believe they have a clear understanding of what deviance is and that deviant individuals know when they are being deviant and plan their actions. Yet there is little empirical evidence to support these beliefs, as the research reported in this chapter shows.

Medical marijuana patient Kay Mitchell, age 82, of Sonoma, joined more than 1,000 people protesting outside the California state capital to rally for state-approved and licensed medical marijuana dispensaries in California, which serve mostly terminally ill patients suffering from cancer, AIDS, and other ailments. The U.S. administration has announced that it will no longer prosecute those using marijuana for legal medical purposes.

Thinking Sociologically

Think of examples in your life that illustrate the relative nature of deviance. For instance, are some of your behaviors deviant in one setting but not in another, or were they deviant when you were younger but not deviant now?

Crime: Deviance That Violates the Law

It is rather easy for a politician to commit illegal acts—*if* he or she does not get caught. Sometimes illegal acts committed by those in office are punished, as in the case of impeached U.S. Governor Rod Blagojevich of Illinois, charged with abusing power and soliciting bribes. When the criminal justice system gets involved and formal penalties are imposed by society, we refer to deviance as crime—deviance that violates criminal law. Laws reflect opinions of what is considered right and wrong or good and bad at a particular time and place in a society. Like all other norms, laws change over time, reflecting changing public opinion based on social conditions or specific events. Still, there are formal sanctions—punishments—that the government imposes for violation of laws, and the stigma associated with these deviant acts results in the perpetrator being identified as "criminal."

At the end of the 1920s, 42 of the 48 U.S. states had laws forbidding interracial marriages (Coontz 2005; see Map 6.1). Legislatures in half of these states removed those restrictions by the 1960s, but the rest of these laws became unconstitutional only after a U.S. Supreme Court ruling in 1968. Today, this legal bar on interracial marriage has been eliminated completely, illustrating that most laws change to reflect the times and sentiments of the majority of people. When members of society are in general agreement about the seriousness of deviant acts, these are referred to as **consensus crimes** (Brym and Lie 2007; Goodman and Brenner 2002). Predatory crimes (premeditated murder, forcible rape, and kidnapping for ransom) are consensus crimes that are considered wrong in and of themselves in most nations.

In contrast, **conflict crimes** occur when one group passes a law over which there is disagreement or that disadvantages another group (Hagan 1993, 1994). Examples include laws concerning public disorder, chemical (drug

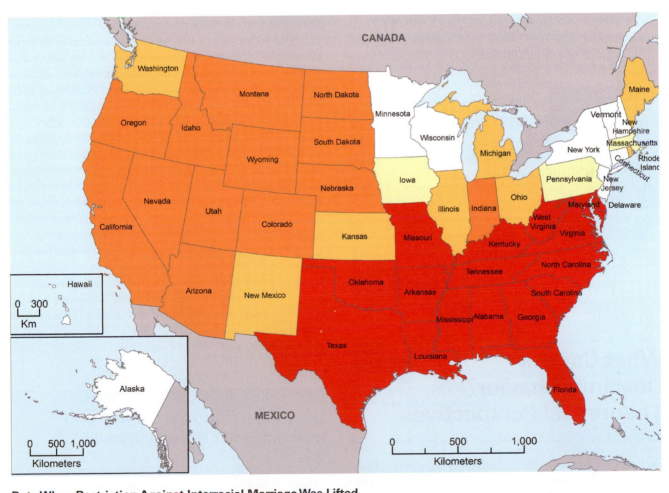

Date When Restriction Against Interracial Marriage Was Lifted

1788–1855	1856–1890	1891–1966	1967	Never had restrictions

Map 6.1 Historical Restrictions on Interracial Marriage in the United States.

Source: Wallenstein (2002:253–254). Map by Anna Versluis.

In the United States, until 1968, this couple would have been violating the law in roughly half of the states, and their family would be "illegitimate." Interracial marriages were illegal until the Supreme Court decided otherwise. Change in definitions of what is illegal has been common in the past 50 years.

and alcohol) offenses, prostitution, gambling, property offenses, and political disenfranchisement (denying voting rights only to some citizens—females, particular ethnic groups, or those without property). Public opinion about the seriousness of these crimes is often divided, based on people's different social class, status, and interests. The severity of societal response also varies, with high disagreement over the harmfulness of conflict crimes. Consensus or conflict about whether the behavior is harmful has implications for the punishment or support experienced by the person who is accused.

Crimes are often thought to be the most threatening forms of deviance, but it is important to recognize that they are still just one type of deviant behavior. We will discuss crime further at a later point in this chapter. Be aware that as we discuss theories in the next section, the theories explain a range of deviant acts, including (but not limited to) crimes.

What Causes Deviant Behavior? Theoretical Perspectives

Helena is a delinquent. Her father deserted the family when Helena was 10, and before that, he had abused Helena and her mother. Now, her mother has all she can cope with; she is just trying to survive financially and keep her three children in line. Helena gets little attention and little support or encouragement in her school activities. Her grades have fallen steadily. As a young teen, she sought attention from boys, and in the process, she became pregnant. Now, the only kids who have anything to do with her are others who have also been in trouble; her friends are other young people who have also been labeled delinquent. Helena's schoolmates, teachers, and mother see her as a delinquent troublemaker, and it would be hard for Helena to change their views and her status.

How did this happen? Was Helena born with a biological propensity toward deviance? Does she have psychological problems? Is the problem in her social environment? Helena's situation is, of course, only one unique case. Sociologists cannot generalize from Helena to other cases, but they do know from their studies that there are thousands of teens with problems like Helena's.

Throughout history, people have proposed explanations for why some members of society "turn bad"—from biological explanations of imbalances in hormones and claims of innate personality defects to social conditions within individual families or in the larger social structure. Biological and psychological approaches focus on personality disorders or abnormalities in the body or psyche of individuals, but they generally do not consider the social context in which deviance occurs.

Social scientists attempt to study questions of deviance scientifically. They examine why certain acts are defined as deviant, why some people engage in deviant behavior, and how other people in the society react to deviance. Sociologists place emphasis on understanding the interactions, social structure, and social processes that lead to deviant behavior, rather than on individual characteristics. They consider the socialization process and interpersonal relationships, group and social class differences, cultural and subcultural norms, and power structures that influence individuals to conform to or deviate from societal expectations. Theoretical explanations about why people are deviant are important because the interpretations influence social policy decisions about what to do with deviants.

This section explores several approaches to understanding deviance and crime. Some theories explain particular categories of crime better than others, and some illuminate micro-, meso-, or macro-level processes better than others. Taken together—as complementary perspectives on a complex dimension of human behavior—these theories help us understand a wide range of deviant and criminal behaviors.

Micro-Level Explanations of Deviance: Rational Choice and Interactionist Perspectives

No one is born deviant. Individuals learn to be law-abiding citizens or to be deviant through the process of socialization. Thus, behavior is acquired during the processes of interaction and socialization as people develop their social relationships. Why do some people learn to become deviant and others learn to follow the norms of society? A rational choice explanation focuses on the cost-benefit analysis of one's choices. Another approach, based in symbolic interaction theory, is that people are exposed to the opportunity to commit delinquent acts through their social relationships with peers and family members, and they come to be labeled deviant. Rational choice and symbolic interaction theories focus primarily on micro-level issues.

Rational Choice

The basic idea behind *rational choice theory* is that when individuals make decisions, they calculate the costs and benefits to themselves. They consider the balance between pleasure and pain. Social control comes from shifting the balance toward more pain and fewer benefits for those who deviate from norms. However, some members of society find crime to be to their advantage within their situations and opportunities, the product of a conscious, rational, and calculated decision made after weighing the costs and benefits of alternatives. Often they choose lives of crime after failure in school or work or seeing others succeed in crime.

Rational choice theorists believe that punishment—imposing high "costs" for criminal behavior, such as fines, imprisonment, or even the death penalty—is the way to dissuade criminals from choosing the path of crime. When the cost outweighs the potential benefit and opportunities are restricted, it deters people from thinking that crime is a "rational" choice (Earls and Reiss 1994; Winslow and Zhang 2008). Even just changing the perception of the cost-benefit balance can be important in lowering the crime rates. Criminals make decisions based on the situational constraints and opportunities in their lives (Schmalleger 2006).

Social Control Theory

One of sociology's central concepts is social control (Gibbs 1989; Hagan 2007). Control theory focuses on why most people conform most of the time and do not commit deviant acts. If human beings were truly free to do whatever they wanted, they would likely commit more deviant acts. Yet to live near others and with others requires individuals to control their behaviors based on social standards and sanctions—in short, social control.

A perpetual question in sociology is the following: How is order possible in the context of rapidly changing society? A very general answer is that social control results from social norms that promote order and predictability in the social world. When people fail to adhere to these norms, or when the norms are unclear, the stability and continuance of the entire social system may be threatened.

Control theory contends that people are bonded to others by four powerful factors:

1. *Attachment* to other people who respect the values and rules of the society. Individuals do not want to be rejected by those to whom they are close or whom they admire.

Rational choice theories hold that people weigh the possible negative consequences of deviant behavior against its benefits, and if the benefits outweigh the costs, then violating official rules or expectations may be worth it. This would suggest that the cost must be increased to deter deviance. This little boy is weighing the costs and benefits of taking cookies, and the benefits are looking pretty sweet!

2. *Commitment* to conventional activities (such as school and jobs) that they do not want to jeopardize

3. *Involvement* in activities that keep them so busy with conventional roles and expectations that they do not have time for mischief

4. *Belief* in the social rules of their culture, which they accept because of their childhood socialization and indoctrination into those conventional beliefs

Should these variables be weakened, there is an increased possibility that the person could commit deviant acts (Hirschi [1969] 2002).

Two primary factors shape our tendency to conform. The first is internal controls, those voices within us that tell us when a behavior is acceptable or unacceptable, right or wrong. The second is external controls—society's formal or informal controls against deviant behavior. Informal external controls include smiles, frowns, hugs, and ridicule from close acquaintances (Gottfredson and Hirschi 1990). Formal external controls come from the legal system through the police, judges, juries, and social workers. In both cases, the cost-benefit ratios shift, making either conformity or deviance a rational choice. The basic idea in rational choice approaches is that when individuals make decisions, they calculate the costs and benefits to themselves. Humans seek to maximize pleasure (benefit) and minimize pain (costs), and the decision regarding whether to conform or deviate from social norms is determined by the individual's assessment and rational decision of the pleasure-pain ratio from their mental calculations in a given situation. Social control comes from shifting the balance toward more pain and fewer benefits for those who deviate from norms.

Positive sanctions reward those behaviors approved by society. This is the reason why schools have honor ceremonies, companies reward their top salespeople, and communities recognize civic leadership with "Citizen of the Year" awards. All these actions enhance the rewards for conventional behavior. Negative sanctions (or punishments) increase the cost to those who have deviated from the norm. They range from fines for traffic violations to prison sentences for serious crimes and even death for acts considered most dangerous to society. If one belongs to a subculture or group whose norms conflict with those of the dominant society, conformity to the subculture may take precedence over conformity to the larger society.

Deterring deviance can be accomplished by increasing the costs (by imposing tougher penalties in the courts), by increasing awareness of the costs that are already in place, by reducing the benefits of being deviant (by lessening social benefits such as admiration), or by changing perception of the cost-benefit balance.

Thinking Sociologically

Think of a time when you committed a deviant act or avoided doing so despite tempting opportunity. What factors influenced whether you conformed to societal norms or engaged in deviance?

Spending time and money shooting drugs is a way of life for some young people. Yet most teens would not know the technique for preparing and injecting illegal drugs, nor would they have learned from associates that this is a fun or acceptable way to spend one's time.

Differential Association Theory

If someone offered you some heroin, what would determine whether you took it? First, would you define sticking a needle in your arm and injecting heroin as a good way to spend your afternoon? Second, do you typically hang around with others who engage in this type of behavior and define it as "the thing to do"? Third, would you know the routine—how to cook the heroin to extract the liquid—if you had never seen it done? You likely would not know the proper technique for how to prepare the drug or how to inject it. Why? It depends on whether you have associated with drug users and whether your family and friends define drug use as acceptable or deviant.

Differential association or *reinforcement theory* refers to two processes that can result in individuals learning to engage in crime. First is association with others who share criminal values and commit crimes, which results in learning how to carry out a criminal act (Sutherland, Cressey, and Luckenbil 1992). Second, social learning also results in reinforcement of criminal behavior (Akers 1992, 1998; Burgess and Akers 1966; Lee, Akers, and Borg 2004). This approach links the learning process with the criminal behavior.

Differential association theory focuses on the process of learning deviance from family, peers, fellow employees, political organizations, neighborhood groups such as gangs, and other groups in one's surroundings (Akers 1992; Akers et al. 1979; Sutherland et al. 1992). This theory is a symbolic interaction approach because the emphasis is on how others shape one's definition of what is normal and acceptable. Helena, for example, came to be surrounded by people who made dropping out of school and other delinquent acts seem normal. If her close friends and siblings were sexually active as teens, her teen pregnancy might not be remarkable and might even be a source of some prestige with her group of peers.

According to differential association theory, the possibility of becoming deviant depends on four factors: the duration, intensity, priority, and frequency of time spent with the deviant group (Sutherland et al. 1992). If deviant behavior exists in people's social context and if they are exposed to deviance regularly and frequently (duration and intensity), especially if they are in close association with a group that accepts criminal behavior, they are more likely to learn deviant ways. Furthermore, individuals learn motives, drives, rationalizations, and attitudes, and they develop techniques that influence behavior and cause them to commit a deviant act.

Some theorists contend that lower-class life constitutes a distinctive subculture in which delinquent behavior patterns are transmitted through socialization. The values, beliefs, norms, and practices that have evolved in lower-class communities over time can often lead to violation of laws. These values and norms have been defined by those in power as deviant. Just as upper-class youth seem to be expected and destined to succeed, lower-class youth may learn other behaviors that those with privilege have defined as delinquent and criminal (Bettie 2003; Chambliss 1973). For instance, in a recent study, Bettie (2003) found that race, class, and gender intersect in important ways to increase the labeling (discussed next) and decrease the opportunities for lower-class and minority high school girls. For some inner-city youth, the local norms are to be tough and disrespectful of authority, to live for today, to seek excitement, and to be "cool"—these are survival techniques. With time, these attitudes and behaviors become valued in and of themselves by their peer group.

Elijah Anderson's (2000) book, *Code of the Street*, describes two types of groups that coexist in poor neighborhoods: "decent people" and "street people." The code of the street often involves norms that are opposed to those of mainstream society, yet many children are socialized in areas where this code provides the dominant norms. "Street-oriented people" hang around with peers on streets and adopt a certain look with their clothes and jewelry—an image expected by the group. Peers become more important than society's social control agents. "Decent families" accept mainstream values and often find support systems in church communities or other organizations. Lower-status youth are more likely to be suspected, watched, and caught for deviant behavior than higher-status youth. Thus, the reported delinquency rates may be higher for this group even if the incidence of violence is not greater (Anderson 2000). The next theoretical approach, labeling, explains why. Today, we know that members of all social classes commit crimes, and no socioeconomic class has a monopoly on violence, graft, corruption, or dishonesty.

Labeling Theory

Labeling theory is also related to the symbolic interaction perspective, for labels (such as "juvenile delinquent") are symbols that have meanings that affect the self. Labeling theory focuses on how people define deviance—what is or is not "normal"—which is a core issue in the symbolic interactionist paradigm. The basic assumption underlying labeling theory is that no behavior or individual is intrinsically deviant. Behavior is deviant because individuals in society label it deviant.

The basic social process of labeling someone is as follows: Members of a society create deviance by defining certain behaviors as deviant—smoking pot, wearing long hair, holding hands in public, or whatever is seen as inappropriate at a particular time and place. They then react to the deviance by rejecting the miscreant or by imposing penalties.

Labeling theorists define two stages in the process of becoming a deviant. **Primary deviance** is a violation of a norm that may be an isolated act, such as a young teenager shoplifting something on a dare by friends. Most people commit acts of primary deviance. However, few of us are initially labeled deviant as a result of these primary acts. Remember how you marked the deviant behavior test that you took at the beginning of this chapter? If you have engaged in deviant acts, you were probably not labeled deviant for the offense. If you had been labeled, you might not be in college or taking this class.

If an individual continues to violate a norm and begins to take on a deviant identity, this is referred to as **secondary deviance**. Secondary deviance becomes publicly recognized, and the individual is identified as deviant, beginning a deviant career. If a

Journal Article Link 6.1
Read an interactionist view of deviance.

Shoplifting is often done by young people who have not been arrested for anything—a form of primary deviance.

teenager like Helena in the opening example is caught, her act becomes known, perhaps publicized in the newspaper. She may spend time in a juvenile detention center, and parents of other teens may not want their children associating with her. Employers and store managers may refuse to hire her. Soon, there are few options open to her, and others expect her to be delinquent. The teen may continue performing the deviant acts and associating with delinquent acquaintances. Society's reaction, then, is what defines a deviant person and may limit options for that person to change the label (Lemert 1951, 1972).

The process of labeling individuals and behaviors takes place at each level of analysis, from individual to society. If community or societal norms define a behavior as deviant, individuals are likely to believe it is deviant. Sanctions against juvenile delinquents can have the effect of reinforcing the deviant behavior by (a) increasing alienation from the social world, (b) forcing increased interaction with deviant peers, and (c) motivating juvenile delinquents to positively value and identify with the deviant status (Kaplan and Johnson 1991).

Self-fulfilling prophesy refers to a belief that becomes a reality. Individuals may come to see themselves as deviant because of harassment, ridicule, rejection by friends and family, and negative sanctions. For example, James is 8 years old and already sees himself as a failure because his parents, teachers, and peers tell him he is "dumb." In keeping with the idea of self-fulfilling prophesy, James accepts the label and acts accordingly. Unless someone—such as an insightful teacher—steps in to give him another image of himself, the label is unlikely to change. Labeling theory also focuses on the micro level: the individual and the formation of the self.

Thinking Sociologically

What labels do you carry, and how do they affect your self-concept and behavior?

Another explanation of why certain individuals and groups are labeled deviant has to do with their status and power in society. Those who are on the fringes, away from power and nonparticipants in the mainstream, are more likely to be labeled deviants—the poor, minorities, members of new religious movements, or those who in some way do not fit into the dominant system. Because the powerful have the influence to define what is acceptable, they protect themselves from being defined as deviants. People from different subcultures, social classes, or religious groups may be accorded deviant labels.

A study by Chambliss (1973) illustrates the process of labeling in communities and groups. Perhaps during your high school years you witnessed situations similar to that described in his study. Chambliss looked at the behavior of two small peer groups of boys and at the reactions of community members to their behavior. The Saints, boys from "good" families, were some of the most delinquent boys at Hanibal High School. Although the Saints were constantly occupied with truancy, drinking, wild driving, petty theft, and vandalism, none was officially arrested for any misdeed during the 2-year study, partly because they had cars and could go out of town for their pranks. The Roughnecks were constantly in trouble with the police and community residents, even though their rate of delinquency was about equal to that of the Saints. Chambliss found that poor kids—like the Roughnecks—may be involved in deviant behavior because the dominant cultural goals seem distant and unattainable. On the other hand, rich kids—like the Saints—indulge in delinquent activities to cope with boredom, to rebel, or to seek visibility among peers.

What was the cause of the disparity between these two groups? Community members, the police, and teachers alike labeled the boys based on their perceptions of the boys' family backgrounds and social class. The Saints came from stable, White, upper middle-class families; were active in school affairs; and were precollege students whom everyone expected to become professionals. The general community feeling was that the Roughnecks would amount to nothing. They carried around a label that was hard to change, and that label was realized. The Saints almost all became professionals, whereas none of the Roughnecks did. Two Roughnecks ended up in prison, two became coaches, and little is known of the others. For these groups of boys, the prophecy became self-fulfilling (Chambliss 1973). The belief that the Roughnecks would "amount to nothing" came true because that was what was expected by the community; their opportunities were affected by their labels, and the boys came to expect nothing for themselves.

The general learning theory of crime and deviance combines elements of both labeling theory and differential association theory. It argues that "labeling effects are mediated by associations with one's peer group, including delinquent peers" (Schmalleger 2006:256; see also Adams 1996). So someone may be labeled, and whether or not the label sticks to that person may have to do with how the peer group responds to that label—perhaps even by claiming the "deviant" designation with some pride.

Labels are powerful and can stigmatize—branding the target as disgraceful or reprehensible. This process can be extended to a number of issues, including fatness, as the next "Sociology in Our Social World" illustrates.

Sociology in Our Social World

Stigmatizing Fatness

By Leslie Elrod

The United States is now the fattest country in the world. "American society has become 'obesogenic,' characterized by environments that promote increased food intake, nonhealthful food, and physical inactivity . . . One in seven low-income preschool children are obese" (Centers for Disease Control and Prevention 2009). The CDC has found that more than 60% of American adults are classified as overweight or obese, and 25% of children are classified as obese. Deviation from the idealized image of physical thinness allows others to judge and condemn non-conforming individuals, resulting in embarrassment, severe isolation, or alienation. According to Cooley's theory of the looking-glass self, because we tend to define ourselves by the attitudes of and interaction with others, the obese may suffer lower self-esteem and have negative self-images, thus creating heightened levels of psychological distress. When a physical attribute is assigned social significance, norm-violators such as the obese are likely to endure negative labeling because of perceived physical imperfections. The obese, labeled as self-indulgent, gluttonous, lazy, sloppy, and mean, experience social condemnation. Obese women tend to experience greater discrimination than obese men.

Women are taught that their physical appearance is a valuable commodity, both in the public and private spheres. Ascertaining the degree to which they fit the media image models of female perfection, women attempt to adapt their appearance to reach this standard of beauty. Holding up an image of female perfection, such as slenderness, daintiness, or being demure, the media insinuates that the woman herself somehow falls short of that perfection. This is exemplified in print ads, magazines, television programming, and movies as well as merchandising directed toward females of all ages. The "feminine failing" not only jeopardizes her happiness but also challenges her femininity. The appearance discrepancy is based on the fact that over the course of the past century, as real women grew heavier, models and "beautiful" women were portrayed as increasingly thinner. An example of the change in media imagery is that of the White Rock mineral girl, portrayed as 5 feet 4 inches tall and 140 pounds in 1950. More recently, she is 5 feet 10 inches tall, weighing 110 pounds (Phipher 1994).

While much of the research on women's obsession with weight assumes that all women and girls are affected by the culture of thinness, there is some evidence to suggest that not all women are affected equally. Obesity rates are highest among minorities, the poor, and the disenfranchised. Yet Powell and Kahn (1995) have noted that "few black women seem to have eating disorders . . . and less emphasis [is placed] on eating and weight in general among black college students compared to white students" (p. 190). When compared to black females, white women are under significantly greater social pressure to be thin. Hesse-Biber and Leavy 2007 finds that eating disorders, an outcome of dissatisfaction with one's body, are no longer confined to upper-class white females, indicating that the effects of body mass on self-esteem may be changing.

This is not to suggest that people of color are not concerned about body image; rather, it suggests that the messages disseminated through the majority culture are mediated in various ways through the experiences and expectations that are associated with distinct social locations. Moreover, since media portrayals are still predominantly white, whether through the use of white or white-featured models—thin lips, thin hips, straight hair, and light complexion—there is less pressure on minorities to relate and compare themselves to the given images because these images do not represent their reference groups.

Because the obese are victims of prejudice and discrimination resulting from social norm violation, they are less likely than their non-obese counterparts to be involved in various organizational and social activities such as extracurricular participation for fear of social rejection. Olson, Schumaker, and Yawn (1994) found that weight-based embarrassment was indicated as a reason that obese people shied away from social obligations. Several clinical studies have documented that obese women delay seeking medical care and participating in preventative medical techniques.

Some obese persons reject the stigmatizing "fat identity," using a variety of coping mechanisms such as avoidance of others who stigmatize them or coping through immersion in supportive subcultures. Those who suffer from low self-esteem may actively seek out activities and relationships that have the capacity to improve their self-esteem. While not all obese persons experience and internalize fat stigmatization, a statistically significant number of overweight and obese juveniles do indicate poor body image and diminished self-esteem. Many experts suggest that individuals should take a proactive approach by seeking medical or psychological help, joining support groups, and dealing with the problem if it is impairing their activities.

Chinese soldiers tried in vain to stop student protesters in China as the students demanded more freedom to make choices. The students were defined by the government as deviant, many were arrested, and some were shot in Tiananmen Square, the main square in Beijing.

Why are some behaviors defined as deviant? Again, when a majority of individuals agree that an act is a violation of norms, it is labeled deviant. In other cases, powerful members of society can label certain behaviors as deviant. While labeling theory is mostly based on symbolic interactionism (a micro-level theory), labeling theorists also point to the role of macro-level social forces—social inequality or lack of access to power—in determining whether people are labeled or whether they can avoid being labeled as deviant. Thus, labeling theory is also sometimes used by conflict theorists. When members of the dominant group in society see certain behaviors as potentially threatening or disruptive to the society or to their privileged statuses, the group in power reinforces its position by creating an impossible situation for minority group members. The minority's nonacceptance of the rules becomes deviant. For instance, dissidents opposed to government restrictions or human rights violations against their groups in China, Myanmar (Burma), and other countries have been thrown in jail because their protests were labeled deviant by those in power.

Thinking Sociologically

You have a friend who is getting into drugs. From what you know about the above theories, what might be the reason why this is happening, and what, if anything, could you do for your friend?

Meso- and Macro-Level Explanations of Deviance: Structural-Functional and Conflict Theories

While interpersonal interaction processes can result in deviance, many sociologists believe that meso- and macro-level analysis creates greater understanding of the societal factors leading to deviance. Meso-level analysis focuses on ethnic subcultures, organizations, and institutions within macro-level nations and global social systems.. We look first at structural-functional theories of deviance, those with the longest history in sociology. They include two themes: (1) anomie, the breakdown of the norms guiding behavior, which leads to social disorganization, and (2) the strain created by the difference between definitions of success (goals) in a society and the means available to achieve those goals.

Anomie and Social Disorganization

Villagers from industrializing countries in Africa, Asia, and Latin America were pushed off marginally productive rural lands and were pulled by the lure of the city: new opportunities, excitement, and a chance to change their lives. They flocked to population centers with industrial opportunities, but when they arrived, they were often disappointed. Poor, unskilled, and homeless, they moved into crowded apartments or shantytowns of temporary shacks and tried to adjust to the new style of life, which often included unemployment.

Many industrializing countries face structural changes as their economies move from agricultural to industrial or service economies. Young men in particular leave behind strong bonds and a common value system that exists in the countryside. In cities, individuals melt into the crowd and live anonymously. Old village norms that provided the guidelines for proper behavior crumble, sometimes without clear expectations emerging to take their places. The lack of clear norms in the rapidly changing urban environment leads to high levels of social disorganization and deviant behavior.

Sociologists use the term **anomie**, or normlessness, to describe the breakdown of norms caused by the lack of shared, achievable goals and the lack of socially approved means to achieve those goals (Merton 1938). When norms are absent or conflicting, deviance increases, as the previous example illustrates. Émile Durkheim (1858–1917) first described this normlessness as a condition of weak, conflicting, or absent norms and values that arises when societies are disorganized. This situation is typical in rapidly urbanizing, industrializing societies, at times of sudden prosperity or depression, during rapid technological change, or when a government is overthrown. Anomie affects urban areas first but may eventually affect the whole society. Thus, macro-level events, such as economic recessions or wars, show how important social solidarity is to an individual's core sense of values.

This general idea of anomie led a group of Chicago sociologists to study the social conditions of that city that are correlated with deviance. The Chicago School, as the research team is known, linked life in transitional slum areas to the high incidence of crime. Certain neighborhoods or zones in the Chicago area—generally inner-city transitional zones with recent settlers—have always had high delinquency rates, regardless of the group that occupied the area. Low economic status, ethnic heterogeneity, residential mobility, family disruption, and competing value systems (because of the constant transitions) led to community disorganization. Although new immigrant groups have replaced the older groups over time, the delinquency rate has remained high because each generation of newcomers experienced anomie (Shaw and McKay 1929). The high in-migration and out-migration in these communities in itself explains the lack of stability in primary families. Peer group norms became influential, and models of nondeviant behavior were scarce for many teenagers and adults (Anderson 2000).

Strain Theory

Most people in a society share similar values and goals, but those with poor education and few resources have less opportunity to achieve those shared goals than others. When legitimate routes to success are cut off, frustration and anger result and deviant methods may be used to achieve goals. Strain theory focuses on the contradictions and tensions between the shared values and goals on the one hand and the opportunity structures of the society on the other.

Strain theory (Merton 1968) suggests that the gap between a society's definitions of goals and the legitimate means, or ways, of attaining those goals can lead to strain in the society. Individuals may agree with the society's goals for success (say, financial affluence) but may not be able to achieve them using the socially prescribed means of achieving that success. The strain that is created can lead to deviance. Merton (1968) uses U.S. society as an example because it places a heavy emphasis on success, measured by wealth and social standing. He outlines five ways by which individuals adapt to the strain. Figure 6.1 shows these five types and their relationship to goals and means. To illustrate these, we trace the choices of a lower-class student who realizes the value of an education, knows it is necessary to get ahead, but has problems financing her education and competing in the middle-class-dominated school setting.

1. *Conformity* means embracing the society's definition of success and adhering to the established and approved means of achieving success. The student works hard despite the academic and financial

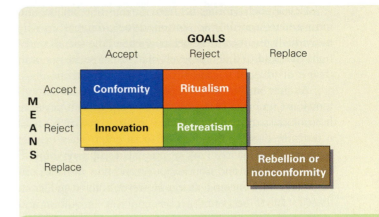

Figure 6.1   Merton's Strain Theory

obstacles, trying to do well in school to achieve success and a good job placement. She uses legitimate, approved means—education and hard work—to reach goals that the society views as worthy.

2. *Innovation* refers to the use of illicit means to reach approved goals. Our student uses illegitimate means to achieve her education goals. She may cheat on exams or get papers from Internet sources. Success in school is all that matters, not how she gets there.

3. *Ritualism* involves strict adherence to the culturally prescribed rules, even though individuals give up on the goals they hoped to achieve. The student may give up the idea of getting good grades and graduating from college but, as a matter of pride and self-image, she continues to try hard and to take classes. She conforms to expectations, for example, but with no sense of purpose. She just does what she is told.

4. *Retreatism* refers to giving up on both the goals and the means. The student either bides her time, not doing well, or drops out, giving up on future job goals. She abandons or retreats from the goals of a professional position in society and on the means to get there. She may even turn to a different lifestyle—for example, a user of drugs and alcohol—as part of the retreat.

5. *Rebellion* entails rejecting the socially approved ideas of success and the means of attaining that success. It replaces those with alternative definitions of success and alternative strategies for attaining the new goals. Rebelling against the dominant cultural goals and means, the student may join a radical political group or a commune, intent on developing new ideas of how society should be organized and what a "truly educated" person should be.

Deviant behavior results from retreatism, rebellion, and innovation. According to Merton (1968), the reasons why individuals resort to these behaviors lie in the social conditions that lead to different levels of access to success, not in their individual biological or psychological makeup.

Anomie and strain theories fall under the structural-functional umbrella of theories. They help explain deviance from a social structural point of view, focusing on what happens if deviance disrupts the ongoing social order. They explore what causes deviance, how to prevent disruptions, how to keep change slow and nondisruptive, and how deviance can be useful to the ongoing society. However, anomie and strain theories fail to account for class conflicts, inequities, and poverty, which conflict theorists argue cause deviance.

Conflict Theory

The Tea Party Express bus rumbled across the United States in 2009, stopping in cities to protest what participants felt were bad policies: bailouts, cap-and-trade legislation, "out of control" spending, government-run health care, and higher taxes. In Kenya, thousands of citizens protested what they felt was the corrupt 2008 election process for a new president. As a result, many Kenyans were displaced or killed in tribal fighting. Greenpeace, an environmental activist group, confronted Japanese whaling vessels in the Southern Ocean Whale Sanctuary in January 2008, preventing them from killing whales in the area. From 2002 to the present, antiwar protests have been held in many major cities around the world against the war in Iraq. Are protesters involved in this sampling of conflict events deviants and criminals, or are they brave heroes? The response depends on who answers the question.

Conflict theorists assume that conflict between groups is inevitable. Because many societies today are pluralistic, heterogeneous groupings of people, the differences (in goals, resources, norms, and values) between interest groups and groups in power often cause conflict. Conflict theory focuses on a macro-level analysis of deviance, looking at deviance as the result of social inequality or of the struggle between groups for power.

Deviance is often related to social class status, interest groups, or cultural conflict between the dominant group and ethnic, religious, political, regional, or gender groups. Wealthy and powerful elites want to maintain their control and their high positions (Domhoff 2009). They have the power to pass laws and define what is deviant, sometimes by effectively eliminating the opposition groups. The greater the cultural difference between the dominant group and other groups in society, the more the possibility of conflict. This is because minority groups and subcultures challenge the norms of the dominant groups and threaten the consensus in a society (Huizinga, Loeber, and Thornberry 1994).

Some conflict theorists blame capitalist systems for the unjust administration of law and argue that the ruling class uses the legal system to further the capitalist enterprise (Quinney 2002). The dominant class defines deviance, applies laws to protect its interests, represses any conflict or protest, and, in effect, forces those in subordinate classes to carry out actions defined as deviant. These actions, in turn, support the ideology that works against the subordinate classes. Activities that threaten the interests and well-being of the wealthy capitalist class become defined as deviant. By subordinating certain groups and then defining them as deviant or criminal, the dominant group consolidates its powerful position. Because the dominant class is usually of one ethnic group and those of other races or ethnicities tend to be in the subordinate class, conflict often has racial and ethnic implications as well as social class dimensions. The fact that for the same offenses, subordinate class or race members are arrested and prosecuted more often than dominant class or race members is provided as evidence by conflict theorists to support this contention (Quinney 2002). When people feel they are not treated fairly by the society, they have less loyalty to the society and to its rules. This may result in activities considered deviant by those in power.

To reduce deviance and crime, conflict theorists agree that we must change the structure of society. For instance, laws in many countries claim to support equal and fair treatment for all, but when one looks at the law in action, another picture emerges. Recall the example of the Saints and Roughnecks; the students from powerful families and higher social classes received favored treatment. Unequal

Handbook Link 6.2
Read about drug use and conflict theory.

A conservative group called the Tea Party Patriots protest against President Barack Obama's health care reform bill in September of 2009. One sign with his image calls him "Parasite in Chief," as thousands of people protest against his policies. The Tea Party has taken a strident oppositional position to stop governmental growth and possible increase in taxes.

treatment of groups that differ from the dominant group—the poor, laboring class and racial or ethnic minorities in particular—is rooted in the legal, political, and occupational structures of societies.

If the structure of society were changed and there were no dominant groups exploiting the subordinate groups, would crime disappear? To answer this, we can look to patterns of crime in societies that have attempted to develop a communist, classless structure. The rate of crime in China and Cuba, for instance, is lower than in many Western democracies, in part because of the less dramatic inequality and the strict social controls on behavior. On the other hand, deviance is still present in noncapitalist societies. So although capitalistic inequality contributes to deviance, it is only one of the many variables at work.

Feminist Theory

The goal of most feminist theorists is to understand and improve women's status, including their treatment by men and those in power. Feminists argue that traditional theories do not give an adequate picture or understanding of women's situations. Although there are several branches of feminist theory, most see the macro-level causes of abuses suffered by women as rooted in the capitalist patriarchal system. Feminist theorists look for explanations in gender relations and societal structures for violence against women and the secondary status of most women. They include the following ideas: (a) women are faced with a division of labor resulting from their sex, (b) the separation between public (work) and private (home) spheres of social activity create a "we" versus "they" thinking between men and women, and (c) socialization of children into gender-specific adult roles has implications for how males and females perceive and relate to each other.

One result of women's status is that they are often victims of crime. The type of victimization varies around the globe, from sex trafficking to rape (Bales 2004, 2007). Women are less often in a position to commit crimes. In fact, deviant acts by women have traditionally fallen into the categories of shoplifting, credit card or welfare fraud, writing bad checks (in developed societies), prostitution, and, in some countries, adultery or inappropriate attire. Many Western feminist theorists contend that until women around the world are on an equal footing with men, crimes against women and definitions of various behaviors of women as deviant are likely to continue.

Consider the case of intimate partner violence, including rape. Until recent years, there have been few serious consequences for the offenders in many countries (especially during times of anomie or war), and women often were blamed or blamed themselves for "letting it happen" (Boy and Kulczycki 2008). In some cultures, women fear reporting violence and may blame themselves for the beating or rape. Yet, from limited studies, we know that 16% to 52%

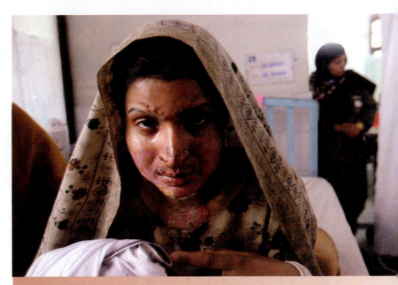

Ishraht Abullah sits in her hospital bed showing the burns inflicted to over 30% of her body after her husband threw sulfuric acid over her during a domestic dispute. Such abuse is the concern of feminist scholars who see women as disproportionately the victims.

of married women in the Middle East were assaulted in 1 year, compared with 1.3% to 12% in Europe and North America (Krug et al. 2002). The next "Sociology Around the World" feature on page 182 illustrates this pattern.

Feminist theorists argue that we learn our gender roles, part of which is men learning to be aggressive. Women's status in society results in their being treated as sex objects—to be used for men's pleasure. Women's race and class identification become relevant in the exploitation of poor, ethnically distinct women from developing countries for human trafficking.

One thing is certain: Women who have been victimized need help from their family and loved ones to feel in control again, but some are unjustly blamed for the rape (McEvoy and Brookings 2008). Keep in mind that each cultural practice evolved for a reason in each society. The meaning of these standards needs to be understood through the eyes of that culture so that we can effectively deal with human rights abuses. Western values make it difficult to understand the reason for certain practices.

According to feminist theory, women's work in the private sphere—including housework, child care, and sexual satisfaction of their husbands—is undervalued, as are the women who carry out these roles. In some societies, women are the property of their husbands, with men's strength and physical force the ultimate means of control over women. Some branches of feminist theory argue that men exploit women's labor power and sexuality to continue their dominance. The system is reproduced through new generations that are socialized to maintain the patriarchy and to view inequality between the sexes as "normal"

Sociology Around the World

Blaming the Victim: An Extreme Case

Every woman fears being raped—being forced into having sex against her will. In most countries, rape is considered a deviant behavior on the part of the perpetrator—a crime punishable by imprisonment. The woman is provided medical help and counseling, yet only a small percentage of estimated rapes are reported. In a few countries or regions in countries, the legal system is based on strict interpretations of religious books by those who practice fundamentalist interpretations of the religion, in an attempt to guard against loss of a woman's virtue, shame, and illegitimate children. Some would also argue that these laws maintain patriarchal control. Recent rape laws proposed in Afghanistan would have permitted marital rape; stones were thrown at protesting women. Cases in other countries show the contentious nature of this issue. Although the following examples are rare, they show the extremes to which communities can go to protect the "virtue" of women and the family. In the first case, excerpted from *the New York Times*, a woman was blamed for sex outside marriage even though she had been raped.

> The evidence of guilt was there for all to see—a newborn baby in the arms of its mother, a village woman named Zafran Bibi. Her crime: She had been raped. Her sentence: death by stoning.
>
> Now, Ms. Zafran, who is about 26, is in solitary confinement in a death row cell in Kohat, a nearby town. The only visitor she is allowed is her baby daughter, now a 1-year-old being cared for by a prison nurse. In photographs, Ms. Zafran is a tall woman with striking green eyes—a peasant woman of the hot and barren hills of Pakistan's North-West Frontier country. . .
>
> Thumping a fat, red statute book, the white-bearded judge who convicted her—Anwar Ali Khan—said he had simply followed the letter of the Koran-based law, known as *hudood*, that mandates punishments. "The illegitimate child is not disowned by her and therefore is proof of *zina*," he said, referring to laws that forbid any sexual contact outside marriage. Furthermore,

he said, in accusing her brother-in-law of raping her, Ms. Zafran had confessed to her crime.

> "The lady stated before this court that, yes, she had committed sexual intercourse, but with the brother of her husband," Judge Khan said. "This left no option to the court but to impose the highest penalty."

Although legal fine points do exist, little distinction is made in court between forced and consensual sex.

When *hudood* was enacted 23 years ago, the laws were formally described as measures to ban "all forms of adultery, whether the offense is committed with or without the consent of the parties," but it is almost always the women who are punished, whatever the facts (Mydans 2002:A3). Zafran Bibi appealed the decision and was subsequently released from prison. She still fears, however, that she will be the victim of violence because she became a public figure through the publicity her case received and because the individuals who opposed her acquittal know where she lives and what she looks like.

In another case, covered extensively by American and European news, a young Pakistani woman, Mukhtar Mai, was ordered to be raped as punishment for her brother who was seen with a woman from another, more powerful tribe. In 2004, Pakistani governments (mostly those of small towns and villages) ordered about 400 rapes as punishment for both sexual and nonsexual offenses. Higher-policing groups do occasionally arrest the rapists in these cases for sexual violation, but this is not uniform. For Mai, 6 of her 14 rapists have been charged with rape, and Mai has asked that the men not be acquitted (BBC News 2005).

In Saudi Arabia, a young woman victim was abducted at knifepoint, gang-raped for being seen with a man who had blackmailed the woman and her family, then beaten by her brother for disgracing the family, and sentenced by the court to 90 lashes for being seen with the man who was blackmailing them and who may have lured her into the trap ("Gang-Rape Victim Faces Lashes" 2007).

and "natural." Women who deviate from the cultural expectations of "normal" behavior are condemned.

No one theory of why deviance occurs can explain all the forms of deviance. Some theories consider the

micro-level processes that shape one's values and self-identity. These approaches examine why certain behaviors and certain individuals are defined as deviant, and they explore the consequences of being labeled deviant. Meso- and macro-level theories attempt to explain the structural factors at the community, national, or even the global level that result in deviance being more common among certain groups, in certain areas, or at certain times. Thus, depending on the level of analysis of the questions sociologists wish to study (micro, meso, or macro), they select the theory that best fits the data they find.

In the following sections, we explore in more detail the micro-meso-macro connections as they apply to one manifestation of deviance—crime. This illustrates how the sociological imagination can be applied to deviance at each level in the social system.

Thinking Sociologically

Meso- and macro-level social forces may be even more powerful than micro-level forces in explaining deviance. What might be the factors that contribute to deviance at the meso and macro levels? Pick a recent example of deviance from your newspaper or television news. Which sociological theories help explain this deviance?

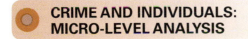

CRIME AND INDIVIDUALS: MICRO-LEVEL ANALYSIS

In this and the following two sections, we will be looking at one type of deviance—crime—at various levels in the social system (micro, meso, and macro). Crime is deviance that (if one is caught) involves formal sanctions from the government. A criminal justice system or court becomes involved in reinforcing conformity. Notice how this varies at the micro, meso, and macro levels of the social system.

Crimes that affect the individual or primary group seem most threatening to us and receive the most attention in the press and from politicians. Yet these micro-level crimes are only a portion of the total crime picture and, except for hate crimes, are not the most dysfunctional or dangerous crimes. In the United States, more than 2,800 acts are listed as federal crimes. These acts fall into several types of crime, some of which are discussed below. First, we consider how crime rates are measured.

How Much Crime Is There?

How do sociologists and law enforcement officials know how much crime there is, especially because not all crime is reported to the police? Each country has methods of keeping crime records. For instance, the official record of crime in the United States is found in the U.S. Federal Bureau of

Investigation's (FBI's) *Uniform Crime Reports* (UCR). The FBI relies on information submitted voluntarily by law enforcement agencies and divides crimes into two categories: Type I and Type II offenses. Type I offenses, also known as *FBI index crimes*, include murder, forcible rape, robbery, aggravated assault, burglary, larceny theft, motor vehicle theft, and arson. There are hundreds of Type II offenses, including fraud, simple assault, vandalism, driving under the influence of alcohol or drugs, and running away from home. Figure 6.2 summarizes UCR crime records on Type I offenses.

To examine trends in crime, criminologists calculate a rate of crime, usually per 100,000 individuals. Recent data indicate that the rate of violent crime in the United States has dropped since the mid-1990s (see Table 6.1 on page 184). In 1985, there were 558 violent crimes per 100,000 residents; in 1995, that number was 684.5; by 2000, the number had dropped to 506.5; and in 2006, it had dropped again to 473.5 (FBI 2006c). The number of violent crime offenses fell in the United States in 2008, according to the FBI. Crime records also show that Black men were six times as likely to be homicide victims as White men (Stout 2009).

Although the UCR data provide a picture of how much crime gets reported to the police and leads to arrest, it does not provide information on how much crime there is in the United States. Sometimes a crime that is reported to the police does not lead to an arrest, or an arrest is made but the case is never prosecuted in court, or a prosecutor will initiate prosecution but the case never comes to trial. Instead, it is plea-bargained—a suspect agrees to plead guilty in exchange for being given a lesser charge, perhaps because the suspect feels guilt, because the person does not have the resources to fight the charges with a good attorney, or because the suspect is willing to exchange information for a lighter sentence. The reduction in the

 Video Link 6.2 Take a look at Hurricane Katrina and crime.

Every 3.2 seconds	1 property crime
Every 4.8 seconds	1 larceny, theft
Every 14.5 seconds	1 burglary
Every 26.8 seconds	1 motor vehicle theft
Every 22.2 seconds	1 violent crime
Every 36.6 seconds	1 aggravated assault
Every 1.2 minutes	1 robbery
Every 5.8 minutes	1 forcible rape
Every 30.9 minutes	1 murder

Figure 6.2   Crime Clock
Source: FBI (2006b) and U.S. Department of Justice (2009).

Table 6.1	**Index of Violent Crime, United States**
Year	Violent Crime Rate (per 100,000 residents)
1985	556.6
1990	731.8
1995	684.5
2000	506.5
2005	469.0
2006	473.5
2007	466.9
2008	454.5

Source: UCR Crime Statistics (2008).

Note: The number of violent crime offenses in the United States in 2008 was 1,382,012.

How crime is measured affects what and how much crime is reported. Although differences in crime reports are often difficult to reconcile, each measurement instrument provides a different portion of the total picture of crime. By using several data-gathering techniques (triangulation), a more accurate picture of crime begins to emerge. Most of the crimes that concern average citizens of countries around the world are violent crimes committed by individuals or small groups. The following are some examples of these micro-level crimes.

Thinking Sociologically

Which source of data discussed above do you think best tells us what the crime rates are? Why might there be a benefit in having more than one method? Why are FBI reports usually given attention by the press?

number of cases at each level of the criminal justice system is just one of the problems of attempting to determine accurate crime rates.

Changes in the UCR to eliminate some of its problems have led to a new measurement, the *National Incident-Based Reporting System* (NIBRS). In this measure, the reporting is incident driven, meaning that the FBI gathers not only information on the crime but also more detailed information on victim and offender characteristics and other, more detailed categories. Reports include the type of offense, whether a weapon was used, the location, whether drugs were a factor, and any motivations related to race, religion, or gender. Ultimately, this system will provide more detailed and accurate crime statistics.

Another technique to assess crime rates is by carrying out self-reporting surveys—asking individuals what criminal acts they have committed. Criminal participation surveys typically focus on adolescents and their involvement in delinquency. Yet another way to assess crime rates is through victimization surveys—surveys that ask people how much crime they have experienced. The most extensively gathered victimization survey in the United States is the National Crime Victimization Survey, conducted by the Bureau of Justice Statistics. According to these records, the tendency to report crime to the police varies by the type of crime, with violent victimizations having the highest reporting rate. The victimization survey corroborates the findings of the Index of Crime, showing that violent crime rates have declined since 1994, although the trend has recently reversed slightly.

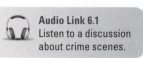

Audio Link 6.1
Listen to a discussion about crime scenes.

Predatory or Street Crimes

Crimes committed against individuals or property are called predatory crimes by law enforcement agencies and are considered the most serious crimes by the public. In the United States, the UCR lists eight serious predatory index crimes used to track crime rates: acts against people (murder, robbery, assault, and rape) and against property (burglary, arson, theft, and auto theft).

Citizens of the United States are increasingly afraid of violent predatory crime, especially by strangers. Surveys show that citizens feel they cannot trust others. Some people keep guns. Others, especially women, African Americans, older Americans, and low-income individuals, are afraid to go out near their homes at night (U.S. Bureau of Justice Statistics 2001). Because one's property and bodily safety are at stake, the public fixates on these crimes as the most feared and serious. However, the percentage of U.S. households experiencing one or more crimes dropped from 25% in 1994 to 14% in 2005 (Klaus 2007). Most criminologists feel there are more serious crimes to be discussed under meso- and macro-level deviance.

Crimes Without Victims

Acts committed by or between consenting adults are known as **victimless** or **public order crimes**. Depending on the laws of countries, these can include prostitution, homosexual acts, gambling, smoking marijuana and using drugs, drunkenness, and some forms of white-collar crime. The participants involved do not consider themselves to be victims, but the offense is mostly an affront to someone else's morals. The behaviors labeled deviant by law fall into the category of conflict crime. These illegal acts may be tolerated as long as they do not become highly visible. Some prostitution is overlooked in major cities of the world, but if it becomes visible or is seen as a public nuisance, authorities crack down, and it is controlled. Even though these acts are called victimless, there is controversy over whether individuals are victims even when consenting to the act and whether others such as family members are victims dealing with the consequences of the illegal activities.

Thinking Sociologically

Can a person be victimized by drugs even if he willingly uses them? Many prostitutes only consent to sex acts because poverty leaves them with few other options and because, like many women without resources, they are vulnerable to domination by men. Are they victims?

Societies respond to victimless crimes such as using and selling drugs with a variety of policies, from execution in Iran and hanging in Malaysia to legalization in Holland. Long prison terms in the United States mean that 3 out of every 10 prison cells are now reserved for the user, the addict, and the drug seller—yet the problem has not diminished (Goode 1997, 2005). Proposals to legalize drugs, gambling, prostitution, and other victimless crimes

A woman smokes a marijuana pipe in Amsterdam, the Netherlands, where smoking pot is legal. The Dutch do not think there is any victim, and therefore there should be no prohibition on the behavior.

meet with strong opinions both for and against. Although in many countries current policies and programs toward drugs are not working, by almost every measure of success, the various consequences of alternative proposals are also uncertain.

Hate Crimes

Ethnic violence around the world results in reports of hate crimes in communities, at workplaces, and on college campuses. Hate crimes are criminal offenses committed against a person, property, or group that are motivated by the offender's bias against a religion, ethnic or racial group, national origin, gender, or sexual orientation. The UCR in the United States indicate that hate crimes account for 11.5% of the total criminal offenses. Most hate crimes are directed against property (84.4%) and involve destruction, damage, or vandalism; 31.3% include direct intimidation, totaling 9,035 hate crimes involving 9,528 victims (FBI 2005; U.S. Bureau of Justice Statistics 2005). In 2008, the most recent data available, there were 7,783 hate crime incidents involving 9,168 offenses: 51% racial bias, 20% religious bias, 18% sexual-orientation bias, 12% nationality bias, and 1% disability bias (UCR Crime Reports 2009).

Research suggests that most hate crimes are spontaneous incidents, often a case of the victim being in the wrong place at the wrong time. Consider the case of Matthew Shepard, the gay college student who was robbed, tied to a fence post, beaten, and left to die in the cold Wyoming night. Nearly 16% of hate crimes are against those with different sexual orientations. Victims often form supportive in-groups to protect themselves from others who create a "culture of hate" (Jenness and Broad 1997; Levin and McDevitt 2003).

Hate crimes are often vicious and brutal because the perpetrators feel rage against the victim as a representative of a group they despise. The crimes are committed by individuals or small vigilante groups. Emotionally based crimes upholding moral codes may threaten a person's own behavior as the most vociferous protestors may be hiding guilt. The targets are usually individuals who happen to have certain traits or are part of a particular community. In the case of some White supremacy movements, philosophical, political, and even religious principles guide their group beliefs (Blee 2008).

The examples above represent only three of the many micro-level crimes, characterized by individual or small-group actions. We now turn to crime in organizations and institutions. Not only is crime rooted in complex organizations at the meso level, but crimes themselves are committed within or by organizations.

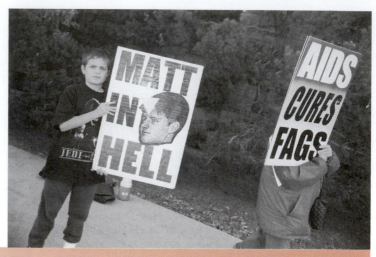

Advocates of a hate-free America (left) express their support for the gay and lesbian community. Others (right) express their sentiment that Matthew Shepard, a gay student who was beaten and left to die in a hate crime, was a deviant who had no moral standing or, seemingly, even the right to live.

CRIME AND ORGANIZATIONS: MESO-LEVEL ANALYSIS

Understanding criminal behavior is especially important if we wish to understand complex modern societies. First, as societies modernize, there is an almost universal tendency for crime rates to increase dramatically due to the anomie that new migrants and the poor experience in urban areas as old norms are no longer relevant (Merton 1938). Second, as societies modernize, they become more reliant on formal or bureaucratic mechanisms of control—in other words, development of a criminal justice system at the meso level of our social world.

Crimes Involving Organizations and Institutions

Audio Link 6.2
Listen to stories about fraud and crime.

We all seek reasons for the alarming rise in health care costs and insurance premiums. Among the many reasons is fraud, and one of the most egregious examples of this is Medicare fraud, estimated at $60 billion a year. For example, in South Florida, criminals open storefronts claiming to sell medical equipment; often these are located in dying strip malls, and the offices for the equipment are usually closed. Once the criminals have sent in false claims for Medicare payments, sometimes amounting to millions of dollars, they close the storefronts and move on so that they cannot be traced. Although the federal government has a small number of investigators, they are hardly a match for the fast-moving criminals with their get-rich-quick schemes ("Medicare Fraud" 2009).

This is but one example of crimes involving organizations. Some crimes are committed by highly organized, hierarchically structured syndicates that are formed for the purpose of achieving their economic objectives in any way possible. These groups intentionally flout the law. On the other hand, some crimes are committed by legitimate corporations that break the law. Their crimes are very serious, but the purpose and the public image of such organizations are not criminal. We will look first at organized criminal organizations and then at crimes committed by people within their legitimate occupations and organizations.

Organized Crime

Organized crime, ongoing criminal enterprises, have the ultimate purpose of personal economic gain through illegitimate means (Siegel 2009). Organized criminals use business enterprises for illegal profit. They engage in violence and corruption to gain and maintain power and profit (Adler et al. 2004). Our image of this type of crime is sometimes glamorized, coming from stereotypes in films such as *No Country for Old Men, The Godfather, Gangs of New York*, and many others. On television, *The Sopranos* is the ultimate media "mob" depiction. Despite the alluring view of these idealized stories, organized crime is a serious problem in many countries. It is essentially a counterculture with a hierarchical structure, from the boss down to the underlings. The organization relies on power, control, fear, violence, and corruption. This type of crime is a particular problem when societies experience anomie and social controls break down.

Marginalized ethnic groups that face discrimination may become involved in a quest to get ahead through organized crime. Early in U.S. history, Italians were especially prominent in organized crime, but today, many groups are involved. Organized crime around the world has gained strong footholds in countries in transition (Siegel and Nelen 2008). For example, in Russia, the transition from a socialist economy to a market economy has provided many opportunities for criminal activity. The *Mafiya* is estimated to be 100,000 people strong, and some estimate that the members control 70% to 80% of all private business and 40% of the nation's wealth (Lindberg and Markovic n.d.; Schmalleger 2006). Organized crime usually takes one of three forms: (1) the sale of illegal goods and services, including gambling, loan sharking, trafficking in drugs and people, selling stolen goods, and prostitution; (2) infiltrating legitimate businesses and unions through threat and intimidation and using bankruptcy and fraud to exploit and devastate a legitimate company; and (3) racketeering—the extortion of funds in exchange for protection (i.e., not being hurt). Activities such as running a casino or trash collection service often appear to be legitimate endeavors on the surface but may be cover operations for highly organized illegal crime rings.

Although the exact cost of organized crime in the United States is impossible to determine, estimates of the annual gross income from organized crime activity range from $50 billion—more than 1% of the gross national product—to $90 billion per year ("Organized Crime" 2009; Siegel 2000).

Transnational organized crime takes place across national boundaries, using sophisticated electronic communications and transportation technologies. Experts identify several major crime clans in the world: (a) Hong Kong–based triads, (b) South American cocaine cartels, (c) Italian mafia, (d) Japanese Yakuza, (e) Russian Mafiya, and (f) West African crime groups. Each operates across borders. Organized crime is responsible for thousands of deaths every year through drug traffic and murders, and it contributes to the climate of violence in many cities (Siegel 2009).

The value of the global illicit drug market is estimated at more than $13 billion at the production level, $90 billion at the wholesale level, and $320 billion at the retail level (based on retail prices and taking seizures and other losses into account). The largest market is cannabis, followed by cocaine, the opiates, and other markets such as methamphetamine, amphetamine, and ecstasy (Common Sense for Drug Policy 2006; Drug War Chronicle 2009; United Nations Development Programme 2005b). Many people survive from the drug trade, from the poppy farmers in Afghanistan, who grow more than 75% of the world's poppies, to street drug dealers. In 2007, the acreage devoted to growing poppies was the highest ever, especially in southern Afghanistan. This problem is not likely to end soon because the farmers are in debt to the Taliban and are therefore forced to continue growing poppies. The Taliban profit from the sales by more than $100 million per year, which helps keep them in power. Thus, Westerners who use opium drugs help in financially sustaining this group (National Public Radio 2008).

Add other types of crimes (transporting migrants, trafficking in women and children for the sex industry, and sales of weapons and nuclear material) and the estimates of profits for international crime cartels are from $750 billion to more than $1.5 trillion a year (United Nations Development Programme 2005b).

Occupational Crime

Although the scandal became public knowledge in December 2008, the details unfolded over the next several months. Bernard (Bernie) Madoff, former chair of the NASDAQ stock exchange, had developed a Ponzi scheme that is probably the largest investment fraud Wall Street has every seen. The scheme defrauded and wrecked thousands of investors, public pension funds, charitable foundations, and universities of billions of dollars, with more than $65 billion missing from investor accounts. Named after Charles Ponzi, the first to be caught, Ponzi schemes involve promises of large returns on investments, paying old investors with money from new investors. Money is shifted between investors ("The Madoff Case" 2009).

The Arthur Andersen accounting firm employee working with Enron shredded documents, covering a trail of shady dealings. This was illegal. The Enron and Arthur Andersen scandal became the largest fraud in American business history, and the taint spread to other companies (Shore 2008). Today, we see many more tales of greed that have brought down Wall Street companies and businesses.

A violation of the law committed by an individual or group in the course of a legitimate, respected occupation or financial activity is called white-collar or occupational crime (Coleman 2006; Hagan 2007). Occupational crime can be committed by individuals from virtually any social class, and it can occur at any organizational level. However, most often this refers to white-collar crimes. In the United States, these are "estimated to be ten times greater than all the annual losses from all the crimes reported to the police" (Coleman 2006:43). Antitrust violations cost $250 billion. Tax fraud costs $150 billion, and health care industry fraud costs $100 billion. Employee theft adds 2% to the retail purchase price of the products we buy (Coleman 2006).

Occupational crime receives less attention than violent crimes because it is less visible, does not always cause obvious physical injury to identifiable people, and is frequently committed by people in positions of substantial authority and prestige. Reports of violent crimes that appear on the television news each night attract more attention. Yet occupational crime is far more costly in currency, health, and lives. Victims of financial scams who have lost their life savings are well aware of this.

In addition to occupational crimes such as embezzlement, pilfering, bribery, tax evasion, price fixing, obstruction of justice, and various forms of fraud, computer crime is adding to the losses of businesses and government. Identity theft, embezzlement, international illegal transfers of money, illegal stock trades, sales of illegal or inferior products, creation of computer viruses, computer hacking—this list is long and will become longer. "As technology advances, it facilitates new forms of behavior . . . new and as yet unimaginable opportunities for criminals positioned to take advantage of it and the power such technology will afford" (Schmalleger 2006:473).

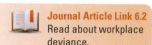

Journal Article Link 6.2
Read about workplace deviance.

Sociologists divide occupational crimes into four major categories: (1) against the company, (2) against the employees, (3) against customers, and (4) against the general public (Hagan 2007).

Crimes against the company include pilfering (using company resources such as the photocopy machine for personal business) and employee theft ("borrowing company property," taking from the till, and embezzlement). Most employees are otherwise upstanding citizens, but those who commit occupational crimes say they do so for several reasons. First, they feel little or no loyalty to the organization, especially if it is large and impersonal. It is like stealing from nobody, they say. Second, workers feel exploited and resentful toward the company. Stealing is getting back at the company. Third, the theft is seen as a "fringe benefit" or "informal compensation" that they deserve. Making personal long-distance calls on company phones or taking paper and pens are examples. Fourth, workers may steal because of the challenge. It makes the job more interesting if they can get away with it. It is important to note that these people do not see themselves as criminals, especially compared with "street" criminals (Altheide et al. 1978).

The next three types of corporate crime are often done on behalf of the company, and the victims are employees or members of the larger society. *Crimes against employees* refer to corporate neglect of worker safety. In the United States, the Occupational Safety and Health Act was passed in 1970 to help enforce regulations to protect workers, but there are still many problems. Government agencies estimate that the death rate each year from job-related illness and injuries is fivefold the number of deaths from street crimes. For example, one out of every five cancer cases has been traced to pollutants in workplaces, and many of these cases were preventable (Simon 2006). Neglect of worker safety is a serious problem in some developing or peripheral countries trying to attract multinational corporations with low taxes, cheap labor, and few regulations.

Why does corporate crime and negligence occur? Several theories of crime are helpful in explaining this pattern.

Organizational crimes by executives take place in environments where profits are expected by investors and by one's coworkers (as explained by differential association theory) and where the benefits of such behavior seem, at the time, to outweigh the costs (which illustrates rational choice theory). The micro-level environment within the larger corporation shapes the decision-making process in a way that fosters crime.

Strain theory points out that the goals of corporations are to make the greatest short-term profits. In fact, it is illegal for a U.S. corporation to do anything contrary to the interests of the stockholders. Thus, to install expensive equipment or safety devices cuts those profits, and many employers are concerned with the bottom line, not the long-term consequences. Although government agencies in many countries are responsible for reducing environmental hazards and workplace dangers, they do not have sufficient staff to police companies for adherence to laws. Internationally, there is little oversight. When agencies do step in, it is usually after the fact—when complaints are lodged against those companies because of serious health and safety problems resulting from their actions. Multinational corporations generally look for the cheapest labor costs and lowest environmental regulations to maximize their profits, and governments of poor countries try to attract foreign corporations to keep the poor populace employed regardless of the environmental or workplace consequences.

Crimes against customers involve acts such as selling dangerous foods or unsafe products, consumer fraud, deceptive advertising, and price-fixing (i.e., setting prices in collusion with another producer). The purpose of advertising is to convince customers, by whatever means, to buy the product—appealing to their vanity, sexual interests, or desire to keep up with their neighbors. Sometimes these techniques cross the line between honesty and deception. The result can be customers purchasing products that are defective and even dangerous—all with the full knowledge of company officials.

Crimes against the public include acts by companies that negatively affect large groups of people. One example is hospitals or medical offices that overbill Medicare (discussed above), which costs U.S. taxpayers an estimated $100 billion a year. The FBI (2006a) estimates that 3% to 10% of the total health care expenditures, both public and private, are fraudulent.

Surreptitiously dumping pollutants into landfills, streams, or the air is another crime against the public. Proper disposal of contaminants can be costly and time-consuming for a company, but shortcuts can cause long-term effects for the public. One example is Love Canal, New York, the illegal dumping ground for toxic chemicals from the Hooker Chemical Corporation. Years after the dumping, the effects of the chemicals were seen in injured children and others. Hooker eventually paid $227 million in damages, but the cleanup cost taxpayers another $280 million (Coleman 2006). Pollutants from industrial wastes have caused high rates of miscarriages, birth defects, and diseases among residents. These cases demonstrate how lethal crimes against the public can be.

After reviewing the evidence, Coleman (2006) draws the conclusion that white-collar crime committed by company executives is by far our most serious crime problem. The economic cost of white-collar crime is vastly greater than the economic cost of street crime. White-collar criminals kill considerably more people than all violent street criminals put together (Coleman 2006).

Thinking Sociologically

Why are meso-level crimes considered more dangerous and more costly to the public than micro-level crimes? Why do they get so much less attention?

NATIONAL AND GLOBAL CRIME: MACRO-LEVEL ANALYSIS

Terrorism refers to "premeditated, politically motivated violence perpetrated against noncombatant targets by subnational groups or clandestine agents, usually intended to influence an audience" (Zalman 2009).

Add to that international terrorism practiced in one or more foreign countries, and terrorism can be seen to be a worldwide problem. The number of international terrorist attacks in 2006 was down to 240 from 310 in 2005 and almost 400 in 2004 (Memorial Institute for the Prevention of Terrorism 2007). In 2004, 1,907 people were killed and 9,300 wounded (U.S. Department of State 2005). Terrorist groups can be religious, state sponsored, left wing or right wing, or nationalist. Table 6.2 shows the types of terrorist groups (Schmalleger 2006:347).

Some beaches in the United States, even in beautiful resort communities, have been closed due to unsafe water, and in some communities, children cannot play outside during the warm months due to risk of injury to their lungs. The U.S. Environmental Protection Agency has documented many cases in which industries violate pollution control laws, and it is the citizenry who suffer. This illustrates corporate crimes against citizens, but it is still not considered a "major" crime in the FBI index crimes or by most journalists.

Table 6.2	**Types of Terrorist Groups**
Nationalist	Irish Republican Army, Basque Fatherland and Liberty, Kurdistan Workers' Party
Religious	Al-Qaeda, HAMAS, Hezbollah, Aum Shinrikyo (Japan)
State sponsored	Hezbollah (backed by Iran), Abu Nidal Organization (Syria, Libya), Japanese Red Army (Libya)
Left wing	Red Brigades (Italy), Baader-Meinhof Gang (Germany), Japanese Red Army
Right wing	Neo-Nazis, skinheads, White supremacists
Anarchist	Some contemporary antiglobalization groups

Source: Schmalleger (2006:347).

Crime is a national and global issue, as illustrated by *state organized crime.* Overlooked by the public and by social scientists, this form of crime includes acts defined by law as criminal but committed by state or government officials. For example, a government might be complicit in smuggling, assassination, or torture, acting as an accessory to national or international crime, which is then justified in terms of "national defense." Government offices may also violate laws that restrict or limit government activities such as eavesdropping. In some countries, including the United States, political prisoners are held for long periods without charges, without access to lawyers, and without trials, or they are tortured, violating both national and international laws. U.S. torture of enemy combatants during the Bush administration raised questions of legality. Some countries have also violated their own laws, but it is difficult to cast blame when the guilty party is the government.

Bribery and corruption are the way of life in many governments, businesses, and police forces. The percentage of persons who said that they had paid a bribe to obtain services is as high as 79% in Nigeria, 72% in Cambodia, and 71% in Albania. Table 6.3 shows comparative corruption rankings as measured by bribes paid to obtain services (Transparency International 2007).

Table 6.3 **Percentage of Respondents Who Said They Had Paid a Bribe to Obtain Services**	
Africa	42
Cameroon	79
Nigeria	40
Asia Pacific	22
Cambodia	72
India	25
Japan	1
Pakistan	44
Latin America	13
Argentina	5
Bolivia	27
European Union	5
Austria	1
Denmark	2
Finland	2
France	1
Netherlands	2
Sweden	1
Switzerland	1
United Kingdom	2
Southeast Europe	12
Albania	71
Kosovo	67
Macedonia	44
North America	2
Canada	1
United States	2

Source: Reprinted from *Transparency International Global Corruption Barometer, 2007.* Copyright © 2007 Transparency International: The Global Coalition Against Corruption. For more information, visit www.transparency.org.

Detainees sit in a holding area at the naval base in Guantánamo Bay, Cuba, in the "temporary" detention facility. Many years later, most of these men were still being held without trial. In several U.S. Supreme Court rulings (2006 and 2008), the verdict was that the rights of these people have been violated by the U.S. administration. The Obama administration promised to shut down the facility in 2010.

Thinking Sociologically

Sometimes government officials and even heads of state are the perpetrators of crimes. Is there a difference if a crime is committed by an official and justified as necessary for national defense? Why or why not? Is it ever justified for a military or intelligence agency to violate its own country's laws?

Cross-National Comparison of Crimes

The vending machine was on the corner near the Ballantines' house in Japan. The usual cola, candy, and sundries were displayed, along with cigarettes, beer, whiskey, sake, and pornographic magazines. Out of curiosity, Jeanne and her family watched to see who purchased what from the machines, and not once did they see teenagers sneaking the beer, cigarettes, or porn. It turns out that the Ballantines were not the only ones watching! The neighbors also kept an eye on who did what—the neighborhood watch being an effective form of social control in Japan. Because of the **stigma**—the disapproval attached to disobeying the expected norms—teens understand the limits, and vigilant neighbors help keep the overall amount of deviance low. The neighborhood watch sends a signal that deviant behavior is unacceptable and provides social control on behaviors of those who might be tempted to commit crimes.

Japan and the United States are both modern, urban, industrial countries, but their crime rates and the way they deal with deviant behavior and crimes are quite different. Japan has 21 violent crimes for every 100,000 individuals (including 1 homicide, 2 rapes, and 5 robberies). That means in a population of 127 million, Japan had 1,391 homicides in 2005. Compare that with the rate in the United States, 637 for every 100,000 individuals (including 6 homicides, 32 rapes, and 149 robberies)—a rate 30 times greater (Greimel 2007; Interpol 2003). Yet the overall crime rate in Japan has increased to 2.27 million cases compared with 1.81 million a decade earlier. The Japanese are concerned with the increase, although compared with the number of homicides in the United States, 16,692 in a population of about 300 million, their rate is still low (Greimel 2007).

How can these differences in crime rates be explained? Researchers look at cultural differences: Japan's low violent crime rate is due in part to Japan's homogeneous society—inequality between citizens is not great; success is not as focused on material possessions and consumption; and there is loyalty to a historic tradition of cooperation that provides a sense of moral order, a network of group relations, strong commitment to social norms, and respect for law and order (Westermann and Burfeind 1991). The example of vending machines in Japan illustrates this idea. In addition, guns are outlawed.

Although Japan's crime rate is roughly one third that of the United States, it is not attained through harsher penalties. The Japanese government actually spends far less of its gross national product on the police, courts, and prisons, and the police in Japan want to be thought of as kind and caring rather than strict in their enforcement of the law. For many crimes in Japan, the offender may simply be asked to write a letter of apology. This is frequently sufficient sanction to deter the person from further violation of the law. The humiliation of writing an apology and the fear of shame and embarrassing one's family are strong enough to curb deviant behavior (Lazare 2004).

Criminologists consider the causes of economic inequality in different countries. If minority status prevents certain individuals and groups from fitting into the dominant society and getting ahead, this helps explain the higher levels of deviance among the disfranchised groups. The overall health of a country's economy—as measured by job opportunities, unemployment, and inflation—also affects the crime rate. When a country has a great income differential between members, the crime rates rise. Research shows that the incidence of homicide is higher in countries with greater income inequality.

Although comparing cross-national data on crime is difficult because there are variations in the definitions of crime and the measurements used, comparisons do give us insight into what types of crimes are committed, under what circumstances, and how often. Two sources of international data are Interpol (the International Criminal Police Organization) and the United Nations. Although these organizations collect and present data, they have no way to check the accuracy of the data they receive from countries.

Table 6.4 in the next "Engaging Sociology" on page 192 provides information on crimes in selected countries. Differences are due in part to the much higher disparity in income between the rich and the poor and the heterogeneity of populations. The size of the country is also provided since that is relevant to the comparison.

Global Crimes

Increasingly, crimes are global in nature. Some crimes are committed by transnational conglomerates and may involve organized crime and the smuggling of illegal goods and humans. Other crimes are committed by countries that violate international laws, treaties, and agreements. Consider international agreements regarding protection of the environment, which some countries and transnational corporations ignore when these agreements act against their own self-interests. Yet these violations of agreements may affect the entire global ecological system. The international community has the capacity to try people, organizations, and countries for violation of human rights or international laws, but the process is difficult and politically charged.

Some scholars use a world systems perspective, arguing that the cause of global crime lies in the global economy, the inequalities between countries, and the competition between countries for resources and wealth. As a result of the capitalist mode of production, an unequal relationship has arisen between core nations (the developed, wealthy nations in the Global North) and periphery nations (the Global South) that results in inequality. Core nations often take unfair advantage of peripheral nations. Peripheral nations, in turn, must find ways to survive in this global system, and they sometime turn to surreptitious methods to achieve their goals (Chase-Dunn and Anderson 2006). Some nations with many resources are semi-periphery nations. Benefiting from

Engaging Sociology

Crime Comparison

The frequency of crimes varies across countries and is influenced by many variables. Examine this table, and then answer the questions below.

Table 6.4 Crime Incidents in Selected Countries

Country	Murders	Rapes	Assaults	Burglaries	Auto Thefts	Population Size (in millions)
Australia	302	15,630	141,124	436,865	139,094	21.3
Canada	489	24,049	233,517	23,065	160,268	33.5
Chile	235	1,250	53,133	13,375	n.a.	16.6
Denmark	58	497	9,796	1,297	32,203	5.5
Finland	148	579	27,820	370,993	16,391	5.3
France	1,051	8,458	106,484	1,885	301,539	64.1
Germany	960	7,499	116,912	n.a.	83,063	82.3
Italy	746	2,336	29,068	n.a.	243,890	58.1
Japan	637	2,260	43,229	3,027	309,638	127.1
New Zealand	45	861	30,177	65,675	21,992	4.2
United Kingdom	850	8,593	450,865	836,027	338,796	61.1
United States	12,658	89,110	2,238,480	2,099,700	1,147,300	307.2

Source: Interpol Data (2007) and World Factbook (2010d).

Note: n.a. = not available.

Engaging:

1. Take the population (in millions) and divide it by the number of crimes in a given category (e.g., murder). If you do that for each country for a particular type of crime, you can see the ratio of crimes per person in the population.

2. Which countries have especially striking crime rates?

3. What can you tell about countries from studying their crime rates?

4. Do any particular rates stand out?

5. How might you explain those rates?

extensive trade, they are less vulnerable than the poorest nations. Map 6.2 helps you see where some of these core, peripheral, and semi-peripheral nations are located.

As you look at this map, note that the developed or affluent countries are almost all located in the Northern Hemisphere. Although some poor countries are north of the equator, the pattern is obvious. To avoid some misleading implications of the words *developed* and *developing*, some scholars prefer the term *Global South* to refer to less affluent nations. If you see or hear the phrase Global South, this map should help you see why it refers to developing or poor countries.

The forms of global corruption are too extensive to catalog here, so we will settle for an illustration of one of the newest manifestations of global crime against people and property: computer crimes. Internet deviance or cyberspace crime is growing faster than a cybergeek can move a mouse. This new world of crime ranges from online identity theft and gambling to cybersex and pornography, to hate sites and stalking, and to hacking into files and terrorism (Thio 2007).

As one team of researchers report, the Internet "is where crime is rampant and every twisted urge can be satisfied . . . Fraudsters can tap into an international audience from

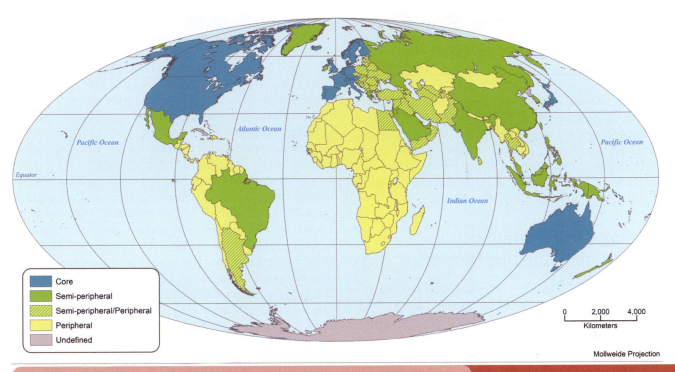

Map 6.2   Core, Semi-peripheral, and Peripheral Countries of the World

Source: Map by Anna Versluis.

Note: Some countries are left undefined (in gray).

anyplace in the world" (Sager et al. 2006:261). The illegal "underground Web" of businesses, such as arms dealing, was estimated at more than $36 billion in 2002. Compare that with legitimate business consumers in the United States spending just over $39 billion on the Internet the same year. Of the fraud complaints received by the U.S. government, more than 70% involved the Internet. Financial fraud costs consumers $22 billion annually, according to *Business Week*, and identity theft is running into $22 billion annually, according to the Identity Theft Resource Center (Sager et al. 2006). "The Underground Web, if unchecked, has the potential to undermine the values of society. It enables— even encourages—ordinary citizens to break the law" (Sager et al. 2006:262).

Even legitimate businesses such as Google, Yahoo!, or eBay can unwittingly support crime by connecting people to illegal operations. Internet auction fraud comprises 44% of official complaints to the FBI, 19% for undelivered merchandize or payment, and 4.9% for check fraud (FBI 2007). Internet fraud in the United States increased 33% between 2007 and 2008, with 275,284 fraud claims and the dollar loss at $265 million (Cratty 2008). Drug trafficking is one of the most common forms of scam. For example, people purchase prescription drugs that are contaminated or diluted and can be life threatening,

find recipes for making illegal methamphetamines, or purchase body-building or date rape drugs (gamma-hydroxybutyric acid [GHB]). Another avenue of illegal Internet usage is music and video downloading and sales (Friedman 2005).

Other crimes have also become easier to commit: The FBI reported an increase of 1,789% in online child porn cases opened between 1996 and 2006. The arrests and summons during the same time period increased from 68 in 1996 to 1,546 in 2006, a 2,174% increase, and the increase in convictions and pretrial diversions was from 68 to 1,018 (FBI 2006d). One policy difficulty is that law enforcement gets gridlocked in both national and international jurisdictional confusion. As many as five different federal U.S. agencies can be involved in preventing financial fraud on the Internet, not to mention the state and local agencies that might play a role. If the fraud involves international cybercrime, the customs services and other branches of governments also may enter the investigation. The resulting confusion and lack of clear authority regarding who should prosecute can play into the hands of lawbreakers. Few local authorities feel that identity theft is within their jurisdiction, but government officials may not have the personnel or the interest to pursue these cases (Sager et al. 2006).

Controlling Crime: Social Policy Considerations

Someone commits a crime, gets caught, has a trial or plea bargain, and goes to jail or prison if found guilty. It sounds straightforward, but it is far from that. Most governments pass laws and make policies to keep deviance from disrupting the smooth functioning of society. This section discusses the mechanisms used by societies to control the amount of deviance and punish deviants.

Dealing With Crime: The Criminal Justice Process

When people are afraid to walk the streets because they might be assaulted and when a significant number of individuals are dropping out of society and taking up deviant lifestyles, deviance becomes a topic of great concern. Every society has a process for dealing with crime and criminals. Sometimes the ground rules and processes of justice respect human rights and represent blind justice, meaning that all people are treated equally, but often they are not.

Structural-functionalists see the justice system as important to maintaining order in society. Some conflict theorists argue that the criminal justice system depicts the threat of crime as a threat from poor people and minorities, which creates fear of victimization in members of society. It is in the interests of those in power to maintain the image that crime is primarily the work of outsiders and the poor. This deflects discontent and hostility from the powerful and helps them retain their positions of power (Reiman and Leighton 2010a, 2010b). Conflict theorists point out that there will always be a certain percentage of crime in society because the powerful will make sure that something is labeled deviant. So policy might focus on how to deter deviant acts, or it could focus on the injustices of the system and the ways in which the criminal justice system protects and sustains the power structure. In either case, prisons and jails—penal institutions—are currently the primary means of controlling individual criminal behavior.

Prisons and Jails

Protecting the public from offenders often means locking criminals in prisons, a form of total institution that completely controls the prisoners' lives and regulates all their activities. Goffman (1961) describes inmates' lives as being drastically changed through the processes of *degradation*,

Video Link 6.3
Watch video about juveniles with life sentences.

which marks the individual as deviant, and *mortification*, which breaks down the individual's original self as the inmate experiences resocialization (see also Irwin 1985). The inmate is allowed no personal property. There is little communication, and verbal abuse of inmates by guards is common. Heterosexual activity is prohibited, uniforms and standard buzz cuts are required, and the inmates' schedules are totally controlled.

Social systems that develop within the prison often involve rigid roles, norms, and privileges. In a famous study that simulated a prison situation, Zimbardo, Haney, Banks, and Jaffe (1973) illustrated the social organization that develops and the roles that individuals play within the prison system. Students were assigned roles as prisoners or prison guards. Within a short time, the individuals in the study were acting out their roles. The students playing the role of "guard" became cruel and sadistic, causing Zimbardo to end the experiment prematurely to prevent problems. Participants had taken their roles so seriously that the abuse was beginning to have alarming consequences (Zimbardo et al. 1973). The recent abuse of prisoners in Iraq and at the Guantánamo Bay prison in Cuba parallel the findings from Zimbardo's earlier study of the roles that develop in these social situations (Zimbardo 2009).

Jails in local communities have been called catchall asylums for poor people. Most people in jails are there for their "rabble existence"—including petty hustlers, derelicts, junkies, "crazies," and outlaws—but they are mostly disorganized and economically marginal members of society (Irwin 1985). Jails in Europe and the United States house disproportionate numbers of immigrants (especially those with non-European features and skin tones), young men, and members of the poorest class of the citizenry.

In June 2008, 2,310,984 prisoners were being held in U.S. federal and state prisons and local jails. Whites comprise 38.8% of the incarcerated population, yet their percentage of the U.S. population is about 68%. African Americans make up more than 34% of all inmates but only about 12.4% of the total population, and Hispanics make up 20% of all inmates and about 14.1% of the total population (Sabol, West, and Cooper 2009; U.S. Census Bureau 2009c). Among women, the number of African Americans incarcerated declined as the number of White women increased from 33 to 48 per 100,000 between 2000 and 2006. Table 6.5 breaks down the incarcerated population by race/ethnicity and sex.

Conflict theorists believe that these figures are strong evidence that jails and prisons are mostly about controlling or "managing" the minorities and poor people, not about public safety. African American males, for example, are 6.6 times more likely to be incarcerated than White men, with more than 10% having been in prison or jail for 25 to 39 years as of June 2008 (Fathi 2009; The Sentencing Project 2006; West and Sabol 2008).

Table 6.5 U.S. State and Federal Prisoners by Gender, Race, and Hispanic Origin, 2008		
	Number	*Total (%)*
Male	1,434,784	93.2
White	562,800	36.5
African American	477,500	31.0
Hispanic/Latino	295,800	19.2
Female	105,252	6.8
White	29,100	1.9
African American	50,700	3.3
Hispanic/Latino	17,300	1.1
Total	1,540,036	100

Source: Sabol et al. (2009).

Jails or prisons are often the formal sanctions applied to enforce the rules passed by legitimate officials. This woman is being arrested for a serious legal infraction.

Overall, the number of incarcerated individuals has increased rather dramatically in the United States. From 2005 to 2006, the increase was 2.8% nationwide, and the average annual growth rate of the prison population from 2000 to 2005 was 1.9% (Sabol 2007). The reasons for the increase in incarceration rates in the United States have to do with get-tough-on-crime policies, preventative detention policies that lock people up for minor offenses, and the "war on drugs," which increases the number of people put in jails and prisons. The increase in inmates in the United States has meant more jails being built and more people being hired to work in the legal system. One in eight African American males between the ages of 25 and 29 (12.6%) are in prison today. Likewise, 3.6% of the Hispanic population is imprisoned, compared with 1.7% of Whites. In some areas such as Washington, D.C., the rate is much higher (The Sentencing Project 2006).

Thinking Sociologically

From what you have learned so far in this chapter, why are the people who get sent to jail disproportionately young, poor immigrants, or racial and ethnic minorities?

The Purposes of Prisons

From the functional perspective, prisons serve several purposes for society: the desire for revenge or retribution, removing dangerous people from society, deterring would-be deviants, and rehabilitating through counseling, education, and work training programs inside prisons (R. Johnson 2002). However, in prison, inmates are exposed to more criminal and antisocial behavior, so rehabilitation and deterrence goals are often undermined by the nature of prisons. Roughly one in five males is sexually assaulted in U.S. prisons every year, often in gang rapes (Banbury 2004). This ongoing problem of assault, rape, and threat of violence in prison so brutalizes inmates that it becomes difficult for them to reenter society as well-adjusted citizens ready to conform to the conventional society that they feel has brutalized them (Hensley, Koscheski, and Tewksbury 2005). Many prisoners suffer from mental health problems and have difficulty reintegrating into society (Fathi 2009; Hanser 2002; Hensley et al. 2005).

Although estimates indicate that only 3% of known criminals go to prison, there has been a tremendous increase in incarceration rates in the United States. Incarceration rates were so high in 2008 that 1 out of every 100 Americans was incarcerated in a jail or prison, a rate that is unprecedented in the nation's history and a tremendous increase since the mid-1970s (Harrison and Karberg 2003; Liptak 2008). Even if we look only at the federal and state imprisonment, the U.S. rate of locking up citizens is the highest in the world and five to eight times higher than that in other industrial nations (International Centre for Prison Studies 2006; The Sentencing Project 2006). Table 6.6 (page 196) shows the countries with the highest incarceration rates and compares the rates of incarceration in industrial countries.

The disturbing reality is that despite the high rates of incarceration in the United States, **recidivism rates**—the

Table 6.6 **World Rates of Incarceration (Rates Per 100,000 people)**			
Top 10 Countries		*Other Industrialized Countries*	
United States	762[a]	United Kingdom	152[a]
Russian Federation	594	Netherlands	127
St. Kitts and Nevis	536	Australia	126
Bermuda	532	Canada	116[a]
Virgin Islands	521	Germany	97
Turkmenistan	489	Italy	97
Cuba	487	France	88
Palau	478	Switzerland	83
Belize	470	Sweden, Denmark, Finland	78–75
Bahamas	462	Japan	63[a]

Source: Fathi (2009) and International Centre for Prison Studies (2006).

a. Figures are for 2008.

Prisoners awaiting death penalty are held in a separate isolation unit known as "death row." Seventy percent of the members of the United Nations have abolished the death penalty, including all the European nations. More than 90% of all executions occurred in six countries: China, Iran, Iraq, Pakistan, Sudan, and the United States.

likelihood that someone who is arrested, convicted, and imprisoned will later be a repeat offender—are also very high in the United States. Three out of four men who do time in prison will be confined again for a crime. This means that as a specific deterrent or for rehabilitation, imprisonment does not work very well (National Center for Policy Analysis 2001). What options does government have? In the following sections, we discuss the death penalty and other alternatives to prisons.

The Death Penalty

Crimes of murder, assault, robbery, and rape usually receive severe penalties because they are the most dangerous. The most controversial (and irreversible) method of control is for the state to put the person to death. The most common argument for using the death penalty, more formally known as capital punishment, is to deter people from crime. The idea is that not only the person who has committed the crime will be punished, but also others will be deterred from committing such a crime because they know that the death penalty is a possibility for them too. Although most developed countries do not use the death penalty, the United States still does. In fact, as you can see from Map 6.3, the United States is one of the few countries with the death penalty. Capital punishment is most common in Asia, the Middle East, and parts of Africa.

By 2007, 133 of the 192 United Nations member states had abolished the death penalty in law or in practice, declaring it cruel and unusual punishment. In 2006, 86 countries had laws against the death penalty, 11 more forbid it except for exceptional crimes (such as war crimes), and 27 additional countries had not executed anyone in 10 or more years, although they had no laws forbidding capital punishment. That means that 133 countries do not actively employ the death penalty. Other countries retain the right to use the death penalty in extraordinary cases, although many of those countries actually do not follow through with the sentence (Amnesty International 2006).

In 2006, there were 1,591 known executions in the world, a drop of 25% from the 2,148 executions in 2005. About 91% of those executions occurred in six countries: China, Iran, Iraq, Pakistan, Sudan, and the United States (Amnesty International 2007). Methods of killing included beheading, electrocution, hanging, lethal injection, shooting, and stoning to death.

U.S. states with the death penalty assume that those contemplating crimes will be deterred by the severe penalty and those who have committed crimes will be justly punished. However, studies on the deterrent effects of capital punishment do not support the first assumption. Fewer than 25% of prison inmates believe that the death penalty would deter violent crime (Steele and Wilcox 2003). Inmates who had committed three or more violent crimes indicated that their crimes were not planned, that they "just happened," that "things went wrong,"

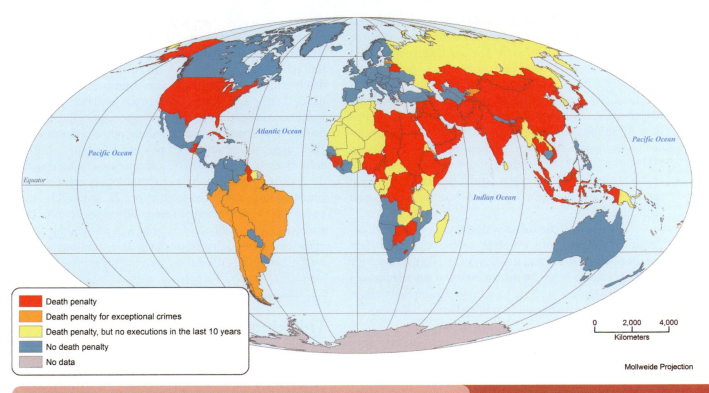

Map 6.3   Global Status of the Death Penalty in 2008

Source: Amnesty International. Map by Anna Versluis.

Legend:
- Death penalty
- Death penalty for exceptional crimes
- Death penalty, but no executions in the last 10 years
- No death penalty
- No data

Mollweide Projection

and that they were not thinking about the possible penalty when committing their crimes (Wilcox and Steele 2003). In 2004, the average murder rate per 100,000 people in states with the death penalty was 5.1, and the murder rate was much less—2.9—in states that do not have the death penalty (Death Penalty Information Center 2009; Hood 2002). So murder is more likely to happen in states with the death penalty, which is not very good evidence to show that this penalty has been a deterrent. However, it does serve as retribution or punishment for a crime (Hood 2002).

Thinking Sociologically

How can you explain the higher murder rates in U.S. states that have the death penalty?

Is the death penalty fairly administered? There is evidence that the death penalty is race and class biased. In most U.S. states with capital punishment, a disproportionate number of minority and lower-class individuals are put to death. African Americans make up 42% of death sentence inmates (Bonczar and Snell 2005). In some jurisdictions, African

Audio Link 6.3
Listen to stories involving DNA evidence.

Americans receive the death penalty at a rate 38% higher than all other groups. Since 1976, 35% of all those executed have been African American, a disproportionate number when considering that they make up less than 13% of the population (Amnesty International 2005; Sarat 2001; Siegel 2006).

Furthermore, the death penalty is usually imposed if a White person has been murdered. Homicides in which African Americans, Latinos and Latinas, Native Americans, and Asian Americans are killed are much less likely to result in a death penalty for the murderer, implying that people in society view their loss of life as less serious (Amnesty International 2006). In addition, mistakes are made. Since 1973, 123 prisoners have been released from death row because they were found innocent. DNA tests are acquitting other death row prisoners and have exonerated people who have already been executed.

A perhaps unexpected fact is that in the United States it cost more to put someone to death in most cases than to sentence them to life in prison. The national average cost for incarceration of an inmate is $25 thousand a year, or about $1 million for 40 years. In Florida, the average cost is $24 million for each execution. The death penalty in California costs taxpayers more than $250 million for each execution. In North Carolina an execution costs the state $2.16 million more than sentencing the person to life imprisonment (Death Penalty

Information Center 2009). The majority of those costs occur at the trial level, with extensive preparations to try to be sure the right person is being convicted. The cost doesn't stop when the trial is over; it increases because death row only has one person per cell, and the laws require individual recreation and meal times, which means more supervision for death row inmates. The cost of death row incarceration jumps from $2 million to $3 million for the years while appeals are under way. New Jersey banned the death penalty in 2007 to help with their budget, and New Mexico followed in 2009. Maryland, Montana, and Colorado are among those considering similar legislation because of the costs (Sunshine 2009).

The cost issue combined with the facts that the death penalty sometimes kills innocent people, that it is often racially discriminatory, and that it is not an effective deterrent have led to a search for alternative means to deter crime and has spurred policy analysts to rethink assumptions about what factors are effective in controlling human behavior.

Alternative Forms of Social Control

Based on the assumptions that most criminal behavior is learned through socialization, that criminals can be resocialized, and that tax dollars can be saved, several sociological theories of crime suggest methods of treatment other than incarceration without rehabilitation. The goal is to reduce both the number of individuals who go to prison and the number who are rearrested after being released—the recidivism rate. Improving the social capital of potential offenders is one approach based in theory.

Social capital refers to social networks within and among groups, access to important resources, and sharing the norms, values, and understandings that facilitate belonging to society (Flavin 2004). Social capital encompasses one's relationships, support systems, and access to community resources (Jarrett, Sullivan, and Watkins 2005). Increasing an individual's social capital by increasing educational attainment, job skills, and the ability to take advantage of available resources can reduce the chances of that person going to prison in the first place and of recidivism, or repeat offenses and incarceration (Faulkner 2006). The case study in "The Applied Sociologist at Work" that follows raises interesting questions about enhancing the social capital of potential deviants.

The tendency to think that the way to control human behavior is through more severe punishments is based on a rational choice theory. If the cost is high enough for committing deviant acts, so the idea goes, people will conform. Yet despite severe punishments, crime rates generally remain higher in the United States than in other countries. What works in one country cannot necessarily be imported directly into another country.

Deterrence is complex. It is influenced by dozens of variables, including the cultural values and meanings attached to specific behaviors. Not many people think that the apology technique used in Japan would work as a deterrent to crimes in many other countries. On the other hand, there is a wide range of options available for dealing with crime other than harsh (and expensive) punishments. Seeing how crime is controlled in other countries may challenge assumptions in one's own country, causing authorities to come up with creative new solutions that do work. For example, many criminologists argue that the United States should concentrate on the serious criminals and reduce the number of minor offenders in jails. They also suggest a number of alternatives to sending minor offenders to jail and prisons, such as community service, work release, and educational training programs.

Thinking Sociologically

Do you think changing the "cost-benefit" ratio so that the costs of crime to the criminal are higher will deter crime, or are other policies or methods more effective in enticing people to be responsible, contributing members of society?

Prison reforms, rehabilitation, training programs, shock probation, work release, halfway houses, and other alternative programs are intended to integrate the less serious offenders into the community in a productive way and help them regain social capital. If we can integrate the potential criminal into the community, reduce discrimination, and teach at-risk youth acceptable behavior patterns, we may reduce crime and gain productive citizens.

If ex-prisoners can turn to alternative behaviors other than crime, if they have educational or job skills, and if they have families to return to, they are less likely to commit further crimes. Therefore, some state penal systems provide education, from basic skills to college courses, and allow conjugal and family stays to help keep families together. More than one in three prisoners in state correctional facilities around the United States were enrolled in academic programs, from adult basic education to college; another third were involved in vocational training; 13% were engaged in counseling or therapy programs; and 8% received drug and alcohol counseling (U.S. Bureau of Justice Statistics 2003).

Other programs included shock probation (releasing first-time offenders early in the hope that the shock of prison life would deter them), community service to help develop citizenship and pay restitution for the offense, and day treatment and halfway houses to help inmates readjust to community life and find jobs. The programs can relieve

The Applied Sociologist at Work— James Faulkner
Reducing Recidivism by Increasing Social Capital

By James Faulkner

James Faulkner is a police department detective. Part of his work is with adults and juveniles, trying to increase their chances of leading productive lives and staying out of prison by increasing their social capital. The following is a case study by Detective Faulkner, at the time a school resource officer, describing his work with one young man.

Ray was a 20-year-old male, African American college student who started life with absolutely no social capital and continues to struggle to increase his chances for success. He was the type of offender who continually violated the law. Ray's father left when he was seven years old, and his mother died when he was eight. The father's whereabouts were no longer known. With no information and no parents, this was a prime example of someone with limited resources.

As a school resource officer, I was approached by a school official who was concerned for Ray's long-term future, due to the complexities of his life. As a member of law enforcement and through my personal experiences and observations, I knew Ray was stealing frequently to eat and live. Ray was living with a disabled aunt in deplorable conditions with no food in the house. When I picked him up to help him move in with yet another relative, there was no electricity, water, or phone.

We used my phone as a light as we gathered his items, and I helped him pack what few clothes he had. I began taking Ray food with the assistance of others, a concept not known to Ray.

With his high school graduation approaching, Ray asked me to help him find a job. A simple endeavor proved to be very difficult. It began with a potential employer's request for his social security card. Not only did Ray not have one, but he had no idea how to get one. Initially thinking that this would be relatively simple to solve, I asked him to bring his birth certificate, and we would go apply for his social security card. It was then that he asked me how one goes about "getting one of those birth certificate things."

After graduation and the following summer, and with the aid of the assistant school superintendent, who took Ray under her wing, we set out to increase Ray's level of social capital. I felt motivated to help Ray because he had been so motivated to try to help himself, yet he had met failure after failure. He continually fell, got back up, and tried something else. This encouraged me to invest in Ray. Small increases in his level of social capital and resources helped Ray establish a network of support for a more successful future. It is my belief that these small increases in Ray's resources will have significant impact on his future lifestyle and reduce his chances for a life of crime. Among other things, we taught him how to apply for loans to get financial help.

With the help of government loans and grants, Ray was admitted and entered college that fall. We helped supply him with housing, toiletries, and clothing. We did our best not to do these things for him but rather show him how to do them himself. There was no family or celebration after his high school graduation, so some school officials and I took Ray to a local steakhouse to celebrate his graduation and entering college, a step he had once perceived as unobtainable. By investing a small amount of social capital in the form of relationships and resources, we were able to steer Ray in the direction of accumulating additional social capital in the form of education.

This could be his ticket out of his previous way of life.

Note: James Faulkner has a master's degree in Applied Social Science/Criminal Justice.

overcrowded prisons and save money by reducing the cost of incarceration. There is some evidence that they reduce recidivism as well.

Work release programs build social capital by placing primarily nonviolent offenders in positions to earn wages and help support their families rather than accumulate debt while in prison. They also provide work experience and keep offenders away from hardened criminals in prison, thus helping reintegrate the offender into the community. A key to the success of such programs is adequate supervision. Transmitters are often used to track offenders and protect concerned community members (The Urban Institute 2004).

Restitution puts the offender in the position of "making it right" with the victim. The offender renders money or service to the victim or community under supervised parole to compensate the victim. This is a positive way of teaching juvenile offenders lessons in responsibility without imprisoning and exposing them to more criminal behavior. Restitution is less costly than long incarceration, and victims are often satisfied with this type of program. The likelihood of repeated offense at a later time is also lower in restitution programs than for those who are sent to prison.

Journal Article Link 6.3
Read about prisoner citizenship.

Another current trend is toward privatization of prisons in an attempt to run them in a more businesslike, cost-effective way. This trend is unlikely to improve the rehabilitation aspects in this age of overcrowded prisons and cost cutting, but several states are experimenting with private facilities, and some federal agencies, such as the Immigration and Naturalization Service, have contracted with private operators to run facilities. Because sociologists and criminologists study prison programs, make recommendations to improve the correction programs, and help find solutions to deviance, they are highly skeptical of privatization. There are many problems in having any public service administered by people whose primary and

perhaps only goal is to make a profit. The current trend seems to be to "warehouse prisoners," with little effort to rehabilitate them or help them reenter society as productive citizens (Irwin 2005).

Thinking Sociologically

Considering what you have read, how has this affected some of your ideas about deviance, crime, and the criminal justice system?

At the beginning of the chapter, we said that some of the material presented in this chapter might surprise you, some commonly held assumptions about deviance might be challenged, and a different way of looking at deviance might emerge. Lack of respect for law and for social conventions is often tied to severe social inequality.

Those without resources have fewer reasons to be committed to the existing system of rules and regulations, and they are more likely to become desperate for resources that they cannot access "by the rules." The next section deals with inequality, and the next chapter focuses on socioeconomic differences.

What Have We Learned?

Perhaps the answers to some of the chapter's opening questions—What is deviance? Why do people become deviant? and What should we do about deviance?—have now taken on new dimensions. Deviance as defined by society, communities, and even religion or subcultural groups has many possible explanations, and there are multiple interpretations about how it should be handled. Deviance and crime are issues for any society, for unless most of the people obey the rules most of the time, there can be real threats to stability, safety, and a sense of fairness, undermining the social structure. The criminal justice system tends to be a conservative force in society because of its focus on ensuring social conformity.

To make the society run more smoothly, we must understand why deviance and crime happen. Good policy must be based on accurate information and careful analysis of the information. We must also understand that deviance and conformity operate at various levels in the social world: micro, meso, and macro. In addition, it is important to understand that there may be positive aspects of deviance for any society, from uniting society against deviants to providing creative new ways to solve problems.

One of the dominant characteristics of modern society is social inequality, and as we have seen, inequality is often an issue in criminal activity. Indeed, many of our social problems are rooted in issues of inequality. Extreme inequality may even be a threat to the deeper values and dreams of a society, especially one that stresses individualism and achievement. In the following three chapters, we look at three types of inequality: socioeconomic, ethnic or racial, and gender-based inequity.

Key Points

- Deviance—the violation of social norms, including those that are formal laws—is a complex behavior that has both positive and negative consequences for individuals and for society. (See pp. 166–169.)

- Deviance is often misunderstood because of simplistic and popular misconceptions. (See pp. 169–170.)

- Many theories try to explain deviance—rational choice, differential association, and labeling theories at the micro level, along with structural explanations, including anomie and disorganization, strain theory, conflict theory, and feminist theory. (See pp. 172–183.)

- Many of the formal organizations concerned with crime (such as the FBI and the media) focus on crimes involving individuals—predatory crimes, crimes without victims, and hate crimes—but the focus on these crimes may blind us to crimes that actually are more harmful and more costly. (See pp. 183–185.)

- At the meso level, organized and occupational crimes may cost billions of dollars and pose a great risk to thousands of lives. Occupational crime may be against the company, employees, customers, or the public. (See pp. 186–189.)

- At the macro level, national governments sometimes commit state-organized crimes, sometimes in violation of their own laws or in violation of international laws. These crimes may be directed against their own citizens (usually the minorities) or people from other countries. (See pp. 189–191.)

- Also at the macro level, some crimes are facilitated by global networks and by global inequities of power and wealth. (See pp. 191–193.)

- Controlling crime has generated many policy debates, from the use of prisons to the death penalty and even to alternative approaches to the control of deviance. (See pp. 194–200.)

Contributing to Our Social World: What Can We Do?

At the Local Level

- *LGBT groups:* College campuses throughout the country have support groups for students who are lesbian, gay, bisexual, and/or transgender (often abbreviated as "LGBT"). The Consortium of Higher Education LGBT Resource Professionals, a national organization of such campus groups, maintains a Web site at www.lgbtcampus .org. Regardless of your identity/orientation, consider contacting your campus LGBT group, attending meetings, and participating in its support and public education activities.

- *Boys and Girls Clubs:* Organizations for youth need interns and volunteers to provide role models for youth. Consider volunteering to help children with homework or activities.

At the Organizational or Institutional Level

- *The U.S. criminal justice system:* This extensive and rapidly growing institution focuses on crime prevention, law enforcement, corrections, and rehabilitation. Identify the aspect of the system that interests you most and, using faculty and community contacts, select an appropriate organization for volunteer work or an internship.

- *The criminal courts:* These are central actors in the administration of criminal justice, and trials are often open to the public. Attending a trial and/or contacting a judge or magistrate could provide a good introduction to a longer-term relationship.

- *DARE:* Volunteer in a prevention program, such as DARE. These are administered by local law enforcement agencies and might provide opportunities for volunteer work and for observing how the system works "from the inside."

- *Juvenile corrections and rehabilitation:* These organizations include halfway houses for teens in trouble or afterschool or weekend programs. These groups provide work one-on-one with juveniles to provide positive role models and increase their social capital.

- *Battered-women's shelters:* Many community programs provide safe houses, counseling, and practical help for women and children in abusive situations.

- *The Date Rape Project:* It provides information and research on date rape on college campuses and in other locations.

At the National and Global Levels

- One of the most serious forms of global organized crime is trafficking in human beings. This often involves kidnapping, slavery, sexual exploitation of children and adults, and even torture and murder.

- *Human Trafficking:* This international organization is engaged in research and action programs intended to end such crimes. Its Web site, at www.humantrafficking .org, discusses several programs in which you can participate, including a special section on activities at academic institutions.

- *The Polaris Project:* This organization works to reduce global trafficking in women and children (www.polaris project.org). Volunteers participate in letter-writing campaigns, support antitrafficking legislation, and conduct research on the problem.

 For chapter-specific resources, including **Frontline**, **TED**, and **YouTube** videos; self-quizzes; web exercises; and more, visit **www.pineforge.com/oswmedia3e.**

PART III

Inequality

Why do some people rise to the top of society with wealth, power, and prestige at their fingertips, and others languish near the bottom? Why are some individuals and countries rich and others poor? These are the underlying questions in the next three chapters that focus on inequality, the process of stratification through which some people "make it" and others do not. At the very bottom of the human hierarchy are those starving and diseased world citizens who have no hope of survival for either themselves or their families. This compares with bankers, corporate executives, and some world politicians or royalty who have billions of dollars at their disposal.

Social inequality is one of the most important processes in modern societies, and the implications extend all the way to global social networks. Sometimes, the inequality is based on socioeconomic status, but the basis of differential treatment is often other characteristics: race, ethnicity, gender, sexual orientation, religion, or age. These differences often result in strong "we" versus "they" thinking. One factor runs throughout these patterns of inequality: They have implications for social interaction at the micro, meso, and macro levels of analysis. In this section, we do not try to cover all forms of inequality; rather, we illustrate the patterns by exploring issues of social class, race or ethnicity, and gender.

CHAPTER 7

Stratification

Rich and Famous— or Rags and Famine?

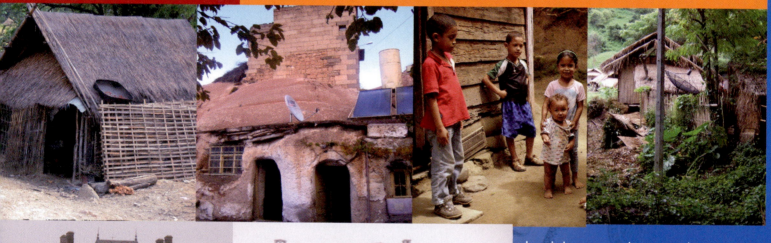

In rich countries, such as the United States, Canada, Japan, and Western European nations, we assume that there are many economic opportunities, and we like to believe that anyone can become rich and famous. The reality, however, is that our social world is very brutal for many people, and what they experience is rags and famine.

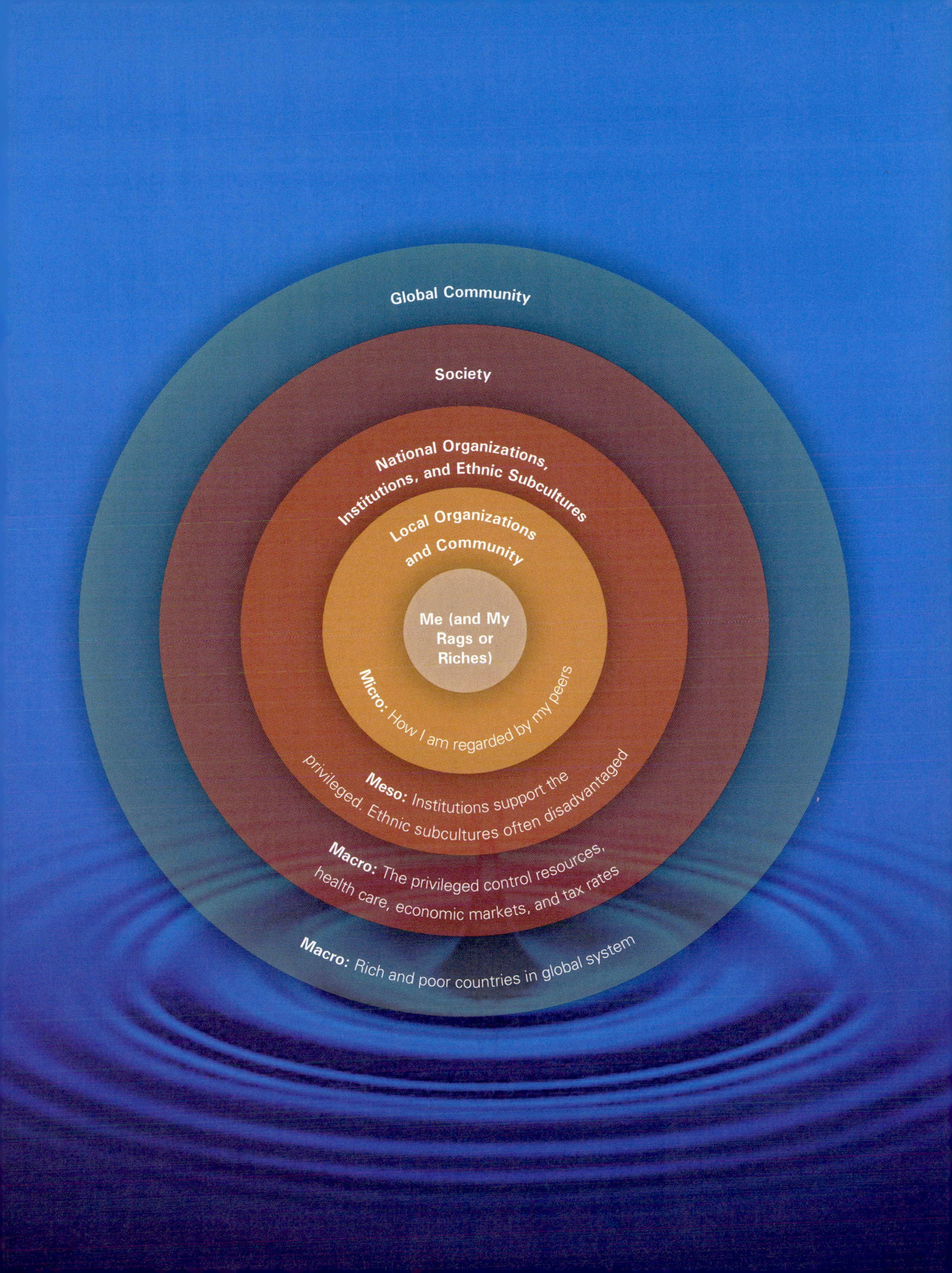

Global Community

Society

National Organizations,
Institutions, and Ethnic Subcultures

Local Organizations
and Community

Me (and My
Rags or
Riches)

Micro: How I am regarded by my peers

Meso: Institutions support the
privileged. Ethnic subcultures often disadvantaged

Macro: The privileged control resources,
health care, economic markets, and tax rates

Macro: Rich and poor countries in global system

Think About It	
Me (and My Inner Circle)	Why do you buy what you buy, believe what you believe, and live where you live?
Local Community	Why are some people in your community rich and others poor?
National Institutions; Complex Organizations; Ethnic Groups	How do institutions—such as education, the family, religion, and the economy—help to keep people in the class they were born into?
National Society	Why are some nations affluent and others impoverished?
Global Community	How does the fact that we live in a global environment affect you and your social position?

Prince Harry of England, second in line to the British throne, was in Afghanistan in 2008 fighting along with the regular grunts, hoping not to be discovered, but when his cover was blown he was pulled out immediately. Because of his royal status, British leaders thought he would be a target for the enemy and a danger to those around him.

Not just anyone can belong to a royal family. One must be born as royalty or marry into it. Members of royal families—such as Prince William and Prince Harry of Britain—grow up in a world of the privileged: wealth, prestige, all doors open to them, or so it appears. Their lifestyles include formal receptions, horse races, polo games, royal hunts, state visits, and other social and state functions. The family has several elegant residences at its disposal. However, like most royalty, William and Harry also live within the confines of their elite status, with its strict expectations and limitations. They cannot show up for a beer at the local pub or associate freely with commoners, and their problems or casual antics are subject matter for front pages of tabloids. In today's world, some royalty are figureheads with little political power; others—such as the Ashanti chiefs in West Africa, King Bhumibol Adulyadej of Thailand, King Sihanok of Cambodia, and Emperor Akihito in Japan—have great influence in state affairs.

In Newport, Rhode Island, spacious mansions are nestled along the coast, with tall-masted sailboats at the docks. These are the summer homes of the U.S. aristocracy. They do not hold royal titles, but their positions allow for a life of comfort similar to that of royalty. Members of this class have an elegant social life, engage in elite sports such as fencing and polo, patronize the arts, and are influential behind the scenes in business and politics.

Hidden from the public eye in each country are people with no known names and no swank addresses; some

Newport, Rhode Island, has long been one of the most affluent cities in North America, a community where mansions and yachts line the sea coast. The vessel in the photo at the right is the largest privately owned yacht in the world, docked in Newport in the summer of 2009.

have no address at all. We catch glimpses of their plight through vivid media portrayals of refugees in Darfur, Sudan, impoverished victims of natural disasters such as Hurricane Katrina in 2005 along the Gulf of Mexico coast, and famines in many countries. They are the poor; many of them live in squalor. Economic hard times have pushed some of them from their rural homes to cities in hopes of finding jobs. However, with few jobs for unskilled and semiskilled workers in today's postindustrial service economies, many of the poor are left behind and homeless. They live in abandoned buildings or sleep in unlocked autos, on park benches, under bridges, on beaches, or anywhere they can stretch out and hope not to be attacked or harassed. Beggars stake out spots on sidewalks, hoping citizens and tourists will give them a handout. In the United States, cities such as Houston, Texas; Los Angeles, California; Washington, D.C.; and New York City try to cope with the homeless by setting up sanitary facilities and temporary shelters, especially in bad weather; cities rely on religious and civic organizations such as churches and the Salvation Army to run soup kitchens.

In some areas of the world, such as sub-Saharan Africa and parts of India, the situation is much more desperate, and many families are starving. At daybreak, a cattle cart traverses the city of Kolkata (Calcutta), India, picking up bodies of diseased and starved homeless people who have died on the streets during the night. Mother Teresa, who won the Nobel Peace Prize for her work with those in dire poverty, established a home in India where these people could die with dignity. She also founded an orphanage for children who would otherwise wander the streets begging or lie on the sidewalk dying. Survival, just maintaining life, is a daily struggle for the 40% of the world's population that lives on 5% of the global income. Of the 2.2 billion children in the world, 1 billion live in poverty. Nearly 400 million children have no access to safe water (1 in 5 in the world), and 1.4 million children die each year due to lack of safe drinking water and adequate sanitation; 270 million children have no access to health services (1 in 7), and 2.2 million die because they are not immunized. Just today, as you are reading these facts, more than 25,000 children died (United Nations Development Programme 2007). These humans are at the bottom of the stratification hierarchy.

This raises the following question: Why do some people live like royalty and others live in desperate poverty? Most of us live between these extremes. We study and work hard for what we have, but we also live comfortably, knowing that starvation is not pounding at our door. This chapter discusses (a) why stratification is important, (b) why people are rich or poor (stratification systems), (c) the importance and consequences of social rankings for individuals, (d) whether one can change social class positions (social mobility), (e) characteristics of major stratification systems, (f) poverty and social policies to address problems, and (g) the global digital divide (patterns of stability and change).

Poor people around the world find shelter wherever they can. A woman and her children displaced by war sit beneath a temporary shelter at a refugee camp in South Darfur. Even in affluent North America, some people are homeless and spend nights on sidewalks, in parks, or in homeless shelters.

The Importance of Social Stratification

Social stratification refers to how individuals and groups are layered or ranked in society according to how many valued resources they possess. Stratification is an ongoing process of sorting people into different levels of access to resources, with the sorting legitimated by cultural beliefs

Journal Article Link 7.1
Read more about inequality.

about why the inequality is justifiable. This chapter focuses on socioeconomic stratification, and subsequent chapters examine ethnic and gender stratification.

Three main assumptions underlie the concept of stratification: (1) people are divided into ranked categories; (2) there is an unequal distribution of desired resources, meaning that some members of society possess more of what is valued and others possess less; and (3) each society determines what it considers to be valued resources. In an agricultural society, members are ranked according to how much land or how many animals they own. In an industrial society, occupational position and income are two of the criteria for ranking. Most Japanese associate old age with high rank, whereas Americans admire and offer high status to some people for their youthful vigor and beauty.

What members of each society value and the criteria they use to rank other members depend on events in the society's history, its geographic location, its level of development in the world, the society's political philosophy, and the decisions of those in power. Powerful individuals are more likely to get the best positions, most desirable mates, and the greatest opportunities. They may have power because of birth status, personality characteristics, age, physical attractiveness, education, intelligence, wealth, race, family background, occupation, religion, or ethnic group—whatever the basis for power is in that particular society. Those with power have advantages that perpetuate their power, and they try to hold onto those advantages through laws, customs, power, or ideologies.

Handbook Link 7.1
Read more about social stratification.

Look at all those forks and knives. Some people know what to do with each of them! Knowing which fork or knife to use for each course of a meal could influence someone's chances of success on a job interview for certain kinds of jobs.

Consider your own social ranking. You were born into a family that holds a position in society—upper, middle, or lower class, for instance. The position of your family influences the neighborhood in which you live and where you shop, go to school, and attend religious services. Most likely, you and your family carry out the tasks of daily living in your community with others of similar position. Your position in the stratification system affects the opportunities available to you and the choices you make in life. The social world model at the beginning of the chapter provides a visual image of the social world and socioeconomic stratification. The stratification process affects everything from individuals' social rankings at the micro level of analysis to positions of countries in the global system at the macro level.

Micro-Level Prestige and Influence

Remember how some of your peers on the playground were given more respect than others? Their high regard may have come from belonging to a prestigious family, having a dynamic or domineering personality, or owning symbols that distinguished them—"cool" clothing, a desirable bicycle, expensive toys, or a fancy car. This is stratification at its beginning stage.

Property, power, and prestige are accorded to those individuals who have *cultural capital* (knowledge and access to important information in the society) and *social capital* (networks with others who have influence). Individual qualities such as leadership, personality, sense of humor, self-confidence, quick-wittedness, physical attractiveness, or ascribed characteristics—such as the most powerful gender or ethnic group—influence cultural and social capital.

Meso-Level Access to Resources

Our individual status is shaped by our access to resources and learned and reinforced in the family through the socialization process. We learn grammar and manners that affect our success in school, for example. Educational organizations treat children differently according to their social status, and our religious affiliation is likely to reflect our social status. Political systems, including laws, courts, and police, reinforce the stratification system. Access to health care often depends on one's position in the stratification system. Our position and connections in organizations have a profound impact on how we experience life and how we interact with other individuals and groups.

Macro-Level Factors Influencing Stratification

The economic system, which includes the occupational structure, level of technology, and distribution of wealth in a

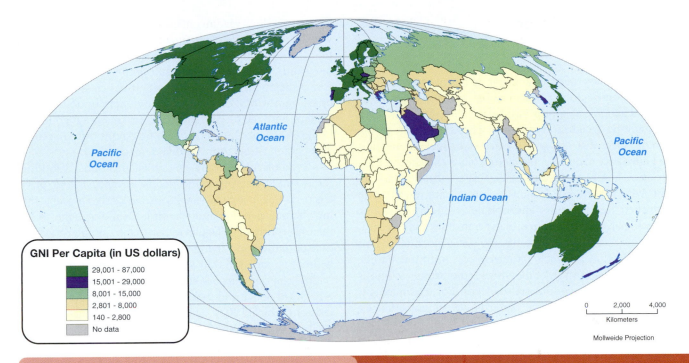

GNI Per Capita (in US dollars)
- 29,001 - 87,000
- 15,001 - 29,000
- 8,001 - 15,000
- 2,801 - 8,000
- 140 - 2,800
- No data

Mollweide Projection

Map 7.1 Gross National Income per Capita in 2006

Source: World Bank. Map by Anna Versluis.

society, is often the basis for stratification (see Map 7.1). Haiti, located on the island of Hispanola, is the poorest country in the Western Hemisphere and one of the poorest countries in the world, with little technology, few resources, and an occupational structure based largely on subsistence farming. Even its forest resources are almost gone as desperately poor people cut down the last trees for firewood and shelters, leaving the land to erode (Diamond 2005). The economy is collapsing, leaving many already poor people still more destitute and on the lowest rungs of the world's stratification system. The economic position and geographic location of nations such as Haiti affect the opportunities available to individuals in those societies. There are simply no opportunities for Haitians to get ahead. Thus, macro-level factors can shape the opportunity structure and distribution of resources available to individuals.

One problem for Haiti is that it has few of the resources that many other countries in the global system take for granted—a strong educational system, well-paying jobs in a vibrant economy, productive land, an ample supply of water, money to pay workers, and access to the most efficient and powerful technology. Almost all societies stratify members, and societies themselves are stratified in the world system, so that each individual and nation experiences the world in unique ways. Stratification is one of the most powerful forces that we experience, but we are seldom conscious of how it works or how pervasive it is in our lives. This is the driving question sociologists ask when developing theories of stratification: How does it work?

Thinking Sociologically

Place yourself in the center of the social world model. Working outward from micro-level interactions toward the macro-level institutions, indicate what has influenced where you fall in the stratification system.

Theoretical Explanations of Stratification

Why do some people have more money, possessions, power, and prestige than others? We all have opinions about this question. Sociologists also have developed explanations—theories that help explain stratification. Recall that theories provide a framework for asking questions to be studied. Just as your interpretation of a question may differ from your friends' ideas, sociologists have developed different explanations for stratification and tested these with research data. These explanations of social rankings range from individual micro-level to national and global macro-level theories.

Micro-Level Theory

Symbolic Interaction

Most of us have been at a social gathering, perhaps at a swank country club or in a local bar, where we felt out of place. Each social group has norms that members learn through the socialization process. These norms are recognized within that group and can make clueless outsiders feel like space aliens. People learn what is expected in their groups—family, peer group, social class—through interaction with others. For instance, children are rewarded or punished for behaviors appropriate or inappropriate to their social position. This process transmits and perpetuates social rankings. Learning our social position means learning values, speech patterns, consumption habits, appropriate group memberships (including religious affiliation), and even our self-concept. For example, students bring their language patterns, values, experiences, and knowledge they have learned at home with them to school. These attributes are referred to as their *cultural capital*. Schools place children into courses and academic groups based in part on the labels they receive due to their cultural capital. Home environments can help children by expanding vocabularies; developing good grammar; experiencing concerts, art, and theater; visiting historical

In India, many people must bathe every day in public in whatever water supply they can find. Even many people with homes would not have their own water supply. Privacy for one's grooming is a symbol of privilege for the affluent.

sites; providing reading materials; and modeling adults who like to read. The parents of higher-class families tend to stress thinking skills as opposed to simply learning to obey authority figures. The result of this learning at home is that members of the middle and upper classes or higher castes get the best education, setting them up to be future leaders with better life chances. In this way, children's home experiences and education help reproduce the social class systems (Ballantine and Hammack 2009).

Symbols often represent social positions. Clothing, for example, sets up some people as special and privileged. Young people wear expensive designer jeans that low-income people cannot afford. Drinking wine rather than beer, driving a Jaguar rather than a simpler mode of transportation, and living in a home that has six or eight bedrooms and is 5,000 square feet is an expression of *conspicuous consumption*—displaying goods in a way that others will notice and that will presumably earn the owner respect (Veblen 1902). Thus, purchased products become symbols that are intended to define the person as someone of high status.

In most of the Global North, one symbol of middle-class "decency" is the right to bathe and do one's grooming in privacy. Indeed, most young people in the United States expect to have their own bedrooms and expect no interruptions when sprucing up for the day. Homeless people in the United States do not have this luxury, and in India, bathing on the streets is not uncommon. So even privacy is a symbol of affluence.

Interaction theories help us understand how individuals learn and live their positions in society. Next, we consider theories that examine the larger social structures, processes, and forces that affect stratification and inequality: structural-functional and various forms of conflict theory.

Meso- and Macro-Level Theories

Structural-Functional Theory

Structural-functionalists (sometimes simply called functionalists) view stratification within societies as an inevitable—and generally necessary—part of the social world. The stratification system provides each individual a place or position in the social world and motivates individuals to carry out their roles. Societies survive by having an organized system into which each individual is born, where each is raised, and where each contributes some part to the maintenance of the society.

The basic elements of the structural-functional theory of stratification were explained by Kingsley Davis and Wilbert Moore (1945), and their work still provides the main ideas of the theory today. Focusing on stratification by considering different occupations and how they are rewarded, Davis and Moore argue the following:

1. Positions in society are neither equally valued nor equally pleasant to perform. Some positions—such as physicians—are more highly valued because people feel they are very important to society. Therefore, societies must motivate talented individuals to prepare for and occupy the most important and difficult positions, such as being physicians.

2. Preparation requires talent, time, and money. To motivate talented individuals to make the sacrifices necessary to prepare for and assume difficult positions such as becoming a physician, differential rewards of income, prestige, power, or other valued goods must be offered. Thus, a doctor receives high income, prestige, and power as incentives.

3. The differences in rewards such as pay in turn lead to the unequal distribution of resources for occupations in society. Therefore, stratification is inevitable. The unequal distribution of status and wealth in society provides societies with individuals to fill necessary positions—such as willingness to undertake the stress of being chief executive officer of a corporation in a highly competitive field.

In the mid-20th century, functional theory provided sociologists with a valuable framework for studying stratification (Tumin 1953), but things do change. In the 21st century, new criteria such as controlling information and access to information systems have become important for determining wealth and status, making scientists and technicians a new class of elites. The society also experiences conflict over distribution of resources that functionalism does not fully explain.

Conflict Theory

Conflict theorists see stratification as the outcome of struggles for dominance and scarce resources, with some individuals in society taking advantage of others. Individuals and groups act in their own self-interest by trying to exploit others, leading inevitably to a struggle between those who have advantages and want to keep them and those who want a larger share of the pie.

Conflict theory developed in a time of massive economic transformation. With the end of the feudal system, economic displacement of peasants, and the rise of urban factories as major employers, a tremendous gap between the rich and the poor evolved. This prompted theorists to ask several basic questions related to stratification: (a) How do societies produce necessities—food, clothing, and shelter? (b) How are relationships between rich and poor people shaped by this process? and (c) How do many people become alienated in their routine, dull jobs in which they have little involvement and no investment in the end product?

Karl Marx (1818–1883), considered the father of conflict theory, lived during this time of industrial transformation. Marx described four possible ways to distribute wealth, according to (1) what each person needs, (2) what each person wants, (3) what each person earns, or (4) what each person can take. It was this fourth way, Marx believed, that was dominant in competitive capitalist societies (Cuzzort and King 2002; Marx and Engels 1955).

Marx viewed the stratification structure as composed of two major economically based social classes: the haves and the have-nots. The haves consisted of the capitalist bourgeoisie, whereas the have-nots were made up of the working-class proletariat. Individuals in the same social class had similar lifestyles, shared ideologies, and held common outlooks on social life. The struggle over resources between haves and have-nots was the cause of conflict (Hurst 2006).

The haves control what Marx called the means of production—money, materials, and factories (Marx [1844] 1964). The haves dominate because the lower-class have-nots cannot earn enough money and power to change their positions. The norms and values of the haves dominate the society because of their power and make the distribution of resources seem "fair" and justified. Social control mechanisms, including laws, religious beliefs, educational systems, political structures and policies, and police or military force, ensure continued control by the haves.

The unorganized lower classes can be exploited as long as they do not develop a *class consciousness*—a shared awareness of their poor status in relation to the means of production (control of the production process). Marx contended that, with the help of intellectuals who believed in the injustice of the exploited poor, the working class would develop a class consciousness, rise up, and overthrow the haves, culminating in a classless society in which wealth would be shared (Marx and Engels 1955).

> **Video Link 7.1**
> See the lifestyle of the very rich.

Unlike the structural-functionalists, then, conflict theorists maintain that money and other rewards are not necessarily given to those in the most important positions in the society. Can we argue that a rock star or baseball player is more necessary for the survival of society than a teacher or police officer? Yet the pay differential is tremendous. This pay differential brings into question the idea of enticing people to make sacrifices to perform the "most important" tasks in the society. In addition, high-prestige positions often go to sons and daughters of elites.

Not all the predictions of Karl Marx have come true. No truly classless societies have developed, but some developments have moved in that direction. Labor unions arose to unite and represent the working class and put them in a more powerful position vis-à-vis the capitalists, managerial and technical positions emerged to create a large middle class, some companies moved to employee ownership, and workers gained legal protection from government legislative bodies in most industrial countries (Dahrendorf 1959).

Taylor Swift (top) was the 2009 Entertainer of the Year, and although she just turned 20 and has little education, she is paid millions of dollars each year to entertain the public. Meanwhile the public school teacher (bottom) would take 30 years of teaching hundreds of children to read before her total cumulative income for her entire career would add up to 1 million dollars.

Even societies that claim to be classless, such as China, have privileged classes and poor peasants. In recent years, the Chinese government has allowed more private ownership of shops, businesses, and other entrepreneurial efforts, motivating many Chinese citizens to work long hours at their private businesses to "get ahead." The only classless societies are a few small hunter-gatherer groups that lack extra resources, which would allow some members to accumulate wealth.

Some theorists criticize Marx for his focus on only the economic system, pointing out that noneconomic factors enter into the stratification struggle as well. Max Weber (1864–1920), an influential theorist, amended Marx's theory by considering other elements in addition to economic forces. He agreed with Marx that group conflict is inevitable, that economics is one of the key factors in stratification systems, and that those in power try to perpetuate their positions. However, he added two other influential factors that he argued determine stratification in modern industrial societies: power and prestige, discussed later in this chapter. Consider these "three Ps": property, power, and prestige.

Recent theorists suggest that using three Ps, we can identify five classes—capitalists, managers, the petty bourgeoisie, workers, and the underclass—rather than just haves and have-nots. *Capitalists* own the means of production, and they purchase and control the labor of others. *Managers* sell their labor to capitalists and manage the labor of others for the capitalists. The *petty bourgeoisie*, such as small shop or business owners, own some means of production but control little of the labor of others; nevertheless, they have modest prestige, power, and property (Sernau 2005). *Workers* sell their labor to capitalists and are low in all three Ps. Finally, the *underclass* has virtually no property, power, or prestige.

In the modern world, as businesses become international and managerial occupations continue to grow, conflict theorists argue that workers are still exploited but in different ways. Owners get more income than is warranted by their responsibilities—for example, the CEO of Oracle received pay and stock options worth $182 million in 2007. Executives at the 500 biggest companies in the United States received a collective 38% pay raise in 2006, cut by 15% in 2007. Nonetheless, they earned a collective $6.4 billion in 2007, an average of $12.8 million each (DeCarlo 2008). The Obama administration's new pay czar is publishing names and salaries of the 25 most highly paid employees in a number of companies, including many of those that received help from the bailout—Citigroup, Bank of America, American International Group (AIG), Graduate Management Admission Council (GMAC), and others ("Pay Czar . . ." 2009).

Many people argue that better educated and skilled people get more income than is warranted by the differential in education (Wright 2000). Moreover, the labor that produces our clothes, cell phones, digital cameras, televisions, and other products is increasingly provided by impoverished people around the world working for low wages at multinational corporations (Bonacich and Wilson 2005). In rich countries, service providers receive low wages at fast-food chains and box stores such as Wal-Mart (Ehrenreich 2001, 2005). One controversial question is whether multinational corporations are bringing opportunity to poor countries or exploiting them, as many conflict theorists contend (Wallerstein 2004).

Thinking Sociologically

Is it possible for a society to be truly "classless" with shared wealth? Why or why not? What evidence might support your position?

The Evolutionary Theory of Stratification: A Synthesis

Evolutionary theory (Lenski 1966; Nolan and Lenski 2008) borrows assumptions from both structural-functional and conflict theories in an attempt to determine how scarce resources are distributed and how that distribution results in stratification. The basic ideas are as follows: (a) to survive, people must cooperate; (b) despite this, conflicts of interest occur over important decisions that benefit one individual or group over another; (c) valued items such as money and status are always in demand and in short supply; (d) there is likely to be a struggle over these scarce goods; and (e) customs or traditions in a society often prevail over rational criteria in determining distribution of scarce resources. After the minimum survival needs of both individuals and the society are met, power determines who gets the surplus: prestige, luxury living, the best health care, and so forth. Lenski believes that privileges (including wealth) flow from having power, and prestige usually results from having access to both power and privilege (Hurst 2006).

Lenski (1966; Nolan and Lenski 2008) tested his theory by studying societies at different levels of technological development, ranging from simple to complex. He found that the degree of inequality increases with technology until it reaches the advanced industrial stage. For instance, in subsistence-level hunting and gathering societies, little surplus is available, and everyone's needs are met to the extent possible. As surplus accumulates in agrarian societies, those who acquire power also control surpluses, and they use this to benefit their friends and relations. However, even if laws are made by those in power, the powerful must share some of the wealth or fear being overthrown. Interestingly, when societies finally reach the advanced industrial stage, inequality is moderated. This happens because people in various social classes enjoy greater political participation

and because more resources are available to be shared in the society.

Lenski's (1966; Nolan and Lenski 2008) theory explains many different types of societies by synthesizing elements of both structural-functional and conflict theory. For instance, evolutionary theory takes into consideration the structural-functional idea that talented individuals need to be motivated to make sacrifices by allowing private ownership to motivate them. Individuals will attempt to control as much wealth, power, and prestige as possible, according to this view, resulting in potential conflict as some accumulate more wealth than others (Nolan and Lenski 2008). The theory also recognizes exploitation leading to inequality, a factor that conflict theorists find in capitalist systems of stratification. The reality is that while some inequality may be useful in highly complex societies, extraordinary amounts of differential access to resources may even undermine productivity by making upward mobility so impossible that the most talented people are not always those in the most demanding and responsible jobs.

The amount of inequality differs in societies, according to evolutionary theorists, because of different levels of technological development. Because industrialization brings surplus wealth, a division of labor, advanced technology, and interdependence among members of a society, no one individual can control all the important knowledge, skills, or capital resources. Therefore, this eliminates the two extremes of haves and have-nots because resources are more evenly distributed.

The symbolic interaction, structural-functional, conflict, and evolutionary theories provide different explanations for understanding stratification in modern societies. These theories are the basis for micro- to macro-level discussions of stratification. Our next step is to look at some factors that influence an individual's position in a stratification system and the ability to change that position.

Thinking Sociologically

According to the theories discussed above, what are some reasons for your position in the stratification system?

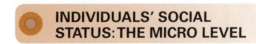

INDIVIDUALS' SOCIAL STATUS: THE MICRO LEVEL

You are among the world's elite. Few people have the opportunity to earn a college degree. However, that number is expanding rapidly as countries such as China provide higher education opportunities to more students to support their growing economies. In 2006, 23 million Chinese students were enrolled, surpassing the U.S. enrollment, with an enrollment rate of 21% of the Chinese population (Jing 2007). Although China has more than 4,000 colleges and universities, only 15% of the nation's college-age population's needs are being met (Porter 2005). However, many Chinese are studying abroad, adding to their opportunities and enhancing China's knowledge of the world. In 2010, the worldwide enrollment in higher education is likely to be 120 million, up from 100 million a few years ago (Daniel, Kanwar, and Uvalic-Trumbic 2006).

Yet being able to afford the time and money for college is a luxury with little relevance to those struggling to survive each day. It is beyond the financial or personal resources of 99% of people in the world. Considered in this global perspective, college students learn professional skills and have advantages that billions of other world citizens will never know or even imagine. Does that give you a new respect for the opportunities you have?

In the United States, access to higher education is greater than in many other countries because there are more levels of entry—technical and community colleges, large state universities, and private 4-year colleges, to name a few. However, with limited government help, most students must have financial resources to help pay tuition and the cost of living. Many students do not realize that the prestige of the college they choose makes a difference in their future opportunities. Those students born into wealth can afford better preparation for entrance exams as well as tutors or courses to increase SAT (Scholastic Aptitude and Reasoning Test) scores. They often attend private prep schools and gain acceptance to prestigious colleges that open opportunities

For some people living in poverty, the standard of wealth is ownership of a single horse. The boys below travel to their village in Afghanistan, where they must work every day rather than going to school.

not available to those attending the typical state university or nonelite colleges (Persell 2005).

Ascribed characteristics, such as gender, can also affect one's chances for success in life. Imbedded gender stratification systems may make it difficult for women to rise in the occupational hierarchy. Many Japanese women earn college degrees but leave employment after getting married and having children (Japan Institute of Labor 2002). Of 2,396 companies surveyed, the number with women directors was just 72 (less than 3%). Furthermore, Japanese women hold only 2% of all corporate board seats, and few are on boards of directors (Globe Women's Business Network 2006). Issues of gender stratification will be examined in more depth in Chapter 9, but they intersect with socioeconomic class and must be viewed as part of a larger pattern of inequality in the social world.

Individual Life Chances

Life chances refer to your opportunities, depending on your achieved and ascribed status in society. That you are in college, probably have health insurance and access to health care, and are likely to live into your late 70s or 80s are factors directly related to your life chances. Let us consider several examples of how placement in organizations at the meso level affects individual experiences and has global ramifications.

Education

Although education is valued by most individuals, the cost of books, clothing, shoes, transportation, child care, and time taken from income-producing work may be insurmountable barriers to attendance from grade school through college. Economically disadvantaged students in most countries are more likely to attend less prestigious and less expensive institutions if they attend high school or university at all.

One's level of education affects many aspects of life, including political, religious, and marital attitudes and behavior. Generally speaking, the higher the education level, the more active individuals are in political life, the more mainstream or conventional their religious affiliation, the more likely they are to marry into a family with both economic and social capital, the more stable the marriage, and the more likely they are to have good health.

Health, Social Conditions, and Life Expectancy

Pictures on the news of children starving and dying dramatically illustrate global inequalities. The poorest countries in the world are in sub-Saharan Africa, where most individuals eat poorly, are susceptible to diseases, have great stress in their daily lives just trying to survive, and die at young ages compared with the developed world. (See the following "Engaging Sociology.")

If you have a sore throat, you go to see your doctor. Yet many people in the world will never see a doctor. Access to health care requires doctors and medical facilities, money for transportation and treatment, access to child care, and released time from other tasks to get to a medical facility. The poor sometimes do not have these luxuries. In contrast, the affluent eat better food, are less exposed to polluted water and unhygienic conditions, and are able to pay for medical care and drugs when they do have ailing health, and live twice as long. Even causes of death illustrate the differences between people at different places in the stratification hierarchy. For example, in the poor Global South, shorter life expectancies and deaths, especially among children, are due to controllable infectious diseases such as cholera, typhoid, tuberculosis, and other respiratory ailments. In contrast, in affluent countries, heart disease and cancer are the most common causes of death, and most deaths are of people above the age of 65. So whether considered locally or globally, access to health care resources makes a difference in life chances. To an extent, the chance to have a long and healthy life is a privilege of the elite. Again, globally speaking, if you are reading this book as part of a college course, you are part of the elite.

The impact of social conditions on life expectancy is especially evident if we compare cross-national data. Countries with the shortest life expectancy at birth illustrate the pattern. These countries lack adequate health care, immunizations, and sanitation; have crises of war and displacement of population resulting in refugees; and experience illnesses, epidemics, and famine. Even a drought has more tragic impact when no other aid resources are available to help families cope. By studying Table 7.1 in the "Engaging Sociology"

Video Link 7.2
See how changes in social conditions have changed class structure.

Engaging Sociology

Health, Life Expectancy, Infant Mortality, and Socioeconomic Factors

Analyzing the meaning of data can provide understanding of the health and well-being of citizens around the world. A country's basic statistics, including life expectancy, per capita gross national product, and infant mortality, tell researchers a great deal about the status of the country.

1. What questions do the data in Table 7.1 raise regarding differences in mortality and life expectancy rates around the world?

2. From what you know from this and previous chapters and from the table below, what are some differences in the lives of citizens in the richest and poorest countries?

Table 7.1 Life Expectancy, per Capita Income, and Infant Mortality for Selected Poor and Rich Countries

Poor Countries	Life Expectancy, 2009 (in years)	Infant Mortality 2009	Per Capita GNP ($) 2008	Rich Countries	Life Expectancy, 2009 (in years)	Infant Mortality 2009	Per Capita GNP ($) 2008
Swaziland	32.0	68.6	4,400	Japan	82.1	2.8	38,980
Angola	38.2	180.2	1,350	Hong Kong	81.9	2.9	43,800
Zambia	38.6	101.2	490	Australia	81.6	4.8	32,220
Mozambique	41.1	105.8	900	Canada	81.2[a]	5.0[a]	39,200
Sierra Leone	41.2	154.4	900	France	81.0	3.3	33,300
Liberia	41.8	138.2	500	Sweden	80.9	2.8	41,060
Afghanistan	44.6	152.0	800	Switzerland	81.9	4.2	42,000
Zimbabwe	45.8	32.3	200	Iceland	80.7	3.2	42,300
Chad	47.7	98.7	1,600	New Zealand	80.4	4.9	27,900
South Africa	49.0	44.2	10,100	Italy	80.7	5.5	31,400
Niger	52.6	116.7	700	United States	78.1[b]	6.3[b]	47,500

Source: *World Factbook* (2010b, 2010c) for infant mortality and life expectancy; *World Factbook* (2010a) for per capita income.

Note: Infant mortality is per 1,000 live births.

a. Canada is 7th in life expectancy and 36th in infant mortality rates.

b. United States is 50th in life expectancy and 45th in infant mortality rates.

People living in poverty around the world often get health care at clinics or emergency rooms, if they have access to care, where they wait for hours to see a health care provider as shown in this mother-child health clinic in Kisumu, Kenya.

box, you can compare life expectancy with two other measures of life quality for the poorest and richest countries: the gross national product (GNP) per capita income—the average amount of money each person has per year—and the infant mortality rates (death rates for babies). Note that average life expectancy in poor countries is as low as 32 years, income as low as $200 a year (many of the people in these populations are subsistence farmers), and infant mortality is as high as 180.2 deaths (estimated) in the first year of life for every 1,000 births and as low as 2.8 in some Global North countries (Geocommons 2009; World Factbook 2010a, 2010b, 2010c). Numbers for the richest countries are dramatically different.

The United States has much larger gaps between rich and poor people than most other wealthy countries, resulting in higher poverty rates (more people at the bottom rungs of the stratification ladder). This is, in turn, reflected in health statistics, with infant mortality rates at 6.26 deaths in the first year of life per 1,000 births (index mundi 2009). Sweden and Japan have the lowest infant mortality rates in the world at 2.8, a measure of their health standards (World Factbook 2007). Deaths of children below 5 years of age are highest in Sierre Leone (270 per 1,000), Angola (260), and Afghanistan (257). More than 25,000 children below 5 years of age die each day on average; that is 1 child every 3 to 5 seconds, 17 to 18 every minute, and approximately 9 million per year (Shah 2009a). The world average infant mortality is 43.5 per 1,000 (Swivel 2007). This evidence supports the assertion that health, illness, and death rates are closely tied to socio-economic stratification. Race and gender interact with social class in ways that often have negative results.

Thinking Sociologically

What are some factors at the micro, meso, and macro levels that affect your life expectancy and that of your family?

Individual Lifestyles

Your attitudes, values, beliefs, behavior patterns, and other aspects of who you are make up your individual **lifestyle**. As individuals grow up, the behaviors and attitudes consistent with their culture and family's status in society become internalized through the process of socialization. Lifestyle is not a simple matter of having money. Acquiring money—say, by winning a lottery—cannot buy a completely new lifestyle (Bourdieu and Passeron 1977). This is because values and behaviors are ingrained in our self-concept from childhood. You may gain material possessions but that does not mean you have the lifestyle of the upper-class rich and famous. Even the way one dresses is often a statement about one's social class, and some people dress up for special occasions to have a "status holiday"—to pretend they are rich and famous for a night. Consider some examples of factors related to your individual lifestyle: attitudes toward achievement, political involvement, and religious membership.

Attitudes Toward Achievement

In Global North countries, opportunity is available for most children to attend school at least through high school and often beyond. However, some students do not learn to value achievement in school due to difficulty in school, peer pressures, lack of support from family members, poor self-concepts, poor role models, poor schools and teaching, language differences, cultural differences, and many other factors (Ballantine and Hammack 2009). Attitudes toward achievement differ by social status and are generally closely correlated with life chances. Motivation to get ahead and beliefs about what you can achieve are in part products of your upbringing and the opportunities you see as available to you. These attitudes differ greatly depending on the opportunity structure around you, including what your family and friends see as possible and desirable. Then, consider the situation of children from poor countries and poor families. Their primary concern may be to help put food on the family's table. Even attitudes toward primary and secondary education reflect the luxury and inaccessibility that schooling is for some children.

Family Life and Child-Rearing Patterns

Attitudes toward achievement are not the only things that differ between socioeconomic groups. Child-rearing

Clothing not only covers our bodies but also acts as a symbol of our social status and reflects our lifestyles. This couple is either from a very affluent family or they are enjoying a night where they pretend to be rich.

patterns are also affected by social class and serve to reinforce one's social position in society. When you were growing up, were your afterschool hours, weekends, and summers filled with adult-organized activities (e.g., formal lessons, youth sports)? In contrast, were you pretty much free to play on your own, watch TV, or hang out with friends or extended family? Sociologist Annette Lareau (2003) reports that a family's social class location shapes "the daily rhythms of family life" (p. 8). Middle-class parents engage in the "concerted cultivation" (p. 238) of their kids. They scheduled their kids in multiple activities, engaged in more elaborate verbal communication with them, and "intervened on their behalf" (p. 238) with school and other authorities. Working-class parents, other than providing daily essentials, tended to be more hands-off, an approach that Lareau labeled the "accomplishment of natural growth" (p. 238). These kids engaged in more casual, unstructured play rather than having their time dominated by adult-organized activities, had fewer linguistic opportunities, and were at the mercy of school and other authorities to a greater degree than middle-class kids. However, when children in the United States from the lower and working class *are* disciplined, their parents tend to use more physical punishment than

middle-class parents, who use guilt, reasoning, time-outs, and other nonphysical sanctions to control children's behavior. These differences may have implications for one's assumptions about how authority is exercised and whether it is acceptable to challenge authority figures.

While there are advantages and disadvantages of each pattern, these differences matter because they lead to the "transmission of differential advantages to children" (Lareau 2003:5). Middle-class children are enabled to navigate the educational and, later, occupational worlds more successfully than are working-class children, thus influencing the social class destinations of each group (Lashbrook 2009).

In addition, in many countries, higher social class correlates with later marriage and lower divorce rates. Members of lower classes tend to marry earlier and have more children. Because of tensions from life stresses including money problems, they often have less stable marriages and more instances of divorce and single parenthood.

Audio Link 7.1
Listen to the ways money can change behavior.

Religious Membership

Religion also correlates with social status variables of education, occupation, and income. For instance, in the United States, upper-class citizens are found disproportionately in Episcopalian, Unitarian, and Jewish religious groups, whereas lower-class citizens are attracted to Nazarene, Southern Baptist, Jehovah's Witnesses, and other holiness and fundamentalist sects. Although there are exceptions, each religious group attracts members predominantly from one social class, as will be illustrated in Chapter 12 on religion (Kosmin and Lackman 1993; Roberts 2004).

Political Behavior

What political preferences one holds and how one votes are also affected by social status. Around the world, upper-middle classes are most supportive of elite or pro-capitalist agendas because these agendas support their way of life; lower working-class members are least supportive (Wright 2000). Generally, the lower the social class, the more likely people are to vote for liberal parties (Kerbo 2008), and the higher the social status, the more likely people are to vote conservative on economic issues consistent with protecting wealth (Brooks and Manza 1997).

In the United States, members of the lower class tend to vote liberal on economic issues, favoring government intervention to improve economic conditions. However, those with lower levels of education and income vote conservatively on many social issues relating to minorities and civil liberties (e.g., rights for homosexuals, gay marriage, and abortion; Gilbert and Kahl 2003; Jennings 1992; Kerbo 2008). In the 2008 election, many voters had to make choices about economic policies they liked and whether those policies were more important than their preferences on some of the social issues.

Status Inconsistency

The reality is that some people experience high status on one trait, especially a trait that is achieved, but may experience low standing in another area. For example, a professor may have high prestige but low income. Max Weber called this unevenness in one's social standing *status inconsistency*. Individuals who experience such status inconsistency, especially if they are treated as if their lowest ascribed status is the most important one, are likely to be very liberal and to experience discontent with the current system (Weber 1946).

Video Link 7.3
Watch video about the affect of recession on New York City residents.

People tend to associate with others like themselves, perpetuating and reinforcing lifestyles. In fact, people often avoid contact with others whose lifestyles are outside their familiar and comfortable patterns. This desire for familiarity also means that most people remain in the same social class because they have learned the "subculture," and it is comfortable and familiar.

Life chances and lifestyles are deeply shaped by the type of stratification system that is prevalent in the nation. Life experiences such as hunger, the unnecessary early death of family members, or the pain of seeing one's child denied opportunities are all experienced at the micro level, but their causes are usually rooted in events and actions at other levels of the social world. This brings us to our next question: Can an individual change positions in a stratification system?

Thinking Sociologically

Describe your own lifestyle and life chances. How do these relate to your socialization experience and your family's position in the stratification system? What difference do they make in your life?

 SOCIAL MOBILITY: THE MICRO-MESO CONNECTION

The Kobe Bryants and Peyton Mannings of the world make millions of dollars—at least for the duration of their playing careers. For professionals in the world of sport, each hoop, goal, or touchdown throw is worth thousands of dollars. These riches give hope to those in rags that if they "play hard" on their local hoops, they too may be on the field or court making millions. The problem is that the chances of making it big are so small that such hopes are some of the cruelest hoaxes faced by young African Americans and others in the lower or working class. Therefore, it is a false promise to think of sports as the road to opportunity as

chances of success or even of moving up through them are very limited (Dufur and Feinberg 2007; Edwards 2000).

Those few minority athletes who do "make it big" and become models for young people experience "stacking," holding certain limited positions in a sport. When retired from playing, few Black athletes rise in the administrative hierarchy of the sports of football and baseball, although basketball has a better record of hiring Black coaches and managers. Thus, when young people put their hopes and energies into developing their muscles and physical skills, they may lose the possibility of moving up in the social class system, which requires developing their minds and technical skills. Misplaced focus thwarts their dreams of upward social mobility.

The whole idea of changing one's social position is called social mobility. **Social mobility** refers to the "extent to which people move up or down in the class system, especially from one generation to the next" (Gilbert 2008:123). What is the likelihood that your status will be different from that of your parents over your lifetime? Will you start a successful business? Marry into wealth? Win the lottery? Experience downward mobility due to loss of a job, illness, or inability to complete your education? What factors at different levels of analysis might influence your chances of mobility? These are some of the questions addressed in this section and the next.

This young street basketball player slamdunks his ball in a milk-crate hoop as he dreams of glory on the courts. Despite grand dreams by young minorities, few experience dramatic social mobility through this avenue.

The four issues that dominate the analysis of mobility are (1) types of social mobility, (2) methods of measuring social mobility, (3) factors that affect social mobility, and (4) whether there is a "land of opportunity."

Types of Social Mobility

Intergenerational mobility refers to change in status compared with one's parents' status, usually resulting from education and occupational attainment. If you are the first to go to college in your family and you become a computer programmer, this would represent intergenerational mobility. The amount of intergenerational mobility in a society measures the degree to which a society has an **open class system**—one that allows movement between classes, meaning that you could move up or down in comparison with your parents in the stratification system.

Intragenerational mobility (not to be confused with *intergenerational mobility*) refers to the change in position in a single individual's life. For instance, if you begin your career as a teacher's aide and end it as a school superintendent, that is upward intragenerational mobility. However, mobility is not always up.

Vertical mobility refers to movement up or down in the hierarchy and sometimes involves changing social classes. You may start your career as a waitress, go to college part-time, get a degree in engineering, and get a more prestigious and higher-paying job, resulting in upward mobility. Alternatively, you could lose a job and take one at a lower status, a reality for many when the economy is doing poorly. In the global economic downturn, people at all levels of the occupational structure are experiencing layoffs, and often having problems finding new positions at comparable levels.

Encyclopedia Link 7.1
Read more about social mobility.

How Much Mobility Is There? Measures of Social Mobility

Can one move up in the class system? One traditional method of measuring mobility is to compare fathers and sons. Surveys ask men about their occupations and those of their fathers or sons. Table 7.2 reflects questions asked of U.S. fathers about their son's and daughter's mobility. Several conclusions can be derived from this table (Gilbert 2008):

Table 7.2	**Outflow From Father's Occupation to Son's Occupation**					
	Son's Occupation (percentage) in *Blue* Daughter's Occupation (percentage) in *Red*					
	Upper-White Collar	*Lower-White Collar*	*Upper Manual*	*Lower Manual*	*Farm*	*Total*
Father's Occupation						
Upper White-Collar	42	31	12	15	1	100
	54	33	9	3	*	
Lower White-Collar	34	33	13	19	1	100
	49	34	11	6	*	
Upper Manual	20	20	29	29	2	100
	35	37	18	8	1	
Lower Manual	20	22	20	36	12	100
	32	39	19	9	1	
Farm	16	18	19	35	3	100
	34	28	22	14	2	
Total (N = 3,398)	27	25	19	27	1	100
	27	25	19	27	3	

Source: Gilbert (2008:124).

Note: Rows but not columns add to 100%. For example, read across the row that begins with "lower manual" on far left to trace the sons of fathers who held unskilled "lower manual jobs." While 20% rose to upper-white-collar (professional or managerial) positions, the largest group (36%) followed their fathers into unskilled manual jobs.

1. There is a high level of occupational inheritance—sons following fathers into jobs at the very same occupational level.

2. The higher the father's occupation level, the better the son's chances for occupational achievement.

3. There is also considerable movement up and down the occupational ladder from one generation to the next.

4. Sons are more likely to move up than down.

5. Daughters are even more likely to move up than sons. (pp. 124–125)

Determining the mobility of women is more difficult because they often have lower-level positions, and their mothers may not have worked full-time, but a conclusion that can be drawn is that both women's and men's occupational attainment is powerfully influenced by class origins.

Factors Affecting an Individual's Mobility

Why are some people successful at moving up the ladder, while others lag behind? Mobility is driven by many factors, from your family's *cultural capital* to global economic variables. One's chances to move up depend on micro-level factors—one's family background, socialization, personal characteristics, and education—and macro-level factors—the occupational structure and economic status of countries, population changes, the numbers of people vying for similar positions, discrimination based on gender or ethnicity, and the global economic situation.

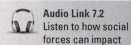
Audio Link 7.2
Listen to how social forces can impact lives.

The study of mobility is complicated because these key variables are interrelated. The macro-level forces (such as the economy, opportunity, and occupational structure in a country) are related to meso-level factors (such as access to education and opportunities) and micro-level factors (such as socialization and family background; Blau and Duncan 1967). An individual's background accounts for nearly half

of the factors affecting occupational attainment (Jencks 1979). Consider a few of the variables that can make a difference in your chances for mobility.

Family Background, Socialization, and Education

Our family background socializes us into certain behavior patterns, language usage, and occupational expectations (Sernau 2005). One example is language. Parents in professional families use three times as many different words at home as parents in low-income families. By the time the children of professional families are 3 years old, they have a vocabulary of about 1,100 words and typically use 297 different words per hour. Children in working-class families have a 700-word vocabulary and use 217 words per hour, while children from low-income families have 500 words accessible to them and use 149 per hour. These numbers represent a gap in the range of words they hear at home (Hart and Risley 2003). How might that difference in one's vocabulary affect one's success in school? How might an expanded vocabulary affect one's opportunities in life?

College is one expectation for upward mobility. Although not all those with a college degree are successful, few in Global North countries have a chance to be successful without a 2- or 4-year college degree (Lareau 2003). College education is the most important factor for high-income status, and the rewards of college degrees have increased. Those with degrees become richer than those without, largely because of changes in occupational structures creating new types of jobs for the computer information age. These "social-cultural specialists" work with ideas, knowledge, and technology rather than manufacturing (Florida 2002; Hurst 2006). We can see from Table 7.3 that most students in the United States with high ability from high-status families go to college, while high-ability students from low-status families go to college less often (83% vs. 51%). Note that a student with top cognitive ability but from the lowest-income families is less likely to enroll in college than someone from the third quartile of cognitive ability but the top socioeconomic quartile of society (51% vs. 57%).

Table 7.3 College Attendance by Social Class and Cognitive Ability (in percentage)

| Cognitive Ability Quartile | Family Socioeconomic Status Quartile | | | |
	Top	Second	Third	Lowest
Top	83	63	74	51
Second	69	42	51	33
Third	57	24	40	23
Lowest	35	13	20	13
Total (*N* = 3,398)	69	33	48	24

Source: Gilbert (2008:142).

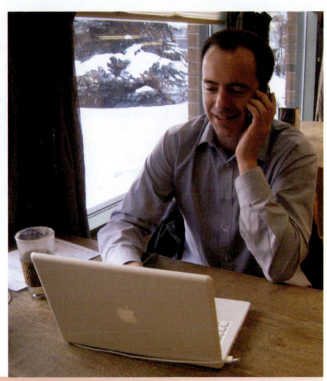

These men hold very different positions in society; one can offer his family more cultural capital that can be spent in influential positions and can provide more opportunities because of his education, family background, and networks with others in positions of influence. One of the two has a law degree.

When we look at actual college degrees, the pattern is more extreme, with diplomas going disproportionately to students in the top-status groups (50%), compared with only 10% of students from the bottom half of income levels. If American society was truly a meritocracy, as is so often claimed, one would expect cognitive ability to be the most important variable (Gilbert 2008).

Even when a young person is admitted to a college or university, she or he may be at a disadvantage in the classroom and alienated from past social ties. The culture of college is the culture of the well-educated upper-middle class, and everything from values to knowledge base to sense of humor may be different and uncomfortable (Dews and Law 1995). This alienation is explored in more detail in the "Engaging Sociology" on pages 222–223.

Many poor people lack education and skills such as interviewing and getting recommendations needed to get or change jobs in the postindustrial occupational structure (Ehrenreich 2001, 2005; McLeod 2004). Isolated from social networks in organizations, they lack contacts to help in the job search. The type of education system one attends also affects mobility. In Germany, Britain, France, and some other European countries, children are "streamed" (tracked) into either college preparatory courses or more general curricula, and the rest of their occupational experience reflects this early placement decision in school. In the United States, educational opportunities remain more

open to those who can afford them—at least this is what is supposed to happen.

Occupational Structure and Economic Vitality

The economic vitality of a country affects the chances for individual mobility, since there will be fewer positions at the top if the economy is stagnant. As agricultural work is decreasing and technology jobs increasing in most areas of the world (Hurst 2006), these changes in the composition and structure of occupations affect individual opportunity. Thus, a country's economy and place in the global system shapes employment chances of individuals. The global economic downturn of 2008 and 2009 illustrates the vulnerability of both macro-level nations whose banks and companies are failing and micro-level individuals living in those nations that are losing jobs.

How possible is upward social mobility? Have recent generations found it harder to move to a higher social class than previous generations of young people entering the workforce? There are a lot of data on the socioeconomic standing and income levels of Americans, but this gives little indication of how people move through their careers and become better off financially. Four scholars tried to remedy this missing link using survey data collected over nearly two decades. Two groups of young men, beginning as teenagers but from different decades (Morris et al. 2001), provided the

Engaging Sociology

First-Generation College Students: Issues of Cultural Capital and Social Capital

Socioeconomic classes develop subcultures that can be quite different from each other, and when one changes sub-cultures, it can be confusing and alienating. College campuses provide an example. Generally, they are dominated by middle-class cultures. Young people from blue-collar backgrounds and those who are first-generation college students often find themselves in a world as alien to them as visiting another country. Students whose parents went to college are more likely to have "cultural or social capital" that helps them adjust and helps them understand their professors who are generally part of the middle-class culture. Answer the following survey questions. How might your own cultural or social capital cause you to feel at home or alienated, privileged or disprivileged, hopeful or despairing?

1. Which of the following experiences were part of your childhood?
   ◊ Had a library of books (at least 50 adult books) at your childhood home
   ◊ Had a subscription to a newspaper that was delivered to your home
   ◊ Had news magazine subscriptions that came to your home (*Time, Newsweek, The Economist*)
   ◊ Listened to music as a family, including classical or instrumental music such as harp or flute
   ◊ Traveled to at least 20 other states or to at least 5 other countries
   ◊ Took regular trips to the library
   ◊ Took regular trips to museums
   ◊ Attended movies
   ◊ Attended plays (theater productions)
   ◊ Attended concerts
   ◊ Played a musical instrument
   ◊ Took dance lessons
   ◊ Listened to National Public Radio (NPR)
   ◊ Watched PBS (Public Broadcasting Station) on television

2. Which of the following *relationships* were part of your childhood?
   ◊ My parents knew at least two influential people in my community on a first name basis—such as the major, members of the city council, the superintendent of schools, members of the school board, the local county sher-iff, the chief of police, the prosecuting attorney, the governor, and the district's representative to Congress.
   ◊ The regional leader of my religious group—church, temple, synagogue, or mosque—knew and respected my family.
   ◊ My parents knew on a first name basis at least three chief executive officers (CEOs) of corporations.
   ◊ When I entered new situations in high school, it was likely that my parents were known by the coaches, music directors, summer camp counselors/directors, or other authority figures who were "running the show."
   ◊ When I came to college, one or more professors and administrators at the college knew my parents, a sibling, or another family member.
   ◊ I have often interacted directly and effectively (in a nonadversarial way) with authority figures.

If you experienced many of the items in #1 at home, you had fairly high cultural capital. If you marked most of the items in #2, you had a lot of social capital. If you did not, you may find the culture of a college campus to be alien and even confusing.

Answer the three questions below and then read the sociological explanations.

1. Which of the following makes a first-generation college student feel most alienated at your college and even within this sociology course: *economic capital* (money), *social capital* (networks with those who have resources), or *cultural capital* (knowledge of important aspects of the culture)? Why?

2. What did "doing well" in school mean in your family? Did they stress education, and if so, how?

3. What did it mean within your family to be "independent" when you were in high school?

Note: The following ideas provide some sociological insight into the above questions.

1. Students who do not have a middle-class cultural capital may find that they are in a strange culture at college as if they entered another country. Students who do not have a strong social capital may find that they do not know how to find advocates or support in difficult situations. If students lack financial capital then they may find themselves as social isolates, because they cannot afford to do the things that are part of the social life of the campus; in addition, they may have to work long hours to pay for their education.

2. Blue-collar definitions of *success in school* often stress

   - Obeying authority and memorizing material
   - Getting the reward (the diploma) is most important, with minimal necessary commitment of effort

   Middle-class definitions of *school success* often emphasize
   - Learn the material and get good grades
   - Become a committed and contributing member of the school

3. Blue-collar definitions of *independence* often emphasize

   - Supporting oneself financially
   - Not taking "crap" from anyone; that is, defending oneself physically

   Middle-class definitions of *independence* typically focus on
   - Being original and creative
   - Thinking things through on your own and challenging authority or "the common wisdom"

In short, social and cultural capital pervade the experiences of students pursuing a college education.

Source: Survey constructed in part using ideas from Morris and Grimes (1997).

---

participants for a longitudinal study. Gathering data from the same people over a period of time allows researchers to see how their lives develop and change. They found several patterns about the structure of employment and how some young men negotiated the transition successfully:

- Changing jobs early in one's career (a) helps one find a position that is best suited for one's training, talents, and personal traits and (b) this enhances one's prospects for greater income. However, this is only true for those with a good deal of education who are entering positions in the middle class or higher. Those with less education did not have the same positive effect from job switching early on.
- The pattern of a man's income is established, and his biggest gains are made relatively early in his career.
- After searching for the "best career and employment fit," stability in the job greatly enhances overall income and upward mobility over the life path. In short, changing employers beyond the first 6 or 8 years seldom increases social mobility. Early job change followed by long tenures was the pattern best suited to upward mobility.
- Upward mobility has been more difficult for the younger generation of men, in large part because of instability in the job market and in corporations.
- Parents' socioeconomic level was a major predictor of the paths toward affluence or poverty. Those who had little social capital (networks) had less upward mobility, and this was even more true of the younger cohort.
- The society seems to be polarizing between rich and poor, and stagnating for all groups. Wage growth is becoming more difficult for all groups, but the American dream of mobility is not a positive dream for those most in need.

Poverty on the Hopi reservation in Arizona makes this town seem like it could be part of the Global South. The poverty is largely due to lack of resources, much of their land having been taken away by the federal government in the 19th century.

The authors conclude that there is a growing "stickiness" in low-wage, high-turnover jobs in the service industries that make it harder to ever "make it in the United States." This is not due to personality traits but to the structure of the service industry: There is a lack of stable positions, career training, or career ladders in these service positions, and this has created a lower-end labor market with few paths to mobility (Morris et al. 2001).

Population Trends

The U.S. nationwide baby boom that occurred following World War II resulted in a flood of job applicants and downward intergenerational mobility for the many who could not find work comparable with their social class at birth. In contrast, the smaller group following the baby boomer generation had fewer competitors for entry-level jobs. Baby boomers hold many of the executive and leadership positions today, so promotion has been hard for the next cohort. As baby boomers retire, opportunities will open up, and mobility should increase. The *fertility rates*, or number of children born at a given time, influence the number of people who will be looking for jobs.

Gender and Ethnicity

Many women and ethnic minority groups, locked in a cycle of poverty, dependence, and debt, have little chance of changing their status. Women in the U.S. workforce, for instance, are more likely than men to be in dead-end clerical and service positions with no opportunity for advancement. In the past three decades, the wage gap between women and men has generally narrowed, and women now earn 77.1% of what men earn for full-time, year-round work, down from 77.8% in 2007. This puts the gender wage gap in the United States at 22.9%. This compares with 60% in 1980 (U.S. Department of Labor 2005). African American men make 72.1% and African American women 63.6% of White men's earnings for comparable jobs. Table 7.4 shows the earnings for White males and the percentage of those earnings for other gender and ethnic groups.

Special circumstances such as war have often allowed women and others who were denied access to good jobs to get a "foot in the door" and has actually enhanced their upward mobility. A recent factor affecting career success of women is that more females than males are earning college degrees (Center for American Progress, 2009).

Some people experience *privilege* (e.g., in the United States, White, European-born, native-speaking males who are in the middle class or higher), whereas some experience *disprivilege* due to socioeconomic status, ethnicity, gender, or a combination of these.

The Interdependent Global Market and International Events

If the Asian stock market hiccups, it sends ripples through world markets. If high-tech industries in Japan or Europe falter, North American companies in Silicon Valley, California, may go out of business, costing many professionals their lucrative positions. In ways such as these, the interdependent global economies affect national and local economies, and that in turn affects individual families.

Whether individuals move from "rags to riches" is not determined solely by their personal ambition and work ethic. Mobility for the individual, a micro-level event, is linked to a variety of events at other levels of the social world, and one cannot assume that the unemployed individual is just lazy or incompetent.

Thinking Sociologically

Do you know individuals who have lost jobs because of economic slowdowns at the meso or macro level or who have gotten jobs because of economic booms and opening opportunities? What changes have occurred in their mobility and social class?

Is There a "Land of Opportunity"? Cross-Cultural Mobility

Remember the case of "balloon boy," the 6-year-old who was thought to be floating through the air in a homemade balloon when all the time he was hiding in an attic? The perpetrator of the hoax hoped that he would get attention and be asked to appear on reality shows; he is now charged with fraud, his "get rich" scheme a total failure. Television shows bombard us with images of rich bachelors and the desirability of marrying a millionaire to improve one's status in life. By playing a game of trivia or being challenged on an island on a TV show, we too might "strike it rich." Another possibility—we might win the lottery by buying a ticket at our local grocery. In reality, these quick fixes and easy get-rich-fast plans are seldom realized, and the chances of us profiting are slim indeed.

Table 7.4 Median Annual Earnings by Race/Ethnicity and Sex		
Race/Gender	Earnings ($)	Wage Ratio (%)
White men	47,814	100.0
White women	35,151	73.5
Black men	34,480	72.1
Black women	30,398	63.6
Hispanic men	27,490	57.5
Hispanic women	24,738	51.7
All men	42,210	
All women	32,649	
Wage gap		77.4

Source: U.S. Census Bureau (2007b).

The question for this section concerns your chances for mobility: Do you have a better chance to improve your status in England, Japan, the United States, or some other country? However, the answer is not simple. If there is a land of opportunity where individuals can be assured of improving their economic and social position, it is not easy to identify, as many variables affect the opportunity structure. Countless immigrants have sought better opportunities in new locations. Perhaps your parents or ancestors did just this. The reality of the "land of opportunity" depends on the historical period and current economic conditions, social events, and political attitudes toward foreigners when the immigrants came, their personal skills, and their ability to blend into the new society. With the recession of 2008–2009, unemployment in many countries around the world is higher and fewer migrants are finding work in new countries. In the United States, not only are there fewer migrants from Latin America entering, but there is some reverse migration as disappointed workers cannot get jobs.

During economic growth periods, many immigrants have found great opportunities for mobility in the United States and Europe. Early industrial tycoons in railroads, automobiles, steel, and other industries are examples of success stories. Fortunes have been made in the high-tech industries of China, India, and other countries, and in energy resources in Russia. The number of millionaires and billionaires in the world is increasing dramatically, yet this is still a very small percentage of the world's population. In 2008, there were an estimated 1,125 billionaires globally; the United States had the most, with Russia rising to 87 billion, moving ahead of Germany (Center for Research on Globalization 2008). China is the dramatic success story, reaching an estimated 260 billionaires, including many women, in 2009, doubling in 1 year. It will soon top the list of countries with billionaires (France 24 International News 2009; Spero News 2009). Such wealth eludes most people, especially immigrants, who must work multiple low-paying jobs just to feed their families and stay out of poverty.

Opportunities for upward mobility have changed significantly with globalization. Many manufacturing jobs in the global economy have moved from the Global North to the Global South with cheap labor, reducing the number of unskilled and low-skilled jobs available in Global North countries. Multinational corporations look for the cheapest sources of labor, mostly in the Global South, which features low taxes, no labor unions, few regulations, and many workers needing jobs, thus draining away low-skilled jobs from the United States. Since the 1970s, the earnings differential between high school graduates and college graduates has widened, leaving high school graduates struggling to find work that will support a family.

Why the changes in the job structure? First, there are fewer demands for manufacturing jobs as service-producing jobs requiring higher education expand. Second, the increase in international trade results in demand for high-tech products from the United States, but fewer manufacturing products, thus reducing manufacturing jobs. New technologies and automation leave low-skilled workers in Global North countries without jobs. The minimum-wage and low-wage jobs are all that is available to lower-skilled workers, and labor unions have less influence on the wages and working conditions of these workers today (Gilbert 2008). High-tech positions are good news for those with college degrees and technical skills, but the replacement of laboring positions with service jobs in fast-food and box store chains (e.g., Walmart, Kmart, Home Depot, Lowe's) means a severe loss of genuine opportunity for living wages.

Although the new multinational industries springing up in Global South countries such as Malaysia, Thailand, and the Philippines provide opportunities for mobility to those of modest origins, much of the upward mobility in the world is taking place among those who come from small, highly educated families with individualistic achievement-oriented values

Video Link 7.4
Watch an explanation of global banking.

and people who see education as a route to upward mobility (Blau and Duncan 1967; Featherman and Hauser 1978; Jencks 1979; Rothman 2005). They are positioned to take advantage of the changing occupational structure and high-tech jobs. As the gap between rich and poor individuals and countries widens, more individuals in the United States begin to move down rather than up in the stratification system. The "Sociology in Our Social World" on the next page illustrates this problem.

Thinking Sociologically

What social factors in your society limit or enhance the likelihood of upward social mobility for you and your generation? Explain.

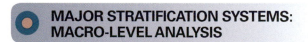

MAJOR STRATIFICATION SYSTEMS: MACRO-LEVEL ANALYSIS

Mansa's family works on a plantation in Mozambique. He tries in vain to pay off the debts left by his father's family. However hard he and his wife and children work, they will always be in debt because they cannot pay the total amount due for their hut or food from the owner's store. Basically, they are slaves—they do not have control over their own labor. They were born into this status, and there they will stay.

Imagine being born into a society in which you have no choices or options in life because of your family background, age, sex, and ethnic group. You cannot select an occupation that interests you, cannot choose your mate,

Sociology in Our Social World

Nickel-and-Dimed

Have you or has someone you know held a minimum-wage job? Did you have to support yourself and maybe other family members on that wage, or was it just pocket money? Millions in the United States live in this world of unskilled laborers, getting minimum wage—if that—for their work, and most rely on these wages to support themselves and their families.

Author Barbara Ehrenreich (2001) asked how individuals and families survive on these wages. To find out, she tried it herself. Living in several cities—Key West, Florida; Portland, Maine; and Minneapolis, Minnesota—she held jobs as a waitress, retail clerk at Walmart, hotel housekeeper, and nursing home aide. Each job was physically and mentally demanding.

After describing the details of each job and the lives of her coworkers, Ehrenreich concludes that people are earning far less than they need to live. Her coworkers struggled to meet minimum housing costs (sometimes living in hotels or cars), bought cheap food, and shopped at thrift stores. They were also consistently struggling with transportation, child care, and health care. Many were also managing large debts.

The number of "working poor" is growing. Many states added work requirements for mothers to remain eligible for welfare benefits. These reforms became federal law when President Bill Clinton replaced Aid to Families with Dependent Children (AFDC) with Temporary Aid to Needy Families (TANF). Beyond work requirements, TANF also added time limits for welfare eligibility and eliminated increased benefits for families that grew while receiving assistance.

The Economic Policy Institute recently reviewed dozens of studies of what constitutes a living wage and came up with an average figure of $30,000 a year for a family of one adult and two children, which amounts to a wage of $14 an hour. (Ehrenreich 2001:214)

This budget includes health insurance, a telephone, and child care, but no extras, and it is more than most minimum-wage workers have. Upward mobility for this large group in the population is difficult if not impossible. Ehrenreich's research makes it clear: To be a society of at least minimal opportunity for all, we must reconsider economic policies to better address underpaid workers as well as the unemployed. Although many states have raised the minimum wage since *Nickel and Dimed* was published—and federal minimum wage incrementally increased to $7.25 as of July 2009—no state currently has a minimum wage that meets minimum living wage requirements by the Economic Policy Institute's calculation. Add to that the increases in costs of gas and food, and many U.S. citizens are struggling to make ends meet.

and cannot live in the part of town you choose. You see wealthy aristocrats parading their advantages and realize that this will never be possible for you. You can never own land or receive the education of your choice.

This situation is reality for millions of people in the world—they are born this way and will spend their lives in this plight. In **ascribed stratification systems**, such characteristics determine one's position in society. In contrast, **achieved stratification systems**, such as class systems, allow individuals to earn positions through their ability and effort. In a class system, it is possible to achieve a higher ranking by working hard, obtaining education, gaining power, or doing other things that are highly valued in that culture.

Ascribed Status: Caste and Estate Systems

Caste systems, the most rigid ascribed systems, are maintained by cultural norms and social control mechanisms that are deeply imbedded in religious, political, and economic institutions. Individuals born into caste systems have predetermined occupational positions, marriage partners, residences, social associations, and prestige levels. A person's caste is easily recognized through clothing, speech patterns, family name and identity, skin color, or other distinguishing characteristics. From their earliest years, individuals learn their place in society through the process of socialization. To behave counter to caste prescriptions would be to go against religion and social custom and to risk not fitting into society. Religious ideas dictate that one's status after death (in Christian denominations) or one's next *reincarnation* or rebirth (in the Hindu tradition) also might be in jeopardy. Stability is maintained by the belief that people can be reborn into a higher status in the next life if they fulfill expectations in their ascribed position in this life. Thus, believers in both religions work hard with the hope of attaining a better life after death or in the next reincarnation. The institution of religion works together with the family, education, and economic and political institutions to shape (and sometimes reduce) both expectations and aspirations and to keep people in their prescribed places in caste systems.

The clearest example of a caste system is found in India. The Hindu religion holds that individuals are born into one of four *varnas*, broad caste positions, or into a fifth group below the caste system, the *outcaste* group. The first and highest varna, called *Brahmans*, originally was made up of priests and scholars but now includes many leaders in society. The second varna, *Kshatriyas* or *Rajputs*, includes the original prince and warrior varna and now embraces much of the army and civil service. The *Vaishyas*, or merchants, are the third varna. The fourth varna, the *Sudras*, include peasants, artisans, and laborers. The final layer, below the caste system, the outcastes encompasses profoundly oppressed and broken people— "a people put aside"—referred to as untouchables, outcastes, *Chandalas* (a Hindu term), and *Dalits* (the name preferred by many "untouchables" themselves). Although the Indian Constitution of 1950 granted full social status to these citizens, and a law passed in 1955 made discrimination against them punishable, deeply rooted traditions are difficult to change. Caste distinctions are still very prevalent, especially in rural areas, as seen in the discussion in "Sociology Around the World."

Estate systems are similarly rigid in stratifying individuals. They are characterized by the concentration of economic and political power in the hands of a small minority of political-military elite, with the peasantry tied to the land (Rothman 2005). Estate systems are based on ownership of land, the position one is born into, or military strength. An individual's rank and legal rights are clearly spelled out, and arranged marriages and religion bolster the system. During the Middle Ages, knights defended the realms and the religion of the nobles. Behind every knight in shining armor were peasants, sweating in the fields and paying for the knights' food, armor, and campaigns. For farming the land owned by the nobility, peasants received protection against invading armies and enough of the produce to survive.

The futures of these Aboriginal boys in Australia are determined by their ethnic group and family of birth, making it unlikely that they will ever experience much affluence in Australian society.

Their life was often miserable. If the yield of crops was poor, they ate little. In a good year, they might save enough to buy a small parcel of land. A very few were able to become independent in this fashion.

Estate systems existed in ancient Egypt, the Incan and Mayan civilizations, Europe, China, and Japan. Today, similar systems exist in some Central and South American, Asian, and African countries on large banana, coffee, and sugar plantations, as exemplified in the description of Mansa's life in Mozambique. Over time, development of a mercantile economy resulted in modifications in the early estate systems, and now peasants often work on the land in exchange for the right to live there and receive a portion of the produce.

Thinking Sociologically

In much of the Global North, individualism is so highly valued that ascribed systems of stratification are rejected. What values—both positive and negative—might support ascribed systems? Why might those values make your society's system seem unacceptable and even offensive to people in other non-industrial societies?

Sociology Around the World

The Outcastes of India

The Dalits—sometimes called "untouchables"—are the most impoverished people in India and some of the most impoverished in the world. These are Dalit children, attending a school that is so poor that they do not have books, pencils, chairs, or desks.

The village south of Chennai (Madras) in the state of Tamil Nadu was on an isolated dirt road, 1 kilometer from the nearest town. It consisted of a group of mud and stick huts with banana leaf–thatched roofs. As our group of students arrived, the Dalit villagers lined the streets to greet us—and stare. Many had never seen Westerners. They played drums and danced for us and threw flower petals at our feet in traditional welcome.

Through our translator, we learned something of their way of life. The adults work in the fields long hours each day, plowing and planting with primitive implements, earning about 8 cents from the landowner, often not enough to pay for their daily bowl of rice. Occasionally, they catch a frog or bird to supplement their meal. In the morning, they drink rice gruel, and in the evening, they eat a bowl of rice with some spices. Women and children walk more than a kilometer to the water well—but the water is polluted during the dry season. There are no privies but the fields. As a result of poor sanitation, inadequate diet, and lack of health care, many people become ill and die from health problems that are easily cured in Western societies. For instance, lack of vitamin A, found in many fruits and vegetables to which they have little access, causes blindness in many village residents. Although the children have the right to go to the school in the closest village, many cannot do so because they have

no transportation, shoes, or money for paper, pencils, and books. Also, the families need them to work in the fields alongside their parents or help care for younger siblings. Many taboos rooted in tradition separate the Dalit from other Indians. For instance, they are forbidden to draw water from the village well, enter the village temple, or eat from dishes that might be used later by people of higher castes. The latter prohibition eliminates most dining at public establishments. About 95% are landless and earn a living below subsistence level.

Dalits who question these practices have been attacked and their houses burned. In one instance, 20 houses were burned on the birthday of Dr. Ambedkar, a leader of the Dalit rights movement. Official records distributed by the Human Rights Education Movement of India state that every hour, two Dalits are assaulted, three Dalit women are raped, two Dalits are murdered, and two Dalit houses are burned (Dalit Liberation Education Trust 1995; Thiagaraj 2006; K. Wilson 1993). This group on the bottom rung of the stratification system has a long fight ahead to gain the rights that many of us take for granted.

A few Dalits have migrated to cities, where they blend in, and some of them have become educated and are now leading the fight for the rights and respect guaranteed by law. Recently, unions and interest groups have been representing the Dalit, and some members turn to religious and political groups that are more sympathetic to their plight, such as Buddhists, Christians, or Communists.

One social activist, Henry Thiagaraj, has committed his life to improving conditions for the Dalits. Thiagaraj works on the micro, meso, and macro levels. On the micro level, he suggests that those in power form Dalit youth and women *sangams* (activist groups) and organize the people who live in Dalit slums. At the meso level, Thiagaraj and other Dalit activists work to initiate micro lending to the Dalits and improve their education and labor training. On the macro level, Thiagaraj works with nongovernmental organizations (NGOs) to increase support for Dalit interests. He also works to improve media coverage of the Dalits to raise awareness of their experiences. Thiagaraj's (2007) book, *Human Rights From the Dalits' Perspective*, provides an outstanding retrospective of how India has addressed caste discrimination since the 1980s.

Achieved Status: Social Class Systems

Social class systems of stratification are based on achieved status. Members of the same social class have similar income, wealth, and economic position. They also share comparable styles of living, levels of education, cultural similarities, and patterns of social interaction. Most of us are members of class-based stratification systems, and we take advantage of opportunities available to our social class. Our families, rich or poor, educated or unskilled, provide us with an initial social ranking and socialization experience. We tend to feel a kinship and sense of belonging with those in the same social class—our neighborhood and work group, our peers and friends. We think alike, share interests, and probably look up to the same people as a reference group. Our social class position is based on the three main factors determining positions in the stratification system: (1) property, (2) power, and (3) prestige.

This is the trio that, according to Max Weber, determines where individuals rank in relation to each other (Weber 1946, 1947). By property (wealth), Weber refers to owning or controlling the means of production. Power, the ability to control others, includes not only the means of production but also the position one holds. Prestige involves the esteem and recognition one receives, based on wealth, position, or accomplishments. Table 7.5 gives examples of households in the upper and lower social classes by illustrating the variables that determine a person's standing in the three areas of the stratification system.

Although these three dimensions of stratification are often found together, this is not always so. Recall the idea of status inconsistency: An individual can have a great deal of prestige yet not command much wealth (Weber 1946). Consider winners of the prestigious Nobel Peace Prize such as Wangari Maathai of Kenya, Rigoberta Menchu of Guatemala, or Betty Williams and Mairead Corrigan of Northern Ireland. None of them is rich, but each has made contributions to the world that have gained them universal prestige. Likewise, some people gain enormous wealth through crime or gambling, but this wealth may not be accompanied by respect or prestige.

Compared with systems based on ascribed status, achieved status systems maintain that everyone is born with common legal status; everyone is equal before the law. In principle, all individuals can own property and choose their own occupations. However, in practice, most class systems pass privilege or poverty from one generation to the next. Individual upward or downward mobility is more difficult than the ideology invites people to believe.

Audio Link 7.3
Think about the three factors when listening to these stories.

The Property Factor

One's income, property, and total assets comprise one's **wealth**. These lie at the heart of class differences. The contrast between the splendor of Newport aristocrats and British royalty with the daily struggle for survival of those in

Table 7.5	**Basic Dimensions of Social Stratification**		
	Class Variables (Economic)	*Prestige Variables*	*Power Variables (Political-Legal)*
	Income Wealth Occupation Education Family stability	Occupational prestige Respect in community Consumption Participation in group life Evaluations of race, religion, ethnicity	Political participation Political attitudes Legislation and governmental benefits Distribution of justice
Households in the upper social class	*Affluence:* economic security and power, control over material and human investment Income from work but mostly from property	More integrated personalities, more consistent attitudes, and greater psychic fulfillment due to deference, valued associations, and consumption	Power to determine public policy and its implementation by the state, thus giving control over the nature and distribution of social values
Households in the lower social class	*Destitution:* worthlessness on economic markets	Unintegrated personalities, inconsistent attitudes, sense of isolation and despair; sleazy social interaction	Political powerlessness, lack of legal recourse or rights, socially induced apathy

Source: Rossides (1997:15).

Note: Contains examples of values in the top and bottom classes within each dimension and examples of subdimensions. For expository purposes, religious and ethnic or racial rankings are omitted.

poverty is an example of the differences extreme wealth or lack thereof creates. Another example is shown in the income distribution in the United States by quintiles (see Table 7.6). Note that there has been minimal movement between the groups over the years, and what little change has occurred has been toward the richest having even more of the assets in the United States. In 2007, the median household income in the United States was $50,233. However, the poverty rate was 37.3 million, or 12.5% of the population. Roughly 47 million, or 15.3% of the U.S. population, had no health insurance (U.S. Census Bureau 2008d).

Although income distribution in the United States has not changed dramatically over time, there has been an increase in overall inequality, as the middle class has decreased by more than 8% since 1969. A majority of the 8% have experienced a downward movement, although a few have moved up in the stratification system (Rose 2000).

Table 7.6	**Share of Household Income in Quintiles**			
	1980	*1990*	*2000*	*2007*
Lowest quintile	4.2	3.8	3.6	3.4
Second quintile	10.2	9.6	8.9	8.7
Third quintile	16.8	15.9	14.9	14.8
Fourth quintile	24.7	24.0	23.0	23.4
Highest quintile	44.1	46.6	49.8	49.7

Source: U.S. Census Bureau (2009d).

The Power Factor

Power refers to the ability to control or influence others, to get them to do what you want them to do. Positions of power are gained through family inheritance, family connections, political appointments, education, hard work, friendship networks, and sometimes force. Two theories dominate the explanations of power—power elite and pluralist theories.

As discussed earlier, the conflict theorists' view is that those who hold power are those who control the economic capital and the means of production in society (Ashley and Orenstein 2009). Consistent with Marx, many recent conflict theorists have focused on a **power elite**—individuals with powerful positions in political, business, and military arenas (Domhoff 2001; Mills 1956). These people interact with each other and have an unspoken agreement to ensure that their power is not threatened. Each tends to protect the power of the other. The idea is that those who are not in this interlocking elite group do not hold real power (Dye 2000).

Pluralist theorists argue that power is not held exclusively by an elite group but is shared among many power centers, each of which has its own self-interests to protect (Ritzer and

Goodman 2004). Well-financed special interest groups (e.g., insurance industry, dairy and cattle farmers, or truckers' trade unions) and professional associations (e.g., the American Medical Association) have considerable power through collective action. Officials who hold political power are vulnerable to pressure from influential interest groups, and each interest group competes for power with others. Creating and maintaining this power through networks and pressure on legislators is the job of lobbyists. For example, in the U.S. debate over health care legislation, interest groups from the medical community, insurance lobbies, and citizens' groups wield their power to influence the outcome, but, because these major interests conflict and no one group has the most power, permanent resolution is hard to reach.

The Prestige Factor

Prestige refers to an individual's social recognition, esteem, and respect commanded from others. An individual's prestige ranking is closely correlated with the value system of society. Chances of being granted high prestige improve if one's patterns of behavior, occupation, and lifestyle match those that are valued in the society. Among high-ranked occupations across nations are scientists, physicians, military officers, lawyers, and college professors. Table 7.7 shows high and low occupational prestige rankings in the United States.

Table 7.7	**Prestige Rankings of 17 Professions and Occupations (in percentage)**	
Occupations (Base: All Adults)	*Very Great Prestige*	*Hardly Any Prestige at All*
Scientist	51	2
Doctor	50	1
Military officer	47	3
Teacher	47	7
Police officer	40	7
Priest/minister/clergyman	36	11
Engineer	34	4
Architect	27	4
Member of Congress	27	11
Athlete	21	15
Entertainer	19	15
Journalist	19	12
Business executive	18	13
Lawyer	15	20
Banker	15	10
Union leader	14	23
Accountant	13	17

Source: Taylor (2002).

Note the correlation between recent events such as 9/11 and the increased rankings of occupations in which people have been portrayed as "heroes" in the United States. For example, 63% of the U.S. population sees firefighters as having "very great prestige," even though their incomes do not reflect this (Schienberg 2006). Being a hero, obtaining material possessions, or increasing one's educational level can boost prestige but in themselves cannot change class standing.

Thinking Sociologically

Describe your own wealth, power, and prestige in society. Does your family have one factor but not others? What difference does each of the factors make in your life?

Social Classes in the United States

In the current U.S. economic structure, most people are middle class and identify themselves as such, but the middle class is shrinking. There is slight movement to the upper class and somewhat more movement to the lower class. As noted previously, the U.S. system allows for mobility within the middle class, but there is little movement at the very top and very bottom of the social ladder. People in the top rung often use their power and wealth to insulate themselves and protect their elite status, and the bottom group is isolated because of vicious cycles of poverty that are hard to break (Gilbert and Kahl 2003). Figure 7.1 illustrates the social class structure in the United States (Gilbert-Kahl Model of Social Class in Gilbert 2008:13).

The middle class, as defined by sociologists, makes up about 30% of the population in the United States, depending on what economic criteria are used. Whereas most people in the United States identify themselves as middle class, two thirds of the British population identify themselves as "working class" (Cashell 2007). How we identify ourselves expresses our feelings about our placement in the stratification system and also our class "culture." Classes have distinctive values, beliefs, and attitudes toward education, religion, politics, and what makes a good life in general. Often, what we define as "normal" is actually what is affirmed by others in our socioeconomic culture. A number of scholars have written about the cultural shock they experienced when moving from their blue-collar experiences as children to becoming professors. The shift in cultures was like entering a new country. Even the differences in vocabulary usage, discussed earlier in this chapter, represent part of the cultural difference (Hart and Risley 2003).

Since the 1970s, wealth has become increasingly concentrated in the hands of the richest 1% of households. The income

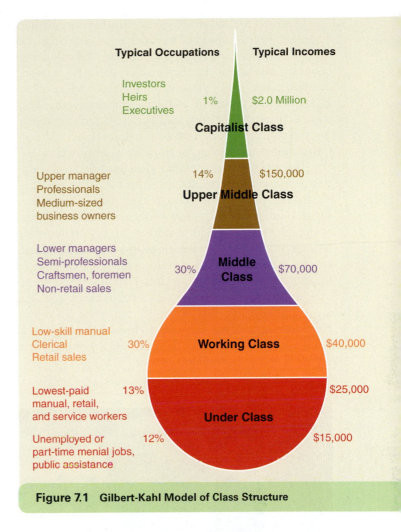

Figure 7.1   Gilbert-Kahl Model of Class Structure

gap between the top 5% and bottom 40% of the U.S. population is increasing, and the number of full-time workers in poverty is rising. There has been no reduction in poverty since the 1970s, yet the proportion of families exceeding $100,000 in annual income continues to grow (Gilbert 2008).

Wages and salaries of the middle classes have declined since the 1980s whereas those of the upper classes have risen. Reasons for middle-class decline include downsizing and layoffs of workers, global shifts in production, technological innovations that displace laborers, competition, trade deficits between countries, and deregulation. All these are macro-level economic forces that mean lower incomes for middle-class workers. The wealthiest 1% earned 21.5% of income gains in the last economic expansion, resulting in two thirds of income gains going to the top 1% (Feller and Stone 2009). Changes in class groups are largely due to changes in the occupational structure and transformations in the global economy. The upward movement among the few who have received huge gains in earning power is causing wages and earnings to become more unequal.

Video Link 7.5
Watch more about class in the United States.

Upper-middle-class families typically have high income, high education, high occupational level (in terms of prestige and other satisfactions), and high participation in political life and voluntary associations. Families enjoy a stable life, stressing companionship, privacy, pleasant surroundings in safe neighborhoods, property ownership, and stimulating associations. They stress internalization of moral standards of right and wrong, taking responsibility for one's own actions, learning to make one's own decisions, and training for future leadership positions.

The *middle to lower middle class* include small businesspeople and farmers, semiprofessionals (teachers, local elected officials, social workers, nurses, police officers, firefighters), middle-management personnel, both private and public, and sales and clerical workers in comfortable office settings. Families in this class are relatively stable. They participate in community life, and although they are less active in political life than the upper classes, they are more politically involved than those in classes below them. Children are raised to work hard and obey authority. Therefore, child-rearing patterns more often involve swift physical punishment for misbehavior than talk and reasoning, which is typical of the upper middle class.

Thinking Sociologically

How does today's popular culture on TV and in films, magazines, and popular music reflect interests of different social classes? How are poor people depicted? Who is responsible for their poverty? Do any of these depictions question the U.S. class system? What kinds of music are class based?

Poverty: Multilevel Determinants and Social Policy

One hardly expects to see hunger in rich countries, yet 4% of U.S. households did not have enough food and were skipping meals in 2008. Demand at food pantries was up

This little boy sits at the feet of an aid worker. How much power do you imagine this little African boy's parents have to make sure their child's needs are met? This boy and his family have personal troubles because the meso and macro systems of his society have failed to work effectively for individual families. Compare his circumstances to that of the little girl with her cell phone in a limousine.

20% (Sells 2008), and the Food Stamp Program had a record 32.2 million recipients in a single month in 2009, a 20% increase over the previous year (Food Research and Action Center 2009). These poor come from rural areas, urban slums, and disprivileged groups such as the homeless, unemployed, single parents, disabled, elderly, and migrant workers. With downturns in employment, low wages, and reduced aid to poor families, hunger and poor health in the United States are likely to continue. Unfortunately, the situation is getting more desperate globally as well. In 2006, there had been 854 million people facing undernutrition. By 2009, 1.02 billion people, or 15% of the world's population, went to bed hungry every night. Of the 10.9 million deaths of children each year, 5 million are directly related to undernutrition (World Hunger Facts 2009).

Most poor people have no property-based income and no permanent or stable work, only casual or intermittent earnings in the labor market. They often depend on help from government agencies or private organizations to survive. In short, they have personal troubles in large part because they have been unable to establish linkages and networks in the meso- and macro-level organizations of our social world. They have no collective power and, thus, little representation of their interests and needs in the political system.

While these men may look impoverished by North American standards, they are relatively well off in comparison with many urban neighbors in India, for they own a method of transportation that can earn a cash income, providing food and shelter for their families. Their poverty is usually not absolute.

Thinking Sociologically

Explain how your family's ability to provide food for its members is connected to the meso and macro levels of society.

Sociologists recognize two basic types of poverty: (1) absolute poverty and (2) relative poverty. **Absolute poverty**, not having resources to meet basic needs, means no prestige, no access to power, no accumulated wealth, and insufficient means to survive. Whereas absolute poverty in the United States is quite limited, the Dalits of India, described earlier in "Sociology Around the World" (The Outcastes of India), provide an example of absolute poverty. Some die of diseases that might be easily cured in other people because their bodies are weakened by chronic and persistent hunger and almost total lack of medical attention.

Relative poverty refers to those whose income falls below the poverty line, resulting in an inadequate standard of living relative to others in a given country. In most industrial countries, relative poverty means shortened life expectancy, higher infant mortality, and poorer health, but not many people die of starvation or easily curable diseases, such as influenza.

The *feminization of poverty* refers to the trend in which single females, increasingly younger and with children, make up a growing proportion of those in poverty. Vicki's situation provides one such example. After her parents divorced, she quit high school to take odd jobs to help her mother pay the bills. At 18, she was pregnant, and the baby's father was out of the picture, so Vicki lived on government aid because without a high school degree, she could not get a job that paid enough to support herself and her baby and certainly not enough to pay for health insurance. She eventually could not pay her rent and lived out of her car, which did not run because she lacked the money to repair it. Her life spiraled out of control, and her daughter has now been placed in foster care.

We do not like to admit that this can happen in affluent North American and European countries, and we try to blame the victim (why did Vicki drop out of high school, get pregnant, not have an abortion). Still, people do what they must to survive. This problem is heightened as many middle-class women are pushed into poverty through divorce. Some of them sacrificed their own careers for husbands and family so their earning power is reduced, yet many are unable to collect child support from the fathers. The numbers in poverty are highest in and around large central cities such as Paris, France; Mexico City, Mexico; Sao Paulo, Brazil; and Caracas, Venezuela. In the United States, numbers are highest in cities such as New York, Chicago, Detroit, Cleveland, and Los Angeles, where the percentage of poor African American families headed by females reaches close to 50% in some cities. Girls who grow up in female-headed households or foster homes, without a stable family model, are more likely to become single teen mothers and to live in poverty, causing disruption in their schooling and setting limits on their employment possibilities and marital opportunities.

Conflict theorists argue that poor women, especially women of color, in capitalistic economic systems are used as a reserve labor force that can be called on when labor is needed and dismissed when not needed (Aguirre and Baker 2007; Ehrenreich 2001). They are an easily exploited group.

Those in poverty live under constant stress that can cause mental or physical breakdowns and alienation from the social system. Some turn to alcohol or drugs to escape the pressure and failure or to crime to get money to pay the bills. Poor physical and mental health, inadequate nutrition, high mortality rates, obesity, low self-esteem, feelings of hopelessness, daily struggle to survive, and dependence on others are a few of the individual consequences of poverty within our social world. In addition, costs to the larger society are great:

- The loss of talents and abilities that these people could contribute
- Expenditure of tax dollars to address their needs or to regulate their lives with social workers and police
- The contradictions of their lives with cultural values: The United States claims that all citizens "are created equal" and are worthy of respect, yet not all can "make it" in U.S. society.

Welfare programs in affluent countries are only one of a number of kinds of government assistance programs. In the United States, such programs are often thought of as unearned giveaways for the poor. However, there are massive programs of government support for people at all levels of the social system: tax breaks for wealthy business owners, farmers, oil companies, and financial institutions; universal health care provided in most affluent countries; university students pay nothing or little to attend college in some countries. Support is clearly not just for the poor. The question is whether affluence and prosperity are viewed as collectively created and shared rather than as individual achievements.

Thinking Sociologically

Why is it that programs to help the poor are often stigmatized in the United States as unearned giveaway programs, whereas tax breaks and other programs for the wealthy often go unnoticed?

For most societies, poverty means loss of labor, a drain on other members in society to support the poor, and extensive health care and crime prevention systems. Those working with people in poverty generally argue that the elimination of poverty takes money and requires choices by policymakers to *do* something about poverty but could save societies in the long run. Some argue that poverty will never be eliminated because poor people are needed in society. Consider the position put forth in the next "Sociology in Our Social World."

Eliminating Poverty: Some Policy Considerations

Government programs in the United States and other countries are designed to help individuals through difficult times, especially during economic downturns. The stated goal of most public and private poverty reduction and welfare programs is to change factors that perpetuate poverty, but this requires money, jobs, and remodeling our social institutions. Some policymakers suggest attacking the problem of poverty institution by institution, offering incentives for family stability, for students to finish high school, and for job training. The Joint Center for Poverty Research, among other think tanks, has set forth policies based on research to reduce poverty (Poverty Research News 2002). Can welfare reform plans "end welfare as we know it" as policymakers claim?

Welfare and Other Aid Programs

Most Global North countries provide assistance to citizens who need help when unemployed, sick, or elderly. Some of the U.S. Great Society programs of the 1960s and 1970s were successful in reducing poverty by attacking the root causes. The Women, Infants, and Children Program provides nutritional help, and Head Start provides early childhood education. Both programs have received good grades for helping poor women and children, but funding to some of these programs has been cut back due to other funding priorities, and as a result, their effectiveness has diminished (which will surely lead to criticism of its ineffectiveness). Other programs—Aid to Families With Dependent Children, Medicaid, Medicare, food stamps—helped many who had short-term problems but were criticized as creating dependence of families on aid (Blank 2002; Corbett 1994–1995; Haskins 2006).

Britain, France, the United States, and other countries have instituted work-incentive programs such as *workfare* that encourage or require recipients of aid to work or attend job training in order to qualify for food stamps. In the United States, able-bodied unemployed or underemployed adults must work 20 to 30 hours a week, be receiving on-the-job training, or be getting education in basic skills or college work to qualify for assistance for up to 5 years. Since

Sociology in Our Social World

The Functions of Poverty: Why We Need Poor People

Surely wealthy countries such as the United States have the means to eliminate poverty if they choose to do so. Its persistence invites debate. Some sociologists argue that poverty serves certain purposes or *functions* for society (Gans 1971, 1995), and these make it difficult to address the problem directly and systematically. Some people actually benefit from having poor people kept poor. Consider the following points:

1. The fact that some people are in poverty provides us with a convenient scapegoat for societal problems. We have individuals to blame for poverty—the poor individuals themselves—and can ignore meso- and macro-level causes of poverty that would be expensive to resolve.

2. Having poor people creates many jobs for those who are not poor, including "helping" professions such as social workers as well as law enforcement jobs such as police, judges, and prison workers.

3. The poor provide an easily available group of laborers to do work, and they serve as surplus workers to hire for undesirable jobs.

4. The poor serve to reinforce and legitimate our own lives and institutions. Their existence allows the rest of us to feel superior to someone, enhancing our self-esteem.

5. Their violation of mainstream values helps remind us of those values, thereby constantly reaffirming the values among the affluent.

This perspective can be extended to poverty on the global scale.

1. Just as poor U.S. laborers can be hired for undesirable jobs, the global poor work at very low wages to provide consumers in wealthy nations with low-cost goods.

2. The gifted and talented individuals in poor societies often migrate to wealthier nations, creating a brain drain that removes human capital from poor states and increases it in wealthy states.

3. The poor of the world are blamed for macro-level social problems such as overpopulation and terrorism. As with our local poor, their existence allows us to overlook the macro-level causes of poverty.

From this perspective, the poor serve a role in the structure of society. Therefore, some groups of people, be it individuals or nations, will always be at the bottom of the stratification ladder.

1996, when welfare reform was legislated, the number of people on welfare has dropped 57% in the United States. Child poverty rates have also dropped, although they are still high compared with other countries (MacDougal 2005).

Work-incentive programs have gained adherents who argue that many welfare recipients would work if provided support and motivation. In addition to micro-level incentives such as child care and work training, success in helping people out of poverty depends on meso-level economic conditions: Are there jobs available at living wages? Are taxpayers, many of whom are attracted to politicians who cut taxes, willing to provide money for social programs to help the "invisible" poor out of poverty as well as subsidies provided for other groups? In fact, institutions such as prisons absorb public funds that could go to poverty reduction, yet crime is often a result of people in poverty feeling that they have no other options for survival.

Information needed by policymakers to establish sound policies is often provided by social research centers. Data collected on social problems such as poverty, drug problems, and welfare affect governmental decisions about how to deal most effectively with problems. The next "The Applied Sociologist at Work" provides an example of one sociology major who became an activist in the welfare rights movement, attempting to influence policymakers.

Video Link 7.6
Consider the affect of aid on poverty.

The Applied Sociologist at Work—Karen Schaumann

The Struggle for Welfare Rights in Michigan

By Jay Weinstein

Drawing on a long history of welfare rights activism at the national, state, and even local levels, Karen Schaumann's involvement in the welfare rights movement at Eastern Michigan University (EMU) began when she returned to school as a recently divorced, low-income single parent. Prior to returning to school, she had looked for employment and was unable to find a job that would even cover day-care expenses for her then 3- and 1-year-old daughters. She notes that "returning to school was the best decision I'd made in some time. However, it was really a struggle dealing with the welfare bureaucracy. If you didn't know your rights, you pretty much had none."

As a graduate student, Karen took a leadership role in creating a local welfare rights union. Later, she became its faculty sponsor and began a campaign that continues to this day to organize and educate welfare recipients about how the welfare system operates. For Karen, "Being able to help generation after generation of low-income Eastern Michigan University students (and staff) achieve a college degree is one of the most rewarding things I've done professionally."

Karen and others in a similar position learned from women in leadership of Michigan Welfare Rights that there was power in their numbers. They found they needed to advocate for each other with the state welfare department where they encountered social class bias. Some agency personnel devalued them, displayed a lack of respect, and stereotyped them and their children. The union organization's main achievement on the micro level was helping families survive and navigate the confusing bureaucracy. Many of those in the core group were able to finish college, although it took them longer than most students.

At the meso level, the union helped to create an advisory board for the Michigan Department of Human Services/Family Independence; it also worked with legal services to create training for recipients and agencies. In cooperation with the Poverty Law Program at the University of Michigan, the group successfully challenged policies that endangered the lives of women escaping domestic violence. The union helped to create a viable advocacy force. Members traveled to Washington, D.C., to lobby against welfare reform, so their actions took on a macro-level dimension as well.

The group set up tent cities in Detroit, Ann Arbor, Flint, and Lansing to protest the elimination of general assistance in the cold winter of 1991. These tent cities became a practical way station for hundreds of ex-recipients who had been evicted from "welfare hotels" into the snowy Michigan winter. Karen recalls that "we saw people who were locked out without coats, boots, or identification. You name it, we saw it. I personally remember a man named Jesse in the Detroit tent city, confined to a wheelchair by the time he reached us. He had lost his feet from frostbite."

Karen continues to help interested college students, faculty members, and community members organize for mutual survival. Karen's work exemplifies applied sociology in that it requires a sociological imagination—the ability to connect private troubles with public issues. Once people realize that they are not alone in their struggle, they have taken an important first step. In this work, the sociologist is "close to the ground" and is well aware of where the problems are. The job is to help to solve those problems, on both the micro and macro levels. When policymakers and legislators claim that welfare reform is a "success," the sociologist is able to point to measures of child well-being and statistics that show that merely declaring a case closed does not mean that a family has moved out of poverty.

Karen Schaumann received her BA and MA degrees in sociology from Eastern Michigan University (EMU) in Ypsilanti. She went on to serve as a lecturer in sociology at EMU and is currently on the faculty of nearby Schoolcraft College. Karen invites sociology teachers and students who are interested in doing something similar to send an e-mail message to her at kschauman@emich.edu. The union will send you a packet called *How to Start a Welfare Rights Union*. Her motto is: "Don't Agonize, Organize!"

Note: Jay Weinstein, professor of sociology, received his doctorate and bachelor's degrees from University of Illinois–Urbana and his master's from Washington University–St. Louis. He currently holds the position of editor-in-chief of *Applied Social Science Journal*.

Thinking Sociologically

Recalling what you have learned about poverty, how would you develop a plan to attack the problem of poverty within your community or country taking into account factors at the different levels—micro, meso, and macro? Are the root causes a matter of job training, family values, breaking the cycle, welfare support, or something else?

NATIONAL AND GLOBAL DIGITAL DIVIDE: MACRO-LEVEL STRATIFICATION

Mamadou from Niger and Eric from Ghana answer their cell phones to the sound of chimes from London's Big Ben clock tower and a Bob Marley song. One speaks in Kanuri and French and the other in Twi to friends thousands of miles away. They are the future generation of elites from the Global South, fluent in the languages of several countries, of computers, and of the digital age. Many of their fellow citizens in Niger and Ghana in Africa are not so fortunate. They live subsistence lives and have little contact with the digital world swirling overhead through satellite connections. This represents the *digital divide*, the gap between those with access to information technology and those without it. The lines of the divide are drawn by socioeconomic status, minority group, and urban versus rural residence (Mehra, Merkel, and Bishop 2004).

The world economic and political institutions are increasingly based on producing and transmitting information through digital technology. Few tools are more important in this process than the computer, Internet, and cell phones. In nearly every salaried and professional position, computer knowledge and ability to navigate the Internet are critical employment skills. Individuals with insufficient access to computers and lack of technical skills face barriers to many professions and opportunities. Because computer skills are important for personal success, this is an important micro-level issue. The digital divide is breaking down for some young and elite members of developing societies such as Mamadou and Eric, but many individuals and Global South countries have insufficient technology and educated population to participate in this new economy (Drori 2006; Nakamura 2004).

The number of Internet users around the globe increased from 16 million in 1995 to 500 million in 2001 to 1.3 billion in 2007 (Drori 2006; Miniwatts Marketing Group 2008), mostly in affluent Global North countries, especially among the young and well educated (Horrigan and Smith 2007).

In Laos where many people live in grass houses such as this one (top), there is no reliable electricity or other support systems for Internet technology. Few people in such communities even know about the resources available through the World Wide Web. That contrasts with homes like the bottom one, where computers are seen as necessary equipment and are taken for granted.

For most users, English is the language, although it is the second most spoken language of more than 200 million users. Chinese is the next most popular language on the Internet, and its use is increasing at a high rate. Access to the Internet is not equal around the world (Gibson 1999). In the United States, one of the most wired countries in the world, many poor people do not have access to computers or mentors to teach them how to use computers. This digital divide is beginning to close, but it still creates barriers for many (Nakamura 2004; Shade 2004).

Comparing countries cross-nationally, only 5% of the total world population is online, but more than 50% of residents in North America and Scandinavia (Sweden, Norway, Finland, Denmark, and Iceland) are connected. About 79% of the online population lives in nations that belong to the Organization for Economic and Cooperative Development—countries that hold 14% of the people on the planet. In contrast, in sub-Saharan Africa and in India, only 4 out of every 1,000 citizens use the Internet (Drori 2006). About 97% of Internet hosts are in the Global North (which has only 16% of the world's population), and 66% of income from royalties and licensing fees goes to two countries: the United States (54%) and Japan (12%). In some countries, the monthly access fee for hooking up to the Internet is stunningly high compared with the average monthly income: in Bangladesh, 191%; in Nepal, 278%; and in Madagascar, 614%. This may be the reason why 35 of the poorest countries in the world have less than 1% of the Internet users (Drori 2006).

An additional difficulty is that most Web sites and e-mail services use English, computer keyboards are designed with a Western alphabet, and some of the digital systems in computers are established on the basis of English symbols and logic—a fact that many of us may not think about as we use the system (Drori 2006). For people who are struggling for the very survival of their culture, the dominance of English may feel like a threat, one more example of Western dominance. So resistance to the use of computers and the Internet is more than a matter of finances or technology. There may be cultural objections as well.

Policy decisions at the international level affect the status of the Global South. The United Nations, the International Monetary Fund, and other international organizations have pressured countries to develop their Internet capacities. Indeed, this is sometimes used as a criterion for ranking countries in terms of their "level of modernization" (Drori 2006). Countries that have not been able to get "in the game" of Internet technology cannot keep pace with a rapidly evolving global economy.

Internet technology has created a digital divide, but it also has had some beneficial economic impacts, stimulating jobs in poor countries. In 1999, computer component parts were a substantial percentage of production in some poor countries: 52% of Malaysia's exports, 44% of Costa Rica's, and 28% of Mexico's. The high-tech revenue for India increased from US$150 million in 1990 to US$4 billion in 1999. On the less positive side, e-waste from electronic equipment is extremely toxic, and it is almost always shipped to poor countries, where extremely poor people must deal with the consequences of toxic pollution (Drori 2006).

Digital technology is an example of one important force changing the micro- and macro-level global stratification system—a spectrum of people and countries from the rich and elite to those that are poor and desperate.

Thinking Sociologically

What evidence of the digital divide do you see in your family, community, nation, and world? For instance, can your grandparents program their VCR? Do they know how to work a cell phone or navigate the Internet? Could they create their own Facebook page if asked to do so?

The Global "Digital Divide" and Social Policy

Bengaluru (Bangalore) is home to India's booming digital industries, which are successfully competing in the global high-tech market. Yet many villages and cities in India provide examples of the contrasts between the caste system and the emerging class system. In traditional rural agricultural areas, change is extremely slow despite laws forbidding differential treatment of outcastes and mandating change. In urban industrial areas, new opportunities are changing the traditional caste structures, as intercaste and intracaste competition for wealth and power is increasing with the changes in economic, political, and other institutional structures. The higher castes were the first to receive the education and lifestyle that create industrial leaders. Now, shopkeepers, wealthy peasants, teachers, and others are vying for power. Within the world system, India is generally economically poor but is developing certain economic sectors rapidly. Thus, India is in transition both internally and in the global world system.

In India and other countries, village access to television programming has increased dramatically, with 30 million Indian households adding cable service between 2001 and 2006. As more women are exposed to images of lifestyles in urban areas and other countries—including stories of women working outside the home, controlling money, and attaining high levels of education—new possibilities are opened. Access to private cable television also has helped promote female autonomy, decreased wife beating, reduced preferences for sons over daughters, increased female school enrollment, and decreased fertility (Jensen and Oster 2007). Technology is bringing the world to remote villages, opening new horizons and options, and changing lifestyles.

As poor countries transition into the electronic age, some such as India are making policies that facilitate rapid modernization. They are passing over developmental stages that rich countries went through. As an illustration, consider the telephone. In 2002, 90% of all telephones in the world were cell phones, many using satellite connections. Some countries never did get completely wired for land lines, thus eliminating one phase of phone technology. With satellite technology in place, some computer and Internet options are available without expensive intermediate steps (Drori 2006). In 20 years, cell phones that originated for the business elite have become a personal item. Use in poor countries has boomed, giving people access to health care and other services. By the beginning of 2007, 68% of the world's cell phone subscriptions were in Global South countries ("Cell phone use" 2007; Klein and Ember 2009; Rodgers 2009). Based on a 2009 UN report, 60% of the world uses mobile phones with 4.1 billion cell phone subscriptions worldwide (Barker 2009). In the United States, 20% of homes use cell phones exclusively and 60% use both cell and landline phones (Seeking Alpha 2009).

Positive efforts are underway to provide cheap technology to Global South countries. Currently, 23% of the world's population uses the Internet; in Africa, the figure is 1 in 20, and in rich nations the figure is much greater (Barker 2009). The "One Laptop per Child" Foundation is helping fund efforts to develop efficient small laptops for children around the world. Linux and Novatium, to name just two companies, are developing $100 computers, and some governments are buying them in large numbers for their schools (Rubenstein 2007). Engineers in India, working through an organization called Simputer Trust, have been designing a simple computer (a "simputer") that will be less expensive and will have more multilingual capacities than the PC. Such efforts will enhance access of poor countries to the computer and Internet and will provide the means for children in poor countries to become part of the competitive global stratification system. Technology is leveling the world playing field (Drori 2006; Friedman 2005).

Journal Article Link 7.2
Read about the digital divide.

We leave this discussion of stratification systems, including class systems, with a partial answer to the question posed in the beginning of this chapter: Why are some people rich and others poor? In the next two chapters, we expand the discussion to include other variables in stratification systems—race, ethnicity, and gender.

By the end of these chapters, the answer to the opening questions—why some are rich—should be even clearer. Socioeconomic status is important as a measure in any society, but it is not the sole basis for stratification. In the next chapter, we look at the role of race and ethnicity in social inequality.

What Have We Learned?

Perhaps your understanding of why you are rich or poor—and what effect your socioeconomic status has on what you buy, what you believe, and where you live—has taken on new dimensions. Perhaps you have gained some insight into what factors affect your ability to move up in the social class system. The issue of social stratification calls into question the widely held belief in the fairness of our economic system. By studying this issue, we better understand why some individuals are able to experience prestige (respect) and to control power and wealth at the micro, meso, and macro levels of the social system, while others have little access to those resources. Few social forces affect your personal life at the micro level as much as stratification. That includes the decisions you make about what you wish to do with your life or who you might marry. Indeed, stratification influenced the fact that you are reading this book.

Key Points

- Stratification—the layering or ranking of people within society—is one of the most important factors shaping the life chances of individuals. This ranking is influenced by micro, meso, and macro forces and resources. (See pp. 207–209.)

- Various theories of stratification disagree on whether inequality is functional or destructive to society and its members. The evolutionary perspective suggests ways stratification can be positive, but much of the inequality currently experienced creates problems for individuals and societies. (See pp. 209–213.)

- For individuals, personal respect (prestige) is experienced as highly personal, but it is influenced by the way the social system works at the meso and macro level—from access to education and the problems created by gender and ethnic discrimination to population trends and the vitality of the global economy. (See pp. 213–214.)

- People without adequate connections to the meso and macro levels are likely to experience less power, wealth, and prestige. (See pp. 214–216.)

- Some macro systems stress ascribed status (assigned to one, often at birth, without consideration of one's individual choices, talents, or intelligence). Other systems purport to be open and based on achieved status (depending on one's contributions to the society and one's personal abilities and decisions). Unlike the caste system, the class system tends to stress achieved status, although it does not always perform openly. (See pp. 216–230.)

- The elements of stratification are complex, with property, power, and prestige having somewhat independent influence on the system of inequality and on one's standing. (See pp. 229–231.)

- Poverty itself is a difficult problem, one that can be costly to a society as a whole. But various solutions at the micro, meso, or macro levels have had mixed results, partially, perhaps, because it is in the interests of those with privilege to have an underclass to do the unpleasant jobs. (See pp. 232–236.)

- Technology is both a contributor and a possible remedy to inequality, as the digital divide creates problems for the poor, but electronic innovations may create new opportunities in the social structure for networking and connections to the meso and macro levels—even for those in the Global South, the poor regions of the world. (See pp. 237–239.)

Contributing to Our Social World: What Can We Do?

At the Local Level

Community shelters for homeless people and soup kitchens: These are locations where homeless and very poor people can get shelter and a free meal. These organizations often need volunteer help or interns. Also, donate leftover food from events to a shelter.

Tip service people in minimum-wage jobs: Hotel housekeeping maids, meal servers at restaurants, and employees at fast-food restaurants may depend on tips to survive.

At the Organizational or Institutional Level

Habitat for Humanity: Participants work with current and prospective home owners in repairing or constructing housing for little or no cost. Habitat projects are under way or planned for many communities in the United States and around the world. See the organization's Web site for more details at www.habitat.org.

AmeriCorps: Founded in the early 1990s, AmeriCorps involves 1 year of service volunteers in a wide range of jobs, including teaching and community service. The experience and contribution to those in need provide rewards. See the AmeriCorps Web site at www.americorps.gov.

At the National and Global Levels

Peace Corps: This involves a serious, long-term commitment, but most who have done it agree that it was well worth the time and energy. The Peace Corps is an independent agency of the U.S. government, founded in 1961. Volunteers work in foreign countries throughout the world, helping local people improve their economic conditions, health, and education. The Peace Corps Web site (www.peacecorps.gov) provides information on the history of the organization, volunteer opportunities, and reports of former and present volunteers.

Sociologists Without Borders (or *Sociólogos sin Fronteras*) requires a shorter-term global commitment and has some paid internships. (Check www.sociologistswithoutborders.org.) This organization promotes human rights globally.

Grameen Bank (www.grameen-info.org or www.grameenfoundation.org): This micro-credit organization was started in Bangladesh by Professor Muhammad Yunus, winner of the 2006 Nobel Peace Prize. It makes small business loans to people who live in impoverished regions of the world and who have no collateral for a loan. Consider doing a local fundraiser with friends for the Grameen Bank or other micro-credit organizations, such as Finca and Care International.

 For chapter-specific resources, including **Frontline**, **TED**, and **YouTube** videos; self-quizzes; web exercises; and more, visit **www.pineforge.com/oswmedia3e.**

Race and Ethnic Group Stratification

Beyond "We" and "They"

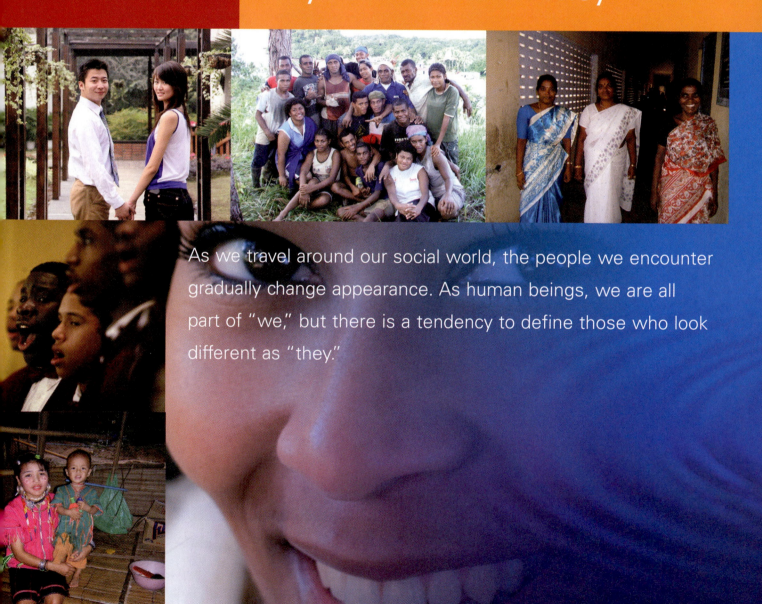

As we travel around our social world, the people we encounter gradually change appearance. As human beings, we are all part of "we," but there is a tendency to define those who look different as "they."

Global Community

Society

National Organizations,
Institutions, and Ethnic Subcultures

Local Organizations
and Community

Me (and My
Minority
Friends)

Micro: Local reference groups:
Exclusion of ethnic group members

Meso: Policies in large organizations that
intentionally or unintentionally discriminate

Macro: Laws or court rulings that
set policy related to discrimination

Macro: Racial and ethnic hostilities resulting
in wars, genocide, or ethnic cleansing

Think About It	
Me (and My Inner Circle)	What makes you look different from those around you? What relevance do these differences have for your life?
Local Community	Why do people in the local community categorize "others" into racial or ethnic groups?
National Institutions; Complex Organizations; Ethnic Groups	How are privilege and disprivilege embedded in institutions—so that they operate independently of personal bias or prejudice?
National Society	Why are minority group members in most countries economically poorer than dominant group members?
Global Community	In what ways might ethnicity or race shape international negotiations and global problem solving? What can you do to make the world a better place for all people?

When Siri wakes, it is about noon. In the instant of waking, she knows exactly who and what she has become . . . the soreness in her genitals reminds her of the 15 men she had sex with the night before. Siri is 15 years old. Sold by her impoverished parents a year ago, she finds that her resistance and her desire to escape the brothel are breaking down and acceptance and resignation are taking their place. . . . Siri is very frightened that she will get AIDS . . . as many girls from her village return home to die from AIDS after being sold into the brothels. (Bales 2002:207–209)

Siri is a sex slave, just like millions of other young women around the world. Slavery is not limited to poor countries: Dora was enslaved in a home in Washington, D.C., and domestic slaves have been discovered in London, Chicago, New York, and Los Angeles. The Central Intelligence Agency (CIA) reports that thousands of women and children are smuggled into the United States and European countries each year as sex and domestic slaves or locked away in sweat shops (Bales 2004). International agencies estimate that more than 1 million children in Southeast Asia have been sold into bondage, mostly into the booming sex trade.

It may be surprising to know that slavery is alive and flourishing around the world (Free the Slaves 2005). An estimated 27 million people, mostly women and children from poor families in poor countries, are slaves, auctioned off or lured into slavery each year by kidnap gangs, pimps, and cross-border syndicates (Bales 2004, 2007; Bales and Trodd 2008). As a global phenomenon, human trafficking in slaves from places such as Ukraine, Myanmar (Burma), Laos, Nepal, and the Philippines, mostly for the commercial sex industry, is so profitable that criminal business people invest in involuntary brothels much as they would in a mining operation (Kyle and Koslowski 2001:1).

International events such as the Olympics and major soccer matches bring new markets for the sex trade. Young

In a red-light district of Kolkata (Calcutta), more than 7,000 women and girls work as prostitutes. Only one group has a lower standing: their children. Zana Briski first began photographing prostitutes in Kolkata in 1998. Living in the brothels for months at a time, she quickly developed a relationship with many of the kids who, often terrorized and abused, were drawn to the rare human companionship she offered. Because the children were fascinated by her camera, Zana taught photography to the children of the prostitutes. Learn more about her organization, Kids With Cameras, at www.kids-with-cameras.org.

foreign girls are brought in from other countries—chosen to be sex slaves because they are exotic and free from AIDS and because they cannot escape due to insufficient money and knowledge of the language of the country to which they are exported (Moritz 2001). Sometimes, poor families sell their daughters for the promise of high wages and perhaps money sent home. As a result, girls as young as 6 are held captive as prostitutes or as domestic workers. Child labor, a problem in many parts of the world, requires poor young children to do heavy labor for long hours in agriculture as well as brickmaking, match-making, and carpet factories. Although they earn little, their income helps families pay debts. Much of the cacao (used to make chocolate) and coffee (unless they are Fair Trade Certified products) that we buy also supports slavery. Cacao especially is grown and harvested at slave camps where young boys are given a choice of unpaid hard labor (with beatings for any disobedience) or death by starvation or shooting (Bales 2000, 2004). Very little chocolate is produced *without* slave labor.

Debt bondage is another form of modern-day slavery. Extremely poor families—often people with differences in appearance or culture from those with power—work in exchange for housing and meager food. Severe debt, passing from generation to generation, may also result when farmers borrow money because they face drought or need cash to keep their families from starving. The only collateral they have on the loan is themselves—put up for bondage until they can pay off the loan. No one but the wealthy landowner keeps accounting records, which results in there being no accountability. The poor families may find themselves enslaved. The lack of credit available to marginal people contributes to slavery. Because those in slavery have little voice and no rights, the world community hears little about this tragedy (Bales 2007). A recent successful international movement in impoverished areas provides women very small loans—called *micro credit*—to help them start small businesses and move out of desperate poverty and slavery. We will read more about this in future chapters.

In the slavery of the 19th century, slaves were expensive, and there was at least some economic incentive to care about their health and survival. In the new slavery, humans are cheap and replaceable. There is little concern about working them to death, especially if they are located in remote cacao or coffee plantations (Bales 2000). By current dollars, a slave in the southern United States would have cost as much as $40,000, but contemporary slaves are cheap. They can be procured from poor countries for an average of $90 (Bales 2004). The cost is $40 in Mali for a young male and $1,000 in Thailand for an HIV-free female (Free the Slaves 2008). Slaves worldwide produce an estimated $1.4 billion in produce and profits for their owners each year. Employers can legally exploit and abuse them with long hours and without legal interference because the slaves owe money.

What is the significance of slavery for our discussion of race and ethnic group stratification? What all these human bondage situations have in common is that poor minority group members are victimized. Because many slaves are members of ethnic, racial, religious, tribal, gender, age, caste, or other minority groups with no cultural capital and have obvious physical or cultural distinctions from the people who exploit them, they are at a distinct disadvantage in the stratification system. Although all humans have the same basic characteristics, few people have a choice about being born into a minority group, and it is difficult to change that minority status. Visible barriers include physical appearance, names, dress, language, or other distinguishing characteristics. Historical conditions and conflicts rooted in religious, social, political, and historical events set the stage for dominant or minority status, and people are socialized into their dominant or subservient group.

Minority- or dominant-group status affects most aspects of people's experiences in the social world. These include status in the community, socialization experience, residence, opportunities for success in education and occupation, the religious group to which they belong, and the health care they receive. In fact, it is impossible to separate minority status from position in the stratification system (Aguirre and Turner 2006; Farley 2009; Rothenberg 2007).

In this chapter, we explore the characteristics of race and ethnic groups that lead to differential placement in stratification systems, including problems at the micro, meso, and macro levels—prejudice, racism, and discrimination. The next chapter considers ascribed status based on gender. The topics in this chapter and the next continue the discussion of stratification: who is singled out for differential treatment, why they are singled out, the consequences for both the individuals and the society, and some actions or policies that deal with differential treatment.

Encyclopedia Link 8.1
Read a history
of slavery.

In India, slaves are used to extract slate from mines, which is then used to make cheap pencils for export. The key to slavery is exploitation of the powerlessness of some humans by those who need cheap labor. Young children who have no family are often sucked into slavery, as these children were.

The Fair Trade Certified symbol signifies that products such as coffee, tea, and chocolate (made from cacao) meet sustainable development goals, help support family farmers at fair prices, and are not produced by slave labor. Much of the work on cacao plantations is done by child slaves smuggled from poor countries.

Thinking Sociologically

Poor people around the world often lose control over their lives. What situations can lead to this condition, and what are the consequences for these people?

What Characterizes Racial and Ethnic Groups?

Migration, war and conquest, trade, and intermarriage have left virtually every geographical area of the world populated by groups of people with varying ethnicities. In this section, we consider the characteristics that set groups apart, especially groups that fall at the lower end of the stratification system.

Minority Groups

Several factors characterize **minority groups** and their relations with dominant groups in society (Dworkin and Dworkin 1999):

1. Minority groups can be distinguished from the group that holds power by factors that make them different—physical appearance, dress, language, or religion.

2. Minority groups are excluded or denied full participation at the meso level of society in economic, political, educational, religious, health, and recreational institutions.

3. Minority groups have less access to power and resources within the nation and are evaluated less favorably based on their characteristics as minority group members.

4. Minority groups are stereotyped, ridiculed, condemned, or otherwise defamed, allowing dominant group members to justify and not feel guilty about unequal and poor treatment.

5. Minority group members develop collective identities to insulate themselves from the unaccepting world; this in turn perpetuates their group identity by creating ethnic or racial enclaves, intragroup marriages, and segregated group institutions such as religious congregations.

Because minority status changes with time and ideology, the minority group may be the dominant group in a different time or society. Throughout England's history, wars and assassinations changed the ruling group from Catholic to Protestant and back several times. In Iraq, Shiite Muslims are dominant in numbers and now also in power, but they were a minority under Saddam Hussein's Sunni rule. Map 8.1 indicates the location of major minority groups in the United States today, although you should be aware that the density of groups in a particular location changes over time.

Dominant groups are not always the numerical majority. In the case of South Africa, possession of advanced European weapons placed the native African Bantu population under the rule of a small percentage of White British and Dutch descendants in what became a complex system of planned discrimination called *apartheid*. Until recently, each major group—White, mixed colored, and Black—had its own living area, and members carried identification cards showing the "race" to which they belonged. In this case, racial classification and privilege were defined by the laws of the dominant group.

Thinking Sociologically

Look again at the list of minority group characteristics above. Explain how some people might be affected at the micro family level, the meso institutional level, and the macro levels of society, depending on their membership in dominant or minority groups.

The Concept of Race

Racial minority is one of the two types of minority groups most common in the social world. The other is ethnic groups. A **race** is a group identified by a society because

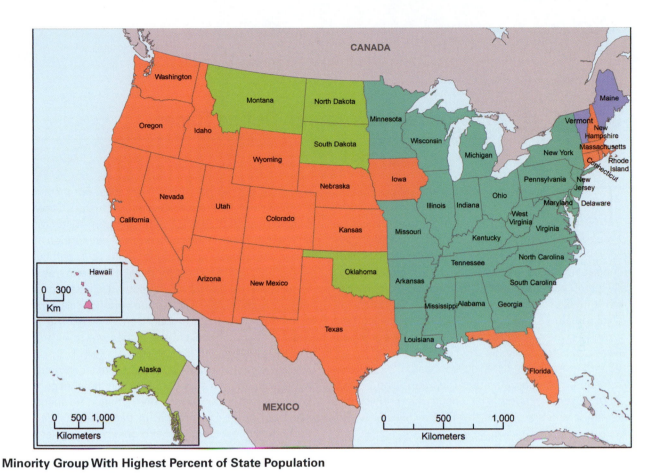

Minority Group With Highest Percent of State Population

Excluding the category "White, not Hispanic"

■ Asian   ■ Black   ■ Hispanic   ■ Native American   ■ Two or more ethnic groups, not Hispanic

Map 8.1   Prevalence of Minority Ethnic Groups in the United States

Source: U.S. Census Bureau 2000. Map by Anna Versluis.

of certain biologically inherited physical characteristics. However, in practice, it is impossible to accurately identify racial types. Most attempts at racial classifications have been based on combinations of appearance, such as skin color and shade, stature, facial features, hair color and texture, head form, nose shape, eye color and shape, height, and blood or gene type. Our discussion of race focuses on three issues: (1) origins of the concept of race, (2) the social construction of race, and (3) the significance of race versus class.

Origins of the Concept of Race

In the 18th and 19th centuries, scientists attempted to divide humans into four major groupings—Mongoloid, Caucasoid, Negroid, and Australoid—and then into more than 30 racial subcategories. In reality, few individuals fit

clearly into any of these types. The "Sociology in Our Social World" on page 248 provides insight into the origins of racial categories that have had a major impact on history and form the basis for many conflicts today.

From their earliest origins in East Africa more than 7 million years ago, humans slowly spread around the globe, south through Africa, north to Europe, and across Asia. Many scholars believe that humans crossed the Bering Straits from Asia to North America around 20,000 BCE and continued to populate North and South America (Diamond 1999). Physical adaptations of isolated groups to their environments originally resulted in some differences in physical appearance—skin color, stature, hair type—but mixing of peoples over the centuries has left few if any genetically isolated people, only gradations as one moves around the world. Thus, the way societies choose to define race has come about largely through what is culturally convenient for the dominant group.

Sociology in Our Social World

Historical Attempts to Define Race

Throughout history, political and religious leaders, philosophers, and even scientists have struggled with the meaning and significance of race. The first systematic classification of all living phenomena was published in 1735 by Carl von Linne (Linnaeus). His hierarchy of species was actually quite complex, including monkeys, elephants, and angels. His work was based on the study of fossil remains of various species, implying evolution of the species over time. Then, in 1758, he published *Systema Naturae*, in which he suggested four human types: Americanus (Native Americans), Asiaticus, Africanus, and Europeanus (Cashmore and Troyna 1990). Other scientists proposed other divisions. Johann Blumenbach was the first to use the word *race* in his 1775 classification system: Caucasian, Mongolian, Ethiopian, American, and Malay.

By the 19th century, race began to take on a biological meaning and to signify inherent physical qualities in humans (Goldberg 1990). From there, it was a short step to theorizing about inherent inequalities between races. For instance, Joseph Arthur, Comte de Gobineau (1816–1882), questioned why once great societies had declined and fallen. He argued that each race has specific characteristics, and he attributed the demise of societies to the inequality of races. His book *Essay on Inequality of the Human Races*, published in 1853–1855, earned him the title "father of modern racism."

A major event in theories of race was the publication of Charles Darwin's *The Origin of Species* ([1858] 1909). Among his many ideas was that human races *might* represent the stages or branches of a tree of evolution. This idea implied that those groups of humans who were biologically best suited to the environment would survive. He argued that "natural selection," or "survival of the fittest," was true of all races in the human species, not of individuals within a species. From Darwin's ideas emerged the concepts of *survival of the fittest* and *ever-improving races.*

These two late-19th-century concepts were taken out of context and became the foundation for a number of theories of superior races. For instance, in 1899, the Brit-turned-German Houston Stewart Chamberlain (1899/1911) published an aristocratic, anti-Semitic work in which he argued that northern and western European populations, Teutonic in particular, were superior. He argued for racial purity, a theme the Nazis of the 1930s and 1940s adopted. Gustaf Kossina introduced the idea of *Volk* in his writings, claiming a commonality of traits among Germans that, he felt, qualified the German people to become the "ruling elite" (Cashmore and Troyna 1990).

Mein Kampf (1939) was Adolf Hitler's contribution to the concept of a superior race. In it, he conceptualized two races, the Aryans and Others. He focused attention on several groups, in particular the Jews. German economic and social problems were blamed on the Jews.

What followed in the name of German purity was the extermination of millions of Jews, Poles, Catholics, Gypsies, homosexuals, and other groups and individuals who were deemed "less human" or who opposed the Nazis. The extent to which Hitler succeeded exemplifies what can happen when one group needs to feel superior to others, blames other groups for its shortcomings, and has the power to act against those minorities. More recent attempts to classify groups have been based not on external characteristics but on blood or gene type, even though blood types or genomes do not always correlate with other traits.

As applied to mammals, the term *race* has biological significance only when it refers to closely inbred groups in which all family lines are alike—as in pure breeds of domesticated animals. These conditions are never realized in humans and are impossible in large populations of any species (Witzig 1996). Many groups have been mislabeled "races" when the differences are actually cultural. Jews, Poles, Irish, and Italians have all erroneously been called "races." In short, when it comes to humans, scientists do not agree about whether race is at all a biological reality.

In the 1970s, the United Nations, concerned about racial conflicts and discrimination, issued a "Statement on Race" prepared by a group of eminent scientists from around the world. This and similar statements by scientific groups point out the harmful effects of racist arguments, doctrines, and policies. The conclusion of their document upheld that (a) all people are born free and equal both in dignity and in rights, (b) prejudice retards personal development, (c) conflicts (based on race) cost nations money and resources, and (d) racism foments international conflict. Racist doctrines lack any scientific basis, as all people belong to the same species and have descended from the same origin. In summary, problems arising from race relations are social, not biological, in origin; differential treatments of groups based on "race" falsely claim a scientific basis for classifying humans. Biologically speaking, a "race" exists in any life form when two groups cannot interbreed, and if they do, the offspring are infertile/sterile. This is not true of any group of human beings. So what is the problem?

Social Construction of Race: Symbolic Interaction Analysis

Why are sociologists concerned about a concept that has little scientific accuracy and is ill defined? The answer is its social significance. The social reality is that people are defined or define themselves as belonging to a group based in part on physical appearance. As individuals try to make meaning of the social world, they may learn from others that some traits—eye or nose shape, hair texture, or skin color—are distinguishing traits that make people different. Jean Piaget, the famous cognitive psychologist, described the human tendency to classify objects as one of our most basic cognitive tools (Piaget and Inhelder [1955] 1999). This inclination has often been linked to the classifying of "racial" groups. Once in place, racial categories provide individuals with an identity based on ancestry—"my kind of people have these traits."

Symbolic interaction theory contends that if people believe something is real, it may become real in its consequences. It does not matter whether scientists say that attempts to classify people into races are inaccurate and that the word is biologically meaningless. People on the streets of your hometown think *they* know what the word *race* means. Moreover, people do look different as we traverse the globe. That people *think* there are differences has consequences. As a social concept, race has not only referred to physical features and inherited genes but has carried over to presumed psychological and moral characteristics, thus justifying discriminatory treatment. The following examples illustrate the complex problems in trying to classify people into "races."

With the enactment of "apartheid laws" in 1948, the White government in South Africa institutionalized differential laws based on their definitions of racial groups and specified the privileges and restrictions allotted to each group (Marger 2009). Bantu populations (the native Africans) and Coloreds (those of mixed blood) were restricted to separate living areas and types of work. Asians—descendants of immigrants from India and other Asian countries—received higher salaries than the Bantu groups but less than Whites, while Whites of European descent, primarily Dutch and English, had the highest living standard and best residential locations. Under the apartheid system, race was determined by tracing ancestry back for 14 generations. A single ancestor who was not Dutch or English might cause an individual to be considered "colored" rather than White. Physical features mattered little. Individuals carried a card indicating their race based on genealogy. Although this system began to break down in the 1990s due to international pressure and under the leadership of the first Black president (Nelson Mandela, elected in 1994), vestiges of these notions of "reality" will take generations to change.

In contrast, in Brazil, an individual's race is based on physical features—skin tone, hair texture, facial features, eye color, and so forth—rather than on the "one drop of blood" rule in South Africa. Brothers and sisters who have the same parents and ancestors may be classified as belonging to different races. The idea of race is based on nearly opposite criteria in Brazil and South Africa, illustrating the arbitrary nature of racial classification attempts (Keith and Herring 1991; Walker and Karas 1993).

Video Link 8.1
Watch an experiment about inequality.

Before civil rights laws were passed in the United States in the 1960s, a number of states had laws that spelled out differential treatment for racial groups. These were commonly referred to as Jim Crow laws. States in the South passed laws defining who was African American or Native American. In many cases, it was difficult to determine to which category an individual belonged. For instance, African Americans in Georgia were defined as people with any ascertainable trace of "Negro" blood in their veins. In Missouri, one eighth or more Negro blood was sufficient, whereas in Louisiana, 1/32 Negro blood defined one as Black. Differential treatment was spelled out in other states as well. In Texas, for example, the father's race determined the race of the child. In Vermont, newborn babies of racially mixed parentage were listed as "mixed" on the birth certificate. In West Virginia, a newborn was classified as "Black" if either parent was considered Black. Until the latter half of the 20th century, several U.S. states still attempted to classify the race of newborns by the percentage of Black blood or parentage (Lopez 1996). Federal law now prohibits discrimination on the basis of "racial" classifications, and most state laws that are explicitly racial have been challenged and dropped.

The Significance of Race Versus Class

From the time of slavery in the Americas until the late 20th century, race has been the determining factor in social

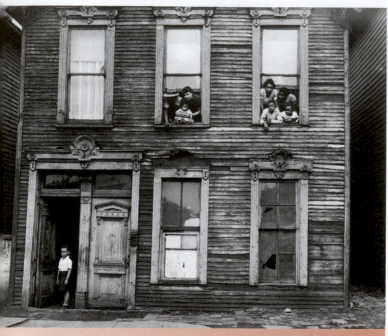

This house in the Chicago slums was not atypical of the quality of homes in segregated America in the 1940s.

stratification and opportunity for people of African descent in the United States, the Caribbean, and Brazil. Whether this is changing in the 21st century is a question that has occupied sociologists, politicians, educators, and other scientists in recent years. Some scholars argue that race is the primary cause of different placement in the stratification system, whereas others insist that race and social class are both at work, with socioeconomic factors (social class) more important than race.

Sociologist William Julius Wilson believes that the racial oppression that characterized the African American experience throughout the 19th century was caused first by slavery and then by a lingering caste structure that severely restricted upward mobility. However, the breakdown of the plantation economy and the rise of industrialism created more opportunities for African Americans to participate in the economy (W. Wilson 1978, 1993a, 1993b).

Wilson (W. 1978) argues that after World War II, an African American class structure developed with characteristics similar to those of the White class structure. Occupation and income took on ever greater significance in social position, especially for the African American middle class. However, as Black middle-class professionals moved up in the stratification structure, lower-class African American ghetto residents became more isolated and less mobile. Limited unskilled job opportunities for the lower class have resulted in poverty and stagnation so severe that some families are almost outside of the functioning economic system. Wilson (1978, 1984, 1993a) calls this group the *underclass*.

Some researchers assert that the United States cannot escape poverty because well-paid, unskilled jobs requiring few skills and little education are disappearing from the economy and because the poor are concentrated in segregated urban areas (Massey 2007; Massey and Denton 1998). Poorly educated African American teenagers and young adults see their job prospects limited to the low-wage sector (e.g., work at fast-food joints at minimum wage), and they experience record levels of unemployment. Movement out of poverty becomes almost impossible (Farley 2009; W. Wilson 1996).

Wilson's point is illustrated by the following: More than 2 in 5 African Americans are middle-class, compared with 1 in 20 in 1940. Thus, many African Americans are now middle-class. On the other hand, many adults in inner-city ghetto neighborhoods are not employed in a typical week. Thus, children in these neighborhoods may grow up without ever seeing someone go to work (W. Wilson 1996). The new global economic system is a contributing factor as unskilled jobs go abroad to cheaper labor (Friedman 2005, 2008; Massey 2007). Without addressing these structural causes of poverty, we cannot expect to reduce the number of people in the underclass—whether they are White, Black, or other minority.

A big debate among scholars surrounds the following question: Has race declined in significance and class become more important in determining placement in the stratification system? Tests of Wilson's thesis present us with mixed results (Jencks 1992). For instance, African Americans' average education level (12.4 years in school) is almost the same as Whites' (12.7 years), suggesting that they have comparable qualifications for employment. However, this equity stops at the high school level; 27.6% of Whites are college graduates, compared with 17.3% of Blacks (U.S. Census Bureau 2005c). More important, African Americans earn less than Whites in the same occupational categories. As Tables 8.1 and 8.2 make clear, income levels for African Americans, Hispanics, and Whites are not even close to being equal. Unemployment and poverty affect a higher percentage of Black families than White ones. Economics alone does not seem a complete answer to who is in the underclass.

Table 8.1	Race/Ethnicity and Family Income		
	White	*Black*	*Hispanic*
Median family annual income	64,427	40,143	40,566
Percentage of White family income		62	63

Source: U.S. Census Bureau (2009e:table 681).

Note: Figures are for 2007.

Education	White	Black	Hispanic
Not a high school graduate	21,464	17,823	18,349
High school graduate	32,083	26,368	23,472
Some college, no degree	32,917	29,308	27,586
College graduate	57,932	47,903	43,676
Master's degree	71,063	55,654	56,486
Professional degree	117,787	101,376	82,627

Table 8.2 Income (in dollars) by Educational Level and Race/Ethnicity

Source: U.S. Census Bureau (2009e:table 224).

Note: Figures are for 2007.

Ethnic enclaves have a strong sense of local community, holding festivals from the old country and developing networks in the new country. Such areas are called "ghettos" and are not necessarily impoverished. The photo depicts a street on the Lower East Side of New York, which was once a transition station and ghetto for recent immigrants.

Although racial bias has decreased at the micro (interpersonal) level, it is still a significant determinant in the lives of African Americans, especially those in the lower class. The data are complex, but we can conclude that for upwardly mobile African Americans, class may be more important than race. Still, the interplay of race, class, and gender is complex, and part contributes to class status; physical traits such as skin color cannot be dismissed (Wallace 2004).

Thinking Sociologically

On what bases do you classify people into social groups? How do you describe someone to another person? Do you use racial terms only for people of color? Why? Are people who are White "just normal"? If so, what does that say?

Ethnic Groups

The second major type of minority group—the **ethnic group**—is based on cultural factors: language, religion, dress, foods, customs, beliefs, values, norms, a shared group identity or feeling, and sometimes loyalty to a homeland, monarch, or religious leader. Members are grouped together because they share a common cultural heritage, often connected with a national or geographical identity. Some social scientists prefer to call racial groups "ethnic groups" because the term *ethnic* encompasses most minorities and avoids problems with the term *race* (Aguirre and Turner 2006).

Visits to ethnic enclaves in large cities around the world give a picture of ethnicity. Little Italy, Chinatown, Greek Town, and Polish neighborhoods may have non-English street signs and newspapers, ethnic restaurants, culture-specific houses of worship, and clothing styles that reflect the ethnic subculture. Occasionally, an ethnic group shares power in pluralistic societies, but most often they hold a minority status with little power.

How is ethnicity constructed or defined? Many very different ethnic groups have been combined in government categories, such as censuses conducted by countries, yet they speak different languages and often have very different religions. For example, in North America, ethnic group members do not view themselves as "Indian" or "Native American." Instead, they use 600 independent tribal nation names to define themselves, including the Ojibwa (Chippewa), Dineh (the Navajo), Lakota (the Sioux), and many others. Likewise, in the U.S. census, Koreans, Filipinos, Chinese, Japanese, and Malaysians come from very different cultures but are identified as *Asian Americans* in the census. People from Brazil, Mexico, and Cuba are grouped together in a category called *Hispanics* or *Latinos*. When federal funds for social services were made available to Asian Americans or American Indians, these diverse people began to think of themselves as part of a larger grouping for political purposes (Esperitu 1992). The federal government essentially created

Journal Article Link 8.1
Read about culture and Mexican restaurants.

an ethnic group by naming and providing funding to that group. If people wanted services (health care, legal rights, and so forth), they had to become a part of a particular group. This process of merging many ethnic groups into one broader category—called *panethnicity*—emphasizes that ethnic identity is itself socially shaped and created.

Biracial and Multiracial Populations: Immigration, Intermarriage, and Personal Identification

Our racial and ethnic identities are becoming more complex as migration around the world brings to distant shores new immigrants in search of safety and a new start in life. Keep in mind that our racial and ethnic identities come largely from external labels placed on us by governments and our associates but reinforced by our own self-identification. The important point is this: *Race is a social construct that can change with conditions in a country.*

Many European countries are now host to immigrants from their former colonies, making them multiracial. France hosts many North and West Africans, and Great Britain hosts large populations from Africa, India, and Pakistan. The resulting mix of peoples has blurred racial lines and created many multiracial individuals. Original migration patterns of early humans, shown in Map 8.2, illustrate that "push" factors drive people from some countries and pull them to other countries. The most common push-pull factors today are job opportunities, the desire for security, individual liberties, and availability of medical and educational opportunities. The target countries of migrants are most often in North America, Australia, or Western Europe, and the highest emigration rates are from Africa, Eastern Europe, Central Asia, and South and Central America.

The United States was once considered a biracial country, Black and White (which of course, disregarded the Native American population). However, the nation currently accepts more new immigrants than any other country. Immigration from every continent has led to a more diverse population, with up to 16% of the U.S. population being foreign born. With new immigration, increasing rates of intermarriage, and many more individuals claiming multiracial identification, the picture is much more complex today, and the color lines have been redrawn (DaCosta 2007; Lee and Bean 2004, 2007). One in forty individuals claims multiracial status today, and estimates are that one in five will do so by 2050

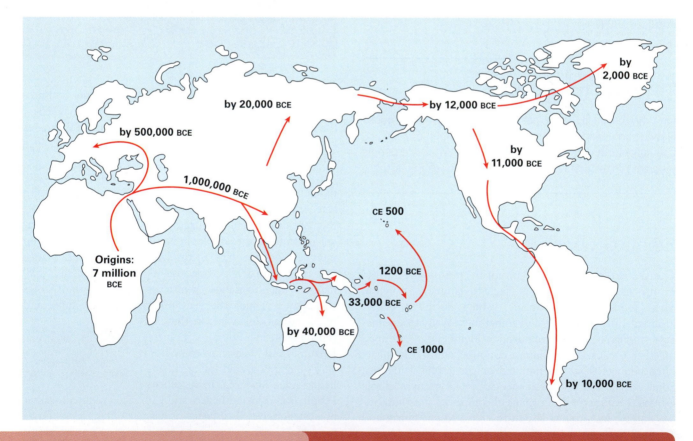

Map 8.2 The Spread of Humans Around the World

Source: Diamond (1999:37).

(Lee and Bean 2004). For the first time, the U.S. has a biracial president, although the application of the "one drop of blood" rule in the United States has caused many people to refer to President Obama as "Black."

Census data are used in countries to determine many characteristics of populations. In the United States, questions about race and ethnic classification have changed with each 10-year study. The important point is that government-determined categories thereafter define the racial and ethnic composition of a country. In the 2000 census, citizens were for the first time given the option of picking more than one racial category. Seven million people or 2.3% of the U.S. population selected two or more racial categories, with White/American Indian being the most common mixed category (Schaefer and Kunz, 2008).

Latinos, sometimes called Hispanics, made up 14% of the population in 2007. This is an increase of more than 50% since the 1990 census, making them the largest and fastest-growing minority group. Among Latinos, Mexicans made up roughly 63%, Puerto Ricans 9%, Cubans 3.5%, Central Americans 7.6%, and South Americans 5.4% (U.S. Census Bureau 2009a). Many Latinos identify themselves as panethnic, identifying with a broad ethnic category ("Hispanic" or "Latino") rather than with a specific ethnic group (e.g., Mexican American or Cuban American; McConnell and Delgado-Romero 2004). Blacks follow Latinos with 12.4% of the population. Whites make up 74%, Asians 4.3%, and Native Americans/Native Alaskans 0.8% of the total U.S. population (U.S. Census Bureau 2009a).

Arbitrary socially constructed classifications such as those in the examples above are frequently used as justification for treating individuals differently despite the lack of scientific basis for such distinctions (Williams 1996). The legacy of "race" remains even in countries where discrimination based on race is illegal. The question remains: Why is a multiracial baby with any African, Native American, or other minority heritage classified by the minority status?

Thinking Sociologically

Identify one dominant and one minority group in your community or on campus. Where do that group's members fall in the stratification system? How are the life chances of individuals in these groups influenced by factors beyond their control?

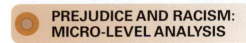

PREJUDICE AND RACISM: MICRO-LEVEL ANALYSIS

Have you ever found yourself in a situation in which you were viewed as different, strange, undesirable, or "less than human"? Perhaps you have felt the sting of rejection, based not on judgment of you as a person but solely because of the ethnic group into which you were born. Then again, you may have been insulated from this type of rejection if you grew up in a homogeneous community or in a privileged group; you may have even learned some negative attitudes about those different from yourself. It is sobering to think that where and when in history you were born determine how you are treated, your life chances, and many of your experiences.

Racial and ethnic minorities experience disproportionate prejudice and racism. Several processes act to keep minority groups among the have-nots of society. Consider the following factors:

Process	Result
Stratification	Minority status
Prejudice	Poor self-concept, negative relations with others
Discrimination	Poor jobs, income, education, housing
Racism	Systems that limit access to resources
Negative contact	Hostilities, war, conflict between groups

Prejudice

When minority groups are present within a society, prejudice influences dominant-minority group relations. **Prejudice** refers to attitudes that prejudge a group, usually negatively and not based on facts. Prejudiced individuals lump together people with certain characteristics as an undifferentiated group without considering individual differences. Although prejudice can refer to positive attitudes and exaggerations (as when a mother is prejudiced in thinking her own child is gifted), in this chapter, we refer to the negative aspects of prejudice. We also focus on the adverse effects brought on minority group members by prejudice. While prejudice can be stimulated by events such as conflicts at the institutional level and war at the societal level, attitudes are held by individuals and can be best understood as a micro-level phenomenon.

When prejudiced attitudes are manifested in actions, they are referred to as **discrimination**—differential treatment and harmful actions against minorities. These actions at the micro level might include refusal to sell someone a house because of the religion, race, or ethnicity of the buyer or employment practices that treat groups differently based on minority status (Feagin and Feagin 2007). Discrimination, such as laws that deny opportunities or resources to members of a particular group, operates largely at the meso or macro level, discussed later in the chapter.

The Nature of Prejudice

Prejudice is an understandable response of humans to their social environment. To survive, every social group or unit—a sorority, a sports team, a civic club, or a nation—needs to mobilize the loyalty of its members. Each organization needs to convince people to voluntarily commit energy, skills, time, and resources so the organization can meet its needs. Furthermore, as people commit themselves to a group, they invest a portion of themselves and feel loyalty to the group.

Individual commitment to a group influences one's perception and loyalties, creating preference or even bias for the group. This commitment is often based on stressing distinctions from other groups and deep preference for one's own group. However, these loyalties may be dysfunctional for out-group members and the victims of prejudice.

One reason people hold prejudices is that it is easier to pigeonhole the vast amount of information and stimuli coming at us in today's complex societies, and to sort information into neat unquestioned categories, than to evaluate each piece of information separately for its accuracy. Prejudiced individuals often categorize large numbers of people and attribute to them personal qualities based on their dress, language, skin color, or other identifying racial or ethnic features. This process is called **stereotyping**.

Stereotypes, or the pictures in our heads, are distorted, oversimplified, or exaggerated ideas passed down over generations through cultures. They are applied to all members of a group, regardless of individual differences, and used to justify prejudice, discrimination, and unequal distribution of power, wealth, and opportunities. Often, the result is unfair and inaccurate judgments about individuals who are members of the stereotyped groups. The problem is that both those stereotyping and those being stereotyped come to believe the "pictures" and act accordingly.

Prejudice is difficult to change because it is rooted in traditions, cultural beliefs, and stereotypes of groups. Individuals grow up learning these ingrained beliefs, which often go unchallenged. Yet when studied scientifically, stereotypes seldom correspond to facts.

Social scientists know, for instance, that prejudice is related to the history and the political and economic climate of a region or country, part of the macro-level cultural and social environment. For instance, in some southern U.S. states where African Americans constitute a majority of the population, there is evidence that White racial attitudes are more antagonistic due to economic and political competition for jobs and power (Farley 2009; Glaser 1994).

In wartime, the adversary may be the victim of racial slurs, or members of the enemy society may be depicted in films or other media as villains. During World War II, American films often showed negative stereotypes of Japanese and German people, stereotypes that likely reinforced the decision to intern more than 110,000 Japanese Americans, the majority of whom were U.S. citizens, in detention camps following the bombing of Pearl Harbor. Similar issues and stereotypes have arisen for American citizens with Middle Eastern ancestry since the attacks on the New York World Trade Center on September 11, 2001.

Sometimes, minority group members incorporate prejudiced views about themselves into their behavior. This process, an example of a *self-fulfilling prophesy*, involves the

Audio Link 8.1
Listen to an account of Muslim Americans after 9/11.

On December 7, 1941, Japan bombed Pearl Harbor in Hawaii, prompting President Franklin D. Roosevelt to sign an executive order designating the West Coast as a military zone from which "any or all persons may be excluded." Although not specified in the order, Japanese Americans were singled out for evacuation, and more than 110,000 were removed from many western states and sent to 10 relocation camps. Barber G. S. Hante points proudly to his bigoted sign against people with Japanese origin.

adoption of stereotypical behaviors (see Chapter 4). No group is born dumb, lazy, dirty, or money hungry, but its members can be conditioned to believe such depictions of themselves or be forced into acting out certain behaviors based on expectations of the dominant group.

Thinking Sociologically

Watch the Oscar-winning movie *Crash*. In what ways does this video raise issues of majority-minority stereotypes? How does it highlight labeling done by each group?

Explanations of Prejudice

We have all met them—people who express hostility toward others. They tell jokes about minorities, curse them, and even threaten action against them. Why do these individuals do this? The following theories have attempted to explain the prejudiced individual.

Frustration-aggression theory. In Greensboro, North Carolina, in 1978, a group of civil rights activists and African American adults and children listened as a guitarist sang freedom songs. A nine-car cavalcade of White Ku Klux Klan (KKK) and American Nazi Party members arrived. The intruders unloaded weapons from the backs of their cars, approached the rally, and opened fire for 88 seconds, then, they left as calmly as they had arrived. Four White men and a Black woman were dead (Greensboro Justice Fund 2005). According to frustration-aggression theory, many of the perpetrators of this and other heinous acts feel angry and frustrated because they cannot achieve their work or other goals. They blame any vulnerable minority group—religious, ethnic, sexual orientation—and members of that group become targets of their anger. Frustration-aggression theory focuses largely on poorly adjusted people who displace their frustration with aggressive attacks on others. Hate groups evolve from like-minded individuals, often because of prejudice and frustration (see Map 8.3).

Scapegoating. When it is impossible to vent one's frustration on the real target—one's boss, teachers, the economic system—this frustration can take the form of aggressive action

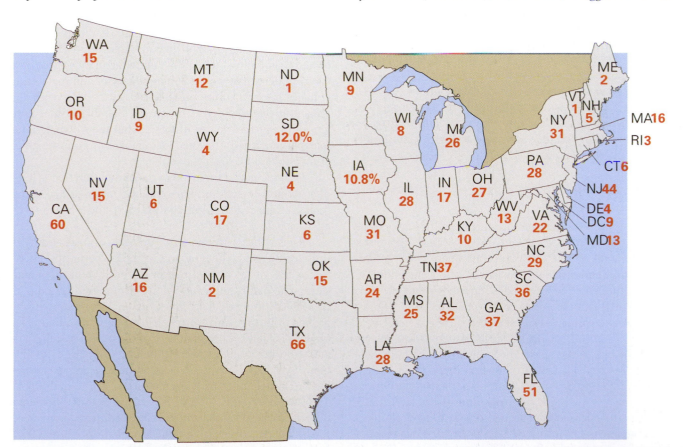

Map 8.3 Active Hate Groups in 2009

Source: Reprinted by permission of the Southern Poverty Law Center.

against minority group members, who are vulnerable because of their low status. They become the scapegoats. The word *scapegoat* comes from the Bible, Leviticus 16:5–22. Once a year, a goat (which was obviously innocent) was laden with parchments on which people had written their sins. The goat was then sent out to the desert to die. This was part of a ritual of purification, and the creature took the blame for others.

Scapegoating occurs when a minority group is blamed for the failures of others. It is difficult to look at oneself to seek reasons for failure but easy to transfer the blame for one's failure to others. Individuals who feel they are failures in their jobs or other aspects of their lives may blame minority groups. From within such a prejudiced mindset, even violence toward the out-group becomes acceptable.

Today, jobs and promotions are harder for young adults to obtain than they were for the baby boom generation, but the reason is mostly demographic. The baby boom of the 1940s and 1950s resulted in a bulge in the population. There are so many people in the workforce at each successive step on the ladder that it will be another few years before those baby boomers retire in large numbers. Until that happens, there will be a good deal of frustration about the apparent occupational stagnation. It is easier—and safer—to blame minorities or affirmative action programs than to vent frustration at the next oldest segment of the population or at one's grandparents for having a large family. Blacks, Hispanics, and other minorities become easy scapegoats.

Although this theory helps explain some situations, it does not predict when frustration will lead to aggression or explain why only some people who experience frustration vent their feelings on the vulnerable and why some groups become targets (Marger 2009).

Racism

Racism is any institutional arrangement that favors one racial group over another, and this favoritism may result in intentional or unintentional consequences for minority groups (Farley 2009). Racism is often embedded in the institutions of society and supported by people who are not aware of the social consequence of their actions. Many people without social science training see racism as a micro-level issue—one involving individual initiative and individual bigotry—whereas most social scientists see the problem as occurring at the meso and macro levels. Still, issues at the micro level continue to be real. *Ideological racism* is an attempt to justify racism on the basis of a pseudo-scientific set of ideas. It involves the belief that humans are divided into innately different groups, some of which are biologically inferior. Those who hold these views see biological differences as the cause of most cultural and social differences, as Hitler's actions against the Jews and other groups illustrate (Marger 2009). (This is illustrated in the discussion "Historical Attempts to Define Race" in "Sociology in Our Social World" on p. 248.)

Klansmen in traditional White robes demonstrate in front of a courthouse in New York City in 1999. They are carrying a flag sewn together from parts of American and Confederate flags, a symbol of their blended loyalties.

In *symbolic racism*, people insist that they are not prejudiced or racist—that they are colorblind and committed to equality—but at the same time, they oppose any social policies that would eliminate racism and make true equality of opportunity possible (Farley 2009). Symbolic racists reject ideological racism as blatant, crude, and ignorant, but they fail to recognize that their own actions may perpetuate institutional inequalities and oppose policies that would correct the problems.

Institutional racism involves discrimination that is hidden within the system, and symbolic racism allows it to remain in place. This will be discussed under meso-level analysis below.

Racism has psychological and social costs, both to those on the receiving end and to the perpetrators. There is a waste of talent and energy of both minorities and those who justify and carry out discriminatory actions. In the 1990s, individual membership in White supremacy groups in Europe and North America grew, as did attacks on Blacks, Jews, immigrants, and those whose religious and cultural practices were different from those of the majority. However, for the past several years, incidents in the United States have declined from 1,554 in 2006 to 1,460 in 2007 and 1,352 in 2008. Anti-Semitic incidents take the form of vandalism, assaults, or threats directed at Jewish citizens or Jewish establishments (Morrison 2009). Unfortunately, until there are better economic opportunities for more people, individual racism is likely to be one result of economic competition for jobs (Feagin, Vera, and Batur 2001).

Journal Article Link 8.2
Read about how students define racism.

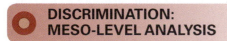
A neo-Nazi protestor makes a White power salute at the opening ceremony for the Illinois Holocaust Museum & Education Center in Skokie, Illinois, in 2009. The group chanted epitaphs expressing their hatred of Jews and other minority groups.

Although social-psychological theories shed light on the most extreme cases of individual or small-group prejudice and racism, there is much that these theories do not explain. They say little about the everyday hostility and reinforcement of prejudice that most of us experience or engage in, and they fail to deal with institutional discrimination.

DISCRIMINATION: MESO-LEVEL ANALYSIS

Dear Teacher, I would like to introduce you to my son, Wind-Wolf. He is probably what you would consider a typical Indian kid. He was born and raised on the reservation. He has black hair, dark brown eyes, and an olive complexion, and, like so many Indian children his age,

he is shy and quiet in the classroom. He is 5 years old, in kindergarten, and I can't understand why you have already labeled him a "slow learner." He has already been through quite an education compared with his peers in Western society. He was bonded to his mother and to the Mother Earth in a traditional native childbirth ceremony. And he has been continuously cared for by his mother, father, sisters, cousins, aunts, uncles, grandparents, and extended tribal family since this ceremony. . . .

Wind-Wolf was strapped (in his baby basket like a turtle shell) snugly with a deliberate restriction on his arms and legs. Although Western society may argue this hinders motor-skill development and abstract reasoning, we believe it forces the child to first develop his intuitive faculties, rational intellect, symbolic thinking, and five senses. Wind-Wolf was with his mother constantly, closely bonded physically, as she carried him on her back or held him while breast-feeding. She carried him everywhere she went, and every night he slept with both parents. Because of this, Wind-Wolf's educational setting was not only a "secure" environment, but it was also very colorful, complicated, sensitive, and diverse.

As he grew older, Wind-Wolf began to crawl out of the baby basket, develop his motor skills, and explore the world around him. When frightened or sleepy, he could always return to the basket, as a turtle withdraws into its shell. Such an inward journey allows one to reflect in privacy on what he has learned and to carry the new knowledge deeply into the unconscious and the soul. Shapes, sizes, colors, texture, sound, smell, feeling, taste, and the learning process are therefore functionally integrated—the physical and spiritual, matter and energy, and conscious and unconscious, individual and social.

It takes a long time to absorb and reflect on these kinds of experiences, so maybe that is why you think my Indian child is a slow learner. His aunts and grandmothers taught him to count and to know his numbers while they sorted materials for making abstract designs in native baskets. And he was taught to learn mathematics by counting the sticks we use in our traditional native hand game. So he may be slow in grasping the methods and tools you use in your classroom, ones quite familiar to his white peers, but I hope you will be patient with him. It takes time to adjust to a new cultural system and learn new things. He is not culturally "disadvantaged," but he is culturally different. (Lake 1990:48–53)

This letter expresses the frustration of a father who sees his son being labeled and discriminated against by the school system without being given a chance. *Discrimination* refers to actions taken against members of a minority group. It can occur at individual and small-group levels but is particularly problematic at the organizational and institutional levels—the meso level of analysis.

Thinking Sociologically

How might schools unintentionally misunderstand Wind-Wolf and other minority children in ways that have negative consequences for the children's success?

Discrimination is based on race, ethnicity, age, sex, sexual orientation, nationality, social class, religion, or whatever other category members of a society choose to make significant (Feagin and Feagin 2007). **Individual discrimination**, actions taken against minority group members by individuals, can take many forms, from avoiding contact by excluding individuals from one's club, neighborhood, or even country to physical violence against minorities, as seen

Handbook Link 8.1
Read about
discrimination in cities.

in hate crime attacks on Asian Americans, who are perceived to be taking jobs away from White Americans.

Institutional discrimination, or meso-level discrimination, is often a normal or routine part of the way an organization operates. It includes both intentional actions, such as laws restricting minorities, and unintentional actions, which have consequences that restrict minorities. Institutional discrimination is built into organizations and cultural expectations in the social world. Even nonprejudiced people can participate in institutional racism quite unintentionally. For example, many schools track students into classes based on standardized test results. Minority children end up disproportionately in lower tracks for a number of reasons (see Chapter 11). Thus, a policy that is meant to give all children an equal chance ends up legitimizing the channeling of some minority group members into the lower-achieving classroom groupings.

Sometimes purposeful discrimination, called de jure discrimination or discrimination by law, is built into the law or is part of the explicit policies of an organization. Jim Crow laws, passed in the late 1800s in the United States, and laws that barred Jewish people in Germany from living, working, or investing in certain places are examples. In contrast, unintentional discrimination results from policies that have the unanticipated consequence of favoring one group and disadvantaging another. This is sometimes called de facto discrimination because there is discrimination "in fact" even if not in intent. It occurs through the meso systems. It can be more damaging than discrimination by individuals at the micro level because it is often implemented by organizational officials who are not the least bit prejudiced and may not recognize the effects of their actions (Merton 1949a). Still, those actions or policies can have sweeping consequences for minorities.

Unintentional discrimination usually occurs through one of two processes: (1) side-effect discrimination or (2) past-in-present discrimination (Feagin and Feagin 2007). **Side-effect discrimination** refers to practices in one institutional area that have a negative impact because they are linked to practices in another institutional area. Figure 8.1 illustrates this idea. Each institution uses information from the other institutions to make decisions. Thus, discrimination in the criminal justice system, which has in fact been well documented, may influence discrimination in the education or health care systems.

Consider the following examples of side-effect discrimination. The first is in the criminal justice and employment systems. In a 1999 interview conducted by one of the authors, a probation officer in a moderate-size city in Ohio said that he had never seen an African American in his county get a not-guilty verdict and that he was not sure it was possible. He had known of cases in which minorities had pleaded guilty to a lesser charge even though they were innocent because they did not think they could receive a fair verdict in that city. When people apply for jobs, however, they are required to report the conviction

Jim Crow laws played out in a Pensacola, Florida, movie house in the 1930s: This was the rear entrance for African Americans.

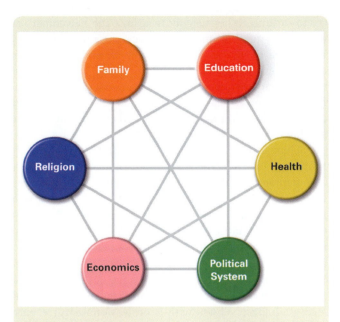

Each circle represents a different institution—family, education, religion, health, political-legal system, and economics. These meso-level systems are interdependent, using information or resources from the others. If discrimination occurs in one institution, the second institution may unintentionally borrow information that results in discrimination. In this way, discrimination occurs at the meso level without awareness by individuals at the micro level.

Figure 8.1 Side-Effect Discrimination

Children play on the porch of their rustic home with no plumbing in the rural Alaska village of Akhiok, among the Aleutian Islands. Finding jobs through the Internet is not an option from this location.

on the application form. By using information about an applicant's criminal record, employers who clearly do not intend to discriminate end up doing so whether or not the individual was guilty. The side-effect discrimination is unintentional discrimination; the criminal justice system has reached an unjust verdict, and the potential employer is swayed unfairly.

Thinking Sociologically

Think of the information that is used in one organization (such as a business that is hiring people) that has been provided by another institution or organization (say, the criminal justice system). How might some of that information be a source of unintended side-effect discrimination for a minority group member?

The second example of side-effect discrimination shows that the Internet also plays a role in institutional

discrimination and privilege. For example, in Alaska, 15.6% of the population is Native, but Natives hold only 5% of state jobs (U.S. Census Bureau 2003). Consider that the State of Alaska uses the Internet as its primary means of advertising and accepting applications for state jobs (State of Alaska 2006). No affordable Internet access is available in the 164 predominantly Native villages in Alaska (Denali Commission 2001). Other options for application include requesting applications by mail, if a person knows about the opening. The usefulness of this process is limited, however, by the reliability and speed of mail service to remote villages and the often short application periods for state jobs. State officials may not intentionally try to prevent Aleuts, Inupiats, Athabaskans, or other Alaska Natives from gaining access to state jobs, but the effect can be institutionalized discrimination. Here, Internet access plays a role in the participation of minorities in the social world (Nakamura 2004).

The point is that Whites, especially affluent Whites, benefit from privileges not available to low-income minorities. The privileged members may not purposely disadvantage others and may not be prejudiced, but the playing field is not level. The discrimination may be completely unintentional (Rothenberg 2008). Put yourself in the position of a person who does not have these privileges (McIntosh 2002:97–101):

I can avoid spending time with people who mistrust people of my color.

I can protect my children most of the time from people who might not like them.

I can criticize our government and talk about how I fear its policies and behavior without being seen as a cultural "outsider."

I can easily buy posters, postcards, picture books, greeting cards, dolls, toys, and children's magazines featuring people of my race.

I can arrange my activities so that I will never have to experience feelings of rejection owing to my race.

Past-in-present discrimination refers to practices from the past that may no longer be allowed but that continue to affect people today. In Mississippi between 1951 and 1952, the average state expenditure to educate a White child was $147 per pupil, whereas the average was $34 per Black pupil in segregated schools (Luhman and Gilman 1980). Such blatant segregation and inequality in the use of tax dollars is no longer legal. This may seem like ancient history, yet some African Americans who were in school in the 1950s and 1960s are now trying to support a family and pay for their children's college expenses. To those who received a substandard education and did not have an opportunity for college, it is not ancient history because it affects their opportunities today.

Why do some minority groups do better than others? New immigrants to the United States from south, central, and Eastern Europe did better than African Americans, but why? Some explanations have focused on skin color and discrimination, yet Japanese and Chinese have fared well too. To address these questions, Stanley Lieberson (1980) did an extensive study and concluded that the new immigrants and Blacks who were arriving in the U.S. North held similar aspirations for education and good jobs, but discrimination against Blacks by employers, labor unions, realtors, and others was intense due to attitudes carried over from the slave period, a case of past-in-present discrimination. Immigrants were given better jobs and chances for mobility. Furthermore, Asians experienced less discrimination because their numbers were small and they were viewed as less of a threat to White jobs, whereas Blacks flooded the job market in large numbers when they moved north and became marginalized as a result. Another factor was the context of intergroup contact. Slaves and Native Americans were forced into contact with Whites, whereas immigrants came voluntarily, usually for economic betterment. Voluntary immigrants perceived the economic conditions to be better because they chose to come. They started out with better economic prospects and more "cultural capital"—education, useful language skills, knowledge of how the social system works, and established kinship or friendship networks (Lieberson 1980). In short, historical patterns made past-in-present discrimination a reality for a very long time.

Remember that prejudice is an attitude, discrimination an action. If neighbors do not wish to have minority group members move onto their block, that is prejudice. If they try to organize other neighbors against the newcomers or make the situation unpleasant once the minority family has moved in, that is discrimination. If minorities cannot afford to live in the neighborhood because of discrimination in the marketplace, that is institutional discrimination. Discrimination can cause prejudice and vice versa, but they are most often found working together, reinforcing one another (Merton 1949a; Myers 2003).

Change has occurred since the election in 2008 of a biracial President of the United States. Conservative commentators and many journalists are fond of saying that this means we are now in a postracial society, that race is now irrelevant. While it is true that President Obama is the nation's first African American president, it is also true that only 1 Senator (out of 100) is Black, and he was appointed rather than elected to the office. We have also seen in Table 8.2 that college-educated African Americans earn significantly less than White college graduates. Whites with a professional degree earn about $117,787 per year, professional African Americans earn $101,376, and Hispanics with the same degree earn $82,627 (U.S. Census Bureau 2009a). Note also that on a typical Sunday morning, Whites and Blacks worship separately, with multiracial churches being a rarity (Marti 2005). As long as these and many other differences continue, it is hard to support the notion that the United States is a "postracial" society.

Thinking Sociologically

Think of some events in history that have an effect on particular groups today. Why might the events cause intergroup hostility? How does discrimination, as discussed above, help us understand world conflicts, such as the intense hostility between Palestinians and Jews in Israel?

 DOMINANT AND MINORITY GROUP CONTACT: MACRO-LEVEL ANALYSIS

Economic hard times hit Germany in the 1930s, following that nation's defeat in World War I. To distract citizens from the nation's problems, a scapegoat was found—the Jewish population. The German states began restricting Jewish activities and investments. Gradually, the hate rhetoric intensified, but even then, most Jews had little idea about the fate that awaited them. Millions perished in gas chambers because the ruling Nazi party defined them as an undesirable *race* (although being Jewish is actually a religious or ethnic identification, not biological).

Japan has a relatively homogeneous population, but one group, the Burakumin (also called "invisible race"), have been treated as outcasts. They make up 2% of the population, about 6 million people. Because their ancestors were relegated to performing work considered ritually unclean—butchering animals, tanning skins, digging graves, and handling corpses—they lived in isolated hamlets. Today, discrimination is officially against the law, but customs persist. Ostracized and kept within certain occupations and neighborhoods, the Burakumin rarely intermarried or even socialized with other Japanese. However, today there is much more intermarriage and blending into the society in large cities (Alldritt 2000; International Humanist and Ethical Union 2009).

Mexico, Guatemala, and other Central American governments face protests by their Indian populations, descendants of the Aztecs, Maya, and Inca, who have distinguishing features and are generally relegated to servant positions. These native groups have been protesting against government policies and their poor conditions—usurping of their land, inability to own land, absentee land ownership, poor pay, and discrimination by the government (DePalma 1995).

These examples illustrate the contact between governments and minority groups. The Jews in Germany faced genocide; the Burakumin in Japan, segregation; and Native Americans, discrimination and population transfer. The form these relations take depends on the following:

1. Which group has more power

2. The needs of the dominant group for labor or other resources (such as land) that could be provided by the minority group, sometimes as slaves

3. The cultural norms of each group, including the level of tolerance of out-groups

4. The social histories of the groups, including their religious, political, racial, and ethnic differences

5. Physical and cultural identifiers that distinguish the groups

6. The times and circumstances (wars, economic strains, recessions)

Where power between groups in a society is unequal, the potential for differential treatment is always present. Yet some groups live in harmony whether their power is equal or not (Kitano, Aqbayani, and de Anda 2005). The Pygmies of the Ituri rainforest have traded regularly with nearby local African settlements by leaving goods in an agreed place in exchange for other needed goods. There is often only minimal direct contact between these groups.

Whether totally accepting or prone to conflict, dominant-minority relations depend on the time, place, and circumstances. Figure 8.2 indicates the range of dominant-minority relationships and policies.

Genocide is the systematic effort of a dominant group to destroy a minority group. Christians were thrown to the lions in ancient Rome. Hitler sent Jews and other non-Aryan groups into concentration camps to be gassed. Iraqis used deadly chemical weapons against the Kurdish people in their own country. Members of the Serbian army massacred Bosnian civilians to rid towns of Bosnian Muslims, an action referred to as ethnic cleansing (Cushman and Mestrovic 1996). From 1975 to 1979, 2 million Cambodians, almost 25% of the population, suffered genocide as a result of leaders instituting new political philosophies. In Rwanda, people of the Tutsi and Hutu tribes carried out mass killings against each other in the mid-1990s. In Darfur, a section of western Sudan in Africa, the ongoing massive genocide is continuing while powerful nations of the world do little to stop it. The United Nations estimates that 2 million Sudanese people have died, disappeared, or become refugees in other countries (R. Smith 2005). Recently, villagers in Kenya, who had lived peacefully alongside their neighbors of different tribes, began killing each other after what was declared a rigged election. Genocide has existed at many points in history, and it still exists today. These examples illustrate the lethal consequences of racism, one group systematically killing off another, often a minority, to gain control and power.

Subjugation refers to the subordination of one group to another that holds power and authority. Haiti and the Dominican Republic are two countries sharing the island of Hispaniola in the Caribbean. Because many Haitians are poor, they are lured by promises of jobs in the sugarcane

Video Link 8.2
Watch an examination of the Balkan War.

Figure 8.2 Types of Dominant-Minority Group Relations

Most Hostile to "Others"				Most Accepting of "Others"
Genocide	**Subjugation**	**Population Transfer**	**Assimilation**	**Pluralism**
Extermination of minorities	Oppression, slavery	Removal to new location	Cultural blending of groups	Groups share power

Beginning in February 2003, there has been a massive genocide in the Darfur region of Sudan (eastern Africa), where the international community has not been effective in stopping the slaughter. Some people have survived in refugee camps with almost no food and little water, in "homes" like these.

fields of the Dominican Republic. However, they are forced to work long hours for little pay and are not allowed to leave until they have paid for housing and food, which may be impossible to do on their low wages.

Slavery is one form of subjugation that has existed throughout history. When the Roman Empire defeated other lands, the captives became slaves. This included ancient Greeks, who also kept slaves at various times in their history. African tribes enslaved members of neighboring tribes, sometimes selling them to slave traders, and slavery has existed in Middle Eastern countries such as Saudi Arabia. As mentioned in the opening story for this chapter, slavery is flourishing today (Bales 2000, 2004, 2007).

Segregation, another form of subjugation, keeps minorities powerless by formally separating them from the dominant group and depriving them of access to the dominant institutions. Jim Crow laws, instituted in the southern United States after the Civil War, legislated separation between groups—separate facilities, schools, and neighborhoods (Feagin and Feagin 2007; Massey and Denton 1998). Around the world, barrios, reservations, squatters' quarters, *favela*, and even regions of a country (e.g., Tibet) are sometimes maintained by the dominant group, usually unofficially but sometimes officially, which serves to isolate minorities in poor or overcrowded areas.

Domestic colonialism refers to exploitation of minority groups within a country (Blauner 1972; Kitano et al. 2005). African Brazilians and Native Americans in the United States and Canada have been "domestically colonized groups"—managed and manipulated by members of the dominant group.

Population transfer refers to the removal, often forced, of a minority group from a region or country. Generally, the

dominant group wants land, or resources, or political and economic power held by the minority. In 1972, Uganda's leader, General Idi Amin, gave the 45,000 Asians in that country, mostly of Indian origin, 36 hours to pack their bags and leave, under threat that they would be arrested or killed. Many found homes in England, while others went to India. For the thousands who were born and raised in Uganda, this expulsion was a cruel act, barring them from their homeland. Because the Asian population had great economic resources, the primary motivation for their expulsion was to regain economic power for Africans. Their departure, however, left the country in economic chaos, with a void in the business class.

Examples of other population transfers are numerous: Native Americans in the United States were removed to reservations. The Cherokee people were forced to walk from Georgia and North Carolina to new lands west of the Mississippi—a "Trail of Tears" along which 40% of the people perished. During World War II, Japanese Americans were forcibly moved to "relocation centers" and had their land and property confiscated. Many Chinese were forced to flee from Vietnam on small boats in the 1970s. Homeless and even nation-less people, they were dubbed "the boat people" by the press. Many Afghani people fled to Pakistan to escape oppression by the ruling Taliban and—in 2001—to escape U.S. bombing. Today, civilians along the Pakistan/Afghanistan border still suffer displacement.

Movements of people and activities "that cross state borders, such as human migrations, flow of ideas and information, and movements of money and credit" are referred to as **transnationalism** (Calhoun 2002). This involves people who fully participate in and have loyalty to two nations and cultures and often hold dual citizenship. An increasing number of naturalized U.S. citizens

In 1988, people in horse-drawn covered wagons and on horseback reenacted the Trail of Tears, the 1,000-mile journey that the Cherokees traveled 150 years earlier.

are also tax-paying members of their countries of origin, and they return often to help families and neighbors with financial needs or immigration plans (Levitt 2001). Yet dual citizenship can create dilemmas of identity and sense of belonging.

Assimilation refers to the social and cultural merging of minority and majority groups, a process by which minority members may lose most of their original identity. Interaction among racial and ethnic groups occurs in housing, schooling, employment, political circles, family groups, friendship, and social relationships (Kitano et al. 2005). Assimilation is often a voluntary process in which a minority group, such as immigrants, chooses to adopt the values, norms, and institutions of the dominant group.

However, forced assimilation occurs when a minority group is compelled to suppress its identity. This happened in Spain around the time of World War II, when the Basque people were forbidden by the central government to speak or study the Basque language. For several centuries—ending only a few decades ago—the British government tried to stamp out the Welsh language from Wales. Assimilation is more likely to occur when the minority group is culturally similar to the dominant group. For instance, in the United States, the closer a group is to being White, English speaking, and Protestant, or what is referred to as WASP (White Anglo-Saxon Protestant), the faster its members will be assimilated into the society, adopting the culture and blending in biologically through intermarriage.

Pluralism occurs when each ethnic or racial group in a country maintains its own culture and separate set of institutions but has recognized equity in the society. For example, Switzerland has three dominant cultural language groups: French, German, and Italian. Three official languages are spoken in the government and taught in the schools. Laws are written in three languages. Each group respects the rights of the other groups to maintain a distinctive way of life. In Malaysia, three groups share power—Malays, Chinese, and Indians. Although the balance is not completely stable because Chinese and Indians hold more political and economic power than the native Malays, there is a desire to maintain a pluralistic society. While tensions do exist, both Switzerland and Malaysia represent examples of pluralist societies. Legal protection of smaller or less powerful groups is often necessary to have pluralism. In the United States, pluralism as a policy was first embraced by the nation's first president, George Washington, as is explained in the "Sociology in Our Social World" on page 264.

Many individuals in the world face disruptions during their lifetimes that change their position in the social structure. The dominant-minority continuum illustrates the range of relations with dominant groups that can affect people's lives as transitions take place.

Thinking Sociologically

Think of examples from current news stories of positive and harmful intercultural contact. Where do your examples fit on the continuum from genocide to pluralism? What policies might address the issues raised in your examples?

Theoretical Explanations of Dominant-Minority Group Relations

Are human beings innately cruel, inhumane, greedy, aggressive, territorial, or warlike? Some people think so, but the evidence is not very substantial. To understand prejudice in individuals or small groups, psychological and social-psychological theories are most relevant. To understand institutional discrimination, studying meso-level organizations is helpful, and to understand the pervasive nature of prejudice and stereotypes over time in various societies, cultural explanations are useful. Although some aspects of macro-level theories relate to micro- and meso-level analysis, their major emphasis is on understanding the national and global systems of group relations.

Conflict Theory

In the 1840s, as the United States set out to build a railroad, large numbers of laborers immigrated from China to do the hard manual work. When the railroad was completed and competition for jobs became stiff, the once welcomed Chinese became targets of bitter prejudice, discrimination, and sometimes violence. Between 1850 and 1890, Whites in California protested against Chinese, Japanese, and Chicano workers. Members of these minority groups banded together in towns or cities for protection, founding the Chinatowns we know today. (Non-Chinese Asian groups suffered discrimination as well because the bigoted generalizations were applied to all Asians [Winders 2004].)

Why does discrimination occur? Conflict theorists argue that creating a "lesser" group protects the dominant group's advantages. Because privileges and resources are usually limited, those who have them want to keep them. One strategy used by privileged people, according to conflict theory, is to perpetrate prejudice and discrimination against minority group members. A case in point is the *Gastarbeiter* (guest workers) in Germany and other western European countries, who immigrate from Eastern Europe, the Middle East, and Africa to fill positions in European economies. They are easily recognized because of cultural

Sociology in Our Social World

Pluralism: A Long-Standing History in the United States

This Jewish synagogue, the oldest in the United States, proudly displays a letter from George Washington enshrining pluralism in the new nation's policies.

It is no mistake that the oldest Jewish synagogue in the United States is in Rhode Island, for separation of church and state and tolerance of other religious traditions was a founding principle of Rhode Island. After George Washington was elected president of the new nation, he received a letter from that early Jewish congregation in Newport, Rhode Island, asking about his policies of pluralism or multiculturalism (though those words had not been coined yet). In response in 1790, Touro Synagogue received a handwritten letter signed by President Washington (and now proudly on display at the synagogue) embracing an open and "liberal" policy to all American citizens, regardless of origins or religious affiliation. In this letter, George Washington affirmed a policy of pluralism from the very beginning of the country's existence as a nation. Passages from that letter follow.

The Citizens of the United States of America have a right to applaud themselves for having given to mankind examples of an enlarged and liberal policy: a policy worthy of imitation. . . . It is now no more that toleration is spoken of, as if it was by the indulgence of one class of people, that another enjoyed the exercise of their inherent natural rights. For happily the Government of the United States, which gives to bigotry no sanction, to persecution no assistance, requires only that they who live under its protection should demean themselves as good citizens.

. . . May the children of the Stock of Abraham, who dwell in this land, continue to merit and enjoy the good will of the other Inhabitants; while every one shall sit in safety under his own vine and fig tree, and there shall be none to make him afraid. May the father of all mercies scatter light and not darkness in our paths, and make us all in our several vocations useful here, and in his own due time and way everlastingly happy.

—G. Washington

and physical differences and are therefore ready targets for prejudice and discrimination, especially in times of economic competition and slowing economies. This helps keep many of them in low-level positions.

Karl Marx argued that exploitation of the lower classes is built into capitalism because it benefits the ruling class. Unemployment creates a ready pool of labor to fill the marginal jobs, with the pool often made up of identifiable minority groups. This pool allows people to remain in their higher-level positions and prevents others from moving up in the stratification system.

Three critical factors contribute to hostility over resources, according to one conflict theorist (Noel 1968): First, if two groups of people are identifiably different in appearance, clothing, or language, then we-versus-they thinking may develop. However, this by itself does not establish long-term hostility between the groups. Second, if the two groups come into conflict over scarce resources that both groups want for themselves, hostilities are very likely to arise. The resources might be the best land, the highest-paying jobs, access to the best schools for one's children, or positions of prestige and power. Conflict over resources is likely to create stereotypes and animosity. If the third element is added to the mix—one group having much more power than the other—then intense dislike between the two groups and misrepresentation of each group by the other is virtually unavoidable.

What happens is that the group with more power uses that power to ensure that its members (and their offspring) get the most valued resources. However, because they do not want to see themselves as unfair and brutish people, they develop stereotypes and derogatory characterizations of "those other people" so that it seems reasonable and justified not to give "them" access to the resources. Discrimination comes first, and prejudiced ideology comes later to excuse the discrimination (Noel 1968). Thus, macro- and meso-level conflicts can lead to micro-level attitudes.

Split labor market theory, a branch of conflict theory, characterizes the labor market as having two levels: The primary market involves clean jobs, largely in supervisory roles, and provides high salaries and good advancement possibilities, whereas the secondary market involves undesirable, hard, and dirty work, compensated with low hourly wages and few benefits or career opportunities. Minorities, especially those from the urban underclass, are most likely to find dead-end jobs in the secondary market. For instance, when Mexicans work for little income picking crops as migrant laborers, they encounter negative stereotypes because they are poor and take jobs for low wages. Prejudice and discrimination build up against the new, cheaper workers, who threaten the next level of workers as the migrant workers seek to move up in the economic hierarchy. Thus, competition for lesser jobs

Chinese men were invited and encouraged to come to North America to help build railroads. However, prejudice was extremely prevalent, especially once the railroads were completed and the immigrants began to settle into various jobs in the U.S. economy.

pits minorities against each other and low-income Whites against minorities. By encouraging division and focusing antagonism between worker groups, employers reduce threats to their dominance and get cheaper labor in the process. Workers do not organize against employers who use this dual system because they are distracted by the antagonisms that build up among themselves—hence, the split labor market (Bonacich 1972, 1976). This theory maintains that competition, prejudice, and ethnic animosity serve the interests of capitalists because that atmosphere keeps the laboring classes from uniting.

Conflict theory has also been used to illuminate issues of ethnic hostility on other continents, for this theory has wide application. Kichiro Iwamoto, who does sociological work on race relations issues in Africa and elsewhere, discusses the conflicts in Africa in the next "Sociology in Our Social World" on page 266.

Video Link 8.3
Watch reflections from a Holocaust survivor.

Conflict theory has taught us a great deal about racial and ethnic stratification. However, conflict theorists often focus on people with power quite intentionally oppressing others to protect their own self-interests. They depict the dominant group as made up of nasty, power-hungry people. As we have seen in the meso-level discussion of side-effect and past-in-present discrimination, privilege and disprivilege are often subtle and unconscious, which means they can continue even without ill will among those in the dominant group. Their privilege has been institutionalized. Conflict theorists sometimes miss this important point.

Structural-Functional Theory

From the structural-functional perspective, maintaining a cheap pool of laborers who are in and out of work serves several purposes for society. Low-paying and undesirable jobs for which no special training is needed—busboys, janitors, nurse's aides, street sweepers, and fast-food service workers—are often filled by minority group members of societies, including immigrant populations seeking to improve their opportunities.

Not only does this cheap pool of labor function to provide a ready labor force for dirty work or menial unskilled jobs, these individuals also serve other functions for society. They make possible occupations that service the poor, such as social work, public health, criminology, and the justice and legal systems. They buy goods others do not want—day-old bread, old fruits and vegetables, secondhand clothes. They set examples for others of what not to be, and they allow others to feel good about giving to charity (Gans 1971, 1994).

Sociologist Thomas Sowell (1994) contends that history and the situation into which one is born create the major differences in the social status of minority groups. Minority individuals must work hard to make up for their disadvantages. Sowell's contentions are controversial in part

Sociology in Our Social World

Violence in Kenya

By Kichi Iwamoto

In January 2008, violence gripped Kenya as rival political leaders representing different ethnic groups fought for control of the country in a contested election. Former Secretary General of the United Nations Kofi Annan said, while visiting western Kenya during the unrest, "What we saw was heart-wrenching. We saw houses burning, grandmothers and children being pushed out of their homes, and people suffering everywhere." He told the rival political leaders to resolve the political conflict as the violence was out of control in the country (UPI 2008).

At a small Assembly of God church in Kiambaa, Kenya, armed men trapped Kikuyu women, children, and elderly people inside, barricaded all the doors, and burned the building down, killing an estimated 50 people. The attackers were reported to be members of a rival tribe, the Kalenjin (Gettleman 2008). The scientific eye of sociology can identify the key variables in this complex, tragic event.

Political conflicts over power can incite age-old rivalries and erupt into genocide, systematic killing of "others." These ethnic differences between the tribal groups in Kenya generated prejudice and negative contact, with the Kalenjin and Kikuyu attacking each other. Tribalism leads to discrimination against other tribes that are viewed as economic and power rivals, "different," and often inferior, and then resentments result in reprisals. The violence is perpetuated in a vicious cycle of "we" versus "they" animosity.

What are some meso- and macro-level sociological factors that could be contributing to this massacre? As in most ethnic conflicts, economic and political factors contribute to a violent racial or ethnic event. In Kenya, the mob violence and social chaos may have been advantageous for those in high political positions as the "reign of terror" kept frightened people from protesting the controversial national election of December 2007. "President Mwai Kibaki's electoral victory, seen by the opposition as fraudulent, triggered days of ugly tribal violence," one report said (*Los Angeles Times* 2008). The tribal violence kept the population fragmented, weakening any opposition and challenge to the current political structure. The situation was also exacerbated by roads that are too dangerous to use so that help could not reach villages, tremendous food scarcity in many parts of the country, and many citizens struggling for survival rather than focusing on immediate political justice.

Some argue that the roots of these (Kenyan) conflicts are not tribal. "A *tribe* in Africa is a particular (social) identity construction created by colonial powers in an effort to more easily dominate the population. Ethnicity is a group of people who share a common identity, rituals, and most commonly, language. There are ethnic differences in Kenya, however constructed, but they are commonly trumped by kinship, class, labor, religion and even geographic identities" (Marcus 2008). Still, it is clear that the horrific violence is rooted in conflicts over scarce resources and defense of the self-interests of one group against another.

because of the implication that institutional discrimination can be overcome by hard work. Conflict theorists counter his argument by saying that discrimination that reduces opportunities is built into institutions and organizations and must be dealt with through structural change. They argue that hard work is necessary but not sufficient for minorities to succeed.

Prejudice, racism, and discrimination are dysfunctional for society, resulting in loss of human resources, costs to societies due to poverty and crime, hostilities between groups, and disrespect for those in power (Schaefer 2008).

Thinking Sociologically

What are some micro-, meso-, and macro-level factors that enhance the chances that minority persons can move up the social ladder to better jobs?

Cultural explanations point out that prejudice and discrimination are passed on from generation to generation through cultural transmission. Stereotypes about groups limit our perceptions of what these groups can do and thereby limit the opportunities available to minority group members. Cultural beliefs are passed on through micro-level socialization processes and macro-level institutional structure, aided by media stereotypes. Even when we see cases of minorities who do not conform to the stereotypes about them, selective perception reinforces the stereotypes, prejudices, and labels we have learned.

Cultural beliefs help explain why racism remains in place and why inequality is sustained over a long period of time. From this perspective, cultural beliefs serve to stabilize inequality once it is created in a society, but beliefs alone do not lead to inequality. The phenomenon of symbolic racism in contemporary North America is a good example: The assertion that a society is already fair prevents an honest look at institutional discrimination, which operates so subtly and so pervasively at the meso and macro levels of society.

The Effects of Prejudice, Racism, and Discrimination

Pictures of starving orphans from Sudan and Ethiopia and broken families from war-torn Bosnia and Darfur remind us of the human toll resulting from prejudice and discrimination. This section discusses the results of prejudice, racism, and discrimination for minority groups and for societies.

The Costs of Racism

Individual victims of racism suffer from the destruction of their lives, health, and property, especially in societies where racism leads to poverty, enslavement, conflict, or war. Poor self-concept and low self-esteem result from constant reminders of a devalued status in society.

Prejudice and discrimination result in costs to organizations and communities as well as to individuals. First, they lose the talents of individuals who could be productive and contributing members. Because of poor education, substandard housing, and inferior medical care, these citizens cannot use their full potential to contribute to society. In 2008, 46.3 million (or 15.4%) of U.S. citizens did not have health insurance (U.S. Census Bureau 2009f). The number of uninsured children is 8.3 million and growing (Center on Budget and Policy Priorities 2006). Yet the United States spends 16% of its gross domestic product (GDP) on health care, the highest expenditure in the world. Still, the inequities in health care coverage are striking: 13% of Whites are without care, but the figure for African Americans is 21% and for Hispanics 34% (James et al. 2007).

Indian women (originally from the state of Rajasthan) inspect red chili peppers and other spices, a niche market to make a living in the United States and Canada.

Sudanese children wait in line to receive food in the Sudanese refugee camp of Narus. A worldwide study by UNICEF reveals that some 5.6 million children die every year in part because they do not consume enough of the right nutrients and 146 million children are at risk of dying early because they are underweight.

Second, government subsidies cost millions in the form of welfare, food stamps, and imprisonment, but they are made necessary in part by the lack of opportunities for minority individuals. Representation of ethnic groups in the U.S. political system can provide a voice for their concerns. Table 8.3 shows the representation of ethnic groups in Congress.

Video Link 8.4
Consider whether race affects votes.

Table 8.3	**Representation in the U.S. Congress, 2009**			
	Native American	*Asian*	*Black*	*Hispanic*
Senate	0	1 (1%)	1 (1%)	3 (3%)
House	2 (0.5%)	6 (1.4%)	39 (9%)	24 (5.5%)
Percentage of Population	0.8	4.3	12.4	14.1

Source: Center on Congress (2009).

Thinking Sociologically

How might lack of health care and insurance affect other aspects of a person's life (work, family life, education)? Give some examples of how one's self-interests might be underrepresented in policy decisions if there is low representation of one's ethnicity in Congress.

Continued attempts to justify racism by stereotyping and labeling groups have cultural costs, too. There are many talented African American athletes who are stars on college sports teams, but very few of them have been able to break into the ranks of coaches and managers, although there has been more opportunity in basketball than in other sports (Eitzen and Sage 2003; Sage 2005). The number of African American and Mexican American actors and artists has increased, but the number of minority playwrights and screenwriters who can get their works produced or who have become directors remains limited. African American musicians have found it much more difficult to earn royalties and therefore cannot compose full-time (Alexander 2003). Because these artists must create and perform their art "as a sideline," they are less able to contribute their talents to society. The rest of us in society are the poorer for it.

Minority Reactions to Prejudice, Discrimination, and Racism

How have minority groups dealt with their status? Five different reactions are common: assimilation, acceptance, avoidance, aggression, and change-oriented actions directed at the social structure. The first four are micro-level responses. They do not address the meso- and macro-level issues.

Audio Link 8.2
Listen to stories about integration.

Assimilation is an accommodation to prejudice and discrimination. Some minority group members attempt to *pass* or assimilate as members of the dominant group so as to avoid bigotry and discrimination. Although this option is not open to many because of their distinguishing physical characteristics, this strategy usually involves abandoning their own culture and turning their back on family roots and ties, a costly strategy in terms of self-esteem and sense of identity. People who select this coping strategy are forced to deny who they are as defined by their roots and to live their lives in constant anxiety, feeling as though they must hide something about themselves.

In the 1960s, popular items advertised in African American magazines included "whitening creams" or "skin bleaches." Light-colored people with African ancestry would bleach their skin to pass as White. Skin-whitening creams can be found today on pharmacy shelves in many countries. Dissatisfaction with one's body can have an impact on one's self-concept.

Passing—pretending to be a member of the privileged group when one is not fully a part of that community—also has been a common response of gays and lesbians who are afraid to come out. Homosexuals experience the costly impact on self-esteem and the constant fear that they may be discovered. Likewise, assimilated Jews have changed their religion and their names to be accepted. Despite the wrenching from their personal history, passing has allowed some individuals to become absorbed into the mainstream and to lose the stigma of being defined as a minority. To these people, this acceptance by the dominant group is worth the high cost.

Acceptance is another common reaction to minority status. Some minority groups have learned to live with their minority status with little overt challenge to the system. They may or may not hold deep-seated hostility, but they ultimately conclude that change in the society is not very likely and acceptance may be the rational means to survive within the existing system.

There are many possible explanations for this seeming indifference. For example, religious beliefs allow poor Hindus in India to believe that if they accept their lot in life, they will be reincarnated in a higher life-form. If they rebel, they can expect to be reincarnated into a lower life-form. Their religion is a form of social control.

Unfortunately, many children are socialized to believe that they are inferior or superior because minority group members are expected by the dominant group to behave in certain ways and often live up to that expectation because of the self-fulfilling prophesy (Farley 2009). Evidence to support stereotypes is easily found in individual cases— "inferior" kids live in shabby houses, dress less well, speak a different dialect. At school and on the job, minority position is reaffirmed by these characteristics.

Avoidance means shunning all contact with the dominant group. This can involve an active and organized attempt to leave the culture or live separately as some political exiles have done. In the United States, Marcus Garvey organized a Back-to-Africa movement in the 1920s, encouraging Blacks to give up on any hope of justice in American society and to return to Africa. Native Americans continually moved west in the 19th century—trying to or being forced to get away from the White Anglo settlers, who brought alcohol and deadly diseases. In some cases, withdrawal may mean dropping out of society as an individual—escaping by obliterating consciousness in drugs or alcohol. The escape from oppression and low self-concept is one reason why drug use is higher in minority ghettos and alcohol abuse is rampant on Native American reservations.

Aggression resulting from anger and resentment over minority status and from subjugation may lead to retaliation or violence. Because the dominant group holds significant power, a direct route such as voting against the dominant group or defeating oppressors in war is not always possible. Indeed, direct confrontation can be very costly to those lacking political or economic power. Suicide bombers from Palestine, Iraq, and Afghanistan represent the many disaffected youth who are frustrated and angry over their situations, with no means to fight back, express their anger, or bring about change.

Aggression usually takes one of two forms, indirect aggression or displaced aggression. Indirect aggression includes biting assertiveness in the arts—literature, art, racial and ethnic humor, and music—and in job-related actions such as inefficiency and slowdowns by workers. Displaced aggression, on the other hand, involves hostilities directed toward individuals or groups other than the dominant group, as happens when youth gangs attack other ethnic gangs in nearby neighborhoods. They substitute aggression against the dominant group by acting against the other minority groups to protest against their frustrating circumstances and limited resources.

The four responses discussed thus far address the angst and humiliation that individual minorities feel. Each strategy allows an individual person to try to cope, but none addresses the structural causes of discrimination. The final strategy is change-oriented action. Minority groups in some countries embrace violent tactics as a means to bring about change—riots, insurrections, hijackings, and terrorist bombings aimed at the dominant group. Their hope is either to destroy the dominant power structure or to threaten the stability of the current macro-level system such that the group in power is willing to make some changes. Sometimes, minority reactions result in assimilation, but often, the goal is to create a pluralistic society in which cultures can be different yet have economic opportunities open to all. Minority groups pursue social change in the meso- and macro-level structures of society.

Nonviolent Resistance: Institutional and Societal Policy for Change

Another technique for bringing about change at the institutional and societal levels is nonviolent resistance by minority groups. The model for this technique comes from India,

Mahatma Gandhi, leader of the Indian civil disobedience revolt, marched to the shore to collect salt, a clear violation of the law, a law that he felt was inhumane and unjust. On the right is Sarojini Naidu, a woman lieutenant in his nonviolent resistance movement.

where, in the 1950s, Mahatma Gandhi led the struggle for independence from Britain. Although Britain clearly had superior weapons and armies, boycotts, sit-ins, and other forms of resistance eventually led to British withdrawal as the ruling colonial power. Jesse Jackson, a U.S. presidential candidate in 1984 and 1988, led his Chicago-based organization, PUSH, in economic boycotts against companies such as Coca-Cola to force them to hire and promote Blacks. Cesar Chavez led boycotts against grape growers to improve the working conditions of migrant workers. This strategy has been used successfully by workers and students to bring about change in many parts of the world.

In the United States, Martin Luther King Jr. followed in the nonviolent resistance tradition of India's Gandhi, who sought to change India's laws so that minorities could have equal opportunities within the society. King's strategy involved nonviolent popular protests, economic boycotts, and challenges to the current norms of the society. The National Association for the Advancement of Colored People (NAACP) sought to bring about legal changes through lawsuits that created new legal precedents supporting racial equality. Often, these lawsuits addressed side-effect discrimination—a meso-level problem. Many other associations for minorities—including the

Anti-Defamation League (founded by Jews) and La Raza Unida (a Chicano organization)—also seek to address problems both within organizations and institutions (meso level) and in the nation as a whole (macro level). Like King, who had an undergraduate degree in sociology, many sociologists have used their training to address issues of discrimination and disprivilege through empowerment and change.

Some other minority individuals have used their sociology degrees in business, both to enhance their own competence in the business world and to help their ethnic communities. One example is the work of David Staddon, who writes about his applications of sociology in consulting, administration, and business. See the next "Applied Sociologist at Work."

The Applied Sociologist at Work— David Staddon   Native American Cultures and Applied Sociology in Business

I have had several positions in Indian Country, beginning with the YMCA of Michigan's Native American Outreach Project. The program worked with every tribe in Michigan and included urban youth leadership development, family enhancement, and the preservation of traditional cultural values and behaviors. I left that position to attend graduate school at Central Michigan University where I eventually became director of their Native American Programs Office. Since then I have worked with a number of indigenous nations, including the Saginaw Chippewa in Michigan and the Northern Arapaho in Wyoming. A person with sociological/intercultural skills can have a distinct advantage in the marketplace, especially considering the changing demographics in the U.S. This is especially true where there are cultural intersections involved, and I experienced many of those working with native nations.

One of the first challenges (of many) that I needed to overcome was the fact that 98% of all our casino customers in Wyoming were tribal members. That really did not help the Arapaho people since we were simply churning money through the local economy. We needed to diversify our customer base and bring in "outside" money. Many organizations currently talk about "re-engineering their corporate culture" to be more friendly and accessible to minority groups. I was faced with the interesting challenge of creating an atmosphere where *non-Indians* felt safe, secure, and comfortable in our gaming environment, rather like "reverse engineering."

The situation was further complicated by the fact that I am from a different tribe than the Arapahos. Most people (including sociologists) have scant understanding of the intercultural differences between Indian tribes—an important factor in having a successful career in Indian Country. So I had to learn to deal with intersections between Arapaho-Ottawa-Mainstream-Male/female-Corporate values, outlooks, and behaviors. My challenge was to build a corporate culture that took all these factors into consideration and led to financial success of the business. So some of my first priorities were in image development and customer service.

Having spoken with many white folks in Riverton, I came away with the distinct view that many (if not all) of them felt that the casino was an unsafe place. I was told, "If I win money, I'll just get knocked in the head in the parking lot." We had to do many things to change the image, including designing a new logo for the casino and providing snazzy uniforms for all the staff. The logo was on everything, so we could unify the corporate image. I instituted customer service training and standards for interaction with customers, installed more lights in the parking lot, and started an escort service (not *that* kind!) where, upon request, our security staff would escort customers to their cars in the parking lot. I also took pictures of our security staff and developed some advertising materials emphasizing friendliness, safety, and security. I got active with the local chamber of commerce, establishing relationships with local business and opinion leaders.

By the time I left, we had experienced a completed turn-around with the business—both from the financial standpoint and its customer base. Our customer base is now over 90% non-Native, and we were bringing millions of dollars into the local native community. Prior to this, the casino had only had two years of profitability out of twelve.

A lot of other peripheral efforts went into developing the organization and improving its image. In short, we worked with "image-management" ideas from Goffman and notions of how people define a situation—a central idea in symbolic interactionism. I was doing applied sociology to help this business venture work—a business venture that also helped a minority community.

My background in social sciences was vital in melding the cultural considerations which contributed to an organizational culture conducive to employee creativity, success, and enjoyment. My training and education in social science has had direct relevance for my various jobs. One interesting aspect of applied social science in business is the examination of corporate culture and its relationship to behavior, public image, policies, planning, and other organizational behavior. A liberal arts education is becoming increasingly important in the U.S. workplace, especially one that emphasizes cross-cultural understanding. For me, coupling this knowledge with my business skills was the key to success.

Note: David Staddon is a member of the Wikwemikong Band of Ottawa Indians, located on Manitoulin Island, Lake Huron, Georgian Bay, Southern Ontario. David has been working with "first-nation" governments most of his working life. With a bachelor's degree in sociology/social science and a master's in administration, he is well prepared to deal with native issues. He now works with the St. Regis Mohawk Tribe near Massena, New York, as their Director of Public Information.

Thinking Sociologically

The discussion above presents five types of responses by minorities to the experience of discrimination and rejection. Four of these are at the micro level and only one at the meso and macro levels. Why do you suppose most of the coping strategies of minorities are at the micro level?

Policies Governing Minority and Dominant Group Relations

Civilians, mostly women, children, and elderly people, are fleeing the Darfur region of Sudan in great numbers, trying to find a degree of safety, food, and shelter after people in their villages have been slaughtered by bullets and machetes. Towns have been pillaged and bombed, and planting fields have been burned (Polgreen 2008). Most of the 45,000 survivors are seeking refuge in camps in eastern Chad, places already crowded with more than 300,000 survivors (United Nations Commission on Human Rights 2006a). Darfur, Sudan, is only one recent site of war resulting in refugees. Kenya is also experiencing internal refugee displacement as a result of conflicts over the recent elections. In the 1990s, residents fled from Albania, Bosnia, Cuba, Haiti, Rwanda, Zaire, and other nations.

These conflicts are complex and represent different ethnic and religious groups fighting for power, land, and resources. For our purposes, the important point is that the refugees come from minority groups in the country, civilians caught in a conflict they cannot control.

War, famine, and economic dislocation force families to seek new locations where they can survive and perhaps improve their circumstances. About 17 countries have policies to host or accept refugees from war-torn countries as new citizens. Refugees who cannot return home may end up in a new country, perhaps on a new continent.

The degree of acceptance children and their families find in their newly adopted countries varies depending on the government's policies, the group's background, and economic conditions in the host country (Rumbaut and Portes 2001). Some formerly refugee-friendly countries are closing their doors to immigration because of the strain on their economy and threats of terrorism. In this section, we consider the policies that emerge as dominant and minority groups come into contact and interact.

Video Link 8.5
Watch President Obama speak about race relations.

Policies to Reduce Prejudice, Racism, and Discrimination

In the preceding pages, we considered some of the costs to individuals, groups, societies, and the global community inflicted by discriminatory behavior and policies. Discrimination's influence is widespread, from slavery and subjugation to unequal educational and work opportunities, to legal and political arenas, and to every other part of the social world. If one accepts the premise that discrimination is destructive to both individuals and societies, then ways must be found to address the root problems effectively. However, finding solutions to ethnic tensions around the world leaves many experts baffled. Consider the ethnic strife in Bosnia and Croatia in Eastern Europe; conflicts between Palestinians and Israelis in the Middle East; conflicts between Shiites and Sunni Muslims in Iraq; tribal genocide in Kenya, Sudan, and Rwanda in Africa; and conflicts between religious groups in Northern Ireland. In places such as these, each new generation is socialized into the prejudice and antagonisms that perpetuate the animosity and violence. Social scientists and policymakers have made little progress in resolving conflicts that rest on century-old hostilities.

From our social world perspective, we know that no problem can be solved by working at only one level of analysis. A successful strategy must bring about change at every level of the social world—individual attitudes, organizational discrimination, cultural stereotypes, societal stratification systems, and national and international structures. However, most current strategies focus on only one level of analysis. Figure 8.3 shows some of the programs enacted to combat prejudice, racism, and discrimination at the individual, group, societal, and global levels.

Individual or Small-Group Solutions

Programs to address prejudice, racism, and stereotypes through human relations workshops, group encounters, and therapy can achieve goals with small numbers of people. For instance, African American and White children who are placed in interracial classrooms in schools are more likely to develop close interracial friendships (Ellison and Powers 1994). Also, the higher the people's education level, the more likely they are to respect and like others and to appreciate and enjoy differences. Education gives a broader, more universal outlook; reduces misconceptions and prejudices; shows that many issues do not have clear answers; and encourages multicultural understanding and focus on individuals, not judging of groups.

Two groups with strong multicultural education programs are the Anti-Defamation League and the Southern Poverty Law Center's Teaching Tolerance Program. Both groups provide schools and community organizations with literature, videos, and other materials aimed at combating intolerance and discrimination toward others.

However, these strategies do not address the social conditions underlying the problems because they reach only a few people. Thus, this approach alone achieves only limited results. It also does not begin to address dilemmas that are rooted in meso- and macro-level discrimination. Micro-level solutions are often blind to the structural causes of problems.

There has been a great deal of controversy about the barbed and razor wire fence along the U.S. border with Mexico. Some people feel it is the only way to enforce immigration laws and to control the growth rate of the country. Others think that walls of this sort foster we-they thinking, are a waste of money, and do not lead to permanent solutions. Many Mexican Americans think such a wall is insulting to Mexican American people. Do you think such a wall is a step in the right direction or not, and why?

Types of Problems at Each Level

Individual level: stereotypes and prejudice

Group level: negative group interaction

Societal level: institutional discrimination

Global level: deprivation of human rights

Types of Solutions or Programs at Each Level

Therapy, tolerance-education programs

Positive contact, awareness by majority of their many privileges

Education, media, legal-system revisions

Human rights movements, international political pressures

Figure 8.3   Problems and Solutions

Group Contact

Many social scientists advocate organized group contact between dominant and minority group members to improve relations and break down stereotypes and fears. Although not all contact reduces prejudice, many studies have shown the benefits of contact. Some essential conditions for success are equal status of the participants, noncompetitive and nonthreatening contact, and projects or goals on which to cooperate (Farley 2009).

In a classic study of group contact, social psychologists Muzafer Sherif and Caroline Sherif (1953) and their colleagues ran summer camps for boys of ages 11 and 12 and studied how groups were established and reestablished. On arrival, the boys were divided into two groups that competed periodically. The more fierce the competition, the more hostile the two cabins of boys became toward each other. The experimenters tried several methods to resolve the conflicts and tensions:

1. *Appealing to higher values (be nice to your neighbors):* This proved of limited value.

2. *Talking with the natural leaders of the groups (compromises between group leaders):* The group leaders agreed, but their followers did not go along.

3. *Bringing the groups together in a pleasant situation (a mutually rewarding situation):* This did not reduce competition; if anything, it increased it.

4. *Introducing a superordinate goal that could be achieved only if everyone cooperated:* This technique worked. The boys were presented with a dilemma: The water system had broken, or a fire needed to be put out, and all were needed to solve the problem. The groups not only worked together, but their established stereotypes eventually began to fade away. Such a situation in a community might arise from efforts to get a candidate elected, a bill passed, or a neighborhood improved. At the global macro level, hostile countries sit together to solve issues.

Programs involving group contact to improve conditions for minorities have been tried in many areas of social life, including integrated housing projects, job programs to promote minority hiring, and busing children to schools, to achieve a higher level of racial and socioeconomic integration. For instance, the Chicago Housing Authority opened a refurbished mixed-income housing experiment with resident participation in decision making. Although many predicted failure, the project thrived, with long waiting lists of families wanting to participate (McCormick 1992). Positive contact experiences tend to improve relations in groups on a micro level by breaking down stereotypes, but to

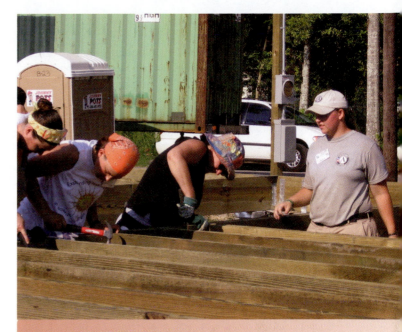

An AmeriCorps volunteer supervises construction on a Habitat for Humanity building in St. Tammany Parish, Louisiana, for people displaced by Hurricane Katrina—many of them minorities. The solution proposed by some nongovernmental organizations (NGOs) such as Habitat is to address problems and suffering with volunteer work and donations. Do you agree?

solidify these gains, we must also address institutionalized inequalities.

Institutional and Societal Strategies to Improve Group Relations

Sociologists contend that institutional and societal approaches to reduce discrimination get closer to the core of the problems and affect larger numbers of people than do micro-level strategies. For instance, voluntary advocacy organizations pursue political change through lobbying, watchdog monitoring, educational information dissemination, canvassing, protest marches, rallies, and boycotts (Minkoff 1995). Groups such as the NAACP and ACLU have filed lawsuits and lobbied legislators for changes in laws that they believed were discriminatory.

The Civil Rights Commission, Fair Employment Practices Commission, and Equal Employment Opportunity Commission are government organizations that protect rights and work toward equality for all citizens. These agencies oversee practices and hear complaints relating to racial, sexual, age, and other forms of discrimination. Legislation, too, can modify behaviors. Laws requiring equal treatment of minorities have resulted in increased tolerance of those who are "different" and have opened doors that previously were closed to minorities.

In the United States, executive action to end discrimination has been taken by a number of presidents. In 1948, Harry Truman moved to successfully end military segregation, and subsequent presidents have urged the passage of civil rights legislation and equal employment opportunity legislation. Affirmative action laws, first implemented during Lyndon Johnson's administration, have been used to fight pervasive institutional racism (Crosby 2004; Farley 2009).

Affirmative Action

One of the most contentious policies in the United States has been affirmative action. The following discussion addresses the intentions and forms of the policy. A societal policy for change, affirmative action actually involves three different policies. Its simplest and original form, which we call *strict affirmative action*, involves taking affirmative or positive steps to make sure that unintentional discrimination does not occur. It requires, for example, that an employer who receives federal monies must advertise a position widely and not just through internal or friendship networks. If the job requires an employee with a college education, then by federal law, employers must recruit through minority and women's colleges as well as state and private colleges in the region. If employers are hiring in the suburbs, they are obliged to contact unemployment agencies in poor and minority communities as well as those in the affluent neighborhoods. After taking these required extra steps, employers are expected to hire the most qualified candidate who applies, regardless of race, ethnicity, sex, religion, or other external characteristics. The focus is on providing opportunities for the best-qualified people. For many people, this is the meaning of affirmative action, and it is inconceivable that this could be characterized as reverse discrimination, for members of the dominant group will be hired if they are in fact the most qualified. These policies do not overcome the problem that qualified people who have been marginalized may be competent but do not have the traditional paper credentials that document their qualifications.

The second policy is a quota system, a requirement that employers *must* hire a certain percentage of minorities. For the most part, quotas are now unconstitutional. They apply only in cases where a court has found a company to have a substantial and sustained history of discrimination against minorities and where the employment position does not have many requirements (if the job entails sweeping floors and cleaning toilets, there would not be an expectation of a specific academic degree or a particular grade point average).

The third policy, and the one that has created the most controversy among opponents of affirmative action, is preference policies. Preference policies are based on the concept of equity, the belief that sometimes people must be treated differently in order to treat them fairly. This policy was enacted to level the playing field, which was not rewarding highly competent people because of institutional racism.

The objectives of preference policies are to (a) eliminate qualifications that are not substantially related to the job but that unwittingly favor members of the dominant group and (b) foster achievement of objectives of the organization that are only possible through enhanced diversity. To overcome these inequalities and achieve certain objectives, employers and educational institutions take account of race or sex by making special efforts to hire and retain workers or accept students from groups that have been underrepresented. In many cases, these individuals bring qualifications others do not possess. Consider the following examples.

A goal of the medical community is to provide access to medical care for underserved populations. There is an extreme shortage of physicians on the Navajo reservation. Thus, a Navajo applicant for medical school might be accepted, even if her scores are slightly lower than another candidate's, because she speaks Navajo and understands the culture. One could argue that she is more qualified to be a physician on the reservation than someone who knows nothing about Navajo society but has a slightly higher grade point average or test score. Some argue that tests should not be the only measure to determine the merit of applicants.

Likewise, an African American police officer may have more credibility in a minority neighborhood and may be able to defuse a delicate conflict more effectively than a White officer who scored slightly higher on a paper-and-pencil placement test. Sometimes, being a member of a particular ethnic group can actually make one more qualified for a position.

A 1996 proposition in California to eliminate affirmative action programs in the state was passed in a popular referendum. The result was that colleges in California are allowed to offer preference to applicants based on state residency, athletic competency, musical skill, having had a parent graduate from the school, and many other factors—but not race or ethnicity. Many colleges and universities admit students because they need an outstanding point guard on the basketball team, an extraordinary soprano for the college choir, or a student from a distant state for geographic diversity. These students are shown preference by being admitted with lower test scores than some other applicants because they are "differently qualified."

A landmark case filed in a Detroit district court in 1997 alleged that the University of Michigan gave unlawful preference to minorities in undergraduate admissions and in law school admissions. In this controversial case, the court ruled that these undergraduate admissions were discriminatory because numbers rather than individualized judgments were used to make the determination (University of Michigan Documents Center 2003). Consider the next "Engaging Sociology" on page 276 and decide whether you think the policy was unfair and whether only race and ethnicity should have been deleted from the preferences allowed.

The question remains, Should preferences be given to accomplish diversity? Some people feel that programs involving any sort of preference result in reverse discrimination. Others believe that such programs have encouraged employers, educational institutions, and government to look carefully at hiring policies and minority candidates and that many more competent minority group members are working in the public sector as a result of these policies.

Global Movements for Human Rights

A unique coalition of world nations has emerged from a recent international event—the terrorist attack of September 11, 2001. In this attack on the World Trade Center in New York City, a center housing national and international businesses and workers, citizens from 90 countries were killed when two hijacked commercial jetliners crashed into the towers. In addition to the worldwide condemnation of the attack, many countries' governments have pledged to fight against terrorism. Yet why did such a heinous act occur? Many social scientists attempting to identify a cause point to the disparities between the rich and poor peoples of the world. The perpetrators likely felt that Muslims were treated as inconsequential players in the global world and their values and way of life were threatened. They struck out to make a dramatic impact on the world community and the United States. The point is that global issues and ethnic conflicts in the social world are interrelated.

The rights granted to citizens of any nation used to be considered the business of each sovereign nation, but after the Nazi holocaust, German officers were tried at the Nuremberg trials, and the United Nations passed the Universal Declaration of Human Rights. Since that time, many international organizations have been established, often under the auspices of the United Nations, to deal with health issues, world poverty and debt, trade, security, and many other issues affecting world citizens—World Health Organization, World Bank, World Trade Organization, and numerous regional trade and security organizations.

Some civil rights or human rights movements have justice issues in other countries as their focal point. Amnesty International is one such movement, which has strong support on many college campuses.

The United Nations, several national governments (Britain, France, and Canada), and privately funded advocacy groups speak up for international human rights as a principle that transcends national boundaries. The most widely recognized private group is Amnesty International, a watchdog group that does lobbying on behalf of human rights and supports political prisoners and ethnic group spokespersons. When Amnesty International was awarded the Nobel Peace Prize in 1997, the group's visibility was dramatically increased. Even some activist sociologists have formed groups such as Sociologists Without Borders, or SSF (*Sociólogos sin Fronteras*; www.sociologistswitoutborders.org), a transnational organization committed to the idea that "all people have equal rights to political and legal protections, to socioeconomic security, to self-determination, and to their personality."

Audio Link 8.3
Listen to a story about race relations in South Africa.

Everyone can make a positive difference in the world, and one place to start is in our community (see "Contributing to Your Social World"). We can counter prejudice, racism, and discrimination in our own groups by teaching children to see beyond "we" and "they" and by speaking out for fairness and against stereotypes and discrimination.

Engaging Sociology

Preference Policies at the University of Michigan

To enhance diversity on the campus—a practice that many argue makes a university a better learning environment and enhances the academic reputation of the school—many colleges have preference policies in admissions. However, the University of Michigan was sued by applicants who felt that they were not admitted because others had replaced them on the roster due to their racial or ethnic background.

The University of Michigan is a huge university, so a numbering system is needed to handle the volume (tens of thousands) of applicants; the authorities cannot make a decision based on personal knowledge of each candidate. Thus, they give points for each quality they deem desirable in the student body. A maximum of 150 points is possible, and a score of a 100 would pretty much ensure admission. The university felt that any combination of points accumulated according to the following formula would result in a highly qualified and diverse student body.

For academics, up to 110 points are possible:

- 80 points for grades (a particular grade point average [GPA] in high school would result in a set number of points: 80 points for a 4.0 GPA, 56 points for a 2.8 GPA)
- 12 points for standardized test scores (ACT or SAT)
- 10 points for the academic rigor of the high school (so all students who went to tougher high schools earned points)
- 8 points for the difficulty of the curriculum (e.g., points for honors curriculum vs. keyboarding courses)

For especially desired qualities, including diversity, up to 40 points are possible for any combination of the following (but no more than 40 in this "desired qualities" category):

- Geographical distribution (10 for Michigan resident, an additional 6 for underrepresented Michigan county)
- Legacy—a relative had attended Michigan (4 points for a parent, 1 for a grandparent or sibling)
- Quality of submitted essay (3 points)
- Personal achievement—a special accomplishment that was noteworthy (up to 5 points)
- Leadership and service (5 points each)
- Miscellaneous (only one of these could be used):

  - Socioeconomic disadvantage (20 points)
  - Racial or ethnic minority (20 points; disallowed by the court ruling)
  - Men in nursing (5 points)
  - Scholarship athlete (20 points)
  - Provost's discretion (20 points; usually for the son or daughter of a large financial donor or a politician)

In addition to ethnicity being given preference, athleticism, musical talent, having a relative who is an alum, or being the child of someone who is important to the university are also considered. Some schools also give points for being a military veteran. The legal challenge to this admissions system was based only on the racial and ethnic preference given to some candidates, not to the other items that are preferenced.

* * * * * *

Answer the following questions:

1. Does this process seem reasonable as a way to get a diverse and highly talented incoming class of students? Why or why not?

2. Does it disadvantage some students? Explain how.

3. How would you design a fair system of admissions, and what other factors would you consider?

Socioeconomic inequality combines with racial and ethnic disprivilege to create some problems for a society. However, a full understanding of inequality also requires insights into discrimination based on gender. In some ways, the most intriguing topic is the issues that arise when we look at the intersection and overlapping of race, class, and gender.

What Have We Learned?

Why are minority group members in most countries poorer than dominant group members? This and other chapter-opening questions can be answered in part by considering the fact that human beings have a tendency to create "we" and "they" categories and to treat those who are different as somehow less human. The categories can be based on physical appearance, cultural differences, religious differences, or anything the community or society defines as important. Once people notice differences with others, they are more inclined to hurt "them" or to harbor advantages for "us" if there is competition over resources that both groups want. Even within a nation, where people are supposedly all "us," there can be sharp differences and intense hostilities.

Key Points

- Although the concept of race has no real meaning biologically, race is a social construction because people *believe* it is real. (See pp. 246–251.)

- Minority group status—having less power and less access to resources—may occur because of racial status or because of ethnic (cultural) factors. (See pp. 251–253.)

- Prejudice operates at the micro level of society and is closest to people's own lives, but it has much less impact on minorities than discrimination. Symbolic racism has become a significant problem—the denial of overt prejudice but the rejection of any policies that might correct inequities. (See pp. 253–257.)

- At the meso level, institutional discrimination operates through two processes: side effect and past-in-present. These forms of discrimination are unintended and unconscious—operating quite separately from any prejudice of individuals in the society. (See pp. 257–260.)

- When very large ethnic groups or even nations collide, some people are typically displaced and find themselves in minority status. (See pp. 260–261.)

- The policies of the dominant group may include genocide, subjugation, population transfer, assimilation, or pluralism. (See pp. 261–264.)

- The costs of racism to society are high, including loss of human talent and resources, and these costs make life more difficult for minority group members. (See pp. 267–268.)

- The coping devices used by minorities include five strategies: assimilation, acceptance, avoidance, aggression, and organizing for societal change. Only one of these, organizing for societal change, addresses the meso- and macro-level causes. (See pp. 268–271.)

- Policies to address problems of prejudice and discrimination range from individual and small-group efforts at the micro level to institutional, societal, and even global social movements. (See pp. 271–274.)

- Affirmative action policies are one approach, but the broad term *affirmative action* includes three different sets of policies that are quite distinct and have different outcomes. (See pp. 274–276.)

Contributing to Our Social World: What Can We Do?

At the Local Level

African American Student Associations, Arab American Student Associations, and Native American Student Associations: Most campuses have student organizations dedicated to fighting racism and promoting the rights of racial minorities. Identify one of these groups on your campus and arrange to attend a meeting. If appropriate, volunteer to help with its work.

At the Organizational or Institutional Level

The Leadership Conference on Civil and Human Rights: This is a national coalition dedicated to combating racism and its effects. It maintains a Web site that includes a directory of more than 100 local chapters (www.civilrights .org). Explore ways in which you can participate in these programs.

Teaching Tolerance (www.splcenter.org/center/tt/teach.jsp): This program of the Southern Poverty Law Center has curriculum materials for teaching about diversity and a program for enhancing cross-ethnic cooperation and dialogue in schools. Check into internships in local primary and secondary schools, and explore with them ways in which the Teaching for Tolerance approach can be incorporated into the curricula.

At the National and Global Levels

American Indian Movement (AIM; www.aimovement.org): This highly activist organization has worked for many years to bring the plight of Native Americans to the attention of the public and the government and to promote the civil/human rights of community members. Explore ways in which you can assist in the community's educational and legislative initiatives.

Cultural Survival and the UN Permanent Forum on Indigenous Issues (www.cs.org and www.un.org/esa/socdev/unpfii): Organizations such as these provide opportunities for combating racism globally. You should also consider purchasing only coffee and, especially, chocolate that are Fair Trade products (packages are clearly marked as such).

Amnesty International (www.amnestyusa.org): This worldwide movement of people campaigns for internationally recognized human rights. It relies heavily on volunteer workers.

 For chapter-specific resources, including **Frontline**, **TED**, and **YouTube** videos; self-quizzes; web exercises; and more, visit **www.pineforge.com/oswmedia3e.**

CHAPTER 9

Gender Stratification

She/He—Who Goes First?

NATIONAL LEAGUE FOR DEMOCRACY

Social inequality is especially evident in gender relations, and although in some societies women are treated with deference, they are rarely given first access to positions of significant power or financial reward. While they may hold many work roles, they often carry the load of child care by themselves, causing more role strains. The photos presented here focus on women's roles.

Global Community

Society

National Organizations,
Institutions, and Ethnic Subcultures

Local Organizations
and Community

Me (and My
Gender
Groups)

Micro: Groups including peers, neighbors,
teachers, religious leaders socializing into gender roles

Meso: Organizations and
institutions limiting access to positions

Macro: National policies provide
sex-based privileges

Macro: Gender status determined
by laws and power structures

Think About It	
Me (and My Inner Circle)	How does being female or male affect your thoughts and behaviors?
Local Community	Why do some people face violence in their homes and communities because of their sexuality?
National Institutions; Complex Organizations; Ethnic Groups	Can anything be done in our organizations and institutions to make men and women more equal?
National Society	Why do women have second class status in your society and in other societies?
Global Community	How is gender inequality an issue in this new age of globalization?

Jocelyn is now retired, but she is having trouble making ends meet. After training in nursing, including a master's degree, she married and dropped her career to raise her family. The marriage did not work, and 15 years after her college training she found herself with no credit, two children, little job experience, and mounting expenses. She is a conscientious and hard worker, but with two children and meager child support from the father, she could not put much away for retirement. Nursing does not pay well in her town in the Midwest, but there had been few other career options for females in the early 1960s when she was getting her education. Moreover, she had worked a full-time job and done all the housework for 22 years, but two decades does not build a very large retirement annuity, and she had never been able to buy a very adequate home on her income. If she had been a male with a master's degree, her lifetime earnings would have been nearly 1 million dollars more in cumulative income (U.S. Census Bureau 2010a). Her life chances were clearly affected by the fact that she was a female.

Jocelyn's granddaughter, Emma, will have a range of opportunities that were beyond consideration for her grandma. Ideas about sex, gender, and appropriate roles for men and women not only transform over time, but they also vary a great deal from one society to the next. Some practices of your own society may seem very strange to women and men in another society. Moreover, gender identities and roles are not stagnant; they change slowly over time, reflecting the economic, political, and social realities of the society. For instance, women in today's India seldom commit *sati* (suicide) on their husband's funeral pyre; however, before the practice of *sati* was outlawed, it was a common way to deal with widows who no longer had a means of support (Weitz 1995).

In this chapter, we will explore the concepts of gender, sexuality, one's sex, and combine these with race and class for further understanding of the stratification system. At the micro level, we consider gender socialization, and at the meso and macro levels, gender stratification, or placement in the society's stratification system. The costs and consequences of gender stratification plus policy implications will end this chapter.

Sex, Gender, and the Stratification System

You name it, and some society has probably done it! Gender relations are no exception. Variations around the world show that most roles and identities are not biological but rather socially constructed. In Chapter 7, we discussed factors that stratify individuals into social groups (castes and classes) and in Chapter 8, we discussed the roles that race and ethnicity play in stratification. Add the concepts of sex and gender, and we have a more complex picture of how class, race and ethnicity, and gender together influence who we are and our positions in society. Consider the following examples from societies that illustrate some unusual human social constructions based on sex and gender. These examples show that gender roles are created by humans to meet the needs of their societies. We will then move to more familiar societies.

Men of the Wodaabe society in Niger, Africa, are nomadic cattle herders and traders who would be defined as effeminate by most Western standards because of their behavior patterns. The men are like birds, showing their colorful feathers to attract females. They take great care in doing their hair, applying makeup, and dressing to attract women. They also gossip with each other while sipping their tea. What are the women doing? They are cooking meals, caring for the children, cleaning, tending to the animals, planting small gardens, and preparing for the next move of this nomadic group (Beckwith 1993; Saharan Vibe 2007). These patterns have developed over time as a way for the group to meet its basic human needs and survive.

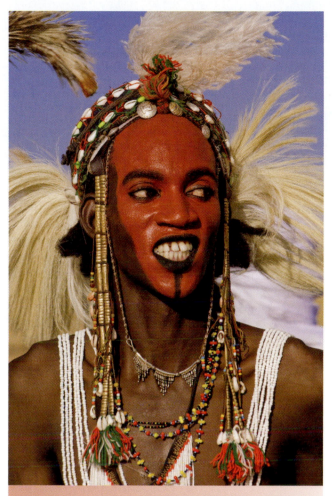

Wodaabe men in Niger (Africa) go to great pains with makeup, hair, and jewelry to ensure that they are highly attractive, a pattern that is thought by many people in North America to be associated with females.

Muslim girls and women in some parts of the world cover their faces when in public. The display of bodies, even in a college classroom, would be immoral to many Muslims. However, this is far from a universal pattern, and in many predominantly Muslim countries, such coverings would be unusual.

People in industrial societies might seem unacceptably aggressive and competitive to people of the Arapesh tribe in New Guinea, where gentleness and nonaggression are the rule for both women and men. Yet nearby, women of the Tchambuli people are assertive, businesslike, and the primary economic providers. Men of the Tchambuli exhibit expressive, nurturing, and gossipy behavior. The Mbuti and !Kung peoples of Africa value gender equality in their division of labor and treatment of women and men, and among the Agta of the Philippines, women do the hunting. In west African societies such as the Ashanti and Yoruba kingdoms, women control much of the market system (Dahlberg 1981; Mead [1935] 1963; Turnbull 1962). Each tradition has evolved over time to meet the basic human needs.

Under the Taliban in Afghanistan, women cannot be seen in public without total body covering that meets strict requirements. Anyone not obeying could be stoned to death. Women cannot hold public positions or work outside their homes. If they become ill, women cannot be examined by a physician because all doctors are male. Instead, they have to describe their symptoms to a doctor through a screen (Makhmalbaf 2003).

Obligations of the youngest daughter in some Mexican households require that she forgo marriage, stay at home, and care for her mother as she ages (Esquivel 2001). In China, women and men work in the factories and fields. Children are cared for in state-run child care settings and schools. Equality between the sexes is the goal, although many women claim that they serve in the public work arena in addition to doing a disproportionate amount of work in the private home setting.

Certain tasks must be carried out by individuals and organizations in each society for members to survive. Someone must be responsible for raising children, someone must provide people with the basic necessities (such as food, clothing, and shelter), someone needs to lead, someone must defend the society, and someone must help resolve conflicts. One's sex and age are often used to determine who holds what positions and who carries out what tasks. Each society develops its own way to meet all the needs, and this results in a wide range of gender role expectations from one society to the next.

Thinking Sociologically

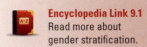

Encyclopedia Link 9.1
Read more about gender stratification.

Why did groups in different corners of the globe develop such radically different ways of organizing their gender roles?

Genetic, Cultural, and Structural Connections—and Divergences

At birth, when doctors say, "It's a . . .," they are referring to the distinguishing primary characteristics that determine **sex**—that is, the penis or vagina. *Sex* is a biological term referring to ascribed genetic, anatomical, and hormonal differences between males and females. Right? Partly. Sex is also "a determination made through the application of socially agreed upon biological criteria for classifying persons as females or males" (West and Zimmerman 1987:127). In other words, sometimes this binary male-female categorization by biological criteria is not clear. Occasionally, people are born with ambiguous genitalia, not fitting the typical definitions of male or female (the *intersexed*). About 1.7% of babies are born with "anomalies of sex chromosomes, internal procreative organs, and external genitalia in a variety of combinations" (Fausto-Sterling 2000:50–54). These babies often undergo surgeries to clarify their gender, with hormonal treatments and possible further surgery at adolescence (Chase 2000). Whether male, female, or intersexed, anatomical differences at birth or chromosomal typing before birth result in cultural attempts to clearly categorize sex.

In many societies, great lengths are taken to assign a sex to an infant. Why is this an issue? The reality is that sex constitutes a major organizing principle in most societies. People's roles and statuses and society's expectations guiding their behavior are largely determined by their sex. Our attraction to others is expressed by our sexuality and our sexual identity. Most people fall into the category of heterosexual (other sex), homosexual (same sex), bisexual (both sexes), or "varied." The term *heteronormativity* defines the cultural expectations held in most societies that a "normal" girl or boy will be sexually attracted to and eventually have sex with someone of the other sex (Lorber and Moore 2007). The point is that sex is not always a straightforward distinction and is as social as it is biological.

In adolescence, secondary characteristics further distinguish the sexes, with females developing breasts and hips and males developing body hair, muscle mass, and deep voices. Individuals are then expected to adopt the behaviors appropriate to their anatomical features as defined by society. In addition to the physical sex differences between males and females, a few other physical conditions are commonly believed to be sex linked, such as a prevalence of color blindness, baldness, learning disabilities, autism, and hemophilia in males. Yet some traits that members of society commonly link to sex are actually learned through socialization. There is little evidence, for instance, that emotions, personality traits, or ability to fulfill most social statuses are determined by inborn physical sex differences.

Although the terms *sex*, *gender*, and *sexuality* are often used interchangeably, it is useful to understand the technical difference. A person's sex—male, female, or other—is a basis for stratification around the globe, used in every society to assign positions and roles to individuals. However, what is defined as normal behavior for a male, female, or intersexed person in one society could get one killed in another.

Gender, which is learned and created, refers to socially constructed notions of masculinity and femininity. **Gender identity** is how individuals form their identity using these categories and negotiating the constraints they entail. The examples at the beginning of this section illustrate some differences in how cultures are structured around gender.

These gender meanings profoundly influence the statuses we hold within the social structure and our placement in the stratification system (Rothenberg 2007). Individuals are expected to fulfill positions appropriate for their sex category. Statuses are positions within the structures of society, and roles are expected behaviors within those statuses. **Gender roles**, then, are those commonly assigned tasks or expected behaviors linked to an individual's sex-determined statuses (Lips 2007). Members of each society learn the structural guidelines and positions expected of males and females (West and Zimmerman 1987:128). Our positions, which affect access to power and resources, are embedded in institutions at the meso level. However, socially appropriate statuses and roles vary greatly across cultures, with each different culture defining what is right and wrong. There is not some global absolute truth governing gender or gender roles. While both vary across cultures, gender is a learned cultural idea, while gender roles are part of the structural system of the society.

Sexuality refers to how cultures shape the meanings of sexuality and sexual acts and how we experience our own bodies and our bodies in relation to others. Strange as it may seem, sexuality is *socially constructed*. A sex act is a "social enterprise," with cultural norms defining what is normal and acceptable in each society, how we should feel, and hidden assumptions about what the act means (Steele 2005). Even what we find attractive is culturally defined. For a period, in China, men found tiny feet a sexual turn-on—hence, the bound feet of women. In some cultures, legs are the attraction, and in others, men are attracted by breasts. In the United States and elsewhere, pornography is a moneymaker because of the way it stimulates people, yet as the next "Sociology in Our Social World" indicates, the stimulation itself is variable by gender.

Consider the ideal male body as depicted in popular magazines in contemporary Western cultures:

Over 6 feet tall, 180 to 200 pounds, muscular, agile, with straight white teeth, a washboard stomach, six-pack abs, long legs, a full head of hair, a large penis (discreetly shown by a bulge), broad shoulders and chest, strong muscular back, clean shaven, healthy, and slightly tanned if White, or a lightish brown if Black or Hispanic. (Lorber and Moore 2007:114)

We grow up learning what is appealing.

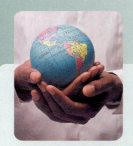

Sociology in Our Social World

Sexuality and Pornography: What Turns You On?

By Michael Norris

Sexuality and arousal is complex and it varies between men and women. Pornography is often used to titillate the viewers sexually, and it has become big business. Adult videos generate more revenue than Hollywood box office cinema; more people visit porn sites on the Internet than prominent news sites; 70% of those who visit porn sites admit doing so at work; and college students have more legal access to pornography than alcohol. So despite objections to the "thingification" of women (or of men) in pornography, it is widely used. However, there are some interesting variations in how people respond to pornographic videos that are seldom understood.

Meredith Chivers and her colleagues (Chivers, Seto, and Blanchard 2007) were interested in gender differences in reaction to sexual videos. The researchers found that for women, sexual activity itself was arousing, whereas men tended to be influenced more by the gender of the actors in the videos. Women were aroused by sexual activity regardless of the gender of the participants and even when the actors were nonhuman primates. Women can apparently be genitally aroused just by cues of sexual activity. On the other hand, heterosexual men were aroused by videos of nude women engaged in nonsexual activities such as exercise. By contrast videos of nude males were no more arousing to heterosexual women than videos of the Himalayan mountain range (Newman 2008).

Chivers and her colleagues (2007) also discovered gender differences in biological arousal and subjective awareness of that arousal. Men were immediately aware of their physiological arousal while women were often not. This gender difference has been verified in previous research, which suggests that biological reactions precede subjective awareness of arousal in women, but not in men. Biological arousal may happen in women without any self-reported arousal at all.

This research adds to a growing body of literature suggesting greater flexibility of women's sexuality in terms of sexual identity, same-sex attraction, and same-sex behavior. Women's greater sexual flexibility may result from a tendency to identify with both male and female targets of sexual activity and greater same-sex emotional attachments than men.

This study also helps explain the fact that for heterosexuals viewing mainstream, commercially available pornography, watching two women having sex is more socially acceptable than watching two men having sex. A popular cultural belief, reinforced by comedians, is that men particularly enjoy "lesbian action" in adult videos. Research suggests that this is not the case. In fact, the adult video industry may include these vignettes because it stimulates women, and this may help to sell their product. Sexuality is complex and involves both biological reactions and socially constructed definitions of sexuality.

Note: Michael Norris is a professor at Wright State University, where he teaches and does research in sociology and criminal justice.

In the 19th century, medical science began to study sexuality and sexual behavior. Most often, sexuality was defined in binary terms (Colligan 2004), and behaviors falling outside heterosexual boundaries were defined as perverse. In the 20th century, researchers such as Kinsey (Kinsey et al. 1953) and Masters and Johnson (1966, 1970) conducted studies that uncovered actual sexual behaviors, not just those defined as normal. These studies considered a range of sexual practices, from premarital sex and homosexuality to orgasm and masturbation (Lindsey 2008).

The struggles that individuals have with their sexual identity are reflected in the studies of *transgender*—when intersexed individuals do not fit clearly into female or male sex classifications (Leeder 2004). Transgender refers to "identification as someone who is challenging, questioning, or changing gender from that assigned at birth to a chosen gender—male-to-female, female-to-male, transitioning between genders, or gender 'queer' (challenging gender norms)" (Lorber and Moore 2007:6). Transgendered individuals are of interest to sociologists because of their ambiguous life—living on the boundaries. Due to the pressure to fit in, most transgendered people change themselves, sometimes through surgery, to fit into their chosen gender. They may "pass" as one sex or engage in social interaction as both men and women.

In summary, although the terms *sex*, *gender*, and *sexuality* are often used interchangeably, they do have distinct meanings. The distinctions between these terms are not always as clear-cut as the definitions would imply. One can be a masculine heterosexual female, a masculine homosexual male, or any of a number of possible combinations. Individuals continually negotiate the meanings attached to gender and sexuality—they are *doing gender*, a concept discussed later in this chapter (Lucal 1999; West and Zimmerman 1987).

Sex, Gender, and Sexuality: The Micro Level

"It's a boy!" brings varying cultural responses. In many Western countries, that exclamation results in blue blankets, toys associated with males (footballs, soccer balls, and trucks), roughhousing, and gender socialization messages. In some Asian societies, boys are sources for great rejoicing, whereas girls may be seen as a burden. In China and India, *female infanticide* (killing of newborn girl babies) is sometimes practiced in rural areas, in part because of the cost to poor families of raising a girl and the diminished value of girls. In China, the male preference system has been exacerbated by the government's edict that a couple may have just one child. Exceptions are made in rural areas and for minorities.

Video Link 9.1
Watch a video about gender socialization of men.

Beginning at birth, each individual passes through many stages. At each, there are messages that reinforce appropriate gender behavior in that society. Although gender socialization differs in each society, proper roles are established by the culture and learned from birth. These gender expectations are inculcated into children by parents, siblings, grandparents, neighbors, peers, and even day care providers. If we fail to respond to the expectations of these significant people in our lives, we may experience negative sanctions: teasing, isolation and exclusion, harsh words, and stigma. To avoid these informal sanctions, children usually learn to conform, at least in their public behavior.

The lifelong process of gender socialization continues once we reach *school age* and become more involved in activities separate from our parents. Other people in the community—teachers, religious leaders, coaches—also begin to influence us. We are grouped by sex in many of these social settings, and we come to think of ourselves as like *this* group and unlike *that* group: boys versus girls, we versus they. Even if our parents are not highly traditional in their gender expectations, we still experience many influences at the micro level to conform to traditional gender notions.

With adulthood, the differential treatment and stratification of the sexes take new forms. Men traditionally have more networks and statuses, as well as greater access to resources outside the home. This has resulted in women having less power, because they depend more on husbands or fathers for resources. Even spousal abuse is related to imbalance of power in relationships. Lack of connections to the larger social system makes it difficult for women to remove themselves from abusive relationships.

The subtitle of this chapter asks, "Who goes first?" When it comes to the question of who walks through a door first, the answer is that in many Western societies, *she* does—or at least, formal etiquette would suggest this is proper. The strong man steps back and defers to the weaker female, graciously holding the door for her (Walum 1974). Yet when it comes to who walks through the metaphorical door to the professions, it is the man who goes first. Women are served first at restaurants and at other micro-level settings, but this seems little compensation for the fact that doors are often closed to them at the meso and macro levels of society. Some scholars argue that language is powerful in shaping the behavior and perceptions of people, as discussed in the chapter on culture. Women often end sentences with tag questions, a pattern that involves ending a declarative statement with a short tag that turns it into a question: "That was a good idea, don't you think?" This pattern may cause male business colleagues to think women are insecure or uncertain about themselves. The women themselves may view it as an invitation to collaboration and dialogue. Yet a perception of insecurity may prevent a woman from getting the job or the promotion. On the flip side, when women stop using these "softening" devices, they may be perceived by men as strident, harsh, or "bitchy" (Wood and Reich 2006).

Other aspects of language may also be important. The same adverb or adjective, when preceded by a male or female pronoun, can take on very different meanings. When one says, "He's easy" or "He's loose," it does not generally mean the same thing as when someone says, "She's easy" or "She's loose." Likewise, there are words such as *slut* or *bitch* for women for which there is no equivalent for men. There is no female equivalent for *cuckold*, the term describing a man whose wife is making a fool of him by having an affair. Why is that? To use another example, the word *spinster* is supposed to be the female synonym for *bachelor*, yet it has very different connotations. Even the more newly coined *bachelorette* is not usually used to describe a highly appealing, perhaps lifelong role. What might be the implications of these differences?

Those who invoke the biological argument that women are limited by pregnancy, childbirth, or breast-feeding from participating in public affairs and politics ignore the fact that in most societies, these biological roles are time limited and that women play a variety of social roles in addition to keeping the home and hearth. They also ignore those societies in which males are deeply involved in nonaggressive and nurturing activities such as child rearing.

Thinking Sociologically

Some people always write *he* first when writing "he and she." Others sometimes put *she* first. Does this influence gender roles or is this just fussiness about insignificant matters? Explain.

Sex, Gender, and Sexuality: The Meso Level

By whatever age is defined as adulthood in a society, members are expected to assume leadership roles and responsibilities in the institutions of society—carrying out family roles, educating the young, providing health care, teaching principles of faith, providing for support through the economic institution, and participating in government. The roles we play in these institutions often differ depending on our sex or gender, which determine our placements and many of our experiences in the social world (Brettell and Sargent 2005).

In most societies, sex and age stipulate when and how we experience *rites of passage*—rituals and formal processes that acknowledge a change of status. These include any ceremonies or recognitions that admit one to adult duties and privileges. Rites of passage are institutionalized in various ways: religious rituals such as bar mitzvah or bat mitzvah ceremonies, which are a bit different for males and females; educational celebrations such as graduation ceremonies, which often involve caps and gowns of gender-specific colors or place females on one side of the room and males on the other; and different ages at which men and women are permitted to marry.

Other institutions also segregate us by sex. Traditional Greek Orthodox Christian churches and Orthodox Jewish synagogues, for example, do not have families seated together. Men sit on one side of the sanctuary and women on the other. Many institutions, including religious, political, and economic organizations, have historically allowed only males to have leadership roles. Only men

Many women today are in major leadership positions. India's recently elected President Pratibha Patil (left) is the first woman to hold the post in her country, and she won the election with about twice the votes of the opposition candidate. Michelle Bachelet (center), the president of Chile, won almost 54% of the popular vote in 2006. Songul Chapouk, trained engineer, teacher, and women's activist (second from right), and Dr. Raja Habib al-Khuzaai, a southern tribal leader (right), are members of the 25-member Governing Council of Iraq, constituting the nation's most prominent leaders.

are to teach the scriptures to the young among traditional Jews, but few men fill that role in contemporary Christian congregations.

Often, women's reduced access to power in micro-level settings has a lot to do with their lack of power and status in meso-level organizations and institutions. This is one reason why policymakers concerned about gender equality have focused so much on inclusion of women in social institutions. For example, micro-credit organizations around the world make small financial loans, primarily to women, to start small businesses to support their families. One of these organizations is described in the next "Sociology Around the World."

Video Link 9.2
What are the macro-, meso-, and micro-level issues in this discussion about abortion rights?

Thinking Sociologically

How might women's lack of positions of authority in organizations and institutions—the meso level of society—influence females at the micro level? How might it influence their involvements at the macro level?

Sociology Around the World

Micro Credits and Empowerment of Women

The 30 village women gather regularly to discuss issues of health, crops, their herds, the predicted rains, goals for their children, and how to make ends meet. They are from a subsistence farming village in southern Niger on the edge of the Sahara desert. Recently, a micro-credit organization was established with a small grant of $1,500 from abroad. With training from Care International, an international nongovernmental organization (NGO), the women selected a board of directors to oversee the loans. Groups of five or six women have joined together to explain their projects to the board and request small loans. Each woman is responsible for paying back a small amount on the loan each week once the project is established and bringing in money.

The women are enthusiastic. In the past they had no funds, and banks charged enormous interest rates on loans.

A loan of between $20 and $50 from the micro-credit organization is a tremendous sum considering that for many of these women, it is equivalent to 6 months' earnings. Strong social norms are instituted to encourage repayment. Women who repay their loans promptly often decide who is eligible for future loans. Participation in the program encourages women and grants them economic and social capital otherwise unavailable to them.

With the new possibilities for their lives, they have big plans: For instance, one group plans to buy a press to make peanut oil, a staple for cooking in the region. Currently, people pay a great deal for oil imported from Nigeria.

Another group will buy baby lambs, fatten them, and sell them for future festivals at a great profit. Yet another group plans to set up a small bakery. Women are also discussing the possibility of making local craft products to sell to foreign fair-trade organizations such as Ten Thousand Villages (a fair-trade organization that markets products made by villagers and returns the profits back to the villagers).

Some economists and social policymakers claim that grassroots organizations such as micro credits may be the way out of poverty for millions of poor families and that women are motivated to be small entrepreneurs to help support their families and buy education and health care for their children (KBYU-TV 2005). Indeed, in 2006, Muhammad Yunus, who founded Grameen Bank—a micro-credit lender for the very poor—received the Nobel Prize for Peace.

Micro-credit lenders build significant social capital for their participants, but critics suggest that there is an underresearched downside to micro lending. As they see it, despite its success, the solution is a micro-level attempt to address a macro-level problem. Macro economists such as Linda Mayoux (2002, 2008) question whether or not the program will address the gender inequalities in the developing nations they target. Also, micro credit shifts the balance of power in marriages as the wife obtains resources; sometimes this results in higher divorce rates. Most economists agree that micro lending works best alongside macro-level initiatives seeking to address national economic problems.

Sex, Gender, and Sexuality: The Macro Level

Going to school, driving a car, and working—people around the world engage in these necessary activities. Yet in some parts of the world, these activities are forbidden for women. When we turn to the national and global level, we again witness inequality between the sexes that is quite separate from any form of personal prejudice or animosity toward women. Patterns of social action that are imbedded in the entire social system may influence women and men, providing unrecognized privileges or disadvantages. This is called *institutionalized privilege* or *disprivilege*.

In hunter-gatherer and agricultural societies, women increase their power relative to men as they age and as people gain respect for their wisdom. Especially within a clan or a household, women become masters over their domains. Men move from active roles outside the home to passive roles after retirement, whereas women often do the opposite.

The winds of change are influencing the roles of women in many parts of the world, as is seen in governing structures. Although women are still denied the right to vote in a few countries, voting is a universal right in most. In the United States, women have voted for a little more than 80 years. Yet in the entire history of the United States, only 35 women have served in the U.S. Senate. As of 2009, the number is at an all-time high, with 17 of the 100 senators being women. Still, the United States is far behind many other countries in women's representation in governing bodies. In fact, the global average for women in national parliaments is 18.4%, so the United States is below the average in female representation. The nation with the highest percentage of women in the national parliament or congress is Rwanda (sub-Saharan Africa)—the only country to exceed 50%. Canada is 52nd among nations, and the United States ranks 88th—between Turkmenistan and San Marino and well below Afghanistan, Sudan, Ethiopia, and Uzbekistan (Inter-Parliamentary Union 2010).

Several factors have been especially effective in increasing women's positions in national parliaments in Africa: the existence of a matriarchal culture (where women may have increased authority and power in decision making), political systems that stress proportional representation, and the adoption of gender quotas for government positions (Yoon 2004, 2008). Yet democratization of governmental systems is sometimes linked to a *decrease* in representation by women, a sad reality for those committed to establishing democracy around the world (Yoon 2001, 2005). Globally, women's access to power and prestige is highly variable, with African and northern European countries having a position of leadership when it comes to gender equity in government (Table 9.1).

Table 9.1 **Women in National Governments (Selected Countries) 2010**

Rank	Country	Lower or Single House: Women (%)	Upper House or Senate: Women (%)
1	Rwanda	56.3	34.6
2	Sweden	46.4	—
3	South Africa	44.5.0	29.6
4	Cuba	43.2	—
5	Iceland	42.9	—
6	Netherlands	42.0	34.7
7	Finland	40.0	—
8	Norway	39.1	—
9	Angola	38.6	—
10	Argentina	38.5	35.2
11	Belgium	38.0	40.8
12	Denmark	38.0	—
13	Costa Rica	36.8	—
14	Spain	36.6	30.8
15	Andorra	35.7	—
16	New Zealand	33.6	—
17	Nepal	33.2	—
18	Germany	32.8	21.7
19	Macedonia	32.5	—
20	Ecuador	32.3	—
28	Mexico	28.1	18.0
33	Afghanistan	27.3	22.5
34	Australia	27.3	35.5
39	Iraq	25.5	—
52	Pakistan	22.2	17.0
53	Canada	22.1	34.4
56	Ethiopia	21.9	18.8
60	China	21.3	—
68	United Kingdom	19.5	19.7
74	France	18.9	21.9
75	Sudan	18.9	6.0
87	Turkmenistan	16.8	—
88	United States of America	16.8	15.3
95	Zimbabwe	14.0	24.2
100	Zambia	14.0	—

Source: Inter-Parliamentary Union (2010). Reprinted with permission of the Inter-Parliamentary Union.

Note: To examine the involvement of women in other countries or to see even more recent figures, go to www.ipu.org/wmn-e/classif.htm.

Men and women are segregated in many social settings, including rituals of various sorts. Here, we see only men attending a funeral service in Cairo, Egypt, while women watch from the side.

Cross-cultural analyses confirm that gender roles either evolve over centuries or are transformed by sweeping reform laws such as voting rights. The fact that women in China generally work outside the home whereas women in some Muslim societies hardly venture from their homes is due to differences in cultural norms about gender roles that are dictated by governments or tradition and learned through the socialization process.

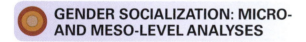

GENDER SOCIALIZATION: MICRO- AND MESO-LEVEL ANALYSES

"Sugar and spice and everything nice—that's what little girls are made of. Snips and snails and puppy dog tails—that's what little boys are made of." As the verse implies, different views of little girls and little boys start at birth, based on gender and stereotypes about what is biologically natural. Behavioral expectations stem from cultural beliefs about the nature of men and women, and these expectations guide socialization from the earliest ages and in intimate primary group settings.

Socialization into gender is the process by which people learn the cultural norms, attitudes, and behaviors appropriate to their gender. That is, they learn how to think and act as boys or girls, women or men. Socialization reinforces the "proper" gender behaviors and punishes the improper behaviors. This process, in turn, reinforces gender stereotypes. In many societies, traits of gentleness, passivity, and dependence are associated with femininity, whereas boldness, aggression, strength, and independence are identified with masculinity. For instance, in most Western societies, aggression in women is considered unfeminine, if not inappropriate or disturbing. Likewise, the gentle, unassertive male is often looked on with scorn or pity, stigmatized as a "wimp." Expectations related to these stereotypes are rigid in many societies (Pollack 1999).

Stages in Gender Socialization

Bounce that rough and tumble baby boy and cuddle that precious, delicate little girl. Thus begins gender socialization, starting at birth and taking place through a series of life stages, discussed in Chapter 4 on socialization. Examples from infancy and childhood show how socialization into gender roles takes place.

Infancy

Learning how to carry out gender roles begins at birth. Parents in the United States describe their newborn daughters as soft, delicate, fine featured, little, pretty, cute, awkward, and resembling their mothers. They depict their sons as strong, firm, alert, and well coordinated (Lindsey 2008; Rubin 1974). Clothing, room decor, and toys also reflect notions of gender. In Spain, parents and grandparents dress babies and their carriages in pink or blue depending on gender, proudly showing off the little ones to friends as they promenade in the evenings. Although gender stereotypes have declined in recent years, they continue to affect the way we handle and treat male and female infants (Karraker 1995).

Childhood

Once out of infancy, research shows that many boys are encouraged to be more independent and exploratory, whereas girls are protected from situations that might prove harmful. More pressure is put on boys to behave in "gender-appropriate" ways. Boys are socialized into "the boy code" that provides rigid guidelines (see "Sociology in Our Social World"). Cross-cultural studies show boys often get more attention than girls because of their behavior, with an emphasis on achievement, autonomy, and aggression for boys (Kimmel and Messner 2009).

Thinking Sociologically

First, read about the Boy Code on the next page. What evidence do you see of the Boy Code when you observe your friends and relatives? What is the impact of the Boy Code? Is there a similar code for girls?

Sociology in Our Social World

The Boy Code

Boys and girls begin to conform to gender expectations once they are old enough to understand that their sex is rather permanent—that boys are not capable of becoming "mommies." They then become even more conscious of adhering to the norms of others in their gender category.

In Chapter 5, we mentioned the Old Boy network in American society—a system that favors adult men through networks. This system actually starts with "the boy code," the rules about boys' proper behavior. Young boys learn "the code" from parents, siblings, peers, teachers, and society in general.

They are praised for adhering to the code and punished for violating its dictates. William Pollack (1999) writes that boys learn several stereotyped behavior models exemplifying the boy code:

1. "The sturdy oak": Men should be stoic, stable, and independent; a man never shows weakness.

2. "Give 'em hell": From athletic coaches and movie heroes, the consistent theme is extreme daring, bravado, and attraction to violence.

3. "The 'big wheel'": Men and boys should achieve status, dominance, and power; they should avoid shame, wear the mask of coolness, and act as though everything is under control.

4. "No sissy stuff": Boys are discouraged from expressing feelings or urges perceived as feminine—dependence, warmth, empathy.

The boy code is ingrained in society; by 5 or 6 years of age, boys are less likely than girls to express hurt or distress. They have learned to be ashamed of showing feelings and of being weak. This gender straitjacket, according to Pollack, causes boys to conceal feelings in order to fit in and be accepted and loved. As a result, some boys, especially in adolescence, become silent, covering any vulnerability and masking their true feelings. This affects boys' relationships, performance in school, and the ability to connect with others. It also causes young males to put on what Jackson Katz (2006) calls the "tough guise"—when young men and boys emphasize aggression and violence to display masculinity.

Pollack (1999) suggests that we can help boys reconnect to nongendered norms by doing the following:

1. Giving some undivided attention each day just listening to boys

2. Encouraging a range of emotions

3. Avoiding language that taunts, teases, or shames

4. Looking behind the veneer of "coolness" for signs of problems

5. Expressing love and empathy

6. Dispelling the "sturdy oak" image

7. Advocating a broad, inclusive model of masculinity

With the women's movement and shifts in gender expectations have come new patterns of male behavior. Some men are forming more supportive and less competitive relationships with other men, and there are likely to be continued changes in and broadening of "appropriate" behavior for men (Kimmel and Messner 2009).

From infancy, messages are sent to children and to visitors so that no one is likely to mistake the sex of the child.

Stereotypes for girls in a majority of societies label feminine behaviors as soft, nonaggressive, and noncompetitive and favor diminutive women. Consider that boys act out their aggressive feelings, but girls are socialized to be nice, nurturing, and not aggressive. In a study about how school girls express aggression, Simmons (2002) finds that girls express "relational aggression"—that is, aggression that affects girls' social contacts indirectly through rumors, name-calling, giggling, ignoring, backbiting, exclusion, and manipulation of victims. Friendship and needing to belong are the weapons rather than sticks and stones. This form of bullying is subtle and hard to detect, but it can have long-lasting effects on girls (Simmons 2002).

Names for children also reflect stereotypes about gender. Boys are more often given strong, hard names that end in consonants. The top 10 boys' names in 2008 include Jacob, Michael, Ethan, Joshua, Daniel, Alexander, Anthony, William, Christopher, and Matthew. Girls are more likely to be given soft pretty names with vowel endings such as most of the top 10: Emma, Isabella, Emily, Madison, Ava, Olivia, Sophia, Abigail, Elizabeth, and Chloe (Social Security Administration 2009).

Alternatively, girls may be given feminized versions of boys' names—Roberta, Jessica, Josephine, Nicole, Michelle, or Donna. Sometimes boys' names are given to girls without first feminizing them. Names such as Lynn, Stacey, Tracey, Faye, Dana, Jody, Lindsay, Robin, and Carmen used to be names exclusively for men, but within a decade or two after they were applied to girls, parents stopped using them for boys. So a common name for males may for a time be given to either

sex, but then, it is given to girls only. The pattern rarely goes the other direction. Once feminized, the names seem to have become tainted (Lieberson, Dumais, and Bauman 2000).

In the early childhood years, children become aware of their own gender identity. As they reach school age, they learn that their sex is permanent, and they begin to categorize behaviors that are appropriate for their sex. As children are rewarded for performing proper gender roles, these roles are reinforced. That reinforcement solidifies gender roles, setting the stage for gender-related interactions, behaviors, and choices in later life.

Meso-Level Agents of Gender Socialization

Clues to proper gender roles surround children in materials produced by corporations (books, toys, games), in mass media images, in educational settings, and in religious organizations and beliefs. In Chapter 4 on socialization, we learned about agents of socialization. Those agents play a major role in teaching children proper gender roles. The following examples demonstrate how organizations and institutions in our society teach and reinforce gender assumptions and roles.

Corporations

Corporations have produced materials that help socialize children into proper conduct. Publishers, for example, produce books that present images of expected gender behavior. Language and pictures in preschool picture books, elementary children's books, and school textbooks are steeped in gender role messages, reflecting society's expectations and stereotypes. In a classic study of award-winning children's books from the United States that have sold more than 3 million copies, Weitzman (Weitzman et al. 1972) made several observations: (a) males appear more often in stories as central characters; (b) activities of male and female characters in books differ, with boys playing active roles and girls being passive or simply helping brothers, fathers, or husbands; and (c) adult women are pictured as more passive and dependent, whereas males are depicted as carrying out a range of activities and jobs.

Although more recent books show some expansion in the roles book characters play, studies confirm a continuing pattern of gender role segregation in children's books (Anderson and Hamilton 2005; Diekman and Murmen 2004). Whether Peter Rabbit, Curious George the Monkey, or Babar the Elephant, the male animal characters in children's books outnumber females; studies of children's books show that males of any species most often are portrayed as adventurous, brave, competent, clever, and fun, whereas female counterparts may be depicted as incompetent, fearful, and dependent on others (Purcell and Stewart 1990). Moreover, even though authors and publishers have begun producing books presenting unbiased gender roles and strong girls and women, the tens of thousands of older, classic books in public and school libraries mean that a parent or child picking a book off the shelf is still likely to select a book that has stereotypical views of boys and girls.

Producers of toys and games also contribute to traditional messages about gender. Store-bought toys fill rooms in homes of children in the Western world, and it is usually quite clear which are boys' rooms and which are girls' rooms. Boys' rooms are filled with sports equipment, army toys, building and technical toys, and cars and trucks. Girls' rooms have fewer toys, and most are related to dolls and domestic roles. Boys have more experience manipulating blocks, Tinker Toys, Legos, and Erector sets—toys paralleling masculinized activities outside the home in the public domain, from constructing and building trades to military roles and sports. Girls prepare for domestic roles with toys relating to domestic activities. Barbie dolls stress physical appearance, consumerism, and glamour. Only a few Barbies are in occupational roles. In contrast, the Ken dolls that Mattel designed to match Barbie (and have now been discontinued) were often doctors or other professionals.

In 2009, Mattel produced Barbie's online dream house, a virtual house that can be decorated and furnished. Barbie's

Girls and boys quickly pick up messages—from parents, from other children, and from the media—about what kinds of toys are appropriate for someone of their sex. Many toys—such as Barbie dolls and construction toys or trucks—have very explicit messages.

At the left is the display for Barbie dolls in a Toys R Us store in Louisville, Kentucky. Mattel's Barbie dolls have been criticized for their extremely traditional and highly sexualized images of young women. The boy at the right looks at toys marketed for boys, and the message he receives is very different.

house was designed with girls as the target market. A complementary target boy program features Hot Wheels cars with car races and uses virtual tools to customize cars. These models differed in more than simple appearance. The life lessons learned from these computer games reinforce gender stereotypes (Snider 2009).

Each toy or game prepares children through anticipatory socialization for future gender roles. Toys that require building, manipulating, and technical skills provide experiences for later life. Choices ranging from college major and occupational choice to activities that depend on visual-spatial and mathematical abilities appear to be affected by these early choices and childhood learning experiences (Tavris and Wade 1984).

Consider the example of "Dungeons and Dragons," a popular game primarily among adolescent boys in Europe, Japan, and North America. The participants role-play their way through scenarios full of demons and dragons, using a vast array of dungeons, weapons, and magical spells. The boys develop characters that they impersonate throughout the game as they negotiate, bargain, create, imitate, and develop a variety of other social or cognitive skills. They must calculate complex mathematical formulae and use logic and imagination—all skills that will aid them in coping with the adult public world. Although more girls are taking up gaming activities, the packaging of this product makes it clear it is a boys' activity.

Mass Media

Have you ever noticed the media coverage of female celebrities who have made poor choices? The men who get

Video Link 9.3
Watch a music video that presents an alternative version of Snow White.

into trouble are slapped on the hand. "Boys will be boys," after all. However, actresses such as Paris Hilton, Lindsey Lohan, and Britney Spears experience intense scrutiny and hostility. Is this because of their class, their gender, or their nontraditional roles and nonconforming behavior? Whatever variables affect the reactions to these women, they are subjects of mass media frenzy.

Mass media in their many forms—magazines, ads, films, music videos, Internet sites—are major agents of socialization into gender roles. Young men and women, desiring to fit in, are influenced by messages from the media. For instance, the epidemic of steroid use among boys and dieting among girls are health concerns driven by ads in the United States (Taub and McLorg 2007). Yet manufacturers advertise such products with promises to remake teens into more attractive people.

Video games that depict women as sex objects teach and perpetuate stereotypes about women. Some video games include content that is violent, degrading, and voyeuristic—a dehumanizing of women. Women in such videos become objects to be exploited. The virtual "rewards" for winning some games include having sex with a

prostitute, raping a Native American woman, and "participating" in nude party games with women warriors wearing skintight skimpy outfits. This makes clear who the producers see as their target audience. Furthermore, when these are "normal" activities in video games, the video industry seems in fact to be encouraging boys and men to view women as objects (Glass 2003).

Some action films produced within the past decade include adventurous and competent girls and women, helping to counter images such as the ones in the video games described above. Hermione in *Harry Potter* is intelligent and creative. Queen of Naboo and Senator Amidala in *Star Wars* and Lyra Belacqua in *The Golden Compass* are strong, brave, intelligent (and beautiful). Lara Croft in *Tomb Raider* holds her own against evil. However, videos depicting highly competent females are few, and most of those few women are unrealistically thin and highly attractive with large breasts.

Television is another powerful socializing agent. By the time they start school, typical English, Canadian, and U.S. children will have spent more time in front of a television than they will in classrooms in the coming 12 years of school, a behavior that contributes to obesity in the United States (Randerson 2008). Television presents a simple, stereotyped view of life, from advertisements to situation comedies to soap operas. Women in soap operas and ads, especially those working outside the home, are often depicted as having problems in carrying out their role responsibilities (Benokraitis and Feagin 1995). Even the extraordinary powers of superheroes on Saturday morning television depict the female characters as having gender-stereotyped skills such as superintuition. Notice the next time you are in a video game room that the fighting characters are typically male and often in armor. When fighting women do appear, they are usually clad in skin-revealing bikini-style attire—odd clothing in which to do battle!

Films and television series in the United States seldom feature average-size or older women (although a greater variety of ages and body types is seen in the British Broadcasting Company productions). Movie stars are attractive and thin, presenting an often unattainable model for young women, making many feel inadequate and feeding the diet frenzy (Kramer 2007; Taub and McLorg 2007). Women who are quite large are almost entirely depicted as comic figures in U.S. television.

How do social scientists know that television affects gender role socialization? Studies have shown that the more television children watch, the more gender stereotypes they hold. From cartoons to advertisements, television in many countries provides enticing images of a world in which youth is glorified, age is scorned, and female and male roles are stereotyped and/or made unattainable (Kilbourne 2000; Tuchman 1996). However, research has also found that these media images have a much greater impact on White girls than on African American teens (Milkie 1999).

Olsen twins Mary-Kate and Ashley (left) pose together in front of their new star on the Walk of Fame in Hollywood. Like most glamour stars, they must conform to the image of very thin, shapely femininity. Kirstie Alley appears at Showtime's Fat Actress premiere (right). When Kirstie gained weight, her range of acting options suddenly became very slim.

Thinking Sociologically

Think of recent mass media examples that you have seen. How do they depict women and men? How might these meso-level depictions affect young men and women individually at the micro level?

Educational Systems

Even centers of learning bolster sex-specific expectations and limitations. Educational systems are socialization agents of children through textbooks, classroom activities, playground games, and teachers' attitudes. For example, boys are encouraged to join competitive team sports and girls to support them (Gilligan 1982; Kramer 2007). These simulate hierarchical adult roles of boss/secretary and physician/nurse. Furthermore, the team sports that the boys learn

teach them strategic thinking—a critical skill that involves anticipating the moves of the opponent and countering with one's own strategy. This is a very useful skill in the business world and is not explicitly taught in other places in the school curriculum. Girls' games rarely teach this skill.

Children's experiences in grade school and middle school reinforce boundaries of "us" and "them" in classroom seating and activities, in the lunchroom, and in playground activities, as girls and boys are seated, lined up, and given assignments by sex (Sadker and Sadker 2005). Those who go outside the boundaries, especially boys, are ridiculed by peers and sometimes teachers, reinforcing stereotypes and separate gender role socialization (Sadker and Sadker 2005; Thorne 1993).

Boys act out and receive more attention in school classrooms than girls do, even though it may be negative attention. Boys are called on more often to do physical chores such as erasing the boards and emptying the trash. Teachers reward girls for being passive and obedient. Boys begin at young ages to work and play together as teams. Girls also join team sports, but their play more frequently involves one-on-one activities. In contrast to girls, boys learn the skills of competition, negotiating, bargaining, aggressiveness, good sportsmanship, and strategic thinking.

Part of the issue of male-female inequality in schools is tied to the issue of popularity, which it seems has less to do with being liked than with being known. If everyone knows a person's name, she or he is popular (Eder, Evans, and

High school and college athletics are much less reliable paths for women to become known on campus because so few people come to the games. Even this college basketball game has sparse attendance (top photo). In contrast, women in very sexy outfits are highly visible and can even become local celebrities when they perform as cheerleaders in front of 80,000 fans at men's sporting events.

Parker 1995). At the middle school level, there are more ways by which boys can become known. Even when there are both boys' and girls' basketball teams, many spectators come to the boys' contests and very few to the girls' games. Thus, few people know the female athletes' names. In fact, a far more visible position is cheerleader—standing on the sidelines cheering for the boys—because those girls are at least visible (Eder et al. 1995). The other major way in which girls are visible or known is physical appearance, a major standard of popularity and esteem (Eder et al. 1995). Generally, there are far more visible positions for the boys than for girls in middle school.

Title IX of the U.S. Educational Amendments Act of 1972 was a major legislative attempt to level the educational and sports playing field. Passed to bar gender discrimination in schools receiving federal funds, this legislation mandates equal opportunity for participation in school-sponsored programs (Lindsey 2008). The law has reduced or eliminated blatant discrimination in areas ranging from admissions and health care to counseling and housing, sex-segregated programs, financial aid, dress codes, and other areas that were of concern. However, the biggest impact of Title IX legislation has been in athletics.

Partly aided by Title IX, the number of women's athletic programs and scholarship opportunities grew in the late 1990s, but it has slowed since 2000 and still lags behind men's levels. From 1995 to 2005, the number of women in college sports at 738 National Collegiate Athletic Association (NCAA) schools surveyed grew by 26,000 to 205,492, while the number of men was 291,797 (Rosen 2007). Some men's sports have been cut back, but others have grown, resulting in a steady number of opportunities for men in sports. One third of high school women participate in sports compared with 45% of males. Overall, 79% of the public supports Title IX and what it has accomplished (Women's Sports Foundation 2005).

Religious Beliefs

Religious beliefs serve as agents of socialization by defining, reinforcing, and perpetuating gender role stereotypes and cultural beliefs. Religious teachings provide explanations of proper male/female roles. Although the specific teachings vary, the three major monotheistic religions that affirm that there is only one God—Christianity, Islam, and Judaism—are traditionally patriarchal, stressing separate female and male spheres (Kramer 2007). The following are examples of some of these traditional role expectations and the status of women in various religions.

Some interpretations of the Adam and Eve creation story in the Hebrew Bible (the Old Testament in the Christian Bible) state that because man was created first, men are superior. Because Eve, created from the rib of man, was a sinner, her sins keep women forever in an inferior, second-class position. For these reasons, in some branches of these religions, women are restricted in their roles within the family and religious organizations. They cannot be priests in Catholic churches and cannot vote on business matters in some religious organizations. However, recent work by feminist scholars is challenging the notion of patriarchy in Judaic and Christian history, pointing out that women may have played a much broader role in religious development than currently recognized (Hunter College Women's Studies Collective 2005). Even *Yahweh*—the name for God in the Hebrew Bible—had both male and female connotations, and when God is referred to as a source of wisdom, feminine pronouns and references were used (Borg 1994). Increasingly, denominations are granting women greater roles in the religious hierarchies, ministries, and priesthood.

Women in Judaism lived for 4,000 years in a patriarchal system where men read, taught, and legislated while women followed (Lindsey 2008). Today, three of the five main branches of Judaism allow women equal participation, illustrating that religious practices do change over time. However, Hasidic and Orthodox Jews have a division of labor between men and women following old laws, with designated gender roles for the home and religious life.

Some Christian teachings have treated women as second-class citizens, even in the eyes of God. For this reason, some Christian denominations have excluded women from a variety of leadership roles and told them they must be subservient to their husbands. Other Christians point to the admonition by Saint Paul that theologically speaking, "There is no such thing as . . . male and female, for you are all one in Christ Jesus." This suggests that women and men are not spiritually different (Galatians 3:28).

Traditional Hindu religion painted women as seductresses, strongly erotic, and a threat to male spirituality and asceticism. To protect men from this threat, women were kept totally covered in thick garments and veils and seen only by men in their immediate families. Today, Hinduism comes in many forms, most of which honor the woman's domestic sphere of life—as mothers, wives, and homemakers—while accepting women in public roles (Lindsey 2008).

Traditional Islamic beliefs also portrayed female sexuality as dangerous to men, although many women in Islamic societies today are full participants in the public and private sphere. The Quran (also spelled Qur'an or Koran), the Muslim sacred scripture, includes a statement that men are superior to women because of the qualities God has given men. Hammurabi's Code, written in the Middle East between 2067 and 2025 BCE, is the earliest recorded legal system. The laws about women's status were written to distinguish between decent women, belonging to one man, and indecent or public women. Some aspects of these traditional beliefs have carried over to present times. Sharia law, strict Islamic law, was recently imposed on a woman in Nigeria who had a child out of wedlock and on another woman in Pakistan who was a rape victim. Both women were sentenced to death by stoning, but their sentences have not been carried out because of protests from within and outside the countries. These women suffer social humiliation, degradation, and potential death, but they also demonstrate the severe penalties for violating the social expectations for others who might stray from the laws (Mydans 2002).

Women in fundamentalist Muslim societies such as Algeria, Iran, Syria, and Saudi Arabia are separated from men (except for fathers and brothers) in work and worship. They generally remain covered. *Purdah*, which means curtain, refers to practices of seclusion and separate worlds for women and men in Islamic cultures. Screens in households and veils in public enforce female modesty and prevent men from seeing women where this is dictated (Ward and Edelstein 2009). Today, some women argue that the veil they wear is for modesty, cosmetic purposes, or to protect them from the stares of men. Others claim that the veil is a symbol of oppression and subservience, showing that women must keep themselves in submissive positions. In Turkey, a secular Muslim society, schools and universities have long forbidden religious representation, including the wearing of scarves. However, recent debates in Turkey have challenged the rulings forbidding scarves in schools, and the president has declared it legal for women to choose (BBC News 2004; Knickmeyer 2008). The debate in Turkey, France, and other countries continues.

Religious laws often provide the justifications to keep women servile, and public shaming and threat of severe punishments reinforce the laws. Meso-level religious systems influence how different societies interpret proper gender roles and how sometimes these belief systems change with new interpretations of scriptures. (Further discussion of the complex relationship between religion and gender appears in Chapter 12.)

Audio Link 9.1
Listen to stories about gender.

All these meso-level agents of socialization reinforce "appropriate" gender roles in each society.

Thinking Sociologically

What are some of the books, toys, games, television shows, school experiences, religious teachings, and peer interactions that have influenced your gender role socialization? In what ways did they do so?

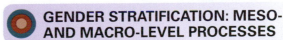

GENDER STRATIFICATION: MESO- AND MACRO-LEVEL PROCESSES

"The **glass ceiling** keeps women from reaching the highest levels of corporate and public responsibility, and the

Engaging Sociology

Masculinity and Femininity in Your Social World

1. Mark each characteristic with an "M" or an "F" depending on whether you think it is generally defined by society as a masculine or feminine characteristic.

　＿＿ Achiever

　＿＿ Aggressive

　＿＿ Analytical

　＿＿ Caring

　＿＿ Confident

　＿＿ Deferential (defers to others, yields with courtesy)

　＿＿ Devious

　＿＿ Dynamic

　＿＿ Intuitive

　＿＿ Loving

　＿＿ Manipulative

　＿＿ Nurturant

　＿＿ Organized

　＿＿ Passive

　＿＿ A planner

　＿＿ Powerful

　＿＿ Sensitive

　＿＿ Strong

　＿＿ Relationship oriented (makes decisions based on how others will *feel*)

　＿＿ Rule oriented (makes decisions based on *abstract procedural rules*)

2. Next, mark an "X" just to the right of 10 characteristics that you think are the essential qualities for a leadership position in a complex organization (business, government, etc.). You might want to ask 20 of your acquaintances to do this, and then add up the scores for "masculinity," "femininity," and "leadership trait."

3. Do you (and your acquaintances) tend to view leadership as having the same traits as those marked "masculine" or "feminine"? What are the implications of this for the glass ceiling?

4. How might correlations between the traits of leadership and gender notions help explain the data on income in Table 9.2?

Table 9.2	**U.S. Income by Educational Level and Sex (in dollars)**	
Education	*Men*	*Women*
Not a high school graduate	24,985	15,315
High school graduate	36,839	24,234
Some college; no degree	39,375	26,527
College graduate (bachelor's)	70,898	43,127
Master's degree	86,966	54,772
Doctorate	108,941	69,251
Professional degree	142,282	83,031

Source: U.S. Census Bureau (2010a: table 227).

'sticky floor' keeps the vast majority of the world's women stuck in low-paid jobs" (Hunter College Women's Studies Collective 2005:393; see also Kimmel 2003). Men, on the other hand, face the "glass escalator," especially in traditionally female occupations. Even if they do not seek to climb in the organizational hierarchy, occupational social forces push them up the job ladder to the higher echelons (Wingfield 2009). Women around the world do two thirds of the work, receive 10% of the world's income, and own 1% of the world's means of production (Robbins 2005). They make up more than 40% of the world's paid workforce but hold only about 20% of the managerial jobs, and for those, they are often compensated at lower pay than their male counterparts. Only 5% of the top corporate jobs are held by women. However, companies with women in leadership positions do realize high profits (Adler 2001; Hunter College Women's Studies Collective 2005). The "Engaging Sociology" on page 298 provides an exercise to think about how our ideas may subtly maintain the glass ceiling.

Women and Men at Work: Gendered Organizations

How can I do it all—marriage, children, education, career, social life? This is a question that women in our college classes ask. They already anticipate a delicate balancing act. Work has been central to the definition of masculinity in U.S. society, and for the past half century, women have been joining the workforce in greater numbers (Kramer 2007). Today, women's proportion of the workforce is almost equal to men in the United States and many other Western countries. Working is necessary for many women, especially single mothers, to support their families, and many women with career education and goals want to work. Among countries of the Global North, Sweden has the highest percentage of women in the labor force (82%) and the lowest percentage of homemakers. Yet even in Sweden, with its parental leave and other family-friendly policies, women feel pressures of work and family responsibilities (Eshleman and Bulcroft 2006). Dual-career marriages raise questions about child rearing, power relations, and other factors in juggling work and family.

Every workplace has a gendered configuration: ratios of female to male workers and matters of who are in the supervisory statuses and how positions are distributed. This, in turn, affects our experiences in the workplace. Consider the example of mothers who are breastfeeding their babies. Must they quit their jobs or alter their family schedules if the workplace does not provide a space for breastfeeding? Some workplaces accommodate family needs, but others do not. Many women have multiple responsibilities: They try to support their families financially and in other ways, by being good mothers and by being responsible employees or employers. Men do not face the same issues because most corporations assume the average worker is male.

Research shows that workers are more satisfied when the sex composition of their work group and the distribution of

Although most public school teachers are disproportionally women and although serving in the classroom is the normal channel for working into high administrative posts, principals and superintendants—who have higher pay and more authority—are disproportionally men. This is an example of a gendered organization.

men and women in power are balanced (Britton 2000:430). Feminists propose ideas to minimize gender differences in organizations—that is, to "degender" organizations so that all members have equal opportunities (Britton 2000).

Thinking Sociologically

If corporate structures were reversed so that women structured and organized the workplace, how might the workplace environment change?

Institutionalized Gender Discrimination

Gender stratification at the meso level—such as race and ethnic stratification—can occur quite independently of any overt prejudice or ill will by others. It becomes part of the social system, and we are not even conscious of it, especially if we are one of the privileged members of society. Most of what has been discussed so far is *de jure discrimination*, done deliberately and justified with laws and ideological beliefs about women's inability to carry out certain tasks. The more subtle process of *de facto discrimination* (which is not intended) also needs attention. When inequality is woven into the web of the macro-level social structure and becomes taken for granted, it is called institutional discrimination. It can include intentional actions such as bank policies requiring single women, compared with single men, to pay as much as three times the money up-front for a house down payment to receive a homeowner's loan, but it can also include unintentional actions with consequences that disadvantage women (Feagin and Feagin 1986, 2007).

You may recall from the previous chapter that *side-effect discrimination* involves practices in one institution that are linked to practices in another institution. The practices in the first institution have an effect in the second one that is not anticipated or even recognized by most people in the society. For example, if roles of women in family life are determined by rigid gender expectations, as research shows, then women find it more difficult to devote themselves to gaining job promotions. In addition, as long as little girls learn through socialization to use their voices and hold their bodies and gesture in ways that communicate deference, employers assume a lack of the self-confidence necessary for major leadership roles. If women are paid less despite the same levels of education (see Table 9.2 on page 298), they are likely to have less access to expensive health care or to be able to afford a $20,000 down payment for a house unless they are married. This makes women dependent on men in a way that most men are not dependent on women.

A factor affecting differences in incomes is the type of academic degrees that men and women receive (e.g.,

engineering rather than education). However, even when these differences are factored in, men still make considerably more on average than women with identical levels of experience and training.

Men often get defensive and angry when people talk about sexism in society because they feel they are being attacked or asked to correct injustices of the past. However, the empirical reality is that the playing field is not level for men and women. Most men do not do anything to intentionally harm women, and they may not feel prejudiced toward women, but sexism operates so that men are given privileges they never asked for and may not even recognize.

Past-in-present discrimination refers to practices from the past that may no longer be allowed but that continue to affect people today. We discussed above the problem that men and women have different pay with similar levels of education. Note that a difference in the typical number of years women have spent in their professional fields is a small part of the difference in income levels. In other words, there are fewer women senior law partners in part because women who are now in their 50s or older were often not admitted to professional graduate programs in the 1960s and 1970s. A policy of the past still influences women's positions and incomes today.

Let us consider another example of the past influencing the present. At an appliance industry in the Midwest investigated by one of the authors, there is a sequence of jobs one must hold to be promoted up the line to foreman. This requirement ensures that the foreman understands the many aspects of the production at the plant. One of the jobs involves working in a room with heavy equipment that cuts through and bends metal sheets. The machine is extremely powerful and could easily cut off a leg or hand if the operator is not careful. Because of the danger, the engineers designed the equipment so it would not operate unless three levers were activated at the same time. One lever was triggered by stepping on a pedal on the floor. The other two required reaching out with one's hands so that one's body was extended. When one was spread-eagled to activate all three levers, there was no way one could possibly have a part of one's body near the blades. It was brilliant engineering.

There was one unanticipated problem: The hand-activated levers were 5 feet, 10 inches off the ground and 5 feet apart. Few women had the height and arm span to run this machine, and therefore, no women had yet made it through the sequence of positions to the higher-paying position of foreman. The equipment cost millions of dollars, so it was not likely to be replaced. Neither the engineers who designed the machine nor the upper-level managers who established the sequence of jobs to become foreman had deliberately tried to exclude women. Indeed, they were perplexed when they looked at their employee figures and saw so few women moving up through the ranks. The cause of women's disadvantage was not mean-spirited men but features

Little girls learn to use their voices and hold their bodies and gesture in ways that communicate deference. This little girl does not look very powerful or confident. When women tilt their heads—either forward or to one side—they also look like they lack confidence, and this hurts their chances of promotion in the corporate world.

of the system that had unintended consequences. The barriers women face, then, are not just matters of socialization or other micro-level social processes. The nature of sexism is often subtle and pervasive in the society, operating at the meso and macro levels as institutional discrimination.

Gender Differences in Internet Use

One specific form of institutionalized difference in access to resources at the global level has to do with the Internet. Knowledge of events in the world, job skills, awareness of job openings, networks that extend beyond national borders, and other resources are available through the Internet. Women like the human connections created by the Internet, whereas men tend to like the experience and financial options it offers. Although women are catching up with men in its usage in some Global North countries, there is a larger-world digital divide in gender here than in the other categories (Drori 2006; Fallows 2005). The difference in Internet use by women as a percentage of all users varies significantly by development levels of countries: Women are roughly 45% of the Internet users in Sweden and Denmark, 46% in Mexico, 49% in South Africa and Thailand each (Drori 2006), a bit more than 40% in Israel, about 30% in China, 17% in Senegal, and 14% in Ethiopia. In the Arab world, women account for only 4% of the online population. Women's usage has climbed to that level only in the past few years. In Kenya, a 1999 survey in two provinces found that 99% of the women had never heard of the Internet.

However, the story is different in the United States, where women have caught up with or outpaced their male age and ethnic group peers. Sixty-seven percent of the U.S. population uses the Internet, including 66% of all women and 68% of men. Between 18 and 29 years of age, more women use the Internet than men—86% women as compared with 80% men. However, in the 65 years and older cohort, more men (34%) than women (21%) are online. In addition, more African American women (60%) than men (50%) are Web savvy. Men tend to use the Internet more often and longer and have more high-speed connections (Fallows 2005). The direction of U.S. usage parallels that of other Global North countries and may predict the future in other countries.

In Chapter 7, we explored global differences in Internet usage and found that the largest variance was based on the wealth of the country and access to technology. The same principle holds for women's usage in the Global North and South. Many African countries may have only half of 1% of the population online, but in none of the African countries cited by Drori (2006) do women have more than 15% of that tiny share. So of the women in most African countries, fewer than 7 out of 10,000 have used the Internet. Clearly, the majority of these women are "out of the digital loop." Yet competency in use of the Internet has become an

In some countries, there is a huge gender digital divide. In others, nearly as many women as men use computers. However, research shows that women tend to use computers in different ways. These women in Iraq are learning computer skills.

extremely important resource in the contemporary global economy. Lack of access and savvy is a handicap.

Internet-related gender stratification exhibits itself not just in terms of *whether* a person uses the Internet but also in terms of *how* a person uses the Internet. Even within industrialized countries such as the United States, women tend to use mostly the e-mail services, with the intent of keeping up with family and friends (Shade 2004). For men, the Internet is used to gather information and to exchange ideas and facts relevant to professional activities. Thus, "women are using the Internet to reinforce their private lives and men are using the Internet for engaging in the public sphere" (Shade 2004:63). The difference also reflects differences in the professional positions men and women hold. For men, the Internet is enhancing their careers. This is far less true for women. However, things do change very rapidly in the world of the Internet.

Video Link 9.4 Consider gender issues in pornography.

Thinking Sociologically

Ask several people from different generations and different genders how they use computer technology and the Internet and how they learned these skills. What do you learn from this?

Gender Stratification: Micro- to Macro-Level Theories

In recent years, some biologists and psychologists have considered whether there are innate differences in the makeup of women and men. For instance, males produce more testosterone, a hormone found to be correlated with aggression. Research shows that in many situations, males tend to be more aggressive and concerned with dominance, whether the behavior is biologically programmed or learned or both. Other traits, such as nurturance, empathy, or altruism, show no clear gender difference (Fausto-Sterling 1992; Pinker 2002).

Although biological and psychological factors are part of the difference between females and males, our focus here is on the major contribution that social factors make in the social statuses of males and females in human society. This section explores social theories that explain gender differences.

Symbolic Interaction Theory: Micro-Level Analysis

Symbolic interactionists look at gender as socially constructed. Sex is the biological reality of different "plumbing" in our bodies, and interactionists are interested in how those physical differences come to be symbols, resulting in different social rights and rewards. This chapter's discussions of micro-level social processes have pointed out that the meaning connected to one's sex produces notions of masculinity and femininity. The symbolic interaction perspective has been forceful in insisting that notions of proper gender behavior are not intrinsically related to a person's sex. The bottom line is that gender is a socially created or constructed idea (Mason-Schrock 1996).

Traditional notions of gender are hard to change. Admitting confusion over proper masculine and feminine roles creates anxiety and even anomie in a society. People want guidelines. Thus, it is easier to adhere to traditional notions of gender that are reinforced by religious dogmas, making those ideas appear sacred, absolute, and beyond human change. Absolute answers are comforting to those who find change disconcerting. Others believe the male prerogatives and privileges of the past were established by men to protect their rights. Any change in concepts of gender or of roles assigned to males and females will be hard to bring about precisely because they are rooted in the meaning system and status and power structures present in the social world.

Symbolic interaction—more than any other theory—stresses the idea of *human agency*—the notion that humans

Some cultures suggest that women are helpless and need the door held for them, and women's stylish attire—such as many forms of shoes and many dresses—actually does make them more vulnerable and helpless in certain situations. In these decisions, men and women are "doing gender." Does this give men more power?

not only are influenced by the society in which they live but also actively help create it (Charon 2007; Hewitt 2007). In a study of elementary children in classrooms and especially on playgrounds, Barrie Thorne (1993) found that while teachers influenced the children, the children themselves were active participants in creating the student culture that guided their play. As children played with one another, Thorne noticed the ways in which they created words, nicknames, distinctions between one another, and new forms of interaction. This is a very important point: Humans do not just passively adopt cultural notions about gender, they *do gender*. They create it as they behave and interact with others in ways that define "normal" male or female conduct (West and Zimmerman 1987). "Doing gender" is an everyday, recurring, and routine occurrence. It is a constant ongoing process that defines each situation, takes place in organizations and between individuals, and becomes part of institutional arrangements. Social movements such as civil rights and the women's movement challenge these arrangements and can bring about change. Understanding the process of doing gender helps us understand why we think and act as we do.

When children are in an ambiguous situation, they may spontaneously define their sex as the most relevant trait about themselves or others. Indeed, even when children act as if gender matters, they are helping to make it a reality for those around them. This process helps make the notion of gender more concrete and real to the other children. As the next child adopts the "definition of reality" from the first, acting as if sex is more important than hair color or eye color, it makes gender the most prominent characteristic in the mind of the next child. Yet each child, in a sense, could choose to ignore gender and decide that something else is more important. The same principle applies to adults. When a person "chooses" to recognize gender as a critical distinction between two individuals or two groups, that person is "doing gender" (Hewitt 2007; O'Brien 2006).

Through interaction, people do gender, and although this process begins at a micro level, it has implications all the way to the global level. The Iowa School of symbolic interactionism places more stress on meso-level reinforcement of social constructions of gender (Carrothers and Benson 2003; Stryker 1980), emphasizing individuals conforming to or rebelling against the messages about gender that pervade our institutions. The next section explores meso- and macro-level forces that shape gender and stratification based on sex.

Thinking Sociologically

How do you *do gender*? How did you learn these patterns of behavior? Are they automatic responses, or do you think about "who opens the door"?

Structural-Functional and Conflict Theories: Meso- and Macro-Level Analyses

Structural-Functional Theory

From the structural-functional perspective, each sex has a role to play in the interdependent groups and institutions of society. Some early theorists argued that men and women carry out different roles and are, of necessity, unequal because of the needs of societies and practices that have developed since early human history. Social relationships and practices that have proven successful in the survival of a group are likely to continue and be reinforced by society's norms and laws. Thus, relationships between women and men that are believed to support survival are maintained. In traditional hunter-gatherer, horticultural, and pastoral societies, for instance, the division of labor is based on sex and age. Social roles are clearly laid out, indicating who performs which everyday survival tasks. The females often take on the primary tasks of child care, gardening, food preparation, and other duties near the home. Men do tasks that require movements farther from home, such as hunting or fishing.

As societies industrialize, roles and relationships change due to structural changes in society. Durkheim ([1893] 1947) described a gradual move from traditional societies held together by mechanical solidarity (common values and emotional ties between members) to modern societies that hold together due to organic solidarity. The glue that holds modern society together is based less on common values and more on division of labor and the interdependence of statuses within the social world. According to early functionalists, gender division of labor exists in modern societies because it is efficient and useful to have different-but-complementary male and female roles. They believed this accomplishes essential tasks and maintains societal stability (Lindsey 2008).

More recent structural-functional theorists describe society as an integrated system of roles that work together to carry out the necessary tasks in society. The female plays the expressive role through childbearing, nursing, and caring for family members in the home. The male carries out the instrumental role by working outside the home to support the family (Anderson 1994; Parsons and Bales 1953). Although this pattern was relevant during the industrial revolution and again after World War II, when men returned to take jobs women had held during the war, it currently characterizes only a small percentage of families in Western industrial and postindustrial societies and less than 10% of families in the United States (Aulette 2002). In reality, gender segregation has seldom been total because in most cultures, women's work has combined their labor in the public sphere—that is, outside the home—with their work in the private sphere—inside the home (Lopez-Garza 2002). Poor minority women in countries around the world must often work in low-paying service jobs in the public sphere and carry the major burden for roles in the private sphere. Gender analysis through a structural-functional perspective stresses efficiencies that are believed to be gained by the specialization of tasks (Waite and Gallagher 2000).

Video Link 9.5
Watch stories about sex slaves.

Conflict Theory

Conflict theorists view males as the haves—controlling the majority of power positions and most wealth—and females as the have-nots. Women have less access to power and have historically depended on males for survival. This is the case even though they raise the next generation of workers and consumers; provide unpaid domestic labor; often grow much of the food; and assure a pool of available, cheap labor during times of crisis, such as war. By keeping women in subordinate roles, males control the means of production and protect their privileged status.

A classical conflict explanation of gender stratification is found in the writings of Karl Marx's colleague, Friedrich Engels ([1884] 1942). In traditional societies, where size and strength were essential for survival, men were often dominant, but women's roles were respected as important and necessary to the survival of the group. Men hunted, engaged in warfare, and protected women. Over time, male physical control was transformed into control by ideology, by the dominant belief system itself. Capitalism strengthened male dominance by making more wealth available to men and their sons. Women became dependent on men, and their roles were transformed into "taking care of the home" (Engels [1884] 1942).

Ideologies based on traditional beliefs and values have continued to be used to justify the social structure of male domination and subjugation of women. It is in the interest of the dominant group, in this case men, to maintain their position of privilege. Conflict theorists believe it unlikely that those in power by virtue of sex, race, class, or political or religious ideology will voluntarily give up their positions as long as they are benefiting from them. By keeping women in traditional gender roles, men maintain control over institutions and resources (Collins 1971).

Feminist Theory

Feminist theorists agree with Marx and Engels that gender stratification is based on power struggles, not biology. Yet some feminist theorists argue that Marx and Engels failed to include a key variable in women's oppression: patriarchy. Patriarchy involves a few men dominating and holding authority over all others, including women, children, and the less powerful men (Arrighi 2000; Lindsey 2008). According to feminist theory, women will continue to be oppressed by men until patriarchy is eliminated.

A distinguishing characteristic of most feminist theory is that it actively advocates a change in the social order, whereas many other theories we have discussed try only to explain the social world (Anderson 2006; Lorber 1998). There are a range of feminist theories. However, all feminist theories argue for bringing about a new and equal ordering of gender relationships to eliminate the patriarchy and sexism of current gender-stratification systems (Kramer 2007).

Feminist theorists try to understand the causes of women's lower status and seek ways to change the systems to provide more opportunities, to improve the standard of living, and to give women control over their bodies and reproduction. Feminist theorists also feel that little change will occur until group consciousness is raised so that women understand the system that limits their options and do not blame themselves for their situations (Sapiro 2003).

As societies become technologically advanced and need an educated workforce, women of all social classes and ethnic groups around the world are likely to gain more equal roles. Women are entering institutions of higher education in record numbers, and evidence indicates they are needed in the world economic system and the changing labor force of most countries. Societies in which women are not

In contrast to the clothing and gestures that create vulnerability in women, men are encouraged to use gestures that communicate strength and self-assurance, and their clothing and shoes allow them to defend themselves or flee danger.

Men who play cards, games, or sports together or who join men-only clubs develop networks that enhance their power and their ability to "close deals." When women are not part of the same networks, they are denied the same insider privileges. Many conflict theorists would argue that this is purposeful, whereas others point to it as a reality even if it is not intentional.

integrated into the economic sphere generally lag behind other countries. Feminist theorists examine these global and national patterns, but they also note the role of patriarchy in interpersonal situations—such as domestic violence.

Violence against women perpetuates gender stratification, as is evident in the intimate environment of many homes. Because men have more power in the larger society, they often have more resources within the household as well (a side-effect discrimination). Women are often dependent on the man of the house for his resources, meaning they must yield on many decisions. Power differences in the meso- and macro-level social systems also contribute to power differentials and vulnerability of women in micro-level settings. In addition, women have fewer options when considering whether to leave an abusive relationship. Although there are risks of staying in an abusive relationship, many factors enter into a woman's decision to stay or leave (Scott, London, and Myers 2002). The following "Sociology in Our Social World" discusses one form of violence around the world that is perpetuated predominantly against women: rape.

In summary, feminist analysis finds gender patterns embedded in social institutions of family, education, religion, politics, economics, and health care. If the societal system is patriarchal, ruled by men, the interdependent institutions are likely to reflect and support this system. Feminist theory helps us understand how patriarchy at the meso and macro level can influence patriarchy at the micro level and vice versa.

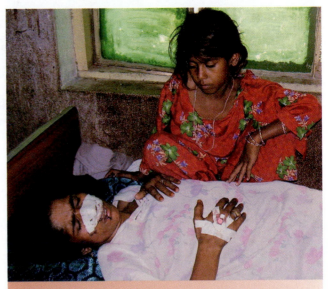

When women have less power at the meso level, they may also be more vulnerable at home. This girl attends to her injured mother at a hospital in Hyderabad, Pakistan, after the woman's husband chopped off her nose with an axe and broke all her teeth. According to the Pakistan Institute of Medical Sciences, more than 90% of married women report being severely abused when husbands are dissatisfied with their cooking or cleaning or when the women give birth to a girl instead of a boy or are unable to bear a child at all.

Thinking Sociologically

Why do women and men stay in abusive relationships? If these behaviors are hurtful or destructive, what might be done to change the situation or what policies might be enacted to address the problems?

The Interaction of Class, Race, and Gender

Zouina is Algerian, but she was born in France to her immigrant parents. She lived with them in a poor immigrant suburb of Paris until she was forced to return to Algeria for an arranged marriage to a man who already had one wife. That marriage ended, and she returned to her "home" in France. Since she returned to France, Zouina has been working wherever she can find work. The high unemployment and social and ethnic discrimination, especially against foreign women, makes life difficult (as shown in the film *The Perfumed Garden*; Benguigui 2000). An estimated 70,000 forced (and illegal) polygamous marriages occurred in 2006 in the immigrant communities of France (Levy 2008).

The situation is complex. Muslim women from Tunisia, Morocco, and Algeria living in crowded slum communities

outside Paris face discrimination in the workplace (da Silva 2004). Expected to be both good Muslim women and good family coproviders—which necessitates working in French society—they face ridicule when they wear their *hijab* (coverings) to school or to work. However, they encounter derision in their community if they do not wear them. They are caught between two cultures.

Journal Article Link 9.2 Read about the veiling of Muslim women.

Because of high unemployment in the immigrant communities, many youth roam around the streets. Gang rapes by North African youth against young women have been on the rise in France and elsewhere abroad. These rapes mean that North African women are faced with rejection and disdain in both the immigrant community and in their original African communities. With the conflicting messages due to their ethnic differences (race), their poor status (class), and their sex, these women attempt to construct their identities under grueling circumstances (Killian 2006).

Feminist theory seeks explanations for the conditions women face. One current trend in feminist interpretation, illustrated in the example above, is to view the social world as an intersection of class, race, and gender (Anderson and Collins 2006; Glenn 1999; Smith 1999). In this way, one can look at the variety of ways by which many common citizens are controlled by those who have a monopoly on power and privilege. The reality is that some women are quite privileged and wealthy. Not all women live in poverty.

Sociology in Our Social World

Rape and the Victims of Rape

For many women around the world, rape is the most feared act of violence and the ultimate humiliation. Rape is a sexual act but closely tied to macho behavior. Rape is often a power play to intimidate, hurt, and dominate women (Sanday and Goodenough 1990) or the act of a hypersexual man who feels entitled to sex (Felson 2002). Rape has been used by "owners" as a method to subdue women slaves (Bales and Trodd 2008; Brown 2001), by military troops in conquests (such as by Serbian army troops to humiliate Bosnian Muslim men who are expected to protect their women), and by prison inmates against other inmates to establish power hierarchies. Some societies are largely free from rape, whereas others are prone toward rape. What is the difference?

Rape provides an example of the impact of cultural practices, beliefs, and stereotypes. When a society is relatively tolerant of interpersonal violence, holds beliefs in male dominance, and strongly incorporates ways to separate women and men, rape is more common (Sanday 1981; Sanday and Goodenough 1990; Shaw and Lee 2005). Rape is also more common when gender roles and identities are changing and norms about interaction between women and men are unclear. What does this say, then, about the United States, where one in four college women will be raped or survive a rape attempt during their college years (One in Four, Inc. 2008), where someone is sexually assaulted or raped every 2 minutes, averaging more than 2,000 rapes daily and 272,350 rapes or sexual assaults annually? These figures are probably much lower than reality because estimates are that only 1 in 10 rapes in the United States are reported (U.S. Department of Justice 2006).

An alarming problem is rape on college campuses in the United States. Researchers report that "nearly one of every four women on college campuses has experienced sexual violence" (Shaw and Lee 2005:424). Women report being sexually assaulted, whereas few males define their behavior as assault. This discrepancy points to the stereotypes and misunderstandings that can occur because of different beliefs and attitudes. Rape causes deep and lasting problems for women victims as well as for men accused of rape because of "misreading" women's signals. Some college men report thinking of gang rape as a form of male bonding. To them, it was no big deal. The woman was just the object and instrument. Her identity was immaterial (Martin and Hummer 1989; Sanday and Goodenough 1990). Sometimes alcohol and roofies (date-rape drugs) are involved in date rape, impairing the judgment of all parties.

Men who hold more traditional gender roles view rape very differently than women and less traditional men. They tend to attribute more responsibility to the female victim of the rape, believe sex rather than power was the motivation for rape, and look less favorably on women who have been raped. In a strange twist of logic, some men actually believe that women want to be forced into having sex. Researchers show that societies with widespread gender stratification report more gendered violence, including rape (Sanday 1996, 2007).

Many citizens and politicians see rape as an individualized, personal act, whereas social scientists also tend to see it as a structural problem that stems from negative stereotypes of women, subservient positions of women in society, and patriarchal systems of power. Until there is a better understanding on the part of both men and women about gender and rape, the culture of rape is likely to continue (McEvoy and Brookings 2008). A number of sociologists and anthropologists believe that rape will not be substantially reduced unless our macho definitions of masculinity are changed (McEvoy and Brookings 2008; Sanday and Goodenough 1990).

However, even privileged women often have less power than their husbands or other men in their lives. It is also true that some women in the world are privileged because of their race or ethnicity (Rothenberg 2007). In many respects, they have more in common with men of their own ethnicity or race than they do with women of less esteemed groups, and they may choose to identify with those statuses that enhance their privilege.

Still, many women are not a part of the privileged classes. In the United States, income for men and women varies significantly depending on ethnicity, and this means that minority women are even more disprivileged. However, even when ethnicity is held constant, women get paid less than men (see Table 9.3).

Table 9.3 Median Earnings in the Past 12 Months of Workers by Race, Sex (in Dollars), and the Percentage of Men's Earnings by Women			
Race and Ethnicity	Male	Female	Women's (%) of Men's Earnings
Asian American	48,693	37,792	77.6
White	46,807	34,190	74.1
African American	34,433	29,588	85.9
Hispanic (any race)	27,380	24,451	89.3

Source: U.S. Census Bureau (2007b).

Race, class, and gender have crosscutting lines that may modify one's subjugation in the society or may intensify it. Sexual orientation, age, nationality, and other factors may have the effect of either diminishing or increasing minority status of specific women, and theorists are paying increasing attention to these intersections (Rothenberg 2007). Chapter 8 discussed the fact that racial and class lines may be crosscutting or parallel. In the case of gender, there are always crosscutting lines with race and social class. However, gender will still affect one's prestige and privilege within that class or ethnic group. Thus, to get a full picture, these three variables should be considered simultaneously (Hossfeld 2006; Kirk and Okazawa-Rey 2007).

Thinking Sociologically

What are some other ways by which race, class, and gender inequality have intersected in your community so that some people receive a double or triple dose of privilege or disprivilege?

Putting these characteristics together suggests that women are indeed a "minority group," subject to stereotypes, prejudice, and discrimination. Women of color can face the triple status determinants of being poor (class) women (gender) of color (race/ethnicity). They may be at risk to their lives when they are first born (see photo) and later in life (see the next "Sociology Around the World" on page 308).

Because daughters are a financial liability in some countries—such as India and China—there is a longstanding preference for sons. This results in extended families in which there are far more boys than girls due to sex-selective abortion and female infanticide.

Gender, Homosexuality, and Minority Status

Sex and sexuality are not binary (male-female) concepts but embrace a broader range of combinations of masculine, feminine, heterosexual, homosexual, and other variations. This range is normal in human sexuality. It is societal expectations developed over time that impose categories on human sexuality.

Audio Link 9.2
Listen to the story behind declassification of homosexuality as a mental disorder.

The movement among gays, lesbians, bisexuals, and transsexuals for equal rights and recognition is not just a North American or European phenomenon. These Nepalese transsexuals are among hundreds from across the country who gathered in Kathmandu, the capital, to demand official recognition and political representation in Nepal. This is a global movement.

Sociology Around the World

Dowry and Death: Some Dangers of Marriage

Dowry is a longstanding tradition in India, Bangladesh, Pakistan, and Sri Lanka, though it has been the practice in many lands. It involves "payment from the bride's family to the groom and groom's family at the time of marriage" and includes the money, goods, and estate or property that a woman brings her husband in marriage (Srinivasan and Lee 2004:1108). When a son is married, the son's family receives a dowry. Though once a practice of the wealthy, it is now most common in poorer families where sons are often more "valuable" than daughters because they can bring a dowry, and a dowry can amount to the equivalent of a year's salary. The idea of dowry is one of reciprocity; that is, the wife's family is also contributing something to the well-being of the younger generation. The bride receives her inheritance at the time of the wedding rather than at the time of death of her parents.

Although dowry payments were prohibited in India by the Dowry Prohibition Act in 1961 (Bradley, Tomalin, and Subramaniam 2009), this traditional practice is still widespread. The problem is that misunderstandings surrounding dowry agreements and payments can result in a form of dowry death called bride burning. These marriages are typically arranged between families and generally do not involve consent or love. It is a business deal. When the business deal fails or results in disagreement, the bride may be found soaked in kerosene or other flammable liquid and burned to death, usually in the kitchen. Authorities often rule these bride burnings as suicides. The husband can then seek another bride and another dowry (Ward and Edelstein 2009). How many bride burnings occur is uncertain because of reporting irregularities, but the National Crime Records Bureau of India confirmed and reported 7,026 cases in 2005 alone (Chinn 2007). Although police receive many calls, there are very few convictions for the crime.

Women's groups in south Asia have formed to protest against both dowries and the problems they bring, especially to poor young women who have no power or options. Some women's shelters and burn wards in hospitals have been established. The Dowry Project, established in 1995, does research on the practice, especially the link between violence and death, or bride burning. However, traditions are strong and poverty great; bride burnings are likely to continue until the penalties make it unprofitable.

Homosexuals face discrimination in some countries. Homosexuality has always existed and has been accepted and even required at some times and places and rejected or outlawed in others. In some cases, homosexuals have been placed in a separate sexual category with special roles. Some societies ignore its existence; a few consider it a psychological illness or form of depraved immorality; and a very few even consider this form of sexuality a crime (as in some Muslim societies today and in most states in the United States during much of the 20th century). In each case, the government or dominant religious group determines the status of homosexuals. The reality is that deviation from a society's gender norms, such as attraction to a member of the same sex, may cause one to experience minority status.

Lesbians—women attracted to other women—do not follow traditional gendered expectations of femininity in many societies; they often experience prejudice and discrimination. Women's status is typically based on their relationship with men, and in most societies, they are economically dependent on men. Therefore, lesbians—who support themselves and each other—may go against norms of societies and are in some instances perceived as dangerous, unnatural, or a threat to men's power (Burn 2005; Ward and Edelstein 2009).

Sexism affects the lives of gay men as well. *Homophobia* (intense fear and hatred of homosexuality and homosexuals) is highly correlated with and perhaps a cause of the traditional notions of gender and gender roles (Pharr 1997; Shaw and Lee 2005). Some homosexuals deviate from traditional notions of masculinity and femininity and therefore from significant norms of many societies. This may result in hostile reactions and stigma from the dominant group. Indeed, homosexual epitaphs are often used to reinforce gender conformity and to intimidate anyone who would dare to be different from the norm. Still, the issue of homophobia focuses on prejudice held and transmitted by individuals.

Heterosexism is the notion that the society reinforces heterosexuality and marginalizes anyone who does not conform to this norm. Heterosexism focuses on social processes that define homosexuality as deviant and legitimize heterosexuality as the only normal lifestyle (Oswald 2000, 2001). In short, heterosexism operates often at the meso and macro levels of society, through privileges such as rights to health care and jobs granted to people who are heterosexual and denied to those who are not.

Homosexuality has been an issue in recent political elections in the United States. As of 2007, almost all states had "Defense of Marriage Acts" or constitutional amendments prohibiting same-sex marriage. This has spawned debates about family life and whether homosexuals should be allowed to marry, to adopt or have children, or to have the same rights as heterosexuals. In short, many institutions in the social world have been influenced by this debate over sexuality and gender. The notion of allowing gays and lesbians the right to a legal marriage has been extremely controversial in the United States, and more than 30 states have passed legislation defining marriage as between a man and a woman, some even approving amendments to their constitutions to ensure that same-sex marriages will not happen in those states (Newman and Grauerholz 2002). As of January 2010, marriage licenses are available to same-sex couples in six states (Massachusetts, Connecticut, Iowa, Vermont, Maine, and New Hampshire). Vermont was the first to pass this policy through the legislature, followed later in 2009 by Maine and New Hampshire. In the other states the law was implemented by court decisions. Similar court decisions have been made in Hawaii, Alaska, and California, but in each case a state referendum has overruled the courts. One reason the lesbigay community is so intent on having same-sex marriage is that same-sex partnerships are "insufficiently institutionalized" (Cherlin 1978; Stewart 2007), making them somewhat less stable and creating ambiguity about their roles and rights. They have been denied the role of spouse, which roots personal relationships in meso-level institutions.

The point here is not to argue for or against same-sex marriage but to note that homosexuals do not have many of the rights that heterosexuals have. The discrepancy is based on sexual characteristics. Heterosexuals in the United States have a variety of rights—ranging from insurance coverage and inheritance rights for lifelong partners to jointly acquired property, hospital visitation rights as family, rights to claim the body of a deceased partner, and rights to have the deceased prepared for burial or cremation. The U.S. federal government confers 1,138 rights to heterosexuals that they normally take for granted, but often, these rights do not extend to same-sex partners in a lifelong relationship. Most states also bestow more than 200 specific rights to persons who "marry," but because most states do not allow same-sex marriages, homosexuals do not have these same rights (U.S. General Accounting Office 2003). In Canada and many European countries, citizens do have a right to same-sex marriage, and this has reduced the number of discrepancies in the rights of homosexuals and heterosexuals.

Thinking Sociologically

The concept of *homophobia* focuses on micro-level processes, whereas the notion of *heterosexism* is attentive to meso- and macro-level forces. Which of these concepts reveals the most about issues faced by the lesbian and gay community? Why?

Costs and Consequences of Gender Stratification

In rapidly changing modern societies, role confusion abounds. Men hesitate to offer help to women, wondering if gallantry will be appreciated or scorned. Women are torn between traditional family roles, on the one hand, and working to support the family and fulfilling career goals, on the other. As illustrated in the examples below, sex-based stratification limits individual development and causes problems in education, health, work, and other parts of the social world.

Video Link 9.6
Watch discussion of children and gender roles.

Psychological and Social Consequences: Micro-Level Implications

For both women and men, rigid gender stereotypes can be very constraining. Individuals who hold highly sex-typed attitudes feel compelled to behave in stereotypic ways, ways that are consistent with the pictures they have in their heads of proper gender behavior (Basow 1992, 2000). However, individuals who do not identify strongly with masculine or feminine gender types are more flexible in thoughts and behavior, tend to score higher on intelligence tests, have greater spatial ability, and have higher levels of creativity. Because they allow themselves a wider range of behaviors, they have more varied abilities and experiences and become more tolerant of others' behaviors. High masculinity in males sets up rigid standards for male behavior and has been correlated with anxiety, guilt, and neuroses, whereas less rigid masculine expectations are associated with emotional stability, sensitivity, warmth, and enthusiasm. Rigid stereotypes and resulting sexism affect everyone and curtail our activities, behaviors, and perspectives.

Superwoman Image

The "superwoman syndrome," a pattern by which women assume multiple roles and try to do all well, takes its toll (Faludi 1993). The resulting strain contributes to depression and certain health problems such as headaches, nervousness, and insomnia (Wood 2008). Women in many societies are expected to be beautiful, youthful, and sexually interesting and interested, while at the same time they must prepare the food, care for the children, keep a clean and orderly home, and sometimes bring in money to help support the family. Some are also expected to be competent and successful in their careers. Multiple, sometimes contradictory, expectations for women cause stress and even serious psychological problems.

Journal Article Link 9.3
Read about steroids, race, and gender.

Women who work outside the home are often expected to keep up with the domestic tasks as well. Evidence indicates that when women enter the labor force, there are no parallel changes or redistribution of responsibilities in family life. On the contrary, working generally leads to an increase in what is expected of women.

Beauty Image

Beautiful images jump out at us from billboards, magazine covers, and TV and movie screens. Some of these images are unattainable by most women because they have been created through surgeries and eating disorders—and even by the use of airbrushing on photographs. Disorders, including anorexia and bulimia nervosa, relate to societal expectations of the ideal woman's appearance. About 1 out of every 100 U.S. women (7 million women compared with 1 million men) suffers from these severe eating disorders, and the numbers have been growing since the 1970s.

Encyclopedia Link 9.2
Read more about body image.

The beauty-image obsession in North America is far more of an issue with White Anglos than African Americans or Latinas, but especially with young White women it results in disorders relative to eating. Some young women are obsessed with thinness, even at the expense of their health.

This dangerous ailment occurs most frequently in females between 12 and 18 years of age, caused by distortions in body image that are brought on by what the women, especially the White middle- and upper-middle-class women, see as societal images of beauty, often images created in magazines that are unattainable in real life (ANRED 2007; Kilbourne 1999; Taub and McLorg 2007).

Thinking Sociologically

If females are expending great energy and attention on how they look—to ensure that they are physically appealing to others—how might this influence their ability to get access to positions of power and prestige?

Men also suffer psychological costs of stereotyping, from eating disorders to fitness magazines that picture the "perfect" male body and advertise exercise equipment and steroids. In addition, men die earlier than women, in part due to environmental, psychological, and social factors. Problems in developed countries such as heart disease, stroke, cirrhosis, cancers, accidents, and suicides are linked in part to the male role that dictates that males should appear tough, objective, ambitious, unsentimental, and unemotional—traits that require men to assume great responsibility and suppress their feelings (Leit, Gray, and Pope 2002).

Societal Costs and Consequences: Meso- and Macro-Level Implications

Gender stratification creates costs for societies around the world in a number of ways. Poor educational achievement of female children leads to the loss of human talents and resources of half the population. Lack of health care coverage affects not only the women but also their children, and social divisiveness leads to alienation, if not hostility. Discrimination and violence against women, whether physical or emotional, has consequences for all institutions in a society (UNESCAP 2007).

Consider how the ratio of women to men in an occupational field affects the prestige of the occupation. As more men enter predominantly female fields such as nursing and library science, the fields gain higher occupational prestige, and salaries tend to increase. It seems that men take their gender privilege with them when they enter female professions (Kramer 2007). However, the evidence indicates that as women enter male professions such as law, the status tends to become lower, making women's chances of improving their position in the stratification system limited.

Gender stratification has often meant loss of the talents and brain power of women, and that is a serious loss to modern postindustrial societies because human capital—the resources of the human population—is central to social prosperity in this type of system. Yet resistance to expanding women's professional roles is often strong. For example, Japanese women make up close to 50% of the workforce, but only 10.1% hold managerial positions (Fackler 2007). Although their education levels are generally high, Japanese and Korean women earn wages that are only about 66% of their male counterparts' wages, the largest wage gap among developed countries in the Organization for Economic Cooperation and Development (OECD), Japan Institute for Labour Policy and Training 2009; Kumlin 2006). Breaking through the glass ceiling continues to be not only a barrier for individual women but also a challenge for entire societies that could benefit from abilities never fully maximized.

Changing Gender Stratification and Social Policy

Policy is informed by social science research. Some applied feminist sociologists have focused on women's issues in North America, working in shelters for battered women, in rape response centers, and with other agencies addressing the needs of girls and women. "The Applied Sociologist at Work" looks at the work of a sociologist who is interested in understanding the progress of and barriers to women pursuing careers in science, technology, engineering, and mathematics.

Many other policy issues have focused on issues for women around the globe. Women in factories in the Global South face dangerous conditions and low pay. Sweatshops exist because poor women have few other job options to support their families and because people in rich countries want to buy

The Applied Sociologist at Work— Lynette Osborne

Gender Inequality and STEM

By Lynette Osborne

Science, Technology, Engineering, and Mathematics Education (STEM) is a government initiative to help girls, women, and ethnic minorities contribute to science, develop stronger global skills, and achieve economic security. The Obama administration is increasing funding for STEM initiatives, and you may see a STEM school in your neighborhood in the near future.

The problem is that women's participation in STEM education has decreased in the past few years, despite increased efforts to recruit and retain women in college STEM majors. Recruitment and retention of low-income and minority women into STEM careers through community colleges has also been challenging. To understand the reasons for these problems, Lynette Osborne participated in several research projects on gender equity in science. She has employed many types of research methods—questionnaires, interviews, and participant observation—to provide answers to her research questions. For instance, when studying the perceptions of women in engineering education, she combined interviews with students and professors, a Web survey, and participant observation of engineering classes to provide a more complete picture. The result helped identify techniques for recruiting low-income and minority women to mid-skilled STEM careers.

Each project incorporated a theoretical framework to guide the research and interpretation. Because Dr. Osborne's research is concerned with gender equity, most often the guiding theoretical perspective she uses is feminist. For example, in her research on women in engineering education, the project was informed by and analyzed using feminist standpoint theory (Harding 2004).

Note: Lynette Osborne earned her master's degree in sociology at Old Dominion University and a PhD in sociology at Purdue University. She is a research associate at the Institute for Women's Policy Research and an adjunct professor at The George Washington University. She worked for a year as a scholar-in-residence at the National Academy of Education's Center for the Advancement of Scholarship on Engineering Education (NAE/CASEE).

the cheap products that perpetuate the multinational corporate system. Just a few years ago, workers in *maquiladoras* (foreign-owned assembly plants) in Mexican border towns worked for 2,000 multinational companies that paid a minimum of $3.40 per *day* compared with $5.15 per *hour* in the United States (CorpWatch 1999). The entry-level wage for low-level jobs along the border with Mexico was about 25% of the hourly wage paid to U.S. workers, and Mexico has a 48-hour work week, reducing extra expenses for overtime work (Burn 2005; Made in Mexico, Inc. 2005). Two thirds of the workers were poor women. As you examine Figure 9.1 on labor costs in the textile industry around the world, note the variation between the nations.

Women in many parts of the world typically earn less than half of what men earn (Burn 2005) and not what is needed to survive in their areas. Yet corporations can pay low wages and, in many cases, continue to maintain poor and even dangerous working environments because these areas have high unemployment, and families have no other options. What can be done about the abusive treatment of women around the world? This is a tough issue: Governments have passed legislation to protect workers, but governments also want the jobs that multinational corporations bring and therefore do little to enforce regulations. International labor standards are also difficult to enforce. Multinationals are so large that it is difficult to influence

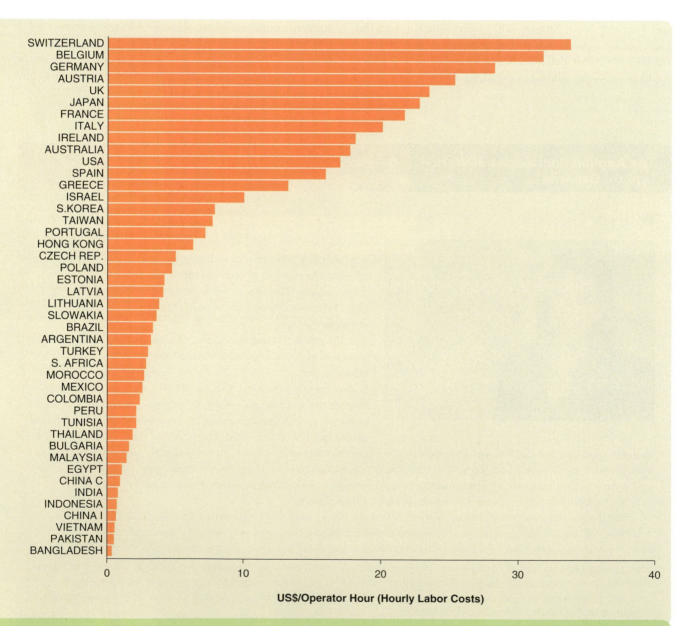

Figure 9.1   Labor Costs in the Textile Industry Around the World

Source: New Twist (2007).

their practices. Trade unions have had little success attracting workers to join because companies squash their recruiting efforts immediately.

One way to begin considering fair wages and conditions for workers is to adopt practices that have worked for other groups facing discrimination in the past. Consider the following possibilities for bringing about change: holding nonviolent protests—sit-down strikes and walkouts—to protest unequal and unfair treatment; working together in support groups to help the children and neighborhoods; using the Internet to carry the message to others; carrying out boycotts against companies that mistreat employees; following traditions that have succeeded in the past such as using the arts, preachers, storytellers, and teachers to express frustration and resistance, educate others, and provide ideas and strategies for resistance; and building on traditions of community and religious activism (Collins 2000). Most of these strategies require organized groups.

Thinking Sociologically

Consider the strategies for change listed in the previous paragraph. Which of these do you think has a realistic chance of bringing constructive change for women working for poverty-level wages? Which approaches would surely fail? Why do you think so?

At women's conferences around the world, policymakers debate the means to create solutions to women's problems. Most UN member countries have at least fledgling women's movements fighting for the improved status of women and their families. The movements attempt to change laws that result in discrimination, poverty, abuse, and low levels of education and occupational status. Although the goals of eliminating differential treatment of women, especially minority women, are jointly affirmed by most women's groups, the means to improve conditions for women are debated between women's groups. For instance, some advocates work within existing institutions to bring about equal rights. Others push for the complete overhauling of existing systems to bring about a new order that would ignore sex as a variable in assigning power. Whether any of these efforts will change women's individual lives and the lives of their children is unknown.

Women in Thailand produce shoes at extremely low rates. These jobs are better than no employment at all, but before pressures from Western societies changed their cultures, most people were able to feed their families quite adequately on farms in small villages. Changes in the entire world system have made that form of life no longer feasible; also, working for multinational corporations keeps them impoverished.

We grow up being socialized into patterns of behavior, even if those patterns include discrimination. In Western countries with relatively high wages, many young women are afraid of change and of the protests implied in being an active feminist. Familiar patterns are comfortable, even if they limit opportunities. Being an activist is risky, especially if one is living a comfortable life. Restrictions caused by gender stratification become clearer as young women enter the public sphere (Hogeland 2004).

We would be too optimistic to predict that grassroots efforts or boycotts against those who are enjoying the fruits of poor women's labor will change the system. The best hope may lie in increased opportunities for women as countries modernize and in efforts of countries (such as Cambodia [Kampuchia]) that strive to enforce labor laws and improve conditions and wages for workers. These efforts will work only if a number of countries join in, if they maintain a competitive labor market, and if buyers support products made in countries with fair labor practices (Better Factories Movement 2006).

Inequality based on class, race, ethnicity, and gender is a process taking place at all levels of analysis and is often entrenched at the meso level within institutions. Major institutions include family, education, religion, politics, economics, and medicine. In complex societies, there are other necessary institutions including health care, science and technology, sport, and the military. We turn now to a discussion of institutions in our social world.

What Have We Learned?

In the beginning of this chapter, we asked how being born female or male affects our lives. Because sex is a primary variable on which societies are structured and stratification takes place, being born female or male affects our public and private sphere activities, our health, our ability to practice religion or participate in political life, our educational opportunities, and just about everything we do. As sociologists with a focus on empirical ways of knowing and scientific methods, we can only focus on a description and analysis of what is. Other disciplines, such as philosophy and theology, may articulate what "ought" to be. Applied sociologists sometimes move from an analysis of empirical data to questions of how to improve the quality of people's lives by suggesting solutions. Likewise, policy recommendations are those that take what is known about gender relations and offer plans for changing and improving the society. Gender inequality clearly exists. What should be done to alleviate the problems is a matter of debate.

Key Points

- Whereas sex is biological, notions of gender identity and gender roles are socially constructed and learned and therefore variable. (See pp. 282–286.)

- Notions of gender are first taught at the micro setting—the intimacy of the home—but they are reinforced and even sacralized at the meso and macro levels. (See pp. 286–289.)

- While "she" may go first in micro-level social encounters (served first in a restaurant or the first to enter a door), "he" goes first in meso and macro settings—with the doors open wider for men to enter leadership positions in organizations and institutions. (See pp. 289–292.)

- Greater access to resources at the meso level makes it easier to have entree to macro-level positions, but it also influences respect in micro settings. (See p. 293.)

- Much of the gender stratification today is unconscious and unintended—not caused by angry or bigoted men who purposefully oppress women. Inequality is rooted in institutionalized privilege and disprivilege. (See pp. 299–301.)

- Various social theories shed different light on the issues of sex roles and inequality. (See pp. 302–306.)

- For modern postindustrial societies, there is a high cost for treating women like a minority group—individually for the people who experience it and for the society, which loses the intelligence, skills, and commitment of highly competent people. (See pp. 309–311.)

Contributing to Our Social World: What Can We Do?

At the Local Level

- *Human Resources (employment) office or affirmative action on your campus:* Schedule an interview with the director or other staff members to learn about your school's policies regarding gender discrimination. What procedures exist for hiring? Do women and men receive the same salaries, wages, and benefits for equal work? Explore the possibility of your working as a volunteer or intern in the office specifically in the area of gender equity.

At the Organizational and National Levels

- *The National Organization for Women (NOW):* This has been the world's leading advocate for gender equity. Its Web site at www.now.org deals with issues such as abortion and reproductive rights, legislative outreach, economic justice, ending sex discrimination, and promoting

diversity. Several internship programs are listed on their Web site, along with contact information and state and regional affiliates and "NOW on Campus" links.

At the Global Level

- *MADRE:* This is an international women's rights organization that works primarily in the less developed countries. Its Web site (www.madre.org) lists numerous opportunities for working on issues of justice, human rights, education, and health.

- *The United Nations Inter-Agency Network on Women and Gender Equality:* This organization works on relevant global issues, including violence against women and women's working conditions. Its WomenWatch Web site at www.un.org/women watch contains news, information, and ideas for contributing to the worldwide campaign for women's rights.

 For chapter-specific resources, including **Frontline**, **TED**, and **YouTube** videos; self-quizzes; web exercises; and more, visit **www.pineforge.com/oswmedia3e.**

PART IV

Institutions

Picture a house, a structure in which you live. Within that house there are processes—the action and activities that bring the house alive. Flip a switch, and the lights go on because the house is well wired. Adjust the thermostat, and the room becomes more comfortable as the structural features of furnace or air-conditioning systems operate. If the structural components of the plumbing and water heating systems work, you can take a hot shower when you turn the knob. These actions taken within the structure make the house livable. If something breaks down, you need to get it fixed so that everything works smoothly.

Institutions, too, provide a framework or *structure* for society. As such, they promote guidelines and stability. *Processes* are the action dimension within institutions—the activities that take place. They include the interactions between people, decision making, conflict, and other actions in society. These processes are often dynamic and can lead to significant change within the structure—like a decision by a new homeowner to remodel the kitchen. Institutions are meso-level structures because they are larger in scope than the face-to-face social interactions of the micro level, and yet they are smaller than the nation or the global system. Institutions—such as family, education, religion, politics, economics, and health care—are also interdependent and mutually supportive, just as the plumbing, heating system, and electricity in a house work together to make a home functional. However, a breakdown in one institution or conflict over limited resources between institutions affects the whole society, just as a malfunction in the electrical system may shut the furnace off and cool down the water heater.

The Importance of Institutions

Institutions are not anything concrete that you can see, hear, or smell. The whole concept of institutions is an abstraction about human activities: It refers to the behavior of thousands of people, which—taken as a whole—form a social structure. Think of your own family. It has unique ways of interacting and raising children, but it is part of a community with many families. Those many families, in turn, are part of a national set of patterned behaviors we call "the family." This pattern meets the basic needs of the society for producing and socializing new members and providing an emotionally supportive environment. Institutions do not dictate exactly how you will carry out the roles of family, but it does specify certain needs families will meet and statuses (husband, wife, child) that will relate to each other in certain mutually caring ways and filling certain seminegotiable roles. An institution provides a blueprint (much like a local builder needs a blueprint to build a house), and in your local version of the institution you may make a few modifications to the plans. Still, through this society-encompassing structure and interlocking set of statuses, the basic needs—for individuals at the micro level and for society at the macro level—are met.

Institutions, then, are *organized, patterned, and enduring sets of social structures* that provide *guidelines for behavior* and help each society *meet its basic survival needs*; while institutions operate mostly at the meso level, they also act to *integrate micro and macro levels of society*. Let us look more deeply at this definition.

1. *Organized, patterned, and enduring sets of social structures* means that institutions are not bricks and mortar of buildings but refer to a complex set of groups or organizations, statuses within those groups, and norms of conduct with which the people comply. These structures ensure socialization of children, education of the young, sense of meaning in life to the distressed, or goods (food, clothing, automobiles, iPods, cell phones) to the members of the society. This is patterned behavior that is important; if it were missing, these needs might not be addressed. At the local level, we may go to a neighborhood school or we may attend worship at a congregation we favor. These are local organizations—local franchises, if you will—of a much more encompassing structure (education and religion) that provides guidelines for education or addresses issues of meaning of life for an enormous number of people. The Catholic Church in your town, for example, is a local "franchise" of an organization that is transnational in scope and global in its concerns.

2. *Guidelines for behavior* help people know how to conduct themselves to meet basic needs. Individuals and local "franchises" actually carry out the institutional guidelines in each culture; the exact ways the guidelines are carried out vary by locality. In local "franchises" of the political system, people know how to govern and how to solve problems at the local level because of larger norms and patterns—the political institution. Individual men and women operate a local hospital or clinic (a local "franchise" of the medical institution) because a national blueprint of how to provide health care informs local expectations and decisions. The specific activities of a local school, likewise, are influenced by the guidelines and purposes of the larger notions of "formal education" in a given nation.

3. *Meeting basic survival needs* is a core component of institutions because societies must meet needs of their members; otherwise the members die or the society collapses. Institutions, then, are the structures that support social life in a large bureaucratized society. Common to all industrialized societies are family, education, religion, economics, politics, and health. These institutions are discussed in the following chapters.

4. *Acting to integrate micro and macro levels of society* is critical because one of the collective needs of society is coherence and stability—including some integration between the various levels of society. Institutions help provide that integration for the entire social system. They do this by meeting needs at the local franchise level (food at the grocery, education at the local school, health care at the local clinic) at the same time they coordinate national and global organizations and patterns.

Again, if all this sounds terribly abstract, that is because institutions *are* abstractions. You cannot touch institutions, yet they are as real as air, love, or happiness. In fact, in the modern world institutions are as necessary to life as is air, and they help provide love and happiness that make life worth living.

The Development of Modern Institutions

If we go all the way back to early hunting and gathering societies, there were no meso or macro levels to their social experience. People lived their lives in one or two villages, and while a spouse might come from another village or one might move to a spouse's clan, there was no national or state governance, and certainly no awareness of a global social system. In those simple times, family might provide whatever education was needed, produce and distribute goods, pay homage to a god or gods, and solved conflicts and disputes through a system of familial (usually patriarchal) power distribution. One social unit served multiple functions. As societies have become more complex and differentiated, not only have multiple levels of the social system emerged but also various new institutions have emerged. Sociology textbooks in the 1950s identified only "five basic institutions": family, economic systems, political systems, religion,

and education (formal public education only having been created in the mid-19th century). These five institutions were believed to be the core structures that met the essential needs of individuals and societies in an orderly way.

Soon thereafter, *medicine* moved from the family and small town doctors to be recognized as an institution. Medicine had become bureaucratized in hospitals, medical labs, professional organizations, and other complex structures that provided health care. *Science* is also now something more than flying kites in thunderstorms in one's backyard. It is a complex system that provides training, funding, research institutes, peer review, and professional associations to support empirical research in the sciences. New information is the lifeblood of an information-based or postindustrial society. Science, discussed in Chapter 14, is now an essential institution. Although it is arguable whether sports are an essential component for social viability, sports have clearly become highly structured in the past 50 years, and many sociologists consider it an institution. The mass media and military also fall into the category of institutions in more advanced countries. There are gray areas as to whether or not something is considered an institution, but the questions to ask are (a) whether the structure meets basic needs of the society for survival, (b) whether it has become a complex organization providing routinized structures and guidelines, and (c) whether it is national or even global in its scope, while also having pervasive local (micro) impact.

The Interconnections Between Institutions

Keep in mind that changes in one institution affect all other institutions, since they are interdependent. For example, the global economic crisis of 2008–2009 illustrates the forces that bring about changes through interconnections between institutions. As described by "the sociological imagination," our individual problems such as loss of a job are tied to the macro-level changes in the economy. So the family is affected, and citizens expect the government to intervene and fix the problem. Religious congregations have increased demands at their food banks, soup kitchens, and thrift shops run for low-income people, yet religious contributions from religious congregants are more difficult to make in tough economic times. Schools also suffer from lack of income from the economic downturn. From a study of Table IV.1, see if you can place other institutions (mass media, military, science, sports) in the framework.

Interconnections between meso-level institutions are a common refrain in this book. As you read these chapters, notice that change in one institution affects others. Sociologists studying the legal system, mass media, medicine, military, science, or sports as institutions would raise similar questions and would want to know how they influence the micro, meso, and macro levels of a society. We begin with the institution of family—that institution which is such an intimate part of our lives and which is often called the "most basic" institution of society.

	Family	Education	Economic Systems	Political Systems	Religion	Medicine
Macro (national and global social systems and trends)	Kin and marriage structures, such as monogamy versus polygamy; global trends in family such as choice of partners rather than arranged marriages	National education system; United Nations Girls' Education Initiative	Spread of capitalism around the world; World Bank; International Monetary Fund; World Trade Organization	National government; United Nations; World Court; G8 (most powerful eight nations in the world)	Global faith-based movements and structures: National Council of Churches; World Council of Churches; World Islamic Call Society; World Jewish Congress	National health care system; World Health Organization; transnational pandemics
Meso (institutions, complex organizations, ethnic subcultures, state/provincial systems)	The middle-class family; the Hispanic family; the Jewish family	State/provincial department of education; American Federation of Teachers*	State/provincial offices of economic development; United Auto Workers*	State/provincial governments; national political parties; each state or province's supreme court	National denominations/movements: e.g., United Methodist Church or American Reform Judaism	HMOs; American Medical Association*
Micro (local "franchises" of institutions)	Your family; local parenting group; local Parents Without Partners; county family counseling clinic	Your teacher; local neighborhood school; local school board	Local businesses; local chamber of commerce; local labor union chapter	Neighborhood crime watch program; local city or county council	Your local religious study group or congregation	Your doctor and nurse; local clinic; local hospital

Table IV.1 The Impact of Institutions at Each Level of Analysis

* These organizations are national in scope and membership, but they are considered meso level here because they are complex organizations *within* the nation.

CHAPTER 10

Family

Partner Taking, People Making, and Contract Breaking

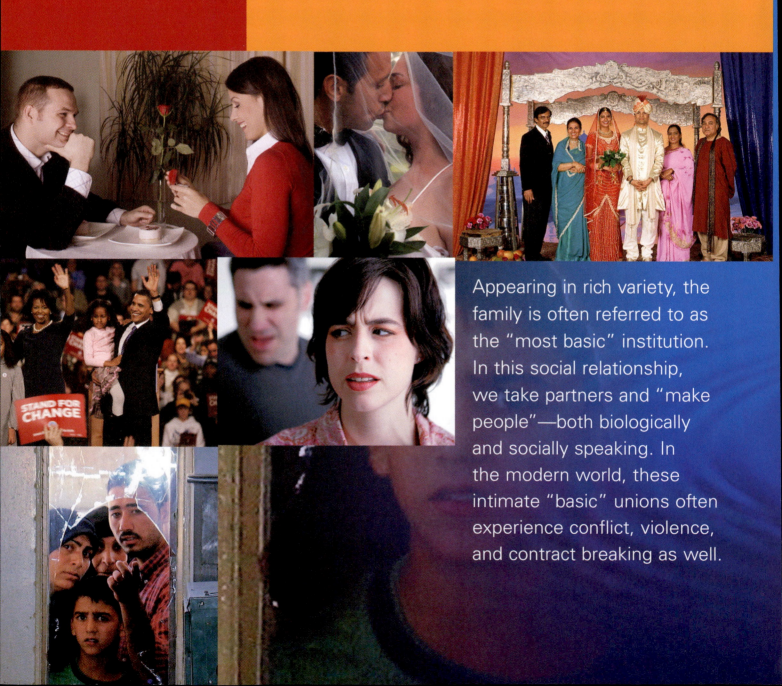

Appearing in rich variety, the family is often referred to as the "most basic" institution. In this social relationship, we take partners and "make people"—both biologically and socially speaking. In the modern world, these intimate "basic" unions often experience conflict, violence, and contract breaking as well.

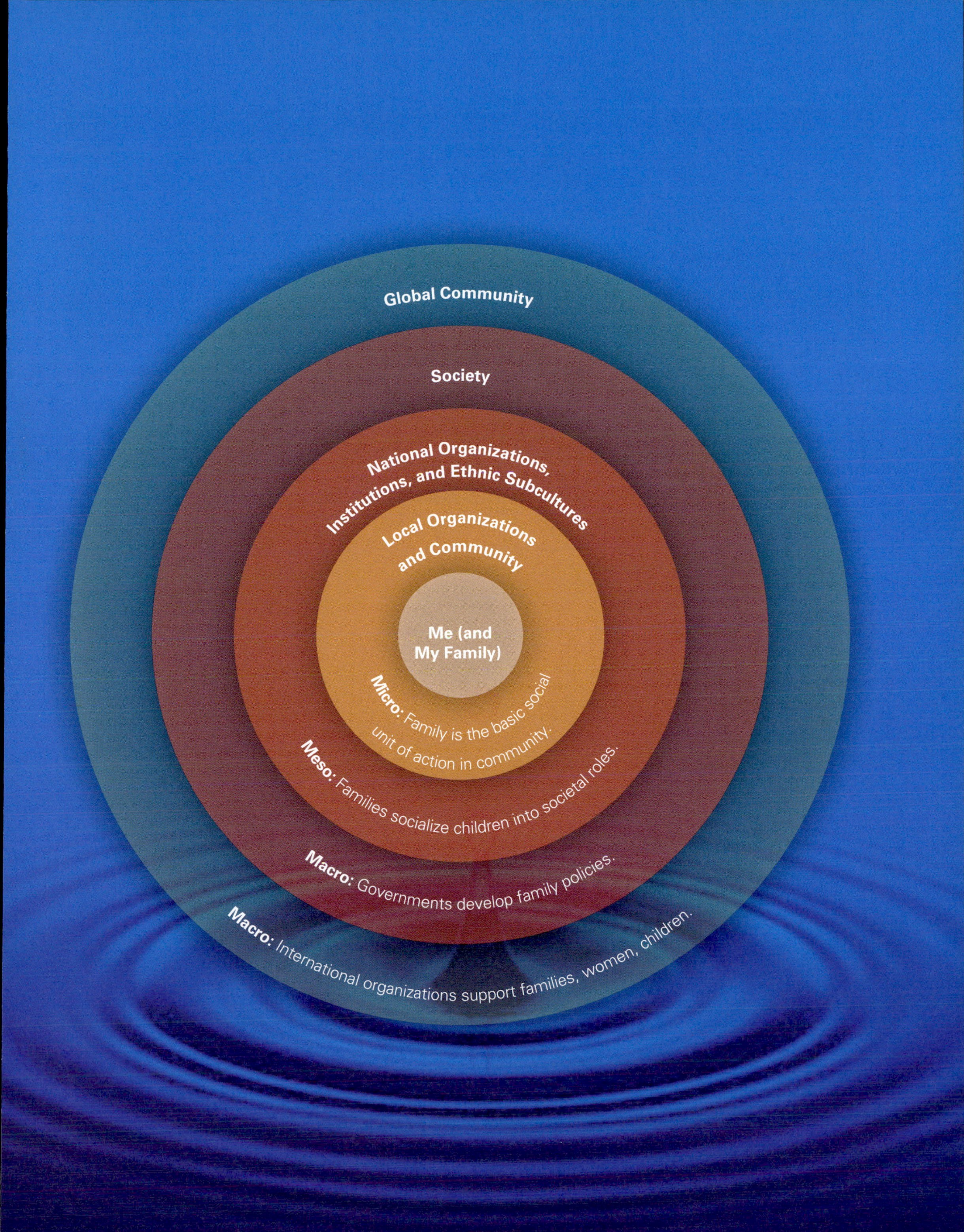

Global Community

Society

National Organizations, Institutions, and Ethnic Subcultures

Local Organizations and Community

Me (and My Family)

Micro: Family is the basic social unit of action in community.

Meso: Families socialize children into societal roles.

Macro: Governments develop family policies.

Macro: International organizations support families, women, children.

In a village in Indonesia, the family is preparing for the day's chores. Daya and Chetana work with other women in the end of the long house that is used for cooking for the entire group. Other rooms along the house are designated for sleeping, greeting guests, and caring for children. Many people of all ages come and go—children, middle-aged adults, and elderly members. In this system, family units live together in an extended family, several generations of blood relatives sharing a single household.

It is morning in Sweden. Anders and Karin Karlsson are rushing to get to their offices on time. The children, a 12-year-old son and an 8-year-old daughter, are being hurried out the door to school. All will return in the evening after a full day of activities and join together for the evening meal. In this dual-career family, common in many postindustrial societies, both parents are working professionals.

The gossip at the African village water well this day is about the rich local merchant, Azi, who has just taken his fourth and last wife. She is a young, beautiful girl of 15 from a neighboring village. She is expected to help with household chores and bear children for his already extensive family unit. Several of the women at the well live in affluent households where the husband has more than one wife.

Tom and Henry recently adopted Ty into their family. The couple share custody of the 5-year-old boy; adoption by gay couples is not legal in some U.S. states, but it is legal for gay couples in some states and for single gay persons in many others (Johnson 2008). Ty's parents attend his school events and teach him what all parents are expected to teach their children. Dora, a single mom, lives next door with her two children. She bundles them off to school before heading to her job. After school, she has an arrangement with other neighbors to care for the children until she gets home.

What do the very different scenes described at the outset of this chapter have in common? Each describes a family, yet there is controversy about what constitutes a family. Those groupings that are officially recognized as families tend to receive a number of privileges and rights, such as health insurance and inheritance rights (Degenova and Rice 2010). In this chapter, we will discuss characteristics of families, theoretical perspectives on family, family dynamics, family as an institution, family issues, and policies regarding marriage and divorce.

Families come in many shapes, sizes, and color combinations. We begin our exploration of this institution with a discussion of what *is* family.

In recent decades, the definition of family has broadened. No longer is it necessarily limited to heterosexual couples. These gay men are parents to this baby.

What Is a Family?

Ma, Pa, and the kids? Not always! Who defines what constitutes a family? Each individual? The government? Religious groups? Let us consider several definitions. The U.S. Census Bureau (2005b) defines the **family** as "a group of two or more people (one of whom is the householder) related by birth, marriage, or adoption and residing together; all such people (including other related family members) are considered as members of the family." Thus, a family in the

United States might be composed of siblings, cousins, a grandparent and grandchild, or other groupings. Some sociologists define family as those sharing economic property, sexual access among the adults, and a sense of commitment among members (Collins and Coltrane 2001). This definition would include same-sex couples as families. Some religious groups define family as a mother, father, and their children, whereas others include several spouses and even parents and siblings living under one roof.

How do you define family? Answering the questions in the "Engaging Sociology" will indicate the complexity of this question.

Engaging Sociology

The Ideal Family

What is "the ideal family"? Does it have one adult woman and one adult man? One child or many? Grandparents living with the family? First, complete the following survey. Then, ask a friend or relative to answer the questions below.

1. How many adults should the ideal family contain? _____

2. How many children should the ideal family contain? _____

3. What should be the sex composition of the adults in an ideal family? (Check all that apply)

    a. One female and one male

    b. Male-male or female-female

    c. Several males and several females

    d. Other (write in) _____

4. What should be the sexes of the child(ren) in the ideal family? _____

5. Who should select the marriage partner? (Check all that apply)

    a. The partners should select each other.

    b. The parents or close relatives should select the partner.

    c. A matchmaker should arrange the marriage.

    d. Other _____

6. What is the ideal number of generations living in the same household?

    a. One generation: partners and no children

    b. Two generations: partners and children

    c. Three or more generations: partners, children, grandparents, and great-grandparents

    d. Other _____

7. Where should the couple live?

    a. By themselves

    b. With parents

    c. With brothers or sisters

    d. With as many relatives as possible

8. What should the sexual arrangements be? (Check all that apply)

    a. Partners have sex only with each other.

    b. Partners can have sex outside marriage if it is not "disruptive" to the relationship.

    c. Partners are allowed to have sex with all other consenting adults.

    d. Male partners can have sex outside marriage.

    e. Female partners can have sex outside marriage.

    f. Other _____

(Continued)

(Continued)

9. Which person(s) in the ideal family should work to help support the family?

  a. Both partners

  b. Male only

  c. Female only

  d. Both, but the mother only after children are in school

  e. Both, but the mother only after children graduate from high school

  f. All family members including children

  g. Other _____

10. Should the couple have sex before marriage if they wish? Yes ___ No ___ Other_____

11. Should physically disabled aging parents

  a. Be cared for in a child's home?

  b. Be placed in a nursing care facility?

  c. Other _____

Why do you hold these particular views of "the ideal family"? Are your answers different from those of your friend or relative? Why might others in your society have answered differently?

Note that all these options are found in some societies.

The family is often referred to as the most basic *institution* of any society. First, it is the place where we learn many of the norms for functioning in the larger society. Second, most of us spend our lives in the security of a family. People are born and raised in families, and many will die in a family setting.

This Romanian family does not have much money, but the children learn many survival skills, and the most basic needs of the children, physical and psychological, are met.

Through good and bad, sickness and health, most families provide for our needs, both physical and psychological. Therefore, families meet our primary, our most basic, needs. Third, major life events—marriages, births, graduations, promotions, anniversaries, religious ceremonies, holidays, funerals—take place within the family context and are celebrated with family members. In short, family is where we invest the most emotional energy and spend much of our leisure time. Fourth, the family is capable of satisfying a range of social needs—belonging to a group, economic support, education or training, raising children, religious socialization, resolution of conflicts, and so forth. One cannot conceive of the economic system providing emotional support for each individual or the political system providing socialization and personalized care for each child. Family carries out these functions (Benokraitis 2010).

The family is the place where we confirm our partnerships as adults, and it is where we *make people*—not just biologically, but socially. In the family, we take an organism that has the potential to be fully human, and we mold this tiny bit of humanity into a caring, compassionate, productive person.

Thinking Sociologically

What purposes does your family serve for its members? What role does each member play in the family? Why might this be important for the larger society?

No other institution can fulfill the functions of the family, but the family can fulfill many functions of other institutions. At the left, family members work together as an economic team to produce food. At the right, a family prays together before lunch.

In most Western societies, individuals are born and raised in the **family of orientation**, which consists of our parent(s) and possibly sibling(s). In this family, we receive our early socialization and learn the language, norms, core values, attitudes, and behaviors of our community and society. When we find a life mate and/or have our own children, we establish our **family of procreation**. The transmission of values, beliefs, and attitudes from our family of orientation to our family of procreation preserves and stabilizes the family system. Because family involves emotional investment, we have strong feelings about what form it should take.

Whether we consider families at micro, meso, or macro levels, sociological theories can help us understand the role of families in the social world.

Theoretical Perspectives on Family

Consider the case of Felice, a young mother locked into a marriage that provides her with little satisfaction. For the first year of marriage, Felice tried to please her husband, Tad, but gradually he seemed to drift further away. He began to spend evenings out. Sometimes, he came home drunk and yelled or hit her. Felice became pregnant shortly after their marriage and had to quit her job. This increased the financial pressure on Tad, and they fell behind in paying the bills.

Then, came the baby. They were both ecstatic at first, but Tad soon reverted to his old patterns. Felice felt trapped. She was afraid and embarrassed to go to her parents. They had

warned her against marrying so young without finishing school, but she was in love and had gone against their wishes. She and Tad had moved away from their hometown, so she was out of touch with her old support network and had few friends in her new neighborhood. Her religious beliefs told her she should try to stick it out, suggesting that the trouble was partly her fault for not being a "good enough wife." Lacking a job or skills to get one, she could not live on her own with a baby. She thought of marriage counseling, but Tad refused to consider this and did not seem interested in trying to work out the problems. He had his reasons for behaving the way he did, including feeling overburdened with the pressure of caring for two dependents. The web of this relationship seems difficult to untangle, but sociological theories provide us with some tools to analyze such family dynamics.

Audio Link 10.1
How might symbolic interaction theory explain expectations about prom?

Micro-Level Theories of Family and the Meso-Level Connection

Symbolic Interaction Theory

Symbolic interaction theory can help us understand Felice's situation by explaining how individuals learn their particular behavior patterns and ways of thinking. Our role relationships are developed through socialization and interaction with others. Felice, for example, developed certain expectations and patterns of behavior by modeling her experiences on her family of orientation, observing others, and developing expectations from her initial interactions with Tad. Tad developed a different set of expectations for his role of husband, modeled after his father's behavior. His father had visited bars after work, had affairs with other women, and expected "his woman" to be at home and to accept this without question. Two related concepts in symbolic interaction theory are the *social construction of reality* and the *definition of a situation*. What we define as real or as normal is shaped by what significant others around us accept as ordinary or acceptable. Our ideas about family, like anything else, are socially shaped by our experiences and our significant others. Children who grow up in homes where adults argue or hit one another or shout at one another with sarcastic put-downs may come to think of this behavior as typical or a normal part of family life. They simply have known no other type of interaction. Thus, without seeing other options, they may create a similar pattern of family interaction in their own families of procreation. Interaction with others, according to this theoretical model, is based on people's shared meanings. Concepts such as *family*, *wife*, or *parenting* carry meaning to you and your siblings but may mean

Handbook Link 10.1
Read about theory and the decision to have children.

something very different to the person sitting beside you in class or to a potential mate.

One of the great challenges of newlyweds is meshing their ideas about division of labor, family holidays, discipline of children, spousal relations, and economic necessities, along with their assumptions about being in a committed relationship. A new couple socially constructs a new relationship, blending the models of life partnership from their own childhood homes or creating an entirely new model as they jointly define their relationship. Furthermore, the meaning of one's identity and one's obligations to others change dramatically when one becomes a parent. The mother and father have to work out what this means for each of them, for their interactions with each other, and with the child. This brings us back to a central premise of symbolic interaction: Humans are active agents who create their social structure through interaction. We not only learn family patterns, we *do family* in the sense that we create roles and relationships and pass them on to others as "normal."

Our individual identities and family patterns are shaped by institutional arrangements at the meso level; for example, corporations, religious bodies, legal systems, and other government entities define the roles of "wife" and "husband." Each U.S. state actually spells out in its legal codes the duties of husbands and wives. Those who do not fulfill these duties may be in "neglect of duty." These family roles are embedded in the larger structure in ways that many people do not realize.

Rational Choice Theory

Rational choice theory can also shed light on Felice's situation, helping us understand why people seek close relationships and why they stay in abusive relationships. As discussed in Chapter 2, rational choice theory evaluates the costs and rewards of engaging in interaction. We look for satisfaction of our needs—emotional, sexual, and economic—through interaction. Patterns in the family are reinforced to the extent that exchanges are beneficial to members. When the costs outweigh the rewards, the relationship is unlikely to continue. Women in abusive relationships weigh the costs of suffering abuse against the rewards of having social legitimacy, income, social and religious acceptance, a home, and companionship. Many factors enter into the complex balance of the exchange. Indeed, costs and benefits of various choices are often established by meso-level organizations and institutions: insurance programs, health care options, and legal regulations that make partnering decisions easy or difficult.

According to rational choice theorists, even the mate selection process is shaped by a calculation of exchange. People estimate their own assets—physical, intellectual, social, and economic—and try to find the "best deal" they can make, with attention to finding someone with at least the level of resources they possess, even if those assets are in different areas. Marrying someone with more assets gives

Introduction of a baby to a household changes the interpersonal dynamics, the topics of conversation, the amount of sleep people are able to get, the sense of responsibility for the future, relationships to the larger community (including schools), and many other aspects of social life.

Photo Essay

Family Interactions

Families vary a great deal from one culture to another, but if they work well together, they provide support for members, a sense of identity, and feelings of belonging and caring.

them more power and forces the other to put up with things that equal partners would not tolerate. Cost/benefit, according to this view, affects the forming of the relationship and the power and influence in the relationship.

Thinking Sociologically

What did you learn about spouse and parenting roles from your family of orientation? How might what you learned affect your current or future family roles?

Meso- and Macro-Level Theories of the Family

Structural-Functional Theory

Structural-functional theory points out the common purposes of family institutions in every society. Despite great variations in form, most human family systems satisfy similar needs, or functions, for their members and for society. Although the families described at the beginning of this chapter vary greatly, their members have a number of common needs and problems. For instance, they all must secure food and shelter, raise children, and care for dependents.

Why do all societies have families? One answer is that families fulfill certain purposes, or functions, for societies and enhance their survival. Traditionally, there have been

at least six ways the family has helped stabilize the society, according to structural-functional theory:

Sexual Regulation. Physically speaking, any adult human could engage in sex with any other human. However, in practice, no society allows total sexual freedom. Every society attempts to regulate the sexual behavior of its members in accordance with its own particular values, often through marriage. Regulation ensures that this strong biological drive is satisfied in an orderly way that does not create ongoing disruption, conflict, or jealousy. Certain people are "taken" and "off limits" (Ward and Edelstein 2009).

Reproduction and Replacement. Societies need children to replace members who die, leave, or are incapacitated. Reproduction is controlled to keep family lineage and inheritance clear. Parent and caretaker roles are clearly defined and reinforced in many societies by ceremonies: baby showers, birth announcements, christenings, and naming ceremonies that welcome the child as a member of the family. In some places, such as New Guinea, procreation is so important that a young girl who has had children is more desirable because she has established her fertility.

Socialization. The family is the main training ground for children. In our families, we begin to learn values and norms, proper behavior, roles, and language. Later socialization in most societies is carried out by schools, religious organizations, and other institutions, but the family remains the most important initial socializing agent to prepare us for roles in society. Much of the socialization is done by parents, but siblings, grandparents, and other relatives are important to socialization as well.

Emotional Support and Protection. Families are the main source of love and belonging in many societies, giving us a sense of identity, security, protection, and safety from harm. It is one place where people may experience unqualified acceptance and feelings of being cherished. Problems of children in youth shelters and incidents of family violence and neglect are reminders that this function is not always successfully provided in families. Still, the family is the environment most capable of meeting this need if all is working well.

Status Assignment. Our family of orientation is the most important determinant of our social status, life chances, and lifestyles. It strongly affects our educational opportunities, access to health care, religious and political affiliations, and values. In fact, in societies with caste systems, the ascribed position at birth is generally the position at death. Although in class societies individuals may achieve new social statuses, our birth positions and the early years of socialization have a strong impact throughout life on who and what we are.

This woman in New Guinea became more attractive to men as a potential wife after she had proven her fertility by having children.

Economic Support. Historically, the family was a unit of production—running a farm, a bakery, or a cobbler shop. Although this function is still predominant in many societies, the economic function carried out in individual families has pretty much disappeared in most Global North families. However, the family remains an economic unit of consumption. Who paid for your clothing, food, and other needs as you were growing up? Who helps many of you pay your college tuition and expenses? Taxing agencies, advertising and commercial enterprises, workplaces, and other social institutions also treat the family as the primary economic unit.

Functional theorists ask about the consequences of what takes place in the family for other parts of the society. They are likely to recognize ways that the micro-level processes of the family (e.g., socialization of Japanese children to be cooperative and members of groups and U.S. children to be competitive and individualistic) are compatible with structural needs of society at the meso and macro levels (e.g., in the United States, the need for motivated workers who thrive on competition). Each part of the system, according to functionalists, works with other parts to create a functioning society.

Changing Family Functions. In some societies, the family is the primary unit for bearing and educating children, practicing religion, structuring leisure time activities, caring for the sick and aged, and even conducting politics. However, as societies modernize, many of these functions are transferred to other institutions.

As societies change, so do family systems. The sociohistorical perspective of family tells us that changes in intimate relationships—sexuality, marriage, and family patterns—have occurred over the centuries. Major transitions from agricultural to industrial to postindustrial societal systems change all the institutions within those societies. The institution of family in agricultural societies is often large and self-sufficient, with families producing their own food and providing their own shelter; this is not the case in contemporary urban societies.

Industrialization and urbanization typical in 18th- and 19th-century Europe and the United States created a distinct change in roles. The wife and child became dependent on the husband who "brought home the bread." The family members became consumers rather than independent and self-supporting coworkers on a farm. This male breadwinner notion of family has not lasted long in the Western world (Coontz 2005). In addition to evolving roles, other changes in society have brought shifts to the family. Improved technology, for example, brought medical advances, new knowledge to be passed on in schools, recreation organized according to age groups and outside the family unit, and improved transportation.

As many families moved to urban areas, the economic function has been transferred to the factory, store, and office. Social prestige is increasingly centered on a family member rather than the family surname. Socialization is increasingly done in schools, and in some cases teachers have become substitute parents. They do a great deal of the preparation of the

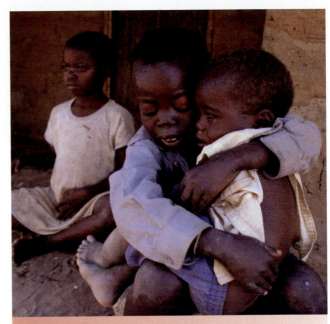

Young AIDS orphans on a doorstep in Chilonga in Zambia. Joseph Mwila comforts his brother Aaron, with their sister Joanna behind. The orphans were cared for by their grandmother Albina.

child for the larger world. The traditional protection and care function has been partially replaced by police, reform schools, unemployment compensation, social security, health care systems (e.g., Medicare and Medicaid), and other types of services provided by the state. Little League baseball, industrial bowling teams, aerobic exercise groups, television, and computer games have replaced the family as the source of leisure activities and recreation. Although many would argue that the family still remains the center of the affection and is the only recognized place for producing children, one does not have to look far to discover that these two functions are also increasingly found outside the boundaries of the traditional family unit.

Audio Link 10.2
Listen to what happens when family roles change.

These changes have made the family's functions more specialized, though still, family remains a critical institution in society. Most families still function to provide stable structures to carry out early childhood socialization and to sustain love, trust, affection, acceptance, and an escape from the impersonal world.

Thinking Sociologically

Does reduction of traditional family functions mean a decline in the importance of family or merely an adaptation of the family to changes in society? Is the modern family—based largely on emotional bonds rather than structural interdependency—a healthier system, or is it more fragile?

Conflict Theory

Conflict theorists study both individual family situations and broad societal family patterns. They argue that conflict in families is natural and inevitable. It results from the struggle for power and control in the family unit and in the society at large. As long as there is an unequal allocation of resources, conflict will arise.

Family conflicts take many forms. For instance, conflicts occur over allocation of resources, a struggle that may be rooted in conflict between men and women in the society: Who makes decisions, who gets money for clothes or a car, who does the dishes? On the macro level, family systems are a source of inequality in the general society, sustaining class inequalities by passing on wealth, income, and educational opportunities to their own members or perpetuating disadvantages such as poverty and lack of cultural capital.

Yet some conflict theorists argue that conflict within the family can be important because it forces constant negotiation among individual family members and may bring about change that can strengthen the unit as a whole. Believing that conflict is both natural and inevitable, these theorists focus on root causes of conflict and how to deal with the discord. For conflict theorists, there is no assumption of a harmonious family. The social world is characterized more by tension and power plays than by social accord.

Feminist Theory

The feminist approach is based on sociological studies done on, by, and for women. Because women often occupy very different places in society than men, feminist theorists argue the need for a feminist perspective to understand family dynamics. Feminist scholars begin by placing women at the center, not to suggest their superiority but to spotlight them as subjects of inquiry and as active agents in the working of society. The biases rooted in male assumptions are uncovered and examined (Eshleman and Bulcroft 2010).

One micro-level branch of feminist theory, the interpretive approach, considers women within their social contexts—the interpersonal relations and everyday reality facing women as they interact with other family members. It does not ignore economic, political, social, and historical factors but focuses on the ways women construct their reality, their opportunities, and their place in the family and community. According to feminist theorists, this results in a more realistic view of family and women's lives than many other theories provide. Applying this feminist approach to understand Felice's situation, for example, the theorists would consider the way she views her social context and the way she assesses her support systems.

Many branches of feminist theory have roots in conflict theory. These theorists argue that patterns of patriarchy and dominance lead to inequalities for women. One of the earliest conflict theorists, Friedrich Engels (Karl Marx's close associate), argued that the family was the chief source of female oppression and that until basic resources were reallocated within the family, women would continue to be oppressed. However, he said that as women become aware of their collective interests and oppression, they will insist on a redistribution of power, money, and jobs (Engels [1884] 1942).

One vivid example of how women and men can be viewed as groups with competing interests is through a feminist analysis of domestic violence. In the United States, one in four (25%) women has experienced domestic violence in her lifetime. With an estimated 1.3 million women assaulted by an intimate partner each year, there is an incident of domestic violence every 25 seconds in the United States. A total of 85% of the victims of those acts of domestic violence are women (Domestic Violence Resource Center 2009). Boys who witness domestic violence are more than twice as likely to abuse their own wives later in life. A total of 1,204 women are murdered each year by boyfriends or husbands (AAUW Dialogue 2008). In most Global North societies, men are under pressure to be successful. When they are not, home may be the place where they vent their frustrations. When socialization results in a hypermasculine sense of identity, and this is combined with an emotional dependency on a female, it is a lethal combination. Cultural messages tell men that they are to be in charge but knowing that they are emotionally and sometimes economically dependent on their wives may result in violence to regain control.

Women are most severely exploited in societies that treat them as property and in which the family is a key political unit for power and status. Where men are the heads of families and women are dependent, women may be treated as less than equal both within the family and in the labor market. A woman's role is clearly prescribed. Consider the practice of *sati* in India. The widow was expected to (or was forced to) throw herself on her husband's funeral pyre because there was no structural place for her in the family after her husband's death. Although outlawed now, the practice lingers in some areas of India.

In some societies such as the Masai of East Africa or communities in Brazil, it is accepted that a husband can beat his wife if he is dissatisfied with her cooking, housekeeping, or child care. In some cultural situations, the woman's life is valuable only as it relates to the economic situation, production of sons, and the needs of men. Changes in the patriarchal family structure, education and employment opportunities for women, and child care availability can lead to greater freedom of choice, equality, and autonomy for women, according to feminist theorists (Shaw and Lee 2005).

FAMILY DYNAMICS: MICRO-LEVEL PROCESSES

The Abubakar family belongs to the Hausa tribe of West Africa. They share a family compound composed of huts or houses for each family unit of one wife and her young children, plus one building for greeting guests, one for cooking, one for the older children, and one for washing. The compound is surrounded by an enclosure. Each member of the family carries out certain tasks: food preparation, washing, child care, farming, herding—whatever is needed for the well-being of the group. Wives live with their husbands' families. Should there be a divorce, the children generally belong to the husband's household because in this tribe the family lineage is through the father's side.

The eldest male is the leader. He makes decisions for the group. When a child is born, the eldest male within the family presides over a ceremony to name and welcome the child into the group. When the child reaches marrying age, the eldest male plays a major role in choosing a suitable mate. On his death, the power he has held passes to his eldest son, and his property is inherited by his sons.

However, Abubakar's eldest son has moved away from the extended family to the city, where he works in a factory to support himself. He lives in a small room with several other migrants. He has met a girl from another tribe and may marry her, but he will have to do so without his family's blessing. He will probably have a small family because of money and space constraints in the city. His lifestyle and even values have already altered considerably. In the social world, the global trend toward the Global North model of industrialization and urbanization is altering cultures around the world and changing family life.

Families are interdependent micro-level social units that make up a meso-level institution and are part of the macro-level social system. Many individual family issues that seem very intimate and personal are actually affected by norms and forces at other levels (such as migration, urbanization, and economic conditions), and decisions of individuals affect meso- and macro-level social structures (such as size of families).

Thinking Sociologically

What kinds of changes in families would you anticipate as societies change from agricultural to industrial to information economies and as individuals move from rural to urban areas? What changes has your family undergone over several generations?

Mate Selection: How Do New Families Start?

At the most micro level, two people get together to begin a new family unit. There are more than six billion people in the world, but it is highly unlikely that your mate was or will be randomly selected from the entire global population. Even in Global North societies, where we think individuals have free choice of marriage partners, mate selection is seldom an entirely free choice. Indeed, mate selection is highly limited by geographical proximity, ethnicity, age, social class, and a host of other variables. As we shall see, micro- and macro-level forces influence each other in the mate selection process.

Norms Governing Choice of Marriage Partners: Societal Rules and Intimate Choices

A number of cultural rules—meso- and macro-level expectations—govern the choice of a mate in any society. Most are unwritten institutional norms. They vary from culture to culture, but in every society we learn them from an early age. One of the cultural rules is **exogamy**, a norm that requires individuals to marry outside their own immediate group. The most universal form of exogamy is the **incest taboo**, including restrictions against father-daughter, mother-son, and brother-sister marriages. Some countries, including about half the U.S. states, forbid first cousins to marry, whereas others, such as some African groups and many Syrian villages, encourage first-cousin marriages to solidify family ties and property holdings. Some societies require village exogamy (marriage outside the village) because it bonds together villages and reduces the likelihood of armed conflict between them.

Reasons given for exogamy range from intuitive recognition of the negative biological results of inbreeding to necessity for families to make ties with outside groups for survival. One clear issue is that rights to sexual access can cause jealousy that rips a social unit apart. If father and son became jealous about who was sleeping with the wife/mother/sister, relationships would be destroyed and parental authority sabotaged. Likewise, if the father was always going to the daughter for sexual satisfaction, the mother and daughter bond would be severely threatened (Williams, Sawyer, and Wahlstrom 2009). No society can allow this to happen to its family system. Any society that has failed to have an incest taboo self-destructed long ago.

On the other hand, norms of **endogamy** require individuals to marry inside certain boundaries, whatever the societal members see as protecting the homogeneity of the group, encouraging group bonding and solidarity, and helping minority groups survive in societies with different cultures. Endogamous norms may require individuals to select mates of the same race, religion, social class, ethnic background, or clan (Endogamy 2007; Williams et al. 2009). For example, strictly endogamous religious groups include the Armenian Iranians, Orthodox Jews, Old Order Amish, Jehovah's Witnesses, and the Parsis of India. The result is less diversified groups but protection of the minority identity (Belding 2004). Whether marriages are arranged or entered into freely, both endogamy and exogamy limit the number of possible mates. In addition to marrying within a group, most people choose a mate with similar social characteristics—age, place of residence, educational background, political philosophy, moral values, and psychological traits—a practice called *homogamy*.

Going outside the limits in mate selection can make things tough for newlyweds who need family and community support. Few take this risk. For instance, in the United States, close to 90% marry people with similar religious values (Williams et al. 2009). About 80% to 90% of Protestants marry other Protestants, and 64% to 85% of Catholics marry within their religious faith. For Jews, the figure has been as high as 90% but has dropped in recent decades to as low as 50% for some Jews, depending on the type of Judaism (Newman 2009). In Canada, only one person in five marries across religious boundaries (British Columbia [B.C.] Ministry of Labour & Citizens' Services 2006). However, with increased tolerance for differences, cross-denominational marriage is more likely today than a century ago.

Interracial marriages also challenge endogamous norms, yet the practice is becoming more common with every passing year. In African nations, men from India often take African wives; in Latin America, Amerindians and Europeans mixed to form Mestizo populations; in the Middle East and North Africa, trading routes brought mixing of populations; and in Japan, 20% of the men are married to non-Japanese women, mostly from Asia. Of interracial marriages in the United States, 5.4% involve a spouse from a different race or ethnic group. Also, one in five has a close relative in a mixed race marriage, and one half of the dating population has dated someone of a different race. The most common pattern is a White American married to someone from a different ethnic or racial group. However, among Hispanics, one in four is married to someone of another Latin ethnicity (e.g., a Mexican American marrying a Cuban American). Among Hispanics, Puerto Ricans are the most likely to marry a non-Hispanic, with 21% of marriages being exogamous. Among Mexicans and Cuban Americans, roughly 12% marry non-Hispanics—usually Whites. Black-White marriages, which represent the lowest intermarriage rate, usually involve Black men and White women. In contrast, Asian American women are more likely to marry exogamously than Asian American men (Lee and Edmonston 2005).

Video Link 10.1 Watch a video on arranged marriages.

Each group may have different definitions of where the exogamy boundary is. For Orthodox Hasidic Jews, marriage to a Reform Jew is exogamy—strictly forbidden. For the Amish, the marriage of a Hostetler Amish woman to a Beachy Amish man is beyond consideration. Marriage of a Hopi to a Navajo has also been frowned on as marriage to an "Other"—even though many Anglos would think of this as an endogamous marriage of two Native Americans.

So cultural norms of societies limit individual decisions about micro-level matters such as choice of a spouse, and they do so in a way that most individuals do not even recognize. Exogamy and endogamy norms and expectations generally restrict the range of potential marriage partners, even though some of these norms are weakening. Still, the question remains: How do we settle on a life partner?

Finding a Mate

In most societies, mate selection is achieved through arranged marriages, free-choice unions, or some combination of the two. In any case, selection is shaped by cultural rules of the society.

Arranged marriages involve a pattern of mate selection in which someone other than the couple—elder males, parents, a matchmaker—selects the marital partners. This method of mate selection is most common in traditional, often patriarchal, societies. Some examples follow.

For many traditional girls in Muslim societies, marriage is a matter of necessity, for her support comes from the family system. Economic arrangements and political alliances between family groups are solidified through marriage. Daughters are valuable commodities in negotiations to secure these ties between families (Burn 2005). Beauty, youth, talent, and pleasant disposition bring a high price and a good match. Should the young people like each other, it is icing on the cake. Daughters must trust that the male elders in their families will make the best possible matches for them. Most often, the men hold the power in this vital decision.

In the Tiwi tribe of Australia, no female child is born without a husband. The father of the child-to-be betroths the unborn to an older man. Should "she" be a "he," the arrangement is cancelled. All females are married *in utero* because it is believed that the female can become pregnant at any time after birth. For a woman to have a child if she is unmarried is a serious offense. At puberty, the girl goes to live with her husband. Should the husband die, the girl is immediately transferred to another man. Although age spans between husbands and their several wives may be great, this arrangement assures everyone a home and security. It has been the tradition for the Tiwi tribe for thousands of years (Nanda and Warms 2010).

Seated front and center with the bride and groom at many Japanese weddings is the matchmaker, the person responsible for bringing the relationship into being. After both families agree to the arrangement, the couple meets over tea several times to decide whether the match suits them. Today, between 25% and 30% of marriages in Japan are still arranged this way, the rest being called "love marriages."

However, some marriages are a mix, combining arrangements with "love" ("Getting Married in Japan" 2007).

Where arranged marriages are the norm, love has a special meaning. The man and woman may never have set eyes on each other before the wedding day, but respect and affection generally grow over time as the husband and wife live together. People from these societies are assured a mate and have difficulty comprehending marriage systems based on love, romance, and courtship, factors that they believe to be insufficient grounds for a lifelong relationship. They wonder why anyone would want to place themselves in a marriage market, with all the uncertainty and rejection. Such whimsical and unsystematic methods would not work in many societies, where the structure of life is built around family systems.

Free-choice marriage, in contrast to arranged marriage, involves the partners selecting each other based primarily on romance and love. Sonnets, symphonies, rock songs, poems, and plays have been written to honor love and the psychological and physiological pain and pleasure that the mating game brings. However impractical romance may seem, marriage choice based on **romantic love** is becoming more prevalent as societies around the world become more Westernized, women gain more rights and freedoms, and families exert less control over their children's choice of mates (Eshleman and Bulcroft 2010). Industrialized societies tend to value love and individualism and tend to have high marriage rates, low fertility rates, and high divorce rates.

Free-choice mate selection is found in most wealthy Global North societies where individualism is emphasized over community interests. Couples in the United States tend to put more emphasis on romantic love and the process of attracting a mate than most other societies. For example, 86% of U.S. college students say they would not marry without love, the figure being higher for men than for women. The old adages about women "hooking a man" and men being "snagged or caught" are challenged by data that suggest men are more likely than women to prefer marriage over the single status for life. In a recent U.S. survey, 66% of men agreed that "it is better to get married" compared with 51% of women (Eshleman and Bulcroft 2006).

The Internet facilitates romance and mate selection in many modern societies, helping people of all ages enter into relationships and find compatible mates. With more than 80 million baby boomers, 30% of whom are single, there is no shortage of Internet mate shoppers who spend more than $900 million a year on online dating. The Internet facilitates what those in arranged marriage systems find bewildering about free-choice systems—How do you meet possible mates? Many of the e-dating services claim that their profiles and processes are based on social science research. The burgeoning business in e-romance introduces people with common interests, backgrounds, ages, and other variables. For example, eHarmony has participants fill out an extensive 436-question personality profile that it claims is a "scientifically proven" compatibility-matching system. More

Japanese weddings are very formal and colorful events, and in many cases they still involve the parental selection of spouse, often with the help of a matchmaker.

than nine million users hope for one or more matches from the system. Many specialized services have sprung up based on race, religion, sexual orientation, and other interests such as Goodgenes.com and conservativematch.com.

Because online dating is relatively new, it is unclear whether it will become a dominant form of mate selection (Gottlieb 2006). Are these services successful in matching up potential mates? A recent study found that one in three respondents was unattached, and 7% were actively looking for partners. About 37% of those had tried online dating sites, and about half had been out on a date as a result of online services. About one third had formed long-term relationships. Once again, the social world model helps us understand that even mate selection processes are shaped by macro-level influences that filter to the national, institutional, community, and individual family levels. A very private and personal process is becoming transformed by global forces and trends (Madden and Lenhart 2006).

Thinking Sociologically

Is e-dating a modern-day form of the matchmaker? Is it replacing other forms of finding a mate? Why or why not?

Starting with the assumption that eligible people are most likely to meet and be attracted to others who have similar values and backgrounds, sociologists have developed various mate selection theories, several of which view dating as a three-stage process (see Figure 10.1).

1. *Stimulus:* We meet someone to whom we are attracted by appearance, voice, dress, similar ethnic background, sense of humor, or other factors. Something serves as a stimulus that makes us take notice. Of course, sometimes the stimulus is simply knowing the other person is interested in us.

2. *Value comparison:* As we learn about the other's values, we are more likely to find that person compatible if she or he affirms our own beliefs and values toward life, politics, religion, and roles of men and women in society and marriage. If values are not compatible, the person does not pass through our filter. We look elsewhere.

3. *Roles and needs stage:* Another filter comes when the couple explores roles of companion, parent, housekeeper, and lover. This might involve looking for common needs, interests, and favored activities. If roles and needs are not complementary to one's own, desire for a permanent relationship wanes.

The mate selection process varies somewhat from person to person, but social scientists believe that a sequential series of decisions, in a pattern such as that described earlier, is often part of the process (Eshleman and Bulcroft 2010; Murstein 1987).

Thinking Sociologically

Conduct a small survey of dating and married couples you know. Ask them about how they became involved in their relationship and their process of deciding to get together or marry. How do their comments mesh with the three-stage process described earlier?

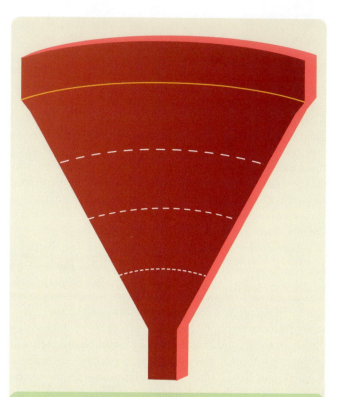

Figure 10.1   Mate Selection "Filtering"
The notion of mate selection described above is sometimes referred to as a filter theory. It is as though you were filtering specs of gold, and the first filter holds out the large stones, the second filter holds back pebbles, the third filter stops sand, but the flakes of gold come through. Each stage in the mate selection process involves filtering some people out of the process. For you there may be other filter factors as well—such as religious similarities or common ethnicity.

Who Holds the Power? Authority Relations in Marriage

Power relations, another micro-level issue shaped by cultural norms at the macro level, affect the interactions and decision making in individual families. Two areas that have received particular sociological attention are decision making in marriage and work roles.

Decision Making in Marriage

Cultural traditions establish the power base in society and family: patriarchy, matriarchy, or egalitarianism. The most typical authority pattern in the world is patriarchy, or male authority. Matriarchy, female authority, is rare. Even where

the lineage is traced through the mother's line, males generally dominate decision making. Some analysts have suggested reasons for male dominance: Males are physically larger, they are free from childbearing, and they are not tied to one place by homemaking and agricultural responsibilities. However, social scientists find no evidence that there are any inherent intellectual or personality foundations for male authority as opposed to female authority (Kramer 2007; Ward and Edelstein 2009).

Egalitarian family patterns—in which power, authority, and decision making are shared between the spouses and perhaps with the children—are emerging, but they are not yet a reality in most households. For example, research indicates that in many U.S. families, decisions concerning vacation plans, car purchases, and housing are reached democratically. Still, most U.S. families are not fully egalitarian. Males generally have a disproportionate say in major decisions (Lindsey 2008).

Resource theory attempts to explain power relations by arguing that the spouse with the greater resources—education, occupational prestige, income—has the greater power. In many societies, income is the most important factor because it represents identity and power. If only one spouse brings home a paycheck, the other is usually less powerful (Tichenor 1999). In families where the wife is a professional, other factors in addition to income such as persuasion and egalitarian values may enter into the power dynamic (Lindsey 2008). Regardless of who has greater resources, men in two-earner couples tend to have more say in financial matters and less responsibility for children and household tasks.

Who Does the Housework?

The *second shift*, a term coined by Hochschild (1989), refers to the housework and child care that employed women do after their first-shift jobs. Studies indicate that women work doing household activities (2.6 hours per day and 18 hours per week) more than men (2 hours per day). Men spend more time doing leisure activities. On an average day, 83% of women and 64% of men spend some time doing housework (U.S. Bureau of Labor Statistics 2009). The following "Engaging Sociology" shows the breakdown in hours spent by men and women at various household activities.

Engaging Sociology

Household Maintenance by Gender

In many households, household tasks are highly gendered. As recently as the 1980s, wives and daughters spent two or three times as much time as fathers and sons in household tasks such as cleaning and laundry and yard work. However, the tides have been shifting, and while they are not entirely equal, they are more balanced (see Figure 10.2).

Questions

1. What is the division of labor (by gender) for household maintenance in your family?
2. How did it evolve?
3. Is it considered fair by all participants?
4. How does it compare with the data in Figure 10.2?

Figure 10.2   Percent of the Civilian Population Engaging in Household Activities, Average per Day by Sex, 2008
Source: Bureau of Labor Statistics (2009).

Employment schedules also affect the amount of time each spouse contributes to household tasks. Husbands who are at home during hours when their wives are working tend to take on more tasks. Employment, education, and earnings give women more respect and independence and a power base for a more equitable division of labor across tasks (Cherlin 2010; Kramer 2007).

In many societies, couples exhibit highly sex-segregated family work patterns. When men do participate in household chores, they tend to do dishes, grocery shopping, repairs, yard work, and care for the car (Bianci et al. 2000). U.S. women spend on average 12 hours a week on child care, whereas men spend about half of that. Married mothers also spend a weekly average of just under 20 hours on housework other than child care, whereas married fathers devote just over 10 hours to such tasks (Newman 2009).

Interestingly, husbands who do an equitable share of the household chores actually report higher levels of satisfaction with the marriage (Stevens, Kiger, and Riley 2001).

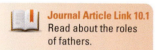

Journal Article Link 10.1
Read about the roles of fathers.

The success or failure of a marriage depends in large part on patterns that develop early in the marriage for dealing with the everyday situations including power relationships and division of labor.

While many women in the world are economically dependent on men, men are often dependent on women emotionally, for they are less likely to have same-sex friends with whom they share feelings and vulnerabilities. Men bond with one another, but they seldom develop truly intimate ties that provide support in hard times. So women are not entirely without power even where they are dependent. It is just that their power frequently takes a different form (and results in fewer privileges; Newman 2009).

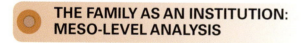

THE FAMILY AS AN INSTITUTION: MESO-LEVEL ANALYSIS

We experience family life at a very personal level, but consider common elements of all families and we have the family as an institution at the meso level of society. In this section, we look at the structure and parts of family as an institution, and the family and its relationship to other institutions. Some of the changes in the family have resulted from—or caused—changes in other institutions.

The Structure and Parts of Family as an Institution

Although the family is an institution in the larger social system, it does vary in interesting ways from one society to another, such as how many mates one should have. Some societies believe that several wives provide more hands to do the work and establish useful political and economic alliances between family groups. They bring more children into the family unit and provide multiple family members for emotional and physical support and satisfaction. On the other hand, having one spouse per adult probably meets most individuals' social and emotional needs very effectively, is less costly, and eliminates the possibility of conflict or jealousy among spouses and shortage of wives. It is also easier to relocate a one-spouse family to urban areas, a necessity for many families in industrialized and postindustrial societies. Let us examine the issue of adult partners in a family. Institutions lay out the general framework for families in any society and include types of marriages, extended and nuclear families, and other structural models of families. Individual families are local expressions of a larger system of families that make up the institution of family in a society.

Types of Marriages

Monogamy and polygamy are the main forms of marriage found around the world. **Monogamy**, the most familiar form to those of us in Global North societies, refers to marriage of two individuals. **Polygamy**, in which a man or woman has more than one spouse, is most often found in agricultural societies where multiple spouses and children mean more help with the farm work. There are two main forms of polygamy—polygyny and polyandry. Anthropologist George Murdock found that *polygyny*, a husband having more than one wife, was allowed (although not always practiced) in 709 of the 849 societies he cataloged in his classic *Ethnographic Atlas*. Only 16% (136 societies) were exclusively monogamous (Barash 2002). Polygyny is limited because it is expensive to maintain a large family, brides must be bought at high prices in some societies, and there are religious and political pressures plus a global movement toward monogamy. Because the numbers of men and women are usually fairly balanced in a society, there are seldom enough extra women to go around. Polygyny does increase at times of war when the number of men is reduced due to war causalities.

Polyandry, a wife having more than one husband, is practiced in less than 1% of the world's societies. Among the Todas of Southern India, for example, brothers can share a wife (O'Connel 1993). The Marquesan Islanders allow wives to have more than one husband. A Tibetan practice originating in the country's system of land ownership and inheritance allows a woman to marry several men, usually brothers (O'Connel 1993). This often happens when the men are poor and must share a single plot of land to eke out a meager livelihood, so they decide to remain a single household with one wife. Murdock found only four societies in the world that practice polyandrous marriage.

Members of Western societies often find the practice of polygamy hard to understand, just as those from polygamous societies find monogamy strange. Some societies insist on strict monogamy: Marriage to one other person is lifelong, and deviation from that standard is prohibited. Yet most Western societies practice what could be called a variation of polygamy—*serial monogamy*. With high divorce and remarriage rates, Western societies have developed a system of marrying several spouses, but one at a time. One has spouses in a series rather than simultaneously.

Extended and Nuclear Families

The typical ma-pa-and-kids monogamous model that is familiar in many industrialized parts of the world is not as typical as it appears. From a worldwide perspective, it is only one of several structural models of family.

Extended families include two or more adult generations that share tasks and living quarters. This may include brothers, sisters, aunts, uncles, cousins, and grandparents. In most extended family systems, the eldest male is the authority figure. This is a common pattern around the world, especially in agricultural societies. Some ethnic groups in the United States, such as Mexican Americans and some Asian Americans, live in extended monogamous families with several generations under one roof. This is financially practical and helps group members maintain their traditions and identity by remaining somewhat isolated from Anglo society.

As societies become more industrialized and fewer individuals and families engage in agriculture, the **nuclear family**, consisting of two parents and their children—or any two of the three—becomes more common. This worldwide trend toward nuclear family occurs because more individuals live in urban areas where smaller families are more practical, mate selection is based on love, couples establish independent households after marriage, marriage is less of an economic arrangement between families, fewer marriages take place between relatives such as cousins, and equality between the sexes increases (Burn 2005; Goode 1970).

The family can be found in many forms. No matter how it manifests itself structurally, a society's family institution is interdependent on each of the other major institutions. For example, if the health care system is unaffordable or not functioning well, families may not get the care they need to prevent serious illness. If the economy goes into a recession and jobs are not available, families experience stress, abuse rates increase, and marriages are more likely to become unstable. When husbands lose jobs, it often makes their primary role in the family ambiguous, causing sense of failure by the husband and stress in the relationship. In single-parent families in which the mother is the custodial parent, the loss of her job can be financially devastating. In worst-case scenarios, families who lose their incomes may become homeless (Staples 1999; Willie 2003).

This polyandrous family poses for a photo in front of their tent in northwest China. Fraternal polyandry means that brothers share a common wife. When children are born, they call the oldest brother father and all other brothers uncle, regardless of who the biological father is. China's marriage law does not officially permit polyandry.

If the government fails to support families, as occurred when Hurricane Katrina hit New Orleans and southern Mississippi in the summer of 2005, families may suffer, be torn apart, and experience wrenching disorientation and dislocation. Interdependence with the economy, the next topic, illustrates this point.

Video Link 10.2
Watch an interview with a polygamist family.

In many societies, the family is still the primary unit of economic production. This family in Myanmar is selling the goods they produced as a family.

Thinking Sociologically

Under what social circumstances would an extended family be helpful? Under what circumstances would it be a burden? What are the strengths and weaknesses of nuclear families?

The Economic Institution and the Family

The family is the primary economic unit of consumption, so what happens when economic times are rough? In the past several years much of the world economy has been troubled, resulting in employment instability and uncertainty, economic strain, and deprivation causing strained family relations. Low-income families, especially single-parent families headed by women, are particularly hard-hit and often have to struggle for survival (Staples 1999; Willie 2003). In some cases, families are so financially devastated that they are homeless, which is difficult, especially for children.

Poverty and Families in the United States

The poverty threshold for a family of four was $22,025 in 2008. For an individual aged 65 years or over, the threshold was $10,326 (Institute for Research on Poverty 2008). In 2007, there were 7.6 million families (9.8%) that lived below the poverty level (U.S. Census Bureau 2008b). Table 10.1 shows the percentage of individuals and families in poverty. Births to unmarried women, the hardest hit group, rose from 18.4% in 1980 to almost 40% in 2007. Table 10.2 shows the increase in single-parent families between 1978 and 2007.

Audio Link 10.3
Listen to stories of family businesses.

The "feminization of poverty," discussed in earlier chapters, is a global problem. It occurs where single motherhood is widespread and where there are few policies to reduce

Table 10.2 Percentage of Births to Unmarried and Married Women: United States

Year	Births to Unmarried Women (%)	Births to Married Women (%)
2007	40.0	60.0
2000	33.2	66.8
1995	32.2	67.8
1990	8.0	72.0
1985	22.0	78.0
1980	18.4	81.6

Source: "Births to Unmarried Women" (2009).

poverty, especially for this group (Williams et al. 2009). Single mothers, whether in capitalist or socialist countries, have some common experiences, including dual roles as workers and mothers, lower earnings than men, irregular paternal support payments, and underrepresentation in policy-making bodies. What differ around the world are governmental policies that help mothers with child support, child care, health care, maternity leave, and family allowances. Single mothers are as prevalent in Sweden as in the United States, but U.S. single mothers are many times more likely to be poor because of fewer support systems from the state (Winkler 2002). For single teens, early motherhood, lack of education, and insufficient income lead to a multiproblem family pattern.

Table 10.1 Poverty Status of U.S. Families by Family Type

Poverty Status and Family Type	Total Percentage Below Poverty Level
Total (all) families	9.8
Married-couple families	4.9 (2.8 million)
Female householder, no spouse present	28.3 (4.1 million)

Source: U.S. Census Bureau (2009g).

Note: Data include families in group quarters.

New York City's homeless population is larger now than it was in the 1980s. The rise is mainly seen in the more than 13,000 children who spend their nights moving from shelter to shelter. Some families board a bus late at night and are taken to a city shelter. Debra Williams and her children receive conditional shelter, but they must leave the site at 6:30 a.m. for school and work. These are not conditions that make for effective parenting.

One reason for the increase in single-parent households among African American women is that there are 1.81 million more African American women than men (U.S. Census Bureau 2007b), due in large part to high mortality and incarceration rates of African American males. Although African Americans value family, many poor men cannot fulfill the economic role of husband and father because the number of jobs available to less-educated men is decreasing (McLeod 2004; Wilson 1987). Although the percentage of births to unmarried women has increased over time, it has leveled off for African Americans in recent years.

Some argue that a culture of poverty, a set of attitudes and values including a sense of hopelessness and passivity, low aspirations, feelings of powerlessness and inferiority, and present-time orientation (concern only for the present and not planning for the future), is passed from one generation to the next (Lewis 1961, 1986). However, many sociological researchers support the argument that poverty itself causes the values and attitudes that develop in poor communities as survival mechanisms (McLeod 2004). In a field study of an African American ghetto community, Carol Stack (1998) found some creative adaptations to unhealthy environmental conditions. Relatives and intimate friends shared money, child care, food, and housing to meet each other's needs in times of crisis. In this example, the notion of family is expanded to include a network of people who provide mutual care. On the flip side, when someone does succeed in escaping the slum, close friends and relatives lean on the person for support and contacts, and the person can get drawn back into the impoverished networks. So the same networks can be both supportive and entrapping.

Dual-Worker Families

A different kind of economic influence can be seen in dual-career marriages. Two incomes may relieve economic strain on a household, but family life in dual-worker families may be quite complicated. Browse through the checkout-line magazine racks next time you are in a grocery store. Note the number of articles offering advice on how to cope with stress and overload or how to budget time, cook meals in minutes, rise to the top, and "make it" together. Stress, role conflict, and work overload are common, but most couples are aware of these strains and have chosen to combine marriage, sometimes children, and the intense involvement required by a career.

With the stress found in juggling the competing home-work responsibilities, some women and men are finding that work provides a haven from their hectic, sometimes unrewarding home life. Women are tending to spend more time at work, but men are not spending more time at home to balance the equation (Hochschild 1997; Schneider and Waite 2005).

In many Global North societies, government and industry support dual-career families with various family-friendly

When both parents have full-time jobs, one solution to the stress is to hire other people to do some of the familial jobs, including care of children. Many people who use child care feel it has been very good for the children, and studies confirm this—depending on the quality of the care individual or agency.

policies: readily available child care facilities, parenting leaves for childbirth and illness, and flexible work hours or telecommuting (working from one's home). These policies allow families to combine both work and family lives with some time for leisure thrown in. The United States has been slower than many other Global North countries to adopt family-friendly policies. The U.S. government passed the Family and Medical Leave Act in 1993, allowing for 12 weeks of unpaid leave for the birth of a baby or care of a newborn, foster care or adoption, serious health issues in the immediate family, or serious medical conditions of the employee (U.S. Office of Personnel Management 2007). However, many corporations in the United States have been slow to respond to dual-career family needs. Company-sponsored day care and paternity leave are still rare. A few businesses are experimenting with family-friendly policies such as flextime, allowing individuals to schedule their own work hours within certain time frames, and job sharing, allowing individuals to split a job, with one family member working in the morning and the other in the afternoon.

Handbook Link 10.2
Read about marriage and poverty.

Family is a diverse and complex social institution. It interacts with other institutions and in some ways reinforces them. Families prepare the next generation. They pray together and talk as families about what happens after death. They provide care of disabled, infirm, or sick members. As a basic institution, the family plays a role in the vitality of the entire nation. So it should not be surprising that at the macro level, many national and global policy decisions concern how to strengthen the family institution.

Thinking Sociologically

What are the challenges facing dual-career families? What might alleviate the stress?

 NATIONAL AND GLOBAL FAMILY ISSUES: MACRO-LEVEL ANALYSIS

The most effective way to explore macro-level issues pertaining to families is to explore policy matters that affect the family or that are intended to strengthen families. After exploring issues of national concern—cohabitation, homosexual relationships, and divorce—we look at some global trends in marriage and family life.

Cohabitation

Cohabitation—living together in a sexual relationship without marriage—is a significant macro-level trend in many countries that has implications for national family laws, tax laws, work benefits, and other macro-level issues. In European and North American countries, cohabitation has been the norm for many groups. For example, in the United States, the number of "unmarried households" reported by the Census has been rising dramatically for several decades. Unmarried couples living together doubled in the 1990s, from 2.9 million in 1990 to more than 6.2 million in 2006 (U.S. Census Bureau 2006a). Between 1960 and 2000, the increase was 10-fold, with 10 million people (8% of U.S. couple households) living with a heterosexual partner. Two thirds of married couples lived together for an average of 2 years before marriage (Jayson 2005b; U.S. Census Bureau 2007a).

Is cohabitation replacing dating? Some argue that a newly emerging pattern for some young adults between 25 and 34 is serial cohabitation (Harms 2000; Jayson 2005a). As Table 10.3 shows, the increases in cohabiting households (same-sex and different-sex couples) in the United States over 20 years are dramatic.

Why do heterosexual couples decide to cohabit? Cohabitors cite a number of reasons:

1. Rejection of the superficial dating game

2. A desire to enter more meaningful relationships with increased intimacy but with freedom to leave the union

3. Emotional satisfaction and reduced loneliness

4. A chance to clarify what individuals want in a relationship and try out a relationship before permanent commitment

5. Financial benefits of sharing living quarters

6. Sexual gratification (the latter cited more often by men than women) and some protection against disease by having one partner (Bumpass and Lu 2000; Lamanna and Riedmann 2010)

For some, cohabitation is part of the mate selection process. In 1987, 33% of the adult population between the ages of 19 and 44 had cohabited at some point (Benokraitis 2004), and by 2009, that percentage had increased to between 60% and 70% (Stanley and Rhoades 2009). However, at any given point in time, only about 9% of the population in the United States is cohabiting (Benokraitis 2008). Countries with the highest percentage of women between 20 and 24 years in cohabiting relationships include Sweden (77%), New Zealand (67%), Austria (64%), France (63%), the Netherlands and Norway (each 57%), and Canada (46%; United Nations 2003). Latin American and Caribbean surveys have indicated that more than one in four women between the ages of 15 and 49 are in relationships they call consensual unions, living together without official sanction. However, such women typically have far less legal protection than European women during or after such unions. The rates of cohabitation seem to be declining in many African countries, where the rates are often below 15% of women (United Nations 2003).

Marriage versus cohabitation rates and reasons vary significantly by ethnicity. For Whites in the United States, cohabitation is often a precursor to marriage. For African Americans, it may be an alternative to marriage. Financial problems encourage cohabitation in African American families because many African American men avoid marriage if they do not think they can support a family and fulfill the breadwinner role. Although childbearing increases the chance of marriage, it is a much stronger impetus for White than for Black cohabitors.

We might assume that cohabiting would allow couples to make more realistic decisions about entering permanent

Table 10.3 **Cohabiting Households in the United States, 1980–2006**	
Year	Number of Cohabiting Households
2006	6,235,000
2000	5,475,768
1995	3,668,000
1990	2,856,000
1985	1,983,000
1980	1,589,000

Source: U.S. Census Bureau (2006a).

relationships. However, studies show that this is not always the case. When couples have different objectives for cohabiting, or have not discussed the relationship before moving in together, problems may arise and divorce may result as indicated in the next "Sociology in Our Social World" (Stanley and Rhoades 2009).

Sociology in Our Social World

Cohabiting: Facts and Fiction

It seems reasonable that if a couple lives together before marriage, they are more likely to have a marriage that lasts. Yet research shows that not all cohabiting unions are the same. While cohabitation can be a pathway to marriage for some (Smock 2004), other research suggests that cohabitation has primarily reached a stage of dating instead of an inevitable path to marriage (Sassler 2010).

Many cohabiting couples never marry. It is more common for a cohabiting couple to have a child together than it is for them to marry (Cherlin 2010). However, some cohabiting couples do choose to marry or fall into marriage. Those who had not talked about the possibility of marriage before moving in together (cohabitation as a stage of dating) are more likely to divorce than couples who saw cohabitation as a step to marriage or couples who did not cohabit prior to marriage (Stanley and Rhoades 2009).

The association between cohabitation before marriage and higher risk of divorce for some couples has intrigued researchers, and several attempts have been made to explain the pattern. Linda Waite and Maggie Gallagher (2000) offer an intriguing interpretation to explain high divorce rates among those who cohabited. They point out that marriage has many benefits. Married people have better physical and mental health, have more frequent and more satisfying sex, and are substantially better off financially by the time of retirement than single people (they have more than double the money invested per person). Interestingly, the same benefits do not accrue to people who cohabit. Much of this is because marriage links two people together in a way that makes them responsible to each other. If one smokes or drinks excessively, the partner has the right to complain about it—to essentially nag that person into better health patterns—because one partner's health has a direct impact on the other's and vice versa.

Likewise, if one partner likes to spend money freely on vacations, the more frugal person is likely to restrain these spending habits. This is acceptable because their financial futures are closely intertwined. As each person restrains the habits of the other, the couple is likely to end up with more savings. At the end of their careers, the couple is likely to have more money put away for retirement. Also, people tend to be more adjusted when they have unqualified and unambiguous emotional support from another person whose life is inextricably tied to their own.

However, there is little relationship between cohabitation and ensuing marital satisfaction, emotional closeness, sharing of roles, or amount of conflict. Some argue that this is because the cohabiting relationship is not grounded in a bargain created by a marriage contract. This is especially true for couples who live together without intending to marry or having discussed marriage. These cohabitors are more likely to keep their finances separate and their options open. Moreover, they do not feel as if they have the right to nag the other person about health habits or finances. Their bond is emotional, but their actions toward one another do not always show that they see their futures as being intertwined. Thus, many of the advantages that come with marriage are lost. Yet inertia may lead them into marriage. When a cohabiting couple does marry, a partner may be shocked to find the other person beginning to nag them or to restrain their spending habits. The relationship is quite different, and partners are irritated by the changed behavior. So cohabitation does not always tell us what life with this other person will be like, if the intent to marry was not present from the outset (Stanley and Rhoades 2009; Waite and Gallagher 2000).

Whether individuals cohabit as an alternative to marriage or as a path to marriage, relationships can be fulfilling, stable, and lifelong (Benokraitis 2008).

Thinking Sociologically

How do you evaluate the argument that cohabitation is a threat to the stability of marriages? Is reducing cohabitation an effective step to strengthening marriage, or is the key the type of cohabitation?

Social analysts such as Waite and Gallagher (2000) and various scholars belonging to the conservative Council on Families in America believe that cohabitation is a threat to the stability of society. The council believes that the government should create more enticements to marry (e.g., tax breaks) and that the society should make cohabitation less acceptable and more stigmatized. This, they believe, would make for a stronger family system.

Same-Sex Relationships and Civil Unions

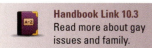

Handbook Link 10.3
Read more about gay issues and family.

A hotly debated macro-level policy matter concerning the family is homosexuality. Policy decisions affect rights and benefits for partners. As same-sex relationships become more widely acknowledged in the Western world, many gay and lesbian couples are living together openly as families. Denmark was the first country to recognize same-sex unions in 1989, granting legal rights to couples, and many countries have followed. In 2001, the Netherlands was the first country to allow same-sex marriages. The 2000 U.S. Census reports 601,209 declared gay or lesbian households, but most scholars acknowledge that this is probably a substantial underreporting because of the stigma in many communities of reporting that one is homosexual (Smith and Gates 2001). Estimates are that 99.3% of all counties in the United States have same-sex couples, and about 3.1 million people live in same-sex relationships. One out of every nine unmarried cohabiting couples are gay or lesbian, and one in three lesbian couples and one in five gay male couples are raising children (Benokraitis 2008; Human Rights Campaign 2003). In some places, these unions are officially recognized by state or religious organizations, but recognition is controversial at the national level. In 2000, Vermont, spurred by a unanimous state Supreme Court ruling that prohibitions against same-sex marriage were discriminatory, passed a law allowing civil unions for gays and lesbians. Other states have followed with similar contract options: Connecticut in 2005, New Jersey in 2007, and New Hampshire and Oregon in 2008 (Human Rights Campaign 2008). In the spring of 2009, the state legislature

approved same-sex marriage, but a referendum reversed that policy the following November. Marriage was approved for gays and lesbians in Massachusetts in 2004. In 2008, the California Supreme Court overruled the state's ban on same-sex marriages, and later that year a state referendum reinstated the ban (Dolan 2008; Ontario Consultants on Religious Tolerance 2008). Currently, same-sex marriage is legal in Massachusetts, Connecticut, Iowa, Vermont, and New Hampshire.

However, many states have amended their state constitutions so that marriage is limited to legal unions between a man and a woman. As of 2008, 44 states had passed laws to not recognize same-sex marriages or civil unions contracted in other states as legally binding. The U.S. public is evenly split on allowing gay and lesbian couples to legally form civil unions. About 52% of the public accept homosexuality as a legitimate lifestyle (Human Rights Campaign 2003), while 90% support equal opportunity for homosexuals on the job (Johnson 2005). Yet in 2003, it was still legal in 36 states to fire someone based on their sexuality (Human Rights Campaign 2003). Many religious groups believe that homosexuality is unacceptable, condemn it in a variety of ways, and deny the right to legal marriage (Robinson 2009).

Despite the mixed messages on civil unions and same-sex marriages, polls in the United States show about 60% public acceptance of homosexuality. A majority believes that gay and lesbian couples should have the same rights as heterosexual married couples and supports marriage benefits and civil rights to gay and lesbian couples. In the mass media, inclusion of gay characters and themes in films such as *Brokeback Mountain* (2005) and *Innocent* (2005), plus television features such as *Ellen* and *Will and Grace*, show popular culture's evolution in acceptance of portraying homosexuality.

In many other countries, same-sex couples are gaining rights that are similar to those of a heterosexual married couple. The Netherlands was the first to approve same-sex marriages in 2001, followed shortly thereafter by Belgium. When Canada approved gay and lesbian marriages in 2005, 8 out of the 10 Canadian provinces had already approved such policies. Spain approved same-sex marriage in 2005, and South Africa followed in 2006. Denmark, France, Germany, Iceland, Norway, Sweden, and Britain offer a legal status similar to Vermont's civil unions, entailing most of the privileges of marriage, such as inheritance rights, health benefits, and family-only visitation rights in hospitals or prisons (Ontario Consultants on Religious Tolerance 2005).

Those who favor gay and lesbian marriages claim that supportive lifelong relationships are good for individuals and good for society. They see the fact that homosexuals want stable socially sanctioned relationships as an encouraging sign about how important the family is to society and how homosexuals want to fit in. Moreover, because many societies offer tax benefits, insurance coverage, and other privileges to married couples, the denial of marriage on the basis of one's gender attraction is seen as discriminatory and may be costly to partners who are denied rights, and to societies that must care for needs of the uninsured or unemployed.

Those opposed insist that marriage has been a function of the church, temple, and mosque for centuries. None of the religious traditions have historically recognized gay relationships as legitimate, although a few are doing so now. Some opponents appeal to biology with the assertion that marriage is a legitimate way to propagate the species. Because homosexual unions do not serve this purpose, they do not serve the society, according to the opponents of same-sex marriage. However, many same-sex couples are providing homes for children, their own or adopted.

Divorce: Contract Breaking

Is the family breaking down? Is it relevant in today's world? Although most cultures extol the virtues of family life, the reality is that not all partnerships work. Support is not forthcoming for the partner, trust is violated, and relationships deteriorate. So we cannot discuss family life without also recognizing the often painful side of family life that results in contract breaking.

Some commentators view divorce rates as evidence that the family is deteriorating. They see enormous problems created by divorce. There are costs to adults who suffer guilt and failure, to children from divided homes, and to the society that does not have the stabilizing force of intact lifelong partnerships. For example, many children around the world are raised without both natural parents present; nearly half of all U.S. children today live at least part of their lives in single-parent families. About 9% of households in the United States are headed by single parents, that is, 12.9 million, with 10.4 million of those single mothers. Just over 67% of children under 18 years live with two married parents, and 33% in single parent or other arrangements (U.S. Census Bureau 2007c).

Others argue that marriage is not so much breaking down as adapting to a different kind of social system. They claim that the family of the 1950s, depicted in television shows such as *Leave It to Beaver*, *Ozzie and Harriet*, and *Father Knows Best* as White, middle class, and suburban, would be ill suited to the societies we have today. Indeed, more people today express satisfaction with marriage than at any previous time period, and there are more golden (50-year) wedding anniversaries now than ever before (Newman and Grauerholz 2002). Even late in the 19th century, the average length of a marriage was only 13 years—mostly because life expectancy was so short. "Til death do us part" was not such a long time then as it is today, when average life expectancy in Global North countries reaches into the 80s (Coontz 2005). There are many misconceptions about divorce in the 21st century as well, and the "Sociology in Our Social World" on page 344 addresses some of those.

Former talk show host Rosie O'Donnell and her longtime girlfriend, Kelli Carpenter, walk down the main steps of San Francisco's City Hall after they tied the knot. This happened during a short window of time in 2004 when San Francisco allowed same-sex marriages, despite state laws to the contrary.

Thinking Sociologically

Micro-level issues of divorce are often rooted in the personalities and relationship factors of the individuals involved. Talk with friends and families of those who have divorced about micro-level factors that contributed. Now, based on the earlier discussion, make a list of meso-level factors (e.g., religious, economic, legal, educational) that contribute to divorce rates or reduce them.

Some factors contributing to divorce are macro-level social problems; these in turn result in micro-level

Journal Article Link 10.2
Read about
marriage contracts.

Sociology in Our Social World

The Top Ten Myths of Divorce

By David Popenoe and Barbara Dafoe Whitehead

1. Half of all marriages end in divorce.

That may have been the case several decades ago, but the divorce rate has been dropping since the early 1980s. If today's divorce rate continues unchanged into the future, the chances that a marriage contracted this year will end in divorce before one partner dies has been estimated to be between 40 and 45 percent.

2. Because people learn from their bad experiences, second marriages tend to be more successful than first marriages.

Although many people who divorce have successful subsequent marriages, the divorce rate of remarriages is in fact higher than that of first marriages.

3. Living together before marriage is a good way to reduce the chances of eventually divorcing.

Many studies have found that those who live together before marriage have a considerably higher chance of eventually divorcing. The reasons for this are not well understood. In part, the type of people who are willing to cohabit may also be those who are more willing to divorce. There is some evidence that the act of cohabitation itself generates attitudes in people that are more conducive to divorce, for example the attitude that relationships are temporary and easily can be ended.

4. Divorce may cause problems for many of the children who are affected by it, but by and large these problems are not long lasting and the children recover relatively quickly.

Divorce increases the risk of interpersonal problems in children. There is evidence, both from small qualitative studies and from large-scale, long-term empirical studies, that many of these problems are long lasting. In fact, they may even become worse in adulthood.

5. Having a child together will help a couple to improve their marital satisfaction and prevent a divorce.

Many studies have shown that the most stressful time in a marriage is after the first child is born. Couples who have a child together have a slightly decreased risk of divorce compared to couples without children, but the decreased risk is far less than it used to be when parents with marital problems were more likely to stay together "for the sake of the children."

6. Following divorce, the woman's standard of living plummets by seventy-three percent while that of the man's improves by forty-two percent.

This dramatic inequity, one of the most widely publicized statistics from the social sciences, was later found to be based on a faulty calculation. A reanalysis of the data determined that the woman's loss was twenty seven percent while the man's gain was ten percent. Irrespective of the magnitude of the differences, the gender gap is real and seems not to have narrowed much in recent decades.

7. When parents don't get along, children are better off if their parents divorce than if they stay together.

A recent large-scale, long-term study suggests otherwise. While it found that parents' marital unhappiness and discord have a broad negative impact on virtually every dimension of their children's well-being, so does the fact of going through a divorce. In examining the negative impacts on children more closely, the study discovered that it was only the children in very high conflict homes who benefited from the conflict removal that divorce may bring. In lower-conflict marriages that end in divorce—and the study found that perhaps as many as two thirds of the divorces were of this type—the situation of the children was made much worse following a divorce. Based on the findings of this study, therefore, except in the minority of high-conflict marriages it is better for the children if their parents stay together and work out their problems than if they divorce.

8. Because they are more cautious in entering marital relationships and also have a strong determination to avoid the possibility of divorce, children who grow up in a home broken by divorce tend to have as much success in their own marriages as those from intact homes.

Marriages of the children of divorce actually have a much higher rate of divorce than the marriages of children from intact families. A major reason for this, according to a recent study, is that children learn about marital commitment or permanence by observing their parents. In the children of divorce, the sense of commitment to a lifelong marriage has been undermined.

9. Following divorce, the children involved are better off in stepfamilies than in single-parent families.

The evidence suggests that stepfamilies are no improvement over single-parent families, even though typically income levels are higher and there is a father figure in the home. Stepfamilies tend to have their own set of problems, including interpersonal conflicts with new parent figures and a very high risk of family breakup.

10. Being very unhappy at certain points in a marriage is a good sign that the marriage will eventually end in divorce.

All marriages have their ups and downs. Recent research using a large national sample found that eighty six percent of people who were unhappily married in the late 1980s, and stayed with the marriage, indicated when interviewed five years later that they were happier. Indeed, three fifths of the formerly unhappily married couples rated their marriages as either "very happy" or "quite happy."

ADDITIONAL MYTH

It is usually men who initiate divorce proceedings

Two-thirds of all divorces are initiated by women. One recent study found that many of the reasons for this have to do with the nature of our divorce laws. For example, in most states women have a good chance of receiving custody of their children. Because women more strongly want to keep their children with them, in states where there is a presumption of shared custody with the husband the percentage of women who initiate divorces is much lower. Also, the higher rate of women initiators is probably due to the fact that men are more likely to be "badly behaved." Husbands, for example, are more likely than wives to have problems with drinking, drug abuse, and infidelity.

Source: From the National Marriage Project *Ten Things to Know* Series, David Popenoe and Barbara Dafoe Whitehead, April 2001. Accessed at http://www.virginia.edu/marriageproject.

individual family problems. Examples of causes include families separated by war or economic problems. One reason for divorce is family violence that often results from problems in the family's environment such as unemployment. Domestic abuse takes many forms: emotional abuse, denial and blame, intimidation, coercion or threats, use of power, isolation, using children as pawns, and economic abuse—including withholding of funds (Mayo Clinic 2007; Straus, Gelles, and Steinmetz 2006).

Children are sometimes the unwitting victims of abuse—beaten, bullied, abused, raped, targeted by predators, and neglected—and this is one factor in marital dissolution. The stress on the family when violence is present means the family is not fulfilling its functions of security and belonging. Mothers may sometimes endure the pain themselves, especially if they feel they are trapped with no alternatives, but the same woman may take action when it is her child who suffers. No wonder families experiencing domestic abuse often end up in a divorce.

If we grant that not everyone is temperamentally suited to sustain a nurturing marriage for 50 years, and if we acknowledge that people do change over time, what would be an acceptable divorce rate for our society—5% of all marriages, 20%, or 30%? This is difficult for governments to decide, but many people feel that the current rate (3.6 per 1,000 people in 2005) is too high (Ahrons 2004; Divorce Magazine 2008; Religious Tolerance 2009a). When people say that more than half of today's marriages will end in divorce, they are pointing out that with upward divorce trends, by the time people now in their 20s reach their 70s, the rates could be 50% to 55%. However, it is also possible that such predictions will not come true. We know that social predictions can become self-negating as people and societies change their behaviors and their policies. In the past two decades, the divorce rate in the United States has been dropping. Still, the long-term divorce trend (over the past century and a half) is clearly in an upward direction (Coontz 2005; U.S. Census Bureau 2008e).

One reason for the increases in the U.S. divorce rate in the past 35 years is a policy change: no-fault divorce laws. For centuries in North America, one had to prove that the other party was in breach of contract. Marriage was a lifelong contract that could only be severed by one party having violated the terms of the contract. Each state spelled out those acts that were so odious that they justified ending such a sacred vow. Even then, if both parties had done something wrong (he was an adulterer, but she did not clean the house and was therefore in "neglect of duty"), the judge was obligated to rule that because they both violated the contract, the divorce would be denied. This resulted in ugly and contested divorces and in people being forced to live together in unloving, non-nurturing relationships.

In 1970, the state of California was the first to initiate no-fault divorce wherein a couple could end a marriage without proving that the other person was in breach of contract. A bilateral no-fault divorce (sometimes called *dissolution*) requires both parties to agree that they want out

A security guard checks people for weapons before they board Miami-Dade County's Family Division Circuit Court bus, which was dubbed "The Divorce Bus." More than two dozen uncontested divorce cases were heard in fewer than 45 minutes. This does seem to give new meaning to the idea of divorce made convenient.

of the marriage. If they agree to the terms of settlement (child custody, child visitation rights, split in property, and so forth), the marriage can be dissolved (Gilchrist 2003). A second form, unilateral no-fault divorce, allows one person to insist that the marriage features irreconcilable differences—the two do not have to agree. Many women feel this arrangement protects vulnerable women from staying in an unloving relationship. They do not have to give up everything to get him to sign the agreement.

All this makes divorce in the United States much easier to obtain. Are divorces being sought for the slightest offense? Some critics believe that this ease has led to a *divorce culture*—a society in which people assume that marriages are fragile rather than assuming that marriages are for life (a *marriage culture*).

Thinking Sociologically

Is divorce really a problem or is it a solution to a worse problem? Does it have lasting consequences? What evidence supports your position?

Divorce and Its Social Consequences

The highest rates of divorce in the world are among young couples. Marriages that occur at later ages have lower divorce rates. In the United States, the highest rates are for women in their teens and men between 20 and 24. The rate of divorce has leveled off and even dropped since the high mark in 1981, as shown in Table 10.4.

Table 10.4	U.S. Divorce Rate Trends
Year	Divorces per 1,000 Population
1950	2.6
1960	2.2
1970	3.5
1980	5.2
1981	5.3 (Highest rate)
1990	4.7
2000	4.1
2006	3.6

Source: U.S. Census Bureau (2008e:table 77).

The emotional aspects of divorce are for many the most difficult. Divorce is often seen as a failure, rejection, or even punishment. Moreover, a divorce often involves a splitting with family and many close friends; with one's church, mosque, or synagogue; and from other social contexts in which one is known as part of a couple (Amato 2000). No wonder divorce is so wrenching. Unlike simple societies, most modern ones have no ready mechanism for absorbing people back into stable social units such as clans.

Adjustment to divorced status varies by gender: Men typically have a harder time emotionally adjusting to singlehood or divorce than women. Divorced men must often leave not only their wives but also their children, and whereas many women have support networks, fewer men have developed or sustained friendships outside marriage. Finances, on the other hand, are a bigger problem for divorced women than for men, especially if women have children to support. White women's standard of living declined 30% for the first 2 years after divorce, African American mothers experienced a 53% decline, whereas men's increased by 10% (Benokraitis 2008; Popenoe 2002). Almost 40% of divorced and widowed women fall into poverty during the first 5 years of being single (McManus and DiPrete 2001).

Video Link 10.3
Watch more about the consequences of divorce.

There are also costs for children, one million of whom experience their parents' divorce each year in the United States. These children's lives are often turned upside down: Many children move to new houses and locations, leave one parent and friends, and must make adjustments to new schools and to reduced resources. In addition, only about 41% of custodial parents receive the full child support payments due them. One-fourth receive less than the specified amount, and one-third receive none at all (U.S. Census Bureau 2006e).

Adjustment depends on the age of the children and the manner in which the parents handle the divorce. Children in families with high levels of marital conflict may be better off long-term if parents divorce (Booth and Amato 2001; Sobolewski and Amato 2007). If the children are torn between two feuding parents or if they are the focus of a bitter custody battle, they may suffer substantial scars. Many studies indicate that divorce lowers the well-being of children in the short-term, affecting school achievement, peer relationships, and behavior. However, more important may be the long-term or lasting effects on their achievement and quality of life as these children become adults (Amato and Sobolewski 2001). The studies offer quite variable findings on this. One study that followed children of divorce for 15 years showed that through adolescence and into adulthood, many children continue to feel anxious and have fears, anger, and guilt (Wallerstein and Blakeslee 2004). Adults may experience depression, lower levels of life satisfaction, lower marital quality and stability, more frequent divorce, poorer relationships with parents, poorer physical health, and lower educational attainment, income, and occupational prestige (Eshleman and Bulcroft 2010). Other studies suggest that later in life, individuals whose parents divorced during their childhood have a higher probability of teen marriage, divorce, peer problems, depression, delinquency, truancy, and other behavior problems (Chase-Lansdale, Cherlin, and Kierman 1995; Newman 2009).

On the other hand, some studies find that children who are well-adjusted to begin with have an easier time with divorce, especially if they can remain in their home and in their familiar school, with both parents part of their lives, and if they maintain their friendship networks. Grandparents, too, can provide stability during these traumatic times. For instance, Ahrons (2004) found that adults whose parents were divorced are actually very well-adjusted and happy. She found no general long-term negative consequences of parental divorce in her extensive longitudinal study that traced people into their middle years. About 79% of her respondents said that their parents' decision to divorce was a good one, and 78% indicated that they were not affected by the divorce. The key, she found, is the nature of the postdivorce relationships. Large numbers of divorced partners have very civil relationships and continue to cooperate and collaborate on behalf of the children. In these cases, there are few, if any, long-term wounds.

Thinking Sociologically

Would making it harder to get a divorce create stronger and healthier families? Would it create more stable but less healthy and nurturing families? If you were making divorce policies, what would you do? What are the positive and negative aspects of your policy?

Marriage, Divorce, and Social Policies

Family systems around the world are changing in similar ways, pushed by industrialization and urbanization, by migration to new countries or refugee status, by changing kinship and occupational structures, and by many other influences from outside the family. The most striking changes include free choice of spouse, more equal status for women, equal rights in divorce, neolocal residency (when partners in a married couple live separate from either set of parents), bilateral kinship systems (tracing lineage through both parents), and pressures for individual equality (Sado and Bayer 2001). However, countermovements in some parts of the world call for strengthening of marriage through modesty of women, separation of the sexes (in both public and private spheres), and rejection of some Global North trends such as high divorce rates.

Global Family Patterns and Policies

National policies can limit families' access to birth control and knowledge about family planning, as in the cases of governments that prohibit birth control in attempts to increase declining populations. These policies in turn affect the economic circumstances of families that are forced to raise many children. One result is more single-parent families created by out-of-wedlock births. In addition, as individuals and couples around the world make decisions such as choosing a spouse based on love, rejecting multiple wives, or establishing a more egalitarian family, the collective impact may rock the foundations of the larger society.

Family life, which seems so personal and intimate, is actually linked to global patterns. Global aid is activated when drought, famine, or other disasters affects communities and a country is not able to provide for families. In such cases, international organizations such as the United Nations, Doctors Without Borders, Oxfam, and the Red Cross mobilize to support families in crises. Support varies from feeding starving children to opposing the slavery that occurs when parents are reduced to selling their children to survive. International crises can lead to war, perhaps removing the main breadwinner from the family or taking the life of a son or daughter who was drafted to fight. Homes and cultivated fields may be destroyed and the families forced into refugee status.

Do marriage and divorce rates indicate that the family is in crisis? To answer this question, we need information on current patterns, historical trend lines, and patterns in various parts of the world. The next "Sociology Around the World" provides cross-cultural data on marriage and divorce ratios.

Global forces, such as ethnic holocausts that create refugees, can strain and destroy families. This is a scene of refugees at a camp called Centro 24 de Julho in Mopeia Sede, Mozambique.

We have been talking about an international trend (divorce rates) regarding an institution (the family) and the impact it has on individuals. Processes at the macro and meso levels affect the micro level of society, and decisions at the micro level (i.e., to dissolve a marriage) affect the community and the nation. The various levels of the social world are indeed interrelated in complex ways. Within each nation, patterns of family affect the trends as shown in the next section on U.S. policies.

Video Link 10.4
Watch a video about family planning in Thailand.

Sociology Around the World

Cross-Cultural Differences in Family Dissolution

s the institution of the family breaking down around the world? Perhaps this is the wrong question. We may, instead, need to consider how the family copes with changing national and global demands. Family conflict and disorganization occur when members of the family unit do not or cannot carry out roles expected of them by spouses, other family members, the community, or the society. This may be due to voluntary departure (divorce, separation, desertion), involuntary problems (illness or other catastrophe), a crisis caused by external events (death, war, depression), or failure to communicate role expectations and needs. Many of these role failures are a direct consequence of societal changes due to globalization. Once again, the social world model helps us understand macro-level trends and patterns that affect us in micro-level contexts.

Divorce is still very limited in some parts of the world, and it may be an option for only one gender. In some Arab countries, only the husband has had the right to declare "I divorce thee" in front of a witness on three separate occasions, after which the divorce would be complete. The wife returns, sometimes in disgrace, to her family of procreation, while the husband generally keeps the children in the patriarchal family and is free to take another wife. Only recently is divorce initiated by the wife coming to be accepted in some countries, though the grounds for divorce by women may be restricted (Khazaleh 2009). Despite a seemingly easy process for men to divorce, the rate remains rather low in many Global South countries because family ties and allegiances are severely strained when divorces take place. Thus, informal pressures and cultural attitudes restrain tendencies to divorce.

Still, when family turmoil and conflict are too great to resolve or when the will to save the family disappears, the legal, civil, and religious ties of marriage may be broken. The methods for dissolving marriage ties vary, but most countries have some form of divorce. Table 10.5 compares marriage and divorce rates in selected industrial countries. Notice that while the divorce rate in countries such as the United States is quite high, the marriage rate is also high.

Table 10.5   Marriage and Divorce Rates in Selected Countries, 1960–2006

Country	Marriages per 1,000 Persons in Population						Divorces per 1,000 Persons in Population					
	1960	1970	1980	1990	2002	2006	1960	1970	1980	1990	2002	2006
United States	8.5	10.6	10.6	9.8	7.8	7.2	2.2	3.5	5.2	4.7	3.9	3.6
Belgium	7.2	7.6	6.7	6.5	3.9	4.3	0.5	0.7	1.5	2.0	3.0	2.8
Canada	—	—	—	—	4.7	—	0.4	1.4	2.6	2.9	2.2	2.2
Denmark	7.8	7.4	5.2	6.1	6.9	6.7	1.5	1.9	2.7	2.7	1.9	2.6
France	7.0	7.8	6.2	5.1	4.7	4.4	0.7	0.8	1.5	1.9	1.9	2.3
Germany	9.4	7.3	5.9	6.5	4.8	4.5	0.8	1.2	1.6	1.9	2.5	2.3
Greece	7.0	7.7	6.5	5.9	5.3	5.2	—	—	—	—	1.0	1.2
Ireland	5.5	7.0	6.4	5.1	5.2	5.2	—	—	—	—	.7	1.2
Italy	7.7	7.3	5.7	5.6	4.7	4.1	—	—	0.2	0.5	0.7	0.8
Japan	—	—	—	—	6.0	5.8	0.7	0.9	1.2	1.3	2.3	2.0
Luxembourg	7.1	6.3	5.9	6.1	4.5	4.1	0.5	0.6	1.6	2.0	2.4	2.5
Netherlands	7.8	9.5	6.4	6.4	5.3	4.4	0.5	0.8	1.8	1.9	2.1	1.9
Portugal	7.8	—	7.4	7.3	5.4	4.5	0.1	0.1	—	0.9	2.7	2.3
Spain	7.7	7.3	5.9	5.7	5.1	4.8	—	—	—	—	1.0	1.7
Sweden	—	—	—	—	4.3	5.0	1.2	1.6	2.4	2.3	2.4	2.2
United Kingdom	7.5	8.5	7.4	6.5	4.9	—	0.5	1.2	3.0	2.9	2.7	—

Source: United Nations (2003 and 2008b: tables 23 and 25).

Note: — = not available.

National Family Patterns and Policies in the United States

Obtaining a divorce in the United States is relatively easy compared with the process in many other countries. All the 50 U.S. states now have no-fault provisions based on "irreconcilable differences" or "irreconcilable breakdown of the marriage" (Benokraitis 2008). The conservative U.S. organization Council on Families in America has argued that the United States should go back to fault divorce to make it less easy to end a marriage in what they consider this "divorce culture." They argue that many couples enter marriages assuming that the marriage will probably not last. An assumption of impermanence is no way to begin a marriage, they believe, insisting that profamily policies promote stability and are a precursor to healthy relationships (Hunter College Women's Studies Collective 2005; Popenoe, Elshtain, and Blankenhorn 1996). Other scholars think that making the divorce process more restrictive would leave many women in highly vulnerable positions in relationships with abusive men, and while such a strategy may create more marriages that stay together, it would not necessarily create healthy ones. Healthy marriages are what help the society, not unhappy ones, say the defenders of no-fault divorce.

A social policy proposal related to healthy marriages aims to change the marriage contract itself. With the new Covenant Marriage Law implemented in Louisiana (1997), Arizona (1998), and Arkansas (2002), people can choose whether they want a standard marriage or an "upgraded" covenant marriage. If they opt for covenant marriage, premarital counseling is required before the wedding, a year of counseling is necessary before a fault divorce is permitted, and the availability of no-fault divorce is restricted by longer requirements of counseling. Twenty-one other state legislatures have considered covenant marriage laws since 2002, but none have implemented it since 2002 (Nock 1999; Nock, Wright, and Sanchez, 2008; Witte and Ellison 2005). Contracts mean marriages are less easily dissolved. "The Applied Sociologist at Work" discusses policies on covenant marriage.

Because legislatures make policies that influence family decisions such as fertility rates, the interaction between policymakers and social scientists can lead to laws based on better information and more comprehensive analysis of possible consequences. This is part of the public contribution of applied sociology—providing accurate information and analysis for wise public policy.

Thinking Sociologically

Would it strengthen marriages to remove all no-fault divorce laws and return to a fault divorce where one member of the couple must prove that the other person was in breach of contract? Why or why not?

The Applied Sociologist at Work— Steven L. Nock

Covenant Marriage

Dr. Steven L. Nock, former professor of sociology at the University of Virginia, specialized in sociology of families. He became intrigued when several states instituted the new legislation—covenant marriage—to try to strengthen and stabilize marriages. This policy initiative is so new that there are very limited data on its successes or failures. At the time of Dr. Nock's death in 2008, his colleagues were still analyzing the data and compiling results.

Nock and his colleagues realized that this legal innovation was the first time in history that individuals would be offered a choice regarding which system of laws would govern their marriages. He wanted to know who desired a more restrictive form of marriage—men or women, rich or poor, Black or White, young or old? Furthermore, he wanted to determine whether government can predictably alter something such as divorce rates through the actions of law.

Nock and his coresearchers conducted interviews with a large number of state power brokers (legislators, governors, and other officials), officials charged with implementing the law and with providing the mandatory counseling (court clerks, judges, clergy, marriage counselors, ministers), and couples who selected covenant or standard marriages. About 350 couples of each type were selected, and both partners in each marriage completed lengthy questionnaires at three points in the first few years of the marriage.

In writing the findings for policymakers, Nock and his associates had to understand the law and the state policies involved. Applied researchers must also be sensitive to the political and economic implications of their findings. (Will implementation require additional taxes? Will policies be acceptable to voters? Will new policies require changes in the existing system of laws in a state? Will they achieve the desired outcome?)

Applied research must be able to convince others that a policy or law will have a predictable consequence. The research must be understandable to the nonsociologist, and it must be done without any appearance of bias or preformed conclusions. Still, Nock did have a policy agenda in his work: strengthening marriages and stabilizing families.

Because of his research, Nock was consulted by legislators and others involved in family policy decisions and passage of laws, especially when they were thinking about implementing covenant marriage in their state. While data about the policy are not yet definitive, Nock knew more about the debates and variations in covenant marriage law than perhaps anyone else. His colleagues are working to maintain his research agenda, finish the data collection efforts and analysis that he started, and release Nock's work. Thus, his impact on marriage and family research survives him. Regarding the challenges and the rewards of this work, Nock wrote this to the authors before he died:

I began my career in sociology with a desire to influence public policy and change social conditions. I saw the field of sociology as offering guidance to those seeking to change our society. My work on covenant marriage, and on marriage more generally, is slowly being incorporated into policy and thinking about policy. There is no doubt that people face many challenges in forming stable relationships in which to raise children. Anything that might help couples should be investigated. The work on covenant marriage takes a small step in this direction. This is one of the most rewarding aspects of my work. The other reward is the chance to collaborate with colleagues who share similar goals and objectives. Working with such valued colleagues is the most rewarding aspect of any research effort.

Note: Dr. Steven L. Nock did his undergraduate work at the University of Richmond, followed by a doctorate in sociology at the University of Massachusetts, Amherst. He worked at the University of Virginia until his death in 2008.

The family is a powerful socializing agent and the first social experience of most human beings. As children grow up and branch out from the embrace of the family, the social environments they experience first are usually the local school and a religious institution. These provide lifelong training for participation in society. It is to the institution of education that we turn next.

What Have We Learned?

Despite those who lament the weakening of the family, the institution of family is here to stay. Its form may alter as it responds and adapts to societal and global changes, and other institutions will continue to take on functions formerly reserved for the family. Still, the family is an institution crucial to societal survival, and whatever the future holds, the family will adapt in response to changes in other parts of the social world. It is an institution that is sometimes vulnerable and needs support, but it is also a resilient institution—the way we partner and "make people" in any society.

Our happiest and saddest experiences are integrally intertwined with family. Family provides the foundation, the group through which individuals' needs are met. Societies depend on families as the unit through which to funnel services. It is the political, economic, health, educational, religious, and sexual base for most people. These are some of the reasons family is important to us.

Key Points

- Families are diverse entities at the micro level, having a wide range of configurations, but families also collectively serve as a core structure of society—institutions—at the meso and macro levels. (See pp. 323–324.)

- The family is sometimes called the most basic unit of society, for it is a core unit of social pairing into groups (partner taking), a primary unit of procreation and socialization (people making), and so important that when it comes unglued (contract breaking), the whole social system may be threatened. (See pp. 324–325.)

- Various theories—rational choice, symbolic interactionism, functionalism, conflict theory, and feminist theory—illuminate different aspects of family and help us understand conflicts, stressors, and functions of families. (See pp. 325–330.)

- At the micro level, people come together in partner-taking pairs, but the rules of partner taking (exogamy/endogamy, free choice/arranged marriage, polygamy/monogamy) are meso level. (See pp. 331–334.)

- Power within a partnership—including distribution of tasks and authority—is assigned through intimate processes that are again largely controlled by rules imposed from another level in the social system. (See pp. 334–339.)

- At the macro level, nations and even global organizations try to establish policies that strengthen families. Issues that are of concern to some analysts include cohabitation patterns that seem a threat to family, same-sex households (including same-sex marriage), and contract breaking (divorce). (See pp. 340–349.)

Contributing to Our Social World: What Can We Do?

At the Local Level

Support groups for married or partnered students: An ever-increasing number of undergraduate students live on or near campus with spouses, partners, and children. If your campus has a support group, arrange to attend a meeting and work with members to help them meet the challenges associated with their family situation. If such a group does not exist, consider forming one.

At the Organizational or Institutional Level

Support groups for immigrants: Many communities of recent immigrants live in extended family households, in which grandparents, parents, children, and possibly other relatives occupy the same home or apartment. Identify a local social service agency that serves such communities. Arrange an interview with a professional to discuss the challenges that these extended households face. Explore the possibility of working with a support group serving these communities.

At the National and Global Levels

Marriage policies: Select a family-related issue about which you feel strongly—pro or con (for example, covenant marriage, no-fault divorce options, or same-sex marriage policies). Find out about the laws of the United States or your state regarding the issue. Next, identify a member of the U.S. Congress, Senate, or your state legislature whose record indicates an interest in the issue. Contact that person via letter or e-mail, stating your views. The Association of Family and Conciliation Courts is an advocacy organization specializing in international family law encompassing a wide range of global issues, including human rights, immigration policy, gender equity, adoption policies, and the rights of children. Its Web site, at www.afccnet.org, includes information about the field and opportunities for volunteer work. Hofstra University maintains a resource site on international family law at http://people.hofstra.edu/lisa_a_spar/intlfam/intlfam.htm where you can learn more about the field.

 For chapter-specific resources, including **Frontline**, **TED**, and **YouTube** videos; self-quizzes; web exercises; and more, visit **www.pineforge.com/oswmedia3e**.

Education

What Are We Learning?

In schools, students are learning a lot besides the three Rs, and sociologists have learned a great deal about what and how they are learning and the place of education within societies. Even the settings in which learning occurs tell us something about what and how students learn.

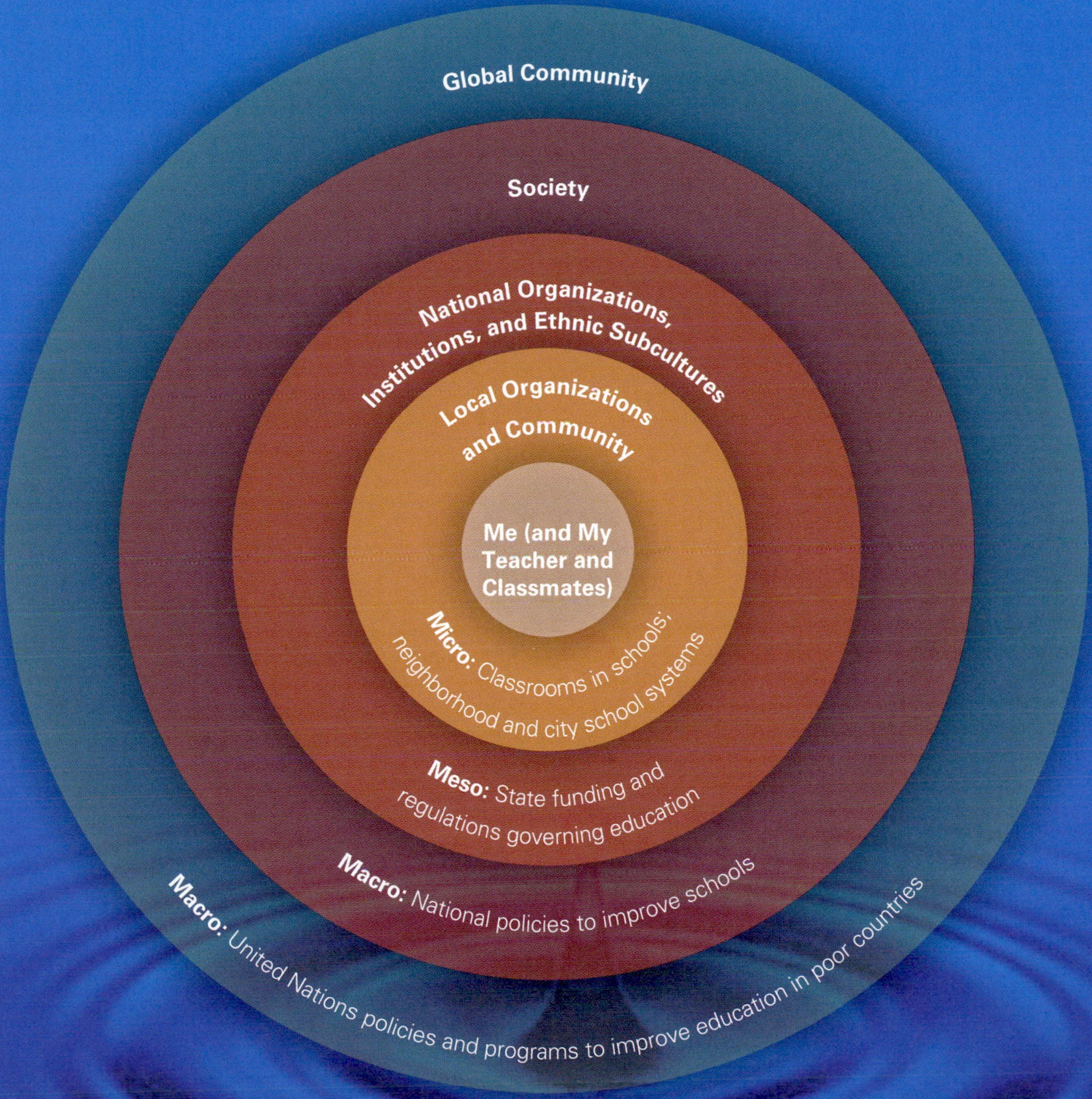

Global Community

Society

National Organizations, Institutions, and Ethnic Subcultures

Local Organizations and Community

Me (and My Teacher and Classmates)

Micro: Classrooms in schools; neighborhood and city school systems

Meso: State funding and regulations governing education

Macro: National policies to improve schools

Macro: United Nations policies and programs to improve education in poor countries

Think About It	
Me (and My Inner Circle)	What did you personally learn—both formally and informally—in school?
Local Community	How do role expectations of people in a local school—student, teacher, and principal—affect the learning that occurs in that school?
National Institutions, Complex Organizations, and Ethnic Groups	Do families help or hurt children's school achievement?
National Society	How is education changing in your nation?
Global Community	Why is education a major concern around the world?

Tomás is a failure. At 9 years of age, he cannot read, write, or get along with his peers, and out of frustration, he sometimes misbehaves. He has been a failure since he was 3, but his failure started earlier than that—his parents say so. They have told Tomás over and over that he will not amount to anything if he does not shape up. His teachers have noticed that he is slow to learn and does not seem to have many friends. They, too, define him as a failure. Tomás believes his parents and teachers, for he has little evidence to contradict their judgment.

Two strikes against him are the judgments of his parents and his teachers. The third strike is Tomás's own acceptance of the label "failure." Tomás is an at-risk child, identified as having characteristics inclining him toward failure in school and society. Probably, he will not amount to anything, and he may even get in trouble with the law unless caring people intervene, encouraging him to realize that he has abilities and is not worthless.

Tomás goes to school in Toronto (Ontario), Canada, but he could live in any country. In every community, there are Tomáses. Although successful children develop a positive self-concept that helps them deal with disappointments and failures, the Tomáses internalize failures. Successful children negotiate the rules and regulations of school, and school provides them with necessary skills for future occupations. Tomás carries a label with him that will largely determine his life chances because, next to home, schools play the biggest role in socializing children into their self-concepts and attitudes toward achievement. What factors could change the educational outcomes for students such as Tomás?

At least Tomás is in the education system. *Schooling*—learning skills such as reading and math in a building via systematic instruction by a trained professional—is a luxury some children will never know. On the other hand, in most urban areas around the world and in affluent countries, formal education is necessary for success—and for survival. Education of the masses in a school setting is a modern concept that became necessary when literacy and math skills became essential to many jobs (even if just to read instructions for operating machinery). Literacy is also necessary for democratic governments, where informed citizenry elect officials and vote on public policies.

Handbook Link 11.1
Read more about education.

In this chapter, we will explore the state of the world's education, micro-level interactions in educational organizations, what happens in schools after the school bell rings, education at the macro level, whether education is the road to opportunity, and educational social policy issues.

State of the World's Education: An Overview

Every society educates its children. In most societies, national education systems are created for this task. Global macro-level organizations concerned with education also contribute. For the past 50 years, UNESCO (United Nations Educational, Scientific, and Cultural Organization) has become the "global center for discussion and implementation of educational ideas and organization models" (Boli 2002:307). It provides teacher training, curricular guidance, and textbook sources, and it gathers international statistics on educational achievement. Many countries have adopted UNESCO standards, including the organizational model of 6 years of primary school and 3 years apiece for intermediate and secondary school, with an emphasis on comprehensive rather than specialized training (Institute for Statistics 2006a).

What is considered essential knowledge to be taught in schools is based largely on a country's level of development, its cultural values and political ideology, and guidelines from international standards. Leaders believe that a literate population is necessary for economic development and expansion, a thriving political system, and the well-being of the citizenry. Global trends in schooling influence education systems in Africa, Asia, Latin America, Europe, and the Middle East, regardless of political system or level of affluence. "Education has become a global social process that both reflects and helps create the global society that is under formation" (Boli 2002:312). Education plays a significant role in the economic growth, social stratification, and political behaviors of countries, regions of the world, and the interdependent global system.

In poor Global South countries, 76% of the population is literate, including 64% of women (UNESCO 2006).

However, there is variation among these countries: Only 38% of the women are literate in South and West Asia. Affluent countries have rates of 99% literacy for men and women, though the highest adult literacy rate, 99.8%, is reported for Cuba, Estonia, and Latvia (Huebler 2008). Eight countries have literacy rates below 40%, with the three lowest being Mali (23%), Chad (26%), and Afghanistan (28%). In total, 24 countries have literacy rates below 60% (see Map 11.1).

As mass education spreads around the world, communication, transportation, and globalization also continue to make countries more interdependent and more accessible to each other. Global North countries influence the levels and types of education worldwide. The national education curriculum of many poor countries is similar to models of mass education used in colonial powers by Global North countries (Chabbott and Ramirez 2000; McEneaney and Meyer 2000). Mathematics, for instance, is taught universally, and science has been taught in most schools since World War II, although more science is taught in countries with a higher standard of living (Baker 2002). Whether this trend toward similar curricula meets the needs of individuals in all countries is a matter of debate.

Education can be studied through several different lenses or perspectives. The next section provides a summary of how various theories attempt to understand and explain education in society.

The Ins and Outs of Local Schools: Micro-Level Interactions in Educational Organizations

The process of education takes place at the micro level in the classrooms, corridors, and on the playgrounds of local schools, with key players who enact the everyday drama of teaching and learning. You probably recall an important learning experience you had in which someone helped you master a skill—a scout leader, grandmother, choir director, coach, neighbor, or teacher. You know how important one-on-one mentoring can be to the learning process, how education often is an intimate exchange between two people. Education has the power to change the way people think about the world, influence their sense of competency, and affect their self-esteem and personal outlooks on self and society.

Schools are important organizations in local communities as well. The school is a source of pride and a unifying symbol of identity. Local communities rally around the success of their school. Moreover, in many communities, the school system is a large employer with real importance to the economic vitality of the area. At the micro level, much sociological analysis has focused on the school as a social setting within a community. At this level, sociologists look

Overcrowding in classrooms is not uncommon in poor countries, such as in this somewhat affluent school in South Africa (top) and in this Darfur refugee camp school (bottom). Note that the students are primarily boys—the situation in many Global South countries.

at roles and statuses in educational settings and the informal norms and interaction patterns that evolve in those settings. First, let us review two micro-level theories, then consider some common in-school interactions.

Micro-Level Theories About Individuals Within Schools

Symbolic Interaction Perspective and the Classroom

The symbolic interaction theory focuses on how people interact based on the meaning they have assigned to various traits, behaviors, or symbols (such as clothing). Children

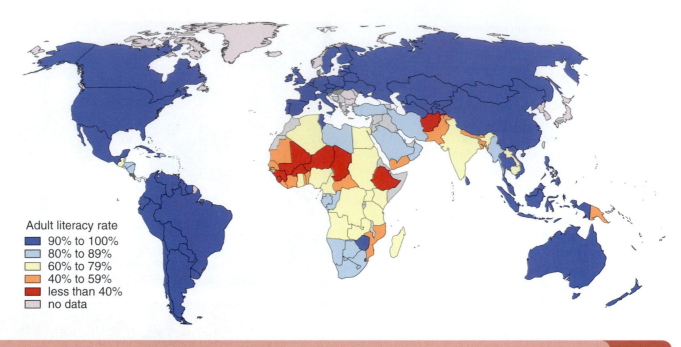

Map 11.1   Adult Literacy Rates by Country, 2007

Source: UNESCO Institute for Statistics, in Huebler 2008; United Nations Development Program Report 2007/2008, p. 226.

actively create distinctions among individuals and groups, becoming agents in determining the social reality in which they live. Popularity, a major issue for many children, especially in middle school years, is mostly a function of being noticed and liked and having everyone know who you are. Students may increase their popularity by being attractive, representing the school in an athletic contest, or being seen in a leadership position. The difficulty is that there are few such positions, leading to a competition in which some individuals are going to be losers. In the United States, the losers are more likely to be children from families that cannot afford to purchase popular clothing or other status symbols or send their children to sports training or camps. Winners have access to material and symbolic resources that give them high visibility. They are given special privileges in the school and are more likely to develop leadership skills and to feel good about themselves—forms of social and cultural capital.

Classrooms are like small societies of peers that reflect the interaction patterns and problems of the larger world (Durkheim 1956). For instance, studies indicate that girls tend to have closely knit and egalitarian friendships, sharing confidences and problems. In contrast, boys tend to have loosely knit associations, with clear status hierarchies based on dominance in a shared activity such as a sport (Wood 2005). Research findings indicate that girls have more struggles with self-esteem than do boys, especially in middle school (American Association of University Women Educational Foundation 2001). One's sense of self—an intensely personal experience—is shaped by the micro interactions of the school. Thus, for young people, from 6 to 18 years of age, the extensive time spent in school means that the status of student has an enormous impact on how individuals see themselves. The image that is reflected back to someone—as student or as teacher, for example—can begin to mold one's sense of competence, intelligence, and likeability.

While Ethiopia shares the commitment to mass education of all young people, its resources are very meager, as we can see from this photo of a crowded impoverished school in an Ethiopian village.

Small-group and interpersonal interactions occur continuously in local schools—such as this tutorial between a young student and a college student involved in a "service learning" tutorial.

Males have many ways of becoming known and respected. Male athletics draw bigger crowds than female athletics, and one can become a local celebrity based on one's skill on the field or court.

The larger school organization creates a structure that influences how individuals make sense of their reality and interact with others. The Iowa School of symbolic interaction emphasizes the link between the self and meso-level positions or statuses (Stryker 2000). Official school positions—such as president of the student council or senior class president or varsity team member—become important elements of one's *self*.

Thinking Sociologically

How do you think teachers affect the sense of self of students? How do you think students affect the sense of the self, the confidence, and the achievement goals of each other and of teachers?

Rational Choice Theory and Educational Settings

Rational choice theory focuses on the cost-benefit analysis that individuals undertake in virtually everything they do. What are the costs—in terms of money, relationships, self-esteem, or other factors—and what are the benefits? If benefits outweigh costs, the individual is likely to continue rewarding activities, but if costs outweigh benefits, the individual is likely to seek other courses of action.

How might weighing costs and benefits influence decisions about education? Students who consider dropping out of school go through some analysis of costs to themselves—for example, a decision may be shaped by battered self-esteem in schools. Similarly, teachers make rational choices about staying in the teaching profession. Roughly half of the new teachers in the United States leave teaching within 5 years, a high rate compared with other professions (Lambert 2006). Rational choice theorists explain teacher retention by looking at perception of benefits, such as rewarding professional practice working with children or adolescents, and perceived costs, such as poor salary for a college graduate; lack of respect from parents, students, and administrators; 12- to 14-hour days for 9 months of the year; and lack of professionalism in treatment of teachers. Teachers compare these costs with the benefits of teaching—the feeling of making a contribution to society and helping children, getting time off in the summer, and enjoying many aspects of teaching, coaching, or directing. The costs today are seen by many teachers as higher than they used to be for professionals in teaching, causing them to leave the profession.

Thinking Sociologically

What other kinds of roles and processes within a school are influenced by costs and benefits, and how? Do you think that most behavior in schools is shaped by this kind of rational choice calculation?

Schools are important organizations in local communities, a source of pride and a unifying symbol of identity. Local communities rally around their school. Moreover, in many communities, the school system is a large employer with real importance to the economic vitality of the area. At the micro level, much of the

In Rwandan secondary schools, as many as 45 students may be in a classroom with little more than benches.

sociological analysis has focused on the school as a social setting within a community. At the meso level, sociologists look at schools as organizations with roles and statuses, informal norms, and interaction patterns that evolve in educational settings.

Statuses and Roles in the Educational System

Students, teachers, staff, and administrators hold major statuses in educational systems. These statuses are part of the larger school organization at the meso level, and individuals are temporary occupants of the statuses during their tenure in the organization. People fill the roles of classroom teachers or local principal at the micro level—in our local schools. The roles associated with each status in educational organizations bring both obligations and inherent problems. When the status holders agree on expected behaviors (role expectations), schools function smoothly. When they do not agree, conflicts can arise. Let us look at several statuses and their accompanying roles in schools.

Students and the Peer Culture of Schools

In the Rwandan secondary school, École des Sciences (High School of Sciences) in Byimana students crowded onto benches are quiet, respectful, and very hardworking. They understand their status and know the roles expected of them. Peer culture supports the rules and norms and reinforces their behavior. They know that they are in a privileged position, and many students are lined up to take their place on the bench should they not carry out their roles, work hard, and succeed. Although they have no written texts, students write down the lectures in their notebooks and memorize the material. The lessons children learn in the classroom are supported by the *student peer culture*, "a stable set of activities or routines, artifacts, values, and concerns that children produce and share in interaction with peers" (Corsaro and Eder 1990:197).

In some countries such as Rwanda, going to high school is a privilege. In others, it is a necessary part of life that many students resist. In either case, children understand the school system well. They know how they must behave to be considered good or bad students, although they do not know how to change a negative label once they have earned it for not carrying out an expected role.

Children's class, race, and gender statuses all affect experiences in school and in their peer culture. In schools around the world, students are assigned a variety of social identities, often given colorful labels. These identities are part of their peer cultures, which have a major effect on their school experience and future roles in society (Waller [1932] 1965). *Nerds* in the United States or *ear 'oles* in Britain are well-behaved, college-bound middle-class students who have an investment in the school system. *Burnouts* or *lads*, on the other hand, are typically working-class students who often feel hostile or alienated in the school environment. They may engage in behaviors that prevent them from succeeding in high school and can lead them to dropping out (Jackson 1968; MacLeod 1995; Willis 1979). Micro-level interaction patterns in school also reflect society's racial and ethnic group patterns. For example, studies in the United States have found that when choosing friends, students are one sixth as likely to choose a cross-race peer as a same-race peer (Grant 2004). Racial inequalities in early schooling affect everything from preparation for jobs to college attendance (Charles, Roscigno, and Torres 2007).

While many experts acknowledge that girls and boys have different experiences in school, a recent debate in Britain and the United States focuses on whether boys and girls should be taught in separate classrooms. Those who argue for separate classrooms, especially in the middle school years, point out the different interests and learning styles of girls and boys at these early-adolescent ages. Others argue that equality requires mixed gender classes. Some parochial schools have long been single sex, and now public school districts are experimenting with single-sex classes. Research such as that presented in the next "Sociology in Our Social World" discusses the concerns that have been raised about gender differences in U.S. schools (Sax 2005; Weil 2008).

Another gender issue in peer culture is sexual harassment (American Association of University Women Educational Foundation 2001). Four out of five students report some type of sexual harassment in school. Compared with boys, girls experience "hostile hallways" in more physically and psychologically harmful ways, and students who identified themselves as gay, lesbian, bisexual, or transgendered experienced high levels of bullying and assaults as well (Gay, Lesbian, and Straight Education Network 2006).

- A total of 83% of girls and 79% of boys report having experienced harassment. More than one in four students experienced it often.
- A total of 76% of students have experienced nonphysical harassment (taunting, rumors, graffiti, jokes, and gestures), while 58% have experienced physical harassment.
- A total of 69% (7 in 10) of students say their school has a policy on sexual harassment compared with only 26% in 1993. Nearly all students (96%) say they know what harassment is, and boys' and girls' definitions do not differ substantially.
- A total of 18% of students are afraid of being sexually harassed or hurt in school some or most of the time. Fewer than half (46%) report never being afraid in school.
- In 2005, slightly more than 75% (three out of four) of high school students heard derogatory sexual labels

frequently or often at school, and 89% reported frequently hearing behavior or appearances described as "gay"—meaning "dumb" or "worthless."

- Nearly 4 of 10 students who identified themselves as gay, lesbian, bisexual, or transgendered experienced physical bullying at school, and half of those students had actually been assaulted because of their sexual orientation (Gay, Lesbian, and Straight Education Network 2006).

Journal Article Link 11.1
Read more about dropouts.

In summary, sexual harassment is experienced every day by boys and girls at school. Adults—parents, teachers, and administrators—need to be aware of the problem and help children know what is and what isn't appropriate (American Association of University Women Educational Foundation 2001).

The environment outside the school also has a powerful affect on students' achievement and behavior within the school. Disorganization in the community and family is related to a lack of school commitment and is reflected in delinquent behavior (Ogbu 1998). The students at highest risk for dropping out of school in Western countries are also at higher risk for joining gangs and committing violent crimes. They often feel the system is stacked against them (Noguera 1996; Willis 1979). Educators are deeply concerned about disruptive students, not only because they disrupt learning and make school unsafe for others but also because many are at risk of dropping out of school and becoming burdens to society rather than contributing to it.

Teachers: The Front Line

The degree of success students experience often depends on their role partners. Teachers serve as gatekeepers, controlling the flow of students, activities, resources, and privileges. One scholar estimated that teachers have more than a thousand interchanges a day in their roles as classroom managers (Jackson 1968).

They also act as timekeepers and traffic managers and spend a great deal of time in nonteaching clerical work. Many teachers complain that they are so bogged down with paperwork and forms that they have little time to address the primary objectives of the school: student learning.

Teachers in the classroom occupy the front line in implementing the goals of the school, community, and the state. As primary socializers and role models for students, they are expected to support and encourage students and at the same time judge their performance—giving grades and recommendations as part of the selection and allocation functions of education. This creates role strain, which can interfere with the task of teaching and contribute to teacher burnout (Dworkin 2007; Dworkin, Saha, and Hill 2003).

Sociology in Our Social World

Where the Boys Are: A Gender Gap

The Notions of the Fragile Girl, The War Against Boys, Failing at Fairness, How America's Schools Cheat Girls, and At Colleges, Women Are Leaving Men in the Dust—these are just a few subjects in a debate about which groups have the biggest advantage or disadvantage in schools in Global North societies. For many years, concern focused on the factors that inhibited minorities' educational attainment in school. Recently, some authors are turning the tables and focusing their concern on dominant groups, but this is controversial, as we shall see. Gender has been one major focus of education disparities.

Statistics indicate that the state of educational achievement varies greatly by sex, age, race or ethnicity, and socioeconomic status. Why is this so? Among the many reasons for the differences, researchers point out the incredible gains made by women and the fact that women tend to study more. In the United States, African American, Hispanic, and low-income males lag behind all other groups, including females from their own ethnic group (King 2000). Asian or Pacific Islanders have a higher high school completion rate (94.9%) than Whites (91.9%), Blacks (85%), or Hispanics (69.2%). However, the gap has been narrowing in recent years (Laird, DeBell, and Chapman 2006; National Center for Education Statistics 2008b), especially when wealth is not a factor (Jez 2008). College attendance rates are shown in Table 11.1.

| Table 11.1 | **College Attendance Rates** |
Race	College Attendance Rate, 2007 (%)
White, non-Hispanic	69.5
Hispanic	64.0
Black	55.7

Source: National Center for Education Statistics (2008b).

A study by the National Urban League (2006) indicates that one third of poorly educated young Black men end up in prison, further reducing their chances for education, good jobs, and a stable family life. They feel disconnected from a society that helps women with children but ignores the vulnerabilities of men (Mincy 2006). The following figures provide a partial picture:

- An estimated two to three million youth between the ages of 16 and 24 are without postsecondary education and are disconnected—neither in school nor employed.
- Among those between the ages of 16 and 24 who are not enrolled in school, only about half are working, and one third are involved with the criminal justice system. Roughly, 3 in 10 will spend some time in prison or jail during their lives.
- As few as 20% of Black teens are employed at any time, and education has not been a path to better jobs for neighbors and family members (Mincy 2006).

Women have surpassed men in college completion (Buchmann and DiPrete 2006), and men, regardless of race or class, get lower grades, take more time to graduate, and are less likely to get a bachelor's degree (Lewin 2006). However, men from the highest income groups attend college at a slightly higher rate than women in that group, and men from low-income families—disproportionately African American and Hispanic in composition—are the most underrepresented in higher education.

The gender gap in favor of females has been most pronounced among low-income Whites and Hispanics. The imbalance is of such concern to college admissions officers that some colleges are turning away more qualified females in favor of males (Britz 2006). Some colleges are even adding activities such as football to attract more male students (Pennington 2006).

Black women earned twice as many bachelor's degrees as Black men (National Center for Education Statistics 2002), yet females who are racial or ethnic minorities lag behind White women (King 2000). Despite the sex differences, some researchers argue that the gender gap is not nearly as significant as the differences for race or ethnicity and social class. Furthermore, men still dominate math and science fields, where jobs pay more money and result in more power. Data indicate that although women do not score as high as men on achievement tests in math and science, women hold higher educational aspirations, are more likely to enroll in college, and in 2008, received 57.9% of the undergraduate diplomas. In addition, in 2008, for the first time, women surpassed men in the number of doctoral degrees received in the United States (National Center for Education Statistics 2008a). Perhaps concern over boys' performance simply reflects nervousness about women's achievements (Lewin 2006).

What do we do? Girls and women face serious educational problems in many developing countries, and women in developed countries are still at a disadvantage in hiring for high-paid jobs and equal wages. The concern about boys is a relatively new twist in the equity issue. Ultimately, we hope to create an educational system that equally benefits all groups.

Photo Essay

What does your social world look like? We want to know. Submit a photo essay and you could win money and a chance to have your work published!

Student and Teacher Roles

Students and teachers in schools play a variety of roles and often are identified by labels. What labels might apply to the teachers and students in these photos, and what were some of the labels applied to students and teachers in your high school?

In Japan, where education is considered extremely important for training future generations, teachers are treated with great respect and honor. They receive salaries competitive with those in industry and professions such as law and medicine (Ballantine and Hammack 2009). In Europe, many high schools are organizationally like universities. Teachers think of themselves as akin to professors. In contrast, in the United States, secondary teachers think of themselves as more like middle school teachers than like university professors (Legters 2001). Many U.S. teachers complain of low salaries, low status of teaching as a profession, regulation of their activities, unmotivated students, problems of discipline in the classroom, a lack of support from students' families and the community, criticism of schools, and interruptions of classroom work for time-consuming special programs. U.S. teachers are held accountable for students' progress as measured on standardized tests, as well as for their own competency as measured in tests to determine their knowledge and skills (Grant and Murray 1999).

The organizational context of the teachers' work is a key source of problems. Studies in Australia and the United States show teachers feel they are unappreciated (Saha and Dworkin 2006). Overcoming poor social standing and lack of respect for teaching require better recruiting, training, and upgrading the status of teachers. Several sociologists suggest that teachers' dissatisfactions can be addressed through organizational and structural changes, allowing teachers more autonomy and control over their environments (Dworkin 2007; Ingersoll and Perda 2008).

Most professionals have some sense of calling and commitment and are motivated not just by money but by prestige, a sense of contribution, and pride in belonging to the profession and serving others. Two key features of being a professional are autonomy on the job and self-regulation by the profession. Incentives from the macro-level federal government in the form of pay increases have been proposed by the new U.S. administration, along with other incentives to improve the quality of teaching. Yet control of teachers often comes from outside teacher organizations (Ingersoll 2004). When government regulates standards for teachers, the quality might actually decrease as teachers—faced with a lack of respect as professionals and a lack of control over their work—opt instead for other occupations. This has the potential to leave schools with less capable and less committed instructors.

Video Link 11.1
Watch the experience of college students.

Thinking Sociologically

Who should enforce high teacher standards? Who should decide what these standards are? How should they be enforced?

Administrators: The Managers of the School System

Key administrators—superintendents, assistant superintendents, principals and assistant principals, or headmasters and headmistresses—hold the top positions in the educational hierarchy of local schools. They are responsible for a long list of tasks: issuing budget reports; engaging in staff negotiations; hiring, firing, and training staff members; meeting with parents; carrying out routine approval of projects; managing public relations; preparing reports for boards of directors, local education councils, legislative bodies, and national agencies; keeping up with new regulations; making recommendations regarding the staff; and many other tasks. Some administrators specialize in overseeing discipline and acting as buffers between parents and teachers when conflicts arise. In some countries, a lay board of education oversees decisions, including the hiring of administrators and expenditures.

Administrators operate one step removed from the actual educational functions of the classroom, and they mediate between the local community school and the larger bureaucracy at the state and national levels. They occupy high-profile leadership positions that may place them in conflict with the interests and goals of students, teachers, parents, or community groups.

Status holders in schools follow many rules and norms, some written and some not. The informal system is as important a part of the educational organization as formal rules, as we will see.

The Informal System: What Really Happens Inside a School?

It is the first day of class, and the professor asks a question. Should you respond or let someone else answer? If you respond, the professor might be impressed, but the other students might think you are showing off or currying favor. What if you answer incorrectly and sound foolish?

The **informal system** of schooling includes the unspoken, unwritten, and implicit norms of behavior that we learn, whether in kindergarten or college. These norms may be created or enforced by teachers or by the student peer culture. The informal system does not appear in written goal statements or course syllabi but nevertheless influences our experiences in school in important ways. Dimensions of the informal system include the hidden curriculum, the educational climate, the value climate, and power dynamics and coping strategies in the classroom.

The **hidden curriculum** refers to the implicit "rules of the game" that students learn in school (Snyder 1971). It includes everything that is not explicitly taught, such as unstated social and academic norms. Students have to learn and respond to these to be socially accepted and to succeed in the education system (Snyder 1971).

Children worldwide begin learning what is expected of them in preschool and kindergarten, providing the basis for schooling in the society (Neuman 2005). For example, Gracey (1967) describes early-school socialization as "academic boot camp." Kindergarten teachers teach children to follow rules, to cooperate with each other, and to accept the teacher as the boss who gives orders and controls how time is spent. All this is part of what young children learn, lessons instilled in students even though it is not yet the formal curriculum of reading, writing, and arithmetic. These less formal messages form the hidden curriculum, examined in more detail in Table 11.2 on page 364.

According to functional theorists, it is through the hidden curriculum that students learn the expectations, behaviors, and values necessary to succeed in school and society. For conflict theorists, the hidden curriculum is a social and economic agenda that maintains class differences. More is expected of elites, and they are given greater responsibility and opportunities for problem solving that result in higher achievement (Brookover and Erickson 1975). Many working-class schools stress order and discipline, teaching students to obey rules and accept their lot as responsible, punctual workers (Willis 1979).

Four-year-old preschoolers recite the Pledge of Allegiance. Developing patriotism is part of the implicit and informal curriculum of schools.

Educational Climate of Schools

Schools can be comfortable and stimulating or cold and unfriendly places. Some have an atmosphere of excitement about learning, with artwork and posters on the walls and

Schools have a formal structure and a culture that affect the classroom. Note the arrangement of desks and the norm of raising a hand before a student may speak. This may seem "normal" to many Americans, but it is far from the universal pattern in schools in North America or around the globe. The formal system is only part of the classroom environment, for every school and classroom also has an informal culture.

excited noises coming from classrooms. Other schools have rules and warnings posted everywhere and hall guards, and uniformed students walk in columns and sit up straight in neat rows. These are aspects of school climate, a general social environment that characterizes a group, organization, or community such as a school (Brookover, Erickson, and McEvoy 1996).

The school's architecture, teachers' expectations, classroom layouts, student groupings by age and ability—all affect the educational and cultural climate of the school. Schools also have ceremonies and rituals that contribute to the climate—logos, symbols, athletic events, pep rallies, and award ceremonies. In some countries, such as Japan, extracurricular activities are held outside school hours, often Saturday afternoons, and are sponsored by private clubs.

Classroom climates are influenced by the teachers' use of discipline and encouragement, the organization of tasks and opportunities for student interaction, and the seating arrangement and classroom furnishings. These nuances can create an atmosphere that celebrates or stifles student achievement (Cohen 1997).

In addition, the friendships students make depend in part on how schools and classrooms are organized and on teachers' policies. Some schools track students on the basis of their tested ability in certain subjects, thus fostering the development of friendship groups within those tracks. Tracking systems also tend to create and maintain racial, ethnic, and social class segregation (Lucas and Berends 2002).

Table 11.2 **Syllabus for the Course**

Actual or Visible Curriculum	Hidden Curriculum
Instructor: Name	What should I call the instructor? (This may be formally established.)
Texts: Names	Do we really have to buy them and read them?
Course topics: Listed	What is the instructor really going to teach? What is he or she really interested in?
Requirements:	
Readings	What do I really have to do to get by?
Projects	Will it help if I speak up in class?
Exams	Will it help if I go see the instructor?
Bibliography	Am I really supposed to use this?

Teachers' responses to class, ethnicity or race, and gender differences create climates that have subtle but profound impacts on students' experiences and learning. Studies indicate that teachers give boys more attention. For example, they call on them more often and give them instructions for accomplishing tasks independently. In contrast, teachers more often do the tasks *for* the girls in the class (Sadker and Sadker 1995; Spade 2004).

Another study found that teachers unconsciously tend to groom White girls for academic attainment in a context of dependence and loyalty while encouraging African American girls to emphasize social relationships over academic work. White boys are groomed for high attainment and high-status social roles, while African American boys are trained for social conformity and are carefully monitored and controlled in the classroom (Grant 2004).

Low achievement is linked to low expectations, and bias is subtle. Do students have equal access to materials and technology? Are all students active and influential participants in the learning process? Goals of equitable teaching and learning are challenged in increasingly diverse classrooms with immigrant students from linguistically and culturally diverse backgrounds. "Different" students tend to end up in lower-ability groups, guaranteeing their poorer achievement (Lucas and Berends 2002). Students' and teachers' perceptions of themselves and the learning environment help shape the school climate and influence achievement. Table 11.3 on the next page discusses teacher expectations.

Table 11.4 on page 366 compares government educational standards with Native American learning styles. It illustrates the problems students from different backgrounds may have in schools that provide unfamiliar experiences. Even the brightest children can be failures in such circumstances.

Value Climate of Schools

The value climate refers to students' motivations, aspirations, and achievements. Why is achievement significantly higher in some schools than in others? How much influence do the values and outlooks of peers, parents, and teachers have on students? Sociologists know that a student's home is influential in determining educational motivation. Recall the opening case of Tomás, who received only negative comments and little encouragement at home and school. Cultural components of the neighborhood racial, ethnic, and class composition also affect the value climate. Researchers have found, for example, that classrooms integrated along ethnic or class lines frequently raise the level of motivation and achievement for members of minorities (Lucas and Berends 2002). Also, students who are expected to do very well generally rise to meet these expectations (Cohen 1997; Morris 2005; Weber and Omotani 1994).

Students perform better if they feel they belong (Smerdon 2002). Students perform less well if they feel their school success is futile or hopeless or if they think that the teachers do not believe in them or are obsessed with discipline. If teachers have negative expectations, students are likely to have lower aspirations and achievement levels (Rosenthal and Jacobson 1968). Others' expectations can become a self-fulfilling prophecy, affecting how children feel about their abilities, which affects their motivation to achieve and ultimately their life chances.

Taking into consideration the finding that teachers' expectations account for 5% to 10% of students' achievements (Brophy 1983), a group of researchers undertook to raise the value climate and expectations of teachers and students in a group of Chicago public schools. They based their plan on three goals for creating an effective academic learning

Table 11.3   Teacher Expectations

Teachers are influenced by the same stereotypes as others, and those mistaken perceptions can lead to lower expectations for some children. The following factors can sometimes create lower expectations for certain groups of students.

Sex	Boys and girls are sometimes the recipients of low academic expectations because of beliefs about boys' maturation and gender assumptions about girl's mathematics skills.
Socioeconomic status	Low expectations are typically held for children from families with low income and education levels, low-status jobs, and an undesirable neighborhood residence.
Race and ethnic identifiers	Teachers are less likely to expect African American, Hispanic, and Native American students to succeed. They are also less likely to expect African American and Hispanic students to attend college. In contrast, school personnel often have high expectations for Asian American students.
The location of the school	Rural and inner-city schools often have lower expectations than suburban schools. This sometime evolves into a negative "can't do anything" climate.
Appearance and neatness	Lower expectations are associated with clothes and grooming that are out of style, made of cheaper material, not branded, or purchased at thrift or discount stores. Poor handwriting and other sloppiness in presentation can also create assumptions about the intellectual abilities of students.
Oral language patterns	Nonstandard English grammar and vocabulary is a basis for holding lower expectations for students.
The halo effect	There is a tendency to label a student's current achievement based on past performance evaluations of the child. Therefore, blind grading—evaluation of student work without knowledge of who wrote the material until after it is graded—is important.
The seating position	Lower expectations are typically transmitted to students who sit on the sides and in the back of a classroom.
Student behavior	Students with nonacademic behaviors that are inappropriate by middle-class standards also tend to receive lower academic expectations from teachers.
Tracking or grouping	Students in lower academic tracks are presumed to have been placed there for a good reason (i.e., they have limited capacities and can never be expected to learn critical knowledge and skills), yet in some cases, placements may have been arbitrary or incorrect.

Source: Adapted from *Creating Effective Schools: An In-Service Program for Enhancing School Learning Climate and Achievement* by Wilbur B. Brookover, Fritz J. Erickson, and Alan W. McEvoy. Copyright © 1997, 1982, Wilbur B. Brookover, Fritz J. Erickson, and Alan W. McEvoy. Published by Learning Publications, Inc.

climate: (1) schools need to be safe and orderly with no violence or disruptions, (2) schools need to be organized so that they become true academic learning communities with no ability groupings that result in large numbers of failures, and (3) schools need to be clear on what students will learn at each level in math, science, social studies, language, and technical skills such as computer literacy.

Although eliminating ability grouping (tracking) is controversial in some school districts, in Chicago, the school achievement levels rose significantly with this plan (Brookover et al. 1996). Another reform plan in Chicago is Renaissance 2010, a movement to create 100 new small schools in neighborhoods across the city to relieve crowding, increase students' feelings of belonging, and bring in new leadership (Ayers and Klonsky 2006; Duncan 2006). These are only two of many plans to improve school

achievement levels. Plans need to take into consideration the educational and value climates of schools in order to be successful. Whether throughout the school or in a particular classroom, the atmosphere that pervades the learning environment and expectations has an impact on students' educational achievement.

Power Dynamics and Coping Strategies in the Classroom

For teachers, getting students to obey or cooperate or take responsibility is a source of pressure. For students, winning some control from teachers or freedom from supervision is often a goal. Both students and teachers develop strategies to cope with pressures and difficult situations. Coping strategies, part of the hidden curriculum, range from complete

Table 11.4 The Mismatch Between the Recent "No Child Left Behind" Programs and the Research Base on Native American Learning

Native American Learning Styles	No Child Left Behind (NCLB) Requirements
Best practices	NCLB programs
Hands-on, experience based	Abstract, "drill and kill"
Use of culturally appropriate materials	Culturally bland/generic
Informal, flexible learning environment	Highly structured, extreme inflexibility
Collaborative, teamwork	Highly individualistic, isolating
Teacher as facilitator or coach	Teacher centered, top-down
High levels of dialogue	Scripted, unnatural interactions
Learning styles (preferences)	NCLB programs
Holistic approach, whole to part	Fragmented learning, part to whole
Reflective meaning making	Rote learning, memorizing
Visual learning mode, including pictures and illustrations	Heavy print emphasis
Culturally appropriate programs	NCLB programs
Based on culture's values and beliefs	Based on dominant culture's values and beliefs
Both approaches (local and global)	Dominant culture only
Begins but does not end with community	Content irrelevant to community
Environmental conditions that support resiliency	NCLB programs
Promotes close bonds	Not addressed in NCLB
Uses high-warmth, low-criticism style of interaction	Failure focused
Sets and enforces clear boundaries using democratic principles	Uses top-down imposed rules
Encourages sharing of responsibilities, service to others, and an expectation of helpfulness	Not addressed in NCLB
Supports development of autonomy/independence	Teacher controlled
Expresses high and realistic expectations	Expectations are low
Encourages personal goal setting and future focus	Not addressed in NCLB
Encourages development of values and life skills	Not addressed in NCLB
Encourages development of leadership, allows for decision making and other opportunities for meaningful participation	Scripted participation and decision making
Appreciates unique talents of each individual	Group focused
Emphasizes creativity	Emphasizes conformity
Encourages development of a sense of humor	Sense of humor absent

Source: Starnes (2006).

compliance to outright rebellion. For instance, college students set priorities for studying various subjects, deciding which test is most important and figuring out where to cut corners. Do the following five strategies sound familiar? They are taken in part from Merton's (1938) strain theory of deviance (see Chapter 6) and represent strategies students use to cope with school pressures:

- *Conformity:* acceptance of goals and means—doing the schoolwork expected
- *Innovation:* finding alternative or unapproved methods to achieve conventional goals—cheating or plagiarizing to pass a course or to win an academic contest
- *Retreatism:* rejection of goals and means—rebelling against school establishment by not conforming or cooperating
- *Ritualism:* indifference toward goals—getting by following rules but not excelling in school
- *Rejection with replacement:* rejection of goals and means in favor of another strategy—being a discipline problem or dropping out of school to pursue other activities (Hammersley and Turner 1980; Merton 1968)

Teachers try to elicit cooperation and participation from students by creating a cost-benefits ratio that favors compliance. Manipulating the classroom is one effective means of control: putting students at tables or in a circle, breaking up groups of chattering friends, or leading a discussion while standing beside the most disruptive child.

Thinking Sociologically

What examples of the informal system can you see in the courses you are currently taking? How do these norms and strategies affect your learning experience?

AFTER THE SCHOOL BELL RINGS: MESO-LEVEL ANALYSIS OF EDUCATIONAL ORGANIZATIONS

Schools can be like mazes, with passages to negotiate, hallways lined with pictures and lockers, and classrooms that set the scene for the educational process. Schools are mazes in a much larger sense as well. They involve complex interwoven social systems at the meso level—the state agencies above the local community that affect a school's operations. At this level, we encounter the formal organization of the school system in a more bureaucratized form.

Formal Education Systems

Formal education came into being in the Western world in 16th-century Europe. Schools were seen as a way for Catholics to indoctrinate people into religious faith and for Lutherans to teach people to read so that they could interpret the Bible for themselves. The first compulsory education was in a Lutheran monastery in Germany in 1619. By the 19th century, schooling was seen as necessary to teach the European lower classes better agricultural methods, skills for the rapidly growing number of factory jobs, national loyalty, and obedience to authorities.

After 1900, national state school systems were common in Europe and its colonial outposts and former colonial empires. These systems shared many common organizational structures, curricula, and methods, as world leaders shared their ideas. The Prussian model, with strict discipline and ties to the military, became popular in Europe in the 1800s, for example, and the two-track system of education that developed—one for the rich and one for the poor—was debated worldwide.

Classrooms are loaded with power dynamics, and as this photo shows, it is very clear who is in charge of the classroom.

Thus, formal education systems came into being when other social institutions required new roles, skills, and knowledge that parents could not teach. Knowledge needed by the young became too complex to be taught informally in families through example, moral lessons, and stories. Industrializing societies required workers with reading and math skills, and eventually, they would need electronic technology skills. Schooling that formerly served only the elite gradually became available to the masses, and some societies began to require schooling for basic literacy (usually third-grade level). Schools emerged as major formal organizations and eventually developed extensive bureaucracies. The postwar period from 1950 to 1992 brought about a rapid rise in education worldwide, as shown in Table 11.5 on the next page.

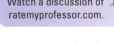

Video Link 11.2
Watch a discussion of ratemyprofessor.com.

Sometimes, differing goals for educational systems lead to conflict. What need, for example, does a subsistence farmer in Nigeria or Kenya have for Latin? Yet Latin was often imposed as part of the standard curriculum in colonialized nations. Some countries are now revising curricula based on the goals and needs of agriculturally based economies.

Table 11.5	**World Educational Enrollment Rates, 1950–1992 and 2000–2005 (in Percentages)**		
Year	*Primary Schooling*	*Secondary Schooling*	*Tertiary Schooling (University)*
1950	36	13	1.4
1960	77	27	6.0
1970	84	36	11
1980	96	45	11
1992	98	53	14
2000–2005[a]	90 (M), 86 (F)	61 (M), 60 (F)	

Source: Boli (2002:309) for figures up to 1992; Institute for Statistics (2006b:table 5).

Note: M, males; F, females.

a. Number of children enrolled in primary/secondary school who are of official school age, expressed as a percentage of the total number of children of official school age.

The Bureaucratic School Structure

The formal bureaucratic atmosphere that permeates many schools arose because it was cost-effective, efficient, and productive. Bureaucracy provided a way to document and process masses of students coming from different backgrounds. Recall Weber's (1947) bureaucratic model of groups and organizations, discussed in Chapter 5:

1. Schools have a division of labor among administrators, teachers, students, and support personnel. The roles associated with the statuses are part of the school structure. Individual teachers or students hold these roles for a limited time and are replaced by others coming into the system.

2. The administrative hierarchy incorporates a chain of command and channels of communication.

3. Specific rules and procedures in a school cover everything from course content to discipline in the classroom and use of the schoolyard.

4. Personal relationships are downplayed in favor of formalized relations among members of the system, such as placement on the basis of tests and grading.

5. Rationality governs the operations of the organization; people are hired and fired on the basis of their qualifications and how well they do their jobs.

One result of bureaucracy is that some children are not helped with personal problems or learning difficulties (Kozol 2006; Sizer 1984). Impersonal rules can lock people into rigid behavior patterns, leading to apathy and alienation. In schools, these feelings cause passivity among students, which

Audio Link 11.1
Listen to a story about bureaucracy in a school district.

in turn frustrates teachers. Children like Tomás in the opening example do not fit into neat cubbyholes that bureaucratic structures invariably create. These children view school not as a privilege but as a requirement imposed by an adult world. Caught between the demands of an impersonal bureaucracy and goals for their students, teachers cannot always give every child the personal help she or he needs. Thus, we see that organizational requirements of educational systems at a meso level can influence the personal student-teacher relationship at the micro level. This is another example of how the social world model helps us understand human behavior in organizations.

These chairs represent the bureaucracy or hierarchy of the school, with every student facing the teacher as though she or he is the only student who is expected to speak and is worthy of undivided attention. Look through other photos in this chapter, especially the photos from Global South countries. Do you notice any differences in the arrangement of students that suggests differences in relationships in the school?

The bottom line is that formal bureaucratic structures can thwart the goals of an education system. Even colleges and universities face controversies over control of decision making and direction of programs. For instance, the funding of the university from business and government grants requires many professors to concentrate on research. In so doing, it takes time away from other functions of the university, such as teaching (Gamson 1998).

Education and the Social Institution of Family

Interconnections between meso-level institutions are a common refrain in this book. There are many interconnections between the institutions of family and education. When children enter kindergarten or primary school, they bring their prior experience, including socialization experiences from parents, brothers, sisters, and other relatives. Family background, according to many sociologists, is the single most important influence on children's school achievement (Jencks 1972). Children succeed in large part because of what their parents do to support them in their educations (MacLeod 1995; Schneider and Coleman 1993).

Most families stress the importance of education, but they do so in different ways. Middle-class parents in the Global North tend to manage their children's education, visiting schools and teachers, having educational materials in the home, and holding high expectations for their children's achievement. In these families, children learn the values of hard work, good grades, and deferred gratification for reaching future goals.

In Korea, for example, parents select an academic or vocational track for their children after middle school. Some send their youngsters to private, competitive, specialized high schools that focus on foreign language, natural sciences, or the arts. At the end of high school, any student who wishes to go on to the university has only one chance to take the difficult competitive entrance exam. Koreans are concerned about the number of suicides among young people who do not pass this high-stakes exam. In Japan, students also take a high-stakes college entrance exam, but students who do not pass the first time have an additional year to retake it. In Israel, students receive either a plain or university-qualifying diploma, also based on an exam (Ayalon and Shavit 2004).

Involvement of parents from lower socioeconomic status and first-generation immigrant families can have a significant impact on their children's educational outcomes (Bankston 2004; Domina 2005), yet these parents tend to look to schools as the authority. They are less involved in their children's schooling, leaving decisions to the school. Yet children who must make educational decisions on their own are more likely to do poorly or drop out of school (Kalmijn and Kraaykamp 1996).

Much of the disadvantage experienced by children from immigrant families, however, is rooted in the core problem—poverty. Shifts in the other institutions—family and the

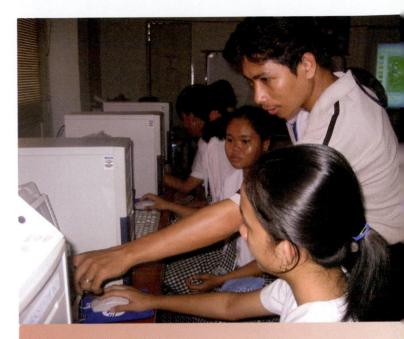

Computer skills are increasingly essential in societies and schools, yet some children come from families that do not have access to computers. Children who have computers at home have a significant advantage. These students are receiving help from their teacher in the Philippines.

economy, for example—can impact educational achievement. Changes in family and work structures put parents under more stress. For example, busy single parents often have little time to help their children with schoolwork. People who work 60- or 70-hour weeks also find that their time for being attentive to their children's learning is limited.

Thinking Sociologically

How do religion, health, politics, economics, and other meso-level institutions influence education and vice versa? Provide some examples of links between schools and other social institutions.

Educational Decision Making at the Meso Level

Who should have the power to make decisions about what children learn? In relatively homogeneous countries such as Japan and Sweden, where centralized goal setting and school decisions are possible, educational decision making typically causes little controversy. Centralized national ministries of education are also common in Latin American, Asian, and African countries, where educational standards and funding are controlled by the national government. In contrast, heterogeneous societies, such as Canada, Israel, and the United States, include many different racial, ethnic, regional, and religious subcultures, each with its own needs and interests. Teachers, administrators, school boards, parents, and interest groups all claim the right to influence the curriculum. Consider the following influences from micro and macro levels on the meso-level organization.

Local-Level Influences

At the U.S. local community level, curricular conflicts occur routinely over the selection of reading material and sex education courses, for example, as well as any content that is thought to contain obscenity, sex, nudity, political or economic bias, profanity, slang or nonstandard English, racism or racial hatred, and antireligious or presumed anti-American sentiment (Delfattore 2004). For example, Family Friendly Libraries, an online grassroots interest group that started in Virginia, argues that the popular *Harry Potter* books should be banned from school libraries. They believe the series promotes the religion of witchcraft (DeMitchell and Carney 2005).

Banned books in the past have included *The Wizard of Oz, Rumpelstiltskin, The Diary of Anne Frank, Madame Bovary, Soul on Ice, Grapes of Wrath, Huckleberry Finn,* Shakespeare's *Hamlet,* Chaucer's *The Miller's Tale,* and Aristophanes's *Lysistrata* (Ballantine and Hammack 2009). Table 11.6 shows the most frequently challenged books in 2008. Off the list this year, but on for several years past, are *Catcher in the Rye,* by J. D. Salinger; *Of Mice and Men,* by John Steinbeck; and *Beloved,* by Toni Morrison.

Decisions about sex education curricula are equally fraught with controversy. The number of sexually active teens in the United States has risen substantially since 1980, increasing the number of citizens advocating sex education. Most sexually active teens have used at least one method of birth control—98% claiming such usage in one survey (Abma et al. 2004). A growing number of large city school districts, concerned with teen pregnancy and sexually transmitted disease, including AIDS, now provide teens with sex education, information about contraception, counseling, and sometimes condoms. Many who oppose sex education in schools claim that it appears to endorse premarital sex rather than abstinence and teaches teens how to have sex. Critics also believe that sex education should be left to families and religious institutions.

National-Level Influences

Because the U.S. Constitution leaves education in the hands of each state, the involvement of the federal government has been

---

Table 11.6   The 10 Most Challenged Books of 2008

The following are the 10 books that were most often challenged in public schools in 2008 and the reasons they were being contested.

Book	Author	Reason
And Tango Makes Three	Justin Richardson/Peter Parnell	Anti-ethnic, sexist, homosexuality, antifamily, religious viewpoint, unsuited to age group
The Chocolate War	Robert Cormier	Sexually explicit, offensive language, violence
TTYL; TTFN; L8R, G8R (series)	Lauren Myracle	Offensive language, sexually explicit, unsuited to age group
Scary Stories (series)	Alvin Schwartz	Occult/Satanism, religious viewpoint, violence
Bless Me, Ultima	Rudolfo Anaya	Occult/Satanism, offensive language, religious viewpoint, sexually explicit, violence
The Perks of Being a Wallflower	Stephen Chbosky	Drugs, homosexuality, nudity, offensive language, sexually explicit, suicidal, unsuited to age group
Gossip Girl (series)	Cecily von Ziegesar	Offensive language, sexually explicit, unsuited to age group
Uncle Bobby's Wedding	Sarah S. Brannen	Homosexuality, unsuited to age group
The Kite Runner	Khaled Hosseini	Offensive language, sexually explicit, unsuited to age group
Flashcards of My Life	Charise Mericle Harper	Sexually explicit, unsuited to age group

Source: American Library Association (2009).

Note: For the top 100 banned books, go to www.ala.org/ala/issuesadvocacy/banned/frequentlychallenged/challengedbydecade/index.cfm.

more limited than in most countries. Yet the federal government wields enormous influence through its power to make federal funds available for special programs, such as mathematics and science, reading, or special education. The government may withhold funds from schools that are not in compliance with federal laws and the U.S. Constitution. For example, the federal government, courts, and public opinion forced all-male military academies to become coeducational, despite the schools' resistance to such change. School changes as a result of the Civil Rights Act and the Americans with Disability Act are other examples of federal government influence on local schools through the enforcement of federal laws. Schools have accommodated people with various disabilities—people who in the past would have been left out of the system. With their classroom experiences and working with other teachers and children, the differently abled can participate fully in society. However, as the following "Sociology in Our Social World" shows, this process is not always smooth.

Audio Link 11.2
Listen to a story about the Supreme Court and special education.

Sociology in Our Social World

Disability and Inequality

By Robert M. Pellerin

L iving with a visual disability for over 40 years has provided me with lived experience. I have also been doing research on experiences of others with disabilities as part of my PhD research. My results show that having a disability puts people at a disadvantage in education, employment, attitudes of others toward those with disabilities, and personal relationships. Technologies for those with disabilities have advanced, legislation has been introduced and sometimes passed, and advocacy for rights abound, but I still have to remind others, including professionals, that due to my visual impairment some methods of communication, such as print media, do not work. Additionally, most of the technology from which those with visual impairment could benefit is unaffordable and most mainstream companies do not include features that would make products disability-friendly. The

bottom line is that many of us are ready, willing, and able to be productive citizens, but we are often precluded from positions because of our disabilities and difficulty obtaining accommodation.

Disability in America has undergone a significant transition since the late 1800s. Most of those who have helped bring disability to the forefront have been American Veterans who were wounded in war and notable figures like Helen Keller who influenced societal perceptions of disability. They have helped define disabilities as being a relative disadvantage instead of a tragedy. Historically, disability has been synonymous with an inability to engage in employment. During the 1800s and early 1900s, people deemed unfit were often warehoused in asylums or institutions and placed in residential schools where they were provided with less than adequate instruction. For several decades in the early 20th century some countries—including the United States—sterilized people with disabilities. However, advocates campaigned during the late 1960s to change such laws and to close asylums for the disabled.

Media portrayals have contributed to false stereotypes that promoted both false beliefs and lowered goal attainment for people with disabilities. Examples of images fostered by the media include miracle cures for people who become religious; foolish tales about superhuman hearing and "face feeling"; stories of blind or visually impaired males who are depicted as wise sages; and images of disabled women who are depicted as pure, vulnerable, and in need of rescue.

The most well known legislation seeking to end exclusion and increase participation in areas of education and employment are the Rehabilitation Act of 1973 and the Americans with Disabilities Act (ADA) of 1990. The 1973 regulations apply federally; the ADA applies to the states and public accessibility (that is, access to jobs, public services, and telecommunications). Despite this legislation, approximately 70% of people with disabilities do not participate in the workforce. Unfortunately, people with disabilities are at higher risk for engaging in drug and alcohol use, sexual promiscuity, higher levels of abuse and suicidal ideation than other groups.

Prior to the 1970s, people with disabilities were excluded from public education. Due to advocacy and legislation, today approximately 75% of school-aged students with disabilities attend public school. Legislation regarding full inclusion has not proven as useful as planned, although exposure to students with disabilities has increased comfort levels of teachers and non-disabled peers. Recent deficiencies in providing equal education include lack of adequate technology and skills needed in college or in vocational or social settings.

Regarding employment, historically people with disabilities have gone from being evaluated on the same standards as nondisabled individuals to being assessed according to how well they know themselves, their accommodation needs, their job qualifications. Despite legislation, courts have generally ruled in favor of employers in discrimination suits. Some social scientists advocate for improving the social capital or human capital of those with disabilities as a way to increase the level of workforce participation. Many employers believe the candidate is responsible for ensuring employment is attained, while some potential employers continue to believe people with disabilities are too difficult to hire and accommodate despite their academic achievement. Employees with disabilities, including myself, concur with recommendations such as improving social and human capital, educating employers about the benefits of hiring people with disabilities, and dispelling misconceptions and negative stereotypes.

The discrimination and inequality experienced by many with disabilities results in a decreased sense of health and wellbeing and increased feelings of isolation. The tragedy here is that people with disabilities, despite their efforts, continue to meet with virtual hoops posed by court decisions, changes in education, and negative labeling. I believe that until society views people as having abilities and strengths as opposed to disabilities, stigma will predominate and society will be deprived of talents and qualities from which all can benefit.

Thus, policy decisions by federal lawmakers influence what and how children learn. This changes with each administration, based on liberal or conservative responses to calls for school reform. Reform reports have variously called for strengthening high school graduation requirements, raising college entrance requirements, emphasizing basic skills, requiring a longer school day and school year, improving the training and status of teachers, holding educators responsible for students' performance, providing the funds necessary to improve the educational system, and holding families accountable for children's achievement.

Since 1965 and the establishment of the U.S. Department of Education, each president has put his mark on the U.S. education system. President George W. Bush's controversial No Child Left Behind (NCLB) initiative is a prime example. It tied school performance to federal funds and required annual competency testing of students. Under NCLB, schools were required to administer achievement tests for accountability—tests that focus on math and reading. Schools failing to meet guidelines were penalized. The result was that 70% of schools reduced instructional time in other subject areas (Center for Education Policy 2006). So even in the decentralized United States, where only 1 out of 14 education dollars comes from the federal government, the macro-level policies have an impact on what happens in the intimate environment of classrooms.

Critics argue that NCLB ignored much of what educators and social scientists know from research about teaching and learning, it overemphasized testing, penalized schools that have proportionally more low-income students and students with disabilities, demoralized schools through unrealistic timetables for improvement, and failed to provide funding necessary to carry out the mandates, further disadvantaging small, rural, and poor school districts (Bracey 2005; Karen 2005).

President Obama and his education secretary, Arne Duncan, are changing the NCLB plan by funding parts of the law that were left unfunded and adding funding for new initiatives as part of the "Race to the Top" agenda, adding new assessment measures of student learning, providing some alternatives to the high-stakes testing, stressing rewards for high-performing teachers, and nationalizing some of the standards that were previously in the hands of states. They plan to place new emphasis on "zero to five" education, expand Head Start funding for preschoolers, and increase parental involvement. Changes are also being considered that would waive or reduce tuition for students who become long-term teachers, and tax credits may be given for college tuition. Still, critics charge that the Obama administration continues with many of the NCLB policies that caused problems in the previous administration, especially the use of high-stakes testing and centralized control ("Plan for Lifetime Success Through Education" 2008).

Thinking Sociologically

What benefits the individual may not be what helps schools or serves as priority for the nation. Who should make decisions about whether individual or societal needs take precedence? Where do you think the primary authority for decision making should be—local, state, or national? Why?

Macro-level political and economic trends outside a country can have a significant impact on the educational system as well. External influences include international relations and events as well as new technologies and new knowledge. In the United States, for example, the terrorist attacks on the World Trade Center and Pentagon on September 11, 2001, reshaped school curricula overnight, as schools added units on terrorism, American values, and Islam.

EDUCATION, SOCIETY, AND THE ROAD TO OPPORTUNITY: EDUCATION AT THE MACRO LEVEL

Carlos Muñoz was born in San Diego, the only child of Rafael and Yolanda Muñoz. Carlos's parents were born in Mexico, but they met and were married in the United States. They divorced several years ago, and Carlos alternates living with his mother and father. His mother has long worked as a teacher's aide in the local school district. She lives in a tidy house in a working-class, mostly Mexican area near downtown San Diego. She periodically takes Carlos on trips to Mexico.

Mrs. Muñoz graduated from a high school in the same district where she is now employed, and she is knowledgeable about the educational system here. She is happy with Carlos's high school, which is not overcrowded and understaffed as his junior high school had been, but she is worried about his school performance. She says that he lacks *ganas* (desire) and is not spending enough time or effort on his studies. "He tries to do

everything fast. . . . He's getting an F in biology and Cs in most other classes," she says. Of her career hopes for Carlos, she says, "It would be perfect for him to be a lawyer, but he needs to work harder. I don't think that he can do it" (Portes and Rumbaut 2001:14–15). His father has now taken a more active role in Carlos's education, hoping to get him on the right track again.

Mrs. Muñoz and millions of other immigrant parents in countries around the world have high hopes for their children, hopes that can be realized through education. Immigrant families from around the globe view education as essential to success in their new cultures. Many groups push their children to achieve in order to improve their opportunities in the new country (Kao 2004). This section focuses on the role of education in the stratification system. Although it has implications regarding individual families' chances to succeed, the reality is that education is deeply interwoven into the macro-level inequalities of the society.

Why Societies Have Educational Systems: Macro-Level Theories

In a rural Indian village in Uttar Pradesh, children gather in a lean-to shelter for their morning lessons before going to the fields to help with the animals. The average number of years of schooling in India is eight (UNESCO 2005). In some rural areas, little more than basic literacy is considered necessary or possible, especially for girls. Basic literacy is a goal for all citizens in most countries, but it is sometimes limited to urban areas in the Global South where basic academic skills (literacy, mathematics, and science) are essential to find employment. Mass education was not even a goal until the 1900s (Benavot, Meyer, and Kamens 1991). It was only then that it became clear that a literate citizenry is necessary for economic development and informed political participation.

Wherever it takes place and whatever the content, education gives individuals the information and skills that their society regards as important and prepares them to live and work in their societies. Education plays a major role in providing children with skills for their adult lives—but how education takes place varies across societies. Village children in many Global South countries around the world go to the community school, tablets in hand, but when the family needs help in the fields or with child care, older children often stay at home. Even though attending several years of school is mandated by law in most countries, not all people become literate. Learning survival skills takes most of an individual's available time and energy—how to grow crops, care for the home, treat diseases, and make clothing—and these essential skills come before formal schooling.

These children, who live near Inle Lake in Myanmar (Burma), take the only available mode of transportation to get to school, a gondola school bus.

Manifest Functions

- Socialize children to be productive members of society.
- Select and train individuals for positions in society.
- Promote social participation, change, and innovation.
- Enhance personal independence and social development.

Latent Functions

- Confine and supervise underage citizens.
- Weaken parental controls over youths.
- Provide opportunities for peer cultures to develop.
- Provide contexts for the development of friendships and mate selection.

Figure 11.1 Key Functions of Education

Education provides hope in this refugee camp in the Central African Republic. The adults created this school for children, even though families often lack food. They view education as a functional necessity for the future of their children.

Functionalist Perspective on the Purposes of Education

Functional theorists argue that formal and informal education serve certain crucial purposes in society, especially as societies modernize (Boli 2002). The functions of education as a social institution are outlined in Figure 11.1. Note that some functions are planned and formalized (manifest functions), whereas others are unintended and unorganized—the informal results of the educational process (latent functions).

Latent functions of schooling are often just as important to the society as manifest functions. For example, schools give parents release time from childrearing responsibilities so that they can perform other roles. Schools also keep children off the streets until they can be absorbed into productive roles in society. They provide young people with a place to congregate and interact among themselves, fostering a "youth culture" of music, fashion, slang, dances, dating, and cliques or gangs. At the ages when social relationships are being established, especially with the opposite sex, schools are the central meeting place for the young—a kind of mate selection market. Education also weakens parental control over youths, helps them begin the move toward independence, and provides experience in large, impersonal secondary groups.

In the functionalist view, the structure and processes within the educational institution remain stable only if basic functions are met. When social functions are not met adequately, an educational system becomes ripe for change. Government proposals for educational reforms are stimulated by new knowledge and technologies and by indications of poor outcomes, such as falling behind in international test comparisons or experiencing high unemployment in an undertrained labor force.

Socialization: Teaching Children to Be Productive Members of Society. Societies use education to pass on essential information of a culture—especially the values, skills, and knowledge necessary for survival. Sometimes this process occurs in formal classrooms and other times in informal places. In west African villages, children may have several years of formal education in a village school, but they learn what is right and wrong, values, and future roles informally by observing their elders and by "playing" at the tasks they will soon undertake for survival. The girls help pound cassava root for the evening meal, while the boys build model boats and practice negotiating the waves and casting nets. In less prosperous countries, formal education beyond basic literacy is reserved mainly for the elite—the sons and daughters of the rulers and the wealthy.

In all postindustrial Global North societies, however, elders and family members cannot teach all the skills necessary for survival. Formal schooling emerged as an institution to meet the needs of industrial and postindustrial societies, furnishing the specialized training required by rapidly growing and changing technology. Schools also teach students culture beyond what families in heterogeneous societies can provide. Diverse groups must learn common rules that maintain the social order, for example (Brint, Contreras, and Matthews 2001).

Selecting and Training Individuals for Positions in Society. Students take standardized tests, receive grades at the end of the term or the year, and ask teachers to write recommendation letters. These activities are part of the selection process prevalent in competitive societies with formal educational systems. Individuals accumulate **credentials**—grade point averages, standardized test scores, and degrees—that determine the colleges or job opportunities available to them, the fields of study or occupations they can pursue, and ultimately their positions in society. In some societies, educational systems enact this social function through tracking, ability grouping, grade promotion and retention, high-stakes and minimum-competency testing, and pull-out programs that contribute to job training, such as vocational education and service learning.

Thus, education outfits people for making a living in their society and contributing to the economy. Individual, family, community, state, and national income and standard of living are linked to educational level. For example, Map 11.2 in the "Engaging Sociology" on page 376 indicates the distribution of college degrees in the United States.

Promoting Change and Innovation. In multicultural societies such as Israel, France, and England, citizens expect schools to help assimilate immigrants by teaching them the language and customs, along with strategies for reducing intergroup tensions. In Israel, for example, many recent Jewish immigrants from Africa and Russia work hard to master Hebrew and to move successfully through the Israeli educational system. In most societies, providing educational opportunity to all groups is a challenge but effective social participation and readiness for change require it.

Institutions of higher education are expected to generate new knowledge, technology, and ideas and produce students with up-to-date skills and knowledge to lead industry and other key institutions in society. In our high-tech age, critical thinking and analytical skills are more essential for problem solving than rote memorization, and this fact is reflected in curriculum change. Thus, the curriculum changes to meet the changing needs of people in new social circumstances. Familiarity with technological equipment—computers, Internet resources, electronic library searches, and so forth—become critical survival skills. Lack of training in these areas fosters further division of social classes and reduced chances for social mobility.

India has top-ranked technical institutes, and the highly skilled graduates are employed by multinational companies around the world. Companies in Europe and the United States also send information to India for processing and receive it back the next morning because of the time difference. Well-trained, efficient engineers and computer experts working in India for lower wages than workers in many highly developed countries have become an essential part of the global economy (Friedman 2005).

Enhancing Personal and Social Development. Do you remember your first day of elementary school? Perhaps it marked a transition between the intimate world of the family and an impersonal school world that emphasized discipline, knowledge and skills, responsibility, and obedience. In school, children learn that they are no longer accepted unconditionally as they typically were in their families. Rather, they must meet certain expectations and compete for attention and rewards.

In school, children are taught educational and social skills and ethical conduct that will enable them to function in society. For example, in addition to the 3 Rs, they learn to get along with others, resolve disputes, stay in line, follow directions, obey the rules, take turns, be kind to others, be neat, tell the truth, listen, plan ahead, work hard, meet deadlines, and so on. Children worldwide begin learning what schools expect of them in preschool and kindergarten, providing the basis for schooling in the society (Neuman 2005); in the functionalist view, the prosocial values and social competencies learned in academic boot camp are necessary for social cohesion and social order (Gracey 1967).

Conflict Perspectives on Stratification and Education

Fortunate students around the world receive elite educations, but many others do not. Why? In part, this is because of class, race, and gender differences between children (Kerckhoff 2001). Attendance

Video Link 11.3
Watch a discussion of segregated schools.

Engaging Sociology

Consequences of High or Low Numbers of Bachelor's Degrees

Percent of Population with a Bachelor's Degree or More

- 36 - 47
- 31 - 35
- 26 - 30
- 21 - 25
- 15 - 20

Map 11.2   Percentage of the U.S. Population Holding a Bachelor's Degree or Higher by State: 2004

Source: U.S. Census Bureau.

Study the preceding map and answer the questions based on it.

1. How does your state rank?

2. How might the economy of a state be affected when an especially low percentage of the population has a college degree?

3. What kinds of businesses, industries, or professionals are more likely to locate in a state with very high percentage of its population having a college education?

4. How might the politics, the health care system, or science be influenced by the high or low levels of education within the state?

5. Look at the states that have especially high or especially low levels of the population with college degrees. What might be some causes for these high or low rates of college graduation? Provide some results. Check the statistics on your state or province.

6. What else might we learn from this map? What else do you notice or what questions does this map raise?

at an elite school is a means of attaining high social status, for example. Graduates of British *public schools*, American preparatory (prep) schools, private high schools, and international schools in countries around the world attend the best universities and become leaders of government, business, and the military. Because elite schools are very expensive and highly selective, affluent members of society have the most access to them and thereby learn class privilege and advantage (Howard 2007; Persell and Cookson 1985), and thus perpetuate their status. Many leaders of former colonized countries have had the opportunity to study abroad, continuing Global North influence in these countries. Those not born into positions of advantage have very limited chances to participate in elite education.

At a macro level, conflict theorists see institutions, including education, as tools of powerful affluent groups to ensure that their self-interests are met. Educational opportunities are manipulated in ways that keep the sons and daughters of the haves in positions of privilege, while lower-class children are prepared for less prestigious and less rewarding positions in society. If schools do not provide equal educational opportunities for all children in a society, as conflict theorists contend, then students cannot compete equally in the job market.

According to this view, when elites of society protect their educational advantages, the result is *reproduction of class*—the socioeconomic positions of one generation passing on to the next. This process takes place in part through the socialization of young people into adult work roles and compliance with the modern corporation and its needs. Schools teach students from lower socioeconomic positions to obey authority and accept the dominant ideology that justifies social inequality. If citizens believe that those with the best educations and jobs in their society personally earned them, they are not motivated to change the system. In these ways, schools serve the interests of the privileged (Bowles and Gintis 2002; Collins 2004).

The cultural values and social norms of the dominant group, such as ideas of etiquette, proper ways of speaking and writing, notions of deference to superiors, and so forth, are transmitted to all social classes and legitimated through formal schooling. Other definitions of reality from other ethnic or socioeconomic groups are marginalized. Studies comparing working-class schools with upper-middle-class schools and private schools with public schools support this view, revealing structural differences in the ways schools are organized that reinforce class differences (Kozol 2005). According to conflict theorists, this process enhances power and confirms the privileges of the dominant group. The educational system is not equally beneficial to all or even to the majority of citizens in society.

Elite preparatory (prep) schools in England, Japan, the United States, and many other countries traditionally have been the training ground for the sons and daughters of the elite. In countries such as Chile, privatization of schools in the form of parental choice and vouchers was seen as a way to broaden educational opportunity, in line with Chile's transition to a market-oriented economy. After 30 years, however, inequality persists in educational opportunity and outcomes, especially in the transition to secondary schools. Advantages come to those in private-voucher and private-paid schools as opposed to public schools (Torche 2005). Proposed choice and voucher plans allowing students and parents to choose schools have been tried in the United States, as well. Critics of choice and voucher plans fear that

Zimbabwe once had one of the best education systems in Africa, but after a severe economic crisis in the country, educational conditions have declined rapidly. Still, some children are privileged over other children, who do not get any education. This system that provides education only for the privileged protects the interests of the elite.

public schools might be left with the least capable students and teachers, further stratifying an already troubled system (Chubb and Moe 1990; Witte and Thorn 1996). Private schools could also become sanctuaries for those who do not want race- and class-integrated schools, perpetuating religious, economic, and racial segregation.

Having explored some lenses through which sociologists analyze educational systems, we now focus on the classrooms, corridors, local schools, and key players where the everyday drama of teaching and learning is played out.

Thinking Sociologically

Consider the community in which you went to high school. Do you think the education there enhances upward social mobility and serves both individuals and the community, or does it mostly serve the affluent, reproducing social class and training people to fulfill positions at the same level as their parents?

Can Schools Bring About Equality in Societies?

Equal opportunity exists when all people have an equal chance of achieving high socioeconomic status in society regardless of their class, ethnicity or race, or gender (Riordan 2004). James Coleman (1968, 1990) describes the goals of equal educational opportunity:

- To provide a common curriculum for all children regardless of background
- To provide that children from diverse backgrounds attend the same school
- To provide equality within a given locality

In the United States, equal opportunity means that children are provided with equal facilities, financing, and access to school programs (Kozol 1991). Schools in poor neighborhoods or in rural villages in the United States and around the world, however, often lack the basics—safe buildings, school supplies and books, and funds to operate. Lower-class minority students who live in these areas fall disproportionately to the bottom of the educational hierarchy. Many children face what seem to be insurmountable barriers to educational success: increasing numbers of children living in poverty, lack of health care and immunizations, school absence due to illness or homelessness, or dropouts to help the family (Kozol 2005).

Two widely cited classical studies on equal educational opportunity, the Coleman Report and Jencks's study of inequality (Coleman et al. 1966; Jencks 1972), have had a major impact on policy in education and stand out because of their comprehensive data collection, analysis, and contribution to the understanding of inequality. Coleman found that the differences in test scores between minority students and White students were due not only to in-school factors but also to parents' education levels and other environmental factors such as segregated schools, economic makeup of schools, and some differences in facilities. Based on these findings, Coleman recommended integration of schools to create a climate for achievement. That recommendation resulted not only in plans to integrate but also in controversy and court challenges (Orfield et al. 1997). Today, busing and other methods to desegregate schools such as magnet schools and choice plans are in place.

The second major study that shaped educational policy in the 1970s (Jencks 1972) argued that schools alone cannot create equal opportunity. Even if schools reduce the educational attainment gap, the economic inequality among adults continues to exist. The bottom line is that most agree schools alone cannot solve the achievement gap between students.

Who Gets Ahead and Why? The Role of Education in Stratification

Education is supposed to be a **meritocracy**, a formal system in which people are allocated to positions according to their abilities and credentials, as in level of education attained. This, of course, is consistent with the principles of a rational or formal bureaucratic social system, where the most qualified person is promoted and decisions are impersonal and based on "credentials" (Charles et al. 2007). Still, in societies around the world, we see evidence that

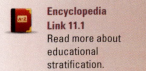

Encyclopedia Link 11.1 Read more about educational stratification.

middle-class and elite children, especially boys in the Global South, receive more and better education than equally qualified poor children. Children do not attend school on an equal footing, and in many cases, meritocracy does not exist. Why is Tomás "unlucky" while others succeed? Explanations go beyond a focus on the children's abilities to the analyses of background factors, the ethnic groups, the placements of their families in the stratification system, and the role of their country in the world system. Conflict theorists, in particular, maintain that education creates and perpetuates inequality. The haves hold the power to make sure that institutions, including schools, serve their own needs and protect their access to privileges (Sadovnik 2007). Elite parents have social and cultural capital—language skills, knowledge of how the social system works, and networks—to ensure that their children succeed (Kao 2004).

A country's level of education is a key indicator of quality of life and placement in the global social world. Industrialized countries want to trade with poor countries, which provide natural resources and new pools of workers and consumers. Education helps enable poorer countries and their citizens to participate and compete in global markets. As a consequence, international organizations such as the United Nations and transnational business communities have become more involved in educational development, especially in programs for training workers in technology.

Sources of Inequality

Three sources of inequality in schools—testing, tracking, and funding—illustrate how schools reproduce and perpetuate social stratification. They also give clues as to what might be done to minimize the repetitious pattern of poverty.

Assessing Student Achievement: Testing. Testing is one means of placing students in schools according to their achievement and merit and of determining progress being made. Critics of standardized testing argue that test questions, language differences, and testing situations are biased against lower-class, minority, and immigrant students, resulting in lower scores and relegating these students to lower tracks in the educational system. In addition, in the case of IQ tests, scientists know that intelligence is complex and that paper-and-pencil tests measure only selected types of intelligence (Gardner 1987, 1999). Other scholars question whether the tests are unbiased for boys and for girls from different class and ethnic backgrounds. Critics of achievement tests point out that higher-class students with better schooling and enriched backgrounds do better on the tests, even if they have not gained as much knowledge. Nonetheless, testing is the means used to evaluate student achievement locally, nationally, and internationally. Table 11.7 in the next "Engaging Sociology" shows differences in ACT (American College Test) and SAT (Scholastic Assessment Test) scores depending on sex, race, and ethnic group. Answer the questions that are posed as you engage with the sociological data.

Engaging Sociology

Test Score Variations by Gender and Ethnicity

Evaluate your testing experiences and compare them with those of other groups:

Table 11.7 ACT and SAT Scores by Sex and Race/Ethnicity

ACT Scores (2007)	Average	SAT Scores (2008)	Average
Composite (total scores)	21.2	Writing (all students)	497
Male	21.2	Male	491
Female	21.0	Female	502
Race/Ethnicity		White	519
African American	17.0	Black/African American	424
American Indian	18.9	Mexican American	447
Hispanic	18.7	Puerto Rican	445
Caucasian	22.1	Other Hispanic	449
Asian American	22.6	Asian American	516
SAT Scores (2008)	**Average**	American Indian	470
Critical reading (all students)	502	Other	494
Male	504	Math (all students)	509
Female	500	Male	527
White	528	Female	499
Black/African American	430	White	537
Mexican American	454	Black/African American	426
Puerto Rican	456	Mexican American	463
Other Hispanic	455	Puerto Rican	453
Asian American	513	Other Hispanic	461
American Indian	495	Asian American	591
Other	496	American Indian	491
		Other	512

Source: Inside Higher Ed (2007) for ACT scores; Inside Higher Ed (2008) for SAT scores.

Note: ACT, American College Testing; SAT, Scholastic Assessment Test.

Questions

1. Were your scores an accurate measure of your ability or achievement? Why or why not?
2. What other factors besides your ability affected your test scores?
3. Have your scores affected your life chances? Are there ways in which you have been privileged or disprivileged in the testing process?
4. What might be some causes for the variation between different groups or categories of students?

Governments compare their students' educational test scores on the International Assessment of Educational Progress and the International Association for the Evaluation of Educational Achievement (IEA) with other countries' scores to determine how their students and educational systems are performing. These are tests of children around the world in literacy, mathematics, science, civic education, and foreign language. For example, recently IEA tested students in the Fourth International Mathematics and Science Study, in which more than 60 countries participated, testing children at the fourth-, eighth-, and 12th-grade levels (IEA 2007). These rankings provide information on the similarities, differences, and effects of development on education (Ballantine and Spade 2008). However, copying educational systems of successful countries is not necessarily the answer to improvement, for education occurs in different cultural contexts (Kagan and Stewart 2005; Zhao 2005).

Educational inequality among countries includes differences in achievement in different parts of the curriculum. For example, some countries rank higher in math and science, but the same countries do not always rank high in reading (Baker 2002). East Asian countries routinely score the highest in math and science achievement. Many educators believe that gleaning ideas and adapting methods from other successful systems will help improve scores, but cultural context determines what will be successful (Houlihan 2005; Zhao 2005).

Student Tracking. Tracking (sometimes called *streaming*) places students in ability groups, allowing educators to address students' individual learning needs. Many sociologists of education have argued against tracking, pointing out that it contributes to the stratification process that perpetuates inequality. Research finds that levels at which students are tracked correlate with factors such as the child's background and ethnic group, language skills, appearance, and other socioeconomic variables (Rosenbaum 1999; Wells and Oakes 1996). In other words, track placement is not always a measure of a student's ability. It can be arbitrary, based on teachers' impressions or questionable test results. Even language differences between teachers and students can affect placement. Over time, differences in children's achievement become reinforced. Students from lower social classes and minority groups are clustered in the lower tracks and complete fewer years and lower levels of school (Lucas and Berends 2002; Oakes et al. 1997). School failure in early adolescence leads to other problems later on that affect employment and socioeconomic status (Chen and Kaplan 2003).

Still, other research indicates that students do better in school when working in groups based on their achievement levels. In comparing Massachusetts middle schools that track students with those that have "detracked" students,

Video Link 11.4
Watch city and suburban students change places.

researchers found that schools that track in math courses have more advanced math students than those that do not (Loveless 2009). The bottom line is that if a school district does track students, it should find ways to eliminate possible race or gender bias and students should be tracked in each subject independently, not in a single track for all subjects.

Some school districts have accomplished both integration and tracking by establishing magnet schools. These plans draw students from around the districts to learning centers of excellence focused on science, the arts, and other subject areas. The Obama administration is funding a number of STEM high schools (Science, Technology, Engineering, and Math) to attract students to the science fields.

In a study of three magnet schools in a Midwestern city (Metz 1986), established to accomplish court-ordered desegregation and stimulate innovative education, the city achieved desegregation without the mandatory reassignment of students. Each of the three magnet schools offered a different type of program to attract students. The first offered Individually Guided Education, with special organization of the curriculum, instructional techniques, and specific roles of staff members. The second offered "open education" developed by the staff. This school offered a highly flexible curriculum that required and encouraged self-directed students. The third school—for gifted and talented students—had a policy of selective admissions and promised an enriched traditional curriculum. The researcher's goal was to understand the character, atmosphere (climate), and influences shaping the lives of these three magnet schools—what really happened in these schools—and to learn about the experiences of the schools' participants. She used multiple research strategies—interviewing, participant observation, and documents—both in the schools and the school district. In addition, Metz considered the historical context of desegregation in which the schools developed, as well as the community climate.

This magnet school concept was only partially successful in desegregating schools. Most children bused were Black, and many parents sent their children to the closest school regardless of the program offered. Yet the magnet schools made desegregation palatable. Many districts struggle to understand how to integrate schools and improve student achievements. Some proposed solutions include magnet schools such as those discussed earlier, charter schools, and publicly owned schools.

School Funding. The amount of money available to fund schools and the sources providing it affect the types of programs offered, an important issue for nations that must compete in the global social and economic system. In some societies, money for education comes from central governments and, in others, from a combination of federal, state, and local government and private sources, such as religious denominations and philanthropies. In countries such as Uganda, the government

This computer class is held at a formerly failing inner-city British school, transformed by new management and increased governmental funding. Many students come from situations that present educational challenges: having refugee status, living in temporary shelters, or being from non-English speaking homes. However, the school is highly successful and has become a "government beacon school" in Britain.

runs the schools, but most of the funding comes from tuition paid by each student or by the student's parents.

Whatever the source, schools sometimes face budget crises and must trim programs. In the United States, unequal school spending results from reliance on local property taxes as well as state and federal funds. About 50% of the money for U.S. schools comes from state funds and most of the rest from property taxes. Spending is closely related to the racial and class composition of schools and to student achievement levels. Schools in low-income communities are particularly disadvantaged by smaller tax bases and fewer local resources (Condron and Roscigno 2003). Wealthier districts, on the other hand, can afford better education for their children because more money is collected from property taxes. Higher-class students have advantages not available in poor districts (Kozol 1991, 2005; Wenglinsky 1997). Controversies over school funding in the United States have reached the courtroom in a number of states, yet overall, the United States spends less money per student on education than most other industrialized nations.

Thinking Sociologically

Were you tracked in any subjects? What effect, if any, did this have? What effect did tracking have on your friends?

Public and Private Schools

In the United States, Catholic parochial schools are the most prevalent type of private schools. Other religiously affiliated schools are the next most common. Private preparatory schools are third. About 10% of U.S. students attend private schools.

Studies of low-income and minority students have found that those attending Catholic schools, especially in inner cities, perform more like White middle-class students than those attending public schools (Morgan

Journal Article Link 11.2
Read a case study of school reform.

2001). In general, private schools are more academically demanding, more stringent, more disciplined, and more orderly. They assign more homework, and they demand more parental involvement than do public schools (Cookson and Persell 1985). They can also expel children who do not perform or are disruptive, an option the public schools often do not have. However, part of the reason private schools have generally had higher levels of achievement is the select population they admit. A massive study released in the summer of 2006 by the U.S. Department of Education compared 7,000

Schoolgirls in Kenya wait for classes to begin. Children like this, whose parents can afford to send them to school, will likely grow up with enough education to have better economic prospects.

"The Little Red School Bus," sponsored by the nonprofit Christian Appalachian Project, helps residents in rural Kentucky prepare for high school equivalency certificates and a better chance of finding a job. This may be the only chance for an education these people will experience.

public schools and 530 private schools (National Assessment of Educational Progress 2006). The study controlled for student socioeconomic backgrounds in a way that is often not done, and it found that children performed roughly on par in the two types of schools, either private or public schools, excelling slightly in either math or reading depending on grade level. The only group that lagged significantly was children attending conservative Protestant Christian schools (Schemo 2006). Another analysis of the data found that private school students scored higher than public school students in most subject areas (except in fourth-grade math where the scores were equal; Peterson and Llaudet 2006).

The proposed choice and voucher plans allowing students and parents to choose their schools have been controversial in part because it is thought that public schools might well be left with the least capable students and teachers, further stratifying an already troubled system (Chubb and Moe 1990). Private schools could also become sanctuaries for those who do not want integrated schools and could perpetuate religious and racial segregation.

Thinking Sociologically

Educational needs at the micro (individual) level, the meso (institutional or ethnic group) level, or the macro (national) level can be very different. This raises the question of who makes decisions and whether individual needs or societal needs take precedence. Where do you think the primary authority for decision making should be—local, state, or national level? Why?

In addition to the structural features of schools as organizations and part of the institutional structure of society, education interplays with national and global forces in interesting and complex ways. We turn next to a macro-level analysis.

Educational and Social Policy Issues

Early in the 21st century, school systems around the world face dramatic changes: pressures for equal educational opportunity for all groups—classes and castes, race and ethnic groups, females and males. The need for technological training of citizenry, increased demand for more access to higher education, changes in the student composition of the classroom, and accountability and testing of students and teachers are but a few of the many issues. Because education reflects societal politics and problems, policies swing from conservative to more liberal and back again, depending on who is in power and what their agenda is for change.

Consider the current concerns about world tensions that are resulting in the internationalization of the classroom (King 2006). Within our lifetimes, we are likely to experience several of these swings. For example, recently in the United States, the issues of accountability, standardized testing, and teaching basic skills have been at the forefront, but movements toward individualization of education and developing the whole child are reappearing (Gamoran 2001). Although the past century brought some improvement in equality in education, much remains to be done to level the playing field. The greatest barrier to equal education in the 21st century, both within and between countries, may prove to be socioeconomic, with many minorities represented in lower classes. Sociologists of education contribute to the policy discussions in their roles as researchers, consultants, policy analysts, and applied sociologists.

Educational Policies in the United States

Today, despite numerous U.S. government policies and reports, the data on school success show a worsening picture. There are 27 million functionally illiterate U.S. citizens, with many 17-year-olds unable to write well or solve mathematical problems and lacking the basic skills needed to enter business and the military. In some major inner cities, only a quarter of students graduate from high school (CBS News 2008).

Each new presidential administration proposes educational reforms to address the same problems. Under the Bush administration plan, NCLB schools were required to administer achievement tests for accountability—tests that focus on math and reading. Schools failing to meet guidelines were penalized. The result was that 70% of schools reduced instructional time in other subjects to teach more reading and math. The greatest reduction was in social studies, followed by science, art, music, and physical education (Center for Education Policy 2006). Critics argue that these are extremely important fields for the 21st century and should not be shortchanged. Numerical gains based on math and reading achievement tests do not measure learning in many other areas, and they certainly do not measure the ability to think critically.

Providing Early-Childhood Education

Early-childhood education has been touted as providing the start that many children need to be successful in school, as discussed later. Compensatory education helps narrow the opportunity gap, and a key part is early-childhood education offered by the Head Start program. Evaluations of the Head Start program in the United States, designed for 3- to 5-year-olds from disadvantaged backgrounds, show that it increases the likelihood that enrolled children stay in school, receive preventive health care, avoid later remedial classes, and do not become juvenile delinquents. Parental

Two young girls use the computers in a classroom during a Head Start program. The Head Start program introduces reading and writing to children who are about to enter elementary school. It is one federal effort in the United States to provide support to children from poor neighborhoods and families.

education is also part of the compensatory education program. Yet fewer than half of the eligible children take part in the program due to fluctuations in support as political administrations change. The Obama administration has worked to increase funding and access for early-childhood programs.

Comparing early-childhood education programs, research in China, India, Brazil, Canada, and Europe demonstrate similar findings:

1. Children from birth to age 5 develop rapidly in linguistic and cognitive abilities, emotional development, social regulatory development, and other capacities.

2. In the child's early years, the growth trajectory in learning, health, and emotional development should not be interrupted.

3. The needs of young children are not always adequately addressed.

4. In developing countries, child survival programs that concentrate on reducing infant mortality rates, increasing immunization rates, improving nutrition, and providing clean water and sanitation services have produced long-term economic benefits (Levine 2005; UNICEF 2004).

> **Audio Link 11.3**
> Listen to a positive transformation of a school.

The value of early-childhood education has been proven, but access is far from universal. Still, applied sociologist

The Applied Sociologist at Work—Geoffrey Canada   Harlem Children's Zone

The United States is "the land of opportunity," but not for residents of Harlem, according to Geoffrey Canada. In Harlem, the goal is to avoid being beaten, shot, or raped. Canada has an ambitious agenda—to break the cycle of poverty and have all young people in the Harlem Children's Zone graduate from college.

Geoffrey Canada's life experience prepared him to work as a social activist and educator. He grew up in the south Bronx, was raised by a single mom, and then had a lucky break. He moved to the suburbs with his grandparents and from there received a college degree from Bowdoin College and a master's from the Harvard Graduate School of Education.

Having been given an opportunity for education, he is now giving back to the community. As president and CEO of the Harlem Children's Zone in New York, he works with students to increase high school and college graduation rates. The Harlem Children's Zone started out as a 24-block area of Harlem but has grown to 97 blocks due to its success. In the 97-block neighborhood, his center follows the academic careers of youth, providing social, medical, and educational services that are free to the 10,000 children who live in the Zone. He has built his own charter school, the Promise Academy, with 1,200 students in grades K to 10th, soon to be through 12th grade. Tuition to the school is free, and admission is done by lottery. For those who do not win the school's admissions lottery, Harlem Children's Zone still provides services to everyone in the Zone, including parenting classes, preschool language classes, school preparation classes, and SAT tutoring.

The Promise Academy has long days and a short summer vacation, a dress code, and strict discipline. The student-teacher ratio is 6 to 1. For students who work hard and achieve, there are rewards. Canada is not apologetic about "buying" the students' cooperation. Some get free trips to Disneyland for good grades, and others get paid for good high school grades.

The Zone is not cheap to run, but Canada points out that the costs of a child ending up in the criminal justice system are much greater, for if a child fails, the community and society have also failed. Therefore, he believes that the investment is sound. The program costs $76 million a year, or $5,000 per child. Much of the funding comes from the business community and Wall Street. That may sound like a lot of money, but the national average in 2006 was more than $9,000 per student and the average expenditure per student for the state of New York was nearly $15,000 (U.S. Census Bureau 2008c). To test the effectiveness of the school and program, a Harvard economics professor studied the data from tests of achievement and other academic indicators. He found that the Promise Academic elementary school had closed the gap in math and reading between its students and students in White or mixed schools, and outperformed many of the comparison schools. Those middle school students who started at the Promise Academy were behind, but they caught up with students in comparison schools. According to the evaluator, the results were "stunning."

The project has been called "one of the biggest social experiments of our time" (Tough 2008). Because of the proven success of the Harlem Children's Zone, U.S. President Obama has taken notice and plans to replicate the model in 20 other cities across the nation.

Note: Geoffrey Canada received his undergraduate degree from Bowdoin College and his master's in education from Harvard. He has written several books and articles, including *Reaching Up for Manhood: Transforming the Lives of Boys in America* (1998).

Geoffrey Canada has had success with implementing programs for poor children in Harlem, from preschool to high school, as discussed in the above "The Applied Sociologist at Work."

Global Policy Issues in Education

Most societies view the education and training of young people as an economic investment in the future. Countries with capitalist economic systems are more likely to have an educational system that stresses individualism and competition, pitting students against one another for the best grades and the best opportunities. The elites often ensure that their own children get a very different education than the children of the laboring class. Socialist and traditional economic systems often encourage cooperation and collaboration among students, with the collective needs of society viewed as more important than those of individuals. The social and economic values of the society are reflected in approaches to learning and in motivation of students (Rankin and Aytaç 2006).

Other studies compare the curricula of nations and changes in those curricula to determine how similar and different they are. Findings generally support a convergence of curricular themes across nations, reflecting the interdependence of nations. However, many researchers question whether that convergence is good for all people in all societies, especially students from peripheral Global South countries.

Video Link 11.5
Watch a discussion on education innovation.

Political and economic trends outside a country can also have an impact on the educational system within the country. Examples of external influences include technological trends, new inventions, and new knowledge. Even an event such as the terrorist attacks on the World Trade Center and the Pentagon on September 11, 2001, shapes the school curricula, as schools give greater weight to patriotism. In addition to loyalty, however, schools often need to teach people to accept those who are different from themselves—that is, to reduce prejudice.

Education of Girls Around the Globe

"One of the silent killers attacking the developing world is the lack of quality basic education for large numbers of the poorest children in the world's poorest countries— particularly girls" (Sperling 2005:213). In 2005, more than 110 million children—60% of them girls from ages 6 to 11—received no schooling at all. Another 150 million dropped out of primary school. About 50% of girls in sub-Saharan Africa do not complete primary school, and only 17% are in secondary school (UNESCO 2005). Of the one sixth of the world's population that is illiterate, two thirds are women (Dobriansky 2006). In Niger, for instance, only 12% of the girls in rural areas are in primary school compared with 83% in the capital city, Niamey. In refugee camps in Africa, only 6% of children receive any secondary education due to hardships from lack of teachers, the impact of AIDS, and orphaned status. Even when children do receive some primary education, the quality is such that many children leave school without basic skills (UNESCO 2005).

The availability of clean drinking water is a major issue in the Global South. Because women and girls must spend as much as 6 hours a day carrying water home (26% of a woman's day in Africa), the daughters are needed to care for children. When wells were built and usable water became more accessible, the school attendance of girls immediately increased by 15% in Bangladesh and by 12% in Tanzania (WaterAid 2004). Indeed, research by WaterAid (2008) estimates that in the Global South, 443 million school days are lost each year due to water-related issues and diseases.

What is clear is that when girls are educated, the consequences are great: "What is striking is the breadth of benefits derived from educating girls—not only economic benefits in terms of higher wages, greater agricultural productivity, and faster economic growth, but also health benefits" (Sperling 2006:274). More educated girls have lower fertility rates; lower maternal, infant, and child mortality; greater protection against HIV/AIDS; increased labor force participation and earnings; and a greater ability to pass on these benefits to the next generation (World Bank 2008).

Sexual activity (as well as marrying at young ages and failing to use contraception) is dramatically reduced when girls are in school and learn about AIDS. We know that girls in Uganda "with some secondary education were

Greg Mortenson founded a nonprofit organization, the Central Asia Institute, that builds schools in Afghanistan and Pakistan. This has been especially important for girls who had previously been a low priority for learning to read and write in this area. These girls work together in one of Mortenson's schools.

three times less likely to be HIV-positive, and those with some primary school [education] were about half as likely to be HIV-positive" (Sperling 2005:214). When school fees were abolished in Uganda, Kenya, and Tanzania in

Recent controversy in France has focused on Islamic girls and women wearing the traditional head covering (hijab) to schools—including a school fair where hula hoops are played. French officials thought the distinctive dress was a contributor to the "we" versus "them" polarization between Muslims and non-Muslims. Many scholars insist that societies work better when there is diversity and tolerance of diversity rather than sameness and conformity.

In Namibia, as elsewhere around the world, education is increasingly necessary as the economy is globalized and skills in literacy and numeracy become critical to survival and hopes of prosperity.

Computer and Internet skills are essential to success in college and most jobs in this globalized social world. Many courses, even degrees, can now be done online.

East Africa, enrollments increased dramatically. Additional incentives to parents to compensate for the loss of labor of their children also increase enrollment, as shown in Bangladesh, Mexico, and Brazil. In China, better-educated citizens hold more egalitarian gender attitudes (Shu 2004), and in Turkey, gender inequalities in education are lessened in metropolitan areas and in less patriarchal families (Rankin and Aytaç 2006). In Taiwan, researchers find that the social class and education level of the parents play a major role in the educational attainment of their children, especially daughters. The education of girls is raising the standards of living for them and their families (Jao and McKeever 2006).

Thinking Sociologically

How might education be important to children in a rural agricultural area? How might education in a local community be affected by global events, such as a war or a worldwide economic recession?

The Future of Education in the Global System

The search for the perfect model of education is neverending. School systems around the world are under pressure to meet the diverse needs of both the societies as a whole and their individual citizens. A major concern in Global North countries in the Information Age is this: What will become of those students who do not complete enough education to fit into the technological and economic needs in the 21st century (Von Holzen 2005)? In these countries, high school used to prepare most young people for a job and marriage. By the 1990s, high school was preparation for college, which was itself necessary to find a decent job in the globalizing world. In the United States, educators, corporations, wealthy individuals, and philanthropies—concerned that minority groups are falling behind—support special programs to reduce cyber segregation of the haves and the have-nots (Attewell 2001), the latter composed of poor and minority families.

Although the cyber gap may be closing in some parts of the world, there are differences in the implementation of new innovations and ways computers are used. Electronic textbooks and materials have potential to give both the affluent Global North and the poor Global South immediate access to new knowledge and ideas that can continually be updated through e-textbooks (Rossman 2005). Video games are used by corporations, the government, and the military to educate. Advocates argue, "They let people participate in the world. They let players . . . *inhabit* roles that are otherwise inaccessible to them" (Shaffer et al. 2005:105). Much learning will take place without walls, clocks, or age segregation as students learn through distance learning and through digital technology on their own time (Lundt 2004). Classrooms of the future will incorporate technological innovations and use information networks.

One form of technology that is having a major impact on the future is the Internet. The next "Sociology Around the World" discusses application of the Internet and other computer technologies to higher education.

Sociology Around the World

Distance Education: Breaking Access Barriers?

By Amy J. Orr

Technology has had a tremendous impact on education. Computers are used in a variety of ways in classrooms around the world for both the consumption and production of knowledge. The Internet, as well as programs such as WebCT and Blackboard, has made the distribution of education around the world much more feasible. Today, thousands of individuals worldwide can obtain a college degree while sitting in front of their computers.

According to the U.S. Department of Education (2004–05), distance learning is defined as "an option for earning course credit at off-campus locations via cable television, Internet, satellite classes, videotapes, correspondence courses, or other means." In 2004–2005, about two thirds of postsecondary institutions in the United States offered distance education courses (National Center for Education Statistics 2006), and the number continues to increase. Around the world, distance education is available in countries such as Australia, Canada, China, India, Japan, Mexico, Thailand, Turkey, and the United Kingdom.

One of the primary purposes of distance learning is to increase access by learners who might not ordinarily be able to obtain a traditional postsecondary education. For example, distance education courses are often heavily used by nontraditional students who wish to continue their education but face barriers such as family or employment. Questions arise, however, regarding the level of accessibility that is truly provided to underrepresented groups throughout the United States and the world. Does distance education provide new opportunities for these groups to attain postsecondary education? Or are new barriers created due to the increasing use of technology to deliver a college curriculum?

In an attempt to address these questions, the National Postsecondary Education Cooperative (NPEC) explored the relationship between distance learning and access to college education in the United States. In a report published in 2004, the NPEC concluded that (1) distance education increases overall access to postsecondary education, (2) a "digital divide" still remains for some groups, such as blacks and Hispanics, (3) a "dearth of germane information, literacy barriers, and limited diversity of content are significant barriers to getting lower income users online," and (4) low-income students are less likely than those with higher incomes to have opportunities to gain the skills required to use the technology (NPEC 2004).

Similar issues arise on a global level. Access to technology differs significantly by nation. Like disadvantaged students in the United States, individuals in the least developed nations may face literacy barriers or find the curriculum irrelevant. An additional concern arises with regard to diversity of cultural contexts and perspectives. Numerous studies report cross-cultural differences in student learning styles as well as diverse preferences for teaching approaches. For example, Weisenberg and Stacey (2005), on reviewing a number of cross-cultural studies, note that Asian students are accustomed to individualized learning techniques and tend to prefer "teacher-centered" teaching styles. Online pedagogies tend to emphasize collaborative learning and "student-centered" techniques. Because distance learning rests on the technological foundations of Western culture, minority cultures around the world may be further marginalized, as the dominant pedagogies may not be responsive to their cultural uniqueness (Smith and Ayers 2006).

Overall, distance education presents a dilemma with regard to the accessibility of postsecondary education. Although it provides unprecedented opportunities to expand access to education, distance education also runs the risk of creating new divides.

Thinking Sociologically

First, read about distance education on the previous page. How might distance education in higher education affect segments of the population—the poor, the working class, the middle class—differently? What implications does it have for equal access to education for ethnic groups? People of color? Men and women? In what ways would it be beneficial, and in what ways might it cause new problems?

The link between school completion and work, or what is referred to as the *school-to-work transition*, is clearly defined and planned by public policy in most European countries and Russia. Schools offer postsecondary options such as vocational school and associate degrees to prepare young people for skilled positions (Kerckhoff 2001), and the numbers of needed engineers or dentists determine the educational slots available in these fields. However, these options are poorly defined in other countries, especially the United States (Altbach and Davis 1999). The mismatch between jobs available and over-educated students seeking work results in dissatisfaction (Brooks and Waters 2010; Levinson 2010).

In the process of governments developing their educational policies, we again see the interconnections of our social world. Curricula respond to global events and international markets and are also shaped by micro-level effectiveness or ineffectiveness of teachers and students in individual classrooms. The macro-level concerns and the micro-level processes come together in education, with the ultimate objective of preparing individuals in each classroom to meet the needs of the community, the state, the nation, and the world.

Education is one of the first institutions after the family that a child encounters, and like the family, it is primarily concerned with the process of socialization of the populace. Another institution that is deeply concerned with socialization and the inculcation of values into young people is religion. Both religion and education tend to address issues of "what" and "why," but whereas education tends to focus on answers that have to do with knowledge—causality and the relationship between facts—religion tends to address questions of ultimate meaning in life. We turn in the next chapter to a sociological perspective on religion.

What Have We Learned?

Educational systems are typically viewed as the channel for reduction of inequality, the source of upward mobility, the way to improve the economy, and the path for reduction of prejudice in societies. However, institutions such as education also have a vested interest in stability. Schools foster patriotism and loyalty toward the political system, families support schools and education, and education is expected to support the economic vitality of the nation. Institutions and organizations are driven by interest in their own survival, and risk-taking behaviors on behalf of change are not necessarily ones that foster survival. Taking risks may threaten those who have power, privilege, and influence. It should not be surprising, therefore, that education does more to enhance stability than to create change. Still, those who seek to improve the society see tremendous potential in education as an agent of change if its influence can be harnessed. It works largely with young minds in the socialization process—carrying out what powerful policymakers feel is important.

Key Points

- Education is one of the primary institutions of society, focusing on the socialization of children and adults into their cultures so that they become contributing members. (See pp. 354–355.)

- At the micro level, various statuses and roles interact within a school, and classrooms develop their own cultures that may or may not enhance learning. (See pp. 355–363.)

- What we learn in schools goes far beyond the formal curriculum. Sometimes these implicit messages support the educational system, but sometimes they sabotage the formal and intended messages. (See pp. 363–367.)

- At the micro level, social theory is attentive to interaction in classrooms and local schools, using concepts of symbolic interaction or cost-benefit analysis to understand the climate of learning. (See pp. 355–358.)

- At the meso level, education can be understood as a formal organization that works toward certain goals (bureaucracy) but that has many of the dysfunctions of other bureaucracies. (See pp. 367–373.)

- At the macro level, national governments often try to see that their national needs are met by shaping educational policy, and their actions often create tension with those administrators and teachers at the meso and micro levels who do the actual work of teaching. (See p. 373.)

- Macro-level theories focus on how education supports the social system (functionalism) or on how education serves the interests of the "haves" and reproduces social inequality (conflict theory). (See pp. 374–382.)

- Educating is also a global concern, with a variety of questions about how to help economic development in the Global South without imposing Western models that are incompatible with the cultures of other countries. (See pp. 384–388.)

Contributing to Our Social World: What Can We Do?

At the Local Level

FIGS (First-Year Interest Groups) program: Some schools have established programs to identify and assist at-risk students at an early point in their studies. Entering students identified as at-risk take special courses, receive tutoring and peer mentoring, meet together to discuss common problems, and in some cases live in the same residence hall. You can volunteer to work as a tutor or in another capacity. Learn more about FIGS at other schools such as the University of Wisconsin (http://figs.wisc.edu), the University of Washington (http://fyp.washington.edu/figs), or the University of Missouri (http://admissions.missouri.edu/housing/academic-interest-based-communities.php), If your school does not have this program, try to initiate one.

At the Organization or Institutional Level

Reading and math tutoring: Most primary schools welcome volunteers and Service Learning students who can read to young students and tutor them in reading and math. Contact a faculty member on your campus who specializes in early-childhood education and investigate the opportunities for such volunteer work.

At the National and Global Levels

Teach for America (www.teachforamerica.org): This is a national organization, modeled along the lines of AmeriCorps and Peace Corps, that places recent college graduates in short-term (approximately 2-year) assignments teaching in economically disadvantaged neighborhood schools. "Teach for America is the national corps of outstanding recent college graduates and professionals of all academic majors and career interests who commit 2 years to teach in urban and rural public schools and become leaders in the effort to expand educational opportunity. . . . Our mission is to build the movement to eliminate educational inequity by enlisting our nation's most promising future leaders in the effort."

At the International Level

UNICEF, Care International, TeachAmerica, Jet program: Consider teaching English abroad through one of many organizations that sponsor teachers. Visit www.globaltesol.com, www.soyouwanna.com, www.teachabroad.com, and related Web sites.

 For chapter-specific resources, including **Frontline**, **TED**, and **YouTube** videos; self-quizzes; web exercises; and more, visit **www.pineforge.com/oswmedia3e.**

Religion

The Meaning of Sacred Meaning

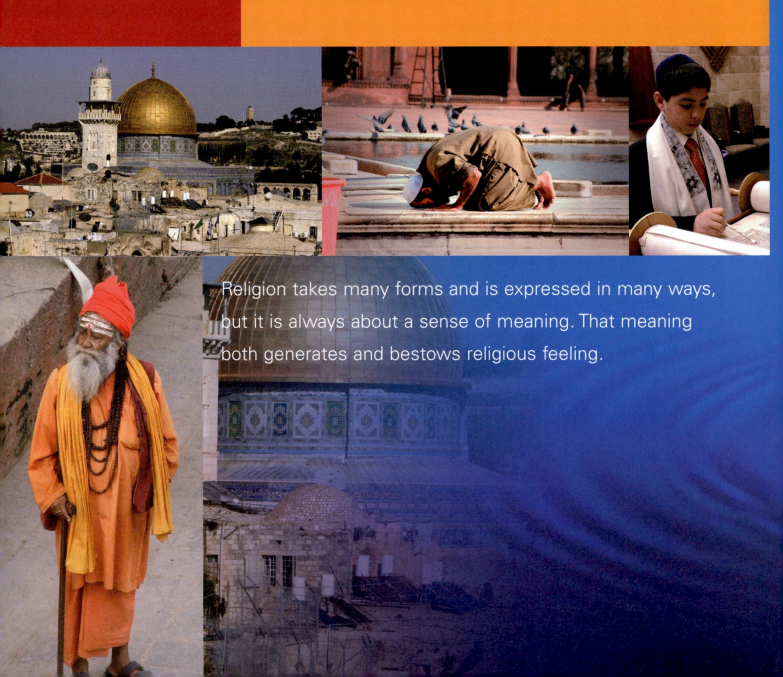

Religion takes many forms and is expressed in many ways, but it is always about a sense of meaning. That meaning both generates and bestows religious feeling.

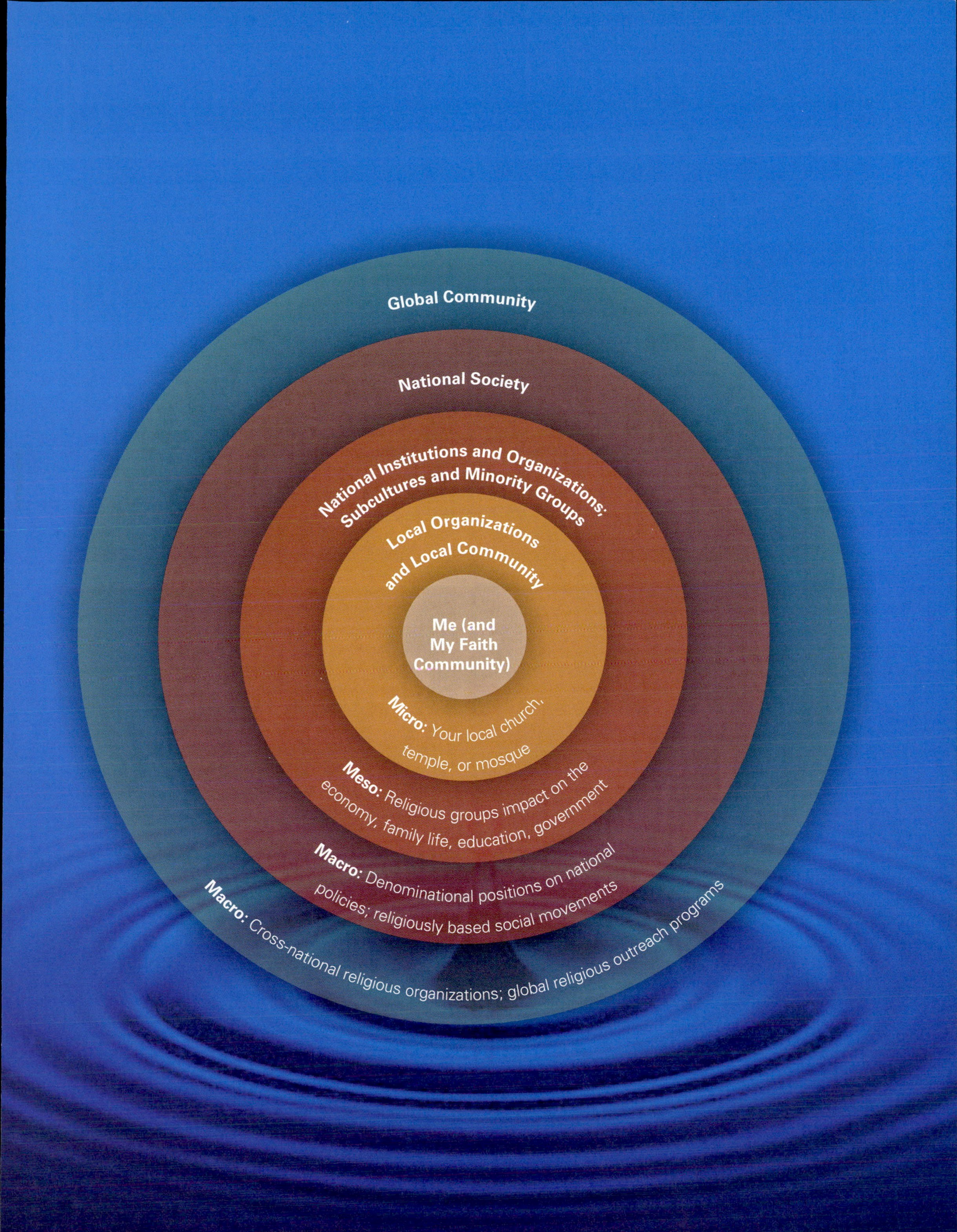

Global Community

National Society

National Institutions and Organizations;
Subcultures and Minority Groups

Local Organizations
and Local Community

Me (and
My Faith
Community)

Micro: Your local church,
temple, or mosque

Meso: Religious groups impact on the
economy, family life, education, government

Macro: Denominational positions on national
policies; religiously based social movements

Macro: Cross-national religious organizations; global religious outreach programs

Think About It	
Me (and My Inner Circle)	How did you become committed to a faith and a church, temple, or mosque, or not become so?
Local Community	How do religious congregations affect the local community?
National Institutions; Complex Organizations; Ethnic Groups	How does the institutionalization of a religion help it survive?
National Society	How do religions provide solidarity or conflict within your country?
Global Community	How do religions help solve world problems (war, poverty, hunger, disease, bigotry) or contribute to them?

Tuneq, knowledgeable Netsilik Eskimo hunter that he is, apologizes to the soul of the seal he has just killed. He shares the meat and blubber with his fellow hunters, and he makes sure that every part of the seal is used or consumed—skin, bones, eyes, tendons, brain, and muscles. If he fails to honor the seal by using every morsel or if he violates a rule of hunting etiquette, an invisible vapor will come from his body and sink through the ice, snow, and water. This vapor will collect in the hair of Nuliajuk, goddess of the sea. In revenge, she will call the sea mammals to her so the people living on the ice above will starve. Inuit religion provides rules that help enforce an essential ecological ethic among these arctic hunters to preserve the delicate natural balance.

Before going to bed, Nandi Nwankwo from Nigeria sets out a bowl of milk and some food for the ancestors who, he believes, are present outside the family's dwelling at night. Respected ancestors protect family members, but they are also a powerful and even frightening force in guiding social behavior. Children are told that they must behave or the ancestors will punish them.

Abu Salmaan, a Muslim father and shopkeeper in Syria, prays frequently in keeping with the commands of the holy book of his faith. Like his neighbors, when the call to prayer is heard, he comes to the village square, faces Mecca, and prostates himself, with his head to the ground, to honor God and to pray for peace. Doing this five times a day is a constant reminder of his ultimate loyalty to God, whom he calls Allah. As part of the larger Abrahamic religious tradition (which includes Judaism, Christianity, and Islam), he is monotheistic and accepts the Hebrew Bible and the authority of Jeremiah, Isaiah, Amos, and Jesus as prophets. He believes that God also revealed Truth through another voice—that of Muhammad. He is devoted, worshipping daily, cherishing his family as directed by his scriptures, giving generously to charities, and making business decisions based on the moral standards of a God-loving Muslim.

Trevor Weaver is a Presbyterian living in Louisville, Kentucky. He attends worship and prays to God in church and during emergencies, when he feels helpless. Trevor had undertaken theological studies at a church-related college, and he has a remarkably strong knowledge of the scriptures. When he makes daily decisions, he thinks about the ethical implications of his behavior as "a member of the larger family of God." He opposes prayer in schools because this would make some children feel ostracized, he values diversity and acceptance of other traditions, and he believes each person needs to "work out his own theology." He thinks of himself as a person of faith, but his evangelical neighbor thinks he is a fallen soul.

These are but a few examples from the world's many and varied religious systems. What they have in common is that each system provides directions for appropriate and expected behaviors and serves as a form of social control for individuals within that society. Whether ancestors, gods, one God, prophets, or elders are watching over us, the sanctions that encourage conformity are strong. Indeed, they are made *sacred*, a realm of existence different from mundane everyday life. Religion, according to Andrew M. Greeley (1989), the well-known Catholic priest and sociologist, pervades the lives of people of faith. It cannot be separated from the rest of the social world. Members of societies believe so strongly in their religions that conquests and wars throughout history have been based on the dissemination or defense of religious beliefs.

Sociologists are interested in these relationships—in the way social relationships and structures affect religion and in the consequences of religion for individuals and for society as a whole. In this chapter, we explore religion as a complex social phenomenon, one that is interrelated with other processes and institutions of society. We investigate what religion does for individuals, how individuals become religious, how religion and modern societies interact, and what religious policies have to say about homosexuality, abortion, and other social issues.

What Does Religion Do for Us?

We began this chapter by looking at examples of daily experiences in which religion and society have enormous power over people. What do people have to gain from religious practices, beliefs, and organizations? In short, they do so because religion meets certain very basic needs.

Human questions about the meaning of life, the finality of death, or whether injustice and cruelty will ever be ended cannot normally be answered by science or by everyday experience. Religion helps explain the meaning of life, death, suffering, injustice, and events beyond our control. As sociologist Émile Durkheim ([1915] 2002) pointed out, humans generally view such questions as belonging to a realm of existence different from the mundane or profane world of experience. He called this separate dimension the *sacred realm*. This sacred realm elicits feelings of awe, reverence, and even fear. It is viewed as being above normal inquiry and doubt. Religious guidelines, beliefs, and values dictate "rights and wrongs," provide answers to the big questions of life, and instill moral codes and ideas about the world in members of each society or subculture. For that reason, religions are extremely important in controlling everyday behavior (Durkheim [1915] 2002).

Thus, religion is more than a set of beliefs about the supernatural. It often *sacralizes* (makes sacred and unquestionable) the culture in which we live, the class or caste position to which we belong, the attitudes we hold toward other people, and the morals to which we adhere. Religion is a part of our lifestyle, our gender roles, and our place in society. We are often willing to defend it with our lives. Around the world, many different people believe quite as strongly as we do that they have found the Truth—the ultimate answers—in their religions. They, too, are willing to die for their faith, which they are convinced is "the only way."

Note the various wars between Hindus and Muslims in India, between Catholics and Protestants in Northern Ireland, or between the two Muslim sects of Sunni and Shi'ite in the Muslim country of Iraq. Although the root causes of these wars are political and economic, religious differences help polarize we-versus-they sentiments. Such conflicts are never exclusively about religion, but religion can convince each group that God is on their side. Religion is an integral part of most societies and is important in helping individuals define reality and determine what is worth living or dying for.

Thinking Sociologically

Consider your own religious tradition. Which of the purposes or functions of religion mentioned above does your religious faith address? If you are not part of a faith community or do not hold religious beliefs, are there other beliefs or groups that fulfill these functions for you?

Components of Religion

Religion normally involves at least three components: (1) a faith or worldview that provides a sense of meaning and purpose in life (which we will call the *meaning system*), (2) a set of interpersonal relationships and friendship networks (which we will call the *belonging system*), and (3) a stable pattern of roles, statuses, and organizational practices (which we will call the *structural system*; Roberts 2004).

Meaning System

The meaning system of a religion includes the ideas and symbols it uses to provide a sense of purpose in life and to help explain why suffering, injustice, and evil exist. It provides a big picture to explain events that would otherwise seem chaotic and irrational. For example, although the loss of a family member through death may be painful, many people find comfort and hope and a larger perspective on life in the idea of life after death. Most religious people find that a deep love of God gives purpose and deep satisfaction to life (discussed later in this chapter).

Because each culture has different problems to solve, the precise needs reflected in the meaning system vary. Hence, different societies have developed different ways of answering questions and meeting needs. In agricultural societies, the problems revolve around growing crops and securing the elements necessary for crops—water, sunlight, and good soil. Meaning systems often reflect these concerns. Among the Zuni of New Mexico and the Hopi of Arizona, water for crops is a critical concern. These Native American people typically grow corn in a climate that averages roughly 10 inches of rain per year, so it is not surprising that the central focus of the dances and the supernatural beings—*kachinas*—is to bring rain. In many societies, the

At this temple in Japan, people write their hopes and wishes on strips of paper, attaching them to ropes and trees as a form of prayer. When their life circumstances seem out of control, people will often appeal to a nonempirical or supernatural source for help, and this provides hope and some sense of meaningful action.

death rate is so high that high fertility has been necessary to perpetuate the group. Thus, fertility goddesses take on great significance. In other societies, strong armies and brave soldiers have been essential to preserve the group from invading forces; hence, gods or rituals of war have been popular. Over time, the meaning systems of religion have reflected the needs of the societies in which the religion is practiced.

Belonging System

Belonging systems are profoundly important in most religious groups. Many people remain members of religious groups not so much because they accept the meaning system of the group but because that is where their belonging system—their friendship and kinship network—is found. Their religious group is a type of extended family. In fact, church membership

Audio Link 12.1
Listen to stories about faith.

increases as people get older and move through the family life cycle of marriage, childbearing, and child rearing, though the increase is slowing in some denominations (Cline 2008; Religious Tolerance 2006; Sherkat and Ellison 1999). A prayer group may be the one area in their lives in which people can be truly open about their personal pain and feel safe to expose their vulnerabilities. Irrespective of the meaning system, a person's sense of identity may be very much tied up with being a Buddhist, a Christian, a Muslim, or a follower of some other religion.

The religious groups that have grown the fastest in recent years are those that have devised ways to strengthen the sense of belonging and to foster friendship networks within the group, including emphasis on endogamy—marrying within one's group. If a person is a member of a small group in which interpersonal ties grow strong—a church bridge club, a Quran study group, or even a working committee—he or she is likely to feel a stronger commitment to the entire organization. In short, the belonging system refers to the interpersonal networks and emotional ties that develop among adherents of a particular faith.

Structural System

A religion involves a group of people who share a common meaning system. However, if each person interprets the beliefs in his or her own way and if each attaches his or her own meanings to the symbols, the meaning system becomes so individualized that *sacralization* of common values can no longer occur. Therefore, some system of control and screening of new revelations must be developed. Religious leaders in designated statuses must have the authority to interpret the theology and define the essentials of the faith. The group also needs methods of designating leaders, of raising funds to support their programs, and of ensuring continuation of the group. To teach the next generation the meaning system, members need to develop a formal structure to determine the content and form of their educational materials, and then they must produce and distribute them. In short, if the religion is to survive past the death of a charismatic leader, it must undergo institutionalization.

Religious institutions embrace several interrelated components: (a) the meaning system, mostly operating at the micro level; (b) the belonging system, critical at the micro level but also part of various meso-level organizations; and (c) the structural system, which tends to have its major impact at the meso and macro levels. These may reinforce one another and work in harmony toward common goals, or there may be conflict between them. When change occurs, it usually occurs because of disruption in one of the systems.

Because religion is one institution in the larger society, it is interdependent and interrelated with the political, economic, family, education, health, and technology

Buddhist monks pray at Bayon Temple in Angkor Thom, Cambodia. Their religious system gives them a sense of meaning and purpose in life, but also provides social ties.

systems. Changes in any one of these areas can bring change to religion, and changes in religion can bring changes to other institutions of society. Consider the furor that is occurring in parts of the United States over the teaching of intelligent design as part of the science curriculum in public schools. The conflict is reverberating in congregations, schools, legislative chambers, courts, and scientific communities.

Although some people dislike the idea of organized religion, the fact remains that a group cannot survive in the modern world unless it undergoes *routinization of charisma*. That is, the religious organization must develop established roles, statuses, groups, and routine procedures for making decisions and obtaining resources (Weber 1947).

At the local level, too, a formal religious structure develops, with committees doing specific tasks, such as overseeing worship, maintaining the building, recruiting religious educators, and raising funds. These committees report to an administrative board that works closely with the clergy (the ordained ministers) and has much of the final responsibility for the life and continued existence of the congregation. The roles, statuses, and committees make up the structural system.

Furthermore, like any other formal organization in society, meso-level religious structures consist of individuals and committees doing specialized tasks. Contemporary Christian denominations in the United States, for example, may have national commissions on global outreach, evangelism, worship, world peace, social justice, and so forth. In addition, bishops, presbyters, or other leaders provide guidelines for the work of several hundred pastors who lead their own congregations. Religious organizations are, among other things, bureaucracies. The formal organization may be caught up in some of the dysfunctions that can plague any organization: goal displacement, the iron law of oligarchy, alienation, and other problems discussed in Chapter 5.

Just as any organization needs data on its effectiveness, religious organizations collect information to help inform policy. "The Applied Sociologist at Work" describes the work of a sociologist who does research within such a denominational structure.

The Applied Sociologist at Work— C. Kirk Hadaway

Research for Religious Organizations

By C. Kirk Hadaway

My interest in research on and for religious institutions began when I worked with my graduate school mentor on a grant studying the growth and decline of denominations. I explored demographic change and church growth, denominational switching, and the impact of new church development on the growth of established denominations.

I am a church research officer, a position that entails everything from mundane gathering of statistics to serious social research. Our office of six persons collects membership, attendance, and giving data from all United Church of Christ (UCC) churches and analyzes those data. We do surveys among our churches, pastors, staff, and lay leaders on a wide variety of topics (issues related to congregational health, leadership, use of denominational resources, beliefs and attitudes, and so forth). I also conduct research on the state of religion/churches in modern society and on social trends that might impact our churches. This research is written up in reports and published in books that give advice to our churches and pastors. I speak to clergy groups regularly on related topics. My clients get an interpretation of data based on broader, sociologically-grounded understanding of the religious trends.

I have studied church trends (patterns of growth and decline) using data from local congregations and studies of religious participation and religious marginality. Also, I have conducted large-scale surveys with pastors from several denominations as key informants. It is particularly gratifying to see theories confirmed with real data on real churches.

The least rewarding facets of my job are grunt work (providing routine information) and other aspects of life in a bureaucracy (forms to fill out, committee meetings, staff retreats, performance evaluations, and having one's work ignored due to other agendas).

The most rewarding aspect of my work is the ability to help church leaders see their situation from a different perspective and use that perspective and information to make a positive difference in their work.

Note: Dr. C. Kirk Hadaway received his PhD in sociology from the University of Massachusetts, Amherst. He has worked for various boards and agencies of the Southern Baptist Convention, has been director of research at the United Church of Christ, and is currently director of research for the Episcopal Church.

Thinking Sociologically

Think about the meaning, belonging, and structural systems of a religion with which you are familiar. Illustrate how these elements influence and are influenced by the larger social world, from individual to national and global systems.

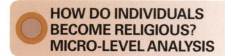
HOW DO INDIVIDUALS BECOME RELIGIOUS? MICRO-LEVEL ANALYSIS

Handbook Link 12.1
Read more about religion.

We are not born religious, although we may be born into a religious group. We learn our religious beliefs through socialization, just as we learn our language, customs, norms, and values. Our family usually determines the religious environment in which we grow up, whether it is an all-pervasive message or a one-day-a-week aspect of socialization. We start imitating religious practices such as prayer before we understand these practices intellectually. Then, as we encounter the unexplainable events of life, religion is there to provide meaning. Gradually, religion becomes an ingrained part of many people's lives.

It is unlikely that we will adopt a religious belief that falls outside the religions of our society. For instance, if

we are born in India, we will be raised in and around the Hindu, Muslim, or Sikh faiths. In most Arab countries, we will become Muslim; in South American countries, Catholic; and in many Southeast Asian countries, Buddhist. However, even if we had been born into the family next door, our religion and politics might be different. Indeed, although our religious affiliation may seem normal and typical to us, no religion has a majority of the people of this world as its adherents, and we may in fact be part of a rather small minority religious group when we think in terms of the global population. Table 12.1 shows this explicitly.

Table 12.1 **Religious Membership Around the Globe**		
Religion	Membership (in millions)	Percentage of World Population
Christian (Total)	2,199.8	33.3
Roman Catholic	1,121.5	17.0
Independents	433.1	6.5
Protestant	381.8	5.8
Orthodox	233.1	3.5
Anglican	82.6	1.2
Unaffiliated	19.5	1.8
Muslim	1,387.5	21.0
Hindu	875.7	13.2
Nonreligious	776.8	11.7
Ethnic/Tribal Religions	652	9.8
Universist (Chinese Folk Religion)	385.6	5.8
Buddhist	385.6	5.8
Atheist	153.4	2.3
New Religious Movements	106.5	1.6
Sikh	22.9	0.3
Jewish	15.0	0.2
Spiritist	13.5	0.2
Baha'i	7.7	0.1
Confucianism	6.4	0.1
Jain	5.3	0.1
Taoism	3.4	0.1
Shintoism	2.8	a
Zoroastrian	0.2	a

Source: Barrett, Johnson, and Crossing (2008). Reprinted with permission from *Encyclopedia Britannica Almanac 2008.* Copyright © 2008 Encyclopedia Britannica, Inc.

Note: Numbers add up to more than the 6 billion people in the world because many people identify themselves with more than one religious tradition. Thus, the percentages will also add up to more than 100%. Percentages are rounded.

a. Less than 0.05%.

Kwanzaa, which means "first fruits of the harvest" in Kiswahili, was initiated in 1966 by Dr. Maulana Karenga. It is an African American celebration of the traditional African values of family, community responsibility, and self-improvement. This family celebrates Kwanzaa, which runs from December 26 to January 1. Such rituals create in children a sense of sacredness about certain values and outlooks on life.

Learning the meaning system of a religious group is both a formal and an informal process. In some cultures, religious faith pervades everyday life. For the Amish, farming without machines or the use of electricity is part of their Christian teachings, which affect their total lifestyle. Formal teaching in most religions takes place primarily in the temple, church, or mosque. The formal teaching may take the form of Bar or Bat Mitzvah classes, Sunday school, or parochial school. Informal religious teaching occurs when we observe others "practicing what they preach."

One church or temple member may be committed to the meaning system, another to the belonging system through strong friendship networks, and a third to the structural system, making large financial donations to a congregation even though he rarely attends services. In most cases, however, commitment to one of these systems will reinforce commitment to the others. They usually go together (see Figure 12.1).

Most people do not belong to a religious group because they accept its belief system. Rather, they come to believe because they want to belong and are socialized to feel they are an integral part of the group (Greeley 1972). People generally accept the explanation of death, injustice, and suffering provided by the religious group. They feel comfortable sharing similar feelings and beliefs.

Research on people who switch religious affiliations or join new religious movements (NRMs) indicates that loyalty to a friendship network usually comes first, followed by commitment to the meaning and structural systems. In many cases, accepting a new meaning system is the final stage rather than the initial stage of change (Roberts 2004).

There is more fluidity in religious membership now than at any time of our history. Historically, most people

The Bat Mitzvah, shown here, is the initiation ceremony into the faith for Jewish girls.

An Amish family enjoys a trip to the beach. Their faith influences every aspect of their lives, including their beach attire.

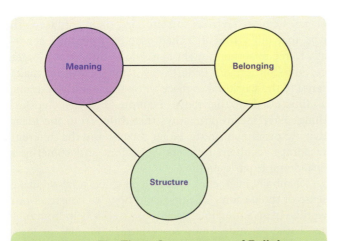

Figure 12.1 The Three Components of Religion

Note: Religious commitment can involve any one or more of these dimensions of religion.

remained part of the same religious group for a lifetime. A Pew Foundation study released in 2008 found that 44% of Americans will change their religious affiliation in their lifetime, just as a very high percentage will change their place of residence, their jobs, and even their spouses (Pew Forum 2008). In fact, the increase in interreligious marriages is a factor in the religious switching, as 27% of current marriages involve spouses with different religious affiliations (Pew Forum 2008). Change is becoming part of the norm in North America, particularly since World War II, and this is affecting religious affiliation as well. Still, the change is likely to be to a new branch of the same religion rather than to an entirely different religious tradition, and when it does involve a more major shift, it is usually because of the increased diversity of our society enabling us to know people from other faith traditions.

Because changing religious groups occurs most often through change of friendship networks, religious groups frequently try to control the boundaries and protect their members from outside influences. The Amish in the United States have done this by living in their own communities and attempting to limit schooling of their children by outside authorities. To help perpetuate religious beliefs and practices, most religious groups encourage endogamy, marrying within the group. For example, Orthodox Jews have food taboos and food preparation requirements that limit the likelihood that they will share a meal with "outsiders."

Religious groups also try to socialize members to make sacrifices of time, energy, and financial resources on behalf of their faith. If one has sacrificed and has devoted one's resources and energy for a cause, one is likely to feel a commitment to the organization—the structural system (Kanter 2005; Sherkat and Ellison 1999). Many young men in the Church of Jesus Christ of the Latter-Day Saints (Mormons) devote 2 years of their lives to being missionaries, and young women devote 1 to 1½ years. They must save money in advance to support themselves. This sacrifice of other opportunities and investment of time, energy, and resources in the church creates an intense commitment to the organization. Few of them later feel that they have wasted those years or that the investment was unwise.

Video Link 12.1
Watch video of religious worship.

The survival of a religious group depends in part on how committed its members are and whether they share freely of their financial and time resources. Most religious groups try, therefore, to socialize their members into commitment to the meaning system, the belonging system, and the structural system of their religion.

A Romanian Gypsy woman uses different tubs to wash upper- and lower-body clothing and men's and women's apparel separately so that they will not become spiritually defiled.

Thinking Sociologically

How did you or individuals you know become religious? Did you think about the process as it occurred?

Symbols and the Creation of Meaning: A Symbolic Interactionist Perspective

Dina is appalled as she looks around the Laundromat. The *gaje* (the term Gypsies use to refer to non-Gypsies) just do not seem to understand cleanliness. These middle-class North American neighbors of hers are very concerned about whether their clothes are *melalo*—dirty with dirt. In contrast, they pay no attention to whether they are *marime*—defiled or polluted in a spiritual sense. She watches in disgust as a woman not only places the clothing of men, women, and children in a single washing machine but also includes clothing from the upper and lower halves of the body together. No respectable Gypsy would allow such mixing, and if it did occur, the cloth could be used only as rags. The laws of spiritual purity make clear that the lower half of the body is defiled. Anything that comes in contact with the body below the waist or that touches the floor becomes *marime* and can never again be considered *wuzho*—truly "clean." Food that touches the floor becomes filthy and inedible.

Ideally, a Gypsy woman would have separate wash tubs for men's upper-body clothing, men's lower-body clothing, women's upper-body clothing, women's lower-body clothing, and children's clothing. Gypsies know too well that the spirit of Mamioro brings illness to homes that are *marime*. The lack of spiritual cleanliness of non-Gypsies causes Gypsies to minimize their contact with *gaje*, to avoid sitting on a chair used by a *gaje*, and generally to recoil at the thought of assimilation into the larger culture (Sutherland 1986; Sway 1988). How we make sense of the world takes place through meaning systems, as illustrated in the above example. For the Gypsies, things have meaning in ways that differ from the ideas that are prominent in the larger society, and the different meanings result in different behaviors and sometimes distancing from "outsiders."

Symbolic interaction theory focuses on how we make sense of the meaning of things and how we construct our worlds. In an ambiguous situation, we seek help from others: Is the situation funny, scary, bizarre, normal, or mysterious? Think about how you feel attracted to, or perhaps put off by, someone who wears a Cross or who has other religious symbols, such as a yarmulke, worn by Orthodox

The yarmulke (skullcap or kippah*) has been worn by Jewish men since roughly the 2nd century CE. It symbolizes respect for and fear of God and serves to remind the wearer of the need for humility: There is always some distance between himself and God. These caps are also a sign of belonging and commitment to the Jewish community.*

Jewish men to cover the crown of the head, or a head scarf worn by Muslim women. Symbols affect micro-level interaction, the way we feel about people and whether we are inclined to form a relationship. Note that a Muslim woman may wear a head scarf, and while she finds it a reassuring reminder of her family's long tradition, others may view it as a symbol of women's oppression or even find it a cause for hatred of the "other."

It is the meaning system that most interests symbolic interactionists—the worldview or conceptual framework by which people make sense of life and cope with suffering and injustice. Religious meaning systems are made up of three elements: myths, rituals, and symbols.

Myths are stories embodying ideas about the world. When sociologists of religion use the word *myth*, they are not implying that the story is untrue. A myth may relate historical incidents that actually occurred, it may involve fictional events, or it may communicate abstract ideas, such as reincarnation. Regardless of the literal truth or fiction of these stories, myths transmit values and a particular outlook on life. If a story, such as the exodus from Egypt by ancient Hebrew people, elicits some sense of sacredness, communicates certain attitudes and values, and helps make sense of life, then it is a myth. The Netsilik Eskimo myth of the sea goddess Nuliajuk (explained in the chapter opener) reinforces and makes sacred the value of conservation in an environment of scarce resources. It provides messages for appropriate behavior in that group. Thus, whether a myth is factual or not is irrelevant. Myths are always "true" in some deeper metaphorical sense.

Rituals are group activities in which myths are reinforced with music, dancing, kneeling, praying, chanting,

storytelling, and other symbolic acts. A number of religions, such as Islam, emphasize devotion to orthopraxy (conformity of behavior) more than orthodoxy (conformity to beliefs or doctrine; Preston 1988; Tipton 1990). Praying five times a day while facing Mecca, mandated for the Islamic faithful, is an example of orthopraxy.

Often, rituals involve an enactment of myths. In some Christian churches, the symbolic cleansing of the soul is enacted by actually immersing people in water during baptism. Likewise, Christians frequently reenact the last supper of Jesus (Communion or Eucharist) as they accept their role as modern disciples. Among the Navajo, rituals enacted by a medicine man may last as long as 5 days. An appropriate myth is told, and sand paintings, music, and dramatics lend power and unique reality to the myths.

The group environment of the ritual is important. Ethereal music, communal chants, and group actions such as kneeling or taking off one's shoes when entering the shrine or mosque create an aura of separation from the everyday world and a mood of awe so that the beliefs seem eternal and beyond question. They become sacralized. Rituals also make ample use of symbols, discussed in Chapter 4.

A **symbol** is anything that can stand for something else. Because religion deals with a transcendent realm, a realm

Muslims pray to God (whom they call Allah) five times a day, removing their shoes and prostrating themselves as they face Mecca. This is an important ritual, and it illustrates that orthopraxy is central for Muslims. Personal devotion, which is expressed in actions, is emphasized in Islam.

Removal of shoes before entering a mosque is an expression of respect for the sacred among Muslims. Hundreds of Iraqi Shiite Muslim pilgrims have arrived to pray at this mosque in northern Baghdad.

that cannot be experienced or proven with the five senses, sacred symbols are a central part of religion. They have a powerful emotional impact on the faithful and reinforce the sacredness of myths.

Sacred symbols have been compared to computer chips, which can store an enormous amount of information and deliver it with force and immediacy (Leach 1979). Seeing a cross can flood a Christian's consciousness with a whole series of images, events, and powerful emotions concerning Jesus and his disciples. Tasting the bitter herb during a Jewish Seder service may likewise elicit memories of the story of slavery in Egypt, recall the escape under the leadership of Moses, and send a moral message to the celebrant to work for freedom and justice in the world today. The mezuzah, a

plaque consecrating a house, fixed to the doorpost of a Jewish home, is a symbol reminding the occupants of their commitment to obey God's commandments and reaffirming God's commitment to them as a people. Because symbols are often heavily laden with emotion and can elicit strong feelings, they are used extensively in rituals to represent myths.

Myths, rituals, and symbols are usually interrelated and interdependent (see Figure 12.2). Together, they form the meaning system—a set of ideas about life or about the cosmos that seem uniquely realistic and compelling. They reinforce rules of appropriate behavior and even political and economic systems by making them sacred. They can also control social relationships between different groups. The Gypsy revulsion at the filthy *marime* practices of middle-class Americans, like the Kosher rules for food preparation among the Jews, create boundaries between "us" and "them" that nearly eliminate prospects of marriage or even of close friendships outside the religious community. Some scholars think that these rituals and symbolic meanings are the key reason why Gypsies and Jews have survived for millennia as distinct groups without being assimilated or absorbed into dominant cultures. The symbols and meanings created barriers that prevented the obliteration of their cultures.

When symbolic interactionists study religion, they tend to focus on how symbols influence people's perception of reality and on the role rituals and myths play in defining what is "really real" for people. Symbolic interactionists stress that humans are always trying to create, determine, and interpret the meaning of events. Clearly, no other institution focuses as explicitly on determining the meaning of life and its events as religion.

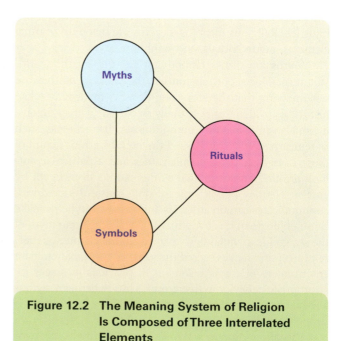

Figure 12.2   The Meaning System of Religion Is Composed of Three Interrelated Elements

Clan totems are part of the cultural and religious tradition of native peoples in northwest North America, from Oregon to Alaska, and totem poles are used to tell stories. This photo from St. John's United Methodist Church in Anchorage, Alaska, is interesting because it blends local cultural and religious symbols with a Christian symbol (the Cross) in a Christian sanctuary. This totem pole tells the Easter story.

Thinking Sociologically

In a tradition with which you are familiar, how do symbols and sacred stories reinforce a particular view of the world or a particular set of values and social norms?

Seeking Eternal Benefits: A Rational Choice Perspective

People with religious freedom make rational choices to belong to a religious group or change to another religion after weighing the costs (financial contributions, time involved) and benefits (eternal salvation, a belonging system, and a meaning system) of belonging (Roger and Stark

This advertisement ran in The Sundial, *the daily paper at California State University, Northridge (CSUN). The church is located only a few miles from the university and hoped to catch, with their student-friendly service (and their targeted marketing), the interest of CSUN students.*

2005; Warner 1993). Rational choice theory is based on an economic model of human behavior. The basic idea is that the process people use to make decisions is at work in religious choices: What are the benefits, and what are the costs? Do the benefits outweigh the costs? The benefits, of course, are nonmaterial when it comes to religious choices—a feeling that life has meaning, confidence in an afterlife, a sense of communion with God, and so forth. This approach views churchgoers as consumers who are out to meet their needs or obtain a "product." It depicts churches as entrepreneurial establishments, or "franchises," in a competitive market, with "entrepreneurs" (ministers) as leaders. Competition for members leads churches to "market" their religion to consumers. Converts, and religious people generally, are thus regarded as active and rational agents pursuing self-interests, and growing churches are those that meet "consumer demand" (Finke 1997; Finke and Stark 2005; Iannaccone 1994). Religious groups produce religious "commodities" (rituals, meaning systems, a sense of belonging, symbols, and so forth) to meet the "demands" of consumers (Sherkat and Ellison 1999).

Rational choice theorists believe that aggressive religious entrepreneurs who seek to produce religious products that appeal to a target audience will reap the benefits of a large congregation. Churches, temples, and mosques are competitive enterprises, and each must make investments of effort, time, and resources to attract and keep potential buyers. There are many religious entrepreneurs seeking to increase their flocks. The challenge is for the various groups to beat the competition by meeting the demand of the current marketplace (Finke and Stark 2005).

For instance, when the United States separated church from state so that most individuals were not automatically members of a state religion, organized religions had to offer a product that would sell to consumers (Moore 1995). Indeed, some scholars argue that where religion is an ascribed identity (adopted based on one's family of birth or the country's official religion), it is likely to be much less vigorous than in places where there is a competitive religious marketplace and religion is an achieved identity chosen freely from many options (Finke and Stark 2005; Iannaccone 1995; Sargeant 2000).

Rational choice theorists believe that when more religious groups compete for the hearts and minds of members, concern about spiritual matters is invigorated and commitment is heightened. Religious pluralism and spiritual diversity increase the rates of religious activity as each group seeks its market share and as more individual needs are met in the society (Finke and Stark 2005; Iannaccone 1995).

Not everyone agrees that religion is a competitive enterprise (Stark 2000). This strictly utilitarian economic analysis of religion seems counter to the way most religious people understand their own behavior. As one religious scholar put it,

It is one thing to describe a person's decision to join a church *as if* the person were trying to maximize his or her benefits; it is something different to claim that the person's *actual* thought in joining measured his or her potential gains against potential losses. (McGuire 2002:298–299)

Thinking Sociologically

Does the rational choice approach seem to you to make sense of religious behavior? Is religious behavior similar to self-interested economic behavior?

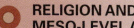

RELIGION AND MODERN LIFE: MESO-LEVEL ANALYSIS

The Yaqui youth was very ill. He had been bitten by a rattlesnake in the hot Arizona desert just outside his village. Although there was a medical clinic staffed by nurses and a visiting doctor, the family decided to use traditional Yaqui medicine, a blend of Native American rituals and what is referred to as *pagan Catholicism*. The medicine man broke eggs, mixed curative potions, and chanted incantations over the sick boy. These familiar rituals gave comfort to the family waiting anxiously for signs of the boy's recovery. After the boy had received the medicine man's treatment, he went to the clinic as well. He recovered, and the people believed that what led to the recovery was adherence to their traditional method of healing. The interaction of traditional religious practices and modern health care institutions illustrates these interconnections at the meso level.

In this section, we explore how religion as an institution interacts with other institutions and what kinds of organizational forms religion takes as it interacts with the larger social environment.

Religion and Other Social Institutions

In traditional societies, religion is not separated from other social institutions, as the Yaqui's religious practice was separate from the clinic, but is an integral part of people's social world. In complex societies, on the other hand, religion denotes a distinctive group or organization. The dominant religion(s) in any complex society generally supports the political system and ideology of the dominant group. It is closely related to the economic system, is linked to the education system, and legitimates the family system through sacred rites of passage for marriage, birth, and death. Even the health system, as shown in the Yaqui example, is closely

Yaqui dancers, who blend Christian and indigenous beliefs, appeal to the supernatural for healing.

linked to religious beliefs about the healing process, disease, and death.

Religion not only supports other institutions but may also experience support or pressure from these other institutions. The Catholic Church has faced increasing criticism from international organizations, political movements, governments, religious groups, and educational institutions for its ban on birth control. Due to rapid population growth, especially in poor Catholic nations, many interested parties are putting pressure on the Catholic Church to ease its strict birth control ban in these countries. The Church cannot ignore these pressures, for they will undermine its legitimacy if they are not addressed or countered. Even if the Church does not change, it must expend considerable effort to defend its position in order to keep from losing credibility in the eyes of members and nonmembers alike. Some Catholic clergy and a number of lay members have defected over the positions of the Church. Let us consider the relationship between religion and three other social institutions: family, politics, and economics.

Audio Link 12.2
Listen to a story about the Catholic Church and condom use.

Iran's supreme leader, Ayatollah Ali Khamenei, speaks to ethnic Arabs during a visit to Dehlavieh in the southern oil province of Khuzestan. Religious leaders in Iran have advocated theocracy in that country—a government operated on the principles of the Quran.

Religion and Family

Everyone was dressed in colorful finery to welcome the baby into the religious community. The naming ceremony in this Nigerian village takes place when the baby reaches 6 weeks and is considered a viable human being. After the ceremony, the bonds of religious community are solidified with food, music, and dancing.

Our parents provide our first contact with religion. They may say prayers, attend worship services, and talk about proper behavior as defined by their religious group. Religious congregations make marriages sacred through ceremonies. Mother's Day, Father's Day, and Grandparents' Day are recognized by many religions and societies, thereby honoring and legitimating parenting. Many of the sacred ceremonies in religion are family affairs: births, christenings or naming of new members, marriages, and funerals. Jews, Muslims, and Latter-Day Saints (Mormons) are especially known for their many ceremonies and gatherings designed specifically for family units, and their moral codes place a high value on family loyalty and responsibility.

Religiosity, a person's degree of religious involvement, is positively associated with moral beliefs and behavior in youth and influences interaction with children and support of spouses in marriages. Some religious groups, such as conservative Protestants and fundamentalist groups of other religions, are involved in child rearing, producing parenting manuals to guide families. Some of these manuals have created controversy because of their emphasis on hierarchical and authority-centered parenting models (Grille 2005). Tensions can arise between family and religion over social control. Among the

Amish, if the bishop orders a member of the Church to be shunned, the family must comply and must refuse to speak to or associate with that person. If the family does not comply, it will be ostracized by the other members of the community. This sometimes leads to intense tension as the Church tries to direct communication patterns and interactions within a family (Clarke 2007; Hostetler 1993).

The New Right and other conservative organizations sometimes argue that if society could reinstate the family and the religious values of the past, today's societal problems would be reduced. They believe that if parents would spend more time instilling proper values in their children, things would be better. However, working parents today often spend more time with their children than parents did in past times. Stereotypes of the families and the religious values of the "good old days" come from a small segment of the total population: those upper-middle-class families in which only one parent had to work (Coontz 1997, 2005). Today, many of the problems and pressures facing families occur at different levels of analysis and are out of the control of the family or the local religious group. However, religiously affiliated organizations and social movements may also attempt to transform or strengthen other institutions. The conservative Christian organization, Focus on the Family, which has a syndicated newspaper column, radio programs, books, DVDs, and a monthly magazine produced by its founder James Dobson, is one example of an effort to strengthen families by restoring the traditional model of family life. Although religion cannot solve all family problems, most religions encourage a stable family life.

Religion and Politics: Theocracies and Civil Religion

Jan, a Swede, belongs to a state religion: Lutheranism. He was raised a Lutheran and does not really think about the possibility of other religious beliefs, although there is a growing Pentecostal movement in Sweden. The Nwankwo family, mentioned in the chapter opening, practices an ancient tribal religion, also with no thought that another religious belief might have something better to offer. Most of us are raised in a particular belief system from childhood and adhere to that religion because it is part of the custom and tradition most familiar to us. We seldom question our "choice."

In a pure **theocracy**, or rule by God, religious leaders rule society in accordance with God's presumed wishes. Iran is one example where religion clearly has a privileged position. In other countries, religion is used as a tool of the state to manipulate the citizenry and to maintain social control. A state religion, on the other hand, has some autonomy but receives support from tax money. Sweden, Britain, and Italy are examples. Some countries, such as the former Soviet Union, outlawed religion altogether so that nothing competed with loyalty to the nation. The continuum in Figure 12.3 shows the possible relationships between church and state.

Countries with diverse religious groups experience multiple pressures on their political systems: religious voting blocs, conflicts over definitions of public morality, and lobbying efforts for policies that have moral implications—abortion, euthanasia, rights for homosexuals, care of the poor, war and peace, and so forth. Sometimes, religious

Journal Article Link 12.1
Read about "civil religion."

groups form the basis for political parties. Even in the United States, which professes separation between church and state matters, religious groups influence policies such as prayer in school, selection of textbooks and reading matter, and abortion. In some countries, religious groups strongly oppose the government and seek to undermine the authority and power of political leaders. In Nazi Germany, some church leaders formulated the Barmen Declaration in opposition to Hitler. Many Christian groups in South Africa opposed apartheid. In some parts of Latin America, church leaders work for human rights and more equitable distribution of land and resources. Although religion often reinforces the power of the state, it may also be a source of conflict and tension on issues regarding morality, justice, and legitimate authority. Indeed, depending on the organizational structures, religion can provide a source of authority that offers a real challenge to the power of the state when that government has become oppressive, as shown in the next "Sociology Around the World."

In simple homogeneous societies, religion serves as a kind of glue, sacralizing the current social system by offering it supernatural legitimacy. In complex and heterogeneous societies, on the other hand, no single religion can provide the core values of the culture. In such circumstances, an alternative form of religion called **civil religion** frequently evolves. Civil religion is based on a set of beliefs, symbols, and rituals that pervade many aspects of secular life and institutions. It involves a shared public faith in the nation and what that nation stands for. Although civil religion lacks the structural system of organized religion, it is often supported by various types of patriotic groups. These small voluntary associations develop intense belonging systems, and civil religion also tends to strengthen the sense of belonging of all citizens as members of that society (Bellah 1992; Roberts 2004).

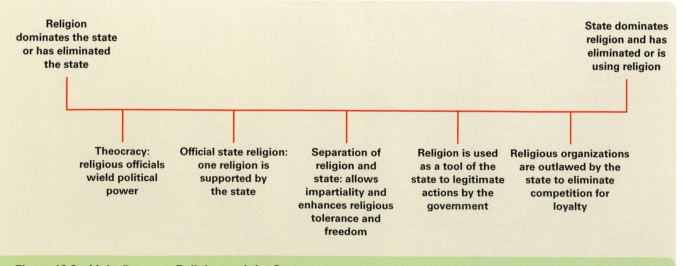

Figure 12.3   Links Between Religion and the State

Sociology Around the World

Transnational Religion: The Catholic Church and Political Systems

The Roman Catholic Church was one of the first complex organizations to be truly transnational, external to any one nation and including representation from many countries. Many religious organizations are contained within a single nation. This type of religious association is not linked to congregations or a denomination in other countries (Roberts 2004).

The Catholic Church is an international body that must be sympathetic to the circumstances of people in many nations, for its membership and its organizational reach span the globe. It cannot align itself with the economic and political interests of one nation or set of nations without risking the alienation of tens of millions of members in another part of the world.

Multinational religious organizations such as the Catholic Church can have a real impact on the social and economic policies within a nation, sometimes protecting the welfare of the people against a tyrannical state. In Poland during the 1970s and 1980s, the citizenry often felt colonized by a foreign power—the Soviet Union. The communist government in Poland was extremely unpopular, and the people had no real way to make the government more responsive to their needs. In 1983, only 3% of Poles who were surveyed felt that the government-dominant political hierarchy represented the interests of the Polish people. In contrast, 60% identified the Catholic Church and the Pope as protecting Polish interests (Tamney 1992).

The Catholic Church became a major power broker in negotiations between unions and the government in Poland (Tamney 1992). Catholic bishops sometimes took on a role akin to union leaders and, in so doing, became major players in the political future of the country. Because those bishops were ultimately responsible to the Pope and had a source of support external to the nation, they experienced a good deal of independence from the communist party that was in power. Clergy supported by a church financed with tax dollars would not have had the same freedom to challenge the government. The global nature of the Catholic Church influenced the role bishops could play in the Polish situation.

Transnationalism can influence the power of religious officials in our complex global environment. It provides an external source of authority that may be seen by citizens as superseding the political authority. In many single-nation religious denominations, the primary function of churches is to support the political power of the particular state or affirm an ethnic or national identity (Turner 1991b). Poland is an especially intriguing case in that a single religion tended to be identified with national pride and culture but that religion was global in its power base. That combination provided an exceptionally strong base for challenging governmental policies that were not in the interests of the citizens (Tamney 1992).

Being a religion that crosses national boundaries can also be a source of suspicion in some circumstances. Roman Catholics were traditionally suspected of lacking national loyalty in the United States. They were derisively called "papists" in the first half of the 20th century. Likewise, Jews have often been accused of maintaining dangerous, subversive ties because of their international networks with others who share their faith. The fact that a religion is more inclusive than just national boundaries can have benefits as well as risks for individuals and the state. This is true of any religious tradition.

Rituals of civil religion include making the pledge of allegiance, saluting the flag, and singing the national anthem. For example, American civil religion is not explicitly Christian, for it must appeal to those who are non-Christian as well (Bellah 1970), but it involves reference to God in many areas of civilian life and a legitimation of the political system. It attempts to give the nation and the government supernatural blessing and authority. It also calls the nation to a higher standard of justice and may be used by change agents such as Martin Luther King Jr. to make social change more acceptable and compelling.

Civil religion blends reverence for the nation with more traditional symbols of faith. Pictured is the chapel at Punchbowl, the Pacific cemetery for U.S. military personnel, located in Hawaii. Note that two U.S. flags are inside the altar area and are more prominent than two of the three religious symbols that also adorn the chancel: the Christian Cross, the Jewish Star of David, and the Buddhist wheel of Dharma.

In Ireland, part of the intense conflict between Protestants and Catholics is over civil religion. Protestants and Catholics not only come from different economic strata and different ethnic backgrounds but also have different visions for the future of the country and different ideas about what gives the country its special place in history. Although civil religion is supposed to unite a country, in Ireland and other divided countries, civil religion can itself be a point of intense conflict (Bellah and Greenspahn 1987; McGuire 2002).

Thinking Sociologically

How does civil religion manifest itself in your country? Give specific examples.

Religion and the Economy: The Protestant Ethic and Capitalism

Why do most of us study hard, work hard, and strive to get ahead? Why are we sacrificing time and money now—taking this and other college courses—when we might spend that money on an impressive new car? Our answers probably have something to do with our moral attitudes about work, about those who lack ambition, and about the proper way to live. Max Weber ([1904–1905] 1958) saw a relationship between the economic system, particularly capitalism, and ideas about work and sacrifice. He gathered information by studying many documents, including the diaries of Calvinists (a branch of Protestantism), sermons and religious teachings, and other historical papers. The following is his argument in a nutshell.

Noting that the areas of Europe where the Calvinists had strong followings were the same areas where capitalism grew the fastest, Weber ([1904–1905] 1958) argued that four elements in the Calvinist Protestant faith created the moral and value system necessary for the growth of capitalism: predestination, a calling, self-denial, and individualism.

1. *Predestination* meant that one's destiny was predetermined. Nothing anyone could do would change what was to happen. Because God was presumed to be perfect, he was not influenced by human deeds or prayer. Those people who were chosen by God were referred to as the *elect* and were assumed to be a small group. Therefore, people looked for signs of their status—salvation or damnation. High social status was sometimes viewed as a sign of being among the elect, so motivation was high to succeed in *this* life.

2. The *calling* referred to the concept of doing God's work. Each person was put on Earth to serve God, and each had a task to do in God's service. One could be called by God to any occupation, so the key was to work very hard and with the right attitude. Because work was a way to serve God, laziness or lack of ambition came to be viewed as a sin. These ideas helped create a society in which people's self-worth and their evaluation of others were tied to a work ethic. The Protestants became workaholics.

3. *Self-denial* involved living a simple life. If one had a good deal of money, one did not spend it on a lavish home, expensive clothing, or various forms of

entertainment. Such consumption would be offensive to God. Therefore, if people worked hard and began to accumulate resources, they simply saved them or invested them in a business. This self-denial was tied to an idea that we now call *delayed gratification*, postponing the satisfaction of one's present wants and desires in exchange for a future reward. The reward they sought was in the afterlife. Because Calvinists believed in predestination, they did not expect to earn salvation, but they believed that they could demonstrate to themselves and others that they were among the elect.

4. *Individualism* meant that each individual faced his or her destiny alone before God. Previous Christian theology had emphasized group salvation, the idea that an entire community would be saved or damned together. The stark individualism of Calvinistic theology stressed that each individual was on his or her own before God. Likewise, in the economic system that was emerging, individuals were on their own. The person who thrived was an individualist who planned wisely and charted his or her own course. Religious individualism and economic individualism reinforced one another.

The Protestant ethic that resulted from these elements stressed hard work, simple living, and rational decision making by daring individualists. Businesspeople and laborers spent long hours working at their calling, and the profits were reinvested for new equipment or expansion of the company. Individualism allowed people to pursue their own course of action and not to feel guilty for doing so. This combination was ideal for the growth of capitalism. Religion led to major changes in cultural values, which, in turn, transformed the economic system. Weber ([1904–1905] 1958) saw both the religious and the economic systems as dynamic, interrelated, and ever-changing.

Gradually, the capitalistic system, stimulated by the Protestant ethic, spread to other countries and to other religious groups. Many of the attitudes about work and delayed gratification no longer have supernatural focus, but they are part of the larger cultural value system nonetheless. They influence our feelings about people who are not industrious and our ideas about why some people are poor. In fact, some religious sects see individuals as responsible for their own fate, believing that the poor and jobless got themselves into their circumstances and should solve their own problems rather than depend on government aid (Davis and Robinson 1999).

Weber recognized that other factors also had to be present for capitalism to arise, but he believed that the particular set of moral values and attitudes that Calvinism instilled in the people was critical. Whereas Marx argued that religion kept workers in their places and allowed the capitalists to exploit the system and maintain their elite positions, Weber focused on the change brought about in the economic system as a result of religious beliefs and values.

Religion interacts with the economy in other ways as well. For one thing, religion is big business. In the United States, 35.5% of the total estimated charitable contributions go to religious organizations, and members of congregations donate an average of $895 per year to religious organizations, with contributions to all religious groups in the United States just under $90 billion by 2005 (Center on Philanthropy 2009). In most countries, religions (a) employ clergy and other people who serve the church, (b) own land and property, and (c) generate millions through collections and fund-raising. Some of this money goes to the upkeep of the building, some to charitable activities, and some to investments. Religious ventures continue to expand into many areas, from shopping centers to homes and apartment buildings for the elderly. In the United States, televangelism and megachurches (congregations with upward of 10,000 members) are multimillion-dollar industries with sophisticated marketing strategies. The televangelism industry, for example, involves the sale of books and tapes; donations of hundreds of millions of dollars by listeners; the establishment of colleges, hospitals, and amusement parks; and the provision of jobs in a wide variety of technical electronic areas. These megachurches become corporations and use information from the corporate world to ensure success.

There are other ways in which religion and economic institutions are linked. When large religious organizations take a moral stand on poverty, they may influence the economy. Moreover, when the economy is especially bad, certain kinds of religious movements are more likely to be spawned: Millenarian movements, which expect the end of the world soon, almost always occur when economic prospects are bleak (Roberts 2004).

Although religion today may not have the power to transform the economy or other social institutions, each institution does affect others. Society also shapes the kind of organization and the relationship to other institutions that the religious group adopts, as discussed in the next section.

Thinking Sociologically

Religion is influenced not only by other institutions in society but also by the media. What messages from the media (movies, TV, music) reflect the state of religion in society?

In the high-tech South Barrington, Illinois, Willow Creek Community Church, images of the pastor can be seen projected on several televisions during a worship service. Megachurches, which sometimes draw 20,000 to 30,000 worshippers on a weekend, offer high-entertainment worship and a range of other services. These churches are run—and marketed—like a business.

Types of Religious Associations

From denominations to sects to NRMs, religious organizations take many forms. The following discussion explores *ideal types*—that is, models that summarize the main characteristics of religious organizations. Any specific religious group may not match all the characteristics exactly. Furthermore, these organizational patterns are particularly relevant to understanding the evolution of Western religious traditions, especially Christianity. The one major world religion that displays a very different pattern is Islam, as discussed in the next "Sociology in Our Social World."

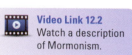

Video Link 12.2
Watch a description of Mormonism.

The Ecclesia

Official state religions are called **ecclesia**, referring to religious groups that claim as members everybody within the

boundaries of a particular society (Roberts 2004). Ecclesia include all members of a society. They try to monopolize religious life in that society, have a close relationship with the power structure, have a formal structure with officially designated full-time clergy, and have membership based on birth into the society.

Many countries have official state religions. Norway and Sweden are Lutheran. Spain, France, Italy, and many Latin American countries are Roman Catholic. Greece is Greek Orthodox. Iran, Egypt, and other Middle Eastern countries are Islamic. England is Anglican. India is predominantly Hindu, although Muslims share power. Because ecclesia represent the interests of the state and those in power, disfranchised groups often seek other religious outlets. In the early 20th century in Britain, 80% of the Welsh people (Wales is the westernmost of the British Isles) affiliated with nonconformist Christianity, not with the Church of England, of which the queen is officially the head. They explicitly rejected the meshing

Sociology in Our Social World

Islam, Mosques, and Organizational Structure

Most mosques in the United States are relatively new, with 87% having been founded since 1970 and 62% since 1980. At the turn of the century, there were 1,209 mosques in the United States (Bagby 2003). Christian congregations tend to be somewhat autonomous entities: supported by members but linked organizationally to a denomination. According to the Islamic scholar Ihsan Bagby (2003:115), "Most of the world's mosques are simply a place to pray. . . . A Muslim cannot be a member of a particular mosque" because mosques belong to God, not to the people. The role of the imam—the minister—is simply to lead prayers five times a day and to run the services on the Sabbath, including delivery of a sermon. Unlike many Christian and Jewish leaders in the United States, the imam does not run an organization and does not need formal training at a seminary. Mosques were historically government supported in other countries, so they had to make major changes in how they operate when they opened in North America. Because they could not depend on government funding, Islamic mosques needed to adapt to the congregational model: members who were loyal to a particular mosque and would support it. They also began to put more emphasis on religious education (which had been managed largely by extended families in the "old country"), religious holidays celebrated at the mosque rather than with families and dinners at a fellowship hall, and life cycle celebrations (births and marriages). This is a major change in the role of the mosque and the imam for many Muslims.

Bagby reports that there are two main categories of mosques: (1) those attended primarily by African Americans and (2) those attended primarily by immigrants. African American mosques represent only 27% of the total, and they are in some important ways different in organizational structure from those attended by immigrants (28% of the remaining American Muslims being from South Asia, 15% being Arab, and 30% having a mixed background). So even the makeup of mosques is unlike anything most Americans might expect. Only 28% of American mosques depend on an imam as the final authority, whereas the majority are led by an executive committee or board of directors (called the *majlis*). More important, 93% of African American mosques are led by an imam, compared with only 38% of immigrant-attended mosques.

About 33% of all mosques in the United States have a paid, full-time imam, and 16% of those imams need to hold a second job. In comparison, 89% of other congregations (Christian and Jewish) have paid ministers. Only 13% of imams have a master's degree in theology, which is the standard expected for most mainstream Christian and Jewish clergy. So despite having exceptionally high levels of adherents in management and the professions, with exceptionally high incomes, and having 58% of adherents with college degrees, Islamic mosques are less bureaucratized, with less emphasis on professional credentials, membership roles, or denominational connections. It is likely that mosques will begin to assimilate to the religious organizational pattern of the larger society, but at this point, it is important to recognize that the discussion of "denominations" and "sects" is not apt for Islam in America. Islam is less rationalized, bureaucratized, and professionalized, with more stress on family and personal connections.

of religious and national loyalty, feeling that religious bodies should have a free and independent voice that is not compromised by politics or patriotism (Davies 1993; Morgan 1981).

In societies that do not have official religions, such as the United States, religion takes several forms: denominations, sects, and NRMs (or cults).

Denominations

In the United States, Congregationalist, Episcopalian, Presbyterian, Lutheran, Baptist, Methodist, and other mainline Christian religious groups are denominations. They all have certain characteristics in common. The denomination is seen as a legitimate form of religious expression but does not have religious dominance or monopoly in the society. Each religious group appeals to a particular segment of the population, often related to class, race, ethnicity, and sometimes regional area. They coexist with and usually are accepting of other denominations (Christiano, Swatos, and Kivisto 2002; Roberts 2004). The largest denominations in the United States are indicated on Map 12.1.

Most denominations have formal bureaucracies with hierarchical positions, specialization of tasks, and official creeds. This hierarchy extends even to the international level in some denominations, such as the Anglicans. The leadership is trained, and there is often a professional church staff. Worship typically involves formal, ritualized, and prescribed ceremonies. Note that the Roman Catholic Church is an ecclesia in Spain because it is the official state religion, but it is a denomination in the United States and Canada, where it is one of many religious groups and is not affiliated with or supported by the state.

Although denominations vary somewhat in the values and beliefs they advocate, they usually support the basic values and social arrangements of the larger society. They may work for moderate changes, but they seldom call for radical or revolutionary restructuring of the society. Thus, the membership tends to be made up of those people who have benefited from the existing social arrangements and who hold positions of power and influence. Most of these denominations are large and financially secure, in part because they attract a middle- and upper-class clientele. This comfortable accommodation between denominations and the existing social order is precisely what made Marx feel that religion was used to keep the social structure from changing.

The key characteristic of a denomination is its accommodation to the state, and thus, disfranchised members of society are more likely to be attracted to sects or cults.

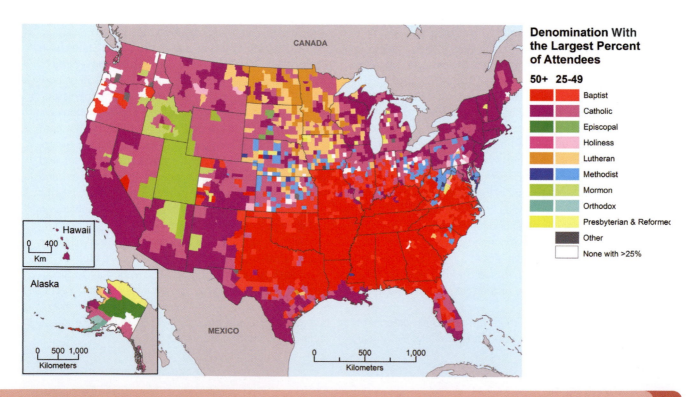

Map 12.1 Denominational Distribution in the United States

Source: Religious Congregations and Membership Study (2000).

Map by Anna Versluis.

Note: This map shows the largest religious denomination by attendance for each county. In some cases, the largest denomination has less than a majority of the county's religious adherents. The map thus underrepresents the diversity in any area, but it does demonstrate regional variation. Only one county—in Virginia—has a majority of adherents that are Muslim; in all other counties with a majority, a Christian denomination is the largest religion.

Sects

John Wesley (1703–1791) began a Church of England renewal movement, now known as the Methodist Church. He wanted to call people back to the basics of the faith. His evangelical revival called followers to lead Christian lives through a method of strict discipline—prayer, worship, study, and mutual support groups. Hence, the name *Methodists* arose—a term that was originally derogatory. It referred to people whose worship was too "enthusiastic" to be decent and orderly—the standard of worship among Anglicans and Presbyterians of the day. Because church authorities disapproved of Wesley's new methods, he was marginalized and refused an Anglican church to lead. He took his movement to the streets. As a person of deep commitment and a skilled organizer, Wesley formed associations in Great Britain and North America. Today, the Methodists have become one of the largest Christian bodies and a mainstream denomination in the United States.

Sects, such as the early Methodists, form in protest against their parent religion. Sometimes they are begun by dissatisfied members who form splinter groups and break away from denominations. Those splitting off do so because of theological concerns or because they feel the church has surrendered to secular authority (Roberts 2004; Stark and Bainbridge 1985). They believe that the true religious doctrines are being abandoned, people are becoming contaminated by worldly ways, and the group must save itself by returning to the true religion. Often, the break has other underlying social dimensions. Sect members may feel the denomination has come to embrace the existing power structure too closely. Part of the membership feels that the unjust social arrangements are condemned by God and should be condemned by the faithful. In other instances, the splinter group is simply alienated by the bureaucracy and hierarchical structure of the parent group (Niebuhr 1929).

There are more than 400 sects in the United States. Tennessee has the highest sect membership per population. The region with the least sectarianism is New England. By comparison, Africa has six times as many sects as the United States (Stark and Bainbridge 1985).

Sects are characterized by their separation from other religious and even social groups (see Table 12.2). There is exclusive commitment to one body of teaching and a claim of monopoly over religious Truth. Sects typically demand total allegiance to the organization (Wilson 1982). An example of an extreme isolationist sect—a type of counterculture—is the Old Believers of the Russian Orthodox Church. In the mid-1600s, the Old Believers were so adamant about not adhering to the reforms of the tsar and the head of the Russian Orthodox Church that when troops approached, they barricaded themselves inside their churches and set themselves on fire rather than accommodate to change (Crummey 1970; Pentikänen 1999; Robson 1995).

Table 12.2 **Distinguishing Sects From Denominations or Ecclesia**
The following are characteristics that distinguish a sect from a denomination or an ecclesia: 1. Exclusive membership policy: Only the saved or those who meet high standards of membership are admitted.   2. Conflict with the host society: The outside secular society is usually viewed as depraved or evil, values of the larger society are rejected, and there is often deep suspicion of the state.   3. Lack of a complex organizational structure: Little or no national organization exists, clergy are often not educated in seminaries and have no formal ordination beyond the local congregation, and there may not be a larger affiliated institution that produces religious education materials.

Source: Yinger (1970).

Tofuni members of the sect of Heavenly Christians kneel in worship during a ceremony. The sect was founded in 1947, in Benin, by Samuel Oshofa and has more than 10 million followers throughout the countries bordering the Gulf of Guinea, Africa.

Members of Christian sects in North America are often socially separated from those of higher social classes. As Liston Pope ([1942] 1965) stated, sectarians "substitute religious status for social status." For those who are less well off, a sect gives the feeling that members are among God's chosen, even if they do not have much social prestige in this world. Because most people who join sects feel deprived, there is a high degree of tension between the values of members and those of the larger society (Roberts 2004; Stark 1985).

There are now a number of Old Believer communities in the Kenai Peninsula of Alaska, such as this Church of St. Nicholas. Some of these Old Believer sects are so isolationist that they are accessible almost entirely by horse or by foot, and they have large "Keep Out" signs as one approaches the community. Commitment to the beliefs of the in-group is intense in this Russian Orthodox sect.

As sects grow in membership, coordination becomes necessary, leadership succession occurs, a hierarchy develops, and members become less alienated as social class positions change. Any of these factors can be the catalyst to move the sect toward becoming a denomination. The process of institutionalization occurs and helps in survival, but it is fraught with difficulties as the intimacy of the small group is overwhelmed by the impersonality of the emerging large organization.

Sects are often formed because groups split from denominations or individuals feel deprived, but over time, most sects become denominations. Few contemporary groups are pure sect or pure denomination. Instead, they are on a continuum between the two and may be moving toward sectarianism or toward denominationalization.

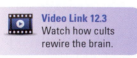
Video Link 12.3
Watch how cults rewire the brain.

New Religious Movements (NRMs) or Cults

NRMs, like sects, are protest or splinter groups. However, unlike sects, if NRMs survive for several generations, become established, and gain some legitimacy, they become new religions rather than new denominations of the existing faith. *Cult* was once the common term for this kind of movement, but the media and the public have so completely misused the word that its meaning has become unclear and often negative. The term *cult*, as sociologists have historically used it, is simply descriptive, not evaluative. Most sociologists of religion now prefer to use the term *NRM* to describe these religious forms (Christiano et al. 2002).

NRMs are founded on a new revelation (or insight) or on a radical reinterpretation of an old teaching. They are usually out of the mainstream religious system, at least in their early days. Christianity, Buddhism, and Islam all began as NRMs or cults. Either Jesus started a new cult, or else we must conclude that Christianity is a denomination of Judaism—an idea that neither Christians nor Jews would likely accept. The estimated number of NRMs in North America at the turn of the century was between 1,500 and 2,000. There could be 10,000 more NRMs in Africa and an undetermined but large number in Asia (Hadden 2006; Religious Worlds 2007).

An NRM is often started by a charismatic leader, someone who claims to have received a new insight, often directly from God. For example, Reverend Sun Myung Moon founded an NRM called the Unification Church, the members of which are often referred to as *Moonies*. Some sensational NRMs have ended in tragedy: Reverend Jim Jones led his devoted followers to a retreat in Guyana, South America, and ultimately to their suicides in the belief that heaven was awaiting them (Lacayo 1993; Wright 1995). A group suicide also occurred in 1997 in California by a band called Heaven's Gate, which thought supernatural beings were coming to take them away in a flying saucer (Wessinger 2000).

Most new religious groups are not dangerous to members. Furthermore, most religious groups that are now accepted and established were stigmatized as weird or evil when they started. Early Christians were characterized by Romans as dangerous cannibals, and in the early decades of the 20th century in the United States, Roman Catholics were depicted in the media as dangerous, immoral, and anti-American (Bromley and Shupe 1981). When we encounter media reports about NRMs, we should listen to and read these with a good dose of skepticism and recognize that not all cults are like the sensational ones.

Many NRMs are short-lived, lasting only as long as the charismatic leader does. The Jim Jones movement died with him and the cyanide poisoning of its members. Only those groups that institutionalize and prepare for their future, as did the early Christians, are likely to survive. So both sects and NRMs find that developing a complex organization enhances survival, but in the process, they are usually transformed religious groups. Figure 12.4 illustrates the parallel evolution of these two types of religious groups.

The social conditions in the late 20th century were ripe for NRMs. Many young people, often from middle-class families in industrialized nations, were attracted to NRMs in their quest to find out who and what they are. These religious communities provide meaning and belonging systems with friendship bonds and clear-cut answers for people seeking meaning and direction in life. Such communities are especially abundant in urban areas and on the west coast of the United States and Canada.

NRMs tend to be hard to study because the members feel they might be persecuted for their faith and beliefs. Witchcraft (or Wicca) is one example of a religion that has been forced to remain secretive, and the next "Sociology in Our Social World" explores the strategies of one sociologist to examine this interesting religious community.

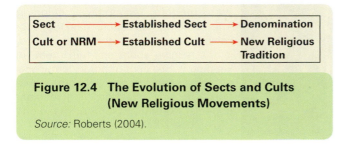

Figure 12.4   The Evolution of Sects and Cults (New Religious Movements)

Source: Roberts (2004).

Thinking Sociologically

What factors might cause the birth and success of NRMs?

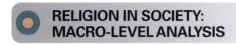

RELIGION IN SOCIETY: MACRO-LEVEL ANALYSIS

As an integral part of society, religion meets the needs of individuals and of the social structure. In this section, we explore functionalist and conflict theories as we consider some functions of religion in society and the role of religion in supporting stratification systems and in various conflicts within societies and in the global system.

The Contribution of Religion to Society: A Functionalist Perspective

Regardless of their personal belief or disbelief in the supernatural, sociologists of religion acknowledge that religion has important social consequences. Functionalists contend that religion has positive consequences—helping people answer questions about the meaning of life and providing part of the glue that helps hold a society together. Let us look at some of the social functions of religion, keeping in mind that the role of religion varies depending on the structure of the society and the time period.

Social Cohesion

Religion helps individuals feel a sense of belonging and unity with others, a common sense of purpose with those who share the same beliefs. It serves to hold any social unit together and gives the members a sense of camaraderie. Durkheim's ([1897] 1964) widely cited study of suicide stresses the importance of belonging to a group. Research shows that religious homogeneity and a high rate of congregational membership in a community are associated with lower rates of suicide (Ellison, Burr, and McCall 1997). Thus, religion serves society well as long as religious views are consistent with other values of society (Bainbridge and Stark 1981). If there are competing religions, cohesion may be reduced and the religions may even be a source of conflict and hatred. Societies with competing religions often develop a civil religion—a theology of the nation—that serves to bless the nation and to enhance conformity and loyalty.

Journal Article Link 12.2
Read about religion and academic achievement.

Legitimating Social Values and Norms

The values and norms of a culture must not be seen as random or arbitrary if they are to be compelling to members of the society. Religion often sacralizes social norms—grounds them in a supernatural reality or a divine command that makes them larger than life. Whether those norms have to do with care for the vulnerable, the demand to work for peace and justice, the immorality of extramarital sex, the sacredness of a monogamous heterosexual marriage, or proper roles for men and women, the foundations of morality from scripture create feelings of absoluteness. This lends stability to society: Agreement on social control of deviant behavior is easier, and the society needs to rely less on coercion and force to get citizens to behave themselves. Of course, the absoluteness of the norms also makes it more difficult to change them as the society evolves. This inflexibility is precisely what pleases religious conservatives and distresses theological liberals, the latter often seeking new ways to interpret the old norms.

Of course, what people say they believe and how they behave are not always compatible, as the "Sociology in Our Social World" on page 415 makes clear.

Sociology in Our Social World

Witchcraft in the United States

Wiccans participate in a lunar ritual in Illinois.

In *A Community of Witches: Contemporary Neo-Paganism and Witchcraft in the United States*, Helen Berger (1999) applies sociological analysis to conduct a fascinating study of contemporary Wicca. She did participant observation in a newly formed coven in New England. A coven is a small congregation of witches, usually having no more than 10 or 12 members. It took considerable effort to establish trust with the members, but this method of gathering data allowed her to experience firsthand the close-knit support group and the actual behaviors and interactions within the group. A national organization provided her with a wealth of printed material produced by Neo-Pagans and allowed her entry to several national Neo-Pagan festivals, where she observed the rituals. She also did in-depth, open-ended interviews with 40 members from a number of covens. By using a variety of methods, Berger was able to gain in-depth information, but she was also able to get an idea of whether her experiences were generalizable to all parts of the country.

Although Berger found Wicca to be a rather healthy and vibrant movement, she also found that it experiences some of the same dilemmas as any other religious congregation. Wicca is feminist, believing in a goddess and emphasizing gender equality. It also celebrates the spiritual unity of humans with nature and therefore has a strong ecology ethic. The religion encourages an intuitive approach to decision making (rather than using logic) and celebrates the senses. This sensuousness embraces sexuality, fertility, and being at one with the universe.

Berger finds that Wicca is a product of the globalized world, for the religion involves bits and pieces selected from religions around the world. It has spread with modern technology, including Internet communication, desktop publishing, and fax machines. Furthermore, it is a religion about self-fulfillment, in keeping with a contemporary emphasis on self-awareness and self-transformation. Wicca is a fast-growing religion, especially among women (Religious Tolerance 2006).

In a more recent book, *Teenage Witches*, Berger worked with an Australian scholar, Douglas Ezzy (Berger and Ezzy 2007), to explore the expansion of witchcraft among teenagers in the English-speaking world. The book is based on interviews that Berger and Ezzy did with 90 young people in the United States, United Kingdom, and Australia (30 from each country). Young people, even more than the generation before them, are attracted by the emphasis on self-transformation. Many of the past generation found their politics, particularly their belief in environmentalism and gender equity, mirrored in Wicca. Unlike the past generation, the new generation of witches are more likely to practice alone—that is, outside the covens. They learn about the religion through books and magazines and online. They may interact with others on Web sites, through blogs, or in Wiccan chat rooms, but they remain solitary practitioners.

The increase in the number of teenagers becoming witches is in part a product of the growth of positive media representations of witchcraft, such as the movie *The Craft* or television shows such as *Sabrina, the Teenage Witch*. However, Berger and Ezzy found that many more young people search online for information about witchcraft or read books about it than actually become witches. Although the media may stimulate interest, it does not cause young people to join. Those who do become witches tend to find that the religion speaks to their personal needs. They are more likely to already have had an interest in the occult and to have felt themselves to be different from their peers. The influx of young people has the potential to significantly change the face of the religion, particularly because so few of them seek coven training and have the traditional ideas and practices passed on to them.

Sociology in Our Social World

Red Sex, Blue Sex

Even sex has political-religious guidelines and implications. The reactions at the 2008 Republican convention to the pregnancy of vice-presidential candidate Sarah Palin's unmarried evangelical 17-year-old daughter were far from what some people might have expected. One delegate said, "I think it's great that she instilled in her daughter the values to have the child and not to sneak off someplace and have an abortion." Another added, "Even though young children are making that decision to become pregnant, they've also decided to take responsibility for their actions and . . . get married and raise this child" (Talbot 2008:1).

For social liberals in the U.S. "blue states," sex education is key. They are not particularly bothered by teens having sex before marriage but would regard a teenage daughter's pregnancy as devastating news. On the other hand, social conservatives in the "red states" generally advocate abstinence-only education and denounce sex before marriage. However, they are relatively unruffled when a teenager does become pregnant, as long as she does not choose to have an abortion.

From a national survey of 3,400 teens from 13 to 17 years old and from a government study of adolescent sexual behavior, the authors of the National Longitudinal Study of Adolescent Health conclude that "religion is a good indicator of attitudes toward sex, but a poor one of sexual behavior, and that this gap is especially wide among teenagers who identify themselves as evangelical" (Regnerus 2007). The vast majority of White evangelical adolescents (74%) say that they believe in abstaining from sex before marriage. (Only half of mainline Protestants and a quarter of Jews say that they believe in abstinence.) Moreover, among the major religious groups,

evangelical virgins are the least likely to anticipate that sex will be pleasurable and the most likely to believe that having sex will cause their partners to lose respect for them. Yet the Adolescent Health research indicated that evangelical teenagers are more sexually active than Mormons, mainline Protestants, and Jews. On average, White evangelical Protestants make their "sexual debut" shortly after turning 16 (Regnerus 2007; Shriver 2007).

Another key difference is that "evangelical protestant teenagers are significantly less likely than other groups to use contraception. This could be because evangelicals are also among the most likely to believe that using contraception will send the message that they are looking for sex" (Talbot 2008:1) and that condoms will not really protect them from pregnancy or venereal disease.

The disconnect between the ideals of one's faith and actual behavior is obvious when we examine the outcomes of abstinence-pledge movements. Roughly 2½ million people have taken a pledge to remain celibate until marriage, usually under the auspices of religiously based movements such as True Love Waits or the Silver Ring Thing. However, more than half of those who take such pledges end up having sex before marriage, usually not with their future spouse. While those who take the pledge tend to delay their first sexual intercourse for 18 months longer than nonpledgers and have fewer partners, communities with high rates of pledging also have very high rates of sexually transmitted diseases (STDs). This could be because fewer people in these communities use condoms when they break the pledge (Regnerus 2007; Talbot 2008).

The main point is that sexual attitudes and behaviors can be linked to our religious affiliations but perhaps not in the ways we expect.

Social Change

Depending on the time and place, religion can work for or against social change. Some religions fight to maintain the status quo or return to simpler times. This is true of many fundamentalist religions—whether they are branches of Christian, Jewish, Hindu, or Islamic faiths—that seek to simplify life in the increasingly complex industrial world. Other religious traditions support or encourage change. Japan was able to make tremendous strides in industrialization

in a short time following World War II, in part because the Shinto, Confucian, and Buddhist religions provided no obstacles and, in fact, supported the changes. In the United States, the central figures in the civil rights movement were nearly all African American religious leaders. As the first nationwide organizations controlled by Black people, African American religious organizations established networks and communication channels that were used by those interested in change (Lincoln and Mamiya 1990; McAdam 1999).

Procession in Bolivia celebrating the Virgin Mary.

This religious procession in Bolivia is a community-uniting event with symbolism representing the synthesis of traditional Christian symbols and local native religions.

Thinking Sociologically

Which religious groups in your community have a stabilizing influence, sacralizing the existing system? Which groups advocate change in the society, pushing for more social equality and less ethnocentrism toward others? Are there mosques, temples, or churches that oppose the government's policies, or do they foster unquestioning loyalty?

The Link Between Religion and Stratification: A Conflict Perspective

 Video Link 12.4
How might conflict theory explain the power of priests?

At times, religions reinforce socially defined differences between people, giving sacred legitimacy to racial prejudice, gender bias, and

inequality. Conflict theory considers the ways in which religion relates to stratification and the status of minority groups. Our religious ideas and values and the way we worship are shaped not only by the society into which we are born but also by our family's position in the stratification system. Religion serves different primary purposes for individuals, depending on their positions in the society. People of various social statuses differ in the type and degree of their involvement in religious groups.

The Class Base of Religion

Conflict theorist Karl Marx ([1844] 1963) states clearly his view of the relationship between religion and class—that religion helps perpetuate the power structure. For the proletariat or working class, religion is a sedative, he asserts, a narcotic that dulls people's sensitivity to and understanding of their plight. He calls religion the "opiate of the people." It keeps people in line and provides an escape from reality—from the tedium, if not suffering, in everyday life. At the same time, it helps those in power keep other people in line because it promises that if laborers serve well in this life, then life in the hereafter or the next incarnation will be better. Some religions justify the positions of those who are better off by saying they have earned it.

Because the needs and interests of socioeconomic groups differ, religion is class based in most societies. In the United States, different denominations and sects show corresponding differences in social class measures such as education, occupation, and income (Pyle 2006; Smith and Faris 2005). The specific links between denominational affiliation and socioeconomic measures in the United States at the beginning of the 21st century are indicated in Table 12.3. The sectarian religions (sects) tend to attract lower- and working-class worshippers because they focus on the problems and life situations faced by people in the lower social classes. People with higher social status attend worship more regularly and know more about the scriptures than do people with less education and income, but people with lower socioeconomic status are more likely to pray and read the holy scriptures daily (Roberts 2004).

Max Weber (1946) referred to this pattern of people belonging to religious groups that espouse values and characteristics compatible with their social status as *elective affinity*. For example, people in laboring jobs usually find that obeying the rules of the workplace and adhering to the instructions of the employer or supervisor are essential for success on the job (Bowles and Gintis 1976; McLeod 2004). The faith communities of the poor and the working class tend to stress obedience, submission to "superiors," and the absoluteness of religious standards. The values of the workplace are reenacted and legitimated in the

Table 12.3 Socioeconomic Profiles of American Religious Groups

Religious Group	Annual Household Income Over $100,000 (%)
Jewish	46
Hindu	43
Episcopal Church in USA	35
Unitarian	26
Buddhist	22
Presbyterian USA	28
Orthodox	28
United Church of Christ	18
Atheist	28
United Methodist	22
Disciples of Christ	20
Evangelical Lutheran in America	17
Nondenominational	18
Latter-Day Saint (Mormon)	15
Catholic	19
Muslim	16
Southern Baptist	15
Seventh Day Adventist	11
Religious but unaffiliated	12
American Baptist	8
Assemblies of God	8
Other Pentecostal	7
Jehovah's Witness	9
Black Baptist	8

Source: Pew Forum (2008:78–80, 84–86).

churches and help socialize children to adapt to noncreative laboring jobs.

Many people in affluent congregations are paid to be divergent thinkers, to be problem solvers, and to break the mold of conventional thinking. They will not do well professionally if they merely obey rules. Instead, they are expected to be rule makers while trying to solve organizational or management problems (Bowles and Gintis 1976). It is not surprising, then, that the denominations of the affluent are more likely to value tolerance of other perspectives, religions, or values and to view factors that limit individual opportunity (e.g., institutional racism and sexism) as evil. They embrace tolerance of differences and condemn rigidity, absolutism, and conventionalism. Critical thinking, creativity, and even a streak of independence are valuable characteristics. Their religious

communities are likely to encourage each member to work out his or her own theology, within limits (Roberts 2004; Roof 1999).

Stratification is found in various world religions, not just Christianity. For example, Hinduism in the upper classes of India conforms much more to the official beliefs of the religion. It is monotheistic and stresses the concept of transmigration of souls (also called reincarnation). The lower castes believe in a sort of Hindu folk religion that is *polytheistic*, having multiple gods. Lower-class Hindus tend to identify Hindu statues as gods in themselves (rather than as symbols), and they believe in heaven and hell rather than in reincarnation (Noss and Noss 1990).

Whatever the particular belief, the relationship between one's religion and one's social status affects everything from life expectancy, the likelihood of divorce, and mental health to attitudes regarding sexual behavior, abortion, and stem cell research.

Thinking Sociologically

How do the social class and religious affiliation of people you know relate to the discussion here? How do denominations in your community whose members have higher than average levels of education (Unitarians, Jews, Episcopalians, Presbyterians, and Congregationalists) differ from those with less educated members?

Racial Bias, Gender Prejudice, and Religion

Most religious groups profess to welcome all comers, yet most have practiced discrimination against some group at some time, often related to political and economic factors in the society. In fact, some studies show positive relationships between religion, prejudice, and discrimination. The American Psychological Association (2007) was concerned enough about religious-based prejudice to pass a resolution condemning it. It is important to recognize that religion has multiple and even contradictory effects on societies. For example, most Christian denominations have formal statements that reject racial prejudice as un-Christian. The meaning system teaches tolerance. However, informal group norms in a local congregation—the belonging system—may be tolerant of ethnic jokes and may foster distrust of certain races (Woodberry and Smith 1998). Among Whites in the United States, for instance, active church members have historically displayed more prejudice than inactive church members or the unchurched (Chalfant and Peck 1983; Roberts 2004).

Prejudice may be perpetuated because promotions to larger churches are usually awarded to those ministers who are well liked, who have growing and harmonious churches, and whose churches are financially sound. Ministers are sometimes reluctant to speak out forcefully on controversial issues or for racial equality for fear of offending their parishioners. Bishops may not promote a minister to a larger church if his or her current congregation is racked with dissention and donations have declined. Even though the denomination's meaning system may oppose prejudice, the structural system may reward clergy who do not defend that meaning system (Campbell and Pettigrew 1959; Roberts 2004).

Women have often been the main volunteers and the most faithful attendees in congregations, and in some denominations, they hold leadership positions (Chaves 2004). This curious phenomenon that women are more spiritual or religious than men is discussed in the next "Engaging Sociology." Despite this, women have often been denied entry into many levels in the hierarchy of religious organizations and are treated differently. In some Christian, Islamic, and conservative Jewish worship services, women must also cover their heads and sit separately from men. Religious rules regarding attire and hair length also help reinforce the differentiation. Men may enter a Christian cathedral in Europe with very few restrictions, but women must cover their heads so that God will not be offended. This symbolizes and communicates the presumed differences between women and men before God as laid out in 1 Corinthians 11:2–16.

Engaging Sociology

Gender and Spirituality

The following table indicates that there is a spirituality gap.

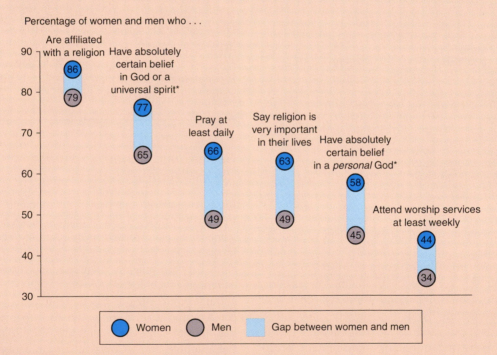

Source: Pew Forum (2009).

Questions

1. Are you convinced by this evidence that women are more spiritual than men? Why or why not?

2. If so, why do you think this is the case? If not, why do the data seem to suggest less involvement of men?

3. Is the message of religious communities and faith traditions (altruism, self-sacrifice, trusting others) less in tune with the everyday experiences of men than of women?

Similarly, men within Islam have more power, although women must be treated with respect. Within this faith tradition, many adherents see this stratification as providing protection for both groups to worship without distraction. All worshippers remove their shoes, but women must cover their heads and sometimes their faces, and they cannot enter certain areas of the mosque when men are present. The literal teachings of many religions legitimate treating women differently, often in ways that disallow leadership opportunities and imply inferiority. This is true of certain groups within all the Abrahamic religious traditions: Judaism, Christianity, and Islam.

Within Christian groups, women have traditionally played one of two roles: (1) silence and obedience to men in religious authority or (2) specialized subordinate roles within the religious group. Many deeply religious women have been concerned over the lack of significant roles for women and have fought for reformation within their religions. Ordination of women is a newly won right in several denominations (Chaves 2004; Religious Tolerance 2009b). Moreover, a study of Seventh-Day Adventists found very positive attitudes toward female pastors, and female Anglican clergy in the United Kingdom felt they brought important skills and strengths to their ministries (Robbins 1998).

By the end of the 20th century, 71% of the public in the United States who express a religious preference favored having women as pastors, ministers, priests, or rabbis, compared with 42% in 1977 (Gallup Poll 2000). Still, some religious groups do not ordain women into the ministry or the priesthood. Because such leadership statuses are important symbolic positions, many women feel that this refusal helps sacralize the social stereotype of women as less capable.

While most mainline Christian denominations now have official statements on the equality of women and formal policies against discrimination in ordaining or hiring women pastors, the official meaning system does not tell the whole story. Local congregational search committees who screen and hire new ministers care deeply about the survival and health of the local church. Studies show that such persons are themselves not opposed to women in the pulpit, but they believe that others in their church would be offended if they hired a woman and would stop coming and giving money to the church. Thus, the local belonging and structural systems of the religion may perpetuate unequal treatment of clergywomen, even if the meaning system says they are equal (Chaves 1999, 2004; Lehman 1985).

Given these frustrations, some women have been uncomfortable working for reform from within and have left traditional religions to form new structures in which they can worship as equals, including NRMs. Indeed, women in the Western world have, throughout history, been more

A Presbyterian minister blesses the cup before offering the sacrament of Communion.

likely than men to opt for unconventional forms of religion (McGuire 2002).

In some instances, religion may reinforce and legitimate social prejudices toward racial groups or toward women. In others, religion may be a powerful force for change and for greater equality in a society. Seldom does religion take a passive or entirely disinterested position on these matters. Consider the conflicts around the world, many of which are based on religious and class differences. People are fighting and dying for their religious beliefs. In Sudan, Muslims fight those with African religions. In Belfast, Ireland, bombs sent civilians to their graves or to hospitals, maimed for life. In India, Muslims and Hindus continue to massacre each other. Protestant against Catholic, Shiite Muslim against Sunni Muslim, Jew against Muslim, Christian against Jew—religion elicits strong emotions and influences people's definition of reality. Ethnocentric attitudes and economically rooted conflicts can be reinforced by religious beliefs. Religion has been the apparent cause of wars and social strife, but it has also been the motivation for altruism and a major contributor to social solidarity.

Thinking Sociologically

From what you know about the status of minority groups and women, how are the problems they face in religion and other institutions (education, politics, economics) similar?

Religion in the Modern World

One issue that continually comes up in the analysis of religion is its role in the modern world, for some issues—such as "creation science," pluralism, and prayer in schools—raise serious questions about the compatibility of the modern scientific world and religious viability. In this section we look at religious vitality, the process of secularization, the role of religion in war and peace, and the expansion of technology, especially Internet technology.

Name almost any religion, and a group representing that belief system can probably be found in the United Kingdom, the United States, Canada, Kenya, and several other countries where religious diversity is the norm. In the

Handbook Link 12.2
Read more about globalization and religion.

United States, religious pluralism has been a founding principle since Roger Williams settled in Rhode Island. This makes for a complex religious pattern. Sociologists of religion have documented the vitality of American religions with empirical data that track religious trends over time (Pew Forum 2008; Stark 2000).

Is Religion Dying or Revitalizing in North America?

Although it seemed at times during the past century that society was becoming secular and religion was fading in influence, religion is a fundamental, integral part of culture and individuals' lives (Christiano et al. 2002; Stark 2000). One third of all Americans currently claim no affiliation with any religious tradition, but one third of that unaffiliated group said that religion or spirituality is important in their lives. So we need to be cautious about how we interpret the numbers (Pew Forum 2008).

Religion in North America adjusts to changes in society and takes on new forms. While the number of Protestants in the United States has declined from two thirds of the population in the 1970s to roughly half in 2008, this does not mean that atheism has increased.

The latter half of the 20th century saw a wide range of religious groups forming and growing in North America, from the occult and astrology to Moonies and from New Age spirituality to Zen Buddhism. Furthermore, middle-class Catholics and Episcopalians were "speaking in tongues," and "the fervent evangelical culture could not be classified as 'marginal' when successive presidents"—Ford, Carter, Reagan, and Bush—openly affirmed being born again and claimed membership in the evangelical community (Marty 1983). Polling data indicate that 41% of U.S. Christians identify themselves as born-again or evangelical Christians (Gallup Poll 2006). The religiosity of President George W. Bush was a political factor in his reelection in 2004 (Green and Silk 2005), and religion and race played a role in the 2008 presidential primary—both with the Mormon candidate Mitt Romney (a Republican) and with controversies over the church membership of the Democrat, Barack Obama.

In addition, the makeup of the United States and Canada is changing in many ways. Although two out of every three native-born U.S. citizens are Protestant, two out of every three Christian immigrants are Catholic. Some other religious faiths are represented among those new Americans as well, so the shift in the country's data on religion may indicate less a decline in religiosity than a shift in its character (Pew Forum 2008). Religion remains strong as an influence in Canadian life as well. Religious adherence in that country has remained at nearly 90% for the past four decades. Half the population reports having had a personal religious experience, three out of four claim to pray at least occasionally, and the overall religious membership in Canada has continued to increase every decade (Bibby 2002). These rates are higher than those in most other religiously pluralistic nations.

About 56% of Americans sampled indicate a high confidence in organized religion, more confidence than they have in politics and other institutions, and religious membership has increased over the past three centuries (Gallup Poll 2001). In the "good old days" of American colonialism, only about 17% of the population belonged to a church. Religious membership rose fairly steadily from the 1770s until the 1960s. Although there has been a modest decline in the past 30 years, membership has fluctuated between 64% and 70% since 1992 (Newport 2006). Membership in mosques, synagogues, or churches was reported at 64% of the adult population in 2005 (Newport 2006). Another measure of religious strength is belief in God. Gallup Poll results for three decades indicated that 93% of the U.S. population believe in God or a universal spirit or higher power (Newport 2004). Tables 12.4a and 12.4b show the results from Gallup Polls regarding indicators of the importance of religion in people's lives. Map 12.2 also shows that Americans report high levels of attendance at religious worship services, but as you can see, there are significant geographical variations. Attendance at weekly worship is shown in Figure 12.5 on page 422.

Table 12.4a Leading Religious Indicators (in percent)	
Belief in God	81[a]
Member of a church	64[a]
Attended church in the past 7 days	35[a]
Religion *very important* in life	61[b]
Religion answers problems	65[c]
High confidence in organized religion	56[c]

Source: Newport (2006) and Bukhari (2003).

a. Gallup Poll (2006).
b. Gallup Poll (2004).
c. Gallup Poll (2001).

Table 12.4b   How Important Is Religion in Your Life (in percent)?

	Very[a]	*Fairly*	*Not Very*
2005	59	25	16
2000	59	29	12
1995	58	29	12

Source: Newport (2006) and Bukhari (2003).

a. These figures vary by religious affiliation. Note, for example, that Muslims rate among the highest—at 79%: *very important*—in a 2001 survey (Bukhari 2003).

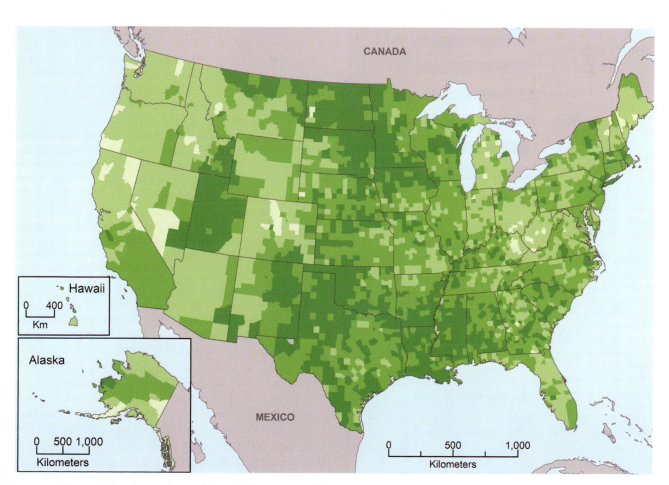

Percent of Population Attending a Church, Mosque, or Temple

0–25   26–50   51–75   76–100

Map 12.2   Percentage of U.S. Population Affiliated With a Church, Mosque, or Temple

Source: Religious Congregations and Membership Study (2000). Map by Anna Versluis.

Note: This map is based on data reported by local congregations and includes both members and other regular attendees; it does not represent weekly attendance. The numbers indicate overreporting, but that does not change the overall geographical pattern of religious affiliation.

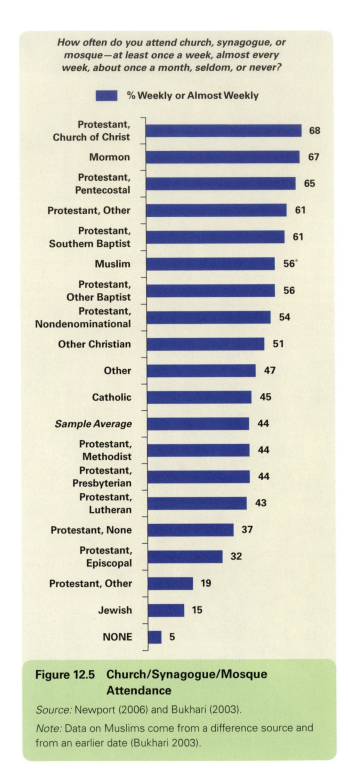

How often do you attend church, synagogue, or mosque—at least once a week, almost every week, about once a month, seldom, or never?

■ % Weekly or Almost Weekly

Protestant, Church of Christ	68
Mormon	67
Protestant, Pentecostal	65
Protestant, Other	61
Protestant, Southern Baptist	61
Muslim	56*
Protestant, Other Baptist	56
Protestant, Nondenominational	54
Other Christian	51
Other	47
Catholic	45
Sample Average	44
Protestant, Methodist	44
Protestant, Presbyterian	44
Protestant, Lutheran	43
Protestant, None	37
Protestant, Episcopal	32
Protestant, Other	19
Jewish	15
NONE	5

Figure 12.5   Church/Synagogue/Mosque Attendance

Source: Newport (2006) and Bukhari (2003).

Note: Data on Muslims come from a difference source and from an earlier date (Bukhari 2003).

The question of what it means to be "religious" is discussed in the next "Engaging Sociology."

Religion and Secularization: Micro-, Meso-, and Macro-Level Discord

Secularization refers to the diminishing influence and role of religion in everyday life. Instead of religion being the dominant institution, it is but one of many. Secularization involves a

Engaging Sociology

Determining What It Means to Be "Religious"

- Study the list of items in Table 12.4a (page 421). Do issues such as belief in God, church membership, or frequency of attendance seem like a good measure of one's religiousness? Why might the answers to those questions be indicating something other than the depth of one's religious faith?

- Look at the variability of attendance indicated in Figure 12.5. Given the fact that attendance varies so much by religious group, does that mean that members of some groups are less religious, or does that mean that attendance is not a very good measure of religiosity for some groups?

- Is asking whether religion is very important in one's life, whether religion answers problems in life, or how much confidence one has in religious organizations good indicators of religiosity? What might be some misleading dimensions of using these as measures of "religiosity"?

- Some scholars have argued that how religious beliefs actually affect one's behavior is a good indicator of religiosity. So in studying Islam, Judaism, or some forms of Christianity, the measure has been how much one gives to charitable causes—including the church but also including help given to those less fortunate. Is this an accurate way to understand levels of religious influence in the society? Why or why not?

movement away from supernatural and sacred interpretations of the world and toward decisions based on empirical evidence and logic. Before the advent of modern science and technology, religion helped explain the unexplainable. However, the scientific method, the emphasis on logical reasoning, and the fact that there are many different religious interpretations rather than one have challenged religious and spiritual approaches to the world. Although religion is still strong in the lives of individuals, it does not have the extensive control over other institutions of education, health, politics, or family that it once did. It is just one institution among others rather than being the dominant one.

Some scholars have argued that secularization is an inevitable and unstoppable force in the modern postindustrial world (Berger 1961; Beyer 2000; Dobbelaere 1981, 2000). Others argue that secularization is far from inevitable and that it has almost reached its limit (Stark 2000; Swatos and Gissurarson 1997; Warner 1993). Our social world model helps us understand that, like religion, secularization is a complex phenomenon that occurs at several levels and affects each society differently (Beyer 2000; Chaves and Gorski 2001; Yamane 1997).

Secularization may be occurring at the societal level, but the evidence suggests that this is not so at the individual level in

North America (Bellah et al. 1996; Chaves and Gorski 2001). Although it is true that 12% to 15% of Americans do not identify with any religious tradition (Pew Forum 2010), 64% do claim membership in a local congregation, and 61% say religion is very important in their lives (Gallup Poll 2006). Religion remains a strong influence in Canadian life as well. Religious adherence in that country has remained at nearly 90% for the past four decades. When religious faith guides people's everyday lives—their conduct on the job, their political choices, their sexual behavior, or their attitudes toward race relations—then secularization at the micro level is weak and religious influence is strong. Faith still matters to many people (Roof 1999).

Video Link 12.5
Watch examination of plastic surgery in Iran.

Within church-related organizations (Baptist hospitals, Presbyterian colleges, Jewish social service foundations), the decisions about how to deliver services or who will be hired or fired are based on systematic policies designed for organizational efficiency. In other words, meso-level secularization is present even within many religious organizations (Chaves 1993). Likewise, policies in the society at large are made with little discussion of the theological implications, decisions being based on human rights arguments rather than on what is sinful, again suggesting that society has become secular at the macro level (Chaves 1993; Dobbelaere 2000; Yamane 1997; see Table 12.5). Debates about prayer in schools, court decisions about "one nation under God" in the Pledge of Allegiance to the flag, and the involvement of religious leaders in political issues suggest that societal-level secularization is a point of controversy in the United States. Still, few will deny that the bureaucratic structures of the United States and virtually every other postindustrial nation are thoroughly secularized. Macro, meso, and micro levels of secularization do not seem to be in harmony, as illustrated in Table 12.5.

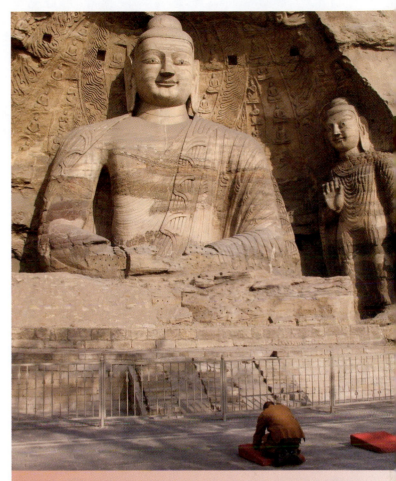

Despite the process of secularization in some parts of the world, the sense of awe before the holy remains strong for many people. This enormous Buddha at the Yungang Buddhist Caves at Wuzhou Mountain in China was built out of a sense of the sacredness of Buddha, and it then became a source of veneration for subsequent generations.

Table 12.5   The Complexity of Secularization in the Social World

	Institutional Differentiation	*Decision Making*
Macro Level	Institutions in the society, including government, education, and the economy, are independent and autonomous of religious organizations.	Decision making about social policies uses logic, empirical data, and cost/benefit analysis rather than scripture, theological arguments, or proclamations of religious authorities.
Meso Level	Organizations look to other social associations for accepted practices of how to operate the organization, not to religious organizations and authorities.	Decision making about an organization's policies is based on analyses of possible consequences, rather than on scripture, theological arguments, or proclamations of religious authorities.
Micro Level	Individuals emphasize being "spiritual rather than religious," formulate their own meaning system or theology, and may believe that spirituality has little to do with other aspects of their lives.	Decision making about life decisions is based on individual self-interest without concern for the teachings of the religious group or the clergy.

Source: Roberts (2004).

Photo Essay

Secularization and Faith in Context

Religious faith is very strong at the micro level in American society, but public policy and the operation of organizations and institutions such as the government and public schools are secularized—based on principles of pluralism, rational deliberation rather than doctrine, and scientific evidence rather than scripture or dogma. Protests arise—such as "See you at the Pole" prayers around the American flag (the symbol of the nation); this sign about the Ten Commandments in Kentucky, where the courts had ruled that the Ten Commandments were not to be posted in the city hall or the courthouse; and crèche scenes displayed on public properties, amid controversies and conflicting court rulings on whether this constitutes endorsement of one religious tradition.

In short, most sociologists of religion believe that religion continues to be a particularly powerful force at the individual level and that it has some influence in the larger culture (at the meso and macro levels). There is a macro-level trend toward secularization in most global North societies, but the trend is neither inevitable nor uniform across societies (Dobbelaere 2000; Lambert 2000; Sommerville 2002; Yamane 1997).

At the global level, no particular theological authority has the power to define reality or determine policies, religious authority structures are minimal, and secularization is well established. Perhaps, this is one reason why conservatives of nearly every religious faith are leery of global processes and global organizations, such as the United Nations. Our global organizations are governed by rational-legal (secular) authority, not religious doctrines.

Thinking Sociologically

What might be the results if a society is secularized at the meso and macro levels but not at the micro level? Is this a problem? Does it create problems in decision making and social coherence? Is separation of church and state with government policies based on secular calculations of the interests of the nation still a good idea? Why or why not?

Religion: Contributor to War or Peace?

Can religion bring peace to the world? Most religious systems advocate living in harmony with other humans and with nature, yet peace is not the reality. Although the meaning systems of all the Abrahamic religions—Christianity, Judaism, and Islam—embrace a world of peace and justice, the structural system does not always reward those who pay attention to the meaning system, as we see in cases of racism and sexism. Christian denominations often foster nationalistic loyalty—with displays of the flag and even pledges of allegiance to the flag during worship. This endorsement of national pride can actually foster we-versus-they thinking and can undermine peace. Congregations that take peace activities seriously may decline in membership and financial stability, whereas those that stir up chauvinistic sentiments attract large numbers. So the structural system may actually undermine the message of the meaning system because growth and financial vitality are major concerns for many local church leaders. Despite the rhetoric, fiscal concerns can actually trump claims to worship the "Prince of Peace."

Still, there is movement toward interfaith and transnational cooperation. Christian, Islamic, Jewish, and other world faiths sponsor a variety of programs aimed at health care, hunger relief, and easing of suffering caused by natural disasters. Prior to the 1700s, remarkably few efforts had been made to reach out to people in other cultures. Moreover, from 1700 until well into the 20th century, outreach programs were aimed almost exclusively at trying to convert the "heathen," those with belief systems that differed (Hunter 1983; Lee 1992).

Liberal theologies suggest that God may speak to people through a variety of channels, including the revelations of other religious traditions. While religious leaders may feel that their beliefs provide the fullest and most complete expression of God's Truth, they recognize that other beliefs also provide paths to Truth. Many global religious programs today are ecumenical and aimed at humanitarian relief rather than proselytizing.

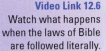
Video Link 12.6
Watch what happens when the laws of Bible are followed literally.

Members of fundamentalist groups—whether they are Orthodox Jews, traditional Muslims, or born-again Christians—generally believe in a literal interpretation of their holy books and a personal experience with Allah or God. They usually believe that they have the only Truth, which they must defend. Some even try to spread "the true Word" by force. This generates ethnocentrism and sometimes hatred, causing people to fight and die to defend their belief systems and way of life. Fundamentalist religious groups use strategies to attempt to preserve their distinctive identity as a people or group (Marty and Appleby 1991, 2004). They seldom believe in pluralism or tolerance of other beliefs but rather believe that they are the only true religion. Consequently, they resist and defend themselves against modernism, which threatens their beliefs and way of life (Ebaugh 2005; Stern 2003; Wessinger 2000). Thus, religious groups may engage in violent acts against others.

Conflict between religious groups is especially intense if ethnic, economic, and religious differences are present. Consider Ireland, where the main landowners are Protestants of Scottish descent. The laborers are predominantly native Irish in ethnicity and are Roman Catholic. Hatred between Protestants and Catholics is exacerbated by the lack of cross-cutting loyalties or friendships (McGuire 2002). The frustrations of groups not in power lead to ethnocentrism and sometimes hatred against others. Those in power similarly develop stereotypes about those unlike themselves, whose ideology and values are different. Cross-cutting social cleavages reduce social hostilities, as Figure 12.6 on page 426 illustrates.

Religion has the greatest potential for reducing hatred between groups when those groups share some type of common identification. If the conflict is over ethnicity and economics, a common religious heritage can lessen the likelihood of violent confrontation. Some religious groups have

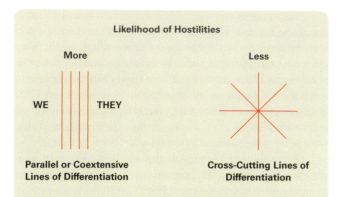

Figure 12.6   Lines of Differentiation Between "We" and "They"

Note: Imagine that each line represents a division in society between groups based on religion, ethnicity, political party, economic status, language spoken, skin color, or other factors. Parallel lines of differentiation divide people in each conflict along the same lines. *Cross-cutting lines* cut the differences, so that people who were part of "they" in a previous antagonism become part of "we" in the present discord. This lessens the likelihood of deep and permanent hostilities within a social unit.

joined together in peaceful enterprises such as attempts to ban nuclear weapons or to address global poverty or climate change. These common purposes provide for cooperation and collaboration, thus lessening animosity and we-versus-they thinking.

The core reason why some countries are secular may be found in their history. The conflicts in Europe between religious groups were very brutal, beginning with the bloodletting in the Hundred Years' War. From that time, "religion was the sixteenth century word for nationalism" (Wallerstein 2005:125). The intense religious in-group loyalties led to a willingness to kill those who were Other. The horrific religious conflicts in European societies did not reach closure until the Enlightenment. At this time, tolerance of other religions became dominant and a primary foundation for determining national policy (Dobbelaere 1981, 2000; Lambert 2000).

As we have seen, the disconnect between micro and macro levels—religious passion at the micro level and secular domination at the macro level—has resulted in severe tensions around the world (Wallerstein 2005). For instance, in the United States, the movement is toward increasing religiosity at the micro level and increasing secularism—with its openness to diversity—at the macro level.

The rise of religious fundamentalism in the 20th century, whether Islamic, Buddhist, Hasidic Jewish, evangelical Christian, or Malaysian Dukway, appears to be a local reaction against global modernization (Davidman 1990; Robertson and Garrett 1991; Shupe and Hadden 1989; Turner 1991a). Rapid global change has resulted in anomie as people confront change—fear of obliteration of their own culture, the increasing secularization of society as the supernatural realm shrinks, the threat to the material self-interests of religious organizations, and fear of interdependence among the powerful nations of the Western world. All these threats have strengthened fundamentalism, which is a reaction to global secularization.

Thinking Sociologically

What specific religious beliefs or behaviors might influence the way in which religions and countries relate to one another? How might religious organizations influence international relations?

Religion, Technology, and the World Wide Web

Technology and the Internet affect not only nations but also religions. From television broadcasts of megachurch services to Muslim chat rooms using technology to communicate, religious messages travel in new ways.

Prior to the wide distribution of religious texts to people who were not ordained ministers, the hierarchies of Christendom controlled what was disseminated as Truth. The common (and typically illiterate) member of the local church did not have any basis for challenging the Pope or other church leaders. Those leaders were the authority. However, Martin Luther used the printed word in many powerful ways. He and other reformers claimed that the Bible alone was the ultimate source of Truth and religious authority. The church leaders were to be believed only insofar as they were faithful to the scriptures. Luther himself used the printed word to spread his version of Christian Truth, and he did so with a vengeance. He not only wrote more than the other dissenters, he outpublished the entire legion of Vatican defenders (Brasher 2004). He published in the common languages of the people rather than in Latin, and the Protestant Reformation was launched. It is doubtful whether this could have happened without the printing press. The printing press had similar revolutionary effects within Judaism (Brasher 2004).

Today, television and multimedia worship have enhanced the marketing of religion, including the modification of the product to meet "consumer" demand (Ebaugh

2005; Roberts 2004; Sargeant 2000). The Internet is the most recent technology with enormous impacts. There are more than a million religion Web sites, and they cover an extraordinarily wide range of religious beliefs and practices (Brasher 2004). Even conservative Christians such as Jerry Falwell, who dubbed the Internet an evil Tower of Babel, have used it to spread their message. The panic over whether the turn of the millennium (Y2K) would result in massive crashes in computers around the world was related to the "end of the world" prophesies by some conservative Christians (Brasher 2004). The computer, in short, was to be the medium to bring an end to life in this world.

The medium of the Internet is fast paced and oriented to the now (Brasher 2004). Technology is often outdated in a few years if not in a few months, and the past hardly seems a source of authority or of Truth. Yet traditional religious communities often excel in maintaining and propagating memories of past events that give meaning to life or that define notions of sacredness and Truth as the world around them changes rapidly. It is too early to tell for sure what impacts these most recent technologies might have on religions around the world, but one thing is clear: The Internet allows instant access to information about religions that otherwise might be obscure or nonexistent for many people.

Social Policy: The Homosexuality Debates

Gays in the church, ordination of gay ministers, same-sex marriage in churches—these issues make for heated debate over church policy and threaten to split some denominations. Most established religious groups assume the normality of heterosexuality.

Marriage is sanctified by religious ceremony in all major religious groups, but recently, some religious bodies have recognized the possibility of officially sanctioned weddings for gays and lesbians. In the Christian tradition, there are six passages in scripture that condemn homosexual relationships, only one of which condemns lesbian relationships (Genesis 19:1–28; Leviticus 18:22, 20:13; Romans 1:26–27; I Corinthians 6:9; I Timothy 1:10). Opposition to homosexuality is especially high among religious fundamentalists. In recent years, there have been strident conflicts in the Presbyterian (U.S.) and United Methodist denominations, but in the most conservative denominations, few questions are even raised about homosexuality because the rightness of absolute heterosexuality is taken for granted.

Liberals in the churches tend to see this issue as one of prejudice against people for a characteristic that is immutable. They assume that homosexuality is an inborn trait. Conservatives argue that homosexuality is a choice that has moral implications. They tend to see homosexuality as a behavior that is acquired through socialization. Therefore, acceptance of homosexuality will likely increase the numbers of people who engage in this lifestyle, they believe. Conservatives see liberal notions about homosexuality and gender roles as a threat to society and the family, a threat to the moral social order, whereas liberals often feel that sexuality within a committed relationship is not a moral issue. The real moral issue for them is bigotry—lack of tolerance for other lifestyles. Thus, the two groups have socially constructed the meaning of morality along different lines.

Some mainstream denominations have developed policies supportive of lesbian, gay, and bisexual persons in local churches: More Light (Presbyterian), Open and Affirming (United Church of Christ and Christian Church), Reconciled in Christ (Lutheran), and Reconciling Congregations (Methodist). These designations apply to about 300 congregations that wish to be known as "gay and lesbian friendly" (www.mlp.org). A new denomination, Universal Fellowship of Metropolitan Community Churches (UFMCC), affirms homosexuality as a legitimate lifestyle for Christians (Rodriguez and Ouellette 2000). It has more than 300 local churches in the United States, with 17 in the conservative state of Texas. There are also congregations on six continents (Metropolitan Community Churches 2008). One study conducted on a UFMCC congregation in New York found that homosexuals affiliated with this church have exceptionally positive personal adjustment. They are more likely to have an integrated self-concept as both a gay person and a religious person (Rodriguez and Ouellette 2000). At the same time, some religious people who are homosexual and members of traditional congregations struggle with their sense of self-integration.

One of the most controversial issues in several mainline denominations is over ordination of homosexuals as ministers. A Gallup Poll shows an overall shift toward acceptance of homosexual clergy by Americans: Whereas only 36% approved in 1977, 56% approved by 2004 (Gallup and Lindsay 1999; Gallup Poll 2004). Still, most denominations do not knowingly ordain homosexuals as ministers and do not allow their ministers to perform marriages or "holy unions" of two gay men or two lesbian women. If ministers do so, they may be defrocked. In one denomination, the Episcopalian Church in the United States, the election in 2003 of the gay clergyman Gene Robinson as bishop created a breach in the international Anglican community, as African churches cut off ties with the Episcopalians in the United States. In the summer of 2008, the Presbyterian

Church (U.S.) also officially voted to change its rules and to approve ordination of gay and lesbian pastors. The decision is highly controversial, but the policy shift has been building for many years (Helfand 2008).

Thinking Sociologically

Are the core issues in same-sex marriage and ordination of homosexual clergy ones of the right of religious communities to decide their own values, or is this a broader civic issue of individual rights? How can this conflict in the definition of the problem be resolved?

Some ministers continue to perform marriage ceremonies as a protest against a policy they think is immoral. They may take a "don't ask, don't tell" position with their bishops. One retired minister estimated that even in his very conservative Midwestern state, there are roughly 50 homosexual holy unions performed by Methodist pastors each year. He stated,

Back in the 1950s, ministers could lose their ordination and ministerial privileges if they married someone in a church wedding who had been divorced. Performing a marriage of someone who had been divorced was a serious offense in the Methodist church—and in most other Protestant churches, too. If a divorced person wanted to marry a second time, a civil wedding was supposedly the only option. Many of us in the pastorate thought that the policy was inhumane. These were people whom we pastored. They had made a mistake in a previous selection of a spouse and wanted to start again. Many clergy secretly went against formal policy of the church, but we did not tell our bishops. By the 1960s, if the church purged all of us who had done this, the Methodist church would have lost more than half of its ministers. In another 20 years, the same thing will be true with holy unions. If you have two people in your congregation who really care for each other and want to ritually affirm their lifelong commitment, how can we not honor that commitment and caring? I think it is a matter of time before this will become widely accepted. (Roberts 2004:299)

One study has documented more acceptance of homosexual rights among religiously committed people (Petersen and Donnenwerth 1998). Even where there are strong reservations about marriage of gays or lesbians, there is support for nondiscrimination in other areas such as jobs.

In our social world, religious organizations influence society, and the larger society influences religious groups. Moreover, attitudes in a local community or a region of the country influence attitudes within a congregation, irrespective of the positions of the official denomination (Koch and Curry 2000). Two catalysts are creating tension for change in religious organizations: (1) the emphasis on the equality of all people before God in Christian theology and (2) an impetus in the larger society that legitimates people in leadership roles based on competence and commitment rather than on traits beyond their control (skin color, gender, or sexual orientation).

Thus, the policy issues for all religious communities are (1) whether a homosexual person can ever have the spiritual qualities to lead a congregation as its minister; (2) whether that faith community should or should not endorse and permit same-sex marriages in its churches, mosques, or temples; and (3) whether faith groups should be involved in government policy regarding the right of the state to grant marriage licenses to homosexuals or licenses for a civil union—a secular equivalent to the marriage contract that would allow more than 1,000 rights and privileges that heterosexuals enjoy. One proposed solution is that because marriage has historically been "owned" by religious communities, the state could grant licenses for civil unions (not marriages) for both homosexuals and heterosexuals. Faith communities alone would decide whether they acknowledge a couple as married. The notion that the state should have any say in the matter of marriage began only with Martin Luther, who insisted that marriage was not a sacrament. These highly contested areas of public policy continue to be contentious.

Thinking Sociologically

How is hostility toward homosexuals similar and different from sexism and racism? Does religion play a role in heterosexism and homophobia? Why or why not?

Religion deals with issues of meaning and, like education, it serves as a core socialization agent in the society. It provides socialization of members of society on important values, which sometimes makes cooperation more possible within a society. However, conflict cannot always be overcome by appeals to values, and sometimes the issues between individuals and groups come down to matters of power and access to resources. In the next chapter, we try to penetrate power and privilege and to understand how penetrating into our lives power and privilege can be. We turn now to the institutions of politics and economics.

What Have We Learned?

Religion is a powerful force in the lives of people around the world. It typically elicits passions and deep loyalties, and in so doing, it can stimulate people to great acts of self-sacrificing charity or it can elicit horrible atrocities and intergroup bigotries. People's religious affiliation is strongly related to their nationality, ethnic and racial group, and lifestyle. Religion is the one institution in most societies that consistently professes a desire for peace and goodwill, yet there may be inconsistencies between what people say and what they do. Religion can provide us with the hope that the world's problems may be dealt with in humanitarian ways.

Religion provides a sense of meaning in life regarding the big questions, and that is why religious symbols come to have sacred meaning. They address our spiritual life and our sense of purpose. Humans in the modern world, however, are not just spiritual. They live in states with massive governmental bureaucracies that hold power and resolve conflicts, and they participate in economic systems that produce and distribute the goods and services needed for survival. The next institutions we will examine are politics and economics—how power relations are negotiated at each level in the social world.

Key Points

- Religion makes our most important values sacred, operating through three interconnected systems: (1) a meaning system, (2) a belonging system, and (3) a structural system. (See pp. 392–393.)

- We become committed through these three systems, by our attachment to a reference group that becomes a belonging system, by making investments in the organization (the structural system), and by holding as real the system of ideas (the meaning system). (See pp. 393–395.)

- At the micro level, symbolic interaction theory illuminates how the meaning system works, with an interaction of myths, rituals, and symbols coming to define reality and making the values and the meaning system sacred. Rational choice theory focuses on the costs and benefits that influence the decisions individuals make about religious commitments, but it also examines how religious organizations go about seeking a "market share" in the competition for members. (See pp. 396–402.)

- At the meso level, religious communities usually have a mutually supportive relationship with other institutions—the family, the political system, and the economy. Religious organizations themselves can evolve into one of several types of structures (or even bureaucracies): ecclesia, denomination, sect, or New Religious Movement (NRM). (See pp. 402–413.)

- At the macro level of analysis, functionalists maintain that religions can serve as a kind of glue to help solidify the country and can meet the basic needs of the populace. In contrast, conflict theorists focus on the ways in which religion reinforces conflicts and inequalities in society, whether socioeconomic, racial, or gender. (See pp. 413–420.)

- In the United States and Canada, secularization is dominant at the meso and macro levels but does not seem to be happening much at the micro level. This is the source of tension in societies. (See pp. 420–424.)

- At the global level, religion can be involved in issues of war and peace (sometimes unwittingly undermining peace) and is currently experiencing interface with the world of technology and the World Wide Web. (See pp. 424–427.)

- Finally, homosexuality, same-sex marriage, and ordination of gay or lesbian clergy are examples of religious policy issues causing considerable controversy. (See pp. 427–428.)

Contributing to Our Social World: What Can We Do?

At the Local Level

Campus religious foundations or ministries: Many organizations such as the Newman Foundation (Roman Catholic) and Hillel Foundation (Jewish) are branches of national organizations. Contact a student representative or faculty sponsor, attend a meeting, become involved in outreach work, and volunteer to assist in this type of initiative, including soup kitchens, food pantries, or thrift stores for the poor.

At the Organizational or Institutional Level

Habitat for Humanity (www.habitat.org): This faith-based organization makes extensive use of volunteers for house building and other projects (see Chapter 7).

American Atheists (www.atheists.org): "Now in its fourth decade, American Atheists is dedicated to working for the civil rights of Atheists, promoting separation of state and church, and providing information about Atheism." Volunteers assist in this work through contributions, research, and legal support.

At the National and Global Levels

Several religious groups are committed to working for justice and peace at the national and global levels.

Tikkun Community (www.tikkun.org): This is an ecumenical organization, started by the Jewish community, to "mend, repair, and transform the world. . . . International community of people of many faiths calling for social justice and political freedom."

The American Friends Service Committee (www.afsc.org): This is "a Quaker organization which includes people of various faiths who are committed to social justice, peace, and humanitarian service." These and similar faith-based organizations sponsor many relief and peace projects around the world.

 For chapter-specific resources, including **Frontline**, **TED**, and **YouTube** videos; self-quizzes; web exercises; and more, visit **www.pineforge.com/oswmedia3e**.

Power and privilege *penetrate* every aspect of our lives. The chapter subtitle has a double meaning, however, for sociology helps us penetrate the sources and the consequences of power and privilege—both political and economic.

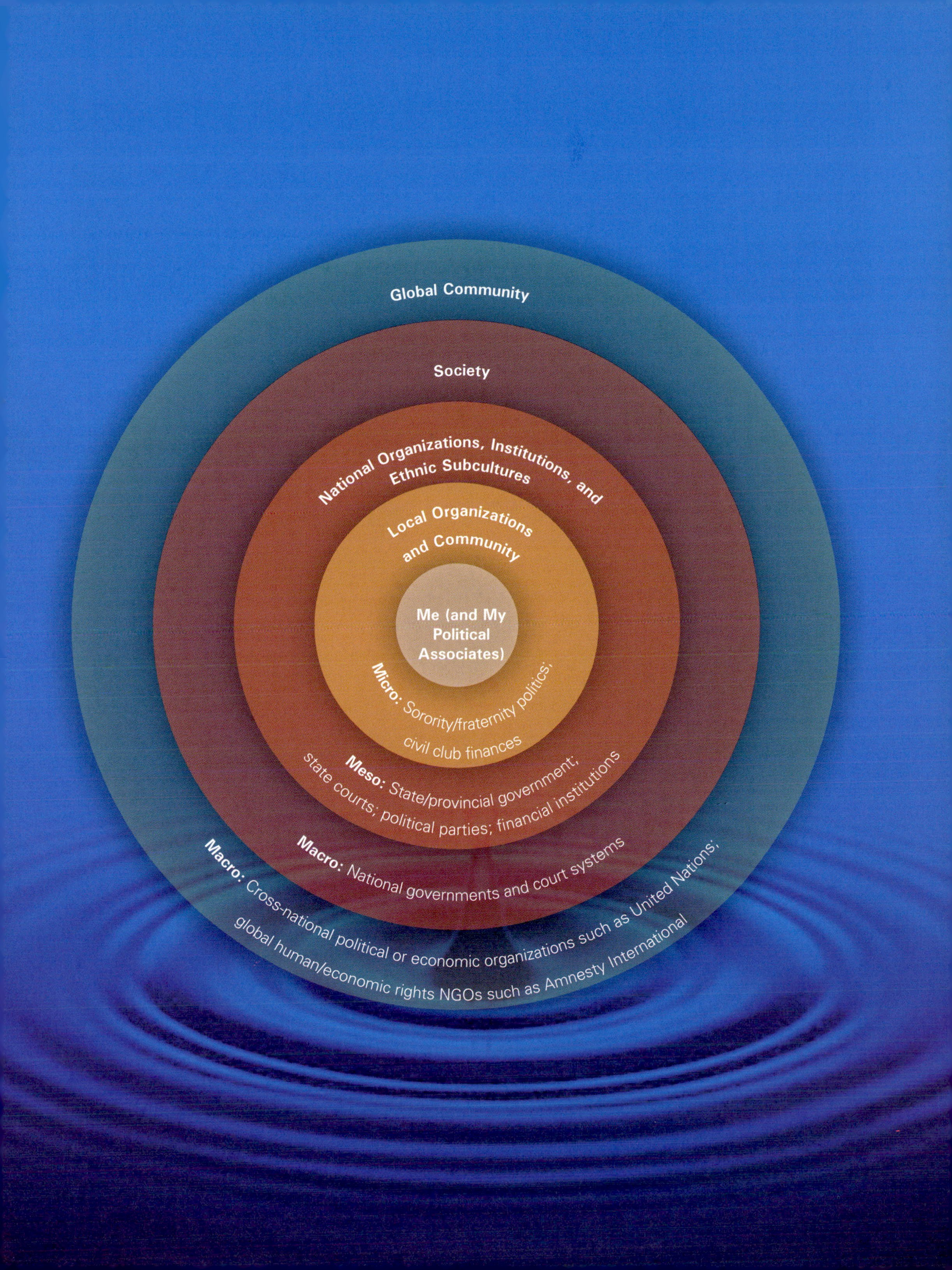

Global Community

Society

National Organizations, Institutions, and
Ethnic Subcultures

Local Organizations
and Community

Me (and My
Political
Associates)

Micro: Sorority/fraternity politics;
civil club finances

Meso: State/provincial government;
state courts; political parties; financial institutions

Macro: National governments and court systems

Macro: Cross-national political or economic organizations such as United Nations;
global human/economic rights NGOs such as Amnesty International

Imagine that a nuclear disaster has struck. The mortality rate is stunning. The few survivors gather together for human support and collectively attempt to meet their basic survival needs. They come from varying backgrounds and have diverse skills. Before the disaster, some—the stockbroker and the business executive, for instance—earned more money and held higher social status than the others, but that is in the past. Faced with the new and unfamiliar situation, different skills are more immediately important for survival.

Where should this group begin? Think about the options. Some sort of organization seems essential, a structure that will help the group meet its needs. Food, shelter, and medical care are paramount. Those with experience in agriculture, building trades, and health care are likely to take leadership roles to provide these initial necessities. As time goes on, the need for clear norms and rules emerges. These survivors decide that all members must work—must contribute their share of effort to the collective survival. At

first, these norms are unwritten, but gradually some norms and rules are declared more important than others and are recorded, with sanctions (penalties) attached for noncompliance. Committees are formed to deal with group concerns, and a semblance of a judicial system emerges. One person is appointed to coordinate work shifts and others to oversee emerging aspects of this small society's life. This scenario could play out in many ways.

What is happening? A social structure is evolving. Not everyone in the group will agree with the structure, and some people will propose alternatives. Whose ideas are adopted? Leadership roles may fall to the physically strongest, or perhaps the most persuasive, or those with the most skills and knowledge for survival. Those who are most competent at organizing may become the leaders, but that outcome is by no means assured.

Political systems that have developed and have been refined over centuries probably went through similar processes under less immediately dire circumstances. However, in our world of power and privilege, a war, an invading power, or revolutionary overthrow of an unstable government can change the form of a political system overnight, necessitating rapid reorganization. The daily news brings stories of governments overthrown by military leaders in coups, with new governments emerging to fill the gap.

The opening scenario and the political activity in our modern society share a common element—power. The concept of power is critical to understanding many aspects of our social world. Our primary focus in this chapter is on the political and economic dimensions of society, since both the political and economic systems enforce the distribution of power in a society. Political systems involve the power relationships between individuals and the larger social institutions. Economic systems produce and distribute goods and services. Not everyone gets an equal share, thus giving some citizens privileges that others do not have.

In this chapter, we will consider the nature of power, politics, and economics at each level in our social world; theoretical perspectives on power and privilege; individuals and power; political systems and the distribution of power and privilege through political and economic institutions; and national and global systems of governance, including international

Politics is about power and about mobilizing support to lead. The 2008 presidential primaries generated a lot of interest as these two U.S. senators—John McCain (left) and Barack Obama (right)—battled for the most powerful political office on the planet—the U.S. presidency.

conflicts, war, and terrorism. Because economics have been explored in many chapters of this book, such as chapters on inequality, more emphasis will be given to political systems and their relation to economic systems.

Thinking Sociologically

A nuclear disaster has killed all but a few people. How would you construct a social system from scratch? What are the issues that would need to be resolved if one were to build a system from scratch?

What Is Power?

Power is an age-old theme in many great scholarly discussions. Social philosophers since Plato, Aristotle, and Socrates have addressed the issue of political systems and power. Machiavelli, an early 16th-century Italian political philosopher, is perhaps best known for his observation that "the end justifies the means." His understanding of how power was exercised in the 15th, 16th, and 17th centuries significantly influenced how monarchs used the powers of the state (the means) to obtain wealth, new territories, and trade dominance (the ends).

The most common definition of power used in social sciences today comes from Max Weber (1947), who saw **power** as the ability of people or groups to realize their own will in group action, even against resistance of others who disagree.

Building on Weber's (1947) idea of power, we can identify various *power arenas*. First, the nation-state (national governments) attempts to control the behavior of individuals through (a) *physical control* (police force) or *outright coercion* (threats and actual violence), (b) *symbolic control* such as intimidation or manipulation of people, and (c) *rules of conduct* that channel behavior toward desired patterns, such as workplace rules. For instance, the military in Haiti used torture, rapes, and death to intimidate workers and families, representing physical force as a mechanism of power.

Second, Weber's definition explains power as the ability to influence social life. Wherever people interact or participate in activities or organizations, power is a consequence (Olsen 1970). Therefore, individuals who have an understanding of interorganizational dynamics and can manipulate organization members are likely to have more power than others in organizational settings.

Third, there is a perspective that focuses on a traditional Marxist approach to class structures, arguing that the control of economic resources and production allows the ruling class to keep ruling (Therborn 1976). People who control economic resources also protect their self-interests by controlling political processes through ideology, economic constraints, and physical coercion or political resources. Among many recent examples, Zimbabwe's leader, Robert Mugabe, used all these methods of controlling political processes to hold onto power. Thus, power is found in all parts of the social world and is an element of every social situation (Domhoff 2005; Kettl 1993). So how does power work at each level?

Thinking Sociologically

How do you, your family members, your boss, or your professors use power? Why does each of these people have power?

Power and Privilege at Various Levels in the Social World

Power can be found at the most micro levels of interaction, from individuals to family groups. In family life, husband-wife relations often involve negotiation and sometimes conflict over how to run a household and spend money. Interactions between parents and children also involve power issues as parents socialize their children. Indeed, the controversies over whether spanking is an effective discipline or an abusive imposition of pain is a question of how parents use their power to teach their children and control their behavior.

At the meso level, power operates in cities, counties, and states and provinces. Governments make decisions about which corporations receive tax breaks to locate their plants within the region. They pass laws that regulate everything from how long one's grass can be before a fine is imposed to how public schools will be funded. State and provincial governments in Global North democracies can also control the way people live and make their living. Therefore, people have an interest in influencing governments by selecting their leaders, contributing to political campaigns, and helping elect the people who support their views. Interest groups such as ethnic or minority groups and national organizations and bureaucracies also wield power and try to influence the political process at the meso level.

At the macro level, international organizations such as the United Nations and World Bank; nongovernmental organizations (NGOs) such as Doctors Without Borders;

Individuals can work to elect the party—and the candidates—that they think will make their lives better and improve conditions in the world. They work at the micro level to influence the meso and the macro systems.

and military, political, and economic alliances such as the North Atlantic Treaty Organization (NATO) are parts of the global system of power.

Thus, power processes pervade the micro, meso, and macro levels. Locally organized groups can force change that influences politics at the local, state/provincial, national, or global levels. Provincial or state laws shape what can and cannot be done at the local level. Laws at the national level influence state, province, or county politics and policies. Global treaties influence national autonomy.

Power can be studied in political structures such as governments, in political parties, and in different types of national political systems. It can also be understood in terms of the allocation of economic resources in a society and what factors influence patterns of resource distribution. Both economic and political systems are important in the sociologist's consideration of power distribution in any society. Let us first consider the theoretical lenses that help us understand power and politics.

Audio Link 13.1
Listen to an account of the 2001 Presidential election.

Theoretical Perspectives on Systems of Power and Privilege

Do you and I have any real decision-making power? Can our voices or votes make a difference, or do leaders hold all the power? Many sociologists and political scientists have studied these questions and found several answers to who holds power and the relationship between the rulers and the ruled.

Among the common theoretical perspectives on power are our familiar ones: interaction, functional, and conflict theories. Interaction theorists focus on symbols and constructions of reality that allow some people to assume power. A core concern is the legitimacy of power, or whether power is accepted by those who are ruled. Functionalists believe that citizens legitimize political systems by supporting them through their votes or traditions. They do this because political systems serve important functions, or purposes, in society. They establish and coordinate societal goals—for example, promoting stability, providing law and order, carrying out societal goals, engaging in relations with other countries, providing protection, and meeting social needs. Conflict theorists believe that the state protects the privileged position of a few, allowing them to consolidate power and perpetuate inequalities that keep them in power. This power elite theory stems from conflict theory's contention that power is concentrated in the hands of the elite, and the masses have little power.

Micro- and Meso-Level Perspectives: Legitimacy of Power

Interaction theorists focus on symbols and constructions of reality that allow some people to assume power. For symbolic interactionists, a central question is how loyalty to the power of the state is created—a loyalty that is so strong that citizens are willing to die for the state in a war. In the founding years of the United States, loyalty tended to be mostly to individual states. Even as late as the Civil War, northern battalions fought under the flag of their own state rather than that of the United States. The Federalist Party, which stressed centralized government in early U.S. history, faded from the scene. The Democratic Republican Party, which evolved into the current Democratic Party, had downplayed the power of the federal government. This has changed. Today, the Democratic Party generally supports a larger role for the federal government than its rival, although Republican President George W. Bush expanded federal powers substantially.

Most people in the United States now tend to think of themselves as U.S. citizens more than Virginians, Pennsylvanians, or Oregonians, and they are willing to defend the whole country. National symbols such as anthems and flags help create loyalty to nations. The treatment of flags is an interesting issue that illustrates the social construction of meaning around national symbols. The next "Sociology in Our Social World" explores this issue.

Sociology in Our Social World

The Flag, Symbolism, and Patriotism

Flags have become pervasive symbols of nations, creating a national identity (Billig 1995). In some countries, loyalty to the nation is taught with daily pledges to the flag at work or school. National loyalty becomes sacred—as does the flag itself. Indeed, the nation is *reified*—it becomes a concrete material reality through this symbol. Durkheim (1947) maintained that one's larger group elicits sacredness and, thereby, becomes *sacralized*. He believed that sacredness actually is a form of respect for that which transcends the individual, including the state.

In the United States, the flag and its construction illustrate key ideas in symbolic interaction theory. For many decades after the nation was founded, Americans had more loyalty to their state than to a federal government, but in the aftermath of the Civil War, a sense of nation began to gel (Answers.Com 2006).

Symbolic interactionists sometimes speak of the externalization, objectification, and internalization of important symbols (Berger and Luckmann 1966). In this case, the symbol was created (*externalized* by Betsy Ross in the summer of 1776), it came to have a life of its own separate from its creator (*objectified* by Presidential Order in 1912 when the official arrangement of stars was established), and it came to be incorporated by people as a symbol that was meaningful (*internalized* as a symbol of "us" for Americans; Independence Hall Association 2008). In places such as Britain and India, a national flag does not have the same symbolic power and internal resonance as a national symbol. This is not because those countries are less loyal to the nation or less proud of their heritage. It is that other symbols, such as royal status, work just as well.

Care of the U.S. flag is an interesting example of symbolism and respect for that symbol. Flag etiquette instructions make it clear that flying a flag that is faded, soiled, or dirty is considered an offense to the flag. We are told to either burn or bury a damaged flag as a way to honor and respect it.

Some propose a constitutional amendment prohibiting burning of the U.S. flag to prevent protestors from using the flag as a protest statement against certain American policies. Because protests show disrespect, some patriots have a visceral reaction of outrage. As recently as June 2006, the Senate came within one vote of sending the flag burning amendment to the individual states for ratification (CNN.com 2006). Supporters want flag burners punished and disrespect

for the flag outlawed. For many, the flag is dear and symbolizes all that is good about the United States (Billig 1995).

Those who oppose this amendment feel that only tyrannical countries limit freedom of speech. They feel that the principle of free speech, central to democracy, must be allowed even if a sacred symbol is at stake. Indeed, opponents of the amendment think passing such a law would be a desecration of what that flag stands for. The two sides have each attached different meanings to what is considered desecration of the national symbol. In the meantime, if you have a tattered or fading flag, burning it is the way you honor that flag—as long as you do so in private!

Other aspects of the U.S. Flag Code, which specifies what is considered official respect for or desecration of the flag, are interesting precisely because many people violate this code while they believe themselves to be displaying their patriotism.

1. The flag should *never* be used for advertising in any manner whatsoever. It should not be embroidered on cushions, handkerchiefs, or scarves, nor reproduced on paper napkins, carry-out bags, wrappers, or anything else that will soon be thrown away.
2. No *part* of the flag—depictions of stars and stripes that are in any form other than that approved for the flag design itself—should ever be used as a costume, a clothing item, or an athletic uniform.
3. Displaying a flag after dark should not be done unless it is illuminated, and it should not be left out when it is raining.
4. The flag should never be represented flat or horizontally (as many marching bands do). It should *always* be aloft and free.
5. The flag should under no circumstances be used as a ceiling covering. (U.S. Flag Code 2008)

According to the standards established by U.S. military representatives and congressional action, any of these forms of display may be considered a desecration of the flag, yet the meaning that common people give to these acts is quite different. Symbolic interactionists are interested in the meaning people give to actions and how symbols themselves inform behavior.

This man no doubt feels he is expressing his patriotism, yet technically he is violating the U.S. Flag Code and "desecrating" the American flag. During the Vietnam War, protesters risked attack for dressing this way, which was viewed as disrespect for the flag and the country.

Thinking Sociologically

Is wearing a shirt or sweater with the U.S. stars and stripes in some sort of artistic design an act of desecration of the flag or a statement of patriotism? Does flying a Confederate flag symbolize disrespect for the national U.S. flag? Why?

Socialization of individuals at the micro level generally includes instilling a strong sense of the legitimacy and authority of the reigning government in a particular society. This includes loyalty to a flag or a monarch that represents the nation.

Legitimacy, Authority, and Power: Social Constructions

Max Weber (1946) distinguished between legitimate and illegitimate power. Legitimate power, which he referred to as **authority**, is recognized as rightful by those subject to it. Governments are given legitimate power when citizens acknowledge that the government has the right to exercise power over them. This is measured by two factors: (1) whether the state can govern without the use or threat of forceful coercion and (2) the degree to which challenges to state authority are processed through normal channels such as the legal system (Jackman 1993). Citizens of Western societies recognize elected officials and laws made by elected bodies as legitimate authority. They adhere to a judge's rulings because they recognize that court decrees are legitimate. In contrast, illegitimate power, or coercion, includes living under force of a military regime or being kidnapped or imprisoned without charge (see Figure 13.1). These distinctions between legitimate and illegitimate power are important to our understanding of how leaders or political institutions establish the right to lead. To Weber (1946), illegitimate power is sustained by brute force or coercion. Authority is granted by the people who are subject to the power, which means that no coercion is needed.

Force + Consent = Power

Force < Consent = Legitimate Power (authority)

Force > Consent = Illegitimate Power (e.g., dictatorship)

Figure 13.1   Weber's Formula Regarding Power

How Do Leaders Gain Legitimate Power?

In constitutional democracies, those with power do not have the right to hold people against their will, to take their property, to demand they make unauthorized payments, or to kill them to protect others. Yet, even in democracies, certain people in power have the right to carry out such duties against people who are determined to be threats to society. How do leaders get these rights? To establish legitimate power or authority, leaders generally gain their positions in one of three ways:

1. *Traditional authority* is passed on through the generations, usually within a family line, so that positions are inherited. Tribal leaders in African societies pass their titles and power to their sons. Japanese and many European royal lines pass from generation to generation. Usually called a monarchy, this has been the most common form of leadership throughout history. Authority is seen as "normal" for a family or a person because of tradition. It has always been done that way, so no one challenges it. When authority is granted based on tradition, authority rests with the position rather than the person. The authority is easily transferred to another heir of that status.

2. *Charismatic authority* is power held by an individual resulting from a claim of extraordinary, even divine, personal

characteristics. Charismatic leaders often emerge at times of change when strong, new leadership is needed. The most vivid examples of charismatic leaders are Jesus, Muhammad, and the founder of the Mormon Church, Joseph Smith. Charismatic political leaders include Mao Zedong in China and Mahatma Gandhi in India. Both men led their countries to independence and had respect from citizens that bordered on "awe." Some women have also been recognized as charismatic leaders, such as Burma's (Myanmar) Aung San Suu Kyi, pro-democracy activist, widely recognized prisoner of conscience, leader of the National League for Democracy of Burma, and winner of the Nobel Peace Prize.

Other charismatic leaders such as Adolf Hitler, leader of Nazi Germany, and Jim Jones, leader of the Jonestown cult that urged its members toward mass suicide, were charismatic but led their followers to negative ends. The key point is that for charismatic leaders, unlike traditional authority leaders, the right to lead rests with the person, not the position. Followers believe power is rooted in the personality of a dynamic individual. This is an inherently change-oriented and unstable form of leadership because authority resides in a single person. Ultimately, as stability reemerges, power will become institutionalized—rooted in stable routine patterns of the organization. Charismatic leaders are effective during transitional periods but are often replaced by rational-legal leaders once affairs of state become stable.

3. *Rational-legal authority* is the most typical in modern nation-states. Leaders have the expertise to carry out the duties of their positions, and the leadership structure is usually bureaucratic and rule bound. Individuals are granted authority because they have proper training or have proven their merit. This is the form of authority most familiar to individuals living in democracies. The rational-legal form of authority often seems entirely irrational and an invitation to chaos to people in tradition-oriented societies. It is important that authority in this system is divided between the position (which establishes criteria and credentials for the position) and the person (who has achieved those credentials for the position).

Each of these three types of authority, according to Weber (1947, 1958), is a "legitimate" exercise of power because the people being governed give their consent, at least implicitly. However, on occasion, leaders overstep their legitimate bounds and rule by force.

Macro-Level Perspectives: Who Rules?

Pluralist Theory

Pluralist theory holds that power is distributed among various groups so that no one group rules. It is primarily

His Royal Highness Charles, Prince of Wales, at his investiture in Caernarvon Castle. Charles is next in line to inherit the throne of England, and his position has legitimacy because the citizenry of England consent to the system. The authority of the throne is traditional.

Protesters against the situation in Burma hold masks with the face of Aung San Suu Kyi outside the Chinese Embassy in London, England, on October 24, 2007. That marked the 12th anniversary of the leader's detention by the country's military regime in Myanmar. (The new dictatorship changed the name of the country as part of the effort to delegitimize her right to govern.) She is a charismatic leader, who is held in high esteem by those who admire her.

through interest groups that you and I influence decision-making processes. Our interests are represented by groups such as unions or environmental organizations that act to keep power from

Audio Link 13.2
Listen to stories about the rise of the GOP.

Pluralist theories see value in having many sources of power in a society, so that no one group can dominate. For workers, this usually means uniting to have a strong voice through unions. Here we see several hundred ironworkers and their supporters in Hong Kong stage a protest against poor pay and working conditions, outside the government's headquarters in 2007.

being concentrated in the hands of an elite few (Dahl 1961; Dye and Zeigler 1983).

Politics involves negotiation and compromise between competing groups. Interest groups can veto policies that conflict with their own interests by mobilizing large numbers against certain legislative or executive actions. Witness the efforts to influence health care reform in the United States and to reform government and industry practices. Greenpeace, Common Cause, Earth First!, Bread for the World, the Christian Coalition, Focus on the Family, various labor unions, and other consumer, environmental, religious, and political action groups have had impacts on policy decisions. According to pluralists, shared power is found in each person's ability to join groups and influence policy decisions and outcomes.

National or international NGOs can have a major impact on global issues and policy making, as exemplified by the Grameen Bank and other micro-credit organizations (Yunus and Jolis 1999). NGOs exert influence on power holders because of the numbers they represent, the money they control, the issues they address, and the effectiveness of their spokespeople or lobbyists. Sometimes they form coalitions around issues of concern such as the environment, human rights, health care, and women's and children's issues. An example is opposition to the U.S. Patriot Act by Libertarians on the far right and the American Civil Liberties Union on the far left. Although the groups differ on many issues, their opposition to infringements of civil liberties and individualism brought them together to contest many aspects of the Patriot Act, which was intended to fight terrorism.

According to pluralists, multiple power centers offer the best chance to maintain democratic forms of government because no one group dominates, and many citizens are involved. Although an interest group may dominate decision making on a specific issue, no one group dictates all policy.

Another major theory counters the pluralists, arguing that the real power centers at the national level are controlled by an elite few and that most individuals like you and me have little power.

Elite Theory

Power elite theorists believe it is inevitable that a small group of elite will rule societies. They argue that this is the nature of individuals and society and that pluralists are imagining a world that does not exist. Individuals have limited power through interest groups (Domhoff 2005, 2008; Dye 2002; Mills 1956), but real power is held by the power elite. They wield power through their institutional roles, make decisions about war, peace, the economy, wages, taxes, justice, education, welfare, and health issues—all of which have serious impact on citizens. These powerful elite attempt to maintain, perpetuate, and even strengthen their rule. Michels ([1911] 1967), a well-known political philosopher, believed that elite rule is inevitable. He described this pattern of elite domination as the **iron law of oligarchy**. In democratic and totalitarian societies alike, leaders have influence over who is elected to succeed them and to whom they give political favors. This influence eventually leads those in elite positions to abuse their power. (Michels [1911] 1967).

The social philosopher Pareto ([1911] 1955) expanded on this idea of abuse of power, pointing out that abuse would cause a counter group to challenge the elite for power. Eventually, as the latter group gains power, its members become corrupt as well, and the cycle—a circulation of the elite—continues. Corruption in many countries illustrates this pattern.

C. Wright Mills (1956) points out another angle, that there is an invisible but interlocking power elite in U.S. society, consisting of leaders in military, business, and political spheres, wielding their power from behind the scenes. They make the key political, economic, and social decisions for the nation. This group manipulates what the public hears (Mills 1956). At the turn of the century, the top U.S. elite included 7,314 people from these three spheres (Dye 2002). For example, in the business sphere, the top corporations control more than half of the nation's industrial assets, transportation, communication, and utilities. They also manage two thirds of the insurance assets. These corporations are controlled by 4,500 presidents and directors. According to the power elite theory, the U.S. upper class provides a cohesive economic-political power structure that represents upper-class interests (Domhoff 2005, 2008).

Private preparatory schools are one example of how elite status is transmitted to the next generation (Howard

2007; Persell and Cookson 1985). Many of those who hold top positions on national committees and boards or in the foreign policy-making agencies of national government attended the same private preparatory schools and Ivy League colleges—Brown, Columbia, Cornell, Harvard, University of Pennsylvania, Dartmouth, Princeton, and Yale.

Domhoff (2008) analyzed the power elite in domestic and foreign policy decision making and found that the elite have the strongest impact on national policy decisions because they run large corporations and financial institutions. Their common characteristics promote a network of connections, or "higher circles," and constitute a pool of potential appointees to top government positions. Key government officials come from industry, finance, law, and universities. They are linked with an international elite that helps shape the world economy. According to this theory, Congress ultimately has minimal power. The elected representatives accede to the power elite. Elite theorists believe that government seldom regulates business. Instead, business co-opts politicians to support their interests by providing financial support needed to run political election campaigns.

Pluralist theorists, however, disagree, believing that one reason we have big government is that a very powerful government serves as a balance to the enormous power of the corporate world. Big business and big government are safety checks against tyranny—and each is convinced that the other is too big. Thus, although middle-level white-collar workers make decisions in specialized areas of interest, their decisions have much less influence on our lives than those made at the macro level by the few at the top.

Thinking Sociologically

Is your national society controlled by pluralist interest groups or a power elite? Can individuals influence the power elite? What evidence supports your view?

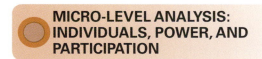

MICRO-LEVEL ANALYSIS: INDIVIDUALS, POWER, AND PARTICIPATION

Whether you have health insurance or are subject to a military draft depends in part on the political and economic decisions made by the government in power. Political systems influence our personal lives in myriad ways, some of which are readily apparent: health and safety regulations, taxation, military draft, regulations on food and drugs that people buy, and even whether the gallon of gas pumped into one's car is really a full gallon. In this section, we explore the impact individuals have on the government and

A Pakistani woman casts her ballot in the 2008 Pakistani national and provincial elections. The elections were considered a crucial step in moving Pakistan from military to civilian rule. Voting is viewed as a wonderful privilege and a source of hope in this setting.

the variables that influence participation in political and economic policy-making processes. A key issue at the micro level is decisions by individuals to vote or otherwise participate in the political system. This private decision is, in turn, affected by where those individuals fall in the stratification system of society, not just by personal choices.

Participation in Democratic Processes

Citizens in democratic countries have the power to vote. Most countries, even dictatorships, have some form of citizen participation. In only a handful of countries are there no elections. Sociologists ask many questions about voting patterns, such as what influences voting and why some individuals do not participate in the political process at all. Social scientists want to know how participation affects (and is affected by) the individual's perception of his or her power in relationship to the state. The "Applied Sociologist at Work" on page 442 discusses the world of a political sociologist as he considers the voting patterns of red, blue, and purple states in the United States.

Handbook Link 13.1
Read more about political sociology.

Ideology and Attitudes About Politics and Economics

Political ideology refers to how people think about power. Let us consider several ways that our beliefs and attitudes affect

The Applied Sociologist at Work— Ruy Teixeira

The Future of Red, Blue, and Purple America

The election of 2008 was exciting and unusual in the political arena. Prominent among those studying the election period is Dr. Ruy Teixeira, a sociologist and specialist in political demography and geography.

Dr. Teixeira's 2008 research was a joint project of the Brookings and American Enterprise Institutes. It considered the U.S. political scene with its red and blue states and, particularly, "purple" or swing states. Dr. Teixeira convened a group of researchers to consider social changes that affected the American political landscape. Each researcher focused on a specific aspect of the political scene. Dr. Teixeira focused particularly on the purple or swing states.

Past elections have been influenced by voters' needs and interests, the advance of suburbanization, the rise of baby boomers, and women's entry into the labor force. In the most recent election, new issues were shaping voter behavior. Seven dominant themes affecting the political landscape emerged from the work of these researchers:

1. The structure of American suburbs and changes in urban living patterns more generally

2. Geographic clustering—the idea that people are increasingly likely to live near, and vote like, those who look, act, and think just like them (Cushing and Bishop 2008)

3. Race and immigration factors, including changes in the numbers and voting patterns of Blacks, Hispanics, and Asians

4. Class structure changes, especially the decline of the White working class and the rise of the mass upper middle class

5. American family modifications, including the decline in the number of married couple households with children and the rise of the proportion of singles

6. Cultural issues that make the nation more secular, more religious, or both (what these changes in religious belief and practice mean for our politics)

7. Aging of the baby boomers, the largest generation in American history, and the rise of the millennials (Teixeira 2008)

According to Teixeira and colleagues, the American class structure has gone through major social shifts since World War II in education levels (more high school graduates and more college-educated citizens), types of occupations (more white-collar jobs), and income levels. Today there are fewer people in the white working class and a rise in the mass upper middle class. These demographic trends, the themes mentioned above, and geographic movements have resulted in new political alignments.

A reality of the first two presidential elections of the 21st century was political polarization enhanced by polarized media hype, gerrymandering of political voting boundaries, and cultural "sorting" of people supporting each major party. See Map 13.1 for the political breakdown of states in the 2004 presidential election. The political orientations of various groups shifted over two or three decades, resulting in deadlock on each side of the political spectrum. However, the researchers believe that this deadlock is likely to begin to ease by the 2016 elections. Growth in Hispanic and Asian groups, shifts of the population not only to different regions of the country but also to suburbs and just beyond the suburbs, changing family structures and shifting women's roles, aging of baby boomers, and the high levels of political engagement by "millennials" (younger people who generally value diversity) combine to suggest major changes by the 2016 election.

Dr. Teixeira predicts that "culture wars"—the polarization and clashes between segments of society over differences in values—will not be as important in the future. Issues such as how to help nontraditional families, improve education, and provide health care will be shared concerns that unite people. Therefore, he predicts that the polarization that has divided some communities will not last.

The range of methodological tools used by sociologists has been essential to Dr. Teixeira's work. Theories that help explain social structure and demographic change guide his research, and working with large data sets results in many of his findings. He is interested in the U.S. government, policy making, and wrestling with issues that face the country. Dr. Teixeira has found that sociology provides exceptionally useful theory and methods to help understand our political world.

Note: Dr. Ruy Teixeira is a Senior Fellow at The Century Foundation and American Progress, a Fellow at the New Politics Institute, and a Visiting Fellow at the Brookings Institution. Being a fellow means you are employed as a scholar to carry out research that meets the goals of the organization or *think tank*.

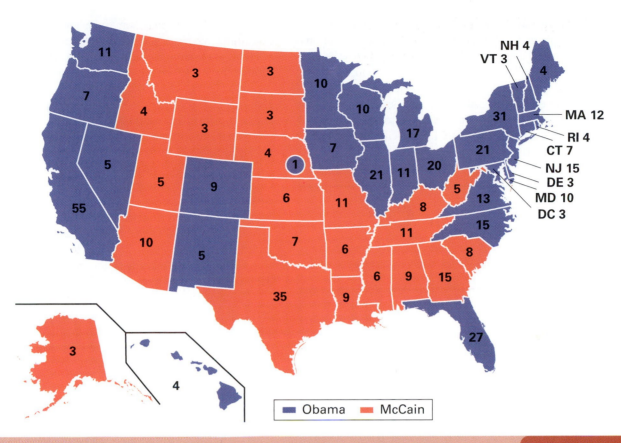

Map 13.1   States that voted Republican (McCain/Palin) or Democratic (Obama/Biden) in the U.S. Presidential Election of 2008. The numbers indicate electoral votes a state gets.

our political ideas. First, what do we believe about the power of the individual versus the power of the state? If we believe that individuals are motivated by selfish considerations and desire for power, we may feel as the 17th-century English philosopher Thomas Hobbes did: Humans need to be controlled, and order must be imposed by an all-powerful sovereign. This is more important than individual freedom and liberty. On the other hand, we might believe, as did John Locke, another 17th-century political philosopher, that human nature is perfectible and rational, that we are not born selfish but learn selfishness through experience with others. Humans, Locke argued, should have their needs and interests met, and among these needs are liberty, ability to sustain life, and ownership of property. He felt that the people should decide who governs them. Thus, we can see that support for democracy is influenced by one's core assumptions about what it means to be human.

Second, do we believe in equal distribution of resources, or do we think that those who are most able or have inherited high status should receive more of the wealth? Some social scientists, politicians, and voters think that individuals have different abilities and are therefore entitled to different rewards. Some are successful, and some are not. (Recall the structural-functional theory discussion in the stratification chapter about the inevitability of inequality.) Others think society should facilitate more equal distribution of resources

simply because all persons are equally deserving of human dignity. Conflict theorists tend to support this view.

In the United States, for example, Republicans (and others on "the right") tend to believe that individuals and local communities should take more responsibility for education, health care, welfare, child care, and other areas of common public concern, feeling that this protects rights to local control and prevents creation of a powerful bureaucracy. Democrats (and those on "the left") are more likely to argue for the federal government's social responsibility to the people. For instance, Democrats have been concerned that leaving policies such as school integration to local communities would perpetuate inequality and discriminatory patterns in some communities. National government involvement, they feel, protects the rights of all citizens. The ongoing debates about the national welfare system and health care policies in the United States reflect these different philosophies. Both parties support government spending and national laws; the question is for what: Military? Social programs? Education? Health care? Abortion? Prisons?

Third, do we believe that change is desirable? Generally, these views fall into two camps: change as a potential threat to stability versus policy change to benefit the general population or segments of the population. Views on change affect how people vote.

Voters in many countries are influenced by issues such as the environment or immigration rather than traditional party ideology. Party affiliation based on ideology is becoming relatively weak in the United States, and an increasing number of people are identifying themselves as independents rather than Democrats or Republicans, either because they do not want to commit themselves to one ideology or because they are more interested in specific issues than in an overriding philosophy of government.

Thinking Sociologically

How might your decision to vote (a micro-level decision) make a difference at the state/provincial, national, or global levels?

Levels of Participation in Politics

The majority of people in the world are uninvolved in the political process because there are few opportunities for them to be meaningfully involved (especially in nondemocratic countries). They feel that involvement can have little relevance for them (apathy) or that they cannot affect the process (alienation from a system that does not value them). However, political decisions may affect people directly, and they may be drawn unwittingly into the political arena. Peasants making a subsistence living may be forced off the land and into refugee camps by wars over issues that have little relevance to them. Their children may be drafted and taken away to fight and be killed in these battles. Religious or ideological factions may force them to help pay for conflicts in which they see no purpose or have no stake. In recent years, such situations have drawn the uninvolved into politics in Guatemala, Uganda, Cambodia (Kampuchea), Haiti, Rwanda, Somalia, India, Iraq, Lebanon, Gaza, and Darfur (Sudan).

Journal Article Link 13.1
Read about youth political involvement.

In representative systems, citizens are encouraged to have a voice, although their levels of involvement vary greatly. While some remain uninvolved, some vote in most elections but otherwise do not participate in politics. Others have contact with government representatives only when they have issues of personal concern. Still others are involved in local politics, actively working on issues or local elections that are of concern to them. The most involved engage in both local and national political campaigns (Verba and Nie 1972).

Political participation is affected by election laws, including those that enfranchise people, that stress voting as a requirement of citizenship, and that structure elections to facilitate representation by historically underrepresented groups. In some countries, voting is an obligation of citizenship and voter turnout is above 90%. In Australia and New Zealand, for example, it is a violation of the law not to vote and the election is extended over many days to ensure that people can get to the polls. Some other countries also make sure that ethnic minorities and women have a voice by structuring elections to ensure broad representation. The next "Sociology Around the World" on page 445 examines the reasons that an African country—the war-torn nation of Rwanda—emerged early in the 21st century with the highest percentage of women in government of any nation in the world.

In the United States, voter turnout went down from 63% of eligible voters in 1960 to 50% in 1996 to 47.3% in 2000. However, in the 2004 presidential election, turnout was 60% (Bergman 2005). More than 70% of citizens of age 45 and older voted in 2004, and 67% of Whites voted in 2004 compared with 60% of African Americans, 47% of Hispanics, and 44% of Asian Americans (Bergman 2005). In 2008, the turnout was 56.8% (Information Please Database 2008; McDonald 2009), and African American participation increased from 11.1% of the total electorate to 13% (Short 2009).

Participation in elections in the United States is the second lowest of the Global North democracies, as indicated in Table 13.1 (see page 446). This means that citizens are not exercising their right to vote. The unusually high number of "inactives" is not an encouraging sign for the vitality of a democracy (Orum 2001). Still, there was a resurgence of interest in politics among those under 30 years old during the 2008 presidential campaign as discussed in the "Sociology in Our Social World" feature on page 447, with the primary elections for nomination of candidates and the November election itself yielding record-breaking turnouts. Of course the fact that Barack Obama is very charismatic, he appealed to young voters with very intentional strategies using the latest technologies, and he is the first African American ever to be on the ballot for a major party made the presidential election an unusual draw for young people and for minorities.

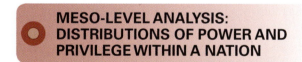

MESO-LEVEL ANALYSIS: DISTRIBUTIONS OF POWER AND PRIVILEGE WITHIN A NATION

A village within the Bantu society of southern Africa has lost its chief. Bantu societies provide for heirs to take on leadership when a leader dies. However, there is no male heir to the position, so a female from the same lineage is appointed. This woman must assume the legal and social roles of a male husband, father, and chief by acting as a male and taking a "wife." The wife is assigned male sexual partners, who become the biological fathers of children. This provides heirs for the lineage, but the female "husband" is their social father because she has socially become a male. This pattern has been common practice in many southern Bantu societies and among many other populations in four separate geographic areas of Africa. Anthropologists interpret this as a means of maintaining public positions of dominance and power in the hands of males in a particular

Sociology Around the World

Women and Political Change in Postgenocide Rwanda

By Melanie Hughes

In 2003, Rwanda became the new global leader in women's political representation. Women were elected to 49% of the seats in Rwanda's Chamber of Deputies, making it the most gender balanced of any national legislature in the history of the world (Paxton and Hughes 2007; see also Table 9.1 (p. 289). For the first time since 1988, a country outside of Scandinavia garnered the top spot in women's political representation, and for the first time in history, the position was held by an African country. From just 10 years earlier, the number of women serving in Rwanda's parliament almost tripled.

Many were particularly surprised about Rwanda's women's involvement, given the country's recent history of economic upheaval and civil war. The instability culminated in 1994, when during a span of 100 days, about 800,000 Rwandans died at the hands of their countrymen and countrywomen in horrific ethnic genocide. The economy and the old power structure were decimated. Many political leaders were killed or were among the more than 100,000 Rwandans imprisoned on charges of war crimes. So, how did Rwanda bounce back within a decade to lead the world in women's political representation? What follows is a brief discussion of what happened to catapult women to the top of Rwandan politics.

At the micro level, research suggests that the behavior of individual women during and after the Rwandan genocide generated support for their empowerment (Hughes 2004). During the civil war, women served on the front lines with men, led military actions, and worked as mediators to help end the insurgency. After conflict subsided, women played key roles in the reconstruction effort. Women took on new roles, becoming heads of their households and taking on traditionally male occupations. Women also adopted some 400,000 orphans from the war (UNIFEM 2002). Interviews with Rwandans suggest that the burdens taken on by women during this period generated both the political will and public support necessary to advance women in politics (Mutamba 2005).

Important changes also occurred at the meso level. Immediately after the killing subsided, women's associations, both new and old, began to step into the void (Longman 2005). Women's organizations took action early on to shape the new state. For example, in 1994, an organization of women's associations drafted a document addressing Rwanda's post-conflict problems and suggesting how women could foster reconciliation (Powley 2003). Building up to the adoption of the new constitution in 2003, women's organizations served as a bridge, taking suggestions from women at the grassroots level into meetings with the transitional government. These groups also made specific recommendations to ensure that the constitution provided space for women to participate in the political process. Women at all levels were supported by international organizations and foreign aid. Rwanda's economic troubles meant that dependence on international funding was unavoidable, and women were well situated to take advantage of foreign monies. The empowerment of women, especially in the Global South, was on the agenda of the United Nations and other global bodies. Therefore, many international organizations helped to advance the idea that women's incorporation into political decision-making positions was essential for sustainable peace. Research suggests that these global-level processes helped generate political change in Rwanda (Hughes 2004).

Action by individual women, native women's associations, and international organizations all helped to encourage the transitional government to adopt female-friendly political institutions. Women's councils and women-only elections were established to guarantee female representation down to the grassroots level. A Ministry for Gender and Women in Development was established, along with gender posts in all other government and ministerial bodies. The new constitution mandated that women fill 30% of all policy-making posts in Rwanda. These women-friendly political institutions, combined with the politicization of women during and after the war, help to explain the success of Rwandan women in politics.

Rwanda today is not a democratic country, but since their election in 2003, women have still been able to leave their mark on Rwandan politics. Women politicians have helped to revise inheritance laws, pass a law banning discrimination against women, and strengthen rape laws (Longman 2005). Some even argue that "women in government are now perceived by Rwandans as more approachable and trustworthy politicians than their male counterparts" (Remmert 2003:25). Skeptics argue that the focus on women diverts attention from the absence of ethnic diversity within government. But clearly, Rwanda has come a long way toward giving women a political voice.

Table 13.1 Voter Turnout Percentages for Elections Since 1945

Country	Voter Participation %
Italy	92.5
Iceland	89.5
New Zealand	86.2
South Africa	85.5
Austria	85.1
Netherlands	84.8
Australia	84.4
Denmark	83.6
Sweden	83.3
Germany	80.6
Greece	80.3
Guyana	80.3
Israel	80.0
Suriname	77.7
Malta	77.6
United Kingdom	74.9
Republic of Korea	74.8
Turkey	73.5
Argentina	70.6
Uruguay	70.3
Philippines	69.6
Papua New Guinea	69.1
Japan	69.0
Dominican Republic	68.7
Canada	68.4
Costa Rica	68.4
France	67.3
Bolivia	61.4
India	60.7
Bangladesh (6)	56.0
Switzerland	49.3
United States	48.3
Mexico	48.1
Peru	48.0
Brazil	47.9
Thailand	47.4
Chile	45.9
Ecuador	44.7
El Salvador	44.3
Colombia	36.2
Guatemala	29.8

Source: International Institute for Democracy and Electoral Assistance (2008).

Note: The figures are averages of voter participation for all elections over a 60-year period. Note that enfranchisement of women and various ethnic minorities has changed in some countries during that time, so these should be viewed as very crude overall indicators of voting patterns. To see the voting participation figures for 172 countries in the world, go to www.idea.int/vt/introduction.cfm.

Among the Bantu of Southern Africa, if a chief dies it is possible for a woman within the family lineage to succeed him, but she must take a "wife" and fulfill the leadership role normally established for males.

family and community (O'Brien 1977). Ruling groups in society, in this case a meso-level tribal society under the jurisdiction of a nation-state, have mechanisms for ensuring a smooth transition of power to keep the controlling structure functioning.

Meso-level political institutions include state or provincial governments, national political parties, and large formal organizations within the nation. Equally important is that meso-level political institutions influence and are influenced by other institutions: family, education, religion, health care, and economics.

Thinking Sociologically

First, read the essay on page 447. How important do you think the youth vote was in the most recent election? Were there other voting blocks—women, African Americans, Latinos, the religious right, blue-collar families, White males—that were more important in the outcome of this election?

What Purposes Do Political and Economic Institutions Serve?

Most of us have had an argument over ownership of property, have been in an accident, have met people who needed help to survive, or have been concerned about wars raging around the world. The political institution addresses these issues and serves a variety of other purposes, or functions, in societies. The economic institution includes the statuses, groups, and processes that ensure the production of goods and services that people in the society need to survive and to thrive.

Sociology in Our Social World

The Youth Vote in the U.S. Presidential Election of 2008

Despite rising levels of education, "young Americans," those under 30 years old, have had a lower rate of turnout than their older counterparts for several decades (Abramson, Aldrich, and Rhode 2007). Political scientists argue that the low rates of youth voters are the primary reason for the generally low turnout rates in American elections (Rosenstone and Hansen 1993). For this reason, the nonpartisan organization Rock the Vote was launched in 1990 in an attempt to stimulate political involvement of young people. Rock the Vote's strategies involved depicting voting as "fashionably subversive" and encouraging young adults to register, including facilitating voter registration online (Rampell 2008). Another nonpartisan movement—Declare Yourself—has used similar strategies. Rock the Vote and Declare Yourself each registered roughly a million young people, resulting in 4.2 million more people in this age group voting in 2004. Rock the Vote estimated that it registered at least 2 million in time for the 2008 presidential election (Smith 2008).

Yet Rock the Vote alone cannot claim all the credit for the major increases in new voters in 2008. According to the Youth Vote Coalition, 64% of young adults were registered to vote in the 2008 presidential election (Romano 2008). In the 2008 presidential primaries, the rate of participation among 18- to 29-year-old voters nearly quadrupled in Tennessee and Missouri (Rampell 2008). What was the reason for this increase in participation?

The 2008 election cycle involved candidates who excited many younger voters. Although he was the oldest person ever to be nominated for a first term as president, John McCain was deeply admired not only as a war hero but as an independent thinker and a "maverick" who stood up against the powerful, regardless of party, when he thought they were wrong (Powell 2008b). To add to the excitement, McCain selected Governor Sarah Palin, a relatively young woman—only the second in the history of the country to be nominated for the vice presidency—as his running mate. She brought to the ticket a reputation for being a courageous reformer and for standing up to the "old boy" system in her state.

On the Democratic side, many young women were drawn to Hillary Clinton as the first woman who seemed to have a realistic chance at the presidency. However, Barack Obama was the primary beneficiary of youth participation. Like John Kennedy in 1960 and his brother, Robert Kennedy, in 1968, Obama entered the race as a young candidate and an agent of change—visionary, charismatic, transcending the rhetoric of we/they politics, and exuding a message of hope (Bristow 2008). Equally important, an exit poll by NBC showed that voters between the ages of 18 and 29 were more likely than their elders to favor government intervention to solve problems, to oppose the Iraq War, and to select energy policy as the most important national issue (Keeter, Horowitz, and Tyson 2008). It is notable that all these preferences correspond with Obama's political strengths, ensuring that Obama's policies communicated the same visionary ideas of change that his personality did.

A third factor is the Obama campaign's incredible success at mobilizing younger voters. Obama's "Yes, we can" mantra was a YouTube video created by Will.i.am of the Black Eyed Peas, and many of Obama's speeches were put on YouTube (Geist 2008). The Obama campaign also used MySpace and Facebook heavily, including use of a Facebook group to encourage users to watch videos, donate money, and volunteer for the campaign (Greist 2008; Sarno 2008). Exit polls by NBC show that these efforts at mobilization paid off: 25% of younger voters were contacted by the Obama campaign, whereas just 13% were contacted by the McCain campaign (Keeter et al. 2008). Once they were contacted, many younger voters became a part of the campaign. David Plouffe, Obama's campaign manager, wrote that "at least 95 percent of our six thousand employees were under the age of thirty, most under the age of twenty-five" (Plouffe 2009:370).

Together, these various appeals added up to a major win among youth for the Obama campaign. Obama secured 66% of the vote among those under 30, compared with just 50% of the vote among those older than 30 (Keeter et al. 2008). Younger voters also rose as a proportion of total voters, particularly in key battleground states such as Indiana, North Carolina, and Virginia (Keeter et al. 2008). It is notable that just 62% of the 18 to 29 age group identifies their race as "White" compared with 79% among those in the 45 to 64 age group (Keeter et al. 2008). This suggests that Obama's strength among youth may have been compounded by the higher percentages of African American and Hispanic voters among the youngest age cohort. Younger voters were also the least likely to identify themselves as part of a religious tradition or attend church regularly, further suggesting that sociological differences played a role in the election's outcome. The 2008 election results show the largest gap between younger and older presidential voters since exit polling began in 1972, leading researchers to declare that "a significant general shift in political allegiance is occurring" (Keeter et al. 2008).

A study from the Harvard University Institute of Politics reports that this is not a one-time phenomenon but rather the "civic reawakening of a new generation" (Cillizza and Murray 2008). The idealism, the desire for national unity, the avoidance of red-state-blue-state polemics, the desire for hope and optimism, and the rejection of explicit racial or gender categories as defining characteristics of leadership have all been traits of this group of younger voters, and those attitudes have matched well with the emphasis of Barack Obama's campaign.

Note: Written with the assistance of Jeremiah Castle.

For most people, interaction with the government begins with a record of their birth and ends with a record of their death. In between, the government is the institutional structure that collects taxes, keeps records of the work activities and wages of citizens, and keeps fingerprints and other personal information on file.

We have learned in earlier chapters that each institution has purposes or functions it serves. Just as family, education, medicine, and religion meet certain societal needs, so do the political and economic systems. The following six activities are typical purposes (functions) of meso-level political and economic institutions. They set the stage for power and privilege carried out at the macro level in national and international arenas.

1. *To maintain social control:* We expect to live in safety, to live according to certain "rules," to be employed in meaningful work, and to participate in other activities prescribed or protected by law. Ideally, governments help clarify expectations and customs and implement laws that express societal values. However, in some cases, governments rule with an iron hand and people live in fear because of the social control imposed by government. This has been the case in Afghanistan under the Taliban, when leaders used armed militia to terrorize the country by imprisoning, torturing, and killing suspected dissenters to make sure the population did the Taliban's bidding.

2. *To serve as an arbiter in disputes:* When disputes arise over property or the actions of another individual or

A boy with a toy rifle sits on his father's shoulders at a pro-Taliban demonstration in late September of 2001 in Pakistan. The protest supported Osama Bin Laden and the Taliban movement in Afghanistan. Sometimes animosities toward a feared "other," such as the United States, are so strong that people will support even oppressive authoritarian regimes.

group, a judicial branch of government can intervene. In some systems, such as tribal groups mentioned above, a council of elders or powerful individuals perform judicial functions. In other cases, elected or appointed judges have the right to hear disputes, make judgments, and carry out punishment for infractions.

3. *To protect citizens of the group:* Governments are responsible for protecting citizens from takeover by external powers or disruption from internal sources. However, they are not always successful. Cities are often violent, gangs roam the streets, terrorists threaten lives, minority groups receive unfair treatment, and governments lose territory or even control of their countries to external forces. While Venezuelan President Hugo Chavez has nationalized some of the nation's oil and other industries to prevent foreign interests from controlling the country's resources, Mexico's President Felipe Calderon is fighting a difficult war against drug cartels (Herman and Peterson 2006; Oliver 2003; Parenti 2006).

4. *To represent the group in relations with other groups or societies:* Individuals cannot negotiate agreements with foreign neighbors. Official representatives deal with other officials to negotiate arms and trade agreements, protect the world's airways, determine fishing rights, and establish military bases in foreign lands, among other agreements. The four functions listed thus far are rather clearly political in nature; the last two are areas of contention between political and economic realms.

5. *To make plans for the future of the group:* As individuals, we have little direct impact on the direction our society takes, but the official governmental body—be it elected, appointed, or imposed through force—shares responsibility with economic institutions for planning in the society. In some socialist societies, this planning dictates what each individual will contribute to the nation: how many engineers, teachers, or nurses they need. They then train people according to these projections. In other societies, power is much less direct. In capitalist systems, for instance, supply and demand is assumed to regulate the system, and there is less governmental planning—especially in economic matters—than in socialist societies. The question of who plans for the future is often a source of stress between the political and economic institutions: Are the planners elected politicians or private entrepreneurs?

6. *To provide for the needs of their citizens:* Governments differ greatly in the degree to which they attempt to meet the material needs of citizens. Some provide for most of the health and welfare needs of citizens, whereas others tend to leave this largely to individuals, families, local community agencies, and other institutions such as religion. Not everyone agrees that providing needs is an inherent responsibility of the state. Their idea is that the economy will produce higher quality goods and in the right proportions for the population if the government gets out

of the way and lets individuals make the decisions based on what is in their self-interests. The debates over a health care system and welfare system in the United States point to the conflicts over who should be responsible—the state or private individuals. Should such services be coordinated by the government or left to "the invisible hand" of market forces?

The ways in which governments carry out these six functions are largely determined by their philosophies of power and political structures. Political and economic institutions, such as family and religious institutions, come in many forms. In essence, these variations in political institutions reflect variations in human ideas of power. The point is that functionalists focus on the positive role of each institution in the lives of people and for the stability of society.

Thinking Sociologically

In an era of terrorist threats, how do you think the "protecting the safety of the citizens" function has affected the ability of governments to meet their other functions?

Meso- and Macro-Level Systems of Power and Privilege

While *politics* refers to the social institution that determines and exercises power relations in society, *economics* is the social institution that deals with production and distribution of goods and services. Both politics and economics focus on questions related directly to the concept of power and power relationships between individuals, organizations, nation-states, and societies. How goods are distributed to the members of society—a major function of economics—is often determined by who has power.

Government officials have a vested interest in the well-being of the economy, for should the economy fail, the state is likely to fail as well. Recessions, depressions, and high rates of inflation put severe strains on governments that need stable economies to run properly. When problems occur, government officials are inclined to increase their roles in the economic sector. Witness the volatile money markets since 2008 and measures such as bailouts taken by governments to stabilize the economy.

In September 2008, the Dow Jones index dropped an unprecedented 777 points in 1 day and fell another 782 points 1 week later. The New York Stock Exchange, usually bustling, was nearly empty, and President Bush and Congress immediately began to look for "stimulus packages" to keep the economy from going into a deep recession. Turning the economy around then became one of the key challenges for President Obama.

The problem of a dramatic drop in financial markets is a loss of confidence so that no one invests, lending institutions are not able to loan money easily, business stagnates, unemployment rates skyrocket, and the entire government may be held responsible for lack of economic vitality. In February of 2009, Elkhart, Indiana, had an unemployment rate of more than 15%—a figure that approached the unemployment rates of the depression (S. Smith 2009).

When a country goes into a recession, the party in power is often held responsible and will not likely be reelected if the recovery takes too long. Economic recessions can destroy the

Video Link 13.1
Watch a video about national debt.

A stable economic system is essential to political stability, and extreme fluctuations in the economy are frightening to those in power. On the day the Dow Jones index dropped dramatically, the New York Stock Exchange, usually bustling with activity, was nearly empty.

careers of politicians but can also create such dissatisfaction that the entire government may be at risk of an uprising from citizens.

Indeed, Dennis Blair, the U.S. Director of National Intelligence, said in February 2009 that the global economic crisis is the most serious national security issue facing the nation (Miller 2009). He pointed out that in the past, countries have been able to export more goods to work their way out of a recession, but that is not possible when the economic slump is global. The result could be a "backlash against American efforts to create free markets," unstable governments, and waves of refugees crossing national borders (Miller 2009). The economic crisis could mean that governments cannot meet their defense obligations or provide the services necessary to their citizens. Therefore Blair called the extreme economic downturn a "bigger threat than Al Qaeda terrorists" (Haniffa 2009).

In many countries, the government is the largest employer, purchaser of goods, controller of exports and imports, and the regulator of industry and of interest rates. In the United States, many government regulatory agencies, such as the Food and Drug Administration, Department of Agriculture, and Justice Department, watch over the economic sector to protect consumers.

Types of Political Systems

The major political systems in the world range from fascist totalitarianism to democracy. However, each culture puts its own imprint on the system it uses, making for tremendous variation in actual practice. Two broad approaches are discussed below to illustrate the point.

Authoritarian Political Systems. The government of Kuwait is a hereditary monarchy based on traditional leadership. After the Persian Gulf War of 1991, it brought to trial and condemned to death a number of its citizens, mostly of Palestinian background, who were accused of collaborating with the Iraqis during the takeover of Kuwait. Although the sentences were commuted, this was a lesson to would-be dissenters. The regime has absolute power, allows little citizen involvement and no criticism of governmental decisions, and determines much of what happens in individuals' lives.

Authoritarian regimes headed by dictators or military *juntas* with absolute power are and have been common forms of government in the world. Some of these regimes are helpful to citizens, but most stamp out dissent. Saddam Hussein ruled in Iraq, Muammar Gaddafi remains in command of Libya, and the current military regime controls Myanmar (Burma), one of the world's most ruthless regimes.

Video Link 13.2
Watch a video about the changing power of the executive branch.

Totalitarian political systems: Russia under Joseph Stalin and Germany under Adolf Hitler were totalitarian dictatorships that followed strong ideologies and demanded adherence to them. Totalitarian states are often based on a specific political ideology and run by a single ruling group or party, referred to as an *oligarchy*. The state often controls the workplace, education, the media, and other aspects of life. All actions revolve around state aims. Dissent and opposition are discouraged or forcefully eliminated as we have seen in Iran in the past several years with violent crackdowns on demonstrators. Interrogation by secret police, imprisonment, and torture are used to quiet dissenters. Terror is used as a tactic to deal with both internal and external dissent, but when it is used by the state to control the citizenry or to terrorize those of another nation, it is called *state terrorism*.

Throughout history, most people have lived under authoritarian or totalitarian systems. Under certain conditions, totalitarian regimes can turn into democratic ones, and of course, democratically elected leaders can become self-proclaimed dictators, as was the case of Ferdinand Marcos in the Philippines. The next "Sociology Around the World" on page 451 provides an example of one totalitarian regime.

Democratic Systems. In contrast to totalitarian regimes, democratic systems are characterized by accountability of the government to the citizens and a large degree of control by individuals over their own lives. Democracies always have at least two political parties that compete in elections for power and that generally accept the outcome of elections. Mechanisms for the smooth transfer of power are laid out in a constitution or other legal document. "Ideal-type" democracies share the following characteristics, although few democracies fit this description exactly:

1.   *Citizens participate in selecting the government:* There are free elections with anonymous ballots cast, widespread suffrage (voting rights), and competition between members of different parties running for offices. Those who govern do so by the consent of the majority, but the political minorities have rights and representation.

2.   *Civil liberties are guaranteed:* These usually include freedom of association, freedom of the press, freedom of speech, and freedom of religion. Such individual rights ensure dissent, and dissent creates more ideas about how to solve problems. These freedoms are therefore essential for a democracy to thrive.

3.   *Constitutional limits are placed on governmental powers:* The government can intrude only into certain areas of individuals' lives. Criminal procedures and police power are clearly defined, thus prohibiting harassment or terrorism by the police. The judicial system helps maintain a balance of power. These limits have caused dissent in the United States in recent years, with debates over whether the Patriot Act inappropriately limits freedoms.

Sociology Around the World

The Khmer Rouge Revolution: A Totalitarian Regime

These skulls are the remains of people massacred by the Khmer Rouge government in the Killing Fields in Cambodia (also called Kampuchia).

When the Khmer Rouge faction took over the government of Cambodia in 1978, they abolished private property, relocated urban dwellers to rural areas, seized personal property, classified some people as peasants, workers, or soldiers—and killed the rest. Their most amazing feat was the total evacuation of the capital city, Phnom Penh. This was done to remove urban civilization and isolate Cambodia from other political influences, such as democracy.

This complete social and economic revolution under the leadership of Pol Pot was planned in Paris by a small group of intellectual revolutionaries. They believed that it would allow Kampuchea, their former name for the country, to rebuild from scratch, eliminating all capitalism, private property, and Western culture and influence.

After urban dwellers were resettled in rural camps, the totalitarian regime tried to break down the family system by prohibiting contact between members, including sexual relations between husbands and wives. Many people, including defeated soldiers, bureaucrats, royalty, businesspeople, intellectuals with opposing views, Muslims, and Buddhist monks were slaughtered for minor offenses—hence the term *the killing fields* to describe the execution sites. The death toll is estimated at more than 1.25 million. However, the Cambodian Genocide Program has uncovered meticulous records kept by Khmer Rouge leaders, and combined with evidence from mass graves, these data may double that number (Crossette 1996; Mydans 2009).

Famine followed the killings, causing many Cambodians to flee their land, traveling by night and hiding by day to reach refugee camps across the border in Thailand. Today, the economy in Cambodia is growing, especially in the areas of garment work and tourism. Thousands of tourists visit the ancient temples of Angkor Wat and the Killing Fields each year. Despite growth, more than 80% of the citizens work in agriculture, and 90% of poverty is in rural areas (Asian Development Bank 2002).

The economy in Cambodia mostly provides sweatshop employment. More than 200,000 young women work in the 200 export garment factories, making clothes for companies such as The Gap. Their wages were $35 a month in 2002. To keep their jobs, they must often work overtime, up to 80 hours a week, with no extra pay (Sine 2002).

Cambodia has never been a country at peace, and that seems to be true today. Violence still exists. The Human Rights Center reports chaos, corruption, poverty, and a reign of terror in Cambodia, as the military kills and extorts money from citizens. Killings, violence, and intimidation surrounded elections in 2002, with more than 14 killings of political activists and candidates (U.S. Department of State 2002). The Khmer Rouge is still a threat to any hopes of democracy, but since the United States government officially recognizes the current government in Cambodia, it will not grant political refugee status to any new refugees from Cambodia.

Within a democracy, individuals have a variety of ways in which they can influence the government such as voting, working for political parties, and protesting policies. Such individual voices are greatly enhanced if one has constitutional guarantees of freedom of speech. In this photo protestors in front of the U.S. White House in Washington, D.C., try to get the attention of President Obama regarding the policies affecting women's rights in Iran.

4. *Governmental structure and process are spelled out:* Generally, some officials are elected whereas others are appointed, but all are accountable to the citizens. Representatives are given authority to pass laws, approve budgets, and hold the executive officer accountable for activities.

5. *Written documents such as constitutions are the basis for the development of legal systems:* The constitutions describe activities in which the government must—or must not—engage. Constitutions can provide some protection against tyrants and arbitrary actions by government. The two main forms of democratic constitutional government are the parliamentary and presidential systems. In typical parliamentary governments, the head of state is often a monarch, and the head of government is a prime minister, chancellor, or premier. These are two different people. Belgium, Canada, Denmark, the United Kingdom, Japan, the Netherlands, Norway, and Sweden have this model. Examples of presidential governments include France, Italy, the United States, and Germany. The presidents in these countries tend to have more autonomy than the heads of parliamentary governments.

▶ **Video Link 13.3**
Watch video about President Obama's Blackberry.

Proportional representation means that each party is given a number of seats corresponding to the percentage of votes it received in the election. In winner-take-all systems, the individual with more than 50% of the votes gets the seat. In the United States, the "winner-take-all" system has come under attack because the winner of the presidential popular vote can lose the electoral vote to an opponent who wins several of the most populous states by narrow margins. This actually happened in the presidential election in the United States: Al Gore received the most votes for president in 2000, but because all but two states (Maine and Nebraska) had a winner-take-all system for electing the Electoral College, George W. Bush became the next president, as elected by the Electoral College. Defenders of this system of choosing the president argue that this protects the voice of each state, even if each individual voice is not given the same weight.

Constitutional governments may have from two to a dozen or more parties, as has been the case in Switzerland. Most have four or five viable ones. In European countries, typical parties include Social Democrats, Christian Democrats, Communists, Liberals, and other parties specific to local or state issues, such as green parties.

Technology and Democracy

In the modern world, there are new challenges and issues that face democracies. Electronic technology—the Internet and other telecommunications technologies—can be a boon to democracy, an opportunity for people around the world to gain information necessary to be an informed electorate, or a burden that hinders thoughtful debate and civic engagement in ideas. The latter are essential ingredients of a functioning democracy (Barber 2006).

The Internet, fax machines, camcorders, and other telecommunications devices have been major instruments for indigenous people, linking them to the outside world and combating oppressive governments. On the other hand, blogs, talk shows, Web pages, and Internet discussions are often known more for sound bites and polemical attacks on opponents than for reasoned debates in which opposing sides express views.

The key contribution that these technologies bring is speed. However, speed is not necessarily good for democracy:

> Democracy takes thought, patience, and reconsideration. That is why parliamentary procedure often requires several readings of a legislative bill prior to passage. The aim is to require time before precipitous action is taken. . . . Both representative and direct democracy are speed-averse, requiring time and patience to implement civic judgment. (Barber 2006:64)

Representative democracy involves citizens electing officials periodically and then letting them make the decisions. In a direct democracy, the voters make major policy decisions, and citizens work in communities to govern their social life, develop civic trust, and create social capital. This, of course, requires a literate and well-informed electorate, which does not always exist.

Rapid communication can help individuals stay in touch with their representatives in a representative democracy—witness the mass text messaging at the 2008 Democratic convention. However, we must be aware of the pros and cons of various technologies for democratic decision making. Several features of technology can produce contradictory outcomes:

1. Speed and the need for careful deliberation in democratic process

2. The tendency of digital media to reduce everything to simplistic binary opposites, as though only two choices are possible

3. The tendency to isolate individuals behind their own keyboards and monitors, so that collaborative skills may wane

4. Pictorial images that sensationalize issues so that decisions are based on emotional responses more than reasoned deliberation

5. Immoderate, impulsive rhetoric, divisive attacks by people who know little or nothing about the history of the problem (as often happens on blogs and talk shows)

6. The tendency for the Internet (and many other media) to be primarily about commerce—creating a consumer mentality rather than a place for debate and problem solving

7. A confounding of information (with which we are sometimes overloaded) with wisdom, which is solely needed

Social policy consideration—careful deliberative reflection—is necessary if we are to have technology benefit and not undermine democratic systems (Barber 2006).

Thinking Sociologically

How can the seven issues of technology be problems for representative democracy? Which are benefits? What effect do they have on direct participatory democracy?

Types of Economic Systems

As societies become industrialized, one of two basic economic systems evolves: planned or market systems. **Planned or centralized systems** involve state-based planning and control of property, whereas **market systems** stress individual planning and private ownership of property, with much less governmental coordination or oversight. These basic types vary depending on the peculiarities of the country and its economy. For instance, China has a highly centralized planned economy

The British system of government is a democracy and parliamentary in form. This is the opening ceremony in 2007 for the Parliament. Note the pomp and circumstance that are used to create a sense of awe for power and authority.

with strict government control, yet some private property and incentive plans exist, and these are expanding. The United States is a market system, yet the government puts many limitations on business enterprises and regulates the flow and value of money. Distinctions between the two major types rest on the degree of centralized planning and the ownership of property. In each type of system, decisions must be made concerning which goods (and in what quantity) to produce, what to do in the event of shortages or surpluses, and how to distribute goods. Who has power to make these decisions helps determine what type of system it is.

Market Systems/Capitalism. The goal of capitalism is profit, made through free competition between competitors for the available markets. It assumes that the laws of supply and demand will allow some to profit, while others fail. Needed goods will be made, and the best product for the price will win out over the others. No planning is needed by any oversight group because the invisible hand of the market will ensure sufficient quality control, production, and distribution of goods. This system also rewards innovative entrepreneurs who take risks and solve problems in new ways, resulting in potential growth and prosperity.

The goal of capitalist manufacturers is to bring in more money than they pay out to produce goods and services. Because workers are a production cost, getting the maximum labor output for the minimum wage is beneficial to capitalists. Thus, for example, multinational corporations look for the cheapest world sources of labor with the fewest restrictions on employment and operations. Marx predicted that there would be victims in such a system—those whom the system exploited. This potential for exploitation leads most governments to exercise some control over manufacturing and the market, although the degree of control varies widely.

Capitalism was closest to its pure form during the Industrial Revolution, when some entrepreneurs gained control of the capital and resources to manipulate those who needed work and became laborers. Using available labor and mechanical innovations, these entrepreneurs built industries. Craftspeople such as cobblers could not compete with the efficiency of the new machine-run shops, and many were forced to become laborers in new industries to survive.

Marx predicted that capitalism would cause citizens to split into two main classes: the **bourgeoisie**, capitalists who own the means of production (the "haves"), and the **proletariat**, those who sell their labor to capitalists (the "have-nots"). He argued that institutions such as education, politics, laws, and religion would evolve to preserve the privileges of the elite. Religious ideology often stresses hard work and deference to authority, allowing entrepreneurs to increase profits that benefit the owners. Furthermore, members of the economic and political elite usually encourage patriotism to distract the less privileged from their conflicts with the elite. According to Marx, the elite want the masses to draw the line between "us" and "them" based on national loyalty, not based on lines of economic self-interests (Gellner and Breuilly 2009). So in Marxist thought, even patriotism is a tool of the elite to control the workers. However, Marx believed that ultimately the workers would realize their plight, develop political awareness or consciousness, and rebel against their conditions. They would overthrow the "haves" and bring about a new and more egalitarian order.

The revolutions that Marx predicted have not occurred in most countries. Labor unions have protected workers from the severe exploitation that Marx witnessed in the early stages of industrialization in England, and capitalist governments have created and expanded a wide array of measures to protect citizens, including social security systems, unemployment compensation, disability programs, welfare systems, and health care systems. Therefore, workers have not been discontent to the point of revolt, but they have expressed frustrations through union walkouts and strikes followed by compromises between workers and capitalist owners.

Some contend that the largest corporations in the United States have such enormous power that they "own the United States." By the onset of this century, the largest 635 corporations controlled three quarters of corporate assets. Moreover, the combined sales of the 200 largest corporations surpass the combined federal budgets of all but 10 countries in the world (Rothenberg 2006a; U.S. Census Bureau 2001). A few elite businesspeople control many top companies through a system of interlocking directorates, giving them enormous power (Domhoff 2005, 2008; Rothenberg 2006). If people running the corporations pursue their own interests, as some corporate heads seemed to do even after they received

millions in "federal rescue money" in 2008 and 2009, the nation and the populace may be in trouble.

The capitalist emphasis on market control encourages a close relationship between U.S. corporations and the government's decision-making apparatus. Business interests often argue that government intervention in markets or regulation of commerce discourages competition, encourages mergers, and causes concentration of wealth and power in fewer and fewer hands. Thus, they argue that it is in the best interests of corporate decision makers to have influence in politics and government. According to power elite theorists, they do!

Thinking Sociologically

Should we be worried that freedom of the press—and therefore democracy—is threatened when a few corporations own a very large number of the nation's radio stations and newspapers? Why or why not?

One of the major criticisms of pure capitalism is that profit is the only value that drives the system. Human dignity and well-being, environmental protection, rights of ethnic groups, and other social issues are important only as they affect profits. This leaves some people deeply dissatisfied with capitalism.

Planned Systems. Planned systems attempt to deemphasize private control of property and economic autonomy and have the government do economic planning. Matters of production and labor are, in theory, governed with the "communal" good in mind. There is deep suspicion of the exploitation that can occur when individuals all pursue their own self-interests. Those who hold to this philosophy believe that the market system also results in oligarchy—a system run by the financial elite in the pursuit of their own self-interests. According to Marxist analysis, when the ideal state is achieved, motivating incentives for individuals such as earning more money are not needed. Each individual contributes to the general welfare of the community or society in exchange for benefits from the system, including food, shelter, employment, schooling, and cultural events. The state oversees the total economy. Monotonous, tedious jobs are shared voluntarily by all. The idea is that this frees individuals to concentrate on the humanistic and culturally important aspects of life. Values other than profits can be protected and affirmed. China, Cuba, and about 24 nations in Africa, Asia, and Latin America have planned economies with industry controlled by the state (Freedom House 2002).

In reality, however, no system is a perfect planned state with the complete elimination of private property or differences in privilege. China, based on a planned and government-controlled system, made rapid progress in tackling hunger, illiteracy, drug addiction, and other problems by using its strong central government to establish 5-year economic development plans. Today, however, the government is experimenting with new economic plans, including limited private entrepreneurship, more imported goods, and trade and development agreements with other countries. Much of China has moved beyond the survival level and can experiment with modifications to the economic system. China has not, however, granted much political freedom to its citizenry.

One key criticism of planned systems is that placing both economic power and political power in the hands of the same people can lead to control by a few leaders, leading to tyranny. Multiple power centers in government, the business world, and the military can balance each other and help protect against dictatorships and tyranny (Heilbroner and Milberg 2007).

Mixed Economies (Democratic Socialism). Some systems are mixed economies, sometimes called "welfare states" or "democratic socialism" because they try to balance societal needs and individual freedoms. **Democratic socialism**, for example, refers to collective or group planning of the development of the society, but within a democratic political system. Private profit is less important than in capitalism, and the good of the whole is paramount. Planning may include goals of creating equality, protecting the environment, or supporting families, but individuals' rights to pursue their own self-interests are also allowed within certain parameters. The system seeks checks and balances so that both political and economic decision makers are accountable to the public. Several countries, including Sweden, the United Kingdom, Norway, Austria, Canada, and France, have incorporated some democratic socialist ideas into their governmental policies, especially in public services (Olsson 1990).

Many western European democracies redistribute income through progressive tax plans that tax according to people's ability to pay. The government uses this tax money to nationalize education, health plans and medical care, pensions, maternity leaves, and sometimes housing for its citizens. Although much of the industry is privately run, the government provides regulations for the industry and assesses high taxes to pay for government programs. Typically, public service industries such as transportation, communications, and power companies are government controlled.

When President Obama was elected, he was faced with a huge economic crisis that was extremely complex, but most analysts believe that a major cause had been deregulation of banks and a system of loans for home mortgages and businesses. The President—like his Republican predecessor, George Bush—pushed a massive stimulus plan through

The China and Vietnam systems have been highly centralized economies in which the government has done the planning. In recent years, both countries have permitted more initiatives by entrepreneurs, rewarding those who would take a risk in the market. This photo is of a bustling street in Ho Chi Minh City in Vietnam.

Congress, this one for $787 billion (Espo 2009). The problem was lack of regulation of the economy, and the solution was support for corporations and businesses on a massive scale. That is not the only form of socialism; so is Social Security, Medicaid, Medicare, farm subsidies, a national parks system that ensures open natural spaces, the idea of public schools to educate the citizenry, policies that limit pollution and protect the environment that all the citizens share, and thousands of other programs that most Americans affirm. So despite hostility to the term *socialism*, any government program that "bails out" the economy or that "protects consumers" is a component of a mixed economy.

Audio Link 13.3 Listen to an economic discussion of Jamaica and Barbados.

Economic systems that attempt to balance market and planned economies are relatively recent experiments in governance, and they remain an idealized vision that has yet to be fully implemented or understood. In some ways, democratic socialist states outproduce capitalist ones, and in some ways, they can seem cumbersome ways to run a complex society. The bottom line in evaluating which system works best comes down to value priorities: individualism and economic growth for the system versus values such as equality, distribution of wealth, and protection of the environment.

Many Marxists in Europe believe that democratic socialism is what Karl Marx really had in mind, not the bureaucratic system that evolved in the Soviet Union,

China, and elsewhere. Marx, after all, felt that the worst of all governments was *state capitalism*—a system in which the state controlled the economy. His early writings, in particular, put much more emphasis on decentralization and even a withering away of the government (Marx 1963). Few social democrats today think that the government will ever wither away, but they think that the public, not just the elite, should have input into economic as well as governmental decisions and planning. The market system (capitalism) and the planned systems (socialism and communism) both have their advocates, but each system also has its shortcomings. The question, then, is whether there is an economic system that can avoid the dangers of each.

More than two centuries ago, it was widely believed, perhaps rightly at that time, that democracy could not work. The notion of self-governance by the citizenry was discredited as a pipe dream. Yet this experiment in self-governance is continuing, despite some flaws and problems. In a speech to the British House of Commons in 1947, then Prime Minister Winston Churchill said that "democracy is the worst form of government, except for all those other forms that have been tried" (Churchill 2009). Some economists and social philosophers have argued that if the people can plan for self-governance, they certainly should be able to plan for economic development in a way that does not put economic power in the hands of a political elite.

The institutions of politics and economics cannot be separated. In the 21st century, new political and economic relationships will emerge as each institution influences the other. Both institutions ultimately have a close connection to power and privilege.

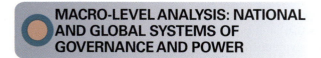

Power and the Nation-State

A **nation-state** is a political, geographical, and cultural unit with recognizable boundaries and a system of government. Boundaries of nation-states have been established through wars, conquests, negotiations, and treaties. These boundaries change as disputes over territory are resolved by force or negotiation. For example, Russia and the country of Georgia had a conflict in 2008 over whether two breakaway provinces of Georgia—Ossetia and Abkhazia—belonged within the national boundaries of Georgia. There are more than 200 nation-states in the world today, 192 of which are represented in the United Nations (United Nations 2007). This number is increasing as new independent nation-states continue to develop in Europe, Asia, Africa, and other parts of the world.

Within each nation-state, power is exerted by the systems that govern people through leaders, laws, courts, tax structure, the military, and the economic system. Different forms of power dominate at different times in history and in different geographical settings.

The notions of the nation-state and of nationalism are so completely internalized as realities that we do not stop to think of them as social constructions of reality, created by people to meet group needs. In historical terms, nationalism is a rather recent or modern concept, emerging only after the nation-state (Gellner 1983, 1993; Gellner and Breuilly 2009).

Medieval Europe, for example, knew no nation-states. One scholar writes that

> throughout the Middle Ages, the mass of inhabitants living in what is now known as France or England did not think of themselves as "French" or "English." They had little conception of a territorial nation (a "country") to which they owed an allegiance stronger than life itself. (Billig 1995:21)

Some argue that the nation-state has "no precedent in history" (Giddens 1987:166) prior to the 16th century and perhaps considerably later than that.

This raises an interesting question: Why did nation-states emerge in Europe and then spread throughout the rest of the world? This is one of the major puzzles of modern history, and it has to do with the change to rational organizational structures (Billig 1995). It is noteworthy that today every square foot of the Earth's land space is thought to be under the ownership of a nation-state. Yet, even today, a sense of nationalism or patriotism linking one's personal identity to the welfare of a nation is a foreign idea to many. People have loyalty to their region, their ethnic or tribal group, their religious group, or their local community, but a sense of being Pakistani, Kenyan, or Afghani is weak at best. Yet, in places such as the United States, having a passionate sense of national loyalty for which one would die is so taken for granted that anyone lacking this loyalty is suspect or deviant. Note the earlier discussion of the role of the flag. The nation is largely an imagined reality, something that exists because we choose to believe that it exists (Anderson 2006; McCrone 1998). Indeed, for some people, belonging to the nation has become the substitute for religious faith or belonging to local ethnic groups (Billig 1995; McCrone 1998).

Revolutions and Rebellions

From the 1980s to the new century, significant social and political changes have taken place throughout the world. The Berlin Wall was dismantled, leading to unification of East and West Germany. The Baltic states of Estonia, Latvia, and Lithuania became independent. In Eastern Europe, political and social orders established since World War II underwent radical change. When the Soviet Union and Yugoslavia broke apart, national boundaries were redrawn. Internal strife resulted from ethnic divisions formerly kept under check by the strong centralized governments in both areas.

Were these changes revolutions? *Revolution* refers to social and political transformations of a nation that result when states fail to fulfill their expected responsibilities (Skocpol 1979). Revolutions can be violent, and they result in altered distributions of power in the society. Revolutions typically occur when the government does not respond to citizen's needs and when leadership emerges to challenge the existing regime. News from around the world frequently reports on nation-states that have been challenged by opposition groups attempting to overthrow the regimes. In 2008 and 2010, Thailand's prime minister faced threats from opposition forces demanding that he resign due to corruption and lack of action on pressing problems, charges not substantiated in a court of law but compelling to the citizenry. Revolutions are also enhanced by new technologies, as is discussed in the next "Sociology Around the World."

Journal Article Link 13.2
Read about revolutionary movements.

The Meso-Macro Political Connection

State or provincial governments and national political parties are meso-level organizations that operate beyond the local community, but they are less encompassing in their influence than national or federal governments or global systems. Still, decisions at the state or provincial government level can have major influences in political processes at the national level. We have already seen some of these debates elsewhere in this book in discussions of state and federal policies on same-sex versus strictly heterosexual marriage. There were likewise controversies in 2009 when some state governors refused the federal funds for the economic stimulus plan—an act that some analysts thought might undermine the recovery. Here we look at another issue: the recent controversies about how to nominate and elect a president within the United States. Although the focus is on the U.S. political system, this discussion should be seen as illustrative of the tensions and peculiarities of the meso-macro link in any complex political system.

In some U.S. states, each political party runs its own caucuses (face-to-face meetings of voters in homes, schools, and other buildings) to discuss policy and to carry out public votes. In caucus states, the political party funds and operates the process of selecting delegates who will nominate the presidential candidate. In contrast, other states have primary elections run by the state government, but even these are not all the same. On the Democratic side, states distribute their delegates based on the proportion of the vote won by a

Revolutions can be violent overthrow of governments or nonviolent events such as this Burmese monk protest that was violently suppressed by the government in Myanmar, formerly Burma.

Zapatista commanders from the state of Chiapis hold a Mexican flag as they attend a mass rally in Mexico City's main square. They are calling for indigenous rights, including clean water and schooling for their children through sixth grade. The Zapatistas wear masks to avoid identification and persecution by the government, despite the fact that they are nonviolent. They are in communication with other human rights movements around the globe.

Sociology Around the World

Social Networking and Political Protests

By Jeremiah Castle

Several political events in 2009 show how social networking Web sites such as Facebook and Twitter can be crucial resources for protestors seeking to mobilize other like-minded individuals and garner attention from the international community. Such was the case in Moldova in 2009, when a group of several hundred citizens accusing the ruling communist party of rigging election used Twitter, Facebook, and text messages to mobilize potential sympathizers, resulting in a crowd of over 10,000 protesters the next day (*NY Times*, April 8, 2009:A1). Their success led the media to nickname the protests "the Twitter Revolution" (Barry 2009; Johnson 2009; Stone and Cohen 2009).

Similarly, when Iran quarantined international reporters following the disputed 2009 election, reporters and Iranian citizens used Twitter and other Web sites to send news to the global community. Tweeters were posting about 30 messages a minute related to Iranian protests, and protesters were flooding government Web sites in an attempt to crash government servers, reportedly with some success (Landler and Stelter 2009). Twitter played such an important role that members of the U.S. State Department asked Twitter to delay scheduled server maintenance to keep the lines of communication open (*NY Times*, June 17, 2009). Other protesters used YouTube to distribute videos of police beating crowds, raiding Tehran University, and shooting women in the streets, causing concerns among the media due to the graphic nature of the videos and the difficulty in verifying their authenticity (Stelter 2009). Despite these concerns, it is clear that social networking Web sites played an enormous role in mobilizing and sustaining the protests.

These subversive uses of the Internet led the Iranian government to attempt to silence protesters by blocking text messages and Facebook, but protesters were able to use proxy servers located in other countries to continue their efforts (*NY Times*, June 16, 2009). Similarly, China attempted to block access to Web sites including Twitter, blogspot.com, and YouTube in an effort to silence dissenters in advance of the 20th anniversary of the government's use of force against protesters in Tiananmen Square. However, some users were able to get around the block, as evidenced by a number of unfavorable tweets regarding the 1989 crackdown on protesters (Twigg 2009). Together, these unsuccessful efforts at blocking access to Web sites demonstrate one of the advantages of using the Internet to coordinate protests: the Internet is so vast that no government can censor every outlet of subversive expression without shutting it down altogether. Thus, evidence suggests that social networking Web sites will continue to "empower people living under less than democratic governments around the world" (*NY Times*, June 16, 2009:A11).

---

candidate in that state. On the Republican side, the delegate selection may be based on the proportion of the vote for each candidate, whereas in other states, it is a winner-take-all system, even if one candidate wins by only a half of a percentage point. One state (Texas) has both a primary election and a party caucus. Still others have a formula by which some delegates are elected in the primary based on proportion of the statewide vote, while others are chosen based on who wins each congressional district (see Table 13.2).

This means that some state governments decide when the primaries will be held, while elsewhere the primaries are "owned" by the political parties. Eleven states have split primaries, so the Democratic and Republican primaries are not on the same day: Hawaii, Idaho, Kansas, Maine, Montana, Nebraska, New Mexico, South Carolina, Washington, West Virginia, and Wyoming. New Hampshire has in its state constitution a clause that the state must have the first presidential primary.

Thinking Sociologically

Is it acceptable that some states never get any say in the nomination of candidates because the process is completed before they vote? Should one state be able to write into its constitution that it must have the first primary election, or should this be a decision that is somehow made at the national level? Who has the authority to tell a state it cannot put that in its constitution?

Table 13.2 Meso-Level Presidential Nomination Variations in the United States

	State-Run Primary (P) Versus Party-Run Caucus (C)	Closed (CL), Semiclosed (SC), Open (O)[1]	Winner-Takes-All (WTA) Proportional (%) Combination (Combo) Purely Advisory (Advisory)[2] Delegate Selection
Alabama	P	O	Rep: Combo; Dem: %
Alaska	C	SC	Rep: %; Dem: %
Arizona	P	CL	Rep: WTA; Dem: %
Arkansas	P	O	Rep: %; Dem: %
California	P	SC	Rep: %; Dem: %
Colorado	C	CL	Rep: %; Dem: %
Connecticut	P	CL	Rep: WTA; Dem: %
Delaware	P	CL	Rep: WTA; Dem: %
Florida	P	CL	Rep: WTA; Dem: %
Georgia	P	SC	Rep: WTA; Dem: %
Hawaii	P	CL	Rep: %; Dem: %
Idaho	P	O	Rep: %; Dem: %
Illinois	P	SC	Rep: %; Dem: %
Indiana	P	O	Rep: WTA; Dem: %
Iowa	C	SC	Rep: %; Dem: %
Kansas	C	Rep: CL; Dem: SC	Rep: %; Dem: %
Kentucky	P	CL	Rep: %; Dem: %
Louisiana	P	CL	Rep: %; Dem: %
Maine	C	CL	Rep: %; Dem: %
Maryland	P	CL	Rep: WTA; Dem: %
Massachusetts	P	SC	Rep: %; Dem: %
Michigan	P	O	Rep: WTA; Dem: %
Minnesota	C	O	Rep: %; Dem: %
Mississippi	P	O	Rep: WTA; Dem: %
Missouri	P	O	Rep: WTA; Dem: %
Montana	P	Rep: CL; Dem: O	Rep: Advisory; Dem: %
Nebraska	C	CL	Rep: Advisory; Dem: %
Nevada	C	CL	Rep: %; Dem: %
New Hampshire	P	SC	Rep: %; Dem: %
New Jersey	P	CC	Rep: WTA; Dem: %
New Mexico	P	CL	Rep: %; Dem: %
New York	P	CL	Rep: WTA; Dem: %
North Carolina	P	CL	Rep: %; Dem: %
North Dakota	C	O	Rep: WTA; Dem: %
Ohio	P	SC	Rep: WTA; Dem: %
Oklahoma	P	CL	Rep: WTA; Dem: %
Oregon	P	CL	Rep: %; Dem: %
Pennsylvania	P	CL	Rep: Advisory; Dem: %
Rhode Island	P	SC	Rep: %; Dem: %
South Carolina	P	O	Rep: WTA; Dem: %
South Dakota	P	CL	Rep: %; Dem: %
Tennessee	P	O	Rep: WTA; Dem: %

(Continued)

(Continued)

	State-Run Primary (P) Versus Party-Run Caucus (C)	Closed (CL), Semiclosed (SC), Open (O)[1]	Winner-Takes-All (WTA) Proportional (%) Combination (Combo) Purely Advisory (Advisory)[2] Delegate Selection
Texas	P and C	Prim: SC; Cauc: CL	Rep: WTA; Dem: %
Utah	P	Rep: CL; Dem: O	Rep: WTA; Dem: %
Vermont	P	O	Rep: WTA; Dem: %
Virginia	P	O	Rep: %; Dem: %
Washington	C	O	Rep: Combo; Dem: %
West Virginia	P	Rep: CL; Dem: O	Rep: Combo; Dem: %
Wisconsin	P	O	Rep: WTA; Dem: %
Wyoming	C	CL	Rep: %; Dem: %
Washington, DC	P	CL	Rep: WTA; Dem: %

Source: BBC News (2008), Bowen (2008), The Center for Voting and Democracy (2008), The Green Papers (2008a), The Green Papers (2008b), National Archives and Records Administration (2008), *The New York Times* (2008), Project Vote Smart (2008), State of Delaware (2008), Voting and Democracy Research Center (2008).

With a contentious U.S. election held in 2008, several controversial questions were raised. Can a political party tell a state when to have its elections and then punish that state if it does not obey by refusing to seat its delegates at the party convention? This is exactly what happened in Michigan and Florida in 2008. However, it gets even more complicated. In Florida, a Republican-dominated legislature moved the date of the primary election. The Democrats from that state were outvoted in the state legislature, but they still lost the right to represent their state at the convention where a presidential candidate is nominated. Can a state legislature—a meso-level political entity—tell a national political party—another meso-level political entity—how to run its nomination process? The answers to these questions are not clear, yet they can have profound effects on who becomes the next president of the most powerful nation on Earth.

In some states, only members of the party can vote. In other states, citizens who are registered as independents can vote in either the Republican or Democratic primary election and help select the party's candidate. In other states, Democrats and Republicans can cross over and vote in the primary for the other party. What are the implications of having different rules in different states about crossover party voting?

Finally, in some states, the Republican primary is a "beauty contest" with no binding outcome. The results are purely advisory, and the delegates from that state are free to ignore the outcome of the election. The delegates are selected by the party insiders in that state, not by the voters. The Democratic Party has only recently passed a national policy banning this kind of primary. On the other hand, the Democratic Party has 915 "super delegates"—party insiders who have not been elected by the populace and who may commit their votes to anyone they please. So both parties allow delegates to vote who are not representing any constituency that elected them. What are the implications for a democracy?

Even selection of the Electoral College, which actually decides who will be president after the general election, is not uniform in policy across the states. Two states—Nebraska and Maine—have proportional distribution of electors and all the others have winner-take-all. If one additional state with large numbers of electors were to shift to proportional distribution of electors, it could change the outcome of our national elections for a long time to come. Should there be consistency between the states in the way the Electoral College is selected? Should state elections all be proportional or all be winner-take-all?

Because the Constitution grants considerable autonomy to states to make these decisions, how does the nation ever get consistency? At the state (meso) level, legislatures are very protective of their right to make their own decisions. Yet governance of the nation and the nation's relationships with the global community may be at stake. The point is this: Meso-level political power can shape power at the macro level, which then influences policies relevant to individual lives. The three levels are intimately linked. This complex link is explored in the next "Engaging Sociology."

Global Interdependencies and Politics

Dependency theorists and world systems theorists point out the inequality between rich core countries and developing peripheral countries that are dependent on the core countries. The more dependent a country is, the more inequality is likely to exist between that country and core countries. The physical quality of life for citizens in dependent countries is also likely to be poor. For example, permitting a foreign company to mine resources in a Global South country may produce a short-term gain in employment for the country and may make some leaders wealthy, but when the exhaustible resources are gone, the dependent country is often left with its natural resources destroyed and an even poorer economy (Wallerstein 1979, 1991).

Young democracies are emerging in peripheral countries in eastern Europe, East Asia, and Latin America. In several Central and Latin American countries formerly ruled by civilian and military dictatorships, democratic governments are taking hold, and elected officials are gaining power. Despite the movement toward political liberalization, democracy, and market-oriented reforms in countries such as Chile, Mexico, Nigeria, Poland, Senegal, Thailand, and Turkey, not all these societies are ready to adopt democratic forms of governance. In a study of the experiences of 26 developing Asian, African, and Latin American countries, the conclusion was that several factors were important for these countries to develop stable democracies: political participation, interest groups, economic growth, control of corruption, and maintenance of order without reducing liberty (Diamond 1992, 2009). In addition, literacy is critical for the citizens of a democracy to be informed voters.

The most affluent countries in the Global North have democracies, but there is some question about how to create a democratic system in poor countries with different cultural values and systems (Etounga-Manguelle 2000). What are the chances that the United States or another powerful nation-state will be successful in attempts to create democracies elsewhere? The odds are probably not good, according to a number of political analysts. Foreign powers can do little to alter the social structure and cultural traditions of other societies, and as indicated, these structures are key to the successful development of democracy. If the imposed system is premature or incompatible with the society's level of development and other institutional

Handbook Link 13.2
Read about global environmental politics.

Engaging Sociology

Political Decisions: Social Processes at the Micro, Meso, and Macro Levels

Imagine that your state legislature is considering a change in the presidential election process. Your electoral college state representatives would be selected according to the percentage of the popular vote in your state going to each candidate (Republican, Democratic, Libertarian, and Green Party). (*Note*: Currently, almost all states distribute their electors on a winner-takes-all basis.)

1. Identify two possible micro-level consequences of this policy change. (For example, how might it affect an individual's decision to vote or how the local board of elections does its job?)

2. Identify three consequences at the macro level. (For example, how might the change affect how presidential candidates spend their resources and time, how might Congress respond to such an initiative, and so forth?)

3. How does this illustrate the influence of meso-level organization on micro and macro levels of the social system? For example, is it a problem for a *national* democracy when the delegate selection system is so complete a variable at the meso level, or does this make elections even more democratic because states can make their own autonomous decisions? Explain your answer.

structures, authoritarian dictatorship rather than democracy may emerge as the traditional authority structure breaks down. Some scholars believe certain preconditions are necessary for the emergence of democracy:

- High levels of economic well-being
- The absence of extreme inequalities in wealth and income
- Social pluralism, including a particularly strong and autonomous middle class
- A market-oriented economy
- Influence in the world system of democratic states
- A culture that is relatively tolerant of diversity and can accommodate compromise
- A literate population informed about issues (Bottomore 1979; Inglehart 1997)

Thinking Sociologically

Why might some analysts believe that Iraq—where the United States is attempting to set up democracy—may not be ready for a successful democratic government at this time? Which of these conditions are in place and which ones are missing in Iraq?

Socioeconomic development strengthens democracy by contributing to social stability (Diamond 1992). Promoting democracy means offering moral, political, financial, and diplomatic support to efforts to replace authoritarian regimes (Diamond 1992, 2003). Thus, an outside power can help establish the structures necessary to support democracy but is seldom successful trying to impose it. If countries in the Global North want more democracies around the world, an important strategy is to support economic development in less affluent countries. Again, politics and economics are intertwined.

Some developing countries see discussions of democracy as a ploy—a cover-up used by dominant affluent nations for advancing their wealth. For example, the Global North nations have combined to form a coalition of nations calling itself the Group of Seven (or the G7—the United States, Japan, Germany, Canada, France, Great Britain, and Italy). Recently, Russia was added, and the group is now the G8. The G8 uses its collective power to regulate global economic policies to ensure stability (and thereby ensure that members' interests are secure). The G8 has the power to control world markets through the World Trade Organization, the World Bank, and the International Monetary Fund (Brecher, Costello, and Smith 2006; Stein 2006; Weidenbaum 2006; Weller and Hersh 2006). Global South nations responded to the G8 with an organization of poor countries that they called the G77. They are attempting to create collective unity so they will have some power

to determine their own destinies (Brecher et al. 2006; Hayden 2006). Map 13.2 shows where the G8 and G77 nations are located.

Political systems can face threats from internal sources such as disaffected citizens, the military, and interest groups vying for power, or they can be challenged by external sources such as other nations wanting land or resources or by coalitions of nations demanding change. This is the situation for North Korea and Iran as coalitions of nations demand that they drop their nuclear enrichment programs. Sometimes these power struggles erupt into violence. The following section discusses how war, terrorism, and rebellion challenge existing systems.

Violence on the Global Level

Once upon a time, gallant knights in shining armor went forth to battle with good luck tokens from their ladies and the cause of their religion or their monarch to spur them on. They seldom died in these battles, and the daily life of the society went on as usual. In contrast, since the invention of modern weaponry, no one has been safe from death and destruction in war. Weapons can destroy whole civilizations. A malfunctioning computer, a miscalculation, a deranged person, a misunderstanding between hostile factions, or a terrorist attack could kill millions of people.

War is armed conflict occurring within, between, or among societies or groups. It is sometimes called

Palestinian schoolchildren take cover under their desks in their classroom during an emergency drill in Israel. This exercise to prepare for war is stimulated by the government's fear of attacks by neighboring enemies. Children in North America today seldom live with such anxieties.

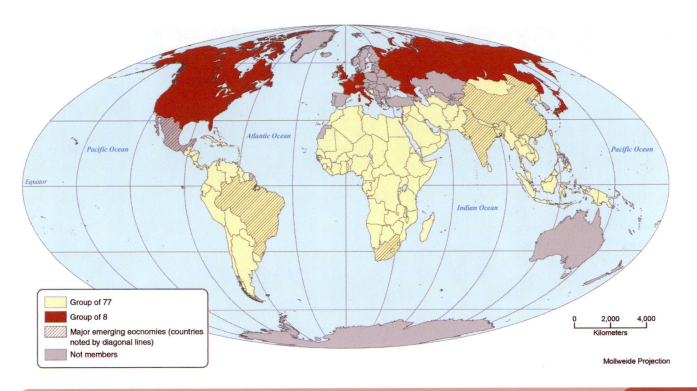

Map 13.2   Countries of the Group of 8, Major Emerging Economies, and Countries of the Group of 77

Source: www.g77.org, retrieved April 2008. Map by Anna Versluis.

"organized mass violence" (Nolan 2002:1803). War is a frequent but not inevitable condition of human existence. Many countries are now engaged in wars that are debilitating and detrimental to their economies and morale. Some of these wars (between India and Pakistan, in the Sudan, between Palestine and Israel, and between rival factions in the Congo) have lasted for years. Others have been short and decisive, such as the "Desert Storm" war with Iraq. Table 13.3 lists ongoing world conflicts as of 2009.

Why Do Nations Go to War?

Leaders use moral, religious, or political ideology to legitimize war, although the cause may be conflicts over economic resources or ethnic tensions. Wars have been waged to support religions through crusades and jihads; to liberate a country from domination by a foreign power; to protect borders, resources, and cultural customs; and to capture resources, including slaves, land, and oil. War can also distract citizens from other problems in their country, and it may therefore be used by politicians intent on staying in power. On the other hand, there are cultures where war is virtually unknown. Groups, often isolated, live in peace and cooperation, with little competition for land and resources. The bottom line is that war is a product of societies and their leaders, created by societies, and learned in societies.

Two familiar sociological theories attempt to explain the social factors that can lead to war. Functional theorists think underlying social problems cause disruptions to the system, including war, terrorism, and revolution. If all parts of the system were working effectively, they contend that these problems would not occur. Agents of social control and a smooth-running system would prevent disruptions. However, some functionalists also argue that war brings a population together behind a cause, resulting in social solidarity.

Conflict theorists see war, terrorism, and revolution as the outcome of oppression by the ruling elite and an attempt to overthrow that oppression. Many businesses profit from wars because their manufacturing power is put to full use. In fact, more money is spent on war than on prevention of disease, illiteracy, hunger, and other human problems. Citizens from the lower classes and racial minorities join the military, fight, and die in disproportionate numbers. Since they are more likely to join the military as an avenue to employment and job training, they join as enlistees who serve on the front lines and are more at risk. Often perceived social inequities lead to wars, such as the conflicts in Northern Ireland where Catholics feel that Protestants have come to control the land that Catholics once called their own.

Table 13.3   Significant Ongoing Armed Conflicts, 2009

Main Warring Parties	Year Began[1]
Middle East	
U.S. and UK vs. Iraq	2003
Israel vs. Palestinians	1948
Yemen: Government forces vs. the rebel group Shabab al-Moumineen (The Youthful Believers)	2004
Turkey: Government forces vs. the Kurdish Workers' Party (PKK)	1999
Asia	
Afghanistan: U.S., UK, and Coalition Forces vs. al-Qaeda and Taliban	2001
India vs. Kashmiri separatist groups/Pakistan	1948
India vs. Assam insurgents (various)	1979
Philippines vs. Mindanaoan separatists (MILF/ASG)	1971
Africa	
Algeria vs. Armed Islamic Group (GIA)	1991
Somalia vs. rival clans and Islamist groups	1991
Sudan vs. Darfur rebel groups	2003
Uganda vs. Lord's Resistance Army (LRA)	1986
Europe	
Russia vs. Chechen separatists	1994
Latin America	
Colombia vs. National Liberation Army (ELN)	1978
Colombia vs. Revolutionary Armed Forces of Colombia (FARC)	1978
Colombia vs. Autodefensas Unidas de Colombia (AUC)	1990

Sources: Project Ploughshares, www.ploughshares.ca, and Information Please Database, (2009).

Note: As of October 2009.

1. Where multiple parties and long-standing but sporadic conflict are concerned, date of first combat deaths is given.

Some nations are more war prone than others, and one cannot tell simply by paying attention to the rhetoric about war and peace. U.S. politicians give much vocal support to peace, but the country has been at war 193 of the 233 years since the colonies declared independence. Indeed, during the entire 20th century, there were only 6 years when the United States was not engaged in some sort of military action around the world (Brandon 2005; Noguera and Cohen 2006).

Video Link 13.4
Explore the relationship between Iran and the U.S.

The conclusion is that war is not a natural or biological necessity. It is in large part a result of leaderships' decisions. Some sociologists believe that war—like incest, slavery, and cannibalism (which at times were thought to be instinctual but have come to be understood as aberrations)—can be "unlearned" (Stoessinger 1993), though not all agree.

How Can Nations Avoid War?

Deterrence is one approach to discourage and perhaps avoid war. Some government officials argue that if a nation is militarily strong, no one will dare attack it, and the country will be secure. Leaders can "negotiate from strength." Believers in this approach argue that nations should become superior to others or maintain a balance with other militaristic nations. However, evidence from ongoing statistical analyses of militarization concludes that deterrence has not been effective in reducing the chance of war. The more militarized a country becomes, the more likely the country is to enter into war. Continual buildup of weapons increases mistrust and raises the potential for misunderstandings, mistakes, or disaster. Furthermore, military personnel often have a vested interest in war—that is, what the military is trained to do and what proves its competence. Business interests and economies may also profit from supporting war.

Deterrence is extremely expensive. As countries develop their military power, the spiral toward bigger, more sophisticated, and expensive technological weaponry such as nuclear weapons in North Korea and Iran continues. Figure 13.2 shows military spending around the world giving rise to what is often called the military-industrial complex. The question is whether *brinkmanship*, expending money and pushing the potential for conflict to the brink, works to deter others. The question has been applied to many international conflicts, including North Korea. Two classic experiments (Deutsch and Krauss 1960; Deutsch and Lewicki 1970) that have been replicated numerous times consider the many possible strategies leading up to brinkmanship and how to reduce threats. The results indicate that parties with similar power or wealth usually do not lock themselves into positions they cannot reverse, especially if they will continue to have interaction with their opponents. Brinkmanship is a high-risk strategy.

World military expenditures in 2009 were $1.46 trillion. The United States accounts for 48% of world military spending, an estimated $675 billion in 2010, not counting nuclear weapons at $23 billion a year (Shah 2009b). Military expenditures are usually at the expense of social programs such as education and health care. Spending for weapons widens the gap between rich and poor countries and diverts money from social causes at home and abroad (Ayers 2006). Still, many people feel that protection of the citizenry is the government's most essential responsibility.

In 2008, 20% of the U.S. budget went to the Defense Department (Runningen and Faler 2008). How the

A soldier, just back from Iraq after finishing his service, looks at boots of nearly 2,000 U.S. soldiers and thousands of Iraqi civilians killed during the Iraq war. The display was at a Military Park in Newark, New Jersey. Those who have served in wartime know better than anyone the agonies and costs of war that statistical tables and pie charts cannot convey.

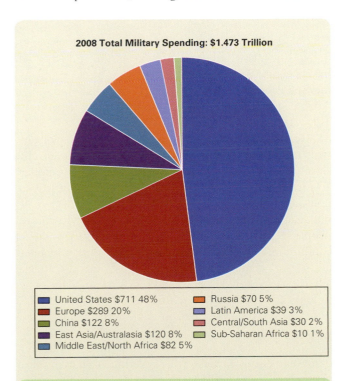

2008 Total Military Spending: $1.473 Trillion

- United States $711 48%
- Europe $289 20%
- China $122 8%
- East Asia/Australasia $120 8%
- Middle East/North Africa $82 5%
- Russia $70 5%
- Latin America $39 3%
- Central/South Asia $30 2%
- Sub-Saharan Africa $10 1%

Figure 13.2   U.S. Military Spending Versus the World, 2008 (in billions of U.S. dollars and percentage of total global)

Source: From *The FY 2009 Pentagon Spending Request—Global Military Spending* by Christopher Hellman and Travis Sharp. Center for Arms Control and Non-Proliferation, February 20, 2008. Reprinted with permission.

military budget percentage is calculated varies depending on whether social security trust fund and other programs are figured into the total annual budget. If they are not, the percentage of spending on the military is dramatically higher. Stockpiles of U.S. weapons have been reduced somewhat in the last year from 10,000 long- and short-range nuclear weapons, enough to annihilate the human race many times over, to 5,200 intact warheads and 2,702 deployed warheads in 2009 ("Current U.S. and Russian Nuclear Weapons Stockpiles"; J. Johnson 2007; R. Johnson 2007; SIPRI Yearbook 2010). There are an estimated 31,000 nuclear warheads deployed or in the stockpiles of eight nations: China, France, United Kingdom, India, Israel, Pakistan, Russia, and the United States. About 13,000 are deployed, and 4,600 are on high alert ready to be launched in minutes (Ware 2008). The debate is over whether such preparations are essential or they actually create the possibility for violence as a way to solve problems. President Obama has pointed out that maintaining "cold war weapons systems" is expensive and can drain a weakened economy (Zeleny 2009). He and President Medvedev of Russia have signed a nuclear arms reduction agreement that must now be approved by the U.S. Senate and the Russian Duma (Nuclear Threat Initiative 2010).

Negotiation is the second approach to avoiding war and resolving conflicts by discussion to reach agreement. For example, diplomacy and treaties have set limits on nuclear weapons and their use. In the 1990s, the superpowers made major efforts to move into a new peaceful era. Peace talks were held in the Middle East, Cambodia, Rwanda, the former Yugoslavia and Bosnia, Ireland, and other countries

International Solidarity Movement (ISM) activists protest against the construction of the Israeli security fence near a Palestinian village. Dozens of people from many nations have put their own bodies on the line to prevent bulldozing of Palestinian homes and construction of the fence. American Rachel Corrie, a member of the ISM, was run over and killed by an Israeli bulldozer on March 16, 2003, when she tried to stop it from destroying a family's home.

war. Peace advocates and veterans of the war often stand and weep together in front of that memorial.

Scholars draw several conclusions from studies of war in the past century: (a) no nation that began a major war in the 20th century emerged a clear winner; (b) in the nuclear age, war between nuclear powers could be suicidal; and (c) a victor's peace plan is seldom lasting. Those peace settlements that are negotiated on the basis of equality are much more permanent and durable. War is often stimulated by inequitable distribution of resources. Therefore, peace that is lasting also requires attention to at least semi-equitable distribution of resources, illustrating that economics are also at the heart of war and peace issues.

In the long run, people around the world would seem to benefit from peace, yet many leaders and citizens hold bitter hatred against their neighbors. Obviously, this is not a climate for peace. As long as there is discrimination, hunger, and poverty in the world, the roots of violence are present. The world is a complex interdependent system. When the linkages between peoples are based on ideologies that stress we/they polarities and power differentials that alienate people, then war, terrorism, and violence will not disappear from the globe.

Terrorism

On September 11, 2001, three commercial airplanes became the missiles of terrorists, two crashing into the twin towers of the World Trade Center in New York City and one into the Pentagon in Washington, D.C., killing more than 3,025 people from 68 nations and injuring countless others. This was an act of terrorists. Why did they do it?

Terrorism refers to the use of indiscriminate violence, which can cause mass fear and panic, intimidate citizens, and advance a group's political goals (Nolan 2002). Terrorism usually refers to acts of violence by private nonstate groups to advance revolutionary political goals, but *state terrorism* is government use of terror to control people. Terrorists are found at all points on the political continuum: anarchists, nationalists, religious fundamentalists, and members of ethnic groups. Terrorist attacks fell 18% in 2008. There were 11,770 terrorist incidents in 2008 compared with 14,506 in 2007. Deaths fell 30% from 22,508 to 15,765 in those same 2 years, mostly due to changes in Iraq (Kellerhals 2009).

What makes terrorism effective? Terrorists strike randomly and change tactics so that governments have no clear or effective way of dealing with them. This unpredictability causes public confidence in the ability of government to protect citizens and deal with crises to waver. Terrorists seldom attack targets in oligarchic or dictatorial societies because these countries ignore their demands despite the risk to innocent civilians and hostages' lives (Frey 2004).

Why do terrorists commit hostile acts? In our anger against terrorists, we sometimes fail to look at why they commit these atrocities. Who are the terrorists, and what have

threatened by tensions and war. Leaders of the United Nations were often involved in diplomatic attempts to resolve conflicts. The inherent problem, however, is that negotiation means a partial win—and a partial loss—for each side. Each gives a little, and each gets a little. Both sides tend to want a win/lose resolution—with the other side losing. Commitment to a win/lose perspective can lead to a lose/lose situation with neither side really winning.

Some citizens are not satisfied to leave peacekeeping efforts to their government leaders. Strong grassroots peace movements in Europe, the Middle East, the United States, South Africa, and other countries are aimed at lessening tensions and conflicts around the world. The widespread demonstrations in many European and U.S. cities by people opposed to the Iraq war are one such example.

Video Link 13.5
Watch people working toward peace.

Many peace groups sponsor educational programs and museum displays. The horrors depicted in the Hiroshima Peace Memorial Museum in Japan; the Killing Fields in Cambodia; the Holocaust Memorial Museum in Washington, D.C.; the Anne Frank Museum in Amsterdam, the Netherlands; and the Korean War and Vietnam Veterans Memorials in Washington, D.C., all help sensitize the public and politicians to the effects of war. Interestingly, most war memorials in the United States glorify the wars and lionize the heroes who fought in them. In Europe, many memorials stress the pathos and agony of war. However, the Vietnam Veterans Memorial sends a message about the sorrows of

they to gain? Without understanding the underlying causes of terrorism, we can do little to prevent it.

Few terrorists act alone. They are members of groups that are highly committed to an ideology or cause—religious, political, or both. One person's terrorist may be someone else's freedom fighter—it is in the eye of the beholder. Terrorists are willing to die to support their group's cause. Class, ethnic, racial, or religious alienation often lie at the roots of terrorism. The ideology of terrorist groups stresses *we* versus *they* perceptions of the world, with *they* being "evil." Those committing terrorist acts often feel that they are the victims of more powerful forces, and sometimes, they see their only weapon to fight back as the ultimate sacrifice—their lives.

Ahmad is a terrorist. All his life, his family has been on the move, forced to work for others for hardly a living wage, controlled by rules made up by other people—ones that he feels are hostile to his group. When he was very young, his family's home was taken away, and the residents of his town scattered to other locations. He began to resent those who he thought had dislocated his family, put some in jail, and separated him from friends and relatives. Ahmad sees little future for himself or his people, little hope for education or a career of his choosing. He feels that he has nothing to lose by joining a resistance organization to fight for what he sees as justice. Its members keep their identities secret. They are not powerful enough to mount an army to fight, so they rely on terrorist tactics against those they see as oppressors.

Ahmad puts the "greater good" of his religious and political beliefs and his group above his individual well-being. When he agrees to commit a terrorist act, he truly believes it is right and is the only way he can retaliate and bring attention to the suffering of his people. If killed, he knows he will be praised and become a martyr within his group.

Continued frustration by those who are alienated is illustrated by ongoing current events: militants setting off bombs in London, Madrid, Pakistan, and Mumbai, India; suicide bombers in Iraq; and terrorist attacks by Palestinian suicide bombers in Israel. These examples are terrorist incidents expressed in a long string of violent, sophisticated, and bloody acts. Those who are attacked feel that they are the real victims and have done nothing to deserve the brutality.

Religious and political beliefs lead some terrorists to commit violent acts. Timothy McVeigh and Terry Nichols were charged with bombing the Alfred P. Murrah Federal Building in Oklahoma City, Oklahoma. Research on their backgrounds shows connections to paramilitary, antigovernment militia groups, many of which opposed government intervention in the private lives of Americans. These patriot groups are antigovernment (despite their fanatic pro-Americanism) and White supremacist. Most patriot paramilitary groups consider themselves to be devoutly Christian, and they believe that their acts are justified by their religion and their "good intentions." They are scattered throughout the United States as shown in Map 8.3 on page 255.

Journal Article Link 13.3
Read about terrorism and national security.

Structural explanations help predict when conditions are right for terrorism. Terrorism and war are unlikely to exist unless there is conflict and strife within and between societal systems. Ahmad learned his attitudes, hatreds, and stereotypes from his family and friends and through media such as the Internet. These beliefs were reinforced by his leaders, religious beliefs, and schools. However, their origin was anger and economic despair.

Conflict theory explanations of terrorism lie in the unequal distribution of world resources and the oppression of groups in the social world. Wealthy countries such as Germany, Japan, and the United States control resources and capital and have considerable economic influence and power over peripheral nations. Citizens of poor countries work for multinational corporations, often for very low wages, and the profits are returned to wealthy countries, helping perpetuate their elite status. The result is that the rich get richer, and the poor get poorer. This inequity results in feelings of alienation, hostilities, and sometimes terrorism against the more powerful country. The attack on the New York City World Trade Center was carried out in part to terrorize and punish the United States.

Reactions to terrorism range from demands for immediate retaliation to frustration with the lack of power and control to fight a "hidden" enemy. People disagree over whether governments should negotiate with the terrorists and try to understand their demands or hold firm by not negotiating or giving in to such coercion. Terrorism, then, is the means by which the powerless can attempt to receive attention to their cause and gain some power in the global system, even if it involves hijackings, bombings, suicides, kidnappings, and political assassinations. The victims of these acts are understandably outraged.

Democracy comes in many forms and structures. If you want to live in a society where you have a voice, get involved in the political system and stay well informed about the policies that your government is considering or has recently enacted. Healthy political systems need diverse voices and critics—regardless of what party is currently in power—to create vibrant societies that represent the citizens. The following two chapters focus on processes of change in societies, often involving political decisions and actions.

What Have We Learned?

The most direct source of power is the political system, with the ability to influence decisions about how society is run. The most direct source of privilege is the economic system, and these two institutions are highly interlinked. There is no one right way to organize a political or an economic system, for each approach has shortcomings. However, some systems do a better job of distributing power and privilege, ensuring accountability, and providing checks on abuses of power.

Key Points

- The study of political and economic processes and systems involves penetrating power—in the sense that we try to penetrate the meanings and consequences of power and that power penetrates every aspect of our lives. Power involves ability to realize one's will, despite resistance. (See pp. 434–435.)
- Power and economics penetrate our intimate (micro-level) lives, our (meso-level) organizations and institutions, and our (macro-level) national and global structures and policies. (See pp. 435–436.)
- Leadership facilitates getting things done in any social group. It can be accomplished through raw power (coercion) or through authority (granted by the populace). Different types of leadership invest authority in the person, the position, or both. (See pp. 436–439.)

- Various theories illuminate different aspects of political power and view the nation's policy-making processes very differently—as dominance of the power elite or as pluralistic centers of power. (See pp. 439–441.)
- At the micro level, a key issue is each citizen's decision to vote or participate in politics. These decisions are not just individualist choices but are shaped by culture and structures of the society. (See pp. 441–444.)
- At the meso level, the political institution (when it functions well) works to resolve conflicts and to address social needs within the political system, and this may be done with authoritarian or democratic structures. Within nations, meso-level policies can also have major implications for national power distribution. (See pp. 444–452.)
- The economic system ensures production and distribution of goods in the society, and the type of economy in a society determines who has the power to plan for the future and who has access to resources. (See pp. 453–456.)
- At the macro level, nation-states have emerged only in the past four or five centuries as part of modernity. (See pp. 456–461.)
- At the global level, issues of power, access to resources, alienation, and ideology shape economic policies, war, terrorism, and the prospects for lives of peace and prosperity for citizens around the planet. (See pp. 461–467.)

Contributing to Our Social World: What Can We Do?

At the Local Level

- *Student government on your campus:* Contact a member or officer and arrange to attend a meeting. Consider running for office, a way to learn the basic principles of the democratic process.
- *Model legislature or Model U.N. program:* Often administered through the department of political science, learn about it and get involved.
- *Campus visit by a local political candidate or office holder:* If this can be done through a sociology club, it would be especially appropriate to have the visitor discuss the political system as a social institution.

At the Organizational or Institutional Level

- *MADD (Mothers Against Drunk Driving):* Consider working for a NGO or volunteering for a political cause such as MADD.

- *Internship with a state/provincial legislator, the governor's office, or a court judge.*
- *Special-interest parties:* Become involved in a special interest group such as the The Green Party (www.gp.org), the Libertarians (www.lp.org), and the Socialist Party (www.sp-usa.org), or any number of others.

At the National and Global Levels

- *Internship with congressional representative or senator:* Explore the possibility of volunteer work with a representative or senator. Each has a Web site that provides local contact information. Several agencies of the *United Nations* hire interns. The general contact for relevant information is www.un.org/Depts/OHRM/sds/internsh/. An agency that uses interns with social science backgrounds is the U.N. Development Program. Contact it at www.undp.org/internships.

 For chapter-specific resources, including **Frontline**, **TED**, and **YouTube** videos; self-quizzes; web exercises; and more, visit **www.pineforge.com/oswmedia3e.**

CHAPTER 14

Medicine

An Anatomy of Health and Illness

Health and illness are social matters, influenced by social interactions, affected by complex organizations intended to provide health care, and shaped by social policies at national and global levels. A true anatomy of health and illness involves comprehension of the social parts of medicine.

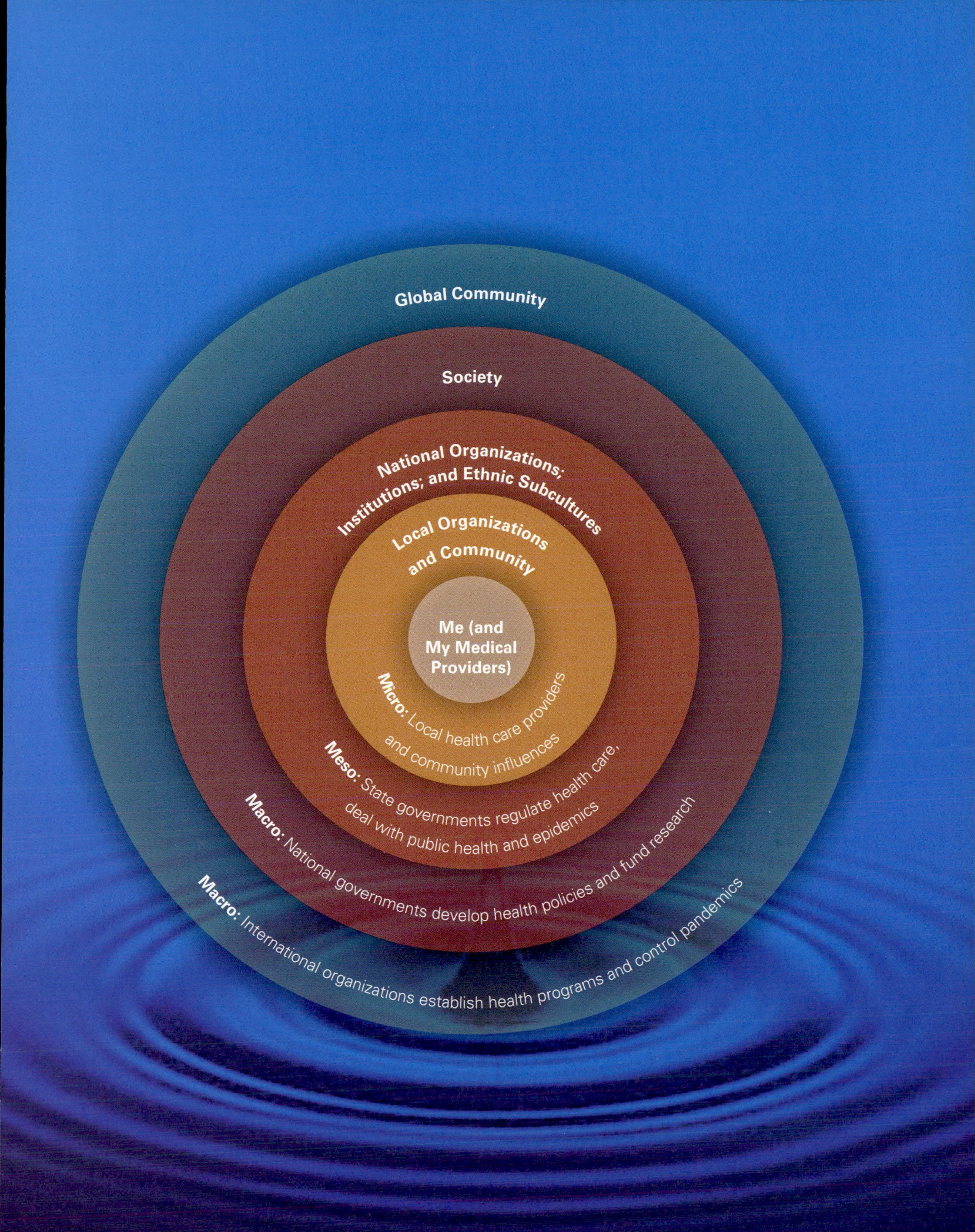

Global Community

Society

National Organizations;
Institutions; and Ethnic Subcultures

Local Organizations
and Community

Me (and
My Medical
Providers)

Micro: Local health care providers
and community influences

Meso: State governments regulate health care,
deal with public health and epidemics

Macro: National governments develop health policies and fund research

Macro: International organizations establish health programs and control pandemics

Think About It	
Me (and My Inner Circle)	What does it mean for you to be sick or healthy? Why is this a social state and not just individual?
Local Community	How does health or illness affect the functioning of your local community?
National Institutions; Complex Organizations; Ethnic Groups	Which health care systems keep people healthiest?
National Society	What are the costs to the nation (and to individuals) of having a national health care system, and what are the costs of not having one?
Global Community	What are variations in health care around the world?

Terri Schiavo died March 31, 2005, after making headlines for months. Though unconscious and in a vegetative state, the controversy surrounding her removal from life support kept the nation's attention. Politicians entered the debate, and then President Bush signed an order to keep her alive. Her husband argued that she would not have wanted to go on in her current state and that it would be a kindness to let her die. However, her parents and court rulings argued to keep her alive through the feeding and oxygen tubes. The case is significant because it raises issues of when and how a person should die—and who has the right to decide. Technology allows us to keep people alive, even in vegetative states so that the patient cannot make

Dr. Kevorkian (left) is accompanied to court in Michigan. He was tried and found guilty of helping people who were in severe pain and who no longer wanted to live to commit suicide.

the choice. Some people choose to sign "Living Wills" and "Do Not Resuscitate" documents stating that they wish no measures be taken to revive them or keep them alive. Still, the lines are often unclear.

Another euthanasia case involved Debbie, a 20-year-old woman in Portland, Oregon, lying in pain and dying from ovarian cancer. She had not eaten or slept for 2 days and was struggling for air. Her words to the physician were, "Let's get this over with." In this case of medical futility, in which treatment "fails to end total dependence on intensive medical care," the physician relieved her suffering with a syringe of morphine sulfate. She began breathing normally and shortly thereafter died as a result of the physician-assisted suicide. These two cases and others like them raise great controversy in medical, legal, and religious communities. One thing is clear: Very personal decisions about health, illness, and death are not just personal. They may be governed or overruled by state laws and even the president of the country.

Allowing individuals to choose death to relieve the irreversible suffering of an incurable disease and allowing physicians to hasten the death of terminally ill patients are actions accepted by proponents of active or voluntary euthanasia (sometimes called "the good death"). This involves aiding the dying individual by prescribing or administering a lethal dose of drugs to patients who request it, usually under legally controlled conditions. Most deaths of terminally ill individuals are planned and sometimes hastened by medical interventions (American Psychological Association 2008). In addition, anyone can sign a living will or "Right to Die" form and "Do Not Resuscitate" form requesting that no extraordinary efforts be made to help keep one alive when death would naturally occur (passive euthanasia). However, opponents see aiding death as a sin or even as murder.

Those who favor euthanasia argue that (a) physicians should be able to create comfortable environments for death to occur, (b) terminally ill individuals have a right—without interference by the state—to determine how they die and to make the decision to die, (c) legal safeguards are available to prevent abuse of physician-assisted suicide, (d) high rates of self-induced suicide already exist among terminally ill patients, (e) a majority of the public favors legalization of physician-assisted suicides, and (f) extending life with no hope of recovery is costly to families as well as to the medical care system.

Those opposed to euthanasia argue that (a) physicians are responsible to sustain life and relieve suffering; (b) medical measures are available to relieve pain, so few have to suffer; (c) religious beliefs affirm the sanctity of life, which means supporting life at every turn; (d) terminally ill individuals who request to die are often acting out of depression, or they may feel pressured to accept a facilitated death to save the family's resources; and (e) a terminally ill patient's acceptance of active euthanasia may make suicide a more acceptable option for those people who are depressed, disabled, elderly, or retarded (Weiss and Lonnquist 2008).

Some countries and states have passed laws legalizing and controlling euthanasia. Euthanasia is legal with very strict regulations in the Netherlands, Belgium, Albania, Luxembourg, and Switzerland; Japan does not criminalize those who carry out euthanasia. In the United States, euthanasia is legal in Oregon, Washington, and Montana. In 2006, the number of deaths in Oregon was 46, a slow increase from 1998 when euthanasia was legalized. The courts require that two or more doctors must agree that the patient has 6 or fewer months to live, and the patient must also ask to die at three different times, the last time in writing, before doctors can act on the request. Doctors have to wait for 15 days before complying with the patient's wishes (Oregon's Euthanasia Law 2010).

The cost of dying differs tremendously, from nothing in many poor Global South countries with no health care for the dying, to an estimated $35,838 for the last 6 months of life in Manhattan, New York (Appleby 2006). On average, the last week of life in the United States costs $2,917, though for those patients who have had end-of-life discussions with their doctors, the average cost is $1,876 because fewer medical interventions take place (Zhang et al. 2009). About 30% of the budget for the U.S. government's Medicare program goes toward the final year of life (Neurological Correlates 2008). In about 12 years, the number of people who are sick, old, and frail will double, and the Medicare system will be under great pressure to cover expenses at the current rate due to increased medical costs and increasing numbers of people living longer (Appleby 2006).

Whereas in the past people died from heart attacks and bad infections, today people who are afflicted with these problems can be kept alive. Policy analysts point out that cost for elder care could be reduced and quality of care improved by providing more in-home services to allow people to die at home rather than in an intensive care unit of a hospital. Some medical ethicists raise questions about large expenses for efforts to prolong life of elderly people with heart failure, provide chemotherapy for advanced cancer, or do expensive procedures for complications from diabetes and other chronic ailments. In a public survey of attitudes toward end-of-life issues, 48% of respondents advocated weighing the costs of keeping a person alive as long as possible, versus 40% who argued to keep the person alive as long as possible regardless of cost (Appleby 2006).

Dying is not something that just happens. How we die, where we die, who is with us when we die, and whether we have a choice about when to die are decisions bound in cultural values, beliefs, and laws. Death and its various issues are but one aspect of the interrelationship between our physical condition and our social system. This chapter illustrates that events surrounding health, illness, and death are social

Handbook Link 14.1
Read more about the sociology of health.

events governed by rules of the social world. In this chapter, we will consider why health is a social issue, and we will examine theoretical perspectives on health and illness, the status and roles of sick people, modern health care systems, and health care policy issues at the national and global levels.

Why Is Health a Social Issue?

In the West African country of Nigeria, fundamentalist religious leaders in the northern part of the country refused to allow international medical teams to immunize children against polio, and there was an outbreak of this crippling disease that had almost been eradicated elsewhere. The religious leaders had little trust in the motives of Western medical teams. When the epidemic broke out, however, and children began dying, the leadership relented and allowed the immunization programs to take place. Since 1989, a worldwide campaign to eradicate polio has reduced victims from 350,000 across 125 countries to less than 2,000, mostly in 4 countries: India, Pakistan, Afghanistan, and Nigeria. Only in Nigeria, where average life expectancy is 45, is polio spreading (Padden 2009; PBS Newshour 2009b). This illustration of health at the global level points out how individual decisions have an effect on health of a community and nation, and shows the importance of medical organizations and their efforts to control world pandemics such as polio, AIDS, SARS, bird flu, swine flu (H1N1), and other illnesses.

Let us explore some of the factors that affect health, illness, and death in the world. **Health** is a state of physical, mental, and social well-being, or the absence of disease. **Illness**, or lack of health, affects the way we perform our individual responsibilities in the social world. Like any key social issue, effective health care affects how individuals and groups carry out their lives at the micro, meso, and macro levels.

Health at the Micro Level

Sociologists are concerned with how our state of health affects our individual ability to carry out social responsibilities. Everyday lives are shaped by our own state of health or illness and that of our loved ones and close associates. If a roommate, significant other, or child is ill, it affects our lives in a number of ways. It alters our schedules, takes time as we deal with the illness, causes us to worry, and costs us in terms of medical care and lost work time. If a parent is dying of cancer or a child has epilepsy, our lives are influenced in profound and disruptive ways.

Video Link 14.1
Watch a video about bipolar disorder in children.

In many societies, communities are responsible for providing adequate health care, sanitation, and clean drinking water to citizens—services that affect the health of citizens. The health of citizens also affects community activities. A serious outbreak of influenza in the public schools may force schools to close for several days, causing repercussions in workplaces throughout the community as parents struggle to deal with child care issues. Thus, health status affects other institutions in the community, from family to schools to the workplace.

Health at the Meso Level

The institution of health care provides for the physical, mental, and social well-being of citizens. This includes prevention, diagnosis, and treatment of illness and regulation of the dispensing of medicine. The health care institution

Other institutions, such as schools, interact with health care systems in a variety of ways. The Chinese school toilet facility shown here indicates a different standard of sanitation and health than what many of us are accustomed to seeing.

works in conjunction with families, education, religion, politics, and economics. What happens in the system of health care affects every part of the social world, as shown in the example of assisted suicide. The economic well-being of individuals in a society relates to health care access and who can pay. This often determines who lives, who dies, who is healthy, and who is not. Education about health care influences health and life expectancy. Well-educated citizens are more likely to develop health-enhancing lifestyles. Families attempt to prevent illness and care for sick individuals and often have responsibility to care for the ill and ailing. Political systems determine standards for health care and regulate medicinal drugs. Religious organizations establish support systems and health services, sometimes offer faith-healing alternatives to supplement the established medical system, and offer solace in times of illness and death. At the meso level, institutions are interconnected.

Health at the Macro Level

Each society has a vested interest in the health of its citizenry because the general state of health affects the quality of life of the people and the state of the economy. Imagine the society in which citizens had "permission" to be sick frequently. How would that society continue to function? Societies have social policies that influence the way medicine is organized and health services are delivered. Beliefs about who is ill with what kinds of illness and for how long vary by society.

Consider the case of the now-dissolved Soviet Union. After the Soviet victory over Czarist Russia in 1917, the new revolutionary government was faced with an underdeveloped nation that essentially still produced its food with human-powered plows and simple hoes. The task of leading the country out of the 16th century and into the 20th was formidable. It called for a total effort from the nation's workforce. Confronted with a severe shortage of labor, the new government determined that absenteeism at work, regardless of excuse, had to be kept very low. Accordingly, they instituted rules that required workers to obtain a certificate allowing them to be absent from work because of illness (Weiss and Lonnquist 2008). These certificates could be obtained only from government clinics, and each clinic could issue a limited number of permits. In some cases, physicians were actively encouraged to compete with one another to see how few certificates they could issue. Thus, absence due to illness was controlled, and the human resources needed for rebuilding the nation were augmented.

Global health focuses on several issues, including possible pandemics of highly contagious diseases, which have become worldwide threats as global travel increases. A *pandemic* is a disease that is prevalent throughout an entire country and may infect a continent or reach around the world. The global nature of the pandemic AIDS is illustrated in Map 14.1. To control such diseases requires cooperation across national boundaries by organizations such as the United Nations. For

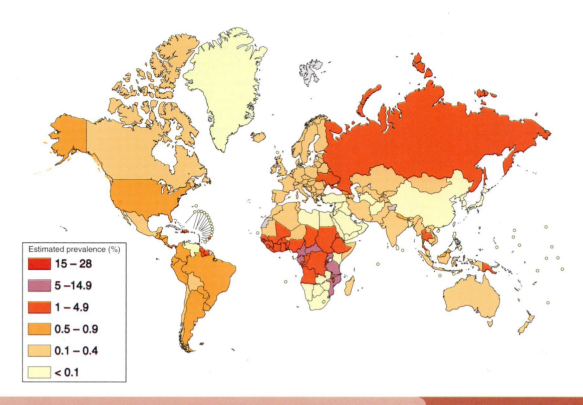

Estimated prevalence (%)

- 15 – 28
- 5 –14.9
- 1 – 4.9
- 0.5 – 0.9
- 0.1 – 0.4
- < 0.1

Map 14.1   Estimated Percentage of Adults Living With HIV in 2005

Source: ©World Health Organization, 2009.

instance, smallpox remained a serious global threat from the Middle Ages until the mid-20th century. The World Health Organization of the United Nations eliminated the disease completely in the 1960s. River blindness afflicted thousands of West Africans but has been eradicated due to international cooperation. Funding by organizations such as the Bill and Melinda Gates Foundation provides for research, treatment, and eradication of killer diseases such as malaria, AIDS, and tuberculosis. However, the threat of bioterrorism has raised the specter of other diseases such as smallpox and polio reappearing.

Illness may seem like an individual problem, but as shown in the above examples, it is far more than that. It is a national and global issue. This chapter examines health care at each level of analysis, from individual behaviors and decisions, to religious, political, and economic aspects, to the effect of stratification and ethnic status on the quality of health care one receives. Keep the social world model in mind as you read about health, illness, and medical care.

Thinking Sociologically

Why do pandemic diseases that affect a local community require international solutions?

A Guatemalan child infected with the HIV/AIDS virus marches outside the site where an AIDS conference was being held in Guatemala City. Hundreds of people from different countries marched to bring attention to the problems of poor medical assistance and lack of government attention for the infected people.

Theoretical Perspectives on Health and Illness

In the analysis of institutions, each major paradigm or perspective in sociology offers a lens for understanding different aspects of the institution; health and illness in a given society and within the global system are no exceptions. Let us consider those major theoretical perspectives as they relate to health and illness.

Micro-Level Theoretical Perspectives

Unruly school children were once considered ill mannered or ill behaved. Now, they are often labeled as hyperkinetic or having attention deficit disorder (ADD), suffering from conditions that can be controlled by appropriate medication. Those with learning disabilities were labeled dumb or lazy. Now we know better thanks to medical science. Heavy gamblers, alcoholics, and drug abusers are now defined as addicts rather than as people lacking self-discipline. How conditions are labeled can result in social stigma of varying degrees and lead to different policies to treat problems.

The Symbolic Interaction Perspective and Labeling Theory

To symbolic interactionists, illness is partly whatever powerful individuals in society, such as doctors, define or label it to be. In recent years, the definition of illness in many Global North societies has expanded to encompass substance abuse and some forms of deviant behavior, giving physicians even more power and authority over broad areas of social life. Illness used to be viewed as a physical condition—germs, viruses, bacteria—causing the body to malfunction. Through the labeling process, behaviors that were once seen as criminal or "bad" are now defined as illness.

Medicalization and Labeling. **Medicalization** refers to the shift in handling of some forms of deviance as well as some normal human functions (such as pregnancy and childbirth) from the familial, legal, or religious arenas to the health care system. In some cases, the shift is away from the issue of individual self-control and toward medical diagnosis and treatment. Consider addictive behaviors such as alcoholism and drug abuse. There is considerable debate about how we define alcoholism because this influences the interpretation of the problem, the physician's role in treatment, whether we hold the patient to blame for the problem, and how it will be treated (Cockerham 2007). Symbolic interactionists emphasize the social definitions or labels such as *alcoholic* or *drug addict* and examine the

effect such labels have on the life of the individual. Consider that medical conditions can be treated, and less stigma may be attached to these illnesses if they are not labeled as moral degeneracy (Conrad 2009). On the other hand, labeling the alcoholic as sick creates another type of stigma that may never be erased, and seeing alcoholism as a medical condition takes away individual responsibility, putting control in the hands of the health care system. The next "Sociology in Our Social World" on page 477 explores the issue of policy toward alcoholism.

Thinking Sociologically

First, read "Sociology in Our Social World." Many of us have a friend or relative who consciously or unconsciously struggles with alcohol problems. Do you see that person being labeled by others? What might you do to help the person?

Social critics argue that once conditions are medicalized, they come to be controlled and exploited by powerful experts. Yet some "problems" may not be problems at all. For example, as a result of movements to "demedicalize" various social behaviors, homosexuality has been removed from the American Psychiatric Association's list of mental disorders. However, some scholars see medicalization of health issues as part of a healthy social system because with stigma removed, the issues can be more effectively addressed.

Having some sense of the issues raised by the symbolic interactionists in the examples above, we turn now to how the experience of illness or health at the micro level is shaped by forces at the meso and macro levels in our social world.

Meso- and Macro-Level Theoretical Perspectives

The institution of health care in Western culture differs dramatically from that of many other cultures around the world. Consider the conflicting ideas of illness between the Hmong culture in the United States, made up of immigrants from Vietnamese hill tribes, and the U.S. medical community. In the book *The Spirit Catches You and You Fall Down*, Anne Fadiman (1997) describes the contrasts between how an immigrant Hmong family views an epileptic child and how the hospital in their U.S. community sees the situation. When the parents take their child for treatment of her epileptic seizures, everything from the concepts of what causes the problem, to the cures, to communication about the disease are problematic. The medical staff treats the

Sociology in Our Social World

Alcoholism, Medicalization, and Policy

Perhaps you know someone who struggles with an alcohol problem. A hotly contested debate in the medical, sociological, and psychological fields is how to define *alcoholism*, for that definition affects everything from treatment procedures to who has responsibility for rehabilitation. Is the alcoholic to be held responsible, or is this a condition beyond the individual's control? The idea that alcoholism is a disease, for instance, was first proposed in the 1930s by two reformed drinkers and later given scientific support (Jellinek 1960). In the aftermath of social and political debates, key professional groups officially labeled alcoholism a disease.

Through this process, referred to as "the medicalization of alcoholism," alcoholism was added to the list of behaviors that were formerly considered morally reprehensible—bad, something sinners did, or a result of weakness—but now considered medical problems over which the individual had little control (Conrad and Schneider 1992; Martin 2006; Tracy 2005). The individual became "sick" rather than "bad." Alcoholism was being defined as a medical problem with medical solutions. In fact, many detoxification clinics use medical interventions and drugs to treat alcoholics. The medical definition of alcoholism came to include three dimensions: biophysical, psychological, and social:

Alcoholism is a primary, chronic disease with genetic, psycho-social, and environmental factors influencing its development and manifestations. The disease is often progressive and fatal. It is characterized by impaired control over drinking, preoccupation with the drug alcohol, use of alcohol despite adverse consequences, and distortions in thinking, mostly denial. Each of these symptoms may be continuous or periodic. (Meyer 1996:163)

The medical view of alcoholism has several implications: Unless there is intervention, alcoholics suffer physical and emotional breakdown and an early death. Those who are vulnerable are characterized by

1. having a physiological predisposition in the way their bodies process alcohol;
2. taking up drinking and thus becoming ill;
3. drinking resulting in consumption of ever greater amounts with increasingly severe consequences;
4. drinking that results in distinctive disability, including the loss of ability to choose when it comes to alcohol consumption; and
5. progressing through a predictable sequence of stages, independent of individual characteristics (Schoeman 1991).

The label alcoholic *has a number of implications, including the fact that the stigma associated with the term may prevent some people from seeking help. This is one reason many alcohol treatment centers have recast alcoholism as a disease, hoping that the redefinition would remove stigma. Other problems arise when the issue is medicalized.*

Many health care professionals, however, are reluctant to treat alcohol as a problem drug (Meyer 1996). Some argue that the disease concept is the wrong approach—that what is really at stake is "heavy drinking" as a way of life. Rather than treating a "disease," they feel that professionals should be concerned with approaches that will change the way in which individuals organize their behaviors. These researchers and practitioners argue that heavy drinkers can become nondrinkers or moderate drinkers and can control their drinking. Some critical sociological theorists see medicalization as one more form of social control. By labeling alcoholism as a medical disease, the medical profession becomes an agent of social control for the state (Conrad and Schneider 1992). Changing the alcoholic by altering perceptions, routines, attitudes, and habits of behavior gives the individual responsibility in a context of supportive family or friends, economic opportunities, and alternative role models.

A third possibility exists—that there is truth in both models based on individual differences. Treatment programs can be found based on both of these models, and the debate about the best approach continues. Recent approaches to alcoholism often combine medical and social-behavioral treatments, some of which have been illustrated in the TV show *Interventions* (About.com: Alcoholism 2009). Key in approaches to alcoholism is to help alcoholics recognize that they need help.

epileptic seizures with Western medical techniques, whereas the Hmong family attributes the seizures to spirits (Fadiman 1997). Concepts of health and disease vary greatly in different ethnic groups. Theories and cross-cultural knowledge help understand this and other cultural differences in approaches to health care.

The Functionalist Perspective

Functional theorists focus primarily on the macro level of the health care system. Studies of suicide, carried out by the early French sociologist Émile Durkheim, illustrate that social conditions and events in the larger society and people's group affiliations affected inclinations to commit suicide. Other studies have linked illnesses such as heart disease, kidney failure, stroke, mental illness, and infant mortality to macro-level processes and trends in societies. For example, economic recessions cause social stress and disruption in lifestyles, which can activate mental problems. These, in turn, can result in health problems.

According to functionalists, social norms define what counts as illness and how to treat it. The purpose of the health care system in society is to maintain the social structure and a harmonious balance between individuals and institutions in society. Illness is potentially disruptive to the balanced social world. The sick role is sometimes considered a deviant one because it "robs" the society of normal role functioning. As we saw in the Soviet example, if too many people claim the sick role at the same time, the tasks necessary to maintain the society cannot be performed. The primary task, or function, of the medical profession is to control illness and prevent individuals from being unable to perform their social roles.

Despite the harmonious view of functionalists, ambivalence does exist in the doctor-patient relationship. Physicians hold power over patients in the doctor-patient relationship,

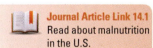

Journal Article Link 14.1
Read about malnutrition in the U.S.

and patients may have contradictory expectations for their treatment (Starr 1982). We turn to conflict theory for a different perspective on the health care system.

Thinking Sociologically

What duties and responsibilities do you relinquish when you occupy a sick role? Which ones do you continue during your illness?

The Conflict Perspective

Poverty, unemployment, low wages, malnutrition, and a host of other economic conditions affect people's access and ability to compete for health care and medicines in many countries. Differential access is a key theme in conflict theorists' approach to health issues. Consider the case of Nkosi, a 4-year-old boy in a rural Ghanaian village. He came down with an infection due to polluted water, causing diarrhea and vomiting. Nkosi was already weakened by malnutrition and parasites, and by the time help came, dehydration was so extensive that he died, one of millions of similar casualties. Why was health care not available?

Nkosi had less access to medical treatment, immunizations, antibiotics, vitamins, and a balanced diet than children in the Global North countries or even in urban areas of the Global South. Children in poor countries around the world suffer from malnutrition and chronic disease before succumbing to pneumonia or other infections, which are normally curable diseases. The explosion in new "emerging infectious diseases" such as AIDS, Brazilian Purpuric fever, new strains of Ebola, various insect- and bird-transported diseases such as SARS and bird flu, and swine flu (H1N1) add to the problems faced by health care workers in the Global South (Farmer 1999). Dr. Paul Farmer, a U.S. infectious disease specialist and anthropologist, set up an organization, "Partners in Health," with the goal of conquering diseases among the world's poor (Kidder 2004). With life expectancy (average length of life) as low as 35 years in some drought-ridden and war-torn countries, the challenge is formidable.

In the world system of rich and poor countries, individuals suffer different illnesses depending on the level of development of their society and their position in it. Poor people in poor countries die from ailments that are curable infectious diseases in rich countries. Consider the case of Swaziland in sub-Saharan Africa, a country of 1.1 million people. Weakened from poor nutrition and hunger because their land has been ravaged by drought, many people in Swaziland die of treatable diseases (UN 2009b). However, the real killer is AIDS. About 25.9% of the adult population are infected with HIV/AIDS. Among pregnant women, the rate of HIV infection is 42.6%, or 220,000 people, including 15,000 below 15 years of age (USAID 2008). The result is that life expectancy at birth in Swaziland was 32 years in 2009 (World Factbook 2009a). By 2010, it is expected to be 30 years. What little governmental health care system exists cannot cope with the crisis. The number of AIDS orphans is growing rapidly. Forget education. Children are concerned with trying to survive on the little food available and to raise their younger siblings. International aid organizations provide most of the meager food they consume.

At the national level, many governments officially proclaim that health care is a basic right of all citizens, although many do not have the means to meet the health needs of citizens. One country that has revolutionized its health care system under the revolutionary government of Hugo Chavez is Venezuela. With oil revenues and tax dollars, the government has built clinics called *Mission Barrio Adentro* to serve those living in urban and rural poverty. Before the Chavez government revolutionized the health delivery system, many poor people had no access to care. Today, each clinic serves a community for free. In the four-tiered system, Tier 1 provides basic care; Tier 2 has some beds, does small surgeries, and treats asthma and similar illnesses; Tier 3 includes small hospitals that accept referrals from the clinics for medical tests such as MRIs and X-rays; and Tier 4 is a hospital for surgeries and other procedures (Witness for Peace 2008). One result of these changes has been that the infant mortality rate has been cut in half, and life expectancy has risen. However, many poor countries do not have oil or other natural resources as Venezuela does to help pay for health care.

Cuba has also developed a system to reach all its citizens, as explained in the "Sociology Around the World" on page 480.

At the global level, multinational companies that build plants in the poor Global South provide examples of the profit motive's influence on health conditions. These businesses are looking for large profit margins and cost-cutting opportunities, so they may seek countries where health and

One way to combat diarrhea diseases in India is through provision of safe drinking water by the government. This is a primary concern of the World Health Organization. However, the World Bank and International Monetary Fund have been pushing for privatization of water, meaning that water would be clean but not affordable for many.

safety standards are lower than those in the Global North, which has more stringent health regulations. Although many multinational companies provide health clinics for workers, lower safety standards can lead to long-term illnesses, eye problems, lung disease, and other debilitating health problems. Moreover, multinational pharmaceutical companies have resisted generic drugs or inexpensive vaccines that are crucial to combating disease in the Global South. Poor countries are places to save money in manufacturing labor costs and raw materials but are not places to provide services because people there can afford little and provide little profit. A few countries such as India are developing their own cheaper versions of drugs for AIDS and other diseases, bypassing international pharmaceutical companies.

A consistent theme in Parsons's (1975) functional model of the sick status is the physician's need for total authority in the relationship to meet the health needs of clients. Some conflict theorists argue that physicians seek this power so that they can decide who they will treat. Some physicians prefer not to locate in poor or rural areas or countries, to treat elderly patients, or to spend time on those with AIDS. The most lucrative positions with the most prestige are generally located in major global urban areas and at well-known clinics, treating people who can pay for private care. This leads some conflict theorists to discuss the doctor-patient relationship as an association in which the doctor exercises social control and loyalty of the doctor to the patient depends in part on the social status of the patient (White 2002).

The point that should be clear is that poverty—whether in the Global North or the Global South—has major impacts on quality of life of the citizens. Individuals who have poor health care or who lack the resources for health insurance are affected in many ways, as the "Engaging Sociology" on page 481 illustrates.

Feminist Theory

For feminist theorists, gender is a key variable that affects health and illness. Feminist theorists argue that the patriarchal control of women carries over to health care systems and reinforces dependence, submission, and definitions of what is illness for women. Women in the Global North are profitable for the health care system because they are seen more often and have more expensive procedures (White 2002). For example, Cesarean section surgery to remove the newborn from the womb tops 31% of births in the United States. Some of these are necessary, but others may be for convenience or to avoid lawsuits (Weiss 2010). According to feminist theorists, controlling women's reproductive health and defining women's normal biological experiences as medical problems are issues rooted in Western society's class interests and in maintaining patriarchal authority. However, in some countries, women

Sociology Around the World

Health Care: Cuba's Pride

One thing all Cubans were promised under the Communist regime of Fidel Castro was access to good health care, which he viewed as a basic right of all people. When Cuba had trading partners and support from the former Soviet Union and allied nations in Europe's eastern bloc, its system was considered a model, especially for a Global South country. Now, the country has lost external support due to the collapse of the Soviet system. Cuba has fallen on hard economic times primarily because of the U.S.-imposed embargo on goods going to Cuba, with the health care system being one victim. Shortages of drugs, diagnostic equipment, and medical supplies have forced Cuba's well-trained doctors to be creative. They use herbal remedies, hypnosis, and acupuncture in place of needed supplies and equipment.

The health care system has the best doctor-patient ratio in the world—1 doctor to every 170 inhabitants (Plant 2007). Hospitals and clinics are spread throughout the country. Infant mortality (deaths per 1,000 live births in the first year) and life expectancy rates (79.9 in 2009) are comparable with those of most Global North developed countries (World Health Organization 2009). However, because of economic hardships and lack of medicine and equipment that could easily control some illnesses and diseases, some experts fear these numbers will begin to slip. Cuba experienced a typhoid fever and tuberculosis outbreak in the early 1990s, even though these diseases were once almost nonexistent in the country. Water contamination in Cuba is increasing. These problems illustrate the interrelationship between health, economic resources, and global links between countries.

Health statistics have a human face; diary entries of a recent visitor to Cuba tell of the impact that economic sanctions have on the health of ordinary citizens:

I visited Dr. Barbara, a young family doctor, in her neighborhood *consultorio* in Havanza, Cuba. Her waiting room was full of young mothers holding plump and healthy babies, sitting against a wall covered with a hand-painted wall mural. A portrait of Fidel Castro (Cuba's head of government) hung next to a painted caricature of Mickey Mouse on the wall behind her desk. Her eyes bright, her long hair bouncing against her shoulders, she said she was very proud to be a Cuban physician and to care for a patient community of 200 families.

However, she added with a pause, sometimes she felt helpless to provide the care that her patients needed. She explained that diagnostic tests were often missed or delayed because of shortages of X-ray film or replacement parts for equipment. Blood work was limited by lack of reagents needed in the labs. Her prescription choices were restricted to the medicines available at the time, a situation that she found very frustrating when her patient had multiple medical problems that dictated the use of one medicine rather than another. Prozac and other state-of-the-art antidepressants were unheard of, and only a few drugs for treating depressive and anxiety disorders were available. Many anticancer medicines were difficult or impossible to get. She said that people were dying sooner than necessary because of these scarcities (Lemkau 2006).

are important and respected healers and doctors. Consider one example, in Gujarat, India, where women medical practitioners hold significant positions of leadership and autonomy in the medical establishment, giving women power and a voice in their health care.

Feminist theorists contend that women have been kept in inferior social positions through much of history because powerful members of society said that their bodies limited them. This is especially true in Global North societies. For instance, drugs to control depression keep women in the situations that caused the depression in the first place. Menopause is treated as an illness or is brushed aside. Women, then, are defined in the medical profession by their reproductive life cycle (White 2002). One result is that more women than men are patients because of medicalization of women's normal life cycles.

Women's risks of maternal death from pregnancy and childbirth complications are much greater in the

Engaging Sociology

Making Decisions That Involve Health Care When One Lives in Poverty

Look at the following list of basic needs. Most of us provide these for our families through our jobs. Now imagine that you and your family are faced with a major financial crisis, and you simply cannot meet all your needs. Which of the items listed below would you give up? If that was still not sufficient to make ends meet, what decisions would you make to balance the budget?

☐ Health care and health insurance
☐ A car or other reliable transportation
☐ Food for the family
☐ Decent shelter
☐ Clothing—especially adequate for cold weather and perhaps appropriate for the breadwinner's occupation
☐ Housing in a safe neighborhood
☐ Access to good schools for the family's children
☐ Other essentials . . .

Many people chose to postpone or sacrifice health care insurance or doctors' visits. If that were the decision, identify how poor health care might affect your income and at least three of the items above.

1. _____
2. _____
3. _____

Perhaps you chose two other items besides health care. Now identify how these items you chose to eliminate might have a long-term impact on three other aspects of your quality of life—including the overall health of family members.

1. _____
2. _____
3. _____

Global South than in the Global North. In Africa, 1 in 19 women die of maternal complications, whereas in the Global North, 1 in 2,976 die. Also in Global South countries, girls are often married at a young age, and having children at a very young age can cause major health problems. The probability that a 15-year-old female will die from complications of pregnancy and childbirth is the highest in Niger, Africa (1 in 7), and lowest in Ireland (1 in 48,000; UN Population Fund 2007). One of the most socially difficult problems for young girls who are married and give birth at a young age is *obstetric fistula*, a childbirth problem in which "torn tissue between the vaginal wall and the bladder or rectum results in incontinence, infections, and ulcerations" (Burn 2005:49). More than 2 million young women are affected, and they are often ostracized and abandoned.

To regain control of women's health, some feminists have formed health organizations concerned with reproductive health: midwifery, natural childbirth, home deliveries, and menopause. With increasing numbers of women physicians, attitudes toward women's health and communication practices between women and physicians are changing.

Conflict theorists argue that the institution of health care creates the conditions that contribute to sickness through low employment opportunities, stress, health hazards at work, poor living conditions, and lack of access to medical care. We now consider the sick role and being sick.

Thinking Sociologically

How might each of the theoretical perspectives deal with conditions such as attention deficit disorder (ADD) or addictions such as gambling, sex, or drugs?

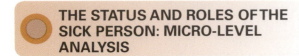

THE STATUS AND ROLES OF THE SICK PERSON: MICRO-LEVEL ANALYSIS

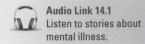

Audio Link 14.1
Listen to stories about mental illness.

What constitutes illness behavior rests on the signs, symptoms, and circumstances defined by our social group rather than on a set of universally recognized bodily malfunctions. Cultural definitions combined with physical symptoms help us understand illness (Weiss and Lonnquist 2008). A poor Central American woman, asked if she has been sick, illustrates this point by commenting that she wished she knew what it meant to be sick. Sometimes she felt so bad she could curl up and die, but she kept going because the kids needed her, and she didn't have money to spend on a doctor. She didn't have time to be sick. She asks, How does one know when someone is sick? Some of us can go to bed almost any time with anything, but many of the world's people can't be sick, not even when they need to be (Koos 1954).

To this woman, being sick was not just a physical condition or how she felt or any physical symptoms she displayed. From a cultural perspective, she had responsibilities that could not be ignored, little access to health care, and no money to buy medicine or care. So who defines the poor woman above as sick? She herself? Her friends and family? Her employer? A health care professional? What is necessary before we can say, from the sociological point of view, that someone is sick?

Illness, or being sick, is a complex matter resulting from changes in the body. Try comparing illness to an iceberg: We do not see the whole iceberg. Similarly, most illness lies under the surface and may never come to public attention unless it forces the person to alter routines or fail in carrying out responsibilities. Generally, physical disorders can be identified, and a health professional can relieve pain or discomfort and return individuals to a healthy state.

However, for the sociologist, the view of illness as only a physical disorder is too limited. A society's definitions influence who is considered sick and under what conditions. Illness, then, is in part socially constructed. The health establishment, schools, and workplaces acknowledge illness only if certain society-defined conditions are present.

Surveys of health in populations around the world indicate that few people are totally free from some degree of physical disorder. Yet the presence of such disorders does not mean that individuals will seek treatment or that the illness will be recognized and treated. Both individual (micro) and structural (meso or macro) factors are important in health care decisions and treatment. The political and economic environment, access to the health care system that provides services, and the predisposition by an individual to seek medical care all enter into health care decisions.

Thinking Sociologically

The Central American woman felt like she could "curl up and die," but she survived. Was she sick? Would you be sick if you felt the way she did? Why might your definition of your situation be different from hers?

The Sick Role

Think of all the social relationships, engagements, and responsibilities that are affected when you are sick. You miss class, have to cancel other engagements, avoid your friends so that you do not infect them with your germs, and cannot carry out your usual responsibilities. Most people are sympathetic for a couple of days, but then, they expect you to get back to your usual routines and responsibilities. Let us consider this "role" of being sick.

Those who are ill occupy a special position or status in society—the **sick role** (Parsons 1975). They are deviant in that they are not carrying out their role expectations. Other members must pick up those responsibilities. Unlike other deviance, however, the sick role is not punished but is

Being sick is more than a physical problem of fever, aches and pains, loss of energy, and other symptoms. Being sick changes relationships, how other people spend their time, and how other people respond to the sick person, including lowered expectations of what that person can do and taking on a new role. The experience of being sick differs across countries. Shown is a health clinic for the poor in Venezuela, where they can obtain free care.

tolerated as long as the sick individual cooperates and acts to overcome illness, returning as soon as possible to fulfill his or her usual social roles (Twaddle 2007).

In an early contribution to the sociology of health, Parsons (1951a) presented a functional theoretical model of the "sick role," outlining four interrelated behavioral expectations—two rights and two obligations:

Right 1: The sick person has the right to be excused from normal social responsibility as needed to be restored to normal functioning in the society. For example, sick students expect to receive permission to miss class or to make up a missed exam.

Right 2: The sickness is not the individual's fault. The sick person did not mean to deviate from normal social expectations and cannot become well by self-decision or by willing it so.

Obligation 1: The sick person should define being sick as undesirable. To avoid the accusation of laziness or malingering, the sick person must not prolong illness unnecessarily to avoid social obligations.

Obligation 2: Those in the sick status are expected to seek technically competent help and cooperate in getting well. In Western countries, the help is most often a medical doctor.

Parsons (1951a) describes the physicians' roles as complementing the "sick role"—to restore routine behavior and "orderliness" in patients. The models presented by Parsons are clearly related to functionalist thought. They focus on integrating all aspects of medical care into a working social system.

One problem is that some individuals might like being excused from tasks and allowed to deviate from social responsibility (such as taking tests or doing an arduous task). Certainly, being sick can be a less demanding lifestyle than going to work or school or taking care of a family. The sick role can also legitimize failure by providing a ready excuse for poor performance at some task (Cole and Lejeune 1972). People who believe they are permanently unable to fulfill their normal social roles may be motivated to define themselves as sick. Yet an excess of sick people could be disruptive to the social fabric, so it is necessary to develop means to control who enters the sick status, as did the Soviet regime, and to guard against misuse of illness as an excuse for avoiding social responsibility.

Individuals make choices about their own health and lifestyles—decisions about leisure time activities; exercise; the amount and type of food they consume; use of alcohol, drugs, and tobacco; and sexual behavior. All these choices affect health. Any of these taken to extremes can result in illness. Health and lifestyle choices are influenced by socialization patterns, family backgrounds, peers, jobs, and cultural expectations.

Eating patterns are a concern for U.S. public health officials. Both children and adults fall into the couch potato syndrome of a sedentary life as flab accumulates into excess weight, a recipe for certain illnesses. Fast food has become a convenient time-saver and a recipe for gaining weight. Health care workers have developed education campaigns to change eating patterns, and schools are removing pop machines from cafeterias. Another concern is the millions of people with negative body images that result in health problems as some men and women abuse their bodies with excessive and unhealthy eating and behavior patterns, such as extreme diets and steroid use.

Many people in industrialized societies, especially in the United States, are extremely overweight, a serious health hazard that brings with it many risks. This is a concern to the society as a whole because it means lowered productivity and increased health care costs.

Thinking Sociologically

Determining who is sick goes beyond physical symptoms and feelings of discomfort. Symptoms such as distress, anxiety, or perceived seriousness of the symptoms often result in seeking health care. Individuals may postpone health action or not seek health care because of lack of availability and affordability or because they deny the existence of the ailment.

Social Factors in Illness and Health

An American Peace Corps volunteer in a South American village could not understand the resigned attitude of the mother, Mónica, as she held her dying baby. He offered to help Mónica get the baby to the clinic 15 miles away, but she seemed resigned to its death. The expectations that shaped Mónica's behavior were learned in her cultural setting. Three of her seven children had died. In this rural Global South setting, as many as half of the babies born will die in infancy because of curable illness, poor sanitation, lack of clean water, and lack of health care and medicine. People come to accept infant deaths, often easily preventable, as normal. Many children are not even named until their parents determine that they are likely to live.

Journal Article Link 14.2
Read about the costs of smoking.

Individual beliefs, experiences, and decisions about health and illness may be deeply rooted in the meso- and macro-level structural factors that shape the availability of medicines and health services as well as in the factors that shape one's lifestyle and attitudes toward health care. Consider some of the social dimensions that affect our individual health.

Cultural Belief Systems and Health. Western scientific medicine centers on physicians who use medical technology to heal those who are sick and return them to society as contributing members. In non-Western parts of the world, quite different healing approaches are used. In North Africa, for example, members of the Azande tribe believe in a spiritual system of healing centered on the activities of the local shaman. Illness occurs, they believe, when an offended individual arranges for a "sickness pellet" to be placed in the body of the offender. Through spiritual ceremonies, the sorcerer sees that the pellet is withdrawn from the body and restores the person to health.

Some Hispanic cultures practice a unique, ancient, and complex system of healing known as *curanderismo*. The origins are found in indigenous herbal medicine, indigenous religious belief systems, witchcraft, and Spanish Catholicism. Good health and a strong body are viewed as God's blessing for the faithful. Illness comes either when one has sinned or as a message from God to help the person learn to be good. The relationship between the *curandero*, or healer, and the patient is close, relying on psychological and spiritual as well as physical treatments. Many Hispanics combine Western medicine and *curanderismo*. For "non-Hispanic illnesses," the physician is the healer of choice. However, for culture-specific conditions such as *susto* (characterized by extreme fright), the *curandero* may be consulted because many believe that such conditions are impervious to even the highest technology of the scientific physician (Weiss and Lonnquist 2008). The role of the *curandero* combines elements of a psychologist and a healer.

Definitions of who is considered mentally ill and who is put away for their own and society's protection vary greatly across societies. Consider the case of Manuel, a schizophrenic who "goes crazy" when the moon is full (the concept of lunacy) and is put in a Nicaraguan mental hospital during that time. Otherwise, he lives a relatively normal life with his parents. In another culture, he might be put in long-term hospital care or given drugs to control the condition. His mental instability might even be given a different definition (Fernando 2002). In rural areas of Goa, India, mental illness, depression, and anxiety are treated by laypeople trained to recognize symptoms. While these problems are most often diagnosed and treated in affluent countries, they exist in all parts of the world. Most often they relate to financial problems, interpersonal conflicts, unemployment, and alcoholism (Luczaj 2008).

Pain is a universal experience, yet how it is perceived, experienced, and reacted to varies by cultural background, ethnic group membership, and socialization experience (Galanti 2008). For example, Asian patients rarely ask for pain medication, but patients from Mediterranean cultures readily ask for help to relieve the slightest pain. Why is there a difference? In a classic U.S. hospital-based study of reactions to pain, researchers observed that patients' responses fell into two main categories: stoic and emotive. Patients with Jewish and Italian cultural backgrounds responded to pain emotionally, while patients of Yankee background were stoical and tried to bravely endure pain. Those of Irish descent denied pain altogether. Although the Jewish American and Italian American patients exhibited similar reactions to pain, their reasons for these reactions were different. The Jewish American patients took a long-term

Gerardo Queupukura, a renowned shaman of the Mapuche tribe in Chile, attends to the line of patients and looks at the urine samples to determine the patients' health status. The medicine man holds consultations twice a week.

view toward pain. They were concerned about its meaning for their future, and their reactions did not subside when pain-relieving drugs were administered. The Italian American patients, on the other hand, were mainly concerned with the pain itself, and drugs both relieved the pain and their complaints (Thomas and Rose 1991; Zborowski 1952).

Other studies have linked expressive, emotive responses to Hispanic, Middle Eastern, and Mediterranean patients, while stoic patients were more often from Northern European and Asian backgrounds (D'Arcy 2009; Galanti 2008). Decisions we make and experiences we have are directly related to our socialization, culture, and definition of reality.

Social Predictors in Individual Health and Illness.

Individual micro-level variables such as age, gender, ethnicity, economic factors, social status, and urban or rural residence are important in determining patterns of health and illness as well. For example, age affects health in several ways. People aged 65 years and above need medical intervention and hospitalization more often than any other age group. They also receive more preventative care than other age groups. As the size of the world's senior population has grown, this age cohort has increased as the population most using the health care system. In the United States, of those citizens 65 years and older, 26.5% had 10 or more visits to the doctor, 36.7% had 4 to 9 visits, 31% had 1 to 3 visits, and 5.7% had no visits (National Center for Health Statistics 2007). Figure 14.1 on page 486 shows the number of visits by females and males to physicians.

Gender patterns are clear, too: In Global North cultures, women report more health problems than do men. They use more physician services on a regular basis and receive more preventive and reproductive care, take more medications, and are more likely to be hospitalized (Weiss and Lonnquist 2008). In contrast, men use emergency services more.

Ethnic groups, meso-level groups, affect the micro level through socialization of individuals into health behaviors and experiences. Recall the cases of Hispanic *curanderismo*, the Hmong concepts of illness, and different experiences of pain discussed earlier. Socialization into possible health care options ranges from modern medical practitioners to alternative medical practitioners (from traditional folk healers to modern chiropractors who are not part of the medical

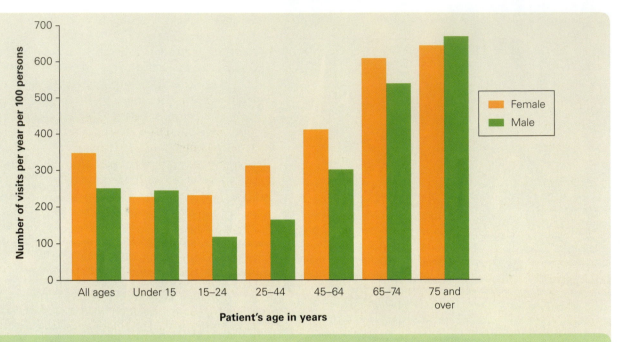

Figure 14.1 Number of Visits per Year by U.S. Females and Males to Physicians

Source: National Center for Health Statistics (2007).

establishment), nonmedical professions (e.g., social workers and clergy), lay advisers, and self-care (Pescosolido 1992).

As we saw in Chapter 8, racial privilege and disprivilege are often rooted in discrimination in organizations and are often not a result of individual prejudice. In the United States, African Americans are less likely to have regular health care providers and more likely to use hospital emergency rooms and health clinics than the majority of the population. Health care is less available in inner cities and rural areas, where there are concentrations of minority residents. Minority women are less likely to receive prenatal care than other women, and the infant mortality gap between Whites, African Americans, and other minorities in the United States (i.e., the number of live-born infants who die in their first year per 1,000 births) is shown in Table 14.1 (National Center for Health Statistics 2007). The high infant-mortality rate of the United States compared with other affluent countries is due largely to social class differentials between the Whites and minorities and differential access to health care in the United States. African Americans also have higher rates of cancers and shorter survival times than Whites at all stages of cancer diagnosis (American Cancer Society 2006; Ries et al. 2000).

Social status affects health because wealthier individuals are more likely to seek professional help early for physical or psychological distress, partly because they can afford treatment. However, contact with physicians is highest among the lowest income categories (7.6 doctor visits

Table 14.1 Infant Deaths per 1,000 Live Births by Race of Mother (in the United States)

Race or Ethnic Origin	Number per 1,000
All racial/ethnic groups	6.9
Black	13.6
Puerto Rican	8.4
American Indian	8.0
White	5.8
Mexican American	5.5
Asian American	4.9
Cuban American	4.4

Source: Mathews and MacDorman (2008).

per year compared with an average of 6 for the entire population; Weiss and Lonnquist 2008). Lower-income citizens' perceptions of necessary health consultation often involve response to crises. The "working poor" who do not qualify for Medicaid but cannot afford private insurance or medical care delay care (Weiss and Lonnquist 2008). About 20% of adults in the United States did not receive the needed health-related services in 2007 because they could not afford a physician visit (National Center for Health Statistics 2007: table 79). Without universal access to health care, income affects health status.

Thinking Sociologically

Why do some people in the world have more access to health care than others? What does this mean for health and productivity of individuals supporting their families and for societies as a whole?

Differences in access to health care relate to meso and macro levels of the social system, as discussed in the next sections.

⊙ MODERN HEALTH CARE SYSTEMS: MESO-LEVEL ANALYSIS

At one time, health care was largely an issue addressed in homes by families. Today, in wealthy countries, health care has become institutionalized. The bustling hospital, the efficient nurses and nurses' aides, and the technically proficient physicians have replaced home care, visiting doctors, folk remedies, and homes as the setting for births, deaths, and many health issues in between. Much of the treatment of diseases depends on research that is funded by governments or foundations, and health delivery is performed by organizations that are bureaucratized corporations. This section explores the institution of medicine: organization of health care systems, hospitals as complex organizations, and changes of professional status for physicians.

The Organization of Health Care Systems

Citizens' access to health care depends on several factors: the cultural values concerning the government's role in providing health care, whether health care is seen as a human right for all citizens or a privilege for those who can pay, the amount and source of funding to provide health care, and the type of health care available. Societies around the world struggle with issues of cost, quality and access to care, and medical technology. In the Global North, these struggles result from aging populations with more health needs and smaller numbers of citizens in the tax-paying working population to support health care programs. Nations in the Global South struggle with problems that result in high death rates from curable diseases and from epidemics. Nations develop health care philosophies and systems based on population needs and their ability to address them.

Video Link 14.2 Watch a discussion about alternative medicine.

Types of National Health Care Systems

The two most common national models for providing health care—socialized medicine and decentralized national health care programs—are based on the philosophy of health care as a human right. Add to that the U.S. fee-for-service plan. Table 14.2 summarizes key aspects of these three most common national models for health care.

Socialized medicine programs provide a government-supported consumer service with equal access to health care for all citizens of a country (Cockerham 2007). The political system controls the organization and financing of health services and owns most facilities, pays providers directly, and allows private care for an extra fee. There are variations in systems. Developed countries that have socialized medicine systems include Canada, Great Britain, Israel, Norway, Sweden, and several other European countries.

Countries with decentralized national health programs have many of the same characteristics, but the government's role is different. The government has less direct control over health care and acts to regulate the system, but not operate it (Cockerham 2007). Countries with decentralized systems include France, Germany, Japan, and the Netherlands. The United States, unique among Global North countries, has a **fee-for-service health care**, in which doctors and hospitals are paid for each service they perform, they typically can order as

Table 14.2 **Types of Health Care Delivery Systems Around the World**			
Role of Government	*Fee-for-Service*	*Socialized Medicine*	*Decentralized National Health*
Regulation	Limited	Direct	Indirect
Payment to providers	Limited	Direct	Indirect
Ownership of facilities	Private and public	Private and public	Private and public
Public access	Not guaranteed	Guaranteed	Guaranteed
Private care	Dominant	Limited	Limited
Source: Cockerham (2007).			

many tests as they feel necessary, and they make lots of money because they decide the prices charged for every service. In the United States, this system is financed by not only a mix of private and public purchasers but also government-run Medicare and Medicaid programs for poor and elderly that are closer to socialized medicine plans.

Most governments in Europe decided to support health care as a human right for all citizens and put these systems into place in the late 1800s and early 1900s. Their motivations were to develop healthier populations, to strengthen their military forces and their economic systems, and to reduce the possibility of revolution by the poor and working classes by providing for basic health care needs. By providing health insurance and protection for the injured or unemployed, financial security in case of illness was increased.

Health care systems in poor countries are often patterned after former colonial systems. However, most countries struggle to provide for basic health care needs, to ensure access to health care for citizens living in rural areas, and to deal with costly diseases such as AIDS. Because of the lack of physicians, especially in rural areas, most countries in the Global South rely on a combination of Western scientific practices and indigenous medical practices using herbs and other local remedies. Trained midwives deliver babies, and health education workers travel to villages to teach about the spread of diseases such as AIDS, sometimes making condoms available. In Ugandan villages, where a high percentage of the adult working population has been infected with or died from AIDS, social workers visit regularly to be sure orphaned children are getting enough to eat and are sowing crops necessary for their survival.

Global health organizations serve many poor countries, but only with humanitarian aid during wars or epidemics, and immunizations. The World Health Organization and other international organizations help provide immunizations and treatment for epidemics, but not for ongoing health needs. For example, Kenya in East Africa has a rapidly growing population, 85% of which lives in rural areas. Kenya has a socialized health care system based on the British model, with a national health service that employs doctors and owns hospitals. However, these services are available primarily in the largest cities of Nairobi and Mombasa. In fact, 80% to 85% of the health care budget goes to these urban areas. Rural areas are served by only 10% of the doctors in the national health system, and citizens in remote areas rely on folk healers and herbalists for care (Cockerham 2007). Recently, some African nations, including Kenya and Rwanda, are experimenting with locally trained health care workers that go door to door to provide medicines and assess health care needs.

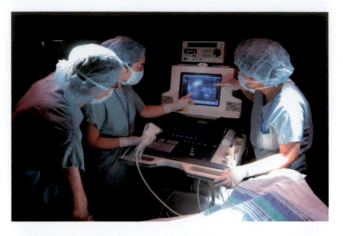

High-tech medical equipment is expensive (top), but in places such as Ethiopia (bottom), hospitals have few resources and physicians must use whatever limited technology is available.

Hospitals as Complex Organizations

Hospitals are places for the care and treatment of the sick and injured, providing centralized medical knowledge and technology for treatment of illnesses and accidents. The Industrial Revolution in Western Europe and the United States caused population shifts to urban areas. These shifts, in turn, precipitated new and threatening environmental and health conditions due to crowding and lack of sanitation. Rational, systematic approaches to health care replaced individual folk remedies. In the late 1800s, there was an explosive growth in the number of hospitals, many of which were sponsored by religious organizations. The focus of these early hospitals was on segregating the destitute and terminally ill, who might be contagious and were likely to die. At this time, most hospitals were still small, but improvements in medical knowledge and competency were changing the old system.

The status of the hospital shifted dramatically in the early 1900s due to advances in medical science. Trained staff, sterile conditions, and more advanced techniques and technology changed hospitals from being the last resort of the urban poor and the dying to places of healing for all classes. Small community hospitals were an essential element of town life. As hospital care has become more available, the structure of hospitals also changed.

The post–World War II period produced huge growth in health care facilities and numbers of employees in the health care system. Medicines and vaccines controlled many infectious diseases that had formerly killed and disabled individuals. This period also saw the growth and funding of medical schools and large medical facilities that provided not only patient care but also education and research. Thus began the dominance of the hospital in providing medical care. Today, many hospitals are centers of medical knowledge and technology, housing not only patients and surgical units but also laboratories and diagnostic centers, specialty clinics, and rehabilitation centers.

Although medical health systems differ across societies, hospitals exhibit many characteristics similar to other large, bureaucratic organizations: hierarchical structures, rules and regulations, positions (doctors, nurses) based on competency and training, hiring and promotion based on merit, and contracts for work performed. Primary-care physicians and other gatekeepers control client access to hospitals.

Historically, hospitals were designed for the convenience of physicians. However, today two rather independent bureaucracies function within modern large-scale hospital organizations. Physicians dominate the medical operations, while lay administrators operate the everyday functioning.

Health care systems are major employers in most affluent nations. In the United States, for instance, more than 14 million people are employed in a variety of hospital jobs as nurses, hospital administrators, pharmacists, physical therapists, physician's assistants, and imaging specialists (those who work with X-rays), and that number is growing. Nurses are the largest group of health care workers, with licensed registered nurses (2,192,400) and licensed practical nurses (619,100) accounting for nearly six nurses per physician (512,500; Bureau of Labor Statistics 2010–2011). In the hospital, the nurse manages the patient care team under the authority of the physician, who is the prime decision maker. Under the nurse's authority in this hierarchical structure come increasing numbers of ancillary personnel.

As hospitals and other medical facilities in the United States are increasingly owned and operated by for-profit corporations, the overwhelming power of the professional or medical line is giving way to powerful corporate management—the lay or administrative line. Physicians have become the customers of the hospital, buying space and time to carry out their functions. Sometimes, the physician's orders contradict those of the administrative line, especially with regard to medical decisions versus cost-saving decisions.

Thinking Sociologically

Who controls the medical facilities in your community? Do you see evidence of hospitals' corporate structures being geared to efficiency and profit? What effect, if any, has this had on service and commitment to clients?

Changing Professional Status of Employees in the Health Care System

Special features distinguish the hospital from other large-scale organizations or bureaucracies. The division of labor in the hospital is extensive and more highly specialized than other formal organizations. The hospital has a hierarchical pecking order based on prestige and power, and hospitals depend on the cooperation of highly skilled people whose work must be coordinated. Not only are patterns of authority rigidly followed, but the clothing and symbols peculiar to particular positions are recognizable and, as in the army, serve as status badges. The physicians, at the top of the stratification ladder, exercise the most power and receive the highest financial and prestige rewards. Signs of their superior status include wearing long white coats or not wearing special uniforms at all.

The physician's position is changing in modern societies. Physicians rank among the most respected professionals in most societies. Although trust and prestige seem to decline each year for all professions, physicians continue to command great respect, based on an assumption that they have special esoteric knowledge and humanitarian intent (Starr 1982; Weiss and Lonnquist 2008).

The widespread acceptance of physician authority is relatively recent. Before the 19th century, too little medical knowledge was established, and too few means of practice were successful to command such recognition. Physicians gained status from the discovery that some diseases were caused by bacteria and could be treated with antiseptics, from the introduction of anesthesia, and from the idea that specially trained people could treat illnesses. Coupled with scientific advances and more sophisticated diagnostic tools, these beliefs began to elevate the status of physicians and scientific medicine (Pescosolido and Boyer 2010).

The transformation of physicians to a position of professional recognition in the United States came when some

Photo Essay

Clothing and Status in the Hospital

Note the difference in how each of these people dresses. The outfits they wear are not insignificant, for they distinguish status, authority, and rights to certain prerogatives within the hospital or clinic.

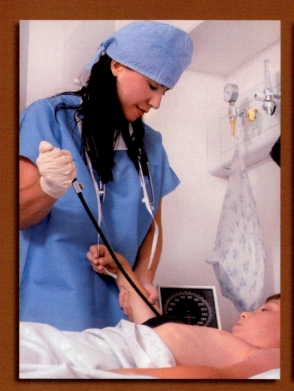

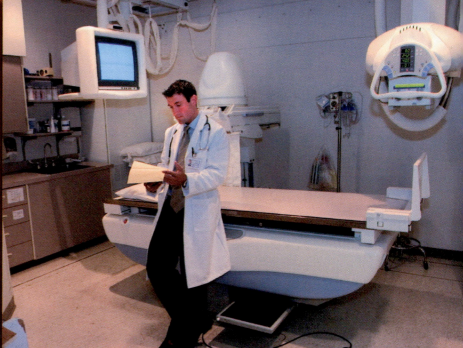

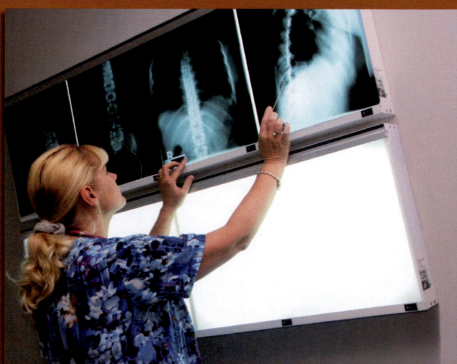

250 physicians meeting in Philadelphia in May 1847 established the American Medical Association (AMA). This umbrella organization became the means to gain legitimacy and power over health care practice (Cockerham 2007). The predominantly female health care areas such as midwifery and other holistic approaches such as osteopathy, chiropractic medicine, and homeopathy were delegitimized by the powerful new AMA. Only one approach was granted credibility: allopathy, the approach involving countersymptomatic treatment used by the dominant groups of physicians in the West.

Physicians entering practice in the United States today are faced with several major challenges. First, health care is now a system shaped by the purchasers of care and the competition for profits where it was once run by doctors who knew their patients and were committed to the Hippocratic oath of healing. Second, there has simultaneously been a decline in the public's trust of physicians, with greater willingness to question them and even outright distrust by some people. Third, an emphasis on specialization and subspecialization has arisen where previously there had been prestige and rewards in primary care (family doctors). Fourth, outpatient care in homes and doctors' offices is once again becoming more common, where the middle part of the 20th century saw an emphasis on hospitalization. Finally, there is a demand by payers (especially insurance companies) for detailed accounts of medical decision making, fixed prepayment rates established by insurers, and less willingness to pay doctors based solely on their decisions about patients' needs (Cockerham 2007; Vanderminden and Potter 2010).

Deprofessionalization means that the work of physicians is increasingly controlled by nonprofessional outside forces—financial concerns, government regulation, technological changes, new medical administrators, and a more knowledgeable public. Many physicians now work for managed care systems, so their own autonomy is limited by the bureaucrats for whom they work (Pescosolido and Boyer 2010). Moreover, bureaucratization of hospitals and controls by insurance companies on doctors' decisions have reduced the autonomy of physicians to make decisions they think are best for the patient, another element of deprofessionalization. Nurses face similar issues that can cause burnout, as discussed in the following "Applied Sociologist at Work."

The Applied Sociologist at Work— James Anderson

The Case of Nurse Burnout

With a shortage of trained nurses in the health care industry and a growing elderly population living in long-term care facilities, the United States does not need to lose nurses to burnout. This problem of nurse burnout in retirement communities is what Dr. James G. Anderson and his ex-doctoral student, Dr. Kathleen Abrahamson, set out to study.

Burnout refers to feeling unappreciated, not respected, having low status, lacking in autonomy to do the job, and being unsupported by the establishments for which they work.

To learn about the experiences of nurses in long-term care facilities, the researchers analyzed interview data from the Partners in Caregiving Study, funded by the National Institute on Aging. A finding that affects many of us is that for nurses, conflict with patients and their families was a leading cause of dissatisfaction and burnout (Abrahamson et al. 2009). Even what might appear to be minor issues such as patients' laundry became irritants. Burnout was highest early in the nurse's career cycle, then leveled off but did not go away. The finding that initial episodes of conflict have a strong influence on nursing staff burnout highlights the importance of interpersonal conflict within nursing homes on both individual and institutional outcomes.

In addition to sampling nursing staff, the researchers used computer simulations to incorporate multiple variables into the equation for burnout, and predict the major causes of burnout. The use of computer simulation modeling allowed the investigators to assess the cumulative effects of conflict between staff and families on staff burnout and test strategies that could be used to reduce the harmful effects of conflict.

Dr. Anderson has a background in engineering that has trained him to use quantitative modeling (structural equation modeling and computer simulation) to test hypotheses on social processes and social structural influences on behaviors. Modeling allows for consideration of multiple equations and variables, and to ask "what if" questions, posing scenarios to be tested. In another research, he has looked at the acceptance of information technology in health care settings, including physicians' willingness to use electronic record keeping technology (Anderson and Aydin 2005).

Note: Dr. James G. Anderson received engineering degrees and a PhD in Sociology and Education at Johns Hopkins University in Baltimore, Maryland. He is a professor of Medical Sociology and Health Communication. Dr. Kathleen Abrahamson, an RN with her PhD from Purdue, is currently an assistant professor, Department of Public Health, Western Kentucky University.

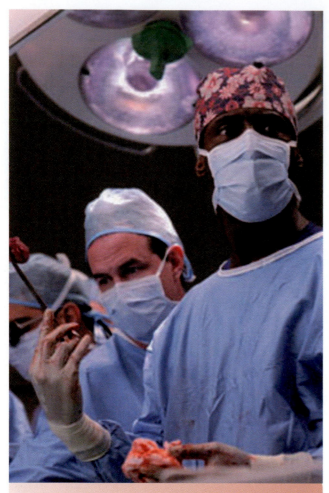

Television shows such as Grey's Anatomy *depict doctors as highly autonomous and respected professionals. Although there is some truth to this, physicians are increasingly working in bureaucratic settings in which the bureaucracy governs many of their decisions, causing deprofessionalization.*

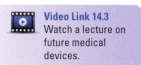

Video Link 14.3
Watch a lecture on future medical devices.

We have explored issues of health care at the micro level (the role of sick people) and at the meso level (organization of health care and hospitals as complex organizations). We now move on to macro-level policy issues at national and global levels.

Thinking Sociologically

Doctors have been depicted in many television shows over the past five decades. How might these depictions affect people's expectations of doctors and hospitals? In what ways are TV doctors and nurses different from real-life doctors and nurses?

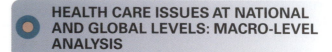

HEALTH CARE ISSUES AT NATIONAL AND GLOBAL LEVELS: MACRO-LEVEL ANALYSIS

The Health Care System in the United States

The United States has the best system—and the worst. It is one of the best in the world in terms of quality medical care, trained practitioners, facilities, and advanced medical technology. People from around the world seek training and care in the United States. It is also the worst system: It requires the highest cost per capita in the world to provide care (discussed in more detail later), does not provide equal access to citizens, is inefficient, has competing interests, and is fragmented.

Eloise knew something was seriously wrong when she lost her appetite, vomited when she ate more than a few bites, and lost her usually abundant energy. Without health insurance and fearing to lose her job if she missed work to sit in the outpatient waiting room of the hospital to see a doctor, she tried home remedies and hoped the symptoms would go away. When she finally did go to the hospital, she was in a serious condition. Eloise spent a few days in intensive care and is now on treatments, but without income from her job, she cannot pay the bills for herself and her child. Similar medical emergencies occur across the United States for more than 46.3 million people who lack medical insurance (U.S. Census Bureau 2009f). Because of cases like Eloise, some critics claim that the U.S. health care system is a social problem. It developed without specific direction and responded to demands piecemeal, allowing practitioners, medical facilities, and insurance and drug companies to establish themselves and then protect their self-interests, sometimes at the expense of citizens. In a discussion of the development of the U.S. health care system (see the next "Sociology in Our Social World" on page 496), Starr uses historical analysis to determine key elements in its transformation.

Health Care Advances

Medical research into gene therapy, understanding of the human genome, and research into new drug and technological therapies make research one of the most rapidly advancing medical fields. New therapies will help people live longer, more comfortable, and productive lives—if they can afford the care. As science moves rapidly, ethical questions about the use of fetal tissue in experiments and treatments, cloning, prolonging life, and other issues challenge ethicists and lawmakers (Mike 2003).

In addition to advances in medical science, there have been achievements in public health and education that prolong lives: motor vehicle safety, safer workplaces, control of infectious diseases, decline in heart problems, healthier foods, healthier mothers and babies, family planning, clean drinking water, and education of citizens about the dangers of tobacco and other substances as health hazards (Morbidity and Mortality Weekly Report 2006).

Problems in the U.S. Health Care System

The fragmented way in which the U.S. health care system has developed has led to two major problems: lack of universal access to health care and constantly escalating health care costs along with a sizeable uninsured population, resulting in lack of health care security (LeBow 2004; Oberlander 2002; Pescosolido and Boyer 2010).

Access to Health Care. No matter how advanced technical-medical skills may be, they are of little use to society if they are not available to those who need them. In the United States, services are not necessarily distributed according to the needs of the people (Quesnal-Vallee and Jenkins 2010).

First, there is a maldistribution of services. The shortage of physicians in rural areas in the United States and many other countries is particularly serious (White 2002), and there is no indication that this will change soon. Some free-enterprise advocates contend that an oversupply of physicians will lead to a trickle-down to rural areas, but data analysis shows that this is not occurring. The expectation that family or primary-care physicians would gravitate to rural areas is not occurring either. The United States has followed the lead of some other countries, which cover physician education costs in exchange for a commitment to work in poor or rural areas for a set time period. Called the National Health Service Corps (NHSC), this strategy encourages better distribution of health services, but also brings less experienced and nonpermanent physicians to poor and rural locations (Gallagher and Johnson 2001; Ginsberg 1999).

Within cities, physicians are concentrated in certain neighborhoods—and outside certain neighborhoods. As a hospital's service area becomes increasingly populated by poorer residents, the facility faces a higher demand for free care. Closure and relocation to more profitable areas are particularly common among for-profit hospitals, and poor minority populations suffer.

Another aspect of maldistribution is the lack of family physicians. Many physicians choose to enter one of more than 30 specialty areas in medicine. The reward system of medicine in terms of prestige, income, and lifestyle makes specialty practice more appealing than general medicine. Moreover, most specialists are found in urban areas. The result of lack of access in rural areas and urban poor areas, especially for the poor and uninsured, is less frequent care, fewer regular physician visits and procedures, and a higher chance of serious costly illness and of dying in a hospital once they do get admitted.

Health Care Cost and Funding. Perhaps the most serious problem for health care systems and consumers in the United

Dr. Nilda Soto, director of the Open Door Health Center in Homestead, Florida, walks with a patient along a hallway. The Open Door Health Center is a free health clinic that assists the uninsured poor. Those who serve the poor often do so with very poor financial compensation for their training. In other countries, governments generally do not expect health care to be provided by altruistic people. Insurance helps pay for medical care in developed countries.

States, however, is the escalating cost of health care. Since 1947, expenditures for health care in the United States (now at 16% of the gross national product) have increased more rapidly than expenditures for other areas of the economy, and the United States spends twice as much per year on health care as other countries. For example, Switzerland spends 10.9% of the gross domestic product (GDP) and Canada 9.7% (National Coalition on Health Care 2008). About 30% of health care costs in the United States go to administration. This cost is much lower in other countries (e.g., it is 16% in Canada; Woolhandler, Campbell, and Himmelstein 2004). Table 14.3 on page 494 shows the increases in costs of health care over time in the United States.

Thinking Sociologically

Develop several hypotheses to explain why health care costs are rising rapidly, focusing on the United States. How would you test these hypotheses?

The United States is now the only developed country in the world that does not have a national health insurance program providing health care coverage for all citizens. Proposals for universal coverage plans have failed primarily because of philosophical differences between politicians and

Table 14.3	**National Health Expenditures: United States**		
Year	In Billion Dollars	Percentage of Gross Domestic Product	Yearly Amount per Capita (in Dollars)
1960	26.9	5.1	141
1970	73.2	7.1	341
1980	247.2	8.9	1,051
1990	699.5	12.2	2,689
2000	1,309.4	13.3	4,670
2007	2,300.0	16	7,600

Source: Centers for Medical and Medicaid Services (2004); National Coalition on Health Care (2008).

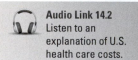

Audio Link 14.2
Listen to an explanation of U.S. health care costs.

opposition from private insurance companies, physicians, and drug companies. The medical profession fought against the first proposed government medical insurance programs—Medicare and Medicaid (Marmor 1999). The programs passed mainly because they allowed physicians to retain their autonomy and to control their financial rewards. Prior to 2009 attempts to nationalize health care in the United States have failed or stalled in large part due to lobbying and public influence ads by insurance and drug companies. The AMA, in contrast, supported the plan in 2009.

Managed health care plans developed quickly to fill the gap after the 1994 national health plan failed to pass in Congress (Pescosolido and Boyer 2010). About 61% of insured patients are in managed health care plans. Health care companies control costs by limiting visits to specific physicians in their network, requiring referrals for specialists, and demanding preauthorization for hospital stays. Each insured individual is guaranteed care in exchange for a monthly sum paid by the employer and employee.

Managed care tries to integrate two goals—efficiency and high-quality care—with two means—financing and health care delivery. Evidence indicates that managed health care plans are making profits. Although surveys show that 43% of consumers have been satisfied with their health care (Burda 2001; Health Confidence Survey 2001; Vandenburgh 2001), 80% are dissatisfied or very dissatisfied with how much it costs.

As health care costs rise, employers are shifting more of the cost to employees by charging higher deductibles, using mail-order and generic prescription programs, and increasing patient co-pays. Workers are now paying an average of $1,400 more in premiums annually than they did in 2000 (National Coalition on Health Care 2008). The problem is that these strategies cannot keep up with the rising costs. These recent developments in administration and cost containment have helped control but not reduced costs because of increased

demand for care, rising numbers of senior citizens who need more health care, and expensive new technologies.

Managed care has its critics who argue that for-profit corporations do not belong in the business of health care because health is a human right. Costs of for-profit care are high and rising, leading to demands for a national health plan that would provide universal coverage at less expense, such as the plan the Clinton administration hoped to develop. Meanwhile, the federal government is passing piecemeal legislation to deal with the problems.

Almost all other Global North countries have national health care systems that cover all citizens, but citizens pay higher taxes for the coverage. However, the cost structure for administration is much less, saving money for individuals and the state. Michael Moore's 2007 documentary film, *Sicko*, and recent books and articles compare health care systems; they look at the high profitability of the U.S. health care industries (including insurance companies, drug manufacturers, and some practitioners) to the free universal health care offered at lower overall cost in countries such as Canada, United

Table 14.4	**National Health Expenditures by Type 2007 (in trillions of dollars)**
National health expenditures	$2.24 trillion
Annual percentage change	6.1% higher
Percentage of gross domestic product	16.2%
Private expenditures	$1,205.5 trillion
Public expenditures	$1,035.7 trillion
Percentage paid by the federal government	72.8%

Source: U.S. Census Bureau (2010b:table 128).

Kingdom, and France (PBS Newshour 2009a; Reid 2009). Table 14.4 shows sources of funding for U.S. health care.

Controversies such as extending health benefits to domestic partners—unmarried cohabiting heterosexual and homosexual couples—have further clouded the issues of insurance coverage. However, some city and state government employees do receive partner benefits. New York City granted benefits to its employees' domestic partners, but in 1999, Pennsylvania voted to deny such benefits to homosexual partners.

Thinking Sociologically

What are the benefits of the U.S. managed health care systems? What are the benefits of national health care systems? What are the problems with each? What is your solution to the health care problems faced by the United States?

Lack of Health Care Security and the New Obama Health Care Plan. The biggest criticism of the U.S. system has been the lack of health insurance for millions, making health security unattainable. One out of three Americans, or 86.7 million below 65 years of age, were uninsured at some point between 2007 and 2008. The estimated uninsured population at any given time since 2007 has been 52 million, or 19.2% of the population (Hiebert-White 2010). With the passage of the 2010 health care bill, many of these uninsured will be covered by or before 2014, and those individuals with preexisting conditions cannot be denied coverage (The White House 2010).

Currently, for clients who cannot pay in the pay-for-service system of health care, options are limited: public hospitals (which are few in number), county and state facilities, and free clinics. Paying for health care was the Number 1 economic concern of 50% of U.S. citizens, and many uninsured citizens delayed health care (National Coalition on Health Care 2008). By the time the uninsured sought help, the situation was often an emergency, costing much more than early intervention. Who paid? Public hospitals have relied on tax dollars from you and me to foot the bill for those who did not have insurance or cash. Not only were there more emergencies, but also health care for the poor costs more because it has been delayed. The new health care system is intended to alleviate such problems.

Of the people in the United States with no insurance, 11% were children below 19 years; 13.2 million young adults were uninsured; 23% of those 30 to 35 years had no insurance, 17% of those 36 to 49 years, and 13% of those 50 to 64 years (Bolduan 2009). After that people qualify for Medicare. A disproportionate number have been unmarried women, often with children, or members of ethnic groups. During recessions, the number of uninsured has grown because families and individuals could not afford insurance premiums. Even in the best of times, roughly 6% of people applying for coverage have been refused (HealthReform.gov 2010), and roughly an

Union members and health care workers demonstrate for national health care and Medicaid. This demonstration in New York City was stimulated by federal cuts in Medicaid that left many people without health care.

equal number are charged significantly higher rates if they have preexisting medical conditions. Insurance companies have been able to deny medical claims to reduce their costs if they deem a procedure unnecessary. This policy will change under the new health care plan. Still, there will likely be unexpected consequences of the new program that no one has foreseen, for that happens with virtually all social policies, regardless of how well intended.

Barriers to health care and lack of health insurance have kept many from using services, even with the payments of Medicare and Medicaid. Table 14.5 shows the differences and disparities in health insurance coverage between groups in the United States. Note the numbers of uninsured, lowest for White citizens at 12.5%, and the number of privately insured, highest for Whites at 79.3%.

Medicare and Medicaid—services for the growing percentage of citizens 65 years and older (estimated to be one in five by 2050) and for the poor—were legislated without cost limits. Whatever the medical profession charged was what

Table 14.5 Health Insurance: Type of Coverage for Persons Below 65 Years of Age				
Insurance Type	Total U.S.	White	Black	Hispanic
Private (%)	71.7	79.3	57.0	46.6
Medicaid	9.4	6.3	19.3	12.5
Other Public	2.1	1.9	3.7	1.0
Uninsured	16.8	10.4	16.0	30.7

Source: Centers for Disease Control (2009).

the government paid. Since the original legislation, Congress has had some success in regulating and limiting charges and the length of hospital stays, but "creative billing" has thwarted government attempts to control the costs of the services. Thus, efforts to reform the system and control costs continue.

Lack of universal access and escalating costs have adversely affected the quality of care offered to some citizens. For example, many uninsured clients such as Eloise, the woman discussed at the beginning of this section, have deferred care due to unaffordable fees. This compounds their health risks, increasing the likelihood of more expensive emergencies later. Financial considerations may also affect the type of services offered to clients. Socioeconomic status influences the decision to perform some surgical procedures, such as Cesarean deliveries.

Paul Starr writes about the development of health care systems in the United States, described in the next "Sociology in Our Social World."

Sociology in Our Social World

The Social Transformation of American Medicine

In his Pulitzer Prize–winning book, Paul Starr (1982) uses historical documents to analyze the development of medicine in America from the 1700s to the 1980s. The research was a massive undertaking. Starr consulted books, journals, historical documents and accounts of medical practice, government reports, public health documents and records of specific diseases, hospital records, medical cost reports, medical school histories and catalogs, information on medical organizations, biographies and autobiographies, and other documents that shed light on the history and development of medicine in the United States. By doing content analysis on each historical period—that is, systematically studying the written materials available about medicine—he pieced together a picture of the themes and trends at different time periods. Starr used many sociological concepts and theories throughout his research to give his analysis depth.

His book represents two long movements: (1) the rise of medical profession sovereignty and (2) the transformation of medicine into an industry with the expansion of corporate influence and state control. Starr examines a number of issues about the institution of medicine. Why, for example, did Americans change from being wary of medicine to being devoted to it? Doctors who were previously deeply divided became united—and prosperous. Why was that? Hospitals, medical schools, clinics, and other medical organizations assumed forms in the United States that were unlike those institutions in other countries, an intriguing difference. In the process, hospitals became the central institutions in medical care while public health became marginalized, unlike other places in the world. Similarly, there is no national health insurance in the United States, and commercial indemnity insurance now dominates the private health insurance market. In an interesting twist, some physicians are now taking part in the creation of corporate health care systems, a new development. Why did they evolve the way they did? Medicine is now a business as well as a cultural phenomenon in the United States, and Starr's investigation helps us understand that reality.

During the early years of U.S. history, the medical profession was not yet established. Many doctors were educated people who had no coursework in the sciences, and hospitals were places where people went to die, not to be healed. With the advent of modern medicine—sanitation and sterilization, understanding of disease, medicines, and vaccines—medicine grew in stature and people turned to doctors and hospitals for their medical needs. Starr documents the changing trends in medicine and ends with a discussion of recent problems with insurance systems and the debates between private insurance, medical systems, and public programs. Concerns today center on privatization of health care, hospital and physician services, insurance, and containment of costs.

By using historical analysis, Starr was able to give both an overview of trends and a detailed account of medicine throughout U.S. history. Only such a long-term perspective could help us deeply understand many of the issues regarding medical care, the status of physicians, and the institutionalization of medicine.

Policy Issues and Social Reforms in the U.S. System

We return to this question: Is medical care a right or a privilege? Some argue that it is a human right that cannot be bought and sold to the highest bidder or richest segments of society. Others argue that it is a privilege, a commodity to be purchased in a free market and that competition will both improve quality and reduce costs. The human rights argument provides the model for most of the Global North, whereas the market-driven system is the main model in the United States for all but the elderly and poor, who qualify for some government insurance (Harrington and Estes 2004).

Recent proposals for reform of the U.S. health care system take several forms:

1. Revise the partly public, partly private system with a mix of governmental and private insurers. This model would be the simplest reform because it is most compatible with the current system.

2. Vote in reforms one at a time. This is currently happening.

3. Pass a comprehensive reform package that would provide national health insurance and government oversight and administration. Some states have already passed programs to provide access and contain costs for their residents.

Many recent attempts to insure more citizens have been carried out at the state level, with some states reaching close to 90% coverage rates. Depending on the success of federal health care reform, states may continue to be the ones actually achieving reform (Pescosolido and Boyer 2010).

Thinking Sociologically

What are the advantages and disadvantages of each proposal mentioned? What effect would each proposal have on different groups of people in a society?

A significant problem for state and federal governments and for individuals is the high cost of drug prescriptions. The pharmaceutical industry does not cap costs in the United States as it does in many other countries, as required by governments, partly due to what they argue are research costs connected with developing new drugs. For this reason also, only brand-label drugs can be sold in the United States for a certain period before similar but cheaper generic drugs can be sold. Many individuals and even states have turned to Canada and other countries for cheaper drugs to control

costs. However, the U.S. administration has upheld bans on purchases outside the United States, pointing out possible problems with quality control.

Social scientists say that three factors must be present for a major social initiative such as universal health insurance to pass the U.S. Congress: common understanding of the problem, general agreement on the approach to solving the problem, and positive political ramifications for legislators taking a position on the problem. The most recent attempt to pass a comprehensive reform plan in the United States in 2010 resulted in a compromise package that accomplished some goals of the Obama administration for meeting health care needs.

Experts in health care predict that several trends will affect the future direction of U.S. health care (Coile 2002; Weber 2003):

1. Response to the threat of bioterrorism means hospitals must be prepared to be first responders in an emergency, and public health officials and the Centers for Disease Control have taken on new importance with the national threats from terrorism.

2. Hospitals are growing to meet increased demand for services, advertising their services, and changing their images to please clients.

3. Use of computer technology for record keeping and medical tests is growing.

4. Medical advances are changing the way physicians and hospitals treat clients. For example, gene testing and therapy, stem-cell therapy, and individualized drugs are imminent.

5. Employers are fighting the rapid increases in health care insurance costs. Many are dropping managed health programs and shifting more cost for health care to employees.

6. The growing numbers of citizens without health insurance and reformers have argued for universal health insurance. Several organizations have pushed for a national plan that would cover everyone (Physicians' Working Group 2003).

Although it is difficult to predict whether change will mean dramatic restructuring or tinkering with the current system, change is inevitable. The health care system of the United States faces three main challenges: (1) what to do about the rising uninsured population; (2) how to control costs, especially in a managed care system; and (3) what the physician-client relationship will be under new structures of health care (Pescosolido and Boyer 2010).

Many reformers look to other countries for ideas; Canada's system is one that is seen as a possible model (see "Sociology Around the World"). The next section looks at change in health care at the global level of the social world.

Sociology Around the World

Comparing Health Care Systems: The Canadian Model

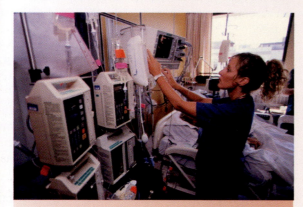

An intensive care nurse checks the monitors for a patient at Lion's Gate Hospital in Vancouver, Canada. In Canada, medical care is guaranteed by citizenship.

Two principles underlie Canada's system: All Canadians should have the right to health care, and financial barriers to care should be eliminated. After World War II, the Canadian government established universal health insurance to improve the health of all Canadians, with costs shared 50-50 by federal and provincial governments (Bolaria and Dickinson 2001). The government, in consultation with the medical professionals, sets prices for services.

Comparing major health indicators in Canada and the United States, Canada has lower infant mortality (4.6 deaths per 1,000 live births in Canada vs. 6.9 in the United States) and higher life expectancy (80.3 years in Canada vs. 78.0 years in the United States; United North America 2008). Canada pays

for the system with taxes that are 10% to 15% higher than the United States, but at 0.33% less cost per capita for health care than the United States. Canada spent 10% of its GDP in 2007 on health care, while the United States commits 15.3% of its GDP (Canadian Institute for Health Information 2007; National Coalition on Health Care 2008). Comparing Canada, United States, Mexico, Japan, and the Netherlands, Table 14.6 shows differences in costs of health care.

Problems of care denied because of lack of insurance, discrimination, and geographic maldistribution—major issues in the U.S. system prior to 2010—have been largely solved. In a comparison of access in the U.S. and Canadian systems, 13% of Americans are unable to get the needed care, many for financial reasons. In Canada, 3.7% cannot get care, almost none for financial reasons.

In addition, controls by insurance companies result in hospital stays in the United States that are 20% to 40% shorter than in most other countries for similar procedures. Some attribute this to the profit motive, which undermines attention to services and to client needs as foremost. Yet, in Canada, waiting periods for nonessential procedures are longer, and tests such as MRI are given less often.

Fewer people in the United States report being satisfied with their health system than in Canada. Concern among conservatives in the United States about government control has helped keep the U.S. system in private hands. Other concerns raised about the Canadian system have to do with access to some types of care, waiting periods for nonessential surgeries, and rationing of care for some procedures (Cockerham 2007). No system is perfect, including the Canadian one. The issue of how to provide better and affordable care to citizenry was a key political topic in the United States 2008 presidential election and continues to be debated in Congress.

Table 14.6	Differences in Costs of Health Care				
	Health spending per capita	Health costs covered by government	Percent GDP spent on health care	Infant deaths per 1,000	Average life expectancy
Japan	$2,581	81.3%	8.1%	3	83
Netherlands	$3,481	80%	9.4%	4	80
Canada	$3,673	70.4%	10%	5	81
United States	$6,719	45.8%	15.3%	7	78
Mexico	$778	44.2%	6.6%	29	74

Source: PBS Newshour (2009a).

Thinking Sociologically

Do profit motive and competition create higher quality in a service field such as health care, as they seem to in production of products? Why or why not? What are some positive and some negative consequences of a competitive system with the "winners" rewarded by higher profits?

Health Care Around the Globe

During a year-long sabbatical in England, the Ballantine family was signed up with a local surgeon, as the British call family physicians. Their sore throats, upset tummies, and bruised feet were taken to the doctor at no direct cost. The school referred their daughter to the hospital eye clinic for glasses at no cost. Their son was diagnosed and treated for "glandular fever" (mononucleosis), again at no cost. In Great Britain, all citizens have access to treatment by family physicians and dentists, to the dispensing of prescribed drugs, to eye care, and to community nursing and health visitor services. Universal health care is covered by taxes.

The demographic makeup, value systems, and financial status of each country will have an effect on how health care is delivered. Global North societies, with a high proportion of elderly and a low proportion of young people, have very different needs from Global South societies with many dependent children. In societies with many elders, special care for chronic illness is more necessary, whereas societies with many children must deal with childhood illnesses.

One global health issue is the maldistribution of physicians, which is illustrated in Map 14.2 in the next "Engaging Sociology." The highest number of physicians, between 425 and 591 per 100,000 people, are found in Cuba, Belarus, Belgium, Estonia, Greece, and the Russian Federation. The lowest numbers are in Global South African countries of Tanzania, Malawi, Niger, Burundi, Ethiopia, Sierra Leone, and Mozambique, all at between 2 and 3 doctors per 100,000 people, and most of these located in urban areas (Human Development Report 2007). In some Global South countries, local rural residents are trained both in emergency medicine and to recognize illnesses. Those needing additional care are taken to regional centers. In Rwanda, for example, health care workers make house calls to inquire about diseases and provide the required treatment (PBS NOW 2009).

Each society organizes its health care system in ways congruous with its culture. Although societies have developed different ways of dealing with illness, Western scientific medicine is spreading throughout the world. Although ideas about health and medicine are moving in more than one direction and each country has a different system, they all face similar problems as they "continue to search for strategies to contain costs, provide access to high-quality and effective care, manage care for chronic illnesses and disabilities and the treatment of old and new infectious diseases, and reconfigure new professional roles and responsibilities" (Pescosolido and Boyer 2010).

Some of the ideas from other parts of the world are now influencing Western approaches to health and illness, as the following example from China illustrates. China mixes traditional with Western medicine.

The People's Republic of China: Medicine in a Communist State

Little was known outside China about China's health care system until the 1970s, when visitors, including health observers, were welcomed by the government. When the "bamboo curtain" that isolated China was raised in 1971, the outside world learned that, despite a background of poverty, a primary network of health services had been established. However, health care delivery faced problems because the country was so large and the population so spread out and rural. The political leaders were determined to bring industrialization and a modern lifestyle to the country in a very short time. Privatization of some aspects of the social system eliminated some government and communal support for primary health care. This put severe pressures on all of China's institutions.

Video Link 14.4
Watch a video on international health care.

Jeanne, one of your coauthors, met Xi (pronounced "She") on a train in China. He was returning to his village after completing a medical training course that covered first aid treatment, immunizations, and recognition of serious symptoms. He was one of more than 1.8 million barefoot doctors or *countryside doctors*—paramedics trained in basic medicine to provide health care for rural residents in China's villages. The program was very successful in curbing infectious diseases. In fact, the program has provided a model for reaching out into the countryside for several Global South countries, including Kenya and Rwanda.

Handbook Link 14.2
Read more about comparative health systems.

Barefoot doctors were generally local peasants selected by fellow members of their agricultural communes. They continued to work on the farm but, after some training, took responsibility for preventive medicine and some aspects of primary care in the local neighborhood. If they passed an exam they could become a village doctor, licensed to carry out additional medical procedures. Their income was determined in the same manner as other agricultural workers. The barefoot doctor was generally the only medical practitioner that many of the 800 million people living in rural China ever saw. From a sociological perspective, a positive feature of these practitioners was their within-culture socialization. Given the homogeneity of peasant neighborhoods, the barefoot doctor had little difficulty

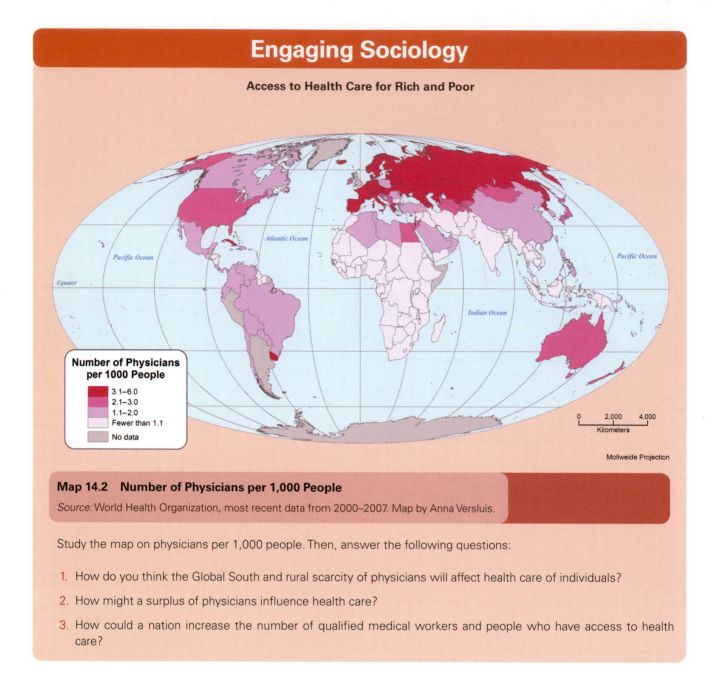

Engaging Sociology

Access to Health Care for Rich and Poor

Number of Physicians per 1000 People

- 3.1–6.0
- 2.1–3.0
- 1.1–2.0
- Fewer than 1.1
- No data

Mollweide Projection

Map 14.2 Number of Physicians per 1,000 People

Source: World Health Organization, most recent data from 2000–2007. Map by Anna Versluis.

Study the map on physicians per 1,000 people. Then, answer the following questions:

1. How do you think the Global South and rural scarcity of physicians will affect health care of individuals?

2. How might a surplus of physicians influence health care?

3. How could a nation increase the number of qualified medical workers and people who have access to health care?

understanding the local culture and their resistance to certain procedures. This program to spread health care to all areas of China began in 1951.

Today this program that provided a model for poor countries has all but collapsed. This process began in the late 1970s with the privatization of agriculture, private enterprises, and rapid growth in China. No longer were there collective farms with groups of people to finance the barefoot doctors and the government was unwilling to train them. This left many villages with no primary care or immunization programs. Diseases that had been thought to be eradicated began to resurface. Since most of the doctors in China are located in urban areas, many people in rural areas must now depend on home remedies (Casella 2009). Recently, the central government has allocated funds to increase basic coverage in regional areas and improve hospitals, and it has a goal of insuring 90% of the population (Wang 2009).

Once introduced, Western-style medicine expanded rapidly in China. From 1978 to 1980, the number of traditional Chinese medical personnel increased slightly, but the number of medical personnel with training in Western medicine increased significantly. Today, some clinics for preventive care, birth control, and first aid are found in rural areas, and the very sick go to regional hospitals. Many health care workers now blend Western medicine practices with Chinese approaches. Increasingly, doctors are trained in both.

Chinese medical practices are also influencing medicine around the world. Consider the example of acupuncture, an ancient Chinese method for treating certain physical problems and relieving pain. It is part of a healing system that understands health and the human body in relation to nature. The body seeks a balance between itself and the world around it. When imbalance occurs, disease results. Thus, part of the goal of Chinese medicine is to restore internal balance to the body.

Acupuncture, along with related treatments, is based on the idea that the body has certain points (700 of them) that ease and control pain and stimulate body functions. The process of inserting fine sharp needles into selected points related to affected organs in the body is essentially painless, and doctors have even done operations without chemical anesthesia using acupuncture to block pain. The procedures are widely practiced in Asia and are gaining popularity in many Western countries.

Although acupuncture has been practiced for more than 5,000 years in China, only in the 1970s, when relations with China improved, did this treatment become known and practiced in the West. Many doctors in the Global North reject the practice as unscientific and ineffective, and some regulating agencies have put limits on its practice. However, many patients feel otherwise. California (among other states) licenses the estimated 15,000 qualified practitioners in the state (China.org 2009). An increasing number of acupuncture pain clinics are opening around the world, and about 8.2 million U.S. adults have used acupuncture (Barnes et al. 2004). Some insurance companies also cover the costs of acupuncture, and the World Health Organization recognizes more than 40 conditions that can be effectively treated by acupuncture (Weiss and Lonnquist 2008). In Australia, 15% of general practitioners offer acupuncture (Lupton 2001). Thus, we see that diffusion of medical knowledge throughout the world brings new practices to all countries.

The Chinese health care system does face problems. In rural areas, many people practice traditional folk medicine. Disease, poor sanitation, pollution, ignorance, and smoking result in lowered life expectancy. Chinese account for about 30% of the world's tobacco consumption, with 360 million smokers—about 31% of the population. Smoking-related deaths, including lung cancer deaths, are increasing. In fact, smoking causes 90% of lung cancer deaths worldwide (Ong et al. 2007). Government efforts to control smoking have been uneven because the government receives needed money from foreign tobacco sales.

Today, China's health care system is financed primarily by the central government, patient fees, and health insurance. Health care expenditures amount to more than 4.7% of the GDP (World Health Organization 2007). China has brought down the death rate and the average life expectancy is now 73.5 years, whereas just after the Chinese Cultural Revolution in 1955, it was 40.8 years (U.S. Census Bureau

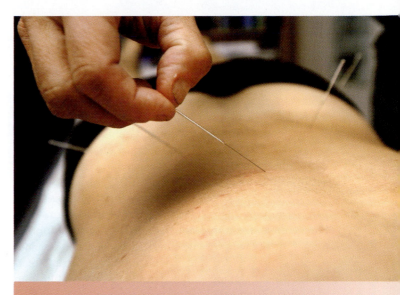

This acupuncturist is inserting needles on the back of his patient. This is an ancient and highly respected medical technique in China, and it has gained adherents in the United States and other Western countries.

2006b). Most significant for the rest of the world is the impact Chinese traditional medical techniques and remedies are having around the world.

Health care systems around the world illustrate the impact of national and global political and economic factors on the health care available to citizens. The political systems of countries and their economic status influence the philosophy toward health care and the money each country puts into health care. International policies such as embargoes between countries influence availability of health care *within* countries. International organizations, such as the World Health Organization, focus on epidemics and pandemics throughout the world.

Thinking Sociologically

What are some positive features of the Chinese approach to health care? What are some drawbacks of their approach? How is it similar and how is it different from the Cuban and Canadian models discussed earlier in the chapter?

Globalization of Medical Problems

A dramatic worldwide health problem illustrating the interconnectedness between countries is the international sale of body parts. In some countries, people at the bottom of the stratification system are so desperately poor that they sell their body parts to help their families survive.

For example, mothers and fathers in some poor slums of Mumbai and other cities in India and Pakistan sell their kidneys for money to pay for housing, food, education for their children, and dowries to marry off their daughters. In the process, their health often deteriorates, and when the money is gone, life is even more difficult. Although laws were passed in India in 1994 banning the sale of human organs, few violators are caught and punished ("Body Parts for Sale" 2008; "Cruellest Cut" 2009; Kumar 2001). As of 2008, the only nation where the sale of body organs was legal was Iran ("Body Parts for Sale" 2008).

Wealthy individuals in need of kidneys buy these body parts to improve their chances of survival and a normal life. For example, the transplant trade attracts medical tourists from Europe, who visit impoverished countries in Latin America and Asia for transplants and other "cheap" treatments. This is a dramatic illustration of world stratification of health care, effects of government policies, the differences in health attitudes, and behavior between rich and poor.

The black market in body parts is spreading to many countries. For example, an international "transplant Mafia" (based in Moldova, which was once part of the Soviet Union) smuggles live donors to the United States to sell their lungs and kidneys because the market for body parts exceeds the supply (Kates 2002). Even officials in coroners' offices have been apprehended harvesting body parts without consent of family members, often making a profit from the sales (Mashberg 2002). Reports from Nigeria indicate that mortuary and cemetery workers are selling body parts at markets (Ananova 2001), and a survey of students in the United Kingdom found that one in four would sell a kidney to help pay for their education (Ananova 2002). This issue emphasizes the global differences between rich and poor people and countries. Where there is a need and a market for goods, those in need will step in to fill the gap, and many sick individuals will pay handsomely for body parts.

The status of a nation's health and medical care are often measured by key international markers—decrease in infant mortality and increase in life expectancy. **Infant mortality** refers to the number of deaths within the first year of life divided by the number of live births in the same year times 1,000. The rate for each country is a good indicator of the availability of and access to prenatal care and care for infants. **Life expectancy** refers to the average number of years people live in a particular society. It shows the overall health conditions in a country. These basic data tell us a great deal about the health and health care of a nation. The infant morality and life expectancy statistics appeared in Table 7.1 on page 215. The low national rate for infant mortality is 2.3 per 1,000 live births and the high is 184. Life expectancy ranges from 32 in Swaziland to more than 82 in Japan.

Note the different causes of death in affluent/Global North versus poor/Global South countries in Table 14.7 (World Health Organization 2002). In the past, people in the Global North died of heart attacks and bad infections.

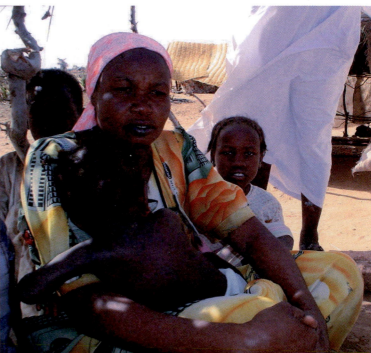

These two women are of similar age, both in their thirties. Health facilities make an enormous difference in one's life chances, health, and how one ages. The woman on the left lives in North America; the woman on the right raises a family in Senegal, West Africa.

Table 14.7	**Leading Causes of Death**			
Poor Countries' Deaths (in Percentage)			*Affluent Countries' Deaths (in Percentage)*	
Lower respiratory infections	11.2		Coronary heart disease	16.3
Coronary heart disease	9.4		Stroke/cerebrovascular disease	9.3
Diarrheal diseases	6.9		Tracheal/bronchal/lung cancers	5.9
HIV/AIDS (leading cause of death for women)	5.7		Lower respiratory infections	3.8
Stroke/cerebrovascular diseases	5.6		Chronic obstructive pulmonary disease	3.5
Chronic obstructive pulmonary disease	3.6		Alzheimer and other dementias	3.4
Tuberculosis	3.5		Colon and rectal cancers	3.3
Perinatal diseases	3.4		Diabetes mellitus	2.8
Malaria	3.3		Breast cancer	2.0
Prematurity, low birth weight	3.2		Stomach cancer	1.8

Source: World Health Organization (2008, Fact Sheet No. 310).

Today, cancer is the leading cause of death (World Health Organization 2009), but many can be kept alive, even cured, extending life expectancy into the 80s. Yet infectious diseases are major killers in the Global South, reducing life expectancy in some poor countries to 40 years or less.

Globalization and the Mobility of Disease

In December 2007, a man boarded an international flight bound for the United States. The passengers and crew did not know that he was carrying a deadly strain of tuberculosis, one that is very difficult to treat with current medicines. The Centers for Disease Control knew he carried the strain, tracked him down, and brought him in for testing. They needed to know if he was contagious. If so, they would need to contact all people on the flight and start preventative measures to reduce the possibility of a pandemic. The media picked up this story, and it blanketed the front pages of newspapers for several days, showing the concern about uncontrollable diseases spreading around the globe.

When the West Nile virus—a deadly mosquito-borne disease—was first discovered in New York City in 1999, it killed seven people before any action could be taken. Within a year, it had spread to 12 states, and within 2 years, it was found not only in mosquitoes but also in 60 species of birds and a dozen different types of mammals (Wilson 2006). Although health officials acted rapidly to stem the spread of this disease and others such as H1N1, pandemics are a constant threat. The world is highly connected, and diseases anywhere in the world can quickly spread to other continents, overpowering the medical communities' ability to diagnose, isolate, and treat diseases. Because both people and infection are highly mobile today, the problem is global. Global change and interconnectedness facilitate the spread of diseases and require countries and world organizations working together to attack health problems.

The density and mobility of the world's population (discussed in Chapter 15) affects human health. For example, use of land and space determines the number of rodents and insects, the water supplies, and the direct contact people have with one another. Currently, about half of the world's people live in urban areas and many in slums surrounding major cities. Problems such as open sewers, inadequate sanitation, lack of electricity, and polluted water pervade these slums. Most infections spread more readily where there is a population of at least 150,000, although more than 1 million is even more favorable for infectious germs by increasing the chances

This woman has just acquired new bed nets, which her family will use to protect themselves from malaria-causing mosquitoes. Often, people are bitten and infected while they sleep.

This sign in a rural area of Ethiopia is an effort to educate local people about the dangers of AIDS and methods to protect oneself.

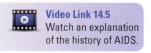

Video Link 14.5
Watch an explanation of the history of AIDS.

people are moving around the globe for business and tourism much more today than in the past, they are exposed to more people in more environments. More than 5,000 airports now host international travelers, and more than 1 million people travel across international borders each day, counting only commercial airline travel (Wilson 2006).

Examples of contagious diseases spread by world travelers include SARS, bird flu, tuberculosis, H1N1, and HIV/AIDS. In 2008, the HIV/AIDS pandemic took the lives of 1.5 million people in sub-Saharan Africa alone, and an additional 1.9 million people in the region became newly infected with HIV (Avert 2009; UNAIDS-Joint United Nations Programme on HIV/AIDS 2009). Sixty-seven percent of the 33 million people living with HIV today are in sub-Saharan Africa. Two million people in the world died of AIDS in 2008, and there are an estimated 14 million AIDS orphans in Africa. Women have 50% of the cases (UNAIDS 2009). In just one country—South Africa—the HIV-infected population grew to 18.8% of the total population, with 5.5 million people infected and 320,000 dead in 2008 (Avert 2009). Local traditions contribute to the spread of AIDS. In sub-Saharan Africa, where AIDS is rampant and only children and elderly people remain in some villages, men travel to urban areas for work and contract AIDS from prostitutes. When they return, they infect their wives. A major problem is the lack of resources for contraception and medications.

When the South African government passed a law that would make life-saving HIV/AID medicines available to the millions of people suffering from the disease in that country, pharmaceutical giants from the Global North united and used their clout to crush the law. Only intense negative publicity caused them to relent. Many places in the world have diseases that are not being controlled due to lack of resources to buy needed medications (Booker and Minter 2006). Some funding comes from international organizations and foundations such as the Bill and Melinda Gates Foundation, which in 2006 funded a new initiative to help combat AIDS and malaria in poor countries. To rephrase the statement of Martin Luther King Jr. about injustice, disease anywhere is disease everywhere.

The issue of global health is not limited to diseases and their treatment. Use of tobacco is a major issue, with perhaps a trillion "sticks"—mostly American made—being sold to and smuggled into countries around the world. Mark Schapiro (2006) documents the active involvement of a number of American tobacco companies in illegal smuggling activity, and the top U.S. tobacco companies now earn more from cigarette sales abroad than at home. These companies have a vested interest in the globalization of their product, which is made difficult if countries bar or severely limit the importation of tobacco products. The World Health Organization considers smuggling tobacco products a major world health issue, and the nations involved also see it as a major health issue. Governments have mixed reactions: They gain tremendous revenue from taxes and tariffs on

that the germs will find hosts that are not already immune (Wilson 2006). Our globe has increasing numbers of cities that exceed 1 million people.

Other factors that help the spread of disease are the growing numbers of settings with shared circulated air (airplanes, domed stadiums, air-conditioned office buildings and hotels), especially because most diseases travel by direct contact with other infected people. A World Health Organization study indicates that of the infections leading to death, 65% are due to person-to-person contact. Another 22% come from food, water, or soil contamination; 13% are transmitted by insects; and just 0.3% are acquired directly from animals (bird flu, rabies, etc.; Wilson 2006). Because

Many people around the world engage in tobacco use, a serious health hazard that brings many risks. This is also a concern to the society as a whole because it means lowered productivity and increased health care costs for all.

tobacco products, but health care costs also increase due to diseases. Criminal justice systems have little leverage over companies that operate abroad, so it is rare that action to curb illegal sales of tobacco products abroad is ever taken (Schapiro 2006).

Indigenous Medicine: Traditional and Modern Medical Practices

In India, an ancient Hindu approach to medical care focuses on the link between mind and body. It suggests that health can be achieved if there is an adequate balance between the two and that balance can be brought about through meditation and medication, a combination of Western medicines and appropriate relaxation and exercise. Such beliefs are consistent with the overall pattern of Indian culture and religion.

In a rural Mexican–Native American village in Arizona, a gravely ill young boy named Yas is being treated by the shaman of the village for a rattlesnake bite. Prayers are chanted by all present as the shaman pours a mixture of herbs and other ingredients over Yas's head. After this procedure, Yas is taken to a local health care clinic for additional Western-style treatment.

An elderly Nicaraguan woman, Lucia, comes to a rural clinic with the complaint of "sadness in my body and fear in my chest." Was this a heart problem? Arthritis? Some other sickness? Knowing the cultural context of the woman's description, the doctor determines her problem. After checking her physical condition, he finds that her complaint is not symptomatic of a heart attack, but rather of missing her children, who have all left to work in foreign countries. For a modest fee based on her income, and with limited access to psychological care, she had found what help she could.

In an African village in Ghana, the local shaman, Kofa, grows his own herbal garden, which produces many of the medicinal plants that he uses for treatment, using recipes passed down through the generations. There are herbal mixtures for infection, impotence, infertility, asthma, stomach ailments, and numerous other problems. Using combinations of traditional and Western treatments, he gains legitimacy. He points out that the herbal medicines he uses are very effective and, in fact, form the basic substances of many Western medicines. Down the road from this shaman, patients can seek treatment from Amma, the priestess, in exchange for a small contribution. The closest role in Western medicine to Amma's services would be a psychologist or psychiatrist. Her visitors include the lovesick, the lonely, the hypochondriacs, and the bereaved. She sings, chants, prescribes potions (mixtures of herbs, often sedatives), and gives advice.

People around the world rely on a variety of medical models and practitioners to meet their needs. As migrations occur, practices spread. Western medicine has borrowed from folk medicine traditions; tested many of the traditional herbal remedies; incorporated acupuncture, pressure point, and massage therapies; and used other procedures adopted from traditional medicine. *Allopathy* (medicine based on remedies that simply reverse one's symptoms) retains dominance over alternative medical practices—homeopathy, chiropractic, acupuncture, and other types of medical practices that Global North medical practitioners sometimes label as quackery. Yet folk medicines in many societies, often combined with Global North medicine, effectively treat people's illnesses in their social contexts. Medicine itself has become globally informed, delivered with awareness of local social settings.

One result of the spread of medical ideas around the world is the "Complementary and Alternative Medicines" movement (CAM) in the United States and other Global North countries. CAM includes health care systems, practices, and products that are used to complement conventional medicine or as alternative medicine used in place of conventional medicine. CAM therapies include

Depicted here is the process of creating traditional medicines, from start to finish, in Ethiopia. First, the plants are cultivated or picked from wild herbs. Then the medicine is extracted from the plants. This is sold in the equivalent by pharmacies or prescribed by traditional healers.

acupuncture and chiropractic, natural products, special diets, and megavitamin therapy. Of interest to sociologists is the spread of practices, along with who accepts alternative practices and who resists them.

In a major survey of U.S. health practices, 38% (4 in 10) of adults and 12% of children said they use some form of CAM for health reasons. The profile of CAM users looks like this: more women than men, those with higher education, those who have been hospitalized, and former smokers. About 12% of the study population sought care from a CAM practitioner such as an acupuncturist or chiropractor (Barnes, Bloom, and Nahin 2008; National Institutes of Health 2007).

Pressures for change in the health care system come from consumers, health care financing, and competition

Encyclopedia Link 14.1
Read more about indigenous medicine.

to keep medical practices profitable. As the population ages and people live longer, as patients look for alternative ways to deal with chronic illness, and as alternative health providers set up shop, more doctors are adding aspects of holistic medicine and CAM to meet consumer demands (Winnick 2006). The medical establishment has incorporated some of these practices, especially if scientific study finds them effective, but others lie outside accepted Western medicine at this time. The most prevalent CAM practices that have been imported to Western countries from traditional medical practices are acupuncture, ayurveda, biofeedback, chelation therapy, chiropractic care, deep breathing exercises, diet-based therapies, energy healing therapy, folk medicine, guided imagery, homeopathic treatment, hypnosis, massage, meditation, megavitamin therapy, natural products, neuropathy, prayer for health reasons, progressive relaxation, Qi gong, Reiki, Tai chi, and Yoga. Figure 14.2 shows the percentages using the 10 most common CAM practices.

Because of the uneven distribution of health care, doctors, and medicines around the world, many preventable and curable diseases go untreated. When the average life expectancy in countries is in the 30s, we know that medical help is not available for common medical problems. For example, dehydration from diarrhea caused by water-borne diseases such as cholera, blindness caused by vitamin A deficiency, malaria

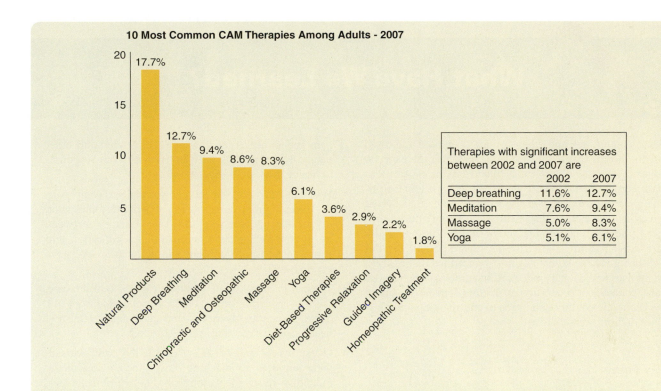

Figure 14.2   The 10 Most Common CAM Therapies Among Adults, 2007

Source: National Institute of Health (2008).

cause by infected mosquitoes, and other preventable diseases are unnecessary afflictions in today's world. Yet many nations in the Global South have few physicians per capita. For instance, in Malawi, there is one doctor for every 100,000 people, in Ethiopia and Niger, three doctors for every 100,000 citizens, and in Mali, four doctors per 100,000 citizens. The few doctors in these countries are located mostly in urban areas (United Nations Development Programme 2005a). Folk remedies are the only health care most of these citizens have.

As long as there is inequality in our social world, adequate health care is unlikely to reach all people and all countries (Garrett 2000). In spite of increasingly sophisticated medical technology and medicines, availability, cost, distribution, and policies of governments are the determinants of who receives health care around the world.

Thinking Sociologically

We live in a global world, yet our most immediate experiences are local. What are benefits you and your family might receive if international agencies resolve health problems in Africa, Asia, and South America?

Our social institutions—from family, education, and religion to politics, economics, and health—maintain stability in societies. However, the world in which we live is a dynamic one. In the final two chapters, we turn to an examination of how change occurs. First, we examine two forces that have changed exponentially in the past two centuries—population patterns and urbanization. We close with an examination of social change in its many manifestations.

What Have We Learned?

When you are sick and when you are diagnosed and cared for, the norms that allow you to be sick and the expectations of you in the sick role may differ from the expectations placed on others around the world. Although health is a private, personal concern, it is also a public concern, delivered through organizations dispensing health care and government practices determining access and funding of health care. Distant from your daily life but important to your well-being are the global health organizations that concern themselves with global epidemics. In addition, whether you have insurance or money to pay doctors depends in part on the economic conditions in society and the global marketplace of health care delivery.

Key Points

- Sociology looks at the anatomy of medicine by examining the social implications of health and illness—from the micro level of individual coping with illness to the meso level of institutional interactions and complex organizations that manage health and illness, to the global issues of controlling spread of diseases around the world. (See pp. 473–475.)

- Whether looking at the medicalization of social problems through labeling or examining functions and socioeconomic conflicts regarding health care in society, various social theories offer alternative lenses for our sociological anatomy of medicine. (See pp. 476–481.)

- At the micro level, we can look at issues of the "sick role," how social and cultural factors affect our responses to pain and ill health, or how our age, gender, and other personal aspects of identity are related to our responses to health and illness. (See pp. 482–487.)

- Hospitals and other elements of organizational complexity, the issues of professionalism and of deprofessionalization of medical personnel, and the linkages between institutions such as the economy, politics, education, and family are all aspects of health care at the meso level. (See pp. 487–492.)

- The national level is often linked to access to health care, the cost as a proportion of the nation's resources, the issues of security of citizens, and questions of reform of health-care delivery. (See pp. 492–496.)

- Questions of policy are also highly controversial, with countries approaching the responsibilities of the individual versus the nation with different philosophies. This has been a particularly contentious issue in the United States. (See pp. 497–499.)

- Globally, we find not only that diseases spread around the planet much faster in our age of rapid travel and migrations but also that curing philosophies and techniques from around the globe are influencing the approaches we each choose in our own local communities. (See pp. 501–505.)

- In summary, the study of anatomy is at the core of preparation for a career in medicine, but sociologists would argue that understanding the anatomy of the social processes that affect health, illness, and the delivery of health care are necessary for a full comprehension of medicine in the modern world. (See pp. 505–507.)

Contributing to Our Social World: What Can We Do?

At the Local Level

Obesity in America (www.obesityinamerica.org): This organization provides information on a wide range of resources, many of which are directly applicable to problems faced by students.

At the Organizational or Institutional Level

Free or low-cost clinics: Most communities provide health screening and other services to uninsured individuals and families. The U.S. Department of Health and Human Services has a locator Web site at http://findahealthcenter.hrsa.gov/Search_HCC.aspx that searches for free clinics by state and city. United Way and larger hospitals have the names and contact persons of these clinics in your community. Most have volunteer and internship opportunities that afford interesting and valuable experiences, especially if you are considering a career in the health care field.

At the National and Global Levels

The Joint United Nations Program on HIV/AIDS (www.unaids.org/en): This organization is seeking volunteer and professional help to conduct research, participate in educational outreach, and raise funds to fight this epidemic.

World Vision (www.worldvision.org): Six thousand children are orphaned daily by HIV/AIDS throughout the world, and especially in the poorer countries in Africa and Asia. The organization's Hope Child program lists several suggestions for getting involved, including sponsorship of a child. AVERT, an international AIDS charity (www.avert.org/worldaid.htm), has designated December 1 as International AIDS Awareness Day. Visit the site for suggestions on getting involved, including organizing AIDS Awareness Day activities on your campus or in your community.

For chapter-specific resources, including **Frontline**, **TED**, and **YouTube** videos; self-quizzes; web exercises; and more, visit **www.pineforge.com/oswmedia3e.**

PART V

Social Dynamics

Social structures such as institutions—family, education, religion, health, politics, and economics—tend to resist change. Yet this entire book shows that societies are dynamic and changing. Institutions and organizations come alive with processes that are fluid and vibrant. Globalization itself, a major theme in this book, is a process bringing transformation to our social world. We do not live in the same sort of world our grandparents inhabited. The macro- and meso-level dimensions of the world have become increasingly powerful, which is exactly why we need a sociological imagination to understand how the events in our own micro worlds are influenced by the larger society.

This section looks at some of those processes that are dynamic, fluid, and vibrant—population changes, urbanization, expansion of technology, social movements, and more. We live in exciting and challenging times, and we will thrive best if we understand the micro-, meso-, and macro-level dimensions of change in our lives and the linkages between parts of our social world. We turn next to population dynamics and urbanization.

CHAPTER 15

Population and Urbanization

Living on Spaceship Earth

The human population is limited to this one moderate-sized sphere, on which it depends for survival. The question is whether human groups can cooperate with each other and use the resources of the planet responsibly. The challenges of controlling migration patterns and the spread of disease add to the need for global cooperation. In the meantime, humans are concentrated in dense urban areas. As the night shot in the background of this page illustrates, bright lights beam from urban centers in Europe but from fewer places in Africa, illustrating the differences in both population density and level of development.

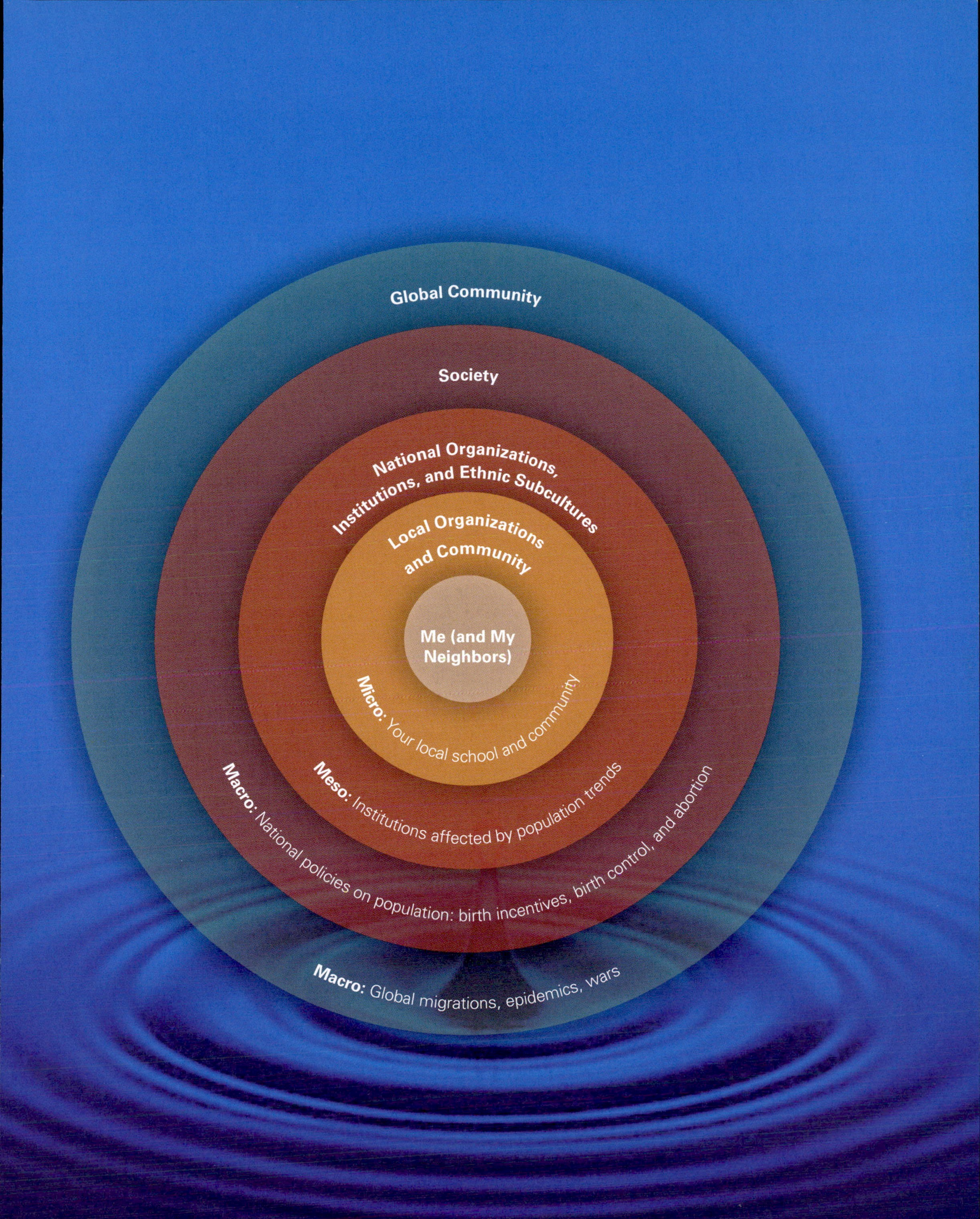

Global Community

Society

National Organizations, Institutions, and Ethnic Subcultures

Local Organizations and Community

Me (and My Neighbors)

Micro: Your local school and community

Meso: Institutions affected by population trends

Macro: National policies on population: birth incentives, birth control, and abortion

Macro: Global migrations, epidemics, wars

Think About It	
Me (and My Inner Circle)	Why is your family the size it is?
Local Community	What characterizes the population composition of your hometown? How do you feel living there?
National Institutions; Complex Organizations; Ethnic Groups	Why do people move from rural areas to urban areas? What problems does urbanization create?
National Society	How might immigration affect the make-up of a nation, and what effect could this have on a nation's policies?
Global Community	How do global issues relating to urbanization, the environment, and technology affect your family and your local community?

What if you were from outer space looking down at a spherical object drifting through space? It appears to be a beautiful mix of greens and blues, and at night, parts of the sphere glow with lights while other parts are dark. That is home to earthlings—our little (relatively speaking) planet. The controlling inhabitants of the planet are humans, all 6.8 billion of them (Population Reference Bureau 2009b), increasing by 211,090 people daily (World Factbook 2008). The topic of this chapter is the life, death, spread, and distribution of those humans living on spaceship Earth (Diamond 1999, 2005).

Since the emergence of *Homo sapiens* in East Africa, human populations have grown in uneven surges and declines due to births, deaths, and migrations. The world Population Clock (see Table 15.1) illustrates the current state of the human population.

The world's human population has grown sporadically over the millennia, so the explosion of human beings on the planet in the past two and a half centuries is stunning. If we collapsed all human history into one 24-hour day, the time period since 1750 would consume 1 minute. Yet 25% of all humans have lived during this 1-minute time period. In the 200 years between 1750 and 1950, the world's population mushroomed from 800 million to 2.5 billion. On October 12, 1999, the global population reached 6 billion. It has now expanded to more than 6.8 billion, growing by 83 million alone in 2008. Estimates put the world population at 7 billion by mid-2011 with most growth in the poorest countries (Population Reference Bureau 2009a). This means that the world is growing each year by the number of people in the country of Germany, Philippines, or Vietnam. Every minute in 2006, for example, 249 children were born and 108 people died around the world, resulting in a net increase of 141 people per minute (U.S. Census Bureau 2006c). Between 2000 and 2050, virtually all the world's growth will occur in Africa, Asia, and Latin America, where 81% of the world's population lives and 90% of each year's births occur (Population Reference Bureau 2008).

Table 15.1 Population Clock, 2009

	World	Global North (More Developed)	Global South (Without China) (Less Developed)
Population (millions)	6,810	1,232	4,246
Births per 1,000 Pop.	20	12	26
Deaths per 1,000 Pop.	8	10	8
Rate of natural increase	1.2%	0.2%	1.7%
Infant mortality rate	46	6	55
Total fertility rate	2.6	1.7	3.1
Percentage of population <15	27	17	33
Percentage of population 65+	8	16	5
Life expectancy at birth	69	77	65
Life expectancy— males	67	74	63
Life expectancy— females	71	81	67

Source: Population Reference Bureau (2009b).

Let us start by focusing on one area of our world, Kenya in East Africa. We focus here partly because East Africa, where Kenya and Tanzania are located, was home to spaceship Earth's earliest human inhabitants. Scientists believe that bones found in the dry Olduvai Gorge area are the oldest remains of *Homo sapiens* ever found. We also focus here because today Kenya is making human history for another reason. With a population of more than 39 million people, a birth rate of 36.6 per 1,000, a death rate of 9.7 per 1,000, resulting in a natural increase of 2.78% annually (World Factbook 2009a), Kenya has one of the most rapidly growing populations on Earth. Kenya is made up of many tribal groups of people. With different religions and value systems, they have clashed in power struggles in recent years. Still, there are several themes that pervade most Kenyan subcultures, as illustrated by the following example.

Wengari, like Kenyan girls of most tribal affiliations, married in her teens. She has been socialized to believe that her main purpose in life is to bear children, to help with the farming, and to care for parents in their old age. Children are seen as an asset in Kenya. Religious beliefs and cultural value systems encourage large families. However, the population of Kenya is 45% dependent: people under 15 or over 65, who rely on working-age citizens to support them (World Factbook 2009a).The working-age population is becoming scarce and cannot continue to feed the growing population. Add to that severe droughts in parts of the country—droughts that are killing animal herds and preventing growth of crops. These facts, however, have little meaning to young women like Wengari, who have been socialized to conform to the female role within their society.

In contrast, to the north in many of the industrialized, urbanized countries of Europe, birth rates are below population replacement levels, meaning population size eventually will begin to drop. In Germany, natural growth rate is 0%, in France 0.4%, and in the United Kingdom 0.2%. Hungary, Latvia, and the Czech Republic are losing population (Rosenberg 2009).

While Asia's share of world population may continue to hover around 55% through the next century, Europe's portion has declined sharply and is likely to drop even more during the 21st century. Africa and Latin America each will gain part of Europe's portion. By 2100, Africa is expected to capture the greatest share. Countries growing by less than 1% annually include Japan, Australia, New Zealand, Russia, and much of Europe (Population Reference Bureau 2006).

In industrialized societies, children in the middle class and above are dependent until they leave home. Typical European young people often wait until their late 20s or even 30s to start a family, postponing children until their education is complete and a job is in hand. Many limit their family size because societal values support small families. It is difficult to house large families in small urban apartments where the majority of the population live. Workers must support and feed their families on earned wages rather than through farming. Both mother and father often work, and unlike many children in the Global South, most children born in Europe will survive to old age. Life expectancy, the average

Changes in the environment and in the global economy make it difficult for this Kenyan family to provide for itself. Some of these children and their cousins may find it necessary to move to urban centers, a worldwide migration trend. Much of the socialization they received in villages will not be relevant to their adult urban lives.

age at death, is 51.8 years in Kenya (World Factbook 2009a). In some European countries, it is older than 81 years.

On yet another continent, China, the country with the largest population in the world (1.31 billion people), had the greatest drop in population growth in the late 20th century due to strict governmental family planning practices (*Time Almanac* 2008). India, the second-largest country, has a population growth rate (increase in a country's population during a specified period of time) of 1.58% a year, just over replacement level (World Factbook 2008).

Although some countries have birth rates below population replacement levels, the world's population continues to grow because of the skyrocketing growth rate in other countries and because of *population momentum* caused by the large number of individuals of childbearing age having children. Even though birth rates per couple drop, the number of women of childbearing age is still very high, resulting in continued growth in population size. Unfortunately, most of the countries with the highest growth rates are in the Global South, where there are fewer resources to support the additional population.

What we have been discussing is the study of human populations, called **demography**. All permanent societies, states, communities, adherents of a common religious faith, racial or ethnic groups, kinship or clan groups, professions, and other identifiable categories of people can be referred to as **populations**. The size, geographical location, and spatial movement of the population, its concentration in certain geographical areas, including urban areas, and changing characteristics of the population are important elements in

Hanoi, Vietnam, is a crowded Asian city. The overcrowding in some cities means that governments have a difficult time providing the infrastructure and services needed for the growing urban population.

the study of demography. With growing populations and limited farmland to support the population, hungry people move to cities in hopes of finding jobs. This pattern of movement is called **urbanization**. The second half of this chapter will consider the evolution, growth, and development of populated areas, including movements from rural areas to cities, the organization of micro-level urban life, the relationship between individuals and the city, and some problems facing cities.

The previous chapters have been organized by moving from micro- to macro-level analysis. Because demographic work has focused on societies and global trends, we will reverse the order in the first section and discuss macro-level patterns in world population growth first, followed by meso-level institutional influences on population, and micro-level population patterns.

Encyclopedia Link 15.1
Read more about population.

Thinking Sociologically

Do you have choice in how many children you have? What factors go into your decision? How might your decision differ if you were in a different country? Should global patterns—which include food shortages and climate change—be a consideration in the size of your family and those of your neighbors? Why or why not?

MACRO-LEVEL PATTERNS IN WORLD POPULATION GROWTH

Early humans roamed the plains of Africa for thousands of years, their survival and growth depending on the environment in which they lived. They mastered fire and tools, then domesticated animals and invented agriculture, and with these skills slowly increased control over the environment, allowing their numbers to expand. This evolution in the growth patterns of human populations is worth closer examination.

Patterns of Population Growth Over Time

Members of the small band of early *Homo sapiens* who inhabited the Olduvai Gorge moved gradually, haltingly, from this habitat into what are now other parts of Africa, Asia, and Europe. The process took thousands of years. At times, births outnumbered deaths and populations grew, but at other times, plagues, famines, droughts, and wars decimated populations. From the beginning of human existence, estimated from perhaps one million years ago until modern times, the number of births and deaths balanced each other over the centuries (Diamond 2005). The large population we see today results from population evolution that consisted of three phases:

1. Humans, because of their thinking ability, competed satisfactorily in the animal kingdom to obtain the basic necessities for survival of the species.

2. With the agricultural revolution that occurred about 10,000 years ago and the resulting food surplus, mortality rates declined, and the population grew as more infants survived and people lived longer.

3. The biggest increase came with the Industrial Revolution, beginning about 300 years ago. Improved medical knowledge and sanitation helped bring the death rate down.

When industrialization made its debut, it not only brought the social and economic changes discussed in Chapter 3 (e.g., machines replacing human labor and mass production using resources in new ways), but it also augmented urbanization of societies. The population explosion began with industrialization in Europe and spread to widely scattered areas of the globe. With trade and migrations came the diffusion of ideas and better medical care, influencing population growth rates in all parts of the world by keeping people alive longer. Figures 15.1 and 15.2 show population growth throughout history. The worldwide *rate* of population growth reached its peak in the 1960s and has

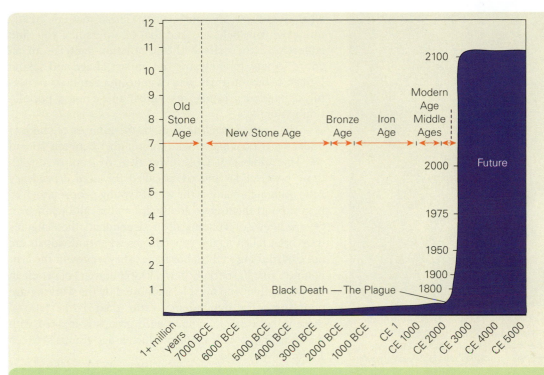

Figure 15.1   The Exponential World Population Growth From About 8000 BCE to 21st Century

Source: Abu-Lughod (2001:50).

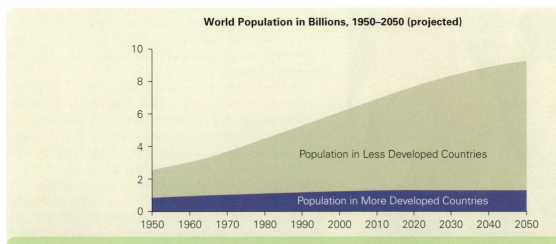

World Population in Billions, 1950–2050 (projected)

Population in Less Developed Countries

Population in More Developed Countries

Figure 15.2   World Population Growth Rate, 1950–2050

Source: Population Reference Bureau (2009a).

decreased to a current rate of about 1.14% per year, resulting in the world population doubling every 61 years (World Factbook 2009c).

Predictors of Population Growth

In some villages in sub-Saharan and East African countries, children are forced to fend for themselves. With large percentages of the working-age population dead (or dying) from AIDS, orphaned children take care of their younger siblings. In some villages in Uganda, for instance, social workers visit periodically to bring limited food for survival and see that children are planting crops. These children must learn survival skills and gender roles at a very young age. They have little chance to experience a childhood typical in other places (Avert 2009).

AIDS has a horrific impact on individuals at the micro level, on families at the meso level, and on entire societies at the macro level. Joseph Mwila comforts his younger brother Aaron in Chilonga in Zambia, with their sister Joanna behind. This is what remains of the family after both parents died of AIDS.

A Palestinian boy carrying the Palestinian flag demonstrates against evictions. With half of the Palestinian population under age 15, younger Palestinians are taking active roles in politics, and many are responsible for helping to support their families.

Think for a moment about the impact that your age and sex have on your position in society and your activities. Are you of childbearing age? Are you dependent on others for most of your needs or are you supporting others? Your status is largely due to your age and sex, and

what they mean in your society. These matters greatly influence your behavior and that of others like you, and collectively, they shape the population patterns of an entire society. In analyzing the impact of age and sex on human behavior, three sets of concepts can be very useful: dependency ratios, sex ratios, and age-sex population pyramids.

The *youth dependency ratio* is the number of children under age 15 compared with the number between 15 and 64. The number of those older than 64 compared with those between 15 and 64 is called the *aged dependency ratio*. Although many of the world's young people under 15 help support themselves and their families, and many over 64 are likewise economically independent, these figures have been taken as the general ages when individuals are not contributing to the labor force. They represent the economic burden (especially in wealthy countries) of people in the population who must be supported by the working-age population. The **dependency ratio**, then, is the ratio of those in both the young and aged groups compared with the number of people in the productive age groups between 15 and 64 years old.

In several resource-poor countries about 9 out of every 20 people are under 15 years of age. These include Benin (43.6%), Rwanda (41.9%), Gaza (Palestine; 47.1%), Liberia (44%), and Ethiopia (43.1%; World Factbook 2008). Working adults in less-privileged countries have a tremendous burden to support the dependent population, especially if a high percentage of the population is urban and not able to be self-supporting through farming.

Similarly, high percentages of older dependent people over 64 are found in most Global North countries. In the European countries of Norway, Sweden, Denmark, the United Kingdom, and Germany, between 15% and 20% of the population is in the age group 65 and older. These countries have low death rates, resulting in the average life expectancy at birth being as high as 81 years (World Factbook 2008).

The percentage of dependent elderly people is growing, especially in affluent countries. Consider the case of Japan, which faces the problem of its "graying" or aging population. In 2009, more than 22% of its population was 65 or older, and the average life expectancy was over 82 years. The Japanese population is graying nearly twice as fast as the population in many other nations, in large part because the birth rate is very low, only 7.6 births per 1,000 in the population; with a death rate of 9.5 per 1,000, there is a negative growth rate of almost −0.2% per year (World Factbook 2009b). There simply are not enough replacement workers to support the aging population. Japan provides a glimpse into the future for other rapidly aging societies, including Germany, the United States, and China (Moffett 2003; see Figure 15.3).

The **sex ratio** refers to the ratio of males to females in the population. For instance, the more females, especially

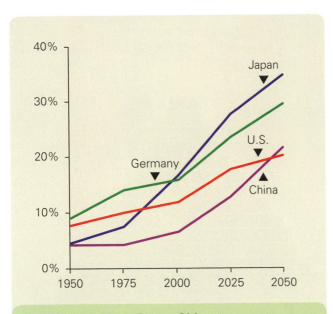

Figure 15.3   Japan Grows Old

Source: Moffett (2003).

Note: Japan's percentage of population over 65 is growing faster than in any other nation.

Japan is an aging society, with life expectancy exceeding 81 and more than 20% of the population over age 65. Ninety-two-year-old Toshi Uechi practices a traditional Japanese dance in Okinawa. An active lifestyle and Spartan diet have helped make Okinawa the home of an exceptionally high percentage of centenarians (those over 100 years)—39.5 per 100,000 residents.

females in the fertile years, the more potential there is for population growth. The sex ratio also determines the supply of eligible spouses. Marriage patterns are affected by economic cycles, wars in which the proportion of males to females may decrease, and migrations that generally take males from one area and add them to another. **Population pyramids** illustrate sex ratios and dependency ratios (see Figure 15.4 on page 520).

The graphic presentation of the age and sex distribution of a population tells us a great deal about that population. The structures are called pyramids because that is the shape they took until several decades ago. By looking up and down the pyramid, we can see the proportion of population at each age level. Looking to the right and left of the centerline tells us the balance of males to females at each age. The bottom line shows us the total population at each age.

The first pyramid shows populations that have fairly low birth and death rates, typical of Global North countries. The second pyramid illustrates populations with high birth rates and large dependent youth populations, typical of Global South countries. The world population has been getting both younger (the Global South) *and* older (the Global North), resulting in large numbers of people dependent on working-age population between 15 and 65 years of age.

As Global South nations have more and more children, they are creating more potential parents in later years, adding momentum to the world's population growth. Today young children survive their early years, whereas in the past they might have died of disease and malnutrition. Fewer deaths

of infants and children, which can be credited to immunizations and disease control, result in lower mortality rates, younger populations, and higher potential numbers of births in the future.

Video Link 15.1
Watch how China is dealing with an aging population.

Thinking Sociologically

Consider your own country's population pyramid. You can find it at http://www.census.gov/ipc/prod/wp02/wp-02004.pdf. What can you tell about your country's level of development by studying the population pyramid? How might societies differ if they have a young versus old population?

Population Patterns: Theoretical Explanations

We find evidence of interest in population size and growth from the earliest historical writings. Scriptures such as the

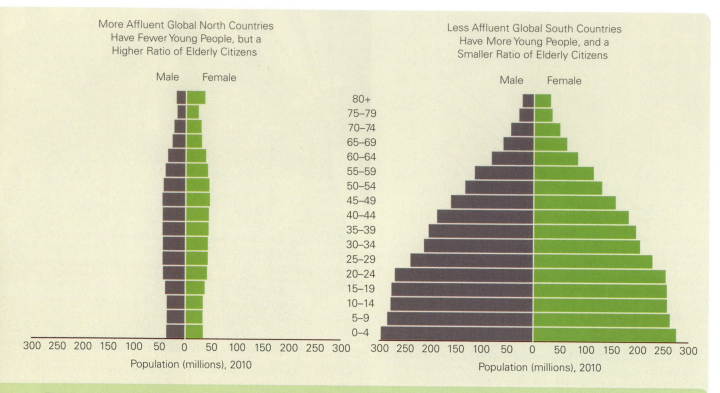

More Affluent Global North Countries Have Fewer Young People, but a Higher Ratio of Elderly Citizens

Less Affluent Global South Countries Have More Young People, and a Smaller Ratio of Elderly Citizens

Figure 15.4   Population Pyramids, by Level of Affluence, 2009

Source: Bremner et al. (2009). Reprinted with permission.

Quran and the Bible have supported population growth to increase the ranks of the faithful. Of course, population expansion made sense at the time these holy tracts were written. Government leaders throughout the ages have adopted various philosophies about the best size of populations. The ancient Greek philosopher Plato (350 BCE/1960) argued that the city-state should have 5,040 citizens and that measures should be taken to increase or decrease the population to bring it in line with this figure. However, the first significant scholarly analysis that addressed global population issues came from Thomas Malthus (1766–1834), an English clergyman and social philosopher.

Malthus's Theory of Population

In his "Essay on the Principle of Population," Malthus ([1798] 1926) argued that humans are driven to reproduce and will multiply without limits if no checks are imposed. An unchecked population increases geometrically: 2 parents could have 4 children, 16 grandchildren, 64 great-grandchildren, and so forth—and that is simply with a continuous average family size of 4 children. Because the means of subsistence (food) increases at best only arithmetically or lineally (5, 10, 15, 20, 25), the end result is a food shortage and possible famine.

Malthus recognized several positive checks on populations, factors that would keep populations from excessive growth, including wars, diseases and epidemics, and food shortages leading to famine (a drastic, wide-reaching

Malthus predicted that if left unchecked, population increases would result in massive famine and disease. This is exactly what has happened in Ethiopia, as this gathering of famished people at a relief camp shows.

shortage of food). Malthus held strong political views based in part on his population theory. He suggested preventive checks on rapid population growth, primarily in the form of delayed marriage and practice of sexual abstinence until one could afford a family. Contraception technology was crude and often unrealistic in his day, and therefore, he did not present it as an option for population control.

Looking at the world today, we see examples of these population checks. War decimated the populations of several countries during the World Wars and has taken its toll on other countries in Eastern Europe, Africa, and the Middle East since then. The AIDS virus, SARS, Ebola, and bird flu have raised fears of new plagues (epidemics of often fatal diseases). Waterborne diseases such as cholera and typhus strike after floods, and the floods themselves are often caused by environmental destruction resulting from too many humans in a geographic area. Recent famines in Ethiopia, Zimbabwe, and countries in the horn of Africa resulted in massive global relief efforts by organizations such as the United Nations, but too little and too late to save thousands who died of starvation. More than 20 million people, many of them children, are experiencing famines in East Africa ("Millions Vulnerable to Famine in Africa" 2006) and part of Sudan and Niger in West Africa. Famines are caused in part by erosion and stripping the Earth of natural protections such as forests and grasslands by people in need of more land to grow food and graze animals and of more firewood to cook. Today, economic factors are also affecting populations as imported cheap food is driving local farmers out of business in some areas.

Four main criticisms have been raised about Malthus's theory. First, Malthus did not anticipate the role capitalism would play in population dynamics, exploiting raw materials and laborers and encouraging excessive consumption patterns in wealthy industrial nations. In fact, having large families made sense to many, who believed having more children provided more workers and more economic security (Robbins 2005). Second, Malthus's idea that food production would grow arithmetically and could not keep up with population growth must be modified in light of current agricultural techniques, at least in some parts of the world. Third, Malthus saw abstinence from sex, even among the married, as the main method of preventing births and did not recognize the potential for contraception. Fourth, poverty has not always proven to be an inevitable result of population growth.

Two neo-Malthusians, scientists who accept much of his theory but make modifications based on current realities, are Garrett Hardin and Paul Ehrlich. Hardin (1968), a biologist, argues that individuals' personal goals are not always consistent with societal goals and needs related to population growth. An individual may decide to have many children, but this could be detrimental to the whole society. If people act solely on their own and have many children, societal tragedy may well ensue.

Scarcity of freshwater and other resources threatens survival, as in these two water sources in Ethiopia. In the 19th century, Thomas Malthus predicted such shortages due to population increases.

Ehrlich and Ehrlich (1990) add to the formula of "too many people and too little food" the problem of a "dying planet" caused by environmental damage. To hold on to economic gains, population must be checked, and to check population, family planning is necessary, they assert. Ehrlichs' ideas can be summed up as follows:

America and other rich nations have a clear choice today. They can continue to ignore the population problem and their own massive contributions to it. Then they will be trapped in a downward spiral that may well lead to the end of civilization in a few decades. More frequent droughts, more damaged crops and famines, more dying forests, more smog, more international conflicts, more epidemics . . . will mark our course. (p. 23)

The neo-Malthusians favor contraception rather than simple reliance on the moral restraint that Malthus proposed. They also acknowledge that much of the environmental damage is caused by corporate pollution and excessive consumption habits in affluent areas such as the United States, Canada, and Europe (Weeks 2005).

Thinking Sociologically

What are contemporary examples of Malthus's checks on population growth—war, disease, famine? Are family planning and contraception sufficient to solve the problem of global overpopulation by humans? Can you think of other alternatives?

Demographic Transition: Explaining Population Growth and Expansion

Why should a change in the economic structure such as industrialization and movement from rural agricultural areas to urban cities have an impact on population size? One explanation is found in the **demographic transition theory**.

The idea of demographic transition involves comparing countries' stages of economic development with trends in birth and death rates. Three stages of development are identified in this theory:

Stage 1: These populations have high birth and death rates that tend to balance each other over time. Births may outpace deaths until some disaster diminishes the increase. This has been the pattern for most of human history.

Stage 2: Populations still have high birth rates, but death rates decline (i.e., more people live longer) because of improvements in health care and sanitation, establishment of public health programs, disease control and immunizations, and food availability and distribution. This imbalance between continuing high births and declining deaths means that the population growth rate is very high.

Stage 3: Populations level off at the bottom of the chart with low birth rates and low death rates. Most industrial and postindustrial societies are in this stage. Population growth rates in these countries are very low because nuclear families are small.

These stages are illustrated in Figure 15.5.

Demographic transition theory helps explain the developmental stage and population trends in countries

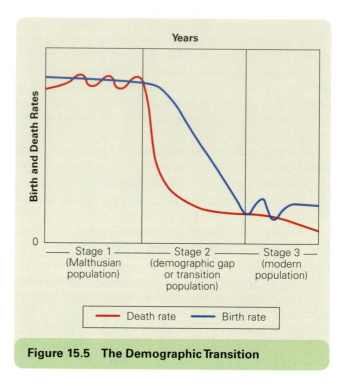

Figure 15.5   The Demographic Transition

around the world, but it does not consider some important factors that affect the size of populations: (1) people's age at marriage determines how many childbearing years they have (late marriage means fewer years until menopause); (2) contraceptive availability determines whether families can control their number of children; (3) a country's resources and land may determine how much population a country can support; (4) the economic structure of a country, religious beliefs, and political philosophies affect attitudes toward birth control and family size; and (5) economic expansion rates influence a country's need for labor.

Not all societies go through the same time frame in transition from one stage to another. For example, demographic transition occurred rapidly in Europe, where notions of modernization, urbanization, and progress evolved naturally from the cultural values. People generally married later, and the value of having children varied with resources available. In addition, many deadly diseases that at one time kept population growth in check were under control.

Critics argue that there is a built-in assumption that modernization in the second and third stages will result in rational choices about family size. Yet unless women gain status by having smaller families, they are likely to continue to have large families (Robbins 2005). However, economic development generally results in a decline in the birth rate. The process of modernization that parallels economic development puts pressure on extended families to break apart into smaller nuclear family units, especially as families move to crowded urban areas. Urban families tend to have fewer children because children are a liability and cannot help support the family. Economic development, modernization, and urbanization did not occur together in all parts of the world, so the outcome of the three-stage transition has not always occurred as predicted in the theory.

The *wealth flow theory* suggests that two strategies are operating in couples' personal decisions about their family size. When wealth flows from children to parents, that is, when children are an asset working on the family farm or laboring, parents have larger families. When wealth flows from parents to children, families are likely to have fewer children (Caldwell 1982). To raise a child born in 2008 to 18 years in the United States, for instance, cost an average of more than $221,190 (USDA 2009).

Conflict Theorists' Explanations of Population Growth

Karl Marx and Fredrick Engels did not agree with Malthus's idea that population growth outstrips food and resources because of people's fertility rates, resulting in poverty. They felt that social and structural factors built into the economic system were the cause of poverty. Capitalist structures resulted in wealth for the capitalists and created overpopulation and poverty for those not absorbed into the system. Workers were expendable, kept in competition for low wages, used when needed, and let go when unprofitable to capitalists. In short, for conflict theorists, inequitable distribution and control of resources are at the heart of the problem.

Socialist societies, Marx argued, could absorb the growth in population so the problem of overpopulation would not exist. In a classless society, all would be able to find jobs, and the system would expand to include everyone. Engels asserted that population growth in socialist societies could be controlled by the central government. This regulation is, in fact, what is happening in most present-day socialist countries through such methods as strict family planning and liberal abortion policies.

Environmental racism and justice has become a pressing issue in many neighborhoods, especially poor minority areas where housing has knowingly been built on contaminated land (United Church of Christ 2007). Toxic dumps and burns, hazardous waste sites, landfills on which people must live because of lack of space, dumping waste in indigenous "First Nations" lands and abandoned chemical plants and mines occur not only in poor countries and but also in poor areas of Global North countries. Regulations in the United States to prevent housing being built on contaminated land are controversial because they require testing and delay development. Conflict between haves and have-nots is clear in such an issue.

One award-winning study in Chicago focused on efforts to have a more eco-friendly or "green" city by doing more recycling. However, there were substantial problems of pollution, disease risk, and other costs to the neighborhoods where this recycling was done. It is sobering to realize that environmentally friendly policies have often been implemented at a cost to those who have fewest resources—people living in poverty and minorities (Pellow 2002).

Overpopulation presents a challenge to food and water resources, and large populations damage the environment and provide little ecological recovery time. Pollution of a stream in Yunnan, China (top). A billboard in Shanghai advertising China's "One Child Only" policy (bottom).

Policy Implications: Population Patterns and Economic Development

Does rapid population growth retard the economic development of a country? This question has been a subject of debate among demographers and policymakers in recent years. It is an important issue because the beliefs of decision makers affect the policies and solutions they advocate. For instance, if policymakers feel that population growth retards economic development, family planning efforts are more likely because economic prosperity is of more immediate concern to political office holders (Solow 2000).

This issue of population growth has caused heated debate at several World Population Conferences. Some socialist and Catholic countries argue that capitalistic economic exploitation and political control, not population growth, cause poverty in Global South countries. Multinational companies and foreign countries exploit poor countries' resources, sometimes with payoffs to government officials, leaving the citizens with no gains. In most nations, policymakers and demographers agree, high population growth contributes to poverty because countries cannot adjust quickly enough to provide the infrastructure (housing, health care, sanitation, education) for so many additional people (United Nations Population Division 2005). Better sex education, access

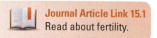

Journal Article Link 15.1
Read about fertility.

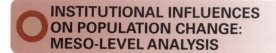

to contraceptives, and birth control advice help reduce population growth and spread of disease. Also important to limiting population growth is providing opportunities for citizens, especially women, to obtain education and jobs.

INSTITUTIONAL INFLUENCES ON POPULATION CHANGE: MESO-LEVEL ANALYSIS

Populations change in size (overall number of people), composition (the makeup of the population, including sex ratio, age distribution, and religious or ethnic representation in the population), and distribution (density or concentration in various portions of the land). The key demographic variables that cause changes are **fertility** (the birth rate), **mortality** (the death rate), and **migration** (movement of people from one place to another). Populations change when births and deaths are not evenly balanced or when significant numbers of people move from one area to another. Migration does not change the size or composition of the world as a whole, but can affect size or makeup in a local micro-level or national macro-level population. The most unpredictable yet controllable population factor in the world or in a nation is fertility.

Factors Affecting Fertility Rates

Jeanne, one of the coauthors, was riding in the back of a "mammy wagon," a common means of transport in Africa. Crowded in with the chickens and pigs and people, she did not expect the conversation that ensued. The man in his late 20s asked if she was married and for how long. Jeanne responded, "Yes, for three years." The man continued, "How many children do you have?" Jeanne answered, "None." The man commented, "Oh, I'm sorry!" Jeanne replied, "No, don't be sorry. We planned it that way!" This man had been married for 10 years to a woman 3 years younger than him and had eight children. The ninth was on the way. In answer to his pointed questions, Jeanne explained that she was not being cruel to her husband and that birth control was what prevented children, and no, it did not make sex less enjoyable. He expressed surprise that limiting the number of children was possible and rather liked the idea. He jumped at the suggestion that he visit the family planning clinic in the city. With his meager income, he and his wife were finding it hard to feed all the little mouths. The point is that knowledge of and access to family planning options are not always available.

Demographers consider micro-, meso-, and macro-level factors in attempting to understand fertility rates around the world. We know that individuals' personal decisions are key. People deciding to marry, couples' decisions

In an urban area in Cambodia (Kampuchia), residents crowd onto this truck, a common form of transportation. With a high fertility rate and migration from rural to urban areas, crowded transportation is common.

to use contraception, their ideas about the acceptability of abortion, and whether they choose to remain childless can have an impact on national and global rates of population change. So choices at the micro level do make a difference at the macro level.

Economic Factors

Overpopulation is complex, related to poverty, the status of women, and exploitation of resources and labor by wealthy individuals and countries. These are just some factors that contribute to overpopulation. Note the cyclical nature of the problem—overpopulation leads to poverty, which leads to overpopulation. The relationship between poverty and population reduction is very complex, which makes agreement about a solution difficult.

Fertility also fluctuates with what is happening in meso-level institutions such as economic, political, and family systems. During depressions, for example, the rate of fertility tends to drop. However, macro-level structural factors also affect fertility: (a) level of economic prosperity within the nation, (b) the government's commitment to providing (or restricting) contraception, (c) changes in norms and values about sexuality within a society, and (d) health care factors, including the availability of food and water.

We know that one of the most significant distinguishing characteristics between the rich Global North and the poor Global South countries is their fertility rates. The worldwide fertility rate has fallen in every major world region, but some still remain very high. In sub-Saharan Africa, the average number of children per woman is 5.4, which is high, but that number has actually dropped since 1950, when the average was 6.7. Worldwide, the number of children per woman fell from 5.0 in 1950 to 2.6 by 2008 (Population Reference Bureau 2008). Figure 15.6 compares fertility rates in the Global North regions of the world with the poorest Global South regions.

Thinking Sociologically

What does Figure 15.6 (fertility rates by development levels) tell you about the lives of individuals in these different regions of the world?

Women's fertile years are roughly from 15 to 44. Women in the Global South countries have 80% of their children between the ages of 20 and 35, with a few below age 20 (United Nations 2006). Still, close to 20% of births in developing regions occur at age 35 or older, ages when there is greater risk in pregnancy, labor, and delivery. An important point in this section is how various organizations, institutions, and government programs affect fertility rates.

Extremely dense populations are often found in poverty-stricken areas. This slum in Kolkata (Calcutta), India, houses many rural migrants who are the lucky ones, having found a spot in the overpopulated sliver of land by a highway where they put up a shelter with whatever materials are available. Others sleep on sidewalks and highway medians.

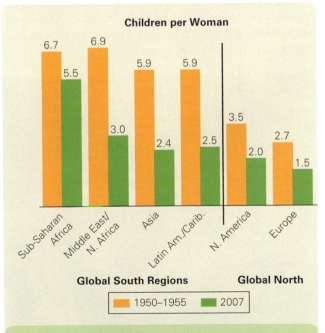

Figure 15.6   Fertility Rates: Comparing Various Regions of the World in the Early 1950s With 2007

Source: Population Reference Bureau (2007a). From Population Reference Bureau, "World Population Highlights," Population Bulletin 62, no. 3 (2007). Reprinted with permission.

Note: Fertility rates have fallen in every major world region but are still highest in sub-Saharan Africa.

Government Influence

Some governments provide incentives to parents to have more children, whereas others discourage high fertility. Thus, meso- and macro-level social policies shape decisions of families at the micro level. Government *pronatalist policies* (those that encourage fertility) or *antinatalist policies* (those that discourage fertility) take several forms: manipulating contraceptive availability; promoting change in factors that affect fertility such as the status of women, education, and degree of economic development; using propaganda for or against having children; creating incentives (maternity leaves, benefits, and tax breaks) or penalties (such as fines); and passing laws governing age of marriage, size of family, contraception, and abortion.

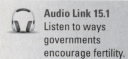

Audio Link 15.1
Listen to ways governments encourage fertility.

Antinatalist policies arise out of concern over available resources and differences in birth rates among population subgroups. Singapore, a country in Asia located off the Malay peninsula, consists of one main island and many smaller islands. It is one of the most crowded places on earth, with 18,645 people per square mile. This is compared with 84 in the United States, 9 in Canada, and 836 in Japan (Infoplease 2009). The entire population of Singapore is urban, and 90% live in the capital city. The country has little unemployment and one of the highest per capita incomes in Asia. However, it depends on imports from other countries for most of its raw materials and food.

A condom mascot offers leaflets to teenagers in Bangkok, Thailand, during a promotional campaign to educate Thai youths on how to use condoms. The issue is partially related to birth control and partially to HIV/AIDS prevention. The effect is an antinatalist effort to lower the fertility rate.

Some years ago, the central government in Singapore started an aggressive antinatalist plan. Birth control was made available, and residents of Singapore who had more than one or two children were penalized with less health care, smaller housing, and higher costs for services such as education. Singapore now claims one of the lowest natural increase rates (the birth rate minus the death rate) in Southeast Asia, at 0.8% a year, just behind China. Singapore's governmental policies have controlled the natural increase rate.

China's antinatalist policy has been in effect since 1962. The government discourages traditional preferences for early marriage, large families, and many sons by using group pressure, privileges for small families, and easy availability of birth control and abortion. The government has reduced the natural increase rate in China, the most populous nation on earth, to only 0.5% annually (Population Reference Bureau 2008). Unfortunately, there are side effects to such a stringent policy among a people who value male children. There has been an increase in selective abortions by couples hoping to have sons, and there are instances of female infanticide—killing of female infants when they are born—so that families can try for a male child.

An example of pronatalist government policies can be seen in Romania. Many Romanian men were killed in World War II, creating a sex imbalance. Marriage and birth rates plummeted. Concerned about the low birth rate, in 1966, the government banned abortions and the importation of most contraceptives. Within 8 months, the birth rate doubled, and within 11 months it tripled.

In the United States, citizens like to think that decisions about fertility are entirely a private matter left to the couple. Indeed, it is sometimes hard to pin a simple label of antinatalist or pronatalist on the administration in power. President George W. Bush reinstated the "gag rule" that Presidents Ronald Reagan and George H. W. Bush had implemented and Presidents Bill Clinton and Barack Obama each eliminated. The rule limits the availability of birth control for teens in the United States unless parents are informed that the teen has applied for contraception. Many experts argue that this policy has contributed to the increased teen pregnancy rates in the United States. The Bush administration also blocked U.S. funding to international family planning groups that, among their many services, offer abortions and abortion counseling (Blackman 2001) and proposed a 19% cut in international family planning contributions for 2006 ("Overseas Population Spending Threatened" 2006). Both limits to contraceptive availability and prohibitions on abortion are pronatalist because they increase fertility. While promoting births may not be the intention of those who oppose birth control and abortion, the policy still has the latent consequence of encouraging population increases. Other governmental policies that might encourage larger families, such as family tax breaks or access to day care centers, are much less available in the United States. Each new administration brings its own policy initiatives and President Obama has rescinded the restrictions on international agencies supported by U.S. funds providing family planning assistance.

Well into the 20th century, other U.S. policies encouraged sterilization of Black women. While White women were being encouraged to have large families in the 1950s, poor women of color were being discouraged from reproducing. The legal scholar Dorothy Roberts has found a continuing legacy of dual treatment of Black and White fertility and motherhood in the United States. This has led to a continuing distrust of governmental family policies in some parts of the African American community (Roberts 1997, 2002).

Thinking Sociologically

Do you think it is appropriate for governments to use enticements or penalties to encourage or discourage fertility? Why or why not? What are positive factors and problems with different policies mentioned above?

Religious and Cultural Norms

Religion is a primary shaper of morality and values in most societies. Norms and customs of a society or subculture also influence fertility. In some cultures, pronatalist norms support a woman having a child before she is married so she can prove her fertility. In other societies, a woman can be stoned to death for having a child or even sex out of wedlock.

Some religious groups oppose any intervention, such as birth control or abortion, in the natural processes of conception and birth. Roman Catholicism, for example, teaches that large families are a blessing from God and that birth control is a sin. The Roman Catholic Church officially advocates the rhythm method to regulate conception, a less reliable method in lessening birth rates than contraception technology. However, a great many Catholics in the Western world are not following these teachings and are little different from their neighbors in use of contraception. Islam also encourages large family size to increase the number of faithful. These policies were created when population growth was kept in check by high death rates.

Nonreligious cultural customs affect fertility as well. Couples may be pressured to delay marriage until they are in their late 20s or even 30s when they are economically secure. In Ireland, the mean age at first marriage for men was 30 and for women 28.2 years (Office of National Statistics UK 2007). Although Ireland is a predominantly Catholic country, delayed marriage helps keep the birth rate down. Another antinatalist custom in some polygamous groups is sexual abstinence after birth of a child, usually

In Indonesia, Nur Azizah binti Hanafiah, 22, receives a caning, having been found by a citizen having illegal sex with her boyfriend at her house. This Aceh region of Indonesia has practiced Islamic Sharia law since 2001. In some societies, she would have been stoned to death for having premarital sex.

during the lactating (breast-feeding) period, which lasts anywhere from 1 to 5 years.

Education

"Women with a secondary school education have substantially smaller families than women with less education" (Population Reference Bureau 2010), illustrating that the higher women's status in society as measured by education level and job opportunities, the lower their fertility. If a country wants to control population growth, raising the status of women is key. Figure 15.7 on page 528 shows the relationship between education and family size in seven Global South countries (Population Reference Bureau 2010). Note in the figure that the higher the educational level, the lower the fertility rate and population growth. So, again, education and reduction of poverty are major variables contributing to moderation in population size.

Studies repeatedly show that investing in education of girls and women raises every index of a country's progress toward economic growth and development. Yet 300 million children are without access to education, two thirds of them girls. Of 771 million illiterate adults in the world, two thirds are women. Although this gender gap has narrowed, it persists in sub-Saharan Africa, Arab states, and South and West Asia where only 6 in 10 adults are literate (Institute for Statistics 2005). Two thirds of the world's illiterate adults live in nine countries, and 45% live in India and China.

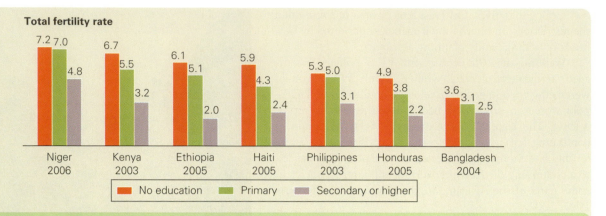

Figure 15.7   Women's Education and Family Size in Selected Countries, 2000s

Source: Population Reference Bureau (2010). Reprinted with permission.

Note: Among women in developing countries, more education often leads to lower fertility.

Availability of contraception may determine a woman's ability to control the number of children she has during the fertile years. Family planning programs and contraceptive availability have resulted in a significant decline in global fertility rates, over and above such factors as education (Rama Rao and Mohanam 2003). For instance, worldwide use of contraception increased from 10% in the 1960s to 62% in 2007, with sharp contrasts between regions (Population Reference Bureau 2007a). An estimated 200 million women do not have access to contraception, resulting in 76 million unplanned births a year (Medical News Today 2009). Usage doubled in Global South countries, resulting in a decline of fertility in all regions and a total world decline from 3.2% to 2.7%. However, availability of contraception is spotty. In Africa, only 27% of married women are using any method of contraception, and only 20% are relying on modern methods. In some parts of Africa, fewer than 5% use modern methods. As a result, the region has the highest levels of fertility (and AIDS) in the world. Globally, 201 million women lack access to effective contraceptives, but many would practice family planning if given the option (United Nations Population Fund 2005).

As seen above, many factors affect fertility rates. Lower population growth means less pressure on governments to provide emergency services for booming populations and means more attention given to services such as schools, health care, and jobs. Most population experts encourage governments and other meso-level institutions in fast-growing countries to act aggressively to control population size. Critics argue that wealthy countries also need to help by curbing resource depletion and pollution. There are consequences of population fluctuations in affluent parts of the world as well as poor parts. The impact of the baby boom in the United States illustrates this, as discussed in the next "Sociology in Our Social World."

Thinking Sociologically

After reading the "Sociology in Our Social World" on page 529, discuss what impact the baby boom and baby boomlet have had on your opportunities for education and a career. How will retirement of baby boomers affect your opportunities?

Factors Affecting Mortality Rates

Life expectancy refers to the average number of years people live in a particular society. It indicates the overall health conditions in a country. In affluent countries, medicines cure many of the diseases that cause death in the Global South. Polluted water also spreads diseases as seen in the cholera epidemic in Zimbabwe in 2008 and 2009.

Imagine living in Sierra Leone, West Africa, where the life expectancy at birth is 41.2 years and the average number of children for each mother is 5.9. Of every 1,000 babies born alive, 154 will die within the first year. A majority of the population lives on less than $900 a year (World Factbook 2009d). At 20, life is almost half over. Close to 70% of men and women are subsistence farmers, working small plots that may not provide enough food to keep their families from starving (United Nations Development Programme 2007/2008). When one plot is overfarmed and the soil depleted so that plants will no longer grow, the family moves to another and clears the land, depleting more arable land. Shortages of food result in malnutrition, making the population susceptible to illnesses and disease. The limited medical care that is available is mostly available in urban areas.

The figures above give us substantial information about the country—its population dynamics and mortality. Some

Sociology in Our Social World

The Significance of the Baby Boom

At the end of World War II, the birth rate shot up temporarily in most countries involved in the war, as many young people who had been forced to delay marriage made up for lost time. The postwar economy was growing, people were employed in relatively well-paying positions, and the norms supported large families. While this baby boom lasted about only 3 years after World War II in Britain, it lasted 17 years in the United States, from 1946 to 1963.

The baby boom phenomenon has had many impacts. During the late 1960s, school boards and contractors were busy building schools to educate the growing number of children. By the 1980s, student numbers declined, and towns were consolidating schools and closing buildings. When the baby boomers entered the job market starting in the mid-1960s, there were great numbers of applicants for jobs, and employers could pay less. The supply was so great they were assured that someone would take the job.

Two decades later, it was much easier for young people to find jobs because there were fewer of them in that age range looking for starting-level positions. However, that generation is finding it hard to get promotions because the baby boomers have dominated so many of the high-level positions. In addition, trends in marketing and advertising have, for years, been dictated by the baby boom generation because they are such a large segment of the consumer public.

By the 1960s, changes in people's views of the ideal family size and the proper age for marriage changed. Zero population growth movements and environmental concerns slowed the rate of growth. The period from the late 1960s to early 1970s has been referred to as a "baby bust" or the "birth dearth." (This fluctuation resulted in a population structure that did not look very much like a pyramid, as shown in Figure 15.8 on page 534.)

In the mid-1970s and into the 1980s, when the baby boom generation started having babies, there was another baby boom—or "baby boomlet"—but it was much smaller because the baby boomers had smaller families. The result is that population growth in many

The 1950s was the era of the baby boom.

developed countries has remained below the replacement level, or the number of births or migrants a location needs to maintain its population. Growth in the overall size of populations in Global North at this point is due largely to immigration. Otherwise, many populations would be declining more significantly.

Population growth also triggers cultural and social change. Generation Xers (or the children of the baby boomers) now look at careers as transient, and they often move from job to job to advance instead of working up the internal labor market of one firm or organization. Similarly, Generation Xers are experiencing "delayed adulthood" (Furstenberg 2003). Unlike their parents, who saw having a family as the major rite of passage for growing up, Gen Xers spend longer attaining education and have delayed partnering and parenting until they achieve fiscal security. These are two strategies societies have made to adapt to population shifts. The point is that extreme fluctuations in fertility rates can affect societies in a number of ways.

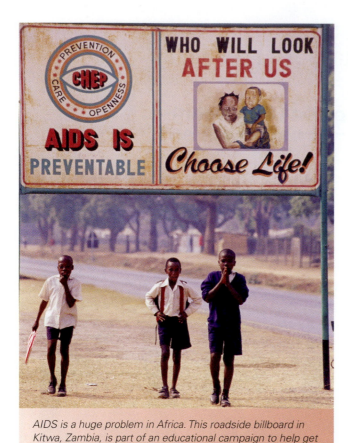

AIDS is a huge problem in Africa. This roadside billboard in Kitwa, Zambia, is part of an educational campaign to help get control of the pandemic.

Table 15.2	**Infant Mortality Rates Around the World**
Region	Infant Mortality Rate[a]
World	49
More affluent (Global North) countries	6
Less affluent (Global South) countries	54
Least affluent (the very poor Global South)	85
Africa	82
North America	7
Latin America	23
Asia	45
Europe	6
Oceania	25

Source: Population Reference Bureau (2008).

a. The infant mortality rate indicates deaths of children under 1 year per 1,000 births.

other African countries face similar situations: life expectancy in Swaziland is 33 years, Lesotho 36 years, Zimbabwe 40 years and dropping, and Zambia 38 years (Population Reference Bureau 2008). Average life expectancy for sub-Saharan Africa as a whole is 49 years.

Why are these societies so dramatically different from Global North countries, many of which have average life expectancies into the 80s? The low life expectancy is due to lack of medical care, high infant mortality, epidemics such as AIDS, wars and civil strife, draughts and famine, malnutrition, and resulting susceptibility to diseases. Table 15.2 shows the infant mortality rate around the world, meaning the number of infant deaths (children under 1 year) per 1,000 births. This is a key indicator of a country's overall well-being.

Migration and Mobility: Why and Where People Move

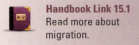

Handbook Link 15.1
Read more about migration.

Most of us have moved one or more times in our lives, a process called migration, the movement of people from one place to another. Perhaps, we have moved to a larger house down the block, maybe to another area for a job opportunity or school, or even to another country altogether. If we have changed our residence, we have been part of the process called **geographic mobility**.

Over the history of the human race, people have migrated to the far reaches of the globe. Because of adaptability to climatic and geographic barriers, humans have dispersed to more areas of the globe than any other species. Even inhospitable locations such as the Arctic North and the South Pole have human settlements.

The *push-pull* model points out that some people are pushed from their original locations by wars, plagues, famine, political or religious conflicts, economic crises, or other factors and pulled to new locations by economic opportunities or political and religious tolerance. Most people do not leave a location unless they have been forced out or they have a viable alternative in the new location and the benefits of moving outweigh the costs (Weeks 2005). In some cases, the push factors are especially strong; in others, the pull factors dominate.

When we are young, we go where our parents go. If a parent receives a lucrative job offer in another location, the family dwelling becomes too small, a relative needs help, or a family member's health requires a different climate, the family moves. Migration is often initiated at the micro level. If an opportunity is present, the individual or family may move. However, if the risks are high, if the information about migration is scarce, or if negative factors such as leaving family behind are present, individuals may decide not to move.

Although the decision to move is often a personal or family one, it is also influenced by the sociocultural environment. History is replete with examples of large groups of people who left an area because of aspirations to improve their life chances, hopes of retaining a way of life, or expulsion by political, economic, or religious forces. Chinese railroad workers came to the United States for economic reasons. Amish and Mennonite settlers from Europe sought religious freedom and preservation of their way of life. The Amish, a group originating in Germany, left Germany *en masse*, and the members of this group now live entirely in North America. Italian immigration to the United States took place in a collective manner. When a family left Italy, they would usually move to a U.S. city where a relative or a previous acquaintance lived. Thus, residents of entire apartment buildings in the North End of Boston were from the same extended family, or entire city blocks of people came from the same town or region of southern Italy (Gans 1962). Also, former colonial powers have numerous immigrants from colonized countries. This has helped make many European cities, such as London and Paris, the multicultural environments they are today.

Those living at the receiving end have not always been welcoming, and in fact have often tried to isolate the newcomers in ghettos, preventing them from moving into neighborhoods. Job opportunities are sometimes limited, especially in difficult economic times when competition for jobs is greatest (Foner 2005). Immigration laws in the United States, for example, reflect the nation's attitudes toward immigrants at different time periods. The Chinese Exclusion Act of 1882 ended Chinese immigration; the National origin system in 1921 targeted southern Europeans and reduced immigration from Greece and Italy; the Immigration and Naturalization Act of 1965 and the Immigration Reform and Control Act of 1986 aimed to keep out less skilled and illegal immigrants but facilitated entry of skilled workers and relatives of U.S. residents (Schaefer 2007). Current stalemates in the U.S. Congress over immigration reform show the contentious nature of policies related to immigration, especially illegal immigrants crossing borders.

Social science studies of the impact of immigration counter some of the negative stereotypes, pointing out the net economic gain for countries. Yet some U.S. states and European cities are burdened with newcomers who are not yet self-sufficient. California Proposition 187, for example, illustrated anger against illegal immigration. Known as "Save Our State" (SOS), this bill denied education, welfare, and nonemergency health care to illegal immigrants (Schaefer 2007). These policies often make life difficult for immigrants, even if they do have official papers.

Migrations can be international, from one country to another, or internal, within a single nation. Moves from rural farm communities to urban areas are a common internal migration pattern found around the world. For people who depend on the land, drought and other adverse environmental conditions force movement. International moves are often influenced by political unrest or discrimination against a group of people such as the Nazi persecutions of the Jewish population or for economic opportunity as we see in the next section.

International Migration

More than 3% of the world's population is "on the go" each year. That is 214 million international migrants in 2009 alone. These migrants change the size and characteristics of populations around the world, from those being expanded to those being left behind (United Nations 2009a). From 1995 to 2000, 2.6 million migrants left the Global South for Global North countries, and more than half of them entered the United States or Canada. An entirely new phenomenon—previously unknown in human history—is also occurring: Cyber-migration is a process by which the Internet creates global Internet connections across physical and cultural borders, allowing for new opportunities for migration.

International migration is especially common where political turmoil, wars, famines, or natural disasters ravage a country. *Refugees*, those "who flee in search of refuge in times of war, political oppression, or religious persecution," numbered 42 million at the end of 2008, and asylum seekers numbered 16 million in 2007. Twenty-six million citizens are also *internally displaced*, forcibly relocated within their own countries by violent conflict or environmental

This ship containing more than 300 immigrants from Eritrea, East Africa, was spotted by an Italian customs police helicopter. Every year, thousands of illegal immigrants departing from the Mediterranean coasts of Africa try to reach Europe through Sicily. The voyage is dangerous, and many immigrants are found dead on the Sicilian shoreline, but the desire for a better future keeps the masses coming.

disaster (www.answers.com/topic/refugee; UNHCR 2006, 2009). The tsunami in Indonesia and the hurricane that hit New Orleans and the Gulf coastal areas are examples of displacement caused by natural disasters. People from war-torn Darfur seek refuge in neighboring Chad. The list of international population movements due to internal crises is extensive and constantly changing. These are not just irrelevant events occurring elsewhere in the world. They involve human beings who are seeking a place to live and may end up as your neighbors, and each migrant has a unique story.

Mohammed from Senegal traverses the streets of Verona, Italy, during the day selling children's books and trying to make enough to live on, hoping he might have some money left to send back to his family. Mohammed speaks five languages and has a high school education, but opportunities in his homeland are limited, and he is an illegal immigrant in Italy. Most Global North countries are desirable destinations for those seeking economic opportunities. European countries, especially those that formerly had colonies, have large populations of immigrants from North Africa and the Middle East. These immigrants often face great peril in their attempts to seek a better life, and many find themselves in crowded, unsanitary housing with little economic opportunity once they arrive in European cities.

Economic opportunities and the demand for cheap labor have brought many guest workers from the Global South to European nations and the Persian Gulf states, where foreign workers make up the majority of the labor force. Women, who make up a growing proportion of those seeking economic opportunities, total 55% of legal immigrants to the United States. This high percentage has to do with the demand for specific types of work (Population Reference Bureau 2007b). In some cases, women and children enter countries illegally due to human trafficking.

Audio Link 15.2
Listen to stories about U.S. immigration law.

Prior to 1914, when World War I began, it was not standard practice for nations to require a passport to enter a country (Friedman 2005). Because most people could not afford intercontinental travel, controlling the flow of people was not an issue. The United States has had a more restrictive stance than Canada or most European countries regarding immigration (Farley 2009). Still, the number of foreign-born people in the United States was 38 million in 2009, a slight decline from 2008 to 12.5% of the population; this number is expected to rise to 48 million by 2025, resulting in 14% of the U.S. population being foreign-born (Morello and Keating 2009). First- and second-generation residents will constitute about one third of the U.S. population by 2025 (Population Reference Bureau 2007b:8). About 11 million illegal migrants from Mexico and other South and Central American countries now live in the United States, and half a million illegal immigrants enter the country each year. Some people are so desperate to cross over to the United States that they risk everything.

Four hundred Mexicans died in 2005 trying to cross the desert to the U.S. border (*The Economist* 2006a, 2006b).

Two factors curb migrations: (1) restrictive immigration laws of receiving countries and (2) economic recessions. During recessions, many countries restrict immigration by passing strict immigration quotas, even for political refugees from war-torn countries. In fact, the number of immigrants to the United States has dropped with the economic downturn by 14%, or 1.7 million people between 2007 and 2009, according to some estimates (Jacoby 2009).

Thinking Sociologically

Think about your own grandparents or great grandparents. How long have your ancestors occupied the same land or lived in the same community? Do they go back more than one generation on the same property? If they have been mobile, what factors were critical to their mobility? How has their mobility or stability influenced your family's experiences? How were they received in their new home?

Since the terrorist attacks of September 11, 2001, the idea that the U.S. borders are porous has been highly divisive as the U.S. Congress and state legislatures struggle to find appropriate policies. The lack of agreement stems from conflicts over how the country feels about immigrants. Some favor the diversity and new ideas brought by skilled, highly educated immigrants, as well as the labor brought by low-skilled immigrants, who work at jobs not filled by U.S. citizens. Conflicts focus on who the migrants are, their religions, economic impact of immigrants, settlement patterns, whether immigrants bring crime, political loyalties of immigrants, moral values, and work habits. Research finds that, for the most part, immigrants are industrious, innovative, and hard working. They pay taxes and contribute to their communities. However, 9/11 affected attitudes about immigration, with a 20% increase in U.S. citizens favoring policies restricting immigration. One such policy that is in progress, for example, is a fence along a length of the Mexican-U.S. border (Inhofe 2008). Completion may be halted by economic constraints or new policies.

As of July 2007, lack of agreement in the United States on a comprehensive nationwide policy has resulted in more than 1,404 bills related to immigration being introduced in the 50 state legislatures; 170 of these bills had been proposed in 2007 alone. In addition, 182 different bills became laws in 43 states. The laws relate to employment eligibility, health care, acceptable identification, drivers' licenses, public benefits, and human trafficking (National Conference of State Legislatures 2007). Many laws protect the rights of immigrant workers and their families to education and health care. Most immigrants are of working age and accounted for 60% of the labor force increase; they will account for all the population increase within 5 to 25 years (Population Reference Bureau 2007b).

The debate in the United States and other countries is intense, and the solutions will not be easy. The Obama administration in the United States has proposed changes that have yet to be enacted into law by Congress, but the new policy is unlikely to be as restrictive as many against immigration would like.

Internal Migration

The rate of internal migration in the United States is high compared with most places in the world. Patterns have primarily involved individual "pull" migration to economic opportunities and better housing. Almost half report housing as the main reason for their relocation: A better apartment or house, owning rather than renting, cheaper housing, and better neighborhood with less crime are primary reasons for moving (U.S. Census Bureau 2006b, 2006d). Table 15.3 provides reasons for moving that fall into several categories.

During different historical periods, movement directions have varied. For many years, rural residents in the United States moved to higher income urban areas. Until the 1950s, people moved out of the southern states and into northern states, especially north central states. Then the pattern reversed, and the flow started south and west. Movement since the 1960s has been toward the Sunbelt, especially to California, Arizona, Texas, and Florida. Movement to the Pacific Coast and even Alaska has also increased due to economic opportunities in these locations.

One major form of internal migration is *urbanization*—movement from rural areas to cities. For people who are seeking economic opportunity, excitement, and anonymity, they are "pulled" to cities. The urbanization process involves a change of lifestyle for individuals that results from living in

cities (Brunn, Williams, and Zeigler 2003:5). This process is so important that the second half of this chapter is devoted to analysis of urbanization of the population across the globe.

Although decisions about family size and migration are individual ones, they are influenced by what happens at the meso and macro levels as we see in the next section.

 Journal Article Link 15.2 Read about migration of older people.

Thinking Sociologically

What are the benefits and costs for individuals and governments of extensive internal migration? What are the advantages and disadvantages of having large numbers of internal immigrants?

 MICRO-LEVEL POPULATION PATTERNS

You might get the impression that population studies are mostly about other places and problems that do not affect your country. However, understanding demography can be extremely important for comprehending social processes very close to your everyday life. While most Global North countries do not have massive famines or population explosions, population fluctuations influence them in many ways. Consider the life choice decisions you as an individual will be making regarding education, employment, and retirement.

In 1969, Keith, one of the coauthors of this book, lived in Boston, and his wife taught in a suburban school system there. The elementary school where she taught had four first-grade classrooms, with 28 children per room—112 first graders in

Table 15.3   Reasons for Moving by Type of Move, 2006 (in percentage)

Reasons for Mobility	All Movers	Intracounty (within a country)	Intercounty (between counties)	From Abroad
Family-related reasons	11,025	6,894	3,759	372
Change in marital status	2,395	1,547	786	62
To establish own household	3,389	2,617	753	19
Other family reasons	5,241	2,730	2,220	290
Work-related reasons	7,328	2,160	4,491	677
New job/job transfer	3,481	538	2,641	302
To look for work/lost job	638	153	319	166
Closer to work/easier commute	1,440	737	701	2
Retired	170	9	159	2
Total	39,837	24,851	13,690	1,296

Source: U.S. Census Bureau (2006b, 2006d).

Note: Reported in thousands.

the school. By the next year, the decline in the fertility rate 6 years earlier was being felt, and the number of first graders declined. Within 4 years, the number of first graders in her school was reduced to 40, with two classrooms and only 20 students per class. Some school systems lost half of their student population in a short time. One year, first-grade teachers were losing their jobs or having to move to another grade, and the next year, it was second-grade teachers who were scrambling. The third year, third-grade teachers were in oversupply, and so forth. With low demand, these were not times for college students to be pursuing teaching careers. A personal decision was being influenced by population trends.

We have already mentioned the impact of the baby boom (the high fertility rates from 1946 to about 1963) and the following baby bust (the drop in fertility for more than a decade following the baby boom). The impact on the population is graphically represented in the population pyramid of the United States (see Figure 15.8). As we can see, the U.S. population no longer looks anything like a pyramid, yet from it we can tell a great deal about job prospects, retirement security, career decisions, and deviance rates, to name only a few of the outcomes. As that bulge for the baby boomer group moves into the senior citizen's category, it is likely to have a real impact on the society.

The decision about your career choice is a deeply personal decision, but population trends also shape that decision. For example, if a business that produces baby products expands its production shortly after a dip in fertility rates, the timing of the business expansion may cause severe financial hardships or even bankruptcy for the company. Smart businesspeople pay a great deal of attention to characteristics of the population. That same information might be relevant to an individual deciding on a career. For example, this is an incredibly good time for students who enjoy working with older people

Video Link 15.2
Watch more on the aging population in the U.S.

(gerontology) or in the medical field to think about a career in gerontology or health care.

Retirement is another topic for which population patterns are critical. Most countries in the Global North are struggling with how young working people are going to support the nonworking aging populations. The number of working people contributing to pensions compared with retirees who depend on support is changing dramatically. Systems in many countries are in trouble because of low birth rates and increasing numbers of nonworking elderly people.

When social security was established in the United States in the 1930s, life expectancy was 59. The number of people in the age-dependent categories of under 15 or over 65 was low. For each person who received social security, 20 paid into the federal coffers. Twenty people each paying $500 a year could easily support a retired person, who might receive $10,000 per year. However, the average life expectancy has shifted, and the age-dependent population increased. Currently in the United States, 13% of the population is over the age of 65 (World Factbook 2009b), as opposed to 4% in the 1930s. Moreover, predictions are that by 2035, 20% of the population will be over 65. When the baby boomers are collecting social security, the people born during the birth dearth will be the ones in their prime earning years, but there are far fewer of them paying into the system. When commentators and politicians say social security is in trouble, therefore, they are not generally saying it has been mismanaged. They are pointing to problems created by changes in the composition of the U.S. population.

In the 1980s, the U.S. administration and Congress saw the problem coming and for the first time began to save funds in a social security account for the baby boomers. They also passed laws requiring baby boomers to work longer before they qualify for social security. That there are so many baby boomers—and that an extremely high percentage of citizens over the age of 65 vote—makes it unlikely that Congress

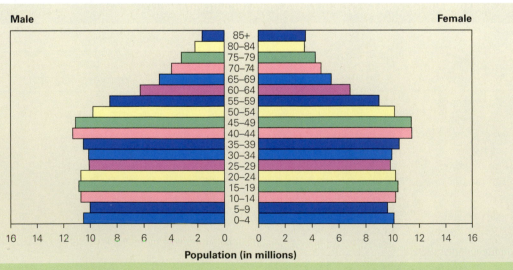

Figure 15.8   United States, 2005
Source: U.S. Census Bureau (2006c).

or the president would cut back on benefits to this group. Still, with the federal budget squeezed by war and natural disasters causing the deficit to grow, some members of Congress have voiced interest in "borrowing" from the social security reserves. Members of the younger generations will be the ones to pay if insufficient funds are available for the baby boomers, and their future pensions may be in jeopardy. The aging population and need for funds could have a profound influence on your own family budget.

Rates of deviance and juvenile delinquency in a local community are also influenced by population patterns. In the 1960s and 1970s, these rates climbed precipitously. When the rates of juvenile delinquency began to decline in the 1980s and 1990s, members of both major U.S. political parties claimed that it was their policies that made the difference. However, most deviant acts are committed by young people in their mid-teens to early 20s.

Thus, when the baby boom generation was in their teens and early 20s, the overall rates of deviance were higher. Many of those same delinquents became upright citizens—even law-and-order conservatives—once they had families and careers. When the birth dearth group was in their teens, overall rates of crime dropped because there were fewer teenagers. So private and personal decisions by thousands of couples (micro level) may result in rise or fall of the crime rates for the entire country 15 years later.

Because population trends will shape your life, understanding those trends can help you use that knowledge to your advantage. To illustrate the power of demographic trends on individual decisions, the next "Engaging Sociology" provides an exercise in problem solving using information from population pyramids of U.S. cities.

Video Link 15.3
Watch a discussion about social security and baby boomers.

Engaging Sociology

Population Pyramids and Predicting Community Needs and Services

Study these three Population Pyramid graphs. Based on what you see, answer the following questions:

1. Which community would be likely to have the lowest crime rate? Explain.

2. Which would be likely to have the most cultural amenities (theaters, art galleries, concert halls, etc.)? Explain.

3. Imagine you were an entrepreneur planning on starting a business in one of these communities.

   a. Name three businesses that you think would be likely to succeed in each community. Explain.
   b. Name one business that you think would be unlikely to succeed in each community. Explain.

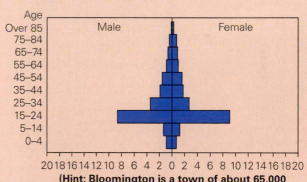

Bloomington, Indiana

(Hint: Bloomington is a town of about 65,000 and is the home of Indiana University, a large Big Ten university.)

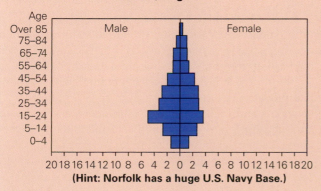

Norfolk, Virginia

(Hint: Norfolk has a huge U.S. Navy Base.)

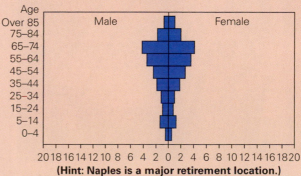

Naples, Florida

(Hint: Naples is a major retirement location.)

Thinking Sociologically

Have you thought about economic security after retirement? What plans can you make now for this long period of life after work? Why is this planning important?

Urbanization: Movement From Rural to Urban Areas

Mumbai (Bombay), India; Caracas, Venezuela; Lagos, Nigeria; Shanghai, China; and New York City, United

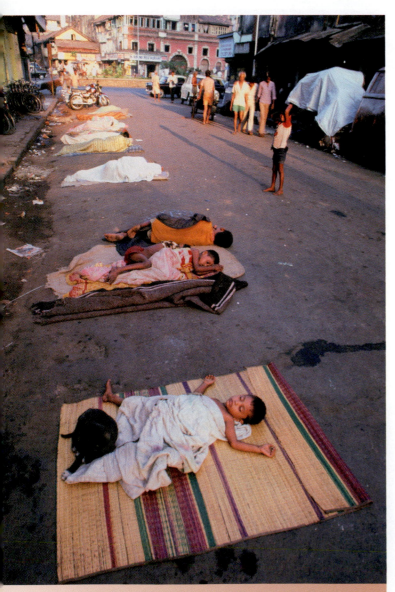

In Mumbai (Bombay) many children have no choice but to sleep on the streets each night.

States—all are bustling megacities (cities with more than 10 million people) with traffic congestion and people rushing to their destinations. Carts, bicycles, and taxis weave in and out of traffic jams. The local spices and other aromas scent the air. Sidewalk merchants display vegetables and fruits unique to the country. Beggars and the homeless, often migrants from rural areas, dot the sidewalks, while merchants sell colorful wares. Cities are vibrant places with diversity and contributions of a variety of ethnic traditions coming together. The amazing sights, sounds, smells, tastes, and cultural activities—from art and theater, to music and night clubs—mean there is always excitement. There is also the draw of possible exciting and high-paying jobs. These options and opportunities lure people to cities.

For people who are seeking economic opportunity, excitement, and anonymity, they are "pulled" to cities. Migration is often from rural areas to urban cities. The urbanization process involves a change of lifestyle for individuals that results from living in cities (Brunn et al. 2003:5). The problem is that the poor, who come to cities to find opportunities, often live with no running water, electricity, or sewage disposal and lack basic services, including health care and education. They set up makeshift shelters of any materials available. Some live on the streets. Countries and cities have little money to provide needed services to the migrants, and migrants often lack the skills needed for success in urban areas. Yet the world continues to become more urbanized as small farms in rural areas cannot support the growing populations.

These megacities around the world are part of a global trend that has gained momentum over several centuries—urbanization. The next "Engaging Sociology" feature invites you to explore some consequences of major urbanization trends in the world (Brunn et al. 2003; United Nations Population Division 2003).

This urbanization process involves "1. the movement of people from rural to urban places, where they engage in primarily non-rural occupations, and 2. the change in lifestyle that results from living in cities" (Brunn et al., 2003:5). Urbanization accompanies *modernization*—transformation from traditional, mostly agrarian societies to contemporary bureaucratized states—and *industrialization*—transformation from an agricultural base and handmade goods to manufacturing industries. We explore urbanization in this section as a very specific demographic trend that has major social implications for how people live and interact.

Most people live their lives in communities: locations that provide dwellings, a sense of identity and belonging, neighbors and friends, social involvements, and access to basic necessities. Our most intimate micro-level interactions take place in these communities. Yet we are connected through our communities to larger meso- and macro-level social structures, such as political and religious organizations, world health organizations, and international relief agencies (e.g., UNICEF). In this section, we consider the

Engaging Sociology

Trends in World Urbanization

World Urbanization Prospects are reports published by the United Nations Population Division. They provide valuable data on past, present, and future urbanization trends in regions and subregions of the world. They also provide data on individual cities and urban areas. Consider the impact of major migration trends on the environment, friends and relatives left behind, dual-career families, maintaining one's culture, the impact of new cultural ideas spreading, and many more impacts. The major findings of the most recent edition follow.

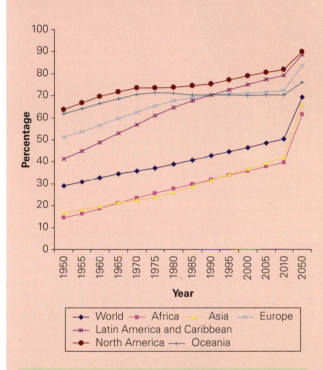

Figure 15.9   Percentage of Population Residing in Urban Areas

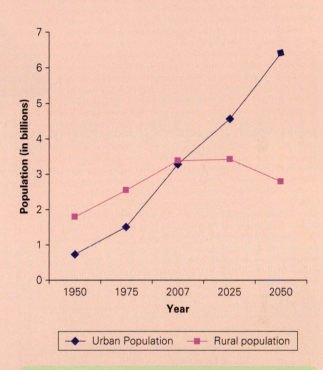

Figure 15.10   Urban and Rural Population of the World, 1950–2050

Answer the following questions about the figures:

- What do you learn from these graphs about world urbanization trends? Which continents seem to be urbanizing most rapidly?
- How might these trends affect people moving to urban areas?

- What might be some effects on global climate change, the possibilities of globally transmitted diseases, political stability or instability, or the global economy?
- How might the global trend toward urbanization affect your own life?
- Identify two positive and two negative consequences of this urbanization trend for a nation.

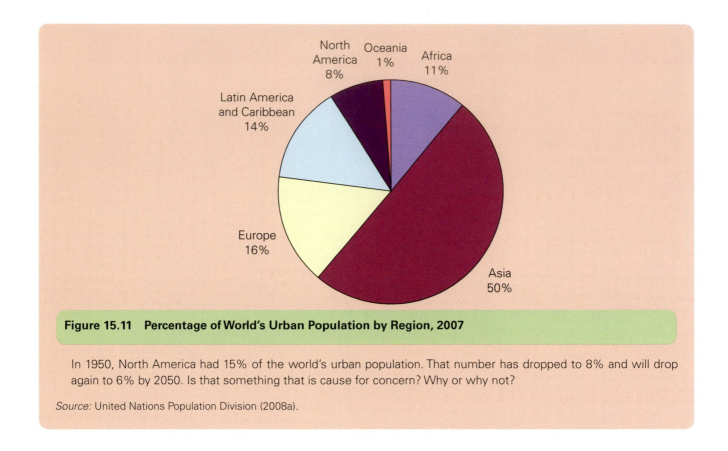

Figure 15.11   Percentage of World's Urban Population by Region, 2007

In 1950, North America had 15% of the world's urban population. That number has dropped to 8% and will drop again to 6% by 2050. Is that something that is cause for concern? Why or why not?

Source: United Nations Population Division (2008a).

development of communities—from rural areas and small towns to urban areas such as megacities.

The second half of this chapter is a continuation of the discussion of demographic patterns. However, we will return here to the pattern used in previous chapters of discussing micro-level analysis first, followed by meso- and macro-level analyses. First, how do urban environments affect us as individuals?

CITIES AS MICRO-LEVEL LIVING ENVIRONMENTS

In the 17th and 18th centuries, when Europe was undergoing dramatic changes, small, bucolic villages contrasted sharply with the rapidly growing urban centers. Tonnies (1855–1936) described these two extreme types on a continuum from **Gemeinschaft**, a German word indicating a small traditional community, to **Gesellschaft**, meaning a large, impersonal urban area. He saw social life as an evolution from family units to rural villages, towns, cities, nations, and finally cosmopolitan urban life (Tonnies [1887] 1963). Family, friendship, relations to the land, common values, traditions, and experiences are key elements of Gemeinschaft. Gesellschaft, a product of urban industrial society, is characterized by formal relations, contracts, laws,

and economies built on money. People in urban areas do not necessarily know one another or share common values. They tend to be employees of bureaucratic organizations, and they tend to be more isolated as individuals rather than members of a collectivity.

A number of other theorists living in the Europe of the 19th century suggested similar contrasts. Durkheim (1858–1917) described the social bonds that held society together and the changes that arose from industrialization and urbanization. **Mechanical solidarity** was his term for the glue that held a society together through shared beliefs, values, and traditions typical of rural areas and simple societies. In mechanical solidarity, social bonds were formed by homogeneity of thought.

Think of any large business in which each employee has a specific task to perform in the division of labor. Similarly, the social glue that holds modern industrial and postindustrial societies and people together is **organic solidarity**, a division of labor with each member playing a highly specialized role in the society. Each person depends on others with interrelated, interdependent tasks. This interdependence of specialized tasks is the key to unity in more complex societies with organic solidarity.

The ways in which order is maintained in society illustrate the differences between the two types of societies. In mechanical solidarity, legal systems are concerned with moral order, upheld by shared beliefs and values and a desire to be well regarded in the community. Organic solidarity stresses making amends for a wrongdoing by paying fines or spending time in jail (Durkheim [1893] 1947). So even the notion of how to maintain social order varies as this transformation in the society occurs.

For most of human history, humans lived in small population centers. Rural areas dominated. *Rural sociology*, which refers to the study of social life in nonmetropolitan areas, considers patterns and behaviors among people at a distance from population centers. In the United States, rural areas have fewer than 1,000 people per square mile. According to the 2000 U.S. census, this constituted 21% of the U.S. population. Some rural residents are in farming or agribusiness and are concerned with the economics of farm production, ranching, and mining. Others live in resort towns or cater to tourists. Popular rural destinations are mountain areas, the Ozarks, coastal regions, and some midwestern areas in Nebraska, Kansas, and surrounding states.

As the years pass, agriculture occupies many fewer citizens. A rural exodus has been under way, with movement to cities that have more economic opportunities and better health care and education. Rural areas face problems just as cities do: environmental degradation from overfarming, overuse of water resources, toxic dumps, and poverty due to reductions in economic opportunities and selling of family farms.

Major population shifts from rural to urban areas came with industrialization in Europe and North America, followed by the same process in other areas of the world. As urbanization continues to sweep the world, many rural areas are disappearing, and those that remain are taking on aspects of metropolitan life as they move away from mechanical and toward organic solidarity. Even the remotest villages are influenced by urban and global concerns. For instance, decisions about what crops to grow are often tied to nonlocal demand. Poor farmers in South America and Afghanistan make more money growing poppies for drug suppliers in big cities than from food crops to feed the local population, making them food dependent.

The early interpretations of urbanization, especially by European sociologists, were made through a rather pessimistic lens. The trend was seen largely as a decline of civil society. However, there are pluses as well as minuses in quality of life as people inhabit more densely populated areas. Many city planners have worked to make cities more inhabitable and "green."

Life in the City

On warm evenings, the residents come out of their oppressive apartments to sit on the front steps. Children play ball in the street or splash in front of open fire hydrants. Neighbors chat about work and politics and other things neighbors share. Across the interstate

Many urban areas now have urban planners who work to make cities beautiful, aesthetically pleasing, and recreation-friendly. This scene in New York City is possible because planners had the foresight to put in several sizeable parks.

highway, the professional couple is having cocktails with friends from work in their renovated, air-conditioned Victorian home. In a nearby suburb, families are returning from sports practices, mowing their lawns, and preparing dinner. Political, economic, and cultural factors help shape these different scenarios in the inner city and its surrounding area, as described by urban residential patterns and suburbanization.

Video Link 15.4
Watch a video about urbanization.

Urban Residential Patterns

Neighborhoods are identifiable areas within the larger metropolitan area. Four characteristics help define neighborhoods:

1. A neighborhood can meet most of the needs of residents: food, schools, religions.

2. Neighborhoods are "natural areas"; that is, to a great degree, residents are homogeneous with respect to income, interests, ethnicity or race, and other shared characteristics.

3. There is a high degree of social interaction among the residents of a neighborhood.

4. There is substantial symbolic commitment, the feeling of belonging to a meaningful sociogeographic area.

Some neighborhoods in cities, especially in ethnic immigrant concentrations, are close-knit. This is especially true when members of extended families live in the same area and provide support for one another (Guest and Stamm 1993; Logan and Spitze 1994). In major cities around the world, ethnic enclaves offer security, familiarity, and protection. For new migrants to cities, neighborhoods provide gradual adaptation to the strange new society and the dominant group. Immigrant groups often attempt to re-create their former, more intimate village-type settings within their urban neighborhood (Gans 1962). Ethnic communities can provide job opportunities and gradual acculturation into language and customs.

Supportive ethnic enclaves are also found in African American inner-city neighborhoods of predominantly single mothers and children. Stack (1998) found that women created support networks—sustaining each other through sharing of child care and resources. However, in some low-income tenement areas, little interaction has been found because of high turnover of residents and fear of violence (Renzetti 2003).

Homogeneous middle-class city and suburban dwellers often have an active neighborhood life as well. A suburb is an area immediately adjacent to a city, extending outward beyond the city limits or the core of the city (Flanagan 2001). The variables that create a sense of community are complex, and generalizations that apply to all types of communities are difficult to make.

City dwellers become accustomed to the fast pace of life, the danger of stepping off the curb to cross the street, the crowds jostling and pushing them along as they rush to work, the impersonal attitudes of clerks, and the impatience with inconveniences. The thrill of city life outweighs the problems for many residents, who are sentimentally attached to the unique nature of life in cities. Let us look at some of the variables that affect how people experience city life.

Human Relationships in Cities

Sociologist Georg Simmel ([1902–1917] 1950) was concerned with the experience of urban life, with what it does to people's thoughts and behavior. He argued that two factors—the intensity and stimulation of city life and the economic effects on urban relations—cause people to have different attitudes, beliefs, and values from those in rural areas. City dwellers have no choice but to be somewhat insensitive, to avoid intense relationships, and to keep social relationships superficial to protect their privacy. However, he did not feel this was necessarily negative. Cities free people from the social constraints of close relationships in

While life in urban areas of North America is typically individualistic and bureaucratic, life in small towns, such as Bhakatapur, Nepal (top), and a Tibetan village (bottom) is more communal and personal, but one has much less privacy.

small towns. Erving Goffman ([1959] 2001) called behaviors of urban dwellers *civil inattention*, elaborate modes of pretending that we do not look, make eye contact, bump into others, pay attention, or listen to what others are doing. Residents show an awareness of others without being conspicuous, threatening, or overly friendly. To visitors or strangers to city life, these behaviors seem callous and cold. However, they offer anonymity and freedom in a crowded environment.

Sociologist Louis Wirth (1964) also contended that because urban residents live in heterogeneous, high-density areas, they develop coping mechanisms for dealing with the situation. They become sophisticated, removed from others to insulate themselves from too many personal claims and expectations of others. The depersonalization that results from lower commitment to a common community "goal" also leads to a higher tolerance for nonconformity in cities, resulting in more individual freedom—and as a result more deviance.

Urban sociologist Claude Fischer (1984) argues that urbanism shapes social life rather than leaving residents as alienated individuals in a sea of traffic, noise, and pollution. City life strengthens social groups, promotes diverse subcultures, and encourages intimate social circles. These urban groups share similar activities or traits. The larger numbers of people make it possible for individuals with similar interests—from ethnic subcultures to gay communities to artist groups—to draw together as clubs, organizations, or neighborhoods. These little social worlds "touch but do not interpenetrate" (Fischer 1984:37). As long as there are enough members of a group, each can maintain its own identity. When different groups come in contact with each other, the result may be positive sharing of cultures, or it may be conflict, causing members to associate all the more closely with their own group. Gangs fall into this latter category. So rather than creating isolated individuals who interact defensively with others, urban life may create choices about lifestyle and enhance a different kind of community base, intensifying the interactions.

Despite these benefits of urban life in countries where cities have substantial resources to provide services, urbanization can have very different consequences, especially in poor regions of the world. Rapidly growing cities in impoverished countries often face challenges to provide services—shelter, water, electricity, sanitation, schools, health care—for the increasing numbers of residents.

Thinking Sociologically

What do you see as the most important impact on individuals or groups of living in urban areas?

Despite the sometimes impersonal environment of cities, local neighborhoods in urban areas often have a sense of community and local traditions. Here we see people playing chess at Washington Square in New York City. This is enough of a community event that it attracts interested spectators.

HOW DID CITIES EVOLVE? MESO-LEVEL ORGANIZATIONAL STRUCTURES

Human settlements have gone through massive transitions over the past 10,000 years, from small agricultural settlements to bustling crowded metropolises with millions of people. The first step in the development of urban life came when those living nomadic lives became more settled. Archeological evidence indicates that there may have been early settlements in southern Russia as early as 15,000 years ago (Zimolzak and Stansfield 1983). Starting about 10,000 years ago with the advent of agriculture, domestication of animals, and the shift from food gathering to food production, small groups established permanent settlements. Among the first was Eridu in Iraq, a settlement of some 25 permanent compounds with a population of up to 200 in each compound and a grain storage facility in the center (see Figure 15.12 on page 542). The people grew wheat and barley and domesticated dogs, goats, and sheep.

These settlements were not cities as we think of them today, however, because they had different cultural and economic structures, and there was little division of labor. Everyone shared roles, worked the land to support the population, and banded together for protection. Cities, in contrast, are large permanent settlements with nonagricultural specialists, a literate elite, and surplus food to support

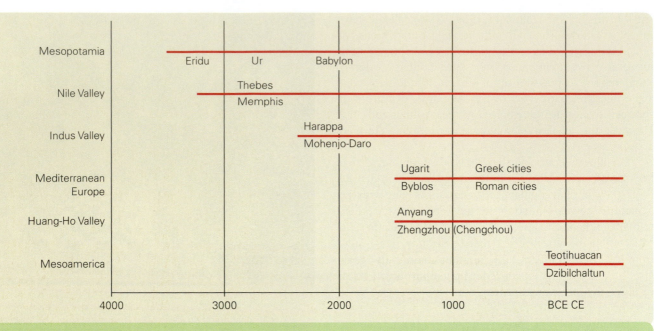

Figure 15.12   Cities in Antiquity

Source: Sjoberg (1965:56–57).

the social classes that are not involved in food production. They have been the source of intense fascination for many social science theorists.

Theories of Urban Development

Among the first sociologists in the United States were urban scholars, dubbed the Chicago School, who studied problems in the city of Chicago. Their studies of urban ecology focused on the patterns of land use and residential distribution of people in urban areas. These theorists pictured the city's growth pattern as a series of circles. Moving out from the center, each circle was dominated by a particular type of activity and residential pattern, from central city ghettoes and rooming houses to working-class apartments and bungalows, to middle-class housing, to upper-class suburbs (Park, Burgess, and McKenzie [1925] 1967). See Figure 15.13 on page 543 for an illustration of this pattern.

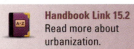

Handbook Link 15.2
Read more about urbanization.

Urban ecologists further refined the Chicago School's original ideas by exploring social, economic, political, and technological systems of cities' spatial patterns (Abu-Lughod 1991). Several processes constantly take place in urban areas: residential segregation; invasion by a new ethnic, religious, or socioeconomic group; and succession by that group. These processes are part of dynamic city life (Berry and Kasarda 1977).

Racial and ethnic segregation is a continuing and troubling issue in many urban areas of the United States. Despite some reductions in racism in the nation, American cities—especially northern cities—have high levels of residential segregation. This segregation affects individual networking, school composition, and access to community resources. The "Engaging Sociology" on page 544 examines the likelihood that someone of a given race will have contacts in their neighborhood that cross racial lines. This figure is based on one city—Chicago, Illinois—but you can easily check the residential patterns in your city by going to www.censusscope.org/segregation.html.

In the past three decades, very new and different theories of urban development have emerged, spurred in part by the decay, riots, and disturbances in cities around the world that dramatized inequalities and prompted sociologists to find new explanations for urban problems. The idea is that urban space is both socially defined and in scarce supply. Therefore, political-economic conflict will arise over how space gets allocated and by whom. Any effective solution to urban problems must address inequalities between groups and allocations of resources in urban areas (Castells 1977; Harvey 1973).

Some conflict theorists see growing city problems as a result of domination by elites, creating poverty and exploitation of the poor (Flanagan 2001; Gottdiener and Hutchison 2006). Cities produce profits for those who buy and sell property and for investors and politicians who redevelop urban areas. Sometimes, poor urban residents are displaced in the process (Hannigan 1998). In short, conflict theorists see urbanization and modernization as a cause of poverty among city residents around the world.

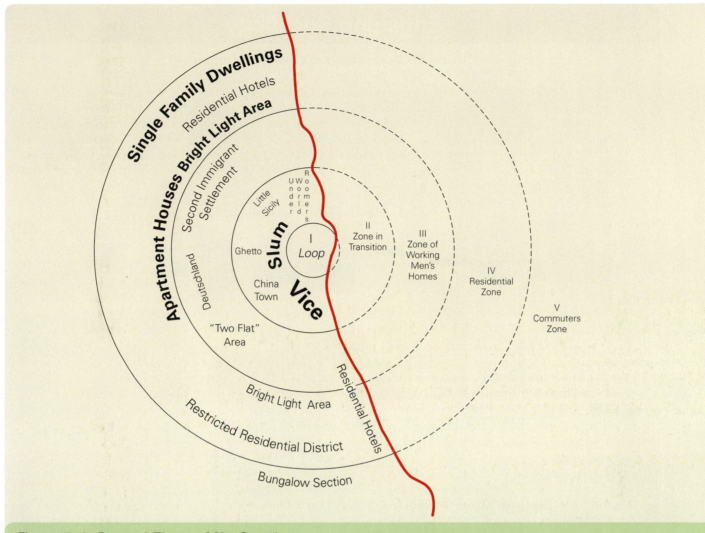

Figure 15.13 Burgess's Theory of City Growth

Source: Park et al. ([1925] 1967:55).

Note: The Chicago School envisioned urban growth as a series of concentric circles, with ethnicity, class, residential patterns, and types of activity evolving with each ring removed from the central city.

Types of Cities

Although organizational structures of cities have changed and evolved over time, in the following section, we will focus on industrial and several variants of postindustrial cities.

Industrial Cities

The onset of industrialization in 17th- and 18th-century Europe started the trend toward urbanized nations, countries in which more than half of the population live in urban areas. Rural peasants migrated to the cities in search of opportunities and to escape the tedium and poverty of agricultural existence and shortage of available farmland. Often,

this resulted in a rapid influx of migrants and an unplanned urbanization process. Cities served the rapidly advancing industrial sector, but crowded conditions, poor sanitation, polluted water supplies, and poor working conditions all contributed to the misery of poor urban residents and to their short life expectancy compared with those living in the countryside. Urban systems became overwhelmed by the large numbers of migrants, and conditions became as desperate as those the people had tried to escape in the rural areas. Today, Global North countries are more than 75% urban, and Global South countries are on average 40% urban. By 2030, this imbalance will be even greater.

Industrial cities became primarily commercial centers motivated by competition, a characteristic that differentiated them from preindustrial cities. The advent of power-driven

Engaging Sociology

Residential Segregation and Cross-Race Contact

Unless there is complete integration, the racial composition of neighborhoods where most Whites live differs from the composition of neighborhoods lived in by ethnic minorities. To examine this, the Census Bureau calculates exposure indices—the average racial composition of neighborhoods experienced by members of each group. This bar graph illustrates typical contact of most residents with members of their own and other races in a metropolitan area. In this graph, the first five columns represent the average racial composition of the neighborhood of a person of a given race. The rightmost column shows the racial composition of the metropolitan area as a whole. Study the line graphs and answer the following questions.

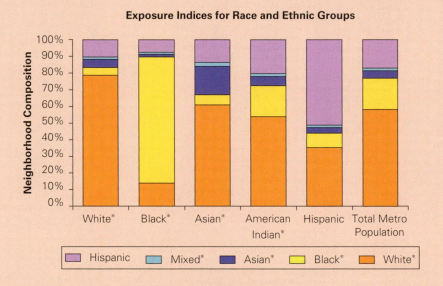

Figure 15.14   Exposure Indices for Race and Ethnic Groups: Chicago

Questions based on the bar graph:

1. How likely are Whites to engage diversity in their neighborhoods compared with the diversity of the city as a whole?
2. Which group experiences the most diversity and is likely to have opportunity to encounter someone unlike himself or herself?
3. Which groups experience the most segregation?
4. What might be some results of living in neighborhoods that are homogeneous? Which group might experience more negative consequences because of the homogeneity? Why?
5. Go to www.censusscope.org/segregation.html and enter a city near you to see how exposure rates fare for various groups in that city. What do you conclude?

Source: Residential Segregation and Cross-Race Contact: Chicago, Illinois. www.censusscope.org/segregation.html.

machinery and the new capitalist factory system transformed and replaced the former craft and cottage industries and guild structures (Abu-Lughod 1991). Roads, waterways, and railroads made travel and communication between towns and cities easier and faster. Cities became fast-paced as mechanical vehicles took to the streets.

By 1850, profound changes began taking place in many European countries and in the United States. A shift from predominantly rural to urban living was under way. In about 1870, Great Britain became the first truly urban nation with more than 50% of the population in urban areas. Economically changing conditions in the British

Isles were conducive to urbanization and industrialization. Parliament had passed "reorganization of land acts" that pushed many rural citizens from the countryside to cities. In addition, raw materials were available from colonies; new technology was rapidly advancing manufacturing techniques; and the banking facilities, credit, stock, and other financing for industry were falling into place (Benevolo 1995; Mumford 1961).

Residential population patterns in the United States are illustrative. About 90% of the U.S. population lived on farms in the 1790s. By 1900, 41% of the labor force worked in agriculture. Today, agricultural workers hold only about 859,000 jobs, and this number, including farmers, those who work with animals, agricultural inspectors, and other related workers, is unlikely to change in the next decade (U.S. Bureau of Labor Statistics 2008–2009). While 17% of the U.S. population is rural, only 1.5% to 1.9% of the U.S. labor force worked in agriculture in 2008 (Answerbag.com 2009; Kusmin 2008). Agribusiness conglomerates have bought out family farmers who could not compete with these large businesses. Young people have moved from farms, leaving the population in rural areas older than that in urban areas.

Between 1940 and 2000, the number of urban areas in the United States increased from 33 to 453 (The Federal Register 2002), and many cities have become global economic centers (Abu-Lughod 2001). Urban growth was aided by an increase in agricultural productivity, which made food available to support urban dwellers, and by the development of an adequate distribution system to get the produce to markets to feed those in urban areas.

With the advent of public transportation in the late 1800s, people in many countries began to escape crowded city conditions by moving out into emerging suburbs. Private automobiles and telephones aided movement to the suburbs. Road systems were developed to accommodate the growing numbers of autos, and more businesses and services relocated to suburban areas.

Since the 1990s, the U.S. Census shows that some rural areas are once again gaining population. This is especially the case in recreation areas, where urban residents relocate to exurbs (rural areas within commuting distance of city jobs), and retired people look for new locations with clean air, space, interpersonal civility, and a slower pace than the city (Johnson and Fuguitt 2000).

Despite the many jobs created, one of the downsides of industrialized cities is phenomenal pollution.

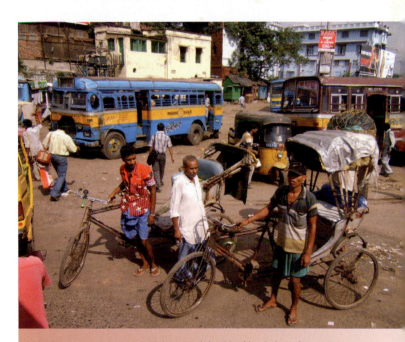

While these men may look impoverished by North American standards, they are relatively well off in comparison to many urban neighbors in India, for they own a method of transportation that can earn a cash income, providing food and shelter for their families. For them, this is life in a postindustrial city.

Postindustrial Cities

Postindustrial cities (Bell [1976] 1999) have a high percentage of employees in the service sector—business headquarters, government and intergovernmental organizations, research and development, tourism, finance, health, education, and telecommunications. They are found in the most technologically advanced, wealthy nations. Washington, D.C., fits most of these characteristics, as does La Defense, an urban center on the outskirts of Paris, built as a commercial, service, and information exchange center to serve France.

Postindustrial cities are closely tied to the economic structures of capitalism, with global production systems and instant exchanges of information (Abu-Lughod 2001; Friedman

2005). In the transformation from industrial to postindustrial economies, from manufacturing to service economies, some people get left behind. There are often severe income disparities between those trained for the new economies and those with less training and in lower-level positions. Cities such as Bengaluru (Bangalore), India, illustrate the disparities between high-tech industries and poor agricultural peasants in the surrounding areas. These high-tech centers attract business from around the world. This book would have been produced in the United States a few years ago, but with the tightening publication market, publishers find it economically prudent to outsource and save on costs.

Video Link 15.5
Watch more on urban planning.

Some urban areas are carefully planned. *New towns*, for example, are cities built from scratch as economically self-sufficient entities with all the needed urban amenities. Urban planners believed that these cities could relieve the congestion of urban areas, provide new economic bases and residences near jobs, and solve many problems faced by older cities. Some new towns have been success stories: Columbia, Maryland; Brasilia, Brazil (the relatively new capital); Canberra, Australia. However, cities around the world have experienced influxes of poor migrants who squat (set up shelter) in any location available—abandoned buildings, cemetery mausoleums, hillsides surrounding cities. The next "Sociology Around the World" discusses archeological research indicating that large planned cities existed in North America before White Europeans even knew the continent existed.

As people move to the suburbs, manufacturing firms, services, commerce, and retail trade follow (Meltzer 1999). These internal migrations lock cities and suburbs into competition over jobs and tax revenues (Stanback 1991). When this happens, farmland and open lands disappear; quality of construction is often shoddy because builders want to make big profits; energy and water demands increase, often straining public utilities; and sprawl leads to vast, crowded freeway systems. Such a suburbanization of industry took place between 1970 and 1990, as many industries relocated out of central city areas, looking for favorable tax rates.

Sociology Around the World

City Planning in Prehistoric Central America: Teotihuacan

Teotihuacan was a Mesoamerican city (between the American continents) created by a society that had no metal tools, had not invented the wheel, and had no pack animals. At its height, Teotihuacan covered 8 square miles (20 square kilometers), which made it larger than imperial Rome. Its central religious monument, the Temple of the Sun, was as broad at its base as the great pyramid of Cheops in Egypt. Its population may have reached 100,000.

Strategically located astride a valley that was the gateway to the lowlands of Mexico, Teotihuacan flourished for 500 years as a great urban commercial center. Yet it was more than that. It was the mecca of the New World, a religious and cultural capital that probably housed pilgrims from as far away as Guatemala. Perhaps most startling, Teotihuacan was a totally planned city. Its two great pyramids, its citadel, its hundred lesser religious structures, and its 4,000 other dwellings were laid out according to an exact design. Streets (and many of its buildings) were organized on a perfect grid aligned with the city center. Even the shape of the river that divided the city was changed to fit the grid pattern.

Planning for the construction of Teotihuacan's major temples must have been an incredible undertaking. The Temple of the Sun, for instance, rises to a height of 215 feet and has a base of 725 square feet. These dimensions mean that it took about one million tons of sun-baked mud bricks to build the temple. When the Spaniards conquered Mexico in the 16th century, they were amazed to find Teotihuacan's ruined temples. Local inhabitants claimed that the temples had been built by giants. They showed the Spaniards the bones of giant elephants (which had lived there in prehistoric times) to prove their point.

Small buildings as well as large ones were cleverly conceived in Teotihuacan. Houses were apparently planned for maximum space and privacy. Apartments were constructed around central patios, with each patio designed to give dwellers light and air, as well as an efficient drainage system. In a Teotihuacan housing complex, a person could indeed have lived in relative comfort (Jordan-Bychkov and Domoch 1998).

In some urban areas, neatly manicured lawns and freshly painted exteriors reflect new directions away from either suburbanization or deterioration of inner-city neighborhoods. The process of **gentrification** refers to low income urban areas that see increases in income and housing prices (Kiviat 2008). Sometimes, this change involves members of the middle and upper classes, mostly young White professionals, buying and renovating rundown properties in central-city neighborhoods. The process begins when affluent urban residents leave their stylish homes and move to suburbs. Poorer residents are left behind to rent once-fashionable homes from absentee owners. Later, affluent professionals buy the rundown homes at bargain rates, renovate them, and live in these newly gentrified areas (Feagin 1983). However, recent research indicates that minority householders, especially those with at least a high school degree, do not all leave. They make up, on average, 33% of the gentrified neighborhoods compared with 20% college-educated Whites. More middle-class minorities, such as Hispanics, also move to gentrified neighborhoods. The bottom line is that all residents tend to do better economically as income and housing prices increase in gentrified areas, and these become more ethnically diverse neighborhoods as well (McKinnish, Walsh, and White 2008).

In recent years, these neighborhoods, which are often adjacent to the central business districts, have become "fashionable" residential areas. Georgetown in Washington, D.C., and German Village in Columbus, Ohio, are examples. Beautiful old classic homes have become affordable to young upper-middle-class professionals and remain within reach of middle-class minorities who decide that they want ready access to the occupational and cultural opportunities of the city. This process of gentrification brings consumers, leadership, and a tax base to the city.

For those low-income people who move because of rising costs, many are pushed into less attractive parts of town with fewer services and recreational areas, and often pay higher rents for less adequate housing. Alternative housing for displaced residents may be difficult to find, contributing to problems of homelessness. Conflict theorists view gentrification and other urban developments that favor the wealthy and displace or exclude the poor to be exploited by real estate capitalists. In contrast, others argue that wealthy residents who choose the lifestyle of the city over suburbia are helping support viable, livable cities (Caulfield 1994).

Thinking Sociologically

What are some positive and negative aspects of gentrification for individuals and cities? Explain.

Megacities

As we look at Earth from space, some areas glow. These urban areas of 10 million or more residents, called megacities, dot the globe. In the 1950s, New York City was the only place in the world that had 10 million people. At that time, there were 75 cities in the world with 1 to 5 million residents, mostly in the Global South. Table 15.4 shows the rapid change in this pattern with the 10 largest population centers in 2000 and 2008.

As the world becomes more congested and cities continue to attract residents, cities start to merge or to become continuous urban areas without rural areas between them. Those who have driven from Boston to Washington, D.C., an area sometimes called Boswash, know the meaning of *megalopolis*, a spatial merging of two or more cities along major transportation corridors (Brunn et al. 2003).

Table 15.4 **The Ten Largest Population Centers (population in millions)**

2000 Rank	Center and Country	Population	2008 Rank	Center and Country	Population
1	Tokyo, Japan	34,450	1	Tokyo, Japan	33,600
2	Mexico City, Mexico	18,066	2	Seoul, Korea	23,400
3	New York/Newark, United States	17,846	3	Mexico City, Mexico	22,400
4	Sao Paulo, Brazil	17,099	4	New York/Newark, United States	21,900
5	Mumbai (Bombay), India	16,086	5	Mumbai (Bombay), India	21,600
6	Kolkata (Calcutta), India	13,058	6	Delhi, India	21,500
7	Shanghai, China	12,887	7	Sao Paulo, Brazil	20,600
8	Buenos Aires, Argentina	12,583	8	Los Angeles, United States	18,000
9	Delhi, India	12,441	9	Shanghai, China	17,500
10	Los Angeles, United States	11,814	10	Osaka, Japan	16,700

Source: United Nations Population Division (2003) and AmO Life (2008).

Global City Variations

Many people around the globe live in cities with long, often glorious histories. Some live in relatively new suburbs surrounding central cities, and others live in new urban areas, recently planned and constructed. Cities' spatial arrangements vary by their histories, as the following examples illustrate.

Kabul, Afghanistan, is an example of a traditional, indigenous city in the Global South. Kabul dates back to between 500 and 300 BCE, and it became the capital of Afghanistan in 1776. In the old section, bazaars and flat-roofed houses crowd the narrow winding streets, which were designed for foot and cart traffic. The newer sections have wide, tree-lined streets. Land use is mixed, with small businesses and residences sharing the same dwellings. Indigenous cities usually predate European cities. In many indigenous cities, certain occupational types occupy distinctive areas. The centers of indigenous cities usually include a market or bazaar, monuments, government buildings, and a religious mosque, church, or temple. Some of the elite live in the heart of these cities, whereas the poor live on the periphery of the city or on the city streets, a pattern vastly different from affluent North America. Global South countries often have dual cities such as Delhi–New Delhi, India, and Abidjan, Ivory Coast, in which a modern Westernized colonial central city is located next to a traditional indigenous city.

Audio Link 15.3
Listen to a story about megacities and earthquakes.

From cities built on ancient foundations to new urban centers, cities are a main organizational structure in modern life. How do these urban areas develop? This leads us to a discussion of macro-level issues.

The hills surrounding Caracas, the capital of Venezuela, are densely packed with migrants from rural areas looking for opportunities in the urban area. Many of these areas lack the most basic services.

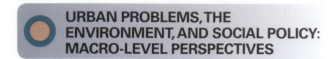

URBAN PROBLEMS, THE ENVIRONMENT, AND SOCIAL POLICY: MACRO-LEVEL PERSPECTIVES

The mountains rise from the sea, dotted with pastel-colored shanties. On the drive from the port city of La Guaira up into the mountains to the capital city of Caracas, Venezuela, one sees settlements nestled into the hillsides. The poor, who have come from throughout the country to find opportunities in the capital, make shelters in the hills surrounding Caracas, often living with no running water, electricity, or sewage disposal. The laundry list of urban problems is overwhelming: excessive size and overcrowding; shortages of services, education, and health care; slums and squatters; traffic congestion; unemployment; and effects of global restructuring, including loss of agricultural land, environmental degradation, and resettlement of immigrants and refugees (Brunn et al. 2003). This section considers several of the many problems facing urban areas such as Caracas.

Rural Migrants and Overcrowding

Barriadas surround the outskirts of Caracas, a situation in many cities where migrants find any available space within or around the city to squat. For example, in Cairo, Egypt, a huge, sprawling graveyard full of large mausoleums, the City of the Dead, has become home to thousands of families transplanted from rural areas. Cities in India such as Chennai (Madras), Mumbai (Bombay), and Kolkata (Calcutta) have thousands of homeless migrants living on the sidewalks, on highway medians, and in river channels that flood during the rainy season.

Overcrowding exists in cities throughout the world but causes special problems in the Global South, where rural residents seek opportunities in urban areas. Squatters with hopes for a better future set up shacks of any material available—tin, cardboard, leaves, mud, and sticks—in settlements known as *barriadas* in Spanish, *shantytowns* in English, *bidonvilles* in French, *favelas* in Portuguese-speaking Brazil, and *bustees* in India. The majority of migrants to the city are young. They are pulled to the city in hopes of finding jobs and often have been pushed from the rural areas because of limited land on which to farm.

In the past three decades, the urban populations in Africa, Asia, and Latin America have begun to grow rapidly, and as Map 15.1 shows, many of the largest cities in the world are now in the Global South. Rural-to-urban migration and development of megacities dominate the economic and political considerations in many countries. The newcomers spill out into the countryside, engulfing towns along the way. Figure 15.15 shows the population living in urban and rural areas by more or less developed regions of the world, indicating trends from 1950 to 2007 and making projections through 2030 (United Nations Population Division 2008a).

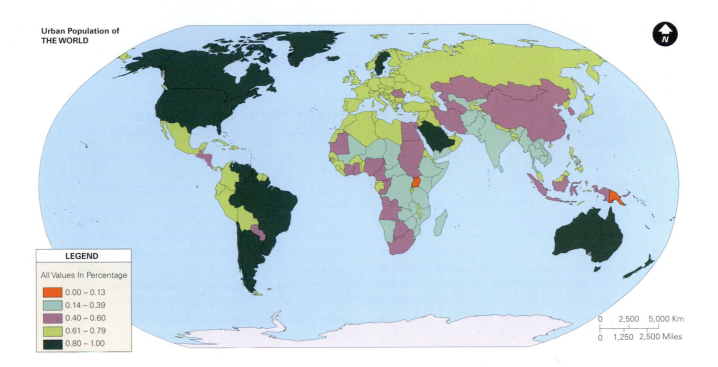

Map 15.1   Percent Urban Population by Country in 2006

Source: World Bank. Map by Anna Versluis.

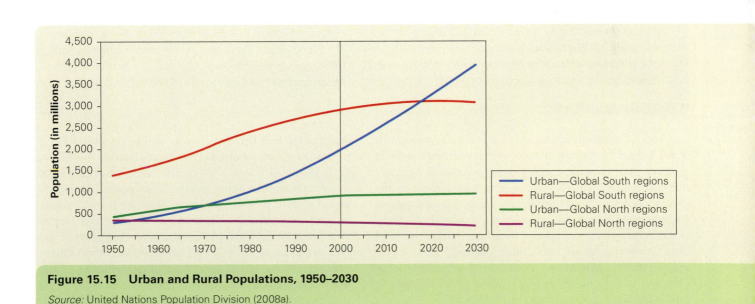

Figure 15.15   Urban and Rural Populations, 1950–2030

Source: United Nations Population Division (2008a).

Countries have little time or money to prepare infra-structures and provide services for the rapidly increasing numbers of urban residents. Technological development, job opportunities, and basic services have not kept up with the large migrations of would-be laborers. Providing services such as water, electricity, sanitation, schools, transportation, and health services to these people has become a major problem—even impossible for some poor governments. Health and disease, especially contagious diseases, cause deadly epidemics due to the lack of services and poor sanitary conditions. The next "Sociology in Our Social World" describes one plague that ravaged much of Europe.

Sociology in Our Social World

"Ring Around the Rosey" and the Plague

Ring around the Rosey, Pockets full of posies, Ashes, Ashes, We all fall down!

Remember this nursery school rhyme? You probably did not understand the meaning of the rhyme as a child. It refers to the bubonic plague, which ravaged England and Europe in the early to mid-1600s, leaving dead and dying people in its wake. One account says that people infected with the plague got red circular sores that smelled very bad. People would put flowers (posies) in their pockets or on their bodies somewhere to cover up the smell. Because people were dying so rapidly, it was difficult to keep up with burials, and the dead were burned to reduce the spread of the disease (ashes, ashes). So many people were sick and dying that "we all fall down." Although there are variations on this story, it is probably true that the rhyme was related to the plague.

From 1603 to 1849, the clergy had the task of recording the deaths, burials, and the cause of deaths that occurred. These were circulated weekly, with a summary put out before Christmas. This process is one of the earliest records of vital statistics. In 1662, John Graunt from London analyzed the records for the first known statistical analysis of demographic data. Among his findings was that "for every 100 people born in London, only 16 were still alive at age 36 and only 3 at age 66" (Weeks 1999:61). The plague had an impact on social relationships, too. Many citizens avoided anyone who was a stranger, and some who contracted the disease died miserable lonely deaths because of others' fears of the disease. As the Industrial Revolution advanced, so did income, housing, sanitation, and nutrition. All these improvements in people's lives reduced the incidence of plague and increased life expectancy. Today, cases of the plague can be found in several places, including India and the rural southwest United States. Antibiotics are effective treatment for people who have access to them, but many poor people cannot afford expensive medications from affluent countries.

Modern plagues, such as avian influenza (bird flu) and Severe Acute Respiratory Syndrome (SARS), have claimed hundreds of lives this decade, but both have significantly smaller impact than the bubonic plague. The World Health Organization is monitoring bird flu and SARS throughout the world to make sure the impact never reaches the tragic levels of the bubonic plague.

Lack of adequate housing is a worldwide problem. It is not helped by high birth rates and lower death rates in resource-poor countries, which cause population increases that are greater than the rate of economic growth or the capacity of society to absorb the migrants into urban areas. Because residents of the squatter settlements hold traditional rural values, adaptation to urban bureaucracy and overcrowding become even more difficult, resulting in *anomie* (normlessness) and exacerbating urban problems. Planning and social policy have failed poor migrants in rapidly growing slums of many world cities.

Environment, Infrastructure, and Urban Ecosystems

Audio Link 15.4
Listen to stories about nature and urban areas.

"Life on Earth in 2050 will be marked by struggles for food, water, and energy security," according to a recent study of the link between human well-being and health of the planet ("Ecosystems Report Links Human Well-Being With Health of Planet" 2006). The study, involving 1,360 scientists from 95 nations, asserts, "Sixty percent of the ecological systems that sustain life on Earth are being degraded or used unsustainably" ("Ecosystems Report Links Human Well-Being With Health of Planet" 2006). Extinction of species, lack of water and water pollution, resource exploitation, collapse of some global fisheries, and new diseases are the likely results of this breakdown. Urbanization by 2050 will stretch resources to their limits. Cities will have no way to dispose of wastes, resulting in epidemics. We cannot address environmental problems in detail here, but humans are contributing to the problems that are killing people now and will kill many in the future. The problems are exacerbated by an increase in natural disasters (e.g., hurricanes), which scientists believe to be a result of global warming. We can ignore the problems or call them nonexistent because life has improved for many people, but this is a short-sighted response. This increase in quality of life is actually magnifying the problems and hastening the demise of cities and the environments that support cities ("Ecosystems Report Links Human Well-Being With Health of Planet" 2006).

Additional infrastructure problems threaten to immobilize cities in the Global South. Traffic congestion and pollution are so intense in some cities that the slow movement of people and goods reduces productivity, jobs, health, and vital services. Pollution of the streets and air are chronic problems, especially with expansion of automobile use around the world. Older cities face deteriorating infrastructures, with water, gas, and sewage lines in need of replacement. In Global South countries, concern for these problems has brought some action and relief, but in impoverished countries where survival issues are pressing, environmental contamination is a low priority. Thus, the worst air pollution is now found in major cities in the Global South, such as Mexico City; Sao Paulo, Brazil; and several Chinese cities, including Beijing, host to the 2008 Olympics.

Water, an essential resource for survival, illustrates the complex urban ecosystem. Cities pipe in millions of gallons of water each day to residents from lakes, rivers, or reservoirs, sometimes located at a distance from the city. Through a complex network of pipes, the water is connected to each establishment. After use—cooking, cleaning, showering, disposing of wastes—the water is discarded and becomes an output. Some of the water is used in products or for industrial uses and some is stored, but most waste water—about 95%—is piped out to sewer plants, rivers, or other disposal sites. Among other plans, environmental scientists are working on methods to purify and recycle greywater (nontoilet waste water) for reuse. External strains from floods, droughts, or various contaminants can cause water supplies to be less than safe (Jordan-Bychkov and Domoch 1998). Water is but one example of the complex urban ecosystem with its interdependent parts.

To understand the urban ecosystem, its growth and its decay, we must understand that there are pressures on the city from both external sources and internal dynamics, as illustrated in the next topic.

Poverty in the World's Cities

Poor people are often invisible. Around the world, they are tucked away in enclaves most affluent people do not see. Until something brings attention to the poor, leaders and most of the citizenry can ignore them. Invisibility of urban poverty results because these residents have little power to make their problems public and little energy beyond that needed for survival. Earlier chapters addressed reasons for poverty and the groups who fall disproportionately into poverty. Urban residential patterns generally reflect the same patterns of poverty. The *permanent underclass* refers to the poor worldwide, people who do not have education or skills to become part of the local or world economy. Children leave school at young ages to help support their families, reducing their opportunities to get out of poverty. However, modernizing economies have little need for unskilled labor.

The *feminization of poverty* refers to the increase of women and their children in the ranks of the impoverished. This is a growing problem in rich and poor countries. The increasing numbers of teenage mothers who have little education, are unemployed, and have few prospects to get out of poverty result in their disproportionate representation among the homeless. (See the "Sociology in Our Social World" on page 552 for a discussion of the circumstances and coping strategies of homeless people.) One cause of feminization of poverty is divorces, which may leave women with small children and poor job prospects. Single-parent homes with a woman as the breadwinner are far more likely than other types of households to be in economic trouble, with poor housing, lack of education, and scant job opportunities.

In some cities, residents are working collectively for survival and improvement in their conditions. In Harlem, New York, some residents live in cooperatives and rental buildings that they manage, taken over after landlords abandoned the buildings. The "community household model" in which residents control their own housing may provide a new method of organization and leadership by tenants and community activists (Leavitt and Saegert 1990).

Crime and Delinquency in the City

Social disruption and crime are not intrinsic to cities. One can walk through many areas of Toronto, London, or Paris at night with little likelihood of problems. Traditional African cities had very low crime rates, but today, they are much less safe because of high numbers of new migrants. When people are transient, when they move frequently, they are more likely to experience *anomie*, to have less commitment to community norms, and to lack a sense of commitment to the norms and the well-being of the local community. Add to that the desperate situation of the very poor, and you have a recipe for crime.

 Journal Article Link 15.3 Read about homicide and urbanization.

As young people move from rural to urban life, juvenile delinquency becomes a problem. In rural communities and tribal cultures, strict norms govern behavior, but in urban areas, cohesiveness of families and ties with tribal groups are lessened. When education, economic security, and social services increase, conformity again becomes a norm for these newcomers, replacing the anomie of the transition.

A key message from the study of urbanization is that people's lives are influenced by the environment in which they live. Applied sociologists can play a role in improving the conditions of urban areas, as described in the "The Applied Sociologist at Work" on page 553.

Sociology in Our Social World

Understanding Urban Homeless People

Migration to urban areas can result in homeless people sleeping under bridges, in parks, in vacant lots, in unused subway tunnels, or even on the sidewalks of main thoroughfares. Although homelessness was frequently observed in Third World countries, it was uncommon in North American and European cities until the early 1980s. The two sociologists, David Snow and Leon Anderson (1993), undertook a study at the macro, meso, and micro levels of analysis to understand the processes of homelessness in America.

In 2009, there were an estimated 124,000 chronically homeless individuals living in the United States compared with 123,833 in 2007, 155,623 in 2006, and 175,914 in 2005. A total of 36.5% were chronic substance abusers, 26.3% were severely mentally ill, and 15% were veterans. On any given night, there are an estimated 664,000 homeless people (Interagency Council on Homelessness 2009). Housing and Urban Development (HUD) officials measure overall homelessness via funding applications for housing services and state that even this number is a large underestimation of the total number of people who experience homelessness (HUD 2008).

In trying to make sense of homelessness, the researchers identified key variables that distinguished different types of homelessness, uncovering a wide range of causes, circumstances, and coping methods. Snow and Anderson's (1993) work was a form of detective work—sorting through information and trying to understand the many dimensions of homelessness. Using macro-level perspectives, they looked at employment trends and wage labor issues in the larger society, social policies of the government designed to address poverty and homelessness. Meso-level issues involved study of family life and caregiving organizations. The researchers also considered the micro culture of street people, how they lend each other support and help each other make sense of their circumstances. They point to many forces at work on the homeless, from global economic trends to the way their families relate to them.

Perhaps the most intriguing findings of this study involved how people affirmed a sense of self in this humiliating situation. After all, to be a person of worth in American society is to (1) own some property, (2) have someone who cares about you enough to take you in if you are really desperate, and (3) occupy a significant status in society by earning some money and having a career or position deserving of respect. The homeless not only lack all these, their master status—"homeless person"—is one that elicits disrespect. "Dignity and worth are not primarily individual characteristics, but instead flow from the roles we play," write the authors (Snow and Anderson 1993:9). To be homeless, then, is far more than to be without a residence or shelter. It is to be without a place to restore one's dignity. So how did the homeless cope?

This research showed a number of coping strategies, only a few of which can be reported here. Sometimes, the homeless people explained away their circumstances as temporary "bad luck" or part of a normal cycle in which they just happened to be on the down end for a while. Sometimes, they would distance themselves from the role of homelessness, pointing out that they were "different" than other homeless people, "didn't really belong," and did not really deserve to be seen as homeless at all. Some people coped by fictive storytelling, pointing to pronounced achievements in the past (often fictionalized or embellished) or creating stories of their phenomenal accomplishments when they finally do get on their feet. By affirming another identity in the past or the future, their self-esteem was salvaged. However, perhaps the most surprising strategy to preserve self-worth was to embrace the role of being homeless with pride—to boast about how one was the best at being a survivor, the best at being a friend to the homeless, or the best at rejecting shallow values of materialism in our commercial society. They could thus affirm themselves for coping skills, for caring qualities, or for deep spirituality. They had defined reality in a way that allowed them to see themselves in a positive light. They had changed the social construction of reality, at least among themselves.

The Applied Sociologist at Work— Jay Weinstein

Improving Quality of Life by Transforming Community Structure

As is true of many urban centers, Detroit, Michigan, has its share of distressed neighborhoods. Dr. Jay Weinstein has been director of an interdisciplinary team attempting to bring about economic, social, and physical restructuring of some of these areas. By developing long-term relationships in several urban neighborhoods, the team has had success working with residents and others to improve conditions. Weinstein calls this approach *relationship brokering*—bringing people together to share perspectives and to clear up misperceptions between residents, local officials, service providers, and police. These efforts have helped empower residents to take action and improve their neighborhoods.

A major project along these lines, which began in 1990 and continues to the present, is in the Detroit suburb of Taylor, Michigan. For decades, residents of Taylor and the surrounding Down River area were painfully aware of the problems of their neighborhood, known by uncomplimentary names such as "Crack Ridge," "Hooker Heaven," and "Sin City." With about 7,500 people packed into an area of one-half square mile, most residents were living in rental units controlled by the U.S. Department of Housing and Urban Development Section 8 program (subsidized private housing).

An influential local newspaper published a series of articles showing that the neighborhood had earned the labels applied to it. The series exposed the high incidences of drug trafficking and use, prostitution, alcoholism, and violent crimes in the neighborhood. The people living in Down River were only too familiar with the situation. Nevertheless, the articles inspired local and federal political leaders to demand action.

Weinstein and his colleagues were awarded an applied research grant by the City of Taylor Department of Community Development. The purposes of the work were to assess the problems by providing reliable data and to make recommendations to improve the community. The fact-finding stage revealed that the residents of the neighborhood were not the main perpetrators. Instead, the area had been under siege by nonresidents who came and went, drifted from apartment to apartment, or illegally occupied residences after threatening to harm the rightful owners.

Based on these and other findings, the research team recommended a plan for a thorough physical, economic, social, and political reconstruction of the neighborhood. Fortunately, city and federal officials understood the value of such sociological expertise. With few reservations, they accepted the recommendations of the sociological team and set out on a 10-year program of implementation. Working with residents of the neighborhood and other citizens of the city, Taylor's mayor, city council, Department of Human Resources, police department, and many others tackled the problem, with Weinstein and his colleagues' help.

Today, the neighborhood has a new name (The Villages of Taylor), a new human services center, a new residential owner (a private nonprofit corporation established by the city), and many new or redesigned buildings. The population density has been reduced by more than 20% and all this without one person being displaced against his or her will, other than drug dealers. The average median income of Taylor is now higher than the national average, and this has led to several new housing developments.

After receiving national attention, Taylor was called "a model for the nation" by the secretary of Housing and Urban Development. Many communities have looked to Taylor to see their plans for redevelopment. In one of the most treasured moments of his life, Weinstein attended the official dedication of The Villages of Taylor.

For Weinstein, sociological theory is at the root of his neighborhood work. He tries to identify the "definitions of reality" held by the residents and then helps residents examine those definitions, a symbolic interaction approach. Only by understanding their definitions can residents begin to act to change the situation.

In his work, Weinstein uses a multiple-methods approach: surveys, participant observation, census data, and other large data sets. Each technique has strengths and limitations. Using a variety of approaches in combination brings him closer to the elusive truths of social life.

Note: Dr. Jay Weinstein, a professor at Eastern Michigan University, specializes in urban sociology, demography, and social change. He received his doctorate from the University of Illinois, Champaign–Urbana. He has been doing private consulting for more than 20 years, with contracts from international and local governments and nonprofit organizations. His studies have included analysis of demographic trends and changes in India, Albania, Bulgaria, and Jamaica.

Urban Planners and Social Policy in the Global Social World

Try planning an ideal city. First, list everything you need to consider. Now think of organization: Who will handle what? Consider services, maintenance, financing, and leadership.

In the urban Global South, many homeless people must bathe every day in public in whatever water supply they can find. Here in Kolkata (Calcutta), India, even some people with homes would not have their own water supply and would have to use fire hydrants on the streets, as this group is doing.

Although cities have many problems, they are exciting bustling places to live or to visit. Some of the liveliness of urban neighborhoods is depicted in this street scene in Bhaktapur, Nepal.

This would be quite a task. The problem is that most urban planners do not have the luxury of starting from scratch. They must work with decaying areas, being cognizant of the meaningful landmarks and treasured sites. Planners may also have to undo hasty or inadequate planning from previous actions. Among other things, they attempt to maximize technical efficiency such as getting water from Point A to Point B.

Planners must meet needs for housing, sanitation, education, food distribution, jobs, family life, and recreation. Planning efforts need to take into consideration what will happen to various groups, including the poor, elderly, women, children, and homeless populations.

In the early 21st century, a number of global trends affected urban planning (Brunn et al. 2003):

1. The process of urbanization—people migrating to cities—will continue, exacerbating the already difficult situation of providing services for many of the world's crowded urban areas.

2. Information and transportation technologies allow people in any part of the globe to be in contact. However, this may also reduce the feelings of belonging to a specific place, reducing commitment to work on city problems.

3. International boundaries will diminish in importance as the flow of information, goods, services, labor, and capital increasingly ignores national boundaries. For example, migration of Asians to cities around the world will continue and will have an impact on these cities.

4. Economies will increasingly rely on brain work, including invention of new technologies, rather than on the brawn work of older manufacturing. Thus, the gap between haves and have-nots is likely to continue.

5. Conflicts between cultural and political groups, including religious and political extremists, will continue to affect urban life.

6. *McDonaldization*—creation of a consumer world dominated by major Western food, music, fashion, and entertainment—will continue, even as we see an increasing diversity of people within Western nations and communities.

Awareness of these trends can help urban planners in their efforts to design cities to meet the needs of the future (Friedman 2006).

In the past, men were designers of cities, but women also experience them. Some analysts believe that women's experiences in the city are quite different from men's. Spaces that have been designed with women in mind emphasize opportunities for participation, involvement in community development, and leisure activities such as informal places for meeting (Hayden and Baron 2007; Renzetti 2003). In the United Kingdom, social science research has informed urban development and renewal with women as consultants (UNESCO 2009). Unfortunately, profit is often the motivation in planning models, and few planning efforts consider cities in a holistic fashion. Urban planners in socialist countries with centralized national plans for urban areas may find it easier to consider the needs of all residents.

Millions of people live satisfying lives in cities, but for others, life is misery. Whether the economic base and urban planners can keep up with the demands for even basic services in the Global South remains to be seen. This is especially true in areas of the world where population is outstripping the amount of land available, and people are flocking to cities for survival. This basic population pattern—urbanization—has consequences at the most global levels and at the most micro levels of human life. Our social world model—which looks at the connections of micro, meso, and macro levels of the social system—makes us cognizant of the consequences of decisions made by millions of individuals and families. It also makes us mindful of the consequences for individuals and for cities of global trends and forces.

Many factors including population dynamics and urbanization create change in a society. Some factors contributing to social dynamics push for innovation and change in a particular direction, and other factors retard change. The next chapter examines the larger picture of social transformation and change in our complex and multileveled social world.

What Have We Learned?

Population trends, including migration resulting in urbanization, provide a dynamic force for change in societies. Whether one is interested in understanding social problems, social policy, or factors that may affect one's own career, demographic processes are critical forces. We ignore them at our peril—as individuals and as a society. Family businesses can be destroyed, retirement plans obliterated, and the health of communities sabotaged by population factors if they are overlooked. If they are considered, however, they can enhance planning that leads to prosperity and enjoyment of our communities. Urban living creates problems, but it can have enormous benefits as well. Urbanization is but a single example of a population trend.

Key Points

- Population analysis (called demography) looks at the composition, distribution, and size of a population as the society is affected by variables of fertility, mortality, and migration. (See pp. 514–516.)

- The planetwide increase in the human population's fertility is stunning. Implications for adequate resources to support life are illustrated in the population pyramids. (See pp. 516–519.)

- Various theories explain causes of the rapid growth, ranging from medical technology to cultural factors. (See pp. 519–523.)

- Many institutions affect and are affected by fertility and mortality rates at the meso level—political policies, religious beliefs, economic factors, education, and health care. (See pp. 523–528.)

- Migration is also an important issue for the society—whether the migration is international or internal—for it can change the size, distribution, and composition of a nation's citizenry. (See pp. 530–533.)

- Population patterns can also affect individual decisions at the micro level, from career choices to business decisions to programs that will affect retirement possibilities. (See pp. 533–536.)

- A major element of population migration has been urbanization. As populations become more densely concentrated, this creates a series of opportunities and problems for meeting human needs. (See pp. 536–538.)

- At the micro level, human relationships are affected by having widespread or dense population concentration. In urban areas, social relations may be less closely knit. On the negative side, this creates anomie and alienation. On the positive side, it provides more choices for people about their social relationships and lifestyles. (See pp. 538–541.)

- Cities themselves are extremely complex meso-level social settings that vary in size and operations. (See pp. 541–548.)

- At the macro level, urban environments must be understood as ecosystems that have dense poverty and homelessness, major pollution issues, and higher crime rates. These are the focus of urban planners, who try to use sociological knowledge to plan for a better future. (See pp. 548–555.)

Contributing to Our Social World: What Can We Do?

At the Local Level

U.S. Census Bureau: Invite a representative to your campus to discuss the bureau's activities.

Local department of urban planning, urban and regional development, or community development: Invite a representative to campus. Discuss how population information is used in planning and service delivery contexts. Consider an internship with one of the listed organizations.

Neighborhood recreation departments, crime watch, or community-organizing agencies: Volunteer to provide services or to help neighbors solve problems and work with local government.

At the Organizational or Institutional Level

Urban planning, urban and regional development, community development, and similar municipal, regional, and state

departments: These organizations often use volunteers and hire interns. Contact one of these organizations and explore the possibility of making a contribution and/or exploring interest in this field.

At the National and Global Levels

Planned Parenthood (www.plannedparenthood.org): This national organization promotes family planning education and outreach programs throughout the United States. The organization uses volunteers and interns, as well as providing long-term employment opportunities.

The Population Council (www.popcouncil.org): This organization conducts research worldwide to improve policies, programs, and products in three areas: HIV and AIDS; poverty, gender, and youth; and reproductive health. Its Web site discusses several ways to get involved, locally as well as globally.

For chapter-specific resources, including **Frontline**, **TED**, and **YouTube** videos; self-quizzes; web exercises; and more, visit **www.pineforge.com/oswmedia3e.**

CHAPTER

16

The Process of Change

Can We Make a Difference?

Individuals are profoundly influenced by the macro structures around them, but people are also capable of creating change, especially if they band together with others and approach change in an organized way. Social movements such as those depicted in the photos above are one powerful way to bring about change.

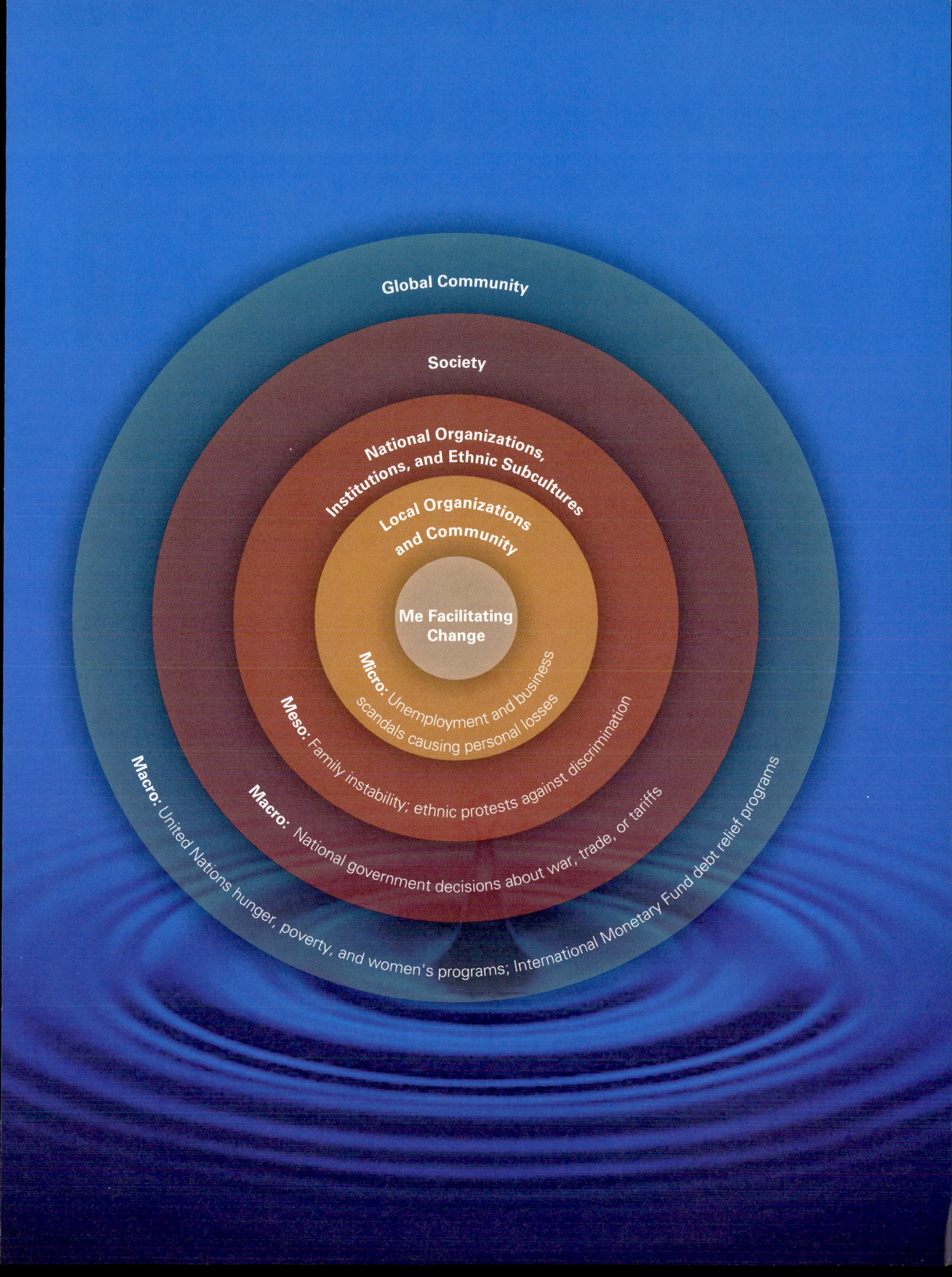

Global Community

Society

National Organizations,
Institutions, and Ethnic Subcultures

Local Organizations
and Community

Me Facilitating
Change

Micro: Unemployment and business
scandals causing personal losses

Meso: Family instability; ethnic protests against discrimination

Macro: National government decisions about war, trade, or tariffs

Macro: United Nations hunger, poverty, and women's programs; International Monetary Fund debt relief programs

Think About It	
Me (and My Inner Circle)	Can you as an individual bring about change in the world?
Local Community	How does change at the micro level of the social world affect change at the other levels?
National Institutions; Complex Organizations; Ethnic Groups	What organizational or ethnic community factors enhance or hinder social change?
National Society	How does the training and support for technological innovation affect the process of change in a country?
Global Community	How do global changes—such as climate change—affect people and societies at each level?

The planet is in peril—according to evidence from the Asian subcontinent to the Arctic and from Africa to the Americas (Intergovernmental Panel on Climate Change 2007; United Nations Climate Change Conference 2009). A major part of this problem is the waste humans create. Wet, dry, smelly, and sometimes recyclable—garbage is a problem. We are running out of space to dispose of our refuse. We dump it in the ocean and see garbage surfacing on beaches and killing fish. We bury it in land fills, and the surrounding land becomes toxic. We sort and recycle it, creating other problems (Pellow 2002). Perhaps your community or campus has separate bins for glass, cans, paper, and garbage. Recycling is a relatively new movement in response to the urgent pleas from environmentalists about our garbage and trash, polluted water sources, dying oceans, and the depletion of renewable resources.

Recycling, salvaging items that can be reused, is part of a social reform movement—the environmental movement. However, few issues have simple solutions. The dumping and recycling have to take place somewhere. Many of the recycling plants and trash dumps are located in areas where poor people and minorities live. Some have referred to this as *environmental racism*, in which ethnic minorities are put at risk by the diseases and pollutants that recycling entails (Black Politics on the Web 2009; Pellow 2002).This illustrates the complexity of global problems: While we may help solve problems at one level of analysis, others may be created. At the micro level, each of us can do our part in the environmental movement to save the planet through responsible personal actions. At the meso level, the environmental movement can help local and regional governments enact policies and plans to reduce the garbage problem, and at the macro level, world leaders need to find responsible ways to dispose of environmental wastes. Yet the solution to this macro-level issue of protecting the earth's resources may have micro-level implications for local minority families. Our social world is, indeed, complex and interdependent.

Turn on the morning or evening news, and there are lessons about other aspects of our changing social world. We see headlines about medical advances and cures for disease; biological breakthroughs in cloning and the DNA code; terrorist bombings in Israel, Iraq, Pakistan, Chechnya, and other parts of the world; famine in drought-afflicted sub-Saharan Africa; disasters such as earthquakes, hurricanes, tsunamis, and floods; and social activists calling for boycott of Wal-Mart, chocolate, coffee, oil companies, or other multinational corporations. Some events seem far away and hard to imagine: thousands killed by a tidal wave in India, hundreds swept away by mud from an erupting volcano in Colombia, massive oil spill in Gulf of Mexico, or a rise in terrorism reflecting divisions in world economic, political, and religious ideologies. Some of these are natural events, but most are the result of human actions.

Social change is defined as variations or alterations over time in the behavior patterns, culture (including norms and values), and structure of society. Some change is controllable, and some is out of our hands, but change is inevitable and ubiquitous. Change can be rapid, caused by some disruption to the existing system, or it can be gradual and evolutionary. Very often, change at one level in the social world occurs because of change at another level. Micro, meso, and macro levels of society often work together in the change process but are sometimes out of sync.

In this chapter, we explore the process of change, the causes of change, and some strategies for bringing about desired change. We consider the complexity of change in our social world, explanations and theories of social change, the role of collective behavior in bringing about change, planned change in organizations, and macro-level social movements, technology, and environmental actions as they affect and are affected by change.

Our social world model is based on the assumption that change, whether evolutionary or revolutionary, is inevitable and ever present in the social world. The impetus for change may begin at the micro, meso, or macro level of analysis. Studies of the change process are not complete, however, until the level under study is understood in relation to other levels in the model, for each level affects the others in a multiplicity of ways.

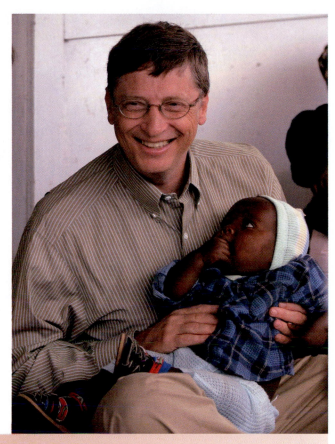

Mother Teresa, an Italian nun who devoted her life to helping the destitute and dying in India, established the orphanage shown here in Kolkata (Calcutta) (left). In the other photo, Bill Gates (right) holds a child who is receiving a trial malaria vaccine at a medical research center in Mozambique. Gates announced a grant of $168 million to fight malaria, a disease that kills more than 1 million people a year, 90% of them children in Africa. Sometimes, social change occurs because of individual initiatives.

Thinking Sociologically

In what ways do you take actions to lessen your impact on the environment? Might your activities be linked to worsening conditions for ethnic minorities or the planet?

The Complexity of Change in Our Social World

The Yir Yorant, a group of Australian aborigines, have long believed that if their own ancestors did not do something, then they must not do it. It would be wrong and might cause evil to befall the group (Sharp 1990). Obviously, these are not a people who favor change or innovation. In contrast, *progress* is a positive word in much of Australia and in other countries where change is seen as normal, even

desirable. The traditions, cultural beliefs of a society, and internal and external pressures all affect the degree and rate of change in society.

Change at the Individual Level: Micro-Level Analysis

One of the nation's top entrepreneurs, Microsoft's Bill Gates, combines intelligence, business acumen, and philanthropy, qualities that appeal to American individualism. Gates has the power to influence others because of his fame, wealth, and personal charisma. He is able to bring about change in organizations through his ability to motivate people and set wheels in motion. Many people have persuasive power to influence decision making, but it is not always based on charisma. For some, it is due to expertise, wealth or privileged position, information, or even the ability to use coercive force. Any of us, if we are diligent and can rally others around an issue of concern, can bring about change in society. Each individual in society has the potential to be a change agent.

Most organizations—schools, businesses, volunteer organizations—use one or more of the following strategies to persuade individuals to accept change: They appeal to individuals' values, they use persuasion by presenting hard data and logic, they convince individuals that the existing benefits of change outweigh the costs, they remove uncooperative individuals from the organization, they provide rewards or sanctions for acceptance of change to alter the cost-benefit ratio, or they compel individuals to change by an order from authority figures. Thus, individuals are active agents who initiate and bring about change.

Change at the Institutional Level: Meso-Level Analysis

The terrorist attacks of September 11, 2001, which killed 3,025 innocent people from 68 nations, resulted in repercussions in many U.S. institutions. Local, state, and national governments responded by putting in place measures to deter any further attacks and to seek out and punish the guilty parties. Religious services had high attendance in the weeks following 9/11 as religious leaders and members tried to make sense of the brutal attacks. Some families lost loved ones. Other families were soon separated as the military and the National Guard were called into action. Security measures were stepped up at airports and other transportation centers.

Encyclopedia Link 16.1
Read more about social movements.

People at the local (micro) level will often try to influence policies at the meso level. At this local community event, people lobby their neighbors on a state referendum in an upcoming election.

These institutions at the meso level—government, religion, the family, the military—guided the response to the attacks.

Terrorism refers to "the use of indiscriminate violence to cause mass fear and panic to intimidate a population and advance one's political goals, whatever they may be" (Nolan 2002a:1648). This usually refers to acts of violence by private nonstate groups. In 2006, there were 14,000 terrorist attacks around the world, which killed 20,000 people. These figures were up 25% from 2005, boosted by the insurgencies in Iraq (CNN.com 2007). Contemporary terrorism is a meso-level phenomenon, even though it has both personal and global ramifications. Most modern terrorist organizations are not nations. They are ethnic, political, or religious subgroups that have elicited passionate loyalty from followers—even to the point of suicide on behalf of the group and its ideology.

Terrorism also has consequences for economies and other institutions. Not only do terrorist acts destabilize economies, but they change the kinds of jobs that are available. Consider the new jobs created in airport and seaport security. In addition to new jobs, investors hesitate to invest if they think the economy will be negatively affected, and this lack of investment can spawn a recession. Economic disruptions or ripple effects are a core motivating factor for terrorists. Furthermore, after 9/11, health care professionals began to make plans for biological and chemical terrorist attacks, changing the way monies are allocated in the health care industry (O'Toole and Henderson 2006). Thus, terrorism is a concern of the medical institution as well.

Change at the National and Global Levels: Macro-Level Analysis

To understand why terrorism occurs around the world, we must look at some of the driving forces. The unequal distribution of world resources has inspired deep anger toward affluent countries among the poor countries, which believe that the rich are using their power to maintain the inequities. High-income countries consume over $22,000 billion in resources (World Resources Institute 2007). That amounts to 76.6% of the world's resources for 20% of the world's people. The world's middle-income countries, with 60% of the world's people, consume 21.9% of the world's resources, and the world's poorest people consume 1.5% of resources (Shah 2009b). U.S. citizens make up only 4.6% of the total world population, yet the United States accounted for 33% of the consumed resources in the world in 2004 (World Resources Institute 2007) and 25% of the world's energy resources (Shah 2009b). The average U.S. citizen consumes six times more energy than the world average (U.S. Department of Energy 2006). This seems grossly unfair to people who can barely feed their families and who have limited electricity, water, and sanitation and minimal shelter for their children. Furthermore, wealthy countries have considerable economic influence over the nations of the Global South because poor countries are dependent on the affluent countries for income, employment, and loans. Citizens of poor countries may work for multinational corporations, often for very low wages. However, the profits are returned to the wealthy countries, helping perpetuate the gross inequity in the distribution of resources. Whether or not we think it is justified, this inequity leads to hostilities and sometimes terrorism as a means of striking out against more powerful countries.

The 9/11 attack was partially motivated by Middle Easterners who were intensely pro-Palestinian and anti-Israeli. Of the hijackers, 15 of the 19 were originally from Saudi Arabia; none was actually Iraqi, and none actually lived in Palestine, but they sympathized with those who had been displaced by the establishment of Israel. From the terrorist perspective, the attack on the New York City World Trade Center was an attempt to strike out at the United States. September 11 was a symbolic date, the day when Britain declared control of Palestine. This set off a chain of events leading to the United Nations granting the land to Jews to establish Israel. Many Middle Easterners felt this was unjust because the Palestinians lost the country in which they had been living. Moreover, the Camp David Accords, which established Israel's right to exist in the Middle East, were signed on September 11, 1979. So on two counts, this date had powerful symbolic meaning for the people who were displaced from Palestine.

The events of September 11 changed the United States as a nation and the core issues, priorities, and spending of the Bush presidency. George W. Bush's administration proposed, and Congress approved, a Patriot Act that channeled resources into heightened security and military preparedness. The provisions of the bill also greatly restricted civil liberties and allowed the government to snoop into the private lives of citizens in ways that had never before been tolerated, from monitoring the home telephone connections of Americans to scrutinizing the books they checked out of the library. Fear for their security led many U.S. citizens to welcome the efforts to prevent further attacks, although the root causes of terrorism were not addressed.

Following September 11, many state governments mandated more intense patriotism training and rituals in schools, with additions to the curriculum and daily loyalty ceremonies. The No Child Left Behind education bill, which was passed by Congress in 2002, also mandated that school personnel turn over personal information about students to military recruiters, including private information that had previously not been available to anyone but the student and the school personnel (Ayers 2006; Westheimer 2006).

Thinking Sociologically

How has terrorism affected institutions and countries with which you are familiar? Has your life been changed by threats of terrorism?

Revolutionary groups with terrorist tactics operate at the meso level, trying to change society by intimidating the citizens and governments so they will change their policies. In this photo, we see the memorial site for victims of the bombing of a federal building in Oklahoma City—a terrorist act by members of a "patriot group" that was opposed to governmental policies. The small chairs are for the deceased children, who were in a day care center in the destroyed building.

Societal-Level Change

To illustrate the increasingly complex and biologically interdependent social world, consider that pollution of the environment by any one country now threatens other countries. Carcinogens, acid rain, and other airborne chemicals carry across national boundaries (Brecher, Costello, and Smith 2006). About 5% of the world's population emits 25% of the heat-trapping gases (Lindsay 2006). Pollutants can also affect the air that surrounds the entire planet, destroying the ozone that protects us from the intense sun rays and warming the planet in ways that could threaten all of us.

 Video Link 16.1 Think about the relationship between media and social change.

In the past century, scientists claim, the earth's surface has warmed by 1°. That does not sound like much until one considers that during the last ice age, the earth's surface was only 7° cooler than today. Small variations can make a huge difference, and we do not know what the consequences might be if the earth's surface temperature increases by another 2° or 3°. Currently, sea ice is melting each year at a rate that equals the size of Maryland and Delaware combined (Cousteau 2008; Lindsay 2006). It is alarming to visit the glaciers on the South Island of New Zealand (closest to Antarctica) and realize that they are melting so fast that they have receded by as much as 10 or 12 miles in just a couple of decades. In a warmer world, there is less snowfall, resulting in smaller mountain icecaps and, thus, a smaller runoff in spring (Struck 2007). This causes major water shortages. While some of the environmental change may be rooted in natural causes, the preponderance of the evidence suggests that human activity—the way we consume and the way we live our lives—is the primary cause (Gore 2006). Even if humans were not a significant cause, the global climate change has consequences that mandate change. What happens when people do not have enough water in their current location to survive? What happens when they try to move into someone else's territory?

Obviously, this is a global issue with implications for nations to work together for change. Yet some nations resist change because they feel controls will impede progress. U.S. President Bush rejected the Kyoto Treaty on global warming because it "does not make economic sense," and his trusted adviser, Condoleezza Rice, bluntly asserted, "Kyoto is dead" (Lindsay 2006:310–311). The Obama administration has reversed this stand and supports dramatic efforts to curb climate change and global warming. At the 2009 Copenhagen Climate Change Conference, December 7 to 18, 2009, nations agreed to a broad framework to reduce carbon emissions and provide help to poor nations dealing with the effects of climate change.

Fixing the environmental issues will be expensive, it may hinder the economy and slow the rate of growth, and it may even stimulate a recession. Because recessions are terrifying for any elected politician who aims to keep the public happy, change is not easy. Still, most of the world's nations have signed the Kyoto Treaty, and there is continuing pressure on the United States to sign. Because nations are still the most powerful units for allocating resources and for setting policy, changes in national policies that address the issues of a shared environment are of critical importance. The two big quandaries are (1) the costs and benefits to various nations of participating in a solution and (2) the question of time—will nations respond before it is too late to make a difference? Currently, most of the cost of pollution is accruing to impoverished countries, while rich nations benefit from the status quo. International treaties could change that.

Global Systems and Change

As the world becomes increasingly interconnected and interdependent, the impetus for change comes from global organizations, national and international organizations and governments, and multinational corporations. New and shifting alliances between international organizations and countries link together nations, form international liaisons, and create changing economic and political systems. The following international alliances between countries, for example, are based primarily on economic ties:

- SADC: Southern African Development Community
- NAFTA: North American Free Trade Agreement
- CEFTA: Central European Free Trade Agreement
- CAFTA: Central American Free Trade Agreement
- ASEAN: Association of Southeast Asian Nations
- WIPO: World Intellectual Property Organization
- G8: Group of Eight
- OPEC: Organization of Petroleum Exporting Countries
- ADP: Asian Development Bank
- EFTA: European Free Trade Association
- EEA: European Economic Area
- APEC: Asia-Pacific Economic Cooperation
- EU: European Union
- SEATO: Southeast Asian Treaty Organization

Consider NAFTA, which was initiated in 1993 to establish a free trade area between Canada, the United States, and Mexico in order to facilitate trade in the region. Promoters, including many global corporations, promised that the agreement would create thousands of new high-wage jobs, raise living standards in each of the countries, improve environmental conditions, and transform Mexico from a poor developing country into a booming new market. Opponents (including labor unions, environmental organizations, consumer groups, and religious groups) argued the opposite—that NATFA would reduce wages; destroy jobs, especially in the United States; undermine democratic policy making in North America by giving corporations a free rein; and threaten health, the environment,

Environmental destruction and global climate change are problems that necessitate cooperation among nations. Air pollution around China's Three Rivers Gorge reduces visibility and creates health hazards.

and food safety (American Cultural Center Resource Service 2004; Public Citizen's Global Trade Watch 2003; U.S. Trade Representative 2003).

Analyses of the agreement show mixed results. There is some indication that tariffs are down and U.S. exports have increased. The treaty countries produced $15.3 billion in goods and services, and trade tripled between 1993 and 2007 to $903 billion. Some Mexican markets are doing well and have weathered global economic crises, and there is growth in manufacturing in Mexico. Some argue that there is improvement in the areas of environmental protection and labor rights, but others argue that these have declined. The truth is hard to determine but probably lies somewhere in between (Amadeo 2009).

On the other hand, it appears that regulations on product quality and environmental pollution have been reduced, U.S. trade deficits have increased, immigration from poorer to wealthier countries has resulted in tensions, income inequality has increased, and perhaps as many as 3 million—1 in 6—manufacturing jobs in the United States have been lost. It is clear that NAFTA has resulted in change at all levels in the social world, from restructuring of economies at the national and global levels to affecting individual job security and availability. The overall verdict on the impact of NAFTA is still out.

The principle is that change at one level of the social world leads to change in other levels, as it did in the global example of NAFTA and the societal, community, and individual examples of terrorism and climate change. Changes at the macro level affect individuals, just as change at the micro level has repercussions at the meso and macro levels.

Different belief systems (political, religious, economic, and social) within a society can also have a major effect on the type and rate of change. For example, some religious groups oppose stem cell research, which uses the cells of fetuses, most of which were created in test tubes. Others within the same congregation believe this research will alleviate the suffering of loved ones and save lives. Although both sides believe they are pro life, the internal strain in the religious group emanates from events and forces in science, medicine, and other institutions.

Stresses, those pressures for change that come from the organization's external environment, can be traced to several sources: the natural environment, population dynamics, actions of leaders, technologies, other institutions, and major historical events.

Video Link 16.2
Watch a lecture about solving social problems.

The natural environment can bring about either slow or dramatic change in a society. Natural disasters such as floods, hurricanes, tsunamis, heavy snows, earthquakes, volcanic eruptions, mud slides, tornadoes, and other sudden events are not planned occurrences, but they can have dramatic consequences. Disease epidemics are often unpredictable, such as the cholera outbreak in Zimbabwe that killed more than 4,000 people in 2008–2009 and a new outbreak due to polluted water that is increasing the death toll (Rusere 2009). Natural disasters are so important that the sociology of disasters has become a specialty field within the discipline, as indicated by one of the classic sociological studies of disasters, reported in the next "Sociology in Our Social World."

Social Change: Process and Theories

The Process of Social Change

Something always triggers a social change. The impetus may come from within the organization, the source known as **strain**. Sometimes, it comes from outside the organization, what sociologists call **stress**. Let us consider two examples of strain: (1) conflicting goals and (2) different belief systems within the organization.

Conflicting goals are seen in the case of the steel industry and its workers. Individual workers' goals are to meet their basic needs for food and shelter for their families by holding jobs. Company goals focus entirely on profit. In Pittsburgh and Cleveland, many steel companies closed down or moved to less costly sites because of lack of profits due to changing economic demands and competition. This created massive unemployment. People who had created hopeful futures for themselves and their families were left without jobs.

Natural disasters—floods, hurricanes, tornadoes, earthquakes, volcanic eruptions—can be the cause of major social changes in a community. As shown in this photo from a community on Lake Pontchartrain near New Orleans, Hurricane Katrina took its toll on Mississippi and Louisiana.

Sociology in Our Social World

Disasters and Their Aftermath

A series of small villages were settled along a mountain creek in West Virginia known as Buffalo Creek. This was mining country, and at the top of the creek, a coal company had poured more than 1 million tons of wastewater and coal waste into a company-created basin. The restraining embankment of shale, clay, slag, and low-quality coal that created the reservoir was referred to by the coal company as an "impoundment," but the people themselves referred to it as a "dam."

Whatever one called it, this restraining wall was weakened by heavy rains in the winter of 1972, and on February 26, it broke, setting forth a massive flood of black sludge and oily, slag-filled wastewater down the valley toward the homes of 5,000 residents in the mountain villages. The first village hit was not just crushed, it disappeared entirely. This meant that the villages farther down the creek bed had not just filthy water coming at them but the remains of homes, churches, stores, vehicles, and bodies. By the time the water subsided, the flood had taken with it almost everything in its path.

Newspapers reported the economic loss and the staggering death toll, but lawyers, psychologists, and sociologists were interested in the human cost to survivors—costs to their sense of self, their mental and emotional well-being, and their family and friendship ties. Here was a community that had had an extraordinarily close-knit social network, where crime was virtually nonexistent, divorces were extraordinary, chemical abuse and mental problems were far below the national norms, and neighborhoods were like extended families. Yet the community had been ripped apart by the flood. Time had not healed the social and emotional wounds, even years after the flood: Few marriages remained intact, problems of deviance and delinquency were rife, and more than 90% of the people interviewed were judged to be in need of psychological counseling.

The federal government's response to the flood in Buffalo Creek dealt mostly with the immediate needs for survival. Thus, mobile homes were brought in, and emergency food was provided, but people were placed in these shelters without taking into account their existing ties with family members, friends, and neighbors. Thus, people found themselves surrounded by strangers at a time when they desperately needed support and when they also had few interpersonal resources to forge new relationships.

The mental health symptoms tied to individual trauma include psychic numbness (feeling mentally blank and emotionally limp), constant anxiety about death, guilt at having survived when so many members of one's family had not, guilt for not having saved people who were seen being swept down the river, loss of the "furniture of self" (the symbols of one's life that might include one's home, family

heirlooms, photographs of loved ones, and other artifacts that connect one to others and to a personal history), and loss of trust in the order of the universe or a loving God, who people believed was in control of life's events.

The "collective trauma" was more important to understand than the individual trauma: "People find it difficult to recover from the effects of individual trauma so long as the community around them remains in shreds" (Erikson 1976:155). The collective trauma included five dimensions:

1. *Disorientation:* Erikson (1976) found that many persons were so socially displaced that they could hardly orient themselves in time and space, even 2 or 3 years after the flood.
2. *Loss of morale and morality:* Following the flood, people were more likely to commit deviant acts and to think they were surrounded by immoral people.
3. *Loss of connection:* Marriages began to disintegrate, and people lost their sense of connection to others. "Members of a family find that intimacy and gentleness are hard to sustain in an emotional atmosphere as dry as this one," reports Erikson (1976:221).
4. *Illness and identity:* People seemed to feel that the land was polluted and untrustworthy, with some people being afraid to till the soil lest they find a body part of a family member or a neighbor buried there. Because the land was polluted, many people felt their own bodies were polluted, too.
5. *Loss of a sense of safety:* People slept in their clothes and boots, and whenever it rained, many residents would run to the creek every hour to check on the water levels.

This disaster at Buffalo Creek indicates how much of our personal mental health rests in the health of the larger community. It helps us understand how anomie (normlessness) can create anxiety and disorientation. Most of all, it helps us understand that natural disasters and human catastrophes, such as the September 11 terrorist attacks, devastating storms such as Hurricane Katrina, and the daily killings in Iraq, can have pervasive effects on individuals and communities. Although Erikson has been a leading figure in outlining what steps to take after a disaster, his work is not always considered when larger policies are made.

Work on collective trauma forces us to be aware of the extent to which we depend on a larger community to regain our footing when a disaster disrupts our lives. We humans are, indeed, profoundly social beings. Changes that disrupt our social ties can have severe and wide-ranging consequences.

Thinking Sociologically

First, read the feature on "Disasters and Their Aftermath." What lessons can we take from Erikson's findings to shed light on recent natural disasters with which you are familiar?

Epidemics such as the SARS (severe acute respiratory syndrome) threat have brought about change in the World Health Organization, global medical reporting systems, and response networks. For instance, the Global Public Health Intelligence Network scans Internet communications for rumors and reports of suspicious diseases. This way, health organizations from the local to global levels can act quickly to contain the spread of deadly epidemics.

Less rapid natural changes also can have incremental but dramatic effects. For example, most scientists predict that the climatic changes resulting from the greenhouse effect are warming our atmosphere, transforming agricultural land areas into deserts, raising sea levels about 1 meter in this century, causing ice sheets to melt, increasing rainfall in currently dry areas, and intensifying the strength of hurricanes. This warming of the earth's atmosphere results from a buildup of carbon dioxide or other gases (Environmental Protection Agency 2004). The majority of scientists are convinced that global warming is a human-generated problem and a genuine threat to our survival. However, policy change is the responsibility of political powers (Lindsay 2006).

Without human intervention to address the causes, change in the climate will affect habitable land areas, very possibly create disasters that cost great amounts of money, and increase the cost of living for ordinary people, thus changing their lifestyles. In the film *An Inconvenient Truth*, former U.S. vice president and presidential candidate Al Gore (2006) addresses the threat and what the world needs to do to save the environment.

Population dynamics—birth and death rates, size of populations, age distribution, and migration patterns—can be important contributors to external stress on organizations. Where populations are growing at extremely rapid rates, strains on government systems result in an inability to meet the basic needs of the people. Values and beliefs regarding childbearing, knowledge of birth control, and the position of women in society are some of the crucial social variables in addressing the ability to meet needs. Immigration due to political upheavals or motivated by anticipated economic opportunities creates stress on the societies that receive the newcomers as they attempt to meet the immigrants' needs. For example, many refugees from the Darfur region in Sudan are fleeing to camps in the nearby country of Chad. Maps 16.1 and 16.2 show visually the global hot spots for refugees and others who have been uprooted or displaced from their homelands.

Leaders or dominant individuals influence change through their policy decisions or the social movements they help generate. India's Mohandas K. (Mahatma) Gandhi taught the modern world ways of bringing about change in political systems through nonviolent methods. The policies of Charles Taylor, former military dictator of Liberia, created long-term war and resulted in thousands of deaths. President Mugabe of Zimbabwe has locked his country in a downward spiral of economic turmoil and disease, killing thousands. These leaders' actions created internal strains in their own countries and external stressors resulting in change in the international community.

Technology also influences societal change. William F. Ogburn (1933) compiled a list of 150 social changes in the United States that resulted from the invention of the radio, such as instant access to information. Other lists could be compiled for cell phones, automobiles, television, and computers. Some of these changes give rise to secondary changes. For example, automobile use led to paved highways, complex systems of traffic patterns and rules, and gasoline stations. The next "Sociology in Our Social World" explores several issues involving the automobile and change.

Thinking Sociologically

First, read "Sociology in Our Social World" on page 569 What might be some long-term social consequences for our individual lives and societies of the expanded use of the computer, the microwave oven, or the cell phone?

New arrivals at Al Salaam camp, in Sudan's Darfur region, make temporary shelters out of household goods they were able to carry with them. A U.S. Agency for International Development (USAID)-supported program at this site is helping register more than 10,000 people who were displaced by violence in their home regions. Migration is a major factor in social change, and in cases like this, it is associated with great suffering and hardship.

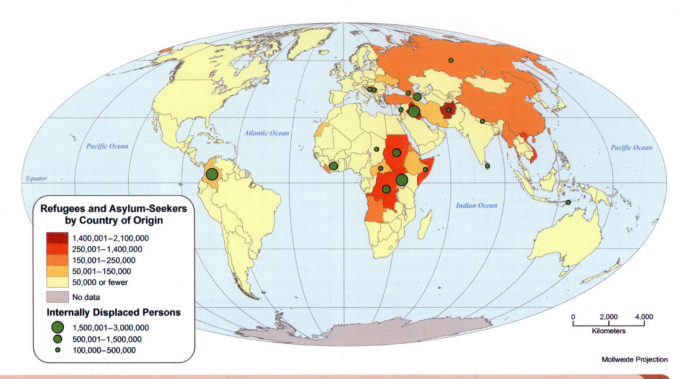

Map 16.1 Refugees, Asylum Seekers, and Internally Displaced People by Their Country of Origin, 2006

Source: United Nations Commission on Human Rights (2006). Map by Anna Versluis.

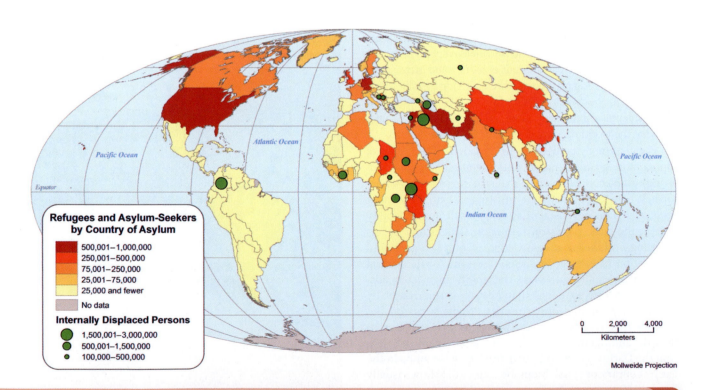

Map 16.2 Refugees, Asylum Seekers, and Internally Displaced People by Their Country of Asylum, 2006

Source: United Nations Commission on Human Rights (2006). Map by Anna Versluis.

Sociology in Our Social World

Technology and Change: The Automobile

Only a century ago, a newfangled novelty was spreading quickly from urban areas to the countryside: the automobile. At the turn of the 20th century, this strange, horseless carriage was often referred to as the "devil wagon" in rural areas. The introduction of this self-propelled vehicle was controversial, and in the 1890s and early 1900s, some cities and counties had rules forbidding motorized vehicles. In Vermont, a walking escort had to precede the car by an eighth of a mile with a red warning flag, and in Iowa, motorists were required to telephone ahead to a town they planned to drive through to warn the community lest their horses be alarmed (Berger 1979; Clymer 1953; Glasscock 1937; Morris 1949). In most rural areas, motorists were expected to pull their cars to a stop or even shut down the motor when a horse-drawn buggy came near. Legislation known as "pig and chicken clauses" meant that the automobilist was liable for any accident that occurred when passing an animal on or near the road, even if the injury was due to the animal having run away in fright (Scott-Montagu 1904). Such norms were considered the decent way to conduct oneself only 100 years ago.

Automobiles were restricted to cities for nearly a decade after their invention because roads were inadequate outside the urban areas and they often slid off muddy roads into ditches or got caught in deep tracks. These conditions had not deterred horses. Owen G. Roberts invented a seatbelt in about 1915 because on a daylong, 80-mile drive westward from Columbus, Ohio, Mary Roberts was knocked unconscious when the rough roads caused her head to hit the roof of the car with great force. Paving of roads became a necessity for automobile travel and, of course, made automobile travel much faster and more common. The expansion was stunning. An estimated 85,000 motored vehicles were in use in rural

America in 1911. By 1930, the number was nearly 10 million (Berger 1979).

Forms of entertainment began to change when people were able to go longer distances in shorter periods of time. As the Model T made cars affordable, families no longer had only each other for socializing. Thus, the complete dependence on family was lessened, possibly weakening familial bonds (Berger 1979). Furthermore, entertainment gradually became available virtually every night of the week, not just on Saturdays and at special events (Berger 1979; McKelvie 1926). Even courting was substantially changed, as individuals could go farther afield to find a possible life partner, couples could go more places on dates, and two people could find more privacy.

Transportation that made traversing long distances easier changed how people related to a number of other institutions as well. Because people could drive farther to churches, they often chose to go to city churches, where the preachers were more skilled as public speakers and where the music was of higher quality. Small country churches began to consolidate or to close down. However, many people found that a country drive was a more interesting way to spend Sunday mornings, and preachers often condemned cars for leading people away from church (Berger 1979). Still, once pastors could afford cars, many people received services such as pastoral calls, which had previously been unknown in rural areas (Wilson 1924). Likewise, motorized buses made transportation to schools possible, and attendance rates of rural children increased substantially (U.S. Department of Interior 1930). Small rural hospitals began to close down, so even the delivery of medical services was changed. The automobile was also a boon to the mental health of isolated farm women, allowing them to visit with neighbors (Berger 1979; McNall and McNall 1983).

As people could live in less congested areas but still get to work in a reasonable amount of time via an automobile, the suburbs began to develop around major cities. No longer did people locate homes close to shopping, schools, and places of worship. Yet a dispersed population needs to use more gasoline, thereby creating pollution. As the wealthy moved to expensive suburbs and paid higher taxes to support outstanding schools, socioeconomic and ethnic stratification between communities increased.

When Owen G. Roberts built one of the first automobiles in Ohio and established a large automobile dealership in Columbus, it was not his intent to heighten segregation, to create funding problems for poor inner-city areas, or to pollute the environment. Yet these are some of the unintended consequences of the spread of the automobile. It sometimes takes decades before we can identify the consequences of the technologies we develop and adopt.

These Ugandan refugees have survived without their parents and must now cope with life as best they can. They were forced to flee from their homes or they would have been killed.

The diffusion or spread of technology throughout the world is likely to be uneven, especially in the early stages of the new technology. For example, computer technology has advanced rapidly, but those advances began in corporate boardrooms, military bases, and university laboratories. Policies of governments and leaders, such as funding for school computers, determine the rate of public access. Thus, only gradually are computers reaching the world's citizenry through schools, libraries, and eventually private homes.

Major historical events—wars, economic crises, assassinations, political scandals, and catastrophes—can change the course of world events. For instance, the triggering event that actually started World War I was the assassination of Archduke Franz Ferdinand of the Austro-Hungarian Empire. This assassination resulted in the German invasion of several other countries and the beginning of the war. So a micro-level act, the murder of an individual, had global ramifications. Clearly, internal strains and external stressors give impetus to the processes of change. The question is "How do these processes take place?"

Video Link 16.3
See how the food crisis is being solved at different levels.

Theories of Social Change

Social scientists seek to explain the causes and consequences of social change, sometimes in the hope that change can be controlled or guided. Theories of change often reflect the events and belief systems of particular historical time periods. Conflict theory developed during periods of change in Europe; it began to gain adherents in the United States during the 1960s, when intense conflict over issues of race and ethnic relations, the morality of the Vietnam War, and changes in social values peaked. Theories that focused on social harmony were of little help.

The major social change theories can be categorized as micro-level (symbolic interaction and rational choice) theories and overlapping meso- and macro-level (evolutionary, functional, conflict, and world systems) theories. As we review these theories, some of them will be familiar to you from previous chapters.

Micro-Level Theories of Change

Symbolic Interactionism. According to symbolic interaction theory, a micro-level theory, human beings are always trying to make sense of the things they experience, figure out what an event or interaction means, and determine what action is required of them. Humans construct meanings that agree with or diverge from what others around them think. This capacity to define one's situation, such as concluding that one is oppressed, even though others have accepted the circumstances as normal, can be a powerful impetus to change. It can be the starting point of social movements, cultural changes, and revolutions.

Some sociologists believe that individuals are always at the core of any social trends or movements, even if those movements are national or global (Blumer 1986; Giddens 1986; Simmel [1902–1917] 1950). After all, it is individuals who act, make decisions, and take action. Corporations, nations, or bureaucracies do not make decisions—people do. The way in which an individual defines the reality he or she is experiencing makes a huge difference in how that person will respond to it.

Social institutions and structures are always subject to maverick individuals "thinking outside the box" and changing how others see things. Individual actions can cause riots, social movements, planned change in organizations, and a host of other outcomes that have the potential to transform society. That people may construct reality in new ways can be a serious threat to the status quo, and those who want to protect the status quo try to ensure that people will see the world the same way they do. If change feels threatening to some members who have a vested interest in the current arrangements, those individuals who advocate change may face resistance. Consider the current state of the world, in which some nations are making rapid technological advances and others are resisting modernization as a threat to their religious cultures and way of life.

Leaders often provide opportunities for group members to participate in suggesting, planning, and implementing change in order to help create acceptance and positive attitudes toward change. This collaborative process is often used when a firm or a public agency is planning a major project, such as the development of a shopping mall or a waste disposal site, and cooperation and support by other parts of the community become essential. Symbolic interactionists would see this as an effort to build a consensus about what the social changes mean and to implement change in a way that is not perceived as threatening to the members.

Rational Choice. To rational choice theorists, behaviors are largely driven by individuals seeking rewards and limiting costs. Because of this, most individuals engage in those activities that bring positive rewards and try to avoid actions that can have negative outcomes. A group seeking change can attempt to set up a situation in which the desired behavior is rewarded. The typology presented in Figure 16.1 shows the relationship between behaviors and sanctions.

Bringing about change may not require a change in costs or rewards. It may be sufficient simply to change people's perception of the advantages and disadvantages of certain actions. Sometimes, people are not aware of all the rewards, or they have failed to accurately assess the expenditures. For example, few citizens in the United States realize all the benefits of marriage. To change the marriage rates, we may not need more benefits to encourage marriage. We may do just as well to change the population's appraisal of the benefits already available.

Meso- and Macro-Level Theories of Change

Social Evolutionary Theories. Social evolutionary theories at the macro level assume that societies move slowly from simple to more complex forms. Early unilinear theories maintained that all societies moved through the same steps and that advancement or progress was desirable and would lead to a better society. These theories came to prominence during the Industrial Revolution, when European social scientists sought to interpret the differences between their own societies and the "primitive societies" of other continents. Europe was being stimulated by travel, exposure to new cultures, and a spawning of new philosophies, a period called the Enlightenment. Europeans witnessed the development of mines, railroads, cities, educational systems, and industries, which they defined as "progress" or "civilization." World travelers reported that other peoples and societies did not seem to have these developments. These reports provided the empirical evidence that early sociologist Auguste Comte used in proposing his theory of unilinear development from simple to complex societies. Unilinear theories came to legitimate colonial expansion and exploitation of other people and lands that were seen as "inferior."

In a more recent version of evolutionary theory, Nolan and Lenski (2008) discuss five stages through which societies progress: hunter-gatherer, horticultural, agrarian, industrial, and postindustrial (see Chapter 3). This does not mean that some stages are "better" than others but that this is the typical pattern of change resulting from new technologies and more efficient harnessing of energy. Despite their claim that this theory does not judge some stages as "better," the authors do use the term *progress*. This word refers to greater technological sophistication rather than to moral superiority. Still, in terms of technology, they do think the later stages are more advanced.

Video Link 16.4
Watch an analysis of Walmart.

Many modern cases do not fit this pattern because they skip steps or are selective about what aspects of technology they wish to adopt. Countries such as India and China are largely agricultural but are importing and developing the latest technology. Furthermore, advocates of some religious, social, and political ideologies question the assumption that "material progress" (which is what technology fosters) is desirable.

Even the phrase *developing countries* has been controversial with some scholars because it might imply that all societies are moving toward the type of social system characterized by the affluent or developed societies. Many now use the term *Global South* because poor countries are disproportionately located south of the 20° N latitude, whereas affluent nations are typically situated north of that line. Note that the term is a metaphor for all poor countries. Some prosperous countries are in the south and some poor ones in the north, but the term is meant to avoid an assumption of inevitable evolution toward Western cultures.

Behavior	Sanction	
	Formal	**Informal**
Positive	Bonuses, advances, fringe benefits, recognition	Praise, smile, pat on the back
Negative	Demotion, loss of salary	Ridicule, exclusion, talk behind back

Figure 16.1   Relationship Between Behaviors and Sanctions

Photo Essay

Transportation Systems and Change

The efficiency and speed of modes of transportation for goods and people vary around the world, often reflecting the level of development of the region or country. "Premodern" modes of transportation cause less pollution and sometimes move more easily through congested streets than gas- or diesel-operated motors. Sometimes, technological progress has a high cost, and resistance to that "progress" may make sense.

Contemporary evolutionary theories are multilinear, acknowledging variations in the way change takes place. The rapid spread of ideas and technologies means that societies today may move quickly from simple to complex, creating modern states. Consider the mass of contradictions in the Middle East today. Due to the world demand for their oil, several countries in this region have among the highest per capita incomes in the world. In 2008, Qatar had a per capita income of $111,000; Kuwait, $57,500; the United Arab Emirates, $44,600; and Bahrain, $37,400 (CIA World Factbook 2008). The urban elite, especially, have access to modern conveniences such as the latest technology, jets, and cell phones. Other Middle Eastern people still live traditional lives as nomads or herders in small villages or earn their living from the desert. Not all segments of society change at the same rate, making categorization of some societies difficult.

Functionalist Theories.

Functional theorists assume that societies are basically stable systems held together by the shared norms and values of their members. The interdependent parts work together to make the society function smoothly. A change in one part of the society affects all the other parts, each changing in turn until the system resumes a state of equilibrium. Change can come from external or internal sources, from contact with other societies or from strains within. Slow, nondisruptive change occurs as societies become more complex, but any change may be seen as threatening to the equilibrium of a system. Rapid change is seen as especially dysfunctional or disruptive. Because sudden, disruptive change is difficult to explain using functional theory and because any change is viewed with some suspicion, some sociologists have turned to conflict theories to help explain change, especially rapid or violent changes.

Conflict Theories.

Conflict theorists assume that societies are dynamic and that change and conflict are inevitable. According to Karl Marx, socioeconomic class conflict is the major source of tension leading to change in any society. Karl Marx and Friedrich Engels ([1848] 1969) predicted that the antagonistic relationship they saw developing between the workers (proletariat) and the owners of the production systems (bourgeoisie) in 19th-century England would lead to social revolution. From this, they believed a new world order would emerge in which the workers themselves would own the means of production. Thus, conflict between the owners and the workers would be the central factor driving social change.

Other conflict theorists study variables such as gender, religion, politics, and ethnic and interest group problems in their analyses, feeling that these factors can also be the grounds for oppression and "we" versus "they" differences (Dahrendorf 1959). Some see conflict as useful for society because it forces societies to adapt to new conditions and leads to healthy change (Coser 1956). Conflicts over slavery and over gender inequality are examples of problems that cause stresses and strains, eventually resulting in an improved society. The recent conflict over health care in the United States is also likely to lead to a better system.

World Systems Theory of Global Change.

World systems theorists focus on the historical development of the whole world and how that development has influenced individual countries today. Capitalist economies first appeared about 1500. Since then, except for a few isolated tribal groupings, almost all societies have been at least indirectly influenced by dominant capitalist world economic and political systems (Wallerstein 1974).

This theory divides the world system into three main parts: the core, semiperipheral areas, and peripheral areas (see Figure 16.2 on page 574). Core countries include some western European states, Australia and New Zealand, Japan, Canada, the United States, and a few others (Wallerstein 1974). Historically, they have controlled global decision making, received the largest share of the profits from the world economic system, and dominated the peripheral areas politically, economically, and culturally by controlling the flow of technology and capital into and out of those countries. Peripheral countries, most of which are in Africa, Asia, and South America, provide cheap labor and raw materials for the core countries' needs. The semiperipheral countries are in an intermediate position, trading with both the core and the peripheral countries. The former republics of the Soviet Union generally are considered semiperipheral. Because most semiperipheral countries are industrializing, they serve as areas to which core-country businesses and multinational corporations can move for continued growth, often in partnerships, as semiperipheral states aspire to join

In this typical situation, these South African miners are all Black and work for low wages, whereas the supervisors and managers are White. These gold miners are part of a multinational corporation and the larger world economic system, with stockholders from around the globe.

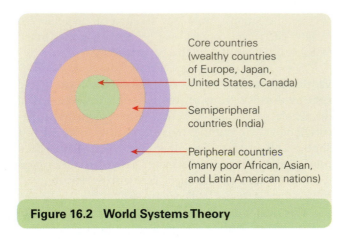

Figure 16.2   World Systems Theory

do even within their own national boundaries, creating debt dependencies on core countries that the poorer countries can never overcome. For example, the IMF has demanded and instituted freezes on salaries and minimum wages in countries such as Greece, Brazil, and Argentina, has mandated the opening of borders to imports, and has unintentionally undermined the economies of some very poor countries. The problem has been one of insisting on the application of economic theories that work in affluent countries but not always in poor ones (The Dollars and Sense Collective 2006; Friedman 2006; Weidenbaum 2006; Weller and Hersh 2006).

In one sense, **world systems theory** is a conflict theory that is global in nature, with core countries exploiting the poor countries. As we might expect from conflict theory, some groups of noncore countries have increased their collective power by forming alliances such as OPEC (Organization of Petroleum Exporting Countries), OAS (Organization of African States), and SEATO (Southeast Asia Treaty Organization). These alliances present challenges to the historically core countries of the world system because of their combined economic and political power. For example, the price we pay at the gas pump reflects the power of OPEC to set prices.

When we understand international treaties and alliances as part of larger issues of conflict over resources and economic self-interests, the animosity of noncore countries toward core countries such as the United States begins to make sense. Likewise, the mistrust of the United States toward countries that seem to be getting U.S. jobs is not entirely unfounded. The problem is an extraordinarily complex system that always leaves the most vulnerable more at risk and the wealthiest even richer.

Sometimes behavior that results in change is unplanned, even spontaneous, as described in the following section.

the core countries. The core and semiperipheral countries process raw materials, often taken from peripheral countries for little return, and may sell the final products back to the peripheral countries. The semiperipheral countries and the peripheral countries need the trade and the resources of the core countries, but they are also at a severe disadvantage in competition and are exploited by those at the core, resulting in an uneasy relationship.

These basic relationships between countries have endured since the 1700s. However, South Korea, Thailand, Taiwan, and China may challenge the existing relationships with their expanding economies (Friedman 2005; Kristoff and WeDunn 2000). Furthermore, since the 1960s, production processes have modified the relationships between the regions of the world. Changes in technology and in international global institutions have allowed corporations to break their production processes into smaller segments. These segments are then scattered over the world to take advantage of the lower manufacturing costs in the periphery. This process creates commodity chains—worldwide networks of labor resources and production processes that create a product. Each piece of the chain can be located in a core, semiperipheral, or peripheral country. Because manufacturing processes are often performed in semiperipheral countries, their share of the world's manufacturing and trade production has risen sharply. In contrast, the distribution of profits from multinational corporations still benefits the core countries.

Core countries have been a major force in the development of global institutions, such as the International Monetary Fund (IMF), that facilitate and attempt to control international capital flow. By increasing the frameworks for debt restructuring for peripheral countries, the IMF attempts to restore sustainability and growth to countries that default on their loans. At least 30 countries have restructured their debt under IMF guidelines (IMF 2003).

However, the IMF leaves countries little economic autonomy. The restructuring plans control what countries

Journal Article Link 16.1
Read about global human rights.

Thinking Sociologically

Where is your clothing made? Did a multinational corporation have it assembled in the Global South? Who benefits from companies buying cheap labor from the Global South: You? The workers? Governments? The companies that manufacture the products? Who, if anyone, is hurt?

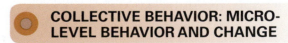

COLLECTIVE BEHAVIOR: MICRO-LEVEL BEHAVIOR AND CHANGE

In June 2009, various cities in Iran, including the capital city of Tehran, saw extensive rioting following an "official" report of the winner of the presidential election. Although Iran's president has limited power, the position remains the highest public office decided by a popular vote. Supporters of the reform candidate, Mir Hossein Mousavi, convinced that there has been extensive voter fraud, vented their anger with both peaceful and violent expressions of contempt for the process. Iranian police and military officers responded with arrests and counterviolence, attempting to control the situation and stop the protests. While not everyone was disheartened by the election, this eruption of anger illustrates the unpredictable nature of collective behavior.

Collective behavior refers to unplanned, spontaneous, unstructured, disorganized actions that often violate norms. It arises when people are trying to cope with stressful situations and unclear or uncertain conditions (Goode 1992; Smelser 1963, 1988). Collective behavior falls into two main types: crowd behavior and mass behavior. It often starts as a response to an event or stimulus. It could begin with a shooting or beating, a speech, a sports event, or a rumor. The key is that as individuals try to make sense of the situations they are in and respond based on their perceptions, collective social actions emerge.

Crowd behaviors—mobs, panics, riots, and demonstrations—are all forms of collective behavior in which a crowd acts, at least temporarily, as a unified group (LeBon [1895] 1960). Crowds are often made up of individuals who see themselves as supporting a just cause. Because the protesters are in such a large group, they may not feel bound by the normal social controls—either internal (normal moral standards) or external (fear of police sanctions).

Mass behavior occurs when individual people communicate or respond in a similar manner to ambiguous or uncertain situations, often based on common information from the news or on the Internet. Examples include public opinion, rumors, fads, and fashions. Unlike social movements, these forms of collective behavior generally lack a hierarchy of authority and clear leadership, a division of labor, and a sense of group action.

Theories of Collective Behavior

Social scientists studying disruptions in the social world have looked at group and crowd dynamics, finding that most members of crowds are respectable, law-abiding citizens, but faced with specific situations, they act out (Berk 1974; Turner and Killian 1993). Several explanations of individual involvement dominate the modern collective behavior literature.

The minimax strategy (Berk 1974) is based on principles of rational choice theory. It suggests that individuals try to minimize their losses or costs and maximize their benefits. People are more likely to engage in behavior if they feel the rewards outweigh the costs. Individuals may become involved in a riot if they feel the outcome—drawing attention to their plight, the possibility of improving conditions, solidarity with neighbors

Suspicion of fraudulent vote counts that reelected an unpopular Iranian president—Mahmoud Ahmadinejad—resulted in extensive rioting, as well as more peaceful protests.

Crowds can stimulate change in a society, but they can also become unruly and unpredictable. Government officials spend a good deal of money and time equipping and training officers to control angry and radicalized members of crowds.

and friends, looting goods—will be more rewarding than the status quo or the possible negative sanctions.

Emergent norm theory (Turner and Killian 1993) points out that the emotions and attitudes that drive the decisions and behaviors of individuals in crowds are quite different from the principles that guide them when they act alone. The theory addresses the unusual situations, involving the breakdown of norms, in which most collective behavior takes place. Unusual situations may call for the development of new norms and even new definitions of what is acceptable behavior. The implication of this theory is that in ambiguous situations, people look to others for clues about what is happening or what is acceptable, and norms emerge in ambiguous contexts that may be considered inappropriate in other contexts.

Audio Link 16.1
Listen to stories about mob mentality.

Value-added theory describes the conditions for crowd behavior and social movements. Key elements are necessary, with each new variable adding to the total situation until conditions are sufficient for individuals to begin to act in common, and collective behavior emerges (Smelser 1963). These are the six factors Smelser (1963) identified:

1. *Structural conduciveness:* Existing problems create a climate that is ripe for change (e.g., the tensions between religious and ethnic groups in Iraq).

2. *Structural strain:* The social structure is not meeting the needs and expectations of the citizens, which creates widespread dissatisfaction with the status quo—the current arrangements (e.g., the Iraqi

government is unable to control violence and provide basic services).

3. *Spread of a generalized belief:* Common beliefs about the cause, effect, and solution of the problem evolve, develop, and spread (e.g., U.S. troops may leave; militias are killing the members of other groups).

4. *Precipitating factor:* A dramatic event or incident occurs to incite people to action (e.g., groups of men from different religious groups are kidnapped, bound, and shot).

5. *Mobilization for action:* Leaders emerge and set out a path of action, or an emergent norm develops that stimulates common action (e.g., citizens gather to protest the killings and the lack of security and services).

6. *Social controls are weak:* If the police, the military, or strong political or religious leaders are unable to counter the mobilization, a social movement or other crowd behavior (e.g., a riot or a mob) is likely to develop.

Some analysts have argued that when all six factors are present, some sort of collective behavior will emerge. Those interested in controlling crowds that are volatile must intervene in one or more of these conditions (Kendall 2004; Smelser 1963).

Thinking Sociologically

Think of an example of crowd behavior or a social movement, preferably one in which you have been involved. Try to identify each of the six factors from Smelser's theory as they operated in your example.

Types of Collective Behavior

Collective behavior ranges from spontaneous violent mobs to temporary fads and fashions. Figure 16.3 shows the range of actions.

Mobs are emotional crowds that engage in violence against a specific target. Examples include lynchings, killings, and hate crimes. Near the end of the U.S. Civil War, self-appointed vigilante groups roamed the countryside in the South looking for army deserters, torturing and killing both those who harbored deserters and the deserters themselves. There were no courts and no laws, just "justice" in the eyes of the vigilantes. The members of these groups constituted mobs. The film *Cold Mountain* (Frazier 1997) depicts these scenes vividly. Unless deterred, mobs often damage or destroy their target.

On the southern outskirts of Basra in Iraq, British soldiers monitor a checkpoint leading into the city, checking people for weapons. A young Iraqi girl experiences the tense and hostile realities of war. This kind of military presence is often scary for residents and is very dangerous work for soldiers. This is an example of the precariousness of maintaining social control in volatile situations.

Spontaneous and often violent ———————————————————— **Less spontaneous and seldom violent**

Crowd behavior				**Mass behavior**		
Mob	Riot	Panic		Rumor	Fad	Fashion

Figure 16.3   Types of Collective Behavior

Riots—an outbreak of illegal violence committed by individuals expressing frustration or anger against people, property, or both—begin when certain conditions occur. Often, a sense of frustration or deprivation sets the stage for a riot—hunger, poverty, poor housing, lack of jobs, discrimination, poor education, or an unresponsive or unfair judicial system. If the conditions for collective behavior are present, many types of incidents can be the precipitating factor setting off a riot. For example, the residents of many towns in Iraq have rioted over lack of jobs, poor pay, and the limited resources available to sustain a decent life. The distinction between riots and mobs is illustrated in Figure 16.4.

Panic occurs when a large number of individuals become fearful or try to flee threatening situations that are beyond their control, sometimes putting their lives in danger. Panic can occur in a crowd situation, such as a restaurant or theater in which someone yells "Fire," or it

can occur following rumors or information spread by the media. Panic started by rumors set off the run on the stock market in October 1929. A large number of actions by individuals caused the stock market crash in the United States, with repercussions around the world. In 2008, the collapse of the global investment banking and securities trader Bear, Stearns and Co. resulted in turmoil in the financial markets. Only with radical intervention by the federal government was the immediate crisis abated. Panics can result in the collapse of financial markets, death due to stampede as people flee a fire, or destruction of property—all the result of group action.

Rumors are a form of mass behavior in which unsupported or unproven reports about a problem, issue, or concern circulate widely throughout the public. Rumors may spread only in a local area, but with electronic means available, rumors are spreading more widely and rapidly. Without authoritative information, ambiguous situations can produce faulty information on which decisions are made and actions are based. *Urban legends*, one example of widely spread but unverified messages, are unsubstantiated stories that sound plausible and become widely circulated. The people telling these stories usually believe them (Henslin 2005). The "Sociology in Our Social World" on page 578 provides an example.

Fads are temporary items or activities that spread rapidly and are copied enthusiastically by large numbers of people. Body modification, especially tattooing, appeals mostly to young people of all social classes. Tattoo artists emblazon IDs, secret society and organization emblems, fraternity symbols, and decorations to order on all parts of the customers' bodies. Body modification has taken place for centuries, but it goes through fads (University of Pennsylvania 2007). Sometimes, fads become institutionalized—that is, they gain a permanent place in the culture. Other fads die out, replaced by the next hot item.

Fashions refer to a social pattern favored by a large number of people for a limited period of time—here today, gone tomorrow. Examples would include clothing styles, music genres, color schemes in home decor, types of automobiles, and architectural designs. Fashions typically last longer than fads but sometimes survive only a season, as

Riots involve dispersed actions expressing frustration (e.g., urban riots over poor conditions).

Mobs involve a group collectively focusing their action on a single individual or location (e.g., a lynch mob).

Figure 16.4   The Difference Between Riots and Mobs

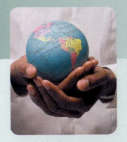

Sociology in Our Social World

Exam Stories: Testing the Truth

College exams are quickly approaching, so it is a good time to take a look at the latest chapter in the tome of teacher-student legend and rumors.

The first one was reported from Calgary, Alberta, by a civil engineering student at the University of Manitoba. This tale says a professor announced an open-book final examination in which the students could "use anything they are able to carry into the exam room." One innovative undergraduate, it is reported, carried in a graduate student who wrote his exam for him.

Another legend came from North Carolina. Supposedly, on the day before the final exam, the professor left his office unattended, with the door open and the examinations left sitting on his desk. A student who came by to ask a question found the room empty and quickly left with one of the exams. However, the professor had printed the exact number of exams that he needed, and the next morning, he counted them again before going to the classroom. Discovering that he was one short, he suspected that it had been stolen, so he trimmed a ½ inch from the bottom of the remaining exams. When the exam papers were turned in, the student whose paper was longer than the others' received a failing grade.

A student procrastinated on writing a paper. Twenty-four hours before the paper was due, he went to the university library and found an old paper on the topic. He copied it and turned it in. A few weeks later, the professor returned the papers and he stopped by the student's desk. He supposedly said to the student, "Twenty-five years ago, when I wrote this paper, it got a B. I always thought it deserved an A." There was an A on the cover, but the professor added, "Try anything like this again, and I'll have you thrown out of school."

Another college legend goes like this: Jack, a less than industrious student, was taking an examination with two blue books, a pen, and a question that had him baffled. Being naturally bright, even if lazy, he solved the problem in the following way. In one of the blue books, he wrote a letter to his mother, telling her that he had finished his exam early but was waiting for a friend to finish and was taking the opportunity to write her a note. He said he had been studying very hard for this instructor, who was a nice guy but had pretty high standards. When the time was up, he handed in one blue book and quickly left with the unused one. When he got to his room, he opened his text, wrote the answer to the exam question, and mailed the blue book to his mother. When the instructor found the letter, he called Jack, who explained that he had written in two blue books and must have gotten them mixed up. The examination essay must be in the mail on the way to Boston where his mother lived, he explained. He offered to call his mother and have her send the envelope back as soon as she got it. He did, she did, and the blue book was returned, with the inner envelope postmarked the day of the test and the outer envelope postmarked Boston.

Finally, in an introductory chemistry class, two guys were taking chemistry, and they had done well on all the quizzes, so that by the last week of class they each had a solid A. These friends were so confident going into the final that for the weekend just before the exam they decided to drive some distance to party at another college. However, after a very good time and hangovers on Monday, they overslept and did not make it back to campus until late on Monday—the day of the exam. They found the professor and told him they missed the final because they had been away, had had a flat tire on the way back to campus, and were without a spare. The professor thought this over and agreed that they could make up the final on the following day. So the two studied intensely that night and went in the next day for the exam. The professor placed them in separate rooms and handed each of them a test booklet and told them to begin. The first problem was simple and was worth 5 points. It looked like it was going to be an easy exam, and they were both relieved. They did the first problem and then turned the page. The next question was "Which tire? (95 points)."

Campus legends such as these help reduce the strain of college life and spread the reputations of legendary professors. Furthermore, they keep alive hopes of someday outfoxing the professors—or the students, depending on which side you are on.

Note: These and other urban legends about exams and college experience can be reviewed at www.snopes.com.

Fashions are established largely at fashion shows, where designers introduce new clothing styles. Fashions cannot occur unless there is a very high level of affluence, where people can afford to throw away perfectly good clothing for something more stylish. For many people in the Global South, it is a gift just to have clean, warm clothing, and the very existence of such displays of consumerism is both amazing and appealing—or sometimes appauling.

can be seen in the clothing industry. Music styles such as "post hard core," "conscious hip hop," and "UK 2-step garage" were popular among some groups as this book was being written and may be passé by the time you read this, replaced by new styles resulting from change in mass behavior.

Each of these forms of collective behavior involves micro-level individual actions that cumulatively become collective responses to certain circumstances. However, ripples are felt in other levels of the social world. Insofar as these various types of collective activity upset the standard routines of society and the accepted norms, they can unsettle the entire social system and cause lasting change.

The separation of each of the forms of change into levels is somewhat artificial, of course, for individuals are

also acting in organizations and in national social movements. However, when we move to meso- and macro-level analyses, the established structures and processes of society become increasingly important. Much of the change at these levels is planned change.

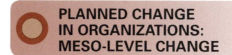

PLANNED CHANGE IN ORGANIZATIONS: MESO-LEVEL CHANGE

The board of trustees of a small liberal arts college has witnessed recent drops in student enrollments that could cause the college to go out of business, but the college has a long tradition of fine education and devoted alumni. How does the college continue to serve future students and current alumni? The problem is how to plan change to keep the college solvent.

A company manufactures silicon chips for computers. Recently, the market has been flooded with inexpensive chips, primarily from Asia, where they are made more cheaply than this North American firm can possibly make them. Does the company succumb to the competition, figure out ways to meet it, or diversify its products? What steps should be taken to facilitate the change? Many companies in Silicon Valley, California, face exactly this challenge.

A Native American nation within the United States faces unemployment among its people due in large measure to discrimination by Anglos in the local community. Should the elders focus their energies and resources on electing sympathetic politicians, boycotting racist businesses, filing lawsuits, becoming entrepreneurs as a nation so they can hire their own people, or beginning a local radio station so they will have a communication network for a social movement? What is the best strategy to help this proud nation recover from centuries of disadvantage?

All these are real problems faced by real organizations. Anywhere we turn, organizations face questions involving change, questions that arise because of internal strains and external stresses. How organizational leaders and applied sociologists deal with change will determine the survival and well-being of the organizations.

How Organizations Plan for Change

If you work for an organization during your lifetime, you will engage in the process of planning for change. Some organizations spend time and money writing long-range strategic plans and doing self-studies to determine areas for ongoing change. Sometimes, change is desired, and sometimes, it is forced on the organization by stresses from society, more powerful organizations, or individuals (Kanter 1983, 2001a, 2001b; Olsen 1968). Moreover, a problem solved in one area can create unanticipated problems some-place else.

Planned change such as strategic planning is the dream of every organizational leader. It involves deliberate, structured attempts, guided by stated goals, to alter the status quo of the social unit (Bennis, Benne, and Chin 1985; Ferhansyed 2008). There are several important considerations when we think about planned change: How can we identify what needs to be changed? How can we plan or manage the change process successfully? What kind of systems adapt well to change? Here, we briefly touch on the topic and outline three approaches advocated by experts to plan change. Keep in mind the levels of analysis as you read about change models. Some applied sociologists devote their careers to combining research and advocacy of change, as illustrated in the "Applied Sociologist at Work" feature.

Models for Planning Organizational Change

Change models fall into two main categories: (1) closed-system models, which deal with the internal dynamics of

the organization, and (2) open-system models (such as our social world model), which consider the organization and its environment. Let us sample a couple of these models.

Closed-system models, often called classical or mechanistic models, focus on the internal dynamics of the organization. The goal of change using closed models is to move the organization closer to the ideal of bureaucratic efficiency and effectiveness. An example is time and motion studies, which analyze how much time it takes a worker to do a certain task and how it can be accomplished more efficiently. Each step in McDonald's process of getting a hamburger to you, the customer, has been planned and timed for the greatest efficiency (Ritzer 2008). In some closed-system models, change is legislated by the top executives and filters down to the workers.

The human relations approach and the *organizational development (OD) movement* both state that participants in the organization should be involved in decision making leading to change. The leadership is more democratic and supportive of workers, and the atmosphere is transparent—open, honest, and accountable to workers and investors. This model emphasizes that change comes about through

The Applied Sociologist at Work— Stephen Steele — Local Community Research Center

Dr. Stephen Steele started using sociology to help a business he was working for solve a problem and bring about needed change. He has been in the business of helping organizations solve problems with sociological knowledge ever since.

"If someone has knowledge and fails to use it, that is a terrible waste," comments Steele. The idea of being involved in social betterment and making a difference were the guiding principles that led Steele to a life of sociological research. In 1978, he used his research skills to help set up a Community Research Center at the local community college. The goals of the nonprofit center were to help community organizations solve their problems, train students to use research skills, help bring about needed change, and provide a service to all. In 1982, he became its director, a position he still holds.

Many students have developed sophisticated analytical and research skills by working on projects in the community, and the center has supported itself by contracting its high-quality, low-cost research services to community organizations. Although the range of the center's research is broad, the main foci have been community change, economic development, and county government issues. For instance, Steele's company, Applied Data Associates, received a federal grant to evaluate an antidrug project and another to evaluate ways to increase the active involvement of Hispanic Americans in community civic organizations.

The interaction between theory and research is crucial in his work. Consider the four basic sociological theories: He looks for systems of interaction (functionalism), for power centers (conflict), for interaction patterns and definitions of reality within corporate cultures (symbolic interactionism), and for the costs and benefits of various choices (rational choice).

Steele likens applied sociology to being a "social plumber"—there is a specific problem, so he uses his tools to fix it. He finds being a social plumber rewarding and exciting, using sociological knowledge and tools to change groups, organizations, and environments and in the process improving the quality of life for people.

Note: Dr. Stephen Steele received his bachelor's and master's degrees from Eastern Michigan University and his doctorate from Catholic University of America. He teaches sociology at Ann Arundel Community College in Maryland and runs his own research center. His students gain practical experience working in the center.

adjusting workers' values, beliefs, and attitudes regarding new demands on the organization. Many variations on this theme have evolved, with current efforts including team building and change of the organizational culture to improve worker morale. Closed-system models tend to focus on group change that occurs from within the organization.

Open-system models combine both internal processes and the external environment. The latter provides the organization with inputs (workers and raw materials) and feedback (acceptability of the product or result). In turn, the organization has outputs (products) that affect the larger society. There are several implications of this model: (1) change is an ever-present and ongoing process, (2) all parts of the organization and its immediate environment are linked, and (3) change in one part has an effect on the other parts. The model in Figure 16.5 illustrates the open system.

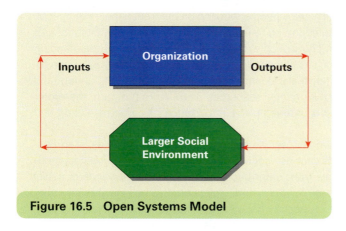

Figure 16.5   Open Systems Model

Thinking Sociologically

Using the model in Figure 16.5, fill in the parts as they relate to your educational institution. For example, inputs might include faculty members and students.

The Process of Planned Change

Nongovernmental organizations (NGOs) plan ways to improve the lives of individuals in many parts of the world. One big issue in the Global South is the availability of clean drinking water. For example, in parts of Africa, women must spend as much as 6 hours a day carrying water to their homes. Because daughters are needed to care for the younger siblings while the mother is away, many girls are unable to attend school. This, in turn, has implications for the continuation of poverty. If estimates are correct—that 443 million school days are lost each year due to water-related diseases—this adds even more to the crisis of continuing poverty (WaterAid 2008).

Clean water is essential for life and for health, but 1 out of 6 people—more than 1 billion humans on this planet—do not have access to it. This affects the quality of their lives and results in more than 2 million deaths per year. With global climate change, the glaciers on top of mountains such as Mount Kenya are melting. Although that mountain peak has been snow covered for more than 10,000 years, the glaciers are expected to be completely gone in perhaps 20 years (Cousteau 2008). When the snow at the mountain top disappears, the water supply for hundreds of thousands of people and animals will disappear (Barnett, Adam, and Lettenmaier 2005; Cyranoski 2005; Struck 2007). One British organization that is bringing about change in this area is WaterAid, launched in 1981. It has grown to become an international NGO that focuses entirely on water and sanitation issues, including hygiene. Communities in poor countries in Zambia and Sri Lanka were the first to receive support, with projects following in Ethiopia, Tanzania, Uganda, Sierra Leone, Ghana, Kenya, Bangladesh, Nepal, India, Gambia, Nigeria, Mozambique, Zambia, Madagascar, and Malawi. Now communities throughout the world are assisted in developing the most appropriate technologies for clean water, given the geographical features and resources of their areas.

WaterAid has helped more than 8½ million people in the poorest parts of the world gain access to one of the most fundamental of human requirements (WaterAid 2008). In 2006, the organization was voted Britain's most admired charity. It all started with a group of people and their vision, some organizational skills, and a passionate commitment to improving the quality of life for people. Some other organizations also working on this issue have employed the skills of sociologists, who use their understanding of social processes that exacerbate or can lessen this problem. This is illustrated by the work of Ruth Meinzen-Dick, which is described in the "Applied Sociologist at Work" on page 582.

This example shows one of the many types of organizations that both changes within itself to meet new conditions and brings about change in the world. The process of planned change is like a puzzle with a number of pieces that differ for each organization but must fit together for the smooth operation of the organization. The goal of most organizations is to remain balanced and avoid threats or conflict. Change is generally perceived as desirable if it is evolutionary or planned. Unplanned change can be disruptive to the system.

At the societal and global macro levels, change is often stimulated by individuals and events outside the chambers of power, and there is much less control over how the change evolves. We turn next to an exploration of change at the macro level.

The Applied Sociologist at Work— Ruth Meinzen-Dick

Natural Resource Management in Developing Countries

What does a sociologist have to say about natural resource management? This is a question Dr. Ruth Meinzen-Dick has often been asked during her career. For 19 years, she has been showing the importance of understanding how farmers are organized and relate to government and other organizations as part of her work at the International Food Policy Research Institute (IFPRI), part of a larger network of international agricultural research organizations.

Her interest came from growing up in a dry part of India, where water was critical. She returned to India to study how small-scale irrigation systems were operated and found that farmers' organizations played an important role, even though the systems were formally under government management. Other students and faculty from different fields at Cornell University were finding similar patterns of farmer-managed irrigation systems in other parts of the world, so Dr. Meinzen-Dick was able to be part of a larger effort to understand the human side of water management. This was not just an academic exercise, as the Cornell program advised USAID. Even while still in graduate school, Dr. Meinzen-Dick had a consultancy with the World Bank to review the extent of farmer participation in their irrigation programs.

During her work at IFPRI, Dr. Meinzen-Dick has been able to continue studying what brings people together to manage water systems in developing countries and to compare this with the factors that encourage collective action for managing forests, rangelands, and other natural resources. This has involved field research in countries such as India, Pakistan, Zimbabwe, Kenya, and Uganda. She has been able to bring all this together by coordinating an international network on Collective Action and Property Rights (CAPRi), which helps people working on different aspects of agricultural research and natural resource management in developing countries to understand that the social institutions of property rights and collective action play a major role in shaping how people use and share resources. Understanding these institutions requires looking beyond simple indicators such as title deeds (for property rights) or formal organizations (for collective action)—it requires a combination of qualitative and quantitative research methods to understand how people in different societies relate to each other and to their natural resources. The CAPRi program, therefore, provides training to researchers and practitioners from many countries on the importance of collective action and property rights and on the research methods to study them.

Much of Dr. Meinzen-Dick's professional life has involved working across disciplines. At times, this has been frustrating, especially when it seemed that more quantitative fields such as economics or engineering were seen as more "rigorous." Still it has also been deeply satisfying when people from other backgrounds see the relevance of social institutions or when principles from economics, political science, or the natural sciences give her insights into why people do (or don't) work together. To achieve this, it has been especially important for her to communicate the findings of sociological research clearly to nonsociologists. Institutional economics and a strong background in quantitative analysis have been especially helpful for her in communicating with her colleagues, who are mostly economists. To achieve impact in terms of changes in government policies or development programs (e.g., to allow farmers to have more voice in water management), it has been important to use sound research methods and then explain the results clearly to policymakers, not just in academic publications but also in research briefs and presentations.

Note: Dr. Ruth Meinzen-Dick received her master's and PhD degrees in development sociology at Cornell University, with minors in agricultural economics and international agriculture. Her training stressed qualitative and quantitative methods, with a strong emphasis on interdisciplinary work, in terms of both coursework in other fields and work with economists, political scientists, and engineers researching water management, which helped prepare her to work across fields in international development.

SOCIAL MOVEMENTS: MACRO-LEVEL CHANGE

Beijing, China, hosted the prestigious summer 2008 Olympics, athletic games that promote peace and goodwill around the globe. The Olympic torch traversed the globe to prepare for and celebrate the event. However, its journey and the opening of the games were far from peaceful and

Video Link 16.5
Watch a discussion of the Coca-Cola controversy in Colombia.

full of goodwill. Protests dogged the torch, and major political leaders refused to attend the opening ceremonies. A social movement was spurred by an uprising in Tibet, a region that was an independent country until the 1950s but is now part of China. The issues—human rights violations by China and autonomy for Tibet—sparked off protests and demonstrations around the world. Will this social movement bring about change in the status of Tibetans? Worldwide attention may aid the cause of those in Tibet seeking improved life conditions, or it may not. However, those people who raised these issues at the games in China were hoping to change more important, life-and-death policies for the people. A social movement tries to bring change, but questions arise: What is a social movement? What brings it about? What might be the results?

What Is a Social Movement?

From human rights and women's rights to animal rights and environmental protection, individuals seek ways to express their concerns and frustrations. **Social movements** are consciously organized attempts outside of established institutions to enhance or resist change through group action. Movements focus on a common interest of members, such as human rights. They have an organization, a leader, and one or more goals that aim to correct some perceived wrongs existing in society or even around the globe. Social movements are most often found in industrial or postindustrial societies made up of diverse groups that advocate for their own goals and interests.

Movements are usually begun by individuals outside the power structure who might not otherwise have an opportunity to express their opinions (Greenberg 1999). The problems leading to social movements often result from the way resources—human rights, jobs, income, housing, money for education and health care, and power—are distributed. In turn, they may stimulate the formation of countermovements—social movements against the goals of the original movement (McCarthy and Zald 1977).

Many individuals join social movements to change the world or their part of the world and affect the direction of history. In fact, social movements have been successful in doing just that. Consider the movements around the world that have protected lands, forests, rivers, and oceans, seeking environmental protection for the people whose survival depends on those natural resources. For example, the Chipko Movement (meaning "embrace") in a number of areas in India has been fighting the logging of forests by commercial industries. Villagers, mostly women, use Gandhi-style nonviolent methods to oppose the deforestation. A movement by local peasants in Bihar, India, fought efforts to control their fishing rights in the Ganges River.

Stages of Social Movements

Why do people become involved in social movements such as PETA (People for Ethical Treatment of Animals), prochoice or prolife movements, or political demonstrations against policies such as war? Social movements begin because of cultural conflicts in society and because people who want to create—or resist—social change come together. Movements take the time and energy of individual volunteers, and these human resources must be focused as the movement evolves. In the preliminary stage, the purpose of the movement is set. Long-standing problems or very recent events may create dissatisfaction and discontent

Protestors hold signs outside the White House in Washington, D.C., during a demonstration organized by Amnesty International. The group was calling on China to respect human rights, using the Olympic Games in Beijing as an occasion to pressure China by damaging its international reputation.

in the general public or a part of the public. This discontent can galvanize people through a single event.

Sociologists have identified several conditions that give rise to the preliminary stage. First, individuals must share some basic values and ideals. They often occupy similar social statuses or positions and share concerns. Second, social movements need to have a "preexisting communication network" that allows alienated or dissatisfied people to share their discontent (Farley 2009). Several recent political movements, such as MoveOn.org and TrueMajority.com, were carried out primarily on the Internet. Third, a strain and a precipitating event galvanize people around the issue. Fourth, effective leadership emerges—leaders who can mobilize people, organize the movement, and garner resources to fund the movement. Finally, the people in the movement develop a sense of efficacy, a sense that they actually can be successful and change the system. Sometimes, as in the case of the civil rights movement, a sense of confidence in success comes from a religious conviction that God will not let the movement fail (Farley 2009).

Journal Article Link 16.2
Read about fundraising for women's organizations.

In the popularization stage, individuals coalesce their efforts, define their goals and strategies, develop recruitment tactics, and identify leaders. The social movement enters the public arena. The leaders present the social problems and solutions as seen by the members of the social movement. Now the social movement enters the institutionalized stage, becoming a formal organization. This organized effort generates the resources and members for the social change efforts.

In some movements, the final stage is fragmentation and demise. The group may or may not have achieved its goals, but fragmentation breaks apart the organization because the resources may be exhausted, the leadership may be inept or may have lost legitimacy, or the leaders may be co-opted by powerful mainline organizations. In this latter case, radical renewal movements may arise among those still strongly committed to the original cause (Mauss 1975).

In the case of the women's movement, interested women were linked into "preexisting communication networks" by serving on state Commissions on the Status of Women (Ferree and Merrill 2000). The refusal of the Equal Employment Opportunities Commission to consider women's rights as equal to those of racial minorities became the strain and precipitating event that led women to form the National Organization for Women (NOW), a group that continues to fight for women's rights today (Freeman 1975). The Equal Rights Amendment (ERA) provided a major issue around which women's groups rallied. Many women spent a tremendous amount of time and effort to have the ERA ratified by the necessary number of states. Spokespersons emerged, and fund-raiser events provided resources. For a long time, the advocates were convinced that the campaign would be successful. However, when the realization of failure came, an era in the women's movement ended. Some women's organizations fragmented and faded from the scene, while others revised their goals and strategies and moved on to new efforts to attain women's empowerment.

Social movements sometimes focus on regional or even organizational modification, but typically, their focus is on national or global issues. For example, Amnesty International's primary interest is human rights violations by nations, and the organization publishes information on violations around the world. Another way to classify social movements is by their purpose or goals.

Types of Social Movements

Stonewall is a gay, lesbian, and bisexual rights movement that began when patrons fought back against a police raid of a gay bar in New York in 1969. After that incident, the concern about gay rights erupted from a small number of activists into a widespread movement for rights and acceptance. Stonewall now has gone global, with chapters in other countries and continents. Proactive social movements, such as the gay rights movement, promote change. Reactive social movements resist change. James Dobson's Focus on the Family and other conservative religious associations have organized lobbying efforts and rallies fighting against the acceptance of homosexuality or giving gay couples equal status to heterosexual married couples, although this is not the organization's only concern. Within the proactive and reactive social movements, there are five main types.

Audio Link 16.2
Listen to stories of young people in social movements.

Expressive movements are group phenomena focused on changing individuals and saving people from corrupt lifestyles. Many expressive movements are religious, such as the born-again Christian movements, Zen Buddhism, Scientology, the Christian Science Church, and Transcendental Meditation. Expressive movements also include secular psychotherapy movements and self-help or self-actualization groups.

Social reform movements seek to change some aspect of society, focusing on a major issue, such as environmental protection, women's rights, same-sex marriage, "non-corporate" and "just" globalization, gay rights, or civil rights. Members generally support the society as a whole but have specific concerns. Typically, these movements use nonviolent, legislative means or appeals to the courts to accomplish their goals. For example, many individuals with disabilities are given little attention, hope, or opportunity to get ahead and are institutionalized or left to languish. However, social reform movements have advocated for legislation to promote the rights of the differently abled. One such movement is the Special Olympics International, begun by Eunice Kennedy Shriver in 1968 to give those with intellectual disabilities an opportunity to excel in sports. Over 3 million athletes from 150 countries now participate in these games (www.specialolympics.org).

The social reform movement ACORN attracted attention for its voter registration drives. The Association of Community Organizations for Reform Now was a grassroots, neighborhood-based antipoverty group. Started in each community by concerned residents, until recently the movement had offices in more than 100 U.S. cities and more than 200,000 members. Community members knocked on doors to register voters, get petitions signed, and get people on the streets to protest against the severe inequality in society. They were funded by foundations, private donations, and organizations working jointly to bring about change. This type of grassroots organization has the potential to be a major force for change in many communities (Eckholm 2006). ACORN was criticized during the 2008 election campaign for signing up fraudulent voters in its voter registration drives, and those opposed to its tactics took the reform movement to court (Merchant 2009). In 2010 it was finally forced out of business.

Revolutionary movements attempt to transform society, to bring about total change in a society by overthrowing existing power structures and replacing them with new ones. These movements often resort to violent means to achieve their goals, as has been the case with many revolutions throughout history. When we read in the paper that there has been a coup, we may be looking at a revolutionary movement that has ousted the government in power. Although it was not violent, Nelson Mandela's African National Congress succeeded in taking power in South Africa in 1994, rewriting the constitution, and purging the apartheid social system, which had oppressed four fifths of the South African population.

Resistance or regressive movements try to protect an existing system or part of a system or return to what a system had been by overthrowing current laws and practices. They see societal change as a threat to values or practices and wish to maintain the status quo or return to a former status by reversing the change process (Inglehart and Baker 2001). The movement to pass a referendum in California to ban gay marriage is one recent example. The Islamic movement under Ayatollah Khomeini in Iran sought to restore fundamentalist Islam and eliminate Western influences.

Global transnational movements take place across societies as international organizations focus on large-scale, often global issues, such as change in the status of women, child labor, rights of indigenous peoples, global warming, and animal rights. Examples include any movement to improve the working conditions and environmental conditions resulting from the actions of multinational corporations (The Durban Accord 2003; Flavin 2001; World Resources Institute 2003). Another example is Free the Slaves, a global antislavery organization started by sociologist Kevin Bales (2000, 2004, 2007). Figure 16.6 summarizes the types of movements and the focus of each, from the micro to the macro level.

Two members of the environmental group Earth First hold a sign in front of the Lincoln Memorial in Washington, D.C., to protest the destruction of the earth's rainforests and to advocate for the rights of various species that are endangered. Such movements use nonviolent protest, legislative means, and appeals to the public or to the courts to accomplish their goals.

Thinking Sociologically

Consider a social movement with which you are familiar. What type of movement is it, and what was or is it trying to accomplish?

Globalization and Social Movements

Social movements are about people trying to improve their situations within their societies. They are intriguing because they provide compelling evidence that humans

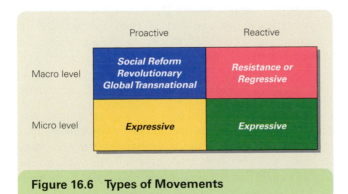

Figure 16.6   Types of Movements

make choices and are capable of countering macro- and meso-level forces. As Eitzen and Zinn (2006) put it,

> Social structures constrain what we do, but they do not determine what we do. While these structures are powerful, human beings are not totally controlled. . . . Individuals acting alone, or with others, can shape, resist, challenge, and sometimes change the social structures that impinge on them. These actions constitute *human agency*. (p. 322)

Since World War II, power in the global system has been dominated by a group of industrial giants called the Group of 8 (or the "G8"). These nations control world markets and regulate economic and trading policies (International Encyclopedia of the Social Sciences 2008). Included among this elite are the dominant three (Japan, representing the East; Germany, representing central Europe; and the United States, representing the Western Hemisphere) and five other important but less dominating powers (Canada, France, Great Britain, Italy, and now Russia). The G8 are the core countries that have the most power in the World Trade Organization (WTO), the World Bank, the IMF, and other regulatory agencies that preside over the global economy. These agencies have often demanded that poor countries adhere to their demands or lose the right to loans and other support. Yet the policies imposed from above (through the World Bank and IMF) have often been disastrous for poor countries, creating situations in which a debt burden is

Nelson Mandela, voting for the first time in South Africa in 1994, participated in the first democratic election open to all races after segregation was abolished. A political prisoner for 26 years, Mandela was held by the apartheid-based government as a dangerous revolutionary for his beliefs in racial equality. He was elected president of his country in this election and was later a corecipient of the Nobel Peace Prize for his work for democracy and equality. His nonviolent movement provided a model for nonviolent revolutionary change, but it did so with the help of pressures from other countries and movements that advocated for racial justice.

Global South nations, calling themselves the G77, are now uniting, rather like a labor union seeking collective unity among workers, in attempts to gain some power and determine their own destinies by challenging what they experience as the tyranny of the G8 (Brecher et al. 2006; Hayden 2006). Map 13.2 on page 463 displays the location of G8 and G77 countries. At the 2009 Climate Change talks in Copenhagen, Denmark, Global South countries joined together to demand that Global North countries do more to alleviate environmental problems since "they started them" with industrialization.

In the competition to find cheaper labor for higher profits, there is a "race to the bottom," as communities must lower standards or else lose jobs to some other part of the world that is even more impoverished. Globalization as it now exists—with corporate profits as the ruling principle of most decision making—has lessened environmental standards, consumer protection, national sovereignty and local control of decisions, and safety and other protections for workers. When jobs move elsewhere, the people who had come to depend on those jobs are devastated and often thrust into poverty and homelessness, and the country loses tax revenue.

Although workers risk losing jobs by participating, one result of globalization has been a rise in countermovements. "Globalization from below" refers to the efforts by common people in small groups and protest movements to fight back. Rather than globalization being controlled solely by the pursuit of profits, these countermovements seek to protect workers, to defend the environment, and to combat the bone-crunching poverty that plagues so much of the Global South. The argument goes like this:

> It is the activity of people—going to work, paying taxes, buying products, obeying government officials, staying off private property—that continually re-creates the power of the powerful. . . . [The system, for all its power and resources, is dependent on common people to do the basic jobs that keep the society running.] This dependency gives people a potential power over the society—but one that can be realized only if they are prepared to reverse their acquiescence. . . . Social movements can be understood as the collective withdrawal of consent to established institutions. (Brecher et al. 2006:337)

The movement against globalization can be understood as the withdrawal of consent from such globalization (Brecher et al. 2006:337). There are thousands of small resistance actions against what are sometimes perceived to be the oppressive policies of G8 transnational corporations. They involve micro-level actions to bring change at the macro level. Consider the following examples:

> Under heavy pressure from the World Bank, the Bolivian government sold off the public water system of its third-largest city, Cochabamba, to a subsidiary of the San Francisco–based Bechtel Corporation, which promptly doubled the price of water for people's homes. Early in 2000, the people of Cochabamba rebelled, shutting down

created that can never be paid off. If these were individuals rather than countries, we would call them indentured servants or slaves (Brecher et al. 2006; Cockburn 2006; Weller and Hersh 2006). This creates nations where hopelessness would seem to reign supreme, yet social movements are arising in precisely these places and are often joining forces across national boundaries (Stein 2006; Weidenbaum 2006). Even some groups within the G8 nations—labor unions, college student groups, and religious bodies concerned about social justice—are joining the movements.

Encyclopedia Link 16.2
Read about antiglobalization.

the city with general strikes and blockades. The government declared a state of siege, and a young protester was shot and killed. Word spread all over the world from the remote Bolivian highlands via the Internet. Hundreds of e-mail messages poured into Bechtel from all over the world, demanding that it leave Cochabamba. In the midst of local and global protests, the Bolivian government, which had said that Bechtel must not leave, suddenly reversed itself and signed an accord accepting every demand of the protestors. (Brecher et al. 2006:341–342)

* * * * *

Concerned groups in Europe, Japan, and the U.S. found that global corporations were increasingly fostering growth of sweatshops in the Global South. They pressured companies like The Gap and Nike to establish acceptable labor and human rights conditions in their factories around the world. Their efforts gradually grew into an anti-sweatshop movement with strong labor and religious support and tens of thousands of active participants. In the U.S., college students took up the anti-sweatshop cause on hundreds of campuses, ultimately holding sit-ins on many campuses to force their college stores to ban the use of college logos on products not produced under acceptable labor conditions. (Brecher et al. 2006:333)

Many concerned citizens in the Global North now buy Fair Trade goods such as coffee, cocoa, and fruits.

Individuals in G8 countries have been extremely generous in donating to international organizations helping victims of disasters and in joining in solidarity with those in dire straits in the Global South. However, governments have often been unsympathetic. During the previous U.S. administration,

Five hundred protesters sitting on the ground are confronted by riot police during a World Trade Organization's (WTO) conference in Seattle, with demonstrators mostly from the G8 countries. The protesters oppose policies that they feel are harmful to common citizens—North or South—and seek a "globalization from below" transnational movement.

0.13% of 1% of the country's gross national product was spent on United Nations programs that address poverty, famine, illiteracy, and disease. That represents a decrease of 90% from the Kennedy administration era, more than 40 years ago. However, many activists believe that actions by individuals and small groups—globalization from below—can have a real impact. Consider how effective you think the actions taken by individuals and local groups can be by thinking about the issues in the next "Engaging Sociology."

Engaging Sociology

Micro to Macro: Change From the Bottom Up

The idea of globalization "from the bottom up" suggests that the actions of a lot of people at the micro or local level can have a significant impact on how things develop at the most macro level of the social world we inhabit. Think about that process and what forces can enhance or retard that kind of change:

1. Are you familiar with cases in which "globalization from below" has made a difference in local, national, or international events? If so, what are those?

2. Identify three structural challenges that might make it hard for people at the micro level to change the national and global forces that interfere with the quality of their lives.

3. Identify three reasons to be optimistic about why change from the bottom up can be successful.

4. Do an Internet search of the Zapatistas or of their leader, Sub-Comandante Marcos. What are the pros and the cons of this movement? Do they have any chance of bringing change to the poor, disenfranchised people of southern Mexico?

In summary, some social change is planned by organizations, some is initiated by groups that are outside the organizational structure (social movements), and some is unplanned and spontaneous (collective behavior). The most important point, however, is that actions taken by individuals affect the larger social world, sometimes even having global ramifications. Likewise, national and international changes and social movements influence the lives of individuals.

Technology, Environment, and Change

At the edge of the town of Bhopal, India, looms a subsidiary plant of the American-based Union Carbide Corporation. The plant provides work for many of the town's inhabitants. However, on December 3, 1984, things did not go as normal. A storage tank from the plant, filled with the toxic chemical liquid methyl isocyanate, overheated and turned to gas, which began to escape through a pressure relief valve. The gas formed a cloud and drifted away from the plant. By the time the sirens were sounded, it was too late for many people.

The deadly gas had done its devastating work: More than 3,000 were dead and thousands ill, many with permanent injuries from the effects of the gas. Put in perspective, the number of casualties was about equal to the number in the terrorist attack on the Twin Towers of New York City on September 11, 2001.

Journal Article Link 16.3
Read about the environmental justice movement.

This example illustrates change at multiple levels of analysis. We see a global multinational company (Union Carbide) in a society (India) that welcomed the jobs for its citizens. A community within that larger society benefited from the jobs until many residents were killed or disabled, leaving shattered families and devastated individual lives. The accident also spawned a number of forms of collective behavior. The immediate aftermath of the accident at Bhopal included panic, as people tried to flee the deadly gas. Later, it resulted in several social movements as activists from India and other countries demanded accountability and safety measures. The disaster also brought about planned change in the way Union Carbide does business and protects workers and citizens.

Technology refers to the practical application of tools, skills, and knowledge to meet human needs and extend human abilities. Technology and environment cannot be separated, as we see from the Bhopal tragedy. The raw products that fuel technology come from the environment, the wastes return to the environment, and technological mistakes affect the environment. This section discusses briefly the development and process of technology, the relationship

Global protests often focus on the actions of Western multinational corporations. Women demonstrators, including the Bhopal gas victims in India, hold a "Wanted" poster of former Union Carbide Chairman Warren Anderson, arguing that he should be tried for criminal negligence at the plant, causing the deaths of more than 3,000 people and injuries for tens of thousands in Bhopal, India.

between technology and the environment, and the implications for change at each level of analysis.

Throughout human history, there have been major transition periods when changes in the material culture brought about revolutions in human social structures and cultures (Toffler and Toffler 1980). For example, the agricultural revolution resulted in the use of the plow to till the soil, establishing new social arrangements and eventually resulting in food surpluses that allowed cities to flourish. With the Industrial Revolution came machines powered by steam and petrol, resulting in mass production, population increases, urbanization, the division of labor in manufacturing, social stratification, and the socialist and capitalist political-economic systems. Today, postindustrial technology, based on the microchip, is fueling the spread of information, communication, and transportation on a global level and the technology to explore outer space and analyze, store, and retrieve masses of information in seconds. However, each wave initially affects only a portion of the world, leaving other people and countries behind and creating divisions between the Global North and the Global South.

According to sociologist William Ogburn ([1922] 1938, 1961, 1964), change is brought about through three processes: discovery, invention, and diffusion. Discovery is a new way of seeing reality. The material objects or ideas have been present, but they are seen in a new light when the need arises or conditions are conducive to the discovery. It is usually accomplished by an individual or a small group, a micro-level activity.

Invention refers to combining existing parts, materials, or ideas to form new ones. There was no light bulb or combustion engine lying in the forest waiting to be discovered. Human ingenuity was required to put together something that had not previously existed. Technological innovations often result from research and the expansion of science, increasingly generated at the meso level of the social system.

Diffusion is the spread of an invention or discovery from one place to another. The spread of ideas such as capitalism, democracy, and religious beliefs has brought about changes in human relationships around the world. Likewise, the spread of various types of music, film technology, telephone systems, and computer hardware and software across the globe has had important ramifications for global interconnectedness. Diffusion often involves expansion of ideas across the globe, but it also requires individuals to adopt ideas at the micro level.

Technology and Science

Science is the systematic process of producing human knowledge. The question "How do we know what we know?" is often answered: "It's science." Whether social, biological, or physical, science provides a systematic way to approach the world and its mysteries. It uses empirical research methods to discover facts and test theories. Technology applies scientific knowledge to solve problems. Early human technology was largely the result of trial and error, not based on scientific knowledge or principles. Humans did not understand why boats floated or fires burned. Since the Industrial Revolution, many inventors and capitalists have seen science and technology as routes to human betterment and happiness. With the increasing emphasis on science, the scientific process is a major social institution in 21st-century industrial and postindustrial societies, providing the bases of information and knowledge for sophisticated technology.

Indeed, one of the major transformations in modern society is the result of science becoming an institution. Prior to the 18th century, science was an avocation. People like Benjamin Franklin experimented in their backyards with whatever spare cash they had to satisfy their own curiosity.

Institutionalization refers to the creation of a stable pattern of roles, statuses, and groups that systematically meet the need for new resources and new ways of understanding the natural world. Science in the contemporary world is

Scientists have developed technologies to ease the looming energy crisis and ward off climate change. Solar panels on this restaurant in Portugal reduce dependence on other sources of energy.

Thomas Edison had more than 1,000 patented inventions, including the light bulb, recorded sound, and movies, but perhaps his most influential invention was the research lab—in which people were paid to invent and to conduct research—at Menlo Park in New Jersey. This was the seminal step in the institutionalization of science.

a social process. It involves mobilizing financial resources and employing the most highly trained people (which in turn requires the development of educational institutions). Innovation resulting in change will be very slow until a society has institutionalized science—providing extensive training and paying some people simply to do research. Specialization in science speeds up the rates of discovery. A researcher focuses on one area and gets much more

Technology has had some unexpected consequences, including a staggering increase in the amount of trash generated. Illustrated here is trash from the fast-food industry in Egypt. The volume of trash has created problems of disposal and pollution control.

1970). Galileo's finding that the earth revolves around the sun and Darwin's theory of evolution are two examples of radical new ideas that changed history. More recently, cumulative scientific knowledge has resulted in engines that power cars and machines and computer technology that have revolutionized communication.

Thinking Sociologically

Imagine what your life would have been like before computers, e-mail, and the Internet. What would be different? (Note that you are imagining the world from only 10 to 20 years ago.) Ask your parents or grandparents what this past world was like.

Technology and Change

The G8 has yearly meetings to regulate global economic policy and markets. The group's power enables those eight countries to dominate technology by controlling raw products such as oil. In the process, they profoundly influence which countries will be rich or poor. Although politicians like to tell us they believe in a free market economy, uninhibited by governmental interference, they actually intervene regularly in the global market.

New technological developments can be a force not only for world integration but also for economic and political disintegration (Schaeffer 2003). The technological revolution in communications has resulted in fiber optic cable and wireless microwave cell phones and satellite technologies that make it easier to communicate with people around the world. We now live in a global village, a great boon for those fortunate enough to have the education and means to take advantage of it (Drori 2006; Howard and Jones 2004; Salzman and Matathia 2000).

However, the changes in technology do not always have a positive effect on less affluent countries. For example, by substituting fiber optic cable for old technologies, the demand for copper, used for more than 100 years to carry electrical impulses for telephones and telegraphs, has bottomed out. Countries such as Zambia and Chile, which depended on the copper trade, have seen major negative impacts on their economies. New developments resulting in artificial sweeteners reduced the demand for sugar, the major source of income for the 50 million people who work in the beet and cane sugar industries around the globe. As new technologies bring substantial benefits to many in the world, those benefits actually harm people in other parts of the interconnected world.

in-depth understanding. Effective methods of communication across the globe mean that we do not need to wait several years for a research manuscript to cross the ocean and to be translated into another language. Competition in science means that researchers move quickly on their findings. Delaying findings may mean that the slowpoke does not get tenure at his or her university, promotion in the research laboratory, or awards for innovation.

We would not have automobiles, planes, missiles, space stations, computers, the Internet, and many of our modern conveniences without the institutionalization of science and without scientific application (technology). Science is big business, funded by industry and political leaders. University researchers and some government-funded science institutes engage in *basic research* designed to discover new knowledge, often on topics that receive funding. Industry and some governmental agencies such as the military and the Department of Agriculture employ scientists to do *applied research* and to discover practical uses for existing knowledge.

Scientific knowledge is usually cumulative, with each study adding to the existing body of research. However, radical new ideas can result in scientific revolutions (Kuhn

Some societies are attempting to replace the old economies with new service industries such as tourism. However, because of violence and terrorist threats, many potential tourists prefer not to travel to peripheral countries. Money spent on travel often goes to airlines, first-class hotels, and cruise ship lines based in the core countries rather than to local businesses in the peripheral countries (Schaeffer 2003). Changes in technology and the economy have forced many individuals to leave their native villages in search of paid labor positions in urban factories and the tourism industry, disrupting family lives.

Rapid technological change has affected generational relationships as well. It is not uncommon for younger generations to have more technological competence than their elders, and this sometimes creates a generational digital divide. In some settings, younger people are looked to for their expertise, whereas in the past, the elders were the source of knowledge and wisdom. Often the older members of a business or group feel devalued and demoralized late in their careers because those with technical competence view the older members as "outdated has-beens." Even networks and forms of entertainment such as the Wii and Nintendo DX further the social distance between generations. With the changes brought about by technology come changes in the nonmaterial culture—values, political ideologies, and human relationships. Clearly, technology can have a variety of social impacts—both positive and negative.

In the opening questions, we asked whether you as an individual can make a difference. In closing, we present in the final "Engaging Sociology" a plan you can follow to make a difference.

Thinking Sociologically

First, read "Making a Difference." Then use the steps to plan how you would bring about a change that would make a difference in your workplace, college, community, region, nation, or in the world. Go to "Contributing to Our Social World: What Can We Do?" at the end of this and other chapters to find ways in which you could be actively involved in bettering society.

Engaging Sociology

Making a Difference

Do you want to develop sociological interventions that will bring about needed change? Applied sociologists and individuals like you can take certain steps to facilitate change (Glass 2004). Because bringing about change requires cooperation, working in a group context is often essential. Flexibility, openness to new ideas, and willingness to entertain alternative suggestions are also key factors in successful change. The following steps provide a useful strategy for planning change:

1. *Identify the issue:* Be specific and focus on what is to be changed. Without clear focus, your target for change can get muddied or lost in the attempt.

2. *Research the issue and use those findings:* Learn as much as you can about the situation or problem to be changed. Use informants, interviews, written materials, observation, existing data (such as Census Bureau statistics), or anything that helps you understand the issues. That will enable you to find the most effective strategies to bring about change.

3. *Find out what has already been done and by whom:* Other individuals or groups may be working on the same issue. Be sure you know what intervention has already taken place. This can also help determine whether attempts at change have been tried, what has been successful, and whether further change is needed.

4. *Change must take into account each level of analysis:* When planning a strategy, you may focus on one level of analysis, but be sure to consider what interventions are needed at other levels to make the change effective or to anticipate the effects of change on other levels.

(Continued)

(Continued)

5. *Determine the intervention strategy:* Map out the intervention and the steps to carry it out. Identify resources needed, and plan each step in detail.

6. *Evaluate the plan:* Get feedback on the plan from those involved in the issue and from unbiased colleagues. If possible, involve those who will be affected by the intervention in the planning and evaluation of the change. When feasible, test the intervention plan before implementing it.

7. *Implement the intervention:* Put the plan into effect, watching for any unintended consequences. Ask for regular feedback from those affected by the change.

8. *Evaluate the results:* Assess what is working, what is not, and how the constituents that experience the change are reacting. Sociological knowledge and skills should help guide this process.

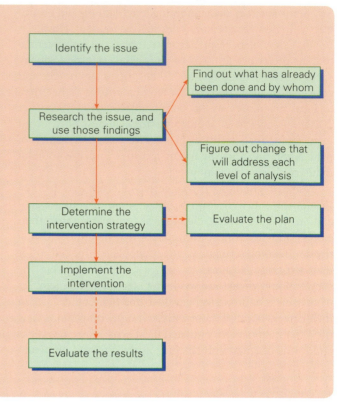

Identify the issue → Research the issue, and use those findings → Find out what has already been done and by whom / Figure out change that will address each level of analysis → Determine the intervention strategy → Evaluate the plan → Implement the intervention → Evaluate the results

What Have We Learned?

Can you change the world? The underlying message of this chapter and the text is that the choices we make facilitate change at each level in our social world. Understanding sociology provides the knowledge and tools to make informed decisions and allows us to work with groups to make a difference. One of the founders of sociology, Émile Durkheim, argued that sociology is not worth a single hour's work if it does not help change the world to a better place (Durkheim 1893/1947).

As you face individual challenges to bring about change in your social world, keep in mind this message: Change at one level affects all other levels. Sociology as a discipline is focused on gathering accurate information about the society in which we live. But sociologists as citizens often use their knowledge to advocate for changes that they think will make a better society, and applied sociologists help organizations bring about change. We hope that through this book and your course you have gained important insights that will help you contribute to the dialogue about how to make our social world a better, more humane place.

Key Points

- Social change—variation or alteration over time in behavior patterns, culture, or structure in a society—typically involves change at one level of the social system that ripples through the other levels, micro, meso, and macro. (See pp. 560–565.)

- Strains within an organization or group can induce change, as can stress that is imposed from the outside environment. (See pp. 565–570.)

- Sociological theories—whether micro or macro—offer explanations for the causes of change. (See pp. 570–574.)

- At the micro level, change is often initiated through collective behavior, which can take several forms: crowds, mobs, riots, rumors, fads, and fashions. (See pp. 574–579.)

- At the meso level, change in organizations is often managed through a planned process. (See pp. 579–582.)

- Social movements often provide impetus for change at the macro level. Social changes can be induced at the micro level, but they have implications even at the global level. (See pp. 582–588.)

- Science and technology can also stimulate change, but science has its greatest impact for change when it is institutionalized. (See pp. 588–590.)

- Social structures constrain what we do, but individuals, especially when acting in concert with others, can challenge, resist, and change the social systems that constrain them. We can change our society through *human agency*. (See pp. 591–592.)

Contributing to Our Social World: What Can We Do?

At the Local Level

Campuswide Movements

- A wide range of social issues, including international peace, environmental issues, human rights, and specific student concerns such as campus safety and rising costs of higher education, may have movements represented on your campus. Consider participating in such activities. If you feel strongly about an issue for which no movement exists, consider organizing one with a few like-minded students.

Community Movements

- Many communities have movements to bring about change. Check with your professors, service learning opportunities, and Chambers of Commerce to find these.

At the Organizational or Institutional Level

Invite a movement leader to campus

- Consider inviting movement leaders to your campus for a lecture, or organize a conference that features several experts in a particular field. Environment, civil rights, and alternative health care are topics that have wide appeal. Through involvement, you can be proactive in shaping the society in which you live.

Volunteer Match

- Volunteer Match seeks to connect individuals with movements of interest to them. Its Web site (www.VolunteerMatch.org) has suggestions for getting involved in your local area.

At the National and Global Levels

International Debt Burden

- Jubilee is a leading organization in the promotion of debt forgiveness—a solution that the U.S. government has embraced in principle. A major obstacle to improvement in living conditions in the less developed countries is the enormous amount of money they owe to banks and governments in the industrialized nations for past-due, development-oriented loans. Named for the commandment in the Old Testament that people are to cancel all debt owed to them every jubilee year (once every 49 years), the organization has legislative programs, research work, and educational outreach activities throughout the world. The Web site of the U.S. branch of Jubilee (www.jubileeusa.org) provides information on ways in which you can get involved, and the international Web site (www.jubilee2000uk.org) includes information about international debt, activities, and the history of the movement.

 For chapter-specific resources, including **Frontline**, **TED**, and **YouTube** videos; self-quizzes; web exercises; and more, visit **www.pineforge.com/oswmedia3e.**

References

AAUW Dialogue. 2008. "Violence Against Women." Oct. 28. Retrieved February 21, 2009 (blog-aauw.org/2008/10/28/violence-against-women).

Abma, J. C., G. M. Martinez, W. D. Mosher, and B. S. Dawson. 2004. "Teenagers in the United States: Sexual Activity, Contraceptive Use, and Childbearing, 2002." *Vital Health Statistics* 23(24). Atlanta, GA: National Center for Health Statistics.

About.com: Alcoholism. 2009. "What Are the Treatments for Alcohol Problems." July 31. alcoholism.about.com/cs/faq/f/prob_faq6.htm.

Abrahamson, K., J. G. Anderson, M. Anderson, J. Suitor, K. Pillemer. 2009. "The Cumulative Influence of Conflict on Nursing Home Staff: A Computer Simulation Approach." *Research in Gerontological Nursing.* Retrieved January 15, 2010 (www.geronurseresearch.com/advanced.asp).

Abramson, Paul R., John H. Aldrich, and David W. Rhode. 2007. *Change and Continuity in the 2004 and 2006 Elections. Washington,* D.C.: CQ Press.

Abu-Lughod, Janet L. 1991. *Changing Cities: Urban Sociology.* New York: Harper Collins.

———. 2001. *New York, Chicago, Los Angeles: America's Global Cities.* Minneapolis: University of Minnesota Press.

Adams, Mike S. 1996. "Labeling and Differential Association: Towards a General Social Learning Theory of Crime and Deviance." *American Journal of Criminal Justice* 20(2):147–64.

Adler, Freda, Gerhard O. W. Mueller, William S. Laufer, and E. Mavis Hetherington. 2004. *Criminology,* 5th ed. New York: McGraw-Hill.

Adler, Patricia A., and Peter Adler. 1991. *Backboards and Blackboards: College Athletes and Role Engulfment.* New York: Columbia University Press.

———. 2004. "The Gloried Self." Pp. 117–26 in *Inside Social Life,* 4th ed., edited by Spencer E. Cahill. Los Angeles: Roxbury.

Adler, Roy D. 2001. "Women in the Executive Suite Correlate to High Profits." *Harvard Business Review* 79(November 16):3.

Aguirre, Adalberto, and David V. Baker. 2007. *Structured Inequality in the United States,* 2nd ed. Englewood Cliffs, NJ: Prentice Hall.

Aguirre, Adalberto, Jr., and Jonathan H. Turner. 2006. *American Ethnicity: The Dynamics and Consequences of Discrimination,* 5th ed. Boston: McGraw-Hill.

Ahrons, Constance. 2004. *We're Still Family.* New York: Harper Collins.

Akers, Ronald. 1992. *Deviant Behavior: A Social Learning Approach,* 3rd ed. Belmont, CA: Wadsworth.

———.1998. *Social Learning and Social Structure: A General Theory of Crime and Deviance.* Boston: Northeastern University Press.

Akers, Ronald L., Marvin D. Krohn, Lonn Lanza-Kaduce, and Marcia Radosevich. 1979. "Social Learning and Deviant Behavior." *American Sociological Review* 44(August):635–54.

Alatas, Syed Farid. 2006. "Ibn Khaldun and Contemporary Sociology." *International Sociology* 21(6):782–95.

Alexander, Victoria D. 2003. *Sociology of the Arts: Exploring Fine and Popular Forms.* Malden, MA: Blackwell.

Alldritt, Leslie D. 2000. "The Burakumin: The Complicity of Japanese Buddhism in Oppression and an Opportunity for Liberation." *Journal of Buddhist Ethics* 7(July).

Altbach, Philip G., and Todd M. Davis. 1999. "Global Challenge and National Response: Note for an International Dialogue on International Higher Education." *International Higher Education* 14:2–5.

Altheide, David, Patricia A. Adler, Peter Adler, and Duane Altheide. 1978. "The Social Meanings of Employee Theft." P. 90 in *Crime at the Top,* edited by John M. Johnson and Jack D. Douglas. Philadelphia: Lippincott.

Amadeo, Kimberley. 2009. "NAFTA Pros and Cons." Retrieved December 20, 2009 (http://useconomy.about.com/b/2008/04/24/nafta-pros-and-cons.htm).

Amato, Paul R. 2000. "The Consequences of Divorce for Adults and Children." *Journal of Marriage and the Family* 62(November):1269–87.

Amato, Paul R., and Juliana M. Sobolewski. 2001. "The Effects of Divorce and Marital Discord on Adult Children's Psychological Well-Being." *American Sociological Review* 63(December):697–713.

American Academy of Pediatrics. 2008. "Fact Sheet: Children's Health Insurance." Retrieved January 9, 2010 (www.aap.org/research/factsheet.pdf).

American Association of University Women Educational Foundation. 2001. "Hostile Hallways: Bullying, Teasing, and Sexual Harassment in School." Retrieved April 17, 2010 (www.aauw.org/research/upload/hostilehallways.pdf).

American Cancer Society. 2006. *Cancer Facts and Figures for African Americans 2005–2006.* Atlanta, GA: Author.

American Cultural Center Resource Service. 2004. "North American Free Trade Agreement." Retrieved September 29, 2006 (http://usinfo.org/law/nafta/chap-01.stm.html).

American Library Association (Office of Intellectual Freedom). 2009. "The Most Frequently Challenged Books of 2008." Retrieved July 10, 2009 (www.ala.org/ala/issuesadvocacy/banned/frequentlychallenged/21stcenturychallenged/2008/index.cfm).

American Psychological Association. 2007. "APA Resolution On Religious, Religion-Based, and/or Religion-Derived Prejudice" August 2007. Retrieved December 24, 2009 (http://wthrockmorton.com/apa-resolution-on-religious-religion-based-andor-religion-derived-prejudice).

———. 2008. "Report From: Working Group on Assisted Suicide and End-of-Life Decisions." Retrieved August 16, 2008 (www.apa.org/pi/aseol/introduction.html).

American Sociological Association. 2006. "'What Can I Do with a Bachelor's Degree in Sociology?' A National Survey of Seniors Majoring in Sociology." Washington DC: American Sociological Association Research and Development Department.

———. 2009. *21st Century Careers With an Undergraduate Degree in Sociology.* Washington, DC: Author.

American Sociological Association Task Force on Institutionalizing Public Sociologies. 2005. "Public Sociology and the Roots of American Sociology: Re-Establishing our Connection to the Public." Washington, DC: Author.

Amnesty International. 2005. "Abolish the Death Penalty: The Death Penalty Is Racially Biased." Retrieved August 4, 2006 (www.amnestyusa.org/abolish/factsheets/racialprejudices.html).

———. 2006. "Facts and Figures on the Death Penalty." Retrieved August 8, 2006 (http://web.amnesty.org/pages/deathpenalty-facts-eng), (http://web.amnesty.org/pages/deathpenaltycountries-eng).

———. 2007. "Stop the Death Penalty: The World Decides." Retrieved July 6, 2008 (www.amnesty.org/en/news-and-updates/news/stop-the-death-penalty-the-world-decides).

AmO Life. 2008. "Top 10 Largest Cities in the World." Retrieved April 12, 2008 (http://amolife.com/great-places/top-10-largest-cities-in-the-world.html).

Ananova. 2001. "Death Workers Sell Body Parts for Extra Christmas Cash." Retrieved December 4, 2005 (www.ananova.com/news/sm_465113.html).

———. 2002. "Students Willing to Sell Body Parts to Fund Education." April 8. Retrieved August 26, 2006 (www.ananova.com).

Anderson, Benedict. 2006. Imagined Communities: Reflections on the Origin and Spread of Nationalism, Rev. ed. London: Verso.

Anderson, David A., and Mykol Hamilton. 2005. "Gender Role Stereotyping of Parents in Children's Picture Books: The Invisible Father." Sex Roles: A Journal of Research 52(3/4):145.

Anderson, Elijah. 2000. Code of the Street: Decency, Violence, and the Moral Life of the Inner City. New York: W. W. Norton.

Anderson, James G., and Carolyn E. Aydin. 2005. Evaluating the Organizational Impact of Health Care Information Systems. New York: Springer.

Anderson, Margaret, and Pat Hill Collins. 2006. Race Class and Gender: An Anthology, 6th ed. Belmont: Wadsworth.

Anderson, Michael. 1994. "What Is New About the Modern Family?" Pp. 67–90 in Time, Family, and Community: Perspectives on Family and Community History, edited by Michael Drake. Oxford, UK: Open University.

ANRED (Anorexia Nervosa and Related Eating Disorders, Inc.). 2007. "Statistics: How Many People Have Eating Disorders?" Retrieved April 17, 2010 (www.anred.com).

Answerbag.com. 2009. "What Percentage of United States Labor Force (People) Works in Agriculture? Industry?" Retrieved January 5, 2010 (www.answerbag.com/q_view/1622383).

Answers.com. 2006. "Flag." Retrieved July 15, 2006 (www.answers.com/flag&r=67).

Anti-Defamation League. 2007. "2006 Audit of Anti-Semitic Incidents." Retrieved January 27, 2008 (www.adl.org/PresRele/ASUS_12/4993-12.htm).

Antoun, Richard T. 2001. Understanding Fundamentalism: Christian, Islamic, and Jewish Movements. Walnut Creek, CA: AltaMira.

Appleby, Julie. 2006. "Debate Surrounds End-Of-Life Health Care Costs." USA Today (October 18). Retrieved April 4, 2008 (www.usatoday.com/money/industries/heaslth/2006-10-18-end-of-life-costs_x.htm).

Armstrong, Karen. 2000. The Battle for God. New York: Knopf.

Arnold, David O., ed. 1970. The Sociology of Subcultures. Berkeley, CA: Glendessary.

Arrighi, Barbara A. 2000. Understanding Inequality: The Intersection of Race, Ethnicity, Class, and Gender. Lanham, MD: Rowman & Littlefield.

Arulampalam, Wiji, Alison L. Booth, and Mark L. Bryan. 2007. "Is there a glass ceiling over Europe? Exploring the gender pay gap across the wages distribution." in Industrial and Labor Relations Review. Vol. 60(1). pp. 163–186.

Aseltine, Robert H., Jr. 1995. "A Reconsideration of Parental and Peer Influences on Adolescent Deviance." Journal of Health and Social Behavior 36(2):103–21.

Ashley, David, and David Michael Orenstein. 2009. Sociological Theory, 7th ed. Boston: Allyn & Bacon.

Asian Development Bank. 2002. "Cambodia's Economy Continues to Gain Ground" (News Release No. 042/02, April 9).

Attewell, Paul. 2001. "The First and Second Digital Divides." Sociology of Education 74(3):252–59.

Aulette, Judy Root. 2002. Changing American Families. Boston: Allyn & Bacon.

Avert. 2009. "Worldwide HIV and AIDS Statistics: Regional Statistics for HIV and AIDS, End of 2008." Retrieved April 13, 2010 (www.avert.org/worldstats.htm).

Ayalon, Hanna, and Yossi Shavit. 2004. "Educational Reforms and Inequalities in Israel: The MMI Hypothesis Revisited." Sociology of Education, 77(2):103–120.

Ayers, William, 2006. "Hearts and Minds: Military Recruitment and the High School Battlefield." Phi Delta Kappan 87(8):594–99.

Ayers, William, and Michael Klonsky. 2006. "Chicago's Renaissance 2010: The Small Schools Movement Meets the Ownership Society." Phi Delta Kappan (February):453–56.

Bagby, Ihsan A. 2003. "Imams and Mosque Organization in the United States: A Study of Mosque Leadership and Organizational Structure in American Mosques." Pp. 113–34 in Muslims in the United States, edited by Philippa Strum and Danielle Tarantolo. Washington, DC: Woodrow Wilson International Center for Scholars.

Bahney, Anna. 2009. "Don't Talk to Invisible Strangers." New York Times March 9, Retrieved August 13, 2009 (www.nytimes.com/2006/03/09/fashion/thursdaystyles/09parents.html).

Bainbridge, William S., and Rodney Stark. 1981. "Suicide, Homicide, and Religion: Durkheim Reassessed." Annual Review of the Social Sciences of Religion 5:33–56.

Baker, David P. 2002. "International Competition and Education Crises: Cross-National Studies of School Outcomes." Pp. 393–98 in Education and Sociology: An Encyclopedia, edited by David L. Levinson, Peter W. Cookson, Jr., and Alan R. Sadovnik. New York: RoutledgeFalmer.

Bales, Kevin. 2000. New Slavery: A Reference Handbook, 2nd ed. Santa Barbara, CA: ABC-CLIO.

———. 2002. "Because She Looks Like a Child." Pp. 207–29 in Global Woman: Nannies, Maids, and Sex Workers in the New Economy, edited by Barbara Ehrenreich and Arlie Russell Hochschild. New York: Henry Holt.

———. 2004. Disposable People: New Slavery in the Global Economy, Rev. ed. Berkeley: University of California Press.

———. 2007. Ending Slavery: How We Free Today's Slaves. Berkeley, CA: University of California Press.

Bales, Kevin, and Zoe Trodd. 2008. To Plead Our Own Cause: Personal Stories by Today's Slaves. Ithaca, NY: Cornell University Press.

Ballantine, Jeanne H., and Floyd M. Hammack. 2009. The Sociology of Education: A Systematic Analysis, 6th ed. Upper Saddle River, NJ: Prentice Hall.

Ballantine, Jeanne H., and Joan Z. Spade. 2008. Schools and Society, 4th ed. Belmont, CA: Cengage/Wadsworth.

Banbury, Samantha. 2004. "Coercive Sexual Behavior in British Prisons as Reported by Adult Ex-Prisoners." The Howard Journal 43(2):113–30.

Bankston, Carl L., III. 2004. "Social Capital, Cultural Values, Immigration, and Academic Achievement: The Host Country Context and Contradictory Consequences." Sociology of Education 77(2):176–80.

Barash, David. 2002. "Evolution, Males, and Violence." The Chronicle Review (May 24):B7.

Barber, Benjamin R. 2006. "The Uncertainty of Digital Politics: Democracy's Relationship with Information Technology" Pp. 61–69 in Globalization: The Transformation of Social Worlds, edited by D. Stanley Eitzen and Maxine Baca Zinn. Belmont, CA: Wadsworth.

Barber, Bonnie L., Jacquelynne S. Eccles, and Margaret R. Stone. 2001. "Whatever Happened to the Jock, the Brain, and the Princes? Young Adult Pathways Linked to Adolescent Activity Involvement and Social Identity." Journal of Adolescent Research 16(5):429–55.

Barker, Colin. 2009. "60% of the World Uses Mobile Phones." March 3. ZD Net UK. Retrieved November 12, 2009 (http://news.zdnet.co.uk/communications/0,1000000085,39621541,00.htm).

Barnes, P. M., B. Bloom, and R. Nahin. 2008. "Complimentary and Alternative Medicine Use Among Adults and Children: US 2007." CDC National Health Statistics Report #12. December.

Barnes, Patricia M., Eve Powell-Griner, Kim McFann, and Richard L. Nahin. 2004. "Complementary and Alternative Medicine Use Among Adults: United States, 2002." CDC Advance Data Report, No. 343.

Barnett, T. P., J. C. Adam, and D. P. Lettenmaier. 2005. "Potential Impacts of a Warming Climate on Water Availability in Snow-Dominated Regions." Nature 438(November 17):303–309.

Barraclough, Geoffrey, ed. 1986. The Times Concise Atlas of World History, Rev. ed. London: Times Books.

Barrett, David B., Todd M. Johnson, and Peter F. Crossing. 2008. "The 2007 Annual Megacensus of Religions." In Time Almanac 2008. Chicago: Encyclopaedia Britannica.

Barry, Ellen. 2009. "Protests in Moldova Explode, With Help of Twitter." New York Times, April 8: A1. Retrieved December 22, 2009 (www.nytimes.com/2009/04/08/world/europe/08moldova.html).

Basow, Susan A. 1992. Gender: Stereotypes and Roles, 3rd ed. Belmont, CA: Wadsworth.

———. 2000. "Gender Stereotypes and Roles." Pp. 101–15 in The Meaning of Difference: American Constructions of Race, Sex and Gender, Social Class, and Sexual Orientation, 2nd ed., edited by Karen E. Rosenblum and Toni-Michelle C. Travis. New York: McGraw-Hill.

Basso, Keith H. 1979. Portraits of the Whiteman: Linguistic Play and Cultural Symbols Among the Western Apache. Cambridge, UK: Cambridge University Press.

BBC's Science and Nature. 2009 "The Ghost in Your Genes." Retrieved November 12, 2009 (www.bbc.co.uk/sn/tvradio/programmes/horizon/ghostgenes.shtml).

———. 2004. "Q and A: Muslim Headscarves." Retrieved April 17, 2010 (www.news.bbc.co.uk/2/hi/europe/3328277.stm).

———. 2005. "Mukhtar Mai—History of a Rape Case." Retrieved July 13, 2008 (http://news.bbc.co.uk/2/hi/south_asia/4620065.stm).

———. 2008. "US Elections Map: State-by-State Guide" (March 5). Retrieved March 21, 2008 (http://news.bbc.co.uk/2/hi/in_depth/629/629/7223461.stm).

B.C. Ministry of Labour & Citizens' Services. 2006 October 6. B.C. Stats Infoline 6(40). Retrieved April 17, 2010 (www.bcstats.gov.bc.ca/releases/info2006/in0647.pdf) OR (www.bcstats.gov.bc.ca/releases/infoline.asp).

Beckwith, Carol. 1983. "Niger's Wodaabe: People of the Taboo." National Geographic 164(4):483–509.

———. 1993. Nomads of Niger. New York: Harry N. Abrams.

Belding, Theodore C. 2004. "Nobility and Stupidity: Modeling the Evolution of Class Endogamy." Retrieved August 7, 2008 (http://arxiv.org/abs/nlin.AO/0405048).

Bell, Daniel. 1973. The Coming of Post-Industrial Society: A Venture in Social Forecasting. New York: Basic Books.

———. [1976] 1999. The Coming of Post-Industrial Society: A Venture in Social Forecasting, Special anniversary edition. New York: Basic Books.

Bellah, Robert N. 1970. "Civil Religion in America." Pp. 168–215 in Beyond Belief: Essays on Religion in a Post-Traditionalist World. New York: Harper & Row.

———. 1992. The Broken Covenant: American Civil Religion in Time of Trial. Chicago: University of Chicago Press.

Bellah, Robert N., and Frederick E. Greenspahn, eds. 1987. Uncivil Religion: Interreligious Hostility in America. New York: Crossroad.

Bellah, Robert N., Richard Madsen, William M. Sullivan, Ann Swindler, and Steven M. Tipton. 1996. Habits of the Heart: Individualism and Commitment in American Life, Updated ed. Berkeley: University of California Press.

Benavot, Aaron, John Meyer, and David Kamens. 1991. "Knowledge for the Masses: World Models and National Curricula: 1920–1986." American Sociological Review 56(1):85–100.

Benderly, Beryl Lieff. 1982. "Rape Free or Rape Prone." Science 82(3):40–43.

Benevolo, Leonardo. 1995. The European City. Cambridge, MA: Blackwell.

Benguigui, Yamina. 2000. The Perfumed Garden. Brooklyn, NY: First Run Icarus Films.

Bennis, Warren G., Kenneth D. Benne, and Robert Chin. 1985. The Planning of Change, 4th ed. New York: Holt, Rinehart Winston.

Benokraitis, Nijole V. 2004. Marriages and Families: Changes, Choices, and Constraints, 5th ed. Englewood Cliffs, NJ: Prentice Hall.

———. 2008. Marriages and Families: Changes, Choices, and Constraints, 6th ed. Englewood Cliffs, NJ: Prentice Hall.

———. 2010. Marriages and Families: Changes, Choices, and Constraints, 12th ed. Englewood Cliffs, NJ: Prentice Hall.

Benokraitis, Nijole V., and Joe R. Feagin. 1995. Modern Sexism: Blatant, Subtle, and Covert Discrimination, 2nd ed. Englewood Cliffs, NJ: Prentice Hall.

Berger, Helen A., 1999. A Community of Witches: Contemporary Neo-Paganism and Witchcraft in the United States. Columbia: University of South Carolina Press.

Berger, Helen A., and Douglas Ezzy. 2007. Teenage Witches: Magical Youth and the Search for the Self. New Brunswick, NJ: Rutgers University Press.

Berger, Michael L. 1979. The Devil Wagon in God's Country: The Automobile and Social Change in Rural America, 1893–1929. Hamden, CT: Archon.

Berger, Peter L. 1961. The Noise of Solemn Assemblies. Garden City, NY: Doubleday.

Berger, Peter L., and Thomas Luckmann. 1966. The Social Construction of Reality. Garden City, NY: Doubleday.

Bergman, Mike. 2005. "U.S. Voter Turnout Up in 2004." U.S. Census Bureau News. Retrieved March 26, 2008 (www.census.gov/Press_Release/www/releases/archives/voting).

Berk, Richard A. 1974. Collective Behavior. Dubuque, IA: Brown.

Berry, Brian J. L., and John Kasarda. 1977. Contemporary Urban Ecology. New York: Macmillan.

Bertman, Stephen. 1998. Hyperculture: The Human Cost of Speed. Westport, CT: Praeger.

Better Factories Movement in Cambodia. 2006. Retrieved April 17, 2010 (www.betterfactories.org).

Bettie, Julie. 2003. Women Without Class: Girls, Race, and Identity. Berkeley: University of California Press.

Beyer, Peter. 2000. "Secularization From the Perspective of Globalization." Pp. 81–93 in The Secularization Debate, edited by William H. Swatos, Jr. and Daniel V. A. Olson. Lanham, MD: Rowman & Littlefield.

Bianci, Suzanne M., Melissa A. Milkie, Liana C. Sayer, and John P. Robinson. 2000. "Is Anyone Doing the Housework? Trends in the Gender Division of Household Labor." Social Forces 79(1):191–228.

Bibby, Reginald W. 2002. Restless Gods: The Renaissance of Religion in Canada. Toronto, Canada: Stoddard.

Billig, Michael. 1995. Banal Nationalism. Thousand Oaks, CA: Sage.

Birdwhistell, Raymond L. 1970. Kinesics and Context: Essays on Body Motion Communication. Philadelphia: University of Pennsylvania Press.

"Births to Unmarried Women Increasing in U.S., Driven by Women in 20s, 30s, Report Shows." 2009. Medical News Today. May 15. Retrieved November 28, 2009 (www.medicalnewstoday.com/articles/150155.php)

Black Politics on the Web. 2009. Retrieved December 22, 2009 (http://blackpoliticsontheweb.com/2009/03/13/environmental-racism-an-unfortunate-reality).

Blackman, Ann. 2001. "Bush Acts on Abortion 'Gag Rule.'" *Time* (January 22). Retrieved September 20, 2006 (www.time.com/time/nation/article/0,8599,96275,00.html).

Blank, Rebecca M. 2002. "Evaluating Welfare Reform in the United States." *Journal of Economic Literature* 40(4):1105–1166.

Blasi, Joseph, Douglas Kruse, and Aaron Bernstein. 2003. *In the Company of Owners.* New York: Basic Books.

Blau, Peter M. 1956. *Bureaucracy in Modern Society.* New York: Random House.

———. 1964. *Exchange and Power in Social Life.* New York: John Wiley.

Blau, Peter, and Otis Dudley Duncan. 1967. *The American Occupational Structure.* New York: John Wiley.

Blauner, Robert. 1972. *Racial Oppression in America.* New York: Harper & Row.

Blee, Kathleen M. 2008. "White Supremacy as Extreme Deviance." Pp. 108–17 in *Extreme Deviance,* edited by Erich Goode and D. Angus Vail. Thousand Oaks, CA: Pine Forge.

Blumer, Herbert. 1969. *Symbolic Interactionism: Perspective and Method.* Englewood Cliffs, NJ: Prentice Hall.

———. 1986. *Symbolic Interactionism: Perspective and Method.* Berkeley: University of California Press.

"Body Parts for Sale." 2008. *Science and Society.* May 6. ABC News. Retrieved January 11, 2010 (blogs.abcnews.com/scienceandsociety/2008/05/body-parts-for.html).

Bolaria, Singh, and Harley D. Dickinson. 2001. "The Evolution of Health Care in Canada: Toward Community or Corporate Control?" Pp. 199–213 in *The Blackwell Companion to Medical Sociology,* edited by William C. Cockerham. Malden, MA: Blackwell.

Bolduan, Kate. 2009. "The Plight of Young Uninsured Americans." CNN Politics.COM. March 7, 2009. Retrieved January 10, 2010 (www.cnn.com/2009/POLITICS/03/07/young.uninsured/index.html).

Boli, John. 2002. "Globalization." Pp. 307–13 in *Education and Sociology: An Encyclopedia,* edited by David L. Levinson, Peter W. Cookson, Jr., and Alan R. Sadovnik. New York: RoutledgeFalmer.

Bonacich, Edna. 1972. "A Theory of Ethnic Antagonism: The Split Labor Market." *American Sociological Review* 37(October):547–59.

———. 1976. "Advanced Capitalism and Black-White Race Relations in the United States: A Split Labor Market Interpretation." *American Sociological Review* 41(February):34–51.

Bonacich, Edna, and Jake B. Wilson. 2005. "Hoisted by Its Own Petard: Organizing Wal-Mart's Logistics Workers." *New Labor Forum* 14:67–75.

Bonczar, Thomas P., and Tracy L. Snell. 2005. "Capital Punishment, 2004." *Bureau of Justice Statistics Bulletin* (NCJ 211349). Washington, DC: U.S. Department of Justice.

Booker, Salih, and William Minter. 2006. "Global Apartheid: AIDS and Murder by Patient." Pp. 517–22 in *Beyond Borders: Thinking Critically About Global Issues,* edited by Paula S. Rothenberg. New York: Worth.

Booth, Alan, and Paul R. Amato. 2001. "Parental Predivorce Relations and Offspring Postdivorce Well-Being." *Journal of Marriage and the Family* 63(February):197–212.

Borg, Marcus J. 1994. *Meeting Jesus Again for the First Time.* San Francisco: Harper San Francisco.

Bottomore, Tom. 1979. *Political Sociology.* New York: Harper & Row.

Boulding, Elise, with Jennifer Dye. 2002. "Women and Development." In *Introducing Global Issues,* 2nd ed., edited by Michael T. Snarr and D. Neil Snarr. Boulder, CO: Lynne Rienner.

Bourdieu, P., and J. C. Passeron. 1977. *Reproduction in Education, Society and Culture.* London: Sage.

Bowen, Debra. 2008. "History Behind California's Primary Election System." Retrieved March 21, 2008 (www.sos.ca.gov/elections/elections_decline.htm).

Bowles, Samuel, and Herbert Gintis. 1976. *Schooling in Capitalist America.* New York: Basic Books.

———. 2002. "Schooling in Capitalist America Revisited." *Sociology of Education* 75(1):1–18.

Boy, Angie, and Andrzej Kulczycki. 2008. "What We Know About Intimate Partner Violence in the Middle East and North Africa." *Violence Against Women* 14(1):53–70.

Bracey, Gerald W. 2005. "The 15th Bracey Report on the Condition of Public Education." *Phi Delta Kappan* (October):138–53.

Bradley, Tamsin, Emma Tomalin, and Mangala Subramaniam. 2009. *Dowry: Bridging the Gap Between Theory and Practice.* London: Zed Books.

Brandon, Mark E. 2005. "War and American Constitutional Order." In *The Constitution in Wartime: Beyond Alarmism and Complacency,* edited by Mark Tushner. Durham, NC: Duke University Press.

Brasher, Brenda E. 2004. *Give Me That On-Line Religion.* New Brunswick, NJ: Rutgers University Press.

Brecher, Jeremy, Tim Costello, and Brendan Smith. 2006. "Globalization and Social Movements." Pp. 330–47 in *Globalization: The Transformation of Social Worlds,* edited by D. Stanley Eitzen and Maxine Baca Zinn. Belmont, CA: Wadsworth.

Bremner, Jason, Carl Haub, Marlene Lee, Mark Mather, and Eric Zuehlke. 2009. "World Population Highlights." *Population Bulletin* 64(3):3. Population Reference Bureau, Retrieved January 10, 2010 (www.prb.org/pdf09/64.3highlights.pdf).

Brettell, Caroline B., and Carolyn F. Sargent. 2001. *Gender in Cross-Cultural Perspective,* 3rd ed. Englewood Cliffs, NJ: Prentice Hall.

———. 2005. *Gender in Cross-Cultural Perspective.* 4th ed. Englewood Cliffs, NJ: Prentice Hall.

Brier, Noah Rubin. 2004. "Coming of Age." *American Demographics* 26(9):16.

Brint, Steven, Mary F. Contreras, and Michael T. Matthews. 2001. "Socialization Messages in Primary Schools: An Organizational Analysis." *Sociology of Education* 74(July):157–80.

Bristow, Jason. 2008. "Can Canadian Youth Be Inspired to Vote?" *The Toronto Sun* (March 6):17.

Britton, Dana M. 2000. "The Epistemology of the Gendered Organization." *Gender and Society* 14(3):418–34.

Britz, Jennifer Delahunty. 2006. "Are Today's Girls Too Successful?" *Dayton Daily News* (March 31):A7.

Bromley, David G., and Anson D. Shupe, Jr. 1981. *Strange Gods: The Great American Cult Scare.* Boston: Beacon.

Brookover, Wilbur B., and Edsel L. Erickson. 1975. *Sociology of Education.* Homewood, IL: Dorsey.

Brookover, Wilbur B., Edsel L. Erickson, and Alan McEvoy. 1996. *Creating Effective Schools: An In-Service Program.* Holmes Beach, FL: Learning Publications.

Brooks, Clem, and Jeff Manza. 1997. "Social Cleavages and Political Alignments: U.S. Presidential Elections, 1960–1992." *American Sociological Review* 62(December):937–46.

Brooks, Rachel, and Johanna Waters. 2010. "Student Mobility as a Response to Labour Market Congestion." Presented at International Sociological Association meetings in Sweden, July 2010.

Broom, Leonard, and Philip Selznick. 1963. *Sociology: A Text With Adapted Readings,* 3rd ed. New York: Harper & Row.

Brophy, Jere E. 1983. "Research on the Self-Fulfilling Prophesy and Teacher Expectations." *Journal of Educational Psychology* 75:631–61.

Brown, Dee. 2001. *Bury My Heart at Wounded Knee: An Indian History of the American West,* 30th anniversary ed. New York: Holt.

Brown, Donald E. 1991. *Human Universals.* Philadelphia: Temple University Press.

Bruner, Jerome. 1996. *The Culture of Education.* Cambridge, MA: Harvard University Press.

Brunn, Stanley D., Jack F. Williams, and Donald J. Zeigler. 2003. *Cities of the World: World Regional Urban Development,* 3rd ed. Lanham, MD: Rowman & Littlefield.

Brym, Robert J., and John Lie. 2007. *Sociology: Your Compass for a New World,* 3rd ed. Belmont, CA: Wadsworth.

Buchmann, Claudia, and Thomas A. DiPrete. 2006. "Gender Specific Trends in the Value of Education and the Emerging Gender Gap in College Completion." *Demography* 43:1–24.

Buechler, Steven. 2008. "What Is Critical About Sociology?" *Teaching Sociology* 36(4).

Bukhari, Zahid H. 2003. "Demography, Identity, Space: Defining American Muslims." Pp. 7–18 in *Muslims in the United States*, edited by Philippa Strum and Danielle Tarantolo. Washington DC: Woodrow Wilson International Center for Scholars.

Bumpass, Larry L., and Hsien-Hen Lu. 2000. "Trends in Cohabitation and Implications for Children's Family Contexts in the United States." *Population Studies* 51(1):29–41.

Burawoy, Michael. 2005. "For Public Sociology." *American Sociological Review* 56(2):4–28.

Burda, D. 2001. "Hospital Operating Margins Hit 5.2%." *Modern Healthcare* 31(45):10.

Bureau of Labor Statistics. 2009. "American Time Use Survey Summary." Retrieved April 17, 2010 (www.bls.gov.news.release/atus.nr0.htm) or (www.bls.gov/tus).

Bureau of Labor Statistics, U.S. Department of Labor. 2010–2011. "Healthcare." Retrieved April 17, 2010 (www.bls.gov/oco/cg/cgs035.htm).

Burgess, Robert, and Ronald L. Akers. 1966. "A Differential Association-Reinforcement Theory of Criminal Behavior." *Social Problems* 14:363–83.

Burn, Shawn Meghan. 2005. *Women Across Cultures: A Global Perspective.* 2nd ed. New York: McGraw-Hill.

Caldwell, John C. 1982. *Theory of Fertility Decline.* New York: Academic Press.

Calhoun. 2002. *Dictionary of the Social Sciences.* New York: Oxford University Press.

California Teen Youngest to Sail Solo Around World. (2009, July 17). *Los Angeles Times.* Retrieved October 7, 2009, http://abclocal.go.com/kabc/story?section=news/local/los_angeles&id=6918605.

Campbell, Ernest Q., and Thomas F. Pettigrew. 1959. *Christians in Racial Crisis.* Washington, DC: Public Affairs Press.

Canadian Institute for Health Information. 2007. "National Health Expenditure Trends, 1975–2007." Retrieved August 26, 2008 (http://secure.cihi.ca/cihiweb/dispPage.jsp?cw_page=PG_876_E&cw_topic=876&cw_rel=AR_31_E).

Cancian, Francesca M. 1992. "Feminist Science: Methodologies That Challenge Inequality." *Gender and Society* 6(4):623–42.

Carrothers, Robert M., and Denzel E. Benson. 2003. "Symbolic Interactionism in Introductory Textbooks: Coverage and Pedagogical Implications." *Teaching Sociology* 31(2):162–81.

Casasanto, Daniel. 2008. "Who's Afraid of the Big Bad Whorf? Crosslinguistic Differences in Temporal Language and Thought." *Language Learning.* 58(1):63–79.

Casella, Alexander. 2009. "Rural China Misses 'Barefoot Doctors.'" *Asia Times* (January 16). Retrieved January 10, 2010 (www.atimes.com/atimes/China/KA16Ad04.html).

Cashell, Brian W. 2007. "CRS Report for Congress: Who Are the Middle Class?" Retrieved April 17, 2010 (www.business.reachinformation.com/middle_class.aspx).

Cashmore, Ellis, and Barry Troyna. 1990. *Introduction to Race Relations.* London: Routledge.

Castells, Manuel. 1977. *The Urban Question: A Marxist Approach.* Cambridge, MA: MIT Press.

Caulfield, Jon. 1994. *City Form and Everyday Life: Toronto's Gentrification and Critical Social Practice.* Toronto, Canada: University of Toronto Press.

CBS News. 2008. "Big Cities Battle Dismal Graduation Rates" (August 18). Retrieved August 23, 2008 (www.cbsnews.com/stories/2008/04/01/national/main3985714.shtml).

"Cell Phone Use Booming Worldwide." 2007. Retrieved April 17, 2010 (www.iro.umontreal.ca/~felipe/IFT6010.../Data/.../mobile_phone).

Center for American Progress. 2009. "Wage Gap by the Numbers." January 6. Retrieved November 11, 2009 (www.americanprogress.org/issues/2009/01/wage_gap_numbers.html).

Center for Education Policy. 2006. *Survey on Hours Spent on Subjects.* Menlo Park, CA: SRI International.

Center for Research on Globalization. 2008. "Russia Has World's Second Largest Number of Billionaires." April 1. Retrieved November 11, 2009 (www.globalresearch.ca/index.php?content=va&aid=8512).

Center for Voting and Democracy. 2008. "Understanding Super Tuesday: State Rules on February 5 and Lessons for Reform." Retrieved March 21, 2008 (www.fairvote.org/?page=27&pressmode=showspecific&showarticle=185).

Center on Budget and Policy Priorities. 2006. "The Number of Uninsured Americans Is at an All-Time High" (August 29). Retrieved March 2, 2008 (www.cbpp.org/8-29-06health.htm).

Center on Congress at Indiana University. 2009. "Learn About Congress." Retrieved January 12, 2009 (www.centeroncongress.org).

Center on Philanthropy. 2009. "Religion and Philanthropy in the United States (2005)." Indiana University-Purdue University, Indianapolis. Retrieved December 24, 2009 (www.philanthropy.iupui.edu/lakefamilyinstitute/past_research.aspx).

Centers for Medical And Medicaid Services. 2004. *Health Care Indicators.* Baltimore, MD: Office of the Actuary, Office of National Health Statistics.

Centers for Disease Control. 2009 National Health Interview Survey. Retrieved January 10, 2010 (www.cdc.gov/nchs/data/nhis/earlyrelease/200906_01.pdf).

Centers for Disease Control and Prevention. 2009 "Overweight and Obesity." July 27–29. Retrieved November 4, 2009 (www.cdc.gov/obesity/index.html).

Chabbott, Colette, and Francisco O. Ramirez. 2000. "Development and Education." Pp. 163–87 in *Handbook of Sociology of Education*, edited by Maureen T. Hallinan. New York: Kluwer Academic/Plenum.

Chalfant, H. Paul, and Charles W. Peck. 1983. "Religious Affiliation, Religiosity, and Racial Prejudice: A New Look at Old Relationships." *Review of Religious Research* 25 (December):155–61.

Chamberlain, Houston Stewart. 1899/1911. *The Foundations of the Nineteenth Century.* Translated by John Lees. London, New York: John Lane.

Chambliss, William J. 1973. "The Saints and the Roughnecks." *Society* 11(December):24–31.

Charles, Camille Z., Vincent J. Roscigno, and Kimberly C. Torres. 2007. "Racial Inequality and College Attendance: The Mediating Role of Parental Investments." *Social Science Research* 36(1):329–52.

Charon, Joel M. 2007. *Symbolic Interactionism: An Introduction, an Interpretation,* 9th ed. Upper Saddle River, NJ: Prentice Hall.

Chase, Cheryl. 2000. "Genital Surgery on Children Below the Age of Consent: Intersex Genital Mutilation." In *Psychological Perspectives on Human Sexuality,* edited by L. Szuchman and F. Muscarella. New York: John Wiley.

Chase-Dunn, Christopher, and E. N. Anderson. 2006. *The Historical Evolution of World-Systems.* New York: Palgrave Macmillan.

Chase-Lansdale, P. Lindsay, Andrew J. Cherlin, and Kathleen E. Kierman. 1995. "The Long-Term Effects of Parental Divorce on the Mental Health of Young Adults: A Developmental Perspective." *Child Development* 66(6):1614–34.

Chaves, Mark. 1993. "Denominations as Dual Structures: An Organizational Analysis." *Sociology of Religion* 54(20): 147–69.

———. 1999. *Ordaining Women: Culture and Conflict in Religious Organizations.* Cambridge, MA: Harvard University Press.

———. 2004. *Congregations in America.* Cambridge, MA: Harvard University Press.

Chaves, Mark, and Philip S. Gorski. 2001. "Religious Pluralism and Religious Participation." *Annual Review of Sociology* 27:261–81.

Chen, Zeng-Yin, and Howard B. Kaplan. 2003. "School Failure in Early Adolescence and Status Attainment in Middle Adulthood: A Longitudinal Study." *Sociology of Education* 76(2):110–127.

Cherlin, Andrew. 1978. "Remarriage as an Incomplete Institution." *American Journal of Sociology* 84(3):634–50.

Cherlin, Andrew J. 2010. *Public and Private Families: An Introduction,* 6th ed. Boston: McGraw-Hill.

China.org. 2009. "Acupuncture, Herbal Medicine Become More Popular in U.S." Retrieved January 10, 2010 (www.china.org.cn/health/2009-06/25/content_18009726.htm).

Chinn, Stacey. 2007. "Bride Burning." Retrieved April 9, 2010 (Search.com. 2009. www.search.com/reference/Bride_burning).

Chivers, M. L., M. C. Seto, and R. R. Blanchard (2007). "Gender and Sexual Orientation Differences in Sexual Response to Sexual Activities Versus Gender of Actors in Sexual Films." *Journal of Personality and Social Psychology* 93(6):1108–1121.

Christiano, Kevin J., William H. Swatos, Jr., and Peter Kivisto. 2002. *Sociology of Religion: Contemporary Developments.* Walnut Creek, CA: AltaMira.

Chubb, John E., and Terry M. Moe. 1990. *Politics, Markets, and America's Schools.* Washington, DC: Brookings Institution.

Churchill, Winston. 2009. In *Churchill by Himself: The Definitive Collection of Quotations,* edited by Richard Langworth. Jackson, TN: Public Affairs.

CIA World Factbook. 2008. "GDP Per Capita." Retrieved December 20, 2009 (www.cia.gov/library/publications/the-world-factbook/rankorder/2004rank.html).

Cillizza, Chris, and Shailagh Murray. 2008. "This Time We Mean It: The Youth Vote Matters." *The Washington Post* (April 27):A8.

Clarke, Anne. 2007. "Amish Traditions—Shunning." EzineArticles.com. June 12. Retrieved December 13, 2009 (http://enzinearticles.com/?Amish-Traditions—-Shunning&id=603322).

Clausen, John A. 1986. *The Life Course: A Sociological Perspective.* Englewood Cliffs, NJ: Prentice Hall.

Cline, Michael E. 2008. "Comparison of Potential Demographic Influences on Church Membership of Two United Methodist Congregations in San Antonio, Texas." Pp. 237–49 in *Applied Demography in the 21st Century,* edited by Steve H. Murdock and David A. Swanson. Springer, Netherlands.

Clymer, Floyd. 1953. *Those Wonderful Old Automobiles.* New York: Bonanza.

CNN.com. 2006. "Flag-Burning Amendment Fails by a Vote" (June 28). Retrieved August 16, 2008 (www.cnn.com/2006/POLITICS/06/27/flag.burning).

———. 2007. "Report: Global Terrorism Up More Than 25 Percent" (April 30). Retrieved April 14, 2008 (www.cnn.com/2007/US/04/30/terror.report/index.html).

Cockburn, Andrew. 2006. "21st Century Slaves." Pp. 299–307 in *Globalization: The Transformation of Social Worlds,* edited by D. Stanley Eitzen and Maxine Baca Zinn. Belmont, CA: Wadsworth.

Cockerham, William C. 2007. *Medical Sociology,* 10th ed. Englewood Cliffs, NJ: Prentice Hall.

Cohen, Elizabeth G. 1997. "Equitable Classrooms in a Changing Society." Chapter 1 in *Working for Equity in Heterogeneous Classroom: Sociological Theory in Practice,* edited by E. Cohen and R. Lotan. New York: Columbia University Press.

Coile, Russell C., Jr. 2002. "Top 10 Trends in Health Care for 2002." *Health Trends* 14(3):2–12.

Cole, Stephen, and Robert Lejeune. 1972. "Illness and the Legitimation of Failure." *American Sociological Review* 37(3):347–56.

Coleman, James S. 1968. "The Concept of Equality of Educational Opportunity." *Harvard Education Review* 38(Winter):7–22.

———. 1990. *Equality and Achievement in Education.* Boulder, CO: Westview.

Coleman, James S., Ernest Q. Campbell, Carol J. Hobson, James McPartland, Alexander M. Mood, Frederic D. Weinfeld, and Robert L. York. 1966. *Equality of Educational Opportunity.* Washington, DC: Government Printing Office.

Coleman, James William. 2006. *The Criminal Elite: Understanding White Collar Crime,* 6th ed. New York: Worth.

Colligan, S. 2004. "Why the Intersexed Shouldn't Be Fixed: Insights From Queer Theory and Disability Studies." Pp. 45–60 in *Gendering Disability,* edited by B. G. Smith and B. Hutchinson. New Brunswick, NJ: Rutgers University Press.

Collins, Patricia Hill. 2000. *Black Feminist Thought: Knowledge, Consciousness, and the Politics of Empowerment,* 2nd ed. New York: Routledge.

———. 2005. *Black Sexual Politics: African Americans, Gender and the New Racism.* New York: Routledge.

Collins, Randall. 1971. "A Conflict Theory of Sexual Stratification." *Social Problems* 19(Summer):2–21.

———. 2004. "Conflict Theory of Educational Stratification." *American Sociological Review* 36:47–54.

Collins, Randall, and Scott L. Coltrane. 2001. *Sociology of Marriage and the Family: Gender, Love, and Property,* 5th ed. Belmont, CA: Wadsworth.

Comarow, Murray. 1993. "Point of View: Are Sociologists Above the Law?" *The Chronicle of Higher Education* (December 15):A44.

Common Sense for Drug Policy. 2006. "Estimating the Illicit Drug Market." Retrieved February 10, 2008 (www.drugwardistortions.org/distortion19.htm).

Condron, Dennis J., and Vincent J. Roscigno. 2003. "Disparities Within: Unequal Spending and Achievement in an Urban School District." *Sociology of Education* 76(January):18–36.

Conrad, Peter. 2009. *The Medicalization of Society: On Transformation of Human Condition Into Treatable Disorders.* Baltimore: Johns Hopkins Press.

Conrad, Peter, and Joseph Schneider. 1992. *Deviance and Medicalization: From Badness to Sickness.* Philadelphia: Temple University Press.

Cook, Karen S., Jodi O'Brien, and Peter Kollock. 1990. "Exchange Theory: A Blueprint for Structure and Process." Pp. 158–81 in *Frontiers of Social Theory: The New Syntheses,* edited by George Ritzer. New York: Columbia University Press.

Cookson, Peter W., Jr., and Caroline Hodges Persell. 1985. *Preparing for Power: America's Elite Boarding Schools.* New York: Basic Books.

Cooley, Charles Horton. 1902. *Human Nature and the Social Order.* New York: Scribner.

———. [1909] 1983. *Social Organization: A Study of the Larger Mind.* New York: Schocken Books.

Coontz, Stephanie. 1997. *The Way We Really Are: Coming to Terms With America's Changing Families.* New York: Basic Books.

———. 2005. *Marriage, a History: From Obedience to Intimacy, or How Love Conquered Marriage.* New York: Viking.

Corbett, Thomas. 1994–1995. "Changing the Culture of Welfare." *Focus* 16(2):12–22.

CorpWatch. 1999. "Maquiladoras at a Glance." Retrieved March 7, 2008 (www.corpwatch.org/article.php?id=1528#wages).

Corsaro, William A., and Donna Eder. 1990. "Children's Peer Cultures." *Annual Review of Sociology* 16:197–220.

Coser, Lewis A. 1956. *The Functions of Social Conflict.* New York: Free Press.

"Cousin Marriages: Marriage License Laws." 2008. Retrieved January 20, 2008 (www.marriage.about.com/cs/marriagelicenses/a/cousin.htm).

Cousteau, Jacques-Yves. 2008. "The Great Ocean Adventure." Lecture at Hanover College, January 15.

Cratty, Carol. 2008. "Internet Crime Jumps by Third Last Year.".com/technology.

Creswell, John W. 2009. *Research Design: Qualitative, Quantitative, and Mixed Methods Approaches,* 3rd ed. Thousand Oaks, CA: Sage.

Crosby, Faye J. 2004. *Affirmative Action Is Dead; Long Live Affirmative Action.* New Haven, CT: Yale University Press.

Crossette, Barbara. 1996. "Angkor Emerges From the Jungle." *The New York Times* (January 28). Retrieved September 9, 2008 (http://query.nytimes.com/gst/fullpage.html?res=9500e0d91139f93ba15752c0a960958260&sec=travel&spon=&pagewanted=1).

"Cruellest Cut—Pakistan's Kidney Mafia." 2009. Retrieved January 11, 2010 (www.youtube.com/watch?v=vi7A_jK64qc).

Crummey, Robert O. 1970. *The Old Believers and the World of Antichrist: The Vyg Community and the Russian State, 1694–1855.* Madison: University of Wisconsin Press.

Curtiss, S. 1977. *Genie: A Psycholinguistic Study of a Modern-Day "Wild Child."* New York: Academic Press.

Cushing, Bill, and Robert G. Bishop. 2008 *The Big Sort: Why the Clustering of Like-Minded America Is Tearing Us Apar.* Boston: Houghton Mifflin Harcourt.

Cushman, Thomas, and Stjepan G. Mestrovic. 1996. *This Time We Knew: Western Responses to Genocide in Bosnia.* New York: New York University Press.

Cuzzort, R. P., and Edith W. King. 2002. *Social Thought Into the Twenty-First Century,* 6th ed. Belmont, CA: Wadsworth.

Cyranoski, David. 2005. "The Long-Range Forecast." *Nature* 438(November 17):275–76.

DaCosta, Kimberly McClain. 2007. *Making Multiracials: State, Family, and Market in the Redrawing of the Color Line.* Stanford, CA: Stanford University Press.

Dahl, Robert A. 1961. *Who Governs?* New Haven, CT: Yale University Press.

Dahlberg, Frances. 1981. *Woman the Gatherer.* New Haven, CT: Yale University Press.

Dahrendorf, Ralf. 1959. *Class and Class Conflict in Industrial Societies.* Palo Alto, CA: Stanford University Press.

Dalit Liberation Education Trust. 1995. *10th Anniversary Newsletter* (May). Madras: Human Rights Education Movement of India.

Danesi, Marcel. 2008. *Popular Culture.* Lanham, MD: Rowman & Littlefield.

Daniel, John, Asha Kanwar, and Stamenka Uvalic-Trumbic. 2006. "A Tectonic Shift in Global Higher Education." *Change* (July/August).

D'Arcy, Yvonne. 2009. "The Effect of Culture on Pain." *Nursing Made Incredibly Easy!* 7(3):5–7.

Darr, Kurt. 2007. "Assistance in Dying: Part II. Assisted Suicide in the U.S." *Hospital Topics* 85(2):31–36.

Darwin, Charles. [1858] 1909. *The Origin of Species.* New York: P. F. Collier.

Da Silva, Marina. 2004. "France: Outsider Women." *Le Monde Diplomatique* (October). Retrieved July 4, 2006 (http://mondediplo.com/2004/10/12women).

Davidman, Lynn. 1990. "Accommodation and Resistance to Modernity: A Comparison of Two Contemporary Orthodox Jewish Groups." *Sociological Analysis* (Spring):35–51.

Davies, John. 1993. *A History of Wales.* London: Penguin.

Davis, Kingsley. 1940. "Extreme Social Isolation of a Child" *American Journal of Sociology.* 45: 554–65.

Davis, Kingsley. 1947. "A Final Note on a Case of Extreme Isolation." *American Journal of Sociology* 52:432–37.

Davis, Kingsley, and Wilbert Moore. 1945. "Some Principles of Stratification." *American Sociological Review* 10(April):242–45.

Davis, Nancy J, and Robert V. Robinson 1999. "Their Brothers' Keepers? Orthodox Religionists, Modernists, and Economic Justice in Europe." *American Journal of Sociology* 104(6):1631–65.

Death Penalty Information Center. 2009. "Facts About the Death Penalty." Retrieved April 17, 2010 (www.deathpenaltyinfo.org/documents/FactSheet.pdf).

DeCarlo, Scott. 2008. "CEO Compensation." Forbes.com. Retrieved November 10, 2009 (www.forbes.com/2008/04/30/ceo-pay-compensation-lead-bestbosses08-cx-sd_0430ceo_land.html).

Degenova, Mary Kay, and Philip F. Rice. 2010. *Intimate Relationships, Marriages, and Families,* 5th ed. New York: McGraw-Hill.

Delfattore, Joan. 2004. "Romeo and Juliet Were Just Good Friends." Pp. 177–83 in *Schools and Society,* 2nd ed., edited by Jeanne H. Ballantine and Joan Z. Spade. Belmont, CA: Wadsworth.

DeMartini, Joseph R. 1982. "Basic and Applied Sociological Work: Divergence, Convergence, or Peaceful Coexistence?" *Journal of Applied Behavioral Science* 18(2):205–206.

Deming, W. E. 2000. *Out of the Crisis.* Cambridge: MIT Press.

DeMitchell, Todd A., and John J. Carney. 2005. "Harry Potter and the Public School Library." *Phi Delta Kappan* (October):159–65.

Denali Commission. 2001. "Telecommunications Inventory Survey." Retrieved June 29, 2006 (www.commonwealth.north.org/transcripts/denalicom.html).

Denzin, Norman K. 1992. *Symbolic Interactionism and Cultural Studies: The Politics of Interpretation.* Cambridge, MA: Blackwell.

DePalma, Anthony. 1995. "Racism? Mexico's in Denial." *The New York Times* (June 11):E4.

Deutsch, M., and R. M. Krauss. 1960. "The Effect of Threat on Interpersonal Bargaining." *Journal of Abnormal and Social Psychology* 61:181–89.

Deutsch, Morton, and Roy J. Lewicki. 1970. "'Locking-In' Effects During a Game of Chicken." *Journal of Conflict Resolution* 14(3):367–78.

Dews, C.L. Barney, and Carolyn Leste Law, eds. 1995. *This Fine Place So Far From Home: Voices of Academics From the Working Class.* Philadelphia: Temple University Press.

Diamond, Jared. 1999. *Guns, Germs, and Steel: The Fates of Human Societies.* New York: W. W. Norton.

———.2005. *Collapse: How Societies Choose to Fail or Succeed.* New York: Viking.

Diamond, Larry. 1992. "Introduction: Civil Society and the Struggle for Democracy." Pp. 1–28 in *The Democratic Revolution: Struggles for Freedom and Pluralism in the Developing World,* edited by Larry Diamond. New York: Freedom House.

———. 2003. "Universal Democracy?" *Policy Review* (June/July). Retrieved August 28, 2008 (www.hoover.org/publications/poicyreview/3448571.html).

———. 2009. *The Spirit of Democracy: The Struggle to Build Free Societies Throughout the World.* New York: Times Books/Henry Holt & Co.

Diekman, Amanda B., and Sarah K. Murmen. 2004. "Learning to Be Little Women and Little Men: The Inequitable Gender Equality of Nonsexist Children's Literature." *Sex Roles: A Journal of Research* 50(5/6):373.

DiversityInc. 2008. "Belonging Nowhere: The Biracial Children of Vietnam Veterans." October 13. Retrieved October 16, 2009 (diversityinc.com/content/1757/article/4574).

Divorce Magazine. 2008 "U.S. Divorce Statistics." Retrieved March 14, 2008 (www.divorcemag.com/statistics/statsUS.shtml).

Dobbelaere, Karel. 1981. *Secularization: A Multidimensional Concept.* Beverly Hills, CA: Sage.

———. 2000. "Toward an Integrated Perspective of the Processes Related to the Descriptive Concept of Secularization." Pp. 21–39 in *The Secularization Debate,* edited by William H. Swatos, Jr. and Daniel V. A. Olson. Lanham, MD: Rowman & Littlefield.

Dobriansky, Paula. 2006. *The Education of Girls in the Developing World.* Washington, DC: U.S. Department of State.

Dolan, Maura. 2008. "California Supreme Court Overturns Gay Marriage Ban." *Los Angeles Times.* Retrieved August 9, 2008 (www.latimes.com/news/local/la-me-gaymarriage16-2008may16,0,6182317.story).

The Dollars and Sense Collective. 2006. "The ABCs of the Global Economy." Pp. 82–92 in *Globalization: The Transformation of Social Worlds,* edited by D. Stanley Eitzen and Maxine Baca Zinn. Belmont, CA: Wadsworth.

Domestic Violence Resource Center. 2009. Domestic Violence Statistics. Retrieved November 28, 2009 (www.dvrc-or.org/domestic/violence/resources/C61).

Domhoff, G. William. 2001. *Who Rules America? Power, Politics, and Social Change,* 4th ed. New York: McGraw-Hill.

———. 2005. *Who Rules America? Power, Politics, and Social Change,* 5th ed. New York: McGraw-Hill.

———. 2008. Who Rules America.net: Power, Politics, and Social Change. Retrieved March 24, 2008 (http://sociology.ucsc.edu/whoruleeesamerica).

———. 2009. *Who Rules America: Challenges to Corporate and Class Dominance.* Upper Saddle River, NJ: Prentice Hall.

Domina, Thurston. 2005. "Leveling the Home Advantage: Assessing the Effectiveness of Parental Involvement in Elementary School." *Sociology of Education* 78(3):233–49.

Dotzler, Robert J., and Ross Koppel. 1999. "What Sociologists Do and Where They Do It—The NSF Survey on Sociologists' Work Activities and Work Places." *Sociological Practice: A Journal of Clinical and Applied Sociology* 1(1):71–83.

Drasfke, Michael and Stan Kossen. 2002. "The Human Side of Organizations, 8th ed. Englewood Cliffs, NJ: Prentice Hall.

———. 2008. *The Human Side of Organizations,* 10th ed. Upper Saddle River, NJ: Prentice Hall.

Drori, Gili S. 2006. *Global E-Litism: Digital Technology, Social Inequality, and Transnationality.* New York: Worth.

Drug War Chronicle. 2009. "Prohibition: UN Drug Chief Says Black Market Drug Profits Propped Up Global Banking System Last Year." Retrieved November 4, 2009 (http://stopthedrugwar.org/chronicle/570/costa_UNODC_drug_trade_banks).

DuBois, W. E. B. [1899] 1967. *The Philadelphia Negro: A Social Study.* New York: Schocken.

Dufur, Mikaela J., and Seth L. Feinberg. 2007. "Artificially Restricted Labor Markets and Worker Dignity in Professional Football." *Journal of Contemporary Ethnography* 36(5):505–36.

Duncan, Arne. 2006. "Chicago's Renaissance 2010: Building on School Reform in the Age of Accountability." *Phi Delta Kappan* (February):457–58.

The Durban Accord. 2003. "Our Global Commitment for People and Earth's Protected Areas" (World Commission on Protected Areas). Retrieved September 16, 2006 (www.iun.org/themes/wcpa/wpc2003/pdfs/outputs/wpc/durbanaccord.doc).

Durkheim, Émile. [1893] 1947. *The Division of Labor in Society.* Translated by George Simpson. New York: Free Press.

———. 1947. *Elementary Forms of Religious Life.* Glencoe, IL: Free Press.

———.1956. *Education and Society.* Translated by Sherwood D. Fox. Glencoe, IL: Free Press.

———. [1897] 1964. *Suicide.* Glencoe, IL: Free Press.

———. [1915] 2002. In *Classical Sociological Theory,* edited by Craig Calhoun. Malden, MA: Blackwell.

Dworkin, Anthony Gary. 2007. "School Reform and Teacher Burnout: Issues of Gender and Gender Tokenism." Pp. 69–78 in *Gender and Education: An Encyclopedia,* edited by Barbara Banks, Sara Delamont, and Catherine Marshall. New York: Greenwood.

Dworkin, Anthony Gary, and Rosalind J. Dworkin. 1999. *The Minority Report: An Introduction to Racial, Ethnic, and Gender Relations,* 3rd ed. Fort Worth, TX: Harcourt Brace.

Dworkin, Anthony Gary, Lawrence J. Saha, and Antwanette N. Hill. 2003. "Teacher Burnout and Perceptions of a Democratic School Environment." *International Education Journal* 4(2):108–120.

Dye, Thomas, R. 2002. *Who's Running America? The Clinton Years.* Upper Saddle River, NJ: Prentice Hall.

Dye, Thomas, and Harmon Zeigler. 1983. *The Irony of Democracy.* North Scituate, MA: Duxbury Press.

Earls, Felton M., and Albert J. Reiss. 1994. *Breaking the Cycle: Predicting and Preventing Crime.* Washington, DC: National Institute of Justice. p. 49.

Ebaugh, Helen Rose Fuchs. 1988. *Becoming an Ex: The Process of Role Exit.* Chicago: University of Chicago Press.

———. 2005. *Handbook of Religion and Social Institutions.* Springer.

Eckert, Penelope. 1989. *Jocks and Burnouts: Social Categories and Identity in High School.* New York: Teacher's College Press.

Eckholm, Erik. 2006. "City by City, an Antipoverty Group Plants Seeds of Change." *The New York Times* (June 26):A12.

The Economist. 2006a. "Immigration: Don't Fence Us Out." (April 1–7):41.

———. 2006b. "The United States and Mexico: Sense, Not Sensenbrenner." (April 1–7):10.

"Ecosystems Report Links Human Well-Being With Health of Planet." 2006. *Popline* 28(January/February):1.

Eder, Donna, Catherine Colleen Evans, and Stephen Parker. 1995. *School Talk: Gender and Adolescent Culture.* New Brunswick, NJ: Rutgers University Press.

Edwards, Harry. 2000. "Crisis of the Black Athlete on the Eve of the 21st Century." *Society* 37(3):9–13.

Ehrenreich, Barbara. 2001. *Nickel and Dimed: On (Not) Getting By in America.* New York: Henry Holt.

———. 2005. *Bait and Switch: The (Futile) Pursuit of the American Dream.* New York: Henry Holt.

Ehrlich, Paul, and Ann Ehrlich. 1990. *The Population Explosion.* New York: Simon and Schuster.

Eitzen, D. Stanley, and George H. Sage. 2003. *Sociology of North American Sport.* Boston: McGraw-Hill.

Eitzen, D. Stanley, and Maxine Baca Zinn, eds. 2006. *Globalization: The Transformation of Social Worlds.* Belmont, CA: Wadsworth.

———. n.d. "Commonsense Sayings." *Sociological Conceptual Tools Room.* (www.angelfire.com/or/sociologyshop/CONCEPTTOOLS.html#css).

Ellens, G. F. S. 1971. "The Ranting Ranters: Reflections on a Ranting Counter-Culture." *Church History* 40(March):91–107.

Ellison, Christopher G., John P. Bartkowski, and Michelle L. Segal. 1996. "Do Conservative Protestant Parents Spank More Often?" *Social Science Quarterly* 77(3):663–73.

Ellison, Christopher G., J. A. Burr, and P. L. McCall 1997. "Religious Homogeneity and Metropolitan Suicide Rates." *Social Forces* 76(1):273–99.

Ellison, Christopher G., and Daniel A. Powers. 1994. "The Contact Hypothesis and Racial Attitudes Among Black Americans." *Social Science Quarterly* 75(2):385–400.

"Endogamy." 2007. University of Michigan. Retrieved April 17, 2010 (www.personal.umich.edu).

Engels, Friedrich. [1884] 1942. *The Origin of the Family, Private Property, and the State.* New York: International Publishing.

Enloe, Cynthia. 2006. "Daughters and Generals in the Politics of the Globalized Sneaker." In *Beyond Borders: Thinking Critically About Global Issues,* edited by Paula S. Rothenberg. New York: Worth.

Environmental Protection Agency. 2004. "Terms of Environment." Retrieved (www.epa.gov/OCEPAterms/gterms.html).

Erikson, Erik H. 1950. *Childhood and Society.* New York: W. W. Norton.

Erikson, Kai T. 1976. *Everything in Its Path: Destruction of Community in the Buffalo Creek Flood.* New York: Simon & Schuster.

———. 1987. "Notes on the Sociology of Deviance." Pp. 9–21 in *Deviance: The Interactionist Perspective,* 5th ed., edited by Earl Rubington and Martin S. Weinberg. New York: Macmillan.

———. [1966] 2005. *Wayward Puritans: A Study in the Sociology of Deviance.* Boston: Pearson Education.

Eshleman, J. Ross, and Richard A. Bulcroft. 2006. *The Family,* 11th ed. Boston: Allyn & Bacon.

———. 2010. *The Family,* 12th ed. Boston: Allyn & Bacon.[Chap 10; Page no. 25].

Esperitu, Yen Le. 1992. *Asian American Panethnicity: Bridging Institutions and Identities.* Philadelphia: Temple University Press.

Espo, David. 2009. "$797 Billion Stimulus Plan Ok'd in Victory for Obama." Los Angeles Daily News February 14. Retrieved February 24, 2009 (www.dailynews.com/search/ci_11703066).

Esquivel, Laura. 2001. *Like Water for Chocolate.* New York: Anchor.

Etounga-Manguelle, Daniel. 2000. "Does Africa Need a Cultural Adjustment Program?" Pp. 65–77 in *Culture Matters: How Values*

Shape Human Progress. Lawrence E. Harrison and Samuel P. Huntington, eds. New York: Basic Books.

Etzioni, Amitai. 1975. *A Comparative Analysis of Complex Organizations.* New York: Free Press.

Europa World Year Book. 2005. London: Europa.

"Facebook Statistics." 2009. Retrieved August 13, 2009 (www .facebook.com/press/info.php?statistics).

Fackler, Martin. 2007. "Career Women in Japan Find a Blocked Path." *The New York Times.* August 6. Retrieved November 8, 2009 (www.nytimes.com/2007/08/06/world/asia/06equal.html).

Fadiman, Anne. 1997. *The Spirit Catches You and You Fall Down.* New York: Noonday.

Fallows, Deborah. 2005. "How Women and Men Use the Internet." Washington, DC: Pew Internet and American Life Project.

Faludi, Susan. 1993. *Backlash: The Undeclared War Against American Women.* New York: Anchor.

Farley, John E. 2009. *Majority-Minority Relations,* 6th ed. Englewood Cliffs, NJ: Prentice Hall.

Farmer, Paul. 1999. *Infections and Inequalities: The Modern Plagues.* Berkeley: University of California Press.

Farrer, Claire R. 1996. *Thunder Rides a Black Horse: Mescalero Apaches and the Mythic Present,* 2nd ed. Prospect Heights, IL: Waveland.

Fathi, David C. 2009. "Prison Nation." Human Rights Watch. April 9. Retrieved April 15, 2009 (www.hrw.org/en/news/2009/04/09/prison-nation).

Faulkner, James B. 2006. "Social Capital, Social Services, and Recidivism." Thesis for Applied Behavioral Science Program, Wright State University.

Fausto-Sterling, Anne. 1992. *Myths of Gender: Biological Theories About Women and Men,* 2nd ed. New York: Basic Books.

———. 2000. *Sexing the Body: Gender Politics and the Construction of Sexuality.* New York: Basic Books.

Feagin, Joe R., 1983. *The Urban Real Estate Game: Playing Monopoly with Real Money.* Englewood Cliffs, NJ: Prentice Hall.

Feagin, Joe R., and Clairece Booher Feagin. 1986. *Discrimination American Style: Institutional Racism and Sexism.* Malabar, FL: Krieger.

———. 2007. *Racial and Ethnic Relations,* 8th ed. Englewood Cliffs, NJ: Prentice Hall.

Feagin, Joe R., Hernan Vera, and Pinar Batur. 2001. *White Racism: The Basics.* New York: Routledge.

Featherman, David L., and Robert Hauser. 1978. *Opportunity and Change.* New York: Academic Press.

Federal Bureau of Investigation. 2005. *Fact Sheet for Hate Crime Statistics* (2004 Uniform Crime Reports). Washington, DC: Author.

———. 2006a. "2006 Financial Crime Report." Retrieved February 8, 2008 (www.fbi.gov/publications/financial/fcs_report2006/financial_crime_2006.htm).

———. 2006b. "Crime Clock." Retrieved February 8, 2008 (www.fbi .gov/ucr/cius2006/about/crime_clock.html).

———. 2006c. "Crime in the United States." Retrieved February 8, 2008 (www.fbi.gov/ucr/cius2006/data/table_01.html).

———. 2006d. "Innocent Images International Task Force." Retrieved February 10, 2008 (www.fbi.gov/publications/innocent.htm).

———. 2007. "Internet Fraud." Retrieved April 15, 2009 (www.fbi .gov/majcases/fraud/internetschemes.htm).

Federal Register. 2002. Office of the Federal Register, National Archives and Records Vol. 67.

Feller, Avi, and Chad Stone. 2009. "Top 1% of Americans Reaped Two-Thirds of Income Gains in Last Economic Expansion" (September 9). Center on Budget and Policy Priorities. Retrieved January 7, 2010 (www.cbpp.org/cms/index.cfm?fa=view&id=2908).

Felson, Richard B. 2002. *Violence and Gender Reexamined.* Washington, DC: American Psychological Association.

Ferhansyed. 2008. "Fundamental Terminology of Planned Change." Retrieved December 21, 2009 (http://organizationdevelopment .wordpress.com/2008/08/10/fundamental-terminology-of-organization-development).

Fernando, Suman. 2002. *Mental Health, Race and Culture,* 2nd ed. New York: Palgrave.

Ferree, Myra Marx, and David A. Merrill. 2000. "Hot Movements, Cold Cognition: Thinking About Social Movements in Gendered Frames." *Contemporary Sociology: A Journal of Reviews* 12:626–48.

Fine, Gary Alan. 1990. "Symbolic Interactionism in the Post-Blumerian Age." Pp. 117–57 in *Frontiers of Social Theory: The New Synthesis,* edited by George Ritzer. New York: Columbia University Press.

Finke, Roger. 1997. "The Consequences of Religious Competition: Supply-Side Explanations for Religious Change." Pp. 45–64 in *Rational Choice Theory and Religion: Summary and Assessment,* edited by L. A. Young. New York: Routledge.

Finke, Roger, and Rodney Stark. 2005. *The Churching of America, 1776–2005: Winners and Losers in Our Religious Economy,* 2nd ed. New Brunswick, NJ: Rutgers University Press.

Finkelhor, David. 2008. *Childhood Victimization: Violence, Crime, and Abuse in the Lives of Young People.* New York: Oxford University Press.

"First Born Children." 2008. Retrieved June 29, 2008 (http://social .jrank.org/pages/261/Firstborn-children.html).

Fischer, Claude S. 1984. *The Urban Experience,* 2nd ed. San Diego: Harcourt Brace Jovanovich.

Fish, Virginia Kemp. 1986. "The Hull House Circle: Women's Friendships and Achievements." Pp. 185–227 in *Gender, Ideology, and Action: Historical Perspectives on Women's Public Lives,* edited by Janet Sharistanian. Westport, CT: Greenwood.

Fiske, Alan Page. 1991. *Structures of Social Life: The Four Elementary Forms of Human Relations.* New York: Free Press.

"Five Rules for Online Networking." 2005, April 1. CNN. Retrieved July 25, 2006 (www.cnn.com/2005/US/Careers/03/31/online .networking).

Flanagan, William G. 2001. *Urban Sociology: Images and Structure,* 4th ed. Boston: Allyn & Bacon.

Flavin, Christopher. 2001. "Rich Planet, Poor Planet." Pp. 1–410 in *State of the World 2001,* edited by Lester R. Brown, Christopher Flavin, and Hilary French. New York: W. W. Norton.

Flavin, Jeanne. 2004. "Employment, Counseling, Housing Assistance . . . and Aunt Yolanda? How Strengthening Families' Social Capital Can Reduce Recidivism." *Fordham Urban Law Journal* 3(2):209–16.

Florida, Richard. 2002. *The Rise of the Creative Class.* New York: Basic Books.

———. 2004. *Cities and the Creative Class.* New York: Routledge.

Foner, Nancy. 2005. *In a New Land: A Comparative View of Immigration.* New York: New York University Press.

Food Research and Action Center. 2009. "New SNAP/Food Stamp Record: 32.2 Million." April 1. Retrieved April 20, 2009 (www .frac.org).

Ford, Clennan S. 1970. *Human Relations Area Files: 1949–1969— A Twenty Year Report.* New Haven, CT: Human Relations Area Files.

France 24 International News. 2009. "Increase in Number of Billionaires Despite Credit Crisis." October 13. Retrieved November 11, 2009 (www.france24.com/en/20091013-global-crisis-china-billionaires-economy-asia-wealthy-rich-list).

Frank, Mark G., and Thomas Gilovich. 1988. "The Dark Side of Self- and Social Perception: Black Uniforms and Aggression in Professional Sports." *Journal of Personality and Social Psychology* 54(1):74–85.

Frazier, Charles. 1997. *Cold Mountain.* New York: Atlantic Monthly Press.

Free the Slaves. 2005. "Modern Slavery." Retrieved June 29, 2006 (www.freetheslaves.net).

———. 2008. Retrieved April 17, 2010 (www.freetheslaves.net).

Freedom House. 2002. *Freedom in the World 2001–2002*. New York: Author.

Freeman, Jo. 1975. *The Politics of Women's Liberation: A Case Study of an Emerging Social Movement and Its Relation to the Policy Process.* New York: McKay.

Freese, J., B. Powell, and L. C. Steelman. 1999. *Rebel Without a Cause or Effect: Birth Order and Social Attitudes.* Washington, DC: American Sociological Association.

Freud, Sigmund. [1923] 1960. *The Ego and the Id.* New York: W. W. Norton.

Frey, Bruno S. 2004. *Dealing With Terrorism:—Stick or Carrot?* Cheltenham, UK. Edward Elgar.

Friedman, Thomas L. 2005. *The World Is Flat: A Brief History of the Twenty-First Century.* New York: Farrar, Straus, & Giroux.

———. 2006. "Opening Scene: The World Is Ten Years Old." Pp. 21–29 in *Globalization: The Transformation of Social Worlds,* edited by D. Stanley Eitzen and Maxine Baca Zinn. Belmont, CA: Wadsworth.

———. 2008. *Hot, Flat and Crowded: Why We Need a Green Revolution—and How It Can Renew America.* New York: Farrar, Straus & Giroux.

Furstenberg, F. F. 2003. "Growing Up in American Society: Income, Opportunities, and Outcomes." Pp. 211–33 in *Social Dynamics of the Life Course: Transitions, Institutions, and Interrelations,* edited by W. R. Heinz and V. W. Marshall. New York: A. deGruyter.

Future for All. 2008. "Future Technology and Society." Retrieved January 14, 2008 (www.futureforall.org).

Galanti, Geri-Ann. 2008. *Caring for Patients From Different Cultures.* 4th ed. Philadelphia, PA: University Pennsylvania Press.

Gallagher, Timothy J., and Robert J. Johnson. 2001. "A Model for Unmet Medical Care Needs." Paper presented at the American Sociological Association meetings, August, Anaheim, CA.

Gallup, George, Jr., and D. Michael Lindsay. 1999. *Surveying the Religious Landscape: Trends in U.S. Beliefs.* Harrisburg, PA: Morehouse.

Gallup Poll. 2000. Retrieved April 17, 2010 (www.gallup.com/poll/indicators/indreligion.asp).

———. 2001. "Gallup Poll Topics: Religion." Retrieved April 17, 2010 (www.gallup.com/poll/indicators/indreligion4.asp).

———. 2004. "Gallup Poll Social Series: Values and Beliefs." Retrieved April 17, 2010 (http://brain.gallup.com/documents/question.aspx?question=152992&Advanced=0&SearchConType=1&SearchTypeAll=homosexual%20clergy).

———. 2006. "Gallup Poll Topics: A–Z." Retrieved April 17, 2010 (http://poll.gallup.com/content/default/aspx?ci=1690&pg=2).

Gamoran, Adam. 2001. "American Schooling and Educational Inequality: A Forecast for the 21st Century." *Sociology of Education* (Extra Issue: Currents of Thought: Sociology of Education at the Dawn of the 21st Century) 60(3):135–55.

Gamson, Zelda F. 1998. "The Stratification of the Academy." Pp. 67–73 in *Chalk Lines: The Politics of Work in the Managed University,* edited by Randy Martin. Raleigh, NC: Duke University Press.

"Gang-Rape Victim Faces Lashes." 2007. Retrieved November 4, 2009 (www.news.com.au/story/0,23599,21332543-2,00.html).

Gans, Herbert J. 1962. *The Urban Villagers: Group and Class in the Life of Italian-Americans.* New York: Free Press.

———. 1971. "The Uses of Poverty: The Poor Pay All." *Social Policy* 2(2):20–24.

———. 1994. "Positive Functions of the Undeserving Poor: Uses of the Underclass in America." *Politics and Society* 22(3):269–83.

———. 1995. *The War Against the Poor.* New York: Basic Books.

———. 2007. "No, Poverty Has Not Disappeared." Reprinted in *Sociological Footprints,* edited by Leonard Cargan and Jeanne Ballantine. Belmont, CA: Wadsworth.

Gardner, Howard. 1987. "The Theory of Multiple Intelligences." *Annual Dyslexia* 37:19–35.

———. 1999. *Intelligence Reframed: Multiple Intelligences for the 21st Century.* New York: Basic Books.

Garrett, Laurie. 2000. *Betrayal of Trust: The Collapse of Global Public Health.* New York: Hyperion.

Gay, Lesbian, and Straight Education Network (GLSEN). 2006. "GLESEN's 2005 National School Climate Survey Sheds New Light on Experiences of Lesbian, Gay, Bisexual and Transgendered (LGBT) Students." Retrieved August 8, 2008 (www.glsen.org/cgi-bin/iowa/all/library/record/1927.html).

Geist, Michael. 2008. "How Obama's Using Tech to Triumph." *The Toronto Star* (February 4):B1.

Gellner, Ernest. 1983. *Culture, Identity, and Politics.* Cambridge, UK: Cambridge University Press.

———.1993. "Nationalism." Pp 409–11 in *Blackwell Dictionary of Twentieth Century Thought,* edited by William Outhwaite and Tom Bottomore. Oxford, UK: Basil Blackwell.

Gellner, Ernest, and John Breuilly. 2009. *Nations and Nationalism,* 2nd ed. Ithaca, NY: Cornell University Press.

Geocommons. 2009. "Infant Mortality Rates, World by Country, 2009." (http://finder.geocommons.com/overlays/11932).

Geoffrey Canada. 1998. *Reaching Up for Manhood: Transforming the Lives of Boys in America.* Boston: Beacon Press.

"Getting Married in Japan." 2007. About.com. Retrieved November 2007 (http://japanese.about.com/library/weekly/aa080999.htm).

Gettleman, Jeffery. 2008. "Mob Sets Kenya Church on Fire, Killing Dozens." *The New York Times* (January 2). Retrieved June 3, 2008 (www.nytimes.com/2008/01/02/world/africa/02kenya.html?pagewanted=1&ref=africa).

Gibbs, Jack P. 1989. *Control: Sociology's Central Notion.* Urbana: University of Illinois Press.

Gibson, William. 1999. "Science and Science Fiction." *Talk of the Nation,* National Public Radio, November 30.

Giddens, Anthony. 1986. *The Constitution of Society.* Berkeley: University of California Press.

Gilbert, Dennis. 2008. *The American Class Structure in an Age of Growing Inequality,* 7th ed. Thousand Oaks, CA: Pine Forge.

Gilbert, Dennis, and Joseph A. Kahl. 2003. *The American Class Structure in an Age of Inequality: A New Synthesis,* 6th ed. Belmont, CA: Wadsworth.

Gilchrist, John. 2003. *Anderson's Ohio Family Law.* Cincinnati, OH: Anderson.

Gilligan, Carol. 1982. *In a Different Voice: Psychological Theory and Women's Development.* Cambridge, MA: Harvard University Press.

Ginsberg, E. 1999. "U.S. Health Care: A Look Ahead to 2025." *Annual Review of Public Health* 20(1):55–67.

Glaser, James M. 1994. "Back to the Black Belt: Racial Environment and White Racial Attitudes in the South." *Journal of Politics* 56(1):21–41.

Glass, John. 2003. "Hunting for Bambi. Hoax? Reality? Does It Matter?" *Common Dreams* (online journal). Retrieved August 5, 2008 (www.commondreams.org/views03/0801-05.htm).

———. 2004. "Developing Sociological Interventions." Retrieved April 17, 2010 (iws.cccd.edu/jglass/how%20to%20Frame%20Sociological%20Interventions.pdf).

Glasscock, C. B. 1937. *The Gasoline Age: The Story of the Men Who Made It.* Indianapolis, IN: Bobbs-Merrill.

Glenn, Evelyn Nakano. 1999. "The Social Construction and Institutionalization of Gender and Race: An Integrative Framework." Pp. 3–43 in *Revisioning Gender,* edited by Myra Marx Ferree, Judith Lorber, and Beth B. Hess. Thousand Oaks, CA: Sage.

Globe Women's Business Network. 2006. "Corporate Women Directors International." Retrieved August 21, 2006 (www.globewomen.com).

Goffman, Erving. [1959] 2001. *Presentation of Self in Everyday Life.* New York: Harmondsworth, UK: Penguin.

———. 1961. *Asylums: Essays on the Social Situation of Mental Patients and Other Inmates.* New York: Anchor.

———. 1967. *Interaction Ritual.* New York: Anchor.

Goldberg, David Theo, ed. 1990. *Anatomy of Racism.* Minneapolis: University of Minnesota Press.

Goode, Erich. 1992. *Collective Behavior.* New York: Harcourt Brace Jovanovich.

———. 1997. *Between Politics and Reason: The Drug Legalization Debate.* New York: St. Martin's Press.

———. 2005. *Drugs in American Society,* 6th ed. Boston: McGraw-Hill.

Goode, William J. 1970. *World Revolution and Family Patterns.* New York: Free Press.

Goodman, Marc D., and Susan W. Brenner. 2002. "The Emerging Consensus on Criminal Conduct in Cyberspace." *International Journal of Law and Information Technology* 10(2):139–223.

Gouldner, Alvin W. 1960. "The Norm of Reciprocity: A Preliminary Statement." *American Sociological Review* 25(2):161–78.

Gordon, Milton. 1970. "The Subsociety and the Subculture." Pp. 150–63 in *The Sociology of Subcultures,* edited by David O. Arnold. Berkeley, CA: Glendessary.

Gore, Al. 2006. *An Inconvenient Truth.* Emmaus, PA: Rodale.

Gottdiener, Mark, and Ray Hutchison. 2006. *The New Urban Sociology,* 3rd ed. Boston: McGraw-Hill.

Gottfredson, Michael R., and Travis Hirschi. 1990. *A General Theory of Crime.* Palo Alto, CA: Stanford University Press.

Gottlieb, Lori. 2006. "How Do I Love Thee?" *The Atlantic* 297(2):58–70.

Gould, Stephen J. 1997. *The Mismeasure of Man.* New York: W. W. Norton.

Gracey, Harry L. 1967. "Learning the Student Role: Kindergarten as Academic Boot Camp." Pp. 215–26 in *Readings in Introductory Sociology,* 3rd ed., edited by Dennis Wrong and Harry L. Gracey. New York: Macmillan.

Grandpa Junior. 2006. "If You Were Born Before 1945." Retrieved July 20, 2006 (www.grandpajunior.com/1945.shtml).

Granovetter, Mark. 2007. "Introduction for the French Reader." *Sociologica* 1(Suppl.):1–10.

Grant, Gerald, and Christine E. Murray. 1999. *Teaching in America: The Slow Revolution.* Cambridge, MA: Harvard University Press.

Grant, Linda. 2004. "Everyday Schooling and the Elaboration of Race-Gender Stratification." Pp. 296–308 in *Schools and Society: A Sociological Approach to Education,* 2nd ed., edited by Jeanne H. Ballantine and Joan Z. Spade. Belmont, CA: Wadsworth.

Greeley, Andrew M. 1972. *The Denominational Society.* Glenview, IL: Scott, Foresman.

———. 1989. *Religious Change in America.* Cambridge, MA: Harvard University Press.

Green, John C., and Mark Silk. 2005. "Why Moral Values Did Count." *Religion in the News* 8(1):5–8.

Greenberg, Edward S. 1999. *The Struggle for Democracy,* 3rd ed. New York: Addison-Wesley.

The Green Papers. 2008a. "Presidential Primaries, Caucuses, and Conventions." Retrieved March 21, 2008 (www.thegreenpapers.com/P08/CO-R.phtml).

———. 2008b. "Presidential Primaries 2008: Republican Delegate Selection and Voter Eligibility." Retrieved March 21, 2008 (www.thegreenpapers.com/P08/R-DSVE.phtml?sort=a).

Greensboro Justice Fund. 2005. "Courage From the Past." *GJF Newsletter* (17, Summer):1.

Greimel, Hans. 2007. "Outbreak of Violent Crime Unnerves Japan." *Associated Press.* Retrieved July 6, 2008 (www.breitbart.com/article.php?id=D8P6V7B80).

Grille, Robin. 2005. "Religious Extremism: A Parenting Style." In *Parenting for a Peaceful World.* Longueville Media.

Guest, Avery M., and Keith R. Stamm. 1993. "Paths of Community Integration." *Sociological Quarterly* 34(4):581–95.

Gumperz and Levinson, eds. 1996. *Rethinking Linguistic Relativity.* Cambridge, UK: Cambridge University Press.

Hadden, Jeffrey K. 2006. "New Religious Movements." Retrieved August 14, 2008 (www.hirr.hartsem.edu/denom/new_religious_movements.html).

Hagan, Frank E. 2007. *Introduction to Criminology,* 6th ed. Belmont, CA: Wadsworth.

Hagan, John L. 1993. "The Social Embeddedness of Crime and Unemployment." *Criminology* 31:465–91.

———. 1994. *Crime and Disrepute.* Thousand Oaks, CA: Pine Forge.

Hall, Edward T. 1959. *The Silent Language.* New York: Doubleday.

———. 1983. *The Dance of Life.* Garden City, NY: Anchor Books/Doubleday.

Hall, Edward T., and Mildred Reed Hall. 1992. *An Anthropology of Everyday Life.* New York: Doubleday.

Hall, Richard H. 2002. *Organizations: Structures, Processes, and Outcomes,* 7th ed. Englewood Cliffs, NJ: Prentice Hall.

Hammersley, Martyn, and Glenn Turner. 1980. "Conformist Pupils." In *Pupil Strategies: Explorations in the Sociology of the School,* edited by Peter Woods. London: Croom Helm.

Handel, Gerald, Spencer Cahill, and Frederick Elkin. 2007. *Children and Society: The Sociology of Children and Childhood Socialization.* New York: Oxford University Press.

Handwerk, Brian. 2004. "Female Suicide Bombers: Dying to Kill." *National Geographic News* (December 13). Retrieved July 5, 2008 (http://news.nationalgeographic.com/news/2004/12/1213_041213_tv_suicide_bombers.html).

Haniffa, Aziz. 2009. "Financial Crisis Bigger Than Al Qaeda, Says U.S. Intelligence Czar." *Rediff India Abroad.* February 13. Retrieved March 17, 2009 (www.rediff.com/money/2009/feb/15bcrisis-financial-crisis-bigger-threat-than-al-qaeda-says-us-intel-chief.htm).

Hannigan, John. 1998. *Fantasy City: Pleasure and Profit in the Postmodern Metropolis.* London: Routledge.

Hansen, Randall, and Katharine Hansen. 2003. "What Do Employers Really Want? Top Skills and Values Employers Seek From Job-Seekers" (Quintessential Careers). Retrieved June 23, 2008 (www.quintcareers.com/job_skills_values.html).

Hanser, Robert D. 2002. "Labeling Theory as a Paradigm for the Etiology of Prison Rape: Implications for Understanding and Intervention." *Professional Issues in Counseling On-line Journal* (April). Retrieved April 17, 2010 (www.shsu.edu/~piic/summer2002/Hanser.htm).

Hardin, Garrett. 1968. "The Tragedy of the Commons." *Science* 162(3859):1243–48.

Harding, Sandra, ed. 2004. *The Feminist Standpoint Reader: Intellectual and Political Controversies.* New York: Routledge.

Harms, William. 2000. "Research Looks at Cohabitation's Negative Effects." *University of Chicago Chronicle* 19(11).

Harrington, Charlene, and Carroll L. Estes. 2004. *Health Policy: Crisis and Reform in the U.S. Health Care Delivery System,* 2nd ed. Sudbury, MA: Jones & Bartlett.

Harris, Judith Rich. 2009. *The Nurture Assumption: Why Children Turn Out the Way They Do,* Revised and Updated Edition. New York: Free Press.

Harris, Marvin. 1989. *Cows, Pigs, War, and Witches: The Riddles of Culture.* New York: Random House.

Harrison, P. M., and J. C. Karberg. 2003. *Prison and Jail Inmates at Midyear 2002.* Washington, DC: U.S. Bureau of Justice Statistics.

Hart, Betty, and Todd R. Risley. 2003. "The Early Catastrophe: The 30 Million Word Gap by Age 3." *American Educator* 27(1):4–9.

Harvey, David. 1973. *Social Justice and the City.* London: Edward Arnold.

Haskins, Ron. 2006. *Work Over Welfare: The Inside Story of the 1996 Welfare Reform Law.* Washington, DC: Brookings Institution Press.

Hayden, Dolores, and Patricia Baron. 2007. "Urban Planning and Women's Needs." *Journal of Planning Education and Research* 26(3):370.

Hayden, Tom. 2006. "Seeking a New Capitalism in Chiapas." Pp. 348–54 in *Globalization: The Transformation of Social Worlds,* edited by D. Stanley Eitzen and Maxine Baca Zinn. Belmont, CA: Wadsworth.

Health Confidence Survey. 2001. "2001 Health Confidence Survey: Summary of Findings" (pp. 1–9). Washington, DC: Health Confidence Survey/Employee Benefit Research.

HealthReform.gov. 2010. "Coverage Denied: How the Current Health Insurance System Leaves Millions Behind." Retrieved January 10, 2010 (www.healthreform.gov/reports/denied_coverage/index.html).

Heilbroner, Robert L., and William Milberg. 2007. *The Making of Economic Society,* 12th ed. Englewood Cliffs, NJ: Prentice Hall.

Heilman Madeline E., and Julie J. Chen, 2003. "Entrepreneurship as a Solution: The Allure of Self-Employment for Women and Minorities." *Human Resource Management Review* 13(2):347–64.

Heilman, Samuel. 2000. *Defenders of the Faith: Inside Ultra-Orthodox Jewry.* Berkeley: University of California Press.

Helfand, Duke. 2008. "Presbyterian Leaders OK Gay Clergy." *Los Angeles Times* (June 28). Retrieved August 18, 2008 (www.latimes.com/news/local/la-me-ordain28-2008jun28,0,7679148.story).

Hendry, Joy. 1987. *Becoming Japanese: The World of the Preschool Child.* Honolulu: University of Hawaii Press.

Henley, Nancy, Mykol Hamilton, and Barrie Thorne. 2000. "Womanspeak and Manspeak: Sex Differences in Communication, Verbal and Nonverbal." Pp. 111–15 in *Sociological Footprints,* edited by Leonard Cargan and Jeanne Ballantine. Belmont, CA: Wadsworth.

Hensley, Christopher, M. Koscheski, and Richard Tewksbury. 2005. "Examining the Characteristics of Male Sexual Assault Targets in a Southern Maximum-Security Prison." *Journal of Interpersonal Violence* 20(6):667–79.

Henslin, James M. 2005. *Sociology: A Down-to-Earth Approach,* 8th ed. Boston: Allyn & Bacon.

Herman, Edward S., and David Peterson. 2006. "The Threat of Global State Terrorism: Retail vs Wholesale Terror." Pp. 252–57 in *Globalization: The Transformation of Social Worlds,* edited by D. Stanley Eitzen and Maxine Baca Zinn. Belmont, CA: Wadsworth.

Hertsgaard, Mark. 2003. *The Eagle's Shadow: Why America Fascinates and Infuriates the World.* New York: Picador.

Hesse-Biber, Sharlene Nagy, and Patricia Lina Leavy. 2007. *Feminist Research Practice: A Primer.* Thousand Oaks, CA: Sage.

Hewitt, John P. 2007. *Self and Society: A Symbolic Interactionism Social Psychology,* 10th ed. Boston: Allyn & Bacon.

Hiebert-White. 2010. "Uninsured Expected to Rise to 52 Million by 2010." *Health Affairs* (June 2). Retrieved January 10, 2010 (http://health affairs.org/blog/2009/06/02/52-million-uninsured-americans-by-2010).

Hill, Christopher. 1991. *The World Turned Upside Down: Radical Ideas During the English Revolution.* New York: Penguin.

Hirschi, Travis. [1969] 2002. *Causes of Delinquency.* New Brunswick, NJ: Transaction.

Hitler, Adolf. 1939. *Mein Kampf.* New York: Reynal & Hitchcock.

Hochschild, Arlie. 1989. *The Second Shift: Working Parents and the Revolution at Home.* New York: Viking.

———. 1997. *The Time Bind: When Work Becomes Home and Home Becomes Work.* New York: Metropolitan Books.

Hogeland, Lisa Maria. 2004. "Fear of Feminism: Why Young Women Get the Willies." Pp. 565–68 in *Women's Voices, Feminist Visions,* 2nd ed., edited by Susan M. Shaw and Janet Lee. Boston: McGraw-Hill.

Holloway, Susan. 2001. "Mothers of Japanese Preschoolers." *GSE Term Paper.* Vol. 8, No. 1. Fall. University of California, Berkeley. Retrieved April 17, 2010 (http://gse.berkeley.edu/admin/publications/termpaper/fall01/fall01/html).

Homans, George C. 1974. *Social Behavior: Its Elementary Forms.* New York: Harcourt, Brace Javanovich.

Hood, Roger. 2002. *The Death Penalty: A World-Wide Perspective,* 3rd ed. Oxford, UK: Clarendon Press.

Horrigan, John B., and Aaron Smith. 2007. "Home Broadband Adoption 2007 Report" (Pew Internet and American Life Project). Retrieved April 17, 2010 (http://pewinternet.org/Reports/2007/Home-Broadband-Adoption-2007.aspx).

Hossfeld, Karen J. 2006. "Gender, Race, and Class in Silicon Valley." Pp. 264–70 in *Beyond Borders: Thinking Critically About Global Issues,* edited by Paula S. Rothenberg. New York: Worth.

Hostetler, John A. 1993. *Amish Society,* 4th ed. Baltimore: John Hopkins University Press.

Houlihan, G. Thomas. 2005. "The Importance of International Benchmarking for U.S. Educational Leaders." *Phi Delta Kappan* (November):217–18.

Housing and Urban Development. 2008. "HUD Reports Drop in the Number of Chronically Homeless Persons" (News Release No. 08–113). Retrieved August 23, 2008 (www.hud.gov/news).

Howard, Adam. 2007. *Learning Privilege: Lessons of Power and Identity in Affluent Schooling.* New York: Taylor & Francis.

Howard, Philip N., and Steve Jones, eds. 2004. *Society On-Line: The Internet in Context.* Thousand Oaks, CA: Sage.

Hozien, Muhammad. n.d. "Ibn Khaldun: His Life and Work." Retrieved May 7, 2009 (www.muslimphilosophy.com/ik/klf.htm).

Huebler, Friedrich. 2008. *International Education Statistics.* Retrieved December 6, 2009 (http://huebler.blogspot.com/2008/11/ptr.html).

Hughes, Melanie M. 2004. "Armed Conflict, International Linkages, and Women's Parliamentary Representation in Developing Nations." Master's Thesis, Department of Sociology, Ohio State University.

Huizinga, David, Rolf Loeber, and Terence P. Thornberry. 1994. "Urban Delinquency and Substance Abuse: Initial Findings." *OJJDP Research Summary.* Washington, DC: Government Printing Office.

Human Development Report. 2007. United Nations. Retrieved January 10, 2010 (hdr.undp.org).

Human Rights Campaign. 2003. *Answers to Questions About Marriage Equality.* Washington, DC: Human Rights Campaign, Family Net Project.

———. 2008. "Questions About Same Sex Marriage." Retrieved February 20, 2008 (www.hrc.org/issues/5517.htm).

Hunter College Women's Studies Collective. 2005. *Women's Realities, Women's Choices: An Introduction to Women's Studies,* 3rd ed. New York: Oxford University Press.

Hunter, James Davidson. 1983. *American Evangelicalism.* New Brunswick, NJ: Rutgers University Press.

Hurst, Charles E. 2006. *Social Inequality: Forms, Causes and Consequences,* 6th ed. Boston: Allyn & Bacon.

Iannaccone, Laurence R. 1994. "Why Strict Churches Are Strong." *American Journal of Sociology* 59(5):1180–1211.

———. 1995. "Voodoo Economics? Reviewing the Rational Choice Approach to Religion." *Journal for the Scientific Study of Religion* 34(1):76–88.

Independence Hall Association. 2008. "Betsy Ross and the American Flag." Retrieved August 16, 2008 (www.ushistory.org/betsy/flagtale.html).

index mundi. 2009. "United States Infant Mortality Rate." Retrieved November 10, 2009 (www.indexmundi.com/united_states/infant_mortality_rate.html).

Infoplease 2009. "Population Density Per Square Mile of Countries." Retrieved January 6, 2010 (www.infoplease.com/ipa/A0934666.html).

Information Please Almanac. 2008. "Languages." Retrieved January 20, 2008 (www.infoplease.com/ipa/A0775272.html).

Information Please Database. 2009. "National Voter Turnout in Federal Elections: 1960–2008." Retrieved March 17, 2009 (www.infoplease.com/ipa/A0781453.html).

Ingersoll, Richard M. 2004. "The Status of Teaching as a Profession." Pp. 102–18 in *Schools and Society: A Sociological Approach to Education,* 2nd ed., edited by Jeanne H. Ballantine and Joan Z. Spade. Belmont, CA: Wadsworth.

Ingersoll, Richard M., and David Perda. 2008. "The Status of Teaching as a Profession." Pp. 119–126 in *Schools and Society: A Sociological Approach to Education*, 3rd ed., edited by Jeanne H. Ballantine and Joan Z. Spade. Thousand Oaks, CA: Pine Forge Press.

Inglehart, Ronald, 1997. *Modernization and Postmodernization: Cultural, Economic, and Political Change in 43 Societies*. Princeton, NJ: Princeton University Press.

Inglehart, Ronald, and Wayne E. Baker. 2001. "Modernization's Challenge to Traditional Values: Who's Afraid of Ronald McDonald?" *The Futurist* 35(2):16–22.

Inhofe, James M. 2008. "Senate Republicans Introduce Package of Immigration Enforcement Bills." Retrieved April 9, 2008 (www. imhofe.senate.gov/public/index.cfm?FuseAction=PresRoom .PressReleases&Co).

Inside Higher Ed. 2007. "More Students and Higher Scores for ACT" (August 15). Retrieved April 2, 2008 (www.insidehighered.com/ news/2007/08/15/act).

———. 2008. "The SAT's Growing Gaps" (August 27). Retrieved October 14, 2008 (www.insidehighered.com/news/2008/08/27/ sat).

Institute for Research on Poverty. 2008. "What Are Poverty Thresholds and Poverty Guidelines?" (www.irp.wisc.edu/faqs/faq1.htm).

Institute for Statistics. 2005. *Fact Sheet: International Literacy Day 2005*. New York: United Nations.

———. 2006a. "Global Education Digest 2006: Comparing Education Statistics Across the World." New York: UNESCO. Retrieved July 28, 2006 (www.uis.unesco.org/TEMPLATE/pdf/ged/2006/ GED2006.pdf).

———. 2006b. "The State of the World's Children 2007." Retrieved August 23, 2008 (www.unicef.org/sowc07/report/report.php).

Interagency Council on Homelessness. 2009. "HUD Awards $1.4 Billion in Grants to Homeless Programs." Retrieved January 7, 2010 (www.ich.gov).

Intergovernmental Panel on Climate Change. 2007. *Climate Change 2007: Synthesis Report*. Retrieved August 29, 2008 (www.ipcc.ch/ pdf/assessment-report/ar4/syr/ar4_syr_spm.pdf).

International Association for the Evaluation of Educational Achievement. 2007. "Trends in International Math and Science Studies." Retrieved August 23, 2008 (www.iea.nl/timss2007 .html).

International Centre for Prison Studies. 2006. "Entire World: Prison Population Rates per 100,000 of the National Population" (King's College, London). Retrieved April 17, 2010 (www.kcl. ac.uk>...>InternationalCenter for PrisonStudies) OR (www.prison studies.org).

International Encyclopedia of the Social Sciences. 2008. Retrieved December 21, 2009 (www.encyclopedia.com/ doc/1G2-3045300884.html).

International Humanist and Ethical Union. 2009. "Untouchability in Japan: Discrimination Against Burakumin." August 21. Retrieved December 4, 2009 (www.iheu.org/untouchability-japan-discrimination-against-burakumin).

International Institute for Democracy and Electoral Assistance. 2008. "Turnout in the World—Country by Country Performance." Retrieved April 17, 2010 (www.idea.int/vt/survey/voter_turnout_ pop2.cfm).

International Monetary Fund. 2003. "Proposal for a Sovereign Debt Restructuring Mechanism: A Factsheet." Retrieved September 29, 2006 (www.imf.org/external/np/exr/facts/sdrm.htm).

Internet World Statistics. 2009. "U.S. Internet Usage and Broadband Usage Report." June. Retrieved October 21, 2009 (www.internet worldstats.com/am/us.htm).

Inter-Parliamentary Union. 2010. "Women in National Parliaments." Retrieved January 30, 2010 (www.ipu.org/wmn-e/classif.htm).

Interpol. 2003. "Drugs and Criminal Organizations." Retrieved August 4, 2006 (www.interpol.int/public/drugs).

———. 2007. "Interpol Funds Recovery Scam." Retrieved February 18, 2008 (www.interpol.int/default.asp).

Irvine, Leslie. 2004. *If You Tame Me: Understanding Our Connection With Animals*. Philadelphia: Temple University Press.

Irwin, John. 1985. *The Jail: Managing the Underclass in American Society*. Berkeley: University of California Press.

———. 2005. *The Warehouse Prison: Disposal of the New Dangerous Class*. Los Angeles: Roxbury.

Jackman, Robert W. 1993. *Power Without Force: The Political Capacity of Nation-States*. Ann Arbor: University of Michigan Press.

Jackson, Philip W. 1968. *Life in Classrooms*. New York: Holt, Rinehart & Winston.

Jacoby, Jeff. 2009. "A Bad Sign Illegal Immigrants Are Leaving." Center for Immigration Studies. September 6. Retrieved April 17, 2010 (www.boston.com/.../2009/.../a_bad_sign_illegal_ immigrants_are_leaving).

James, Cara, Megan Thomas, Marsha Lillie-Blanton, and Rachel Garfield. 2007. "Key Facts: RACE, Ethnicity, and Medical Care" The Kaiser Family Foundation. Retrieved December 19, 2009 (www.kff.org/minorityhealth/upload/6069-02.pdf).

James, William. [1890] 1934. *The Principles of Psychology*. Mineola, NY: Dover.

Jao, Jui-Chang, and Matthew McKeever. 2006. "Ethnic Inequalities and Educational Attainment in Taiwan." *Sociology of Education* 79(2):131–52.

Japan Institute of Labor. 2002. "Women's Work Patterns and the M-Shaped Curve." Retrieved August 22, 2006 (www.jil.go.jp/ index-e.htm).

Japanese Institute for Labour Policy and Training. 2009. "The Gender Gap in the Japanese Labor Market." February 26. Retrieved November 8, 2009 (www.ikjeld.com/en/news/91/the-gender-gap-in-the-labor-market).

Jarrett, R. L., P. J. Sullivan, and N. D. Watkins. 2005. "Developing Social Capital Through Participation in Organized Youth Programs: Qualitative Insights From Three Programs." *Journal of Community Psychology* 33(1):41–55.

Jayson, Sharon. 2005a. "Cohabitation Is Replacing Dating." *USA Today* (July 17). Retrieved April 3, 2008 (www.usatoday.com/ life/lifestyle/2005-07-17-cohabitation_x.htm).

———. 2005b. "Divorce Declining, But So Is Marriage." *USA Today* (July 18):3A.

Jellinek, E. M. 1960. *The Disease Concept of Alcoholism*. New Haven, CT: Hillhouse.

Jencks, Christopher. 1972. *Inequality: A Reassessment of the Effects of Family and Schooling in America*. New York: Basic Books.

———, ed. 1979. *Who Gets Ahead? The Determinants of Economic Success in America*. New York: Harper & Row.

———. 1992. *Rethinking Social Policy: Race, Poverty, and the Underclass*. Cambridge, MA: Harvard University Press.

Jenness, Valerie, and Kendal Broad. 1997. *Hate Crimes*. New York: Aldine de Gruyter.

Jennings, Jerry, T. 1992. "Voting and Registration in the Election of November 1992." *Current Population Reports* (P-20–466). Washington, DC: U.S. Department of Commerce, Economics and Statistics Administration, U.S. Bureau of the Census.

Jensen, Robert, and Emily Oster. 2007. *The Power of TV: Cable Television and Women's Status in India* (NBER Working Paper No. 13305). Cambridge, MA: National Bureau of Economic Research.

Jez, Su Jin. 2008. "The Influence of Wealth And Race in Four-Year College Attendance." A SERU Project Research Paper. Retrieved December 13, 2009 (http://cshe.berkeley.edu/publications/docs/ ROPS-Jez-Wealth-Race-11-13.pdf).

Jing, Tang. 2007. "The Popularizing of China's Higher Education and Its Influence on University Mathematics Education." *Educational Studies in Mathematics*. V66, #1. September. Pp. 77–82.

Johnson, David W. and Frank P. Johnson. 2006. *Joining Together: Group Theory and Group Skills,* 9th ed. Boston: Allyn & Bacon.

Johnson, Jeff. 2007. "U.S. Presses for New Nuclear Weapons." *Chemical and Engineering News* 85(12):34–37.

Johnson, Kenneth M., and Glenn V. Fuguitt. 2000. "Continuity and Change in Rural Migration Patterns, 1950–1995." *Rural Sociology* 65(1):27–49.

Johnson, Paul. 2005. "Majority of Americans Believe Homosexuality Should Not Be Illegal, Support Partner Rights: Gallup Poll." Retrieved August 22, 2006 (www.sodomylaws.org/usa/usnews141.htm).

Johnson, Ramon. 2008. "Where Is Gay Adoption Legal?" Gay Life. Retrieved January 2, 2010 (gaylife.about.com/od/gayparentingadoption/a/gaycoupleadopt.htm).

Johnson, Rebecca. 2007. "NPT Challenges in 2010: Decoding Signals From the 2007 NPT PrepCom." Washington, DC: Carnegie Endowment for International Peace (June 25). Retrieved April 10, 2010 (www.carnegieendowment.org/events/?fa=eventDetail&id=1024).

Johnson, Robert. 2002. *Hard Time: Understanding and Reforming the Prison.* Belmont, CA: Wadsworth/Thompson Learning.

Johnson, Steven. 2009. "How Twitter Will Change the Way We Live (In 140 Characters or Less)." *Time,* June 15: 32–37.

Jordan-Bychkov, Terry G., and Mono Domoch. 1998. *The Human Mosaic,* 8th ed. New York: W. H. Freeman.

Kagan, Sharon Lynn, and Vivien Stewart. 2005. "A New World View: Education in a Global Era." *Phi Delta Kappan* (November):185–87.

Kaiser Family Foundation. 2005. *Generation M: Media in the Lives of 8 to 18 Year-Olds—Report.* Retrieved July 20, 2006 (www.kff.org/entmedia/7251.cfm).

Kalmijn, Matthijs, and Gerbert Kraaykamp. 1996. "Race, Cultural Capital, and Schooling: An Analysis of Trends in the United States." *Sociology of Education* 69(1):22–34.

Kanter, Rosabeth Moss. 1977. *Men and Women of the Corporation.* New York: Basic Books.

———. 1983. *The Change Masters: Innovation for Productivity in the American Corporation.* New York: Simon & Schuster.

———. 2001a. "Creating the Culture for Innovation." In *Leading for Innovation: Managing for Results,* edited by Frances Hesselbein, Marshall Goldsmith, and Iain Somerville. San Francisco: Jossey-Bass.

———. 2001b. "From Spare Change to Real Change: The Social Sector as Beta Site for Business Innovation." *Harvard Business Review on Innovation* 77(3):122–33.

———. 2005. *Commitment and Community.* Cambridge, MA: Harvard University Press.

Kao, Grace. 2004. "Social Capital and Its Relevance to Minority and Immigrant Populations." *Sociology of Education* 77:172–76.

Kaplan, Howard B., and Robert J. Johnson. 1991. "Negative Social Sanctions and Juvenile Delinquency: Effects of Labeling in a Model of Deviant Behavior." *Social Science Quarterly* 72(1):117.

Karen, David. 2005. "No Child Left Behind? Sociology Ignored!" *Sociology of Education* 78(2):165–82.

Karraker, Katherine Hildebrant. 1995. "Parent's Gender-Stereotyped Perceptions of Newborns: The Eye of the Beholder Revisited." *Sex Roles* 33(9/10):687–701.

Kates, Brian. 2002. "Black Market in Transplant Organs." *New York Daily News* (August 25).

Katz, Jackson. 2006. *The Macho Paradox: Why Some Men Hurt Women and How All Men Can Help.* Naperville, IL: Sourcebooks.

KBYU-TV, producer. 2005. *Small Fortunes: Microcredit and the Future of Poverty.* Provo, Ut: Author.

Keeter, Scott, Juliana Horowitz, and Alec Tyson. 2008. "Young Voters in the 2008 Election." Pew Research Center for the People & the Press. November 12 Retrieved July 11, 2009 (http://pewresearch.org/pubs/1031/young-voters-in-the-2008-election).

Keith, Verna M., and Cedric Herring. 1991. "Skin Tone and Stratification in the Black Community." *American Journal of Sociology* 97(3):760–78.

Kellerhals, Merle David. 2009. "Terrorist Attacks Fell 18% in 2008" (April 30). Retrieved April 17, 2010 (www.uspolicy.be/Article.asp?ID=A9DFE100-8F5A-48AF-8D98).

Kendall, Diane. 2004. *Sociology in Our Times: The Essentials,* 4th ed. Belmont, CA: Wadsworth.

Kerbo, Harold R. 2008. *Social Stratification and Inequality,* 7th ed. Boston: McGraw-Hill.

Kerckhoff, Alan C. 2001. "Education and Social Stratification Processes in Comparative Perspective." *Sociology of Education* (Extra Issue: Currents of Thought: Sociology of Education at the Dawn of the 21st Century):3–18.

Kettl, Donald F. 1993. *Sharing Power: Public Governance and Private Markets.* Washington, DC: Brookings.

Khazaleh Lorenz. 2009. "Internet Fatwas Cautiously Support Divorce Among Women" *CULCOM* (October 29). Retrieved January 4, 2010 (www.culcom.uio.no/english/news/2009/bogstad.html).

Kidder, Tracy. 2004. *Mountains Beyond Mountains.* New York: Random House.

Kilbourne, Jean. 1999. *Deadly Persuasion: Why Women and Girls Must Fight the Additive Power of Advertising.* New York: Free Press.

———. 2000. *Killing Us Softly, III* (Video). Northampton, MA: Media Education Foundation.

Killian, Caitlin. 2006. *North African Women in France: Gender, Culture, and Identity.* Palo Alto, CA: Stanford University Press.

Kim, Min-Sun, Katsuya Tasaki, In-Duk Kim, and Hye-ryeon Lee. 2007. "The Influence of Social Status on Communication Predispositions Focusing on Independent and Interdependent Self-Construals." *Journal of Asian Pacific Communication* 17(2):303–329.

Kimmel, Michael, S. 2003. *The Gendered Society,* 2nd ed. New York: Oxford University Press.

Kimmel, Michael S., and Michael A. Messner. 2009. *Men's Lives,* 8th ed. Boston: Allyn & Bacon.

King, Edith W. 2006. *Meeting the Challenges of Teaching in an Era of Terrorism.* Belmont, CA: Thomson.

King, Jacqueline E. 2000. *Gender Equity in Higher Education.* Washington, DC: American Council on Education, Center for Policy Analysis.

Kinsey, Alfred E., Wardell B. Pomeroy, Clyde E. Martin, and H. Gephard. 1953. *Sexual Behavior in the Human Female.* Philadelphia: Saunders.

Kirk, Gwyn, and Margo Okazawa-Rey. 2007. *Women's Lives: Multicultural Perspectives,* 4th ed. Boston: McGraw-Hill.

Kitano, Harry H., Pauline Aqbayani, and Diane de Anda. 2005. *Race Relations,* 6th edition. Englewood Cliffs, NJ: Prentice Hall.

Kiviat, Barbara, 2008. "Gentrification: Not Ousting the Poor?" *Time* (June 29). Retrieved January 5, 2010 (www.time.com/time/business/article/0,8599,1818255,00.html).

Klaus, Patsy. 2007. *Crime and the Nation's Households, 2005* (National Crime Victimization Survey, NCJ 217198). Washington, DC: U.S. Department of Justice, Bureau of Justice Statistics.

Klein, Barbara, and Steve Ember. 2009. "Technology Increases Income, Reduces Poverty in Developing Countries." Voice of America. Retrieved April 17, 2010 (www.unsv.com/voanews.com/specialenglish/article/go.asp?act=next).

Knapp, Mark L., and Judith A. Hall. 1997. *Nonverbal Communication in Human Interaction,* 4th ed. Fort Worth: Harcourt Brace.

Knickmeyer, Ellen. 2008. "Turkey's Gul Signs Head Scarf Measure" (February 23). Retrieved April 17, 2010 (www.washingtonpost.com/>world).

Koch, Jerome R., and Evans W. Curry. 2000. "Social Context and the Presbyterian Gay/Lesbian Debate: Testing Open Systems Theory." *Review of Religious Research* 42(2):206–214.

Kodish, Bruce I. 2003. "What We Do With Language—What It Does With Us." *ETC: A Review of General Semantics* 60:383–95.

Kohlberg, Lawrence. 1971. "From Is to Ought." Pp. 151–284 in *Cognitive Development and Epistemology,* edited by T. Mischel. New York: Academic Press.

Kohn, Melvin. 1989. *Class and Conformity: A Study of Values,* 2nd ed. Chicago: University of Chicago Press.

Koos, Earl. 1954. *The Health of Regionville.* New York: Columbia University Press.

Korte, Charles, and Stanley Milgram. 1970. "Acquaintance Networks Between Racial Groups." *Journal of Personality and Social Psychology* 15:101–108.

Kosmin, Barry A., and Seymour P. Lackman. 1993. *One Nation Under God: Religion in Contemporary American Society.* New York: Harmony Books.

Kozol, Jonathan. 1991. *Savage Inequalities: Children in America's Schools.* New York: Crown.

———. 2005. "Confections of Apartheid: A Stick-and-Carrot Pedagogy for the Children of Our Inner-City Poor." *Phi Delta Kappan* (December):265–75.

———. 2006. *The Shame of the Nation: The Restoration of Apartheid Schooling in America.* New York: Crown.

Kramer, Laura. 2007. *The Sociology of Gender: A Brief Introduction,* 2nd ed. New York: Oxford University Press.

Kristoff, Nicholas D., and Sheryl WeDunn. 2000. *Thunder From the East.* New York: Vintage Books (Random House).

Krug, E., L. Dahlberg, J. Mercy, A. Zwi, and R. Lozano. 2002. *World Report on Violence and Health.* Geneva, Switzerland: World Health Organization.

Kübler-Ross, Elizabeth. 1997. *Death, the Final Stage of Growth,* Rev. ed. New York: Scribner.

Kuhn, Manford. 1964. "Major Trends in Symbolic Interaction Theory in the Past Twenty-Five Years." *Sociological Quarterly* 5:61–84.

Kuhn, Thomas. 1970. *The Structure of Scientific Revolutions,* 2nd ed. Chicago: University of Chicago Press.

Kumar, Sanjay. 2001. "Despite Ban, Organs Still Sold in India." *Reuters Health* (March 9). Retrieved September 20, 2006 (www.geocities .com/somewherereal/bodyparts.html).

Kumlin, Johanna. 2006. "The Sex Wage Gap in Japan and Sweden: The Role of Human Capital, Workplace Sex Composition, and Family Responsibility." *European Sociological Review: Advance Access Published online on Dec. 18, 2006.* Retrieved April 17, 2010 (http://esr.oxfordjournals.org/cgi/content/ abstract/23/2/203).

Kusmin, Lorin. 2008. "Rural America at a Glance, 2008 Edition." Economic Information Bulletin No. (EIB-40) (October). Retrieved January 6, 2010 (www.ers.usda.gov/publications/eib40).

Kyle, David, and Rey Koslowski, eds. 2001. *Global Human Smuggling: Comparative Perspectives.* Baltimore, MD: Johns Hopkins University Press.

Lacayo, Richard. 1993. "Cult of Death." *Time* (March 15):36.

Laird, J. S. Lew, M. DeBell, and C. Chapman. 2006. *Dropout Rates in the United States: 2002 and 2003* (NCES 2006–062). Washington, DC: U.S. Department of Education, National Center for Education Statistics.

Lake, Robert. 1990. "An Indian Father's Plea." *Teacher Magazine* 2(September):48–53.

Lamanna, Mary Ann, and Agnes Riedmann. 2010. *Marriages and Families: Making Choices Throughout the Life Cycle,* 10th ed. Belmont, CA: Wadsworth.

Lambert, Lisa. 2006. "Half of Teachers Quit in Five Years: Working Conditions, Low Salaries Cited." *Washington Post* (May 9):A7.

Lambert, Yves. 2000. "Religion in Modernity as a New Axial Age: Secularization or New Religious Forms?" Pp. 95–125 in *The Secularization Debate,* edited by William H. Swatos, Jr. and Daniel V. A. Olson. Lanham, MD: Rowman & Littlefield.

Landau, Elizabeth. 2009. "Life Expectancy Could Be Topic in Health Care Debate" (June 11). Retrieved April 17, 2010 (www.cnn .com/2009/HEALTH/06/.../life.expectancy.health.care).

Landler, Mark, and Brian Stelter. 2009. "Washington Taps Into a Potent New Force in Diplomacy." *New York Times,* June 17: A12. Retrieved December 22, 2009 (www.nytimes.com/2009/06/17/ world/middleeast/17media.html).

Lareau, Annette. 2003. *Unequal Childhoods: Class, Race, and Family Life.* Berkeley: University of California Press.

Lashbrook, Jeffrey. 2009. "Social Class Differences in Family Life." P. 224 in *Our Social World,* 2nd ed., edited by Jeanne H. Ballantine and Keith A. Roberts. Thousand Oaks: Sage.

Lazare, Aaron. 2004. *On Apology.* New York: Oxford University Press.

Leach, Edmund R. 1979. "Ritualization in Man in Relation to Conceptual and Social Development." Pp. 333–37 in *Reader in Comparative Religion,* 3rd ed., edited by William A. Lessa and Evon Z. Vogt. New York: Harper & Row.

Leavitt, Jacqueline, and Susan Saegert. 1990. From *Abandonment to Hope: Community-Households in Harlem* (Columbia History of Urban Life). New York: Columbia University Press.

LeBon, Gustave. [1895] 1960. *The Crowd: A Study of the Popular Mind.* New York: Viking.

LeBow, Bob. 2004. *Health Care Meltdown: Confronting the Myths and Fixing Our Failing System.* Chambersburg, PA: Alan C. Hood.

Lechner, Frank J., and John Boli. 2005. *World Culture: Origins and Consequences.* Malden, MA: Blackwell.

Lee, B. C., and J. L. Werth. 2000. *Observations on the First Year of Oregon's Death With Dignity Act.* Washington, DC: American Psychological Association.

Lee, Gang, Ronald L. Akers, and Marian J. Borg. 2004. "Social Learning and Structural Factors in Adolescent Substance Use." *Western Criminology Review* 5(1):17.

Lee, Jennifer, and Frank D. Bean. 2004. "America's Changing Color Lines: Immigration, Race/Ethnicity, and Multiracial Identification." *Annual Review of Sociology* 30(August):222–42.

———. 2007. "Redrawing the Color Line?" *City and Community* 6(1):49–62.

Lee, Richard B. 1984. *The Dobe!Kung.* New York: Holt, Rinehart & Winston.

Lee, Richard Wayne. 1992. "Christianity and the Other Religions: Interreligious Relations in a Shrinking World." *Sociological Analysis* (Summer):125–39.

Lee, Sharon M., and Barry Edmonston. 2005. "New Marriages, New Families: U.S. Racial and Hispanic Intermarriage." *Population Bulletin* 60(2). Retrieved August 7, 2008 (www.prb.org/ pdf05/60.2NewMarriages.pdf).

Leeder, Elaine J. 2004. *The Family in Global Perspective: A Gendered Journey.* Thousand Oaks, CA: Sage.

Legters, Nettie E. 2001. "Teachers as Workers in the World System." Pp. 417–26 in *Schools and Society: A Sociological Approach to Education,* edited by Jeanne H. Ballantine and Joan Z. Spade. Belmont, CA: Wadsworth.

Lehman, Edward C., Jr. 1985. *Women Clergy: Breaking Through Gender Barriers.* New Brunswick, NJ: Transaction.

Leit, R. A., J. J. Gray, and H. G. Pope. 2002. "The Media's Representation of the Ideal Male Body." *International Journal of Eating Disorders.* (doi.wiley.com).

Lemert, Edwin M. 1951. *Social Pathology.* New York: McGraw-Hill.

———. 1972. *Human Deviance, Social Problems, and Social Control,* 2nd ed. Englewood Cliffs, NJ: Prentice Hall.

Lemkau, Jeanne Parr. 2006. "Fences, Volcanoes, and Embargoes." Unpublished manuscript.

———. 2010. "Fences, Volcanoes, and Embargoes." Unpublished Manuscript.

Lengermann, Patricia M., and Jill Niebrugge-Brantley. 1990. "Feminist Sociological Theory: The Near-Future Prospects." Pp. 316–44 in *Frontiers of Social Theory: The New Synthesis,* edited by George Ritzer. New York: Columbia University Press.

Lenski, Gerhard E. 1966. *Human Societies.* New York: McGraw-Hill.

Lerner, Richard M. 1992. "Sociobiology and Human Development: Arguments and Evidence." *Human Development* 35(1):12–51.

Leslie, Gerald R., and Sheila K. Korman. 1989. *The Family in Social Context,* 7th ed. New York: Oxford University Press.

Leung, K., S. Lau, and W. L. Lam. 1998. *Parenting Styles and Academic Achievement: A Cross-Cultural Study.* Detroit, MI: Wayne State University Press.

Levin, Jack, and Jack McDevitt. 2003. *Hate Crimes Revisited: America's War on Those Who Are Different.* Boulder, CO: Westview.

Levine, Michael H. 2005. "Take a Giant Step: Investing in Preschool Education in Emerging Nations." *Phi Delta Kappan* (November):196–200.

Levinson, David L. 2010. "Grand Solution or Grab Bag?" *The American Prospect.* November. Pp. 14–17 (www.prospect.org).

Levinson, Stephen C. 2000. "Yeli Dnye and the Theory of Basic Color Terms." *Journal of Linguistic Anthropology* 1:3–55.

Levitt, Peggy. 2001. *The Transnational Villagers.* Berkeley: University of California Press.

Levy, Audrey. 2008. "No to Forced Marriages!" *France Diplomatie.* Retrieved April 17, 2010 (www.diplomatie.gouv.fr/...no.../seen-from-france_4737.html).

Lewin, Tamar. 2006. "At Colleges, Women Are Leaving Men in the Dust." *The New York Times* (July 9):A1, 18.

Lewis, Oscar. 1961. *The Children of Sánchez: Autobiography of a Mexican Family.* New York: Random House.

———. 1986. *La Vida: A Puerto Rican Family in the Culture of Poverty.* New York: Irvington.

Lieberson, Stanley. 1980. *A Piece of the Pie: Blacks and White Immigrants Since 1880.* Berkeley: University of California Press.

Lieberson, Stanley, Susan Dumais, and Shyon Bauman. 2000. "The Instability of Androgynous Names: The Symbolic Maintenance of Gender Boundaries." *American Journal of Sociology* 105(5):1249–87.

Lincoln, Erik, and Laurence Mamiya. 1990. *The Black Church in the African American Experience.* Durham, NC: Duke University Press.

Lindberg, Richard, and Vesna Markovic. n.d. "Organized Crime Outlook in the New Russia: Russia Is Paying the Price of a Market Economy in Blood." Retrieved January 4, 2001 (www.search-international.com/Articles/crime/russiacrime.htm).

Lindsay, James M. 2006. "Global Warming Heats Up." Pp. 307–13 in *Globalization: The Transformation of Social Worlds,* edited by D. Stanley Eitzen and Maxine Baca Zinn. Belmont, CA: Wadsworth.

Lindsey, Linda L. 2008. *Gender Roles: A Sociological Perspective,* 4th ed. Englewood Cliffs, NJ: Prentice Hall.

Linton, Ralph. 1937. *The Study of Man.* New York: D. Appleton-Century.

Lips, Hilary M. 2007. *Sex and Gender: An Introduction,* 6th ed. Boston: McGraw-Hill.

Liptak Adam. 2008. "1 in 100 U.S. Adults Behind Bars, New Study Says." *New York Times,* February 28, 2008. Retrieved December 20, 2009 (www.nytimes.com/2008/02/28/us/28cnd-prison.html).

Logan, John R., and Glenna D. Spitze. 1994. "Family Neighbors." *American Journal of Sociology* 100(2):453–76.

Longman, Timothy. 2005. "Rwanda: Achieving Equality or Serving an Authoritarian State?" Pp. 133–150 in *Women in African Parliaments,* edited by Gretchen Bauer and Hannah Britton. Boulder, CO: Lynne Reinner.

Lopez, Ian F. Haney. 1996. *White by Law.* New York: New York University Press.

Lopez-Garza, Marta. 2002. "Convergence of the Public and Private Spheres: Women in the Informal Economy." *Race, Gender, and Class* 9(3):175–92.

Lopreato, Joseph 2001. "Sociobiological Theorizing: Evolutionary Sociology" Pp. 405–33 in *Handbook of Sociological Theory,* edited by Secaucus, NJ: Springer.

Lorber, Judith. 1998. "Reinventing the Sexes: The Biomedical Construction of Femininity and Masculinity." *Contemporary Society* 27(5):498–99.

Lorber, Judith, and Lisa Jean Moore. 2007. *Gendered Bodies.* Los Angeles, CA: Roxbury.

Los Angeles Times. 2008. "Kenyans Recall the Screams of the Dying in Burning Church" (January 3). Retrieved June 3, 2008 (http://articles.latimes.com/2008/jan/03/world/fg-church3).

Loveless, Tom. 2009. "Tracking and Detracking: High Achievers in Massachusetts Middle Schools." Thomas B. Fordham Institute, Retrieved April 17, 2010 (http://edexcellence.net/.../news_tracking-and-detracking-high-achievers-in-massachusetts-middle-schools).

Lucal, Betsy. 1999. "What It Means to Be Gendered Me." *Gender and Society.* (13: 6): 781–797.

Lucas, Samuel R., and Mark Berends. 2002. "Sociodemographic Diversity, Correlated Achievement, and De Facto Tracking." *Sociology of Education* 75(4):328–48.

Luczaj, Sarah. 2008. "Depression and Anxiety Across Cultures." Retrieved January 9, 2010 (counsellingresource.com/features/2008/03/14/depression-anxiety-crosscultural).

Luhman, Reid, and Stuart Gilman. 1980. *Race and Ethnic Relations: The Social and Political Experience of Minority Groups.* Belmont, CA: Wadsworth.

Lukunka, Barbra. 2008. "Ethnocide." *Online Encyclopedia of Mass Violence.* American University, Washington, DC. Retrieved October 16, 2009 (www.massviolence.org/ethnocide).

Lumsden, Charles J., and Edward O. Wilson. 1981. *Genes, Mind, and Culture: The Coevolutionary Process.* Cambridge, MA: Harvard University Press.

Lundt, John C. 2004. "Learning for Ourselves: A New Paradigm for Education." *The Futurist* (November–December):22.

Lupton, Deborah. 2001. "Medicine and Health Care in Australia." Pp. 429–40 in *The Blackwell Companion to Medical Sociology,* edited by William C. Cockerham. Malden, MA: Blackwell.

MacDougal, Gary. 2005. *Make a Difference: A Spectacular Breakthrough in the Fight Against Poverty.* New York: St. Martin's Press.

Machalek, Richard, and Michael W. Martin. 2010. "Evolution, Biology, and Society: A Conversation for the 21st Century Classroom." *Teaching Sociology* 38(1):35–45.

Macionis, John. 2007. *Sociology,* 11th ed. Upper Saddle River, NJ: Prentice Hall.

MacLeod, Jay. 1995. *Ain't No Makin' It: Aspirations and Attainment in a Low-Income Neighborhood.* Boulder, CO: Westview.

Madden, Mary, and Amanda Lenhart. 2006. "Online Dating." Pew Internet and American Life Project. Retrieved January 3, 2010 (www.pewinternet.org/Reports/2006/Online-Dating.aspx).

Made in Mexico, Inc. 2005. "What Are Maquiladoras? The Maquiladora Industry." Retrieved March 7, 2008 (www.madeinmexicoinc.com/maquiladoras_industry.htm).

"The Madoff Case: A Timeline." 2009. *The Wall Street Journal.* March 12. Retrieved November 5, 2009 (http://online.wsj.com/article/SB112966954231272304.html?mod=googlenews.wsj).

Makhmalbaf, Mohsen, producer. 2003. *Kandahar: The Sun behind the Moon* (Film).

Malthus, Thomas R. [1798] 1926. *First Essay on Population 1798.* London: Macmillan.

Marcus, Richard R. 2008. "Kenya's Conflict Isn't 'Tribal.'" *Los Angeles Times* (January 24). Retrieved June 3, 2008 (www.latimes.com/news/opinion/la-oew-marcus24jan24,0,4231203.story).

Marger, Martin N. 2009. *Race and Ethnic Relations: American and Global Perspectives,* 8th ed. Belmont, CA: Wadsworth/Cengage Learning.

Marmor, Theodore R. 1999. *The Politics of Medicare,* 2nd ed. Hawthorne, NY: Aldine de Gruyter.

Marti, Gerardo. 2005. *A Mosaic of Believers: Diversity and Innovation in a Multiethnic Church.* Bloomington: Indiana University Press.

Martin, Patricia Yancey, and Robert A. Hummer. 1989. "Fraternities and Rape on Campus." *Gender and Society* 3(4):457–73.

Martin, Scott C. 2006. *From Temperance to Alcoholism in America.* Baltimore, MD: Johns Hopkins University Press.

Marty, Martin E. 1983. "Religion in America Since Mid-Century." Pp. 273–87 in *Religion and America,* edited by Mary Douglas and Stephen Tipton. Boston: Beacon.

Marty, Martin E., and R. Scott Appleby, eds. 1991. *Fundamentalism Observed.* Chicago: University of Chicago Press.

———. 2004. *Accounting for Fundamentalism: The Dynamic Character of Movements.* Chicago: University of Chicago Press.

Marx, Karl. [1844] 1963. "Contribution to the Critique of Hegel's Philosophy of Right." Pp. 43–59 in *Karl Marx: Early Writings.* Translated and edited by T. B. Bottomore. New York: McGraw-Hill.

———. [1844] 1964. *The Economic and Philosophical Manuscripts of 1844.* New York: International Publishers.

Marx, Karl, and Friedrich Engels. 1955. *Selected Work in Two Volumes.* Moscow: Foreign Language Publishing House.

———. [1848] 1969. *The Communist Manifesto.* Baltimore: Penguin.

Mashberg, Tom. 2002. "Med Examiner's Office Has Secret Body-Parts Deal." *Boston Herald* (May 20):1.

Mason-Schrock, Douglas. 1996. "Transsexual's Narrative Construction of the 'True Self.'" *Social Psychology Quarterly* 59(3):176–92.

Massey, Douglas S. 2007. *Categorically Unequal: The American Stratification System.* New York: Russell Sage.

Massey, Douglas S., and Nancy A. Denton. 1998. *American Apartheid: Segregation and the Making of the Underclass.* Cambridge, MA: Harvard University Press.

Masters, William H., and Virginia Johnson. 1966. *Human Sexual Response.* Boston: Little, Brown.

———. 1970. *Human Sexual Inadequacy.* Boston: Little, Brown.

Mathews, T.J., and Marian F. MacDorman. 2008. "Infant Mortality Statistics From the 2005 Period Linked Birth/Infant Death Data Set" *National Vital Statistics Reports* 27(2). Retrieved January 23, 2010 (www.cdc.gov/nchs/data/nvsr/nvsr57/nvsr57_02.pdf).

Mauksch, Hans. 1993. "Teaching of Applied Sociology: Opportunities and Obstacles." Pp. 1–7 in *Teaching Applied Sociology: A Resource Book,* edited by C. Howery. Washington, DC: American Sociological Association Teaching Resources Center.

Mauss, Armand. 1975. *Social Problems as Social Movements.* Philadelphia: Lippincott.

Mayo Clinic. 2007. "Domestic Violence Toward Women: Recognize the Patterns and Seek Help." Retrieved April 17, 2010 (www.mayoclinic.com/health/domestic-violence/WO00044).

Mayoux, Linda. 2002. "Women's Empowerment or Feminisation of Debt? Towards a New Agenda in African Microfinance." Report at the One World Action Conference in London, March 21–22.

———, ed. 2008. *Sustainable Learning for Women's Empowerment: Ways Forward in Micro-Finance.* Warwickshire, UK: ITDG Publishing.

McAdam, Doug. 1999. *Political Process and the Development of Black Insurgency, 1930–1970,* 2nd ed. Chicago: University of Chicago Press.

McCaghy, Charles H., Timothy A. Capron, J. D. Jamieson, and Sandra Harley Carey. 2006. *Deviant Behavior: Crime, Conflict, and Interest Groups,* 7th ed. Boston: Allyn & Bacon.

McCarthy, John D., and Mayer N. Zald. 1977. "Resource Mobilization and Social Movements: A Partial Theory." *American Journal of Sociology* 82(6):1212–41.

McConnell, E. D., and E. Delgado-Romero. 2004. "Latinos, Panethnicity, and Census 2000: Reality or Methodological Construction." Retrieved February 24, 2008 (www.allacademic.com/meta/p109991_index.html).

McCormick, John. 1992. "A Housing Program That Actually Works." *Newsweek* (June 22):61.

McCrone, David. 1998. *The Sociology of Nationalism.* London: Routledge.

McDonald, Michael. 2009. "2008 General Election Turnout Rates." Retrieved July 11, 2009 (http://elections.gmu.edu/Turnout_2008G.html).

McEneaney, Elizabeth H., and John W. Meyer. 2000. "The Content of the Curriculum: An Institutionalist Perspective." Pp. 189–211 in *Handbook of the Sociology of Education,* edited by Maureen T. Hallinan. New York: Kluwer Academic/Plenum.

McEvoy, Alan W., and Jeff B. Brookings. 2008. *If She Is Raped: A Guidebook for the Men in Her Life,* 4th ed., abridged. Tampa, FL: Teal Ribbon Books.

McGuire, Meredith. 2002. *Religion: The Social Context,* 5th ed. Belmont, CA: Wadsworth.

McIntosh, Peggy. 2002. "White Privilege: Unpacking the Invisible Knapsack." Pp. 97–101 in *White Privilege: Essential Readings on the Other Side of Racism,* edited by Paula S. Rothenberg. New York: Worth.

McKelvie, Samuel R. 1926. "What the Movies Meant to the Farmer." *Annals of the American Academy of Political and Social Science* 128(November):131.

McKinnish, Terra, Randall Walsh, and Kirk White. 2008. "Who Gentrifies Low Income Neighborhoods?" Retrieved April 17, 2010 (papers.ssrn.com/so13/papers.cfm?abstract_id=1139352).

McLeod, Jay. 2004. *Ain't No Makin' It: Aspirations and Attainment in a Low-Income Neighborhood,* 2nd ed. Boulder, CO: Westview.

McManus, Patricia A., and Thomas A DiPrete. 2001. "Losers and Winners: The Financial Consequences of Separation and Divorce for Men." *American Sociological Review* 66(April):246–68.

McNall, Scott G, and Sally Allen McNall. 1983. *Plains Families: Exploring Sociology Through Social History.* New York: St. Martin's Press.

Mead, George Herbert. [1934] 1962. *Mind, Self, and Society.* Chicago: University of Chicago Press.

Mead, Margaret. [1935] 1963. *Sex and Temperament in Three Primitive Societies.* New York: William Morrow.

Medical News Today. 2009. "Women's Health." September 4. Retrieved January 6, 2010 (www.medicalnewstoday.com/articles/162997.php).

"Medicare Fraud: A $60 Billion Crime." October 25, 2009. Retrieved April 17, 2010 (www.cbsnews.com/stories/2009/10/23/.../main.5414390.shtml).

Mehan, Hugh. 1992. "Understanding Inequality in Schools: The Contribution of Interpretive Studies." *Sociology of Education* 65(1):1–20.

Mehra, Bharat, Cecelia Merkel, and Ann P. Bishop. 2004. "The Internet for Empowerment of Minority and Marginalized Users." *New Media and Society* 6:781–802.

Meltzer, B. 1978. "Mead's Social Psychology." Pp. 15–27 in *Symbolic Interactionism: A Reader in Social Psychology,* 3rd ed., edited by J. Manis and B. Meltzer. Boston: Allyn & Bacon.

Meltzer, Bernard N., John W. Petras, and Larry T. Reynolds. 1975. *Symbolic Interactionism: Genesis, Varieties and Criticism.* London: Routledge & Kegan Paul.

Meltzer, Jack. 1999. *Metropolis to Metroplex: The Social and Spatial Planning of Cities.* Baltimore: Johns Hopkins University Press.

Memorial Institute for the Prevention of Terrorism. 2007. "Number of Terrorist Attacks." MIPT Terrorism Knowledge Database. Retrieved April 14, 2009 (www.publicagenda.org/charts/number-international-terrorist-attacks).

Merchant, Nomaan. 2009. "Law Blocking Acorn Funding Raises Constitutional Question." *The Wall Street Journal* December 18. Retrieved December 21, 2009 (http://online.wsj.com/article/SB126110280150596545.html?mod=WSJ_hpp_MIDDLENextto WhatsNewsSecond).

Merton, Robert K. 1938. "Social Structure and Anomie." *American Sociological Review* 3(October):672–82.

———. 1942/1973. *The Sociology of Science: Theoretical and Empirical Investigations.* Chicago: University of Chicago Press.

Merton, Robert K. 1949. "Discrimination and the American Creed." Pp. 99-126 in Discrimination and American Welfare, edited by Robert M. MacIver. New York: Harper.

———. 1968. Social Theory and Social Structure, 2nd ed. New York: Free Press.

Metropolitan Community Churches. 2008. "Churches." Retrieved March 1, 2008 (www.mccchurch.org/AM/Template.cfm?Section=Find_an_MCC).

Metz, Mary Haywood. 1986. Different by Design: The Context and Character of Three Magnet Schools. New York: Routledge & Kegan Paul.

Meyer, R. 1996. "The Disease Called Addiction: Emerging Evidence in a Two Hundred Year Debate." The Lancet 347(8995):162–66.

Michels, Robert. [1911] 1967. Political Parties. New York: Free Press.

Mike, Valerie. 2003. "Evidence and the Future of Medicine." Evaluation and the Health Professions 26(2):127–52.

Milgram, Stanley. 1967. "The Small World Problem." Psychology Today 1:61–67.

Milkie, Melissa. 1999. "Social Comparisons, Reflected Appraisals, and Mass Media. The Impact of Pervasive Beauty Images on Black and White Girl's Self Concept." Social Psychology Quarterly 62(2):190–210.

Miller, Greg. 2009. "Global Economic Crisis Called Biggest U.S. Security Threat." Los Angeles Times. Retrieved February 13, 2009 (http://articles.latimes.com/2009/feb/13/nation/na-security-threat13).

Mills, C. Wright. 1956. The Power Elite. New York: Oxford University Press.

———. 1959. The Sociological Imagination. New York: Oxford University Press.

Mills, Theodore M. 1984. The Sociology of Small Groups, 2nd ed. Englewood Cliffs, NJ: Prentice Hall.

Mincy, Ronald B. 2006. Black Males Left Behind. Washington, DC: Urban Institute Press.

Miniwatts Marketing Group. 2008. "Internet World Stats." Retrieved July 7, 2008 (www.internetworldstats.com/stats.htm).

Minkoff, Debra C. 1995. Organizing for Equality. New Brunswick, NJ: Rutgers University Press.

Misztal, Bronislaw, and Anson D. Shupe. 1998. Fundamentalism and Globalization: Fundamentalist Movements at the Twilight of the Twentieth Century. Westport, CT: Praeger.

Moffett, Sebastian. 2003. "Going Gray: For Ailing Japan, Longevity Begins to Take Its Toll." The Wall Street Journal (February 11):A1, 12.

Molotch, Harvey. 2003. Where Stuff Comes From: How Toasters, Toilets, Cars, Computers, and Many Other Things Come to Be as They Are. London: Routledge.

Moore, Laurence. 1995. Selling God: American Religion in the Marketplace of Culture. New York: Oxford University Press.

Moore, Valerie Ann. 2001. "Doing Racialized and Gendered Age to Organize Peer Relations: Observing Kids in Summer Camp." Gender and Society 15(6):835–58.

Morbidity and Mortality Weekly Report. 2006 "Tobacco Use Among Adults—United States, 2005." October 27, 55(42):1145–48. Retrieved January 23, 2010 (www.cdc.gov/mmwr/preview/mmwrhtml/mm5542a1.htm).

Morello, Carol, and Dan Keating. 2009. "Number of Foreign-Born U.S. Residents Drops." September 22. Retrieved January 5, 2010 (www.washingtonpost.com/wp-dyn/content/article/2009/09/21/AR2009092103251.html).

Morgan, Kenneth O. 1981. Rebirth of a Nation: Wales, 1880–1980. Oxford, UK: Oxford University Press.

Morgan, Stephen L. 2001. "Counterfactuals, Causal Effect Heterogeneity, and the Catholic School Effect on Learning." Sociology of Education 74(4):341–73.

Moritz, Owen. 2001. "Trafficking in Humans Is Thriving Business in Africa." New York Daily News (April 17):4.

Morris, Edward W. 2005. "From 'Middle Class' to 'Trailer Trash': Teachers' Perceptions of White Students in a Predominately Minority School." Sociology of Education 78(2):99–121.

Morris, Joan M., and Michael D. Grimes. 1997. Caught in the Middle: Contradictions in the Lives of Sociologists From Working Class Backgrounds. Westport, CT: Praeger.

Morris, Lloyd R. 1949. Not So Long Ago. New York: Random House.

Morris, Martina, Mark Stephen Handcock, Marc A. Scott, and Annette D. Bernhardt. 2001. Divergent Paths: Economic Mobility in the New American Labor Market. New York: Russell Sage.

Morrison, Barry. 2009. "What Do Statistics Tell Us About Hate in America in 2009?" December 24, 2009. Retrieved April 8, 2010 (www.adl.org/ADL_Opinions/Civil_Rights/PhilJewishExp_12242009.htm).

Mumford, Lewis. 1961. The City in History: Its Origins, Transformations, and Prospects. New York: Harcourt, Brace, & World.

Murstein, Bernard I. 1987. "A Clarification and Extension of the SVR Theory of Dyadic Pairing." Journal of Marriage and the Family 49(November):929–33.

Mutamba, John. 2005. "Strategies for Increasing Women's Participation in Government." Expert Group Meeting on Democratic Governance in Africa, Nairobi, Kenya, December 6–8.

Mydans, Seth. 2002. "In Pakistan, Rape Victims Are the 'Criminals.'" The New York Times (May 17):A3.

———. 2009. "For Khmer Rouge Guard, It Was Kill or Be Killed." March 1. Retrieved July 11, 2009 (www.nytimes.com/2009/03/01/world/asia/01iht-guard.1.20501994.html).

Myers, John P. 2003. Dominant-Minority Relations in America: Linking Personal History With the Convergence in the New World. Boston: Allyn & Bacon.

Myrdal, Gunnar. 1964. An American Dilemma. New York: McGraw-Hill.

Nagel, Joane. 1994. "Constructing Ethnicity: Creating and Recreating Ethnic Identity and Culture." Social Problems 41(1):152–76.

Nakamura, Lisa. 2004. "Interrogating the Digital Divide: The Political Economy of Race and Commerce in the New Media." Pp. 71–83 in Society On-Line: The Internet in Context, edited by Philip N. Howard and Steve Jones. Thousand Oaks, CA: Sage.

Nanda, Serena, and Richard L. Warms. 2010. Cultural Anthropology, 10th ed. Belmont, CA: Wadsworth.

National Archives and Records Administration. 2008. "What Is the Electoral College?" Retrieved March 21, 2008 (www.archives.gov/federal-register/electoral-college/about.html).

National Assessment of Educational Progress. "Comparing Private Schools and Public Schools Using Hierarchical Linear Modeling." NCES, U.S. Department of Education. NCES 2006–461. Retrieved April 17, 2010 (www.nytimes.com/packages/pdf/national/2006715report.pdf) or (nces.ed.gov/pubinfo.asp?pubid=2006461).

National Center for Education Statistics. 2002. Digest of Education Statistics 2002. Table 207. Washington, DC: U.S. Department of Education.

———. 2006. 2004 Integrated Postsecondary Education Data System (IPEDS), previously unpublished tabulation.

———. 2008a. Degrees Conferred by Degree-Granting Institutions, by Level of Degree and Sex of Student (Table 268). Retrieved January 6, 2010 (http://nces.ed.gov/programs/digest/d08/tables/dt08_268.asp).

———. 2008b. Recent High School Completers and Their Enrollment in College, by Race/Ethnicity: 1960 through 2007 (Table 201). Retrieved January 6, 2010 (http://nces.ed.gov/programs/digest/d08/tables/dt08_201.asp).

National Center for Health Statistics. 2007. Health, United States, 2007: With Chartbook on Trends in the Health of Americans. Hyattsville, MD: Author. Retrieved August 16, 2008 (www.cdc.gov/nchs/data/hus/hus07.pdf).

National Center for Policy Analysis. 2001. "Crime and Gun Control." Retrieved April 17, 2010 (www.ncpa.org/pi/crime/pd042501e.html), (www.ncpa.org/sub/dpd/index.php?Article_Category=14).

National Coalition on Health Care. 2008. "Health Insurance Cost." Retrieved April 17, 2010 (www.nchc.org OR www.whitehouse2.org/.../305-facts-from-the-national-coalition-on-health-care).

National Conference of State Legislatures. 2007. "2007 Enacted State Legislation Related to Immigrants and Immigration." Retrieved April 17, 2010 (www.ncsl.org/default.aspx?tabid=13106 (OR 13134)).

National Health Expenditures by Type. 1990–2007. Retrieved April 17, 2010 (www.cms.hhs.gov/NationalHealthExpendData), (www.census.gov/compendia/statab/2010/tables/10s128.pdf).

National Institutes of Health. 2007. "The Use of Complementary and Alternative Medicine in the United States." Retrieved April 4, 2008 (http://nccam.nih.gov/news/camsurvey_fs1.htm).

———. 2008. "10 Most Common CAM Therapies Among Adults" nccam.nih.gov/news/camstats/2007/72_dpi_CHARTS/chart4.htm.

National Parent Information Network. 2000, May–June. "Kids and Media at the New Millennium." *Parents News*.

National Postsecondary Education Cooperative. 2004. "How Does Technology Affect Access In Postsecondary Education? What Do We Really Know?" (NPEC 2004–831), prepared by Ronald A. Phipps for NPEC Working Group on Access-Technology. Washington, DC.

National Public Radio. "Poppy Growing in Afghanistan." *Morning Edition*, February 9, 2008.

National Science Foundation. 2005. *Children, TV, Computers and More Media: New Research Shows Pluses, Minuses.* Retrieved July 20, 2006 (www.eurekalert.org/pub_releases/2005-02/nsf-ctc021005.php).

National Urban League. 2006. *The State of Black America.* New York: Author.

"National Voter Turnout in Federal Elections: 1960–2008." Retrieved July 11, 2009 (www.infoplease.com/ipa/A0781453.html).

Neuman, Michelle J. 2005. "Global Early Care and Education: Challenges, Responses, and Lessons." *Phi Delta Kappan* (November):188–92.

Neurological Correlates. 2008. "The 30% on Medicare Spent of Last-Year-of-Life Care: Let's Not Forget We're Humans." Retrieved January 8, 2010 (neurologicalcorrelates.com/wordpress/2008/03/12/about-30-of-medicare-is-spent-on-end-of-life-care-what-should-we-do-about-it).

Newman, Andy. 2008. "What Women Want (Maybe)." *The New York Times* (June 12):E6.

Newman, David. 2009. *Families: A Sociological Perspective.* New York: McGraw-Hill.

Newman, David M., and Liz Grauerholz. 2002. *Sociology of Families,* 2nd ed. Thousand Oaks, CA: Pine Forge.

Newport, Frank. 2004. "A Look at Americans and Religion Today." Retrieved July 7, 2006 (http://speakingoffaith.publicradio.org/programs/godsofbusiness/galluppoll.shtml).

———. 2006. "Mormons, Evangelical Protestants, Baptists Top Church Attendance List" (Gallup Poll). Retrieved April 17, 2010 (www.gallup.com/.../mormons-evangelical-protestants-baptists-top-church-attendance-list.aspx).

News of Future. 2007. "Future News in Technology." Retrieved January 14, 2008 (www.newsoffuture.com/technology).

New Twist. 2007. "International Comparison of the Hourly Labor Cost in the Primary Textile Industry, 2007" New Twist (3) May 18. Retrieved November 24, 2009 (www.werner-newtwist.com/en/newsl-vol-003/index.htm#International_Comparison_of__the_Hourly_Labor_Cost_in_the_Primary_Textile_Industry_2007).

New York Times. 2008. "Primary Calendar: Democratic Nominating Contests." Retrieved March 30, 2008 (http://politics.nytimes.com/election-guide/2008/primaries/democraticprimaries/index.html).

Nguyen, Nathalie Huynh Chau. 2005. "Eurasian/Amerasian Perspectives: Kim Lefevre's *Metisse blanche,* and Kien Nguyen's *The Unwanted." Asian Studies Review* 29(June):107–22.

Niebuhr, H. Richard. 1929. *The Social Sources of Denominationalism.* New York: Henry Holt.

———. 1932. *Moral Man and Immoral Society.* New York: Scribner.

Nightingale Alliance. 2007. "Fast Facts." Retrieved January 20, 2008 (www.nightingalealliance.org/cgi-bin/home.pl?section=3).

Nock, Steven L. 1999. "The Problem With Marriage." *Society* 36(5):20–27.

Nock, Steven L., James D. Wright, and Laura Sanchez. 1999. "America's Divorce Problem." *Society* 36(4):43–52.

Nock, Steven L., Laura Ann Sanchez, and James D. Wright. 2008. *Covenant Marriage: The Movement to Reclaim Tradition in America.* Piscataway, NJ: Rutgers University Press.

Noel, Donald. 1968. "A Theory of the Origin of Ethnic Stratification." *Social Problems* 16(Fall):157–72.

Noguera, Pedro, A. 1996. "Preventing and Producing Violence: A Critical Analysis of Responses to School Violence." *Sociology of Education* 56(3):189–212.

Noguera, Pedro, and Robby Cohen. 2006. "Patriotism and Accountability: The Role of Educators in the War on Terrorism." *Phi Delta Kappan* 87(8):573–78.

Nolan, Cathal J. 2002. "Terrorism." Pp. 1648–49 and "War" in *The Greenwood Encyclopedia of International Relations.* London: Greenwood.

Nolan, Patrick, and Gerhard Lenski. 2008. *Human Societies.* Boulder, CO: Paradigm.

Noss, David S., and John B. Noss. 1990. *A History of the World's Religions.* New York: Macmillan.

Nuclear Threat Initiative. 2010. "Obama's Nuclear Nonproliferation and Disarmament Agenda: Building Steam or Losing Traction" (January 15). Retrieved April 10, 2010 (www.nti.org/e_research/e3_obama_administration_agenda.html).

Oakes, Jeannie, Amy Stuart Wells, Makeba Jones, and Amanda Datnow. 1997. "Detracking: The Social Construction of Ability, Cultural Politics, and Resistance to Reform." *Teacher's College Record* 98(3):482–510.

Oberlander, Jonathan. 2002. "The U.S. Health Care System: On a Road to Nowhere?" *Canadian Medical Association Journal* 167(2):163–69.

O'Brien, Denise. 1977. "Female Husbands in Southern Bantu Societies." In *Sexual Stratification: A Cross-Cultural View,* edited by Alice Schlegel. New York: Columbia University Press.

O'Brien, Jody. 2006. *The Production of Reality,* 4th ed. Thousand Oaks, CA: Pine Forge.

O'Brien, Patrick K., ed. 1999. *Atlas of World History.* New York: Oxford University Press.

"O Come All Ye Faithful: Special Report on Religion and Public Life." 2007. *The Economist* (November 3):6.

O'Connel, Sanjida. 1993 "Meet My Two Husbands." *Guardian* (March 4, Sec. 2):12.

Office of National Statistics UK. 2007. "Marriages: Age at Marriage by Sex and Previous Marital Status, 1991, 2001, and 2003–2005." Population Trends 127. Retrieved January 6, 2010 (www.statistics.gov.uk/STATBASE/ssdataset.asp?vlnk=9599).

Ogbu, John U. 1998. "Understanding Cultural Diversity and Learning." *Educational Researcher* 21(8):5–14.

Ogburn, William F. 1933. *Recent Social Trends.* New York: McGraw-Hill.

———. [1922] 1938. *Social Change, With Respect to Culture and Original Nature.* New York: Viking.

———. 1950. *Social Change.* New York: Viking.

———. 1961. "The Hypothesis of Cultural Lag." Pp. 1270–73 in *Theories of Society: Foundations of Modern Sociological Theory,* Vol. 2, edited by Talcott Parsons, Edward Shils, Kaspar D. Naegele, and Jesse R. Pitts. New York: Free Press.

———. 1964. In *On Culture and Social Change: Selected Papers,* edited by Otis Dudley Duncan. Chicago: University of Chicago Press.

Oliver, Arnold. 2003. "Iran and the Forgotten Anniversary." *Foreign Policy in Focus* (August 29).

Oller, Kimbrough. 2006. "Development and Evolution in Human Vocal Communication." *Biological Theory* 1(4):349–51.

Olsen, Marvin E. 1968. *The Process of Social Organization.* New York: Holt, Rinehart, & Winston.

———. 1970. "Power as a Social Process." Pp. 2–10 in *Power in Societies,* edited by Marvin Olsen. New York: Macmillan.

Olson, C. L., H. D. Schumaker, and B. P. Yawn. 1994. "Overweight Women Delay Medical Care." *Archives of Family Medicine* 3(10).

Olsson, Sven E. 1990. *Social Policy and the Welfare State in Sweden.* Stockholm: Swedish Institute for Social Research.

One in Four, Inc. 2008. Retrieved November 6, 2009 (www.oneinfourusa.org).

Ong, Michael, et al. 2007. "360 Million Smokers in China and High Prevalence of Smoking Among Physicians." *American Journal of Preventative Medicine* (August 8). Retrieved April 17, 2010 (www.ucla.edu) or (www.news-medical.net/news/2007/08/08/28574.aspx).

Ontario Consultants on Religious Tolerance. 2004. "'Fundamentalism' in Christianity and Islam." Retrieved July 5, 2008 (www.religioustolerance.org/reac_ter9.htm).

———. 2005. "Homsexuality and Bisexuality." Retrieved August 23, 2008 (www.religioustolerance.org/hom_mar6.htm).

———. 2008. "Prohibiting Same-Sex Marriages in the U.S.: Federal and State 'Doma' Legislation." Retrieved August 7, 2008 (www.religioustolerance.org/hom_mar6.htm).

Oregon's Euthanasia Law. 2010. Law Library. Retrieved January 11, 2010 (http://law.jrank.org/pages/6602/Euthanasia-Oregon-s-Euthanasia-law.html).

Orfield, Gary, Mark D. Brachmeier, David R. James, and Tamela Eitle. 1997. "Deepening Segregation in American Public Schools." *Equity and Excellence in Education* 30(2):5–24.

"Organized Crime." 2009. Retrieved November 4, 2009 (http://law.jrank.org/pages/11951/Organized-Crime.html).

Orum, Anthony M. 2001. *Introduction to Political Sociology,* 4th ed. Upper Saddle River, NJ: Prentice Hall.

Oswald, Ramona Faith. 2000. "A Member of the Wedding? Heterosexism and Family Ritual." *Journal of Social and Personal Relationships* 17(June):349–68.

———. 2001. "Religion, Family, and Ritual: The Production of Gay, Lesbian, and Transgendered Outsiders-Within." *Review of Religious Research* 43(December):39–50.

O'Toole, Tara, and Donald A. Henderson. 2006. "A Clear and Present Danger: Confronting the Threat of Bioterrorism." Pp. 239–45 in *Globalization: The Transformation of Social Worlds,* edited by D. Stanley Eitzen and Maxine Baca Zinn. Belmont, CA: Wadsworth.

"Overseas Population Spending Threatened." 2006. *Popline* 29(March/April):1.

Padden, Brian. 2009. "Nigeria Still Fighting False Rumors About Polio Vaccine" (February 17). Retrieved April 17, 2010 (www.voanews.com/english/archive/2009-02-17-voa48.cfm?CFID=172187621).

"A Painful Tradition." 1999. *Newsweek* (July 5):32–33.

Papalia, Diane E., Sally Wendkos Olds, and Ruth Duskin Feldman. 2006. *A Child's World: Infancy Through Adolescence,* 10th ed. Boston: McGraw-Hill.

Parenti, Michael. 2006. "Mass Media: For the Many, by the Few." Pp. 60–72 in *Beyond Borders: Thinking Critically About Global Issues,* edited by Paula S. Rothenberg. New York: Worth.

Pareto, Vilfredo. [1911] 1955. "Mathematical Economics." In *Encyclopedie des Sciences Mathematique.* New York: Macmillan.

Park, Robert Ezra, Ernest W. Burgess, and Roderick D. McKenzie. [1925] 1967. *The City.* Chicago: University of Chicago Press.

Parkinson, C. Northcote. 1957. *Parkinson's Law.* Boston: Houghton Mifflin.

Parsons, Talcott. 1951a. *The Social System.* New York: Free Press.

———. 1951b. *Toward a General Theory of Action.* New York: Harper & Row.

———. 1975. "The Sick Role and Role of the Physician Reconsidered." *Milbank Memorial Fund Quarterly* 53(3):257–78.

Parsons, Talcott, and Robert F. Bales. 1953. *Family, Socialization, and Interaction Process.* Glencoe, IL: Free Press.

Paulhus, D. L., P. D. Trapnell, and D. Chen. 1999. *Birth Order Effects on Personality and Achievement Within Families.* Malden, MA: Blackwell.

Paxton, Pamela, and Melanie M. Hughes. 2007. *Women, Politics, and Power: A Global Perspective.* Thousand Oaks, CA: Pine Forge.

"Pay Czar Said to Plan to Disclose Top Salaries." 2009. Retrieved November 10, 2009 (dealbook.blogs.nytimes.com/2009/09/17/pay-czar-seen-disclosing-top-executive-salaries).

PBS Newshour 2009a. "Comparing International Health Care Systems" (October 6). Retrieved January 25, 2010 (www.pbs.org/newshour/globalhealth/july-dec09/insurance_1006.html).

———. 2009b. "Health Workers Renew Fight Against Polio in Nigeria" (April 13). Retrieved January 8, 2010 (www.pbs.org/newshour/bb/africa/jan-june09/nigeria_04-13.html).

PBS NOW. 2009. "Africa: House Calls and Health Care." Aired December 18, 2009.

Pellow, David Naguib. 2002. *Garbage Wars: The Struggle for Environmental Justice in Chicago.* Cambridge: MIT Press.

Pennington, Bill. 2006. "Small Colleges, Short of Men, Embrace Football." *The New York Times* (July 12):A1.

Pentikänen, Juha. 1999. *"Silent as Waters We Live": Old Believers in Russia and Abroad.* Helsinki, Finland: Finnish Literature Society.

Persell, Caroline Hodges, 2005. "Race, Education, and Inequality." Pp. 286–24 in *Blackwell Companion to Social Inequalities,* edited by M. Romero and E. Margolis. Oxford, UK: Blackwell.

Persell, Caroline Hodges, and Peter W. Cookson, Jr. 1985. "Chartering and Bartering: Elite Education and Social Reproduction." *Social Problems* 33(2):114–29.

Pescosolido, Bernice A., 1992. "Beyond Rational Choice: The Social Dynamics of How People Seek Help." *American Journal of Sociology* 97(4):1113.

Pescosolido, Bernice A., and Carol A. Boyer. 2010. "The American Health Care System: Beginning the 21st Century With High Risk, Major Challenges, and Great Opportunities." Pp. 391–411 in *The New Blackwell Companion to Medical Sociology,* edited by William C. Cockerham. Malden, MA: Wiley-Blackwell.

Petersen, Larry R., and Gregory V. Donnenwerth. 1998. "Religion and Declining Support for Religious Beliefs About Gender Roles and Homosexual Rights." *Sociology of Religion* 59(4):353–71.

Peterson, Paul E., and Elena Llaudet. 2006. "On the Public-Private School Achievement Debate." Programs on Education Policy and Governance, Harvard University. Retrieved December 14, 2009 (www.hks.harvard.edu/pepg/PDF/Papers/PEPG06-02-PetersonLlaudet.pdf).

Pew Forum. 2009. "The Stronger Sex-Spiritually Speaking." Retrieved December 22, 2009 (http://pewforum.org/docs/?DocID=403).

———. 2010. "U.S. Religious Landscape Survey." Retrieved January 1, 2010 (http://religions.pewforum.org/reports).

Pew Forum on Religion and Public Life. 2008. "U.S. Religious Landscape Survey, 2008." Retrieved March 2, 2008 (http://religions.pewforum.org/pdf/report-religious-landscape-study-full.pdf).

Pew Internet and American Life Project. 2004. "Tracking Survey, February 3 to March 1, 2004." Retrieved January 9, 2008 (www.infoplease.com/ipa/A0921872.html).

———. 2009. "Generations Online in 2009." (Sydney Jones and Susannah Fox. January 28).

Pharr, Suzanne. 1997. *Homophobia: A Weapon of Sexism,* Expanded ed. Berkeley, CA: Chardon.

Phipher, Mary. 1994. *Reviving Ophelia: Saving the Selves of Adolescent Girls.* New York: Ballantine Books.

Physicians' Working Group for Single-Payer National Health Insurance. 2003. "Proposal of the Physicians' Working Group for Single-Payer National Health Insurance." *Journal of the American Medical Association* 290(13):798–805.

Piaget, Jean. 1989. *The Child's Conception of the World.* Savage, MD: Littlefield, Adams Quality Paperbacks.

Piaget, Jean, and Barbel Inhelder. [1955] 1999. *Growth of Logical Thinking.* London: Routledge & Kegan Paul.

Pickard, Ruth, and Daryl Poole. 2007. "The Study of Society and the Practice of Sociology." Previously unpublished essay.

Pieterse, Jan Nederveen. 2004. *Globalization and Culture.* Lanham, MD: Rowman & Littlefield.

Pinker, Steven. 2002. *The Blank Slate: The Denial of Human Nature.* New York: Viking.

"Plan for Lifetime Success Through Education." 2008. Retrieved April 17, 2010 (www.barackobama.com/pdf/issues/Prek-12 EducationFactSheet.pdf) or (www.americanthinker.com/2008/.../obamas_national_public_educati.html).

Plant, Hanna. 2007. "The Challenges of Health Care in Cuba." Retrieved January 8, 2010 (www.global-politics.co.uk/issue9/hanna).

Plato. [ca. 350 BCE] 1960. *The Laws.* New York: Dutton.

Plouffe, David. 2009. *The Audactiy to Win: The Inside Story and Lessons of Barack Obama's Historic Victory.* New York: Viking.

Polgreen, Lydia. 2008. "Scorched-Earth Strategy Returns to Darfur." *The New York Times.* (March 2):1A, 10A.

Pollack, William. 1999. *Real Boys: Rescuing Our Sons From the Myths of Boyhood.* New York: Owl Books.

Pope, Liston. [1942] 1965. *Millhands and Preachers.* New Haven, CT: Yale University Press.

Popenoe, David. 2002. "Debunking Divorce Myths." *National Marriage Project.* New Brunswick, NJ: Rutgers. Retrieved November 30, 2009 (health.discovery.com/centers/loverelationships/articles/divorce.html).

Popenoe, David, Jean Bethke Elshtain, and David Blankenhorn. 1996. *Promises to Keep: Decline and Renewal of Marriage in America.* Lanham, MD: Rowman & Littlefield.

Population Reference Bureau. 2006. "Human Population: Fundamentals of Growth: Population Growth and Distribution." Retrieved April 17, 2010 (www.prb.org) OR (www.cepnet.org/.../USPopulationEnergyandClimateChangeReportCEP.pdf).

———. 2007a. "Migration." *Population Bulletin* 62:3.

———. 2007b. "World Population Data Sheet." Retrieved April 9, 2008 (www.prb.org).

———. 2008. "World Population Data Sheet." Retrieved August 23, 2008 (www.prb.org/Publications/Datasheets/2008/2008wpds.aspx).

———. 2009a. "2009 World Population Data Sheet." Retrieved January 8, 2010 (www.prb.org/pdf09/09wpds_eng.pdf).

Population Reference Bureau. 2009b. "Population Clock 2009." Retrieved January 5, 2010 (www.prb.org/Articles/2009/worldpopulationclock2009.aspx).

———. 2010 "Human Population: Women." Retrieved January 8, 2010 (www.prb.org/Educators/TeachersGuides/HumanPopulation/Women.aspx).

Porter, Susan. 2005. "Higher Education in China: The Next Super Power Is Coming of Age." *American Council on Education.*

Portes, Alejandro, and Ruben G. Rumbaut. 2001. *Legacies: The Story of the Immigrant Second Generation.* Berkeley: University of California Press.

Poverty Research News. 2002. Retrieved April 17, 2010 (www.jcpr.org/newsletters/index.html).

Povik, Fili. 1994. *Zlata's Diary: A Child's Life in Sarajevo.* New York: Viking.

Powell, Andrea D., and Arnold S. Kahn. 1995. "Racial Differences in Women's Desires to Be Thin." *International Journal of Eating Disorders* 17(2):191–95.

Powell, Michael. 2008a. "Campaigns Try to Lure the Facebook Generation." *International Herald Tribune* (January 9):5.

———. 2008b. "Tidal Wave of Youth Buoys 2 Campaigns." *International Herald Tribune* (January 9):2.

Powley, Elizabeth. 2003. "Strengthening Governance: The Role of Women in Rwanda's Transition." In *Women Waging Peace,* edited by S. N. Anderlini. Washington, DC: Hunt Alternatives Fund.

Preston, David L. 1988. *The Social Organization of Zen Practice: Constructing Transcultural Reality.* Cambridge, UK: Cambridge University Press.

Project Vote Smart. 2008. "State Presidential Primary and Caucus Dates." Retrieved April 17, 2010 (www.votesmart.org/election_president_state_primary_dates.php).

Public Citizen's Global Trade Watch. 2003. "The Ten Year Track Record of the North American Free Trade Agreement: U.S. Workers' Jobs, Wages and Economic Security." Retrieved September 29, 2006 (www.citizen.org/documents/NAFTA_10_jobs.pdf).

Purcell, Piper, and Lara Stewart. 1990. "Dick and Jane in 1989." *Sex Roles* 22(3/4):177–85.

Putnam, Robert D. 1995. "Bowling Alone, Revisited." *The Responsive Community* (Spring):18–33.

———. 2001. *Bowling Alone: The Collapse and Revival of American Community.* New York: Simon & Schuster.

Pyle, Ralph E. 2006. "Trends in Religious Stratification: Have Religious Group Socioeconomic Distinctions Declined in Recent Decades?" *Sociology of Religion* 67(Spring):61–79.

Quesnal-Vallee and Jenkins. 2010. "Social Policies and Health Inequalities." Pp. 455–83 in *The New Blackwell Companion to Medical Sociology,* edited by William C. Cockerham. Malden, MA: Wiley/Blackwell.

Quinney, Richard. 2002. *Critique of Legal Order: Crime Control in Capitalist Society.* New Brunswick, NJ: Transaction.

Radcliffe-Brown, A. R. 1935. "On the Concept of Functional in Social Science." *American Anthropologist* 37(3):394–402.

Rama Rao, Saumya, and Raji Mohanam. 2003. "The Quality of Family Planning Programs: Concepts, Measurements, Interventions, and Effects." *Studies in Family Planning* 34(4):227–48.

Rampell, Catherine. 2008. "Why Obama Rocks the Vote." *The Washington Post* (March 30):B7.

Randerson, James. 2008. "Cutting TV Time Makes Children Healthier, Says U.S. Study." *The Guardian* (March 4).

Rankin, Bruce H. and Is,ik A. Aytaç. 2006. "Gender Inequality in Schooling: The Case of Turkey." *Sociology of Education* 79(1):25–43.

Regnerus, Mark D. 2007. *Forbidden Fruit: Sex and Religion in the Lives of American Teenagers.* New York: Oxford University Press.

Reid, Scott A., and Sik Hung Ng. 2006. "The Dynamics of Intragroup Differentiation in an Intergroup Social Context." *Human Communication Research* 32:504–525.

Reid, T.R. 2009. *The Healing of America: A Global Quest for Better, Cheaper, and Fairer Health Care.* Penguin Press; PBS Newshour. "Comparing International Health Care Systems." Aired October 6. Retrieved January 14, 2010 (www.pbs.org/newshour/globalhealth/july-dec09/insurance_1006.html).

Reiman, Jeffrey, and Paul Leighton. 2010a. *The Rich Get Richer and the Poor Get Prison: Ideology, Class, and Criminal Justice,* 9th ed. Boston Pearson.

Reiman, Jeffrey, and Paul Leighton. 2010b. *The Rich Get Richer and the Poor Get Prison: A Reader.* Boston: Allyn & Bacon.

Religious Congregations and Membership Study. 2000. "Association of Religion Data Archives (ARDA) Collected by the Association of Statisticians of American Religious Bodies." Retrieved August 26, 2006 (www.thearda.com/Archive/Files/Descriptions/RCMSCY.asp). [Chap 12; Page no. 44].

Religious Tolerance. 2006. "Trends Among Christians in the U.S." Retrieved December 13, 2009 (www.religioustolerance.org/chr_tren.htm).

———. 2009a. "U.S. Divorce Rates for Various Faith Groups, Age Groups, and Geographic Areas." Retrieved April 17, 2010 (www.religious tolerance.org/chr_dira.htm).

———. 2009b. "Women as Clergy." Retrieved December 24, 2009 (www.religioustolerance.org/femclrgy.htm).

Religious Worlds. 2007. "New Religious Movements." Retrieved August 14, 2008 (www.religiousworlds.com/newreligions.html).

Remmert, Consuelo. 2003. "Women in Reconstruction: Rwanda Promotes Women Decision-makers." *UN Chronicle* 4(3):25.

Renzetti, Claire. 2003. "Urban Violence Against Women." Speech, September 30, Dayton, Ohio, Wright State University.

Residents of Hull House. [ca. 1895] 1970. *Hull House Maps and Papers*. New York: Arno.

Riehl, Carolyn. 2001. "Bridges to the Future: Contributions of Qualitative Research to the Sociology of Education." *Sociology of Education* (Extra Issue):115–34.

Ries, L. A. G., M. P. Eisner, C. L. Kossary, B. F. Hankey, B. A. Miller, and B. K. Edwards, eds. 2000. *SEER Cancer Statistics Review, 1973–1997*. Bethesda, MD: National Cancer Institute.

Riordan, Cornelius. 2004. *Equality and Achievement: An Introduction to the Sociology of Education*. Upper Saddle River, NJ: Prentice Hall.

Riska, Elianne. 2010. "Health Professions and Occupations." Pp. 391–411 in *The New Blackwell Companion to Medical Sociology*, edited by William C. Cockerham. Malden, MA: Wiley/Blackwell.

Ritzer, George, 1998. *The McDonaldization Thesis: Explorations and Extensions*. Thousand Oaks, CA: Pine Forge.

———. 2004. *The Globalization of Nothing*. Thousand Oaks, CA: Pine Forge.

———. 2008. *The McDonaldization of Society*, 5th ed. Thousand Oaks, CA: Pine Forge.

Ritzer, George, and Douglas J. Goodman. 2004. *Sociological Theory*, 6th ed. New York: McGraw-Hill.

Roach, Ronald. 2004. "Survey Reveals 10 Biggest Trends in Internet Use." *Black Issues in Higher Education* (October 21).

Robbins, Mandy. 1998. "A Different Voice: A Different View." *Review of Religious Research* 40(1):75–80.

Robbins, Richard H. 2005. *Global Problems and the Culture of Capitalism*, 3rd ed. Boston: Allyn & Bacon.

Robinson, Bruce. 2009. "The Impact of Religion on Homosexuality and Bisexuality." Religious Tolerance, Retrieved January 4, 2009 (www.religioustolerance.org/homosexu3.htm).

Roberts, Dorothy. 1997. *Killing the Black Body: Race, Reproduction, and the Meaning of Liberty*. New York: Pantheon.

———. 2002. *Shattered Bonds: The Color of Child Welfare*. New York: Basic Books.

Roberts, Judith C., and Keith A. Roberts. 2008 "Deep Reading, Cost/Benefit, and the Construction of Meaning: Enhancing Reading Comprehension and Deep Learning in Sociology Courses" (co-authored with Judith Conkle Roberts). *Teaching Sociology*. April (36:2): 125–140.

Roberts, Keith A. 2003. Interviews with Ohio residents in communities considering tax levies. Unpublished Manuscript.

———. 2004. *Religion in Sociological Perspective*, 4th ed. Belmont, CA: Wadsworth.

Roberts, Keith A., and Karen A. Donahue. 2000. "Professing Professionalism: Bureaucratization and Deprofessionalization in the Academy" *Sociological Focus* 33(4):365–83.

Robertson, Roland. 1992. *Globalization: Social Theory and Global Culture*. London: Sage.

———. 1997. "Social Theory, Cultural Relativity and the Problem of Globality." Pp. 69–90 in *Culture, Globalization and the World System*, edited by Anthony King. Minneapolis: University of Minnesota Press.

Robertson, Roland, and William R. Garrett, eds. 1991. *Religion and Global Order*. New York: Paragon.

Robinson, Bruce. 2007. "Physician Assisted Suicide." Religious Tolerance, June 2. Retrieved October 20, 2009 (www.religious tolerance.org/euth_us2.htm).

Robinson, Bruce. 2009. "The Impact of Religion on Homosexuality and Bisexuality" Religious Tolerance, www.religioustolerance.org/homosexu3.htm (Retrieved January 4, 2009).

Robson, Roy R. 1995. *Old Believers in Modern Russia*. DeKalb: Northern Illinois University Press.

Rodgers, Bill. 2009. "Developing Countries Employ 'Leapfrog Technology' With Cell Phones" *The Cutting Edge*. March 9 Retrieved April 28, 2009 (www.thecuttingedgenews.com/index.php?article=11174&pageid=28&pagename=Sci-Tech).

Rodriguez, Eric M., and S. C. Ouellette. 2000. "Gay and Lesbian Christians: Homosexual and Religious Identity Integration in the Members of a Gay-Positive Church." *Journal for the Scientific Study of Religion* 39(3):333–47.

Roethlisberger, Fritz J., and William J. Dickson. 1939. *Management and the Worker*. Cambridge, MA: Harvard University Press.

Romano, Lois. 2008. "Generation Y: Ready to Rock the 2008 Election." *The Washington Post* (January 10):C1.

Roof, Wade Clark. 1999. *Spiritual Marketplace: Baby Boomers and the Remaking of American Religion*. Princeton, NJ: Princeton University Press.

Rose, Stephen. 2000. *Social Stratification in the United States*. New York: New Press.

Rosen, Karen. 2007. "Women Still Lag in College Sports" (June 6). Retrieved March 7, 2008 (www.oxfordpress.com/sports/content/shared/sports/stories/2007/WOMEN_SPORTS_0606_COX.html).

Rosenbaum, James E. 1999. "If Tracking Is Bad, Is Detracking Better? A Study of a Detracked High School." *American Schools* (Winter):24–47.

Rosenberg, Matt. 2009. "Population Growth Rates." About.Com:Geography (October 15). Retrieved April 14, 2010 (http://geography.about.com/od/populationgeography/a/populationgrow.htm).

Rosenstone, Steven J., and John Mark Hansen. 1993. *Mobilization, Participation, and Democracy in America*. New York: Macmillan.

Rosenthal, Robert, and Lenore Jacobson. 1968. *Pygmalion in the Classroom*. New York: Holt, Rinehart & Winston.

Rossi, Alice S. 1984. "Gender and Parenthood." *American Sociological Review* 49(February):1–19.

Rossides, Daniel W. 1997. *Social Stratification: The Interplay of Class, Race, and Gender*. Englewood Cliffs, NJ: Prentice Hall.

Rossman, Parker. 2005. "Beyond the Book: Electronic Textbooks Will Bring Worldwide Learning." *The Futurist* 39(January/February):18–23.

Rothbard, Nancy P., and Jeanne M. Brett. 2000. "Promote Equal Opportunity by Recognizing Gender Differences in the Experience of Work and Family." In *The Blackwell Handbook of Principles of Organizational Behavior*, edited by Edwin A. Locke. Malden, MA: Blackwell.

Rothenberg, Paula S. 2006a. *Beyond Borders: Thinking Critically About Global Issues*. New York: Worth.

———. 2007. *Race, Class, and Gender in the United States: An Integrated Study*, 7th ed. New York: Worth.

———. 2008. *White Privilege: Essential Readings on the Other Side of Racism*, 3rd ed. New York: Worth Publishers.

Rothman, Robert A. 2005. *Inequality and Stratification: Race, Class, and Gender*, 5th ed. Englewood Cliffs, NJ: Prentice Hall.

Rubenstein, Grace. 2007. "Computers for Peace: The $100 Laptop." Retrieved April 21, 2009 (www.edutopia.org/computers-peace).

Rubin, Jeffrey Z. 1974. "The Eye of the Beholder: Parents' Views on Sex of Newborns." *American Journal of Orthopsychiatry* 44(4):512–19.

Rumbaut, Ruben G., and Alejandro Portes. 2001. *Ethnicities: Children of Immigrants in America*. Los Angeles: University of California Press.

Runningen, Roger, and Brian Faler. 2008. "Bush Boosts Defense Spending in $3.1 Trillion Budget" (February 4). Retrieved September 2, 2008 (www.bloomberg.com/apps/news?pid=206 01103&sid=azGB.29vVkzA8&refer=us).

Rusere, Patience. 2009. "Rainy Season Brings New Cholera Outbreaks in Zimbabwe, Five Deaths Reported." *Voice of America News.* November 16. Retrieved December 20, 2009 (www1.voanews .com/zimbabwe/news/a-13-56-74-2009-11-16-voa48-70422597 .html).

Sabol, William J. 2007. *Prisoners in 2006.* Washington, DC: U.S. Department of Justice, Bureau of Justice Statistics.

Sabol, William J., Heather C. West, and Matthew Cooper. 2009. "Prisoners in 2008." *Bureau of Justice Statistics Bulletin.* U.S. Department of Justice. December 2009. Retrieved December 20, 2009 (bjs.ojp.usdoj.gov/content/pub/pdf/p08.pdf).

Sadker, Myra, and David Sadker. 1995. *Failing at Fairness: How Our Schools Cheat Girls.* New York: Touchstone.

———. 2005. *Teachers, Schools, and Society,* 7th ed. New York: McGraw-Hill.

Sado, Stephanie, and Angela Bayer. 2001. "Executive Summary: The Changing American Family" (Population Resource Center). Retrieved April 17, 2010 (www.prcdc.org/summaries/family/ family/html).

Sadovnik, Alan R. 2007. *Sociology of Education: A Critical Reader.* New York: Routledge.

Sage, George H. 2005. "Racial Inequality and Sport." Pp. 266–75 in *Sport in Contemporary Society,* 7th ed., edited by Stanley D. Eitzen. Boulder, CO: Paradigm.

Sager, Ira, Ben Elgin, Peter Elstrom, Faith Keenan, and Pallavi Gogoi. 2006. "The Underground Web." Pp. 261–70 in *Globalization: The Transformation of Social Worlds,* edited by D. Stanley Eitzen and Maxine Baca Zinn. Belmont, CA: Wadsworth.

Saha, Lawrence, and A. Gary Dworkin. 2006. "Educational Attainment and Job Status: The Role of Status Inconsistency on Occupational Burnout." Paper presented at the International Sociological Association, July 23–29, Durban, South Africa.

Saharan Vibe. 2007. "Wodaabe Beauty Ceremony." February 19. Retrieved November 6, 2009 (saharanvibe.blogspot. com/2007/02/wodaabe-beauty-ceremony.html).

Salzman, Marian, and Ira Matathia. 2000. "Lifestyles of the Next Millennium: 65 Forecasts." Pp. 466–71 in *Sociological Footprints,* edited by Leonard Cargan and Jeanne Ballantine. Belmont, CA: Wadsworth.

Samovar, Larry A., and Richard E. Porter. 2003. *Intercultural Communication.* Belmont, CA: Wadsworth.

Sanday, Peggy Reeves. 1981. "The Socio-Cultural Context of Rape: A Cross-Cultural Study." *Journal of Social Issues* 37(4):5–27.

———. 1996. *A Woman Scorned: Acquaintance Rape on Trial.* Berkeley: University of California Press.

———. 2007. *Fraternity Gang Rape: Sex, Brotherhood, and Privilege on Campus.* New York: New York University Press.

Sanday, Peggy, and Ruth Gallagher Goodenough, eds. 1990. *Beyond the Second Sex.* Philadelphia: University of Pennsylvania Press.

Sapir, Edward. 1929. "The Status of Linguistics as a Science." *Language* 5:207–214.

———. 1949. In *Selected Writings of Edward Sapir in Language, Culture, and Personality,* edited by David G. Mandelbaum. Berkeley: University of California Press.

Sapiro, Virginia. 2003. *Women in American Society: An Introduction to Women's Studies,* 5th ed. Mountain View, CA: Mayfield.

Sarat, Austin. 2001. *When the State Kills: Capital Punishment and the American Condition.* Princeton, NJ: Princeton University Press.

Sargeant, Kimon Howland. 2000. *Seeker Churches: Promoting Traditional Religion in a Nontraditional Way.* New Brunswick, NJ: Rutgers University Press.

Sarno, David. 2008. "Looking for the Youth Vote? It's Online." *Los Angeles Times* (January 13):E42.

Sassler, Sharon. 2010. "Partnering Across the Life Course: Sex, Relationships, and Mate Selection." Forthcoming. *Journal of Marriage and the Family.*

Sassler, Sharon, and Amanda Miller. (forthcoming). "Waiting to Be Asked: Gender, Power, and Relationship Progression Among Cohabiting Couples." *Journal of Marriage and Family.*

Sax, Leonard. 2005. *Why Gender Matters: What Parents and Teachers Need to Know About the Emerging Science of Sex Differences.* New York: Doubleday.

Scarce, Rik. 1999. "Good Faith, Bad Ethics: When Scholars Go the Distance and Scholarly Associations Do Not." *Law and Social Inquiry* 24(4):977–86.

Schaefer, Richard T, 2007. *Racial and Ethnic Groups,* 11th ed. Upper Saddle River, NJ: Prentice Hall.

Schaefer, Richard T. and Jenifer Kunz. 2007. *Racial and Ethnic Groups.* Upper Saddle River, NJ: Pearson/Prentice Hall.

Schaeffer, Robert K. 2003. *Understanding Globalization: The Social Consequences of Political, Economic, and Environmental Change,* 2nd ed. Lanham, MD: Rowman & Littlefield.

Schapiro, Mark. 2006. "Big Tobacco." Pp. 271–84 in *Globalization: The Transformation of Social Worlds,* edited by D. Stanley Eitzen and Maxine Baca Zinn. Belmont, CA: Wadsworth.

Schemo, Diana Jean. 2006. "Public Schools Close to Private in U.S. Study." *The New York Times* (July 15):A1, 10.

Schienberg, Jonathan. 2006. "Firefighters, Doctors and Nurses Considered Most Prestigious Occupations." *CNNMoney.com* (July 31). Retrieved July 7, 2008 (http://money.cnn.com/2006/07/26/ news/economy/prestigious_professions).

Schmalleger, Frank. 2006. *Criminology Today: An Integrative Introduction.* 4th ed. Upper Saddle River, NJ: Prentice Hall.

Schneider, Barbara, and James S. Coleman. 1993. *Parents, Their Children, and Schools.* Boulder, CO: Westview.

Schneider, Barbara, and Linda J. Waite. 2005. *Being Together, Working Apart: Dual-Career Families and the Work-Life Balance.* Cambridge University Press.

Schneider, Linda, and Arnold Silverman. 2006. *Global Sociology,* 4th ed. Boston: McGraw-Hill.

Schoeman, Ferdinand. 1991. "Book Review: Heavy Drinking: The Myth of Alcoholism as a Disease." *The Philosophical Review* 100(3):493–98.

Scott, Ellen K., Andrew S. London, and Nancy A. Myers. 2002. "Dangerous Dependencies: The Intersection of Welfare Reform and Domestic Violence." *Gender and Society* 16(6):878–97.

Scott-Montagu, John. 1904. "Automobile Legislation: A Criticism and Review." *North American Review* 179(573):168–77.

Seeking Alpha. 2009. "Wireless vs. Landlines: Past the Point of No Return." Retrieved November 12, 2009 (http://seekingalpha.com/ article/136416-wireless-vs-landlines-past-the-point-of-no-return).

Sells, Heather. 2008. "Hunger in America a Growing Reality." CBNnews.com. Retrieved April 20, 2009 (www.cbn.com/cbn news/485723.aspx).

The Sentencing Project. 2006. "International Rates of Incarceration 2003." Retrieved August 4, 2006 (www.sentencing project.org/ pdfs/pub9036.pdf).

Sernau, Scott. 2005. *Worlds Apart: Social Inequalities in a New Century,* 2nd ed. Thousand Oaks, CA: Pine Forge.

Shade, Leslie Regan. 2004. "Bending Gender Into the Net: Feminizing Content, Corporate Interests, and Research Strategy." Pp. 57–70 in *Society On-Line: The Internet in Context,* edited by Philip N. Howard and Steve Jones. Thousand Oaks, CA: Sage.

Shaffer, David Williamson, Kurt R. Squire, Richard Haverson, and James P. Gee. 2005. "Video Games and the Future of Learning." *Phi Delta Kappan* (October):95–112.

Shah, Anup. 2009a. "Today, Over 25,000 Children Died Around the World." March 22. Retrieved November 10, 2009 (www.globalissues.org/article/715/today-over-25000-children-died-around-the-world).

———. 2009b. "World Military Spending." Retrieved December 17, 2009 (www.globalissues.org/article/75/world-military-spending).

Sharp, Henry S. 1991. "Memory, Meaning, and Imaginary Time: The Construction of Knowledge in White and Chipewayan Cultures." *Ethnohistory* 38(2):149–73.

Sharp, Lauriston. 1990. "Steel Axes for Stone-Age Australians." Pp. 410–24 in *Conformity and Conflict,* 7th ed., edited by James P. Spradley and David W. McCurdy. Glenview, IL: Scott Foresman.

Shaw, Clifford R., and Henry D. McKay. 1929. *Delinquency Areas.* Chicago: University of Chicago Press.

Shaw, Susan M., and Janet Lee. 2005. *Women's Voices, Feminist Visions: Classic and Contemporary Readings,* 3rd ed. Boston: McGraw-Hill.

Shepherd, William R. 1964. *Historical Atlas,* 9th ed. New York: Barnes & Noble.

Sherif, Muzafer, and Carolyn Sherif. 1953. *Groups in Harmony and Tension.* New York: Harper & Row.

Sherkat, Darren E., and Christopher G. Ellison. 1999. "Recent Developments and Current Controversies in the Sociology of Religion." *Annual Review of Sociology* 25:363–94.

Shore, Cris. 2008. "Corruption Scandals in America and Europe: Enron and EU Fraud in Comparative Perspective." Pp. 191–98 in *Deviance Across Cultures,* edited by Robert Heiner. New York: Oxford University Press.

Short, Katherine. 2009. "Voter Participation Rate, 2008." Retrieved April 17, 2010 (www.askquestions.org/details.php?id=21094) or (www.census.gov/Press-Release/www/releases/.../013995.html).

Shriver, Eunice Kennedy. 2007. *Add Health Study.* Washington, DC: National Institute of Child Health and Human Development. Retrieved December 24, 2009 (www.nichd.nih.gov/health/topics/add_health_study.cfm).

Shu, Xiaoling. 2004. "Education and Gender Egalitarianism: The Case of China." *Sociology of Education* 77(4):311–36.

Shupe, Anson, and Jeffrey K. Hadden. 1989. "Is There Such a Thing as Global Fundamentalism?" Pp. 109–22 in *Secularization and Fundamentalism Reconsidered,* edited by Jeffrey K. Hadden and Anson Shupe. New York: Paragon.

Siegel, Dina, and Hans Nelen, eds. 2008. *Organized Crime: Culture, Markets, and Policies. Series: Studies in Organized Crime,* Vol. 7. New York: Springer.

Siegel, Larry J. 2000. *Criminology,* 7th ed. St. Paul, MN: West.

———. 2006. *Criminology,* 9th ed. Belmont, CA: Wadsworth.

———. 2009. *Criminology: Theories, Patterns, and Typologies.* 10th ed. Belmont, CA: Thomson/Wadsworth.

"Significant Ongoing Armed Conflicts 2009." Retrieved March 26, 2008 (www.infoplease.com/ipa/A0904550.html).

Simmel, Georg. [1902–1917] 1950. *The Sociology of Georg Simmel.* Translated by Kurt Wolff. Glencoe, IL: Free Press.

———. 1955. *Conflict and the Web of Group Affiliation.* Translated by Kurt H. Wolff. New York: Free Press.

Simmons, Rachel. 2002. *Odd Girl Out: The Hidden Culture of Aggression in Girls.* Orlando, FL: Harcourt.

Simon, David R. 2006. *Elite Deviance,* 8th ed. Boston: Allyn & Bacon.

Sine, Richard. 2002. "Garment Workers Say Gap Aided in Cambodian Strife." Retrieved September 2, 2008 (http://laborcenter.berkeley.edu/press/sfchronicle_dec02.shtml).

SIPRI Yearbook: Armaments, Disarmament and International Security. 2010. Retrieved April 10, 2010 (www.sipri.org/research/armaments/nbc/nuclear/usa).

Sizer, Theodore R. 1984. *Horace's Compromise: The Dilemma of the American High School.* Boston: Houghton Mifflin.

Sjoberg, Gideon. 1965. "The Origin and Evolution of Cities." *Scientific American* 213(September):56–57.

Skocpol, Theda. 1979. *States and Social Revolutions: A Comparative Analysis of France, Russia, and China.* Cambridge, UK: Cambridge University Press.

Smelser, Neil J. 1963. *Theory of Collective Behavior.* New York: Free Press.

———. 1988. "Social Structure." Pp. 103–29 in *Handbook of Sociology,* edited by Neil J. Smelser. Newbury Park, CA: Sage.

Smelser, Neil J. 1992. "The Rational Choice Perspective: A Theoretical Assessment." *Rationality and Society* 4:381–410.

Smerdon, Becky A. 2002. "Students' Perceptions of Membership in Their High Schools." *Sociology of Education* 75(4):287–305.

Smith, Barbara Ellen. 1999. "The Social Relations of Southern Women." Pp. 13–31 in *Neither Separate Nor Equal,* edited by B. E. Smith. Philadelphia: Temple University Press.

Smith, Brent L. 1994. *Terrorism in America: Pipe Bombs and Pipe Dreams.* New York: State University of New York Press.

Smith, Christian, and Robert Faris. 2005. "Socioeconomic Inequality in the American Religious System: An Update and Assessment." *Journal for the Scientific Study of Religion* 44(1):95–104.

Smith, Daniel R., and David F. Ayers. 2006. "Culturally Responsive Pedagogy and Online Learning: Implications for the Globalized Community College." *Community College Journal of Research and Practice* 30.

Smith, David M., and Gary J. Gates. 2001. *Gay and Lesbian Families in the United States: Same-Sex Unmarried Partner Households: A Preliminary Analysis of 2000 United States Census Data.* Washington, DC: Human Rights Campaign.

Smith, Heather. 2008. "Galvanizing Young Voters." *The Washington Post* (April 5):A13.

Smith, Russell. 2005. "How Many Have Died in Darfur?" *BBC News* (February 16). Retrieved February 16, 2005 (http://news.bbc.co.uk/2/hi/africa/4268733.stm).

Smith, Scott. 2009. "Obama Touts Stimulus in Elkhart." *Kokomo Tribune.* February 9. Retrieved February 24, 2009 (www.kokomotribune.com).

Smock, Pamela J. 2004. "The Wax and Wane of Marriage: Prospects for Marriage in the 21st Century." *Journal of Marriage and Family* 66(November):966–73.

Snarr, Michael T., and D. Neil Snarr. 2008. *Introducing Global Issues,* 4th ed. Boulder, CO: Lynne Rienner.

Snider, Mike. 2009. "Mattell Gives Barbie Online Dream House" (January 27). *USA Today.* Retrieved April 17, 2010 (www.usatoday.com/.../2009-oi-26-mattel-website-main_N.htm).

Snow, David A., and L. Anderson. 1993. *Down on Their Luck: A Study of Homeless Street People.* Berkeley: University of California Press.

Snyder, Denson R. 1971. *The Hidden Curriculum.* New York: Alfred A. Knopf.

Sobolewski, Juliana M., and Paul R. Amato. 2007. "Parents' Discord and Divorce, Parent-Child Relationships, and Subjective Well-Being in Early Adulthood: Is Feeling Close to Two Parents Always Better Than Feeling Close to One?" *Social Forces* 85(3) March:1105–1124.

Social Security Administration. 2009. "Popular Baby Names." Retrieved November 6, 2009 (www.ssa.gov/OACT/babynames).

Solow, Robert M. 2000. *Growth Theory: An Exposition,* 2nd ed. New York: Oxford University Press.

Sommerville, C. John. 2002. "Stark's Age of Faith Argument and the Secularization of Things: A Commentary." *Review of Religious Research* (Fall):361–72.

Sowell, Thomas. 1994. *Race and Culture: A World View.* New York: Basic Books.

Spade, Joan Z. 2004. "Gender in Education in the United States." Pp. 287–95 in *Schools and Society: A Sociological Approach to Education,* 2nd ed., edited by Jeanne H. Ballantine and Joan Z. Spade. Belmont, CA: Wadsworth.

Sperling, Gene B. 2005. "The Case for Universal Basic Education for the World's Poorest Boys and Girls." *Phi Delta Kappan* (November):213–16.

———. 2006. "What Works in Girls' Education." PBS Wide Angle. Retrieved July 11, 2009 (www.pbs.org/wnet/wideangle/episodes/time-for-school-series/essay-what-works-in-girls-education/274).

Spero News. 2009. "China: Good News From Beijing, the Number of Billionaires Is Rising, So Is the Economy." October 13. Retrieved November 11, 2009 (www.speronews.com/a/20830/china—good-news-from-beijing-the-number-of-billionaires-is-rising-so-is-the-economy).

Srinivasan, Padma, and Gary R. Lee. 2004. "The Dowry System in Northern India: Women's Attitudes and Social Change." *Journal of Marriage and Family.* 66:1108–17.

Stack, Carol B. 1998. *All Our Kin: Strategies for Survival in a Black Community* (Reissued). New York: Harper & Row.

Stanback, Thomas M. 1991. *The New Suburbanization: Challenge to the Central City.* Boulder, CO: Westview.

Stanley, Scott M., and Galena K. Rhoades. 2009. "Marriages at Risk: Relationship Formation and Opportunities for Relationship Education." Pp. 21–44 in *What Works in Relationship Education,* edited by Harry Benson and Samantha Callan. Doha, Qatar: Doha International Institute for Family Studies and Development.

Staples, Robert. 1999. *The Black Family: Essays and Studies,* 6th ed. Belmont, CA: Wadsworth.

Stark, Rodney. 1985. "Church and Sect." Pp. 139–49 in *The Sacred in a Secular Age,* edited by P. Hammond. Berkeley: University of California Press.

———. 2000. "Secularization, R.P.I." Pp. 41–66 in *The Secularization Debate,* edited by William H. Swatos, Jr., and Daniel V. A. Olson. Lanham, MD: Rowman & Littlefield.

Stark, Rodney, and William Sims Bainbridge. 1985. *The Future of Religion: Secularization, Revival, and Cult Formation.* Berkeley: University of California Press.

Starnes, Bobby Ann. 2006. "What We Don't Know Can Hurt Them: White Teachers, Indian Children." *Phi Delta Kappan* (January):384–92.

Starr, Paul D. 1982. *The Social Transformation of American Medicine.* New York: Basic Books.

"State Laws Regarding Marriages Between First Cousins." 2010. Retrieved March 25, 2010 (About.com http://marriage.about.com/od/cousinmarriages/Cousin_Marriages.htm).

State of Alaska. 2006. "Workplace Alaska: How to Apply." Retrieved July 5, 2006 (http://notes3.state.ak.us/WA/MainEntry.nsf/WebData/HTMLHow+to+Apply/?open).

Steele, Stephen F., and Jammie Price. 2004. *Applied Sociology: Terms, Topics, Tools, and Tasks.* Belmont, CA: Wadsworth.

Steele, Tracey L. 2005. *Sex, Self, and Society: The Social Context of Sexuality.* Belmont, CA: Thomson Wadsworth.

Steele, Tracey, and Norma Wilcox. 2003. "A View From the Inside: The Role of Redemption, Deterrence, and Masculinity on Inmate Support for the Death Penalty." *Crime and Delinquency* 49(2):285–313.

Stein, Nicholas. 2006. "No Way Out." Pp. 293–99 in *Globalization: The Transformation of Social Worlds,* edited by D. Stanley Eitzen and Maxine Baca Zinn. Belmont, CA: Wadsworth.

Stelter, Brian. 17 June 2009. "In Coverage of Iran, Amateurs Take the Lead." [Mediadecoder Weblog] *New York Times,* Retrieved December 22, 2009 (http://mediadecoder.blogs.nytimes.com).

Stern, Jessica. 2003. *Terror in the Name of God: Why Religious Militants Kill.* New York: HarperCollins.

Stevens, Daphne, Gary Kiger, and Pamela J. Riley. 2001. "Working Hard and Hardly Working: Domestic Labor and Marital Satisfaction Among Dual-Earner Families." *Journal of Marriage and the Family* 63(May):514–26.

Stewart, Susan D. 2007. *Brave New Stepfamilies: Diverse Paths Toward Stepfamily Living.* Thousand Oaks, CA: Sage.

Stoessinger, John. 1993. *Why Nations Go to War.* New York: St. Martin's Press.

Stone, Brad, and Noam Cohen. 2009. "Social Networks Spread Defiance Online." *The New York Times.* June 16. Retrieved June 30, 2009 (www.nytimes.com/2009/06/16/world/middleeast/16media.html?_r=1&ref=world).

Stone, Norman, ed. 1991. *The Times Atlas of World History,* 3rd ed. Maplewood, NJ: Hammond.

Stout, David. 2009. "Violent Crime Fell in 2008, F.B.I. Report Says." *The New York Times.* September 14. Retrieved November 4, 2009 (www.nytimes.com/2009/09/15/us/15crime.html).

Straus, Murray, and Richard J. Gelles. 1990. *Physical Violence in American Families.* New Brunswick, NJ: Transaction.

Straus, Murray A., Richard J. Gelles, and Suzanne K. Steinmetz. 2006. *Behind Closed Doors: Violence in the American Family.* New Brunswick, NJ: Transaction.

Stringer, Donna M. 2006. "Let Me Count the Ways: African American/European American Marriages." Pp. 170–76 in *Intercultural Communication: A Reader,* edited by Larry A. Samovar, Richard E. Porter, and Edwin R. McDaniel. Belmont, CA: Wadsworth.

Struck, Doug. 2007. "Warming Will Exacerbate Global Water Conflicts." *Washington Post* August 20. Retrieved August 21, 2008 (www.washingtonpost.com/wp-dyn/content/article/2007/08/19/AR2007081900967.html).

Stryker, Sheldon. 1980. *Symbolic Interactionism: A Social Structural Version.* Menlo Park, CA: Benjamin Cummings.

———. 2000. "Identity Competition: Key to Differential Social Involvement." Pp. 21–40 in *Identity, Self, and Social Movements,* edited by Sheldon Styker, Timothy Owens, and Robert White. Minneapolis: University of Minnesota Press.

Stryker, Sheldon, and Anne Stratham. 1985. "Symbolic Interaction and Role Theory." Pp. 311–78 in *Handbook of Social Psychology,* edited by Gardiner Lindsey and Eliot Aronson. New York: Random House.

Stutz, Fredrick P., and Barney Warf. 2005. *The World Economy.* Upper Saddle River, NJ: Prentice Hall.

Sunshine, Rebecca. 2009. "One State Looks to Cut the Death Penalty, Put Money Elsewhere." (www.ktiv.com/Global/story.asp?S=9790524).

Sutherland, Anne. 1986. *Gypsies: The Hidden Americans.* Prospect Heights, IL: Waveland.

Sutherland, Edwin H., Donald R. Cressey, and David Luckenbil. 1992. *Criminology.* Dix Hills, NY: General Hall.

Swatos, William H., Jr., and Luftur Reimur Gissurarson. 1997. *Icelandic Spiritualism: Mediumship and Modernity in Iceland.* New Brunswick, NJ: Transaction.

Sway, Marlene. 1988. *Familiar Strangers: Gypsy Life in America.* Urbana: University of Illinois Press.

Sweet, Stephen. 2001. *College and Society: An Introduction to the Sociological Imagination.* Boston: Allyn & Bacon.

Swivel. 2007. "Infant Mortality." Retrieved February 26, 2008 (www.swivel.com/data_sets/spreadsheet/1006156).

Talbot, Margaret. 2008. "Red Sex, Blue Sex." *The New Yorker.* November 3. Retrieved December 24, 2009 (www.newyorker.com/reporting/2008/11/03/081103fa_fact_talbot).

Tamney, Joseph B. 1992. *The Resilience of Christianity in the Modern World.* Albany: State University of New York Press.

Taub, Diane E., and Penelope A. McLorg. 2007. "Influences of Gender Socialization and Athletic Involvement on the Occurrence of Eating

Disorders." Pp. 81–90 in *Sociological Footprints*, 10th ed., edited by Leonard Cargan and Jeanne Ballantine. Belmont, CA: Wadsworth.

Tavris, Carol, and Carol Wade. 1984. *The Longest War*, 2nd ed. San Diego: Harcourt Brace Jovanovich.

Taylor, Humphrey. 2002. "Scientists, Doctors, Teachers, and Military Officers Top the List of Prestigious Occupations." *The Harris Poll* October 16. Retrieved August 22, 2006 (Harrisinteractive.com/harris_poll/index.asp?Pollyear=2002).

Teixeira, Ruy. 2008. "The Decline of the White Working Class and the Rise of a Mass Upper Middle Class." Brookings Institution. Retrieved June 27, 2008 (www.brookings.edu/experts.aspx).

Therborn, Goran. 1976. "What Does the Ruling Class Do When It Rules?" *Insurgent Sociologist* 6:3–16.

Thiagaraj, Henry. 2006. *Minority and Human Rights From the Dalits' Perspective*. Chennai, India: Oneworld Educational Trust.

———. 2007. *Human Rights From the Dalits' Perspective*. New Delhi, India: Gyan Publications.

Thio, Alex. 2007. *Deviant Behavior*, 9th ed. Boston: Allyn & Bacon.

Thoits, Peggy A., and Lyndi N. Hewitt. 2001. "Volunteer Work and Well-Being." *Journal of Health and Social Behavior* 42(June):115–31.

Thomas, P. 2009. "Zac Sunderland Completes Solo Sail Around World." *Los Angeles Times* July 17. Retrieved October 7, 2009, (from http://latimesblogs.latimes.com/outposts/2009/01/post-4.html).

Thomas, V. J., and F. D. Rose. 1991. "Ethnic Differences in the Experience of Pain." *Social Science and Medicine* 32(9):1063–1066.

Thorne, Barrie. 1993. *Gender Play: Girls and Boys in School*. New Brunswick, NJ: Rutgers University Press.

Thumma, Scott, and Dave Travis. 2007. *Beyond Megachurch Myths: What We Can Learn From America's Largest Churches*. Hoboken, NJ: Jossey-Bass.

Tichenor, Veronica Jaris. 1999. "Status and Income as Gendered Resources: The Case of Marital Power." *Journal of Marriage and the Family* 61(August):638–50.

Time Almanac. 2008. "China" (pp. 277–80). Chicago: Encyclopedia Britannica.

Tipton, Steven M. 1990. "The Social Organization of Zen Practice: Constructing Transcultural Reality." *American Journal of Sociology* 96(2):488–90.

Toffler, Alvin, and Heidi Toffler. 1980. *The Third Wave*. New York: Morrow.

Tolbert, Pamela S., and Richard H. Hall. 2008. *Organizations: Structures, Processes, and Outcomes*, 10th ed. Upper Saddle River, NJ: Prentice Hall.

Tonnies, Ferdinand. [1887] 1963. *Community and Society*. New York: Harper & Row.

Torche, Florencia. 2005. "Privatization Reform and Inequality of Educational Opportunity: The Case of Chile." *Sociology of Education* 78(4):316–43.

Tough, Paul. 2008. *Whatever It Takes: Geoffrey Canada's Quest to Change Harlem and America*. Boston: Houghton Mifflin Harcourt.

Tracy, Sarah W. 2005. *Alcoholism in America: From Reconstruction to Prohibition*. Baltimore: Johns Hopkins University Press.

Transparency International. 2007. *Transparency International Global Corruption Barometer*. Transparency International: The Global Coalition against Corruption. Retrieved April 14, 2009 (www.transparency.org).

Travers, Jeffrey, and Stanley Milgram. 1969. "An Experimental Study of the Small World Problem." *Sociometry* 32:425–43.

Tuchman, Gaye. 1996. "Women's Depiction by the Mass Media." Pp. 11–15 in *Turning It On: A Reader on Women and Media*, edited by Helen Baehr and Ann Gray. London: Arnold.

Tumin, Melvin M. 1953. "Some Principles of Social Stratification: A Critical Analysis." *American Sociological Review* 18(August):387–94.

Turnbull, Colin M. 1962. *The Forest People*. New York: Simon & Schuster.

Turner, Bryan S. 1991a. "Politics and Culture in Islamic Globalism." Pp. 161–81 in *Religion and Global Order*, edited by Roland Robertson and William R. Garrett. New York: Paragon.

———. 1991b. *Religion and Social Theory*. London: Sage.

Turner, Jonathan H. 2003. *The Structure of Sociological Theory*, 7th ed. Belmont, CA: Wadsworth.

Turner, Ralph H., and Lewis M. Killian. 1993. "The Field of Collective Behavior." Pp. 5–20 in *Collective Behavior and Social Movements*, edited by Russell L. Curtis, Jr. and Benigno E. Aguirre. Boston: Allyn & Bacon.

Twaddle, Andrew C. 2007. "Sick Role." In *Blackwell Encyclopedia of Sociology*, edited by George Ritzer. Hoboken, NJ: Blackwell.

Twigg, Krassimira. 2009. "Twitterers Defy China's Firewall." BBC News Online (June 10). Retrieved April 9, 2010 (http://news.bbc.co.uk).

UCR Crime Statistics. 2008. "The Disaster Center." www.disastercenter.com/crime/uscrime.htm.

UNAIDS 2009. "AIDS Epidemic Update" (November). Retrieved January 11, 2010 (www.avert.org/worldstats.htm).

UNESCAP. 2007. "Gender Inequality Continues—at Great Cost." The Economic and Social Survey for Asia and the Pacific 2007. Retrieved April 9, 2010 (www.unescap.org/survey2007/backgrounder/gender_inequality.asp).

UNESCO. 2005. *Education for All Global Monitoring Report 2005: The Quality Imperative*. Paris: Author.

———. 2006. *Education for All Global Monitoring Report 2006: The Quality Imperative*. Paris: Author.

———. 2009. "Women and Accessibility in Town Centers: Open Sesame Project, UK." Retrieved January 6, 2010 (www.unesco.org/most/westeu23.htm).

UNHCR. 2006. "2005 Global Refugee Trends: Statistical Overview of Populations of Refugees, Asylum-Seekers, Internally Displaced Persons, Stateless Persons, and Other Persons of Concern to UNHCR." Retrieved April 17, 2010 (www.unhcr.org/4486ceb12.html).

———. 2009. "UNHCR Annual Report Shows 42 Million People Uprooted Worldwide." Retrieved January 5, 2010 (www.unhcr.org/4a2fd52412d.html).

UNHCR Statistical Yearbook. 2006. "Asylum and Refugee Status Determination" (Chapter 5). Retrieved March 2, 2008 (www.unhcr.org/doclist/statistics/4148094d4.html).

UNICEF. 2004. *Progress for Children: A Child Survival Report Card, No. 1*. New York: Author.

UNIFEM. 2002. "Report of the Learning Oriented Assessment of Gender Mainstreaming and Women's Empowerment Strategies in Rwanda." Retrieved April 7, 2008 (www.unifem.org/attachments/products/rwanda_assessment_report_eng.pdf).

Uniform Crime Reports. 2009. "Hate Crime Statistics, 2008: Incidents and Offenses." Retrieved December 20, 2009 (www.fbi.gov/ucr/hc2008/incidents.html).

United Church of Christ. 2007. "Toxic Waste and Race at Twenty: 1987–2007." Environmental Justice/Environmental Racism. Retrieved April 22, 2009 (www.ejnet.org/ej).

United Nations. 2003. "Demographic Yearbook: 2003." Retrieved August 22, 2006 (http://unstats.un.org/unsd/demographic/products/dyb/dyb2.htm).

———. 2006. "Demographic Yearbook: 2006." Retrieved April 17, 2010 (www.unstats.un.org/unsd/demographic/products/dyb/dyb2006.htm).

———. 2007. "UN Member States." Retrieved March 26, 2008 (www.un.org/members/list.shtml).

———. 2008a. *Economic & World Urbanization Prospects: The 2007 Revision*. New York: United Nations Department of Economic and Social Affairs, Population Division. February 2008. Retrieved April 24, 2009 (www.un.org/esa/population/publications/wup2007/2007WUP_Highlights_web.pdf).

———. 2008b. "Marriage and Crude Marriage Rates: 2002–2006," "Divorce and Crude Divorce Rates: 2002–2006." Retrieved December 2, 2009 (unstats.un.org/unsd/demographic/products/dyb/dyb2006/Table25.pdf).

———. 2009a. "214 Million People Living Outside Country of Birth." November. UN Global Forum on Migration and Development, Athens. Retrieved April 17, 2010 (www.waccglobal.org/...2085:wacc-statement-on-international-migrants-day.html).

———. 2009b. "World Food Program: Swaziland" (November). Retrieved April 13, 2010 (www.wfp.org/countries/swaziland).

United Nations Climate Change Conference. 2009. Retrieved Dec 22, 2009 (http://en.cop15.dk/about+cop15).

United Nations, Development Programme. 2005a. "Human Development Indicators." *Human Development Report*. Retrieved April 17, 2010 (http://hdr.undp.org/en/reports/global/hdr2005).

———. 2005b. United Nations Office on Drugs and Crime. *World Drug Report 2005*. Retrieved April 17, 2010 (www.unodc.org/pdf/WDR_2005/volume_1_web.pdf).

———. 2007/2008. *Human Development Report: Country Fact Sheets*. New York: Author.

United Nations, Population Division. 2003. "World Urbanization Prospects: The 2003 Revision." Retrieved September 29, 2006 (www.un.org/esa/population/publications/wup2003/WUP2003Report.pdf).

———. 2005. "World Urbanization Prospects: The 2005 Revision." Retrieved April 17, 2010 (http://un.org/esa/population/.../WUP2005/2005wup.htm).

United Nations, Population Fund. 2005. "State of the World Population 2005." Retrieved September 29, 2006 (www.unfpa.org/swp/2005/pdf/en_swp05.pdf).

———. 2007. *State of the World*. "Maternal Mortality Figures." Retrieved April 17, 2010 (unic.un.org/imucms/LegacyDish.aspx?loc=11&pg=795).

United North America. 2008. "Similarities and Differences Between Canada & United States." Retrieved August 26, 2008 (www.unitednorthamerica.org/simdiff.htm).

United Press International. 2008. "Annan Says Kenyan Conflict 'Evolving'." January 27. Retrieved June 3, 2008 (www.upi.com/NewsTrack/Top_News/2008/01/27/annan_says_kenyan_conflict_evolving/1912).

University of Michigan Documents Center. 2003. "Documents in the News—1997/2003: Affirmative Action in College Admissions." Retrieved April 17, 2010 (www.lib.umich.edu/files/libraries/govdocs/pdf/affirm/pdf).

University of Pennsylvania. 2007. "Bodies of Cultures: A World Tour of Body Modification." Retrieved April 17, 2010 (www.museum.upenn.edu/new/exhibits/online_exhibits/body_modification/querypublic.shtml) and (www.docstoc.com/docs/6227283/Earring).

The Urban Institute. 2004. "Family Support, Substance Abuse Help, and Work Release Programs Are Essential as Ex-Prisoners Restart Lives in Baltimore." Retrieved April 17, 2010 (www.urban.org/url.cfm?ID=900688).

USAID. 2008. Retrieved January 8, 2010 (www.usaid.gov/our_work/global_health/aids/Countries/africa/swaziland.html).

"U.S. Broadband Penetration Jumps to 45.2%; Internet Access Nearly 75%." 2004. (WebSiteOptimization.com).

U.S. Bureau of Justice Statistics. 2001. *National Crime Victimization Survey Report*. Washington, DC: U.S. Department of Justice.

———. 2002, 2003, 2004, 2005, 2006. *Sourcebook of Criminal Justice Statistics*. Washington, DC: U.S. Department of Justice.

U.S. Bureau of Labor Statistics. 2008–2009. "Occupational Outlook Handbook, 2008–09 Edition." Retrieved April 9, 2008 (www.bls.gov/oco/ocos285.htm).

U.S. Census Bureau. 2001. *Current Population Survey, 2001*. Washington, DC: Government Printing Office.

———. 2003. "2001 Annual Report: The Status of Equal Employment Opportunity and Affirmative Action in Alaska State Government." Retrieved September 29, 2006 (http://factfinder.census.gov/servlet/ACSSAFFFacts?_event=&geo_id=04000US02&_geoContext=01000US%7C04000US02&_street=&_county=&_cityTown=&_state=04000US02&_zip=&_lang=en&_sse=on&ActiveGeoDiv=&_useEV=&pctxt=fph&pgsl=040).

———. 2005a. "Computer and Internet Use in the United States: 2003." *Current Population Reports*. Washington, DC: Author.

———. 2005b. "Housing Vacancies and Housing Ownership." *Annual Statistics 2005*. Retrieved September 15, 2006 (www.census.gov/hhes/www/housing/hvs/annual05/ann05def.html).

———. 2005c. *Statistical Abstracts of the United States: 2004–2005*, 124th ed. Washington, DC: Government Printing Office. Retrieved August 26, 2006 (www.census.gov/Press-Release/www/releases/archives/labor_table597.pdf).

———. 2006a. "America's Families and Living Arrangements 2006." Retrieved February 20, 2008 (www.census.gov/population/www/socdemo/hh-fam/cps2005.html).

———. 2006b. "Geographical Mobility Between 2004 and 2005." *Population Profile of the United States*. Washington, DC: Author.

———. 2006c. "International Database." Retrieved April 17, 2010 (www.census.gov/ipc/www/idb/worldpop.php).

———. 2006d. "Movers by Type of Move and Reason for Moving 2006." *Statistical Abstracts 2008* (Table 0031). Retrieved August 23, 2008 (infochimps.org/dataset/statab2008_0031_moversbytypeofmoveandreasonformovin).

———. 2006e. "Poverty Thresholds." Retrieved April 17, 2010 (www.census.gov/hhes/www/poverty/threshld).

———. 2007a. "America's Families and Living Arrangements: 2007." Retrieved February 21, 2009.

———. 2007b. "Median Earnings in the Past 12 Months of Workers by Sex and Women's Earnings as a Percentage of Men's Earnings" (Table 5). *Income, Earnings, and Poverty Data From the 2005 American Community Survey*. Washington, DC: Author.

———. 2007c. "National Population Estimates: Characteristics." Retrieved August 11, 2008 (www.census.gov/popest/national/asrh/NC-EST2007-srh.html).

———. 2007d. "Single-Parent Households Showed Little Variation Since 1994, Census Bureau Reports" (March 27). Retrieved April 17, 2010 (www.census.gov/Press-Release/.../households/009842.html).

———. 2008a. "Mean Earnings by Highest Degree Earned: 2005." *Statistical Abstracts of the United States, 2008* (Table 220). Washington, DC: Author. Retrieved April 9, 2010 (www.census.gov/compendia/statab/cats/education.html).

———. 2008b. "Number of Poor Families." Retrieved April 17, 2010 (www.census.gov/Press-Release/www/.../012528.html).

———. 2008c. *Public Education Finances: 2006*. Retrieved January 7, 2010 (www2.census.gov/govs/school/06f33pub.pdf).

———. 2008d. "Selected Measures of Household Income Dispersion." Aug. 26. www.census.gov/hhes/www/income/histinc/ie1.html (Retrieved April 20, 2009).

———. 2008e. "Statistical Abstract of the United States: 2007 (Table 77)." Retrieved February 9, 2008 (www.census.gov/compendia/statab/tables/08s0077.xls).

———. 2009a. American Factfinder. Retrieved April 17, 2010 (http://factfinder.census.gov/servlet/SAFFPopulation).

———. 2009b. "Educational Attainment by Selected Characteristic: 2007, for Persons 25 Years Old and Over Reported in Thousands." Statistical Abstract of the United States. Retrieved June 23, 2009 (www.census.gov/compendia/statab/cats/education/educational_attainment.html).

———. 2009c. "Factfinder." Retrieved December 20, 2009 (www.census.gov).

———. 2009d. "Historical Income Tables—Households." Retrieved April 26, 2009 (www.census.gov/hhes/www/income/histinc/h02AR.html).

———. 2009e. "Money Income of Families—Median Income by Race and Hispanic Origin." Retrieved December 19, 2009 (www.census.gov/compendia/statab/2010/tables/10s0681.pdf) and (www.census.gov/compendia/statab/2010/tables/10s0224.pdf).

———. 2009f. Number of Americans Without Health Insurance Rises to 46.3 Million." NY Daily News (September 10). Retrieved April 17, 2010 (www.nydailynews.com/.../2009/.../2009-09-10_number_of_Americans_without_health_insurance_rises_to_463m.html).

———. 2009g. "Weighted Average Poverty Thresholds 2008." September. Retrieved November 28, 2009 (www.irp.wisc.edu/faqs/faq1.htm).

———. 2010a. "Mean Earnings by Level of Highest Degree (Dollars)." Statistical Abstracts Table 227. Retrieved April 13, 2010 (www.census.gov/compendia/statab/cats/health_nutrition.html).

———. 2010b. National Health Expenditure by Type. Statistical Abstracts Table 228. Retrieved April 13, 2010 (www.census.gov/compendia/statab/cats/health_nutrition.html).

USDA. 2009. "USDA Releases Annual Study Which Notes That Child Born in 2008 Will Cost $221,190 To Raise." Release No. 0365.09, August 4. Retrieved January 6, 2010 (www.usda.gov/wps/portal/!ut.p/_s.7_0_a/7_0_10B?contentidonly).

U.S. Department of Agriculture. 2008. "Rural America at a Glance." Economic Information Bulletin No. (EIB-40). Retrieved March 30, 2010 (www.ers.usda.gov/publications/eib40).

U.S. Department of Education. 2004–05. "Integrated Postsecondary Education Data System: Glossary." Retrieved July 10, 2009 (http://nces.ed.gov/ipeds/glossary/?charindex=D).

U.S. Department of Energy. 2006. "Energy Consumption: Energy Kids Page." Retrieved November 8, 2006 (www.eia.doe.gov/kids/energyfacts/saving/efficiency/savingenergysecondary.html).

U.S. Department of Interior, Office of Education. 1930. Availability of Public School Education in Rural Communities (Bulletin No. 34, edited by Walter H. Gaummitz). Washington, DC: Government Printing Office.

U.S. Department of Justice. 2006. National Crime Victimization Survey. Washington, DC: Bureau of Justice Statistics.

———. 2009. "Crime Clock." Retrieved November 5, 2009 (http://ovc.ncjrs.gov/ncvrw2009/pdf/crime_clock_hr.pdf).

U.S. Department of Labor. 2005. Current Population Survey. Washington, DC: Bureau of Labor Statistics.

U.S. Department of State. 2002. "Curbing Violence Against Political Activists in Cambodia" (Press release). Retrieved September 9, 2008 (www.state.gov/r/pa/prs/ps/2002/15978.htm).

U.S. Department of State. 2005. Patterns of Global Terrorism 1985–2005. Washington DC: Berkshire Publishing Group.

U.S. Environmental Protection Agency. 2009. "Ag101: Demographics." Retrieved March 30, 2010 (www.epa.gov/oecaagct/ag101/demographics/html).

U.S. Flag Code. 2008. "U.S. Flag Code (4 US Code 1)." Retrieved August 28, 2008 (http://suvcw.org/flag.htm).

U.S. General Accounting Office. 2003. "Defense of Marriage Act—Update to Prior Report." Retrieved August 18, 2006 (www.gao.gov/new.items/d04353r.pdf).

U.S. Office of Personnel Management. 2007. "Family Leave Policies." Retrieved April 4, 2008 (www.opm.gov/OCA/LEAVE).

U.S. Trade Representative. 2003. "North American Free Trade Agreement: Overview." Retrieved September 29, 2006 (www.ustr.gov/regions/whemisphere/overview.shtml).

Vandenburgh, Henry. 2001. "Emerging Trends in the Provision and Consumption of Health Services." Sociological Spectrum 21(3):279–92.

Vanderminden, Jennifer, and Sharyn J. Potter. 2010. "Challenges to the Doctor-Patient Relationship in the 21st Century." In The New Blackwell Companion to Medical Sociology, edited by William C. Cockerham. Malden, MA.: Wiley/Blackwell.

Veblen, Thorstein. 1902. The Theory of the Leisure Class: An Economic Study of Institutions. New York: Macmillan.

Verba, Sidney, and Norman H. Nie. 1972. Participation in America: Political Democracy and Social Equality. New York: Harper & Row.

Victor, Barbara. 2003. Army of Roses: Inside the World of Palestinian Women Suicide Bombers. Emmaus, PA: Rodale Books.

Von Holzen, Roger. 2005. "The Emergence of a Learning Society." The Futurist 39(January–February):24–25.

Voting and Democracy Research Center. 2008. "Primaries: Open and Closed." Retrieved March 21, 2008 (www.fairvote.org/?page=1801).

Waite, Linda J., and Maggie Gallagher. 2000. The Case for Marriage: Why Married People Are Happier, Healthier, and Better Off Financially. New York: Doubleday.

Walker, Henry A., and Jennifer A. Karas 1993. "The Declining Significance of Color: Race, Color, and Status Attainment." Paper presented at the annual meeting of the American Sociological Association, Miami, FL.

Wallace. G. 2004. "Revisiting the Race vs. Class Debate: Does Race, Class or Another Explanation Best Account for the Black/White Gap in Earnings?" Presented at the annual meeting of the American Sociological Association, August 14, San Francisco.

Wallenstein, Peter. 2002. Tell the Court I Love My Wife: Race, Marriage, and Law—An American History. New York: Macmillan.

Waller, Willard. [1932] 1965. Sociology of Teaching. New York: Russell & Russell.

Wallerstein, Immanuel. 1974. The Modern World System. New York: Academic Press.

———. 1979. The Capitalist World Economy. London: Cambridge University Press.

———. 1991. Geopolitics and Geoculture: Essays on the Changing World-system. Cambridge, MA: Cambridge University Press.

———. 2004. World Systems Analysis: An Introduction. Durham, NC: Duke University Press.

———. 2005. "Render Unto Caesar? The Dilemmas of a Multicultural World." Sociology of Religion 66(2):121–33.

Wallerstein, Judith. 1996. Surviving the Breakup: How Children and Parents Cope With Divorce. New York: Basic Books.

Wallerstein, Judith S., and Sarah Blakeslee. 1996. The Good Marriage: How and Why Love Lasts. New York: Warner Books.

———. 2004. Second Chances: Men, Women and Children a Decade After Divorce, 15th ed. Boston: Houghton Mifflin.

Walum, Laurel Richardson. 1974. "The Changing Door Ceremony: Some Notes on the Operation of Sex Roles in Everyday Life." Urban Life and Culture 2(4):506–515.

Wang, Tina. 2009. "China Health Care Markets." Forbes (January 22). Retrieved January 10, 2010 (www.forbes.com/2009/01/22/china-health-care-markets-econ-cx_twdd_0122markets04.html).

Ward, Martha C. 1996. A World Full of Women. Boston: Allyn & Bacon.

Ward, Martha C., and Monica Edelstein. 2009. A World Full of Women, 5th ed. Boston: Allyn & Bacon.

Ware, Alyn. 2008. "Nuclear Stockpiles" (Project of the Nuclear Age Peace Foundation). Retrieved September 3, 2008 (www.nuclearfiles.org/menu/key-issues/nuclear-weapons/basics/nuclear-stockpiles.htm).

Warner, R. Stephen. 1993. "Work in Progress Toward a New Paradigm for the Sociological Study of Religion in the United States." American Journal of Sociology 98(5):1044–1093.

WaterAid. 2004. "No Water, No School." Oasis (Spring/Summer). Retrieved February 25, 2008 (www.wateraid.org/international/about_us/oasis/springsummer_04/1465.asp).

———. 2008. "WaterAid's Key Facts and Statistics." Retrieved February 25, 2008 (www.wateraid.org/international/what_we_do/statistics/default.asp).

Weber, B. J., and L. M. Omotani. 1994. "The Power of Believing." *The Executive Educator* 19(September):35–38.

Weber, David. 2003. "25 Health Care Trends: What's Hot, What's Not, and What Does the Future Hold." *Physician Executive* 29(1):6–14.

Weber, Max. 1946. *From Max Weber: Essays in Sociology.* Translated and edited by Hans H. Gerth and C. Wright Mills. New York: Oxford University Press.

———. 1947. *The Theory of Social and Economic Organization.* Translated and edited by A. M. Henderson and Talcott Parsons. New York: Oxford University Press.

———. [1904–1905] 1958. *The Protestant Ethic and the Spirit of Capitalism.* Translated by Talcott Parsons. New York: Scribner.

Weeks, John R. 1999. *Population: An Introduction to Concepts and Issues,* 7th ed. Belmont, CA: Wadsworth.

———. 2005. *Population: An Introduction to Concepts and Issues,* 9th ed. Belmont, CA: Wadsworth.

Weidenbaum, Murray. 2006. "Globalization: Wonderland or Waste Land?" Pp. 53–60 in *Globalization: The Transformation of Social Worlds,* edited by D. Stanley Eitzen and Maxine Baca Zinn. Belmont, CA: Wadsworth.

Weil, Elizabeth. 2008. "Teaching to the Testosterone." *The New York Times Magazine* (March 2):38.

Weisenberg, Faye, and Elizabeth Stacey. 2005. "Reflections on Teaching and Learning Online: Quality Program Design, Delivery, and Support Issues From a Cross-Global Perspective." *Distance Education,* 26(3).

Weiss, Gregory L., and Lynne E. Lonnquist. 2008. *The Sociology of Health, Healing, and Illness,* 6th ed. Englewood Cliffs, NJ: Prentice Hall.

Weiss, Robin Elise. 2010. "Pregnancy and Childbirth." Retrieved January 9, 2010 (pregnancy.about.com/od/cesareansections/ss/cesarian.htm).

Weitz, Rose. 1995. "What Price Independence? Social Reactions to Lesbians, Spinsters, Widows and Nuns." Pp. 448–57 in *Women: A Feminist Perspective,* edited by Jo Freeman. Mountain View, CA: Mayfield.

Weitzman, Lenore J., Deborah Eifler, Elizabeth Hokada, and Catherine Ross. 1972. "Sex-Role Socialization in Picture Books for Preschool Children." *American Journal of Sociology* 77(May):1125–50.

Weller, Christian E., and Adam Hersh. 2006. "Free Markets and Poverty." Pp. 69–73 in *Globalization: The Transformation of Social Worlds,* edited by D. Stanley Eitzen and Maxine Baca Zinn. Belmont, CA: Wadsworth.

Wells, Amy Stuart, and Jeannie Oakes. 1996. "Potential Pitfalls of Systemic Reform: Early Lessons From Research on Detracking." *Sociology of Education* 69(Extra Issue):135–43.

Wenglinsky, Harold. 1997. "How Money Matters: The Effect of School District Spending on Academic Achievement." *Sociology of Education* 70(3):221–37.

Wessinger, Catherine. 2000. *How the Millennium Comes Violently: From Jonestown to Heaven's Gate.* New York: Seven Bridges.

West, Candace, and Don H. Zimmerman. 1987. "Doing Gender." *Gender and Society* 1(2):125–51.

West, Heather C., and William J. Sabol. 2008 "Prisoners in 2007." Bureau of Justice Statistics Bulletin. U.S. Department of Justice. Retrieved December 23, 2008 (www.ojp.usdoj.gov/bjs/pub/pdf/p07.pdf).

Westermann, Ted D., and James W. Burfeind. 1991. *Crime and Justice in Two Societies: Japan and the United States.* Pacific Grove, CA: Brooks/Cole.

Westheimer, Joel. 2006. "Patriotism and Education: An Introduction." *Phi Delta Kappan* 87(8):569–72.

The White House, 2010. "Health Care." Retrieved April 13, 2010 (www.whitehouse.gov/issues/health-care).

White, Kevin. 2002. *An Introduction to the Sociology of Health and Illness.* London: Sage.

Whorf, Benjamin Lee. 1956. *Language, Thought, and Reality.* New York: John Wiley.

Whyte, William H. 1956. *The Organization Man.* New York: Simon and Schuster.

Wilcox, Norma, and Tracey Steele. 2003. "Just the Facts: A Descriptive Analysis of Inmate Attitudes Toward Capital Punishment." *The Prison Journal* 83(4):464–82.

Williams, Brian K., Stacey C. Sawyer, and Carl M. Wahlstrom. 2009. *Marriages, Families, and Intimate Relationships,* 2nd ed. Boston: Allyn & Bacon.

Williams, Gregory H. 1996. *Life on the Color Line: The True Story of a White Boy Who Discovered He Was Black.* New York: Dutton.

Williams, Robin Murphy, Jr. 1970. *American Society: A Sociological Interpretation,* 3rd ed. New York: Alfred Knopf.

Willie, Charles Vert. 2003. *A New Look at Black Families,* 5th ed. Walnut Creek, CA: AltaMira.

Willis, Paul. 1979. *Learning to Labor: How Working Class Kids Get Working Class Jobs.* Aldershot, Hampshire, England: Saxon House.

Wilson, Bryan. 1982. *Religion in Sociological Perspective.* Oxford, UK: Oxford University Press.

Wilson, Edward O. 1980. *Sociobiology.* Cambridge, MA: Belknap.

———. 1987. *The Coevolution of Biology and Culture.* Cambridge, MA: Harvard University Press.

Wilson, Edward O., Michael S. Gregory, Anita Silvers, and Diane Sutch. 1978. "What Is Sociobiology?" *Society* 15(6):1–12.

Wilson, K. 1993. *Dialectics of Consciousness: Problems of Development, the Indian Reality.* Madras: Oneworld Educational Trust.

Wilson, Mary E. 2006. "Infectious Concerns: Modern Factors in the Spread of Disease." Pp. 313–19 in *Globalization: The Transformation of Social Worlds,* edited by D. Stanley Eitzen and Maxine Baca Zinn. Belmont, CA: Wadsworth.

Wilson, Warren H. 1924. "What the Automobile Has Done to and for the Country Church." *Annals of the American Academy of Political and Social Science* 116(November):85–86.

Wilson, William Julius. 1978. *The Declining Significance of Race: Blacks and Changing American Institutions.* Chicago: University of Chicago Press.

———. 1984. "The Black Underclass." *The Wilson Quarterly* (Spring):88–89.

———. 1993a. *The Ghetto Underclass: Social Science Perspectives.* Newbury Park, CA: Sage.

———. 1993b. "The New Urban Poverty and the Problem of Race." *The Tanner Lecture on Human Values,* October 22 (printed in *Michigan Quarterly Review,* 247–73).

———. 1996. *When Work Disappears.* New York: Alfred A. Knopf.

Winders, Bill. 2004. "Changing Racial Inequality: The Rise and Fall of Systems of Racial Inequality in the U.S." Paper presented at the Annual Meeting of the American Sociological Association, San Francisco.

Wingfield, Adia Harvey. 2009. "Racializing the Glass Escalator: Reconsidering Men's Experiences With Women's Work." *Gender and Society.* 23(5):5–26.

Winkler, Celia. 2002. *Single Mothers and the State: The Politics of Care in Sweden and the United States.* London: Rowman and Littlefield.

Winkler, Karen J. 1991. "Revisiting the Nature vs. Nurture Debate: Historian Looks Anew at Influence of Biology on Behavior." *Chronicle of Higher Education* (May 22):A5, 8.

Winnick, Terri A. 2006. "Medical Doctors and Complementary and Alternative Medicine: The Context of Holistic Practice." *Health: An Interdisciplinary Journal for the Social Study of Health, Illness and Medicine* 10(2):149–73.

Winslow, Robert W., and Sheldon X. Zhang. 2008. *Criminology: A Global Perspective.* Upper Saddle River, NJ: Pearson Prentice Hall.

Wirth, Louis. 1964. "Urbanism as a Way of Life." *American Journal of Sociology* 44(1):1–24.

Witness for Peace. March 2008. Venezuelan Delegation on Health Care. (Personal communication; interviews with members of the delegation).

Witte, John F., and Christopher A. Thorn. 1996. "Who Chooses? Voucher and Interdistrict Choice Programs in Milwaukee." *American Journal of Education* 104(May):186–217.

Witte, John Jr., and Eliza Ellison 2005 *Covenant Marriage in Comparative Perspective* Grand Rapids, MI: Wm. B. Eerdmans.

Witzig, Ritchie. 1996. "The Medicalization of Race: Scientific Legitimation of a Flawed Social Construct." *Annals of Internal Medicine: American College of Physicians* 125(8):675–76.

Women's Sports Foundation. 2005. "Women's Sports: Title IX Q and A" (May). Retrieved April 17, 2010 (www.womenssportsfoundation .org/.../Title-IX/.../Briefing-Paper-Five).

Wood, Julia T. 2005. *Gendered Lives: Communication, Gender, and Culture,* 6th ed. Belmont, CA: Wadsworth.

———. 2008. *Gendered Lives: Communication, Gender, and Culture,* 8th ed. Belmont, CA: Wadsworth.

Wood, Julia T., and Nina M. Reich. 2006. "Gendered Communication Styles." Pp. 177–86 in *Intercultural Communication,* 11th ed., edited by Larry A. Samovar, Richard E. Porter, and Edwin R. McDaniel. Belmont, CA: Wadsworth.

Woodberry, Robert D., and Christian S. Smith. 1998. "Fundamentalism et al: Conservative Protestants in America." *Annual Review of Sociology* 24:25–26.

Woolhandler, Steffie, Terry Campbell, and David U. Himmelstein. 2004. "Health Care Administration in the United States and Canada: Micromanagement, Macro Costs." *International Journal of Health Services* 34(1):65–78.

World Bank. 2008. "Girls' Education: A World Bank Priority." Retrieved March 29, 2009 (www.worldbank.org/education/girls).

World Factbook. 2007. "World Health Statistics 2007." Retrieved April 4, 2008 (http://www.who.int/countries/swz/en) and (http://www.who.int/whosis/database/core/core_elect_process .cfm?country=chn&indicators).

———. 2008. "World." Retrieved August 23, 2008 (www.cia.gov/ library/publications/the-world-factbook/geos/xx.html).

———. 2009a. "Kenya, Africa." Retrieved January 6, 2010 (www.cia .gov/library/publications/the-world-factbook/geos/ke.html).

———. 2009b. "Percentage of the Population Over 65." Retrieved January 6, 2010 (www.cia.gov/library/publications/the-world-factbook/geos/ke.html).

———. 2009c. "Population Growth Rate." Retrieved January 6, 2010 (www.cia.gov/library/publications/the-world-factbook/geos/ ke.html).

———. 2009d. "Population: Sierra Leone." Retrieved January 6, 2010 (www.cia.gov/library/publications/the-world-factbook/ geos/ke.html).

———. 2009e. "World's 50 Most Populous Countries: 2009." Retrieved July 12, 2009 (www.infoplease.com/world/statistics/ most-populous-countries.html).

———. 2010a. "Country Comparison: GDP—per capita." Retrieved January 26, 2010 (www.cia.gov/library/publications/the-world-factbook/rankorder/2004rank.html).

———. 2010b. "Country Comparison: Infant Mortality Rate." Retrieved January 23, 2010 (www.cia.gov/library/publications/ the-world-factbook/rankorder/2091rank.html).

———. 2010c. "Country Comparison: Life Expectancy at Birth." Retrieved January 23, 2010 (www.cia.gov/library/publications/ the-world-factbook/rankorder/2102rank.html).

———. 2010d. "Country Comparison: Population." Central Intelligence Agency, Retrieved February 1, 2010 (www.cia.gov/library/ publications/the-world-factbook/rankorder/2119rank.html).

World Health Organization. 2002. "The World Health Report: Reducing Risks, Promoting Healthy Life." *The World Health Report 2002.* Retrieved September 29, 2006 (www.who.int/whr/2002/ en/whr02_en.pdf).

———. 2007. "Universal Coverage and Health Financing From China's Perspective." Bulletin of the World Health. Retrieved April 13, 2010 (Organization.www.who.int/bulletin/ volumes/86/11/08-060046/n).

———. 2008. Fact Sheet No. 310. "The Top Ten Causes of Death." Retrieved April 13, 2010 (www.who.int/mediacentre/factsheets/ fs310_2008.pdf).

———. 2009. Retrieved April 17, 2010 (apps.who.int/whosis/ database/core/WHO2009–12–27–151422.csv).

World Hunger Facts. 2009. Retrieved November 11, 2009 (www .worldhunger.org/articles/Learn/world%20hunger%20facts%20 2002.htm).

World Resources Institute. 2003. "Coalition of Twelve Major U.S. Corporations and WRI Announce Largest Corporate Green Power Purchases in U.S." Retrieved September 17, 2006 (www .thegreenpowergroup.org/groupevents.html).

———. 2007. "Ask Earth Trends: How Much of the World's Resource Consumption Occurs in Rich Countries?" *EarthTrends.* Retrieved April 14, 2008 (http://earthtrends.wri.org/updates/node/236).

WorldWideLearn. 2007. "Guide to College Majors in Sociology." Retrieved June 23, 2008 (www.worldwidelearn.com/online-education-guide/social-science/sociology-major.htm).

Wright, Erik Olin. 2000. *Class Counts: Comparative Studies in Class Analysis,* Student ed. Cambridge, MA: Cambridge University Press.

Wright, John W., ed. 2007. *The New York Times Almanac 2008.* New York: Penguin Reference.

Wright, Stuart A. 1995. *Armageddon in Waco: Critical Perspectives on the Branch Davidian Conflict.* Chicago: University of Chicago Press.

Yablonski, Lewis. 1959. "The Gang as a Near-Group." *Social Problems* 7(Fall):108–117.

Yamane, David. 1997. "Secularization on Trial: In Defense of a Neosecularization Paradigm." *Journal for the Scientific Study of Religion* 36(1):109–122.

Yinger, J. Milton. 1970. *The Scientific Study of Religion.* New York: Macmillan.

Yinger, J. Milton. 1960. "Contraculture and Subculture." *American Sociological Review* 25(October):625–35.

Yoon, Mi Yung. 2001. "Democratization and Women's Legislative Representation in Sub-Saharan Africa." *Democratization* 8(2):169–90.

———. 2004. "Explaining Women's Legislative Representation in Sub-Saharan Africa." *Legislative Studies Quarterly* 29(3):447–68.

———. 2005. "Sub-Saharan Africa." Chapter 7 in *Sharing Power: Women, Parliament, Democracy,* edited by Manon Tremblay and Yvonne Galligan. Aldershot, UK: Ashgate.

———. 2008. "Special Seats for Women in the National Legislature: The Case of Tanzania." *Africa Today.* (55:1) Fall:61–85.

youthxchange. 2007. "Women's Literacy." (youthxchange.net/utils/ download.asp?filename...pdf).

Yunus, Muhammad, and Alan Jolis. 1999. *Banker to the Poor: Micro-Lending and the Battle Against World Poverty.* New York: Public Affairs.

Zalman, Amy. 2009. "About.com: Terrorism Issues." *The New York Times Company.* Retrieved November 5, 2009 (http://terrorism. about.com/od/whatisterroris1/ss/DefineTerrorism_2.htm).

Zborowski, Mark. 1952. "Cultural Components in Response to Pain." *Journal of Social Issues* 8(4):16–30.

Zeleny, Jeff. 2009. "Obama Vows, 'We Will Rebuild' and 'Recover'." New York Times. February 25. Retrieved February 25, 2009 (www.nytimes .com/2009/02/25/us/politics/25obama.html?scp=1&sq=obama%20 vows%20we%20will%20rebuild&st=cse).

Zhang, Baohui, Alexi A. Wright, Haiden A. Huskamp, Matthew E. Nilsson, Matthew L. Maciejewski, Craig C. Earle, Susan D. Block, Paul K. Maciejewski, and Holly Prigerson. 2009. "Health Care Costs in the Last Week of Life." *Archives of Internal Medicine.* 16(5):480–488.

Zhao, Yong. 2005. "Increasing Math and Science Achievement: The Best and Worst of the East and West." *Phi Delta Kappan* (November):219–22.

Zimbardo, Philip C. 2004. "Power Turns Good Soldiers Into 'Bad Apples.'" *Boston Globe* (May 9). Retrieved July 5, 2008 (www.boston. com/news/globe/editorial_opinion/oped/articles/2004/05/09/ power_turns_good_soldiers_into_bad_apples).

Zimbardo, Philip. 2009. "The Stanford Prison Experiment: A Simulation Study of the Psychology of Imprisonment Conducted at Stanford University." Video at www.prisonexp.org.

Zimbardo, Philip C., Craig Haney, Curtis Banks, and David Jaffe. 1973. "The Mind Is a Formidable Jailer: A Pirandellian Prison." *The New York Times* (April 8):38–60.

Zimolzak, Chester E., and Charles A. Stansfield, Jr. 1983. *Human Landscape,* 2nd ed. Columbus, OH: Merrill.

Credits

Photo 9.3, page 280. © Mansir Petrie

Photo 9.4, page 280. © Mansir Petrie

Photo 9.5, page 280. © iStockphoto.com/Jo Ann Snover

Photo 9.6, page 280. © Jeanne Ballantine

Photo 9.7, page 280. © David Van Der Veen/epa/Corbis

Photo 9.8, page 283. © Atlantide Phototravel/Corbis

Photo 9.9, page 283. © Thomas Strange/iStockphoto.com

Photo 9.10a, page 287. © epa/Corbis

Photo 9.10b, page 287. © Matthew Cavanaugh/epa/Corbis

Photo 9.10c, page 287. © Marco Di Lauro/Stringer/Getty Images

Photo 9.11, page 289. © Jeanne Ballantine

Photo 9.12, page 291. © www.iStockphoto.com/Zsolt Nyulaszi

Photo 9.13, page 292. © Jostein Hauge/iStockphoto.com

Photo 9.14, page 293. © Keith Roberts

Photo 9.15a, page 293. © Keith Roberts

Photo 9.15b, page 293. © Keith Roberts

Photo 9.16a, page 295. © Hubert Boesl/dpa/Corbis

Photo 9.16b, page 295. © Lawrence Lucier/FilmMagic

Photo 9.17a, page 296. Photo by Joe Robbins; courtesy of Hanover College

Photo 9.17b, page 296. © G Newman Lowrance/Getty

Photo 9.18, page 299. © iStockphoto.com/Aldo Murillo

Photo 9.19, page 300. © Pathathai Chungyam/iStockphoto.com

Photo 9.20, page 301. © USAID

Photo 9.21, page 302. © Trinette Reed/Brand X/Corbis

Photo 9.22, page 304. © Adrian Weinbrecht/Getty Images

Photo 9.23, page 304. © Jeanne Ballantine

Photo 9.24, page 306. © Nadeem Khawer/epa/Corbis

Photo 9.25, page 308. © Kate Ballantine

Photo 9.26, page 308. © Narendra Shrestha/epa/Corbis

Photo 9.27, page 310. © goodshot/thinkstock

Photo 9.28, page 311. © Lynette Osborne

Photo 9.29, page 313. © UNESCO, photo by Dominique Rogers.

Chapter 10

Photo 10.1, page 320. © Akram Saleh/Reuters/Corbis

Photo 10.2, page 320. © iStockphoto.com/

Photo 10.3, page 320. © iStockphoto.com/Radu Razvan

Photo 10.4, page 320. © iStockphoto.com/Nancy Louie

Photo 10.5, page 320. © SAUL LOEB/AFP/Getty Images

Photo 10.6, page 320. © iStockphoto.com/Fred Palmieri

Photo 10.7, page 324. © Elena Korenbaum

Photo 10.8, page 325. © Kate Ballantine

Photo 10.9a, page 325. © Kate Ballantine

Photo 10.9b, page 326. © iStockphoto.com/Glenda Powers

Photo 10.10, page 327. © iStockphoto.com/Joshua Black

Photo 10.11, page 327. © Kate Ballantine

Photo 10.12, page 327. © iStockphoto.com/Jelani Memory

Photo 10.13, page 327. © Andrew Sacks/Corbis

Photo 10.14, page 327. © Jaren Wicklund/iStockphoto.com

Photo 10.15, page 327. © Kate Ballantine

Photo 10.16, page 328. © Wolfgang Kaehler/CORBIS

Photo 10.17, page 329. © Carla Howery

Photo 10.18, page 333. © Radu Razvan/iStockphoto.com

Photo 10.19, page 337. © China Photos/Getty Images

Photo 10.20, page 338. © Elise Roberts

Photo 10.21, page 338. © Mark Peterson/Corbis

Photo 10.22, page 339. © Thinkstock

Photo 10.23, page 343. © Justin Sullivan/Getty Images

Photo 10.24, page 345. © David Adame/Getty Images

Photo 10.25, page 347. © Mansir Petrie

Chapter 11

Photo 11.1, page 352. © iStockphoto.com

Photo 11.2, page 352. © Jared Embree

Photo 11.3, page 352. Photo courtesy of Hanover College

Photo 11.4, page 352. © Jeanne Ballantine

Photo 11.5, page 352. © Elise Roberts

Photo 11.6, page 352. Photo courtesy of Hanover College

Photo 11.7a, page 355. © USAID

Photo 11.7b, page 355. Courtesy of Mia Farrow

Photo 11.8, page 356. © Jared Embree

Photo 11.9, page 357. © JupiterImages/Thinkstock

Photo 11.10, page 357. © iStockphoto.com/Brandon Laufenberg

Photo 11.11, page 358. © Jeanne Ballantine

Photo 11.12, page 360. © iStockphoto.com/Kevin Russ

Photo 11.13, page 361. © iStockphoto.com/Bonnie Jacobs

Photo 11.14, page 361. © Keith Roberts

Photo 11.15, page 361. © iStockphoto.com/Charles Silvey

Photo 11.16, page 361. © Keith Dannemiller/D70s/Corbis

Photo 11.17, page 361. © USAID

Photo 11.18, page 361. © Keith Roberts

Photo 11.19, page 362. © Keith Roberts

Photo 11.20, page 363. © Najlah Feanny/Corbis

Photo 11.21, page 367. © Bonnie Jacobs/iStockphoto.com

Photo 11.22, page 369. © Keith Roberts

Photo 11.23, page 369. © USAID

Photo 11.24, page 371. N/A

Photo 11.25, page 374. © Elise Roberts

Photo 11.26, page 374. © miafarrow.org

Photo 11.27, page 377. © Gideon Mendel/Corbis

Photo 11.28, page 381. © Gideon Mendel/Corbis

Photo 11.29, page 382. © Karen Kasmauski/Corbis

Photo 11.30, page 382. © Karen Kasmauski/Corbis

Photo 11.31, page 383. © Najlah Feanny/Corbis

Photo 11.32, page 385. Image courtesy Central Asia Institute

Photo 11.33, page 385. © Alain Nogues/Corbis

Photo 11.34, page 386. © Anthony Bannister/Corbis

Photo 11.35, page 386. Courtesy of Hanover College

Chapter 12

Photo 12.1, page 390. © iStockphoto.com/Steven Allen

Photo 12.2, page 390. © iStockphoto.com/Nancy Louie

Photo 12.3, page 390. © iStockphoto.com

Photo 12.4, page 390. © Elise Roberts

Photo 12.5, page 394. © Jeanne Ballantine

Photo 12.6, page 394. © Christophe Boisvieux/Corbis

Photo 12.7, page 396. © Corbis

Photo 12.8, page 397. © iStockphoto.com/Graham Graham

Photo 12.9, page 397. © Kevin Fleming/Corbis

Photo 12.10, page 398. © Peter Turnley/CORBIS

Photo 12.11, page 399. © iStockphoto.com/Matthias Wassermann

Photo 12.12, page 399. © Antoine Gyori/CORBIS SYGMA

Photo 12.13, page 400. © AHMAD AL-RUBAYE/AFP/Getty Images

Photo 12.14, page 401. © Keith Roberts

Photo 12.15, page 401. Used with permission from the First Presbyterian Church of Granada Hills.

Photo 12.16, page 402. Ken Matesich, photographer. Courtesy of the Arizona State Museum and the University of Arizona.

Photo 12.17, page 403. © AFP/Getty

Photo 12.18, page 406. © Keith Roberts

Photo 12.19, page 408. © JOHN GRESS/Reuters/Corbis

Photo 12.20, page 411. © Juan Echeverria/Corbis

Photo 12.21, page 412. © Keith Roberts

Photo 12.22, page 414. © Scott Olson/Getty Images

Photo 12.23a, page 416. © Virginia Caudill

Photo 12.23b, page 416. © Virginia Caudill

Photo 12.24, page 419. © Keith Roberts

Photo 12.25, page 423. © Elise Roberts

Photo 12.26, page 425. © Brand X Pictures/Thinkstock

Photo 12.27, page 425. © Keith Roberts

Photo 12.28, page 425. © www.iStockphoto.com/Marcin Pawinski

Chapter 13

Photo 13.1, page 432. © Mark Poprocki

Photo 13.2, page 432. © iStockphoto.com/Ann Steer

Photo 13.3, page 432. © iStockphoto.com/Tony Tremblay

Photo 13.4, page 432. © USAID

Photo 13.5, page 432. © Keith Roberts

Photo 13.6, page 434. © Larry W. Smith/epa/Corbis

Photo 13.7, page 436. © Eric Thayer/Getty Images

Photo 13.8, page 438. © iStockphoto.com

Photo 13.9, page 439. © Anwar Hussein/Getty Images

Photo 13.10, page 439. © Cate Gillon/Getty Images

Photo 13.11, page 440. © ANDREW ROSS/AFP/Getty Images

Chapter 14

Chapter 15

Chapter 16

Glossary/Index

Bell, D., 73
Belonging need, 364, 365
Belonging systems, 394, 413, 417
Benin, 411
Berger, Helen, 414
Berlin Wall, 456
Bhopal gas disaster, 588
Big box stores, 152, 153, 213, 225
Bigotry, 268
Bill and Melinda Gates Foundation, 475, 504
Binge drinking, 12
Biosocial theories, 107
Bioterrorism, 475
Biracial populations, 252–253
Bird flu, 473, 478, 504, 521
Birth control, 347, 370, 403, 524, 526, 527, 528
Birth rates, 514–515, 514 (table), 519, 522
    See also Fertility; Populations
Blaming the victim, 22, 181, 182, 233, 306
Blindness, 475, 506
Blogs, 136
Blue Cross/Blue Shield, 151
Boat People, 262
Body modification fads, 577
Body parts trade, 501–502
Bolivia, 586–587
Born again. See Religious fundamentalism
Borneo, 99, 100
Bosnia, 261, 267, 272
Botswana, 70
Bourgeoisie. Karl Marx term for capitalists; the
    "haves" who own the means of production,
    55, 56–57, 454
Boy code, 290, 291
Boycotts, 269, 313, 560
Brain Computer Interfaces, 74
Brain-computer interfaces, 74
Brazil, 19, 32, 40, 42, 50, 51, 53, 84, 139, 249,
    330, 383, 386, 478, 574
Bread for the World, 440
Bribery, 152, 167, 190, 190 (table)
Bride burning, 308
Brinksmanship, 464–465
Britain. See Great Britain
Bubonic plague, 550
Buddhist beliefs, 170, 394, 415, 584
Buffalo Creek disaster, 56
Bulimia nervosa, 310
Bullying, 359
Burakumin, 26
Bureau of Justice Statistics (BJS), 184
Bureaucracies. Specific types of large formal
    organizations that have the purpose of
    maximizing efficiency; they are characterized
    by formal relations between participants,
    clearly laid out procedures and rules, and
    pursuit of shared goals, 59, 70, 152
    alienation in, 156, 157
    alternative organizational structures and,
        157–158
    authority structure in, 156, 157
    automatic growth in, 157
    characteristics of, 154–155
    cost-benefit analysis and, 156

creative productivity and, 156
degree of bureaucratization, measurement of, 155
dissatisfaction in, 157
diverse workforces in, 157
division of labor in, 155, 157
economic systems and, 455–456
external rewards vs. internal motivations
    and, 156
goal displacement and, 157
ideal-type bureaucracies, characteristics of, 155
individuals in, 156–157
inefficiencies/red tape and, 157
informal structure/norms of, 155
minorities in, 156
modern bureaucracies, movement to, 152–153
oligarchic structure in, 157
organizational needs, primacy of, 156
Parkinson's law and, 157
problems in, 156–158
professionals/professionalism in, 156
rational choice theory and, 156
rationalization process and, 151, 152
self-preservation, core value of, 156
women in, 156, 157
workers' productive behavior, influences
    on, 157
    See also Corporations; Organizations; Social
        interaction
Bureaucratic school structure, 368–369
Burglary, 183
Burma, 169, 439, 450
    See also Myanmar
Burnout, 14, 15, 359, 491
Burnouts, 359
Bush, President George H. W., 526
Bush, President George W., 372, 383, 436, 452,
    455, 472, 526, 563, 564
Business groups. See Bureaucracies; Corporations;
    Occupational crime; Professionals
Calderon, President Felipe, 448
Calvinism, 406–407
Cambodia, 190, 261, 313, 451
Cambodian Genocide Program, 451
Canada, 80, 455, 573
    distance education and, 387
    divorce rate in, 9
    early-childhood education and, 383
    educational regulation and, 369–370
    health care system in, 498, 498 (table)
    religion, modern world and, 420, 423
    same-sex relationships and, 342
    socialized medicine in, 487
    value systems conflict and, 84
Canada, Geoffrey, 383, 384
Cancer, 473, 503, 503 (table)
Cannibalism, 81, 85
Capital punishment, 196–197, 197 (map)
Capitalism, 55, 453–454, 573
    bureaucratic organizations and, 59
    conflict theory and, 180, 304
    core principles of, 55
    gender stratification and, 304
    haves vs. have-nots and, 55, 454
    labor-management conflict and, 55

legal system, subversion of, 180
lower class, exploitation of, 264, 524
means of production and, 55
middle class, development of, 56
overthrow of, 56
population dynamics and, 521, 523
postindustrial cities and, 545–546
privilege systems, elites and, 454
production costs and, 453–454
profit motive, 188, 453, 455, 463, 479, 545
Protestant work ethic and, 406–407
real estate capitalists, 547
religious ideology and, 454
state capitalism and, 456
subordinate groups, unequal treatment of,
    180–181
victims of, 454
women, abuse of, 181
    See also Corporations; Economic systems;
        Market systems/capitalism; Profit motive
Capitalist class, 212, 231 (figure)
Career choice decisions, 534
Caste systems. The most rigid ascribed
    stratification systems; individuals are born
    into a status, which they retain throughout
    life; that status is deeply imbedded in
    religious, political, and economic norms and
    institutions, 210, 226–227, 228, 238, 261,
    417
Castro, Fidel, 480
Catholics/Catholic Church, 147, 170, 248, 367,
    381, 392, 403, 405, 406, 419, 463, 484,
    524, 527
Cause-and-effect relationships. Relationships
    that occur when there is a causal relationship
    between variables, 33, 36–37
Celebrities. See Media effects
Cell phone use, 127, 134, 237, 239, 590
Census data, 322, 342
Center for the Advancement of Scholarship on
    Engineering Education (CASEE), 311
Center for Education Policy, 372, 383
Centers for Disease Control (CDC), 177,
    497, 503
Central America, 82, 253, 261, 482, 532, 546
Central American Free Trade Agreement
    (CAFTA), 564
Central Asia Institute, 18, 385
Central European Free Trade Agreement
    (CEFTA), 564
Centralized economy. See Economic systems;
    Planned/centralized systems
Cerebrovascular disease, 503 (table)
Chad, 66, 532
Change process, 7, 20, 560
    changing cultures, social policy and, 99–100
    complexity of change, 561–565
    diffusion of invention/discovery and, 589
    discovery and, 589
    environmental problems and, 563–564, 565
    global systems and, 564–565
    individuals, change agents, 561–562, 591
    institutional-level change, 562
    invention and, 589

technological individualizing process and, 154
See also Culture; Groups; Neighborhood groups; Social interaction; Society; Urbanization
Community household model, 551
Community Research Center, 580
Competition, 81, 100
self-interest/self-preservation motivations and, 20
split labor market theory and, 265
value systems conflict and, 84
See also Capitalism; Corporations; Profit motive
Complementary and Alternative Medicine (CAM) movement, 505–506, 507 (figure)
Compromise, 100, 440
Computer games, 293–294
Computer hackers, 192
Computers:
access inequalities and, 73–74
Brain Computer Interfaces, 74
computer automation/computer-controlled robots, 74
computer-based communications, 134
computer-based crime, 188
digital divide and, 237–239, 301, 591
global education system, future of, 386–387
simputers, 239
social change and, 570
socialization process and, 124–125, 124 (table), 126–127
telecommuting, 339
third technological revolution and, 73
See also Computer literacy for sociology; Internet; Media effects
Comte, A., 47, 48, 571
Concentrated animal feeding operations (CAFOs), 99
Confidentiality, 45, 46
Conflict, 7, 18, 20, 100
countercultures and, 94–95
dominant culture-subculture tensions, 94, 95, 98–99
dominant-minority group relations and, 263–265
educational systems and, 377
functionalist assumption about, 55
inter-group contact and, 273
socialization process and, 109–110
values mismatch and, 84, 99
See also Conflict crimes; Conflict theory; Feminist theory; Terrorism
Conflict crimes. Examples include laws concerning public disorder, chemical offenses, prostitution, gambling, property offenses, and political disfranchisement; public opinion about the seriousness of these crimes is often divided, based on people's differing social class, status, and interests, 171–172, 185
Conflict groups, 56
Conflict theory. Theory that focuses on societal groups competing for scarce resources:
conflict groups and, 56, 99
critique of, 57
deviant behavior and, 180–181

dominant culture-subcultural tensions and, 98–99
family and, 330
gender stratification and, 303–304
haves vs. have-nots and, 55, 56–57, 59
health systems and, 478–479
human rights, advocacy for, 56
inequality/injustice, roles of, 55
interest groups and, 56–57
modern conflict theory, 55
population growth and, 523
quasi-groups and, 56
race-based conflict, 56
religious systems, social stratification and, 416–419
reserve labor force, permanent insecurity and, 55
resolution of conflict, group loyalty and, 57
resource/power distribution inequities and, 55
social change and, 573
social change process and, 56–57, 99
social stratification and, 211–213
socialization process and, 109–110
split labor market theory and, 265
war, rationales for, 463
See also Conflict; Conflict crimes; Theoretical perspectives; World systems theory
Conformity, 167, 173–174, 179, 179 (figure), 366, 541
Confucian beliefs, 415
Congo, 7, 55
Connections. *See* Groups; Interaction; Interpersonal skills; Organizations; Social interaction; Social networks
Consensus, 54, 99
Consensus crimes. Examples include predatory crimes (premeditated murder, forcible rape, and kidnapping for ransom); members of society are in general agreement about the seriousness of these deviant acts, 171
Conspicuous consumption, 210
Constitution. *See* Democratic rule; Election politics
Consumption. *See* Conspicuous consumption; Goods
Contagious disease. *See* Illness; Infectious diseases
Content analysis, 40, 41
coding systems and, 40
See also Data collection; Research process
Continuous urban areas, 547
Contraception, 370, 385, 521, 525, 526, 527, 528
Control group. In a controlled experiment, the group in which the subjects are not exposed to the variable the experiment wants to test.
See also Research process; Social control
Control theory. *See* Social control
Controlled experiments. Experiments in which all variables except the one being studied are controlled so researchers can study the effects of the variable under study, 39–40
Controls. Steps used by researchers to eliminate all variables except those related to the hypothesis—especially those variables that might be spurious, 37
Cooley, Charles H., 110–111
Cooperative perspective:
value systems conflict and, 84
See also Collective behavior

Copenhagen Climate Change Conference, 564, 586
Corporations, 18
agribusiness practices, 99
developing nations and, 160
dual-career family needs and, 339
executive crime and, 188
gender socialization process and, 292–294
government regulation and, 454
health care services and, 489, 494
human dignity/well-being and, 454
invisible power elite and, 440
local health conditions and, 479
multinational corporations, 73, 158, 188, 213, 225, 312–313, 453, 467, 479, 524, 585, 588
pharmaceutical corporations, 479, 497, 504
political power of, 441, 454
profit motive and, 188, 453, 454, 479
tax breaks for, 234, 435
welfare programs for, 234
See also Bureaucracies; Capitalism; Occupational crime; Organizations; Organized crime; Work
Correlation. Relationships between variables, with change in one variable associated with change in another, 36
Corruption, 152, 167, 186, 190, 192–193, 440
Coser, Lewis, 57
Cost-benefit analysis, 141, 156, 173, 174, 328, 357, 367, 562
Costa Rica, 238
Cottage industries, 48
Council on Families in America, 342, 349
Counterculture. Groups with expectations and values that contrast sharply with the dominant values of a particular society, 94–95, 96, 186, 411
Countryside doctors, 499–500
Courtship practices, 90
Covenant marriage, 349
See also Marriage
Craftspeople, 454
Creativity, 74, 75, 156, 169, 417
Credentials (Credential Society). Grades, test scores, and degrees that determine the college or job opportunities available to a member of society, even though credentials may be irrelevant to the work required, 375, 378, 439
Crime. Deviant actions for which there are severe formal penalties imposed by the government, 183
blaming the victim, 22, 181, 182
body parts trade, 501–502
conflict crimes, 171–172, 185
consensus crimes, 171
cost-benefit analysis and, 173
crime control, social policy considerations and, 194–200
deviance, violation of law and, 171–172
differential association/reinforcement theory and, 174–175
early defiance and, 15
fear of reporting and, 181
financial fraud, 187
general learning theory of crime/deviance and, 176

Mechanical solidarity. European theorist Émile Durkheim's term for the glue that holds a society together through shared beliefs, values, and traditions; typical of rural areas and simple societies, 69, 303, 538–539

Media effects, 7
  gender socialization process and, 294–295
  interactional bonds and, 125
  messages, behavioral effects of, 125
  political polarization, 442
  same-sex relationships and, 342
  socialization process and, 120, 124–125, 124 (table), 126–127
  See also Computers; Internet

Medicaid, 234, 329, 455, 486, 494, 495

Medical care, 473
  basic right of, 478
  cesarean section surgery, 479
  contemporary challenges in, 491, 497
  cultural belief systems and, 484–485
  deprofessionalization of physicians' work and, 491
  doctor-patient relationship, ambivalence in, 478, 479
  elder care, 473, 479, 485, 486 (figure)
  end-of-life care, 473
  health care institution and, 474
  hospitals and, 91, 93, 488–489, 495
  immunizations, 473
  medicalization of deviance and, 476
  Muslim societies and, 283
  nurse burnout and, 491
  office visit patterns, 485–486, 486 (figure)
  pain, 484–485
  patient social status and, 479
  physician authority and, 479, 489, 496
  preventive care, 485
  reproductive health and, 479–481
  rewards of medical practice, 493
  social stratification and, 208, 215, 300
  uninsured/underinsured patients and, 495–496, 495 (table)
  universal health care, 486, 494, 496
  See also Death; Health; Health systems; Illness; National health care systems; Sick role

Medical marijuana, 170

Medicalization. The shift in handling some forms of deviance: familial, legal, religious, and health care systems, 476

Medicalization of deviance, 476, 477

Medicare, 186, 188, 234, 329, 455, 473, 494, 495

Medicine. *See* Health; Health system; Illness; Medical care

Medieval Europe, 456

Megachurches, 149, 407, 408, 426

Megacities, 536, 547, 547 (table)

Megalopolis, 547

Meinzen-Dick, Ruth, 582

Mennonites, 93, 530–531

Menopause, 480

Mental illness, 484

Mental processes, 12

Merchant class, 72

Meritocracy. A social group or organization in which people are allocated to positions

according to their abilities and credentials, as in level of education attained, 59, 378

Meso-level analysis. Analysis of intermediate-size social units, smaller than the nation but large enough to encompass more than the local community or region, 21–22, 21 (table), 23 (figure), 50
  countercultures and, 94–95
  socialization process and, 109–110
  subcultures and, 93–94
  See also Theoretical perspectives

Meso-level discrimination. *See* Institutional discrimination

Message boards, 136

Mexican Americans, 93, 253, 268, 337

Mexico, 80, 84, 98, 238, 261, 283, 301, 312, 386, 387, 448, 457, 461, 498, 505, 532, 546, 564, 565

Michels, Robert, 157

Micro-lending organizations, 288, 440

Micro-level analysis. Analysis with a focus on individual or small-group interaction in specific situations, 21, 21 (table), 23 (figure), 50
  cultural theory and, 96–97
  microcultures and, 91–93
  socialization process and, 109
  See also Theoretical perspectives

Microculture. The culture of a group or organization that affects only a small segment of one's life or influences a limited period of one's life, 91–93

Middle Ages, 46, 47, 170, 227, 456, 475

Middle class, 56, 122, 210, 211, 217, 221, 231, 231 (figure), 232, 250, 369, 515, 540
  See also Social class system; Social stratification

Middle East, 4, 7, 80
  agricultural revolution in, 71
  conflict theory and, 55
  Hammurabi's Code, 297
  Islamic beliefs in, 46
  McDonaldization process and, 160
  national cultures and, 95
  Neolithic Revolution and, 71
  oil industry and, 82, 573
  ongoing armed conflict, 464 (table)
  slave trade and, 262
  women's illiteracy rates in, 9
  See also Muslim beliefs; Terrorism

Migrant workers, 530

Migration. In terms of demographic processes, refers to the movement of people from one place to another, 524, 530
  collective migrations, 531
  colonized countries, exodus from, 531
  disease mobility, globalization and, 503–505
  early human migration patterns, 252, 252 (map)
  economic opportunity and, 532
  en masse migrations, 531
  guest workers and, 532
  immigration and, 531, 532
  industrial cities and, 543
  internal migration, 533, 533 (table), 546, 547
  internally displace people, 531–532
  international migration, 531–533
  job opportunities and, 531
  Middle Ages and, 47

migrants, geographic isolation of, 531
  passport requirements and, 532
  push-pull model of, 530
  refugees and, 531
  restriction of, 532
  sociocultural factors in, 530–531
  transnationalism and, 125
  urban areas, in/out-migration and, 179
  worker migration, 72, 100, 178
  See also Population trends; Populations; Urbanization

Milgram, Stanley, 135

Militant groups, 160

Military dictatorship, 169, 170, 438, 450

Military draft, 116

Military forces:
  military spending worldwide, 464–465, 465 (figure)
  segregation in, 274
  socialization process and, 109
  vested interest in war and, 464
  See also War

Military juntas, 450

Military recruiters, 563

Military-industrial complex, 464–465, 465 (figure)

Militia groups, 94, 467

Millenarian movements, 407

Mills, C. W., 9, 440

Mind. *See* Mental disorders; Mental processes

Minimax strategy, 575

Minority groups. Groups in a population that differ from others in some characteristics and are therefore subject to less power, fewer privileges, and discrimination, 246
  acceptance and, 268
  assimilation and, 268
  avoidance and, 268–269
  bureaucracies and, 156
  characteristics of, 246
  environmental racism and, 523, 560
  frustration-aggression theory and, 255
  human rights advocacy and, 56
  lower-class life, delinquency and, 175
  nonviolent resistance and, 269–270
  obesity rates and, 177
  passing and, 268
  reactions to prejudice/discrimination/racism, 268–271
  self-fulfilling prophesy and, 254–255
  slavery and, 244–246
  United States, minorities in, 246, 247 (map)
  women and, 307, 308
  See also Discrimination; Dominant-minority group relations; Ethnic groups; Prejudice; Race; Racial/ethnic stratification; Subcultures

Mission Barrio Adentro, 478–479

Mobile phones, 134, 239

Mobility. *See* Migration; Social mobility

Mobs. Emotional crowds that engage in violence against a specific target; lynchings, killings, and hate crimes are examples, 186, 576, 577 (figures)

Racism. Any attitude, belief, or institutional arrangement that favors one racial group over another, 249, 256
attempted justifications for, 268
cultural beliefs, socialization process and, 267
economic competition for jobs and, 256
environmental racism, 523, 560
ideological racism, 256
institutional racism, 256
language, color-quality associations and, 89
minority reactions to, 268–271
psychological/social costs of, 256
reduction of, social policies for, 271–275
religion-based prejudice and, 419
sterilization policy and, 527
symbolic racism, 256
See also Prejudice; Race; Racial/ethnic stratification
Racketeering. *See* Organized crime
Radical fundamentalism, 87, 160
Random samples, 42
Rape, 23, 166, 181, 183, 306
blaming the victim and, 181, 182, 306
college campus rape, 306
cultural/societal attitudes toward, 306
culture of rape, 23
date rape drugs, 193, 306
gang rapes, 305, 306
macho behavior/power plays and, 306
masculine roles/personality and, 23
Rational choice (exchange) theory. A theory that focuses on humans as fundamentally concerned with self-interests, making rational decisions based on weighing costs and rewards of the projected outcome, 51–52
bureaucracies and, 156
cost-benefit analysis and, 141
critique of, 52
deviance and, 173, 198
economic model of human behavior and, 401
educational systems and, 357–358
family and, 326, 328
human behavior, rational decisions about, 52
minimax strategy and, 575
punishment and, 173
reciprocity and, 70, 141
religious systems, eternal benefits and, 401–402
self-interest and, 52
social change and, 571, 571 (figure)
social interaction processes and, 52, 141
See also Exchange theory/rational choice; Theoretical perspectives
Rational-legal authority, 439
Rationality. In the management of organizations, the trend of attempting to reach maximum efficiency with rules that are rationally designed to accomplish goals, 151
bureaucratic organizations and, 59, 151
See also Rational choice/exchange theory
Rationalization, 151, 152, 158, 160
Reagan, President Ronald, 526
Real culture. The way things in society are actually done.
Reasoning. *See* Deductive reasoning; Inductive reasoning; Rational choice/exchange theory

Rebellion, 179, 179 (figure), 456–457
Rebirth, 117, 417
Recidivism rates. The likelihood that someone who is arrested, convicted, and imprisoned will later be a repeat offender, 195–196, 198, 199
Reciprocity, 70, 141
Recycling, 523, 560
Red Cross, 151, 154, 347
Reference groups. Groups comprised of members who act as role models and establish standards against which members evaluate their conduct, 149–150
Reform movements. *See* Educational systems; Social reform movements
Refugees, 19, 125, 271, 451, 531, 567, 568 (maps)
Regressive movements. *See* Resistance/regressive movements
Rehabilitation Act of 1973, 372
Reincarnation, 84, 117, 228, 417
Reinforcement theory, 174–175
Rejection. *See* Social rejection
Relative poverty. Occurs when one's income falls below the poverty line, resulting in an inadequate standard of living relative to others in the individual's country, 233
Relief agencies, 521
Religious conflict, 392, 406, 419, 425
class-based religious practice and, 416–417
common religious heritage, moderation of hatreds and, 425–426
ethnic/economic/religious differences and, 425, 426 (figure)
fundamentalist groups and, 425, 426
homosexuality debates and, 427–428
interfaith/transnational cooperation and, 425
liberal theologies and, 425
nationalistic loyalties and, 425
racial bias/gender prejudice and, 417–419
secular nations and, 426
See also Religious fundamentalism; Religious systems
Religious cults. *See* NRMs/New Religious Movements or cults
Religious fundamentalism, 87, 149, 297, 415, 420, 425, 426, 427, 473, 584, 585
Religious systems, 319 (table), 392
agents of socialization and, 119
big business approach/consumer demand and, 407, 426–427
boundary vigilance and, 398
calling to God's work, 406
caste systems and, 227
church-related organizations and, 423, 423 (table)
class-based practices, elective affinity and, 416–417
components of, 393–395, 397, 397 (figure), 398
conflict perspective and, 416–419
creative/independent thought and, 417
data collection, policy decisions and, 395
death, afterlife/rebirth and, 117
denominations, 409–410, 410 (map)
dysfunctions in, 395

early sociological thought and, 46
ecclesia and, 408–409, 410
economic system, Protestant work ethic and, 406–407
entrepreneurial activity, consumer demand and, 401–402
eternal benefits, rational choice perspective and, 401–402
expressive social movements, 584
faith-healing, 474
family systems and, 403
fertility rates and, 515, 520, 527
folk religion and, 417
functionalist perspective, societal contributions of religion, 413–415
funding of, 407, 425
gender prejudice and, 417–419
gender socialization process and, 296–297
health services/support systems and, 474
heretics, 170
homosexuality debates and, 427–428
homosexuals, status of, 308
ideal types of religious associations, 408
individual religious affiliations and, 396–398, 396 (table), 401–402
individualism and, 407
institutionalization process and, 412
labor politics and, 454
leadership roles in, 394, 418, 419, 427–428
legitimation of social values/norms and, 413–414
meaning systems of, 393–394, 400
megachurches and, 149, 407, 408, 426
modern world, role of religion in, 420–427, 421 (map, tables), 422 (figure)
monotheism and, 417
mosques, Islam in United States, 409
myths and, 399, 400
pluralism/spiritual diversity and, 402, 425
politics, theocracies/civil religion and, 404–406, 404 (figure)
polytheism and, 417
predestination and, 406
racial bias and, 419
reincarnation/transmigration of souls and, 84, 117, 228, 417
religious membership, social stratification and, 217
rites of passage and, 287
rituals and, 399
routinization of charisma and, 395
scriptures, reinterpretation of, 297
sects and, 408, 411–412
secularization process and, 422–425, 423 (table), 426
self-denial and, 407
sexual attitudes/behaviors and, 415
social change and, 415
social cohesion function of, 413
social institutions and, 402–407, 410
social stratification and, 416–420
socioeconomic status, religious groups and, 416–417, 417 (table)
structural system and, 394–395
subordination to states and, 47
symbols, meaning creation and, 398–400, 400 (figure)

manifest functions/planned outcomes and, 54
mechanical solidarity and, 69, 303
organic solidarity and, 69, 303
social stratification and, 210–211, 213
socialization process and, 109
societal consensus, social order and, 54
summary of, 54
See also Anomie; Functional theory/structural-
functional perspective; Strain theory;
Theoretical perspectives
Student roles in education, 358–359, 360
Styles. See Collective behavior; Fashions
Sub-Saharan Africa. See Africa
Subculture. The culture of a meso-level
subcommunity that distinguishes itself from
the dominant culture of the larger society,
93–94, 95, 175, 541
Subjugation. The subordination of one group
to another that holds power and authority,
261–262, 261 (figure)
domestic colonialism, 262
segregation, 262
slavery, 262
women's oppression, 2
Subsistence living, 528
Substance abuse. See Alcohol abuse; Drug traffic/abuse
Suburbanization, 539, 540, 546, 569
Sudan, 7, 66, 261, 267, 272, 419, 521, 567
Suicide:
anomic suicide, 147
anomie and, 147–148
cult-based suicides, 412, 439
egoistic suicide, 147
group expectations, nonconformity and, 120
high-stakes exams and, 369
physician-assisted suicide, 117–118
social factors in, 147
Suicide bombings, 55, 166
Sumatra, 22
Summer camp groups, 91, 121
Superstitions, 12
Superwoman syndrome, 309–310
Support. See Networks; Social networks
Survey method. Research method used by
sociologists who want to gather information
directly from a number of people regarding
how they think or feel or what they do; two
common survey forms are the interview and
the questionnaire, 38, 60
interviews, 39
questionnaires, 39
school dropout study example, 39
See also Data collection; Research process
Survivalist groups, 94
Swaziland, 478, 530
Sweatshops, 311–312
anti-sweatshop codes, 11
global social movements and, 587
Sweden, 238, 301, 338, 342, 369, 404, 455, 487
Swine flu (H1N1), 473, 478, 503, 504
Switzerland, 263
Symbolic interaction theory. Sees humans as
active agents who create shared meanings of
symbols and events and then interact on the
basis of those meanings, 50–51
Chicago School of, 51
critique of, 51

culture, development of, 97
definition of a situation and, 326
dramaturgy and, 109
educational systems and, 355–357
family and, 325–326
gender stratification and, 302–303
health/illness, labeling theory and, 476
human agency and, 50–51, 302
individual identity, organizational roles/
positions and, 51
interpretation function and, 51
Iowa School of, 51
modern symbolic interaction perspective, 51
personal/collective histories, creation of, 97
power, legitimacy of, 436–439
race, social construction of, 249
reality, social construction of, 326
reflexive behavior and, 113
religious systems and, 398–400, 400 (figure)
self, development of, 110–113
social change and, 570, 571
social interaction processes and, 141
social stratification and, 210, 213
See also Labeling theory; Language; Self;
Theoretical perspectives
Symbolic racism, 89, 256
Symbols. Actions or objects that represent
something else and therefore have meaning
beyond their own existence; flags and
wedding rings are examples, 50, 51
color symbolism, 89
creation of, 97
dramaturgy and, 109
internalization of, 97
national symbols, loyalty/patriotism and,
436–438
objectification of, 97
religious symbols, meaning creation and,
398–400, 400 (figure)
role-taking and, 113
social positions and, 210
See also Language; Symbolic interaction theory
Syria, 297, 392

Taboos, 85–86, 86 (table)
Taiwan, 386, 574
Taliban, 262, 283
Tanzania, 53, 70, 385, 499, 514, 581
Tattoos, 167, 577
Taureg tribe, 67, 69
Taxation:
corporate tax breaks, 234, 435
progressive tax plans, 455
Taylor, Charles, 567
The Tea Party Express bus, 180
Teacher roles in education, 359, 361–362
Teaching Tolerance Program, 272
Teasing, 121
Technological individualizing process, 154
Technologically-based societies, 73
Technology. The practical application of tools,
skills, and knowledge to meet human needs
and extend human abilities:
agricultural revolution and, 71, 588
automobile use, 567, 569
democratic systems and, 452–453
diffusion of, 570

digital divide and, 237–239, 301, 386, 591
election politics and, 458
future developments in, 74
generational relationships and, 591
leveled playing field and, 239
plow, introduction of, 71
pop culture and, 76–77
postindustrial technology, 588
printing press, 426
religious practice and, 426–427
science and, 589–590
social change process and, 100, 567, 570,
588–591
social networking and, 458
societal complexity and, 70
third technological revolution, 73
See also Industrial Revolution; Internet
Teen pregnancy, 234, 370, 415, 526
Telecommunications. See Communication; Internet
Telecommuting, 339
Televangelism industry, 407, 426–427
Television:
access to, 238
gender socialization process and, 294
religious practice and, 407, 426–427
socialization process and, 124–125, 124 (table),
126–127
See also Media effects
Terrorism. Premeditated, politically motivated
violence perpetrated against noncombatant
targets by subnational groups or clandestine
agents, usually intended to influence an
audience, 81, 96, 189, 562
alienation and, 467
bioterrorism, 475
chemical weapons and, 261
civil society and, 5
conflict theory and, 467
cyber crime and, 192
defensive isolation and, 127–128
definition of, 466
dominant power structure and, 269
economic disruption and, 562
effectiveness of, 466
freedom fighters and, 467
greater-good beliefs and, 467
ideology and, 467
nonstate groups and, 562
rationales for, 466–467, 562–563
reactions to, 467
refugee-friendly countries and, 271
September 11, 2001 attacks, 4–5, 127, 275,
373, 466, 467, 532, 562, 563
state terrorism, 450, 466
suicide bombings, 55, 166
tourism and, 591
traditional cultures, challenges/threats
to, 100, 160
types of terrorist groups, 189 (table)
See also Crime; National/global crime; War
Thailand, 225, 301, 387, 461, 574
Theft, 183
Theocracy. Religion in which religious leaders rule
society in accordance with God's presumed
wishes, 404, 404 (figure)
Theoretical perspective. The broadest theories
in sociology; overall approaches to

SAGE Research Methods Online

The essential tool for researchers

Sign up now at
www.sagepub.com/srmo
for more information.

An expert research tool

- An **expertly designed taxonomy** with more than 1,400 unique terms for social and behavioral science research methods

- **Visual and hierarchical search tools** to help you discover material and link to related methods

- Easy-to-use navigation tools
- Content organized by complexity
- Tools for citing, printing, and downloading content with ease
- Regularly updated content and features

A wealth of essential content

- The most comprehensive picture of quantitative, qualitative, and mixed methods available today

- More than **100,000 pages of SAGE book and reference material** on research methods as well as editorially selected material from SAGE journals

- More than **600 books** available in their entirety online

Launching 2011!

 SAGE research methods online